W9-BVH-931

The first all-new Latin-English dictionary compiled in the United States in the last 60 years— The first Latin dictionary ever to be compiled on the basis of modern lexicographical principles.

THE NEW COLLEGE
LATIN & ENGLISH DICTIONARY

COMPREHENSIVE: More than 40,000 words and phrases.

DEFINITIVE: Based on the foremost Classical authorities and organized to achieve the utmost clarity, precision, and convenience.

MODERN: Obsolete definitions have been replaced by fresh translations that correspond to current English usage.

A NEW LANDMARK
IN LATIN-ENGLISH DICTIONARIES
FOR THE MODERN STUDENT!

John C. Traupman, author of *The New College Latin & English Dictionary*, is Chairman of the Classics Department of St. Joseph's College, Philadelphia. Professor Traupman took his A.B. at Moravian College and his Ph.D. at Princeton. He served as President of the Philadelphia Classical Society and of the Pennsylvania Classical Association.

THE BANTAM NEW
COLLEGE DICTIONARY SERIES
Edwin B. Williams, General Editor

Edwin B. Williams, A.B., A.M., Ph.D., Doct. d'Univ.,
LL.D., L.H.D. has been Chairman of the Department of
Romance Languages, Dean of the Graduate School, and
Provost of the University of Pennsylvania. He is a member
of the American Philosophical Society and the
Hispanic Society of America and the author of *THE
BANTAM NEW COLLEGE SPANISH & ENGLISH
DICTIONARY* and the Holt *Spanish and English Dictionary*
and many other works on the Spanish, Portuguese,
and French languages.

THE
NEW COLLEGE
LATIN & ENGLISH
DICTIONARY

John C. Traupman, Ph.D.

St. Joseph's College,
Philadelphia

THE NEW COLLEGIATE LATIN & ENGLISH DICTIONARY

Bantam Language Library edition / April 1966

2nd printing .... *May 1966*	9th printing .... *August 1971*
3rd printing .. *September 1967*	10th printing .... *June 1973*
4th printing .. *September 1968*	11th printing .... *April 1974*
5th printing .... *December 1968*	12th printing .... *July 1975*
6th printing .... *August 1969*	13th printing ...... *February 1977*
7th printing .... *May 1970*	14th printing .... *May 1978*
8th printing .... *August 1970*	15th printing .... *June 1979*

Library of Congress Catalog Card Number: 66-12159

ISBN 0–553–13252–0

Published simultaneously in the United States and Canada

Bantam Books are published by Bantam Books, Inc. Its trade-
mark, consisting of the words "Bantam Books" and the por-
trayal of a bantam, is Registered in U.S. Patent and Trademark
Office and in other countries. Marca Registrada. Bantam
Books, Inc., 666 Fifth Avenue, New York, New York 10019.

PRINTED IN THE UNITED STATES OF AMERICA

INTRODUCTION

Both Latin and English entry words, as well as illustrative phrases under entry words, are treated in strictly alphabetical order.

Adverbs on the Latin-English side are inserted as separate entries and translated in that position without cross-reference to the corresponding adjective.

Adverbs on the English-Latin side ending in -ly are listed under their adjectives

Compound words are generally given in their assimilated forms, e.g., accurrō rather than adcurrō. Cross-references are provided as guides for those using texts which employ the unassimilated forms.

The letter j has been used in place of consonantal i because some recent texts have begun to use the former again and because students can thus more readily distinguish the consonant from the vowel.

If a feminine substantive, singular or plural, of the first declension, a neuter substantive, singular or plural, of the second declension, or a masculine substantive of the second declension falls alphabetically more than one word before or after the corresponding adjective, it is inserted as a separate entry and translated in that position, and a cross-reference to it is given under the adjective; for example, nāt·a -ae *f* occurs fifteen entries before nāt·us -a -um *adj* ... ; *f* see nata.

If such a substantive does not fall alphabetically more than one word before or after the corresponding adjective, it is treated under the adjective.

Many of the variations in spelling of Latin words are indicated by means of cross-references, e.g., sēpiō see saepio.

Only those past participles are listed as separate entries whose difference in form from the first person singular present indicative warrants such listing, provided they fall alphabetically more than one word before or after the first person singular present indicative.

Only the first person singular present indicative and the present infinitive of regular active verbs of the first conjugation are given; in the case of deponent verbs, the perfect is added. For the other three conjugations and for irregular and defective verbs, all principal parts in use are given.

Discriminations between two or more meanings of the entry word are often shown by means of English words in parentheses.

Transitive and intransitive verbs, with their dependent

constructions, are clearly differentiated and are presented in a fixed order of transitive first and intransitive second.

Centered periods within entry words indicate division points at which inflectional elements are to be added.

All source words and phrases are printed in boldface type.

On the English-Latin side a boldface dash represents the vocabulary entry.

On the Latin-English side, the twofold purpose in marking the quantity of vowels is (1) to indicate accentuation of words and (2) to provide the basis for scansion of Classical Latin verse. Thus, all vowels that are long by nature and occur in open syllables are marked, whereas vowels in closed syllables, whether long or short by nature, are not marked, since the syllable in either case is long. However, since a vowel followed by a mute and a liquid can be open or closed, its quantity is marked when it is long. As a further aid to pronunciation, in words of three or more syllables, the short vowel of the penult is marked.

On the English-Latin side, Latin vowels have been marked to distinguish:

(a) words otherwise spelled alike: lēvis, levis
(b) the genitive singular and the nominative and accusative plural from the nominative singular of the fourth declension
(c) the ablative singular from the nominative singular of nouns of the first declension whenever the distinction is not clear from the context
(d) the nominative and genitive singular from the accusative plural of *i*-stem words of the third declension
(e) the infinitive of verbs of the second conjugation from the infinitive of verbs of the third conjugation.

On the English-Latin side, the genitive of the nouns of the fourth declension is provided in order to distinguish these nouns from nouns of the second declension ending in -us.

John C. Traupman

PRONUNCIATION

Vowels

	CLASSICAL METHOD	ECCLESIASTICAL METHOD
ă	Like *a* in *ago*: **compărō**	(Generally as in the Classical Method. However, in practice the different values of the vowels are frequently not rigidly adhered to.)
ā	Like *a* in *father*: **imāgō**	
ĕ	Like *e* in *pet*: **propĕrō**	
ē	Like *a* in *late*: **lēnis**	
ĭ	Like *i* in *hit*: **ĭdem**	
ī	Like *ee* in *keen*: **amīcus**	
ŏ	Like *o* in *often*: **mŏdus**	
ō	Like *o* in *hope*: **nōmen**	
ŭ	Like *u* in *put*: **ŭt**	
ū	Like *u* in *rude*: **ūtor**	
ў	Like *ü* in German *Hütte*: **mўrīca**	
ȳ	Like *ü* in German *über*: **Tȳdeus**	

Diphthongs

	CLASSICAL METHOD	ECCLESIASTICAL METHOD
ae	Like *y* in *by*: **caecus**	Like *a* in *late*: **caecus**
au	Like *ow* in *now*: **nauta**	As in the Classical Method
ei	Like *ey* in *grey*: **deinde**	As in the Classical Method
eu	Like *eu* in *feud*: **Orpheus**	Like *eu* in Italian *neutro*: **euge**
oe	Like *oi* in *oil*: **coepit**	Like *a* in *late*: **coepit**
ui	Like *uey* in *gluey*: **cui** After **q**, like *wee* in *week*: **qui**	As in the Classical Method

Consonants

	CLASSICAL METHOD	ECCLESIASTICAL METHOD
b	As in English	As in English
c	Always like *c* in *can*: **cīvis, cantō, actus**	Before **e, i, ae,** or **oe** like *ch* in *cherry*: **excelsis, civis, caelum, coepit,** but before other letters like *c* in *can*: **cantō, actus**
d	As in English	As in English
f	As in English	As in English
g	Always like *g* in *go*: **genus, gula, gallīna, grātus**	Before **e** or **i** like *g* in *gentle*: **genus, regīna,** but before other letters except **g** and **n** (see under Consonant Groups) like *g* in *go*: **gula, gallīna, fugō, grātus**
h	As in English	As in English
j	Like *y* in *yes*: **jungō, jam**	As in the Classical Method
k	As in English	As in English
l	As in English	As in English
m	As in English, but in verse final **m** before an initial vowel in the following word was presumably not pronounced	As in English
n	As in English	As in English
p	As in English	As in English
q	As in English and used only before consonantal **u**	As in English
r	Trilled as in the Romance languages	As in the Classical Method
s	Always like *s* in *sing*: **miser, mors**	Like *s* in *sing*: **salūs,** but when standing between two vowels or when final and preceded by a voiced consonant, like *z* in *dozen*: **miser, mors**
t	Like English *t*, but unaspirated	As in the Classical Method

CLASSICAL METHOD	ECCLESIASTICAL METHOD
u Like *w* in *w*ine, when unaccented, preceded by **q**, sometimes by **s**, and sometimes by **g**, and followed by a vowel: **qui·a, suā·vis** (but **su·ŏ·rum**), **dis·tin·guō** (but **ex·i·gŭ·us**)	As in the Classical Method
v Like *w* in *w*ine: **vīvō**	As in English
x Like *x* (= ks) in si*x:* **exactus**	Like *x* (=ks) in si*x:* **pax**; but in words beginning with **ex** and followed by a vowel, **h**, or **s**, like *x* (= gz) in e*x*haust: **exaudī, exhālō, exsolvō**
z *Like dz* in a*dz*e: **zōna**	As in the Classical Method

Consonant Groups

CLASSICAL METHOD	ECCLESIASTICAL METHOD
bs Like *ps* in a*ps*e: **obsĭdĕō, urbs**	Like *bs* in o*bs*ession: **obsĭdĕō**, but in the final position, like *bs* in o*bs*erve: **urbs**
bt Like *pt* in ca*pt*ain: **obtinēre**	Like *bt* in o*bt*ain: **obtinēre**
cc Like *kk* in book*k*eeper: **ecce, occīdō, occāsum, occlūdō**	Before **e** or **i** like *tch* in ca*tch*: **ecce, occīdō**; but before other letters, like *kk* in book*k*eeper: **occāsum, occlūdō**
ch Like *ch* in *ch*aotic: **pulcher**	As in the Classical Method
gg Like *gg* in le*g g*uard: **agger**	Before **e** or **i** like *dj* in a*dj*ourn: **agger**; but before other letters, like *gg* in le*g g*uard: **aggrĕgō**
gn As in English	Like *ny* in ca*ny*on: **dignus**
gu See consonant **u**	As in the Classical Method
ph Like *p-h* in to*p-h*eavy: **phōca**	Like *ph* in *ph*oenix: **phōca**
qu See consonant *u*	As in the Classical Method
sc Like *sc* in *sc*ope; **sciō, scūtum**	Before **e** or **i** like *sh* in *sh*in: **ascendō, sciō**; but before other letters, like *sc* in *sc*ope: **scandō, scūtum**
su See consonant **u**	As in the Classical Method
th Like *t* in *t*ake: **theātrum**	As in the Classical Method
ti Like *ti* in English pa*ti*o: **nātĭŏ**	When preceded by **s**, **t**, or **x** or when followed by a consonant, like *ti* in English pa*ti*o: **hostĭa, admixtĭō, fortĭter**; but when unaccented, followed by a vowel, and preceded by any letter except **s, t,** or **x**, like *tzy* in ri*tzy*: **nātĭō, pretĭum**

SYLLABIFICATION

1. Every Latin word has as many syllables as it has vowels or diphthongs: **ae·ger, fī·lī·us, Bai·ae**

2. When a word is divided into syllables:
   a) a single consonant between two vowels goes with the following syllable (h is regarded as a consonant; **ch, ph, th, qu,** and somtimes **gu** and **su** are regarded as single consonants)*: **a·ger, ni·hil, a·qua, ci·cho·rē·um**
   b) the first consonant of a combination of two or more consonants goes with the preceding vowel: **tor·men·tum, mit·tō, mon·strum**
   c) a consonant group consisting of a mute (**b, d, g, p, t, c**) followed by **l** or **r** is generally left undivided and goes with the following vowel: **pa·trēs, a·cris, du·plex.** In Classical poetry this combination is often treated like any other pair of consonants: **pat·rēs, ac·ris, dup·lex**
   d) prefixes form separate syllables even if the division is contrary to above rules: **ab·est, ob·lā·tus, abs·ti·nē·ō, ab·stō**

3. A syllable ending in a vowel or diphthong is called *open*; all others are called *closed*

4. The last syllable of a word is called the *ultima*; the next to last is called the *penult*; the one before the penult is called the *antepenult*

---

* The double consonant **x** goes with the preceding vowel: **dix·it**

QUANTITY OF VOWELS

1. A vowel is **long** (**lēvis**) or *short* (**lĕvis**) according to the length of time required for its pronunciation

2. A vowel is long:
   a) before **ns, nf,** (and perhaps **gn**): **ingēns, īnfāns, (māgnus)**
   b) when resulting from a contraction: **nil = nihil, cōgō = cŏăgō, iniquus = inaequus**

3. A vowel is short:
   a) before another vowel or **h: dĕa, trăhō**
   b) generally before **nd** and **nt: amăndus, amănt**

4. Diphthongs are long: **causae**

QUANTITY OF SYLLABLES

1. Syllables are distinguished as *long* or *short* according to the length of time required for their pronunciation

2. A syllable is long:
   a) if it contains a long vowel or a diphthong: **vĕ·nī, scrī·bō, cau·sae** (such a syllable is said to be *long by nature*)
   b) if it contains a short vowel followed by **x, z,** or any two consonants except a mute (**b, d, g, p, t, c**) followed by **l** or **r: sax·um, gaz·a, mit·tō, cur·sor** (such a syllable is said to be *long by position*, but the vowel is pronounced *short*)

3. A syllable is short:
   a) if it contains a short vowel followed by a vowel or by a single consonant (**h** is regarded as a consonant; **ch, ph, th, qu,** and sometimes **gu** and **su** are regarded as single consonants): **me·us, ni·hil, ge·rit, a·qua**
   b) if it contains a short vowel followed by a mute (**b, d, g, p, t, c**) plus **l** or **r**, but it is sometimes long in verse: **flă·grans, ba·ră·thrum, ce·lĕ·brō** (such a syllable is said to be *common*)

NOTE: In this dictionary, long vowels are marked except before **x, z,** or two or more consonants unless the two consonants are a mute plus a liquid. Only the short penult of words of three or more syllables is marked.

ACCENT

1. Words of two syllables are accented on the first syllable: **om′nēs, tan′gō, ge′rit**

2. Words of more than two syllables are accented on the penult if it is long: **a·mī′ous, re·gun′tur** and on the antepenult if the penult is short: **fa·mil′li·a, ge′ri·tur**

3. These rules apply to words with enclitics appended (-ce, -dum, -met, -ne, -que, -ve): **vos′met, lau·dat′ne, de′ā·que** (nominative), **de·ā′que** (ablative)

4. In the second declension, the contracted genitive and the contracted vocative of nouns in -ius and the contracted genitive of those in -ium retain the accent of the nominative: **Vir·gi′lī, in·gē′nī**

5. Certain words which have lost a final -e retain the accent of the complete forms: **il·līc′** for **il·lī′ce, tan·tōn′** for **tan·tō′ne**

6. Certain compounds of **faciō**, in which a feeling for the individuality of the components was preserved, retain the accent of the simple verb: **be·ne·fā′cit**

ABBREVIATIONS

abbr	abbreviation	*interrog*	interrogative
abl	ablative	*loc*	locative
acc	accusative	*m*	masculine noun
adj	adjective	*masc*	masculine
adv	adverb	*math*	mathematics
astr	astronomy	*med*	medicine
bot	botany	*mil*	military
c.	circa, about	*m pl*	masculine plural noun
cent.	century	*mus*	music
coll	colloquial	*n*	neuter noun
com	commercial	*neut*	neuter
comp	comparative	*nom*	nominative
conj	conjunction	*n pl*	neuter plural noun
d.	died	*p*	participle
dat	dative	*phil*	philosophy
defect	defective	*pl*	plural
eccl	ecclesiastical	*pol*	politics
esp.	especially	*pp*	past participle
f	feminine noun	*prep*	preposition
fem	feminine	*pres*	present
fig	figurative	*pron*	pronoun
fl	floruit	*reflex*	reflexive
f pl	feminine plural noun	*rel*	relative
fut	future	*rhet*	rhetoric
genit	genitive	*s*	substantive
gram	grammar	*singl*	singular
impers	impersonal	*subj*	subjunctive
impv	imperative	*superl*	superlative
indecl	indeclinable	*v defect*	defective verb
indef	indefinite	*vi*	intransitive verb
inf	infinitive	*v impers*	impersonal verb
interj	interjection	*vt*	transitive verb

A

ā *interj* ah!

ā or ab *prep* (with *abl*) (of agency) by; (of time) since, after, from; (of space) from, away from; at, on, in; **a latere** on the side; **a tergo** in the rear

abactus *pp* of **abigo**

abăc·us -ī *m* cupboard; game board; abacus, counting board; panel; tray

abaliēnāti·ō -ōnis *f* transfer of property

abaliēn·ō -āre *vt* to alienate, estrange; to sell; to separate

Abantiăd·ēs -ae *m* descendant of Abas

Ab·ās -antis *m* king of Argos, father of Acrisius and grandfather of Perseus

abăv·us -ī *m* great-great-grandfather

abdicāti·ō -ōnis *f* abdication, renunciation, resignation

abdĭc·ō -āre *vt* to abdicate, renounce, resign; to disinherit; **se magistratu abdicare** to resign from office

ab·dīcō -dīcĕre -dixī -dictum *vt* (in augury) to disapprove of, forbid

abdĭtē *adv* secretly, privately

abdĭt·us -a -um *adj* hidden, secret

ab·dō -dĕre -dĭdī -dĭtum *vt* to hide; to remove, withdraw; to plunge (*e.g., a sword*)

abdōm·en -ĭnis *n* abdomen, belly; (fig) gluttony, greed

ab·dūcō -dūcĕre -duxī -ductum *vt* to lead away, take away; to seduce; to alienate

ab·eō -īre -ĭī -ĭtum *vi* to go away, depart; to vanish, disappear; to pass away, die; (of time) to pass, elapse; to change, be changed; to retire

abequĭt·ō -āre *vi* to ride off

aberrāti·ū -ōnis *f* wandering, escape, relief

aberr·ō -āre *vi* to wander, go astray; to deviate, differ

abesse *inf* of **absum**

abhinc *adv* ago

abhorr·ĕō -ēre -ŭī *vi* to shrink back; (with **ab** + *abl*) **a** to be averse to; **b** to be inconsistent with, differ from; **c** to be free from

abiegn·us -a -um *adj* fir

abĭ·ēs -ĕtis *f* fir; ship; spear; writing tablet

ab·ĭgō -igĕre -ēgī -actum *vt* to drive away, get rid of; to banish, expel

abĭt·us -ūs *m* departure; outlet; end

abjectē *adv* abjectly, meanly

abject·us -a -um *adj* abject, mean; downhearted

ab·jĭcĭō -jicĕre -jēcī -jectum *vt* to throw away, throw down; to slight; to give up; to humble, debase

abjūdĭc·ō -āre *vt* to take away (*by judicial decree*)

ab·jungō -jungĕre -junxī -junctum *vt* to unyoke; to detach

abjūr·ō -āre *vt* to deny on oath

ablātīv·us -a -um *adj* & *m* ablative

ablātus *pp* of **aufero**

ablēgāti·ō -ōnis *f* sending away, sending off; banishment

ablēg·ō -āre *vt* to send away; to remove, banish; to dismiss

abligurr·ĭō or **abligūr·ĭō** -īre -īvī or -ĭī -ītum *vt* to squander, waste

ablŏc·ō -āre *vt* to lease, rent out

ab·lūdō -lūdĕre -lūsī -lūsum *vi* to be unlike; (with **ab** + *abl*) to differ from

ab·lŭō -luĕre -lŭī -lūtum *vt* to wash away, cleanse, remove

ablūti·ō -ōnis *f* washing, cleansing

abnĕg·ō -āre *vt* to refuse, turn down

abnĕp·ōs -ōtis *m* great-great-grandson

abnept·is -is *f* great-great-granddaughter

abnoct·ō -āre *vi* to stay out all night, sleep out

abnorm·is -e *adj* irregular, unorthodox

ab·nŭō -nuĕre -nŭī -nūtum *vt* to refuse, deny

abol·ĕō -ēre -ēvī -ĭtum *vt* to abolish, destroy, annihilate

abol·escō -escĕre -ēvī *vi* to decay, vanish, die out

aboliti·ō -ōnis *f* abolition

abōmĭn·or -ārī -ātus sum *vt* to detest

aborīgĭn·ēs -um *m pl* aborigines, original inhabitants

ab·orĭor -orīrī -ortus sum *vi* to miscarry; to fail; (of stars, etc.) to set

abortĭ·ō -ōnis *f* miscarriage

abortīv·us -a -um *adj* prematurely born

abort·us -ūs *m* miscarriage

ab·rādō -rādĕre -rāsī -rāsum *vt* to scrape off, shave; (fig) to squeeze out, rob

ab·rĭpĭō -ripĕre -ripŭī -reptum *vt* to take away by force, carry off; to squander

ab·rōdō -rōdĕre -rōsī -rōsum *vt* to gnaw off

abrogātī·ō -ōnis f repeal

abrŏg·ō -āre vt to repeal, annul

abrotŏn·um -ī n southernwood (aromatic, medicinal plant)

ab·rumpō -rumpĕre -rūpī -ruptum vt to break off; to tear, sever

abruptē adv abruptly, rashly

abruptī·ō -ōnis f breaking off; divorce

abrupt·us -a -um pp of **abrumpo**; adj abrupt, steep; n precipice

abs prep (with abl), confined almost exclusively to the combination **abs te**) by, from

abs·cēdō -cēdĕre -cessī -cessum vi to go away, depart; to retire; to desist

abscessī·ō -ōnis f diminution

abscess·us -ūs m departure, absence, remoteness

abs·cīdō -cīdĕre -cīdī -cīsum vt to cut off, chop off; to cut short

ab·scindō -scindĕre -scĭdī -scissum vt to tear off, break off; to divide

abscīs·us -a -um pp of **abscido**; adj steep, precipitous; concise; abrupt

abscondĭtē adv secretly; obscurely; profoundly

abscondĭt·us -a -um adj concealed, secret

abs·condō -condĕre -condī or **-condĭdī -condĭtum** vt to hide; to lose sight of, leave behind; to bury (weapon)

abs·ens -entis pres p of **absum**; adj absent

absentĭ·a -ae f absence

absĭl·ĭō -īre -ĭī or **-ŭī** vi to jump away

absĭmĭl·is -e adj unlike; (with dat) unlike

absinth·ĭum -ĭī or **-ī** n wormwood

abs·is -īdis f vault, arch; orbit (of a star)

ab·sistō -sistĕre -stĭtī vi to withdraw, depart; to cease, lay off

absolūtē adv perfectly

absolūtī·ō -ōnis f acquittal; perfection, completeness

absolūtōrĭ·us -a -um adj of acquittal, granting acquittal

absolūt·us -a -um adj perfect, complete, unqualified

ab·solvō -solvĕre -solvī -solūtum vt to release, set free, detach; to acquit; to finish off; to pay off, discharge

absŏn·us -a -um adj discordant, incongruous, incompatible

absorb·ĕō -ēre -ŭī vt to swallow, devour; to engross

absque prep (with abl) without, apart from, but for; **absque me foret** if it had not been for me

abstēmĭ·us -a -um adj abstemious, temperate, sober

abs·tergĕō -tergĕre -tersī -tersum vt to wipe off, wipe dry; to expel, banish

absterr·ĕō -ēre -ŭī -ĭtum vt to

scare away, deter

abstĭn·ens -entis adj temperate, forbearing; continent, chaste

abstinenter adv with restraint

abstinentĭ·a -ae f abstinence, self-control

abs·tĭnĕō -tĭnēre -tĭnŭī -tentum vt to withhold, keep away; vi to abstain, refrain; (with genit, abl, or with **ab** + abl, with inf, with **quin** or **quominus**) to refrain from

abst·ō -āre vi to stand at a distance, stand aloof

abs·trăhō -trahĕre -traxī -tractum vt to pull away, drag away, remove, detach

abs·trūdō -trūdĕre -trūsī -trūsum vt to push away; to conceal

abstrūs·us -a -um adj hidden, deep, abstruse; reserved

absum abesse afŭī vi to be away, be absent, be distant; (with abl or **ab** + abl) to be removed from, keep aloof from, be disinclined to; (with **ab** + abl) a to be different from, be inconsistent with; b to be free from; c to be unsuitable to, be unfit for; (with dat) to be of no help to

ab·sūmō -sūmĕre -sumpsī -sumptum vt to take away, diminish; to consume, use up, waste; to destroy, ruin

absurdē adv out of tune; absurdly

absurd·us -a -um adj out of tune; absurd, illogical, senseless, silly

Absyrt·us -ī m son of Aeëtes, king of Colchis, killed by his sister Medea when she eloped with Jason

abund·ans -antis adj overflowing, abundant; rich, affluent

abundanter adv copiously

abundantĭ·a -ae f abundance, wealth

abundē adv abundantly, amply

abund·ō -āre vi to overflow; to abound; to be rich

abūsĭ·ō -ōnis f incorrect use (of figure of speech)

abusque prep (with abl) all the way from

ab·ūtor -ūtī -ūsus sum vi (with abl) a to use up; b to misuse, abuse

Abўd·os or **Abўd·us -ī** f town on Hellespont, opposite Sestos

ăc conj (usually used before consonants) and, and also, and moreover, and in particular; (in comparisons) than, as

Acadēmĭ·a -ae f Academy (where Plato taught); Platonic philosophy; Cicero's villa near Puteoli

Acadēmĭc·us -a -um adj Academic; m Academic philosopher; n pl Cicero's treatise on Academic philosophy

acalanth·is -ĭdis f thistlefinch

acanth·us -ī m acanthus

Acarnānĭ·a -ae f district of N.W. Greece

Acast·us -ī m son of Pelias

ac·cēdō -cēdĕre -cessī -cessum *vi* to come near, approach; (with *dat* or **ad** + *acc*) to assent to, agree with, approve of; **b** to come near in resemblance, be like, resemble; **c** to be added to; (with **ad** or **in** + *acc*) to enter upon, undertake; **accedit ut** or **quod** there is the additional fact that

accelĕr·ō -āre *vt* to speed, quicken; *vi* to hurry

ac·cendō -cendĕre -cendī -censum *vt* to light up, set on fire; (fig) to kindle, inflame, excite, awaken

accens·ĕō -ēre -uī -um *vt* to reckon, regard

accens·us -ī *m* attendant, orderly; *m pl* rear-echelon troops

accent·us -ūs *m* accent

acceptĭ·ō -ōnis *f* accepting, receiving

accept·ō -āre *vt* to accept, receive

accept·or -ōris *m* recipient, approver

acceptr·ix -īcis *f* recipient (*female*)

accept·us -a -um *pp* of **accipio**; *adj* welcome, pleasing; *n* receipt; credit side (*in account books*)

accers·ō -ĕre -īvī -ītum *vt* to call, summon; to bring, procure

accessĭ·ō -ōnis *f* approach; passage, entrance; admittance

ac·cīdō -cīdĕre -cīdī -cīsum *vt* to cut down; to impair, weaken; to eat up

ac·cĭdō -cidĕre -cĭdī *vi* to fall; to happen, occur; (with *dat*) to happen to, befall; (with **in** + *acc*) to fall on, fall upon; (with *dat* or **ad** + *acc*) to fall before, fall at (*e.g., someone's feet*); **aures** or **auribus** or **ad aures accidere** to reach or strike the ears

ac·cingō -cingĕre -cinxī -cinctum *vt* to gird; to arm, equip, furnish; to make ready; **accingi** or **se accingere** (with *dat* or with **ad** or **in** + *acc*) to prepare oneself for, to enter upon, to undertake

ac·cĭō -cīre -cīvī -cītum *vt* to call, send for, invite

ac·cĭpĭō -cipĕre -cēpī -ceptum *vt* to take, receive, accept; to admit, let in; to welcome, entertain; to hear, learn, understand; to interpret, explain; to undertake, assume, undergo; to approve of, assent to

accipĭt·er -ris *m* hawk, falcon

accīs·us -a -um *pp* of **accido**; *adj* impaired, ruined; troubled, disordered

accīt·us -ūs *m* summons, call

Acc·ius -iī or **-ī** *m* Roman tragic poet (170-85? B.C.)

acclāmātĭ·ō -ōnis *f* shout, acclamation

acclām·ō -āre *vt* to hail, acclaim; *vi* to shout, cry out; (with *dat*) to shout at

acclār·ō -āre *vt* to make clear, make known

acclīnāt·us -a -um *adj* prostrate; sloping; (with *dat*) sloping toward

acclīn·is -e *adj* (with *dat*) a leaning on or against; **b** inclined toward, disposed to

acclīn·ō -āre *vt* (with *dat* or **in** + *acc*) to lean or rest (*something*) against; **se acclinare** (with **ad** + *acc*) (fig) to be inclined toward

acclīv·is -e *adj* sloping upwards, uphill, steep

acclīvit·ās -ātis *f* slope, ascent

accŏl·a -ae *m* neighbor

ac·cŏlō -colĕre -coluī -cultum *vt* to dwell near

accommodātē *adv* suitably, fittingly

accommodātĭ·ō -ōnis *f* adjustment, compliance, accommodation

accommŏdāt·us -a -um *adj* (with *dat* or **ad** + *acc*) fit for, adapted to, suitable to

accommŏd·ō -āre *vt* (with *dat* or **ad** + *acc*) to adjust or adapt or apply (*something*) to; **se accommodare** (with **ad** + *acc*) to apply or devote oneself to

accommŏd·us -a -um *adj* fit, suitable; (with *dat*) fit for, adapted to, suitable to

ac·crēdō -crēdĕre -crēdĭdī -crēdĭtum *vi* (with *dat*) to believe, give credence to

ac·crēscō -crēscĕre -crēvī -crētum *vi* to grow larger, increase, be added

accrētĭ·ō -ōnis *f* increase

accubitĭ·ō -ōnis *f* reclining at table

accūb·ō -āre *vi* to lie nearby; to recline at table; (with *dat*) to lie near

accūd·ō -ĕre *vt* to coin

ac·cumbō -cumbĕre -cubuī -cubĭtum *vi* to take one's place at table

accumulātē *adv* abundantly

accumulāt·or -ōris *m* hoarder

accumŭl·ō -āre *vt* to heap up, amass; to load, overwhelm

accūrātē *adv* carefully, accurately, exactly

accūrātĭ·ō -ōnis *f* carefulness, accuracy

accūrāt·us -a -um *adj* careful, accurate, exact, studied

accūr·ō -āre *vt* to take care of, attend to

ac·currō -currĕre -currī -cursum *vi* to run up; (with **ad** or **in** + *acc*) to run to

accurs·us -ūs *m* running, concourse

accūsābĭl·is -e *adj* blameworthy

accūsātĭ·ō -ōnis *f* accusation; indictment, bill of indictment

accūsātīv·us -a -um *adj & m* accusative

accūsāt·or -ōris *m* accuser, prosecutor; informer

accūsātōrĭē *adv* like an accuser or prosecutor

accūsātōrĭ·us -a -um *adj* accuser's, prosecutor's

accūsātr·ix -īcis *f* accuser (*female*)

accūsĭt·ō -āre *vt* to keep on accusing

accūs·ō -āre vt to accuse, prosecute; to reproach, blame

ac·er -ēris n maple tree

ăc·er -ris -re adj sharp, pointed; pungent, stinging, penetrating, piercing, shrill; sagacious, keen, judicious; energetic, enthusiastic, ardent, brave; passionate, fierce, violent; severe, vigorous

acerbē adv bitterly, harshly

acerbĭt·ās -ātis f bitterness, harshness, sharpness, sourness; distress

acerb·ō -āre vt to embitter, aggravate

acerb·us -a -um adj bitter, harsh, sour; unripe; severe; morose, rough; untimely, premature; painful, troublesome; sad

acern·us -a -um adj maple

acerr·a -ae f incense box

acersecŏm·ēs -ae m young man, youth

acervātim adv in heaps; briefly

acerv·ō -āre vt to heap or pile up

acerv·us -ī m heap, pile; multitude; (in logic) sorites

acescō acescĕre acŭī vi to turn sour

Acest·ēs -ae m mythical king of Sicily

acētābŭl·um -ī n vinegar bottle

acēt·um -ī n sour wine, vinegar; (fig) pungent wit, shrewdness

Achaemĕn·ēs -is m first king of Persia, grandfather of Cyrus

Achaemenĭ·us -a -um adj Persian

Achae·us -a -um adj & m Achaean; Greek

Achai·a or **Achāi·a -ae** f province in northern part of the Peloponnesus on Gulf of Corinth; Greece

Achāĭc·us -a -um adj & m Achaean; Greek

Achāt·ēs -ae m companion of Aeneas; river in Sicily

Achelō·us -ī m river in N.W. Greece; river god

Achĕr·ōn -ontis or **Achĕr·os -ī** m river in Hades

Achill·ēs -is m Greek warrior, son of Peleus and Thetis

Achille·us -a -um adj of Achilles

Achillĭd·ēs -ae m descendant of Achilles

Achīv·us -a -um adj Achaean; Greek

Acīdali·a -ae f Venus

acĭd·us -a -um adj sour, tart; (of sound) harsh, shrill; sharp, keen, pungent; unpleasant, disagreeable

aci·ēs -ēī f sharpness, sharp edge; keenness of vision, glance; eyesight, eye, pupil; mental power; battle line, battle array, battlefield, battle; debate

acīnăc·ēs -is m scimitar

acĭn·um -ī n or **acĭn·us -ī** m berry, grape; seed in berry

acipens·er -ēris or **acipens·is -is** m sturgeon

Ăc·is -ĭdis m son of Faunus, loved by Galatea, changed into a river

acl·ys -ўdis f small javelin

aconīt·um -ī n wolf's-bane; strong poison

ac·or -ōris m sour taste, sourness

acqui·escō -escĕre -ēvī -ētum vi to become quiet; to rest; to die; (with abl, dat, or with **in** + abl) to find rest in, acquiesce in, be content with, find pleasure in, rejoice in

ac·quīrō -quīrĕre -quīsīvī -quīsītum vt to acquire, obtain, gain, win

Acrăg·ās -antis m town on S.W. coast of Sicily

acrēdŭl·a -ae f bird (perhaps owl or nightingale)

ācrĭcŭl·us -a -um adj irritable, peevish

ācrimōnĭ·a -ae f sharpness, pungency; irritation; energy

Acrisiōnĭăd·ēs -ae m descendant of Acrisius; Perseus

Ācris·ius -ĭī or **-ī** m king of Argos, father of Danaë

ācrĭter adv sharply, keenly, vehemently, severely

acroām·a -ātis n entertainment; entertainer

Acrocerauni·a -ōrum n pl promontory on the Adriatic Sea in Epirus

Acrocorinth·us -ī f citadel of Corinth

act·a -ae f seashore, beach

act·a -ōrum n pl deeds, actions; public acts; proceedings of the senate; records, minutes; journal

Actae·ōn -ōnis m grandson of Cadmus, changed into a stag

Actae·us -a -um adj Attic, Athenian

actĭ·ō -ōnis f doing, performance, action, activity; proceedings; (law) suit, process, action, permission for a suit; delivery, gesticulation; plot, action (of play)

actĭt·ō -āre vt to plead (cases) often; to perform (plays) often

Act·ium -ĭī or **-ī** n promontory in Epirus (where Octavian defeated Antony and Cleopatra in 31 B.C.)

actīv·us -a -um adj (gram) active; practical (opposite of contemplative)

act·or -ōris m doer, performer; (law) plaintiff, pleader, advocate; agent, manager; player, actor; **actor summarum** cashier, accountant

Act·or -ōris m companion of Aeneas

actuārĭŏl·um -ī n small barge

actuārĭ·us -a -um adj swift; m stenographer; f swift ship; n swift ship

actuōsē adv energetically

actuōs·us -a -um adj energetic, very active

actus pp of **ago**

act·us -ūs m act, performance; driving, motion, impulse; right of way; public business; presentation, delivery, gesture, recital; act (of play)

actūtum adv instantly, immediately

acŭl·a -ae f rivulet

aculeat·us -a -um *adj* prickly; (fig) stinging, sharp, subtle

aculē·us -ī *m* barb, sting; point; sarcasm

acūm·en -inis *n* point, sharpness; sting (*of insect*); pungency; shrewdness, ingenuity, cunning

acūō acuēre acuī acūtum *vt* to make sharp or pointed, to whet; to exercise; to stimulate; to give an edge to, enhance; to tease

ac·us -ūs *f* needle, pin; **acu rem tangere** to hit the nail on the head

acūtē *adv* acutely, sharply, keenly

acūtŭl·us -a -um *adj* somewhat sharp, rather subtle

acūt·us -a -um *pp* of **acuo**; *adj* sharp, pointed; shrill; intelligent

ad *prep* (with *acc*) (of space) to, towards, near, at; (of time) toward, about, until, at, on, by; (with numbers) about, almost, for the purpose of, to; according to, in consequence of; with respect to; compared with

adactĭ·ō -ōnis *f* enforcing

adactus *pp* of **adigo**

adact·us -ūs *m* bringing together; snapping (*of jaws*)

adaequē *adv* equally

adaequ·ō -āre *vt* to make level; to equal, match; (fig) to put on the same level; *vi* to be on the same level, be equal; (with *dat*) to be level with

adamantē·us -a -um *adj* made of steel

adamantĭn·us -a -um *adj* hard as steel, adamantine

adăm·ās -antis *m* adamant; steel; diamond

adambŭl·ō -āre *vi* (with **ad** + *acc*) to walk about near

adăm·ō -āre *vt* to fall in love with

ad·aperĭō -aperīre -aperŭī -apertum *vt* to uncover, throw open

adăqu·ō -āre *vt* to water; *vi* to fetch water

adauct·us -ūs *m* growth

ad·augĕō -augēre -auxī -auctum *vt* to increase, aggravate

adaugesc·ō -ĕre *vi* to begin to grow

ad·bĭbō -bĭbēre -bĭbī -bĭbitum *vt* to drink in; to listen attentively to

adbīt·ō -ĕre *vi* to come near, approach

adc- = **acc-**

ad·dēcet -decēre *v impers* it becomes

addens·ĕō -ēre or **addens·ō -āre** *vt* to close (*ranks*)

ad·dīcō -dīcĕre -dixī -dictum *vt* to assign; to doom; to dedicate, devote; *vi* (in augury) to be favorable

ad·discō -discĕre -didĭcī *vt* to learn in addition

additāment·um -ī *n* addition

ad·dō -dĕre -dĭdī -dĭtum *vt* to add, increase; to impart, bestow

ad·docĕō -docēre -docŭī -doctum *vt* to teach in addition

addubĭt·ō -āre *vt* to call into doubt; *vi* to begin to feel doubt; to hesitate

ad·dūcō -dūcĕre -duxī -ductum *vt* to lead up, bring up; to draw together, wrinkle; to prompt, induce, persuade, move

adduct·us -a -um *adj* drawn tight, strained; narrow, tight (*place*); strict, serious, stern (*character*)

ad·edō -esse -ēdī -ēsum *vt* to nibble at; to eat up, consume; to waste

ademptĭ·ō -ōnis *f* taking away

ad·eō -īre -iī or **-īvī -ĭtum** *vt* to approach; to attack; to consult, apply to; to visit; to undertake, set about, undergo; *vi* to go up, come up; (with **ad** + *acc*) **a** to go to, approach; **b** to enter upon, undertake, set about, submit to

adĕō *adv* to such a degree, so; (following pronouns and numerals, to give emphasis) precisely, exactly, quite, just, chiefly; (at the beginning of sentence) thus far, to such an extent; even, indeed, truly

ad·eps -ĭpis *m* or *f* fat; corpulence

adeptĭ·ō -ōnis *f* obtaining, attainment

adeptus *pp* of **adipiscor**

adequĭt·ō -āre *vi* to ride up; (with *dat* or **ad** + *acc*) to ride up to, ride towards

adesse *inf* of **adedo** or of **adsum**

adēsur·ĭō -īre -īvī *vi* to be very hungry

adēsus *pp* of **adedo**

ad·haerĕō -haerēre -haesī -haesum *vi* (with *dat* or *abl* or with **in** + *abl*) **a** to cling to, stick to; **b** to keep close to, hang on to

ad·haerescō -haerescĕre -haesī -haesum *vi* to stick; to falter; (with *dat* or *abl*, with **ad** + *acc*, or with **in** + *abl*) **a** to stick to, cling to; **b** to be devoted to; **c** to correspond to, accord with

adhaesĭ·ō -ōnis *f* clinging, adhesion

adhaes·us -ūs *m* adhering, adherence

adhĭb·ĕō -ēre -ŭī -ĭtum *vt* to bring, put, add; to summon, invite; to apply; to use, employ; to consult; to handle, treat

adhinn·ĭō -īre -iī or **-īvī -ītum** *vt* to whinny after, lust after; *vi* (with *dat* or with **ad** or **in** + *acc*) **a** to whinny after, lust after, crave; **b** to whinny in delight at

adhortātĭ·ō -ōnis *f* exhortation, encouragement

adhortāt·or -ōris *m* cheerer, supporter

adhort·or -ārī -ātus sum *vt* to cheer on, encourage

adhūc *adv* thus far, hitherto; till now; as yet, still; besides, in addition, moreover

ad·ĭgō -ĭgĕre -ēgī -actum *vt* to drive; to drive home, thrust; to compel; to inflict; to bind (*by oath*)

ad·ĭmō -ĭmĕre -ēmī -emptum *vt* to withdraw, take away; to carry off

adipāt·us -a -um *adj* fatty, greasy; gross, bombastic; *n* pastry (*made in fat*)

ad·ipiscor -ipiscī -eptus sum *vt* to reach, get, obtain, win

aditiāl·is -e *adj* inaugural

aditi·ō -ōnis *f* approach

adit·us -ūs *m* approach, access; entrance; admittance, audience, interview; beginning, commencement; chance, opportunity

adjac·eō -ēre -uī *vt* to adjoin; *vi* (with *dat* or **ad** + *acc*) **a** to lie near or at; **b** to border on, be contiguous with

adjectī·ō -ōnis *f* addition, annexation

adjectīv·us -a -um *adj* adjectival

ad·jiciō -jicĕre -jēcī -jectum *vt* to add, increase; (with *dat* or **ad** + *acc*) **a** to throw (*weapon*) at; **b** to add (*something*) to; **c** to turn or direct (*eyes, mind, etc.*) to; (with **in** + *acc*) to hurl (*weapon*) at

adjūdic·ō -āre *vt* to adjudge, award; to ascribe, assign

adjūment·um -ī *n* aid, help, support

adjunct·a -ōrum *n pl* accessory circumstances

adjunctī·ō -ōnis *f* joining, union; addition; (rhet) repetition

ad·jungō -jungĕre -junxī -junctum *vt* (with *dat*) to yoke or harness (*animal*) to; (with *dat* or **ad** + *acc*) **a** to add, attach, join (*something*) to; **b** to apply, direct (*mind, attention, etc.*) to

adjūr·ō -āre *vt* to swear to, confirm by oath; *vi* to swear

adjūtābil·is -e *adj* helpful

adjūt·ō -āre *vt* to help, assist; *vi* (with *dat*) to be of assistance to

adjūt·or -ōris *m* helper, assistant, promoter; aide, adjutant, deputy, secretary; supporting actor

adjūtōr·ium -iī *or* **-ī** *n* help, support

adjūtr·ix -īcis *f* helper, assistant (*female*)

ad·jūvō -juvāre -jūvī -jūtum *vt* to help, encourage, sustain; *vi* to be of use, be profitable

adl- = all-

admātūr·ō -āre *vt* to bring to maturity; to hasten, expedite

ad·mētior -mētīrī -mensus sum *vt* to measure out

Admēt·us -ī *m* king of Pherae in Thessaly, husband of Alcestis

admigr·ō -āre *vi* (with **ad** + *acc*) **a** to go to; **b** to be added to

adminicul·ō -āre *or* **adminicul·or -ārī -ātus sum** *vt* to prop, support

adminicul·um -ī *n* prop, support, stake, pole; rudder; aid; assistant

administ·er -rī *m* assistant, attendant

administr·a -ae *f* assistant, attendant (*female*)

administrātī·ō -ōnis *f* help, aid; administration, management, government

administrāt·or -ōris *m* administrator, manager, director

administr·ō -āre *vt* to administer, manage, direct

admīrābil·is -e *adj* admirable, wonderful; strange, surprising, paradoxical

admīrābilit·ās -ātis *f* admiration, wonder, wonderfulness

admīrābilĭter *adv* admirably; astonishingly, paradoxically

admīrātī·ō -ōnis *f* admiration, wonder, surprise

admīrāt·or -ōris *m* admirer

admīr·or -ārī -ātus sum *vt* to admire, wonder at, be surprised at

ad·misceō -miscēre -miscuī -mixtum *vt* to mix, add; to involve, implicate; to join, mingle; (with *dat*, with **ad** *or* **in** + *acc*, *or* with **cum** + *abl*) to add (*something*) to, to mix or mix up (*something*) with; **se admiscere** to get involved, to meddle

admissār·ius -iī *or* **-ī** *m* stallion, stud; lecherer

admissi·ō -ōnis *f* interview, audience

admiss·um -ī *n* crime

ad·mittō -mittĕre -mīsī -missum *vt* to let in, admit; to let go, let loose; to put at a gallop; to allow; to commit (*crime*)

admixtī·ō -ōnis *f* admixture

admixtus *pp* of **admisceo**

admoderātē *adv* appropriately

admŏdum *adv* to the limit; very, quite, fully; (with *numbers*) just about; (with *negatives*) at all; (in *answers*) quite so, yes

admoen·iō -īre *vt* to besiege, blockade

admōl·ior -īrī -ītus sum *vt* to bring up, move up; **admoliri** (with *inf*) to strive to, struggle to

admon·eō -ēre -uī -itum *vt* to admonish, remind, suggest; to warn; to urge

admonitī·ō -ōnis *f* admonition, reminder, suggestion

admonit·or -ōris *m* admonisher, reminder

admonitr·ix -īcis *f* admonisher, reminder (*female*)

admonit·um -ī *n* admonition

admonit·us -ūs *m* suggestion; reproof

ad·mordĕō -mordēre -momordī -morsum *vt* to bite at, gnaw at; (fig) to fleece

admōtī·ō -ōnis *f* moving, movement

ad·moveō -movēre -mōvī -mōtum *vt* to move up, bring up, bring near; to lead on, conduct; (with *dat* or **ad** + *acc*) **a** to move or bring (*something*) to; **b** to apply (*something*) to; **c** to direct (*attention, etc.*) to; *vi* to draw near, approach

admūg·iō -īre *vi* (with *dat*) to low to, bellow to

admurmurātī·ō -ōnis *f* murmuring

admurmur·ō -āre *vi* to murmur (in *approval or disapproval*)

admutil·ō -āre *vt* to clip close; (fig) to clip, cheat

adn- = ann-

ad·oleō -olēre -oluī -ultum vt to magnify; to honor, worship; to sacrifice, burn; to pile up (altars); to sprinkle (altars)

adol·eō -ēre vi to smell

adolesc·ens -entis m young man; f young woman

adol·escō -escēre -ēvī vi to grow, grow up; to be kindled, burn

Adōn·is -is or -idis m son of Cinyras, king of Cyprus, loved by Venus

adoper·iō -īre -uī -tum vt to cover up; to close

adopīn·or -ārī vi to suppose, conjecture

adoptātī·ō -ōnis f adopting (of child)

adoptī·ō -ōnis f adoption (of child)

adoptiv·us -a -um adj adoptive, by adoption

adopt·ō -āre vt to adopt; to select; to graft (plants)

ad·or -ōris or -ōris n spelt

adōrātī·ō -ōnis f adoration, worship

adōrě·a -ae f reward for valor; praise, glory

adōrě·us -a -um adj of spelt

ad·orior -orīrī -ortus sum vt to rise up against, attack, assault; to attempt; to undertake

adorn·ō -āre vt to equip, get ready; to adorn

adōr·ō -āre vt to implore, entreat; to ask for; to adore, worship

adp- = app-

ad·rādō -rādēre -rāsī -rāsum vt to scrape, shave; to lop off

Adrast·us -ī m king of Argos, father-in-law of Tydeus and Polynices

adr- = arr-

adsc- = asc-

adse- = ass-

adsi- = assi-

adso- = asso-

adsp- = asp-

adst- = ast-

adsu- = assu-

ad·sum -esse -fuī vi to be near, be present; to appear; to be at hand; to be of assistance; (with dat) to share in, participate in, stand by, assist; animo or animis adesse to pay attention; to cheer up

adt- = att-

adūlātī·ō -ōnis f fawning, cringing, servility, flattery

adūlāt·or -ōris m flatterer

adūlātōrī·us -a -um adj flattering

adulesc·ens -entis adj young

adulesc·ens -entis m young man; f young woman

adulescenti·a -ae f youth, young people

adulescentŭl·a -ae f little girl

adulescentŭl·us -ī m young man

adūl·ō -āre vi to fawn

adūl·or -ārī -ātus sum vt to flatter (in a servile manner); vi (with dat) to kowtow to

adult·er -ĕra -ĕrum adj adulterous,

unchaste; m adulterer; f adulteress

adulterīn·us -a -um adj adulterous; forged, counterfeit

adulter·ium -iī or -ī n adultery; adulteration

adultěr·ō -āre vt to defile, corrupt; to falsify; vi to commit adultery

adult·us -a -um adj grown, mature, adult

adumbrātim adv in outline

adumbrātī·ō -ōnis f sketch, outline

adumbrāt·us -a -um adj shadowy, sketchy, unreal, fictitious, dim, imperfect

adumbr·ō -āre vt to shade, overshadow; to sketch; to represent

aduncit·ās -ātis f curvature

adunc·us -a -um adj curved, hooked

adurg·ĕō -ēre vt to pursue closely

ad·ūrō -ūrēre -ussī -ustum vt to set on fire; to scorch; to nip, freeze; (fig) to inflame

adusque adv entirely, throughout

adusque prep (with acc) all the way to, as far as, right up to

adustī·ō -ōnis f burning

adust·us -a -um pp of aduro; adj scorched; sunburned

advecticī·us -a -um adj imported, foreign

advectī·ō -ōnis f transportation

advect·ō -āre vt to keep on conveying

advect·us -ūs m conveyance

ad·vehō -vehĕre -vexī -vectum vt to carry, convey, transport; (equo) advehi (with ad or in + acc) to ride to; (nave) advehi (with ad + acc) to sail to

advēl·ō -āre vt to veil; to wreathe

advěn·a -ae m or f stranger, foreigner

ad·veniō -venīre -vēnī -ventum vi to arrive; (with ad or in + acc or with acc of limit of motion) to arrive at, come to, reach

adventicī·us -a -um adj foreign, strange, extraneous; unusual, extraordinary; unearned

advent·ō -āre vi to keep coming closer, approach

advent·or -ōris m visitor, guest; customer

advent·us -ūs m arrival, approach

adversārī·us -a -um adj (with dat) turned towards, opposed to, opposite; m & f adversary, enemy, rival; n pl journal, notebook, memoranda; assertions (of opponent)

adversātr·ix -īcis f opponent (female)

adversī·ō -ōnis f directing, direction

advers·ō -āre vt to direct (attention)

advers·or -ārī -ātus sum vi (with dat) to oppose, resist

adversum or adversus adv in the opposite direction; prep (with acc) facing, opposite, towards; compared with, contrary to

advers·us -a -um adj opposite, in front; facing; unfavorable, hostile;

adverso flumine upstream; *n* misfortune; opposite

ad·vertō or **ad·vortō -vertĕre -vertī -versum** *vt* (with *dat* or **in** + *acc*) **a** to turn or direct (*something*) to; **b** to steer (*ship*) to; **animum** or **animos advertere** to pay attention; **animum** or **animos advertere** (with *dat* or **ad** + *acc*) to give attention to, attend to, heed, observe; *vi* to land; (with **in** + *acc*) to punish

advesper·ascit -ascĕre -āvit *v impers* evening approaches

advigil·ō -āre *vi* to be vigilant, keep watch; (with *dat*) to keep watch over, bestow attention on; (with *pro* + *abl*) to watch out for

advocātī·ō -ōnis *f* legal assistance; legal counsel; the bar; period of time allowed to procure legal assistance; delay, adjournment

advocăt·us -ī *m* witness; advocate, counsel; helper, friend

advŏc·ō -āre *vt* to call, summon; to consult

advŏl·ō -āre *vi* (with *dat* or with **ad** or **in** + *acc*) **a** to fly to; **b** to dash to

ad·volvō -volvĕre -volvī -volūtum *vt* (with *dat* or **ad** + *acc*) to roll (*something*) to or toward; **advolvi** or **se advolvere genua** or **genibus** (with *genit*) to fall prostrate before

advor- = adver-

adȳt·um -ī *n* sanctuary; tomb

Aeacĭd·ēs -ae *m* descendant of Aeacus

Aeāc·us -ī *m* king of Aegina, father of Peleus, Telamon, and Phocus, and judge of the dead

aed·ēs or **aed·is -is** *f* shrine, temple; building; *f pl* rooms, apartments; house

aedicŭl·a -ae *f* chapel, shrine; small room, closet; small house; *f pl* small house

aedificātī·ō -ōnis *f* constructing, building; structure, building

aedificātiuncŭl·a -ae *f* tiny building

aedificăt·or -ōris *m* builder, architect

aedific·ĭum -iī or **-ī** *n* building

aedific·ō -āre *vt* to build, construct, establish

aedilĭci·us -a -um *adj* aedile's; *m* ex-aedile

aedīl·is -is *m* aedile

aedīlĭt·ās -ātis *f* aedileship

aedis see **aedēs**

aedĭtŭ·us or **aeditĭm·us** or **aeditŭm·us -ī** *m* temple attendant, sacristan

Aeēt·ēs -ae *m* king of Colchis and father of Medea

Aegae·us -a -um *adj* Aegean; *n* Aegean Sea

Aegăt·ēs -um *f pl* three islands W. of Sicily

aeg·er -ra -rum *adj* sick, infirm, unsound; dejected; painful

Aeg·eus -ĕī *m* king of Athens, father of Theseus

Aegĭd·ēs -ae *m* Theseus

Aegīn·a -ae *f* island off Attica; mother of Aeacus

aeg·is -ĭdis *f* shield of Minerva and of Jupiter; aegis, protection

Aegisth·us -ī *m* son of Thyestes, seducer of Clytemnestra, and murderer of Agamemnon

aegrē *adv* painfully; with difficulty; reluctantly; hardly, scarcely

aegr·ĕō -ēre *vi* to be sick

aegr·escō -escĕre *vi* to become sick; to be aggravated, get worse; to be troubled

aegrimōni·a -ae *f* sorrow, anxiety, trouble

aegritūd·ō -ĭnis *f* sickness; sorrow

aegr·or -ōris *m* illness

aegrŏtātĭ·ō -ōnis *f* sickness, disease

aegrŏt·ō -āre *vi* to be sick; to languish

aegrŏt·us -a -um *adj* sick

Aegypt·us -ī *f* Egypt; *m* mythical king of Egypt, whose 50 sons married the 50 daughters of his brother Danaüs

aelĭn·os -ī *m* dirge

aemŭl·a -ae *f* rival (*female*)

aemulātĭ·ō -ōnis *f* emulation, rivalry

aemulāt·or -ōris *m* rival, imitator

aemulāt·us -ūs *m* rivalry

aemŭl·or -ārī -ātus sum *vt* to emulate, rival; *vi* (with *dat*) to be envious of, be jealous of

aemŭl·us -a -um *adj* (with *genit* or *dat*) emulous of, envious of, jealous of, striving after; *m* rival

Aeneăd·ēs -ae *m* descendant of Aeneas; Trojan; Roman; Augustus

Aenē·ās -ae *m* son of Venus and Anchises, and hero of Virgil's epic

Aenē·is -ĭdis or **-ĭdos** *f* Aeneid (*Virgil's epic*)

aēnĕ·us or **ahēnĕ·us -a -um** *adj* bronze

aenigm·a -ătis *n* riddle, mystery

aēnĭp·ēs -ĕdis *adj* bronze-footed

aēn·us or **ahēn·us -a -um** *adj* bronze; (fig) firm, invincible; *n* cauldron

Aeoli·a -ae *f* realm of Aeolus, king of winds; group of islands near Sicily

Aeolĭ·ī -ōrum or **Aeŏl·ēs -um** *m pl* Aeolians (*inhabitants of N.W. Asia Minor*)

Aeŏl·is -ĭdis *f* Aeolia, N.W. part of Asia Minor

Aeŏl·us -ī *m* god of winds

aequābĭl·is -e *adj* equal, alike; consistent, uniform; fair, impartial

aequābĭlĭt·ās -ātis *f* equality; uniformity; impartiality

aequābĭlĭter *adv* equally; uniformly

aequaev·us -a -um *adj* of the same age

aequāl·is -e *adj* equal; even, level; of the same age, contemporary aequāl·is -is *m* or *f* comrade; contemporary

aequālit·ās -ātis *f* equality; evenness; smoothness

aequāliter *adv* equally; evenly

aequanimit·ās -ātis *f* calmness, patience; kindness; impartiality

aequāti·ō -ōnis *f* equal distribution; aequatio bonorum communism

aequē *adv* equally; justly, fairly; aeque . . . ac or atque or et just as, as much as, as; aeque . . . ac si just as if; aeque . . . quam as . . . as, in the same way as

Aequ·ī -ōrum *m pl* people of central Italy

aequilibrit·ās -ātis *f* balance

aequilibr·ium -iī or -ī *n* horizontal position; equilibrium

aequinoctiāl·is -e *adj* equinoctial

aequinoct·ium -iī or -ī *n* equinox

aequiperābil·is -e *adj* (with *dat* or cum + *abl*) comparable to

aequiper·ō or aequipăr·ō -āre *vt* to compare; to equal, rival, come up to; (with *dat*, with ad+ *acc*, or cum + *abl*) to compare (*something*) to; *vi* (with *dat*) a to become equal to, be equal to; b to attain to

aequit·ās -ātis *f* evenness, conformity, symmetry, equity; calmness

aequ·or -ōris *n* level surface; sea, ocean

aequorē·us -a -um *adj* of the sea, marine

aequ·us -a -um *adj* level, even, flat; favorable, friendly; fair, just; calm; *n* level, plain; justice, fairness

ā·ēr -ēris *m* air, atmosphere, sky; weather; mist

aerāment·um -ī *n* bronze vessel or utensil

aerāri·us -a -um *adj* copper, bronze; of mines; financial, fiscal; *m* coppersmith; low-class Roman citizen; *f* mine; smelting furnace; *n* treasury

aerāt·us -a -um *adj* bronze; rich

āĕrĕ·us -a -um *adj* aerial, airy, lofty, high

aerĕ·us -a -um *adj* bronze

aerif·er -ĕra -ĕrum *adj* carrying cymbals

aerip·ēs -ĕdis *adj* bronze-footed

āĕri·us -a -um *adj* aerial, airy, lofty, high

Aěrŏp·ē -ēs or Āĕrŏp·a -ae *f* wife of Atreus, mother of Agamemnon and Menelaus

aerūginōs·us -a -um *adj* rusty

aerūg·ō -īnis *f* copper rust, verdigris; corroding passion, envy, greed

aerumn·a -ae *f* need, want, trouble, hardship, calamity

aerumnābil·is -e *adj* full of troubles, calamitous

aerumnōs·us -a -um *adj* full of troubles, wretched, distressed

aes aeris *n* crude metal, copper, bronze; bronze object; armor, statue, utensil; trumpet; money; payment; reward; *n pl* wages, soldier's pay; aes alienum debt

Aeschýl·us -ī *m* Athenian tragic poet (525-456 B.C.)

Aesculāp·ius -iī or -ī *m* god of medicine, son of Apollo and Coronis

aesculēt·um -ī *n* oak forest

aesculē·us -a -um *adj* oak

aescŭl·us -ī *f* Italian oak

Aes·ōn -ōnis *m* Thessalian prince, father of Jason, restored to youth by Medea

aest·ās -ātis *f* summer; summer heat

aestif·er -ĕra -ĕrum *adj* heatbearing, sultry

aestimābil·is -e *adj* valuable

aestimāti·ō -ōnis *f* appraisal, assessment; esteem

aestimāt·or -ōris *m* appraiser

aestim·ō -āre *vt* to appraise, rate, value, estimate; to esteem, judge, hold

aestīv·a -ōrum *n pl* summer camp; campaign season, campaign; summer pastures

aestīv·ō -āre *vi* to pass the summer

aestīv·us -a -um *adj* summer

aestuār·ium -iī or -ī *n* tidal waters, lagoon, estuary, marsh; air shaft

aestŭ·ō -āre *vi* to boil, seethe; to burn, glow; to undulate, swell, be tossed, heave; to waver, hesitate; to be excited

aestuōsē *adv* hotly, impetuously

aestuōs·us -a -um *adj* sultry; billowy

aest·us -ūs *m* agitation; glow, heat, sultriness; surge, billows, ebb and flow; tide; raging, seething, passion; uncertainty, irresolution

aet·ās -ātis *f* lifetime, age, generation

aetātŭl·a -ae *f* tender age

aeternit·ās -ātis *f* eternity, immortality

aetern·ō -āre *vt* to perpetuate, immortalize

aeternum *adv* forever; constantly, perpetually

aetern·us -a -um *adj* eternal, everlasting, immortal, imperishable

aeth·ēr -ēris or -ĕros *m* upper air, sky, heaven

aetheri·us -a -um *adj* ethereal, heavenly, celestial; of the upper world

Aethi·ops -ŏpis *m* Ethiopian; Negro; blockhead

aethr·a -ae *f* ether, pure air, serene sky; air, sky, heavens

Aetn·a -ae or Aetn·ē -ēs *f* volcano in Sicily

Aetōli·a -ae *f* district in N. Greece

aevit·ās -ātis *f* age, lifetime

aev·um -ī *n* or aev·us -ī *m* age, lifetime, life; time, period; generation; eternity

Āf·er -ra -rum *adj & m* African

affābil·is -e *adj* affable, courteous, kind

affābilit·ās -ātis *f* affability, courtesy

affăbrē *adv* in a workmanlike manner, cunningly

affătim *adv* sufficiently, enough, satisfactorily

affāt·us -ūs *m* address, discourse

affectātī·ō -ōnis *f* eager desire; affectation, conceit

affectāt·or -ōris *m* affected person

affectāt·us -a -um *adj* choice, select; farfetched, studied

affectī·ō -ōnis *f* disposition, state of mind; inclination, partiality; affection, love

affect·ō -āre *vt* to grasp, seize; to pursue, strive after, aim at; to try to win over; to affect, feign

affect·us -a -um *adj* furnished, provided, gifted; weakened, impaired, sick; affected, moved, touched

affect·us -ūs *m* state, disposition, mood; feeling, passion, emotion; affection

affĕrō afferre attŭlī allātum *vt* to bring, carry, convey; to report, announce; to introduce, apply, employ, exert, exercise; to produce, cause, occasion, impart; to allege, assign; to contribute, help; **manus afferre** (with *dat*) to lay hands on, attack, do violence to, rob, plunder

af·ficiō -ficere -fēcī -fectum *vt* to treat, handle, manage; to affect, move, influence, impress; to attack, afflict; to impair, weaken; (*abl* and verb may be rendered by the verb corresponding to the *abl*): **cruce afficere** to crucify; **honoribus afficere** to honor; **supplicio afficere** to punish

af·fīgō -fīgĕre -fixī -fixum *vt* (with *dat* or *ad* + *acc*) to fasten, attach, affix, annex (*something*) to; (with *dat*) to impress (*something*) upon (*mind*)

af·fingō -fingĕre -finxī -fictum *vt* to form, fashion besides; to make up, invent, (with *dat*) to attach, affix, add, join, contribute (*something*) to

affīn·is -e *adj* adjoining, neighboring; related by marriage; (with *dat* or *ad* + *acc*) taking part in, privy to, associated with

affīn·is -is *m* or *f* in-law

affīnĭt·ās -ātis *f* relationship by marriage

affirmātē *adv* with solemn assurance, positively, certainly

affirmātĭ·ō -ōnis *f* affirmation, assertion, declaration

affirm·ō -āre *vt* to strengthen; to confirm, encourage; to aver, assert

afflāt·us -ūs *m* breeze, blast, breath; inspiration

aflĭ·eō -ēre *vi* to weep

afflictātĭ·ō -ōnis *f* physical pain, torture

afflictō -āre *vt* to shatter, damage, harass, injure; to trouble, vex, distress, torment

afflict·or -ōris *m* destroyer, subverter

afflict·us -a -um *adj* damaged, shattered; cast down, downhearted; vile

af·flīgō -flīgĕre -flixī -flictum *vt* to knock, strike down; (fig) to crush

afflĭ·ō -āre *vt* (with *dat*) **a** to breathe (*something*) upon; **b** to impart (*something*) to; *vi* (with *dat*) **a** to breathe upon; **b** to be favorable to

afflŭ·ens -entis *adj* flowing; rich, affluent; abounding, numerous

afflŭenter *adv* lavishly, abundantly

afflŭentĭ·a -ae *f* abundance

af·flŭō -flŭĕre -fluxī -fluxum *vi* (with *dat* or *ad* + *acc*) **a** to flow to, flow towards, glide by; **b** to hasten to, flock to; (with *abl*) to abound in

af·for -fārī -fātus sum *vt* to address, accost, pray to

afföre = **adfutūrus esse**

affōrem -ō -āre = **adessem**

afförmīd·ō -āre *vi* to be afraid

af·fulgĕō -fulgēre -fulsī *vi* to shine, beam, dawn, appear; (with *dat*) to shine on

af·fundō -fundĕre -fūdī -fūsum *vt* (with *dat*) **a** to pour, sprinkle, scatter (*something*) on; **b** to send or despatch (*someone*) to; **affundī** or **se affundere** (with *dat*) to throw oneself at, prostrate oneself before

Afric·us -a -um *adj* African; *m* S.W. Wind; *f* originally the district of Carthage, made a Roman province in 146 B.C.; continent of Africa

Agamemn·ōn -ŏnis *m* king of Mycenae, son of Atreus and of Aërope, brother of Menelaus, and commander in chief of Greek forces at Troy

Aganipp·ē -ēs *f* fountain on Mount Helicon, sacred to the Muses

agās·ō -ōnis *m* driver, groom; lackey

agĕdum *interj* come on!; well!

agell·us -ī *m* little field, plot

agēm·a -ătis *n* corps or division (*of soldiers*)

Agēn·or -ŏris *m* son of Belus, king of Phoenicia, father of Cadmus and Europa, and ancestor of Dido

Agēnorĭd·ēs -ae *m* descendant of Agenor; Cadmus; Perseus

ag·er -rī *m* field, ground, arable land, farm, estate; territory, district

agg·er -ĕris *m* fill dirt, rubbish, soil, mound; rampart, dike, dam, pier; fortification; causeway; funeral pile

aggĕr·ō -āre *vt* to pile up, fill up, amass, increase; stimulate

ag·gĕrō -gĕrĕre -gessī -gestum *vt* to bring forward, utter; (with *dat* or *ad* + *acc*) to bring, convey (*something*) to

aggest·us -ūs *m* accumulation

agglomĕr·ō -āre *vt* to wind up (*as on a ball*); to annex; **se agglomare** (with *dat*) to attach oneself to, join

agglūtĭn·ō -āre *vt* to glue, paste, solder, cement

aggravesc·ō -ĕre *vi* to grow heavy

aggrăv·ō -āre *vt* to make heavier; to make worse, aggravate

ag·gredior -grĕdī -gressus sum *vt* to approach; to address; to attack; to undertake, begin

aggrĕg·ō -āre vt to assemble, collect; to attach, join, include, implicate

aggressĭ·ō -ōnis f attack, assault; introduction

agĭl·is -e adj easily moved, agile, nimble, quick; busy, active

agĭlĭt·ās -ātis f mobility, agility, nimbleness, quickness, activity

agĭtābĭl·is -e adj easily moved, light

agĭtātĭ·ō -ōnis f motion, movement, agitation; activity, pursuit; prosecution

agĭtāt·or -ōris m driver, charioteer

agĭt·ō -āre vt to set in motion, drive on, impel; to hunt, chase, pursue; to drive, urge, support, insist on; to practice, exercise; to observe, keep, celebrate; to obey, carry out; to spend, pass (time); to shake, toss, disturb; to vex, distress; to stimulate, excite; to deride, insult; to criticize; to consider, deliberate on; to discuss, debate; vi to live, dwell, be

Aglaur·ŏs -ī f daughter of Cecrops, changed by Mercury into a stone

agm·en -ĭnis n herd, flock, troop, crowd; body, mass; army (on march), procession, train

agn·a -ae f ewe, lamb (female)

ag·nascor -nascī -nātus sum vi to be born (after the father has made his will)

agnātĭ·ō -ōnis f blood relationship (on father's side)

agnāt·us -ī m relative (on father's side)

agnell·us -ī m little lamb

agnīn·a -ae f mutton

agnĭtĭ·ō -ōnis f recognition, acknowledgment, admission; knowledge

ag·noscō -noscĕre -nōvī -nĭtum vt to recognize, identify, acknowledge

agn·us -ī m lamb

agō agĕre ēgī actum vt to drive, lead, conduct; to chase, hunt; to drive away, steal; to spend (time); to do, act, perform; to manage, administer, carry on; to plead, transact, discuss, propose; to play, act the part of; to accuse, impeach; to exercise, practice, perform, deliver, pronounce; to treat; **agī** to be at stake; **se agere** to behave, deport oneself

ag·ōn -ōnis m contest, combat (in public games)

agrārĭ·us -a -um adj agrarian; m pl land-reform party

agrest·is -e adj rustic; boorish, wild, savage

agrĭcŏl·a -ae m farmer, peasant

Agrĭcŏl·a -ae m father-in-law of Tacitus

agricultūr·a -ae f agriculture

Agrĭgent·um -ī n city on south coast of Sicily (sometimes called Acragas)

agripĕt·a -ae m colonist, settler

Agripp·a -ae m son-in-law of Augustus, husband of Julia, and father of Agrippina

Agrippīn·a -ae f wife of Tiberius; daughter of Agrippa and Julia, and mother of Caligula

āh interj ah!, ha!, oh!

aha interj aha!

ai interj (denoting grief) alas!

āin = aisne (see aio)

aiō vt & vi (used mainly in present and imperfect indicative) I say; I say yes, I say so; I affirm, assert, tell, relate; **ain (= aisne) tandem?, ain tu?, ain tute?,** or **ain vero?** (colloquial phrase, expressing surprise) do you really mean it?, you don't say!, really?

Aj·ax -ācis m son of Telamon, king of Salamis; son of Oileus, king of the Locri

āl·a -ae f wing; armpit; squadron (of cavalry); flank (of battle line)

alăc·er -ris -re adj lively, brisk, quick, eager, active, cheerful

alacrĭt·ās -ātis f liveliness, briskness, eagerness, cheerfulness

alăp·a -ae f slap; emancipation (of slave)

ālārĭ·ī -ōrum m pl auxiliaries, allies

ālār·is -e adj (mil) on the flank, of the flank

ālārĭ·us -a -um adj (mil) on the flank, of the flank

ālāt·us -a -um adj winged

alaud·a -ae f lark

alāz·ōn -ŏnis m boaster

Alb·a -ae f town, also called Alba Longa, mother city of Rome, founded by Ascanius, son of Aeneas

albāt·us -a -um adj dressed in white

alb·ĕō -ēre -ŭī vi to be white

albesc·ō -ĕre vi to become white, whiten; to dawn

albĭc·ō -āre vt to make white, whiten vi to be white

albĭd·us -a -um adj white, whitish

Albĭ·ōn -ōnis f Britain

albĭtūd·ō -ĭnis f whiteness

Albŭl·a -ae f Tiber River

albŭl·us -a -um adj whitish

alb·um -ī n white; white tablet, record, list, register

Albŭnĕ·a or **Albūn·a -ae** f fountain at Tibur; nymph of the fountain

alb·us -a -um adj dead white, white, bright; favorable

Alcae·us -ī m Greek lyric poet of Lesbos, contemporary with Sappho (610 B.C.)

alcēd·ō -ĭnis f kingfisher, halcyon

alcēdŏnĭ·a -ōrum n pl halcyon days; (fig) deep calm, tranquillity

alc·ēs -is f elk

Alcĭbĭăd·ēs -is m Athenian politician, disciple of Socrates (450?-404 B.C.)

Alcīd·ēs -ae m Hercules

Alcĭmĕd·ē -ēs f wife of Aeson and mother of Jason

Alcĭnŏ·ŭs -ī m king of the Phaeacians, by whom Ulysses was entertained

Alcmēn·a or **Alcumēn·a** -ae or **Alcmēn·ē** -ēs *f* wife of Amphitryon and mother of Hercules by Jupiter

ālĕ·a -ae *f* dice game; chance, risk, venture

āleāt·or -ōris *m* dice player, gambler

āleātōrĭ·us -a -um *adj* of dice, gambling

ālĕ·ō -ōnis *m* gambler

āl·es -ĭtis *adj* winged; swift

āl·es -ĭtis *m* or *f* winged creature, fowl, bird; *m* poet; *f* augury, omen, sign

al·escō -escĕre *vi* to grow up, increase

Alexand·er -rī *m* Paris, son of Priam and Hecuba; Alexander the Great, king of Macedon

Alexandrē·a or **Alexandrī·a** -ae *f* city in Egypt, founded by Alexander the Great

alg·a *f* seaweed

al·gĕō -gēre -sī *vi* to be cold, feel cold

al·gescō -gescĕre -sī *vi* to catch cold; to become cold

algĭd·us -a -um *adj* cold

alg·or -ōris *m* cold, chilliness

alg·us -ūs *m* cold

alĭā *adv* by another way

alĭās *adv* at another time; **alias . . . alias** at one time . . . at another, sometimes . . . sometimes

alĭbī *adv* elsewhere; otherwise, in other respects; **alibi . . . alibi** in one place . . . in another, here . . . there

alicŭbī *adv* at any place, somewhere, anywhere

alicunde *adv* from somewhere, from any place, from someone else

aliēnātĭ·ō -ōnis *f* transfer (*of property*); separation, alienation; aversion, dislike

aliēnĭgen·a -ae *m* foreigner, alien, stranger

aliēn·ō -āre *vt* to make strange, transfer, sell; to alienate, set at variance; to remove, separate; to make insane, drive mad

aliēn·us -a -um *adj* another's; foreign; contrary, hostile; strange, unsuitable, incongruous, inconsistent, inconvenient; *m* stranger, foreigner

ālĭ·ger -gĕra -gĕrum *adj* wearing wings, winged

alimentārĭ·us -a -um *adj* alimentary

aliment·um -ī *n* nourishment, food, provisions; fuel

alimōnĭ·a -ae *f* or **alimōn·ĭum** -ĭī or -ī *n* nourishment, food, support

aliō *adv* to another place, elsewhere

alĭōquī or **alĭōquīn** *adv* otherwise, in other respects, for the rest; besides; in general; in any case

aliorsum or **aliorsus** *adv* in another direction; in another manner, in a different sense

ālĭp·ēs -ĕdis *adj* wing-footed, swift-footed

alipt·ēs or **alipt·a** -ae *m* wrestling trainer

aliquā *adv* somehow, in any direction

aliquam *adv* in some degree

aliquamdīū *adv* for some time

aliquandō *adv* sometime or other, once; at any time, ever; sometimes, now and then; for once, now; finally, now at last

aliquantisper *adv* for a while, for a time

aliquantō *adv* somewhat, a little, rather

aliquantŭlum *adv* somewhat

aliquantŭl·us -a -um *adj* little, small

aliquantum *adv* somewhat, a little, rather

aliquant·us -a -um *adj* considerable

aliquātĕnus *adv* for some distance, to a certain extent, somewhat; in some respects, partly

ali·quī -qua -quod *adj* some, any

aliquid *adv* to some extent, at all

ali·quid -cūjus *pron* something, anything; something important

ali·quis -cūjus *pron* someone, somebody, anyone; someone important

aliquō *adv* to some place, somewhere

aliquot (indecl) *adj* some, several, a few

aliquotĭens *adv* several times

aliquōvorsum *adv* to some place, one way or another

aliter *adv* otherwise, else, differently

aliŭbī *adv* elsewhere; **aliubi . . . aliubi** here . . . there

āl·ĭum -ĭī or -ī *n* garlic

aliunde *adv* from another source, from elsewhere

ali·us -a -ud *adj* another, other, different; *pron* another; **alii . . . alii** some . . . others; **alius . . . alius** one . . . another, the one . . . the other; **alius ex alio** one after another

al·lābor -lābī -lapsus sum *vi* to glide, slide, slip; to flow

allabōr·ō -āre *vi* to work hard

allacrĭmō -āre *vi* to weep, shed tears

allaps·us -ūs *m* stealthy approach

allātr·ō -āre *vt* to revile; (*of sea*) to break against, dash against

allātus *pp* of **affero**

allaud·ō -āre *vt* to praise highly

all·ēc -ēcis *n* fish sauce

Allectō (indecl) *f* one of the three Furies

allect·ō -āre *vt* to allure, entice

allēgātĭ·ō -ōnis *f* sending, despatching

allēg·ō -āre *vt* to commission, deputize, despatch; to allege; to instigate

al·lĕgō -legĕre -lēgī -lectum *vt* to select, elect

allevāment·um -ī *n* alleviation, relief

allevāti·ō -ōnis *f* raising, elevating; easing

allĕv·ō -āre *vt* to lift up, raise; to alleviate; to comfort; to lighten

all·ex -īcis *m* (the) big toe; midget

al·līciō -licĕre -lexī -lectum *vt* to attract

al·līdō -līdĕre -līsī -līsum *vt* (with *dat* or with **ad** or **in** + *acc*) to dash (*something*) against; **allidi** to be wrecked

allĭg·ō -āre *vt* to bind, fetter; to bandage; to hinder, detain; to impugn, accuse; (with **ad** + *acc*) to bind (*something*) to

al·līnō -linĕre -lēvī -lĭtum *vt* to smudge; (with *dat*) to smear (*something*) on

all·ĭum -ī or **-ī** *n* garlic

Allobrŏg·ēs -um *m pl* Gallic tribe living between the Rhone and the Isère

allocūti·ō -ōnis *f* address; consoling, comforting

alloqu·ĭum -ī or **-ī** *n* address, conversation; encouragement, consolation

al·lŏquor -lŏquī -locūtus sum *vt* to speak to, address; to exhort, rouse; to console, comfort

allūdi·ō -āre *vi* to play, jest

al·lūdō -lūdĕre -lūsī -lūsum *vi* to play, joke; (of *waves*) (with *dat*) to play against

al·lŭō -luĕre -luī *vt* to wash

alluvi·ēs -ēī *f* inundation, pool (*left by flood waters*); alluvial land

alluvi·ō -ōnis *f* inundation; alluvial land

alm·us -a -um *adj* nourishing; genial, kind, propitious, indulgent, bountiful

aln·us -ī *f* alder tree; ship

al·ō -ĕre -ŭī -tum or **-ĭtum** *vt* to feed, nourish, rear; to support, maintain; to promote; to increase, strengthen

alŏ·ē -ēs *f* aloe; bitterness

nlogī·a -ae *f* folly

Alp·ēs -ĭum *f pl* Alps

alpha (indecl) *n* alpha (*first letter of Greek alphabet*)

Alphē·us or **Alphē·os -ī** *m* chief river of the Peloponnesus

Alpĭc·us -a -um *adj* Alpine

Alpīn·us -a -um *adj* Alpine

alsi·us or **als·us -a -um** *adj* chilly, cool, cold

altār·ĭa -ĭum *n pl* altar top, altar, high altar

altē *adv* high, on high, highly, deeply, far, remotely; loftily, profoundly

alt·er -ĕra -ĕrum *adj* one (*of two*); a second, the second, the next; *pron* one (*of two*), the one, the other; a second one, the second one, the next one; another (*one's fellow man*); **alter . . . alter** the one . . . the other, the former . . . the latter

altercāti·ō -ōnis *f* debate, dispute, discussion

alterc·ō -āre or **alterc·or -ārī**

-ātus sum *vi* to quarrel, wrangle, bicker

alternīs *adv* by turns, alternately

altern·ō -āre *vt* to do by turns; to exchange; *vi* to alternate

altern·us -a -um *adj* one after another, alternate, mutual, every other

alterŭt·er -ra -rum (*f* also: **altĕra utra**; *n* also: **altĕrum utrum**) *adj* one (*of two*), either, one or the other; *pron* one, either one, one or the other

Althae·a -ae *f* daughter of Thestius, wife of Oeneus, king of Calydon, and mother of Meleager

alticinct·us -a -um *adj* active, busy, energetic

altĭl·is -e *adj* fattened, fat, full; rich

altisŏn·us -a -um *adj* high-sounding; sounding from on high

altĭtŏn·ans -antis *adj* thundering on high

altitūd·ō -ĭnis *f* height; depth; (fig) depth, reserve, secrecy

altĭvŏl·ans -antis *adj* high-flying

alt·or -ōris *m* foster father

altrinsĕcus *adv* on the other side

altr·ix -īcis *f* nourisher, foster mother

altrŏvorsum *adv* on the other side

alt·us -a -um *adj* high; deep, profound; ancient, remote (*lineage*); *n* high seas, the deep; heaven; **ab alto** from on high, from heaven; **ex alto** farfetched

ālŭcĭn·or -ārī *vi* to indulge in small talk, ramble

alumn·a -ae *f* foster daughter; pupil

alumn·us -ī *m* foster son; pupil

alūt·a -ae *f* soft leather; shoc; purse

alveār·ĭum -ī or **-ī** *n* beehive

alveŏl·us -ī *m* tray, basin; bed of a stream; game board

alvĕ·us -ī *m* hollow, cavity; tub; bathtub; riverbed; hull of boat, boat; game board; beehive

alv·us -ī *m* belly, bowels, stomach; womb; boat; beehive

amābĭl·is -e *adj* lovable, lovely, attractive, pleasant

amābĭlĭt·ās -ātis *f* charm

amābĭlĭter *adv* lovingly, delightfully

Amalthē·a -ae *f* nymph who fed infant Jupiter with goat's milk; sibyl at Cumae

āmandāti·ō -ōnis *f* sending away

āmand·ō -āre *vt* to send away, remove

am·ans -antis *adj* loving, affectionate; **amans patriae** patriotic; *m* lover

amanter *adv* lovingly, affectionately

amārāc·us -ī *m* or *f* marjoram

amarant·us -ī *m* amaranth

amārē *adv* bitterly

amārĭti·ēs -ēī *f* bitterness

amārĭtūd·ō -ĭnis *f* bitterness; sadness, sorrow, trouble

amār·or -ōris *m* bitterness

amār·us -a -um *adj* bitter; *n pl* disappointments

amās·ĭus -ĭī or **-ī** *m* lover

amāti·ō -ōnis f love affair

amāt·or -ōris m lover, friend; **ama-tor patriae** patriot

amātorcŭl·us -ī m poor little lover

amātōri·us -a -um adj erotic, love; n love charm

amātr·ix -īcis f mistress, girl friend

Amāz·ōn -ŏnis or Amāzōn·is -ĭdis f Amazon (member of mythical female warrior tribe dwelling in the Caucasus)

ambact·us -ī m vassal

ambāg·ēs -is f winding, labyrinth; double-talk, evasion, digression; ambiguity, obscurity; **per ambages** enigmatically

amb·ēdō -esse -ēdī -ēsum vt to eat up; (of fire) to char; to waste

ambĭg·ō -ĕre vt to go around, avoid; vi to waver, hesitate, be undecided; to argue, debate, wrangle; **ambigitur** it is uncertain

ambiguē adv doubtfully, indecisively

ambiguit·ās -ātis f ambiguity, double meaning

ambigŭ·us -a -um adj wavering, changeable; uncertain, doubtful; disputed; unreliable, untrustworthy; ambiguous, dark, obscure; n doubt, uncertainty, paradox

amb·ĭō -īre vt to go around, encircle; (pol) ot canvass; to entreat, solicit, court

ambiti·ō -ōnis f (pol) campaigning (by lawful means); popularity, flattery; ambition (in good or bad sense); partiality, favortism; pomp, ostentation

ambitiōsē adv ostentatiously; from a desire to please

ambitiōs·us -a -um adj winding, entwining; publicity-conscious, eager for popularity, ambitious; ostentatious

ambĭt·us -ūs m winding, revolution; circuit, circumference, border, orbit; (pol) illegal campaigning, bribery; pomp, ostentation; circumlocution; (rhet) period

amb·ō -ae -ō adj both, two; pron both, the two

Ambraci·a -ae f district of Epirus in N.W. Greece

ambrosi·us -a -um adj ambrosial, divine, immortal; f food of the gods

ambūbāi·a -ae f Syrian flute player

ambulācr·um -ī n walk, avenue

ambulāti·ō -ōnis f (act) walk; (place) walk

ambulātiuncŭl·a -ae f short walk; (place) small promenade

ambulāt·or -ōris m peddler; idler

ambŭl·ō -āre vt to traverse, travel; vi to walk, take a walk; to march, travel; to strut

amb·ūrō -ūrĕre -ussī -ustum vt to burn up, scorch, singe; to consume; to numb, nip

amell·us -ī m wild aster

ām·ens -entis adj out of one's mind; mad; foolish, stupid

āmenti·a -ae f madness; folly

āment·ō -āre vt to fit (a javelin) with a strap

āment·um -ī n strap

am·es -ĭtis m pole for fowler's net

amethystĭn·us -a -um adj dressed in purple; n pl purple garments

amethyst·us -ī f amethyst

amīc·a -ae f girl friend, lady friend

amīcē adv in a friendly manner

amic·ĭō -īre -ŭī -tum vt to wrap around; to cover, clothe, wrap

amīcĭter adv in a friendly way

amīcĭti·a -ae f friendship

amict·us -ūs m wrap, cloak; style, fashion (in dress)

amīcŭl·a -ae f girl friend

amīcŭl·um -ī n wrap, mantle

amīcŭl·us -ī m pal, buddy

amīc·us -a -um adj friendly; m friend; patron

āmĭgr·ō -āre vi to move away, emigrate

āmissi·ō -ōnis f loss

amīt·a -ae f aunt (father's sister)

ā·mittō -mittĕre -mīsī -missum vt to lose, let slip; **fidem amittere** to break one's word

amnicŏl·a -ae m or f riverside plant (e.g., willow tree)

amnicŭl·us -ī m brook

amn·is -is m river; **secundo amni** downstream

am·ō -āre vt to love, like, be fond of; to fall in love with; **amabo** or **amabo te** (coll) please

amoenē adv charmingly

amoenĭt·ās -ātis f charm

amoen·us -a -um adj charming, pleasant; n pl charming sights

amōl·ior -īrī vt to remove; to put aside, put away; **se amoliri** to remove oneself, clear out

amōm·um -ī n amomum plant (aromatic shrub)

am·or or am·ōs -ōris m love, affection; object of affection, love; Cupid; m pl love affair

āmōti·ō -ōnis f removal

ā·moveō -movēre -mōvī -mōtum vt to remove, withdraw, put away, put aside; to steal; **se amovere** to retire, withdraw

Amphiarā·üs -ī m famous Greek seer

amphibolĭ·a -ae f (rhet) ambiguity

Amphī·ōn -ōnis m son of Antiope by Jupiter, twin brother of Zethus, king of Thebes, and husband of Niobe

amphitheātr·um -ī n amphitheater

Amphitrў·ō or Amphitrў·ōn -ōnis m husband of Alcmena

Amphitrўōniăd·ēs -is m Hercules

amphŏr·a -ae f amphora; liquid measure (about 7 gallons)

amplē adv largely, abundantly, broadly, spaciously; splendidly

am·plector -plectī -plexus sum vt to embrace, entwine, enclose, encircle; to grab, get hold of; to understand, comprehend; to embrace, include, comprise; to sum up; to embrace affectionately, esteem, cling to; (mil) to occupy, cover

amplex·ō -āre or **amplex·or -ārī -ātus sum** vt to embrace; to honor, esteem

amplex·us -ūs m circuit; embrace, caress

amplificātī·ō -ōnis f extension, enlargement; (rhet) amplification, development

amplificāt·or -ōris m enlarger, amplifier

amplificē adv splendidly

amplific·ō -āre vt to enlarge, extend, widen; to increase; (rhet) to enlarge upon, develop

amplī·ō -āre vt to widen, enlarge; to enhance; to postpone (judgment), adjourn (court, in order to gather further evidence); to remand

ampliter adv splendidly

amplitūd·ō -inis f width, size, bulk, extent; greatness, dignity, importance, high rank; (rhet) development, amplification

amplius adv any further, any more, any longer, besides; further, more, longer; **amplius uno die** one day longer; longer than one day; **nec amplius** no longer

amplius adj (neuter comparative of **amplus**) more, further, else; (with numerals) more than; **hoc amplius** this further point; **nihil amplius** nothing further, no more; **quid amplius** what more, what else; n more, a larger amount; **amplius negoti** more trouble

ampl·us -a -um adj ample, large, wide, spacious; strong, great, powerful; grand, imposing, splendid; eminent, prominent, illustrious, distinguished

ampull·a -ae f bottle, jar, flask; bombast

ampullār·ius -iī or -ī m flask maker

ampull·or -ārī -ātus sum vi to be bombastic

amputātī·ō -ōnis f pruning

amput·ō -āre vt to lop off, prune; to curtail, shorten; **amputata loqui** to speak disconnectedly

Amūl·ius -iī or -ī m king of Alba Longa, brother of Numitor, and granduncle of Romulus and Remus

amurc·a -ae f dregs of oil

amygdăl·a -ae f almond tree

amygdăl·um -ī n almond

amyst·is -ĭdis f drinking bottoms up

an conj (introducing the latter clause of a disjunctive direct or indirect question) or

anabăthr·a -ōrum n pl bleachers

Anăcrě·ōn -ŏntis m famous lyric poet of Teos (fl 540 B.C.)

anadēm·a -ătis n fillet, headband

anagnost·ēs -ae m reader, reciter

analectr·is -ĭdis f shoulder pad (to improve the figure)

anapaest·us -a -um adj anapestic; m anapest; n poem in anapestic meter

an·as -ătis f duck; **anas fluvialis** wild duck

anaticŭl·a -ae f duckling

anatīn·us -a -um adj duck's

anatocism·us -ī m compound interest

Anaxagŏr·ās -ae m Greek philosopher of Clazomenae, teacher of Pericles and Euripides (500?-428 B.C.)

Anaximand·er -rī m Greek philosopher of Miletus (610-547 B.C.)

Anaximĕn·ēs -is m Greek philosopher of Miletus (fl 544 B.C.)

an·ceps -cipĭtis adj two-headed; two-edged; twin-peaked; amphibious; double, twofold; doubtful, undecided, ambiguous; hazardous, critical; n danger, peril

Anchīs·ēs -ae m son of Capys and father of Aeneas

Anchīsiăd·ēs -ae m son of Anchises, Aeneas

ancīl·e -is n oval shield said to have fallen from heaven in reign of Numa, second king of Rome

ancill·a -ae f maidservant

ancillār·is -e adj maidservant's

ancillŭl·a -ae f young slave (female)

ancŏr·a -ae f anchor

ancorāl·e -is n cable

ancorārĭ·us -a -um adj of an anchor

Ancyr·a -ae f Ankara, capital of Galatia

andabăt·a -ae m blindfold gladiator

And·ēs -ĭum f pl village near Mantua, birthplace of Virgil

androgyn·us -ī m or **androgyn·ē -ēs** f hermaphrodite

Andromăch·a -ae or **Andromăch·ē -ēs** f Hector's wife

Andromĕd·a -ae f daughter of Cepheus and Cassiope, rescued from a sea monster by Perseus

andr·ōn -ōnis m corridor

Andronīc·us -ī m Lucius Livius Andronicus (fl 241 B.C., first epic and dramatic poet of the Romans)

Andr·os -ī f Aegean island

ānell·us -ī m little ring

anēth·um -ī n anise, dill

anfract·us -ūs m curve, bend (of road); orbit; digression, prolixity

angell·us -ī m small corner

angīn·a -ae f tonsillitis, inflamation of the throat

angiport·us -ūs m or **angiport·um -ī** n alley

ang·ō -ĕre vt to choke, throttle; to distress, tease, trouble

ang·or -ōris m strangling, suffocation; anguish

anguicŏm·us -a -um adj snake-haired

anguicŭl·us -ī m small snake

anguif·er -ĕra -ĕrum adj snaky

anguigĕn·a -ae m offspring of a dragon; Theban

anguill·a -ae f eel

anguinĕ·us -a -um adj snaky; serpent-like

anguīn·us -a -um adj snaky

anguip·es -ĕdis *adj* serpent-footed

angu·is -is *m* or *f* snake, serpent

Angu·is -is *m* or *f* Dragon, Hydra (*constellation*)

Anguitĕn·ens -entis *m* Ophiuchus (*constellation*)

angulār·is -e *adj* angular

angulāt·us -a -um *adj* angular

angŭl·us -ī *m* angle, corner; nook, recess; **ad parīs angulos** at right angles

angustē *adv* within narrow limits, closely, hardly, scarcely; briefly, concisely

angusti·ae -ārum *f pl* narrow place, defile; narrow passage, strait; (*fig*) shortness; scarcity, want, deficiency; difficulty, tight spot, perplexity, distress, straits; narrow-mindedness

angusticlāvi·us -a -um *adj* wearing a narrow purple stripe

angust·ō -āre *vt* to make narrow

angust·us -a -um *adj* narrow, close, short, brief (*time*); scanty (*means*); difficult, critical; narrow-minded; base, mean; *n* narrowness; critical condition, danger

anhēlit·us -ūs *m* panting, difficulty in breathing, puffing; breath, breathing; vapor

anhēl·ō -āre *vt* to breathe out; to pant after; *vi* to pant, puff; to exhale; (*of fire*) to roar

anhēl·us -a -um *adj* panting, puffing

anicŭl·a -ae *f* little old woman, silly old woman

Aniēns·is -e or **Aniēn·us -a -um** *adj* of the Anio (*tributary of the Tiber*)

anīl·is -e *adj* of an old woman

anīlit·ās -ātis *f* old age (*of women*)

anīliter *adv* like an old woman

anĭm·a -ae *f* air, wind, breeze; breath; breath of life, life; soul (*as the principle of life, opposed to* **animus** *as the principle of thought and feelings*); spirit, ghost

animadversi·ō -ōnis *f* attention, observation; reproach, criticism; punishment

animadvers·or -ōris *m* observer

animad·vertō or **animad·vortō -vertĕre -vertī -versum** *vt* to pay attention to, attend to; to notice, observe, realize; to reproach, criticize; to punish

anĭm·al -ālis *n* animal; living creature

animāl·is -e *adj* consisting of air; animate, living

anĭm·ans -antis *adj* living, animate; *m & f & n* living being; animal

animātī·ō -ōnis *f* living being

animāt·us -a -um *adj* courageous; inclined, disposed; (with **erga** or **in** + *acc*) disposed toward

anĭm·ō -āre *vt* to make alive, to animate; to encourage

animōsē *adv* courageously; eagerly

animōs·us -a -um *adj* full of air,

airy; full of life, living, animate; blowing violently; full of courage, bold, spirited, undaunted; proud

animŭl·a -ae *f* little soul, life

animŭl·us -ī *m* darling

anĭm·us -ī *m* soul (*as principle of intellection and sensation, whereas* **anima** *is soul as principle of life*); intellect, understanding, mind, thought, reason; memory; knowledge; sense, consciousness; judgment, opinion; imagination; heart, feelings, passions; spirit, courage, morale; disposition, character; pride, haughtiness; will, purpose, desire, inclination; pleasure, delight; confident hope; **aequo animo** patiently, calmly; **animi causā** for amusement; **bono animo esse** to take heart; **ex animo** from the bottom of the heart, sincerely; **ex animo effluere** to slip one's mind; **in animo habere** (*with inf*) to intend to; **meo animo** in my opinion

Aniō -ēnis *m* tributary of the Tiber

An·ius -iī or **-ī** *m* king and priest on Delos who welcomed Aeneas

annāl·is -e *adj* lasting a year, annual; **lex annalis** law fixing minimum age for holding public offices; *m pl* annals, chronicle

annāt·ō -āre *vi* (with *dat* or **ad** + *acc*) to swim to

anne *conj* (pleonastic form of **an**) or

an·nectō -nectĕre -nexŭī -nexum *vt* (with *dat* or **ad** + *acc*) to tie, connect, annex (*something*) to; (with *dat*) to apply (*something*) to

annex·us -ūs *m* connection

annicŭl·us -a -um *adj* one year old, yearling

an·nītor -nītī -nīsus sum or **nixus sum** *vi* (with *dat* or **ad** + *acc*) to press against, lean on; (with **ut** or *inf*) to strive to

anniversāri·us -a -um *adj* annual, yearly

ann·ō -āre *vi* (with *dat*, with **ad** + *acc*, or with *acc* of limit of motion) to swim to or towards; (with *dat*) to swim with or along with

annōn *conj* or not

annōn·a -ae *f* year's crop; grain; price of grain; cost of living; high price

annōs·us -a -um *adj* aged, old

annotātī·ō -ōnis *f* notation, remark

annōtīn·us -a -um *adj* last year's

annŏt·ō -āre *vt* to write down, note down; to comment on; to observe, perceive

annumĕr·ō -āre *vt* (with *dat*) to count out (*money*) to; (with *dat* or **in** + *acc*) to add (*something*) to, to include (*someone*) among

annuntī·ō -āre *vt* to announce, make known, proclaim

an·nŭō -nuĕre -nŭī -nūtum *vt* to designate by a nod; to indicate, declare; (with *dat*) to promise, grant (*something*) to; *vi* to nod, nod assent; (with *dat*) to nod assent to, to be favorable to, smile on

ann·us -ī *m* year; season; age, time of life; year of office; **ad annum** for the coming year, a year hence; **annum** or **in annum** for a year; **per annos** year to year

annŭ·us -a -um *adj* lasting a year; annual, yearly; *n pl* yearly pay, pension

an·quīrō -quīrĕre -quīsīvī -quīsītum *vt* to search carefully; to examine, inquire into; (with *genit* or *abl* of the charge) to accuse (*someone*) of; *vi* to hold an inquest

ans·a -ae *f* handle; opportunity

ansāt·us -a -um *adj* having handles; **homo ansatus** man with arms akimbo

ans·er -ĕris *m* gander

ante *adv* before, previously; in front, forwards

ante *prep* (with *acc*) before; more than, above

antĕā *adv* before, previously, formerly

ante·capĭō -capĕre -cēpī -ceptum *vt* to receive beforehand; to take possession of beforehand, preoccupy; to anticipate

ante·cēdō -cēdĕre -cessī -cessum *vt* to precede, to excel, surpass; *vi* (with *dat*) a to have precedence over; b to excel, surpass

antecessĭ·ō -ōnis *f* antecedent cause

antecess·or -ōris *m* (mil) scout; *m pl* advance guard

antecurs·or -ōris *m* (mil) scout; *m pl* advance guard

ante·ĕō -īre -ĭī *vt* to precede; to excel, surpass; to anticipate, prevent; *vi* to precede; to take the lead; (with *dat*) a to go before; b to excel, surpass

ante·fĕrō -ferre -tŭlī -lātum *vt* to prefer; to anticipate

antefix·us -a -um *pp* of **antefigo**; *n pl* images, statues, etc., affixed to roofs and gutters of homes or temples

ante·gredĭor -grĕdī -gressus sum *vt* to precede

antehab·ĕō -ēre *vt* to prefer

antehāc *adv* before this time, before now, formerly

antelātus *pp* of **antefero**

antelūcān·us -a -um *adj* before dawn

antemerīdiān·us -a -um *adj* before noon

ante·mittō -mittĕre -mīsī -missum *vt* to send out ahead

antenn·a -ae *f* yardarm, sail yard

Antēn·or -ōris *m* Trojan who after the fall of Troy went to Italy and founded Patavium

antepīlān·ī -ōrum *m pl* front ranks, front line

ante·pōnō -pōnĕre -posŭī -positum *vt* to prefer; to serve (*food*)

antepŏt·ens -entis *adj* very wealthy

antĕquam or **ante . . . quam** *conj* before

Antĕr·ōs -ōtis *m* avenger of unrequited love

ant·ēs -ĭum *m pl* rows (*e.g., of vines*)

antesignān·us -ī *m* soldier who fought in front of the standards to defend them; leader, commander

ante·stō or **anti·stō -stāre -stĕtī** *vi* to excel, be distinguished; (with *dat*) to be superior to

antest·or -ārī -ātus sum *vt* to call as witness

ante·venĭō -venīre -vēnī -ventum *vt* to anticipate, thwart; to surpass, excel; *vi* to become more distinguished; (with *dat*) a to anticipate; b to surpass, excel

ante·vertō -vertĕre -vertī -versum *vt* to go or come before, precede; to anticipate; to prefer

antevŏl·ō -āre *vi* to dash out ahead

anticipātĭ·ō -ōnis *f* preconception, foreknowledge

anticĭp·ō -āre *vt* to anticipate

antīc·us -a -um *adj* front, foremost

Antigŏn·ē -ēs *f* daughter of Theban king Oedipus; daughter of Trojan king Laomedon

Antilŏch·us -ī *m* son of Nestor, killed by Hector at Troy

Antiphāt·ēs -ae *m* king of the Laestrygones, who sank the fleet of Greeks returning from Troy with Ulysses

antiquārĭ·us -a -um *adj & m* antiquarian

antīquē *adv* in former times; in the good old style

antiquit·ās -ātis *f* antiquity; men of former times, the ancients; the good old days

antiquĭtus *adv* in former times, of old; from ancient times; in the old style

antiqu·ō -āre *vt* to reject (*law, bill*)

antīqu·us -a -um *adj* old, ancient; oldfashioned, venerable; *m pl* ancients, ancient authors; *n* antiquity; old custom

antist·es -ĭtis *m* priest presiding over temple, high priest

antist·es -ĭtis or **antistīt·a -ae** *f* priestess presiding over temple, high priestess

Antisthĕn·ēs -is or **-ae** *m* pupil of Socrates and founder of Cynic philosophy

antithĕt·on -ī *n* (rhet) antithesis

antr·um -ī *n* cave, cavern

ānulār·ĭus -ĭī or **-ī** *m* ring maker

ānulāt·us -a -um *adj* wearing a ring

ānŭl·us -ī *m* ring, signet ring

ān·us -ī *m* anus, rectum; ring

an·us -ūs *f* old woman; hag

anxĭē *adv* uneasily

anxĭet·ās -ātis *f* anxiety, trouble

anxif·er -ĕra -ĕrum *adj* causing anxiety

anxĭ·us -a -um *adj* worried, troubled; disquieting

apăge *interj* go on!; scram!

apēliōt·ēs -ae *m* east wind

Apell·ēs -is *m* famous Greek painter (*fl 4th cent.* B.C.)

ap·er -rī *m* boar

aper.iō -īre -ŭī -tum *vt* to uncover, open, lay bare, disclose, reveal; to prove, demonstrate; to explain, recount

apertē *adv* openly, frankly, candidly

apert·ō -āre *vt* to keep on laying bare

apert·us -a -um *pp of* aperio; *adj* bare, uncovered, exposed; without decks; clear (*style*); frank, candid (*character*); manifest, plain, evident; accessible, unobstructed; *n* open space; **in aperto** in the open; **in aperto esse** to be clear, evident, well known, notorious

ap·ex -icis *m* point, top, summit; hat, cap, crown; crowning glory

aphract·us -ī *f or* **aphract·um -ī** *n* ship without deck

apiăr·ius -iī *or* **-ī** *m* beekeeper

apicŭl·a -ae *f* little bee

ap·is -is *f* bee

ap·iscor -iscī -tus sum *vt* to pursue; to take, reach, gain, get

ap·ium -iī *or* **-ī** *n* celery

aplustr·e -is *n* stern

apoclēt·ī -ōrum *m pl* select committee (*of Aetolian League*)

apodytēr·ium -iī *or* **-ī** *n* dressing room (*at a bath*)

apolactiz·ō -āre *vt* to kick aside, scorn

Apoll·ō -inis *m* son of Jupiter and Latona, twin brother of Diana, god of the sun, divination, archery, healing, poetry, and music

Apollodōr·us -ī *m* famous rhetorician, teacher of Augustus; famous Athenian grammarian and author of an extant work on mythology (*fl* 140 B.C.)

apolog·us -ī *m* story, fable

apophorēt·a -ōrum *n pl* presents for house guests

aposphrāgism·a -ătis *n* device on signet ring, seal

apothēc·a -ae *f* warehouse, storehouse, magazine

apparātē *adv* with much preparation, sumptuously

apparāti·ō -ōnis *f* preparation

apparāt·us -a -um *adj* prepared, well prepared; sumptuous

apparāt·us -ūs *m* getting or making ready, preparing, providing; equipment, apparatus, paraphernalia; pomp, magnificence

appār·ĕō -ēre -ŭī -ītum *vi* to appear, become visible; to be seen, show oneself; (with *dat*) to wait on, serve; **apparet** it is evident, clear, certain

apparĭti·ō -ōnis *f* attendance, service; *f pl* household servants

apparĭt·or -ōris *m* servant; attendant of public official (*e.g.*, aide, lictor, secretary)

appăr·ō -āre *vt* to prepare, make ready, provide

appellāti·ō -ōnis *f* addressing; appeal; naming, calling by name; name, title; pronunciation

ap·pellō -pellĕre -pŭlī -pulsum *vt* (with *dat or* ad + *acc*) to drive (*something*) to, steer (*ship*) to; *vi* (*of ship*) to land

appell·ō -āre *vt* to accost, address; to appeal to; (law) to sue; to name, call; to mention by name; to pronounce

appendicŭl·a -ae *f* small addition

append·ix -icis *f* addition, supplement

ap·pendō -pendĕre -pendī -pensum *vt* to weigh; to pay out; (fig) to weigh, consider

appĕt·ens -entis *adj* greedy, avaricious; (with *genit*) eager for, craving

appetenter *adv* eagerly, greedily

appetenti·a -ae *f* craving, desire; (with *genit*) craving for, desire for

appetīti·ō -ōnis *f* grasping, craving; (with *genit*) grasping at, craving for

appetīt·us -ūs *m* craving, desire; *m pl* appetites, passions

appĕt·ō -ĕre -īvī -ītum *vt* to try to reach; to lay hold of; to make for, head for; to attack, assail, assault; *vi* to approach, draw near

apping·ō -ĕre *vt* to paint; to write

ap·plaudō -plaudĕre -plausī -plausum *vt* (with *dat*) to strike (*something*) against; *vi* to applaud

applicāti·ō -ōnis *f* applying, application

applicāt·us -a -um *adj* (with ad + *acc*) inclined to; (with *dat*) lying close to, attached to

applicĭt·us -a -um *adj* (with *dat*) applied or joined to, attached to

applic·ō -āre -āvī *or* **-ŭī -ātum** *or* **ĭtum** *vt* to bring in close contact; (with *dat or* ad + *acc*) **a** to apply, attach, add, join (*something*) to; **b** to steer (*ship*) toward; **c** to devote (*attention, mind*) to

applōr·ō -āre *vt* to deplore, lament

ap·pōnō -pōnĕre -posŭī -positum *vt* to serve (*food*); (with *dat or* ad + *acc*) to put or lay (*something*) near, at, or beside; (with *dat*) **a** to set (*food*) before; **b** to appoint or designate (*someone*) to (a *duty, task*); **c** to reckon (*something*) as

apporrect·us -a -um *adj* stretched out

apport·ō -āre *vt* to carry or bring up; to cause; (with *dat*) to carry (*something*) to

apposc·ō -ĕre *vt* to demand in addition

appositē *adv* appropriately, pertinently

apposĭt·us -a -um *pp of* appono; *adj* fit, suitable, appropriate; (with *dat*) situated near, continuous with, bordering on; (with ad + *acc*) suited to, fit for

appōt·us -a -um *adj* drunk

apprĕc·or -ārī -ātus sum vt to pray to, worship

appre·hendō -hendĕre -hendī -hensum vt to seize, take hold of; (mil) to occupy

apprimē adv chiefly, especially

ap·primō -primĕre -pressī -pressum vt (with dat) to press (something) close to

approbāti·ō -ōnis f approbation, approval; proof

approbāt·or -ōris m one who seconds or approves

approbē adv very well

approb·ō -āre vt to approve; to prove

apprōmitt·ō -ĕre vt to promise in addition

apprŏpĕr·ō -āre vt to hasten, speed up; vi to hurry

apprōpinquāti·ō -ōnis f approach

apprōpinqu·ō -āre vi to approach; (with dat or ad + acc) to come near to, approach

appugn·ō -āre vt to fight, attack

appuls·us -ūs m landing, approach

aprīcāti·ō -ōnis f basking in the sun

aprīc·or -ārī vi to bask, sun oneself

aprīc·us -a -um adj sunny; n sunny spot

Aprīl·is adj of April; **mensis Aprilis** April, month of April

aprugn·us -a -um adj of a wild boar

aps- = abs-

apsūmēd·ō -īnis f devouring

aptē adv closely; suitably

apt·ō -āre vt to fasten, fit, adjust; to make ready, equip

apt·us -a -um adj suitable, adapted, appropriate, proper

apud prep (with acc) at, by, near, among; at the house of; before, in the presence of; in the writings of; over, (with influence) over

Āpūli·a -ae f district in S.W. Italy

aqu·a -ae f water; f pl baths, spa; **aquā et igni interdicere** to outlaw; **aquam praebere** (with dat) to entertain (guests)

aquaeduct·us -ūs m aqueduct

aquālicŭl·us -ī m belly, stomach

aquāl·is -e adj of water; m & f wash-basin

aquāri·us -a -um adj of water; m water-conduit inspector

Aquār·ius -iī or **-ī** m Aquarius (constellation; sign of the Zodiac)

aquātic·us -a -um adj growing in water; watery, moist, humid

aquātil·is -e adj living or growing in water, aquatic

aquāti·ō -ōnis f fetching water; water hole

aquāt·or -ōris m water carrier

aquĭl·a -ae f eagle (bird; Roman legionary standard); (fig) legion; gable of house

aquil·ex -ēgis m water finder, dowser; water-conduit inspector

aquilif·er -ĕrī m standard-bearer

aquilīn·us -a -um adj eagle's

aquil·ō -ōnis m north wind; north

aquilōnĭ·us -a -um adj northerly

aquĭl·us -a -um adj swarthy

Aquīn·um -ī n town of the Volsci, birthplace of Juvenal

Aquītāni·a -ae f province in S.W. Gaul

aqu·or -ārī -ātus sum vi to fetch water

aquōs·us -a -um adj rainy, humid, full of water

aquŭl·a -ae f small stream, brook

ār·a -ae f altar

Ār·a -ae f Altar (constellation)

arabarch·ēs -ae m customs officer in Egypt

Arabi·a -ae f Arabia

Arabĭc·us or **Arabĭ·us** or **Arāb·us -a -um** adj Arabian

Arachn·ē -ēs f Lydian girl whom Minerva changed into a spider

arānĕ·a -ae f spider; cobweb

arāneŏl·a -ae f small spider

arāneŏl·us -ī m small spider

arāneōs·us -a -um adj full of cobwebs

arānĕ·us -a -um adj spider's; m spider; n spider web

Ar·ar -āris m tributary of the Rhone

arāti·ō -ōnis f cultivation, tilling, agriculture; arable land

arātiuncŭl·a -ae f small plot, small farm

arāt·or -ōris m farmer; m pl farmers on state-owned land

arātr·um -ī n plow

Arāt·us -ī m Greek author of poem on astronomy (fl 270 B.C.)

arbĭt·er -rī m eyewitness; arbiter, judge, umpire; ruler, director, controller

arbĭtr·a -ae f eyewitness (female)

arbitrāriō adv uncertainly

arbitrāri·us -a -um adj uncertain

arbitrāt·us -ūs m decision; inclination, pleasure; direction, guidance

arbitr·ium -iī or **-ī** n decision, judgment; mastery, power, control, authority

arbĭtr·or -ārī -ātus sum vt & vi to decide or judge (as an arbiter); to testify; to think, suppose

arb·or or **arb·ōs -ōris** f tree; mast, oar, ship; gallows

arborĕ·us -a -um adj of a tree; tree-like

arbust·us -a -um adj wooded, planted with trees; n orchard; vineyard planted with trees; n pl trees

arbutĕ·us -a -um adj of arbutus

arbŭt·um -ī n fruit of arbutus

arbŭt·us -ī f arbutus, strawberry tree

arc·a -ae f chest, box, safe; coffin; prison cell

Arcadĭ·a -ae f district of central Peloponnesus

arcānō adv in secret, privately

arcān·us -a -um adj secret, concealed, private; n secret; sacred mystery

arc·ĕō -ēre -ŭī vt to shut up, enclose; to keep at a distance, keep off; to hinder, prevent; (with *abl* or **ab** + *abl*) to keep (*someone*) off, away from

arcessīt·us -a -um *pp* of **arcesso**; *adj* farfetched

arcessīt·us -ūs *m* summons

arcess·ō -ĕre -īvī -ītum *vt* to send for, fetch, summon; (law) to arraign; to derive

archetȳp·us -a -um *adj* & *n* original

Archilŏch·us -ī Greek iambic poet of Paros (c. 714-676 B.C.)

archimagīr·us -ī *m* chief cook

Archimēd·ēs -is *m* scientist and mathematician of Syracuse (287-212 B.C.)

archipīrāt·a -ae *m* pirate captain

architect·ōn -ōnis *m* architect, master builder; master in cunning

architect·or -ārī -ātus sum *vt* to build, construct

architectūr·a -ae *f* architecture

architect·us -ī *m* architect; deviser, author, inventor, contriver

arch·ōn -ōntis *m* archon (*chief magistrate in Athens*)

arcitĕn·ens -entis *adj* holding a bow, wearing a bow

Arcitĕn·ens -entis *m* Archer (*constellation*)

Arctophȳl·ax -ăcis *m* Boötes (*constellation*)

Arct·os -ī *m* the Great and Little Bear (*double constellation*)

arct·os -ī *m* North Pole; North; north wind; night

Arctūr·us -ī *m* brightest star in Boötes

arcŭl·a -ae *f* small box, jewelry box; (rhet) ornament

arcŭ·ō -āre *vt* to curve

arc·us -ūs *m* bow; rainbow; curve; arch, triumphal arch

Ardĕ·a -ae *f* town in Latium

ardĕ·a -ae *f* heron

ardeli·ō -ōnis *m* busybody

ard·ens -entis *adj* blazing, burning, hot, fiery; gleaming, glittering; smarting, burning; (of emotions) glowing, hot, ardent

ardenter *adv* ardently, eagerly, passionately

ardĕō ardēre arsī *vi* to be on fire, burn, blaze; to flash, glow; to smart, burn

ardesc·ō -ĕre *vi* to catch fire; to gleam, glitter; (of passions) to become more intense, increase in violence

ard·or -ōris *m* heat, flame; flashing, brightness; heat (*of passions*); loved one, flame

ardŭ·us -a -um *adj* steep, high; difficult; *n* difficulty

ārĕ·a -ae *f* open space; park, playground; building site; threshing floor

arēna see **harena**

ār·eō -ēre *vi* to be dry; to be thirsty

ārĕŏl·a *f* small open space

Arēopăg·us -ī *m* criminal court in Athens; hill where criminal court met

Ar·ēs -is *m* Greek god of war

āresc·ō -ēre *vi* to become dry; to wither

aretālŏg·us -ī *m* braggart

Arethūs·a -ae *f* nymph pursued by river god Alpheus in Peloponnesus and changed by Diana into a fountain; fountain near Syracuse

Argē·ī -ōrum *m pl* consecrated places in Rome ascribed to Numa; figures of men, made of rushes and thrown annually into the Tiber

argentāri·us -a -um *adj* silver; financial, pecuniary; *m* banker; *f* banking; bank; silver mine

argentāt·us -a -um *adj* plated or ornamented with silver

argentĕŏl·us -a -um *adj* made of pretty silver

argentĕ·us -a -um *adj* silver, silvery

argent·um -ī *n* silver; silver plate; money

Argē·us or **Argīv·us** or **Argolic·us** -a -um *adj* Argive; Greek

Arg·ī -ōrum *m pl* Argos, town in N.E. Peloponnesus

Argīlēt·um -ī *n* district in Rome between the Quirinal and Capitoline

argill·a -ae *f* clay

Arg·ō -ūs *f* Jason's ship

Argŏl·is -ĭdis *f* district around Argos

Argonaut·ae -ārum *m pl* argonauts

Argos *n* (only *nom* and *acc*) Argos

argūmentāti·ō -ōnis *f* argumentation; proof

argūment·or -ārī -ātus sum *vt* to adduce as proof; (with **de** + *abl*) to conclude from; *vi* to bring evidence

argūment·um -ī *n* evidence, proof, argument; theme, plot; topic; subject, motif (*of artistic representation*)

arg·ŭō -uĕre -ŭī -ūtum *vt* to prove; to reveal, betray; to accuse, charge, impeach (*person*); find fault with (*thing*)

Arg·us -ī *n* many-eyed monster set over Io and killed by Mercury

argūtē *adv* subtly; craftily

argūti·ae -ārum *f pl* subtlety; brightness, genius, cunning, shrewdness

argūtŭl·us -a -um *adj* somewhat subtle

argūt·us -a -um *adj* clearcut, clear, bright, distinct; penetrating, piercing; chatty; acute, subtle; bright, smart, witty; cunning, sly

argyrasp·is -ĭdis *adj* wearing a silver shield

Ariadn·a -ae *f* daughter of Minos, king of Crete, who extricated Theseus from the labyrinth

Arīci·a -ae *f* town in Latium on the Via Appia

āridŭl·us -a -um *adj* somewhat dry

ărĭd·us -a -um *adj* dry, parched; withered; meager; (of style) dry, dull

arĭ·ēs -ĕtis *m* ram; battering ram; beam (*used as breakwater*)

Arĭ·ēs -ĕtis *m* Aries (*sign of the Zodiac*)

arĭĕt·ō -āre *vt* & *vi* to butt, ram

Ariobarzān·ēs -is *m* king of Cappadocia

Arĭ·ōn -ŏnis *m* early Greek poet and musician, rescued from drowning by dolphin

arist·a -ae *f* ear of grain

Aristarch·us -ī *m* Alexandrine critic and scholar (*fl* 156 B.C.); stern critic

aristolochĭ·a -ae *f* birthwort

Aristophăn·ēs -is *m* the most famous Greek comic poet (*c.* 444-380 B.C.)

Aristotĕl·ēs -is *m* Aristotle (384-322 B.C.)

arithmētĭc·a -ōrum *n pl* arithmetic

ārĭtūd·ō -ĭnis *f* dryness

arm·a -ōrum *n pl* armor, defensive arms, arms; warfare; camp life; armed men; equipment, tools

armāment·a -ōrum *n pl* ship's gear

armāmentār·ĭum -ĭī or **-ī** *n* arsenal, armory

armārĭŏl·um -ī *n* little chest, little closet

armār·ĭum -ĭī or **-ī** *n* cupboard, chest

armātūr·a -ae *f* outfit, equipment, armor; light-armed troops

armāt·us -a -um *adj* armed, equipped; *m* armed man

Armenĭ·a *f* country in N.E. Asia Minor

armenĭăc·um -ī *n* apricot

armenĭăc·us -ī *f* apricot tree

armentāl·is -e *adj* of a herd

armentār·ĭus -ĭī or **-ī** *m* herdsman

arment·um -ī *n* herd

armĭf·er -ĕra -ĕrum *adj* armed

armĭg·er -ĕra -ĕrum *adj* armed; producing warriors; *m* armed person; armor-bearer

armill·a -ae *f* armlet, bracelet

armillāt·us -a -um *adj* wearing a bracelet

armĭpŏt·ens -entis *adj* powerful in arms, warlike

armĭsŏn·us -a -um *adj* reverberating with arms

arm·ō -āre *vt* to furnish with arms, to arm; to rouse to arms

arm·us -ī *m* shoulder, shoulder blade, upper arm; flank (*of animal*)

ar·ō -āre *vt* to plow, till

Arpīn·um -ī *n* town in Latium, birthplace of Marius and Cicero

arquāt·us -a -um *adj* jaundiced

arrect·us -a -um *pp of* **arrigo; adj** upright; steep, precipitous

arrēp·ō -ĕre -sī *vi* (with *dat* or **ad** + *acc*) to creep towards, steal up on

arrhăb·ō -ōnis *m* deposit (*of money*)

ar·rīdĕō -rīdēre -rīsī -rīsum *vt* to smile at; *vi* (with *dat*) **a** to smile at

or on, laugh with; **b** to be favorable to; **c** to be pleasing to, please

ar·rĭgō -rĭgĕre -rexī -rectum *vt* to erect, raise; to rouse, excite

ar·rĭpĭō -rĭpĕre -rĭpŭī -reptum *vt* to snatch, seize; (fig) to grasp quickly; (law) to arrest, arraign; to satirize

ar·rōdō -rōdĕre -rōsī -rōsum *vt* to gnaw at

arrŏg·ans -antis *adj* arrogant

arrŏganter *adv* arrogantly

arrŏgantĭ·a -ae *f* assumption, presumption; arrogance

arrŏg·ō -āre *vt* to question; to associate; to assume for oneself, claim

ars artis *f* skill; craft, trade; method, way, manner, means; artificial means; work of art; science, theory; manual, textbook; *f pl* cunning; moral qualities, character

artē *adv* closely, tightly; (to love) deeply, dearly; (to sleep) soundly

Artĕm·is -ĭdis *f* Greek counterpart of Diana

artērĭ·a -ae *f* artery; windpipe

arthrītĭc·us -a -um *adj* arthritic

articŭlātim *adv* piecemeal; (to speak) articulately, distinctly

articŭl·ō -āre *vt* to utter distinctly, articulate

articŭl·us -ī *m* joint, knuckle; finger; limb; (gram) clause; turning point; **in ipso articulo temporis** in the nick of time

artĭf·ex -ĭcis *adj* skillful, ingenious; artistic; broken, trained (*horse*); *m* craftsman, artist, master; originator, contriver, author

artĭfĭcĭōsē *adv* skillfully

artĭfĭcĭōs·us -a -um *adj* skillful, ingenious, accomplished; artificial

artĭfĭc·ĭum -ĭī or **-ī** *n* skill, workmanship; artistic work, work of art; art, profession; cleverness, cunning; theory

art·ō -āre *vt* to pack closely; to compress, contract; to limit

artolagăn·us -ī *m* cake

artopt·a -ae *f* baker; bread pan (*to bake in*)

art·us -a -um *adj* close, tight; confined, restricted; dense, firm; scanty, small, needy; strict, severe; sound, deep (*sleep*); stingy; *n* narrow space; tight spot, difficulty

art·us -ūs *m* joint; *m pl* joints, limbs

ārŭl·a -ae *f* small altar

arund·ō -ĭnis *f* reed; shaft, arrow; pipe, flute; pen; fishing rod; hobbyhorse; (in weaving) comb

arvīn·a -ae *f* grease

arv·us -a -um *adj* arable; *n* arable land, soil, land, plain, region; grain

arx arcis *f* fortress, stronghold, citadel, castle, protection, refuge, mainstay; height, summit; **arcem facere e cloaca** to make a mountain out of a molehill

ās assis *m* pound (*divisible into twelve ounces*); bronze coin; **heres ex asse** sole heir

Ascăn·ĭus -ĭī or **-ī** *m* son of Aeneas and Creusa and founder of Alba Longa

ascendō ascendĕre ascendī ascensum *vt* to climb; to mount (*horse*); to board (*ship*); *vi* to climb up, ascend; (of voice) to rise; (with **ad** or **in** + *acc*) to climb, climb up to; (with **super** or **supra** + *acc*) to rise above, surpass

ascensĭ·ō -ōnis *f* climbing up, ascent

ascens·us -ūs *m* climbing up, ascent; means of ascending, approach; step, degree; (fig) climb, rise

ascĭ·a -ae *f* ax; mason's trowel

ascĭō -īre *vt* to associate with oneself, admit

asc·iscō -iscĕre -īvī -ītum *vt* to adopt, approve (*bill*); to adopt (*custom*); to assume, claim, arrogate; to receive, admit (*e.g.*, as ally, citizen, etc.); (with **in** + *acc*) to admit (*someone*)

ascīt·us -a -um *adj* acquired (*as opposed to innate*)

Ascr·a -ae *f* birthplace of Hesiod in Boeotia

a·scrībō -scrībĕre -scripsī -scriptum *vt* to add (*by writing*); to impute, ascribe, attribute; to enroll, register; to reckon, number, class

ascriptĭcĭ·us -a -um *adj* enrolled, registered

ascriptĭ·ō -ōnis *f* addition (*in writing*)

ascriptīv·us -ī *m* (mil) reserve

ascript·or -ōris *m* supporter

asell·a -ae *f* little ass

asell·us -ī *m* little ass

Āsĭ·a -ae *f* Roman province; Asia Minor; Asia

asīl·us -ī *m* gadfly

asĭn·us -ī *m* ass; fool

Ās·ĭs -ĭdis *f* Asia

asōt·us -ī *m* playboy

asparăg·us -ī *m* asparagus

aspargō see **aspergo**

aspectābĭl·ĭs -e *adj* visible

aspect·ō -āre *vt* to look at, gaze at; to look with respect at; to face, lie in the direction of; to observe

aspect·us -ūs *m* look, sight, glance; sense of sight; manner of appearance, appearance, countenance

aspellō -ĕre *vt* to drive away

asp·er -ĕra -ĕrum *adj* rough, uneven; harsh, severe, stormy (*climate*); harsh, grating, hoarse (*sound*); pungent, strong (*smell*); rough, hard, unkind, rude (*character*); austere, rigid (*person*); wild fierce, savage (*animal*); rough, annoying, adverse (*circumstances*) rugged (*style*)

aspērē *adv* roughly; (fig) harshly, sternly, severely

a·spergō -spergĕre -spersī -spersum *vt* to sprinkle, scatter, taint; (with *dat*) to sprinkle (*something*) on

asperg·ō -ĭnis *f* sprinkling; spray

asperit·ās -ātis *f* unevenness, roughness; severity, fierceness; difficulty, trouble

aspernātĭ·ō -ōnis *f* disdain, contempt

aspern·or -ārī -ātus sum *vt* to disdain, despise, reject

aspĕr·ō -āre *vt* to make rough or uneven, roughen; to make fierce, exasperate; to excite

aspersĭ·ō -ōnis *f* sprinkling; laying on of colors

a·spicĭō -spicĕre -spexī -spectum *vt* to catch sight of, spot; to look at; to examine closely, inspect; to observe, consider

aspīrātĭ·ō -ōnis *f* breathing, blowing; evaporation, exhalation; (gram) aspiration

aspīr·ō -āre *vi* to breathe, blow; (with *dat* or with **ad** or **in** + *acc*) to aspire to, desire to reach or obtain, come near to obtaining; (with *dat*) to favor

asp·ĭs -ĭdis *f* asp

asportātĭ·ō -ōnis *f* removal

asport·ō -āre *vt* to carry away

asprēt·a -ōrum *n pl* rough terrain

assēcl·a -ae *m* hanger-on

assectātĭ·ō -ōnis *f* (respectful) attendance

assectāt·or -ōris *m* attendant, escort; disciple

assect·or -ārī *vt* to follow, tail after

assecŭl·a -ae *m* hanger-on

assensĭ·ō -ōnis *f* assent, approval; *m pl* expressions of approval; (phil) realism

assens·or -ōris *m* backer, supporter

assens·us -ūs *m* assent, approval; *m pl* expressions of approval; (phil) realism; echo

assentātĭ·ō -ōnis *f* assent, agreement; flattery

assentātĭuncŭl·a -ae *f* base flattery

assentāt·or -ōris *m* flatterer

assentātōrĭē *adv* flatteringly

assentātr·ix -īcis *f* flatterer (*female*)

as·sentĭō -sentīre -sensī -sensum *vi* to agree; (with *dat*) to assent to, agree with, approve

as·sentĭor -sentīrī -sensus sum *vi* to agree; (with *dat*) to assent to, agree with, approve

assent·or -ārī -ātus sum *vi* to agree always; (with *dat*) to agree with always, to flatter

as·sĕquor -sĕquī -secūtus sum *vt* to pursue, catch up to, reach; to gain, obtain, procure; to come up to, equal, match; to comprehend, understand

ass·er -ĕris *m* pole, stake, post

as·sĕrō -serĕre -sēvī -situm *vt* (with *dat*) to plant (*something*) near

assĕr·ō -ĕre -ŭī -tum *vt* to set free, liberate (*slave*); to protect, defend; to claim, appropriate; **in servitutem asserere** to claim (*someone*) as one's slave

assertĭ·ō -ōnis f declaration of civil status

assert·or -ōris m defender, champion

asserv·ĭō -īre vi (with dat) to serve, assist

asserv·ō -āre vt to preserve, keep, watch over, guard

assessĭ·ō -ōnis f company, companionship

assess·or -ōris m companion, assistant; (law) assistant to a judge, counselor

assess·us -ūs m company, companionship

assevēranter adv emphatically

assevērātĭ·ō -ōnis f assertion, protestation; firmness, earnestness

assevēr·ō -āre vt to assert strongly, affirm, insist on

as·sīdĕō -sīdēre -sēdī -sessum vi to seat nearby; (with dat) **a** to sit near, stand by, attend upon, take care of, keep (someone) company; **b** to be busily engaged in; **c** to attend to, mind; **d** to be near (in some respect), be like, resemble

as·sīdō -sīdēre -sēdī vi to sit down; (with acc) to sit down beside

assĭdŭē adv assiduously, continually, incessantly

assĭdŭĭt·ās -ātis f constant presence or attendance; persistence; frequent recurrence

assĭdŭō adv continually

assĭdŭ·us -a -um adj continually present; persistent, tireless, incessant, busy; m taxpayer; rich man

assignātĭ·ō -ōnis f allotment (of land)

assign·ō -āre vt to mark out, allot, assign (land); to assign, confer; to ascribe, attribute; to consign; to seal

as·silĭō -silīre -silŭī -sultum vi to jump; (with dat) to jump upon, leap at; (with ad + acc) a to jump to; **b** to have recourse to

assimĭlĭter adv in like manner

assimĭl·is -e adj similar; (with dat) like

assimŭlātĭ·ō -ōnis f likeness, similarity

assimŭlāt·us -a -um adj similar; counterfeit

assimŭl·ō -āre vt to consider as similar, compare; to imitate, counterfeit

as·sistō -sistĕre -stĭtī vi to stand nearby; (with ad + acc) to stand at or by; (with dat) to assist, defend

assĭtus pp of assero

assol·ĕō -ēre vi to be usual

assŏn·ō -āre vi to echo; (with dat) to sound in response to, to echo (a sound)

assŭē·facĭō -facĕre -fēcī -factum vt to train; (with dat, with ad + acc, or with inf) to accustom (someone) to

assŭ·escō -escĕre -ēvī -ētum vt (with dat) to accustom (someone) to, make (someone) familiar with, familiarize (someone) with; vi (with dat, with ad + acc, or with inf) to become used to

assuētūd·ō -ĭnis f habit, custom

assuēt·us -a -um pp of assuesco; adj accustomed, customary, usual; (with abl) trained in; (with dat, with ad or in + acc, or with inf) accustomed to, used to

as·sūgō -ēre — -suctum vt to suck in

assŭl·a -ae f splinter, chip, shaving

assŭlātim adv in splinters, in fragments, piecemeal

assult·ō -āre vt to assault, attack; vi to jump; (with dat) to jump to, jump at

assult·us -ūs m assault, attack

as·sūmō -ēre -sumpsī -sumptum vt to take up, adopt, accept; to usurp, claim, assume; to receive, obtain, derive

assumptĭ·ō -ōnis f taking, receiving, assumption; adoption; (in logic) minor premise

assumptīv·us -a -um adj resting on external evidence, extrinsic

assŭ·ō -ēre vt (with dat) to sew (e.g., patch) on (e.g., clothes)

as·surgō -surgĕre -surrexī -surrectum vi to rise up, rise, stand up; to mount up, increase, swell; (with dat) to yield to, stand up for (out of respect)

ass·us -a -um adj roasted; n roast; n pl steam bath, sweat bath

ast conj (older form of at) but

Astart·ē -ēs f Syro-Phoenician goddess, counterpart of Venus

a·sternō -sternĕre vt (with dat) to strew (something) on; asterni (with dat) to throw oneself down upon

astipŭlāt·or -ōris m legal assistant; supporter

astipŭl·or -ārī -ātus sum vi (with dat) to agree with

a·stō -stāre vi to stand erect, stand up, stand nearby; (with dat) to assist

Astraē·a -ae f goddess of justice

astrĕp·ō -ĕre -ŭī -ĭtum vi to roar; to make a noise; to applaud; (with dat) to assent loudly to, applaud

astrictē adv concisely; strictly

astrict·us -a -um pp of astringo; drawn together, tight, stingy; tight; concise

a·stringō -stringĕre -strinxī -strictum vt to tighten, bind fast; to put under obligation, obligate, oblige; (fig) to draw closer; to compress, abridge; to occupy (attention); to embarrass

astrologĭ·a -ae f astronomy

astrolŏg·us -ī m astronomer; astrologer

astr·um -ī n star; constellation; n pl stars, sky, heaven; immortality

astū (indecl) n city

astŭp·ĕō -ēre vi (with dat) to be amazed at

ast·us -ūs m cunning, cleverness

astutē *adv* slyly

astūti·a -ae *f* skill, dexterity; cunning, astuteness

astūt·us -a -um *adj* clever; sly, cunning

Astyăn·ax -actis *m* son of Hector and Andromache

asȳl·um -ī *n* refuge, sanctuary, asylum

at *conj* but; (in a transition) but, but on the other hand; (in anticipation of an opponent's objection) but, it may be objected; (in an ironical objection) but really, but after all; (after a negative clause, to introduce a qualification) but at least; **at contra** but on the contrary; **at tamen** and yet, but at least

Atăbŭl·us -ī *m* sirocco, southeast wind

Atalant·a -ae *f* daughter of King Schoeneus, defeated by Hippomenes in a famous footrace; daughter of Iasius and participant in the Calydonian boar hunt

atat *interj* (expressing surprise, pain, warning) oh!

atāv·us -ī *m* great-great-great-grandfather; ancestor

Atell·a -ae *f* Oscan town in Campania

Atellān·us -a -um *adj* Atellan; **Atellana** or **fabula Atellana** comic farce which originated in Atella

āt·er -ra -rum *adj* (opposed to **ni-ger** glossy black) dead black, black; dark, gloomy, eerie; black, unlucky; malicious; poisonous

Athăm·ās -antis *m* king of Thessaly, father of Helle and Phrixus by Nephele, and of Learchus and Melecerta by Ino

Athēn·ae -ārum *f pl* Athens

athě·os -ī *m* atheist

athlēt·a -ae *m* athlete, wrestler

athlēticē *adv* athletically

athlētic·us -a -um *adj* athletic

Atl·ās -antis *m* giant supporting the sky, son of Iapetus and Clymene

atŏm·os -ī *f* indivisible particle, atom

atque *conj* (denotes closer internal connection than is implied by **et** and gives prominence to what follows) and, as well as, together with, and even, and . . . too; (after words of comparison) as, than; **atque . . . atque** both . . . and; **atque adeo** and in fact

atquī *conj* but yet, but anyhow, however, rather, and yet

ātrāment·um -ī *n* ink

ātrāt·us -a -um *adj* clothed in black

Atr·eus -eī *m* son of Pelops, brother of Thyestes, father of Agamemnon and Menelaus

Atrīd·ēs -ae *m* descendant of Atreus

ātriēns·is -is *m* butler

ātriŏl·um -ī *n* small hall, anteroom

ātrīt·ās -ātis *f* blackness

ātr·ium -iī or **-ī** *n* main room, entrance room (*of Roman house*); hall (*of temples or public buildings*)

atrōcit·ās -ātis *f* hideousness, repulsiveness (*of form, appearance*); fierceness, brutality, cruelty (*of character*); severity, rigidity (*of law*)

atrōciter *adv* horribly, fiercely, cruelly, grimly

Ātrŏp·os -ī *f* one of the three Fates

atr·ox -ōcis *adj* horrible, hideous, frightful; savage, cruel, fierce; harsh, stern, unyielding, grim

attactus *pp* of **attingo**

attact·us -ūs *m* touch, contact

attăg·ēn -ēnis *m* woodcock

attagēn·a -ae *f* woodcock

Attalic·us -a -um *adj* of Attalus; Pergamean; rich, splendid; *n pl* gold-brocaded garments

Attăl·us -ī *m* king of Pergamum in Asia Minor, who bequeathed his kingdom to Rome

attāmen *conj* but still, but yet

attat or **attătae** *interj* (indicating surprise, joy, dismay) oh!

attegī·a -ae *f* hut, cottage

attemperātē *adv* on time, in the nick of time

attempt·ō -āre *vt* to try, attempt; to test; to tempt, try to corrupt; to attack

at·tendō -tendĕre -tendī -tentum *vt* to notice, mark; to pay attention to, mind, consider; (with *dat* or **ad** + *acc*) to direct (*mind, attention*) to; *vi* to pay attention, listen

attentē *adv* attentively

attentī·ō -ōnis *f* attention, attentiveness

attentō see **attempto**

attent·us -a -um *pp* of **attendo**; *adj* attentive; careful, frugal, industrious

attenuātē *adv* (rhet) without flowery language, simply

attenuāt·us -a -um *adj* weak, weakened; shortened, brief; over-refined, affected; plain, bald (*style*)

attenŭ·ō -āre *vt* to make weak, weaken; to thin, attenuate; to lessen, diminish; to humble

at·tĕrō -terĕre -trīvī -trītum *vt* to rub, wear away, wear out, weaken, exhaust; to waste, destroy

attest·or -ārī -ātus sum *vt* to attest, confirm, corroborate, prove

attex·ō -ĕre -ŭī -tum *vt* to weave; to add

Atth·is -ĭdis *f* Attica

Attic·a -ae *f* district of Greece, of which Athens was the capital

atticē *adv* in the Attic or Athenian style

atticiss·ō -āre *vi* to speak in the Athenian manner

Attic·us -a -um *adj* Attic, Athenian; *m* T. Pomponius Atticus (*friend of Cicero*, 109–32 B.C.)

attigō see **attingo**

at·tineō -tinēre -tinŭī -tentum *vt* to hold tight, hold on to, hold, detain, hold back; to reach for; *vi* (with ad + *acc*) to pertain to, relate to, refer to, concern; **quod ad me attinet** as far as I am concerned

at·tingo -tingĕre -tīgī -tactum *vt* to touch, come in contact with; to reach, arrive at; to touch (*food*), taste; to touch, lie near, border; to touch upon, mention lightly; to touch, strike, attack; to touch, affect; to undertake, engage in, take in hand, manage; to resemble; to concern, belong to

Att·is -ĭdis *m* priest of Phrygian goddess Cybele

attoll·ō -ĕre *vt* to lift up, raise; to exalt, extol

at·tondĕō -tondēre -tondī -tonsum *vt* to clip, shave, shear; to prune; to crop; to clip, fleece, cheat

attonĭt·us -a -um *adj* thunderstruck, stunned, amazed, dazed, astonished; inspired; frantic

attorquĕō -ēre *vt* to hurl up

at·trahō -trahĕre -traxī -tractum *vt* to attract, draw, drag by force

attrect·ō -āre *vt* to touch, handle; to appropriate to oneself

attrepĭd·ō -āre *vi* to hobble along

attrib·uō -uĕre -uī -ūtum *vt* to allot, assign, bestow, give, annex; to impose (*taxes*)

attribūtĭ·ō -ōnis *f* payment of a debt; (*gram*) predicate

attribūt·us -a -um *pp* of **attribuo**; *n* (*gram*) predicate

attrīt·us -a -um *pp* of **attero**; *adj* worn away, wasted; shameless

au *interj* ouch!

an·ceps -cŭpis *m* fowler, bird catcher; spy, eavesdropper

auctār·ium -ĭī or **-ī** *n* addition

auctĭfĭc·us -a -um *adj* increasing

auctĭ·ō -ōnis *f* increase; auction

auctĭōnārĭ·us -a -um *adj* auction

auctĭōn·or -ārī -ātus sum *vi* to hold an auction

auctĭt·ō -āre *vt* to increase greatly

auct·ō -āre *vt* to increase, augment

auct·or -ōris *m* originator, author; writer, historian; reporter, informant (*of news*); authority (*for statement or theory*); proposer, backer, supporter; progenitor (*of race*); founder (*of city*); model, example; adviser, counselor; teacher; guarantor, security; leader, statesman

auctōrāment·um -ī *n* contract; pay, wages

auctōrĭt·ās -ātis *f* origination, source, cause; view, opinion, judgment; advice, counsel, encouragement; might, power, authority, weight, influence, leadership; importance, significance, worth, consequence; example, model, precedent; authority (*for establishing a fact*); document, record; decree (*of senate*); right of possession

auctōr·ō -āre *vt* to bind; **auctorari** or **se auctorare** to hire oneself out

auctus *pp* of **augeo**

auct·us -ūs *m* increase, growth, abundance

aucŭp·ium -ĭī or **-ī** *n* fowling; trap; eavesdropping; **aucupia verborum** quibbling

aucŭp·ō -āre or **aucŭp·or -ārī -ātus sum** *vt* to lie in wait for, watch for, chase, strive after, catch; *vi* to catch birds

audācĭ·a -ae *f* (in good sense) boldness, courage, daring; (in bad sense) recklessness, effrontery, audacity; bold deed; *f pl* adventures

audacter *adv* boldly, audaciously

aud·ax -ācis *adj* (in good sense) bold, daring; (in bad sense) reckless, rash, foolhardy

aud·ens -entis *adj* bold, daring, courageous

audentĭ·a -ae *f* daring, boldness

audĕō audēre ausus sum *vt* to dare, venture, risk; **vix ausim** (*old perf subj*) **credere** I could scarcely dare to believe; *vi* to dare, be bold

audĭ·ens -entis *m* hearer, listener; *m pl* audience

audientĭ·a -ae *f* hearing, attention; **audientiam facere** to command attention, to command silence

aud·ĭō -īre -īvī or **-ĭī itum** *vt* to hear, listen to, give attention to; to hear, be taught by, learn from; to hear, listen, to grant; to accept, agree with, approve, yield to, grant, allow; to listen to, obey; to be called, be named, be reported, be regarded

audītĭ·ō -ōnis *f* hearsay, rumor, report, news

audītōr·ium -ĭī or **-ī** *n* lecture hall; the audience

audīt·us -ūs *m* sense of hearing; a hearing; report, rumor

auferō auferre abstŭlī ablātum *vt* to bear or take away, bear off, remove, withdraw; to snatch away, steal, rob; to sweep away, kill, destroy; to gain, obtain, receive, get; to learn, understand; to mislead, lead into a digression; **auferri e conspectu** to disappear from sight

Aufĭd·us -ī *m* river in Apulia

au·fugĭō -fugĕre -fūgī *vt* to escape, flee from; *vi* to escape, run away

Augĕ·ās -ae *m* king of Elis whose stables Hercules cleaned by diverting the River Alpheus through them

augĕō augēre auxi auctum *vt* to increase, enlarge, augment, spread; to magnify, extol, exalt; to exaggerate; to enrich; to honor, advance, promote; to feed (*flame*)

augesc·ō -ĕre *vi* to begin to grow; to become larger, increase

aug·ur -ŭris *m* or *f* augur (*priest who foretold the future by observing the flight of birds, lightning, etc.*), prophet, seer

augurāl·is -e *adj* of divination; augur's; n area in Roman camp where the general took auspices

augurāti·ō -ōnis f prophesying

augurātō adv after taking the auguries

augurāt·us -ūs m office of augur

augur·ium -iī or **-ī** n observation of omens, interpretation of omen, augury; sign, omen; prophesy, prediction, forecast; foreboding

auguri·us -a -um adj of augurs; **jus augurium** the right to take auguries

augŭr·ō -āre or **augur·or -ārī -ātus sum** vt to consult by augury; to consecrate by augury; to conjecture, imagine; to foretell, predict, prophesy; vi to act as augur; to take auspices; to play augur

August·a -ae f (in imperial period) mother, wife, daughter, or sister of the emperor

Augustāl·is -e adj of Augustus; n pl games in honor of Augustus; **sodales Augustales** priests of deified Augustus

Augustān·us -a -um adj Augustan; imperial

augustē adv reverently

august·us -a -um adj august, sacred, venerable; majestic, magnificent

August·us -a -um adj Augustan, imperial; cognomen of Octavius Caesar and of subsequent emperors; **mensis Augustus** August

aul·a -ae f inner court, hall (of house); palace; royal court; people of the royal court, the court

aulae·um -ī n curtain, canopy; theater curtain; bed cover, sofa cover, tapestry

aulic·us -a -um adj courtly, princely; n pl courtiers

Aul·is -is or **-idis** f port in Boeotia from which the Greeks sailed for Troy

auloed·us -ī m singer (accompanied by flute)

aur·a -ae f breeze, breath of air, wind; air, atmosphere; heights, heaven; upper world; odor, exhalation; daylight, publicity; **ad auras ferre** to make known, publicize; **ad auras venire** to come to the upper world; **auram captare** to sniff the air; **aura popularis** popular favor; **auras fugere** to hide; **aura spei** breath of hope

aurāri·us -a -um adj of gold, golden, gold; f gold mine

aurāt·us -a -um adj decorated with gold, made of gold, gold-plated, golden; glittering

aureŏl·us -a -um adj gold; splendid

aurĕ·us -a -um adj of gold, golden; gilded; beautiful, magnificent, splendid; m gold coin

auricŏm·us -a -um adj golden-haired; with golden foliage

auricŭl·a f external ear, ear

aurif·er -ĕra -ĕrum adj producing

or containing gold; (of tree) bearing golden apples

aurif·ex -icis m goldsmith

aurīg·a -ae m or f charioteer, driver; (fig) pilot

Aurīg·a -ae m Auriga, Wagoner (constellation)

aurigĕn·a -ae m offspring of gold (i.e., Perseus)

aurīg·er -ĕra -ĕrum adj gold-bearing; gilded

aurīg·ō -āre vi to drive a chariot, compete in chariot race

aur·is -is f ear; f pl listeners; critical ears; **aurem admovere** to listen; **auribus servire** to flatter; **auris adhibere** to be attentive, pay attention; **in aurem dextram** or **in aurem utramvis dormire** to sleep soundly, i.e., to be unconcerned

aurītŭl·us -ī m ass

aurīt·us -a -um adj long-eared; attentive; nosey; **testis aurītus** witness by hearsay only; m rabbit

aurŏr·a -ae f morning, dawn, daybreak; the Orient, the East

Aurŏr·a -ae f goddess of dawn

aur·um -ī n gold; color of gold, golden luster; gold cup; gold necklace; gold jewelry; gold plate; golden fleece; gold money; Golden Age

auscultāti·ō -ōnis f obedience

auscultāt·or -ōris m listener

auscult·ō -āre vt to hear (with attention), listen to; to overhear; vi (with dat) to obey, listen to

ausim see audeo

Ausŏn·ēs -um m pl Ausonians (ancient inhabitants of central Italy)

Ausonĭd·a -ārum m pl Italians

Ausonĭ·us -a -um adj Ausonian, Italian; m pl Ausonians, Italians; f Ausonia, Italy

ausp·ex -icis m augur, soothsayer; author, founder, leader, director, protector; m pl witnesses (at marriage ceremony)

auspicātō adv after taking the auspices; under good omens, at a fortunate moment

auspicāt·us -a -um adj consecrated (by auguries); auspicious, favorable, lucky

auspic·ium -iī or **-ī** n divination (through observation of flight of birds), auspices; sign, omen, premonition; command, leadership, guidance, authority; right, power, will, inclination; **auspicium habere** to have the right to take auspices; **auspicium facere** (of birds) to give a sign, to yield an omen

auspic·or -ārī -ātus sum vt to begin, take up; vi to take auspices; to make a start

aust·er -rī m south wind; the South

austērē adv austerely, severely

austērit·ās -ātis f austerity

austēr·us -a -um adj austere, stern, harsh (person); pungent (smell); harsh (taste); drab, dark (color); serious (*talk*); gloomy, sad, hard (*circumstances*)

austrāl·is -e *adj* southern; **cingulus, regio,** or **ora australis** torrid zone

austrīn·us -a -um *adj* from the south, southerly; southern

aus·us -a -um *pp* of **audeo**; *n* daring attempt, enterprise, adventure

aut *conj* or; (correcting what precedes) or, or rather, or else; (adding emphatic alternative) or at least; **aut . . . aut** either . . . or

autem *conj* (regularly follows an emphatic word) but, on the other hand, however; (in a transition) but, and now

autheps·a -ae *f* cooker, boiler (*utensil*)

autogrăph·us -a -um *adj* written with one's own hand, autograph

Autolўc·us -ī *m* father of Anticlea, maternal grandfather of Ulysses, and famous robber

automăt·on -ī *n* automaton

automăt·us -a -um *adj* automatic, spontaneous, voluntary

Automĕd·ōn -ontis *m* charioteer of Achilles

Antonŏ·ē -ēs *f* daughter of Cadmus, wife of Aristaeus, and mother of Actaeon

autumnāl·is -e *adj* autumn, autumnal

autumn·us -a -um *adj* autumn, autumnal; *m* autumn

autŭm·ō -āre *vt* to assert, affirm, say

auxiliār·ēs -ĭum *m pl* auxiliary troops

auxiliār·is -e *adj* auxiliary

auxiliāri·us -a -um *adj* auxiliary

auxiliāt·or -ōris *m* helper, assistant

auxiliāt·us -ūs *m* aid

auxili·or -ārī -ātus sum *vi* (with *dat*) a to help, aid, assist; b to relieve, heal, cure

auxil·ium -ĭī or -ī *n* help, aid, assistance; *n pl* auxiliary troops, auxiliaries; military force, military power; **auxilio esse** (with *dat*) to be of assistance to

avārē *adv* greedily

avārĭter *adv* greedily

avārĭti·a -ae *f* greed, selfishness, avarice; gluttony

avārĭti·ēs -ēī *f* avarice

avār·us -a -um *adj* greedy, covetous, avaricious; (with *genit*) desirous of, eager for

avē see **aveo**

ă·vĕhō -vehĕre -vexī -vectum *vt* to carry away; **avehi** to ride away, sail away

ă·vellō -vellĕre -vellī (or -vulsī or -volsī) -vulsum (or -volsum) *vt* to pull or pluck away; to tear off; to separate, remove; **avelli** or **se avellere** (with ab + *abl*) to tear oneself away from, withdraw from

avēn·a -ae *f* oats; reed, stalk, a straw; shepherd's pipe

Aventīn·us -a -um *adj* Aventine; *m* & *n* Aventine Hill (*one of the seven hills of Rome*)

av·eō -ēre *vt* to wish, desire, long for, crave; (with *inf*) to wish to, long to; *vi* to say good-bye; **avē!** or **avetē!** hail!, hello!; good morning!; farewell!, good-bye!

Avernāl·is -e *adj* of Lake Avernus

Avern·us -a -um *adj* without birds; of Lake Avernus; *m* Lake Avernus (*near Cumae, said to be an entrance to the lower world*)

ăverrunc·ō -āre *vt* to avert

ăversābĭl·is -e *adj* abominable

ăvers·or -ārī -ātus sum *vt* to repulse, reject, refuse, decline, shun, avoid, send away; *vi* to turn away (*in displeasure, contempt, shame, etc.*)

ăvers·or -ōris *m* embezzler

ăvers·us -a -um *adj* turned away (*in flight*); rear, in the rear; disinclined, alienated, unfavorable, hostile; (with *dat* or *ab* + *abl*) averse to, hostile to, opposed to, estranged from; *n* the back part, the back; *n pl* the back parts, the back; hinterland; **in adversum** backwards

ă·vertō (or **ă·vortō**) -vertĕre -vertī -versum *vt* to turn away, avert; to embezzle, misappropriate; to divert; to alienate; **se avertere** to retire; *vi* to withdraw, retire

avi·a -ae *f* grandmother; old wives' tale

ăvi·a -ōrum *n pl* pathless, lonely places

aviāri·us -a -um *adj* of birds; bird; *n* aviary; haunt of wild birds

avĭdē *adv* eagerly, greedily

avidĭt·ās -ātis *f* eagerness, longing, great desire; avarice

avĭd·us -a -um *adj* eager, earnest, greedy; hungry, greedy, voracious, gluttonous, insatiable; (with *genit* or *dat* or with **in** + *acc*) desirous of, eager for

av·is -is *f* bird; sign, omen; **avis alba** rarity

avīt·us -a -um *adj* grandfather's, ancestral; old

ăvi·us -a -um *adj* out-of-the-way, lonely; trackless, pathless, untrodden; wandering, straying; going astray

ăvocāment·um -ī *n* diversion, recreation

ăvocăti·ō -ōnis *f* distraction, diversion

ăvŏc·ō -āre *vt* to call away; to divert, remove, withdraw; to divert, amuse

ăvŏl·ō -āre *vi* to fly away; to hasten away, dash off

ăvulsus *pp* of **avello**

avuncŭl·us -ī *m* mother's brother, maternal uncle; **avunculus magnus** great-uncle; **avunculus major** great-great-uncle

av·us -ī *m* grandfather; forefather, ancestor
Axēn·us -ī *m* Black Sea
axicǐ·a -ae *f* scissors

axill·a -ae *f* armpit
ax·is -is *m* axle; chariot, wagon; axis, pole; North Pole; sky; the heavens; region, country; board, plank

B

babae *interj* wonderful!, strange!
Babyl·ōn -ŏnis *f* city on Euphrates
Babylōnǐ·a -ae *f* country between Tigris and Euphrates
bāc·a -ae *f* berry; olive; fruit; pearl
bācāt·us -a -um *adj* adorned with pearls
bacc·ar -ǎris *n* cyclamen (*plant whose root yields fragrant oil*)
Bacch·a -ae *f* bacchante, maenad
bacchābund·us -a -um *adj* raving, riotous
Bacchān·al -ālis *n* place sacred to Bacchus; *n pl* bacchanalian orgies
bacchātǐ·ō -ōnis *f* orgy; revelry
bacch·or -ārī -ātus sum *vi* to celebrate the festival of Bacchus; to revel, rave, rage
Bacch·us -ī *m* god of wine; (fig) vine; (fig) wine
bācǐf·er -ěra -ěrum *adj* bearing berries or olives
bacill·um -ī *n* small staff, wand; lictor's staff
bacǔl·um -ī *n* or **bacǔl·us -ī** *m* stick; staff; scepter
badiss·ō -āre *vi* to go, walk
Baetǐc·us -a -um *adj* of the Baetis; *f* Baetica (*Roman province*)
Baet·is -is *m* river in Spain
Bāǐ·ae -ārum *f pl* resort town at northern extremity of Bay of Naples
bājǔl·ō -āre *vt* to carry, bear
bājǔl·us -ī *m* porter; day laborer
bālaen·a -ae *f* whale
balanāt·us -a -um *adj* anointed with balsam; embalmed
balǎn·us -ī *m* or *f* acorn; date; balsam; shell-fish
balātr·ō -ōnis *m* jester, buffoon
bālāt·us -ūs *m* bleating
balb·us -a -um *adj* stammering
balbūt·ǐō -īre *vt & vi* to stammer, stutter
balině·um -ī *n* bath
ballist·a -ae *f* large military device for hurling stones; heavy artillery
ballistār·ǐum -ǐī or **-ǐ** *n* artillery emplacement
balně·ae -ārum *f pl* baths
balneārǐ·us -a -um *adj* of a bath; *n pl* baths
balneāt·or -ōris *m* bath superintendent
balneŏl·ae -ārum *f pl* baths
balneŏl·um -ī *n* small bath
balně·um -ī *n* bath
bāl·ō -āre *vi* to bleat
balsǎm·um -ī *n* balsam; balsam tree

baltě·us -ī *m* belt; baldric; girdle
baptister·ǐum -ǐī or **-ǐ** *n* bath; swimming pool
barāthr·um -ī *n* abyss, chasm, pit; lower world
barb·a -ae *f* beard
barbǎrē *adv* in a foreign language; barbarously, cruelly
barbarǐ·a -ae or **barbarǐ·ēs -ēī** *f* foreign country, strange land; rudeness, want of culture
barbarǐc·us -a -um *adj* foreign, outlandish
barbarǐēs see **barbaria**
barbǎr·us -a -um *adj* foreign; barbarous, savage, uncivilized, rude; *m* foreigner; barbarian
barbātǔl·us -a -um *adj* wearing a small beard
barbāt·us -a -um *adj* bearded; adult; old-time; *m* old-timer; philosopher, longhair; goat
barbǐg·er -ěra -ěrum *adj* wearing a beard, bearded
barbǐt·os -ī *m* lyre; lute
barbǔl·a -ae *f* small beard
bard·us -a -um *adj* stupid, dull
bard·us -ī *m* bard
bār·ō -ōnis *m* dunce, blockhead
barr·us -ī *m* elephant
bāsǐātǐ·ō -ōnis *f* kissing; kiss
basilǐc·us -a -um *adj* royal; splendid; *f* public building, basilica (*used as law court and exchange*); portico
bāsǐ·ō -āre *vt* to kiss
bas·is -is *f* base, foundation, support; pedestal
bās·ǐum -ǐī or **-ǐ** *n* kiss
Bassǎr·eus -ěī *m* Bacchus
batill·um -ī *n* brazier
battǔ·ō -ěre -ǐ *vt* to beat, pound
beātē *adv* happily
beātǐt·ās -ātis *f* happiness
beātitūd·ō -ǐnis *f* happiness
beāt·us -a -um *adj* happy; prosperous, rich; fertile; abundant; *n* happiness
Bēlǐd·ēs -um *f pl* descendants of Belus, the Danaids, who killed their husbands on their wedding night
bellārǐ·a -ōrum *m pl* dessert
bellāt·or -ōris *adj* warlike; valorous; spirited; *m* warrior
bellātr·ix -īcis *adj* warlike, skilled in war; *f* warrior (*female*)
bellē *adv* prettily, neatly, nicely, well
Bellerŏph·ōn -ontis *m* slayer of Chimaera and rider of Pegasus
bellǐcōs·us -a -um *adj* warlike, martial, valorous

bellic·us -a -um adj war, military; warlike, fierce; n bugle; bugle call

bellig·er -ĕra -ĕrum adj belligerent, warlike, aggressive; martial; valiant

belligĕr·ō -āre or **belligĕr·or -ārī -ātus sum** vi to wage war, fight

bellipŏt·ens -entis adj mighty or valiant in war; m Mars

bell·ō -āre or **bell·or -ārī -ātus sum** vi to wage war, fight

Bellōn·a -ae f Roman goddess of war

bellŭl·us -a -um adj pretty, lovely, cute, fine

bell·um -ī n war; battle

bēlŭ·a -ae f beast, monster, brute

bēluōs·us -a -um adj full of monsters

Bēl·us -ī m Baal; king of Tyre and father of Dido; king of Egypt, father of Danaus and Aegyptus

bene adv well; thoroughly; very, quite

bene·dīcō -dīcĕre -dīxī -dictum vt to speak well of, praise; (eccl) to bless

beneficentī·a -ae f beneficence, kindness

beneficiāri·ī -ōrum m pl soldiers exempt from menial tasks

benefic·ium -iī or **-ī** n kindness, favor, benefit, service; help, support, promotion; right, privilege

benefic·us -a -um adj generous, liberal, obliging

Benevent·um -ī n town in Samnium in S. Italy

benevŏlē adv kindly

benevŏl·ens -entis adj kindhearted, obliging

benevolentī·a -ae f benevolence, kindness, goodwill; favor

benevŏl·us -a -um adj kind, friendly; devoted, faithful

benignē adv in a friendly manner, kindly, courteously; mildly, indulgently; liberally, generously

benignit·ās -ātis f kindness, friendliness, courtesy; liberality, bounty

benign·us -a -um adj kind-hearted; mild, affable; liberal; favorable; bounteous, fruitful

be·ō -āre vt to make happy; to bless; to enrich; to refresh

Berecynt·us -ī m mountain in Phrygia sacred to Cybele

bēryll·us -ī m precious stone, beryl

bēs bessis m two thirds

besti·a -ae f beast, wild beast

bestiāri·us -a -um adj of wild beasts; m wild-beast fighter

bestiŏl·a -ae f little beast

bēt·a -ae f beet

bēta (indecl) n second letter of Greek alphabet

bibliopōl·a -ae m bookseller

bibliothēc·a -ae f library

bibliothēcār·ius -iī or **-ī** m librarian

bib·ō -ĕre -ī vt to drink; to visit, reach, live near (river); (fig) to take in, absorb, listen eagerly to

bibŭl·us -a -um adj fond of drinking; absorbent; thirsty

bi·ceps -cipĭtis adj two-headed; twin-peaked

biclīn·ium -iī or **-ī** n table for two

bicŏl·or -ōris adj two-colored

bicorn·is -e adj two-horned; two-pronged

bid·ens -entis adj with two teeth; with two points; two-pronged; m hoe, mattock; sacrificial animal; sheep

bident·al -ālis n place struck by lightning

bidŭ·um -ī n period of two days; two days

bienn·ium -iī or **-ī** n period of two years; two years

bifārīam adv on both sides, twofold, double, in two parts, in two directions

bifāri·us -a -um adj double, twofold

bif·er -ĕra -ĕrum adj bearing fruit twice a year; of twofold form

bifĭd·us -a -um adj split in two, forked, cloven

bifŏr·is -e adj having two doors; having two holes or openings; double

biformāt·us -a -um adj double, having two forms

biform·is -e adj double, having two forms

bifr·ons -ontis adj two-headed; two-faced

bifurc·us -a -um adj two-pronged, forked

bīg·a -ae f or **bīg·ae -ārum** f pl span of horses, team; two-horse chariot

bijŭg·ī -ōrum m pl team of horses; two-horse chariot

bijŭg·is -e adj yoked two together; drawn by a pair of horses

bijŭg·us -a -um adj yoked two together; two-horse

bilĭbr·is -e adj two-pound

bilingu·is -e adj two-tongued; bilingual; hypercritical, deceitful, false

bīl·is -is f gall, bile; wrath, anger; **bīlis atra** melancholy; madness

bimăr·is -e adj situated between two seas

bimarīt·us -ī m bigamist

bimāt·er -ris adj having two mothers

bimembr·is -e adj half man, half beast

bimembr·is -is m centaur

bimestr·is -e adj two-month-old; lasting two months

bimŭl·us -a -um adj two-year-old

bīm·us -a -um adj two-year-old; for two years

bīn·ī -ae -a adj two by two; two to each, two each; two at a time; a pair of

binoct·ium -iī or **-ī** n two nights

binōmin·is -e adj having two names

bipalm·is -e adj two spans long

bipart·iō -īre — -ītum vt to divide into two parts; to bisect

bipartītō *adv* in two parts

bipăt·ens -entis *adj* open in two directions

bipedāl·is -e *adj* two feet long, broad, thick, or high

bipennĭf·er -ĕra -ĕrum *adj* wielding a two-edged ax

bipenn·is -e *adj* two-edged; *f* two-edged ax

bip·ēs -ĕdis *adj* two-footed, biped

birēm·is -e *adj* two-oared; with two banks of oars; *f* ship with two banks of oars

bis *adv* twice

Bistŏn·ēs -um *m pl* fierce tribesmen in Thessaly

bisulc·us -a -um *adj* split, cloven; forked

bīt·ō -ĕre *vi* to go

bitūm·en -ĭnis *n* bitumen, asphalt

bivi·us -a -um *adj* two-way; *n* crossroads, intersection

blaes·us -a -um *adj* lisping; indistinct

blandē *adv* flatteringly; courteously

blandiloquenti·a -ae *f* flattery

blandiloquentŭl·us -a -um *adj* smooth-tongued

blandīment·um -ī *n* flattery, compliment; charm

bland·ior -īrī -ītus sum *vt* to flatter; to coax; to allure; to please

blandīter *adv* flatteringly

blanditi·a -ae *f* caress, flattery, compliment; charm

blandītim *adv* flatteringly

bland·us -a -um *adj* smooth; flattering, fawning; alluring, charming, winsome, pleasant

blatĕr·ō -āre *vi* to talk foolishly, to babble

blatt·a -ae *f* cockroach; moth

blenn·us -ī *m* idiot, blockhead

blitĕ·us -a -um *adj* silly; tasteless

blit·um -ī *n* tasteless vegetable, kind of spinach

boāri·us -a -um *adj* cattle

Boeotĭ·a -ae *f* district north of Attica in central Greece, the capital of which was Thebes

bōlēt·us -ī *n* mushroom

bol·us -ī *m* throw (*of the dice*); cast (*of the net*); (fig) haul, piece of good luck, gain; choice morsel

bombax *interj* strange!; indeed!

bomb·us -ī *m* booming; buzzing, humming

bombўcīn·us -a -um *adj* silk, silken

bomb·ўx -ўcis *m* silkworm; silk; silk garment

Bon·a De·a (*genit:* **Bon·ae De·ae**) *f* goddess of chastity and fertility

bonĭt·ās -ātis *f* goodness, integrity; kindness, benevolence

bon·us -a -um *adj* good; honest, virtuous; faithful, patriotic; fit, suitable; able, clever; brave; noble; auspicious, favorable; useful, advantageous; *n* good; profit, advantage; *n pl* goods, property

bo·ō -āre *vi* to cry aloud; to roar

Boōt·ēs -ae *m* constellation containing the bright star Arcturus

borĕ·as -ae *m* north wind

borĕ·us -a -um *adj* north, northern

bōs bovis *m* or *f* ox, bull; cow

Bospŏr·us -ī *m* strait between Thrace and Asia Minor, connecting Propontis and Black Sea

botŭl·us -ī *m* sausage

bovil·e -is *n* ox stall

bovill·us -a -um *adj* cattle

brāc·ae -ārum *f pl* pants, trousers

brācāt·us -a -um *adj* wearing trousers; foreign, barbarian; effeminate

bracchiāl·is -e *adj* of the arm

bracchiŏl·um -ī *n* dainty arm

bracch·ĭum -ĭī or **-ī** *n* arm, lower arm; claw; bough; tendril; arm of the sea; sail yard

bractĕ·a -ae *f* gold leaf; gold foil

bractĕŏl·a -ae *f* very thin gold leaf

brassĭc·a -ae *f* cabbage

breviār·ĭum -ĭī or **-ī** *n* summary, abridgement; statistics

brevĭcŭl·us -a -um *adj* rather short

brevĭlŏqu·ens -entis *adj* brief (*in speech*)

breviloquenti·a -ae *f* brevity

brevĭ *adv* briefly, in a few words; shortly, in a short time

brĕv·is -e *adj* short, little, brief; concise; small; shallow; narrow; *n pl* shoals, shallows

brevĭt·ās -ātis *f* brevity; smallness; shortness

brevĭter *adv* shortly, briefly

Britanni·a -ae *f* Britain; British Isles

Brom·ĭus -ĭī or **-ī** *m* Bacchus

brūm·a -ae *f* winter solstice; winter; winter's cold

brūmāl·is -e *adj* wintry

Brundĭs·ĭum -ĭī or **-ī** *n* port in S.E. Italy on Adriatic Sea

Bruttĭ·ī -ōrum *m pl* inhabitants of toe of Italy

Brūt·us -ī *m* Lucius Junius Brutus (*credited with having driven out the last Roman king, Tarquinius Superbus*); Marcus Junius Brutus (*one of the murderers of Julius Caesar*)

brūt·us -a -um *adj* heavy, unwieldy; dull, stupid

būbĭl·e -is *n* ox stall

būb·ō -ōnis *m* owl

būbŭl·a -ae *f* beef

bubulcĭt·or -ārī -ātus sum *vi* to / be a herdsman; to ride herd

būbulc·us -ī *m* cowherd; plowman

būbŭl·us -a -um *adj* of cows or oxen

būcaed·a -ae *m* flogged slave

bucc·a -ae *f* cheek; loudmouthed person; trumpeter; parasite; mouthful

buccell·a -ae *f* small mouthful; morsel

buccŭl·a -ae *f.* little cheek; visor

buccŭlent·us -a -um *adj* loudmouthed

būcĕr(ĭ)·us -a -um *adj* horned

būcĭn·a -ae *f* (curved) trumpet; war trumpet; shepherd's horn

būcĭnāt·or -ōris *m* trumpeter

būcolĭc·us -a -um *adj* pastoral, bucolic

būcŭl·a -ae *f* heifer

būf.ō -ōnis *m* toad

bulb.us - *m* onion

būl.ē -ēs *f* (Greek) council, senate

būlent. -ae *n* councilor

būleuter.ium -iī *or* **-ī** *n* meeting place of Greek council

bull.a -ae *f* bubble: boss, stud, knob; amulet badge (*symbol of boyhood*)

bullāt.us -a -um *adj* inflated, bombastic; studded; wearing a bulla, i.e., still a child

būmast.us -ī *f* species of grape with large clusters

būr.is -is *m* curved handle of plow

bustirāp.us -ī *m* ghoul, grave robber

bustuārī.us -a -um *adj* of a tomb or pyre

bust.um -ī *n* pyre; tomb, sepulcher

buxif.er -ĕra -ĕrum *adj* producing boxwood trees

bux.um -ī *n* boxwood; (spinning) top; comb; writing tablet (*made of boxwood*)

bux.us -ī *f* boxwood tree

Byzant.ium -iī *or* **-ī** *n* city on the Bosporus, later named Constantinople

C

caball.us -ī *m* pack horse, nag, hack

cachinnāti.ō -ōnis *f* loud or immoderate laughter

cachinn.ō -āre *vi* to laugh loud; to roar (*with laughter*)

cachinn.ō -ōnis *m* scoffer

cachinn.us -ī *m* loud laugh; jeering; rippling roaring

cac.ō -āre *vt* to defile; *vi* to defecate

cacoeth.es -is *n* malignant disease, itch

cacūm.en -inis *n* point, tip, top, peak

cacūmin.ō -āre *vt* to make pointed; to sharpen

Cāc.us -ī *m* son of Vulcan, a giant who lived on the Aventine Hill, killed by Hercules

cadāv.er -ĕris *n* corpse, carcass

cadāveros.us -a -um *adj* cadaverous, ghastly

Cadmē.us -a -um *adj* Cadmean; Theban, *f* citadel of Thebes

Cadm.us -ī *m* son of Phoenician king Agenor, brother of Europa, and founder of Thebes

cad.ō cadĕre cecidī cāsum *vi* to fall, sink, drop: to be slain, die, be sacrificed; to happen; to belong, refer, be suitable, apply; to abate, subside, flag, decline, decay, vanish, fail, cease; to end, close

cadūceāt.or -ōris *m* herald

cadūcĕ.us -ī *m* herald's staff, caduceus

cadūcif.er -ĕra -ĕrum *adj* with herald's staff

cadūc.us -a -um *adj* falling, fallen; inclined to fall; frail, perishable, transitory; vain, futile, ineffectual; (law) lapsed, without heir

cad.us -ī *m* jar, flask, jug

caecigĕn.us -a -um *adj* born blind

caecit.ās -ātis *f* blindness

caec.ō -āre *vt* to make blind; to make obscure

Caecūb.um -ī *n* famous wine from S. Latium

caec.us -a -um *adj* blind; invisible; vague, random, aimless, uncertain, unknown; making invisible, blind-

ing; dark, gloomy, obscure

caed.ēs -is *f* murder, slaughter, massacre; bloodshed, gore; the slain

caed.ō caedĕre cecīdī caesum *vt* to hack at, chop; to strike, beat; to fell, cut down, cut off, cut to pieces; to kill, murder

caelām.en -inis *n* engraving, basrelief

caelāt.or -ōris *m* engraver

caelātūr.a -ae *f* engraving

cael.ebs -ibis *adj* unmarried, single (*whether bachelor or widower*)

cael.es -itis *adj* heavenly, celestial

caelest.ia -ium *n pl* heavenly bodies

caelest.is -e *adj* heavenly, celestial; divine, supernatural

caelest.is -is *m* deity

caelibāt.us -ūs *m* celibacy

caelicŏl.a -ae *m* god

caelif.er -ĕra -ĕrum *adj* supporting the sky

caelipŏt.ens -entis *adj* powerful in heaven

caelīt.es -um *m pl* inhabitants of heaven, gods

Cael.ius Mon.s (*genit:* **Cael.iī** *or* **-ī Mon.tis**) *m* Caelian Hill in Rome

cael.ō -āre *vt* to engrave in relief, to emboss, to carve; to cast; to fashion, compose; to adorn

cael.um -ī *n* sky, heaven, heavens; air, climate, weather; engraver's chisel, burin

caement.um -ī *n* quarry stone; rubble; cement

caenōs.us -a -um *adj* dirty, filthy, muddy

caen.um -ī *n* dirt, filth, mud, mire

caep.a -ae *f* or **caep.e -is** *n* onion

Caere (indecl) *n* city in Etruria

caerimōni.a -ae *f* rite: ritual, religious ceremony; sanctity, sacredness; awe, reverence, veneration

caerŭl.a -ōrum *n pl* sea

caerŭlĕ.us *or* **caerŭl.us -a -um** *adj* blue, azure, dark-blue, green, dark-green; dark, gloomy

Caes.ar -ăris *m* C. Julius Caesar (102?-44 B.C.)

caesariăt·us -a -um *adj* long-haired

caesarĭ·ēs -ēī *f* hair

caesicĭ·us -a -um *adj* bluish, dark blue

caesim *adv* by cutting; in short clauses, in a clipped style

caesĭ·us -a -um *adj* bluish-grey; blue-eyed; gray-eyed; cat-eyed

caesp·es -ĭtis *m* sod, turf, grass; altar of sod

caest·us -ūs *m* boxing glove

caetr·a -ae *f* short Spanish shield

caetrāt·us -a -um *adj* armed with a shield

Caiēt·a -ae *f* nurse of Aeneas; town on coast of Latium

Caius see Gaius

Calăb·er -ra -rum *adj* Calabrian

Calabrĭ·a -ae *f* S.W. peninsula of Italy

Cală·is -is *m* son of Boreas and Orithyia, and brother of Zetes

calamist·er -rī *m* hair curler, curling iron; (rhet) flowery language

calamistrāt·us -a -um *adj* curled (*with a hair curler*)

calamistr·um -ī *n* curling iron

calamit·ās -ātis *f* loss, injury, damage; misfortune, calamity, disaster; military defeat

calamitōsē *adv* unfortunately

calamitōs·us -a -um *adj* disastrous, ruinous, destructive; exposed to injury, suffering great damage, unfortunate

calăm·us -ī *m* reed, stalk; pen; arrow; fishing rod; pipe

calathisc·us -ī *m* small wicker basket

calăth·us -ī *m* wicker basket; milk pail; wine cup

calăt·or -ōris *m* servant, attendant

calc·ar -āris *n* spur; stimulus

calcārĕ·um -ī *n* heel

calceāment·um -ī *n* shoe

calceāt·us -ūs *m* sandal, shoe

calcĕ·ō -āre *vt* to furnish with shoes, to shoe

calceolār·ĭus -ĭī or -ī *m* shoemaker

calceŏl·us -ī *m* small shoe, half-boot

calcĕ·us -ī *m* shoe, half-boot

Calch·ās -antis *m* Greek prophet at Troy

calcĭtr·ō -āre *vi* to kick; to resist; to be stubborn; to kick up one's heels

calcĭtr·ō -ōnis *m* blusterer

calc·ō -āre *vt* to tread, tread under foot; to trample on, oppress; to scorn, abuse

calculāt·or -ōris *m* arithmetic teacher; accountant, bookkeeper

calcŭl·us -ī *m* pebble, stone; kidney stone; counter of an abacus; stone used in games; stone used in voting; vote, sentence, decision

caldār·ĭus -a -um *adj* warm-water; *n* hot bath

caldus see calidus

Calēdonĭ·a -ae *f* Highlands of Scotland

cale·facĭō or cal·facĭō -facĕre

-fēcī -factum *vt* to warm, heat; to rouse up, excite, make angry

calefact·ō -āre *vt* to warm, heat

Calend·ae -ārum *f pl* first day of Roman month, calends

calendār·ĭum -ĭī or -ī *n* account book

cal·ĕō -ēre -ŭī *vi* to be warm, hot; to feel warm; to glow; to be hot with passion; to be troubled, be perplexed; to be zealously pursued; to be new or fresh

Cal·ēs -ĭum *f pl* Campanian town famous for its wine

cal·escō -escĕre -ŭī *vi* to get warm or hot; to become excited, be inflamed

calĭd·a or cald·a -ae *f* warm water

calĭdē *adv* quickly, promptly

calĭd·us or cald·us -a -um *adj* warm, hot; eager, rash, hasty, hotheaded, vehement; quick, ready, prompt; *n* warm drink; *f* see calida

caliendr·um -ī *n* wig (*for women*)

calĭg·a -ae *f* shoe, soldier's boot; soldier

caligāt·us -a -um *adj* wearing soldier's boots; (of a peasant) wearing clodhoppers

cālĭg·ō -ĭnis *f* mist, vapor, fog; gloom, darkness, obscurity; mental blindness; calamity, affliction

cālĭg·ō -āre *vt* to veil in darkness, to obscure; to make dizzy; *vi* to steam, reek; to be wrapped in mist or darkness; to be blind, grope

calĭgŭl·a -ae *f* small military boot

Calĭgŭl·a -ae *m* pet name given by the soldiers to Gaius Caesar when he was a small boy

cal·ix -ĭcis *m* cup; pot; (fig) wine

callaĭn·us -a -um *adj* turquoise

call·ĕō -ēre -ŭī *vt* to know by experience or practice, to understand; (with *inf*) to know how to; *vi* to be callous, to be thick-skinned; to be insensible; to be experienced, clever, skillful

callĭdĭt·ās -ātis *f* skill; shrewdness; cunning, craft

callĭdē *adv* skillfully, expertly, shrewdly; well; cunningly

callĭd·us -a -um *adj* expert, adroit, skillful; ingenious, prudent, dexterous; clever, shrewd; sly, cunning, crafty, calculating

Callimăch·us -ī *m* famous Alexandrine poet and grammarian (*c.* 270 B.C.)

Calliŏp·ē -ēs or Calliopē·a -ae *f* Calliope (*muse of epic poetry*)

call·is -is *m* stony, uneven footpath; mountain path; cattle trail; mountain pasture; mountain pass, defile

Callist·ō -ūs *f* daughter of Lycaon, king of Arcadia, who was changed into the constellation Helice or Ursa Major

callōs·us -a -um *adj* hard-skinned; thick-skinned, callous; solid, hard, thick

call·um -ī m hard or thick skin; insensibility, stupidity

cal·ō -āre vt to call out, proclaim; to convoke

cāl·ō -ōnis m soldier's servant; menial servant, drudge

cal·or -ōris m warmth, heat, glow; passion, love; fire, zeal, impetuosity, vehemence

calth·a -ae f marigold

calthŭl·a -ae f yellow robe

calumni·a -ae f trickery; pretense, evasion; false statement, misrepresentation, fallacy; false accusation, malicious charge; conviction for malicious prosecution

calumniāt·or -ōris m malicious prosecutor, perverter of the law, pettifogger

calumni·or -ārī -ātus sum vt to accuse falsely; to misrepresent, calumniate; to blame unjustly; to put in a false light

calv·a -ae f scalp, bald head

calvit·ium -iī or **-ī** n baldness

calv·us -a -um adj bald

cal·x -cis f heel; (fig) foot, kick; **calcibus caedere** to kick

cal·x -cis f pebble; limestone, lime; finish line (marked with lime), goal; **ad calcem pervenīre** to reach the goal; **ad carcerēs a calce revocari** to be recalled from the finish line to the starting gate; to have to start all over again

Calўd·ōn -ōnis f town in Aetolia, scene of the famous boar hunt led by Meleager

Calyps·ō -ūs f nymph, daughter of Atlas, who entertained Ulysses on the island of Ogygia

camell·a -ae f drinking cup

camēl·us -ī m camel

Camēn·a -ae f Muse; poem; poetry

camēr·a -ae f vault, arched roof, arch; houseboat

Camerīn·um -ī n town in Umbria

Camill·a -ae f Volscian female warrior who assisted Turnus against Aeneas

Camill·us -ī m M. Furius Camillus, who freed Rome from the Gauls

camīn·us -ī m fireplace; furnace; forge; **oleum addere camino** to pour oil on the fire

cammār·us -ī m lobster

Campāni·a -ae f district on E. coast of central Italy

campest·er -ris -re adj flat, level; overland (march); (of city) situated in a plain; (of army) fighting in a plain; (of sports, elections, etc.) held in the Campus Martius; n shorts (worn in sports); n pl flat lands

camp·us -ī m flat space, plain; sports field; level surface, surface (of sea); **Campus Martius** field near the Tiber used for sports, elections, military exercises, etc.

cam·ur -ūra -ūrum adj crooked, concave

canāl·is -is m pipe, conduit, gutter

cancell·ī -ōrum m pl railing, grating; barrier (at sports, public events); boundaries, limits

canc·er -rī m crab; the South; tropical heat; cancer (disease)

Canc·er -rī m Cancer (northern zodiacal constellation; sign of the zodiac)

cande·faciō -facĕre -fēcī -factum vt to make dazzling white; to make glow, make red-hot

candēl·a -ae f candle, torch, taper; waxed cord; **candelam apponere valvis** to set the house on fire

candelābr·um -ī n candlestick, candelabrum, chandelier; lamp stand

cand·ens -entis adj shining white, glittering, dazzling, glowing

cand·ĕō -ēre vi to be shining white, glitter, shine; to be white-hot

cand·escō -escĕre -ŭī vi to become white, begin to glisten; to get red-hot

candidātōri·us -a -um adj of a candidate, candidate's

candidāt·us -a -um adj clothed in white; m candidate for office

candidē adv in dazzling white; clearly, simply, sincerely

candidŭl·us -a -um adj pretty white

candid·us -a -um adj (cf albus) shiny white, white, bright, dazzling, gleaming, sparkling; fair, radiant (complexion); candid, open, sincere, frank (person); bright, cheerful (circumstances); clear, bright (day); (of winds) bringing clear weather; white, silvery (poplar, hair, etc.); clear, unaffected (style); clothed in white; **candida sententia** vote of acquittal

cand·or -ōris m glossy whiteness, brightness, radiance; candor, sincerity; naturalness (of style); brilliance (of discourse)

cān·ens -entis adj grey, white

cān·ĕō -ēre -ŭī vi to be grey, be white

cānesc·ō -ĕre -ŭī vi to grow white, become grey; to grow old; (of discourse) to lose force, grow dull

can·ī -ōrum m pl grey hair

canīcŭl·a -ae f small dog, pup; (as term of abuse) little bitch

Canīcŭl·a -ae f Canicula, Sirius, Dog Star (brightest star in Canis Major)

canīn·us -a -um adj canine; snarling, spiteful, caustic; **canina littera** letter R

can·is -is m or f dog, hound; (term of reproach to denote vile person, enraged person, hanger-on, etc.) dog; worst throw (in dice)

Can·is -is m Canis Major (constellation, of which the brightest star is Canicula)

canistr·um -ī n wicker basket (for bread, fruit, flowers, etc.)

cānitĭ·ēs (genit not in use) f greyness; grey hair; old age

cann·a -ae f reed; reed pipe, flute

cannăb·is -ae f or **cannăb·um -ī** n hemp

Cann·ae -ārum f pl village in Apulia, where Hannibal won great victory over Romans in 216 B.C.

canō canĕre cecinī cantum vt to sing; to play; to speak in a singsong tone; to sing the praises of, celebrate; to prophesy, predict, foretell; (mil) to blow, sound; **signa canere** to sound the signal for battle; vi to sing; to play; (of birds) to sing; (of roosters) to crow; (of frogs) to croak; **receptui canere** to sound retreat; **tibiā canere** to play the flute

can·or -ōris m tune, sound, melody, song; tone (of instruments)

canŏr·us -a -um adj melodious, musical; singsong, jingling; n melody, charm (in speaking)

Cantabr·ĭa -ae f district in N.W. Spain

cantăm·en -ĭnis n incantation, spell

cantăt·or -ōris m singer

canthăr·is -ĭdis f beetle; Spanish fly

canthăr·us -ī m wide-bellied drinking vessel with handles, tankard

canthēr·ĭus or **cantēr·ĭus -ĭī** or **-ī** m gelding; eunuch

canth·us -ī m iron tire; wheel

cantic·um -ī n song; aria in Roman comedy; (in delivery of speech) singsong

cantilēn·a -ae f old song, gossip; **cantilenam eandem canere** to sing the same old song, harp on the same theme

cantĭ·ō -ōnis f singing; incantation, charm, spell

cantĭt·ō -āre vt to keep on singing or playing, to sing or play repeatedly

cantiuncŭl·a -ae f catchy tune

cant·ō -āre vt to sing; to play; to sing of, celebrate, praise in song; to harp on, keep repeating; to predict; to drawl out; (of actor) to play the part of; vi to sing, to play; (of instruments) to sound; to drawl; (of rooster) to crow; **ad surdas aures cantare** to preach to deaf ears

cant·or -ōris m singer, poet; eulogist; actor, player; musician

cantr·ix -īcis f musician, singer (female)

cant·us -ūs m tune, melody, song; playing; incantation; prediction; magic spell

cān·us -a -um adj white, grey; aged, old venerable

capācĭt·ās -ātis f capacity

cap·ax -ācis adj capacious, spacious, wide, roomy; (of mind) able to grasp, receptive, capable

capĕd·ō -ĭnis f cup or bowl used in sacrifices

capĕduncŭl·a -ae f small cup or bowl used in sacrifices

capell·a -ae f she-goat, nanny goat

Capell·a -ae f Capella (star of the first magnitude in Auriga)

Capēn·a -ae f Porta Capena (a gate in the Servian Wall which marked the start of the Via Appia)

cap·er -rī m he goat, billy goat

caperr·ō -āre vt & vi to wrinkle

capess·ō -ĕre -īvī or **-ĭī -ītum** vt to try to reach, make for, seize, get hold of, snatch at; to take up, undertake, engage in; **capessere rem publicam** to be engaged in politics

capillāt·us -a -um adj having hair, hairy; **bene capillātus** having a fine head of hair

capill·us -ī m hair

capĭō capĕre cēpī captum vt (archaic fut: capso) to take hold of, grasp, seize; to occupy; to take up, assume (office); to catch, capture; to captivate, charm; to cheat, seduce, mislead, delude; to defeat, overcome (in suite); to convince (in a dispute); to reach, arrive at, land at; to exact, extort, accept as a bribe; to take, obtain, get, enjoy, reap (profit, advantage); to acquire, cherish, cultivate, adopt (habits, etc.); to form, conceive, come to, reach (conclusions, plans, thoughts, resolutions, purposes); to take, derive, draw, obtain (examples, proofs, instances); to entertain, conceive, receive, experience (impressions, feelings); (of feelings, experiences) to seize, overcome, occupy, take possession of; to suffer, be subjected to (injury); to hold, contain, be large enough for; to comprehend, grasp

cap·is -ĭdis f bowl (with one handle, used in sacrifices)

capistr·ō -āre vt to muzzle

capistr·um -ī n halter, muzzle

capĭt·al or **capit·āle -ālis** n capital offense

capitāl·is -e adj relating to the head or life; (law) affecting a man's life or civil status; (of crime) punishable by death, punishable by loss of civil rights, capital; dangerous, deadly, mortal; chief, preeminent, distinguished, of first rank

capĭt·ō -ōnis m big-head

Capitōlīn·us -a -um adj Capitoline; m Capitoline Hill; m pl persons in charge of the Capitoline games

Capitōl·ĭum -ĭī or **-ī** n the Capitol (temple of Jupiter on the summit of Mons Tarpeius); the Capitoline Hill (including temple and citadel); citadel (of any city)

capitulātim adv briefly, summarily

capitŭl·um -ī n small head; (as term of endearment) dear fellow

Cappadocĭ·a -ae f country in Asia Minor between the Taurus and Pontus

capr·a -ae f she-goat, nanny goat; body odor of armpits

caprĕ·a -ae f wild goat, roe

Caprĕ·ae -ārum f pl island at S. end of Bay of Naples off Sorrento

capreŏl·us -ī *m* roebuck, chamois; prop, support

Capricorn·us -ī *m* Capricorn (*sign of the zodiac*)

caprific·us -ī *f* wild fig tree

caprigĕn·us -a -um *adj* of goats; **caprigenum pecus** herd of goats

caprimulg·us -ī *m* rustic

caprīn·us -a -um *adj* of goats, goat; **de lana caprina rixari** to argue over nothing

caprĭp·ēs -ĕdis *adj* goat-footed

caps·a -ae *f* holder, container, box, case (*esp. for book rolls*)

capsō see **capio**

capsŭl·a -ae *f* small box

capt·a -ae *f* captive, prisoner (*female*)

captātĭ·ō -ōnis *f* hunt, quest; **captatio verborum** verbalism, sophistry

captāt·or -ōris *m* (fig) hound; **aurae popularis captator** publicity hound

captĭ·ō -ōnis *f* taking, catching; fraud; loss, disadvantage; sophism

captiōsē *adv* slyly, insidiously, deceptively

captiōs·us -a -um *adj* deceitful; captious, sophistical; dangerous, harmful

captiuncŭl·a -ae *f* quibble, sophism

captīvĭt·ās -ātis *f* captivity; conquest, capture

captīv·us -a -um *adj* caught, taken captive; prisoner's; captured, conquered; *mf* prisoner of war, captive

capt·ō -āre *vt* to catch at eagerly; to keep reaching for; to try to catch, chase after; to strive after, long for, desire earnestly; to try to hear; to try to trap, entice, allure; to adopt (*plan*); to try to cause (*laughter*); to watch for (*opportunity*); to begin (*conversation*)

captūr·a -ae *f* capture; quarry

capt·us -a -um *pp* of **capio**; *adj* **oculis et auribus captus** blind and deaf; **mente captus** mad, crazy; *m* captive, prisoner

capt·us -ūs *m* mental grasp, mental capacity; notion

Capŭ·a -ae *f* chief city of Campania

capulār·is -e *adj* with one foot in the grave

capŭl·us -ī *m* coffin; hilt, handle

cap·ut -itis *n* head; top, summit, point, extremity; source (*of river*); root (*of plant*); top (*of tree*); head, leader; capital (*of country*); main point (*of discourse*); chapter, principal division, heading; substance, summary; (com) capital; main course; life, civil status; **capitis accusare** to accuse of a capital offense; **capitis damnare** to condemn to death; **capitis res** matter of life and death; **diminutio capitis** loss of civil rights; **dim'nutio capitis maxima** condemnation to death or slavery; **diminut'o capitis media** loss of citizenship; **di-**

minutio capitis minima change of status (*as by adoption or, in the case of women, by marriage*)

Cap·ys -ўos *m* son of Assaracus and father of Anchises; companion of Aeneas; eighth king of Alba Longa

carbasĕ·us -a -um *adj* linen, canvas

carbăs·us -ī *f* (*pl:* **carbās·a -ōrum** *n*) fine Spanish flax; linen garment; sail, canvas; awning

carb·ō -ōnis *m* charcoal

carbōnār·ius -iī or **-ī** *m* charcoal burner, collier

carbuncŭl·us -ī *m* small piece of coal; grief, sorrow; precious stone, garnet

carc·er -ĕris *m* prison, jail; prisoner; (term of reproach) jailbird; *m pl* starting gate (*at racetrack*); **ad carceres a calce revocari** to have to start all over again

carcerārĭ·us -a -um *adj* prison

carchēs·ium -iī or **-ī** *n* drinking cup (*slightly contracted in the middle*); upper part of mast (*similarly formed*)

cardĭāc·us -ī *m* dyspeptic

card·ō -ĭnis *m* hinge; turning point, crisis; (astr) axis, pole; **cardo rerum** critical juncture, crisis

cardŭ·us -ī *m* thistle

cārē *adv* at a high price, dearly; highly

cārect·um -ī *m* sedge

cār·ĕō -ēre -ŭī *vi* (*with abl or genit*) a to be without; b to miss; c to be free from; d to keep away from, be absent from; e to abstain from

cār·ex -icis *f* sedge

Cārĭ·a -ae *f* province in S.W. Asia Minor

carĭ·ēs (*genit not in use*) *f* decay, rot

carīn·a -ae *f* bottom of ship, keel; ship

Carīn·ae -ārum *f pl* the Keels (*district in Rome Between the Caelian and Esquiline Hills*)

carīnār·ius -iī or **-ī** *m* dyer of yellow

cariōs·us -a -um *adj* rotten, decayed, crumbled; wrinkled

cār·is -ĭdis *f* crab

cārĭt·ās -ātis *f* dearness, costliness, high price, high cost of living; affection, love

carm·en -ĭnis *n* song, tune; lyric poetry, poetry; incantation, charm; oracular utterance; ritual formula, legal formula; adage

Carment·a -ae or **Carment·is -is** *f* Roman goddess of prophecy, the mother of Evander, who came with him from Arcadia to Latium

Carmentāl·is -e *adj* of Carmenta; **Porta Carmentalis** gate at Rome near temple of Carmenta (*also called* **Porta Scelerata**, *i.e., ominous gate*)

carnār·ium -iī or **-ī** *n* meat hook; pantry

Carneăd·ēs -is *m* famous philosopher, born at Cyrene, and founder of the New Academy (215-130 B.C.)

carnif·ex -icis *m* hangman, executioner; murderer, butcher; scoundrel

carnifioin·a -ae *f* execution; torture, torment

carnific·ō -āre *vt* to mutilate, cut to pieces, behead

car·ō -nis or **carn·is -is** *f* flesh, meat; **caro ferina** venison; **caro putida** carrion; (fig) rotten egg

car·ō -ēre *vt* to card (*wool*)

Carpăth·us -ī *f* island between Crete and Rhodes

carpatin·us -a -um *adj* of rough leather; *f* crude shoe

carpent·um -ī *n* two-wheeled covered carriage (*esp. used by women on holidays*)

carp·ō -ēre -sī -tum *vt* to pluck, pick, cull; to carp at, criticize, take apart; to enjoy, make use of; to crop, browse on (*grass*); to pick, gather (*fruit*); to separate into parts, divide; (mil) to harass, weaken (*esp. by repeated attacks*); **auras vitales carpere** to breathe the breath of life; **diem carpere** to make the most of the present; **gyrum carpere** to go in a circle; **iter** or **viam carpere** to make one's way, pick one's way, travel; **vellera carpere** to spin

carptim *adv* piecemeal, separately, in parts; at different times; at different points; gradually

carpt·or -ōris *m* carver (*of food*)

Carrh·ae -ārum *f pl* town in Mesopotamia where Crassus was defeated and killed by the Parthians (53 B.C.)

carrūc·a -ae *f* four-wheeled carriage

carr·us -ī *m* four-wheeled wagon

Carthāginiens·is -e *adj & mf* Carthaginian

Carthāg·ō -inis *f* Carthage (*city in N. Africa, founded as a Phoenician colony in 9th cent. B.C.*)

caruncŭl·a -ae *f* little piece of meat

cār·us -a -um *adj* dear, high-priced, expensive, costly; dear, beloved, esteemed; loving, affectionate

cas·a -ae *f* cottage, cabin, hut

casc·us -a -um *adj* old, primitive

căseŏl·us -ī *m* small piece of cheese

căse·us -ī *m* cheese

casi·a -ae *f* mezereon (*fragrant plant with purple flowers*)

Cassandr·a -ae *f* daughter of Priam and Hecuba who had the gift of prophecy but was believed by no one

cass·ēs -ium *m pl* hunting net, snare; spider web

cassid·a -ae *f* metal helmet

Cassiŏp·ē -ēs or **Cassiopē·a -ae** *f* wife of Cepheus and mother of Andromeda, afterwards made a constellation

Cass·ius -ii or **-ī** *m* C. Cassius Longinus (*one of the murderers of Caesar*)

cass·is -idis *f* metal helmet

cass·ō -āre *vi* to totter, trip

cass·us -a -um *adj* empty, hollow; (fig) empty, groundless, vain, pointless; (with *abl*) deprived of, devoid of, without; **cassus lumine** without life, dead; **in cassum** to no purpose, pointlessly

Castăl·is -idis *adj* Castalian; **sorores Castalides** Muses; *f* Muse

Castali·us -a -um *adj* Castalian; *f* fountain on Mt. Parnassus, sacred to Apollo and the Muses

castanĕ·a -ae *f* chestnut tree; chestnut

castē *adv* purely, chastely, spotlessly; virtuously; devoutly, piously

castellān·us -a -um *adj* of a fort, of a castle; *m* occupant of a castle or fortress; *m pl* garrison (*of a fortress*)

castellātim *adv* one fortress after another; **castellatim dissipati** (troops) stationed in various fortresses

castell·um -ī *n* fort, fortress, stronghold, castle; (fig) defense, shelter, refuge

castēri·a -ae *f* rowers' quarters

castīgăbil·is -e *adj* punishable

castīgāti·ō -ōnis *f* correction, punishment; censure, reproof

castīgăt·or -ōris *m* corrector, critic

castīgātŏri·us -a -um *adj* reproving

castīgāt·us -a -um *adj* small, contracted, slender

castīg·ō -āre *vt* to correct, make right, blame, reprove, censure, chide, find fault with, punish; to correct, amend; to hold in check, restrain

castimōni·a -ae *f* purity, morality; chastity, abstinence

castit·ās -ātis *f* purity, chastity

cast·or -ōris *m* beaver

Cast·or -ōris *m* son of Tyndareus, twin brother of Pollux, brother of Helen and Clytemnestra, and patron of sailors

castorĕ·um -ī *m* bitter, strong-smelling secretion of beavers

castrens·is -e *adj* camp, military

castr·ō -āre *vt* to castrate

castr·um -ī *n* fort, fortress, castle; *n pl* military camp; day's march; the service, army life; (pol) party; (phil) school; **bina castra** two camps; **castra facere** or **habere** to encamp; **castra movere** to break camp; **castra munire** to construct a camp; **castra ponere** to pitch camp; **castra una** one camp

cast·us -a -um *adj* (morally) pure, chaste, spotless, guiltless, virtuous; religious, pious, holy, sacred

casŭl·a -ae *f* little hut, little cottage

căs·us -ūs *m* falling; (fig) fall, downfall, overthrow, end; chance, event, happening, occurrence, emergency; occasion, opportunity; misfortune, mishap, accident, calamity; fall, death; fate; (gram) case; **non consulto sed casu** not on purpose but by chance

catagelasīm·us -a -um adj bantering, jeering; exposed to ridicule

catagrāph·us -a -um adj painted, colored

cataphract·ēs -ae m coat of mail

cataphract·us -a -um adj mail-clad

catāpl·us -ī m arrival of ship; arriving ship or fleet

catapult·a -ae f catapult; (fig) missile

catapultārī·us -a -um adj catapulted, shot (from catapult)

cataract·a or **catarract·a** or **cataract·ēs -ae** f waterfall, cataract (esp. on the Nile); floodgate; drawbridge

cataractrī·a -ae f spice

catast·a -ae f stage on which slaves were displayed for sale

catē adv skillfully, wisely

catēi·a -ae f javelin

catell·a -ae f puppy (female); small chain

catell·us -ī m puppy; small chain

catēn·a -ae f chain; series; barrier, restraint, bond

catēnāt·us -a -um adj chained

caterv·a -ae f crowd, throng, band, mob; troop (of actors); (mil) troop, horde

catervātim adv in companies, by troops; in crowds or flocks (of plague-stricken people)

cathēdr·a -ae f armchair, cushioned seat; litter, sedan; professional chair

Catilīn·a -ae m L. Sergius Catiline (Roman patrician whose conspiracy was exposed by Cicero in 63 B.C.)

catill·ō -āre vi to lick the plate

catill·us -ī m plate

catīn·us -ī m plate, pot, bowl

Cat·ō -ōnis m M. Porcius Cato (model of Roman aristocratic conservatism, 239-149 B.C.); M. Porcius Cato Uticensis (grandson of Porcius Cato, inveterate enemy of Caesar, 95-45 B.C.)

catōn·ium -iī or **-ī** n lower world

Catull·us -ī m C. Valerius Catullus (lyric and elegiac poet of Verona, 86-54 B.C.)

catūl·us -ī m puppy; whelp, cub

cat·us -a -um adj sharp, shrewd, keen; sly, cunning

Caucăs·us -ī m Caucasus mountains

caud·a -ae f tail (of animal); penis; **caudam jactare** (with dat) to flatter; **caudam trahere** to be mocked

caudě·us -a -um adj of wood, wooden

caud·ex or **cōd·ex -icis** m trunk (of tree); block (of wood to which one was tied for punishment); book, ledger; blockhead

caudicāl·is -e adj of wood cutting

Caud·ium -iī or **-ī** n town in Samnium

caul·ae -ārum f pl hole, opening passage; sheepfold, pen

caul·is -is f stalk, stem; cabbage stalk, cabbage

caup·ō -ōnis m innkeeper

caupōn·a -ae f inn, tavern; retail shop

caupōnī·us -a -um adj of a shop or tavern

caupōn·or -ārī -ātus sum vt to trade in or traffic in

caupōnūl·a -ae f small inn or tavern

caus·a or **causs·a -ae** f (law) lawsuit, case; grounds, cause, motive, purpose, reason; good reason, just cause; pretext, pretense; inducement, occasion, opportunity; side, party, faction, cause; condition, situation, position; (rhet) matter of discussion, subject matter; matter, business, concern; commission, charge; personal relationship, connexion; **causā** (with genit) for the sake of, on account of; **causā cadere** to lose a case; **causam agere, causam dicere,** or **causam orare** to plead a case; **causam cognoscere** to examine a case (as judge); **vestrā causā** in your interests; **per causam** (with genit) under the pretext of; **sine causā** without good reason

causārī·us -a -um adj sick; m (mil) malingerer, goldbrick

causi·a -ae f Macedonian hat (with wide brim)

causidic·us -ī m pleader, lawyer; shyster

causific·or -ārī -ātus sum vi to make excuses

caus·or -ārī -ātus sum vt to pretend, give as a reason

caussa see **causa**

causŭl·a -ae f petty lawsuit; minor cause

cautē adv cautiously, carefully; with security

cautēl·a -ae f precaution

caut·ēs -is f rock, crag

cautim adv warily, cautiously

cauti·ō -ōnis f caution, wariness; guarantee, provision; (law) bond, security, bail, warranty; **mea cautio est** I must see to it; **mihi cautio est** I must take care

caut·or -ōris m wary person; bondsman, surety

caut·us -a -um adj cautious, careful; safe, secure

cavaed·ium -iī or **-ī** n inner court of Roman house

cavě·a -ae f cavity; enclosure for animals: cage, den, stall, beehive, bird cage; auditorium, theater; **prima cavea** section of auditorium for nobility; **ultima cavea** section for lower classes

cavě·ō cavēre cāvī cautum vt to guard against, beware of; to keep clear of; to stipulate, decree, order; to guarantee; vi to be careful, look out, be on one's guard; (with abl or

ab + abl) to be on one's guard against; (with **ab + abl**) to get a guarantee from; (with **dat**) **a** to guarantee, give a guarantee to; **b** to provide for, take care of; **cave tangere** (= **noli tangere**) do not touch

cavern·a -ae f hollow, cavity, cave, cavern; vault; hold (of ship)

cavill·a -ae f jeering, scoffing

cavillāti·ō -ōnis f banter, scoffing, raillery; sophistry, quibbling

cavillāt·or -ōris m scoffer; quibbler, sophist

cavill·or -ārī -ātus sum vt to scoff at, mock, criticize, satirize; vi to scoff, jeer; to quibble

cav·ō -āre vt to hollow out, excavate; to pierce, run through

cav·us -a -um adj hollow, hollowed; concave, vaulted; deep-channeled (river); m & n hole, cavity, hollow

-ce demonstrative enclitic appended to pronouns and adverbs (like colloquial English here, there, with this or that); **hice** (for **hicce**) this (here); **hujusce** of this (here); (when followed by the enclytic -**ne**, the form becomes -**ci: hicine, sicine)**

Cecrŏpĭd·ae -ārum m pl descendants of Cecrops, Athenians

Cecrŏp·is -ĭdis f female descendant of Cecrops (esp. Aglauros); Procne; Philomela; Athenian woman

Cecr·ops -ŏpis m first king of Athens

cēdō cēdĕre cessī cessum vt to grant, concede, yield, give up; vi to go, move, walk, walk along; to go away, depart, withdraw; (of time) to pass; (of events) to turn out; to pass away, die; (mil) to retreat; (with **dat**) **a** to befall, fall to the lot of, accrue to; **b** to yield to, submit to, give in to; **c** to yield (in rank) to, be inferior to; **d** to comply with, conform to, obey; (with **in + acc**) to be changed into, become; (with **pro + abl**) to pass for, be the equivalent of, be the price of; **bonis or possessionibus alicui cedere** to give up or cede one's property to someone; **foro cedere** to go bankrupt

cedo (pl: **cette**) (old impv) here with, bring here, give here; let's hear, tell, out with; look at; **cedo dum!** all right!; come now!; **cedo ut inspiciam** let me look

cedr·us -ī f cedar, juniper; cedar wood; cedar oil

Celaen·ō -ūs f daughter of Atlas and one of the Pleiades; one of the Harpies; greedy woman

cēlāt·um -ī n secret

celĕb·er -ris -re adj crowded, populous, frequented; well-attended; famous; well-known, common, usual; solemn, festive; numerous, repeated, frequent

celebrāti·ō -ōnis f large assembly; festival, celebration; f pl throngs

celebrāt·us -a -um adj much-frequented, much-visited, crowded, populous; celebrated, famous, renowned; customary, usual, frequent; solemn, festive; trite, familiar, often-repeated

celebrĭt·ās -ātis f throng, crowd, multitude, large assembly; publicity; repetition, frequency; fame, renown; celebration

celĕbr·ō -āre vt to frequent, crowd, fill, visit in crowds; to repeat, practice, exercise; to publicize, advertise, honor, glorify; to escort, attend; to cause to resound

cel·er -ĕris -ĕre adj swift, speedy, quick, rapid, hurried; rash, hasty

celĕrĕ adv quickly

Celĕr·ēs -um m pl mounted bodyguards of Roman kings

celerĭp·ēs -ĕdis adj swift-footed

celerĭt·ās -ātis f speed, quickness, rapidity

celerĭter adv quickly, speedily

celĕr·ō -āre vt to quicken, speed up, accelerate; vi to be quick, rush, speed

cell·a -ae f storeroom, storehouse, grain elevator, silo; cheap apartment, garret; sanctuary (of temple, where the cult image stood); cell (of beehive)

cellāri·us -a -um adj of a storeroom; m storekeeper, butler

cellŭl·a -ae f small storeroom, small apartment

cēl·ō -āre vt to hide, conceal; to veil (feelings); to keep (something) secret, keep quiet about; (with acc of thing and acc of person from whom one conceals) to keep (someone) in the dark about, hide (something) from (someone); **celari** (with **de + abl**) to be kept in ignorance of

cel·ox -ōcis adj swift, quick; f swift-sailing ship, cutter, speedboat

cels·us -a -um adj high, lofty, towering, prominent, erect; lofty, elevated (thoughts); high (rank); proud, haughty

Celt·ae -ārum m pl Celts (who occupied most of W. Europe); (in more restricted sense) inhabitants of central Gaul

Celtibĕr·ī -ōrum m pl Celtiberians (early people of Central Spain)

cēn·a -ae f principal meal, dinner; dish, course; company at dinner

cēnācŭl·um -ī n dining room (usually on an upper floor); attic

cēnātĭc·us -a -um adj dinner

cēnātĭ·ō -ōnis f dining room

cēnāt·us -a -um adj having dined; spent in feasting

cēnĭt·ō -āre vi to dine habitually, dine often

cēn·ō -āre vt to make a meal of, dine on, eat; vi to dine, eat dinner

cens·ĕō -ēre -ŭī -um vt to assess, rate, estimate, tax; to esteem, appreciate, value; (of senate) to decree, resolve; to propose, move, vote, argue, suggest, advise; to think, believe, hold, suppose, imagine, expect

censi·ō -ōnis f rating, assessment, taxation; opinion

cens·or -ōris m censor (one of two Roman magistrates who took the census and exercised general control over morals, etc.); severe judge of morals, critic

censōri·us -a -um adj of the censors; subject to censure; rigid, stern, austere; **homo censorius** ex-censor; **lex censoria** contract (drawn up by censors) for leasing buildings

censūr·a -ae f office of censor, censorship; criticism

cens·us -ūs m census; register of the census; income bracket; wealth, property; rich presents, gifts; **censum agere** or **habere** to hold a census; **censu prohibere** to exclude from citizenship, disenfranchise

centaurē·um -ī n centaury (medical herb)

Centaur·us -ī m centaur (creature fabled to be half man and half horse); **Centaurus** (southern constellation between the Southern Cross and Hydra)

centēn·ī -ae -a adj one hundred each; **deciens centena milia passum** ten hundred thousand paces, one million paces

centēsim·us -a -um adj hundredth; f hundredth part, one percent; (com) 1% monthly (12% per annum)

centi·ceps -cipitis adj hundred-headed

centiēs or **centiens** adv a hundred times; (fig) a great many times

centimān·us -a -um adj hundred-handed

cent·ō -ōnis m patchwork, quilt

centum (indecl) adj hundred

centumgemin·us -a -um adj hundredfold

centumpl·ex -icis adj hundredfold

centumpond·ium -iī or **-ī** n hundred pounds, hundred-pound weight

centumvirāl·is -e adj of the centumviri

centumvir·ī -ōrum m pl panel of one hundred (jurors chosen annually to try civil suits under a quaestor, esp. concerning inheritances)

centuncul·us -ī m piece of patchwork, cloth of many colors, saddle cloth

centuri·a -ae f (mil) company, century (theoretically composed of one hundred men); (pol) century (one of the 193 groups into which Servius Tullius divided the Roman people)

centuriātim adv by companies, by centuries

centuriāt·us -a -um adj divided into companies or centuries; **comitia centuriata** centuriate assembly

(legislative body which met in the Campus Martius to elect high magistrates, decree war, etc.)

centuri·ō -ōnis m centurion (commander of an infantry company)

centuri·ō -āre vt to divide into centuries

centuriōnāt·us -ūs m election of centurions

centuss·is -is m a hundred aces (bronze coins)

cēnul·a -ae f little dinner

Cephăl·us -ī m husband of Procris, whom he unintentionally shot

Cephēus -ĕī m king of Ethiopia, husband of Cassiope and father of Andromeda

Cephīs·us -ī m river in Attica; river in Phocis and Boeotia

cēr·a -ae f wax; writing tablet (covered with wax); wax seal; wax bust of an ancestor; cell (of beehive)

Ceramīc·us -ī m cemetery of Athens

cērār·ium -iī or **-ī** n fee for affixing a seal

cerast·ēs -ae m horned serpent

ceras·us -ī f cherry tree; cherry

cērāt·us -a -um adj waxed

Cerběr·us -ī m three-headed dog which guarded the entrance to the lower world

cercopithēc·us -ī m long-tailed monkey

cercūr·us -ī m swift-sailing ship, cutter

cerd·ō -ōnis m workman, laborer

Cereāl·ia -ium n pl festival of Ceres (April 10th)

Cereāl·is -e adj of Ceres; of grain; **arma Cerealia** utensils for grinding and baking

cerebrōs·us -a -um adj hot-headed

cerĕbr·um -ī n brain; head, skull; understanding; hot temper

Cer·ēs -ĕris f goddess of agriculture and mother of Proserpine; grain bread, food

cērĕ·us -a -um adj of wax, waxen; wax-colored; soft, pliant; m candle

cērinth·a -ae f wax flower

cērin·us -a -um adj wax-colored; n pl wax-colored clothes

cernō cernēre crēvī crētum vt (of sight) to discern, distinguish, make out, see; (of mind) to discern, see, understand; to decide, decree, determine; **hereditatem cernere** to formally declare oneself heir to an inheritance, accept an inheritance

cernŭ·us -a -um adj with face turned toward the earth, stooping forwards

cērōm·a -ătis n wrestler's oil

cērōmatic·us -a -um adj smeared with oil, oily, greasy

cerrīt·us -a -um adj crazy, frantic

certām·en -inis n contest; match; rivalry; (mil) battle, combat

certātim adv with a struggle, in rivalry

certāti·ō -ōnis f contest; rivalry, discussion, debate

certē adv surely, certainly, unquestionably, undoubtedly, of course; (in answers) yes, certainly; (to restrict an assertion) at least, at any rate

certō adv for certain, for sure; surely, in fact, really

cert·ō -āre vi to fight, contend, struggle, do battle; to compete; (law) to debate; (with inf) to strive to

cert·us -a -um adj certain, determined, resolved, fixed, settled; specific, particular, certain, precise, definite; faithful, trusty, dependable; sure of aim, unerring; unwavering, inexorable; **certiorem facere** to inform; **certum est mihi** (with inf) I am determined to; **certum habere** to regard as certain; **pro certo** for sure; **pro certo habere** to be assured

cērūl·a -ae f piece of wax; **cerula miniata** red pencil (of a critic)

cērussa·a -ae f ceruse, white paint

cērussāt·us -a -um adj painted white

cerv·a -ae f hind, deer

cervīc·al -ālis n pillow, cushion

cervīcūl·a -ae f slender neck

cervīn·us -a -um adj of a stag or deer

cerv·ix -īcis f neck; nape of the neck; **in cervicibus nostris esse** to be on our necks., i.e., to have (something or someone unpleasant) on our hands; **a cervicibus nostris avertere** to get (someone) off our neck, get rid of (someone); **cervicibus sustinere** to shoulder (responsibility)

cerv·us -ī m stag, deer; (mil) palisade

cessātī·ō -ōnis f letup, delay; inactivity, idleness, cessation

cessāt·or -ōris m idler, loafer

cessī·ō -ōnis f surrendering, relinquishment

cess·ō -āre vi to let up, slack off, become remiss, stop; to be inactive, be idle, do nothing; to lie fallow

cestrosphendŏn·ē -ēs f artillery piece for hurling stones

cest·us or **cest·os -ī** m girdle (esp. of Venus)

cētăr·ium -iī or **-ī** n fish pond

cētăr·ius -iī or **-ī** m fish dealer

cētĕra adv otherwise, in all other respects, for the rest

cētĕrōqui or **cētĕrōquin** adv otherwise, in all other respects, for the rest

cētĕrum adv otherwise, in all other respects, for the rest; but, yet, still, on the other hand

cētĕr·us -a -um adj the other, the remaining, the rest of; pron m pl & f pl the others, all the rest, everybody; n the rest

Cethēg·us -ī m C. Cornelius Cethegus (fellow conspirator of Catiline)

cette see cedo

cēt·us -ī (pl: **cēt·ē**) m sea monster; whale, shark, seal, dolphin

ceu conj (in comparisons) as, just as; (in comparative conditions) as if, just as if; **ceu cum** as when

cēv·ĕō -ēre vi (cf criso) (of a male) to move the haunches

Cē·yx -ўcis m king of Trachis, who was changed into a kingfisher, as was his wife Alcyone

Chaldae·us -a -um adj Chaldaean; m astrologer, fortune-teller

chalybēi·us -a -um adj steel

Chalŷb·es -um m pl people of Pontus in Asia Minor noted as steelworkers

chal·ybs -ўbis m steel

Chāŏn·es -um m pl a tribe in Epirus

Chāonī·us -a -um adj Chaonian; of Epirus; f Chaonia (district of Epirus)

Cha·os -ī n chaos, the unformed world, empty space, shapeless mass from which the world was formed; a **Chao** from the beginning of the world

char·a -ae f wild cabbage

charistī·a -ōrum n pl Roman family festival

Charĭt·es -um f pl the Graces

Char·ōn -ontis m ferryman of the lower world

chart·a -ae f sheet of papyrus; sheet of paper; writing, letter, poem; book; record

chartŭl·a -ae f sheet of paper; letter, note

Charybd·is -is f whirlpool between Italy and Sicily, personified as a female monster

Chatt·ī -ōrum m pl people of central Germany

Chēl·ae -ārum f pl the Claws (of Scorpio); Libra (constellation into which Scorpio extends)

chelŷdr·us -ī m water snake

chely·s (genit not in use; acc: **che-lyn**) f tortoise; lyre

cheragr·a -ae f arthritis in the hand

chĭliarch·ēs -ae or **chĭliarch·us -ī** m commander of 1000 men; Persian chancellor (highest office next to the king)

Chimaer·a -ae f fire-breathing monster, with lion's head, goat's body, and dragon's tail

Chĭ·os -ī f island off coast of Asia Minor, famous for its wine

chīrogrăph·um -ī n handwriting; autography; document; **falsa chirographa** forgeries

Chīr·ōn -ōnis m Chiron (centaur, tutor of Aesculapius, Hercules, and Achilles, and famous for his knowledge of medicine and prophecy)

chironŏm·os -ī or **chironŏm·ōn -untis** m pantomimist

chīrurgī·a -ae f surgery

Chĭ·us -a -um adj & mf Chian; n Chian wine; n pl Chian cloth

chlamydāt·us -a -um adj wearing a military uniform

chlam·ys -ȳdis *f* military cloak; gold-brocaded mantle

Choeril·us -ī *m* incompetent Greek panegyrist of Alexander the Great

chorāg·ium -iī or **-ī** *n* choreography

chorāg·us -ī *m* choragus (*man who finances the chorus*)

ohoraul·ēs -ae *m* flute player who accompanied the choral dance

chord·a -ae *f* gut string, string (*of musical instrument*); cord, rope

chorē·a -ae *f* dance

chorē·us -ī *m* trochee

chor·us -ī *m* chorus; choir

Chrem·ēs -ētis or **-is** or **-ī** *m* miserly old man (*in Roman comedy*)

Christiān·us -ī *m* Christian

Christ·us -ī *m* Christ

Chrȳsē·is -īdis *f* Agamemnon's slave girl, daughter of Chryses

Chrȳs·ēs -ae *m* priest of Apollo

Chrysipp·us -ī *m* famous Stoic philosopher (290-210 B.C.)

chrȳsolith·os -ī *m* chrysolite, topaz

chrȳs·os -ī *m* gold

cibāri·us -a -um *adj* of food; common, coarse (*food of slaves*); *n pl* rations, provisions, food allowance

cibāt·us -ūs *m* food

cib·ō -āre *vt* to feed

cibōr·ium -iī or **-ī** *n* drinking cup

cib·us -ī *m* food; feed; (fig) food, nourishment

cioād·a -ae *f* locust, harvest fly

cicātricōs·us -a -um *adj* scarred, covered with scars

cicātr·ix -īcis *f* scar

cicc·us -ī *m* core of pomegranate; something worthless, trifle

cic·er -ēris *n* chick-pea

Cicer·ō -ōnis *m* M. Tullius Cicero (*orator and statesman*, 106-43 B.C.)

cīchorē·um -ī *n* endive

Cicōn·es -um *m pl* Thracian tribe

cicōni·a -ae *f* stork

cic·ur -ŭris *adj* tame

cicūt·a -ae *f* hemlock tree; hemlock poison; pipe, flute (*carved from hemlock tree*)

cieō ciēre cīvī citum *vt* to set in motion, move; to stir, agitate; to call for, send for; to summon for help; to invoke, appeal to; to call on by name, mention by name; to start, bring about; to renew (*combat*)

Cilici·a -ae *f* country in S. Asia Minor

Cilici·us -a -um *adj* Cilician; *n* garment of goat's hair

Cil·ix -īcis *adj & m* Cilician

Cimbr·ī -ōrum *m pl* Germanic tribe (*defeated by Marius in 101 B.C.*)

cīm·ex -īcis *m* bug

Cimmeri·ī -ōrum *m pl* people in the Crimea; mythical people living in perpetual darkness in caves at Cumae

cinaedic·us -a -um *adj* lewd

cinaed·us -ī *m* sodomite; lewd dancer

cincinnāt·us -a -um *adj* curly-haired

Cincinnāt·us -ī *m* L. Quinctius Cincinnatus (*famous Roman hero, dictator in 458 B.C.*)

cincinn·us -ī *m* curled hair, artificial curl (*of hair*); (rhet) highly artificial expression

cinctícul·us -ī *m* small belt or sash

cinctŭr·a -ae *f* belt, sash

cinct·us -ūs *m* tucking up; belt, sash; **cinctus Gabinius** Gabinian style of wearing toga (*usually employed at religious festivals*)

cinctūt·us -a -um *adj* wearing a belt or sash; old-fashioned

cinefact·us -a -um *adj* reduced to ashes

cinerār·ius -iī or **-ī** *m* curling iron, hair curler

cingō cingĕre cinxī cinctum *vt* to surround, encircle; to wreathe (*head*); to tuck up (*garment*); (mil) to beleaguer, invest; to cover, protect; **cingi in proelia** to prepare oneself for battle, get ready for battle; **ferrum cingi** to put on one's sword

cingŭl·a -ae *f* belt; sash (*worn by women*); girth (*worn by horses, etc.*); sword belt; chastity belt

cingŭl·um -ī *m* belt; sword belt; sash (*worn by women*); girdle, chastity belt

cingŭl·us -ī *m* zone (*of the earth*)

ciniflō -ōnis *m* hair curler

cin·is -ĕris *m* ashes; ruin, death

Cinn·a -ae *m* L. Cornelius Cinna (*consul 87-84 B.C. and supporter of Marius, d. 84 B.C.*)

cinnamōm·um or **cinnām·um -ī** *n* cinnamon; *n pl* cinnamon sticks

Cinȳr·ās -ae *m* father of Myrrha and Adonis

cipp·us -ī *m* stake, post, pillar; gravestone; (mil) palisade

circā *adv* around, round about, all around, in the vicinity; *prep* (with *acc*) (of place) around, surrounding, about, among, through, in the neighborhood of, near; attending, escorting (*persons*); (of time) at about, around, towards; (with numerals) about, nearly, almost; concerning, in respect to

circamoer·ium -iī or **-ī** *n* area on both sides of a city wall

Circ·ē -ēs or **-ae** *f* daughter of Helios and Perse, famous for her witchcraft

circens·is -e *adj* of the racetrack; *m pl* races

circin·ō -āre *vt* to make round; to circle

circĭn·us -ī *m* (geometer's) compass, pair of compasses

circĭter *adv* (of time and number) nearly, about, approximately; *prep* (with *acc*) about, near

circlus see **circulus**

circuĕō see **circumeo**

circuitiō see **circumitio**

circuĭt·us or **circumĭt·us -ūs** *m* circuit; going round, revolution; detour; circumference; circumlocution; (rhet) period

circulāt·or -ōris *m* peddler, vendor

circŭl·or -ārī -ātus sum *vi* to gather around (*for conversation*); to stroll about

circŭl·us or **circl·us** -ī *m* circle, circuit; ring, hoop; social circle; (astr) orbit

circum *adv* about, all around; *prep* (*with acc*) around, about; in the neighborhood of

circum·ăgō -agĕre -ēgī -actum *vt* to turn around; to sway (*emotionally*); **circumagi** or **se circumagere** to go out of one's way, go in a round about way; (*of time*) to pass away, roll around

circumăr·ō -āre *vt* to plow around

circumcaesŭr·ā -ae *f* contour, outline

circum·cīdo -cīdĕre -cīdī -cīsum *vt* to cut around, trim; to cut short, cut down on; to abridge, shorten; to circumcise

circumcircā *adv* all around

circumcīs·us -a -um *pp* of **circumcido**; *adj* steep; inaccessible; abridged, short

circum·clūdō -clūdĕre -clūsī -clūsum *vt* to shut in, hem in, enclose, surround

circumcŏl·ō -ĕre *vt* to live near

circumcurs·ō -āre *vt* & *vi* to run around

circum·dō -dare -dĕdī -dătum *vt* to surround, enclose, encircle; (*with dat*) to place or put (*something*) around

circum·dūcō -dūcĕre -duxī -ductum *vt* to lead around, draw around; (*with double acc*) to lead (*someone*) around to; **aliquem omnia praesidia circumducere** to take someone around to all the garrisons

circum·ěō or **circu·ěō** -īre -īvī or **ĭī** -ĭtum *vt* to go around, go around to, visit, make the rounds of; to surround, encircle, enclose, encompass; to get around, circumvent, deceive, cheat; *vi* to go around, make a circuit

circumequit·ō -āre *vt* to ride around

circum·fěrō -ferre -tŭlī -lātum *vt* to carry around, hand around; to publicize, spread abroad; to purify; **circumferri** to revolve; **oculos circumferre** to look around, glance about

circum·flectō -flectĕre -flexī -flexum *vt* to turn around, wheel about

circumfĭ·ō -āre *vt* to blow around; (fig) to buffet

circum·flŭō -fluĕre -fluxī *vt* to flow around; to surround; to overflow; *vi* to be overflowing, abound

circumflŭ·us -a -um *adj* flowing around; surrounded (*by water*)

circumforănĕ·us -a -um *adj* strolling about from market to market,

itinerant; around the forum

circum·fundō -fundĕre -fūdī -fūsum *vt* to pour around; to surround, cover, envelop; **circumfundi** or **se circumfundere** to crowd around; **circumfundi** (*with dat*) to cling to

circumgěm·ō -ĕre *vt* to growl around (*e.g., a sheepfold*)

circumgest·ō -āre *vt* to carry around

circum·gredior -grĕdī -gressus sum *vt* to surround

circumĭtĭ·ō or **circuĭtĭ·ō** -ōnis *f* going round; patrolling; circumlocution

circumĭtus see **circuĭtus**

circumjac·ĕō -ēre *vi* (*with dat*) to lie near, border on, be adjacent to

circum·jicĭō -jicĕre -jēcī -jectum *vt* to throw or place around; to surround; (*with dat*) to throw (*something*) around (*someone or something*); **fossam circumjicere** to dig a trench all around

circumject·us -a -um *adj* surrounding, adjacent; (*with dat*) adjacent to; *n pl* neighborhood

circumject·us -ūs *m* surrounding; embrace

circumlātus *pp* of **circumfero**

circumlĭg·ō -āre *vt* to bind; (*with dat*) to bind or fasten (*something*) to

circum·lĭnō -linĕre — -lĭtum *vt* to smear all over; to anoint

circumlŭ·ō -ĕre *vt* to flow around

circumlŭvĭ·ō -ōnis *f* island (*formed by a river flowing in a new channel*)

circum·mittō -mittĕre -mīsī -missum *vt* to send around

circummūn·ĭō or **circummoen·ĭō** -īre *vt* to fortify

circummūnĭtĭ·ō -ōnis *f* investment (*of town*); circumvallation

circumpadān·us -a -um *adj* situated along the Po River

circumpend·ěō -ēre *vi* to hang around

circumplaud·ō -ĕre *vt* to applaud from every direction

circum·plector -plectī -plexus sum *vt* to clasp, embrace, surround

circumplic·ō -āre *vt* to wind; (*with dat*) to wind (*something*) around

circum·pōnō -pōnĕre -posŭī -positum *vt* (*with dat*) to place or set (*something*) around

circumpōtātĭ·ō -ōnis *f* round of drinks

circumrēt·ĭō -īre -īvī -ītum *vt* to snare

circum·rōdō -rōdĕre -rōsī *vt* to nibble all around; to hesitate to say; to slander, backbite

circumsaep·ĭō or **circumsēp·ĭō** -īre -sī -tum *vt* to fence in, enclose

circumscind·ō -ĕre *vt* to strip off

circum·scrībō -scrībĕre -scripsī -scriptum *vt* to draw a line around, mark the boundary of; to limit, restrict; to set aside; to defeat the purpose of; to trap, defraud

circumscriptē *adv* comprehensively; (rhet) in periods

circumscriptǐ·ō -ōnis *f* encircling; circle; circuit, limit, boundary; comprehensive statement; cheating, deceiving; (rhet) period

circumscript·or -ōris *m* cheat

circumscript·us -a -um *pp of* **circumscribo**; *adj* restricted, limited; (rhet) periodic

circumsěc·ō -āre *vt* to cut around

circum·sedĕō -sedĕre -sēdī -sessum *vt* to beset, besiege, invest, blockade

circumsēpǐō see **circumsaepio**

circumsessǐ·ō -ōnis *f* besieging, blockading

circumsǐd·ō -ěre *vt* to besiege

circumsǐl·ǐō -īre *vi* to hop around, dance around

circum·sistō -sistěre -stětī *vt* to stand around, surround

circumsǒn·ō -āre *vt* to make resound, fill with sound; *vi* to resound everywhere; (with *dat*) to resound to

circumsǒn·us -a -um *adj* noisy

circumspectātr·ix -īcis *f* spy (female)

circumspectǐ·ō -ōnis *f* looking around; circumspection, caution

circumspect·ō -āre *vt* to search attentively, watch for; *vi* to keep looking around, look around anxiously

circumspect·us -a -um *pp of* **circumspicio**; *adj* well-considered; guarded (*words*); circumspect, cautious (*person*)

circumspect·us -ūs *m* consideration; view

circum·spicǐō -spicěre -spexī -spectum *vt* to look around for, survey, see; to consider, examine; *vi* to be circumspect, be cautious, be on the watch; **se circumspicere** to think highly of oneself

circumstant·ēs -ium *m pl* bystanders

circum·stō -stāre -stětī *vt* to surround, envelop; (of terror, etc.) to grip, confront, overwhelm; *vi* to stand around

circumstrěp·ō -ěre *vt* to surround with noise or shouts

circumsurg·ō -ěre *vi* (of mountains) to rise all around

circumtent·us -a -um *adj* tightly covered

circumtěr·ō -ěre *vt* to rub shoulders with, crowd around

circumtext·us -a -um *adj* with embroidered border

circumtǒn·ō -āre -ǔī *vt* to crash around (*someone*)

circumtons·us -a -um *adj* clipped

circum·vādō -vāděre -vāsī *vt* to attack on every side; (of terror, etc.) to grip, confront

circumvǎg·us -a -um *adj* flowing around, encircling

circumvall·ō -āre *vt* to blockade, invest

circumvectǐ·ō -ōnis *f* carting around (*of merchandise*); revolution (*of sun*)

circumvect·ō -āre *vt* to carry around

circumvect·or -ārī -ātus sum *vt* to ride or cruise around; to describe; *vi* to ride about, cruise about

circum·věhor -věhī -vectus sum *vt* to ride or cruise around; to describe, express by circumlocution; *vi* to ride about, cruise about

circumvēl·ō -āre *vt* to veil, envelop, cover

circum·venǐō -venīre -vēnī -ventum *vt* to encircle, surround; to go around to; to surround (*in a hostile manner*), invest; to distress, afflict, oppress; to circumvent, cheat, deceive

circumvert·ō -ěre *vt* to turn (*something*) around; **circumverti** to turn oneself around, turn around; **circumverti axem** to turn around an axle

circumvest·ǐō -īre *vt* to clothe, wrap

circumvinc·ǐō -īre *vt* to bind, tie up

circumvǐs·ō -ěre *vt* to look around, glare around at

circumvolit·ō -āre *vt & vi* to fly around, dash about, rove around; to hover around

circumvǒl·ō -āre *vt* to fly around, hover about, flit about

circum·volvō -volvěre — -volūtum *vt* to wind, roll around; **circumvolvi** or **se circumvolvere** (with *dat* or *acc*) to revolve around, wind oneself around

circ·us -ī *m* circle; racetrack; (astr) orbit

Circ·us Maxǐm·us (*genit:* **Circī Maxǐm·ī**) *m* oldest racetrack in Rome, between the Palatine and Aventine, alleged to have been built by Tarquinius Priscus

cirrāt·us -a -um *adj* curly-haired

Cirrh·a -ae *f* town near Delphi, sacred to Apollo

cirr·us -ī *m* lock, curl; forelock; fringe

cis *prep* (with *acc*) on this side of; within

Cisalpīn·us -a -um *adj* Cisalpine, on the Roman side of the Alps

cis·ǐum -ǐī or **-ī** *n* light two-wheeled carriage

Cissē·is -ǐdis *f* Hecuba

Ciss·eus -ěī *m* king of Thrace and father of Hecuba

cist·a -ae *f* box, chest

cistell·a -ae *f* small box

cistellātr·ix -īcis *f* female slave in charge of a money box

cistellǔl·a -ae *f* small box

cistern·a -ae *f* cistern, reservoir

cistophǒr·us -ī *m* Asiatic coin

cistǔl·a -ae *f* small box

citātim *adv* quickly, hastily

citāt·us -a -um *adj* quick, speedy, rapid; **citato equo** at full gallop

citeri·or -us *adj* on this side; nearer to earth, more down to earth, more mundane

Cithaer·ōn -ōnis *m* mountain range dividing Attica from Boeotia

cithăr·a -ae *f* zither, lyre, lute; art of playing the zither, lyre, or lute

citharist·a -ae *m* zither player, lute player

citharistrĭ·a -ae *f* zither player, lutist (*female*)

cithariz·ō -āre *vt* to play the zither, lyre, or lute

citharoed·us -ī *m* singer accompanied by zither, lyre, or lute

citĭm·us -a -um *adj* nearest

citius *adv* sooner, rather; **dicto citius** no sooner said than done; **serius aut citius** sooner or later

cito *adv* quickly; soon

cit·ō -āre *vt* to excite, rouse; to call, summon, cite; to call to witness, appeal to

citrā *adv* on this side, on the near side; **citra cadere** to fall short; *prep* (with *acc*) on this side of, on the near side of; (of time) since, before; short of, less than

citrĕ·us -a -um *adj* of citrus wood

citrō *adv* to this side, this way; **ultro citro, ultro citroque,** or **ultro et citro** to and fro, up and down; mutually

citr·us -ī *f* citrous tree; citron tree

cit·us -a -um *pp* of **cieo**; *adj* quick, rapid, swift

cīvic·us -a -um *adj* civil; civic; **corona civica** oak-leaf crown awarded for saving a fellow soldier's life

cīvīl·is -e *adj* civil; civic; political; civilian; democratic; polite; **jus civile** rights as a citizen, civil rights; **ratio civilis** political science

cīvīlit·ās -ātis *f* politics; courtesy

cīvīliter *adv* like a citizen; as an ordinary citizen would; politely

cīv·is -is *m* or *f* citizen; fellow citizen; private citizen

cīvit·ās -ātis *f* citizenship; state, commonwealth, community

clād·ēs -is *f* disaster, ruin, damage, loss; (mil) defeat; (fig) scourge

clam *adv* secretly, privately, in secret; stealthily; *prep* (with *abl* or *acc*) without the knowledge of, unknown to; **clam habere aliquem** to keep someone in the dark; **neque clam me est** nor is it unknown to me

clāmāt·or -ōris *m* loudmouth

clāmitāti·ō -ōnis *f* bawling, noise, racket

clāmĭt·ō -āre *vt & vi* to cry out, yell

clām·ō -āre *vt* to call out, call upon; to proclaim, declare; to invoke; *vi* to cry out, yell, shout

clām·or -ōris *m* shout, cry, call; acclamation, applause; outcry, complaint; war cry; noise, sound, echo

clāmōs·us -a -um *adj* clamorous, noisy

clancŭlum *adv* secretly, privately; *prep* (with *acc*) unknown to

clandestīnō *adv* secretly

clandestīn·us -a -um *adj* clandestine, secret, hidden

clang·or -ōris *m* clang, din, shrill cry

clārē *adv* distinctly, clearly; brightly; with distinction

clār·ĕō -ēre *vi* to be clear, be bright, be distinct; to be evident; to be famous

clār·escō -escĕre -ŭī *vi* to become clear, become distinct, become bright; to become obvious; to become famous

clārigāti·ō -ōnis *f* demand for satisfaction, ultimatum; fine

clārĭg·ō -āre *vi* to give an ultimatum

clārisŏn·us -a -um *adj* clear-sounding, loud

clārĭt·ās -ātis *f* clarity, distinctness; clearness (of *style*); celebrity, distinction

clārĭtūd·ō -ĭnis *f* brightness; distinction, fame

clār·ō -āre *vt* to make clear, explain, illustrate; to make famous; to illuminate

Clar·os -ī *f* town in Asia Minor near Colophon, famous for a temple and an oracle of Apollo

clār·us -a -um *adj* clear, distinct, bright; plain, manifest; famous, renowned; notorious

classiāri·us -a -um *adj* naval; *m pl* marines

classicŭl·a -ae *f* flotilla

classic·us -a -um *adj* first-class; naval; *m pl* marines; *n* battle signal; bugle

class·is -is *f* fleet; army; (pol) class

clāthr·ī or **clātr·ī -ōrum** *m pl* bars, cage, lattice

clātrāt·us -a -um *adj* barred

claud·ĕō -ēre or **claud·ō -ēre** *vi* to limp; to falter, hesitate, waver

claudicāti·ō -ōnis *f* limping

claudic·ō -āre *vi* to be lame, limp; to waver; to be defective

Claud·ius -iī or **-ī** *m* Appius Claudius Caecus (*censor* in 312 B.C. *and builder of the Appian aqueduct and the Appian Way*); Roman emperor, 41-54 A.D.

claudō claudĕre clausī clausum *vt* to bolt, bar, shut, close; to bring to a close, conclude; to lock up, imprison; to blockade, hem in; to limit, restrict; to cut off, block; **agmen claudere** to bring up the rear; **numeris** or **pedibus claudere** to put into verse; **transitum claudere** to block traffic

claud·us -a -um *adj* lame, limping; crippled, imperfect, defective; wavering, untrustworthy

claustr·a -ōrum *n pl* lock, bar, bolt; gate, dam, dike; barrier, barricade; cage, den; fortress, defenses

clausŭl·a -ae *f* close, conclusion, end; (rhet) close of a period

claus·us -a -um *pp* of **claudo**; *n* enclosure

clāv·a -ae *f* cudgel, club, knotty branch

clāvār·ium -iī or **-ī** *n* allowance to soldiers for shoe nails

clāvicŭl·a -ae *f* tendril

clāvĭg·er -ĕra -ĕrum *adj* carrying a club; carrying keys; *m* club bearer (*Hercules*); key bearer (*Janus*)

clāv·is -is *f* key; **clavis adimere uxori** to take the keys away from a wife, get a divorce

clāv·us -ī *m* nail; rudder, helm; purple stripe (*on a tunic, broad for senators, narrow for knights*); **clavus anni** beginning of the year; **clavus trabalis** spike; **trabali clavo figere** to nail down, clinch

Cleanth·ēs -īs *m* Stoic philosopher, pupil of Zeno (300?-220 B.C.)

clēm·ens -entis *adj* gentle, mild, merciful, kind, compassionate; mitigated, qualified, toned down

clēmenter *adv* gently, mildly, mercifully, kindly, compassionately; by degrees, gradually

clēmenti·a -ae *f* mildness, mercy, clemency, compassion

Cle·ōn -ōnis *m* Athenian demagogue after death of Pericles in 429 B.C.

Cleopătr·a -ae *f* queen of Egypt (68-31 B.C.)

clep·ō -ĕre -sī -tum *vt* to steal

clepsydr·a -ae *f* water clock; (fig) time (*allotted to speakers*); **clepsydram dare** (with *dat*) to give (*someone*) the floor; **clepsydram petere** to ask for the floor

clept·a -ae *m* thief

cli·ens -entis *m* client, dependant (*freeman protected by a patron*); follower, retainer; companion, favorite; vassal

client·a -ae *f* client (*female*)

clientēl·a -ae *f* clientele; patronage, protection; *f pl* allies, dependants; clienteles

clientŭl·us -ī *m* poor client

clīnām·en -inis *n* swerve

clīnāt·us -a -um *adj* bent, inclined

Clī·ō -ūs *f* Muse of history

clipeāt·us -a -um *adj* armed with a shield

clipĕ·um -ī *n* or **clipĕ·us -ī** *m* round bronze Roman shield; medallion; disc (*of sun*)

clītell·a -ae *f* saddlebag; *f pl* packsaddle

clītellāri·us -a -um *adj* carrying a packsaddle

clīvōs·us -a -um *adj* hilly, full of hills; steep

clīv·us -ī *m* slope, ascent, hill; slope, pitch; **adversus clivum** uphill; **primi clivi** foothills

Clīv·us Sac·er (*genit:* **Clīv·ī Sac·rī**) *m* part of the Via Sacra ascending the Capitoline Hill, also called Clivus Capitolinus

cloāc·a -ae *f* sewer, drain; **cloaca maxima** main sewer (*draining the valley between the Capitoline, Palatine, and Esquiline*)

Cloācīn·a -ae *f* Venus

Clōdi·a -ae *f* sister of Publius Clodius Pulcher and thought to be the person called Lesbia in Catullus' poems

Clōd·ius -iī or **-ī** *m* Publius Clodius Pulcher (*notorious enemy of Cicero who caused the latter to be exiled in 58 B.C. and was himself killed by Milo in 52 B.C.*)

Cloelĭ·a -ae *f* Roman girl who was given as hostage to Porsenna and escaped by swimming the Tiber

Clōth·ō (*genit* not in use; *acc:* **-ō**) *f* one of the three Fates

clu·ĕō -ēre or **clu·ĕor -ērī** *vi* to be named, be spoken of, be reputed, be famous

clūn·is -is *m* or *f* buttock

clūrīn·us -a -um *adj* of apes

Clūs·ium -iī or **-ī** *n* ancient Etruscan town

Clūs·ius -iī or **-ī** *m* Janus

Clymĕn·ē -ēs *f* wife of Merops and mother of Phaëthon

Clytaemnestr·a -ae *f* wife of Agamemnon, sister of Helen, Castor, and Pollux, and mother of Electra, Iphigenia, and Orestes, the latter of whom killed her

Cnid·us -ī *f* town in Caria, famous for worship of Venus

coacervātĭ·ō -ōnis *f* piling up, accumulation

coacerv·ō -āre *vt* to pile up, accumulate

coac·escō -escĕre -ŭī *vi* to become sour

coact·ō -āre *vt* to force

coact·or -ōris *m* collector (*of money*); **agminis coactores** rearguard elements

coactus *pp* of **cogo**; *adj* forced, unnatural, hypocritical; *n* felt

coact·us -ūs *m* coercion, compulsion

coaedific·ō -āre *vt* to build up (*an area*), fill with buildings; **loci coaedificati** built-up areas

coaequ·ō -āre *vt* to level off, make level, bring down to the same level

coagmentātĭ·ō -ōnis *f* combination, union

coagment·ō -āre *vt* to join, glue, cement

coagment·um -ī *n* joint

coāgŭl·um -ī *n* rennet

coal·escō -escĕre -ŭī -ĭtum *vi* to grow firm, take root; to increase, become strong; become established, thrive

coangust·ō -āre *vt* to contract, compress; to limit, restrict

coarct· = coart·

coargŭ·ō -ĕre -ī *vt* to prove conclusively, demonstrate; to refute, prove wrong or guilty; (with *genit* of the charge) to prove (*someone*) guilty of

coartātĭ·ō -ōnis *f* crowding together

coart·ō -āre *vt* to crowd together, confine; to shorten, abridge

coccĭnāt·us -a -um *adj* clothed in scarlet

coccĭnĕ·us or **coccĭn·us -a -um** *adj* scarlet

cocc·um -ī *n* scarlet

coclĕ·a or **cochlĕ·a -ae** *f* snail

coclĕar·e -is *n* spoon

cocl·es -ĭtis *m* person blind in one eye

Cocl·es -ĭtis *m* Horatius Cocles (*famous for defending the Pons Sublicius against Porsenna's army*)

coctĭl·is -e *adj* baked; brick

coct·us -a -um *pp* of **coquo**; *adj* well-considered

Cōcȳt·us -ī *m* river of the lower world

cōdex see **caudex**

cōdĭcill·ī -ōrum *m pl* small trunks of trees, fire logs; note; petition; codicil

Codr·us -ī *m* last king of Athens, who sacrificed his life for an Athenian victory (1160-1132 B.C.)

coel- = cael-

co·ĕmō -emĕre -ēmī -emptum *vt* to buy up

coēmptĭ·ō -ōnis *f* marriage (*contracted by fictitious sale of contracting parties*); fictitious sale of an estate (*to relieve it of religious obligations*)

coēmptĭōnāl·is -e *adj* of a fictitious marriage; used in a mock sale; worthless

coen- = caen-

co·eō -īre -īvī or **-ĭī -ĭtum** *vt* **societatem coire** to enter an agreement, form an alliance; *vi* to come or go together; to meet, assemble; to be united, combine; to mate, copulate; to congeal, curdle; to agree; to conspire; to clash (*in combat*); (*of wounds*) to close, heal up

coep·ĭō -ĕre -ī -tum *vt & vi* to begin

coept·ō -āre *vt* to begin eagerly; to try; (*with inf*) to try to; *vi* to begin, make a beginning

coept·us -a -um *pp* of **coepio**; *n* beginning; undertaking

coept·us -ūs *m* beginning

coēpŭlōn·us -ī *m* dinner guest

coērc·eō -ēre -ŭī -ĭtum *vt* to enclose, confine, hem in; to limit; to restrain, check, control

coērcĭtĭ·ō -ōnis *f* coercion; right to punish

coēt·us -ūs *m* coming together, meeting; crowd, company

Coe·us -ī *m* Titan, father of Latona

cōgĭtātē *adv* deliberately

cōgĭtātĭ·ō -ōnis *f* thinking, deliberating; reflection, meditation; thought, plan, design; reasoning power, imagination

cōgĭt·ō -āre *vt* to consider, ponder, reflect on; to imagine; (*with inf*) to intend to; *vi* to think, reflect, meditate

cōgĭtāt·us -a -um *adj* well-considered, deliberate; *n pl* thoughts, ideas

cognātĭ·ō -ōnis *f* relationship by birth; agreement, resemblance, affinity; relatives, family

cognāt·us -a -um *adj* related by birth; related, similar, connected; *mf* relative

cognĭtĭ·ō -ōnis *f* learning, acquiring knowledge; notion, idea, knowledge; recognition; (*law*) inquiry, investigation, trial; (*with genit*) knowledge of, acquaintance with

cognĭt·or -ōris *m* advocate, attorney; defender, protector; witness

cognĭtus *pp* of **cognosco**; *adj* acknowledged

cognōm·en -ĭnis *n* surname, family name (*e.g., Caesar*); name

cognōment·um -ī *n* surname; name

cognōmĭnāt·us -a -um *adj* synonymous

cognōmĭn·is -e *adj* like-named, of the same name

co·gnoscō -gnoscĕre -gnōvī -gnĭtum *vt* to become acquainted with, get to know, learn; to recognize, identify; to inquire into, investigate; to criticize, appreciate; to reconnoiter; **cognovisse** to know

cō·gō -gĕre -ēgī -actum *vt* to gather together, collect, convene; to thicken, condense, curdle; to pressure, bring pressure upon; to compel, force; to coax; to exact, extort; to infer, conclude; **agmen cogere** to bring up the rear

cohaer·ens -entis *adj* adjoining, continuous; consistent; harmonious

cohaerentĭ·a -ae *f* coherence, connection

co·haerĕō -haerēre -haesī -haesum *vi* to stick or cling together; cohere; to be consistent, be in agreement; (*with abl*) to consist of, be composed of; (*with cum + abl*) to be closely connected with, be in harmony with, be consistent with; **inter se cohaerere** to be consistent

co·haerescō -haerescĕre -haesī *vi* to cling together, cohere

cohēr·es -ēdis *m* or *f* coheir

cohĭb·eō -ēre -ŭī *vt* to hold together, hold close, confine; to hold back, repress, check, stop

cohonest·ō -āre *vt* to do honor to, celebrate

cohorr·escō -escĕre -ŭī *vi* to shiver all over

cohor·s -tis *f* yard (*esp. for cattle or chickens*); train, retinue, escort; (*mil*) cohort (*comprising 3 maniples or 6 centuries and forming one tenth of a legion*)

cohortātĭ·ō -ōnis *f* encouragement

cohortĭcŭl·a -ae *f* small cohort

cohort·or -ārī -ātus sum *vt* to encourage, cheer up, urge on

coītĭ·ō -ōnis *f* conspiracy, coalition; agreement

coĭt·us -ūs *m* meeting; sexual union

colăph·us -ī *m* slap, blow with a fist

Colch·is -ĭdis f country on E. end of the Black Sea; Medea

cōlĕ·us -ī m sack, scrotum

cōl·is -is m stalk, cabbage

collabasc·ō -ĕre vi to waver, totter

collabefact·ō -āre vt to shake hard

collabe·fīō -fĭerī -factus sum vi to collapse, be ruined, fall to pieces

col·lābor -lābī -lapsus sum vi to collapse, fall to pieces

collacerāt·us -a -um adj torn to pieces

collacrĭmātĭ·ō -ōnis f weeping

collacrĭm·ō -āre vt to cry bitterly over; vi to cry together

collactĕ·a -ae f foster sister

collār·e -is n collar

Collātĭ·a -ae f old town in Latium

Collātīn·us -ī m husband of Lucretia

collātĭ·ō -ōnis f bringing together; contribution of money, collection; comparison, analogy; **signorum collatio** clash of troops

collāt·or -ōris m contributor

collātus pp of confero

collaudātĭ·ō -ōnis f warm praise

collaud·ō -āre vt to praise highly

collax·ō -āre vt to make loose

collect·a -ae f contribution of money

collectĭcĭ·us -a -um adj hastily-gathered

collectĭ·ō -ōnis f gathering; summing up, recapitulation; inference

collectus pp of colligo

collect·us -ūs m collection

collēg·a -ae m colleague, partner (in office); associate, companion; fellow member (of a club)

collēg·ium -ĭī or -ī n association in office; official body, board, college, guild, company, corporation, society

collibert·us -ī m fellow freedman

collĭb·et or **collŭb·et** -ēre -ŭit -ĭtum v impers it pleases

col·līdō -līdĕre -līsī -līsum vt to smash to pieces, shatter, crush; to cause to clash, set at variance

colligātĭ·ō -ōnis f binding together, connection

collĭg·ō -āre vt to tie together, connect; to unite, combine; to fasten, chain; to stop, hinder

col·lĭgō -lĭgĕre -lēgī -lectum vt to pick up, gather together, collect; to contract, compress, concentrate; to acquire gradually; to infer, conclude, gather; to assemble, bring together; to enumerate; to gather, repair; to check, control (horse); **animum colligere, mentem colligere,** or **se colligere** to collect or compose oneself, muster one's courage, rally, come to, come around; **vasa colligere** to pack up (for the march)

Collīn·a Port·a (genit: **Collīn·ae Port·ae**) f Colline Gate (near the Quirinal Hill)

collīnĕ·ō -āre vt to aim straight; vi to hit the mark

col·līnō -linĕre -lēvī -lĭtum vt to smear; to defile

colliquefact·us -a -um adj dissolved, melted

coll·is -is m hill

collocātĭ·ō -ōnis f arrangement; giving in marriage

collŏc·ō -āre vt to place, put in order, arrange; to station, deploy; to give in marriage; to lodge, quarter; to occupy, employ; **se collocare** to settle, settle down (in a place)

collocuplēt·ō -āre vt to enrich, make quite rich

collocūtĭ·ō -ōnis f conversation, conference

colloqu·ium -ĭī or -ī n conversation, conference

col·lŏquor -lŏquī -locūtus sum vt to talk to; vi to talk together, converse, hold a conference

collŭbet see **collĭbet**

collūc·ĕō -ēre vi to shine brightly, be entirely illuminated; (fig) to be resplendent

col·lūdō -lūdĕre -lūsī -lūsum vi to play together; to be in collusion; (with dat) to play with

coll·um -ī n neck

col·lŭō -lŭĕre -lŭī -lūtum vt to wash out, rinse, moisten; **ora colluere** to wet the mouth, quench the thirst

collūsĭ·ō -ōnis f collusion

collūs·or -ōris m playmate; fellow-gambler

collustr·ō -āre vt to light up; to survey, inspect; (in painting) to represent in bright colors

collutulent·ō -āre vt to soil, defile

colluvĭ·ō -ōnis or **colluvĭ·ēs** (genit not in use) f dregs, impurities, filth; rabble

collўb·us -ī m conversion of currency; rate of exchange

collўr·a -ae f noodles, macaroni

collўr·ium -ĭī or -ī n eyewash

colō colĕre colŭī cultum vt to till, cultivate, work; to live in (a place); to guard, protect; to honor, cherish, revere, worship; to adorn, dress; to practice, follow; to experience, live through, spend

colocāsĭ·a -ae f lotus, water lily

colōn·a -ae f peasant woman

colōnĭ·a -ae f colony, settlement; colonists, settlers

colōnĭc·us -a -um adj colonial

colōn·us -ī m settler; farmer

col·or or **col·ōs** -ōris m color, hue, tint; external condition; complexion; tone, style; luster; grace; colorful pretext

colōrāt·us -a -um adj colored, tinted; healthily tanned

colōr·ō -āre vt to color, tan; (fig) to give a certain tone to

colossē·us -a -um adj colossal

coloss·us -ī m gigantic statue, colossus

colostr·a -ae f or **colostr·um** -ī n first milk after delivery, colostrum colŭb·er -rī m snake, adder

colŭbr·a -ae f snake, adder (female)

colubrĭf·er -ĕra -ĕrum adj snaky

colubrīn·us -a -um adj snaky; wily, sly

cōl·um -ī n strainer

columb·a -ae f pigeon, dove (female)

columb·ar -āris n collar

columbār·ĭum -iī or -ī n pigeonhole; (fig) vault with niches for cinerary urns

columbīn·us -a -um adj of a dove or pigeon; m little dove

columb·us -ī m pigeon, dove

columell·a -ae f small column

colŭm·en -ĭnis n height, summit, peak; gable; pillar; head, leader; support, prop

column·a -ae f column, pillar, post; (fig) pillar, support; waterspout; ad columnam (i.e., Maeniam) pervenire or ad columnam adhaerescere to be brought to punishment (because at the Columna Maenia in the Roman forum criminals and debtors were tried); f pl display columns (in bookshop); bookshop

Column·a Maenĭ·a (genit: Column·ae Maenĭ·ae) f column in the Roman forum, possibly of the Basilica Porcia supporting a projecting balcony (maenianum), at which thieves and slaves were whipped and to which debtors were summoned for trial; whipping post

columnār·ĭum -iī or -ī n tax on house pillars

columnār·ĭus -iī or -ī m criminal debtor (punished at the Columna Maenia)

colurn·us -a -um adj made of hazel wood

col·us -ī or -ūs m or f distaff

cōlўphĭ·a -ōrum n pl choice cuts of meat, loin cuts

com·a -ae f hair (of the head); mane (of horse or lion); fleece; foliage; grass; sunbeams

com·ans -antis adj hairy, longhaired; plumed (helmet); leafy; comans stella comet

cōmarch·us -ī m chief burgess

comāt·us -a -um adj long-haired; leafy

combĭb·ō -ĕre -ī vt to drink up; to absorb; to swallow, engulf; to repress, conceal (tears); to imbibe, acquire (knowledge)

combĭb·ō -ōnis m drinking partner

comb·ūrō -ūrĕre -ussī -ustum vt to burn up, consume; (fig) to ruin

com·ĕdō -edĕre (or -esse) -ēdī -ēsum (or -estum) vt to eat up, consume, devour; to waste, squander, dissipate, spend; se comedere to pine away

com·es -ĭtis m or f companion, fellow traveler; associate, comrade; attendant, retainer, dependant; concomitant, consequence

comēt·ēs -ae m comet

cōmĭcē adv like a comedy

cōmĭc·us -a -um adj of comedy, comic; comicum aurum stage money; m actor (of comedy); playwright (of comedy)

cōm·is -e adj courteous, polite; kind, friendly; (with dat or with erga or in + acc) friendly toward

cōmissābund·us -a -um adj parading in a riotous bacchanalian procession; carousing

cōmissātĭ·ō -ōnis f riotous bacchanalian procession; wild drinking party

cōmissāt·or -ōris m drinking partner, reveler, guzzler

cōmiss·or or cōmīs·or -ārī -ātus sum vi to join in a bacchanalian procession; to revel, guzzle

cōmĭt·ās -ātis f politeness, courteousness; kindness, friendliness

comitāt·us -ūs m escort, retinue; imperial retinue, court; company (traveling together), caravan

cōmĭter adv politely, courteously; kindly

comitĭ·a -ōrum n pl comitia, popular assembly; elections; comitia consularia or comitia consulum election of consuls; comitia praetoria election of praetors

comitiāl·is -e adj of the assembly; of the elections, election

comitiāt·us -ūs m assembly of the people in the comitia

comit·ĭum -iī or -ī n comitium, assembly place

comĭt·ō -āre or comĭt·or -ārī -ātus sum vt to accompany, attend, follow

commacŭl·ō -āre vt to spot, stain; to defile

commanipulār·is -is m comrade in the same brigade

commarīt·us -ī m fellow husband

commeāt·us -ūs m passage, thoroughfare; leave of absence, furlough; transport, passage, convoy; (mil) lines of communication; (mil) supplies; in commeatu esse to be on a furlough

commedĭt·or -ārī -ātus sum vt to practice; to imitate

commemĭn·ī -isse vt & vi to remember well

commemorābĭl·is -e adj memorable, worth mentioning

commemorātĭ·ō -ōnis f recollection, remembrance; mentioning, reminding

commemŏr·ō -āre vt to keep in mind, remember; to bring up (in conversation), to mention, recount, relate; vi (with de + abl) to be mindful of

commendābĭl·is -e adj commendable, praiseworthy

commendātĭcĭ·us -a -um adj of recommendation, of introduction; litterae commendaticiae letter of introduction or of recommendation

commendāti·ō -ōnis f recommendation, recommending; commendation, praise; excellence, worth

commendāt·or -ōris m backer, supporter

commendātr·ix -īcis f backer, supporter (female)

commendāt·us -a -um adj commended, recommended, acceptable, approved

commend·ō -āre vt to entrust, commit; to recommend; to render acceptable

commentāriŏl·um -ī n short treatise

commentār·ĭum -iī or **-ī** n or **commentār·ius -iī** or **-ī** m notebook, journal, diary, notes, memorandum; (law) brief; pl memoirs

commentāti·ō -ōnis f careful study, deep reflection; preparation; essay, treatise

commenticĭ·us -a -um adj thought out; invented, fictitious, imaginary; ideal; forged, false; legendary

comment·or -ārī -ātus sum vt to think over, consider well, study; to invent, contrive, make up; to prepare, produce (writings); to discuss, write about; to imitate, adopt the language of; vi to meditate, deliberate, reflect; to experiment in speaking, attempt to speak

comment·or -ōris m inventor

comment·us -a -um pp of **commīniscor**; adj fictitious, feigned, invented, pretended; n invention, fiction, fabrication; device, contrivance

commĕ·ō -āre vi to come and go; to go back and forth; to travel repeatedly; to make frequent visits

commerc·ĭum -iī or **-ī** n trade, commerce; right to trade; dealings, business; communication, correspondence; **belli commercia** ransom

commerc·or -ārī vt to deal in, purchase

commer·ĕo -ēre -uī -ĭtum or **commer·ĕor -ērī -ĭtus sum** vt to earn, merit, deserve fully; to be guilty of

com·mētior -mētīrī -mensus sum vt to measure; (with **cum** + abl) to measure (something) in terms of

commēt·ō -āre vi to go often

commigr·ō -āre vi to move, migrate

commīlit·ĭum -iī or **-ī** n comradeship, companionship, fellowship

commīlit·ō -ōnis m fellow soldier, army buddy

commināti·ō -ōnis f threatening, menacing; f pl violent threats

com·mingō -mingĕre -minxī -mictum vt to urinate on; to wet (bed); to defile, pollute; **commictum caenum** (term of reproach) dirty knave

com·miniscor -miniscī -mentus sum vt to contrive, invent, devise

commin·or -ārī -ātus sum vt to threaten violently

commin·ŭō -uĕre -ŭī -ūtum vt to lessen considerably, diminish; to break up, shatter; to weaken, impair; to humble, crush, humiliate

comminus adv hand to hand, at close quarters; near at hand, near; **comminus conferre signa** to engage in hand-to-hand fighting

com·miscĕō -miscēre -miscŭī -mixtum vt to mix together, mix up, join together; to unite, bring together, mingle

commiserāti·ō -ōnis f pitying; (rhet) appeal to compassion

commiseresc·ō -ĕre vi (with genit) to feel pity for; v impers (with genit) **me commiserescit ejus** I pity him

commisĕr·or -ārī -ātus sum vt to feel sympathy for; vi (rhet) to try to evoke sympathy

commissĭ·ō -ōnis f beginning (of fight, game, etc.)

commissūr·a -ae f connection; joint

commiss·us -a -um pp of **committō**; n offense, crime; secret; undertaking

commītīg·ō -āre vt to soften up

com·mittō -mittĕre -mīsī -missum vt to connect, unite; to match (for a fight, etc.); to start, commence; to undertake; to commit, perpetrate; to entrust, commit; to engage in (battle); to incur (penalty); **se committere** (with dat or in + acc) to venture into

commodĭt·ās -ātis f proportion, symmetry; aptness of expression; convenience, comfort; right time; pleasantness (of personality); courtesy, kindness

commŏd·ō -āre vt to adjust, adapt; to bestow, supply, lend, give; vi to be obliging; (with dat) to adapt oneself to, be obliging to

commodŭlē or **commodŭlum** adv nicely, conveniently

commŏdum adv at a good time, in the nick of time; **commŏdum cum** just at the time when

commŏd·us -a -um adj adapted, suitable, fit, convenient; opportune (time); convenient, comfortable, advantageous; agreeable, obliging, pleasant (person); **quod commodum est** just as you please; n convenience, opportunity; profit, advantage; privilege, favor; loan; pay, reward; **commodo tuo** at your convenience

commōl·ior -īrī -ītus sum vt to set in motion

commone·faciō -facĕre -fēcī -factum vt to recall, call to mind; (with acc of person and genit of thing) to remind (someone) of

common·ĕō -ēre -ŭī -ĭtum vt to remind, warn; (with genit or de + abl) to remind (someone) of

commonstr·ō -āre vt to point out clearly

commorāti·ō -ōnis f delaying, staying; residence, sojourn; (rhet) dwelling (on some point)

com·morior -mōrī -mortŭus sum vi (with dat or with cum + abl) to die with, die at the same time as

commŏr·or -ārī -ātus sum vt to stop, detain; vi to linger, stay, stop off; (with apud + acc) to stay at the house of; **in sententia commorari** to stick to an opinion

commōtĭ·ō -ōnis f commotion; **animi commotio** excitement

commōtiuncŭl·a -ae f minor inconvenience

commōt·us -a -um adj excited, angry; deranged, insane; impassioned, lively (style)

com·movĕō -movēre -mōvī -mōtum vt to stir up, agitate, shake; to disturb, unsettle, disquiet, excite, shake up; to arouse, provoke; to stir up, generate, produce; to start, introduce (novelties); to displace, dislodge (enemy); to refute

commūn·e -is n community, state; **in commune** for general use, for all; in general

commūnicātĭ·ō -ōnis f imparting, communicating

commūnic·ō -āre or commūnic·er -ārī vt to make common; to communicate, impart, share; to share in, take part in; to unite, connect, join

commūnĭ·ō -ōnis f sharing in common

commūn·ĭō -īre -īvī or -iī -ītum vt to fortify, strengthen, barricade

commūn·is -e adj common, public, universal, general; familiar; courteous, affable; democratic; **loca communia** public places; **loci communes** commonplaces, general topics; **sensus communis** common sense; n see **commune**

commūnĭter adv in common, together

commūnītĭ·ō -ōnis f road building; (rhet) introduction

commurmŭr·ō -āre or commurmŭr·or -ārī vi to murmur, grumble

commūtābĭl·is -e adj changeable, subject to change; interchangeable

commūtātĭ·ō -ōnis f changing, change, alteration

commūtāt·us -ūs m change, alteration

commūt·ō -āre vt to change, alter; to interchange, exchange; (with abl or cum + abl) to exchange (something) for

cōm·ō -ere -psī -ptum vt to comb, arrange; braid; to adorn, deck out

cōmoedĭ·a -ae f comedy

cōmoedĭcē adv as in comedy

cōmoed·us -ī m comic actor

comōs·us -a -um adj with long hair, hairy; leafy

compact·a -a -um pp of compingo; adj compact, well built; n agreement

compāg·ēs -is f joining together, joint, structure, framework

compāg·ō -inis f connection

comp·ar -āris adj equal, on an equal level; (with dat) matching

comp·ar -āris m or f comrade; playmate; perfect match; spouse

comparābĭl·is -e adj comparable

comparātĭ·ō -ōnis f comparison; arrangement; acquisition, preparation, provision; relative position (of planets)

comparātīv·us -a -um adj comparative

compār·ĕō -ēre -ŭī vi to be visible, be plain, be evident, appear; to be at hand, be present

compār·ō -āre vt to put together, get together, provide; to prepare, arrange; to match; to compare; to procure, get, obtain, collect; to appoint, establish, constitute; **se comparare** (with ad or in + acc) to prepare oneself for, get ready for

comp·ascō -ascĕre — -astum vt & vi to feed together

compascŭ·us -a -um adj of public grazing

compec·iscor -iscī -tus sum vi to come to an agreement

compect·us -a -um adj in agreement, agreed; n agreement; **compecto** by agreement, according to the agreement

comped·ĭō -īre — -ītum vt to shackle

compellātĭ·ō -ōnis f rebuke, reprimand

compell·ō -āre vt to summon, call; to call to account, bring to book; to reproach; (law) to arraign

com·pellō -pellĕre -pŭlī -pulsum vt to drive together; to crowd, concentrate; to compel, force, urge, drive on

compendiārĭ·us -a -um adj short, abridged; **via compendiaria** shortcut

compend·ĭum -ĭī or -ī n careful weighing; saving (of money); profit; shortening, abridging; shortcut; **compendi facere** to save; **compendi fieri** to be brief; **suo privato compendio servire** to serve one's own private interests

compensātĭ·ō -ōnis f compensation, recompense

compens·ō -āre vt to compensate, make up for

com·percō -percĕre -persī vt to save, hoard up

comperendinātĭ·ō -ōnis f or **comperendināt·us -ūs** m (law) two-day adjournment

comperendin·ō -āre vt to adjourn (court) for two days; to put off (defendant) for two days

comper·ĭō -īre -ī -tum or comper·ior -īrī -tus sum vt to find out, ascertain, learn; **compertum habeo or compertum mihi est**

I have ascertained, I know for certain

compert·us -a -um *adj* discovered, well authenticated; (with *genit*) convicted of

comp·ēs -ĕdis *f* shackle (*for the feet*); (fig) bond

compesc·ō -ĕre -ŭī *vt* to confine, restrain, suppress, check, chain down

competīt·or -ōris *m* competitor, rival

competītr·ix -īcis *f* competitor, rival (*female*)

compĕt·ō -ĕre -īvī or **-ĭī -ītum** *vi* to coincide, come together, meet; to be adequate, be suitable; (with **ad** + *acc*) to be capable of

compīlātĭ·ō -ōnis *f* pillaging, plundering; (contemptuously said of a collection of documents) compilation

compīl·ō -āre *vt* to pillage, plunder

com·pingō -pingĕre -pēgī -pactum *vt* to put together, frame, compose; to confine, lock up, put (*in jail*)

compitāl·ia -ium or **-iōrum** *n pl* festival celebrated annually at the crossroads in honor of the Lares of the crossroads on a day appointed by the praetor

compitālĭcĭ·us -a -um *adj* of the crossroads

compitāl·īs -e *adj* of the crossroads

compĭt·um -ī *n* crossroads, intersection

complacĕ·ĕō -ēre -ŭī or **-ĭtus sum** *vi* (with *dat*) to be quite pleasing to, suit just fine

complān·ō -āre *vt* to make even or level; to raze to the ground, pull down

com·plector -plectī -plexus sum *vt* to embrace, clasp; to comprise; (of writings) to include; to grasp, understand; to display affection for, display esteem for; to enclose (*an area*); to seize, take possession of

complēment·um -ī *n* complement

complĕ·ō -ēre -ēvī -ētum *vt* to fill, fill up; (mil) to bring (*legion, etc.*) to full strength; (mil) to man; to complete; to impregnate; to fill with sound, make resound; to supply fully, furnish

complēt·us -a -um *adj* complete; perfect

complexĭ·ō -ōnis *f* combination, connection; conclusion in a syllogism; dilemma; (rhet) period

complex·us -ūs *m* embrace; (fig) love, affection; close combat; **in complexum alicujus venire** to come to close grips with someone

complicāt·us -a -um *adj* complicated, involved

complĭc·ō -āre *vt* to fold up

complōrātĭ·ō -ōnis *f* or **complōrāt·us -ūs** *m* groaning, lamentation, wailing

complōr·ō -āre *vt* to mourn for

complūr·ēs -ium *adj* several; a good many

complūriens or **complūrĭēs** *adv* several times, a good many times

compluscŭl·ī -ae -a *adj* a fair number of

compluv·ium -iī or **-ī** *n* rain trap (*quadrangular open space in middle of Roman house towards which the roof sloped so as to direct the rain into a basin, called impluviun, built into the floor*)

com·pōnō -pōnĕre -posŭī -posĭtum *vt* to put together, join; to construct, build; to compose, write; to arrange, settle, agree upon, fix, set; to match, pair, couple; to compare, contrast; to put away; take down, lay aside; to lay out, bury (*the dead*); to compose, pacify, allay, calm, appease, quiet, reconcile; to feign, invent, concoct, contrive

comport·ō -āre *vt* to carry together, bring in, collect, gather, accumulate

comp·os -ōtis *adj* (with *genit* or *abl*) in possession of, master of, having control over; having a share in, participating in; **compos animi** or **compos mentis** sane; **compos sui** self-controlled; **compos voti** having one's prayer answered

composĭtē *adv* in an orderly manner, orderly, regularly; **composite dicere** to speak logically

composĭtĭ·ō -ōnis *f* putting together, connecting, arranging, composition; matching (*of gladiators, etc.*); reconciliation (*of friends*); orderly arrangement (*of words*)

composĭt·or -ōris *m* composer, author

composĭtūr·a -ae *f* connection

composĭt·us -a -um *pp* of **compono**; *adj* compound (*words, etc.*); prepared, well arranged, orderly; made-up, feigned, false; adapted; composed, calm, settled; *n* agreement, compact; **composito** or **ex composito** by agreement, as agreed, as had been arranged

compotātĭ·ō -ōnis *f* drinking party

compot·ĭō -īre -īvī -ītum *vt* (with *acc* of person and *abl* of thing) to make (*someone*) master of, put (*someone*) in possession of

compōt·or -ōris *m* drinking partner

compōtr·ix -īcis *f* drinking partner (*female*)

comprans·or -ōris *m* dinner companion, fellow guest

comprecātĭ·ō -ōnis *f* public supplication

comprĕc·or -ārī -ātus sum *vt* to pray earnestly to, implore, supplicate

compre·hendō -hendĕre -hendī -hensum or **compren·dō -dĕre -dī -sum** *vt* to bind together, unite; to take hold of, grasp, seize, catch, apprehend; to attack, seize, arrest, capture, apprehend; to detect, discover; to occupy (*places*); to grasp, perceive, comprehend, take in; to express, describe, narrate, recount; **ignem comprehendere** to catch fire; **memoriā comprehendere** to remember; **numerō comprehendere** to enumerate, count

comprehensibil·is -e *adj* comprehensible, conceivable, intelligible

comprehensi·ō -ōnis *f* seizing, laying hold of; arrest; comprehension, perception; combining; (*rhet*) period

comprendō see comprehendo

compressi·ō -ōnis *f* pressing closely; embrace; (*rhet*) compression

compress·us -ūs *m* compression; embrace

com·primō -primĕre -pressī -pressum *vt* to press together, bring together, compress, close; to embrace; to check, curb, restrain; to keep back, suppress, withhold, conceal; **animam comprimere** to hold the breath; **compressis manibus sedere** to sit on folded hands, to not lift a hand; **ordines comprimere** to close ranks

comprobāti·ō -ōnis *f* approbation, approval

comprobāt·or -ōris *m* enthusiastic backer

comprŏb·ō -āre *vt* to approve, sanction, acknowledge; to prove, establish, make good, confirm, verify

comprōmiss·um -ī *n* mutual agreement to abide by arbiter's decision

comprō-mittō -mittĕre -mīsī -missum *vi* to agree to abide by an arbiter's decision

compt·a -um *pp* of **como**; *adj* neat, elegant

compt·us -ūs *m* hairdo

com·pungō -pungĕre -punxī -punctum *vt* to puncture, prick; to tattoo; to prod

compūt·ō -āre *vt* to compute, count

computresc·ō -ĕre *vi* to become putrid, rot

Cŏm·um -ī *n* Como (*town N. of the Po and birthplace of Pliny the Younger*)

cōnām·en -ĭnis *n* effort, struggle; support, prop; **conamen mortis** attempt at suicide

cōnāt·um -ī *n* effort, exertion; attempt, undertaking, venture

cōnāt·us -ūs *m* effort; endeavor; impulse, inclination, tendency; undertaking

concăc·ō -āre *vt* to defile with excrement

concaed·ēs -ĭum *f pl* log barricade

concale·faciō -facĕre -fēcī -factum *vt* to warm up

concal·escō -escĕre -ŭī *vi* to grow hard; to become insensible; to become shrewd

concastīg·ō -āre *vt* to punish severely

concăv·ō -āre *vt* to curve, bend

concăv·us -a -um *adj* concave, hollow; curved, arched, bent, vaulted; deep (*valley*)

con·cēdō -cēdĕre -cessī -cessum *vt* to give up, relinquish, cede; to pardon, overlook; to allow, grant; *vi* to go away, give way, depart, withdraw, retire; (with *dat*) **a** to yield to, submit to, give way to, succumb to; **b** to submit to, comply with; **c** to make allowance for, pardon; **d** to be inferior to; (with **in** + *acc*) to pass over to, be merged in; **fato concedere, naturae concedere, or vitā concedere** to die

concelĕbr·ō -āre *vt* to frequent, fill; to pursue (*studies*); to fill with life, enliven; to celebrate; to make widely known, proclaim, publish

concēnāti·ō -ōnis *f* dining together

concenti·ō -ōnis *f* singing together, harmony

concenturi·ō -āre *vt* to marshal by the hundreds; (with *dat*) to bring (*fear*) to

concent·us -ūs *m* concert, symphony; harmony; choir; concord, agreement, harmony

concepti·ō -ōnis *f* conception (*becoming pregnant*); (*law*) composing legal formulas

conceptīv·us -a -um *adj* movable (*holidays*)

concept·us -ūs *m* conception (*becoming pregnant*), pregnancy

concerp·ō -ĕre -sī -tum *vt* to tear up, tear to shreds; (*fig*) to cut up, abuse, revile

concertāti·ō -ōnis *f* controversy, dispute

concertāt·or -ōris *m* rival

concertātōri·us -a -um *adj* controversial

concert·ō -āre *vi* to fight it out; to quarrel, debate

concessi·ō -ōnis *f* concession; admission (*of guilt with plea for mercy*)

concess·ō -āre *vt* (with *inf*) to stop (*doing something*)

concess·us -a -um *pp* of **concedo**; *n* concession (*thing allowed*)

concess·us -ūs *m* permission, leave

conch·a -ae *f* clam, oyster, mussel, murex; clam shell, oyster shell, mussel shell; pearl; purple dye; trumpet (*of Triton*); vessel (*containing ointments, etc.*); vulva

conch·is -is *f* bean

conchīt·a -ae *m* clam digger, conch digger

conchȳliāt·us -a -um *adj* purple

conchȳl·ium -iī or **-ī** *n* shellfish, clam, oyster; murex; purple dye; purple; purple garments

concĭd·ō -ĕre -ī *vi* to collapse; to fall (*in battle*); (*fig*) to decline, fail, fall, decay, perish, go to ruin; (*of winds*) to subside

con·cīdō -cīdĕre -cīdī -cīsum *vt* to cut up, cut to pieces, kill; to beat severely; (*fig*) to crush (*with arguments*); (*rhet*) to chop up (*sentences*)

con·ciĕō -ciēre -cīvī -cītum or **-ciō**

-cîre -cîvî -cîtum vt to assemble; to shake, stir up; (fig) to rouse, stir up, provoke

concîliābŭl·um -ī n public meeting place

concîliātī·ō -ōnis f union, bond; conciliating, winning over; inclination, bent, desire

concîliāt·or -ōris m mediator, promoter

concîliātrīcŭl·a -ae f procuress, madame

concîliātr·ix -īcis f mediator, promoter, match maker (female)

concîliāt·us -a -um adj (with ad + acc) endeared to, favorable to

concîliāt·us -ūs m union, connection, combination

concîli·ō -āre vt to bring together, unite, connect; to unite (in feeling), make friendly, win over; to bring about (by mediation); to acquire, win

concîl·ium -iī or -ī n gathering, meeting, assembly; council; combination, union

concinnē adv nicely, elegantly

concinnĭt·ās -ātis or concinnitūd·ō -ĭnis f finish, elegance, symmetry (of style)

concinn·ō -āre vt to make symmetrical, get right, adjust; to bring about, produce, cause; to make (e.g., insane)

concinn·us -a -um adj symmetrical; neat, elegant; courteous, agreeable, nice; polished (style)

concin·ō -ĕre -ŭī vt to sing, celebrate; to prophesy; vi to sing or play together, harmonize; (fig) to agree, harmonize

conciō see conciēo

conciō see contio

concipĭl·ō -āre vt to carry off

con·cipĭō -cipĕre -cēpī -ceptum vt to take hold of, take up, take, receive; to take in, absorb; to imagine, conceive, think; to understand, comprehend, perceive; to catch (fire); to entertain (hope); to draw up in formal language; to announce in formal language

concîsē adv concisely

concîsĭ·ō -ōnis f (rhet) dividing a sentence into short phrases

concîs·us -a -um pp of concīdo; adj cut up, short, concise

concĭtātē adv vigorously, vividly

concĭtātĭ·ō -ōnis f rapid movement; excitement; sedition, agitation

concĭtāt·or -ōris m instigator, ringleader; rabble-rouser

concĭtāt·us -a -um adj rapid, swift; excited

concĭt·ō -āre vt to stir up, rouse, urge; to cause, occasion

concĭt·or -ōris m instigator, ringleader; rabble-rouser

conclāmātĭ·ō -ōnis f loud shouting, yell; acclamation

conclāmĭt·ō -āre vi to keep on shouting, keep on yelling

conclām·ō -āre vt to shout, yell; to call to (for help); to call repeatedly by name, bewail (the dead); to exclaim; jam conclamatum est all's lost; vasa conclamare to give the signal to pack up (for the march); vi to shout, yell, cry out; ad arma conclamare to sound the alarm (for an attack)

conclāv·e -is n room; bedroom; dining room; cage, stall, coop

con·clūdō -clūdĕre -clūsī -clūsum vt to shut up, enclose; to include, comprise; to round off, conclude (letter, speech); to end rhythmically; to deduce, infer, conclude

conclūsē adv (rhet) in rhythmical cadence

conclūsĭ·ō -ōnis f blockade: end, conclusion; conclusion (of a speech), peroration; conclusion (of syllogism); (rhet) period

conclūsiuncŭl·a -ae f false conclusion

conclūs·us -a -um pp of conclūdo; adj confined; n logical conclusion

concŏl·or -ōris adj of the same color

concomĭtāt·us -a -um adj escorted

con·cŏquō -cŏquĕre -coxī -coctum vt to cook thoroughly; to boil down; to digest; to stomach, put up with; to cook up, concoct (plans); to weigh seriously, reflect upon, consider well; to prepare, ripen

concordĭ·a -ae f concord, harmony, good rapport; union

concordĭter adv harmoniously

concord·ō -āre vi to be of one mind, be in harmony, agree

concor·s -dis adj of the same mind, concordant, agreeing, harmonious

concrēbr·escō -escĕre -ŭī vi to grow strong

concrēd·ō -ĕre -ĭdī -ĭtum vi to entrust, commit, consign

concrĕm·ō -āre vt to burn to ashes, burn up

concrĕp·ō -āre -ŭī -ĭtum vi to rattle, creak, grate, clash, sound, make noise; digitis concrepare to snap the fingers

con·crescō -crescĕre -crēvī -crētum vi to grow together; to congeal, curdle, clot; to stiffen; to take shape, grow, increase

concrētĭ·ō -ōnis f condensing, congealing; matter, substance

concrēt·us -a -um pp of concresco; adj grown together, compounded; condensed, congealed, curdled, thick, stiff, hard; frozen; inveterate; dim (light); n hardness, solid matter

concrīmĭn·or -ārī vi to make bitter charges

concrucĭ·ō -āre vt to torture

concubīn·a -ae f concubine

concubīnāt·us -ūs m concubinage, free love

concubīn·us -ī m adulterer

concubĭt·us -ūs m reclining together (at table); sexual intercourse

concubĭ·us -a -um adj used only in

the expression **concubiā nocte** early in the night, at bedtime; *n* bedtime

conculc·ō -**āre** *vt* to trample under foot, despise, treat with contempt

con·cumbō -**cumbĕre** -**cubŭī** -**cubĭtum** *vi* to lie together; (with **cum** + *abl*) to sleep with, have intercourse with

concup·iscō -**iscĕre** -**īvī** -**ītum** *vt* to long for, covet; to aspire to, strive after

concūr·ō -**āre** *vt* to take good care of

con·currō -**currĕre** -**currī** or -**cucurrī** -**cursum** *vi* to run together, flock together; to unite; to strike one another, crash; (mil) to clash, engage in combat; to happen at the same time, coincide; (with **ad** + *acc*) to have recourse to, run for help to; **concurritur** the armies meet, there is a clash

concursātĭ·ō -**ōnis** *f* running together; rushing about; (mil) skirmishing

concursāt·or -**ōris** *m* (mil) skirmisher

concursĭ·ō -**ōnis** *f* meeting, concurrence; (rhet) repetition for emphasis

concurs·ō -**āre** *vt* to run around to; **domos concursare** to run from house to house; *vi* to rush about excitedly, dash up and down; (mil) to skirmish

concurs·us -**ūs** *m* running together, concourse, assembly; union, combination; collision; (mil) rush, charge, clash

concuss·us -**ūs** *m* shaking, concussion

con·cutĭō -**cutĕre** -**cussī** -**cussum** *vt* to strike together, bang together; to convulse; to strike, shake, shatter; to shock; to wave (*the hand*); to brandish (*weapon*); to shake out, ransack, examine; to shake, alarm, trouble, terrify

condal·ĭum -**ĭī** or -**ĭ** *n* slave's ring

condĕc·et -**ēre** *v impers* it befits, it becomes

condecŏr·ō -**āre** *vt* to grace, honor, adorn

condemnāt·or -**ōris** *m* accuser, prosecutor

condemn·ō -**āre** *vt* to condemn, convict, find guilty, sentence, doom; to blame, condemn; to prosecute successfully, bring a conviction against

condens·ō -**āre** *vt* to press close together, condense

condens·us -**a** -**um** *adj* close together, thick, crowded

condicĭ·ō -**ōnis** *f* arrangement, settlement, agreement; stipulation, terms, condition; state, situation; circumstances, rank, place; marriage contract, marriage; **ea condicione ut** on condition that; **sub condicione** conditionally; **vitae condicio** way of life, living conditions

con·dīcō -**dīcĕre** -**dīxī** -**dīctum** *vt*

to talk over, arrange together; to promise; **cenam condicere** (with *dat*) or **ad cenam condicere** (with *dat*) to make a dinner engagement with (*someone*)

condignē *adv* very worthily

condign·us -**a** -**um** *adj* fully deserving; (with *abl*) fully worthy of

condiment·um -**ī** *n* seasoning, spice

cond·ĭō -**īre** -**īvī** or -**ĭī** -**ītum** *vt* to preserve, pickle (*fruits, vegetables*); to season; to embalm (*the dead*); (fig) to spice, give spice to

condiscipulāt·us -**ūs** *m* companionship at school

condiscipŭl·us -**ī** *m* schoolmate, school companion, fellow student

con·discō -**discĕre** -**didicī** *vt* to learn by heart

conditĭō see **condicio**

condītĭ·ō -**ōnis** *f* preserving (*of fruits, etc.*); seasoning, spicing

condĭt·or -**ōris** *m* founder, builder; author, composer

conditōr·ĭum -**ĭī** or -**ĭ** *n* coffin, cinerary urn; tomb

condīt·us -**a** -**um** *pp* of **condio**; *adj* seasoned, spicy; polished (*style*)

con·dō -**dĕre** -**didī** -**ditum** *vt* to build, found; to write, compose (*poetry*); to establish (*an institution*); to store, treasure, hoard; to preserve, pickle; to bury; to conceal, hide, suppress; to shut (*eyes*); to sheathe (*sword*); to place (*soldiers*) in ambush; to plunge, bury (*sword*); to imprison; to memorize; to store up

condoce·facĭō -**facĕre** -**fēcī** -**factum** *vt* to train well

condoc·ĕō -**ēre** -**ŭī** -**tum** *vt* to teach, instruct thoroughly

condol·escō -**escĕre** -**ŭī** *vi* to begin to ache, get very sore

condōnātĭ·ō -**ōnis** *f* donating, donation

condōn·ō -**āre** *vt* to give, present, deliver, abandon, surrender; to adjudge; (with double *acc*) to make (*someone*) a present of; (with *acc* of thing and *dat* of person) to forgive, pardon (*someone an offense*); **condonare alicui pecunias creditas** to remit someone's debt

condorm·ĭō -**īre** *vi* to sleep soundly

condorm·iscō -**iscĕre** -**īvī** *vi* to fall sound asleep

condūcibĭl·is -**e** *adj* advantageous, profitable; (with **ad** + *acc*) just right for

con·dūcō -**dūcĕre** -**dūxī** -**ductum** *vt* to draw together, collect, assemble; to connect, unite; to hire, rent, borrow; to bribe; to employ; to induce; to contract for; *vi* to be of use; (with *dat*) to be useful to, profitable to; (with **ad** or **in** + *acc*) to be conducive to

conductici·us -**a** -**um** *adj* hired, mercenary

conductĭ·ō -**ōnis** *f* bringing together; recapitulation; hiring, renting

conduct·or **-ōris** *m* contractor; lessee, tenant

conduct·us **-a -um** *pp* of **conduco**; *m pl* hired men; (mil) mercenaries; *n* rented apartment, rented house

conduplicātī·ō **-ōnis** *f* doubling; (humorously) embrace

conduplic·ō **-āre** *vt* to double; **corpora conduplicare** (humorously) to embrace

condūr·ō **-āre** *vt* to harden, make very hard

cond·us **-ī** *m* storeroom manager

cō·nectō **-nectēre** **-nexŭi -nexum** *vt* to tie; to connect, join, link; to state as a conclusion; (with *dat*) to implicate (*someone or something*) in; (with *dat* or **cum** + *abl*) to join (*something*) to, connect (*something*) with

cōnexi·ō **-ōnis** *f* logical conclusion

cōnex·us **-a -um** *pp* of **conecto**; *adj* connected, joined; **per affinitatem conexus** (with *dat*) related by marriage to; *n* necessary inference, logical connection, necessary consequence

cōnex·us **-ūs** *m* combination

confābŭl·or **-ārī -ātus sum** *vt* to discuss; *vi* to converse, have a talk

confarreātī·ō **-ōnis** *f* solemn marriage ceremony in the presence of the Pontifex Maximus and ten witnesses

confarrĕ·ō **-āre** *vt* to marry with solemn rites

confātāl·is **-e** *adj* bound by the same fate

confectī·ō **-ōnis** *f* completion, successful completion; chewing, mastication

confect·or **-ōris** *m* finisher, executor; destroyer, consumer

con·ferciō **-fercīre** — **-fertum** *vt* to stuff, cram, pack together; to stuff full

con·ferō **-ferre -tŭli -lātum** *vt* to bring together; to contribute (*money, etc.*); to condense, compress; to bring together (*plans, ideas, etc.*), discuss, talk over; to bear, convey, direct; to devote, apply, confer, bestow, give, lend, grant; to ascribe, attribute, impute, assign; to put off, defer, postpone; (with **in** + *acc*) to change or transform (*someone or something*) into; to compare, contrast; **capita conferre** to put heads together, confer; **gradum conferre** (with **cum** + *abl*) to walk together with; **lites conferre** to quarrel; **pedem cum pede conferre** to fight toe to toe; **se conferre** (with **in** + *acc*) a to go to, head for; **b** to have recourse to; **c** to join (*a group, etc.*); **sermones conferre** (with **cum** + *abl*) to engage in conversation with, to engage (*someone*) in conversation; **signa conferre** to engage in combat, begin fighting

confertim *adv* (mil) shoulder to shoulder

confert·us **-a -um** *pp* of **confercio**; *adj* crowded, packed, thick, dense; (mil) shoulder to shoulder

confervĕfac·iō **-ĕre** *vt* to make glow, make melt

con·fervescō **-fervescĕre -ferbŭī** *vi* to begin to boil, grow hot

confessī·ō **-ōnis** *f* confession, acknowledgment

confess·us **-a -um** *pp* of **confiteor**; *adj* acknowledged, incontrovertible, certain; *m* self-acknowledged criminal; *n* admission; **ex confesso** admittedly, beyond doubt; **in confessum venire** to be generally admitted

confestim *adv* immediately, without delay, suddenly

confici·ens **-entis** *adj* productive, efficient; (with *genit*) productive of; efficient in; *n pl* (with *genit*) sources of

con·ficiō **-ficĕre -fēcī -fectum** *vt* to make, manufacture, construct; to make ready, prepare, bring about, complete, accomplish, execute, fulfill; to bring about, cause; to bring together, collect; to get together, secure, obtain; to use up, wear out, exhaust; to finish off, weaken, sweep away, destroy, kill; to run through (*money, inheritance*); to chew (*food*); to complete, finish, spend, pass (*time*)

confictī·ō **-ōnis** *f* fabrication, invention (*of an accusation*)

confīd·ens **-entis** *adj* trustful; self-confident; presumptuous, smug

confīdenter *adv* confidently; smugly

confīdentī·a **-ae** *f* confidence; self-confidence, smugness

confīdentilŏqu·us **-a -um** *adj* speaking confidently

con·fīdō **-fīdĕre -fīsus sum** *vi* to have confidence, be confident, be sure; (with *dat*) to confide in, rely on, trust, believe; **sibi confidere** to rely on oneself, have self-confidence

con·fīgō **-fīgĕre -fixī -fixum** *vt* to fasten, join together; to pierce, transfix; (fig) to paralyze

con·fingō **-fingĕre -finxī -fictum** *vt* to make up, invent, fabricate

confīn·is **-e** *adj* having common boundaries, adjoining; (fig) closely related, akin

confīn·ium **-ĭī** or **-ī** *n* common boundary, frontier; (fig) borderline; *n pl* neighbors; confines

confirmātī·ō **-ōnis** *f* confirmation, encouragement; affirmation, verification, corroboration; (rhet) presentation of evidence

confirmāt·or **-ōris** *m* guarantor, surety

confirmāt·us **-a -um** *adj* resolute, confident, courageous; established, certain

confirmīt·ās **-ātis** *f* firmness; stubbornness

confirm·ō -āre vt to strengthen, reinforce; to confirm, sanction, ratify; to encourage; to corroborate; to assert positively; **se confirmare** to recover, get back one's strength

confisc·ō -āre vt to deposit in a bank; to confiscate

confīsī·ō -ōnis f confidence, assurance

con·fīteor -fitērī -fessus sum vt to confess, acknowledge, admit; to reveal; vi to confess

conflāgr·ō -āre vi to burn, be on fire; (fig) to burn

conflicti·ō -ōnis f conflict

conflict·ō -āre vt to beat down, strike down; to ruin; **conflictari** to be afflicted, be tormented; vi to contend, struggle, fight

conflict·or -ārī -ātus sum vi to struggle, wrestle

conflict·us -ūs m striking together; wrestling, struggle

con·flīgō -flīgere -flīxī -flīctum vt to throw or knock together; (with **cum** + abl) to contrast (something) with, compare (something) with; vi to come into conflict, clash, fight, battle; (with **cum** + abl) to come into conflict with, clash with; (with **adversus** + acc or **contra** + acc) to fight against; **inter se confligere** to collide, collide with one another

confl·ō -āre vt to kindle, ignite; to inflame (passions); to melt down (metals); to bring together, get up, raise (army, money, etc.); to forge, invent (accusation); to bring about, cause, occasion, produce

conflu·ens -entis m confluence, junction (of rivers); m pl confluence

con·fluō -fluere -fluxī vi to flow or run together; (fig) to pour in together, come together in crowds

con·fodiō -fodere -fōdī -fossum vt to dig up (soil); to stab; (fig) to stab

conformāti·ō -ōnis f shape, form, fashion; idea, notion; arrangement (of words); expression (in the voice); (rhet) figure of speech

conform·ō -āre vt to shape, fashion, put together; to modify, educate

confoss·us -a -um pp of **confodio**; adj full of holes

confractus pp of **confringo**

confragōs·us -a -um adj rough, rugged (terrain); n pl rough terrain

confrēm·ō -ere -uī vi to grumble

confric·ō -āre vt to rub vigorously, rub in; **genua confricare** to nag, pester

con·fringō -fringere -frēgī -fractum vt to smash, crush; to break down, destroy

con·fugiō -fugere -fūgī vi to flee, take refuge, run for help; (with **ad** + acc) (fig) a to resort to, have recourse to; **b** to appeal to

confug·ium -iī or **-ī** n place of refuge, shelter

confulg·eō -ēre vi to glitter, sparkle

con·fundō -fundere -fūdī -fūsum vt to pour together, blend, mingle; to mix up, jumble together, confuse, bewilder, perplex; to spread, diffuse

confūsē adv in disorder, in confusion

confūsi·ō -ōnis f mixing, blending; confusion, mixup, trouble; **confūsio oris** blush

confūs·us -a -um pp of **confundo**; adj confused, perplexed; troubled, confused (look)

confūt·ō -āre vt to prevent (water, etc.) from boiling over; to repress, stop; to silence, confute

congel·ō -āre vt to cause to freeze up, freeze, harden; **in lapidem congelare** to petrify; vi to freeze, freeze up

congemināti·ō -ōnis f doubling

congemin·ō -āre vt to double

congem·ō -ere -uī vt to deplore deeply; vi to gasp, sigh, or groan deeply

cong·er -rī m eel

congeri·ēs -ēī f heap, pile, mass; funeral pile; accumulation

con·gerō -gerere -gessī -gestum vt to bring together; to heap up, build up; to keep up, multiply, repeat (arguments); (with **in** + acc) **a** to shower (weapons) upon, send a barrage of (weapons) upon; **b** to heap (curses, favors, etc.) upon

conger·ō -ōnis m thief

congerr·ō -ōnis m playmate

congestīcī·us -a -um adj piled up

congest·us -ūs m heap, mass, accumulation

congiāl·is -e adj holding a gallon

congiāri·us -a -um adj holding a gallon; n gift of one gallon (e.g., of oil) apiece to the people; bonus to the army; gift of money to the Roman people; gift of money among private friends

cong·ius -iī or **-ī** m Roman liquid measure equaling six sextarii, i.e., about six pints

conglaci·ō -āre vi to freeze up

conglisc·ō -ere vi to blaze up

conglobāti·ō -ōnis f massing together

conglob·ō -āre vt to make round, form into a ball, roll up

conglomer·ō -āre vt to roll up, group together, crowd together; **se in forum conglomerare** to crowd into the forum

conglūtināti·ō -ōnis f gluing together; (fig) combining (of words)

conglūtin·ō -āre vt to glue, cement; (fig) to weld together, cement

congraec·ō -āre vt to squander like the Greeks

congrātul·or -ārī -ātus sum vi to offer congratulations

con·gredior -gredī -gressus sum vt to meet, accost, address, associate with; to fight; vi to come together, meet; to fight; (with **cum** + abl) **a**

to meet with; **b** to associate with; **c** to fight against

congregābil·is -e *adj* gregarious

congregāti·ō -ōnis *f* flocking together, congregation, union, association

congrĕg·ō -āre *vt* to herd together; to unite, associate

congressi·ō -ōnis *f* meeting, conference

congressus *pp of* **congredior**

congress·us -ūs *m* meeting, association, society, union; hostile encounter, contest, fight

congrŭ·ens -entis *adj* coinciding, corresponding; suitable, consistent; self-consistent, uniform, harmonious

congruenter *adv* consistently; (with *dat* or **ad** + *acc*) in conformity with; **congruenter naturae vivere** to live in conformity with nature

congruenti·a -ae *f* consistency, symmetry

congrŭ·ō -ĕre -ŭī *vi* to coincide; to correspond, agree, be consistent; (with **ad** + *acc* or with **cum** + *abl*) to coincide with; (with *dat* or **cum** + *abl*) to correspond to, agree with, be consistent with; (with *dat* or **in** + *acc*) to agree (in *feeling, opinion*) with

congrŭ·us -a -um *adj* agreeing, agreeable

cōniciō or **cōiciō** see **conjicio**

cōnif·er -ĕra -ĕrum *adj* coniferous

cōnig·er -ĕra -ĕrum *adj* coniferous

cō·nitor -nītī -nixus sum or **-nīsus sum** *vi* to make a great effort, struggle, exert oneself; (with **in** + *acc*) to struggle toward, press on toward, try to reach

cōnīv·ĕō -ēre -ī *vi* to close the eyes (*in sleep, from light, from fear, etc.*), to blink; (of sun or moon) to be darkened, be eclipsed; (fig) to be drowsy; (with **in** + *abl*) to connive at, wink at, overlook

conjecti·ō -ōnis *f* throwing, barrage (*of missiles*); conjecture, interpretation

conject·ō -āre *vt* to conjecture, infer, conclude, guess

conject·or -ōris *m* interpreter of dreams, seer

conjectr·ix -īcis *f* interpreter of dreams, seer (*female*)

conjectūr·a -ae *f* conjecture, guess, inference; interpretation

conjectūrāl·is -e *adj* conjectural

conject·us -ūs *m* throwing together; crowding together; connecting; heap, crowd, pile; throwing, casting, hurling; turning, directing (*eyes*); casting (*a glance*); barrage (*of stones, weapons*); **ad** or **intra teli conjectum venire** to come within range of a weapon

con·jiciō -jicĕre -jēcī -jectum *vt* to pile together (*e.g., baggage*); to

conclude, infer, conjecture; to interpret (*omen*); to throw, fling, cast; to throw in (*e.g., words in a letter or speech*); **se in fugam** or **se in pedes conjicere** to take to one's heels

conjugāl·is -e *adj* conjugal

conjugāti·ō -ōnis *f* etymological relationship (*of words*)

conjugāt·or -ōris *m* uniter (*said of Hymen, god of marriage*)

conjugiāl·is -e *adj* marriage

conjug·ium -ī or **-ī** *n* union (*e.g., of body and soul*); marriage, wedlock; mating (*of animals*); (fig) husband, wife, spouse

conjŭg·ō -āre *vt* to form (*friendship*); **verba conjugata** cognates

conjunctē *adv* conjointly; at the same time; (in logic) conditionally, hypothetically; **conjuncte vivere** to live intimately together

conjunctim *adv* jointly

conjuncti·ō -ōnis *f* combination, union; association, connection; friendship; intimacy; marriage; relationship (*by blood or by marriage*); sympathy, affinity; (gram) conjunction

conjunct·us -a -um *adj* (with *dat* or *abl*) bordering upon, near; (with *dat* or *abl*, or with **cum** + *abl*) connected with; **b** agreeing with, conforming with; *n* connection

con·jungō -jungĕre -junxī -junctum *vt* to join together, connect, unite; to unite in making (*war*); to unite or join in marriage; to unite (*by bonds of friendship*); (with *dat*) to add (*e.g., words*) to (*e.g., a letter*)

con·junx or **con·jux -jŭgis** *m* married person, spouse, husband; *m pl* married couple; *f* married person, spouse, wife; fiancee; bride; the female (*of animals*)

conjūrāti·ō -ōnis *f* conspiracy, plot; alliance

conjūrāt·us -a -um *adj* bound together by an oath, allied, associate; (mil) sworn in; *m pl* conspirators

conjūr·ō -āre *vi* to take an oath together; to plot, conspire

conjux see **conjunx**

conl- = coll-

conm- = comm-

Con·ōn -ōnis *m* famous Athenian admiral (*fl* 400 B.C.); famous mathematician and astronomer of Samos (283-222 B.C.)

cōnōpē·um or **cōnōpĕ·um -ī** *n* mosquito net

cōn·or -ārī -ātus sum *vt* to try, endeavor, venture, attempt

conquassāti·ō -ōnis *f* severe shaking; disturbance

conquass·ō -āre *vt* to shake hard; (fig) to shatter, upset, disturb

con·quĕror -quĕrī -questus sum *vt* to complain bitterly about, deplore; *vi* to complain, complain bitterly

conquesti·ō -ōnis *f* complaining, complaint; (rhet) appeal for sympathy; (with *genit*, with **de** + *abl*, or with **adversus** + *acc*) complaint about

conquest·us -ūs *m* loud complaint

conquī·escō -escĕre -ēvī -ētum *vi* to rest, take a rest; to find rest, find recreation; to keep quiet, remain inactive; to slacken, flag; to lie dormant; to take a nap; to stop, pause

conquīnisc·ō -ĕre *vi* to squat, stoop down

con·quīrō -quīrĕre -quīsīvī -quīsītum *vt* to search for, look for; to procure, bring together, collect; (fig) to search for, go after (*pleasures, etc.*)

conquīsītĭ·ō -ōnis *f* search; procuring, collection; (mil) conscription, draft, recruitment

conquīsīt·or -ōris *m* recruiting officer

conquīsīt·us -a -um *pp* of **conquīro**; *adj* chosen, select

conr- = corr-

consaep·ĭō or **consēp·ĭō -īre -sī -tum** *vt* to fence in, hedge in, enclose

consaept·um -ī *n* enclosure

consalūtātĭ·ō -ōnis *f* exchange of greetings

consalūt·ō -āre *vt* to greet (*as a group*), greet cordially; *vi* **inter sē consalūtāre** to greet one another, exchange greetings

consān·escō -escĕre -ŭī *vi* to heal up; to recover

consanguinĕ·us -a -um *adj* related by blood; *m* brother; *m pl* relatives; *f* sister

consanguinīt·ās -ātis *f* blood relationship; **consanguinitāte propinquus** closely related

consaucĭ·ō -āre *vt* to wound severely

conscelerāt·us -a -um *adj* wicked, depraved, criminal; (fig) rotten to the core

conscelĕr·ō -āre *vt* to stain with guilt, dishonor, disgrace

con·scendō -scendĕre -scendī -scensum *vt* to climb up, mount, ascend; to board (*ship*); **aequor navibus conscendere** to go to sea; *vi* to climb; to go aboard, board; (with **in** + *acc*) to go aboard (*ship*)

conscensĭ·ō -ōnis *f* embarkation; **in navis conscensĭo** boarding the ships

conscientĭ·a -ae *f* joint knowledge; consciousness, knowledge; moral sense, conscience; good conscience; bad conscience; scruple; sense of guilt, remorse

con·scindō -scindĕre -scīdī -scissum *vt* to tear up, tear to pieces; (fig) to tear to pieces, abuse

conscĭ·ĭō -īre *vt* to become conscious of (*wrong*)

consc·iscō -iscĕre -īvī or **-ĭī -ītum** *vt* to approve or decide upon; (**sibi**) **mortem consciscere** to decide

upon death for oneself, commit suicide

conscĭ·us -a -um *adj* sharing knowledge with another; cognizant, conscious, aware; (with *genit* or *dat*) having knowledge of, aware of, privy to; *mf* partner, accomplice, confidant(e), confederate

conscrĕ·or -ārī -ātus sum *vi* to clear the throat

con·scrībō -scrībĕre -scripsī -scriptum *vt* to enlist, enroll; to write, write up, compose; to prescribe

conscriptĭ·ō -ōnis *f* document, draft; record, report

conscript·us -a -um *pp* of **conscribo**; *m* senator; **patres conscriptī** members of the senate

consĕc·ō -āre -ŭī -tum *vt* to cut up into small pieces, dismember

consecrātĭ·ō -ōnis *f* consecration; deification (*of emperors*)

consĕcr·ō -āre *vt* to make holy, consecrate, dedicate to a god; to dedicate to the gods below, doom to destruction, execrate; to immortalize, deify

consectārĭ·us -a -um *adj* logic; *n pl* conclusions, inferences

consectātĭ·ō -ōnis *f* eager pursuit

consectātr·ix -īcis *f* pursuer (*female*)

consectĭ·ō -ōnis *f* cutting up

consect·or -ārī -ātus sum *vt* to follow eagerly, go after; to follow up, pursue, chase, hunt; to overtake; to imitate, follow

consecūtĭ·ō -ōnis *f* effect, consequences; (rhet) order, sequence

consen·escō -escĕre -ŭī *vi* to grow old, grow old together; to become gray; to become obsolete; to waste away, fade, decline; to degenerate, sink

consensĭ·ō -ōnis *f* agreement, unanimity; harmony; plot, conspiracy

consens·us -ūs *m* agreement, unanimity; agreement, harmony; plot, conspiracy; **consensū** with one accord; **in consensum vertere** to become a general custom; **omnium vestrum consensu** with the agreement of all of you, as you all agree

consentānĕ·us -a -um *adj* (with *dat* or **cum** + *abl*) agreeing with, according to, in accord with, proper for; **consentaneum est** it is reasonable; *n pl* concurrent circumstances

consentĭ·ens -entis *adj* unanimous

con·sentĭō -sentīre -sensī -sensum *vt* **bellum consentire** to agree to war, vote for war; *vi* to agree; (with *inf*) to agree, plot, conspire to; (with **cum** + *abl*) to harmonize with, fit in with, be consistent with

consēp- = consaep-

consĕqu·ens -entis *adj* reasonable;

corresponding, logical, fit, suitable; *n* consequence, conclusion

consequentl·a -ae *f* consequence, natural sequence

con·sēquor -sēquī -secūtus sum *vt* to follow, follow up, pursue, go after; to catch up with, catch, reach, attain to, arrive at; (fig) to follow, copy, imitate; to obtain, get, acquire; to understand, perceive, learn; (of speech) to be equal to, do justice to; (of time) to come after, follow; to result from, be the consequence of, arise from

con·sĕrō -serĕre -seruī -sertum *vt* to entwine, tie, join, string together; **manum** or **manūs conserere** to fight hand to hand, engage in close combat; **proelium conserere** to begin fighting

con·sĕrō -serĕre -sēvī -situm *vt* to sow, plant

consertē *adv* in close connection, connectedly

conserv·a -ae *f* fellow slave (*female*)

conservāti·ō -ōnis *f* keeping, preserving

conservāt·or -ōris *m* preserver, defender

conservit·ium -iī or **-ī** *n* servitude

conserv·ō -āre *vt* to keep safe, preserve, maintain; (fig) to keep intact

conserv·us -ī *m* fellow slave

consess·or -ōris *m* table companion; fellow spectator; (law) assessor

consess·us -ūs *m* assembly, court

consīderātē *adv* with caution, deliberately

consīderātī·ō -ōnis *f* contemplation, consideration

consīderāt·us -a -um *adj* circumspect, cautious; well considered, deliberate

consīder·ō -āre *vt* to look at closely, inspect, examine, survey; to consider, contemplate; reflect upon

con·sīdō -sīdĕre -sēdī -sessum *vi* to sit down, be seated, settle; (of assemblies) to hold sessions, be in session; (mil) to encamp, take up a position; to settle, stay (*in residence*); to settle, sink down, subside; (fig) to settle, sink, be buried; to diminish, subside, abate, die out

consign·ō -āre *vt* to seal, sign; to certify, attest, vouch for; to note, register, record

consil·escō -escĕre -uī *vi* to become still, calm down

consiliāri·us -a -um *adj* counseling; *m* counselor, adviser; interpreter, spokesman

consiliāt·or -ōris *m* counselor

consiliō *adv* intentionally, purposely

consili·or -ārī -ātus sum *vi* to take counsel, consult; (with *dat*) to give counsel to, advise

consil·ium -iī or **-ī** *n* consultation, deliberation; deliberative body, council; council of war; plan, measure, stratagem; decision; purpose, intention, design, policy; judgment, wisdom, prudence, discretion, sense;

cabinet; advice, counsel; **consilium capere** or **consilium inīre** or **consilium suscipere** to form a plan, come to a decision, decide, determine; **consilium est mihi** (with *inf*) I intend to; **non est consilium mihi** (with *inf*) I don't mean to; **prīvātō consiliō** for one's own purposes

consimil·is -e *adj* quite similar; (with *genit* or *dat*) completely similar to, just like

consip·iō -ĕre *vi* to be sane

con·sistō -sistĕre -stitī -stitum *vi* to come to a stop, come to rest, stop, pause, halt, take a stand, stand still; to grow hard, become solid, set; (mil) to take up a position, be posted, make a stand; (of ships) to come to anchorage, to ground; (of travelers) to halt on a journey; to be firm, be steadfast, continue, endure; to be, exist, occur, take place; (with *abl* or with **in +** *abl*) to consist of, depend on

consitī·ō -ōnis *f* sowing, planting

consit·or -ōris *m* sower, planter

consitūr·a -ae *f* sowing, planting

consōbrīn·a -ae *f* first cousin (*daughter of a mother's sister*)

consōbrīn·us -ī *m* first cousin (*son of mother's sister*)

consociāti·ō -ōnis *f* association, society

consociāt·us -a -um *adj* held in common, shared

consoci·ō -āre *vt* to associate, join, unite, connect, share

consōlābil·is -e *adj* consolable

consōlātī·ō -ōnis *f* consolation, comfort; encouragement; alleviation

consōlāt·or -ōris *m* comforter

consōlātōri·us -a -um *adj* comforting; **litterae consolatoriae** letter of condolence

consōl·or -ārī -ātus sum *vt* to console, comfort, reassure, soothe, encourage, cheer up; to relieve, alleviate, mitigate

consomni·ō -āre *vt* to dream about

conson·ō -āre -uī *vi* to sound together, ring, resound, reecho; (with *dat* or with **cum +** *abl*) to harmonize with, agree with; **inter se consonare** to agree, harmonize

conson·us -a -um *adj* harmonious; (fig) fit, suitable

consōp·iō -īre *vt* to put to sleep

consor·s -tis *adj* having a common lot, of the same fortune; common; shared in common; *mf* partner, associate; *m* brother; *f* wife; sister

consortī·ō -ōnis *f* partnership, association, fellowship

consort·ium -iī or **-ī** *n* partnership; participation; (with *genit*) partnership in

conspect·us -a -um *pp* of **conspicio**; *adj* visible; in full sight; conspicuous, striking

conspect·us -ūs *m* look, sight, view; sight (*power of seeing*); mental view;

being seen, appearance on the scene; **conspectu in medio** before all eyes

con·spergō -spergĕre -spersī -spersum vt to sprinkle, splatter

conspiciend·us -a -um adj worth seeing; distinguished

conspicill·um -ī n (with genit) keeping an eye on

con·spiciō -spicĕre -spexī -spectum vt to look at attentively, observe, fix the eyes upon; to catch sight of, spot; to look at with admiration; to face (e.g., the forum); to perceive, see, discern; **conspici** to be conspicuous, be noticed, be admired, attract attention

conspic·or -ārī -ātus sum vt to catch sight of, spot, see

conspicŭ·us -a -um adj visible, in sight; conspicuous, striking, remarkable, distinguished

conspīrātĭ·ō -ōnis f agreement, unanimity, harmony, concord; plot, conspiracy

conspīrāt·us -a -um adj conspiring, in conspiracy

conspīr·ō -āre vi to breathe together, blow together, sound together; to act in unison, to agree; to plot together, conspire

conspons·or -ōris m coguarantor

con·spŭō -spuĕre — -spūtum vt to spit on; **nive conspuere** to sprinkle with snow

conspurc·ō -āre vt to defile, mess up

conspūt·ō -āre vt to spit on in contempt

constabil·ĭō -īre -īvī -ītum vt to establish, confirm

const·ans -antis adj constant, uniform, steady, fixed, stable, regular, invariable, persistent; consistent, harmonious; (fig) faithful, constant, trustworthy

constanter adv constantly, steadily, uniformly, invariably; consistently; calmly

constantĭ·a -ae f steadiness, firmness, constancy, perseverance; harmony, symmetry, consistency; steadfastness; self-possession

consternātĭ·ō -ōnis f consternation, dismay, alarm; disorder, disturbance; mutiny; wild rush, stampede

con·sternō -sternĕre -strāvī -strātum vt to spread, cover; to pave; to thatch; **constrata navis** ship with deck

constīp·ō -āre vt to crowd together

constit·ŭō -uĕre -ŭī -ūtum vt to set up, erect, establish; to settle (e.g., a people in a place); to set up, establish (authority); to settle, determine, fix (date, price, penalty); to arrange, set in order, organize; to construct, erect; to designate, select, assign, appoint; to decide, arbitrate, decree, judge; (mil) to station, post, deploy

constitūtĭ·ō -ōnis f constitution, nature; disposition; regulation, ordinance, order; definition; (rhet) issue, point of discussion

constitūt·us -a -um pp of constituo; adj ordered, arranged; **bene constitutum corpus** good constitution; n agreement, arrangement

con·stō -stāre -stītī -stātum vi to stand together; to agree, correspond; to stand firm, remain unchanged, be constant; to stand still, stand firm; to be in existence; (of facts) to be established, be undisputed, be well known; (com) to tally, be correct; (with abl of price) to cost; **non mihi satis constat** I have not quite made up my mind; **ratio constat** the account tallies, is correct

constrāt·us -a -um pp of consterno; n flooring

con·stringō -stringĕre -strinxī -strictum vt to tie up; to shackle, chain; (fig) to bind, restrain; (rhet) to condense, compress

constructĭ·ō -ōnis f building, construction; arrangement (of words)

con·strŭō -strŭĕre -struxī -structum vt to heap up, pile up; to construct, build up; (gram) to construct

constuprāt·or -ōris m rapist

constŭpr·ō -āre vt to rape

consuād·ĕō -ēre vi (with dat) to advise strongly

Consuāl·ĭa -ĭum n pl feast of Consus, ancient Italian god of fertility, celebrated on August 21st

consuās·or -ōris m adviser

consūcid·us -a -um adj very juicy

consūd·ō -āre vi to sweat profusely

consuē·facĭō -facĕre -fēcī -factum vt to accustom, inure

consu·escō -escĕre -ēvī -ētum vt to accustom, inure; vi to become accustomed; (with inf) to become accustomed to; (with **cum + abl**) to cohabit with

consuētĭ·ō -ōnis f sexual intercourse

consuētūd·ō -ĭnis f custom, habit; usage, idiom; social intercourse, social ties; sexual intercourse; **ad consuetudinem** (with genit) according to the custom of; **consuetudine** or **ex consuetudine** according to custom, from habit; **pro consuetudine mea** according to my habit, as is my habit; **ut fert consuetudo** as is usual

consuēt·us -a -um pp of consuesco; adj usual, regular, customary

con·sul -sŭlis m consul (one of the two highest magistrates of the Roman republic); **consul designatus** consul-elect; **consulem creare, dicere,** or **facere** to elect a consul; **consul ordinarius** consul who entered office on the first of January; **consul suffectus** consul chosen in the course of the year to fill a vacancy in the consulship

consulār·is -e adj consular; **aetas**

consularis minimum legal age for election to consular office; **comitia consularia** consular elections; *m* ex-consul

consulāriter *adv* like a consul, in a manner worthy of a consul

consulāt·us -ūs *m* consulship; **consulatum petere** to run for the consulship; **se consulatu abdicare** to resign from the consulship

consŭl·ō -ĕre -ŭī -tum *vt* to consult, ask advice of; to consider; to advise (*something*), offer as advice; **boni consulere** to regard favorably; *vi* to deliberate, reflect; (with **ad** or **in** + *acc*) to reflect on, take into consideration; (with *dat*) to look after; (with **in** + *acc*) to take measures against; (with **de** + *abl*) to pass sentence on

consultātī·ō -ōnis *f* mature deliberation, consideration; consulting, inquiry; subject of consultation, case

consultē *adv* deliberately, after due consideration

consultō *adv* deliberately, on purpose

consult·ō -āre *vt* to reflect on, consider maturely; to ask (*someone*) for advice, consult; *vi* to deliberate, reflect; (with *dat*) to take into consideration, look after, care for; **in medium consultare** to look after the common good

consult·or -ōris *m* counselor, adviser; advisee, client

consultr·ix - īcis *f* protectress

consult·us -a -um *pp* of **consulo**; *adj* skilled, experienced; *m* expert; **juris consultus** legal expert, lawyer; *n* deliberation, consideration; decree, decision, resolution; response (*from an oracle*)

consummāt·us -a -um *adj* consummate, perfect

consumm·ō -āre *vt* to sum up; to finish, complete, accomplish, perfect

con-sūmō -sūmĕre -sumpsī -sumptum *vt* to use up, consume, exhaust; to devour; to squander; to wear out, destroy; to spend, waste (*money, time, effort*)

consumptī·ō -ōnis *f* consumption, wasting

consumpt·or -ōris *m* destroyer

con-suō -suĕre -suī -sūtum *vt* to stitch together, sew up

con-surgō -surgĕre -surrexī -surrectum *vi* to stand up; to rise in a body; (with **ad** or **in** + *acc*) to aspire to

consurrectī·ō -ōnis *f* rising up, standing up in a body

Cons·us -ī *m* ancient Italian deity of agriculture and fertility

consusurr·ō -āre *vi* to whisper together

contābĕfac·iō -ĕre *vt* to wear out completely, consume, waste

contāb·escō -escĕre -ŭī *vi* to waste away

contabulātī·ō -ōnis *f* flooring; story

contabŭl·ō -āre *vt* to cover with boards; to build with (*several*) stories

contact·us -ūs *m* touch, contact; contagion; (fig) contagion, infection

contāg·ēs -is *f* touch, contact

contāgi·ō -ōnis *f* touching; touch; contact; contagion, infection; moral contagion, bad example

contāg·ium -iī or **-ī** *n* touch, contact; contagion; moral contamination

contāmināt·us -a -um *adj* polluted, contaminated, impure, vile, degraded; *m pl* perverted youths

contāmin·ō -āre *vt* to bring into contact, mingle, blend; to corrupt, defile; (fig) to corrupt, stain, taint, spoil

contechn·or -ārī -ātus sum *vi* to devise plots, think up tricks

con-tĕgō -tegĕre -texī -tectum *vt* to cover up; to hide; to protect

contemĕr·ō -āre *vt* to defile

con-temnō -temnĕre -tempsī -temptum *vt* to think little of, depreciate, slight, belittle, disregard; to despise, defy

contemplātī·ō -ōnis *f* viewing, surveying, contemplation

contemplāt·or -ōris *m* contemplator, observer

contemplāt·us -ūs *m* contemplation

contempl·ō -āre or **contempl·or -ārī -ātus sum** *vt* to observe, survey, gaze upon, contemplate

contemptim *adv* contemptuously

contemptī·ō -ōnis *f* belittling, despising; **in contemptionem venire** (with *dat*) to become an object of contempt to

contempt·or -ōris *m* or **contemptr·ix -īcis** *f* scorner, despiser

contempt·us -a -um *pp* of **contemno**; *adj* contemptible, despicable

contempt·us -ūs *m* belittling, despising, scorn; **contemptui esse** to be an object of contempt

con-tendō -tendĕre -tendī -tentum *vt* to stretch, draw tight; to tune (*instrument*); to aim, shoot, hurl; (fig) to strain, stretch, exert; to hold, assert, maintain; to compare, contrast; to direct (*course*); *vi* to exert oneself; to compete, contend, fight; to travel, march; (with *inf*) to be in a hurry to; (with **in** + *acc*) to rush to, head for; (with **ad** + *acc*) to strive for, aspire to

contentē *adv* with great effort, earnestly; closely, scantily, sparingly

contentī·ō -ōnis *f* competition, struggle, dispute; straining, exertion, effort; contrast, comparison, antithesis

content·us -a -um *pp* of **contendo**; *adj* tense, tight, taut, strained; eager, intense

content·us -a -um *pp* of **contineo**; *adj* content, satisfied

contermin·us -a -um *adj* (with *dat*) bordering upon

con·těrō -terěre -trīvī -trītum *vt* to grind to powder, pulverize, crumble; (fig) to wear away, wear out, use up; to consume, waste *(time)*

conterr·ěō -ěre -ůī -ĭtum *vt* to frighten, scare the life out of

contest·or -ārī -ātus sum *vt* to call to witness; (fig) to prove, attest; **lītem contestari** to open a lawsuit by calling witnesses

contex·ō -ěre -ůī -tum *vt* to weave together; to brace together; to connect; to devise, build; to compose *(writings)*; to dream up *(a charge)*

contextē *adv* in a coherent manner

context·us -a -um *pp* of **contexo**; *adj* connected

context·us -ūs *m* connection, coherence

contic·escō or **contic·iscō -escěre -ůī** *vi* to become quite still, fall completely silent, hush; to keep silence; (fig) to cease, abate

conticinnō *adv* in the evening

contignāti·ō -ōnis *f* floor, story

contign·ō -āre *vt* to lay a floor on

contigů·us -a -um *adj* touching, adjoining; within reach; (with *dat*) bordering on, near

contin·ens -entis *adj* contiguous, adjacent; unbroken, uninterrupted; self-controlled, continent; (with *dat*) bordering on, contiguous with, adjacent to

contin·ens -entis *f* continent, mainland

contin·ens -entis *n* chief point, main point *(of a speech)*

continenter *adv* in unbroken succession; without interruption; (sitting) close together; moderately, temperately

continenti·a -ae *f* self-control; continence

con·tiněō -tiněre -tinůī -tentum *vt* to hold or keep together; to keep within bounds, confine; to contain, comprise, include; to control, repress

con·tingō -tingěre -tǐgī -tactum *vt* to come into contact with; (fig) to touch, affect; to touch, border on; to reach, reach to; to contaminate; *vi* to happen, turn out, come to pass; (with *dat*) a to touch, border on; b to happen, to befall

continuāti·ō -ōnis *f* unbroken series, succession; (rhet) period

continů·ō -āre *vt* to make continuous, join together, connect; to extend; to continue, carry on, draw out, prolong; to pass, occupy *(time)*; **continuari** (with *dat*) a to be contiguous with, adjacent to; b to follow closely upon

continůō *adv* immediately, without delay; as a necessary consequence, necessarily

continů·us -a -um *adj* continuous, unbroken; successive; **dies continuos quinque** for five successive days

conti·ō -ōnis *f* meeting, rally; public meeting *(of the people or of soldiers)*; speech, pep talk, harangue

contiōnābund·us -a -um *adj* haranguing

contiōnāl·is -e *adj* typical of a public assembly; demagogic

contiōnāri·us -a -um *adj* mob-like

contiōnāt·or -ōris *m* demagogue, public agitator, rabble-rouser

contiōn·or -ārī -ātus sum *vi* to hold forth at a rally, to harangue; to come to a rally; to make a statement at a rally

contiuncůl·a -ae *f* short harangue, trifling speech

contoll·ō -ěre *vt* to bring together

contōn·at -āre *v impers* it is thundering hard

contor·quěō -quěre -sī -tum *vt* to whirl, twist; to throw hard; to twist *(words)* around

contortē *adv* intricately

contortiōn·es -um *f pl* intricacies *(of language)*

contort·or -ōris *m* perverter; **contortor legum** pettifogger

contortůl·us -a -um *adj* rather complicated

contortuplicāt·us -a -um *adj* all twisted up

contort·us -a -um *pp* of **contorqueo**; *adj* involved, intricate; vehement *(speech)*

contrā *adv* in opposition, opposite, in front, face to face; in turn, in return, on the other hand, on the other side; reversely, in the opposite way, the other way; on the contrary, conversely; **contra atque** or **ac** contrary to, otherwise than; **contra dicere** to reply, say in reply; to raise objections; **contra dicitur** the objection is raised; **contra ferire** to make a counterattack; **contra qua fas est** contrary to divine law; **contra quam senatus consulisset** contrary to what the senate would have decided, contrary to the senate resolution; **quin contra** nay on the contrary, in fact it's just the opposite

contrā *prep* (with *acc*) opposite, opposite to, facing, towards, against; in answer to, in reply to; (in hostile sense) against, with, in opposition to, as the opponent of; against, injurious to, unfavorable to; contrary to, the reverse of; in violation of; against, in defiance of; **contra ea putare** to think otherwise; **quod contra** whereas, while; **valere contra** to counterbalance

contracti·ō -ōnis *f* drawing together, contraction; shortening *(of syllable)*; despondency

contractiuncůl·a -ae *f* slight mental depression

contract·us -a -um *pp* of **contraho**; *adj* contracted; narrow, limited (*place*); brief; pinching (*poverty*); in seclusion; **res contracta** contract

contract·us -ūs *m* shrinking

contrā·dīcō -dīcĕre -dixī -dictum *vi* (with *dat*) to contradict, speak against

contrādictī·ō -ōnis *f* objection, refutation

con·trăhō -trahĕre -traxī -tractum *vt* to draw together, collect, assemble; to contract, shorten, narrow, abridge, lessen, diminish; to wrinkle; (*fig*) to bring about, accomplish, cause, produce, incur; to conclude (*bargain*); to transact (*business*); to settle (*an account*); to complete (*business arrangements*)

contrāriē *adv* in opposite ways, in a different way

contrāri·us -a -um *adj* opposite; contrary, conflicting, hostile, antagonistic; from the opposite direction; (with *dat*) opposed to, contrary to; *n* the opposite, the contrary, the reverse; antithesis; **ex contrariō** on the contrary, on the other hand; **in contrāria** in opposite directions; **in contrāria versus** changed into its opposite

contrectābil·iter *adv* appreciably, tangibly

contrectātī·ō -ōnis *f* handling, touching

contrect·ō -āre *vt* to touch, handle; (*fig*) to defile; (*fig*) to dwell upon, consider

contrem·iscō -iscĕre -uī *vt* to shudder at; *vi* to tremble all over; to waver

contrĕm·ō -ĕre -uī *vi* to tremble all over; to quake

contrib·uō -uĕre -uī -ūtum *vt* to bring together, enroll together, associate, unite, incorporate; to contribute, add

contrist·ō -āre *vt* to sadden, cover with gloom; (*fig*) to darken, cloud

contrīt·us -a -um *pp* of contero; *adj* worn out, common, trite

contrōversi·a -ae *f* controversy, quarrel, dispute, debate; civil lawsuit, litigation; subject of litigation; contradiction; question; **sine contrōversiā** indisputably

contrōversiōs·us -a -um *adj* much disputed, controversial

contrōvers·us -a -um *adj* disputed, controversial, questionable, undecided

contrucīd·ō -āre *vt* to cut down, cut to pieces, massacre; (*fig*) to wreck, make a mess of

con·trūdō -trūdĕre -trūsī -trūsum *vt* to crowd together

contrunc·ō -āre *vt* to hack to pieces

contubernāl·is -is *m* army comrade, army buddy; junior staff officer; (*coll*) husband (*of slave*); personal attendant; comrade, companion, associate; colleague; *f* (*coll*) wife (*of slave*)

contubern·ium -iī or **-ī** *n* military companionship; common war tent; concubinage; marriage (*of slaves*); hovel (*of slaves*)

con·tuĕor -tuērī -tuītus sum *vt* to look at attentively, regard, survey

contuīt·us or **contūt·us -ūs** *m* sight, observation

contumāci·a -ae *f* stubbornness, defiance, willfulness; constancy, firmness

contumāciter *adv* stubbornly, defiantly

contŭm·ax -ācis *adj* stubborn, defiant

contumēli·a -ae *f* mistreatment, rough treatment; outrage, insult, abuse, affront

contumēliōsē *adv* abusively

contumēliōs·us -a -um *adj* bringing dishonor; insulting, abusive; reproachful, insolent

contumŭl·ō -āre *vt* to bury

con·tundō -tundĕre -tŭdī -tūsum *vt* to crush, grind, pound, bruise; (*fig*) to crush, destroy, break, subdue; to baffle

conturbātī·ō -ōnis *f* confusion, consternation

conturbāt·us -a -um *adj* confused, distracted, disordered, in confusion

conturb·ō -āre *vt* to confuse, throw into confusion; to disquiet, disturb; to upset (*plans*); **rationes** or **rationem conturbare** to be bankrupt; *vi* to be bankrupt

cont·us -ī *m* pole

cōnūbiāl·is -e *adj* marriage, connubial

cōnūb·ium -iī or **-ī** *n* intermarriage; right to intermarry according to Roman law; marriage; sexual intercourse; **jus conubi** right to intermarry

cōn·us -ī *m* cone; apex (*of helmet*)

convăd·or -ārī -ātus sum *vt* to subpoena

conval·escō -escĕre -uī *vi* to grow strong; to regain strength, convalesce; (*fig*) to improve

convall·is -is *f* valley

convās·ō -āre *vt* to pack up, pack

convect·ō -āre *vt* to heap together; to bring home

convect·or -ōris *m* fellow passenger

con·vĕhō -vehĕre -vexī -vectum *vt* to collect, bring in (*esp. the harvest*)

con·vellō -vellĕre -vellī -vulsum *vt* to tear away, pull off, pluck, wrest; to tear to pieces, dismember; to break, shatter; (*fig*) to turn upside down, subvert, overthrow; **convellere signa** to break camp

convĕn·ae -ārum *m pl* or *f pl* strangers; refugees, vagabonds

convĕni·ens -entis *adj* agreeing, harmonious, consistent; appropriate; (with *dat* or with **cum + abl**) consistent with, appropriate to; (with **ad + acc**) appropriate for, suitable for

convenienter *adv* consistently; suitably; (with **cum** + *abl* or with **ad** + *acc*) in conformity with

convenienti·a -ae *f* agreement, accord, harmony; conformity

con·veniō -venīre -vēnī -ventum *vt* to meet, go to meet; to interview; *vi* to come together, meet, gather, come in a body; to coincide; to unite, combine; to come to an agreement, agree; (with **ad** + *acc*) to fit (*as a shoe fits the foot*); (with *dat*, with **ad** or **in** + *acc*, or with **cum** + *abl*) to be applicable to, appropriate to, fit; **convenit** it is fitting, proper; **convenit inter sē** (with *dat*) there is harmony among

conventīcī·us -a -um *adj* coming together, gathering together; *n* fee for attending the assembly

conventīcŭl·um -ī *n* small gathering; meeting place

conventī·ō -ōnis *f* agreement, contract

convent·us -a -um *pp* of **conveniō**; *n* agreement, contract

convent·us -ūs *m* gathering, assembly; congress; district court; company, corporation; agreement; **ex conventu** by agreement; of one accord; **conventum agere** to hold court

con·verrō or **con·vorrō -verrĕre -verrī -versum** *vt* to sweep together, sweep up; to brush thoroughly; (fig) to scoop up (*e.g.*, *an inheritance*)

conversātī·ō -ōnis *f* social intercourse; conversation

conversi·ō -ōnis *f* revolving, revolution; (fig) alteration, change; (rhet) repetition of word at end of clause; (rhet) balancing of phrases

convers·ō -āre *vt* to turn around; **sē conversāre** to revolve

con·vertō or **con·vortō -vertĕre -vertī -versum** *vt* to cause to turn, turn back, reverse; (fig) to turn, direct (*laughter*, *attention*); to convert, transform; to translate; to attract (*attention*); (mil) **sēsē convertere** to retreat; *vi* to return; to change, be changed, turn; (with **in** + *acc*) to be changed into, turn into

convestī·ō -īre *vt* to clothe, cover

convex·us -a -um *pp* of **convehō**; *adj* rounded off; arched, convex; concave; sloping down; *n* vault, arch

conviciāt·or -ōris *m* reviler

convīcī·or -ārī -ātus sum *vt* to revile

convīc·ium -iī or **-ī** *n* noise, chatter; wrangling; jeers, invective, abuse; cry of protest; reprimand; **conviciīs consectari aliquem** to keep after someone with abuses

convictī·ō -ōnis *f* companionship; companions

convict·or -ōris *m* bosom friend

convict·us -ūs *m* association, so-

cializing; close friends; feast, banquet

con·vincō -vincĕre -vīcī -victum *vt* to refute, prove wrong; to convict, prove guilty; to prove true, demonstrate clearly

convīs·ō -ĕre *vt* to examine, search; to shine on

convīv·a -ae *m* guest, table companion

convīvāl·is -e *adj* convivial, festive

convīvāt·or -ōris *m* master of ceremonies; host

convīv·ium -iī or **-ī** *n* banquet, dinner; dinner party; *n pl* dinner guests; **convivium agitare** to throw a party

con·vīvō -vīvĕre -vixī *vi* to live together; (with **cum** + *abl*) to feast with

convīv·or -ārī -ātus sum *vi* to feast together, have a party

convocātī·ō -ōnis *f* calling together

convŏc·ō -āre *vt* to call together, assemble

convŏl·ō -āre *vi* to flock together; (fig) to flock together, gather hastily

con·volvō -volvĕre -volvī -volūtum *vt* to roll together; to roll up (*a scroll*); to fasten together, interweave; to wrap; **sē convolvere** to roll along; to go in a circle

convŏm·ō -ĕre *vt* to vomit on, vomit all over

convortō see **converto**

convulnĕr·ō -āre *vt* to wound seriously

convulsus *pp* of **convello**

coöper·iō -īre -ŭī -tum *vt* to cover; to overwhelm

coöptātī·ō -ōnis *f* cooption, election of a colleague by vote of incumbent members

coöpt·ō -āre *vt* to coopt

coör·ior -īrī -tus sum *vi* to rise, rise suddenly; (fig) (of war) to break out; (of wind) to arise

coört·us -ūs *m* rising, originating

cōp·a -ae *f* barmaid

cophĭn·us -ī *m* basket

cōpi·a -ae *f* abundance, supply, store, plenty; multitude, large number; wealth, prosperity; opportunity, means; command of language, fluency, richness of expression; (with *genit*) power over; (with *dat*) access to; **pro copia** according to opportunity, according to ability; *f pl* troops, armed forces; provisions, supplies

cōpiŏl·ae -ārum *f pl* small contingent of troops

cōpiōsē *adv* abundantly, plentifully; (rhet) fully, at length

cōpiōs·us -a -um *adj* plentiful; well supplied, rich, wealthy; eloquent, fluent (*speech*); (with *abl*) abounding in, rich in

cōp·is -e *adj* rich, well supplied

cōpŭl·a -ae *f* cord, string, rope, leash; (fig) tie, bond cōpulātĭ·ō -ōnis f coupling, joining, union; combining (of words)

cōpŭl·ō -āre vt to couple, join; (fig) to unite; (with dat or with cum + abl) to couple with, join to, combine with

cōpŭl·or -ārī -ātus sum vt to join, clasp; dexteras copulari to shake hands

coqu·a -ae f cook (female)

coquĭn·ō -āre vi to be a cook

co·quō -quĕre -xī -ctum vt to cook; to fry, roast, bake, boil; to prepare (a meal); to burn, parch; to ripen, mature; to digest; to disturb, worry, disquiet; to plan, concoct, dream up

coqu·us or coc·us -ī m cook

cor cordis n heart; mind, judgment; (as seat of feelings) heart, soul; dear friend; n pl persons, souls; cordi esse (with dat) to please, be dear to, to be agreeable to

cōram adv in person, personally; publically, openly; in someone's presence, face to face; prep (coming before or after abl) before, in the presence of, face to face with

corb·is -is m or f wicker basket

corbīt·a -ae f slow-sailing merchant ship

corbŭl·a -ae f small basket

curcŭl·um -ī n little heart; sweetheart; poor fellow

Corcȳr·a -ae f island off the coast of Epirus, identified with Scheria, the island of Alcinous

cordātē adv wisely, prudently

cordŏl·ium -iī or -ī n heartache

Corfĭn·ium -iī or -ī n town in Central Italy which served as headquarters of Italian allies during the Social War against Rome in 90–89 B.C.

coriandr·um -ī n coriander

Corinthĭ·us -a -um adj Corinthian; aes Corinthium alloy of gold, silver, and copper, used in making expensive jewelry, etc.; m pl Corinthians; n pl costly Corinthian products

Corinth·us -ī f Corinth

Coriŏl·ī -ōrum m pl town in Latium, capital of the Volsci, from the capture of which, in 493 B.C., C. Marcius received the surname of Coriolanus

cor·ium -iī or -ī n or cor·ius -iī or -ī m skin, hide; bark; leather

Cornēlĭ·us -a -um adj Cornelian; gens Cornelia Cornelian tribe (famous Roman tribe, especially for the Scipios, the Gracchi, and Sulla); f Cornelia (daughter of Scipio Africanus Major and mother of the Gracchi)

cornĕŏl·us -a -um adj horny

cornĕ·us -a -um adj horny; of the cornel tree; of cornel wood

cornic·en -ĭnis m horn blower

cornīc·or -ārī -ātus sum vi to caw

cornĭcŭl·a -ae f poor little crow

corniculār·ĭus -iī or -ī m soldier decorated with a horn-shaped medal for bravery; adjutant to a centurion

cornĭcŭl·um -ī n little horn; hornshaped decoration, awarded for bravery

cornĭg·er -ĕra -ĕrum adj horn-bearing, horned

cornĭp·ēs -ĕdis adj hoofed

corn·ix -īcis f crow (whose appearance on one's left side was considered a favorable omen and whose cries were regarded as a sign of rain)

corn·ū -ūs or corn·um -ī n horn; horn, trumpet; lantern; funnel; oil cruet; hoof; bill (of bird); horn (of moon); branch (of river); arm (of bay); tongue (of land); crest socket (of helmet); roller end (of book); (mil) wing, flank; cornua addere (with dat) to give courage to, add strength to; cornua sumere to gain strength

corn·um -ī n cornel cherry

corn·us -ī f cornel cherry tree; dogwood tree; spear, shaft, javelin

coroll·a -ae f small garland

corollar·ĭum -iī or -ī n garland; gilt wreath given as reward to actors; gift, gratuity

corōn·a -ae f crown, garland; circle of bystanders; (mil) cordon of besiegers; ring of defense; corona civica decoration for saving a life, corona muralis decoration for being the first to scale an enemy wall; corona navalis decoration for naval victory; sub corona vendere to sell (captives) as slaves; sub corona venire (of captives) to be sold at public auction

Corōn·a -ae f Ariadne's crown, Corona Borealis (constellation)

corōnārĭ·us -a -um adj for a crown; aurum coronarium gold collected in the provinces for a victorious general

Corōnē·ā -ae f town in Boeotia

Corōn·eus -ĕī m king of Phocis whose daughter was changed into a crow

Corōnĭd·ēs -ae m Aesculapius, the son of Coronia

Corōn·is -ĭdis f daughter of Phlegyas and mother of Aesculapius

corōn·ō -āre vt to crown, wreathe; to enclose, encircle, shut in

corporĕ·us -a -um adj physical, of the body; corporeal, substantial; of flesh

corpulent·us -a -um adj corpulent

corp·us -ŏris n body; matter, substance; flesh; trunk; corpse; person, individual; body, frame, structure; framework; community; corporation; particle, grain

corpuscŭl·um -ī n puny body; particle, atom; (as term of endearment) little fellow

cor·rādō -rādĕre -rāsī -rāsum vt to scrape together, rake up; (fig) to scrape (e.g., money) together

correctĭ·ō -ōnis f correction, improvement, amendment; rhetorical restatement

correct·or -ōris m reformer; censor, critic

correctus pp of **corrigo**

cor·rēpō -rēpĕre -repsī vi to creep, slink; **in dūmeta correpere** (fig) to beat around the bush, indulge in jargon

correptĭus adv more briefly; **correptius exire** to end in a short vowel, have a short vowel

correptus pp of **corripio**

corrīd·ĕō -ēre vi to laugh out loud

corrĭgĭ·a -ae f shoelace

cor·rĭgō -rĭgĕre -rexī -rectum vt to make straight, straighten out; to smooth out; to correct, improve, reform; to make up for (delay); to make the best of

cor·rĭpĭō -rĭpĕre -rĭpŭī -reptum vt to seize, snatch up, carry off; to speed up, rush; to steal, carry off; to attack; to shorten, contract; to reprove, accuse, reproach; to cut (a period of time) short

corrōbŏr·ō -āre vt to strengthen, invigorate, corroborate; (fig) to fortify, encourage

cor·rōdo -rōdĕre -rōsī -rōsum vt to gnaw, chew up

corrŏg·ō -āre vt to go asking for, collect, drum up, solicit

corrōsus pp of **corrodo**

corrūg·ō -āre vt to wrinkle, corrugate; **nares corrugare** (with dat) to cause (someone) disgust

cor·rumpō -rumpĕre -rūpī -ruptum vt to burst; to break to pieces, smash; to destroy completely, ruin, waste; to mar, corrupt, adulterate; to falsify, tamper with (documents); to bribe; to seduce, corrupt

corrŭ·ō -ĕre -ī vt to shatter, wreck, ruin; vi to fall down, tumble, sink; (fig) to fall, fail, sink, go down

corruptē adv corruptly, perversely; in a lax manner

corruptēl·a -ae f corruption, seduction; bribery; seducer, misleader

corruptĭ·ō -ōnis f corrupting, ruining, breaking up; corrupt condition

corrupt·or -ōris m or **corruptr·ix -īcis** f corrupter, seducer, briber

corrupt·us -a -um pp of **corrumpo**; adj corrupt, spoiled, bad, ruined

cort·ex -ĭcis m or f bark, shell, hull, rind; cork; **nare sine cortice** to swim without a cork life preserver; to be on one's own

cortīn·a -ae f kettle, caldron; tripod; (fig) vault of heaven

corŭlus see **corylus**

corusc·ō -āre vt to shake, brandish; vi to flit, flutter, to oscillate; to tremble; to flash, gleam

corusc·us -a -um adj oscillating, vibrating, tremulous; flashing, gleaming, glittering

corv·us -ī m raven; (mil) grapnel

Corybant·ēs -ĭum m pl Corybantes (priests of Cybele)

Corybantĭ·us -a -um adj of the Corybantes

cōrў·us -ī m punching bag

corylēt·um -ī n cluster of hazel trees

corўl·us or **corŭl·us -ī** f hazel tree

corymbĭf·er -ĕra -ĕrum adj wearing or bearing clusters of ivy berries; m Bacchus

corymb·us -ī m cluster (esp. of ivy berries)

coryphae·us -ī m leader, head

cōryt·os or **cōryt·us -ī** m quiver (for arrows)

cōs cōtis f flint; grindstone, whetstone

Cō·s or **Co·ūs -ī** f small island in the Aegean Sea, famous for its wine and fine linen

cosmēt·a -ae m slave in charge of the wardrobe

cost·a -ae f rib; (fig) side, wall

cost·um -ī n perfume

cothurnāt·us -a -um adj wearing the tragic buskin; suitable to tragedy; tragic, of tragedy

cothurn·us -ī m high boot; hunting boot; buskin (worn by tragic actors); subject of tragedy; tragedy; lofty style of Greek tragedy

cōtĭd- = **cottid-**

cottăb·us -ī m game which consisted in flicking drops of wine on a bronze vessel

cottăn·a or **cottŏn·a -ōrum** n pl Syrian figs

cottīdĭānō adv daily

cottīdĭān·us or **cotīdĭān·us -a -um** adj daily; everyday, ordinary

cottīdĭē or **cōtīdĭē** adv daily, every day

coturn·ix -īcis f quail

Cotyttĭ·a -ōrum n pl festival of Cotytto

Cotytt·o -ūs f Thracian goddess of lewdness

Coūs see **Cos**

Cō·us -a -um adj Coan; n Coan wine; n pl Coan garments

covinnār·ĭus -ĭī or **-ī** m soldier who fought from a chariot

covinn·us -ī m war chariot of the Britons and the Belgae; coach

cox·a -ae f hipbone

coxend·ix -īcis f hip

crābr·ō -ōnis m hornet; **irritare crabrones** (fig) to stir up a hornet's nest

cramb·ē -ēs f cabbage; **crambe repetita** warmed-over cabbage; same old story

Crant·or -ōris m Greek Academic philosopher of Soli in Cilicia (fl 300 B.C.)

crāpŭl·a -ae f drunkenness; hangover

crāpulārĭ·us -a -um adj for (i.e., to prevent) a hangover

crās adv tomorrow; (fig) in the future

crassē *adv* thickly; rudely; confusedly; dimly

crassitūd·ō -inis *f* thickness, density; dregs

crass·us -a -um *adj* thick, dense; dense, dull, stupid

Crass·us -ī *m* L. Licinius Crassus (*famous orator, d* 90 B.C.); M. Licinius Crassus (*triumvir, together with Caesar and Pompey,* 112?-53 B.C.)

crastin·us -a -um *adj* tomorrow's; (old *abl* form) **die crastini** tomorrow; *n* tomorrow; **in crastinum differre** to put off till tomorrow

crāt·ēr -ēris *m* or **crātēr·a -ae** *f* mixing bowl; bowl; crater

Crāt·ēr -ēris *m* Bowl (*constellation*)

crāt·is -is *f* wickerwork; harrow; ribs of shield; (mil) faggots (*for filling trenches*); joint, rib (*of body*); honeycomb

creāti·ō -ōnis *f* election

creāt·or -ōris *m* creator; procreator, father; founder

creātr·ix -īcis *f* creatress; mother

crēb·er -ra -rum *adj* luxuriant, prolific (*growth*); numerous, crowded; repeated; frequent

crēbr·escō or **crēb·escō -escēre -uī** *vi* to increase, become frequent; to gain strength

crēbrit·ās -ātis *f* frequency

crēbrō *adv* repeatedly, frequently, again and again

crēdibil·is -e *adj* credible, trustworthy

crēdibiliter *adv* credibly

crēdit·or -ōris *m* creditor, lender

crēd·ō -ēre -idī -itum *vt* to lend, loan; to entrust, consign; to believe; to think, believe, suppose, imagine; *vi* (with *dat*) to believe, put faith in, have trust or confidence in; **credās** one would image; **satis creditum est** it is believed on good evidence

crēdulit·ās -ātis *f* credulity, trustfulness

crēdul·us -a -um *adj* credulous, trustful, gullible; (with *dat* or in with *acc*) trusting in

crem·ō -āre *vt* to burn to ashes; to cremate

Cremōn·a -ae *f* town in N. Italy, which became a Roman colony in 209 B.C.

crem·or -ōris *m* juice obtained from animal or vegetable substances; broth

cre·ō -āre *vt* to create, produce; to elect to office; to cause, occasion; to beget, bear

Cre·ō or **Cre·ōn -ontis** *m* brother of Jocaste and brother-in-law of Oedipus; king of Corinth who gave his daughter in marriage to Jason

crep·er -era -erum *adj* dark; (fig) uncertain, doubtful

crepid·a -ae *f* slipper, sandal

crepidāt·us -a -um *adj* sandal-wearing

crepid·ō -inis *f* base, pedestal; quay, pier; dam, dike, causeway

crepidul·a -ae *f* small sandal

crepit·ō -āre *vi* to make noise, rattle, crackle, creak, chatter, rumble, rustle

crepit·us -ūs *m* noise, rattle, creak, chatter, rumble, rustle

crep·ō -āre -uī -itum *vt* to make rattle; to talk noisily about, chatter about; *vi* to make noise, rattle, crackle, creak, chatter, rumble, rustle

crepundi·a -ōrum *n pl* rattle; toys

crepuscul·um -ī *n* dusk, twilight; dimness, obscurity; *n pl* darkness

crescō crescēre crēvī crētum *vi* to come into being, arise; to grow, grow up; to increase, swell; to prosper, thrive; to become great, attain honor

crēt·a -ae *f* chalk; white clay; cosmetic

Crēt·a -ae *f* Crete

crētāt·us -a -um *adj* chalked; dressed in white (*as candidate for office*)

crēte·us -a -um *adj* of chalk, of clay

crēti·ō -ōnis *f* (law) formal acceptance of an inheritance

crētōs·us -a -um *adj* abounding in chalk or clay

crētul·a -ae *f* white clay (*used for seals*)

crētus *pp* of **cerno**; *pp* of **cresco**

Creūs·a -ae *f* daughter of Priam and wife of Aeneas; daughter of Creon, king of Corinth and wife of Jason

crībr·um -ī *n* sieve; **imbrem in crībrum gerere** to carry coals to Newcastle

crīm·en -inis *n* charge, accusation; reproach; guilt, crime; **esse in crimine** to be accused

crīmināti·ō -ōnis *f* accusation; slander, false charge

crīmināt·or -ōris *m* accuser

crīmin·ō -āre or **crīmin·or -ārī -ātus sum** *vt* to accuse; to slander; to complain of, denounce

crīminōsē *adv* by way of accusation, accusingly, reproachfully

crīminōs·us -a -um *adj* accusing, reproachful, slanderous

crīnāl·is -e *adj* for the hair; *n* hairpin

crīn·is -is *m* hair; (fig) tail of a comet

crīnīt·us -a -um *adj* long-haired; **stella crinita** comet

cris·ō -āre *vi* (of women) to wiggle the buttocks

crisp·āns -antis *adj* curled, wrinkled

crisp·ō -āre *vt* to curl, wave (*hair*); to swing, wave, brandish (*a weapon*)

crisp·us -a -um *adj* curled, waved (*hair*); curly-headed; curled, wrinkled; tremulous, quivering

crist·a -ae *f* cock's comb; crest, plume

cristāt·us -a -um *adj* crested, plumed

critic·us -ī *m* critic

croce·us -a -um *adj* of saffron; saffron-colored, yellow, golden

crocīn·um -ī *n* saffron

crōc·iō -īre *vi* to croak

crocodīl·us -ī *m* crocodile

crocōtāri·us -a -um *adj* of saffron-colored clothes

crocōtŭl·a -ae *f* saffron-colored dress

croc·us -ī *m* or croc·um -ī *n* crocus; saffron; saffron color

Croes·us -ī *m* king of Lydia, famous for his wealth (590?-546 B.C.)

crotalistri·a -ae *f* castanet dancer

crotăl·um -ī *n* castanet

cruciābilitāt·ēs -um *f pl* torments

cruciābiliter *adv* with torture

cruciāment·um -ī *n* torture

cruciāt·us -ūs *m* torture; mental torment; instrument of torture; (humorously) calamity

cruci·ō -āre *vt* to put to wrack, torture, torment; (fig) to grieve, torment

crūdēl·is -e *adj* cruel, hardhearted; (with in + *acc*) cruel toward

crūdēlit·ās -ātis *f* cruelty

crūdēliter *adv* cruelly

crūd·escō -escĕre -ŭī *vi* to grow violent, grow worse

crūdit·ās -ātis *f* indigestion

crūd·us -a -um *adj* bloody, bleeding; uncooked, raw; unripe, green; undressed (*hide*); undigested; suffering from indigestion; hoarse; fresh, vigorous (*old age*); cruel, merciless

cruent·ō -āre *vt* to bloody, stain with blood; (fig) to wound

cruent·us -a -um *adj* gory, bloodstained; bloodthirsty, cruel; bloodred

crumēn·a or crumīn·a -ae *f* purse, pouch; (fig) money

crumill·a -ae *f* purse

cru·or -ōris *m* gore, blood; *m pl* bloodshed, murder

crūppellāri·ī -ōrum *m pl* mail-clad combatants

crūrifrag·ius -iī or -ī *m* slave with broken shins

crūs crūris *n* leg, shin

crust·a -ae *f* crust, shell, rind, bark; inlaid work, mosaic; stucco

crustŭl·um -ī *n* cooky

crust·um -ī *n* pastry

crux crucis *f* cross, gallows; trouble, misery; gallows bird; tormentor; i in malam crucem (coll) go hang yourself

crypt·a -ae *f* underground passage, covered gallery

cryptoportic·us -ūs *f* covered walk

crystallin·us -a -um *adj* made of crystal; *n pl* crystal vases

crystall·us -ī *f* or crystall·um -ī *n* crystal

cubiculār·is -e *adj* bedroom

cubiculāri·us -a -um *adj* bedroom; *m* chamberlain

cubicŭl·um -ī *n* bedroom; emperor's box in the theater

cubīl·e -is *n* bed, couch; marriage bed; lair, nest, hole; kennel; avaritiae cubilia (fig) den of greediness

cubit·al -ālis *n* elbow cushion

cubitāl·is -e *adj* of the elbow; one cubit long

cubīt·ō -āre *vi* to be in the habit of lying down; (with cum + *abl*) to go to bed with, have intercourse with

cubĭt·um -ī *n* elbow; cubit

cubĭt·us -ūs *m* lying down; intercourse

cub·ō -āre -ŭī or -āvī -ĭtum *vi* to lie, lie down; to recline at table; to lie in bed; to lie sick; (of roof) to slope; (of towns, etc.) to lie on a slope

cucull·us -ī *m* cowl, hood

cucŭl·us -ī *m* cuckoo; lazy farmer

cucŭm·is -ĕris *m* cucumber

cucurbĭt·a -ae *f* gourd; (med) cupping glass

cūd·ō -ĕre *vt* to strike, beat, pound; thresh; to forge; to coin, stamp

cuicuimŏdī or quoiquoimŏdī *adj* any kind of

cuj·ās -ātis *pron* from what country

culcĭt·a -ae *f* mattress, feather tick; cushion, pillow

culcitell·a -ae *f* little cushion

cūlĕus see culleus

cul·ex -ĭcis *m* or *f* gnat

culīn·a -ae *f* kitchen; cuisine

cullĕ·us or cūlĕ·us -ī *m* leather bag (*for holding liquids*); scrotum

culm·en -ĭnis *n* stalk; top, summit; roof; (fig) height, pinnacle, zenith

culm·us -ī *m* stalk, stem; straw, thatch

culp·a -ae *f* fault, blame; immorality; in culpa esse or in culpa versari to be at fault

culpĭt·ō -āre *vt* to blame, find fault with

culp·ō -āre *vt* to blame, reproach, censure, find fault with, complain of

cult·a -ōrum *n pl* plantation; grain fields

cultē *adv* elegantly, sophisticatedly, with refinement

cultell·us -ī *m* small knife

cult·er -rī *m* knife; razor; plowshare

cultĭ·ō -ōnis *f* cultivation; tilling of the ground, agriculture

cult·or -ōris *m* tiller, planter, cultivator, farmer; inhabitant; supporter; worshiper

cultr·ix -īcis *f* cultivator (*female*); inhabitant (*female*); (fig) nurse

cultūr·a -ae *f* tilling, cultivating; agriculture; care, cultivation (*of the mind*); (with *genit*) playing up to (*e.g., influential friends*)

cult·us -a -um *pp* of colo; *adj* tilled, cultivated; neat, well dressed, prim; cultivated, refined, civilized (*person*); cultured, refined (*mind*)

cult·us -ūs *m* tilling, cultivation (*of land*); care, tending, keeping (*of flocks, etc.*); care (*of body*); training, education; culture, refinement, civilization; high style of living; luxury;

style of dress, fancy clothes; fancy outfit; worship, reverence, veneration

culull·us -ī *m* drinking cup

cūl·us -ī *m* buttock

cum *prep* (with *abl*) (accompaniment) with, together with, in company with; (time) at the same time with, at the time of, at, with; (circumstance, manner, etc.) with, under, in, in the midst of, among, in connection with; **cum eo quod** or **cum eo ut** on condition that; **cum pace** peacefully; **cum prima luce** at dawn; **cum primis** especially, particularly; **mecum** at my house

cum, quum, or **quom** *conj* when, at the time when; whenever; when, while, as; since, now that, because; although; **cum maxime** just when; especially when, just while; just then, just now; **cum primum** as soon as; **cum . . . tum** both . . . and, not only . . . but also, while . . . so too; **praesertim cum** or **cum praesertim** especially since, especially as; **quippe cum** since of course; **utpote cum** seeing that

Cūm·ae -ārum *f pl* town on coast of Campania and oldest Greek colony in Italy, famous as the residence of its Sibyl

Cūmān·us -a -um *adj* Cumaean; *n* Cicero's estate near Cumae

cumb·a or **cymb·a -ae** *f* boat, skiff

cumĕr·a -ae *f* bin

cumīn·um -ī *n* (*medicinal plant, said to produce paleness*) cumin

cumque, cunque, or **quomque** *adv* at any time

cumulātē *adv* fully, completely, abundantly, copiously

cumulāt·us -a -um *adj* increased, augmented; filled, full, perfect, complete

cumŭl·ō -āre *vt* to heap up, pile up; to amass, accumulate; to overload; to make complete, make perfect, crown

cumŭl·us -ī *m* heap, pile; increase, addition

cūnābŭl·a -ōrum *n pl* cradle

cūn·ae -ārum *f pl* cradle; nest

cunctābund·us -a -um *adj* hesitant, loitering, delaying

cunct·ans -antis *adj* hesitant, reluctant, dilatory

cunctanter *adv* hesitantly, slowly

cunotāti·ō -ōnis *f* hesitation, reluctance, delay

cunctāt·or -ōris *m* dawdler, slowpoke

cunct·or -ārī -ātus sum *vi* to hesitate, delay, linger, be in doubt; **cunctatus brevi** after a moment's hesitation

cunct·us -a -um *adj* all together, the whole, all, entire

cuneātim *adv* in the form of a wedge

cuneāt·us -a -um *adj* wedge-shaped

cunĕ·ō -āre *vt* to fasten with a wedge; (*fig*) to wedge in, squeeze in

cunĕ·us -ī *m* wedge; wedge-form sections of seats in the theater; (mil) troops formed up in the shape of a wedge

cunīcŭl·us -ī *m* rabbit; burrowing underground; (mil) mine

cunque see **cumque**

cūp·a -ae *f* vat

cuped- = **cupped-**

cupīdē *adv* eagerly

cupīdit·ās -ātis *f* eagerness, enthusiasm, desire; passion, lust; ambition; greed, avarice; partisanship

cupīd·ō -īnis *m* eagerness, desire, longing; passion, lust; greed, avarice

Cupīd·ō -īnis *m* Cupid (*son of Venus*)

Cupīdinĕ·us -a -um *adj* Cupid's

cupīd·us -a -um *adj* eager, enthusiastic, desirous, longing; ambitious; (with *genit*) desirous of, longing for, fond of, attached to

cupi·ens -entis *adj* eager, enthusiastic; (with *genit*) desirous of, longing for, fond of, enthusiastic about

cupienter *adv* eagerly, enthusiastically

cup·iō -ĕre -īvī or **iī -ītum** *vt* to wish, be eager for, long for, desire

cupīt·or -ōris *m* daydreamer

cuppēdi·a -ōrum *n pl* or **cupēdi·a -ae** *f* delicacies; sweet tooth

cuppēdinār·ius or **cupēdinār·ius -iī** or **-ī** *m* confectioner

cupped·ō -īnis *f* desire, longing

cupp·ēs -ēdis *adj* fond of delicacies

cupressēt·um -ī *n* cypress grove

cupressĕ·us -a -um *adj* cypress

cupressif·er -ĕra -ĕrum *adj* cypress-bearing

cupress·us -ī or **-ūs** *f* cypress tree; box of cypress

cūr or **quor** *adv* why

cūr·a -ae *f* care, concern, worry; care, pains, attention; heartache; object of concern; sweetheart; administration, management, charge; trusteeship, guardianship; means of healing, cure, treatment; guardian, keeper; study, reflection; literary effort, literary work; **curae esse** (with *dat*) to be of concern to

cūrābil·is -e *adj* troublesome

cūral·ium -iī or **-ī** *n* coral

cūrāti·ō -ōnis *f* management, administration; office; treatment, cure

cūrātius *adv* more carefully

cūrāt·or -ōris *m* superintendent, manager; (law) guardian, keeper

cūrātūr·a -ae *f* care, attention; dieting

cūrāt·us -a -um *adj* cared-for, attended-to; anxious, earnest

curcŭli·ō -ōnis *m* weevil

curculiuncŭl·us -ī *m* little weevil; (fig) trifle

Cur·ēs -ium *m pl* ancient Sabine town

Cūrēt·ēs -um *m pl* mythical people of Crete who attended Jupiter at his birth

cūrǐ·a -ae f curia, ward *(one of the thirty parts into which Romulus divided the Roman people)*; meeting place of a curia; senate building

cūrǐāl·ǐs -ǐs m member of a curia or ward

cūrǐātim adv by curiae, by wards

cūrǐāt·us -a -um adj composed of curiae or wards; passed by the assembly of curiae; **comitia curiata** assembly of the curiae

cūrǐ·ō -ōnis m ward boss; **curio maximus** chief ward boss

cūrǐ·ō -ōnis adj lean, emaciated

cūrǐōsē adv carefully; curiously; (of style) affectedly

cūrǐōsǐt·ās -ātǐs f curiosity

cūrǐōs·us -a -um adj careful, diligent; curious, prying, inquisitive; careworn

cur·ǐs or **quir·ǐs -ǐtǐs** f spear

cūr·ō -āre vt to take care of, look after, attend to, trouble oneself about; to take charge of, see to; to provide for the payment of, settle up; to attend to *(the body with food, washing, etc.)*; to cure; to worry about; **cura ut** see to it that; (at the end of a letter) **cura ut valeas** take care of yourself

curricǔlō adv at full speed, quickly

curricǔl·um -ī n race; lap *(of race)*; racetrack; racing chariot; (fig) career

currō currěre cucurrī cursum vt to run over, skim over, traverse; vi to run, dash, hurry; to sail; to move quickly, flow along; to fly; (of a speech) to move along; (of night, day) to pass away

curr·us -ūs m chariot, car; war chariot; triumphal car; triumph; racing chariot; plow wheel; ship

cursim adv on the double

cursǐt·ō -āre vi to keep running around, run up and down; to vibrate

curs·ō -āre vi to run around, run up and down

curs·or -ōris m runner, racer; courier; errand boy

cursūr·a -ae f running; haste, speed

curs·us -ūs m running, speeding, speed; trip; course, direction; suitable time or weather for travel; rapid movement, speed, flow; flow, progress; **magno cursu** at top speed; **cursus honorum** political career

curt·ō -āre vt to shorten; to circumcise

curt·us -a -um adj shortened; gelded, castrated; circumcised; broken; defective

cūrǔl·ǐs -e adj official, curule; **aedilis curulis** patrician aedile; **sella curulis** curule chair, official chair *(used by consuls, praetors, and patrician aediles)*

curvām·en -ǐnis n curve, bend

curvātūr·a -ae f curvature; **curvatura rotae** rim of a wheel

curv·ō -āre vt to curve, bend, arch; (fig) to affect, move, stir

ourv·us -a -um adj curved; bent; crooked; concave, arched, hollow; winding *(stream, shore)*; (fig) crooked; n wrong, crookedness

cusp·ǐs -ǐdǐs f point, pointed end; bayonet; spearhead; spear, javelin; trident; scepter; sting *(of scorpion)*

custōdēl·a -ae f watch, guard, care

custōdǐ·a -ae f watch, guard, care; sentry, guard; sentry post; custody, prison; **custodiam agitare** to keep guard, be on guard; **in libera custodia** under surveillance, under house arrest

custōd·ǐō -īre -īvī or **-ǐī -ītum** vt to guard, watch over, protect, defend; to hold in custody; to keep an eye on; to keep carefully, preserve; **memoriā custodire** to keep in mind, remember well

cust·ōs -ōdǐs m guard, guardian, watchman; protector, bodyguard; jailer, warden; (mil) sentinel; spy; m pl garrison; f guardian; protectress; box, container

cutǐcǔl·a -ae f skin, cuticle

cut·ǐs -ǐs f skin; **cutem curare** (fig) to look after one's own skin

Cyān·ē -ēs f nymph who was changed into a fountain

cyathǐss·ō -āre vi to serve wine

cyáth·us -ī m ladle; liquid measure *(one-twelfth of a sextarius, i.e., a half pint)*

cybae·a -ae f merchant ship

Cybǎl·ē or **Cybēl·ē -ēs** f originally a Phrygian goddess of fertility, later worshiped in Rome as Ops or Mater Magna

Cyclǎd·es -um f pl Cyclades *(group of islands in Aegean Sea)*

cycl·as -ǎdǐs f woman's formal gown

cyclǐc·us -a -um adj cyclic; **poeta cyclicus** cyclic poet *(one of a group of poets treating the epic sagas revolving around the Trojan War)*

Cycl·ops -ōpǐs m mythical one-eyed giant of Sicily, esp. Polyphemus

cycnē·us -a -um adj swan's

cycn·us or **cygn·us -ī** m swan; (fig) poet

Cycn·us or **Cygn·us -ī** m king of the Ligurians, son of Sthenelus, changed into a swan, and placed among the stars; son of Neptune, changed into a swan

Cydōnǐ·us -a -um adj Cretan; n quince

cygnus see **cycnus**

cylindr·us -ī m cylinder; roller *(for rolling ground)*

Cyllēn·ē -ēs or **-ae** f mountain in Arcadia where Mercury was born

Cyllēnǐ·us -a -um adj of Mt. Cyllene; m Mercury

cymb·a -ae f boat, skiff

cymbǎl·um -ī n cymbal

cymb·ǐum -ǐī or **-ǐ** n small cup

Cynicē *adv* like the Cynics

Cynic·us -a -um *adj* Cynic, relating to the Cynic philosophy; *m* Cynic philosopher, esp. Diogenes, its founder (412-323 B.C.)

cynocephăl·us -ī *m* dog-headed ape

Cynosŭr·a -ae *f* Cynosure (*the northern constellation Ursa Minor*)

Cynthi·us -a -um *adj* of Mt. Cynthus; Cynthian; *m* Apollo; *f* Diana

Cynth·us -ī *m* mountain of Delos, famous as the birthplace of Apollo and Diana

cypariss·us -ī *f* cypress tree

Cypri·us -a -um *adj* Cypriote; *f* Venus

Cypr·us or **Cypr·os -ī** *f* Cyprus (*island off the coast of Asia Minor*)

Cypsěl·us -ī *m* despot of Corinth (655-625 B.C.)

Cyrēn·ē -ēs *f* or **Cyrēn·ae -ārum** *f pl* chief city of Greek settlement in N.E. Africa

Cyr·us -ī *m* founder of the Persian monarchy in 559 B.C. (*d.* 529 B.C.); Cyrus the Younger (*under whom Xenophon served, d.* 401 B.C.)

Cyt·ae -ārum *f pl* town in Colchis, birthplace of Medea

Cytae·is -ĭdis *f* Medea

Cythēr·a -ōrum *n pl* island off the S. coast of the Peloponnesus, famous for worship of Venus

Cythērē·is -ĭdis *f* Venus

Cythērēi·us -a -um *adj* Cytherean; heros Cythereius Aeneas; *f* Venus

Cythērē·us -a -um *adj* Cytherean; *f* Venus

cytīs·us -ī *m* or *f* clover

Cytōriăc·us -a -um *adj* of Cytorus, Cytorian; pecten Cytoriacus comb made of boxwood

Cytōr·us or **Cytōr·os -ī** *m* mountain of Paphlagonia, famous for its boxwood

Cyzĭc·um -ī *n* or **Cyzĭc·us** or **Cyzĭc·os -ī** *f* town on Sea of Marmora

---

D

Dāc·ī -ōrum *m pl* Dacians (*people of the lower Danube*)

dactylĭc·us -a -um *adj* dactylic

dactýl·us -ī *m* dactyl

daedăl·us -a -um *adj* skillful, artistic, artfully constructed

Daedăl·us -ī *m* mythical builder of the labyrinth in Crete and the first to build wings and fly

Damascēn·us -a -um *adj* of Damascus

Damasc·us -ī *f* Damascus (*capital of Coele-Syria*)

damm·a or **dām·a -ae** *f* deer; venison

damnātĭ·ō -ōnis *f* condemnation

damnātōri·us -a -um *adj* guilty (*verdict*)

damnāt·us -a -um *adj* criminal; hateful

damnifĭc·us -a -um *adj* harmful, injurious, pernicious

damnigerŭl·us -a -um *adj* harmful, injurious

damn·ō -āre *vt* to find guilty, sentence, condemn; to disapprove of, reject, blame; to consecrate, offer as a sacrifice, doom to the gods below; (*with genit* or *abl* of charge or punishment) to find (*someone*) guilty of; capite or capitis damnare to condemn to death; de majestate damnare to find guilty of treason; voti damnare to oblige (*someone*) to fulfill a vow

damnōsē *adv* destructively, so as to bring ruin

damnōs·us -a -um *adj* damaging, injurious, destructive, pernicious; prodigal; canes damnosi crap (*worst throw of the dice*); *m* spendthrift

damn·um -ī *n* loss, damage, harm, injury; misfortune; fine, penalty; fault; defect

Dană·ē -ēs *f* daughter of Acrisius and mother of Perseus

Danaĭd·ēs -um *f pl* daughters of Danaus who killed their husbands on their wedding night, with the exception of Hypermnestra, and as punishment were made to carry water in the lower world

Dană·us -ī *m* king of Argos and father of fifty daughters; *m pl* Greeks

danist·a -ae *m* money lender, banker

danistĭc·us -a -um *adj* money-lending, banking, of bankers

danō see **dō**

Dānuv·ius -ĭī or **-ī** *m* Danube

Daphn·ē -ēs *f* nymph pursued by Apollo and changed into a laurel tree

Daphn·is -ĭdis *m* handsome young Sicilian shepherd, the inventor of pastoral song

dapĭn·ō -āre *vt* to serve (*food*)

dap·s -is *f* ceremonial feast; sumptuous meal, banquet; simple food, poor meal

dapsĭl·is -e *adj* sumptuous, costly

Dardăn·us -a -um *adj* Dardanian, Trojan; Roman (*descendant of Aeneas*); *m* son of Jupiter and Electra and ancestor of the Trojan race; *m pl* people of Upper Moesia (*on Danube*)

Darē·us -ī *m* Darius (*king of Persia, 521-485 B.C.*); Darius Ochus or

Nothus (*king of Persia*, 424-405 B.C.); Darius Codomanus (*last king of Persia*, 336-331 B.C.)

datārĭ·us -a -um *adj* to be handed out, to give away

datătim *adv* giving in turn, passing from one to another

datĭ·ō -ōnis *f* giving, alloting; (law) right of alienation

datĭv·us -a -um *adj* & *m* dative

dat·ō -āre *vt* to keep giving away, be in the habit of giving

dat·or -ōris *m* giver

dat·us -ūs *m* giving

Daul·is -ĭdis *f* town in Phocis, famous for the fable of Procne and Philomela

Daun·us -ī *m* king of Apulia and ancestor of Turnus, the opponent of Aeneas

dē *prep* (with *abl*) (of space) down from, from, away from, out of; (of origin) from, of, descended from, derived from; (of separation) from among, out of; (of time) immediately after; about, concerning, of, in respect to; for, on account of, because of; according to, in imitation of; **de improviso** unexpectedly; **de industria** on purpose; **de integro** afresh, all over again; **de novo** anew

de·a -ae *f* goddess

dealb·ō -āre *vt* to whiten, whitewash, plaster

deambulātĭ·ō -ōnis *f* strolling, walking about, stroll, walk

deambŭl·ō -āre *vi* to go for a walk, take a stroll

deăm·ō -āre *vt* to be in love with; to be much obliged to

dearm·ō -āre *vt* to disarm

deartŭ·ō -āre *vt* to tear limb from limb, dismember; (fig) to waste, wreck

deascĭ·ō -āre *vt* to smooth with an ax; (coll) to cheat, con

dēbacch·or -ārī -ātus sum *vi* to rant and rave

dēbellāt·or -ōris *m* conqueror

dēbell·ō -āre *vt* to fight it out with, wear down, subdue; *vi* to fight it out to the end; to bring a war to an end

dēb·ĕō -ēre -ŭī -ĭtum *vt* to owe; to be responsible for; (with *inf*) **a** to have to, be bound to, be obliged to; **b** to be destined to, be fated to; (with *dat*) to owe (*e.g.*, *a favor*) to, be indebted to (*someone*) for; **deberi** (with *dat*) to be due to

dēbĭl·is -e *adj* lame, crippled, frail, feeble, paralyzed

dēbĭlĭt·ās -ātis *f* lameness, debility, weakness, helplessness

dēbilitātĭ·ō -ōnis *f* disabling, paralyzing

dēbĭlĭt·ō -āre *vt* to lame; to disable, debilitate, weaken; to unnerve; to paralyze

dēbĭtĭ·ō -ōnis *f* debt

dēbĭt·or -ōris *m* debtor; person under obligation

dēbĭt·um -ī *n* debt; obligation

dēblatĕr·ō -āre *vt* to blurt out

dēcant·ō -āre *vt* to repeat monotonously; *vi* to sing on to the end; to stop singing

dē·cēdō -cēdĕre -cessī -cessum *vi* to withdraw, clear out, depart; to retire, retreat, fall back, abandon a position; to give place, make way, make room, yield; to depart, disappear, die; to abate, subside, cease; to go wrong, go awry; (with *dat*) to yield to, give in to; (with **de** + *abl*) to give up, relinquish, abandon

decem (indecl) *adj* ten; (fig) large number of

Decemb·er -ris *adj* & *m* December

decemjŭg·is -is *m* ten-horse chariot

decempĕd·a -ae *f* ten-foot measuring rod, ten-foot rule

decempedāt·or -ōris *m* surveyor

decemplex -ĭcis *adj* tenfold

decemprīm·ī or **decem prīm·ī -ōrum** *m pl* board of ten (*governing Italian towns*)

decemscalm·us -a -um *adj* tenoared

decemvirāl·is -e *adj* decemviral; **leges decemvirales** laws passed by the decemviri

decemvirāt·us -ūs *m* decemvirate

decemvir·ī -ōrum *m pl* decemviri, ten-man commission (*appointed in Rome at different times and for various purposes*); **decemviri legibus scribundis** commission to codify the laws (451 B.C.); **decemviri sacris faciundis** commission for attending to religious matters

decenn·is -e *adj* ten-year, lasting ten years

dec·ens -entis *adj* proper, becoming; handsome, pretty; decent, proper

decenter *adv* becomingly, decently, properly, with propriety

decentĭ·a -ae *f* propriety, decency

dē·cernō -cernĕre -crēvī -crētum *vt* to sift, separate; to decide, settle, determine, decree, resolve, vote; to decide by combat, fight out; to fight, combat; *vi* to contend, compete, struggle; to put forward a proposal; (with **de** or **pro** + *abl*) to fight over, fight for (*in court*)

dēcerp·ō -ĕre -sī -tum *vt* to pluck off, tear away, break off, gather, crop; to derive, enjoy (*e.g.*, *benefits, satisfaction*); **aliquid de gravitate decerpere** to detract somewhat from the dignity

dēcertātĭ·ō -ōnis *f* decision, decisive struggle

dēcert·ō -āre *vi* to fight it out, decide the issue

dēcessĭ·ō -ōnis *f* withdrawing; retirement, departure (*from a province*); decrease; disappearance

dēcess·or -ōris *m* retiring official, predecessor in office

dēcess·us -ūs *m* withdrawal; retirement (*of official from a province*); decease, death

dec·et -ēre -ŭit (used only in 3d *sing & pl*) *vt* to befit, be becoming to; (with *inf*) it is fitting to (*someone*) to, it is proper for (*someone*) to; *vi* to be fitting, be proper; (with *dat & inf*) it is fitting for (*someone*) to, it is proper for (*someone*) to

dēcĭd·ō -ēre -ī *vi* to fall down; to fall dead, die; to fall, drop, sink, fail, perish

dē-cīdō -cīdĕre -cīsī -cīsum *vt* to cut off, cut away; to cut short, terminate, put an end to, decide, settle; **pennas decidere** (fig) to clip (*someone's*) wings

deciens or **decies** *adv* ten times; **deciens centena milia** or **deciens** million

decimānus see **decumanus**

decim·us or **decum·us -a -um** *adj* the tenth; **cum decimo** tenfold; **cum decimo effecit ager** the field produced a tenfold return; **decimum** for the tenth time

dē-cipĭō -cipĕre -cēpī -ceptum *vt* to deceive, cheat; to snare, mislead, beguile; to escape the notice of; **aliquem laborum decipere** to make one forget his troubles; **laborum decipi** to be freed of troubles, forget one's troubles

dēcīsĭ·ō -ōnis *f* decision, settlement

decīsum *pp* of **dēcīdō**

Dec·ius -iī or **-ī** *m* P. Decius Mus (*Roman hero who voluntarily gave his life in battle during the Latin War in 340 B.C. to bring victory to the Roman army; his son who likewise gave his life in Samnite War in 295 B.C.*)

dēclāmātĭ·ō -ōnis *f* practice in public speaking; theme or subject matter in rhetorical exercise; loud talking, shouting, hubbub

dēclāmāt·or -ōris *m* elocutionist, declaimer; ranter

dēclāmātōrĭ·us -a -um *adj* rhetorical

dēclāmĭt·ō -āre *vt* to plead (*cases*); *vi* to practice public speaking; to bluster

dēclām·ō -āre *vt* to recite; *vi* to practice public speaking

dēclārātĭ·ō -ōnis *f* disclosure, declaration

dēclār·ō -āre *vt* to make clear, make evident, disclose; to proclaim, announce officially; to show, prove, demonstrate; to mean, express, signify; to declare (*as chosen for office*)

dēclīnātĭ·ō -ōnis *f* leaning away, bending aside, swerving; shunning, avoiding; digression; (gram) declension

dēclīn·ō -āre *vt* to deflect; to parry, avoid; to decline, conjugate; *vi* to deviate; to digress

dēclīv·e -is *n* declivity, slope

dēclīv·is -e *adj* sloping, steep, downhill

dēclīvĭt·ās -ātis *f* sloping terrain

dēcoct·a -ae *f* cold drink

dēcoct·or -ōris *m* bankrupt; (coll) old rake

dēcoct·us -a -um *pp* of **decoquo**; *adj* boiled down; mellow (*style*)

dēcoll·ō -āre *vt* to behead

dēcōl·ō -āre *vi* to trickle away, come to naught, fail

dēcŏl·or -ōris *adj* off-color, faded; dark, tanned; degenerate

dēcolōrātĭ·ō -ōnis *f* discoloring

dēcolōr·ō -āre *vt* to discolor, stain, deface

dē-cŏquō -coquĕre -coxī -coctum *vt* to boil down, boil thoroughly; to bring to ruin; *vi* to go bankrupt

dec·or -ōris *m* beauty, grace, elegance, charm; ornament

decōrē *adv* beautifully, gracefully; suitably, properly

decŏr·ō -āre *vt* to beautify, adorn, embellish; to decorate, honor

decōr·us -a -um *adj* beautiful, graceful, adorned; decorous, proper, suitable; fine, handsome; noble; *n* grace, propriety

dēcrepĭt·us -a -um *adj* decrepit, broken down, worn out

dē-crescō -crescĕre -crēvī -crētum *vi* to grow less, become fewer, diminish, subside, wane

dēcrēt·us -a -um *pp* of **decerno**; *n* decision, decree; principle, doctrine

decum·a or **decim·a -ae** *f* tenth part, tithe, land tax; largess to the people

decumān·us or **decimān·us -a -um** *adj* paying tithes; of the tenth cohort, of the tenth legion; *m* tax collector; *m pl* men of the tenth legion; *f* tax collector's wife; **porta decumana** main gate of a Roman camp on the side turned away from the enemy

decumāt·ēs -ĭum *adj* subject to tithes

dē-cumbō -cumbĕre -cubŭi *vi* to lie down; to recline at table; to fall (*in battle*)

decūm·ō or **decĭm·ō -āre** *vt* to decimate

decurĭ·a -ae *f* decuria, group of ten; tenth part (*of a curia*); division, class (*without reference to number*); panel (*of judges*); social club

decuriātĭ·ō -ōnis *f* dividing into decuries

decuriāt·us -ūs *m* dividing into decuries

decurĭ·ō -āre *vt* (pol) to divide into groups of ten; (fig) to divide into groups

decurĭ·ō -ōnis *m* decurion (*head of a decuria*); (mil) cavalry officer (*in charge of ten men*); senator of a municipality or colony

dē-currō -currĕre -cucurrī or **-currī -cursum** *vt* to pass over, run over, traverse; to pass through (*life*); to get over (*troubles*); to discuss, treat; *vi* to run down; (mil) to parade, maneuver; (of river, ship) to run down to the sea; to run for help; to sail; to land; **eo decursum est ut** it got to the point where

dēcursǐ·ō -ōnis f (mil) dress parade; maneuvers; raid, descent

dēcurs·us -ūs m running down; downward course; (mil) dress parade; (mil) maneuvers; (mil) raid; end of course, completion; **decursus honorum** completion of political career

dēcurtāt·us -a -um adj cut down, cut off short, mutilated; clipped (style)

dec·us -ǒris n beauty, glory, honor, dignity; virtue, worth; source of glory; n pl great deeds, distinctions

dēcuss·ō -āre vt to divide crosswise (in the form of an X)

dē·cutǐō -cutěre -cussī -cussum vt to shake off, beat off, strike down; to chop off (head); to break down (wall with battering ram)

dē·decet -decēre -decuit (used only in 3d sing & pl) vt it ill becomes, ill befits; (with inf) it is a disgrace to

dēdecǒr·ō -āre vt to disgrace, dishonor, bring shame to; to make a sham of

dēdecǒr·us -a -um adj disgraceful, dishonorable, unbecoming

dēdec·us -ǒris n disgrace, dishonor, shame; vice, crime, outrage; (mil) disgraceful defeat; **dedecori esse** (with dat) to be a source of disgrace to; **dedecus admittere** to incur disgrace; **per dedecus** disgracefully

dēdicātǐ·ō -ōnis f dedication, consecration

dēdic·ō -āre vt to dedicate, consecrate, set aside; to declare (property in a census return)

dēdign·or -ārī -ātus sum vt to scorn, disdain, look down on; (with double acc) to scorn (someone) as; **aliquem maritum dedignari** to regard someone as an unworthy husband

dē·discō -discěre -didicī vt to forget

dēditǐc·ǐus -ǐī or **-ī** m captive; m pl prisoners of war

dēditǐ·ō -ōnis f surrender, capitulation

dēdǐt·us -a -um pp of **dedo**; adj (with dat) given to, devoted to, addicted to; (with **in** + abl) absorbed in; m pl prisoners of war, captives

dē·dō -děre -dǐdī -dǐtum vt to give up, surrender; to devote; to apply; to abandon; **aliquem hostibus in cruciatum dedere** to hand someone over to the enemy to be tortured; **deditā operā** on purpose, intentionally; **neci** or **ad necem dedere** to put to death

dēdoc·ěō -ēre -ǔī -tum vt to cause to forget; (with inf) to teach (someone) not to

dēdǒl·ěō -ēre -ǔī vi to grieve no more

dēdǒl·ō -āre vt to chop away; to chop smooth

dē·dūcō -dūcěre -duxī -ductum vt to lead or draw down; to launch (ship); to accompany, escort; to lead out (colonists to new colony); to conduct (bride to her husband), give away (bride); to evict; to subtract, deduct, diminish; to summon (as witness); to divert, mislead; to derive (name); to compose (poetry); to dissuade; to spin out (thread); to comb out (hair)

dēductǐ·ō -ōnis f leading or drawing off; settling (of colonists); (law) eviction; reduction; inference; **rationis deductio** train of reasoning

dēduct·us -a -um pp of **deduco**; adj drawn down; bent inwards, concave; lowered, modest; subtle, well wrought (poem)

deerr·ō -āre vi to go astray, wander away; **a vero deerrare** (fig) to stray from the truth

dēfaec·ō -āre vt to cleanse of dregs; to wash; (fig) to clear up, make clear

dēfatīgātǐ·ō -ōnis f exhaustion

dēfatīg·ō -āre vt to wear out, exhaust

dēfatiscor see **defetiscor**

dēfectǐ·ō -ōnis f failure; defection, desertion; weakening, exhaustion; eclipse; **defectio animi** mental breakdown; **in defectione esse** to be up in revolt

dēfect·or -ōris m defector, deserter; rebel

dēfect·us -a -um pp of **deficio**; adj weak, worn out

dēfect·us -ūs m failing, failure; desertion; revolt; eclipse

dē·fendō -fenděre -fendī -fensum vt to repel, beat off, avert; to defend, protect, guard; to keep off (the cold); to answer (a charge); to champion (a cause); to support, uphold, maintain (an argument); to play the part of (a character); (law) to defend

dēfensǐ·ō -ōnis f defense

dēfensǐt·ō -āre vt to defend often; **causas defensitare** to be a lawyer

dēfens·ō -āre vt to defend, protect

dēfens·or -ōris m defender, protector; (law) defense lawyer; (law) guardian; champion (of people); m pl garrison

dēfensus pp of **defendo**

dē·ferō -ferre -tǔlī -lātum vt to bring or carry down; to bear off, carry away; to throw (ship) off course; to offer, confer, grant; to inform against, indict; to give an account of, announce, report; to recommend; to register; **ad aerarium deferre** to recommend (someone) for a monetary reward (because of outstanding service to the State); **ad consilium deferre** to take into consideration

dē·fervescō -fervescěre -fervī or **-ferbǔī** vt & vi to cool off, calm down; (of a speech) to lose momentum; (of passions) to die out

dēfess·us -a -um *adj* weary, worn out, exhausted

dē·fetiscor or dē·fatiscor -fetiscī -fessus sum *vi* to become weary, tired

dē·ficiō -ficĕre -fēcī -fectum *vt* to fail, disappoint; to desert, abandon; *vi* to fail, be a failure; to defect, desert; to secede; (of arms, food, etc.) to run short, run out; (of strength, morale, etc.) to fail, grow weak, droop, sink; (of sun, moon) to be eclipsed; (of fire) to die out; (com) to be bankrupt

dē·fīgō -fīgĕre -fīxī -fīxum *vt* to fix, fasten down; to drive down; to fix, concentrate (*eyes, attention*); to root to the spot, astound, stupefy; to bewitch, enchant; **in terra defīgere** to stick, plant, set up (*something*) in the ground

dē·fingō -fingĕre -finxī *vt* to form, mold; to portray; to disfigure, deface

dēfīn·iō -īre -īvī -ītum *vt* to set bounds to, limit; (fig) to limit, define, explain; to fix, determine, appoint; to delimit, bring to a finish, end; to assign, prescribe

dēfīnītē *adv* precisely

dēfīnīti·ō -ōnis *f* boundary; (fig) marking out, prescribing; definition

dēfīnītīv·us -a -um *adj* explanatory

dēfīnīt·us -a -um *adj* definite, precise

dē·fīō -fĭerī *vi* to fail, be lacking

dēflagrāti·ō -ōnis *f* conflagration

dēflāgr·ō -āre *vt* to burn down; *vi* to burn down, go up in flames; to perish, be destroyed; (of passions) to cool off, be allayed, subside

dē·flectō -flectĕre -flexī -flexum *vt* to deflect, bend aside, turn away, divert; (fig) to turn away, lead astray; *vi* to turn away, digress, deviate

dēfl·eō -ēre -ēvī -ētum *vt* to cry bitterly for; to mourn as lost; *vi* to cry bitterly

dēfloccāt·us -a -um *adj* stripped of wool, shorn; bald (*head*)

dēflōr·escō -escĕre -uī *vi* to shed blossoms; (fig) to fade, droop

dēflŭ·ō -ĕre -xī *vi* to flow or float down; to glide down, slide, fall; to flow out, run dry; to vanish, pass away, disappear, cease; to go out of style, become obsolete

dē·fodiō -fodĕre -fōdī -fossum *vt* to dig down; to hollow out; to bury, hide, conceal

dēfōre = dēfutūrum esse

dēformāti·ō -ōnis *f* disfiguring, defacing

dēform·is -e *adj* shapeless, amorphous; misshapen, disfigured, ugly; degrading; degraded; unbecoming, humiliating

dēformit·ās -ātis *f* deformity, ugliness, hideousness; vileness, turpitude

dēformiter *adv* without grace, without beauty

dēform·ō -āre *vt* to form from a pattern; to sketch, delineate; to deform, disfigure, mar

dēfossus *pp* of defodio

dēfraud·ō or defrūd·ō -āre *vt* to defraud, rob; to cheat; **genium suum defraudare** to deny oneself some pleasure

dēfrēnāt·us -a -um *adj* unbridled, uncontrolled

dēfric·ō -āre -ŭī -ātum *vt* to rub down; to brush (*teeth*); (fig) to satirize

dē·fringō -fringĕre -frēgī -fractum *vt* to break off, break to pieces

dēfrūdo see defraudo

dēfrŭt·um -ī *n* new wine

dē·fugiō -fugĕre -fūgī *vt* to run away from, avoid, shirk; to evade (*e.g., authority, law*); *vi* to run off, escape

dēfunct·us -a -um *pp* of defungor; *adj* finished; dead

dē·fundō -fundĕre -fūdī -fūsum *vt* to pour out; to empty (*e.g., bucket*)

dē·fungor -fungī -functus sum *vi* (with *abl*) **a** to perform, finish, be done with; **b** to have done with, get rid of; **defunctus jam sum** I'm safe now; **defungi vitā** or **defungi** to die; **parvo victu defungi** to do with or be content with little food

dēfūsus *pp* of defundo

dēgĕn·er -ĕris *adj* degenerate; unworthy; ignoble

dēgenĕr·ō -āre *vt* to disgrace, dishonor, fall short of; *vi* to be inferior to one's ancestors, be degenerate; (fig) to fall off, degenerate, decline

dēgĕr·ō -ĕre *vt* to carry off, carry away

dēg·ō -ĕre -ī *vt* to spend, pass (*time, life*); **aetatem degere** to live; *vi* to live

dēgrandĭnat *v impers* it is hailing hard

dēgrăv·ō -āre *vt* to weigh down; (fig) to burden, distress, inconvenience, overpower

dē·gredior -grŏdī -gressus sum *vi* to march down, go down, walk down, descend; **ad pedes degredi** to dismount

dēgrunn·iō -īre *vi* to grunt hard, grunt out loud

dēgust·ō -āre *vt* to taste; (fig) to taste, sample, try, experience; (of weapon) to graze

dehinc *adv* from here; from now on; then, next; hereafter

dehisc·ō -ĕre *vi* to part, divide, gape, yawn

dēhonestāment·um -ī *n* blemish, disfigurement, dishonor, disgrace

dēhonest·ō -āre *vt* to dishonor, disgrace

dēhort·or -ārī -ātus sum *vt* to advise to the contrary, dissuade

Dēianīr·a -ae *f* daughter of Oeneus and wife of Hercules

dein see **deinde**

deinceps adv one after another, in succession, in order; in regular order, without interruption

deinde or **dein** adv (of place) from that place, from there; (of time) then, thereafter, thereupon, afterwards; (in enumerating facts, presenting arguments) secondly, next in order, in the next place

Dēiotăr·us -ī m king of Galatia (defended by Cicero before Caesar in the latter's house)

Dēiphŏb·us -ī m son of Priam and Hecuba, and husband of Helen after Paris' death

dējecti·ō -ōnis f (law) eviction

dēject·us -a -um pp of **dejicio**; adj low, depressed, sunken (place); discouraged, downhearted, despondent

dēject·us -ūs m felling (of trees); steep slope

dējēr·ō or **dējūrō** -āre vi to swear solemnly

dē·jiciō -jicĕre -jēcī -jectum vt to throw down, fling down; to fell, bring low, kill; to depose (from office); to lower (eyes); to drive off course; (law) to evict; (mil) to dislodge, drive out; to deprive; (with abl or de + abl) to deprive (someone) of, prevent (someone) from obtaining, rob (someone) of; **oculos dejicere** (with ab + abl) to divert the eyes from; to turn away from

dējung·ō -ĕre vt to unyoke; to sever

dējūrō see **dejero**

dōjŭv·ō -āre vt to fail to help

dē·lābor -lābī -lapsus sum vi to slip down, fall down, sink down; to glide down, float down; (fig) to come down, sink; (fig) to stoop, condescend; (with ad + acc) to be inclined toward, be partial to, tend toward; (with in + acc) to sneak in among

dēlacĕr·ō -āre vt to tear to pieces

dēlāment·or -ārī -ātus sum vt to grieve deeply for

dēlass·ō -āre vt to tire out, weary

dēlāti·ō -ōnis f reporting; informing, denouncing; **nominis delatio** indicting of a person

dēlāt·or -ōris m reporter; informer; denouncer

dēlātus pp of **defero**

dēlectābĭl·is -e adj delightful, enjoyable

dēlectāment·um -ī n delight, amusement, pastime

dēlectāti·ō -ōnis f delight, pleasure, charm, amusement, satisfaction

dēlect·ō -āre vt to delight, amuse, charm; to attract, allure; **delectari** (with abl) to be delighted by, delight in; v impers **me ire delectat** I like to go, I enjoy going

dēlect·us -a -um pp of **deligo**; adj picked, choice, select

dēlect·us -ūs m choosing, choice

dēlēgāti·ō -ōnis f substitution, dele-

gation (of one person for another); payment (of debt)

dēlēg·ō -āre vt to assign, transfer; to attribute, impute, ascribe

dēlēnĭfĭc·us -a -um adj soothing, seductive

dēlēnĭment·um -ī n palliative, solace, comfort; allurement, bait

dēlēn·iō or **dēlĭn·iō** -īre -īvī -ītum vt to soothe, calm down, console, appease; to allure, seduce, win over

dēlēnīt·or -ōris m charmer, cajoler

dēl·ĕō -ēre -ēvī -ētum vt to destroy, annihilate, overthrow, extinguish, raze; to blot out, erase, obliterate (writing); to annul, put an end to, abolish, finish

dēlētr·ix -īcis f destroyer

Dēlĭăc·us -a -um adj Delian, of or from Delos

dēlībĕrābund·us -a -um adj deliberating maturely

dēlībĕrātī·ō -ōnis f considering, weighing; deliberation, consultation; **habet res deliberationem** the matter requires thought, needs consideration

dēlībĕrātīv·us -a -um adj deliberative; requiring deliberation

dēlībĕrāt·or -ōris m thoughtful person

dēlībĕrāt·us -a -um adj resolved upon, determined

dēlībĕr·ō -āre vt to weigh well, ponder; to resolve, determine; to consult (oracle); vi to reflect, deliberate; (with de + abl) to think seriously about, think over well

dēlīb·ō -āre vt to sip, take a sip of; to taste, take a taste of, nibble at; to take away, detract, subtract, remove

dēlībr·ō -āre vt to strip the bark off (trees); to peel

dēlībūt·us -a -um adj anointed; defiled, stained, smeared; steeped

dēlĭcātē adv delicately, softly, luxuriously

dēlĭcāt·us -a -um adj delicate, dainty, tender, soft; pampered, spoiled; dainty, fastidious

dēlĭcĭ·ae -ārum f pl allurements, enticements, delights; whims, pet ideas, fanciful ideas; voluptuousness; favorite, sweetheart, darling; **delicias facere** to play tricks; **delicias facere** (with dat) to play around with (a girl); **esse in deliciis** (with dat) to be the pet or favorite of; **habere in deliciis** to have as a pet or favorite

dēlĭcĭŏl·ae -ārum f pl darling

dēlĭc·ĭum -ĭī or -ī n sweetheart; favorite

dēlĭc·ō -āre vt to make clear, explain

dēlĭct·um -ī n fault, offense, wrong, transgression, defect

dēlĭcŭ·us -a -um adj lacking, wanting

dēlĭg·ō -āre vt to tie up, bind together, bind fast

dē·lĭgō -lĭgĕre -lēgī -lectum vt to

choose, select, pick out, single out, elect; to gather, gather in

dē·lingō -lingĕre -linxī *vt* to lick off; to have a lick of

dēlīni- = delēni-

dē·linquō -linquĕre -līquī -lictum *vi* to fail, be wanting, fall short; to do wrong, commit a fault or crime

dē·liquēscō -liquēscĕre -licŭī *vi* to melt, melt away, dissolve; to pine away

dēliquĭ.ō -ōnis *f* failure; (with *genit*) failure to get

dēliqu·ĭum -ī or **-ī** *n* failure

dēliqu·ō or **dēlic·ō -āre** *vt* to clear up, explain

dēlīrāment·um -ī *n* nonsense, absurdity

dēlīrātĭ·ō -ōnis *f* silliness, folly, madness; infatuation; dotage

dēlīr·ō -āre *vi* to be off the beam, be crazy, be mad; to drivel

dēlīr·us -a -um *adj* crazy, demented, silly; in dotage

dēlit·ēscō -ēscĕre -ŭī *vi* to conceal oneself, lie hidden, lurk

dēlītīg·ō -āre *vi* to rant

Dēlĭ·us -a -um *adj* Delian, of Delos

Dēl·os -ī *f* sacred island in the Cyclades, where Apollo was born

Delph·ī -ōrum *m pl* town in Phocis, in Central Greece, famous for the shrine and oracle of Apollo; inhabitants of Delphi

delphīn·us -ī or **delph·īn -īnis** *m* dolphin

Delphīn·us -ī *m* Dolphin (*constellation*)

Deltōt·on -ī *n* Triangulum (*constellation*)

dēlūbr·um -ī *n* shrine, temple, sanctuary

dēluct·ō -āre or **dēluct·or -ārī -ātus sum** *vi* to wrestle

dēlūdificō -āre *vt* to make fun of

dē·lūdō -lūdĕre -lūsī -lūsum *vt* to dupe, mock, deceive, delude

dēlumb·is -e *adj* enervated, enfeebled, weakened

dēmad·ēscō -ēscĕre -ŭī *vi* to become drenched; to be moistened

dēmand·ō -āre *vt* to hand over, entrust

dēmarch·us -ī *m* demarch (*chief of a village in Attica*); (fig) tribune of the people

dēm·ens -entis *adj* out of one's mind, demented, distracted, mad; senseless, wild, reckless

dēmensus *pp* of dēmetior; *n* ration, allowance

dēmenter *adv* insanely

dēmentĭ·a -ae *f* insanity, madness; *f pl* follies

dement·ĭō -īre *vi* to be mad

dēmer·ĕō -ēre -ŭī -ĭtum or **dēmer·ĕor -ērī -ĭtus sum** *vt* to earn, merit, deserve; to serve well, do a service to

dē·mergō -mergĕre -mersī -mersum *vt* to sink, plunge, submerge; (fig) to plunge, cast down, overwhelm

dēmessus *pp* of dēmeto

dē·mētior -mētīrī -mensus sum *vt* to measure off, measure out

dē·mētō -metĕre -messŭī -messum *vt* to mow, reap, cut off, cut down, harvest

dēmigrātĭ·ō -ōnis *f* emigration

dēmigr·ō -āre *vi* to migrate, emigrate, move, depart; (fig) to depart, die

dēmin·ŭō -ŭĕre -ŭī -ūtum *vt* to make smaller, lessen, diminish; (fig) to remit, reduce, lessen; **capite dēminuere** to deprive of citizenship

dēminūtĭ·ō -ōnis *f* lessening, diminution, abridging; (law) right of disposing of property; **capitis dīminutio** loss of civil rights; **provinciae diminutio** shortening of term of office

dēmīr·or -ārī -ātus sum *vt* to be surprised at, to be amazed at

dēmissē *adv* low; humbly, modestly; abjectly, meanly

dēmissīcĭ·us -a -um *adj* allowed to hang down, flowing

dēmissĭ·ō -ōnis *f* letting down, sinking, lowering; **demissio animi** low morale

dēmiss·us -a -um *pp* of dēmitto; *adj* low, low-lying (*place*); drooping (*lips, etc.*); bent (*head*); allowed to hang down, flowing, loose (*hair*); downhearted, dejected, shy, unassuming, retiring, humble; poor, humble

dēmītīg·ō -āre *vt* to make mild; **dēmitigari** to grow more lenient

dē·mittō -mittĕre -mīsī -missum *vt* to drop, let drop, let sink, lower; to bring downstream; to land (*ship*); to grow (*beard*); to move down (*troops from higher place*); **se dēmittere** to descend; to stoop, bend down

dēmiurg·us or **dāmiurg·us -ī** *m* chief magistrate in a Greek state

dēm·ō -ĕre -psī -ptum *vt* to take away, remove, withdraw, subtract; (with *dat* or with **de** + *abl*) to take away from, subtract from, withhold from

Dēmocrit·us -ī *m* famous philosopher of Abdera, in Thrace, founder of the atomic theory (460-361 B.C.)

dēmōl·ĭor -īrī -ītus sum *vt* to demolish, pull down

dēmōlītĭ·ō -ōnis *f* pulling down (*of statues*)

dēmonstrātĭ·ō -ōnis *f* pointing out; explanation

dēmonstrātīv·us -a -um *adj* showy

dēmonstrāt·or -ōris *m* indicator

dēmonstr·ō -āre *vt* to point out clearly; to state precisely, explain, describe; to mention, speak of; to demonstrate, prove, establish

dē·morior -mŏrī -mortŭus sum *vi* to die, die off

dēmŏr·or -ārī -ātus sum *vt* to delay, detain; to hinder, block; *vi* to wait

Dēmosthěn·ēs -is m greatest Greek orator (384-322 B.C.)

dē·mověō -movēre -mōvī -mōtum vt to remove, move away, dispossess, expel; to remove, discharge (from office); (fig) to divert, turn away

demptus pp of demo

dēmūgīt·us -a -um adj bellowing, lowing

dē·mulcěō -mulcēre -mulsī vt to stroke lovingly, to caress

dēmum adv at last, finally; not till then; (to give emphasis) precisely, exactly, just; (to give assurance) in fact, certainly, to be sure, as a matter of fact; **decimo demum anno** not till the tenth year; **modo demum** only now, not till now; **nunc demum** now at last, now till now; **post demum** not till after; **sic demum** thus finally; **tum demum** then at length, not till then

dēmurmŭr·ō -āre vt to grumble right through (e.g., a performance)

dēmūtātī·ō -ōnis f changing, perversion, degeneracy

dēmūt·ō -āre vt to change, alter; to make worse; vi to change one's mind

dēnār·ius -iī or **-ī** m Roman silver coin, originally containing ten aces, later eighteen, approximately equivalent to twenty-five cents; money

dēnarr·ō -āre vt to recount in detail

dēnās·ō -āre vt to bite the nose off (the face)

dēnăt·ō -āre vi to swim downstream

dēněg·ō -āre vt to deny, refuse, turn down; vi to say no, give a flat refusal

dēn·ī -ae -a adj in sets of ten, ten each, in tens; ten; tenth

dēnicāl·is -e adj purifying from death; **feriae denicales** purification service (after death in the household)

dēnique adv finally, at last; in short, in a word, briefly; (for emphasis) just, precisely; (ironical) of course; **octavo denique mense** not till after the eighth month; **tum denique** then at last, only then, not till then

dēnōmĭn·ō -āre vt to name, designate

dēnorm·ō -āre vt to make crooked or irregular; to disfigure, spoil

dēnŏt·ō -āre vt to mark down, specify; to take careful note of, observe closely

den·s -tis m tooth; ivory; point, prong, fluke; (fig) tooth (of envy, hatred, time, etc.); **albis dentibus deridere aliquem** to laugh heartily at someone; **dens Indus** elephant's tusk

densē adv closely, thickly; in quick succession, repeatedly

densĭt·ās -ātis f closeness, thickness

dens·ō -āre or **dens·ěō -ēre — -ētum** vt to make thick, thicken; to press close together; to close

(ranks); to condense (a speech)

dens·us -a -um adj dense, close, crowded, thick; frequent, continuous; intense (love, cold); concise (style)

dentāl·ia -ium n pl plow beam

dentāt·us -a -um adj toothed, having teeth; serrated; polished (paper)

dentifrangĭbŭl·us -a -um adj tooth-breaking; m thug; n fist

dentilěg·us -ī m toothpicker (one who picks up teeth after they have been knocked out)

dent·iō -īre vi to teethe, cut one's teeth

dē·nūbō -nūbĕre -nupsī -nuptum vi (of a woman) to marry beneath one's rank

dēnūd·ō -āre vt to denude, strip naked, strip bare; (fig) to lay bare (facts)

dēnuntiātī·ō -ōnis f intimation, warning, threat; announcement, proclamation; **senatūs denuntiatio** senate ordinance; **testimoni denuntiatio** summons to testify

dēnunti·ō -āre vt to intimate; to give notice of; to announce officially; to give official warning to; (mil) to report to, give an official report to; to warn, threaten; **denuntiare testimonium** (with dat) to give (someone) a summons to testify

dēnŭō adv anew, afresh, once more, all over again

deoněr·ō -āre vt to unload

deorsum or **deorsus** adv downwards, down; (of position) below

deoscŭl·or -ārī -ātus sum vt to kiss warmly, kiss up and down

dēpaciscor see depeciscor

dēpact·us -a -um adj lashed down; driven tight

dēparc·us -a -um adj very stingy

dē·pascō -pascĕre -pāvī -pastum or **dē·pascor -pascī -pastus sum** vt to feed off, graze on; to consume; to destroy, waste; (fig) to prune off (excesses of style)

dēpec·iscor or **dēpac·iscor -iscī -tus sum** vt to agree upon, bargain for, settle by bargaining

dē·pectō -pectĕre — -pexum vt to comb, curry; to curry (one's hide), flog

dēpeculāt·or -ōris m embezzler, plunderer

dēpecŭl·or -ārī -ātus sum vt to embezzle, plunder

dē·pellō -pellĕre -pŭlī -pulsum vt to drive off, drive away, drive out, expel; to avert; (mil) to dislodge; (with **quin** or with **de** or **ab** + abl) to avert, deter, dissuade, wean from; (with abl) to dislodge from; vi to deviate

dēpend·ěō -ēre vi to hang down; (with abl) to be derived from; (with **de** + abl) to depend upon; (with **ex** + abl) to hang down from

dē·pendō -pendĕre -pendī -pen-

sum vt to pay up; **poenam dependere** (with dat) to pay the penalty to

dēper·dō **-děre** **-dǐdǐ** **-dǐtum** vt to lose completely; to ruin, destroy

dēper·ěō **-īre** **-ǐī** vt to be hopelessly in love with; vi to go to ruin, perish; to be lost, finished

dē·pingō **-pingěre** **-pinxī** **-pictum** vt to paint, portray; to embroider; to portray, describe, represent (in words or thoughts)

dē·plangō **-plangěre** **-planxī** vt to grieve over, cry one's heart out over

deplex·us **-a** **-um** adj gripping firmly, grasping

deplōrābund·us **-a** **-um** adj weeping bitterly, sobbing

deplōr·ō **-āre** vt to cry over, mourn; to despair of; vi to take it hard, cry bitterly

deplǔ·it **-ěre** **-it** v impers it is raining hard, pouring down

dē·pōnō **-pōněre** **-posǔī** **-posǐtum** vt to lay down; to put down, put aside, get rid of; to bet, wager; to deposit; (with **apud** + acc) to entrust to, commit to the care of; **bellum deponere** to give up war; **imperium deponere** to relinquish power, renounce power

dēpopulātǐ·ō **-ōnis** f ravaging, pillaging

dēpopulāt·or **-ōris** m pillager, marauder

dēpopǔl·ō **-āre** or **depopǔl·or** **-ārī** **-ātus sum** vt to ravage, pillage, lay waste; to depopulate; (fig) to waste, destroy, wreck

dēport·ō **-āre** vt to carry down; to carry away; to bring home (victory); to transport; to banish; (fig) to win

dē·poscō **-poscěre** **-poposcī** vt to demand, require; to request earnestly; to challenge; **sibi deposcere** to claim (something) for oneself

dēposit·us **-a** **-um** pp of depono; adj despaired of; n deposit (of money as first payment); deposit (for safe keeping)

dēprāvātē adv perversely

dēprāvātǐ·ō **-ōnis** f distorting; (fig) distortion

dēprāv·ō **-āre** vt to make crooked, distort; to pervert, corrupt, seduce; to misrepresent

dēprecābund·us **-a** **-um** adj imploring

dēprecātǐ·ō **-ōnis** f supplication; deprecation, averting by prayer; invocation, earnest entreaty; (with genit) intercession against (danger, etc.)

dēprecāt·or **-ōris** m intercessor (generally against rather than for)

dēprec·or **-ārī** **-ātus sum** vt to pray against, avert by prayer; to pray for, beg for; to intercede in behalf of; to plead in excuse

dēpre·hendō **-henděre** **-hendī** **-hensum** or **dēpren·dō** **-děre** **-dī** **-sum** vt to get hold of; to arrest, intercept; to surprise, catch in the act; to detect, discover, find out; to perceive, understand; to embarrass

dēprehensǐ·ō **-ōnis** f detection

dēpress·us **-a** **-um** pp of deprimo; adj low, suppressed (voice); low (land)

dē·primō **-priměre** **-pressī** **-pressum** vt to depress, press down, weigh down; to plant deep; to dig (e.g., a trench) deep; to sink (a ship)

dēproelǐ·or **-ārī** **-ātus sum** vi to fight it out, battle fiercely

dē·prōmō **-prōměre** **-prompsī** **-promptum** vt to take down; to bring out, produce

dēproper·ō **-āre** vt to make in a hurry; vi to hurry

deps·ō **-ěre** **-ǔī** **-tum** vt to knead

dēpǔd·et **-ěre** **-ǔit** v impers eum depudet he has no sense of shame

dēpūg·is or **dēpȳg·is** **-is** adj without buttocks, with thin buttocks

dēpūgn·ō **-āre** vi to fight hard; to fight it out; (with **cum** + abl) to be in a death struggle with

dēpulsǐ·ō **-ōnis** f averting; (rhet) defense

dēpuls·ō **-āre** vt to push aside; **de via depulsare** to push out of the way

dēpuls·or **-ōris** m averter

dēpulsus pp of depello

dēpung·ō **-ěre** vt to mark off, designate

dēpurg·ō **-āre** vt to clean

dēpǔt·ō **-āre** vt to prune; to reckon, consider

dēpȳgis see depugis

dēque adv down, downwards

dērect·us **-a** **-um** pp of derigo; adj straight, direct, level, upright, perpendicular; (fig) straightforward, direct, simple, right

dērelictǐ·ō **-ōnis** f dereliction, disregarding, neglecting

dēre·linquō **-linquěre** **-līquī** **-lictum** vt to leave behind, forsake, abandon

dērepente adv suddenly

dērēp·ō **-ěre** **-sī** vi to creep down

dēreptus pp of deripio

dē·rīděō **-rīděre** **-rīsī** **-rīsum** vt to deride

dērīdicǔl·us **-a** **-um** adj quite ridiculous; n derision, mockery; absurdity; **deridiculo** esse to be the object of derision, be the butt of ridicule

dērig·escō **-escěre** **-ǔī** vi to grow stiff, grow rigid; to curdle

dē·rigō **-rigěre** **-rexī** **-rectum** vt to direct, aim; to steer (ship); to draw up in battle line; (fig) to direct, guide, regulate; (with dat or with **ad** or **in** + acc) to direct or aim at, guide to; (with **ad** + acc) to regulate (e.g., life) according to

dē·ripǐō **-ripěre** **-ripǔī** **-reptum** vt to tear down, tear off, pull down

dērīs·or **-ōris** m scoffer, cynic

dērīs·us -ūs *m* derision

dērīvātī·ō -ōnis *f* diversion, diverting (*of river from its course*)

dērīv·ō -āre *vt* to draw off, divert; to derive

dērŏg·ō -āre *vt* to propose to repeal in part; to restrict, modify; to take away, diminish, impair

dērōs·us -a -um *adj* gnawed away, nibbled

dēruncin·ō -āre *vt* to plane off; to cheat

dēru·ō -ĕre -ŭī *vt* to throw down, overthrow, demolish; to detract

dērupt·us -a -um *adj* rough, steep, broken; *n pl* crevasses

dēsaev·iō -īre -iī *vi* to rage furiously; to run wild

dēsalt·ō -āre *vi* to dance

dē-scendō -scendĕre -scendī -scensum *vi* to climb down, descend, come or go down; to dismount; to fall, sink, sink down, penetrate; (fig) to go down, sink, sink down, penetrate; (fig) to lower oneself, stoop, yield; (mil) to march down

dēscensī·ō -ōnis *f* going down; **descensio Tiberina** sailing down the Tiber

descens·us -ūs *m* climbing down, descent; slope, descent

desc·iscō -iscĕre -īvī or **-iī -ītum** *vi* to revolt, desert; (fig) to depart, deviate, fall off; (with **ab** + *abl*) **a** to revolt from, break allegiance with; **b** to deviate from, fall away from

dē-scrībō -scrībĕre -scripsī -scriptum *vt* to write out, transcribe, copy; to describe, represent, portray, draw, design, sketch

descriptē see **discriptē**

descriptī·ō -ōnis *f* copy; representation, diagram, sketch, map; description

descriptus *pp of* **describo**

dēsĕc·ō -āre -ŭī -tum *vt* to cut off

dēsĕr·ō -ĕre -ŭī -tum *vt* to desert, abandon, forsake; (law) to forfeit

dēsert·or -ōris *m* deserter

dēsert·us -a -um *pp of* **desero**; *adj* deserted; unpopulated, uninhabited; *n pl* wilderness, desert

dēserv·iō -īre *vi* (with *dat*) to be a slave to, serve devotedly

dēs·es -ĭdis *adj* sitting down, sitting at ease; lazy; apathetic, lifeless, idle

dēsicc·ō -āre *vt* to dry up; to drain

dē-sidĕō -sidĕre -sēdī *vi* to sit idle, remain inactive

dēsiderābil·is -e *adj* desirable

dēsiderātī·ō -ōnis *f* missing, feeling the absence; **desideratio voluptatum** the missing of pleasures, yearning for pleasures

dēsider·ium -iī or **-ī** *n* longing, missing, feeling of loss; want, need, necessity; request, petition; **ex desiderio laborare** to be homesick; **me desiderium tenet** (with *genit*)

I miss, am homesick for

dēsidĕr·ō -āre *vt* to miss, long for, feel the want of; (mil) to lose (*men*) as casualties; **desiderari** (mil) to be missing, be lost, be a casualty

dēsidi·a -ae *f* idleness, inactivity; laziness; apathy

dēsidiābŭl·um -ī *n* place to lounge, hangout

dēsidiōsē *adv* idly

dēsidiōs·us -a -um *adj* idle, indolent, lazy; causing idleness or laziness; spent in idleness

dē-sīdō -sīdĕre -sēdī *vi* to sink, settle down; (fig) to sink, deteriorate

dēsignātī·ō -ōnis *f* specification; designation, election to office

dēsignātor see **dissignator**

dēsign·ō -āre *vt* to mark out, point out, designate, define, trace; to denote, describe, represent; to appoint, choose, elect; **consul designatus** consul-elect

dē-siliō -silīre -silŭī -sultum *vi* to jump down, alight; **ab equo desilire** to dismount; **de nave desilire** to jump overboard; (fig) to venture forth

dē-sinō -sinĕre -siī -situm *vt* to give up, abandon; **furere desinere** to stop raging; *vi* to stop, come to a stop, end; (with **in** + *acc*) to end in; **similiter desinere** to have similar endings

dēsipi·ens -entis *adj* foolish, silly

dēsipienti·a -ae *f* folly, foolishness

dēsip·iō -ĕre *vi* to be silly, act foolishly

dē-sistō -sistĕre -stitī -stitum *vi* to stop, desist; to get stuck, stick; (with *abl* or with **ab** or **de** + *abl*) to desist from, abandon, give up (*an action begun*); **desistere a defensione** to give up the defense

dēsitus *pp of* **desino**

dēsōl·ō -āre *vt* to leave desolate, leave alone, forsake, abandon; **dēsolātus** (with *abl*) deprived of

despect·ō -āre *vt* to look down on, overlook, command a view of; to look down on, despise

despect·us -a -um *pp of* **despicio**; *adj* contemptible

despect·us -ūs *m* commanding view, view

dēspēranter *adv* hopelessly

dēspērātī·ō -ōnis *f* desperation, despair

dēspērāt·us -a -um *adj* despaired of; hopeless; desperate, hopeless

dēspēr·ō -āre *vt* to despair of; *vi* to despair, give up hope; (with **de** + *abl*) to despair of

despicātī·ō -ōnis *f* contempt; *f pl* feelings of contempt

despicāt·us -a -um *adj* despicable; **aliquem despicatum habere** to hold someone in contempt

despici·ens -entis *adj* contemptuous; (with *genit*) contemptuous of

despicienti·a -ae *f* despising, contempt

de·spiciō -spicĕre -spexī -spectum vt to despise, look down on, express contempt for; vi to look down; (with **in** + acc) to look down on, have a view of

despĭc·or -ārī -ātus sum vt to despise, disdain

despoliāt·or -ōris m robber, plunderer, marauder

despolĭ·ō -āre vt to strip, rob, plunder

de·spondĕō -spondēre -spondī -sponsum vt to pledge, promise solemnly; to promise in marriage; to give up, lose; **animum despondēre** or **animos despondēre** to lose heart

despūm·ō -āre vt to skim off, skim; vi to stop foaming

despŭ·ō -ĕre vt to spit upon, show contempt for; vi to spit (on the ground)

desquām·ō -āre vt to take the scales off, to scale (fish); (fig) to peel off

destill·ō -āre vt to drip, distil; vi to trickle down, drip

destimŭl·ō -āre vt to goad on, stimulate

destinātĭ·ō -ōnis f establishing; resolution, determination, purpose, design

destināt·us -a -um adj fixed, determined; **destinatum est mihi** (with inf) I have made up my mind to; n pl designs, intentions

destin·ō -āre vt to lash down, secure; (fig) to fix, determine, resolve; to design, destine; to appoint, designate; to take aim at

destit·uō -uĕre -ŭī -ūtum vt to set apart; to set down, place; to forsake, abandon; to leave in the lurch, leave high and dry, betray, desert; (with **ab** + abl) to rob of, leave destitute of

destitūtĭ·ō -ōnis f forsaking, abandonment; disappointment

district·us -a -um adj severe, rigid

de·stringō -stringĕre -strinxī -strictum vt to strip; to unsheathe; to give (someone) a rubdown; to brush gently against, skim; (of weapon) to graze; (fig) to criticize, satirize

destructĭ·ō -ōnis f pulling down (e.g., of walls); destruction, demolition; refutation

de·struō -struĕre -struxī -structum vt to pull down, demolish, destroy; (fig) to ruin

dēsubĭtō or **dē subĭtō** adv suddenly

dēsūdasc·ō -ĕre vi to begin to sweat all over

dēsūd·ō -āre vi to sweat; (with dat) (fig) to sweat over, work hard at

dēsŭe·fīō -fĭerī -factus sum vi to become unused or unaccustomed

dēsu·escō -escĕre -ēvī -ētum vi to become unaccustomed

dēsuētūd·ō -ĭnis f disuse, lack of use

dēsuēt·us -a -um pp of **desuesco**; adj unused, out of use, obsolete; out of practice; (with dat) unused to, unfamiliar with

dēsult·or -ōris m circus rider who leaps from one horse to another; **amoris desultor** (fig) fickle lover

dēsultōrĭ·us -a -um adj of a circus rider; **equus desultorius** show horse

dēsultūr·a -ae f leaping down (from horse), dismounting

dē·sum -esse -fŭī -futūrus vi to fall short, fail; to fail in one's duty; to be absent, be missing; (with dat) to be absent from, be missing from, be lacking from; **sibi deesse** to cheat oneself, sell oneself short; **tempori deesse** or **occasioni temporis deesse** to pass up the opportunity, pass up the chance

dē·sūmō -sūmĕre -sumpsī -sumptum vt to pick out, choose; to assume, undertake; **sibi hostem desumere** to take on an enemy

dēsŭper adv from above, from overhead

dēsurg·ō -ĕre vi to rise; **cenā desurgere** to get up from the table

dē·tegō -tegĕre -texi -tectum vt to detect, uncover, expose, lay bare; to reveal, disclose, betray; **formidine detegi** to be betrayed by fear

dē·tendō -tendĕre — -tensum vt to unstretch; to take down (tent)

dētentus pp of **detineo**

dē·tergĕō -tergēre -tersī -tersum vt to wipe off, wipe away, wipe clean; (fig) to wipe clean; **mensam detergere** to eat up everything on the table

dēterĭ·or -us adj inferior, worse, poorer, meaner; less favorable, worse (time); degenerate (person); (mil) weaker (e.g., in cavalry)

dēterĭus adv worse

dēterminātĭ·ō -ōnis f boundary; conclusion, end; end (of speech)

dētermin·ō -āre vt to bound, limit, prescribe; to determine, settle

dē·terō -terĕre -trīvī -trītum vt to rub away, wear away; to wear out; to lessen, weaken, detract from; **calces alicujus deterere** to tread on someone's heels

dēterr·ĕō -ēre -ŭī -ĭtum vt to deter, frighten away, discourage; (with abl, or with ab or dē + abl, or with **ne, quin,** or **quominus**) to deter or discourage from; **deterruit quominus hostes persequerentur** he discouraged them from pursuing the enemy

dētersus pp of **detergeo**

dētestābil·is -e adj detestable, abominable

dētestātĭ·ō -ōnis f execration, curse; averting (by sacrifices or prayers)

dētest·or -ārī -ātus sum vt to curse, execrate; to invoke (the gods); to avert; to plead against; to detest, loathe, abhor; (with **in** + acc) to call down (*e.g.*, *vengeance*) upon; **invidiam detestari** to avert envy, avoid unpopularity

dē·tex·ō -ĕre -ŭī -tum *vt* to weave, finish weaving; (fig) to finish, finish off

dē·tĭnĕō -tinēre -tinŭī -tentum *vt* to hold back, keep back; to hold up, detain; to occupy, keep occupied; (with **ab** or **de** + *abl*) to keep back from; (with *abl* or with **in** + *abl*) to occupy (*e.g.*, *day, mind*) with, keep (*someone*) busied with

dē·tondĕō -tondēre -totondī or **-tondī -tonsum** *vt* to cut off, clip off, shear off (*hair, wool*); (fig) to strip

dētŏn·ō -āre -ŭī *vi* to stop thundering; (of Jupiter) to thunder down

dētonsus *pp* of **detondeo**

dē·torquĕō -torquēre -torsī -tortum *vt* to twist or bend aside; to twist out of shape; to turn aside; to turn, direct; to avert (*eyes*); to divert, pervert; to distort, misrepresent (*words*)

dētractĭ·ō -ōnis *f* taking away, wresting; removal; (rhet) ellipsis

detractō see **detrecto**

detract·or -ōris *m* detractor

dē·trăhō -trahĕre -traxī -tractum *vt* to drag down, drag away, pull down, pull away; to remove, withdraw; to take away, deprive, rob, strip; to induce to come down, draw down (*e.g.*, *an enemy from a strong position*); to disparage, detract, slander; (with *dat* or **de** + *abl*) to take away from (*someone*), rob (*someone*) of

dētrectātĭ·ō -ōnis *f* drawing back, avoidance; **militiae detrectatio** draft dodging

dētrectāt·or -ōris *m* detractor, disparager

dētrect·ō or **detract·ō -āre** *vt* to draw back from, shirk, decline, reject, refuse; to disparage, depreciate; to demean; **militiam detrectare** to dodge the draft

dētrīmentōs·us -a -um *adj* detrimental, harmful

dētrīment·um -ī *n* detriment, loss, damage; **detrimentum accipere** or **detrimentum capere** to incur or suffer harm; **detrimentum inferre** or **detrimentum afferre** to cause harm

dētritus *pp* of **detero**

dē·trūdō -trūdĕre -trūsī -trūsum *vt* to push down, push away, push off; (mil) to dislodge; (law) to evict; to postpone, put off; **aliquem de sua sententia detrudere** to force someone to change his mind

detrunc·ō -āre *vt* to cut off, chop off; (fig) to mutilate, behead

dēturb·ō -āre *vt* to beat down, expel, tear down, strike down; (mil) to dislodge, force to come down; to eject, dispossess; **aliquem de sani-**

tate deturbare to drive a person mad

Deucalĭ·ōn -ōnis *m* son of Prometheus, who, together with his wife Pyrrha, was the sole survivor of the Deluge

de·unx -uncis *m* eleven twelfths; **heres ex deunce** heir to eleven twelfths

dē·ūrō -ūrĕre -ussī -ustum *vt* to burn up, destroy; (of frost) to nip

de·us -ī (*nom pl*: **deī** or **dī**; *genit pl*: **deōrum** or **deum**) *m* god, deity; (of a person) god, divine being; *m pl* (of persons in high places) the powers that be; **dī boni!** good heavens!; **di hominesque** all the world; **di meliora!** Heaven forbid!; **dis volentibus** with the help of the gods; **di te ament!** bless your little heart!

deustus *pp* of **deuro**

de·ūtor -ūtī -ūsus sum *vi* (with *abl*) to mistreat

dēvast·ō -āre *vt* to devastate, lay waste

dē·vĕhō -vehĕre -vexī -vectum *vt* to carry down, carry away, carry off; **devehi** to ride down, sail down

dē·vellō -vellĕre -vellī or **-volsī -vulsum** *vt* to pluck off

dēvēl·ō -āre *vt* to unveil

dēvenĕr·or -ārī -ātus sum *vt* to reverence, worship; to avert by prayer

dē·venĭō -venīre -vēnī -ventum *vi* to come down, arrive; (with *acc* of extent of motion or with **ad** or **in** + *acc*) to arrive at, reach; (with **ad** + *acc*) to happen to, befall

dēverbĕr·ō -āre *vt* to thrash soundly

dēvers·or -ārī -ātus sum *vi* to stay as a guest; (with **apud** + *acc*) to stay at the house of

dēvers·or -ōris *m* guest

dēversōrĭŏl·um -ī *n* small inn, motel

dēversōrĭ·us or **dēvorsōrĭ·us -a -um** *adj* of an inn; fit to stay at; **taberna deversoria** inn; *n* inn, hotel

dēverticŭl·um or **dēvorticŭl·um -ī** *n* side road, detour; digression; inn, hotel, tavern; low haunt, dive; refuge

dē·vertō (or **dē·vortō**) **-vertĕre -vertī -versum** or **dē·vertor -vertī -versus sum** *vi* to turn aside, turn away; to stay as guest, spend the night; (with **ad** or **apud** + *acc*) to stay with or at the house of; (with **ad** + *acc*) to have recourse to, resort to

dēvex·us -a -um *adj* inclining, sloping, steep; (with **ad** + *acc*) prone to, inclined to

dē·vincĭō -vincīre -vinxī -vinctum *vt* to tie up, clamp; (fig) to bind fast, obligate, unite closely; **se vino devincire** (coll) to get tight

dē·vincō -vincĕre -vicī -victum *vt* to conquer, subdue

dēvinct·us -a -um *pp* of **devincio**; *adj* (with *dat*) strongly attached to

dēvītātǐ·ō -ōnis *f* avoidance

dēvīt·ō -āre *vt* to avoid

dēvǐ·us -a -um *adj* out of the way, off the beaten track; devious; living apart, solitary, sequestered; inconsistent

dēvǒc·ō -āre *vt* to call down; to call off, recall, call away; to allure, seduce; **deos ad auxilium devocare** to invoke the gods for help

dēvǒl·ō -āre *vi* to fly down; to fly away; to hasten down, hasten away

dē·volvō -volvěre -volvī -volūtum *vt* to roll down; **ad spem inanem pacis devolvi** to fall back on false hopes of peace; **devolvi** to roll down, go tumbling down, sink down

dēvǒr·ō -āre *vt* to devour, gulp down; to consume, waste, squander (*money, etc.*); (of the sea) to engulf, swallow up; to swallow, mumble (*words*); to repress (*tears*); to bear with patience

dēvor- = dever-

dēvortǐ·a -ōrum *n pl* side roads, detour

dēvōtǐ·ō -ōnis *f* self-sacrifice; cursing, outlawing; incantation, spell; **capitis devotio** or **vitae devotio** sacrifice of one's life

dēvōt·ō -āre *vt* to lay a spell on, bewitch, jinx

dēvōt·us -a -um *pp* of **devoveo**; *adj* devoted, faithful; accursed; (with *dat*) a devoted to, faithful to; **b** addicted to, given to (*wine, drinking*)

dē·voveō -vovēre -vōvī -vōtum *vt* to devote, vow, sacrifice, dedicate; to mark out, doom, destine; to curse, execrate; to bewitch; **se devovere dis** to devote oneself to death

dēvulsus *pp* of **devello**

dext·ans -antis *m* five sixths

dextell·a -ae *f* little right hand; right-hand man

dext·er -ěra -ěrum or **-ra -rum** *adj* right, on the right side; handy, dexterous; lucky, propitious, favorable; opportune, right; *f* right hand; right side, the right; **a dextra laevaque** to the right and left, right and left, everywhere; **dextrā** with the right hand; (fig) with valor; **dextrā** (with *acc*) to the right of; **dextram dare** or **dextram tendere** to give a pledge of friendship; **dextram renovare** to renew a solemn pledge

dextěrē or **dextrē** *adv* dexterously, skillfully; **dextre fortunā uti** (fig) to play the cards right

dexterit·ās -ātis *f* dexterity, adroitness; readiness

dextrorsus or **dextrorsus** or **dextrōvorsum** *adv* to the right, towards the right side

dī see **deus**

Dī·a -ae *f* ancient name of the island of Naxos; mother of Mercury

diabathrār·ǐus -ǐī or **-ī** *m* shoemaker

diadēm·a -ātis *n* diadem

diaet·a -ae *f* diet; living room

dialectǐcē *adv* logically

dialectǐc·us -a -um *adj* dialectical; *m* dialectician; *f* dialectics, logic; *n pl* dialectics, logical discussions

dialect·os -ī *f* dialect

Diāl·is -e *adj* of Jupiter; of Jupiter's high priest; **apex Dialis** high priest's miter; **conjux Dialis** high priest's wife; **flamen Dialis** high priest of Jupiter

dialǒg·us -ī *m* dialogue, conversation

Diān·a or **Dīān·a -ae** *f* Diana (*goddess of hunting, patroness of virginity, of the moon as Luna, of childbirth as Lucina, and of incantations and magic as Hecate*); (fig) Diana's temple; (fig) moon; **iracunda Diana** lunacy

diārǐ·a -ōrum *n pl* daily ration

dibǎph·us -ī *f* crimson robe; official robe of magistrate

dic·a -ae *f* lawsuit, case, judicial process, judicial proceedings; **dicam scribere** (with *dat*) **to sue** (*oomeone*); **sortiri dicas** to select a jury

dicācǐt·ās -ātis *f* wittiness, sarcasm

dicǎcǔl·us -a -um *adj* quick-witted, sharp

dicātǐ·ō -ōnis *f* declaration of intent of becoming a citizen

dic·ax -ācis *adj* witty, sharp, sarcastic, caustic; pert

dichorē·us -ī *m* double trochee

dicǐ·ō -ōnis *f* jurisdiction, sway, authority, control, rule, dominion, sovereignty; **in dicione esse** (with *genit*) or **sub dicione esse** (with *genit*) to be under the control of, be subject to, be under the jurisdiction of; **in dicionem redigere** (with *genit*) or **dicioni subjicere** (with *genit*) to bring (*someone*) under the control of

dicis causā or **grātiā** *adv* for show, for the sake of appearances

dic·ō -āre *vt* to dedicate, consecrate; to deify; to inaugurate; to set apart, devote; (with *dat*) to devote (*e.g., time, energy*) to; **se dicare** (with *dat* or **in** + *acc*) to dedicate oneself to

dīcō dīcěre dixī dictum *vt* to say, tell; to indicate, mention, specify, point out; to nominate, appoint; to fix, set, appoint (*day or date*); to speak, deliver, recite; to pronounce, utter, articulate; to call, name; to assert, affirm; to describe, relate, celebrate; to tell, predict; (with double *acc*) to appoint (*someone*) as; **causam dicere** to plead or defend a case; **diem dicere** (with *dat*) to set a date for; **facete dictum!** well put!; **sententiam dicere** to express an opinion; **testimonium dicere** to give evidence

dicrŏt·um -ī n bireme

dictamn·us -ī f dittany (wild marjoram, growing in abundance on Mt. Dicte in Crete)

dictāt·a -ōrum n pl lessons, rules; dictation

dictāt·or -ōris m dictator (emergency magistrate in Rome with absolute authority, legally appointed for a maximum six-month term); chief magistrate (of Italic town)

dictātōri·us -a -um adj dictatorial

dictātr·ix -īcis f mistress of ceremonies

dictātūr·a -ae f dictatorship

Dict·ē -ēs f mountain in Crete where Jupiter was hidden in a cave from his father Saturn

dicti·ō -ōnis f saying, speaking, uttering; diction, style; conversation; oracular response, prediction; **dictio causae** defense of a case; **dictio testimoni** right to give testimony; **juris dictio** administration of justice; jurisdiction

dictit·ō -āre vt to keep saying, to state emphatically; **causas dictitare** to practice law; **ut dictitabat** as he used to say, as he continually alleged

dict·ō -āre vt to say repeatedly, reiterate; to dictate; to compose; to suggest, remind

dict·us -a -um pp of **dīco**; n saying word, statement; witticism; maxim, proverb; prediction, prophecy; order, command, instruction; promise, assurance

Dictynn·a -ae f Diana

dī·dō or **dis·dō -děre -dīdī -dĭtum** vt to publicize, broadcast, disseminate; to distribute, hand out

Dīd·ō -ūs (acc: **Dīdō**) f daughter of Tyrian king Belus, sister of Pygmalion, foundress and queen of Carthage, also called Elissa

dī·dūcō -dūcĕre -duxī -ductum vt to draw apart, part, sever, separate, split; to undo, untie; to divide, distribute; to scatter, disperse; (in mathematics) to divide; **animus dīductus** (with abl) the mind torn between (alternatives)

diēcŭl·a -ae f little while

diērect·us -a -um adj (coll) finished, done for; **i dierectus** or **abi dierectus!** go to the devil!

di·ēs -ēī m or f day; time, period, space of time, interval; daylight, light of day; anniversary; daybreak; season; **dicere diem** (with dat) to impeach, bring an accusation against; **diem ex die** from day to day, day after day; **diem noctemque** day and night, uninterruptedly; **dies meus** my birthday; **in diem** for the moment; for a future day; **in dies** (more and more) every day; **multo denique die** not till

late in the day; **postridie ejus diei** the day after that; **post tertium ejus diei** two days after that

Diespit·er -ris m Jupiter

diffām·ō -āre vt to divulge (something); to defame (someone)

differenti·a -ae f difference, diversity; specific difference, species

differit·ās -ātis f difference

diffĕrō differre distŭlī dīlātum vt to carry in different directions; to scatter, disperse; to publicize, spread around, divulge; to defer, postpone, delay; to humor; to get rid of, put off; to distract, disquiet; vi to differ, be different, be distinguished; (with ab + abl) to differ from

differt·us -a -um adj stuffed, crowded, overcrowded

difficĭl·is -e adj difficult, hard; surly, cantankerous; hard to manage, hard to please

difficĭliter adv with difficulty, barely

difficult·ās -ātis f difficulty, hardship, trouble, distress; surliness; poverty, financial embarrassment

difficulter adv with difficulty, barely

diffīd·ens -entis adj diffident, anxious, nervous

diffīdenter adv without confidence, distrustfully

diffīdenti·a -ae f diffidence, mistrust, distrust

dif·fīdō -fīdĕre -fīsus sum vi (with dat) to distrust, despair of

dif·findō -findĕre -fĭdī -fissum vt to split, split apart, divide; (law) **diem diffindere** to cut short the business day; (fig) to detract

dif·fingō -ĕre vt to form differently, remodel; to alter

diffissus pp of **diffindo**

diffit·ĕor -ērī vt to disavow, disown

diffl·ō -āre vi to blow away; to disperse

diffŭ·ō -ĕre vi to flow in different directions, flow away; to dissolve, melt away, disappear; (with abl) to wallow in (luxury, vice)

dif·fringō -fringĕre — -fractum vt to shatter, break apart, smash

dif·fugiō -fugĕre -fūgī vi to flee in different directions; to disperse; to disappear

diffug·ĭum -iī or **-ī** n dispersion

diffundit·ō -āre vt to pour out, scatter; to waste

dif·fundō -fundĕre -fūdī -fūsum vt to pour, pour out; to scatter, diffuse, spread, extend; to give vent to; to cheer up, gladden

diffūsē adv diffusely; fully, at length, in detail

diffūsil·is -e adj diffusive, expanding

diffūs·us -a -um pp of **diffundo**; adj spread out, spread abroad; wide; prolix; protracted

diffutūt·us -a -um adj exhausted by excessive sexual indulgence

Dīgentĭ·a -ae f small stream on Horace's Sabine farm

dī·gĕrō -gĕrĕre -gessī -gestum vt to spread about, distribute, divide; to arrange, assort, catalogue; to interpret; to digest

dīgestĭ·ō -ōnis f arrangement; (rhet) enumeration

dīgestus pp of **digero**

dīgĭtŭl·us -ī m little finger

dīgĭt·us -ī m finger; inch (one sixteenth of a Roman foot); toe; **caelum digito attingere** to reach the heights of happiness, be thrilled; **digitis concrepare** to snap the fingers; **digito uno attingere** to touch lightly, touch tenderly; **digitum intendere** (with **ad** + acc) to point the finger at; **digitus pollex** thumb; **in digitos arrectus** on tiptoe; **minimus digitus** little finger

dīglădĭ·or -ārī -ātus sum vi to fight hard

dīgnātĭ·ō -ōnis f esteem, respect; dignity, honor

dīgnē adv worthily, fitly

dīgnĭt·ās -ātis f worth, worthiness; dignity; authority, rank, reputation, distinction, majesty; self-respect; dignitary; political office; dignity (of style)

dīgn·ō -āre or **dīgn·or -ārī -ātus sum** vt to think worthy; (with abl) to think worthy of; (with double acc) to think (someone) worthy of being (e.g., a son)

dīgnōsc·ō or **dīnōsc·ō -ĕre** vt to distinguish; (with abl) to distinguish (someone) from; **dominum ac servum dignoscere** to know the difference between master and slave

dīgn·us -a -um adj worthy, deserving (person); fit, adequate, suitable, deserved, proper; (with abl) worthy of

dī·grĕdĭor -grĕdī -gressus sum vi to move apart, separate; to deviate; to digress

dīgressĭ·ō -ōnis f parting, separation; deviation; digression

dīgressus pp of **digredior**

dīgress·us -ūs m departure; digression

dījūdĭcātĭ·ō -ōnis f decision

dījūdĭc·ō -āre vt to decide, settle; **vera et falsa dijudicare** or **vera a falsis dijudicare** to distinguish between truth and falsehood

dījun = **disjun**

dī·lābor -lābī -lapsus sum vi to fall apart, break up; (of ice, etc.) to break up, dissolve; to disperse; to break up, decay; (of time) to slip away; (of water) to flow in different directions

dīlacĕr·ō -āre vt to tear to pieces

dīlāmĭn·ō -āre vt to split in two; **nuces dilaminare** to crack nuts

dīlanĭ·ō -āre vt to tear to pieces

dīlăpĭd·ō -āre vt to demolish (a structure of stone); to squander

dīlapsus pp of **dilabor**

dīlarg·ĭor -īrī -ītus sum vt to hand out generously, lavish

dīlātĭ·ō -ōnis f postponement, delay

dīlāt·ō -āre vt to dilate, stretch, broaden, extend, enlarge; (fig) to amplify, spread, extend; to drawl out

dīlāt·or -ōris m procrastinator, slowpoke

dīlātus pp of **differo**

dīlaud·ō -āre vt to praise enthusiastically

dīlect·us -a -um pp of **diligo**; adj beloved

dīlect·us -ūs m selection; (mil) selective service, draft; draftees; recruitment; **dilectum habere** to conduct a draft; **legiones ex novo dilectu conficere** to bring the legions to full strength with new draftees

dīlĭg·ens -entis adj careful, conscientious, accurate; exacting, strict; thrifty, industrious; (with genit) observant of; (with **ad** + acc or with **in** + abl) careful in, careful to, conscientious about

dīlĭgenter adv carefully, diligently, industriously

dīlĭgentĭ·a -ae f diligence, care, industry, attentiveness, faithfulness; economy, frugality; (with genit) regard for

dī·lĭgō -lĭgĕre -lexī -lectum vt to single out; to esteem, love, value, prize; to approve, be content with, appreciate

dīlōrīc·ō -āre vt to tear open

dīlū·ĕō -ĕre vi to be clear, be evident; (with dat) to be obvious to

dī·lūcescō -lūcescĕre -luxī vi to grow light, dawn

dīlūcĭdē adv clearly, distinctly, plainly

dīlūcĭd·us -a -um adj clear, distinct, plain, evident

dīlūcŭl·um -ī n daybreak, dawn

dīlūd·ĭum -ĭī or **-ī** n intermission

dīl·ŭō -ŭĕre -ŭī -ūtum vt to wash away, break up, separate; to dilute; to get rid of (worries, annoyances); to atone for; to explain, solve

dīluvĭ·ēs -ēī f inundation, flood, deluge

dīluvĭ·ō -āre vt to inundate, flood, deluge

dīluv·ĭum -ĭī or **-ī** n flood, deluge; (fig) destruction

dīmān·ō -āre vi to flow in different directions; (fig) to spread around

dīmensĭ·ō -ōnis f measurement

dī·mētĭor -mētīrī -mensus sum vt to measure out, measure off; to count off

dīmēt·ō -āre or **dīmēt·or -ārī -ātus sum** vt to measure out, mark out (area)

dīmĭcātĭ·ō -ōnis f fight, combat, struggle; contest, rivalry

dīmic·ō -āre *vi* to fight, struggle; to be in conflict, run a risk, be in peril; (with **cum** + *abl*) to fight against; **de capite dimicare** or **de vita dimicare** to fight for one's life

dīmidiāt·us -a -um *adj* half, in half

dīmidi·us -a -um *adj* half; broken in two, broken; **dimidius patrum, dimidius plebis** half patrician, half plebeian; *n* half; **dimidium quam** half as many soldiers as

dīmissi·ō -ōnis *f* dismissal, discharging, sending out

dī·mittō -mittĕre -mīsī -missum *vt* to send away, send around, send out, scatter, distribute; to break up, dismiss, disband; (mil) to discharge; to let loose; to divorce (*wife*); to leave, desert, abandon, give up, relinquish; to let go, let slip, forgo, forsake, renounce; to remit

dīminnū·ō or **dīminŭ·ō -ĕre** *vt* to break to pieces, smash, shatter

dī·moveō -movēre -mōvī -mōtum *vt* to move apart, part, separate; to disperse, dismiss, scatter; to lure away

Dindymēn·ē -ēs *f* Cybele (*also called Magna Mater by the Romans*)

Dindym·us -ī *m* or **Dindym·a -ōrum** *n pl* mountain in Asia Minor, sacred to Cybele

dīnoscō see **dignosco**

dīnumerāti·ō -ōnis *f* enumeration, counting up

dīnumer·ō -āre *vt* to enumerate, count up, compute; to count out, pay

diōbolār·is -e *adj* costing two obols

Diodŏt·us -ī *m* Stoic philosopher and tutor of Cicero (*d. 59 B.C.*)

dioecēs·is -is *f* district, governor's jurisdiction

dioecēt·ēs -ae *m* treasurer; secretary of revenue

Diogĕn·ēs -is *m* famous Ionic philosopher and pupil of Anaximenes (*5th cent. B.C.*); Cynic philosopher, born at Sinope, in Pontus (412?-323 B.C.)

Diomēd·ēs -is *m* son of Tydeus and king of Argos; hero at Troy

Diōn·ē -ēs or **Diōn·a -ae** *f* mother of Venus

Dionȳsi·a -ōrum *n pl* Greek festival of Bacchus

Dionȳsi·us -ī *m* tyrant of Syracuse (430-367 B.C.); Dionysus the Younger (397-330?)

Dionȳs·us or **Dionȳs·os -ī** *m* Bacchus

diōt·a -ae *f* two-handled wine jar

diplōm·a -ătis *n* official letter of recommendation

Dipȳl·on -ī *n* N.W. gate at Athens

Dīr·a -ae *f* a Fury; *f pl* the Furies (*goddesses of revenge and remorse*)

dir·ae -ārum *f pl* curse, execration

Dircae·us -a -um *adj* Dircean, Boeotian; **cycnus Dircaeus Dir-**

cean or Boeotian swan (*i.e., Pindar, famous lyric poet from Boeotia, 522?-442 B.C.*)

Dirc·ē -ēs *f* famous fountain in Boeotia

direct·us -a -um *pp* of **dirigo**; *adj* straight, direct; straightforward

diremptus *pp* of **dirimo**

dirempt·us -ūs *m* separation

direpti·ō -ōnis *f* plundering, pillaging; *f pl* acts of pillage

dirept·or -ōris *m* plunderer

direptus *pp* of **diripio**

dirib·ĕō -ēre — -ĭtum *vt* to sort (*votes taken out of the ballot box*)

diribiti·ō -ōnis *f* sorting

diribĭt·or -ōris *m* sorter (*of ballots*)

diribitōr·ium -lī or **-ī** *n* sorting room

dī·rĭgō -rigĕre -rexī -rectum *vt* to put in order, arrange, line up, deploy

dir·imō -imĕre -ēmī -emptum *vt* to take apart, part, separate, divide; to break off, disturb, interrupt; to separate, dissolve; to put off, delay; to break off, end, bring to an end; to nullify, bring to naught

dī·ripiō -ripĕre -ripŭī -reptum *vt* to tear apart, tear to pieces; to lay waste, pillage, plunder, ravage; to snatch away, tear away; to whip out (*sword*); to steal

dīrĭt·ās -ātis *f* mischief; misfortune; cruelty

dī·rumpō or **dis·rumpō -rumpĕre -rupī -ruptum** *vt* to break to pieces, smash, shatter; to break off (*friendship*); to sever (*ties*); **dirumpi** to burst (*with laughter, envy, indignation, etc.*)

dirŭ·ō -ĕre -ī -tum *vt* to pull apart, demolish, destroy, overthrow; to scatter, disperse; (mil) to break up (*enemy formation*); to bankrupt

dīr·us -a -um *adj* fearful, awful; ominous, ill-omened; dreadful, awful, abominable; cruel, relentless, fierce; **temporibus diris** in the reign of terror; **venena dira** deadly poisons

dī·s -tis *adj* rich, wealthy; rich, fertile (*land*); rich, generous, expensive (*offerings*); (with *abl*) abounding in

Dī·s -tis *m* Pluto (*king of the lower world*)

dis·cēdō -cēdĕre -cessī -cessum *vi* to go away, depart; to separate, be severed; to disperse, scatter, be dissipated, disappear; (mil) to march off, break camp; to come off (*victorious, etc.*); to deviate; to swerve; to pass away, vanish, cease; (with **ab** + *abl*) **a** to forsake (*e.g., friends*); **b** to deviate from, swerve from; **c** to abandon, give up; (with **ex** or **de** + *abl*) to go away from, depart from; (with **ad** + *acc*) to depart for; (with **in** + *acc*) to vote for; **discedere in Catonis sen-**

tentiam to vote for Cato's proposal

disceptāti·ō -ōnis f dispute, difference of opinion; discussion, debate

disceptāt·or -ōris m or **disceptā-tr·ix -īcis** f arbitrator

discept·ō -āre vt to debate, dispute, discuss, treat; to decide, settle (controversies, wars); vi to act as umpire; to be at stake

dis·cernō -cernĕre -crēvī -crētum vt to separate, mark off, divide; to keep apart; to distinguish between; to discern, make out, distinguish

dis·cerpō -cerpĕre -cerpsī -cerptum vt to tear to pieces, mangle, mutilate; (fig) to tear apart (with words, arguments)

discessi·ō -ōnis f separation, division; separation, divorce; (in the senate) division, formal vote; **discessio sine ulla varietate** unanimous vote

discess·us -ūs m separation, parting; going away, departure; banishment; marching away, marching off

discid·ium -iī or **-ī** n parting, separation; discord, dissension, disagreement; divorce

discīd·ō -ĕre vt to cut to pieces, cut up

discinct·us -a -um pp of **discingo**; adj without a girdle; dissolute, loose; effeminate, voluptuous

di·scindō -scindĕre -scīdī -scissum vt to tear apart, tear open, rend, tear; **amicitias discindere** to break off ties of friendship

dis·cingō -cingĕre -cinxī -cinctum vt to take off, ungird; to loose; (fig) to relax

disciplīn·a -ae f instruction, training, teaching, education; learning, knowledge, science; discipline; custom, habit; system; **militaris disciplina** basic training; **rei publicae disciplina** statesmanship

discipŭl·us -ī m or **discipŭl·a -ae** f pupil, student; disciple, follower

discissus pp of **discindo**

dis·clūdō -clūdĕre -clūsī -clūsum vt to keep apart, divide, shut off; **iram et cupiditatem locis discludere** to assign anger and passion to their proper places

discō discĕre didĭcī vt to learn, learn to know, become acquainted with; to be told (e.g., the truth); (with inf) to learn how to

discobŏl·us -ī m discus thrower

discŏl·or -ōris adj of a different color; different; (with dat) different from

discondūc·ō -ĕre vi to be unprofitable

disconven·iō -īre vi to disagree; to be inconsistent

discordābĭl·is -e adj discordant, disagreeing

discordi·a -ae f discord, dissension, disagreement; mutiny

discordiōs·us -a -um adj prone to discord, seditious

discord·ō -āre vi to quarrel, disagree; (with dat or ab + abl) to be out of harmony with, be opposed to

discor·s -dis adj discordant, inharmonious; disagreeing, at variance; contradictory, inconsistent; warring (winds, etc.); (with abl) inconsistent with, at variance with, different from

discrepantĭ·a -ae f discrepancy, dissimilarity, difference

discrepāti·ō -ōnis f disagreement, dispute

discrepit·ō -āre vi to be completely different

discrep·ō -āre -ŭī vi to be different in sound, sound different; to be out of tune; to disagree, be different, be inconsistent, vary, differ; to be disputed; (with dat or abl or with ab or cum + abl) to disagree with, be different from, be inconsistent with; v impers there is a difference of opinion, it is undecided, it is a matter of dispute; **discrepat inter scriptores rerum** there is a difference of opinion among historians

di·scrībō -scrībĕre -scripsī -scriptum vt to distribute, classify, divide; to assign, apportion; (with in + acc) to distribute among, divide among

discrīm·en -ĭnis n dividing line; interval, intervening space, division, distance, separation; discrimination, difference, distinction; critical moment, turning point; decision, determination; crisis, jeopardy, peril, danger, risk; decisive battle

discrimin·ō -āre vt to divide, separate; to apportion

discriptē adv orderly, lucidly, distinctly

discripti·ō -ōnis f distribution, classification

discript·us -a -um pp of **discribo**; adj well arranged; secluded

discrucĭ·ō -āre vt to torture; to distress, torment

dis·cumbō -cumbĕre -cubŭī -cubitum vi to take their places at the table; (of several) to go to bed

discup·iō -ĕre vt (coll) to want badly; (with inf) (coll) to be dying to

dis·currō -currĕre -cucurrī or **-currī -cursum** vi to run in different directions, scamper about, run up and down, dash around

discurs·us -ūs m running up and down, running about; (mil) pincer movement

disc·us -ī m discus

dis·cutiō -cutĕre -cussī -cussum vt to knock apart; to smash to pieces, shatter; to break up, disperse, scatter, dispel; to frustrate, bring to naught; to suppress, destroy

disertē or **disertim** adv eloquently

disert·us -a -um adj fluent, well-spoken; clear, articulate

disject·ō -āre vt to toss about

disject·us -a -um pp of **disjicio**; adj scattered; dilapidated

disject·us -ūs m scattering

dis·jiciō -jicĕre -jēcī -jectum vt to drive apart, scatter, break up; to tear to pieces; to ruin, destroy; to thwart, frustrate, wreck; (mil) to break up (*enemy formation*)

disjuncti·ō or **dijuncti·ō -ōnis** f separation, alienation; diviation, variation; dilemma; asyndeton (*succession of clauses without conjunctions*)

disjunct·us -a -um adj separate, distinct; distant, remote; disjointed, disconnected, incoherent (*speech*); logically opposed; n pl opposites

dis·jungō or **di·jungo -jungĕre -junxī -junctum** vt to unyoke; to sever, divide, part, remove; to separate, part, estrange, disunite, alienate

dispalesc·ō -ĕre vi to be divulged, spread

dispāl·or -ārī -ātus sum vi to wander about, straggle

dis·pandō (or **dis·pendō**) **-pandĕre — -pansum** (or **dis·pennō -pennĕre — -pessum**) vt to stretch out, extend; to spread out, expand

dis·pār -păris adj different, unlike; unequal, ill-matched; unequal, of different lengths

disparíl·is -e adj different, dissimilar

disparíliter adv differently

dispăr·ō -āre vt to separate, segregate

dispartiō or **dispartior** see **dispertio**

dispectus pp of **dispicio**

dis·pellō -pellĕre -pŭlī -pulsum vt to disperse, scatter; to drive away, dispel

dispend·ium -iī or **-ī** n expense, cost; loss

dispendō see **dispando**

dispennō see **dispando**

dispensāti·ō -ōnis f weighing out, doling out; management, superintendence, direction, administration; position of superintendent or treasurer

dispensāt·or -ōris m household manager, chief butler; cashier, treasurer

dispens·ō -āre vt to weigh out, pay out; to distribute, manage (*household stores*); to regulate, manage, superintend

dispercut·iō -ĕre vt to knock out; cerebrum dispercutere (with dat) (coll) to knock out (*someone's*) brains

disper·dō -dĕre -didī -ditum vt to spoil, ruin; to squander

disper·eō -īre -iī vi to go to ruin; to go to waste; to be undone, perish; disperiil (coll) I'm finished; dispeream si (coll) I'll be darned if

di·spergō -spergĕre -spersī -sper-sum vt to scatter about, disperse; to splatter; to distribute, scatter (*e.g., men*) without organization; to spread, extend (*war, rumor, etc.*)

disperse adv here and there; occasionally

dispersus pp of **dispergo**

dispert·iō -īre -īvī or **-iī -ītum** or **dispert·ior** or **dispart·ior -īrī -ītus sum** vt to distribute, divide; to assign (*e.g., gates, areas*) as posts to be guarded

dispessus pp of **dispando**

di·spiciō -spicĕre -spexī -spectum vt to see clearly, make out, distinguish, detect; to consider carefully, perceive, detect, discern, discover, reflect on

displic·eō -ēre -uī -itum vi to be unpleasant, be displeasing; (with dat) to displease; sibi displicere to be dissatisfied with oneself; to be in a bad humor

dis·plōdō -plōdĕre — -plōsum vi to explode

dis·pōnō -pōnĕre -posŭī -positum vt to place here and there; to distribute, arrange, set in order; to station, post, assign; to adjust, order, dispose; diem disponere to arrange the day's schedule

dispositē adv orderly, methodically

dispositi·ō -ōnis f orderly arrangement, development (*of theme, essay*)

dispositūr·a -ae f orderly arrangement

disposít·us -a -um pp of **dispono**; adj well arranged; methodical, orderly

disposít·us -ūs m orderly arrangement

dispŭd·et -ēre -ŭit v impers (with inf) it is a great shame to

dispulsus pp of **dispello**

dis·pungō -pungĕre -punxī -punctum vt to check, balance, audit (*an account*)

disputāti·ō -ōnis f arguing; argument, debate

disputāt·or -ōris m disputant, debater

dispŭt·ō -āre vt to dispute, discuss; (com) to estimate, compute; to examine, treat, explain

disquīr·ō -ĕre vt to examine in detail

disquīsīti·ō -ōnis f inquiry, investigation

disrumpō see **dirumpo**

dissaep·iō -īre -sī -tum vt to separate, wall off, fence off

dissaept·um -ī n partition, barrier

dissāvi·or or **dissuāvi·or -ārī -ātus sum** vt to kiss passionately

dissĕc·ō -āre -uī -tum vt to cut apart, dissect

dissēmin·ō -āre vt to disseminate

dissensi·ō -ōnis f difference of opinion, disagreement; dissension; conflict, incompatibility

dissens·us -ūs m dissension, discord

dissentāne·us -a -um *adj* disagreeing, contrary

dis·sentiŏ -sentīre -sensī -sensum *vi* to differ in opinion, disagree, dissent; to differ, be in conflict, be inconsistent; (with *dat* or with **ab** or **cum** + *abl*) to differ with, disagree with; (with **ab** + *abl*) to differ from, be opposed to

disserēn·at -āre *v impers* it is clearing up

dis·serŏ -serĕre -sēvī -situm *vt* to scatter; to sow here and there; to stick in the ground at intervals

disser·ō -ĕre -ŭī -tum *vt* to arrange; to examine; to discuss, argue, treat

disserp·ŏ -ĕre *vi* to creep about; to spread gradually

dissertī·ō -ōnis *f* gradual abolition, severance

dissert·ō -āre *vt* to discuss, treat

dissertus *pp* of **dissero** (to arrange)

dis·sidĕō -sidēre -sēdī -sessum *vi* to be located far apart, be distant, be remote; to disagree, be at variance; to differ, be unlike; (of a garment) to be on crooked; (with **ab** or **cum** + *abl*) to disagree with

dissignāti·ō -ōnis *f* arrangement

dissignāt·or -ōris *m* master of ceremonies; usher (*at the theater*); undertaker

dissign·ō -āre *vt* to regulate, arrange; to contrive

dissil·iō -īre -ŭī *vi* to fly apart, split, break up, burst; to be dissolved

dissimil·is -e *adj* dissimilar, unlike, different; (with *genit* or *dat* or with **atque** or **ac**) to be dissimilar to, different from

dissimiliter *adv* differently

dissimilitūd·ō -inis *f* difference

dissimulanter *adv* secretly, slyly

dissimulanti·a -ae *f* faking, hiding, dissembling

dissimulāti·ō -ōnis *f* concealing, disguising; Socratic irony

dissimulāt·or -ōris *m* dissembler, faker

dissimul·ō -āre *vt* to dissemble, conceal, disguise; to keep secret; to pretend not to see, ignore

dissipābil·is -e *adj* diffusible, dispersible

dissipāti·ō -ōnis *f* scattering, dispersal, dissipation; destruction

dissip·ō or **dissup·ō -āre** to scatter, disperse; to break up (*enemy formation*); to demolish, overthrow; to squander, dissipate; to circulate, spread; to drive away (*worries*)

dissit·us *pp* of **dissero** (to scatter)

dissociābil·is -e *adj* separating, estranging; incompatible

dissociāti·ō -ōnis *f* separation

dissoci·ō -āre *vt* to dissociate, separate; to ostracize; to set at variance, estrange; to divide into factions; to detach

dissolūbil·is -e *adj* dissoluble, separable

dissolūtē *adv* disconnectedly, loosely; carelessly

dissolūti·ō -ōnis *f* dissolution, dissolving, breaking up; abolishing, destruction; refutation; looseness, dissoluteness; asyndeton (*succession of clauses without conjunctions*)

dissolūt·us -a -um *adj* disconnected, loose; careless, negligent, remiss; loose, licentious, dissolute; *n* asyndeton (*succession of clauses without conjunctions*)

dis·solvŏ -solvĕre -solvī -solūtum *vt* to dissolve, break up, loosen; to free, release; (fig) to break up; to pay; to refute; to unite; **animam dissolvere** to die; **legem dissolvere** to abrogate or annul a law; **poenam dissolvere** to pay the penalty

dissŏn·us -a -um *adj* dissonant, discordant, jarring, confused (*sounds, voices*); different; (with *abl*) differing from, different from

dissor·s -tis *adj* having a different fate; unshared

dis·suādĕō -suādēre -suāsī -suāsum *vt* to advise against, dissuade, object to, oppose

dissuāsi·ō -ōnis *f* dissuasion; (with *genit*) opposition to, objection to

dissuās·or -ōris *m* objector, opponent

dissuāvior *see* **dissavior**

dissult·ō -āre *vi* to fly apart, burst

dis·suŏ -suĕre — -sūtum *vt* to unstitch; to untie, undo, unfasten

dissūpō *see* **dissipo**

distaed·et -ēre *v impers* it makes (*one*) tired; (with *genit*) it makes (*one*) tired of; **me distaedet loqui** I'm sick and tired of speaking

distanti·a -ae *f* distance, remoteness; difference, diversity

dis·tendŏ (or **dis·tennŏ**) **-tendĕre -tendī -tentum** *vt* to stretch apart, stretch out; to distend, swell; to distract, perplex

distent·us -a -um *pp* of **distendo**; *adj* distended; *pp* of **distineo**; *adj* busy, occupied, distracted

distermin·ō -āre *vt* to separate by a boundary, divide, limit

distich·on -ī *n* couplet

distinctē *adv* distinctly, clearly, with precision

distincti·ō -ōnis *f* distinction, differentiation, discrimination; difference; (gram) punctuation

distinct·us -a -um *pp* of **distinguo**; *adj* distinct, separate; studded, adorned; varied, diversified; lucid (*speaker*); eminent

distinct·us -ūs *m* difference, distinction

dis·tinĕō -tinēre -tinŭī -tentum *vt* to keep apart, separate; to detain, hold back, hinder; to employ, engage, divert; to put off, delay; (mil) to keep (*troops*) from meeting; to keep divided; to stand in the way of (peace, victory, etc.); to distract

di·stinguō -stinguĕre -stinxī -stinctum vt to mark off; to separate, part; to set off (with colors, gold, etc.); to distinguish, specify; to punctuate

dist·ō -āre vi to stand apart, be separate, be distant; to differ, be different; (with dat or ab + abl) to differ from; v impers there is a difference, it is important, makes a difference

dis·torqueō -torquēre -torsī -tortum vt to twist, distort; to curl (lips); to roll (eyes)

distortī·ō -ōnis f twisting; contortion

distort·us -a -um pp of distorqueo; adj distorted, misshapen, deformed; perverse

distractī·ō -ōnis f pulling apart; dividing; discord, dissension

distract·us -a -um adj severed, separate

dis·trahō -trahĕre -traxī -tractum vt to pull or drag apart, separate forcibly; to tear away, drag away, remove; to distract; to sever, break up; to estrange, alienate; to prevent, frustrate; to end, settle (e.g., disputes); to sell at retail, sell (e.g., land) in lots

distrib·uō -uĕre -uī -ūtum vt to distribute

distribūtē adv methodically

distribūtī·ō -ōnis f distribution, apportionment, division

district·us -a -um adj drawn in opposite directions; distracted, busied, engaged

di·stringō -stringĕre -strinxī -strictum vt to draw apart; to distract, draw the attention of

distrunc·ō -āre vt to cut in two, hack apart

disturbātī·ō -ōnis f destruction

disturb·ō -āre vt to throw into confusion; to smash up, demolish; to break up (a marriage); to frustrate

dītesc·ō -ĕre vi to grow rich

dīthyrambīc·us -a -um adj dithyrambic; m dithyramb (song in honor of Bacchus)

dīthyramb·us -ī m dithyramb

dītī·ae -ārum f pl wealth

dīt·ō -āre vt to make rich, enrich; ditari to get rich

diū adv by day, in the daytime; long, for a long time; in a long time; diu noctuque by day and by night, continually; iam diu this long; satis diu long enough

diurn·us -a -um adj of the day, by day, day, daytime; daily, of each day; day's, of one day; acta diurna daily newspaper; merum diurnum daytime drinking; n account book; n pl record, journal, diary

dī·us -a -um adj godlike, divine, noble

diūtĭnē adv for a long time

diūtĭn·us -a -um adj long, lasting

diūtissĭmē adv for a very long time; longest; iam diutissime long, long ago

diūtĭus adv longer, still longer; paulum diutius a little too long

diūturnĭt·ās -ātis f length of time, long duration; durability

diūturn·us -a -um adj long, longlasting

dīv·a -ae f goddess

dīvārĭc·ō -āre vt to stretch out, spread

dī·vellō -vellĕre -vellī -vulsum vt to tear apart, tear to pieces; to tear away; to untie; to wrest, remove, separate; to estrange

dī·vendō -vendĕre — -vendĭtum vt to sell piecemeal, retail

dīverbĕr·ō -āre vt to zip through, fly through

dīverb·ium -iī or -ī n dialogue, verbal exchange

dīversē or **dīvorsē** adv in different directions; differently

dīversĭt·ās -ātis f diversity, difference; contradiction, direct opposite

dīvers·us or **dīvors·us** -a -um pp of diverto; adj in different directions; apart, separate; different; remote, opposite, diametrically opposed; hostile; unsettled, irresolute; dissimilar, distinct; m pl individuals; n opposite direction, different quarter, opposite side, opposite view

dī·vertō or **dī·vortō** -vertĕre -vertī -versum vi to go different ways; to turn off; to stop off, stay

dīv·es -ĭtis adj rich, wealthy; costly, precious; sumptuous; plentiful, abundant; (with genit or abl) rich in, abounding in

dīvex·ō -āre vt to plunder; to violate

dīvidĭ·a -ae f worry, trouble, nuisance; dissension, antagonism

dī·vidō -vidēre -vīsī -vīsum vt to divide, force apart; to divide, distribute, share; to break up, destroy; to arrange, apportion; to separate, distinguish; to separate, segregate, keep apart; to accompany (songs with music); sententiam dividere to break down a proposal (so as to vote on each part separately)

dīvidŭ·us -a -um adj divisible; divided, separated

dīvīnātī·ō -ōnis f clairvoyance; forecasting, predicting, divination; (law) selection of the most suitable prosecutor

dīvīnē adv through divine power; prophetically, by divine inspiration; divinely, gorgeously

dīvīnĭt·ās -ātis f divinity, godhead; prophetic power, clairvoyance; excellence

dīvīnĭtus adv from heaven, from god; providentially; prophetically; divinely, in a godlike manner; excellently

divin·ō -āre *vt* to divine, predict, prophesy, foresee, dread

divin·us -a -um *adj* divine, heavenly; divinely inspired, prophetic; godlike, superhuman, excellent, gorgeous; **divinum jus** natural law; **divinum jus et humanum** natural and positive law; **divinum scelus** sacrilege; **rerum divinarum et humanarum scientia** physics and ethics; **rem divinam facere** to worship; to sacrifice; **res divina** worship; sacrifice; **res divinae** religious affairs; religion; *m* prophet; *n* offering; *n pl* divine matters; religious duties; **agere divina humanaque** to perform religious and secular duties; **divina humanaque** things divine and human, the whole world

divisi·ō -ōnis *f* division, distribution

divis·or -ōris *m* distributer; person hired by a candidate to distribute bribes

divis·us -a -um *pp* of **divido**; *adj* separate, distinct

divis·us -ūs *m* distribution; **divisui facilis** easily divided, easy to divide

diviti·ae -ārum *f pl* riches, wealth; richness (*of soil*); costly things

divolg- = divulg-

divor- = diver-

divort·ium -iī or **-ī** *n* separation; divorce; fork (*of road or river*); **divortium facere cum aliqua** to divorce some woman

divulgāt·us -a -um *adj* common, widespread

divulg·ō -āre *vt* to divulge, spread among the people; to publish (*a book*); to spread, publicize, advertise

divulsus *pp* of **divello**

div·us -a -um *adj* divine; deified; *m* god, deity; *n* sky; the open; **sub divo** out in the open, under the open sky; **sub divum rapere** to bring out in the open

dō dare dedī datum (danit = dat; danunt = dant; dane = dasne; duim = dem) *vt* to give; to offer; to offer, dedicate; to give out, pay (*money*); to bestow, confer; to permit, grant, concede, allow; to give up, hand over; to communicate, tell; to ascribe, impute, assign; to cause, produce, make; to furnish, afford, present; to grant, admit; to administer (*medicine*); to utter, give expression to, announce; **legem dare** to enact a law; **locum dare** (with *dat*) to make way for; **nomen dare** to enlist; **operam dare** to pay attention; **operam dare** (with *dat*) to pay attention to, give or devote attention to, look out for; **poenam** or **poenas dare** to pay the penalty; **se dare** to present oneself; to plunge, rush; **velum dare** to set sail; **veniam dare** to grant pardon

doc·eō -ēre -uī -tum *vt* to teach, instruct; to instruct, give instructions

to; (with double *acc*) to teach (*someone something*); **fabulam docere** to teach a play (*to the actors*), produce a play, put on a play

dochm·ius -iī or **-ī** *m* dochmaic foot (*consisting of a trochee and a cretic*)

docil·is -e *adj* docile, easily taught, teachable; docile, tractable

docilit·ās -ātis *f* docility, aptitude for learning

doctē *adv* learnedly, skillfully; shrewdly, cleverly

doct·or -ōris *m* teacher

doctrin·a -ae *f* teaching, instruction, education, training; lesson; erudition, learning; science

doct·us -a -um *pp* of **doceo**; *adj* learned, skilled, experienced, clever, trained; cunning, shrewd; (with *abl*, with **ad** + *acc*, or in + *abl*) skilled in, experienced in, clever at

document·um -ī or **docūm·en -inis** *n* example, model, pattern; object lesson, warning; evidence, proof

Dōdōn·a -ae *f* town in Epirus, famous for the oracular oak tree sacred to Jupiter

Dōdōnae·us -a -um *adj* of Dodona

dodr·ans -antis *m* three fourths; **heres ex dodrante** heir entitled to three fourths of the estate

dogm·a -ātis *n* doctrine, tenet

dolābr·a -ae *f* picker, mattock

dol·ens -entis *adj* painful, smarting; distressing

dolenter *adv* painfully; with sorrow

dol·eō -ēre -uī -itum *vt* to give pain to, hurt; *vi* to feel pain, be sore, ache, smart; to grieve, be sorry, be hurt; take offense; (with *dat*) to give pain to, afflict, hurt; **caput mihi dolet** I have a headache

dōliār·is -e *adj* fat, tubby

dōliōl·um -ī *n* small barrel

dōl·ium -iī or **-ī** *n* large wine jar

dol·ō -āre *vt* to chop; to beat, beat up, drub; (fig) to hack out (*e.g., a poem*)

dol·ō or **dol·ōn -ōnis** *m* pike; string; fore topsail

Dol·ō -ōnis *m* Dolon (*Trojan spy*)

Dolŏp·es -um *m pl* a people of Thessaly

dol·or -ōris *m* pain, ache, smart; pain, grief, distress, anguish; indignation, resentment, chagrin; pathos; object of grief; **capitis dolor** headache; **dentis dolor** toothache; **esse dolori** (with *dat*) to be a cause of grief or resentment to

dolōsē *adv* shrewdly, slyly

dolōs·us -a -um *adj* wily, cunning, deceitful

dol·us -ī *m* trick, device; deceit, cunning, trickery; **dolus malus** (law) intentional deceit, willful wrong, fraud, malice

domābil·is -e *adj* tameable

domesticātim *adv* at home

domestic·us -a -um *adj* of the house or home; domestic, household;

familiar, private, personal; domestic, native, of one's own country; **bellum domesticum** civil war; *m pl* members of the household or family

domī *adv* at home

domicil·ium -iī or **-ī** *n* residence, home

domin·a or **domn·a -ae** *f* lady of the house; mistress, owner; lady; sweetheart; wife

domin·ans -antis *adj* ruling, holding sway; **nomen dominans** word in its literal sense; *m* ruler

domināti·ō -ōnis *f* mastery; tyranny, despotism, absolute power; *f pl* control, supremacy; rulers

domināt·or -ōris *m* ruler, lord

dominātr·ix -īcis *f* ruler, mistress

domināt·us -ūs *m* absolute rule, sovereignty, tyranny; control, mastery

dominic·us -a -um *adj* of a lord, lord's, master's

Dominic·us -a -um *adj* (eccl) the Lord's

domin·ium -iī or **-ī** *n* absolute ownership; banquet, feast

domin·or -ārī -ātus sum *vi* to be master, be lord, have dominion; to play the master, domineer; (with **in** + *acc* or **in** + *abl*) to lord it over, tyrannize

domin·us -ī *m* owner, proprietor, possessor, master, ruler, lord; ruler, despot, tyrant; commander, chief; entertainer, host

Domin·us -ī *m* (eccl) Lord, Master

domiport·a -ae *f* snail

Domitiān·us -ī *m* T. Flavius Domitianus (*son of Vespasian, brother of Titus, and Roman emperor, 81-96 A.D.*)

domit·ō -āre *vt* to train, break in

domit·or -ōris *m* or **domitr·ix -īcis** *f* tamer

domit·us -ūs *m* taming

dom·ō -āre -uī -itum *vt* to tame, break in; to domesticate; to master, subdue, vanquish, conquer

dom·us -ūs or **-ī** (*dat:* **domuī** or **domō**; *abl:* **domō** or **domū**; *locat:* **domī** rarely **domō** or **domū**; *genit pl:* **domuum** or **domōrum**) *f* house, building, mansion, palace; home, residence, family; native country; philosophical sect; **domī** at home; **domī militiaeque** at home and in the field, in peace and in war; **domum** homewards, home

dōnābil·is -e *adj* worthy of a gift

dōnar·ium -iī or **-ī** *n* gift repository of a temple; sanctuary; altar; votive offering

dōnāti·ō -ōnis *f* donation

dōnatīv·um -ī *n* (mil) bonus

dōnec *conj* while; as long as; until

dōn·ō -āre *vt* to present, bestow, grant, confer; to forgive, pardon; to give up, sacrifice; **aliquem civitate donare** to present someone with citizenship; **civitatem ali-**

cui donare to bestow citizenship on someone

dōn·um -ī *n* gift, present; votive offering, sacrifice; **ultima dona** funeral rites, obsequies

dorc·as -ādis *f* gazelle

Dōr·ēs -um *m pl* Dorians (*one of the four Hellenic tribes*)

Dōric·us or **Dōrici·us -a -um** *adj* Dorian; Greek

Dōr·is -idis *f* daughter of Oceanus, wife of Nereus, and mother of fifty sea nymphs

dorm·iō -īre -īvī or **-iī -ītum** *vi* to sleep; to be inactive, be idle, be lazy

dormītāt·or -ōris *m* dreamer

dormīt·ō -āre *vi* to be sleepy, be drowsy; to nod, fall asleep

dormītōri·us -a -um *adj* for sleeping; **cubiculum dormitorium** bedroom

dors·um -ī *n* back; ridge; reef

dōs dōtis *f* dowry

Dossenn·us -ī *m* hunchback, clown (*well-known character in early Italic comedy*)

dōtāl·is -e *adj* of a dowry, given as a dowry, dotal

dōt·ō -āre *vt* to endow

drachm·a or **drachŭm·a -ae** *f* drachma (*Greek coin approximately the value of a denarius*)

drac·ō -ōnis *m* dragon; huge serpent

Drac·ō -ōnis *m* Dragon (*constellation*); Draco (*Athenian lawgiver, notorious for his severity, c. 621 B.C.*)

dracōnigĕn·us -a -um *adj* sprung from a dragon; **urbs draconigena** Thebes

drāpĕt·a -ae *m* runaway slave

drom·as -ădis *m* dromedary, camel

drom·os -ī *m* Spartan racetrack

Druīd·ēs -um or **Druīd·ae -ārum** *m pl* Druids (*priests and sages of the Gauls and Britons*)

Drūsill·a -ae *f* Livia Drusilla (*second wife of Augustus and mother of Tiberius, 63 B.C.-29 A.D.*)

Drūs·us -ī *m* Livius Drusus (*tribune of the people with C. Gracchus in 122 B.C.*); M. Livius Drusus (*former's son, famous orator and tribune of the people in 91 B.C.*); Nero Claudius Drusus (*son of Livia, brother of Tiberius, 38-9 B.C.*)

Dry·ad -ădis *f* dryad (*wood nymph*)

Dryŏp·es -um *m pl* people of Epirus

dubiē *adv* doubtfully; **haud dubie** undoubtedly, indubitably

dubitābil·is -e *adj* doubtful

dubitanter *adv* doubtingly, hesitantly

dubitāti·ō -ōnis *f* doubt, uncertainty; wavering, hesitancy, irresolution; hesitation, delay; (rhet) pretended embarrassment (*to win over the sympathy of the audience*)

dubit·ō -āre *vt* to doubt; to consider, ponder; *vi* to be doubtful, be in doubt, be uncertain, be perplexed;

to deliberate; to waver, hesitate, delay

dubi·us -a -um *adj* wavering, doubtful, dubious, uncertain, irresolute; dubious, undermined; precarious, critical, adverse, difficult; dim (*light*); overcast (*sky*); indecisive (*battle*); *n* doubt, question; **haud pro dubio habere** to regard as beyond doubt; **in dubium venire** to come in question; **in dubium vocare** to call in question; **procul dubio** beyond doubt, undoubtedly

ducēnāri·us -a -um *adj* receiving a salary of 200,000 sesterces

ducēn·ī -ae -a *adj* two hundred each

ducentēsim·a -ae *f* half percent

ducent·ī -ae -a *adj* two hundred

ducentiēns or **ducentiēs** *adv* two hundred times

dūcō dūcĕre duxī ductum *vt* to lead, guide, direct, conduct; to lead, command; to lead, march; to draw, pull, haul; to draw out, protract, prolong; to put off, stall (*someone*); to pass, spend (*time*); to pull at (*oars*); to mislead, take in, fool, trick; to draw, attract; to draw (*lots*); to draw in, breathe in, inhale; to suck in, drink; to draw, trace; to construct, form, fashion, shape; to run (*a wall from one point to another*); to assume, get (*name*); to lead home, marry (*a woman*); to calculate, compute; to regard, consider, hold, account; to derive, trace (*lineage*); to spin (*wool*); (of a road) to lead, take (*someone*)

ductim *adv* in a continuous stream

ductit·ō -āre *vt* to take home, marry (*a woman*); to lead on, trick, deceive, cheat

duct·ō -āre *vt* to lead; to draw; to accompany, escort

duct·or -ōris *m* leader, commander, general; guide, pilot

duct·us -ūs *m* drawing, conducting; line, row; leadership, command; **oris ductus** facial expression

dūdum *adv* a short time ago, a little while ago; just now; once, formerly; **cum dudum** just as; **haud dudum** not long ago, just now; **jam dudum** for some time; **jam dudum eum exspecto** I have been expecting him; **quam dudum** how long; **ut dudum** just as

Duill·ius or **Duīl·ius -iī** or **-ī** *m* Roman consul who won Rome's first naval engagement against the Carthaginians off Sicily in 260 B.C.

duim see **do**

dulcēd·ō -inis *f* sweetness; pleasantness, charm, delightfulness

dulc·escō -escĕre -uī *vi* to become sweet

dulcicul·us -a -um *adj* rather sweet

dulcif·er -ĕra -ĕrum *adj* full of sweetness, sweet

dulc·is -e *adj* pleasant, charming,

delightful; dear, friendly, kind; sweet

dulciter *adv* agreeably, pleasantly, sweetly

dulcitūd·ō -inis *f* sweetness

dūlicē *adv* like a slave

Dūlich·ium -iī or **-ī** *n* or **Dīlichi·a -ae** *f* island in the Ionian Sea, belonging to the realm of Ulysses

dum *adv* up to now, yet, as yet; now; **age dum!** or **agite dum!** come now!; all right!; **nemo dum** no one yet, no one as yet; **non dum** not yet, not as yet

dum *conj* while, during the time in which; as long as; until; provided that, if only; **dum modo** or **dummodo** provided that, if only; **exspectabam dum rediret** I was waiting for him to return

dūmēt·um -ī *n* thicket, underbrush

dummŏdo *conj* provided that, if only

dūmōs·us -a -um *adj* overgrown with bushes, bushy

dumtaxat *adv* strictly speaking, at least; only, simply, merely

dūm·us -ī *m* bush, bramble

du·o -ae -o *adj* two

duodeciēns or **duodeciēs** *adv* twelve times

duodēcim (indecl) *adj* twelve

duodecim·us -a -um *adj* twelfth

duodēn·ī -ae -a *adj* twelve each, twelve apiece, twelve; a dozen; **duodenis assibus** at twelve percent

duodēquadrāgēsim·us -a -um *adj* thirty-eighth

duodēquadrāgintā (indecl) *adj* thirty-eighth

duodēquinquāgēsim·us -a -um *adj* forty-eighth

duodētrīciens or **duodētrīciēs** *adv* twenty-eight times

duodētrīgintā (indecl) *adj* twenty-eight

duodēvīcēn·ī -ae -a *adj* eighteen each

duodēvīgintī (indecl) *adj* eighteen

duoetvīcēsimān·ī -ōrum *n pl* soldiers of the twenty-second legion

duoetvīcēsim·us -a -um *adj* twenty-second

dnovirī see **duumvirī**

dupl·a -ae *f* double the price

dupl·ex -icis *adj* twofold, double; divided into two; in double rows; double, twice as big, twice as long; complex, compound; two-faced, double-dealing, false

duplicār·ius -iī or **-ī** *m* soldier receiving double pay

dupliciter *adv* doubly, on two accounts

duplic·ō -āre *vt* to double; to bend double; to enlarge, lengthen, increase

dupl·us -a -um *adj* double, twice as much, twice as large; *n* double price; **in duplum** twice the amount, double; **in duplum ire** to pay twice as much, pay double

dupond·ius -iī or **-ī** *m* or **dupond·ium -iī** or **-ī** *n* two-ace coin, worth about five cents

dūrābil·is -e *adj* durable, lasting

dūrām·en -ĭnis *n* hardness

dūrătē·us -a -um *adj* wooden

dūrē or **dūrĭter** *adv* hard, sternly, rigorously, roughly; stiffly, awkwardly

dūr·escō -escĕre -uī *vi* to grow hard, harden

dūrit·ās -ātis *f* hardness, toughness, harshness

dūrĭter see **dure**

dūrĭti·a -ae or **dūritĭ·ēs -ēī** *f* hardness; austerity; strictness, harshness, rigor; oppressiveness; insensibility, callousness

dūriuscŭl·us -a -um *adj* somewhat hard, rather harsh

dūr·ō -āre *vt* to make hard, harden, solidify; (fig) to harden, inure, toughen up; to make insensible, to dull, blunt; to bear, endure; *vi* to be inured, be tough; to endure, last, remain, continue, hold out; (of hills) to continue unbroken, extend

dūr·us -a -um *adj* hard; lasting; rough (*to the senses*); tough, hardy, hale; rough, rude, uncouth; shameless, brazen; harsh, cruel, callous,

insensible; severe, oppressive; parsimonious, miserly

duum·vir -vĭrī *m* member of a commission or board of two

duumvĭrāt·us -ūs *m* duumvirate, office of a duumvir

duumvĭr·ī -ōrum or **duovĭr·ī -ōrum** *m pl* two-man commission; **duumvĭrī ad aedem faciendam** two-man commission for the construction of a temple; **duumvĭrī jūrī dīcundō** two-man board of colonial magistrates; pair of judges; **duumvĭrī navāles** two-man commission to equip the navy; **duumvĭrī perduellĭōnis** criminal court; **duumvĭrī sacrōrum** two-man commission in charge of the Sibyline books

dux ducis *m* or *f* conductor, guide; leader, head, author, ringleader; general

Dym·ās -antis *m* father of Hecuba, the queen of Troy

dynăm·is -is *f* store, plenty

dynast·ēs -ae *m* ruler, prince, petty monarch

Dyrrach·ium -iī or **-ī** *n* Adriatic port in Illyria which served as landing place for those who sailed from Italy

E

ē see **ex**

eā *adv* there, that way

eā ejus *f pron* she

eādem *adv* by the same way, the same way; at the same time; likewise, by the same token

eāpropter *adv* therefore

eapse see **ipse**

eātĕnus *adv* to such a degree, so far

ebēnus see **hebenus**

ēbĭb·ō -ĕre -ī *vt* to drink up, drain; to absorb; to spend in drinks, squander

ēbland·ior -īrī -ītus sum *vt* to coax out, obtain by flattery

Eborăc·um or **Eburăc·um -ī** *n* town of the Brigantes in Britain, York

ēbrĭĕt·ās -ātis *f* drunkenness

ēbrĭŏl·us -a -um *adj* tipsy

ēbrĭōsĭt·ās -ātis *f* habitual drunkenness, heavy drinking

ēbrĭōs·us -a -um *adj & m* drunk

ēbrĭ·us -a -um *adj* drunk; drunken (*acts, words*), of a drunk; (fig) intoxicated (*e.g., with love, power*)

ēbull·ĭō -īre *vt* to brag about; *vi* to bubble up, boil over

ebŭl·um -ī *n* or **ebŭl·us -ī** *m* danewort, dwarf elder

eb·ur -ŏris *n* ivory; ivory objects; statue, flute, scabbard; elephant

eburăt·us -a -um *adj* inlaid with ivory

eburneŏl·us -a -um *adj* ivory

eburnĕ·us or **eburn·us -a -um** *adj* ivory; white as ivory; **ensis eburneus** sword with ivory hilt; **dentes eburnei** tusks (*of elephant*)

ēcastor *interj* by Castor!

ecca see **ecce**

eccam see **ecce**

ecce *interj* see!, look!, look here!, here!; ecce me here I am; (colloquially combined with the pronouns **is**, **ille**, and **iste**): ecca (i.e., ecce + ea) or eccam (i.e., ecce + eam) here she is; eccilla or eccistam there she is; eccillum or eccum here he is; eccos here they are

eccerē *interj* there!

eccheum·a -ătis *n* pouring out

ecclēsĭ·a -ae *f* Greek assembly of people; (eccl) church, congregation

ecdĭc·us -ī *m* legal representative of a community

ecf- = eff-

echidn·a -ae *f* viper

Echidn·a -ae *f* hydra; **Echidna Lernaea** Lernaean hydra; monstrous mother of Cerberus, half woman and half serpent

Echĭnăd·es -um *f pl* cluster of small islands off Acarnania

echīn·us -ī *m* sea urchin; dishpan

Echĭ·ōn -ŏnis *m* hero who sprang from the dragon's teeth sown by

Cadmus, married Agave, and became father of Pentheus

Ech·ō **-ūs** *f* nymph who was changed by Hera into an echo

eclŏg·a **-ae** *f* literary selection; eclogue

eclogāri·ī **-ōrum** *m pl* excerpted literary passages

ecquandō *adv* ever, at any time; (in indirect questions) whether ever

ecquī *conj* whether

ecqu·ī **-ae** or **-od** *adj* any

ec·quid **-cūjus** *pron* anything; (in indirect questions) whether, if at all

ec·quis **-cūjus** *pron* any, anyone; (in indirect questions) whether anyone

ecquō *adv* anywhere

ecul·eus **-ī** *m* foal, colt; small equestrian statue; wooden torture rack

edācit·ās **-ātis** *f* gluttony

ed·āx **-ācis** *adj* gluttonous; (fig) devouring, destructive

ēdent·ō **-āre** *vt* to knock the teeth out of

ēdentŭl·us **-a** **-um** *adj* toothless, old

edēpol *interj* by Pollux!, gad!

edēra see hedera

ē·dīcō **-dīcěre** **-dixī** **-dictum** *vt* to proclaim, announce, decree, ordain, appoint

ēdicti·ō **-ōnis** *f* edict, order

ēdict·ō **-āre** *vt* to proclaim, publish

ēdict·um **-ī** *n* decree, edict, proclamation; edict of a praetor listing rules he would follow in his capacity as judge; order, command

ē·discō **-discěre** **-didicī** *vt* to learn by heart, learn thoroughly

ēdissěr·ō **-ěre** **-ŭī** **-tum** *vt* to explain in detail, analyze fully

ēdissert·ō **-āre** *vt* to explain fully, explain in all details

ēditīci·us **-a** **-um** *adj* set forth, proposed; **judices editicii** panel of jurors (*subject to challenge by the defendant*)

ēditi·ō **-ōnis** *f* statement, account, published statement; publishing, publication; edition (*of a book*); (law) declaration (*of the form of judicial procedure to be followed*)

ēdit·us **-a** **-um** *adj* high; (with *abl*) descended from; *n* height; command, order

e·dō **-děre** **-dĭdī** **-dĭtum** *vt* to give out, put forth, bring forth, emit; to give birth to, bear; to publish; to tell, announce, declare, disclose; to show, display, produce, perform; to bring about, cause; to promulgate

edō **eděre** (or **esse**) **ēdī** **ēsum** *vt* to eat; (fig) to devour, consume, destroy; **pugnos edere** to eat fists, to get a good beating

ēdoc·ěō **-ēre** **-ŭī** **-tum** *vt* to teach thoroughly; to instruct clearly; to inform; to show clearly; (with double *acc*) to teach (*someone something*) well

ēdŏl·ō **-āre** *vt* to chop out, hack out; to finish, prepare

ēdŏm·ō **-āre** **-ŭī** **-ĭtum** *vt* to conquer, subdue

Edōn·ī **-ōrum** *m pl* Thracian tribe noted for its heavy drinking

Edōn·is **-ĭdis** *adj* Edonian; *f* bacchante

ēdorm·iō **-īre** **-īvī** or **iī** *vt* to sleep off; **crapulam edormire** to sleep off a hangover; *vi* to sleep soundly

ēdormisc·ō **-ěre** *vt* to sleep off; **crapulam edormiscere** to sleep off a hangover

ēducāti·ō **-ōnis** *f* rearing; education

ēducāt·or **-ōris** *m* foster father; tutor, instructor

ēducātr·ix **-ícis** *f* nurse

ēdŭc·ō **-āre** *vt* to bring up; to train, educate, develop; to produce

ē·dūcō **-dūcěre** **-duxī** **-ductum** *vt* to draw out; to take away; to draw (*sword*); to draw out, spend (*time*); to lead out, march out (*army*); to summon (*to court*); to hatch; to rear, bring up, educate, train; to raise, erect

edŭl·is **-e** *adj* edible

ēdŭr·ō **-āre** *vi* to last, continue

ēdŭr·us **-a** **-um** *adj* hard, tough; (fig) tough

Eëtī·ōn **-ōnis** *m* father of Andromache and king of Thebe in Cilicia

effarciō see effercio

effāt·us **-a** **-um** *pp* of effor; *adj* solemnly pronounced; solemnly dedicated; *n* axiom; prediction

effecti·ō **-ōnis** *f* accomplishment, performing; efficient cause

effectīv·us **-a** **-um** *adj* producing, practical

effect·or **-ōris** *m* or **effectr·īx** **-īcis** *f* producer, author

effect·us **-a** **-um** *pp* of efficio; *adj* finished, complete; *n* effect

effect·us **-ūs** *m* effecting, completion; operation; effect, result, consequence

effēmināte *adv* effeminately, like a woman

effēmināt·us **-a** **-um** *adj* effeminate

effēmin·ō **-āre** *vt* to make a woman of; to represent as a woman; to effeminate, enervate

efferāt·us **-a** **-um** *adj* wild, brutal, savage

ef·ferciō or **ec·ferciō** or **ef·farciō** **-fercīre** — **-fertum** *vt* to stuff; to fill in (*e.g., a ditch*)

efferit·ās **-ātis** *f* wildness, barbarism

effěr·ō **-āre** *vt* to make wild, brutalize; to exasperate

efferō or **ecferō** **efferre** **extŭlī** **ēlātum** *vt* to carry out, bring out, bring forth; to utter, express; to publish, spread (*news*); to carry out for burial, bury; to produce, bear; to name, designate; to lift up, raise; to promote, advance; to bring out, expose; to praise, extol; to sweep off one's feet; **efferri** (fig) to be carried away; **se efferre** to be haughty, be proud, be conceited

effert·us -a -um *pp* of **effercio**; *adj* full, crammed, bulging

effèr·us -a -um *adj* wild, fierce, savage

ef·fervescō -fervescĕre -fervī *vi* to boil, boil over; to burst forth

efferv·ō -ĕre *vi* to boil over; (of bees) to swarm out; (of volcano) to erupt

effèt·us -a -um *adj* effete, spent; vain, delusive; (with *genit*) incapable of

efficācit·ās -ātis *f* efficiency

efficāciter *adv* efficiently, effectively

effic·ax -ācis *adj* efficient, effective, efficacious

effici·ens -entis *adj* efficient, effective; **res efficientes** causes

efficienter *adv* efficiently

efficienti·a -ae *f* efficiency, efficacy, influence

ef·ficiō -ficĕre -fēcī -fectum *vt* to bring about, bring to pass, effect, cause, produce; to make, form; to finish, complete, accomplish; (of a field) to yield, produce; (of numbers) to amount to; to prove, show; **ita efficitur ut** thus it follows that

effictus *pp* of **effingo**

effigi·ēs -ēī *or* **effigi·a -ae** *f* effigy, likeness, semblance; opposite number; copy, imitation; image; statue, figure, portrait; ghost, phantom

ef·fingō -fingĕre -finxī -fictum *vt* to mold, form, fashion; to imitate; to wipe out, wipe clean; to represent, portray; to imagine

effiō passive of **efficio**

efflāgitātī·ō -ōnis *f* urgent demand

efflāgitāt·us -ūs *m* urgent request; **efflagitatu meo** at my insistence

efflāgit·ō -āre *vt* to demand, insist upon

efflictim *adv* (to love, desire) desperately

efflict·ō -āre *vt* to strike dead

ef·flīgō *or* **ecf·flīgō -flīgĕre -flixī -flictum** *vt* to strike dead, exterminate

effl·ō *or* **ecfl·ō -āre** *vt* to breathe out; **animam efflare** to expire

efflōr·esco -escĕre -ŭī *vi* to bloom, blossom, flourish

effluŭ·ō *or* **ecfluŭ·ō -ĕre -xī** *vi* to flow out, flow forth, run out; to slip away, drop out, disappear; (of a rumor) to get out, circulate; **ex pectore effluere** to be forgotten

effluv·ium -iī *or* **-ī** *n* outlet; **effluvium lacūs** outlet of a lake

ef·fodiō *or* **ecf·fodiō -fodĕre -fōdī -fossum** *vt* to dig up; to gouge out (*eyes*); to root out, gut; to excavate

ef·for *or* **ecf·for -fārī -fātus sum** *vt* to speak out, say out loud, tell; (in augury) to mark off, consecrate (*area*); *vi* to state a proposition

effossus *pp* of **effodio**

effrēnātē *adv* without restraint, out of control

effrēnātĭ·ō -ōnis *f* impetuosity

effrēnāt·us -a -um *adj* unbridled; (fig) unbridled, unrestrained

ef·fringō *or* **ec·fringō -fringĕre -frēgī -fractum** *vt* to break open, smash, break off; to break in (*door*)

ef·fugiō -fugĕre -fūgī *vt* to escape; to escape the notice of; *vi* to escape; (with *abl* or with **ab** or **ex** + *abl*) to escape from

effug·ium -iī *or* **-ī** *n* escape, flight; means of escape; avoidance

ef·fulgĕō -fulgēre -fulsī *vi* to shine forth, gleam, glitter

effult·us -a -um *adj* propped up, supported

ef·fundō *or* **ec·fundō -fundĕre -fūdī -fūsum** *vt* to pour out, pour forth; to fling (*weapon*); to give up, let go, abandon, resign; to throw down; to produce in abundance; to lavish, waste, squander, run through; to empty out (*bags, etc.*); to given vent to, pour out; **effundi** *or* **se effundere** to pour out, rush out; to yield, indulge

effūsē *adv* far and wide; at random, in disorder; lavishly; immoderately

effūsĭ·ō -ōnis *f* outpouring, rushing out; shedding; effusion; profusion, lavishness, extravagance; *f pl* excesses

effūs·us -a -um *pp* of **effundo**; *adj* spread out, extensive, broad, wide; relaxed, loose; disheveled; lavish; straggly, disorderly; lavish; loose, dissolute

effūt·iō -īre — -ītum *vt* & *vi* to blab, babble, chatter

ef·futiō *or* **ec·futiō -futuĕre -futŭī -futūtum** *vt* to exhaust through excesses

ēgelid·us -a -um *adj* chilly, cool; lukewarm

eg·ens -entis *adj* needy, poor; (with *genit*) in need of

egēn·us -a -um *adj* needy, destitute; (with *genit* or *abl*) in need of

eg·ĕō -ēre -ŭī *vi* to be needy, suffer want; (with *genit* or *abl*) **a** to be in need of; **b** to lack, be without; **c** to want, desire, miss

Ēgeri·a -ae *f* nymph whom King Numa visited at night for advice

ē·gĕrō -gerĕre -gessī -gestum *vt* to carry out, take away, remove; to discharge, vomit, emit

egest·ās -ātis *f* need, want, poverty; (with *genit*) lack of

ēgestĭ·ō -ōnis *f* squandering

ēgestus *pp* of **egero**

ego *pron* I

egŏmet *pron* I personally, I and nobody else

ē·gredior -grĕdī -gressus sum *vt* to go beyond, pass; to quit; (fig) to go beyond, surpass; *vi* to go out, come out; to march out; to set sail, put out to sea; to disembark, land; to go up, climb; to digress

ēgregiē *adv* exceptionally, singularly, uncommonly, splendidly

ēgrēgi·us -a -um *adj* exceptional, singular, uncommon; distinguished, illustrious; *n* honor, distinction

ēgressus *pp of* **egredior**

ēgress·us -ūs *m* departure; way out, exit; disembarking, landing; mouth (*of river*); digression; *m pl* comings and goings

ēgurgit·ō -āre *vt* to pour out, lavish

ehem *interj* (expressing pleasant surprise) ha!, aha!

eheu *interj* (expressing pain) oh!

eho *interj* (expressing rebuke) look here!, see here!; **eho dum!** look here now!

ei *interj* (expressing fear or dismay) golly!

ēia or **hēia** *interj* (expressing joy or surpise) ah!, ah ha!; good!; (expressing haste) quick!, come on!

ējacul·or -ārī -ātus sum *vt* to squirt (*e.g.*, water); **se ejaculari** to squirt

ējectāment·a -ōrum *n pl* refuse; jetsam

ējecti·ō -ōnis *f* ejection; banishment, exile

ēject·ō -āre *vt* to spout forth; to keep throwing up (*e.g.*, blood)

eject·us -ūs *m* emission

ējēr·ō or **ējūr·ō āre** *vt* to refuse upon oath, abjure, forswear; to deny on oath; to resign, abdicate; to disown, abandon

ē·iciō -jicĕre -jēcī -jectum *vt* to throw out, drive out, put out, eject, expel; to banish, drive into exile; to utter; to run aground; to reject, disapprove; to boo (*someone*) off the stage; **ejici** to be stranded; **se ejicere** (*of passions*) to break out, come to the fore

ējulāti·ō -ōnis *f* wailing, lamenting

ējul·ō -āre *vi* to wail, lament

ējūrō see **ejero**

ē·lābor -lābī -lapsus sum *vi* to glide off; to slip away, escape; to pass away, disappear; (with *abl* or with **super** + *acc*) to glance off

ēlabōrāt·us -a -um *adj* studied, overdone; elaborate, finished

ēlabōr·ō -āre *vt* to work out, elaborate; to produce; *vi* to make a great effort, take great pains; (with *inf*) to strive to

ēlāmentābil·is -e *adj* pathetic

ēlangu·escō -escĕre -ī *vi* to slow down, slacken, let up

ēlapsus *pp of* **elabor**

ēlātē *adv* proudly

ēlāti·ō -ōnis *f* elation, ecstasy

ēlātr·ō -āre *vt* to bark out

ēlāt·us -a -um *pp of* **effero**; *adj* high, elevated; exalted; haughty, proud

ē·lāvō -lavāre -lāvī -lautum or **-lōtum** *vt* to wash out; (coll) to clean out, rob

Elĕ·a -ae *f* town in Lucania in S. Italy, birthplace of Eleatic philosophy

Eleātic·ī -ōrum *m pl* Eleatics, Eleatic philosophers

ēlecĕbr·a -ae *f* snare; seductress

ēlectē *adv* tastefully

ēlectil·is -e *adj* choice, dainty

ēlecti·ō -ōnis *f* choice; *f pl* selection

ēlect·ō -āre *vt* to select, choose; to wheedle out, coax out (*a secret*)

Ēlectr·a -ae *f* Pleiad, daughter of Atlas and Pleione and the mother of Dardanus by Jupiter; daughter of Agamemnon and Clytemnestra

ēlectr·um -ī *n* amber; electrum (*alloy of gold and silver*); *f pl* amber beads

ēlect·us -a -um *pp of* **eligo**; *adj* select, picked, choice; (mil) elite

ēlect·us -ūs *m* choice

ēlĕg·ans -antis *adj* fine, elegant, refined; choosy; fine, choice, select

ēleganter *adv* tastefully, neatly, elegantly

ēlegant̆i·a -ae *f* elegance, refinement, taste, propriety

ēlĕg·ī -ōrum *m pl* elegiac verses

elegi·a or **elegē·a -ae** *f* elegy

Elĕl·eus -ěī *m* (epithet of) Bacchus

elementāri·us -a -um *adj* elementary; **senex elementarius** old schoolteacher

element·um -ī *n* first principle, element; *n pl* elements, rudiments; beginnings; ABC's

elench·us -ī *m* pearl

elephantomăch·a -ae *m* fighter mounted on an elephant

elephant·us -ī or **elĕph·ās -antis** *m* elephant; (fig) ivory

Eleus·in -īnis *f* Eleusis (*sacred city in Attica, famous for its cult of Demeter*)

Eleusīn·us -a -um *adj* Eleusinian; **Eleusina mater** Ceres

ēlĕv·ō -āre *vt* to lift up, raise; to alleviate; to lessen, diminish; to make light of, disparage

ē·liciō -licĕre -licuī -licitum *vt* to elicit, draw out; to lure out, entice; to conjure up

Ēlic·ius -iī or **-ī** *m* (epithet of) Jupiter

ē·līdō -līdĕre -līsī -līsum *vt* to knock out, strike out, tear out, force out; to shatter, smash to pieces, crush; to force out, stamp out; (fig) to stamp out

ē·ligō -ligĕre -lēgī -lectum *vt* to pluck out; to pick out, choose

ēlimin·ō -āre *vt* to carry outside; to spread abroad

ēlim·ō -āre *vt* to file; to finish off, perfect

ēlingu·is -e *adj* without tongue, speechless; (fig) inarticulate

ēlingu·ō -āre *vt* (coll) to tear out the tongue of

El·is or **Al·is -ĭdis** *f* district and town on the W. coast of the Peloponnesus in which Olympia is located

Eliss·a or **Elīs·a -ae** *f* Dido

ēlisus *pp of* **elido**

ēlix·us -a -um *adj* wet through and through, soaked

ellam = ecce + illam

elleborōs·us -a -um *adj* crazy

ellebŏr·us or hellebŏr·us -ī *m* or ellebŏr·um -ī *n* hellebore (*plant used for mental illness*)

ellips·is -is *f* ellipsis

ellum = ecce + illum

ēlŏc·ō -āre *vt* to lease out, rent out

ēlocūtī·ō -ōnis *f* style of speaking, delivery

ēlog·ium -iī or -ī *n* saying, maxim; inscription, epitaph; clause (*in a will*)

ēlŏqu·ens -entis *adj* eloquent

ēloquenter *adv* eloquently

ēloquenti·a -ae *f* eloquence

ēlŏqu·ium -iī or -ī *n* eloquence

ē·lŏquor -lŏquī -locūtus sum *vt* to speak out, declare; *vi* to give a speech

ēlōtus *pp* of elavo

ē·lūcĕō -lūcēre -luxī *vi* to shine forth; to glitter

ēluct·or -ārī -ātus sum *vt* to struggle out of, struggle through (*e.g., deep snow*); to surmount; *vi* to force a way out

ēlūcŭbr·ō -āre or ēlūcŭbr·or -ārī -ātus sum *vt* to compose by lamp light

ē·lūdō -lūdĕre -lūsī -lūsum *vt* to elude, parry, avoid; to escape, shun; to delude, deceive; to make fun of; to get the better of, outmaneuver; *vi* to end the game

ē·lūgĕō -lūgēre -luxī *vt* to mourn for; to cease to mourn

ēlumb·is -e *adj* loinless; bland (*style*)

ē·lŭō -luĕre -luī -lūtum *vt* to wash off, wash clean; to wash away; (fig) to wash away, remove, get rid of

ēlūsus *pp* of eludo

ēlūt·us -a -um *pp* of eluo; *adj* washed out, watery, insipid

ēluvĭ·ēs -ēī *f* inundation, overflow; sewage

ēluvĭ·ō -ōnis *f* deluge

Ēlys·ium -iī or -ī *n* realm of the blessed in the lower world

em *interj* (expressing wonder or emphasis) there!

emācĭt·ās -ātis *f* fondness for shopping

ēmancĭpātĭ·ō or ēmancŭpātĭ·ō -ōnis *f* emancipation; transfer of property

ēmancĭpāt·us -a -um *adj* made over, sold

ēmancĭp·ō or ēmancŭp·ō -āre *vt* to transfer; to declare (*a son*) free and independent, emancipate; to surrender, abandon

ēmān·ō -āre *vi* to flow out; to trickle out, leak out; to become known

Ēmathĭ·a -ae *f* Macedonia

Ēmăth·is -ĭdis *adj* Macedonian; *f pl* the Pierides (*daughters of the Macedonian king Pierus*)

ēmātūr·escō -escĕre -uī *vi* to begin to ripen; to soften; (fig) to soften

em·ax -ācis *adj* fond of shopping

emblēm·a -ātis *n* mosaic, inlaid wood

embol·ium -iī or -ī *n* interlude

ēmendābil·is -e *adj* capable of correction

ēmendātē *adv* faultlessly

ēmendātĭ·ō -ōnis *f* emendation, correction

ēmendāt·or -ōris *m* or ēmendātr·ix -īcis *f* corrector

ēmendāt·us -a -um *adj* faultless

ēmendīc·ō -āre *vt* to obtain by begging

ēmend·ō -āre *vt* to emend, correct; to reform, improve, revise; to atone for

ēmensus *pp* of emetior

ēment·ĭor -īrī -ītus sum *vt* to falsify, fabricate, feign; *vi* to tell a lie

ēmerc·or -ārī -ātus sum *vt* to buy up; to bribe

ēmer·ĕō -ēre or ēmer·ĕor -ērī -ītus sum *vt* to merit fully; to lay under obligation; (mil) to serve out (*term of service*); aliquem emerere to do someone a favor or favors

ē·mergō -mergĕre -mersī -mersum *vt* to raise (*from the water*); emergi or se emergere to raise oneself up, rise; *vi* to emerge; to rise (*in power*); to extricate oneself; (with ex + *abl*) to get clear of

ēmerĭt·us -a -um *pp* of emereor; *adj* worn out, unfit for service; *m* veteran

ēmersus *pp* of emergo

emetĭc·a -ae *f* emetic

ē·mētĭor -mētīrī -mensus sum *vt* to measure out; to traverse, travel over; to live through; to impart, bestow

ēmĕt·ō -ĕre *vt* to mow down

ēmĭc·ō -āre -uī -ātum *vi* to dart out, shoot out, dash out; to flash out; (fig) to shine, be prominent

ēmigr·ō -āre *vi* to move out, depart; e vita migrare to pass on, die

ēmĭn·ens -entis *adj* projecting out, prominent, high; eminent

ēminentĭ·a -ae *f* projection, prominence; (in painting) highlights

ēmĭn·ĕō -ēre -uī *vi* to stand out, project; to be conspicuous, stand out; (in painting) to be highlighted

ēmĭn·or -ārī -ātus sum *vt* to threaten

ēmĭnus *adv* out of range, at a distance; from afar

ēmīr·or -ārī -ātus sum *vt* to be greatly surprised at, stand aghast at

ēmissār·ium -iī or -ī *n* drain, outlet

ēmissār·ius -iī or -ī *m* scout, spy

ēmissīcĭ·us -a -um *adj* prying, spying

ēmissĭ·ō -ōnis *f* discharge, hurling, shooting; releasing, letting off

ēmissus *pp* of emitto

ēmiss·us -ūs *m* emission

ē·mittō -mittĕre -mīsī -missum *vt* to sound out; to hurl, discharge, shoot; to let go, let slip, let loose, drop, release, let out; to send out, publish; to allow to escape; to emancipate, set at liberty; to utter; to pass up (*an opportunity*); **animam emittere** to give up the ghost; **emitti** or **se emittere** (with **ex** + *abl*) to break out of (*e.g., jail*)

emō emĕre ēmī emptum *vt* to buy; to pay for; to gain, obtain, acquire; to bribe; **bene emere** to buy cheap; **in diem emere** to buy on credit; **male emere** to pay dearly for

ēmodĕr·or -ārī -ātus sum *vt* to moderate

ēmodŭl·or -ārī -ātus sum *vt* to sing the praises of, celebrate in song

ēmŏl·ior -īrī -ītus sum *vt* to accomplish

ēmoll·iō -īre -īvī or **-iī -ītum** *vt* to soften; to make mild; to enervate

ēmŏl·ō -ĕre — -ĭtum *vt* to grind up; to consume

ēmolumentum -ī *n* profit, gain, advantage

ēmon·ĕō -ēre *vt* to advise, admonish

ē-morior -mŏrī -mortŭus sum *vi* to die, die off; (fig) to die out; **ēmortnālis -e** *adj* of death; **dies emortualis** day of one's death

ēmortŭus *pp* of **ēmorior**

ē-movĕō -movēre -mōvī -mōtum *vt* to move out, remove, expel; to dislodge; to shake (*e.g., foundations of wall*)

Empĕdŏcl·ēs -is *m* philosopher of Sicily who is said to have jumped into the crater of Mt. Aetna (*fl* 444 B.C.)

emphăs·is -is *f* emphasis, stress

empīric·us -ī *m* self-trained physician

empor·ium -iī or **-ī** *n* market town, market, mart

emptiō -ōnis *f* buying, purchase; thing purchased, purchase

emptĭt·ō -āre *vt* to be in the habit of buying

empt·or -ōris *m* buyer, purchaser

emptus *pp* of **emo**

ēmūg·iō -īre *vt* to bellow out

ē-mulgĕō -mulgēre — -mulsum *vt* to drain out; to exhaust

ēmunct·us -a -um *adj* discriminating; **naris emunctae esse** to have discriminating tastes

ē-mungō -mungĕre -munxī -munctum *vt* to blow the nose of; to swindle; (with *abl*) to cheat (*someone*) of; **emungi** to blow one's nose

ēmūn·iō -īre -īvī or **-iī -ītum** *vt* to build up; to fortify; to make a road through (*woods*)

ēn *interj* (in questions) really?; (in commands) come on!; (to call attention) look!, see!

ēnarrābil·is -e *adj* describable, intelligible

ēnarrāti·ō -ōnis *f* description; analysis

ēnarr·ō -āre *vt* to explain in detail, describe; to interpret

ē-nascor -nascī -nātus sum *vi* to grow out, sprout, arise

ēnăt·ō -āre *vi* to swim away, escape by swimming; (fig) to get away with it

ēnātus *pp* of **enascor**

ēnāvig·ō -āre *vt* to sail over, traverse; *vi* to sail away; (fig) to escape

Encelăd·us -ī *m* one of the giants whom Jupiter buried under Aetna

endrŏm·is -ĭdis *f* athlete's bathrobe

Endymi·ōn -ōnis *m* handsome young man with whom Luna fell in love and who was doomed to everlasting sleep on Mt. Patmos in Caria

ē·nĕcō (or **ē·nĭcō**) **-necāre -necŭī** (or **-nicāvī**) **-nectum** (or **-necātum**) *vt* to kill, kill off; to exhaust, wear out; (coll) to kill, pester to death

ēnervāt·us -a -um *adj* without sinews; without energy or force

ēnerv·is -e *adj* weak, feeble

ēnerv·ō -āre *vt* to weaken, enervate, render impotent

ēnĭcō see **eneco**

enim *conj* namely, for instance; yes, indeed, certainly; in fact, to be sure; (in replies) of course, no doubt; for, because

enimvērō *adv* yes indeed, to be sure, certainly; (ironical) of course

Enĭp·eus -ĕī *m* tributary of the Peneus in Thessaly

ēnisus *pp* of **enitor**

ēnit·ĕō -ēre -ŭī *vi* to shine out, sparkle; to be distinguished or conspicuous

ēnitescō -ĕre *vi* to begin to shine, begin to brighten, become conspicuous

ē-nītor -nītī -nisus or **nixus sum** *vt* to work one's way up, climb; to give birth to; *vi* to exert oneself, make an effort; (with *inf*) to struggle to, strive to

ēnixē *adv* strenuously, earnestly

ēnix·us -a -um *pp* of **enitor**; *adj* strenuous, earnest

Enni·us -ī *m* father of Latin literature, writer of tragedy, comedy, epic, and satire, born at Rudiae in Calabria (239-169 B.C.)

Ennosigae·us -ī *m* (epithet of Neptune) Earthshaker

ēn·ō -āre *vi* to swim out, swim away, escape by swimming

ēnōdātē *adv* without knots; plainly, clearly

ēnōdāti·ō -ōnis *f* solution, explanation

ēnōd·is -e *adj* without knots; plain, clear

ēnōd·ō -āre *vt* to explain, clarify

ēnorm·is -e *adj* irregular; enormous

ēnormĭt·ās -ātis *f* irregular shape

ēnōt·escō -escĕre -ŭī *vi* to become known

ēnŏt·ō -āre *vt* to take notes of, note down

ensĭcŭl·us -ī m small sword

ensīf·er -ĕra -ĕrum adj with a sword, wearing a sword

ensĭg·er -ĕra -ĕrum adj with a sword, wearing a sword

ens·is -is m sword

enthȳmēm·a -ătis n thought, reflection; condensed syllogism

ē·nūbō -nūbĕre -nupsī vi (said of a woman) to marry out of one's rank

ēnucleātē adv plainly

ēnucleāt·us -a -um adj pure, clean; straightforward; simple, clear (style)

ēnuclĕ·ō -āre vt (fig) to give in a nutshell, explain to the point

ēnumerātĭ·ō -ōnis f enumeration

ēnumĕr·ō -āre vt to count up; to pay; to recount, relate, detail, describe

ēnuntiātĭ·ō -ōnis f (in logic) proposition

ēnuntĭ·ō -āre vt to disclose, reveal, betray; to say, assert, express

ēnuptĭ·ō -ōnis f right to marry outside the clan

ēnutr·ĭō -īre -īvī or -iī -ītum vt to nourish, raise, bring up (children)

eō īre īvī or iī ītum vi to go; to go, walk, sail, ride; (mil) to march; (of time) to pass; (of events) to go on, happen, turn out; in sententiam īre to vote for a bill

eō adv there, to that place; to that end, to that purpose; so far, to such an extent, to such a pitch; on that account, for that reason, with that in view; eo ero brevior I will be all the briefer; eo magis all the more; eo maxime quod especially because; eo quo to the place to which; eo . . . quo the . . . the . . .; eo quod because; eo . . . ut to such an extent . . . that

eōdem adv to the same place, purpose, or person

Ēōs (nom only) f Dawn

Ēō·us -ī m morning star; inhabitant of the East, Oriental; one of the horses of the sun

Epamīnond·ās -ae m famous Theban general who fought against the Spartans (d. 362 B.C.)

Epaph·us -ī m son of Jupiter and Io

ēpast·us -a -um adj eaten up

Epē·us or Epī·us -ī m builder of the Trojan horse

ephēb·us -ī m young man (18 to 20 years of age)

ephēmĕr·is -ĭdis f diary, journal

Ephĕs·us -ī f city in Asia Minor with famous temple of Diana

ephippiāt·us -a -um adj riding a saddled horse

ephipp·ium -iī or -ī n saddle

ephor·us -ī m ephor (Spartan magistrate)

Ephȳr·a -ae or Ephȳr·ē -ēs f ancient name of Corinth

Epicharm·us -ī m Greek philosopher and writer of early comedy (540-450 B.C.)

epichȳs·is -is f jug

epicrŏc·us -a -um adj transparent, thin

Epicūr·us -ī m Greek philosopher, born on Samos (342-270 B.C.)

epīc·us -a -um adj epic

epidictĭc·us -a -um adj for display

epidipn·is -ĭdis f dessert

epigramm·a -ătis n inscription; short poem, epigram

epilŏg·us -ī m epilogue, peroration

epimēni·a -ōrum n pl month's rations

Epimēth·eus -ĕī m son of Iapetus and brother of Prometheus

epirēd·ium -iī or -ī n trace

epistol·ium -iī or -ī n note

epistŭl·a -ae f letter

epitaph·ium -iī or -ī n eulogy

epithalam·ium -iī or -ī n wedding song

epithēc·a -ae f addition, increase

epitŏm·a -ae or epitŏm·ē -ēs f epitome, abridgment

epitȳr·um -ī n olive salad

epŏd·es -um m pl seafish

ep·ops -ōpis m hoopoe

epos (nom & acc only) n epic

ēpōt·us or expōt·us -a -um adj drained to the dregs; drunk dry

epŭl·ae -ārum f pl courses, dishes; sumptuous meal, banquet; epulae regum dinner fit for a king

epulār·is -e adj at dinner, of a dinner; sermo epularis talk at dinner

epŭl·ō -ōnis m dinner guest, guest at a banquet; Tresviri or Septemviri Epulones college of priests who superintended the state dinner to the gods

epŭl·or -ārī -ātus sum vt to feast on; vi to attend a dinner; (with abl) to feast on

epŭl·um -ī n banquet, feast

equ·a -ae f mare

equ·es -ĭtis m rider; (mil) trooper, cavalryman; cavalry; m pl cavalry

Equ·es -ĭtis m knight; capitalist (member of Roman middle class); equestrian order, bourgeoisie

equest·er -ris -re adj cavalry; equestrian; middle class, bourgeois, capitalist

equĭdem adv truly, indeed, in any event; (with first person) for my part, as far as I am concerned; of course, to be sure

equīn·us -a -um adj horse's

equīrĭ·a -ōrum n pl horse race

equĭtāt·us -ūs m cavalry

equĭt·ō -āre vi to ride, ride a horse

equŭlĕ·us -ī m foal, colt; small equestrian statue; torture rack

equ·us -ī m horse; equis virisque or equis viris (fig) with might and main; equo merere to serve in the cavalry; equo vehī to ride, to ride a horse; equus bipes sea horse; **in equo** mounted; *m pl* (fig) chariot

er·a -ae *f* mistress of the house

ērādīc·ō or **exrādīc·ō -āre** *vt* to root out, uproot, destroy

ē·rādō -rādĕre -rāsī -rāsum *vt* to scratch out, erase, obliterate

erān·us -ī *m* mutual insurance society

Erātō (*nom* only) *f* Muse of erotic poetry; Muse

Eratosthĕn·ēs -is *m* famous Alexandrine geographer, poet, and philosopher (276-196 B.C.)

erc- see **herc-**

Erĕb·us -ī *m* god of darkness, son of Chaos and brother of Night; lower world

Erechth·eus -ĕī *m* mythical king of Athens, son of Hephaestus

ērect·us -a -um *pp* of **erigo**; *adj* erect, upright; noble, elevated, lofty; haughty; attentive, alert, tense; resolute, courageous

ē·rēpō -rēpĕre -repsī *vt* to crawl through (*field*); to crawl up (*mountain*); *vi* to crawl out

ēreptī·ō -ōnis *f* robbery

ērept·or -ōris *m* robber

ēreptus *pp* of **eripio**

ergā *prep* (with *acc*) to, towards; against

ergastŭl·um -ī *n* prison; *n pl* inmates

ergō *adv* therefore, consequently; (resumptive) well then, I say, as I was saying; (with *imperatives*) then, now; **quid ergo?** why then?; *prep* (with preceding *genit*) for the sake of; **illius ergo** for his sake

Erichthon·ius -iī or **-ī** *m* mythical king of Athens, son of Dardanus, father of Tros, and king of Troy

ēric·ius -iī or **-ī** *m* hedgehog; (mil) beam with iron spikes

Eridăn·us -ī *m* Po river (*so called by the Greeks*)

erifŭg·a -ae *m* runaway slave

ē·rigō -rigĕre -rexī -rectum *vt* to set up straight, straighten out (*e.g., tree*); to set up, erect; to cheer up, encourage; to arouse, excite; (mil) to deploy troops on a slope; **erigi** or **se erigere** to raise oneself, arise

Erigŏn·ē -ēs *f* Virgo (*constellation*)

eril·is -e *adj* master's, mistress's

Erīn·ys -ўos *f* Fury; (fig) frenzy

Eriphyl·a -ae or **Eriphyl·ē -ēs** *f* wife of the seer Amphiaraus and the mother of Alcmaeon, who killed her for betraying Amphiaraus

ē·ripiō -ripĕre -ripŭī -reptum *vt* to snatch away, pull out, tear out; to deliver, rescue; to rob; (with *dat* or with **ab** or **ex** + *abl*) to take away from, wrest from, rescue from; **se eripere** to escape

ērogātī·ō -ōnis *f* paying out, payment

ērogĭt·ō -āre *vt* to try to find out

ērŏg·ō -āre *vt* to allocate, expend; to bequeath; (with **in** + *acc*) to allocate to, expend on; **b** to bequeath to

Er·ōs -ōtis *m* Cupid

errābund·us -a -um *adj* wandering, straggling

errātĭc·us -a -um *adj* erratic, roving, wandering

errātĭ·ō -ōnis *f* wandering

errāt·um -ī *n* error, mistake

errāt·us -ūs *m* roving, wandering about

err·ō -āre *vi* to wander, lose one's way, stray, roam; to waver; to err, make a mistake, be mistaken; (with **in** + *abl*) to be mistaken about

err·ō -ōnis *m* vagrant, vagabond

err·or -ōris *m* wandering, wavering, uncertainty; error; cause of error, deception; maze, winding, intricacy

ērub·escō -escĕre -ŭi *vt* to blush at; to be ashamed of; to respect; *vi* to grow red, redden; to blush

ērūc·a -ae *f* colewort

ēruct·ō -āre *vt* to belch, vomit, throw up; (fig) to belch

ērud·iō -īre -īī -ītum *vt* to educate, teach, instruct

ērudĭtē *adv* learnedly

ērudĭtī·ō -ōnis *f* instructing, instruction; erudition

ērudĭtŭl·us -a -um *adj* somewhat experienced, somewhat skilled

ērudīt·us -a -um *adj* educated, learned, accomplished

ē·rumpō -rumpĕre -rūpī -ruptum *vt* to cause to break out; to give vent to; **iram in hostes erumpere** to vent one's wrath on the enemy; *vi* to burst out, break out

ē·ruō -ruĕre -ruī -rutum *vt* to root up, uproot, dig out; to undermine, demolish, destroy; to draw out, elicit; to rescue; to plow up

ēruptĭ·ō -ōnis *f* eruption; (mil) sortie, sally

ēruptus *pp* of **erumpo**

er·us -ī *m* master of the house, head of the family; lord, owner, proprietor

ērŭtus *pp* of **eruo**

erv·um -ī *n* pulse, vetch

Erycīn·us -a -um *adj* of Mt. Eryx (*in Sicily*); of Venus; Sicilian; *f* Venus

Erymanth·is -ĭdis *f* Callisto (*changed into a bear and made a constellation*)

Erymanth·us -ī *m* mountain range in Arcadia, where Hercules killed a boar

Erysichth·ōn -ōnis *m* son of Thessalian king Triopas, punished with insatiable hunger for having cut down a grove sacred to Ceres

erythīn·us -ī *m* red mullet

Er·yx -ўcis or **Erўc·us -ī** *m* mountain on W. coast of Sicily, famous for its temple to Venus

esc·a -ae *f* dish; food; bait

escāri·us -a -um *adj* of food; of bait; *n pl* dishes, courses

e·scendō -scendĕre -scendī -scensum *vt & vi* to climb, climb up

escensi·ō or exscensi·ō -ōnis *f* climb, climbing

esculent·us -a -um *adj* edible; *n pl* edibles

esculētum see aesculetum

escūlus see aesculus

ēsīt·ō -āre *vt* to be accustomed to eating

Esquili·ae -ārum *f pl* Esquiline Hill in Rome

Esquilīn·us -a -um *adj* Esquiline; *f* Esquiline gate

essedāri·us -iī or -ī *m* soldier fighting from a chariot

esse *inf* of sum; *inf* of edo

essēd·um -ī *n* combat chariot (*used by Gauls and Britons*)

essenti·a -ae *f* essence

estr·ix -īcis *f* glutton (*female*)

essīt·ō -āre *vt* to be accustomed to eating

ēsuriāl·is -e *adj* of hunger

ēsur·iō -īre — -ītum *vt* to be hungry for; *vi* to be hungry

ēsuriti·ō -ōnis *f* hunger

ēsus *pp* of edo

et *adv* besides, also; even, I mean

et *conj* and; (for emphasis) and even, yes and; (antithetical) however, but; et . . . et both . . . and, not only . . . but also

etĕnim *conj* for, and as a matter of fact

etēsi·ae -ārum *m pl* periodic winds (*on the Aegean Sea*)

ēthic·ē -ēs *f* ethics

ēthologi·a -ae *f* portrayal of character

ētholŏg·us -ī *m* impersonator

etiam *conj* also, and also, besides, likewise; (of time) yet, as yet, still, even now; (in affirmation) yes, yes indeed, certainly, by all means; (emphatic) even, rather; (with emphatic imperatives) but just; etiam atque etiam again and again, repeatedly

etiamnunc or etiamnum *adv* even now, even at the present time, still

etiamsī *conj* even if, although

etiamtum or etiamnumo *adv* even then, till then, still

Etrūri·a -ae *f* district N. of Rome

Etrusc·us -a -um *adj & mf* Etruscan

etsī *conj* even if, although

etymologi·a -ae *f* etymology

eu *interj* well done!, bravo!

Euan or Euhan *m* Bacchus

Euand·er or Euandr·us -rī *m* Evander (*Arcadian who founded Pallanteum at the foot of the Palatine hill*)

eu·ans or euh·ans -antis *adj* crying Euan or Euhan (*Bacchic cry*)

euax *interj* hurray!

Euboe·a -ae *f* island off the E. coast of Attica and Boeotia

Euēn·us -ī *m* river in Aetolia

euge or eugĕpae *interj* well done!, terrific!

euh·ans -antis *adj* shouting Euan (*Bacchic cry*)

Euhēmĕr·us -ī *m* Greek writer who attempted to prove that all the ancient myths were actually historical events (*fl* 316 B.C.)

Euh·ius -iī or -ī *m* Bacchus

Euhoe or Euoe *interj* ecstatic cry of revelers at festival of Bacchus

Eu·ius -iī or -ī *m* Bacchus

Eumenid·es -um *f pl* Erinyes or Furies (*goddesses of vengeance*)

eunūch·us -ī *m* eunuch

Euoe see Euhoe

Euphorb·us -ī *m* brave Trojan warrior whose soul Pythagoras asserted had transmigrated to himself

Euphrāt·ēs -is *m* Euphrates River

Eupŏl·is -idis *m* famous Athenian comic poet (446?-411 B.C.)

Eurīpīd·ēs -is *m* Athenian tragic poet (485-405 B.C.)

Eurīp·us -ī *m* strait between Boeotia and Euboea; channel, canal

Eurōp·a -ae or Eurōp·ē -ēs *f* daughter of Agenor and mother of Sarpedon and Minos by Jupiter; he, in the shape of a bull, carried her off to Crete

Eurōt·as -ae *m* chief river in Laconia

Eur·us -ī *m* S.E. wind; east wind; wind

Eurydic·ē -ēs *f* wife of Orpheus

Eurypȳl·us -ī *m* Greek warrior who fought at Troy

Eurysth·eus -ĕī *m* son of Sthenelus, grandson of Perseus, and king of Mycenae, who imposed the twelve labors of Hercules

Eurȳt·is -idis *f* Iole (*with whom Hercules fell in love*)

Eurȳt·us -ī *m* king of Oechalia and father of Iole

euschēmē *adv* gracefully

Euterp·ē -ēs *f* Muse of lyric poetry

Euxin·us Pont·us or Euxin·us -ī *m* or Pont·us -ī *m* Black Sea

ē·vādō -vādĕre -vāsī -vāsum *vt* to pass, pass by; to pass through, escape; *vi* to go out; to turn out, become, prove to be, turn out to be; to get away, escape; to rise, climb

ēvăg·or -ārī -ātus sum *vt* to stray beyond, transgress; *vi* (mil) to maneuver; (fig) to spread

ēval·escō -escĕre -uī *vi* to grow strong; to increase; (of a word or expression) to gain currency; (with *inf*) to be able to; (with in + *acc*) to develop into

ēvān·escō -escĕre -uī *vi* to vanish, pass away, die away; (of wine) to become vapid; to be forgotten, perish

ēvānĭd·us -a -um *adj* vanishing

ēvast·ō -āre *vt* to devastate, wreck completely

evasus *pp* of evado

ē·věhō -vehĕre -vexī -vectum vt
to carry out, convey out; to carry
abroad, spread abroad; to lift up,
raise; **evehi** to ride, sail, drift

ē·vellō -vellĕre -vellī or -vulsī
-vulsum vt to tear or pluck out;
to eradicate

ē·veniō -venīre -vēnī -ventum vi
to come out, come forth; to come
to pass, happen; to follow, result,
turn out, end; v impers it happens

ēvent·um -ī n event, occurrence; result, effect, consequence; fortune,
experience

ēvent·us -ūs m event, accident, fortune, lot, fate; good fortune, success; issue, consequence, result

ēverbĕr·ō -āre vt to strike hard; to
beat violently

ēverricŭl·um -ī n broom; dragnet

ē·verrō -verrĕre -verrī -versum
vt to sweep out; (fig) to clean out,
strip

ēversi·ō -ōnis f overthrow, subversion, destruction

ēvers·or -ōris m subverter, destroyer

ēversus pp of everro; pp of everto

ē·vertō or ē·vortō -vertĕre -vertī
-versum vt to overturn, turn upside down; to overthrow, upset; to
turn out, expel, eject; to subvert,
destroy, ruin

ēvestīgāt·us -a -um adj tracked
down

ēvictus pp of evinco

ēvid·ens -entis adj evident, visible,
plain

ēvidenter adv evidently, plainly,
clearly

ēvidenti·a -ae f distinctness, clearness (in speech)

ēvigil·ō -āre vt to watch through
(the night); to work through the
night writing (e.g., books); vi to be
wide-awake; (fig) to be on one's
toes

ēvil·escō -escĕre -uī vi to depreciate, become worthless

ē·vinciō -vincīre -vinxī -vinctum
vt to tie up; to crown, wreathe

ē·vincō -vincĕre -vīcī -victum vt
to conquer completely, trounce; to
prevail over

ēvinctus pp of evincio

ēvir·ō -āre vt to unman, castrate

ēviscĕr·ō -āre vt to disembowel; to
mangle

ēvitābil·is -e adj avoidable

ēvītāti·ō -ōnis f avoidance

ēvīt·ō -āre vt to avoid, escape

ēvocāt·ī -ōrum m pl veterans called
up again; reenlisted veterans

ēvocāt·or -ōris m recruiter

ēvŏc·ō -āre vt to call out, summon;
to challenge; (mil) to call up (for
service); to evoke, excite, stir

ēvolgō see evulgo

ēvŏl·ō -āre vi to fly out, fly away; to
rush out, dash out; (fig) to soar

ēvolūti·ō -ōnis f unrolling a book;
(fig) reading

ē·volvō -volvĕre -volvī -volūtum
vt to roll out, unroll, unfold; to
spread; to unroll, read, study; to
unfold, disclose; to free, extricate;
to repel; to evolve, develop

ē·vŏmō -vomĕre -vomuī -vomi-
tum vt to vomit, spew out, disgorge

ēvulg·ō or ēvolg·ō -āre vt to divulge, make public

ēvulsi·ō -ōnis f pulling out, extraction (of a tooth)

ēvulsus pp of evello

ex or ē prep (with abl) (of space) out
of, from; down from; up from,
above; (of time) from, from . . . onward, immediately after, following,
since; (cause or origin) from,
through, by, on account of, by reason of; (transition) from, out of;
from being; (conformity) after, according to, in conformity with;
(means) with, by means of; (parti-
tive) out of, from among, among;
made of, out of

exacerb·ō -āre vt to exasperate,
provoke

exacti·ō -ōnis f driving out, expulsion; supervision; exaction, collection; tax, tribute

exact·or -ōris m expeller; supervisor; tax collector

exact·us -a -um pp of exigo; adj
exact, precise

exa·cŭō -cŭĕre -cŭī -cūtum vt to
sharpen; to sharpen, stimulate, excite, inflame

exadversum or exadvorsum or
exadversus adv on the opposite
side; prep (with dat or acc) across
from, right opposite

exaedificāti·ō -ōnis f construction

exaedific·ō -āre vt to finish building, build, construct; (fig) to complete

exaequāti·ō -ōnis f leveling; uniformity

exaequ·ō -āre vt to level, make level; (fig) to equal, regard as equal;
exaequari (with dat) to be put on
the same level with

exaestū·ō -āre vi to seethe, boil; to
ferment

exaggerāti·ō -ōnis f (fig) elevation,
enlargement; **animi exaggeratio**
broadening of the mind

exaggĕr·ō -āre vt to pile up; to enlarge; to enhance

exagitāt·or -ōris m critic

exagit·ō -āre vt to stir up, keep on
the move; to scare away; to criticize, satirize; to irritate; to excite,
stir up (feelings)

exagōg·a -ae f exportation

exalb·escō -escĕre -uī vi to turn
pale

exām·en -inis n swarm; crowd;
tongue of scale; weighing, consideration; examination

exāmin·ō -āre vt to weigh; to consider; to try, test, examine

examussim adv exactly

exancl·ō -āre vt to draw off, drain; to drain to the dregs

exanimāl·is -ē adj dead, lifeless; deadly

exanimātī·ō -ōnis f breathlessness; terror, panic

exanim·is -e or **exanim·us -a -um** adj breathless, terrified; dead, lifeless; fainting (e.g., from fear)

exanim·ō -āre vt to knock the breath out of; to wind, tire, weaken; to deprive of life, kill; to scare out of one's wits; to dishearten; to agitate

exanimus see exanimis

ex·ardescō -ardescĕre -arsī -arsum vi to catch fire; to flare up; (fig) to flare up, be provoked, be exasperated

exār·escō -escĕre -ŭī vi to become quite dry, dry up

exarm·ō -āre vt to disarm

exār·ō -āre vt to plow up; to raise, produce; to write (on wax with a stylus), write down, note; to furrow, wrinkle; **frontem rugis exarare** to knit one's brow

exasciāt·us -a -um adj hewn out; properly planned, properly worked out

exaspĕr·ō -āre vt to make rough, roughen; to exasperate

exauctōr·ō -āre vt (mil) to discharge, cashier

exaud·iō -īre -īvī -ītum vt to hear clearly; to discern; to perceive, understand; to listen to; to grant

exaug·ĕō -ēre vt to increase; to confirm

exaugurātī·ō -ōnis f desecration, profaning

exaugŭr·ō -āre vt to desecrate, profane

exauspic·ō -āre vi to find the omens good

exballist·ō -āre vt to put an end to, finish off

exbĭbō see ebibo

excaec·ō -āre vt to blind; to stop up (a river, pipe, etc.); to darken

excandescenti·a -ae f mounting anger, outburst of anger

excand·escō -escĕre -ŭī vi to grow white hot; to reach a pitch (of emotion)

excant·ō -āre vt to charm away

excarnifĭc·ō -āre vt to tear to pieces, torture to death

excăv·ō -āre vt to hollow out

ex·cēdō -cēdĕre -cessī -cessum vt to exceed, pass, surpass; vi to go out, go away, withdraw, depart, disappear; to die; **e medio excedere** or **e vita excedere** to depart from life, die

excell·ens -entis adj excellent, outstanding, distinguished, superior

excellenter adv excellently

excellenti·a -ae f excellence, superiority

ex·cellō -cellĕre vi to excel, be superior

excelsē adv high, loftily

excelsĭt·ās -ātis f loftiness

excels·us -a -um adj high, lofty; eminent; n height; high social status; **in excelso aetatem** or **vitam agere** to be in the limelight

exceptĭ·ō -ōnis f exception, restriction, limitation; (law) objection raised by a defendant against an accuser's statement

except·ō -āre vt to catch, catch up to

exceptus pp of excipio

ex·cernō -cernĕre -crēvī -crētum vt to sift out, separate

ex·cerpō -cerpĕre -cerpsī -cerptum vt to pick out, extract; to pick out, choose, gather; to leave out, omit, except

excerpt·um -ī n excerpt

excess·us -ūs m departure; death; digression

excētr·a -ae f snake

excidĭ·ō -ōnis f destruction

excid·ium -ī or **-ī** n overthrow, destruction; cause of destruction

ex·cĭdō -cidĕre -cĭdī vi to fall out; (of an utterance) to slip out, escape; to pass away, perish; to degenerate; to disappear; to be forgotten; (with in + acc) to degenerate into; (with abl or ex + abl) a to be deprived of, lose; b to forget, miss; (with dat or de + abl) a to fall from; b to escape from (lips); **e memoria excidere** to slip the memory

ex·cĭdō -cidĕre -cĭdī -cīsum vt to cut out, cut off, cut down; to raze, demolish; (fig) to banish, eliminate

excĭĕō see excio

exc·iō -īre -īvī or **-iī -ītum** or **exci·ĕō -ēre** vt to call (someone) out, summon; to awaken (from sleep); to disturb; to frighten; to stir up, excite; to produce, occasion

ex·cipĭō -cipĕre -cēpī -ceptum vt to take out, remove; to rescue; to exempt; to take, receive, catch, capture; to follow, succeed; to catch, intercept; to be exposed to; to incur; to receive, welcome; to take up eagerly; to listen to, overhear; to except, make an exception of; to reach (a place); to mention in particular; to take on, withstand

excīsĭ·ō -ōnis f destruction

excīsus pp of excīdo

excĭtāt·us -a -um adj excited, lively, vigorous; loud

excĭt·ō -āre vt to wake, rouse; to raise, stir up; to erect, construct, produce; to cause, occasion; (fig) to arouse, awaken, incite, inspire, stimulate, enliven, encourage; to startle

excĭtus pp of excio

exclāmātĭ·ō -ōnis f exclamation

exclām·ō -āre vt to exclaim; vi to shout, yell

ex·clūdō -clūdĕre -clūsī -clūsum vt to exclude, shut out, shut off; to remove, separate; to hatch; (coll) to knock out (an eye); to prevent

exclūsi·ō -ōnis f exclusion

exclūsus pp of **exclūdo**

excoctus pp of **excoquo**

excōgitāti·ō -ōnis f thinking out, inventing, contriving

excōgitāt·us -a -um adj choice

excōgit·ō -āre vt to think out, devise, contrive

ex·cōlō -colere -coluī -cultum vt to tend, cultivate, work carefully; to refine, ennoble, perfect, improve; to worship

ex·coquō -coquere -coxī -coctum vt to cook out, boil away; to dry up, bake thoroughly; to harden, temper (steel)

excor·s -dis adj senseless, silly, stupid

excrēment·um -ī n excretion

excrēō see **exscreo**

ex·crescō -crescere -crēvī -crētum vi to grow out; to grow up, rise up

excruciābil·is -e adj deserving torture

excruci·ō -āre vt to torture, torment; to trouble, harass, distress

excubi·ae -ārum f pl standing guard; sentry; watchfire

excubit·or -ōris m sentry

excūb·ō -āre -uī -itum vi to sleep out of doors; to stand guard; to be attentive, be on the alert

ex·cūdō -cūdere -cūdī -cūsum vt to beat or strike out; to hammer out; to forge; (fig) to hatch (eggs); (fig) to hammer out, write up, hammer into shape

exculc·ō -āre vt to kick out; to tread down on; to stomp

excultus pp of **excolo**

excūrāt·us -a -um adj carefully attended to

ex·currō -currere -cucurrī or **-currī -cursum** vi to run or dash out; (mil) to sally forth, make an incursion; to project, extend; (fig) to fan out, expand

excursi·ō -ōnis f sally, sortie; inroad, invasion; outset, opening (of a speech)

excurs·or -ōris m skirmisher, scout

excurs·us -ūs m reconnoitering, running out ahead; raid, charge, attack, invasion; digression

excūsābil·is -e adj excusable

excūsātē adv excusably, without blame

excūsāti·ō -ōnis f excuse

excūsāt·us -a -um adj free from blame, exempt

excūs·ō -āre vt to free from blame, excuse; to exempt; to make excuses for, apologize for; to allege in excuse, plead as an excuse

excussus pp of **excutio**

excūsus pp of **excudo**

ex·cutiō -cutere -cussī -cussum vt to shake out, shake off, shake loose; to knock out (e.g., teeth); (of

horse) to throw, throw off; to shake out (garment); to jilt, give a cold shoulder to; to toss, throw; to shake out, search; to examine, investigate; (fig) to shake off, discard, banish

exdorsu·ō -āre vt to fillet

exec- see **exsec-**

ex·edō -esse -ēdī -ēsum vt to eat up, consume; to destroy; to prey on; to hollow; to wear away, corrode

exēdr·a -ae f sitting room; lecture room; hall

exēdr·ium -iī or **-ī** n sitting room, parlor, living room

exempl·ar or **exempl·āre -āris** n copy; likeness; pattern, model, ideal

exemplār·is -e adj following a model

exempl·um -ī n sample, example, typical instance; precedent; pattern, make, character; model, pattern (of conduct); object lesson; warning; copy, transcript; portrait

exemptus pp of **eximo**

exenter·ō -āre vt to disembowel; to empty, exhaust; to torture, torment

ex·eō -īre -iī -itum vt to pass beyond, cross; to parry, ward off, avoid; (fig) to exceed; vi to go out, go forth; to go away, withdraw, depart, retire; to march out; to disembark; to pour out, gush out, flow out; to escape, be freed; to pass away, perish; (of time) to run out, expire; to get out, become public; to burgeon forth; (of hills) to rise; **ex urna exire** to come out of, fall out of the urn (said of lots)

exeq- = **exseq-**

exerc·eō -ēre -uī -itum vt to exercise, train; (mil) to drill, exercise, train; to keep (someone) busy, keep (someone) going; to supervise; to cultivate, work (the soil); to engage, occupy (the mind); to practice, follow (a trade, occupation); to carry into effect; to disturb, worry

exercitāti·ō -ōnis f exercise, practice, experience, training; (with genit) practice in

exercitāt·us -a -um adj experienced, trained, disciplined; troubled, worried, distressed

exercit·ium -iī or **-ī** exercise, training

exercit·ō -āre vt to keep in training, exercise

exercit·or -ōris m trainer

exercit·us -a -um pp of **excerceo**; adj disciplined; experienced; trying, tough, harassing; harassed, vexed

exercit·us -ūs m army; infantry; (pol) assembly of the people; army of followers; swarm, flock, multitude

exerō see **exsero**

exēs·or -ōris m corrosive factor, underminer

exēsus pp of **exedo**

exhālāti·ō -ōnis f exhalation, vapor

exhāl·ō -āre vt to exhale, breathe out; vi to steam; to breathe one's last, expire

ex·hauriō -haurīre -hausī -haustum *vt* to draw out, empty, exhaust; to take away, remove; to drain dry; to bring to an end; to undergo, endure (*troubles*); to discuss fully

exhērēd·ō -āre *vt* to disinherit

exhēr·ēs -ēdis *adj* disinherited

exhib·ēō -ēre -uī -ītum *vt* to hold out; to present, produce; to display, exhibit; to cause, occasion; to render, make

exhilăr·ō -āre *vt* to cheer up

exhorr·escō -escĕre -uī *vt* to shudder at; *vi* to be terrified

exhortātĭ·ō -ōnis *f* encouragement; *f pl* words of encouragement

exhort·or -ārī -ātus sum *vt* to encourage

ex·igō -igĕre -ēgī -actum *vt* to drive out, push out, thrust out, expel; to demand, exact, collect, require; to pass, spend, complete, close (*life, time*); to finish, complete, conclude; to ascertain, determine; to weigh, consider, estimate, examine, try, test; to dispose of

exiguē *adv* briefly, slightly, sparingly, barely

exiguĭt·ās -ātis *f* shortness, smallness, meagerness, scantiness, scarcity

exigŭ·us -a -um *adj* short, small, meager, scanty, poor, paltry, inadequate; a little, a bit of

exiliō see **exsilio**

exil·is -e *adj* thin, small, meager, feeble, poor; cheerless, dreary; depleted (*ranks*); worthless, insincere; dry, flat (*style*)

exilĭt·ās -ātis *f* thinness; meagerness, dreariness

exiliter *adv* drily, drearily, jejunely

exilium see **exsilium**

exim see **exinde**

eximĭē *adv* exceptionally

eximĭ·us -a -um *adj* taken out, exempted; exempt; select, special, exceptional

ex·imō -imĕre -ēmī -emptum *vt* to take out, take away, remove; to exempt; to free, release, let off; to make an exception of; to waste, lose (*time*); to banish (*e.g., worries*)

exin see **exinde**

exinān·iō -īre -ĭī -ītum *vt* to empty completely; to plunder; (fig) to clean out, fleece

exinde or **exim** or **exin** *adv* from that place, from that point; (in enumerating) after that, next, then; (of time) from that point, after that, then, furthermore, next; accordingly

existimātĭ·ō -ōnis *f* appraisal, judgment, estimate, opinion, decision, verdict; reputation, good name, character; (com) credit; **vulgī existimatio** public opinion

existimāt·or -ōris *m* critic, judge

existim·ō or **existŭm·ō -āre** *vt* to appraise, evaluate, value, estimate;

to think, judge, consider, regard; **in hostium numero existimare** to regard as an enemy

existō see **exsisto**

exitiābil·is -e *adj* deadly, fatal, destructive; (with *dat*) fatal to

exitiāl·is -e *adj* deadly, fatal

exitĭ·ō -ōnis *f* going out, exit

exitiōs·us -a -um *adj* deadly, destructive

exit·ium -ĭī or **-ī** *n* destruction, ruin; cause of destruction

exit·us -ūs *m* going out, exit, departure; way out, outlet, exit; end, close, conclusion; **ad exitum adducere** to bring to a close

exlecēbra see **elecebra**

ex·lex -lēgis *adj* without law, bound by no law; lawless, heedless of laws

exobsĕcr·ō or **exopsĕcr·ō -āre** *vi* to make an earnest entreaty

exocŭl·ō -āre *vt* to knock the eyes out of

exod·ium -ĭī or **-ī** *n* farce (*presented after the main feature*)

exol·escō -escĕre -ēvī -ētum *vi* to decay, fade; to become obsolete

exolēt·us -a -um *adj* full-grown; *m* (fig) old rake

exonĕr·ō -āre *vt* to unload; (fig) to relieve, free, exonerate

exoptābil·is -e *adj* highly desirable, long-awaited

exoptāt·us -a -um *adj* longed-for, welcome, desired

exopt·ō -āre *vt* to long for, wish earnestly, desire greatly

exōrābil·is -e *adj* accessible, sympathetic, placable

exōrābŭl·a -ōrum *n pl* enticements, bait, arguments

exōrāt·or -ōris *m* lucky petitioner

ex·ordior -ordīrī -orsus sum *vt & vi* to begin, start, commence

exord·ium -ĭī or **-ī** *n* beginning, start, commencement, origin; introduction

ex·orior -orīrī -ortus sum *vi* to come out, come forth, rise, appear; to begin, arise, be caused, be produced

exornātĭ·ō -ōnis *f* embellishment

exorn·ō -āre *vt* to fit out, furnish, equip, provide, supply; to adorn, embellish, decorate, set off, give luster to

exōr·ō -āre *vt* to prevail upon, win over; to gain or obtain by entreaty; to appease

exorsus *pp* of **exordior**; *n pl* beginning, commencement; introduction, preamble

exors·us -ūs *m* beginning, commencement; introduction

exortus *pp* of **exorior**

exort·us -ūs *m* rising; the East, the Orient

ex·os -ossis *adj* boneless

exoscŭl·or -ārī -ātus sum *vt* to kiss lovingly, kiss tenderly

exoss·ō -āre *vt* to bone, take the bones out of

exostr·a -ae *f* movable stage; **in exostra** in public

exōs·us -a -um *adj* hating, detesting; hated, detested

exōtic·us -a -um *adj* foreign, exotic

expall·escō -escĕre -ŭī *vt* to turn pale at, dread; *vi* to turn pale

expalliăt·us -a -um *adj* robbed of one's cloak

expalp·ō -āre *vt* to coax out

ex·pandō -pandĕre -pandī -pansum *vt* to spread out, unfold, expand

expătr·ō -āre *vt* to waste, squander

expav·escō -escĕre -ŭī *vt* to panic at; *vi* to panic

expect- = **exspect-**

expecŭliăt·us -a -um *adj* stripped of property

exped·iō -īre -īī or **-īvī -ītum** *vt* to unfetter, extricate, disentangle; to get out, get ready; to clear for action; to clear (*roads of obstacles*); to free, extricate (*from troubles*); to put in order, arrange, settle, adjust, set right; to explain, unfold, clear up, disclose, recount, relate; **expedit** *v impers* it is expedient, useful, advantageous

expedītē *adv* without obstacles, without difficulty, quickly, promptly

expedītī·ō -ōnis *f* expedition, campaign, special mission

expedīt·us -a -um *adj* unencumbered, unhampered, unobstructed; (mil) lightly equipped; ready, prompt; ready at hand, convenient; **in expedito habere** to have at hand

ex·pellō -pellĕre -pŭlī -pulsum *vt* to drive out, eject, expel; to disown

ex·pendō -pendĕre -pendī -pensum *vt* to weigh out; to pay out, pay down, lay out, expend; to rate, estimate; to ponder, consider; to pay (*penalty*)

expens·us -a -um *adj* paid out, spent; *n* payment, expenditure

expergē·faciō -facĕre -fēcī -factum *vt* to awaken, wake up; to arouse, excite

exper·giscor -giscī -rectus sum *vi* to wake up; to be alert

expergō -ĕre -ī -ītum *vt* to awaken, wake up

experi·ens -entis *adj* enterprising, active; (with *genit*) ready to undergo

experienti·a -ae *f* test, trial, experiment; experience, practice; effort

experīment·um -ī *n* test, experiment, proof; experience

exper·ior -īrī -tus sum *vt* to test, try, prove; to experience, endure, find out; to try to do, attempt; to measure strength with; *vi* to go to court

experrectus *pp* of **expergiscor**

exper·s -tis *adj* (with *genit*) having no share in, devoid of, free from, without

expert·us -a -um *pp* of **experior**;

adj tried, proved, tested; (with *genit*) experienced in

expetess·ō -ĕre *vt* to desire, long for

expĕt·ō -ĕre -īvī or **-īī -ītum** *vt* to ask for, demand; to aim at, head for; to desire, long for, wish; *vi* (with **in** + *acc*) to befall; to fall upon, assail

expiātī·ō -ōnis *f* expiation, atonement; satisfaction

expictus *pp* of **expingo**

expīlātī·ō -ōnis *f* pillaging, plundering, ransacking

expīlăt·or -ōris *m* plunderer, robber

expīl·ō -āre *vt* to pillage, plunder, rob, ransack; to plagiarize

ex·pingō -pingĕre -pinxī -pictum *vt* to paint up; to depict; to paint true to life

expi·ō -āre *vt* to purify, cleanse ritually; to atone for, expiate; to avert (*curse, bad omen*)

expīrō see **exspiro**

expisc·or -ārī -ātus sum *vt* to fish for (*information*), ferret out, try to find out

explānātē *adv* plainly, clearly, distinctly

explānātī·ō -ōnis *f* explanation; clear pronunciation

explānăt·or -ōris *m* explainer; interpreter

explānāt·us -a -um *adj* plain, distinct

explān·ō -āre *vt* to explain, make clear; to pronounce clearly

ex·plaudō -plaudĕre -plausī -plausum *vt* to boo at, hiss at; to reject

explōment·um -ī *n* filling, stuffing

ex·plĕō -ēre -ēvī -ētum *vt* to fill out, fill up; to complete; to satisfy (*desires*); to make good, repair (*losses*); to fulfill, perform, accomplish, discharge

explōtī·ō -ōnis *f* satisfying

explēt·us -a -um *adj* full, complete, perfect

explicātē *adv* clearly, plainly

explicātī·ō -ōnis *f* unfolding, uncoiling; analysis; interpretation

explicăt·or -ōris *m* or **explicătr·ix -īcis** *f* explainer

explicāt·us -a -um *adj* plain, clear-cut

explicāt·us -ūs *m* unfolding; explanation, interpretation

explicit·us -a -um *adj* disentangled; simple, easy

explic·ō -āre -āvī or **-ŭī -ātum** or **-ītum** *vt* to unfold, unroll; to spread out; to loosen, undo; (mil) to exceed, deploy; to set free, release; to set in order, arrange, adjust, settle; to set forth, exhibit, explain

ex·plōdō or **ex·plaudō -plōdĕre -lōsī -plōsum** *vt* to drive off by clapping; to boo (*off the stage*); to disapprove, discredit

explōrātē *adv* after careful examination; for sure, for certain

explōrātī·ō -ōnis f exploration, examination

explōrāt·or -ōris m scout, spy

explōrāt·us -a -um adj sure, certain

explōr·ō -āre vt to explore, investigate; (mil) to reconnoiter; to probe, search; to test, try, try out

explōsī·ō -ōnis f booing (of an actor)

expol·iō -īre -īvī or **-iī -ītum** vt to polish; (fig) to polish, refine, adorn

expolītī·ō -ōnis f polishing, finishing off, embellishing

expolīt·us -a -um adj polished, lustrous; refined

ex·pōnō -pōnere -posuī -positum or **-postum** vt to put out; to expose, abandon; to expose, lay open; to reveal, publish; to exhibit, relate, explain; to offer, tender; to set on shore, disembark, land

expor·rigō -rigere -rexī -rectum vt to stretch out, spread, spread out; **exporge frontem** (coll) smooth out your brow, quit frowning

exportātī·ō -ōnis f exportation

export·ō -āre vt to carry out; to export

ex·poscō -poscere -poposcī vt to demand, beg, insist upon; to demand the surrender of

expositīcī·us -a -um adj foundling

expositī·ō -ōnis f exposing; (rhet) narration, explanation (of details of a case)

exposit·us -a -um pp of **expono**; adj accessible; accessible, affable

expostulātī·ō -ōnis f insistent demand; complaint

expostul·ō -āre vt to demand, insist on; to complain of; (with **cum +** abl of person) to complain of (something) to (someone); vi to lodge a complaint; (with **cum +** abl) to lodge a complaint with

expostus pp of **expono**

expōtus see **epotus**

express·us -a -um adj distinct, clear, express; distinct, real

ex·primō -primere -pressī -pressum vt to press out, squeeze out; (fig) to squeeze out, wring, extort; to model, form, portray; to represent, imitate, copy, describe, express; to translate; to pronounce, articulate

exprobrātī·ō -ōnis f reproach

exprobr·ō -āre vt to reproach, find fault with; (with dat) to cast (something) up to, put the blame for (something) on; vi (with dat) to complain to

ex·prōmō -prōmere -prompsī -promptum vt to bring out, fetch out; to give vent to; to disclose, display, exhibit; to give utterance to, utter, express, state

expugnābil·is -e adj vulnerable to attack, pregnable

expugnācī·or -us adj more potent

expugnātī·ō -ōnis f assault; (with genit) assault on

expugnāt·or -ōris m attacker; **expugnator pudicitiae** assailant

expugn·ō -āre vt to assault, storm; to conquer (persons) in war; (fig) to conquer, overcome; (fig) to achieve, accomplish; (fig) to wrest, extort

expulsī·ō -ōnis f expulsion

expuls·ō -āre vt to drive out, expel

expuls·or -ōris m expeller

expulsus pp of **expello**

expultr·ix -īcis f expeller (female)

ex·pungō -pungere -punxī -punctum vt to expunge; to cancel; to remove

expurgātī·ō -ōnis f justification, excuse

expurg·ō -āre vt to cleanse, purify; to cure; to vindicate, excuse, justify

expūtesc·ō -ere vi to rot away

expūt·ō -āre vt to prune, lop off; to consider; to comprehend

ex·quīrō -quīrere -quīsīvī -quīsitum vt to investigate, scrutinize; to search for, look for; to ransack; to devise

exquīsītē adv carefully, accurately; exquisitely

exquīsīt·us -a -um pp of **exquiro**; adj carefully considered, choice, exquisite

exrādīcitus adv from the very roots

exsaev·iō -īre vi to cease raging, calm down

exsangu·is -e adj bloodless; pale; feeble; causing paleness

ex·sarciō or **ex·serciō -sarcīre — -sartum** vt to patch up; (fig) to repair

exsatī·ō -āre vt to satiate, satisfy fully, glut

exsaturābil·is -e adj appeasable

exsatur·ō -āre vt to satiate, satisfy completely

exsce- = **esce**

ex·scindō -scindere -scīdī -scissum vt to annihilate, destroy

exscre·ō -āre vt to cough up, spit out

ex·scrībō -scrībere -scripsī -scriptum vt to write out; to write out in full; to copy; (fig) to copy, take after, resemble

exsculp·ō -ere -sī -tum vt to carve out; to scratch out, erase; (fig) to extort

ex·sec·ō or **exsic·ō -āre -uī -tum** vt to cut out, cut away, cut off; to castrate; to deduct

exsecrābil·is -e adj accursed; bitter, merciless, deadly; execrating, cursing

exsecrātī·ō -ōnis f curse, execration; solemn oath

exsecrāt·us -a -um adj accursed, detestable

exsecr·or -ārī -ātus sum vt to curse, execrate; vi to take a solemn oath

exsectī·ō -ōnis f cutting out

exsecūtǐ·ō -ōnis f execution, performance; discussion

exsecūtus pp of **exsequor**

exsequǐ·ae -ārum f pl funeral procession, funeral rites

exsequiālǐ·is -e adj funeral; **carmina exsequialia** dirges

ex·sĕquor -sĕqui -secūtus sum vt to follow out; to accompany to the grave; to perform, execute, accomplish, carry out; to follow up, investigate: to pursue, go after; to avenge, punish; to say, tell, describe, relate

exsĕr·ō -ĕre -ŭī -tum vt to untie, disconnect; to stretch out (one's arms); to stick out (the tongue in disdain); to bare, uncover

exsert·ō -āre vt to keep on stretching or sticking out

exsertus pp of **exsero**; adj uncovered, bare; protruding

exsibǐl·ō -āre vt to hiss off the stage

exsiccāt·us -a -um adj dry, uninteresting

exsicc·ō -āre vt to dry up; to drain dry

exsicō see **exseco**

exsign·ō -āre vt to mark down exactly, write down in detail

ex·silǐō -silīre -silŭī vi to jump out, leap up; to start; **exsilire gaudio** to jump for joy

exsil·ium -ǐī or **-ī** n exile, banishment (voluntary or involuntary); place of exile

ex·sistō -sistĕre -stǐtī -stǐtum vi to come out, come forth; to appear, emerge; to exist, be; to arise, proceed; to turn into, become; to be visible

ex·solvō -solvĕre -solvī -solūtum vt to loosen, untie; to release, free, set free; to discharge, pay; to keep, fulfill; to satisfy (hunger); to break open, wound; to solve, explain; to throw off, get rid of; to repay, requite; to give out (awards, punishment)

exsomn·is -e adj sleepless

exsorb·ĕō -ēre -ŭī vt to suck up, drain; to drain, exhaust; to grasp at eagerly, welcome

exsor·s -tis adj without lots; chosen specially; (with genit) having no share in, free from

exspatǐ·or -ārī -ātus sum vi to go off course; to digress

exspectābǐl·is -e adj expected, anticipated

exspectātǐ·ō -ōnis f expectation, suspense; **exspectationem facere** to cause suspense

exspectāt·us -a -um adj expected, awaited, desired

exspect·ō -āre vt to await, wait for, look out for; to hope for, long for, anticipate

ex·spergō -spergĕre — -spersum vt to sprinkle, scatter

exspēs adj hopeless, forlorn; (with genit) without hope of

exspīrātǐ·ō -ōnis f breathing out, exhalation

exspīr·ō -āre or **expir·ō -āre** vt to breathe out, exhale, emit; vi to expire, breathe one's last; (fig) to come to an end, cease

exsplend·escō -escĕre -ŭī vi to glitter, shine

exspolǐ·ō -āre vt to strip; to pillage

es·spŭō -spuĕre -spŭī -spūtum vt to spit out; (fig) to banish (e.g., worries)

exstern·ō -āre vt to startle, scare; to terrify; to stampede (horses)

exstǐll·ō -āre vi to drop, trickle out; to melt

exstimulāt·or -ōris m instigator

exstǐmŭl·ō -āre vt to instigate, goad on

exstinctǐ·ō -ōnis f extinction

exstinct·or -ōris m extinguisher; suppressor; destroyer

ex·stinguō -stinguĕre -stinxī -stinctum vt to extinguish, put out; to destroy, kill; to abolish, annul; **extingui** to die, die out; to be forgotten

exstirp·ō -āre vt to extirpate, root out, eradicate

exst·ō -āre vi to stand out, protrude, project; to stand out, be prominent, be conspicuous; to be visible; to appear; to exist, be extant

exstructǐ·ō -ōnis f erection

ex·struō -struĕre -struxī -structum vt to pile up, heap up; to build, erect

exsuct·us -a -um pp of **exsugo**; adj dried up

exsūd·ō -āre vt to sweat; (fig) to sweat out, sweat over; vi to pour out

ex·sūgō -sūgĕre -suxī -suctum vt to suck out

exs·ul or **ex·ul -ŭlis** m or f exile, refugee

exsǔl·ō -āre vi to be an exile, be a refugee

exsultātǐ·ō -ōnis f exultation, jumping for joy

exsultim adv friskily

exsult·ō or **exult·ō -āre** vi to jump up; to frisk about; (of horses) to rear, prance; to exult, rejoice, jump for joy; to revel, run riot; to boast; (of speech) to range freely

exsuperābǐl·is -e adj climbable; superable

exsuperantǐ·a -ae f superiority

exsupĕr·ō -āre vt to surmount; to exceed, surpass; to overpower; vi to rise; (of flames) to shoot up; to be superior, excel, be conspicuous, prevail

exsurd·ō -āre vt to deafen; (fig) to dull

ex·surgō -surgĕre -surrexī vi to get up, rise, stand up; (fig) to rise, recover strength; **foras exsurgere** to get up and go out

exsuscǐt·ō -āre vt to rouse from sleep; to fan (fire); to excite, stir up

ext·a -ōrum n pl vital organs (of sacrificial animals)

extāb·escō -escĕre -ŭī vi to waste away, pine away; to disappear

extār·is -e adj used for cooking the sacrificial victim; sacrificial

extemplō or **extempŭlō** adv immediately, right away; on the spur of the moment

ex·tendō -tendĕre -tendī -tentum or **-tensum** vt to stretch out, spread out, extend; to enlarge, increase; to widen, broaden; to prolong, continue; to pass, spend; to exert, strain; **extendī** to stretch out, extend; **labellum extendere** to pout

extent·ō -āre vt to exert, strain

extent·us -a -um pp of **extendo**; adj extensive, wide; **extentis itineribus** by forced marches

extenuāti·ō -ōnis f extenuation; thinning out

extenuāt·us -a -um adj thinned, reduced; trifling; weak, faint

extenŭ·ō -āre vt to thin out; to lessen, diminish, extenuate, detract from

exter or **extĕr·us -a -um** adj external, outward; foreign, strange

extĕrebr·ō -āre vt to bore out; to extort

ex·tergēō -tergēre -tersī -tersum vt to wipe out, wipe clean; (fig) to wipe out, plunder

exterī·or -us adj outer, exterior

exterīus adv on the outside

extermin·ō -āre vt to drive out, banish; to put aside, put away, remove

extern·us -a -um adj external, outward; foreign, strange; m foreigner, stranger, foreign enemy; n pl foreign goods

ex·tĕrō -terĕre -trīvī -trītum vt to rub out, wear away; (fig) to crush

exterr·ĕō -ēre -ŭī -ĭtum vt to frighten, terrify

extersus pp of **extergeo**

extĕrus see **exter**

extex·ō -ĕre vt to unweave; (fig) to cheat

extim·escō -escĕre -ŭī vt to become terribly afraid of, dread; vi to become afraid

extĭm·us -a -um adj outermost, farthest, most remote

extisp·ex -ĭcis m soothsayer, diviner (who makes predictions by inspecting the entrails of animals)

extoll·ō -ĕre vt to lift up; to erect; to postpone; to extol, praise; to raise, exalt; to beautify; **animos extollere** to raise the morale

ex·torquĕō -torquēre -torsī -tortum vt to wrench, wrest; to dislocate; to extort

extorr·is -e adj driven out of one's country, banished, exiled

extort·or -ōris m extorter

extortus pp of **extorqueo**; adj deformed

extrā adv outside, on the outside; **extra quam** except in the case that; **extra quam si** unless; prep (with acc) outside, outside of, beyond; apart from, aside from; contrary to; except, besides; without; **extra jocum** all joking aside

ex·trāhō -trahĕre -traxī -tractum vt to pull out, drag out; to drag out, prolong; to waste (time); to extricate, release, rescue; to remove

extrānĕ·us -a -um adj extraneous, external, irrevelant, strange; m stranger

extrāordinārī·us -a -um adj extraordinary

extrārī·us -a -um adj outward, external; unrelated (by family ties)

extrēm·a -ōrum n pl end (e.g., of a marching column, of strip of land, of life)

extrēmĭt·ās -ātis f extremity, end

extrēmō adv finally, at last

extrēmum adv finally, at last; for the last time

extrēm·us -a -um adj extreme, outermost, on the end; latest, last; (of degree) utmost, extreme; lowest, meanest; **extrema aetas** advanced old age; **extrema cauda** tip of the tail; **extremā lineā amare** to love at a distance; **extrema manus** final touches; **extremis digitis attingere** to touch lightly; to touch lightly on; to hold tenderly; **extremus ignis** flickering flame; **in extremo libro secundo** at the end of the second book; n end; extremity; **ad extremum** at last; at the end; utterly; **in extremo** in mortal danger, in a crisis

extrīc·ō -āre or **extrīc·or -ārī -ātus sum** vt to extricate; to clear up; to obtain with difficulty

extrīnsĕcus adv from outside, from abroad; on the outside, outside

extrītus pp of **extero**

ex·trūdō -trūdĕre -trūsī -trūsum vt to thrust out, drive out; to get rid of

extum·ĕō -ēre vi to swell up

ex·tundō -tundĕre -tŭdī -tūsum vt to beat out, hammer out; to fashion; to devise; to extort

exturb·ō -āre vt to drive out, chase out, drive away; to divorce; to knock out

exŭbĕr·ō -āre vi to grow luxuriantly; to abound

exulcĕr·ō -āre vt to make sore, aggravate; to exasperate

exulŭl·ō -āre vt to invoke with cries; vi to howl

exunctus pp of **exungo**

exund·ō -āre vi to overflow; **in litora exundare** to wash up on the shores

ex·ungō -ungĕre — -unctum vt to oil down, rub with oil

ex·ŭo -ŭĕre -ŭī -ūtum *vt* to take off, pull off; to shake off; to unclothe; to strip, deprive; to cast aside, cast off; to bare

exurg·ĕō -ēre *vt* to squeeze out

ex·ūrō -ūrĕre -ussī -ustum *vt* to burn out, burn up; to dry up; to consume, destroy; (fig) to inflame

exustĭ·ō -ōnis *f* conflagration

exustus *pp* of **exuro**

exūtus *pp* of **exuo**

exuvĭ·ae -ārum *f pl* clothing; equipment; arms; hide; slough; booty, spoils

---

F

fab·a -ae *f* bean

fabāl·is -e *adj* bean; **stipulae fabales** bean stalks

fābell·a -ae *f* short story; fable, tale; short play

fab·er -ra -rum *adj* skilled; *m* craftsman; smith; carpenter; (mil) engineer; **faber ferrarius** blacksmith; **faber tignarius** carpenter

Fab·ĭus -iī or **-ī** *m* Quintus Fabius Maximus Cunctator, elected consul five times and appointed dictator in 217 B.C. to conduct the war against Hannibal (d. 203 B.C.); Quintus Fabius Pictor, first Roman historian to use prose (*fl* 225 B.C.)

fabrē *adv* skillfully

fabrē·faciō -facere -fēcī -factum *vt* to build, make; to forge

fabric·a -ae *f* trade, industry; workshop, factory; piece of work, structure, production; **fabricam fingere** (with **ad** + *acc*) (coll) to pull a trick on

fabricātĭ·ō -ōnis *f* structure, construction

fabricāt·or -ōris *m* builder, architect, producer, creator

fabric·or -ārī -ātus sum or **fabric·ō -āre** *vt* to build, construct, produce, forge; to prepare, form; to coin (*words*)

fabrīl·is -e *adj* craftman's, carpenter's, sculptor's; *n pl* tools

fābul·a -ae *f* story, tale; talk, conversation, conversation piece; small talk; affair, matter, concern; myth, legend; drama, play; dramatic poem; **fabulae!** (coll) baloney!; **lupus in fabula!** (coll) speak of the devil!

fābulār·is -e *adj* legendary

fābul·or -ārī -ātus sum *vt* to say, invent; *vi* to talk, chat, gossip

fābulōs·us -a -um *adj* legendary

fābul·us -ī *m* small bean

facess·ō -ĕre -īvī -ītum *vt* to do eagerly, perform, accomplish; to bring on, cause, create; **negotium alicui facessere** to cause someone trouble; *vi* to go away, depart

facētē *adv* facetiously, humorously, wittily, brilliantly

facētĭ·ae -ārum *f pl* clever thing, clever talk, witticism, humor

facēt·us -a -um *adj* witty, humorous; fine, polite; elegant; brilliant

faciēs -ēī *f* make, form, shape; face, look; look, appearance; nature, character; external appearance, pretense, pretext

facil·is -e *adj* easy; nimble; suitable, convenient; ready, quick; easy, easygoing, good-natured; favorable, prosperous; gentle (*breeze*); easilyborne, slight (*loss*); **ex** or **e facili** easily; **in facili esse** to be easy; **facilis victu** prosperous, well-off, well-to-do

facile *adv* easily, without trouble; unquestionably, by far, far; quite, fully; promptly, readily, willingly; pleasantly, well; **non facile** hardly

facilit·ās -ātis *f* facility, easiness, ease; readiness; fluency; suitability; good nature, affability, courteousness; levity

facinorōs·us or **facinerōs·us -a -um** *adj* & *m* criminal

facin·us -ŏris *n* deed, action; crime, villany

faciō facĕre fēcī factum (**faxim** = **fēcĕrim**; **faxō** = **fēcĕrō**) *vt* to make, fashion, frame, create, build, erect; to do, perform; to make, produce, compose; to bring about, cause, occasion; to acquire, gain, get, accumulate; to incur, suffer; to render, grant, give, confer; to grant, admit; to assume, suppose; to assert, say, represent, depict; to choose, appoint; to follow, practice; to regard, prize, value; **certiorem facere** to inform; **copiam facere** to afford the opportunity; **fac ita esse** suppose it were so, granted that it is so; **fidem facere** to give one's word; **pecuniam facere** or **stipendium facere** to make money, earn money; **promissum facere** to fulfill a promise; **sacra facere** to sacrifice; **verbum facere** to speak; **viam facere** (with *dat*) to make way for; *vi* to do, act; to take part, take sides; (with *dat* or with **ad** + *acc*) to be satisfactory for, be fit for, do for

factĕon = **faciendum**

factĭ·ō -ōnis *f* doing; making; party, faction; partisanship; company, social set, association, class; oligarchy; (with *genit*) right to make (*e.g., a will*)

factiōs·us -a -um *adj* busy; partisan; oligarchical; factious, revolutionary, seditious

factit·ō -āre vt to keep doing or making; to practice (e.g., trade); (with double acc) to declare (someone) to be (e.g., heir)

fact·or -ōris m (in playing ball) batter

fact·us -a -um pp of **facio**; n deed, act; accomplishment, exploit

facŭl·a -ae f little torch

facult·ās -ātis f opportunity, means; feasibility; ability, capacity, mental resources; material resources, means, supplies, abundance

fācundē adv eloquently

fācundi·a -ae f eloquence

fācundit·ās -ātis f eloquence

fācund·us -a -um adj eloquent, fluent

faecě·us -a -um adj morally impure, morally rotten

faecŭl·a -ae f wine lees

faenēbr·is -e adj of interest, regarding interest; **res faenebris** indebtedness

faenerāti·ō -ōnis f lending at interest, investment

faenerātō adv with interest

faenerāt·or -ōris m money lender, investor, capitalist

faenēr·or -ārī -ātus sum or **faenēr·ō -āre** vt to lend at interest; to invest; to ruin through high interest rates; vi to bring interest, bring profit; **faeneratum beneficium** (fig) a favor richly repaid

faeně·us -a -um adj made of hay

faenīl·ia -ium n pl hayloft

faenisēc·a -ae m peasant

faen·um or **fēn·um -ī** n hay; **faenum habet in cornu** (fig) he's crazy

faen·us or **fēn·us -ōris** n interest; debt (as result of heavy interest); capital; (fig) profit, gain, advantage

faenuscŭl·um or **fēnuscŭl·um -ī** n a little interest

fae·x -cis f dregs, sediments, grounds, lees; (fig) dregs

fāgině·us or **fāgin·us** or **fāgě·us -a -um** adj beech

fāg·us -ī f beech tree

fal·a or **phal·a -ae** f movable wooden siege tower; scaffold

falāric·a or **phalāric·a -ae** f incendiary missile

falcār·ius -iī or **-ī** m sickle maker

falcāt·us -a -um adj fitted with scythes, scythed; sickle-shaped, curved

falcif·er -ěra -ěrum adj scythe-bearing

Falern·us -a -um adj Falernian; **ager Falernus** district in N. Campania, famous for its wine; n Falernian wine

Falisc·ī -ōrum m pl a people of S.E. Etruria

fallāci·a -ae f deception, deceit, trick

fallācĭter adv deceptively, deceitfully, fallaciously

fall·ax -ācis adj deceptive, deceitful, fallacious

fallō fallěre fefellī falsum vt to cause to fall, trip; to lead into error; to deceive, trick, dupe, cheat; to fail to live up to, disappoint; to wile away; to escape the notice of, slip by; **fidem fallere** to break one's word; **me fallit** I do not know; **nisi** or **ni fallor** unless I'm mistaken; **opinionem fallere** (with genit) to fail to live up to the expectations of

falsē adv falsely

falsidic·us -a -um adj speaking falsely, lying

falsific·us -a -um adj acting dishonestly

falsijūri·us -a -um adj swearing falsely

falsilŏqu·us -a -um adj lying

falsimōni·a -ae f trick

falsipăr·ens -entis adj bastard

falsō adv mistakenly, wrongly, erroneously; falsely, deceitfully, untruly

fals·us -a -um pp of **fallo**; adj mistaken, wrong, erroneous; false, untrue; lying, deceitful; vain, groundless, empty; spurious, sham, fictitious; n error; lying, perjury; lie, untruth, falsehood

fal·x -cis f sickle; pruning hook, pruning knife; (mil) hook for pulling down walls

fām·a -ae f talk, rumor, report; saying, tradition; reputation; fame, renown, glory, name; infamy, notoriety; public opinion

famēlic·us -a -um adj famished, starved

fam·ēs -is f hunger, starvation; poverty; famine; greed; (rhet) bald style, poverty of expression

fāmigerāti·ō -ōnis f rumor

fāmigerāt·or -ōris m gossip, rumormonger

famili·a -ae or **-ās** f household slaves, domestics; household; house, family; family estate; fraternity; sect, school; **familiam ducere** to be the head of a sect; **pater familias** head of the household

familiār·is -e adj domestic, family, household; familiar, intimate; (in augury) one's own (part of the sacrificial animal); m servant, slave; acquaintance, friend, companion

familiārit·ās -ātis f familiarity, intimacy; association, friendship

familiāriter adv on friendly terms

fāmōs·us -a -um adj much talked of; famous, renowned; infamous, notorious; slanderous, libelous; **carmen famosum** lampoon

famŭl·a -ae f slave, maid, maidservant

famulār·is -e adj of slaves, of servants

famulāt·us -ūs m servitude, slavery

famŭl·or -ārī -ātus sum vi to be a slave; (with dat) to serve

famŭl·us -a -um adj serviceable; m servant, attendant

fānātic·us -a -um adj fanatic, enthusiastic, inspired; wild, frantic

fān·um -ī n shrine, sanctuary, temple

fār farris n spelt; coarse meal, grits; sacrificial meal; bread; dog biscuit; n pl grain

far·ciō -cīre -sī -tum vt to stuff, cram

farfăr·us or **farfĕr·us -ī** m coltsfoot (plant)

farīn·a -ae f flour; powder; character, quality

farrāg·ō -ĭnis f mash (for cattle); medley, hodgepodge

farrāt·us -a -um adj filled with grain; made with grain

fart·is -is f stuffing, filling, mincemeat; **fartim facere ex hostibus** to make mincemeat of the enemy

fart·or -ōris m fattener of fowls

fartus pp of **farcio**

fās (indecl) n divine law; sacred duty; divine will, fate; right; **fas est** it is right, it is lawful, it is permitted

fascĭ·a -ae f bandage, swathe; girth; fillet; wisp of cloud

fasciātim adv in bundles

fascĭcŭl·us -ī m small bundle

fascĭn·ō -āre vt to cast an evil eye on, bewitch, jinx; to envy

fascĭn·um -ī n or **fascĭn·us -ī** m evil eye; jinx; witchcraft; charm, amulet; penis

fasciŏl·a -ae f small bandage

fasc·is -is m bundle, pack, parcel, fagot; load, burden; baggage; m pl fasces (bundle of rods and ax, carried before high magistrates by lictors as symbols of authority); high office, supreme power, consulship

fassus pp of **fateor**

fast·ī -ōrum m pl calendar, almanac; annals; register of higher magistrates

fastīd·iō -īre -īvī or **-iī -ītum** vt to disdain, despise, snub, turn up the nose at; vi to feel disgust, feel squeamish; to be snobbish, be haughty

fastīdiōsē adv fastidiously, squeamishly; disdainfully, snobbishly

fastīdiōs·us -a -um adj fastidious, squeamish; disdainful, snobbish; refined, delicate

fastīd·ium -iī or **-ī** n fastidiousness, squeamishness, distaste, disgust, loathing; snobbishness, haughtiness, contempt

fastīgātē adv sloped (like a gable), sloping up, sloping down

fastīgāt·us -a -um adj rising to a point; sloping down

fastīg·ium -iī or **-ī** n gable; pediment; roof, ceiling; slope; height, elevation, top, edge; depth, depression; finish, completion; rank, dig-

nity; main point, heading, highlight (of story, etc.)

fast·us -a -um adj legal (day); **diēs fastus** court day

fast·us -ūs m disdain, contempt, arrogance; m pl brash deeds; calendar

fātāl·is -e adj fateful, destined, preordained; fatal, deadly; **deae fatales** the Fates

fātālĭter adv according to fate, by fate

fatĕor fatērī fassus sum vt to admit, acknowledge; to disclose, reveal

fātĭcăn·us or **fātĭcĭn·us -a -um** adj prophetic

fātĭdĭc·us -a -um adj prophetic

fātĭf·er -ĕra -ĕrum adj fatal, deadly

fatīgātĭ·ō -ōnis f fatigue, weariness

fatīg·ō -āre vt to fatigue, weary, tire; to worry, torment, harass, wear down; to importune, pray to constantly

fātĭlŏqu·a -ae f prophetess

fatisc·ō -ĕre or **fatisc·or -ī** vi to split, crack, give way; (fig) to crack, break down, collapse from exhaustion

fatuĭt·ās -ātis f silliness

fāt·um -ī n divine utterance, oracle; fate, destiny, doom; calamity, mishap, ruin; death; **ad fata novissima** to the last; **fato obire** to meet death, die; **fatum proferre** to prolong life

fātus pp of **for**

fatŭ·us -a -um adj silly, foolish; clumsy; m fool

fauc·ēs -ium f pl upper part of the throat, throat, gullet; strait, channel; pass, defile, gorge; (fig) jaws; **fauces premere** (with genit) to choke, throttle

Faun·us -ī m mythical king of Latium, father of Latinus, and worshiped as the Italian Pan; m pl Fauns, woodland spirits

faustē adv favorably, auspiciously

faustĭt·ās -ātis f fertility; good fortune, happiness

Faustŭl·us -ī m shepherd who raised Romulus and Remus

faust·us -a -um adj auspicious, favorable, fortunate, lucky

faut·or or **favĭt·or -ōris** m promoter, patron, supporter, fan

fautr·ix -īcis f patroness, protectress

favĕ·a -ae f favorite girl, pet slave girl

favĕō favēre fāvī fautum vi (with dat) to be favorable to, favor, support, side with; (with inf) to be eager to; **favere linguis** or **favere ore** to observe a reverent silence

favill·a -ae f ashes, embers; (fig) spark, beginning

favĭtor see **fautor**

Favŏn·ius -iī or **-ī** m west wind (also called Zephyrus)

fav·or -ōris m favor, support; applause; appreciation (*shown by applause*)

favōrābil·is -e adj popular

fav·us -ī m honeycomb

fa·x -cis f torch; wedding torch; wedding; funeral torch; funeral; meteor, shooting star, comet; firebrand; fire, flame; guiding light; instigator; flame of love; stimulus, incitement; cause of ruin, destruction; **dicendi faces** fiery eloquence; **dolorum faces** pangs of grief

faxim see **facio**

febrĭcŭl·a -ae f slight fever

febr·is -is f fever

Februˑa -ōrum n pl Roman festival of purification and expiation, celebrated on February 15th

Februāri·us -a -um adj & m February

februˑum -ī n purgation, purification

fēcundĭt·ās -ātis f fertility, fruitfulness; (rhet) overstatement

fēcund·ō -āre vt to fertilize

fēcund·us -a -um adj fertile, fruitful; abundant, rich; fertilizing; (with *genit* or *abl*) rich in, abounding in

fe·l -llis n gallbladder; gall, bile; bitterness, animosity; poison

fēl·ēs -is f cat

fēlicĭt·ās -ātis f fertility; luck, good fortune, piece of luck; felicity, happiness

fēliciter adv fruitfully, abundantly; favorably, auspiciously; luckily; happily; successfully

fēl·ix -icis adj fruit-bearing; fruitful, fertile; favorable, auspicious; lucky; happy; successful

fēmell·a -ae f girl

fēmin·a -ae f female; woman

fēmināt·us -a -um adj effeminate

fēminē·us -a -um adj woman's; effeminate, unmanly

fēminīn·us -a -um adj (gram) feminine

fem·ur -ŏris or **-ĭnis** n thigh

fēn- = faen-

fenestr·a -ae f window; hole (*for earrings*); (fig) opening, opportunity; (mil) breach (*in a wall*)

fer·a -ae f wild beast, wild animal

ferācĭus adv more fruitfully

Fērāl·ia -ium n pl festival of the dead, celebrated on February 17th or 21st

fērāl·is -e adj funeral; deadly; fatal; gloomy, dismal

fer·ax -ācis adj fertile, fruitful; (with *genit*) productive of

fercŭl·um -ī n food tray; dish, course; litter for carrying spoils in a victory parade or cult images in religious processions

fercŭl·us -ī m litter bearer

ferē or **fermē** adv approximately, nearly, almost, about, just about; generally, as a rule, usually; (with

negatives) practically; **nemo fere** practically no one

ferentār·ius -iī or **-ī** m light-armed soldier; eager helper

Feretr·ius -iī or **-ī** m epithet of Jupiter

ferĕtr·um -ī n litter, bier

fēri·ae -ārum f pl holidays, vacation; (fig) leisure

fēriāt·us -a -um adj vacationing, taking it easy, relaxing, taking time off

ferīn·us -a -um adj of wild animals; **caro ferina** venison; f game, venison

fer·iō -īre vt to strike, hit, shoot, knock; to kill; to slaughter, sacrifice (*an animal*); to coin; (fig) to strike, reach, affect; (fig) to cheat, trick; **cornu ferire** to butt; **foedus ferire** to make a treaty; **securi ferire** to behead; **verba ferire** to coin words

ferĭt·ās -ātis f wildness, fierceness

fermē see **fere**

ferment·um -ī n yeast; beer; (fig) ferment, provocation, vexation, anger, passion

fer·ō ferre tulī or **tetŭlī lātum** vt to bear, carry; to bear, produce, bring forth; to bear, endure; to lead, drive, conduct, direct; to bring, offer; to receive, acquire, obtain, win; to take by force, carry off, plunder, ravage; to manifest, display, make known, report, relate, say, tell; to propose, bring forward; to allow, permit; to cause, create; to set in motion; to call, name; (in accounting) to enter; **aegre ferre** to be annoyed at; **caelo supinas manus ferre** to raise the hands heavenward in prayer; **ferri** to move, rush; to sail; to fly; to flow along; (fig) to be carried away (*e.g., with ambition, greed*); **ferri** or **se ferre** to rush, flee; **iter ferre** to pursue a course; **laudibus ferre** to extol; **legem ferre** to propose a bill; **moleste ferre** to be annoyed at; **pedem ferre** to come, go, move, get going; **prae se ferre** to display, manifest; **se ferre obviam** (with *dat*) to rush to meet; **repulsam ferre** to experience defeat (*at the polls*); **sententiam ferre** to pass judgment; to cast a vote; **signa ferre** (mil) to begin marching; **ventrem ferre** to be pregnant; vi to say, e.g., **ut ferunt** as people say, as they say; to allow, permit, e.g., **si occasio tulerit** if occasion permit; to lead, e.g., **iter ad oppidum ferebat** the road led to the town

ferōci·a -ae f courage, bravery, spirit; ferocity, barbarity; presumption

ferōcĭt·ās -ātis f courage, spirit, fierceness, aggressiveness; ferocity, barbarity; pride, presumption

ferociter *adv* bravely, courageously, aggressively; defiantly; haughtily

Ferōnı̆·a -ae *f* early Italic goddess of groves and fountains, and patroness of ex-slaves

fer·ox -ōcis *adj* brave, intrepid, warlike; defiant; overbearing, haughty, insolent

ferrāment·um -ī *n* tool, implement

ferrāri·us -a -um *adj* iron; **faber ferrarius** blacksmith; *m* blacksmith; *f pl* iron mines, iron works

ferrātĭl·is -e *adj* fit to be chained

ferrāt·us -a -um *adj* iron-plated; iron-tipped; in chains; in armor; **calx ferrata** spur; *m pl* soldiers in armor

ferrĕ·us -a -um *adj* iron, made of iron; hardhearted, cruel; firm, unyielding

ferricrepĭn·us -a -um *adj* (coll) clanking chains

ferriter·ĭum -iī or **-ī** *n* (coll) brig, jug

ferritĕr·us -ī *m* (coll) glutton for punishment

ferritrīb·ax -ācis *adj* (coll) chainsore (*sore from dragging chains*)

ferrūgĭnĕ·us or **ferrūgĭn·us -a -um** *adj* rust-colored, dark, dusky

ferrūg·ō -ĭnis *f* rust, verdigris, dark red; dark color; gloom

ferr·um -ī *n* iron; tool, implement; iron object: sword, dart, arrowhead, ax, plowshare, crowbar, spade, scissors, curling iron; **ferro atque igni** with fire and sword; **ferro decernere** to decide by force of arms

fertĭl·is -e *adj* fertile, fruitful, productive; fertilizing; (with *genit*) productive of

fertĭlit·ās -ātis *f* fertility, fruitfulness

ferŭl·a -ae *f* reed, stalk; rod, whip

fer·us -a -um *adj* wild; uncultivated, untamed; savage, uncivilized; rude, cruel, fierce; wild, desert (*place*); *m* wild beast, wild horse, lion, stag; *f* wild beast

fervĕ·faciō -facĕre -fēcī -factum *vt* to heat, boil

ferv·ens -entis *adj* seething, burning, hot; (fig) hot, heated, violent, impetuous

ferventer *adv* (fig) heatedly, impetuously

ferv·ĕō -ēre or **ferv·ō -ĕre -ī** *vi* to boil, seethe, steam; to foam; to swarm; to be busy, bustle about; (fig) to burn, glow, rage, rave

fervesc·ō -ĕre *vi* to become boiling hot, begin to boil, grow hot

fervĭd·us -a -um *adj* boiling, seething, hot; fermenting (*grapes*); hot, highly spiced; (fig) hot, fiery, violent, impetuous, hot-blooded

fervō see **ferveo**

ferv·or -ōris *m* heat, boiling heat; boiling; fermenting; fever; raging (*of the sea*); (fig) heat, vehemence, ardor, passion

Fescennĭ·a -ae *f* town in Etruria

Fescennīn·us -a -um *adj* Fescennine, of Fescennia; *m pl* Fescennine verses (*rude form of dramatic dialogue*)

fess·us -a -um *adj* tired, exhausted, worn out

festīnanter *adv* quickly

festīnātĭ·ō -ōnis *f* hurrying, haste, hurry

festīnātō *adv* hurriedly

festīn·ō -āre *vt & vi* to rush, hurry, accelerate; **jussa festinare** to carry out orders promptly

festīn·us -a -um *adj* hasty, quick, speedy

festīvē *adv* gaily; humorously

festīvit·ās -ātis *f* gaiety, fun; humor

festīv·us -a -um *adj* holiday, festal; gay, merry; agreeable, pleasing, pretty; humorous

festūc·a -ae *f* stalk; rod with which slaves were tapped when freed

fest·us -a -um *adj* joyous, festive, in holiday mood; *n* holiday; feast; **festum agere** to observe a holiday

fētiāl·is -is *m* member of a college of priests who performed the ritual in connection with declaring war and making peace

fētiāl·is -e *adj* negotiating, diplomatic; fetial, of the fetial priests

fetĭd·us -a -um *adj* fetid, stinking

fetūr·a -ae *f* breeding, bearing; offspring, young

fēt·us -a -um *adj* pregnant, breeding; fruitful, teeming, productive

fēt·us -ūs *m* breeding; (of plants) producing, bearing; offspring, young, brood; fruit, produce; (fig) growth, production

fi *interj* (expressing disgust at a bad smell) phew!

fib·er -rī *m* beaver

fibr·a -ae *f* fiber, filament; *f pl* entrails

fibŭl·a -ae *f* clasp, pin, brooch, buckle; brace, clamp

fīcedŭl·a or **fīcēdŭl·a -ae** *f* beccafico (*small bird*)

fīctē *adv* falsely, fictitiously

fictĭl·is -e *adj* clay, earthen; *n* jar; clay statue; *n pl* earthenware

fictĭ·ō -ōnis *f* forming, formation; disguising; supposition; fiction

fict·or -ōris *m* sculptor, molder, shaper

fictr·ix -īcis *f* maker, creator (*female*)

fict·um -ī *n* falsehood, fiction, pretense

fictūr·a -ae *f* shaping, fashioning

fict·us -a -um *pp* of **fingo**; *adj* false, fictitious; **vox ficta** falsehood

fīcŭl·us -ī *m* little fig

fīculn·us or **fīculnĕ·us -a -um** *adj* of a fig tree

fīc·us -ī or **-ūs** *f* fig; fig tree

fideīcommiss·um -ī *n* or **fideīcommiss·um -ī** *n* trust fund

fidēlĭ·a -ae *f* earthen pot, pail,

bucket; **duo parietes de eadem fidelia dealbare** to whitewash two walls with one pail, to kill two birds with one stone

fidēl·is -e *adj* faithful, loyal; trusty, trustworthy, true, sure, safe (*ship, port, advice, etc.*); (with *dat* or **in** + *acc*) faithful to; *m* confidant

fidēlit·ās -ātis *f* faithfulness, loyalty, fidelity

fidēliter *adv* faithfully, loyally; securely, certainly

Fidēn·ae -ārum *f pl* ancient town in Latium

fīd·ens -entis *adj* confident; resolute; bold

fīdenter *adv* confidently; resolutely; boldly

fīdenti·a -ae *f* self-confidence, boldness

fīd·ēs -ēī *f* trust, faith, reliance, confidence; credence, belief; trustworthiness, conscientiousness, honesty; promise, assurance, word, word of honor; protection, guarantee; promise of protection, safe conduct; (com) credit; confirmation, proof, fulfilment; **dē fidē malā** in bad faith, dishonestly; **Dī vostram fidem!** for heaven's sake! **ex fidē bonā** in good faith, honestly; **fidem dare** to give one's word, offer a guarantee; **fidem facere** to inspire confidence; **fidem fallere** to break one's word; **fidem habēre** (with *dat*) to have confidence in; to convince; **fidem servāre** to keep one's word; **prō fidem deum!** for heaven's sake! **res fidesque** capital and credit

fīd·ēs -is *f* string (*of a musical instrument*); *f pl* stringed instrument: lyre, lute, zither

fīdic·en -inis *m* lutist, lyre player; lyric poet

fīdicin·us -a -um *adj* stringed-instrument; *f* lutist, lyre player (*female*)

fīdicŭl·a -ae *f* or **fīdicŭl·ae -ārum** *f pl* small lute

fīdissimē *adv* most faithfully

Fīd·ius -ii or **-ī** *m* epithet of Jupiter; **medius fīdius!** honest to goodness!

fīdō fīdere fīsus sum *vi* (with *dat* or *abl*) to trust, put confidence in

fīdūci·a -ae *f* trust, confidence, reliance; self-confidence; trustworthiness; (law) deposit, pledge, security, mortgage

fīdūciāri·us -a -um *adj* held in trust

fīd·us -a -um *adj* trusty, dependable; certain, sure, safe

figlīn·us or **figulīn·us -a -um** *adj* potter's

figō fīgĕre fīxī fīxum *vt* to fix, fasten, affix, attach, nail; to drive in; to pierce; to erect, set up; to build; to post up, hang up

figulār·is -e *adj* potter's

figŭl·us -ī *m* potter; bricklayer

figūr·a -ae *f* figure, shape, form;

phantom, ghost; nature, kind; figure of speech

figūrāt·us -a -um *adj* figurative

figūr·ō -āre *vt* to shape, form, mold, fashion; to train, educate

fīlātim *adv* thread by thread

fīli·a -ae *f* daughter

fīlicāt·us -a -um *adj* engraved with fern patterns

fīliŏl·a -ae *f* little daughter

fīliŏl·us -ī *m* little son

fīl·ius -iī or **-ī** *m* son; **terrae fīlius** a nobody

fil·ix -icis *f* fern

fīl·um -ī *n* thread; fillet; string, cord; wick; figure, shape (*of a woman*); texture, quality, style (*of speech*)

fimbri·ae -ārum *f pl* fringe, border, end

fim·us -ī *m* dung, manure; mire

findō findĕre fidī fissum *vt* to split, split in half

fingō fingĕre finxī fictum *vt* to shape, form; to mold, model (*in clay, stone, etc.*); to arrange, dress, trim; to imagine, suppose, think, conceive; to contrive, invent, pretend, feign; to compose (*poetry*); to disguise (*looks*); to trump up (*charges*); (with double *acc*) to represent as, depict as; **ars fingendī** sculpture; **linguā fingĕre** to lick; **se fingĕre** (with **ad** + *acc*) to adapt oneself to; to be subservient to

fīnient·ēs -ium *m pl* horizon

fīn·iō -īre -īvī or **-iī -ītum** *vt* to limit; (fig) to set bounds to, limit, restrain; to mark out, fix, determine; to put an end to, finish complete; **fīnīrī** to come to an end, end; *vi* to come to an end; to die

fīn·is -is *m* or *f* boundary, border, limit; end; purpose, aim; extreme limit, summit, highest degree; starting point; goal; death; **fīne** (with *genit*) up to, as far as; **finem facere** (with *genit* or *dat*) to put an end to; **quem ad finem** how long, to what extent; *m pl* boundaries, country, territory, land

fīnītē *adv* to a limited degree

fīnītim·us or **fīnītūm·us -a -um** *adj* neighboring, bordering; (with *dat*) a bordering upon; **b** (fig) bordering upon, akin to; *m pl* neighbors

fīnīt·or -ōris *m* surveyor

fīnīt·us -a -um *adj* limited; (rhet) rhythmical

fīō fĭĕrī factus sum *vi* to come into being, arise; to be made, become, get; to happen; **fierī nōn potest quīn** it is inevitable that; **fierī potest ut** it is possible that; **ita fit ut** or **quō fit ut** thus it happens that

firmām·en -inis *n* prop, support

firmāment·um -ī *n* prop, support; support, mainstay; main point

firmāt·or -ōris *m* establisher, promoter

firmē adv firmly, steadily

firmĭt·ās -ātis f firmness, strength; steadfastness, stamina, endurance

firmĭter adv firmly, steadily

firmĭtūd·ō -ĭnis f firmness, strength, durability; (fig) stability, constancy

firm·ō -āre vt to strengthen, fortify, support; to encourage, strengthen, fortify, assure, reinforce; to establish, prove, confirm; to declare, aver

firm·us -a -um adj firm, strong, hardy, stable; (fig) firm, steadfast, trusty, true, faithful, lasting; firmus ad bellum toughened for combat

fiscāl·is -e adj fiscal

fiscell·a -ae f small basket

fiscĭn·a -ae f small basket

fisc·us -ī m basket; money box; state treasury; imperial treasury, emperor's privy purse, imperial revenues

fissĭl·is -e adj easy to split; split

fissĭ·ō -ōnis f dividing, splitting

fiss·us -a -um pp of findo; adj cloven; n slit, fissure

fistūc·a -ae f mallet

fistŭl·a -ae f pipe, tube; water pipe; hollow stalk or reed; flute; fistula, ulcer

fisus pp of fido

fix·us -a -um pp of figo; adj fixed, immovable; permanent

flābellĭfĕr·a -ae f female slave who waved a fan

flābell·um -ī n fan

flābĭl·is -e adj of air

flābr·a -ōrum n pl gusts of wind; breezes, winds

flacc·ĕō -ēre vi to be flabby; to lose heart; (of a speech) to get dull

flacc·escō -escĕre -ŭī vi to become flabby; to wither, droop

flaccĭd·us -a -um adj flabby; languid, feeble

flacc·us -a -um adj flabby

flagell·ō -āre vt to whip

flagell·um -ī n whip; scourge; riding crop; young shoot, sucker; arm (of a polypus); sting (e.g., of conscience)

flāgĭtātĭ·ō -ōnis f demand

flāgĭtāt·or -ōris m persistent demander

flāgĭtĭōsē adv shamefully, disgracefully

flāgĭtĭōs·us -a -um adj shameful, disgraceful, profligate

flāgĭt·ium -ĭī or -ī n shame, disgrace, scandalous conduct, scandal; rascal, good-for-nothing

flāgĭt·ō -āre vt to demand; (with double acc or with acc of thing or ab + abl of person) to demand (something) from (someone)

flagr·ans -antis adj blazing, flaming, hot; shining, glowing, glittering; ardent, hot, vehement, eager

flagranter adv vehemently, ardently

flagrantĭ·a -ae f blazing, glow; flagiti flagrantia utter disgrace

flagritrīb·a -ae m (coll) (said of a slave) victim of constant whipping

flagr·ō -āre vi to blaze, be on fire; (with abl) a to glow with, flare up in; b to be the victim of (e.g., envy)

flagr·um -ī n whip

flām·en -ĭnis m flamen (priest of a specific deity); flamen Dialis priest of Jupiter

flām·en -ĭnis n gust, gale; breeze

flāmĭnĭc·a -ae f wife of a flamen

Flāmĭnīn·us -ī m T. Quintus Flamininus (consul of 198 B.C., and conqueror of Philip of Macedon at Cynoscephalae, in Thessaly, in 197 B.C.)

flāmĭn·ĭum -ĭī or -ī n office of flamen, priesthood

Flāmĭnĭ·us -a -um adj Flaminian; via Flaminia road leading from Rome to Ariminum; m Gaius Flaminius (conqueror of Insubrian Gauls in 223 B.C., builder of the Circus Flaminius and the Flaminian highway in 220 B.C., and casualty in the battle at Lake Trasimenus in 217 B.C.)

flamm·a -ae f flame, fire, blaze; star; torch; flame of passion, fire of love, glow, passion; sweetheart; danger, destruction; flamma fumo est proxima where there's smoke there's fire; flammam concipere to catch fire

flammārĭ·us -ĭī or -ī m maker of bridal veils

flammĕŏl·um -ī n bridal veil

flammesc·ō -ĕre vi to become inflamed, become fiery

flammĕ·us -a -um adj flaming, fiery; flashing (eyes); flame-covered; n bridal veil

flammĭf·er -ĕra -ĕrum adj fiery

flamm·ō -āre vt to set on fire; (fig) to inflame, incense; vi to burn, glow, blaze

flammŭl·a -ae f little flame

flāt·us -ūs m blowing, breathing, breath; breeze, wind; snorting; arrogance

flāv·ens -entis adj yellow, golden

flāvesc·ō -ĕre vi to become yellow, become golden-yellow

Flāvĭ·us -a -um adj Flavian; gens Flavia Flavian clan (to which the emperors Vespasian, Titus, and Domitian belonged)

flāv·us -a -um adj yellow, blond, reddish-yellow, golden

flēbĭl·is -e adj pitiful, pathetic, deplorable; crying, tearful

flēbĭlĭter adv tearfully, mournfully

flectō flectĕre flexī flexum vt to bend, curve; to turn, wheel about, turn around; to wind, twist, curl; to direct, avert, turn away (eyes, mind, etc.); to double, sail around (a cape); to modulate (voice); to change (the mind); to persuade, move, appease; viam or iter flectere (with ad + acc) to make one's way toward, head toward; vi to turn, go, march

flēmĭn·a -um n pl swollen, bloody ankles

flĕ·ĕ̄ -ēre -ēvī -ētum vt to cry for, mourn for; vi to cry

flēt·us -ūs m crying; m pl tears

flexănĭm·us -a -um adj moving, touching

flexibĭl·is -e adj flexible; shifty, fickle

flexĭl·is -e adj flexible, pliant

flexĭlŏqu·us -a -um adj ambiguous

flexĭ·ŏ -ōnis f bending, turning; modulation (of the voice)

flexĭp·ĕs -ĕdis adj creeping (ivy)

flexŭŏs·us -a -um adj winding (road)

flexūr·a -ae f bending, winding

flexus pp of **flecto**

flex·us -ūs m bending, turning, winding; shift, change, transition, crisis

flict·us -ūs m clashing, banging together

flŏ·ŏ̄ -āre vt to blow, breathe; to coin (money); vi to blow

flocc·us -ī m lock (of hair, wool); down; **flocci facere** to think little of, disregard, not give a hoot about

Flōr·a -ae f goddess of flowers, whose festival was celebrated on April 28th

flōr·ens -entis adj blooming; prosperous; flourishing, in the prime; (with abl) in the prime of, at the height of

flōr·ĕŏ -ēre -ŭī vi to bloom, blossom; to be in one's prime; (of wine) to foam, ferment; to be prosperous, be eminent; (with abl) a to abound in; b to swarm with, be filled with

flōr·escŏ -escēre -ŭī vi to begin to bloom, begin to blossom

flōrĕ·us -a -um adj flowery; made of flowers

flōrĭd·us -a -um adj flowery; fresh, pretty; florid (style)

flōrĭf·er -ĕra -ĕrum adj flowery

flōrĭlĕg·us -a -um adj (of bees) going from flower to flower

flōr·us -a -um adj luxuriant

flŏ·ŏs -ōris m flower; bud, blossom; best (of anything); prime (of life); youthful beauty, innocence; crown, glory; nectar; literary ornament

floscŭl·us -ī m little flower, floweret; flower, pride, glory

fluctĭfrăg·us -a -um adj wavebreaking (shore), surging

fluctuātĭ·ŏ -ōnis f wavering, vacillating

fluctŭ·ŏ -āre or **fluctŭ·or -ārī -ātus sum** vi to fluctuate, undulate, wave; to be restless; to waver, vacillate, fluctuate

fluctuŏs·us -a -um adj running (sea)

fluct·us -ūs m wave, billow; flowing, undulating; turbulence, commotion; disorder, unrest; **fluctus in simpulo** tempest in a tea cup

flu·ens -entis adj loose, flowing; (morally) loose; effeminate; fluent

fluent·a -ōrum n pl flow, stream, river

fluenter adv like a wave

fluĭd·us or **flūvĭd·us -a -um** adj flowing, fluid; soft; relaxing

fluĭt·ŏ or **flŭt·ŏ -āre** vi to float, swim; to sail; to toss about; to hang loose, flap; to be uncertain, waver; to stagger

flūm·en -ĭnis n flowing, stream, river, flood; fluency; (fig) flood (e.g., of tears, words, etc.); **flumine adverso** upstream; **secundo flumine** downstream

flūmĭnĕ·us -a -um adj river

flu·ŏ -ēre -xī -xum vi to flow; to run down, drip; to overflow; (of branches) to spread; to sink, drop, droop; to pass away, vanish, perish; to be fluent; to be monotonous; to spring, arise, proceed

flūtŏ see **fluito**

fluvĭāl·is -e adj river, of a river

fluvĭātĭl·is -e adj river, of a river

flūvĭdus see **fluidus**

fluv·ĭus -ĭī or **-ĭ** m river; running water, stream

flux·us -a -um adj flowing, loose; careless; loose, dissolute; frail, weak; transient, perishable

fŏcāl·e -is n scarf

fŏcĭll·ŏ -āre vt to warm, revive

focŭl·um -ī n stove

focŭl·us -ī m brazier; (fig) fire

foc·us -ī m hearth, fireplace; brazier; funeral pile; altar; home, family

fodĭc·ŏ -āre vt to poke, nudge

fodĭŏ fodĕre fōdī fossum vt to dig, dig out; (fig) to prod, goad, prick

foecund- = fecund-

foedē adv foully, cruelly, shamefully

foederāt·us -a -um adj confederated, allied

foedĭfrăg·us -a -um adj treacherous, perfidious

foedĭt·ās -ātis f foulness, hideousness

foed·ŏ -āre vt to make hideous, disfigure; to pollute, defile, disgrace

foed·us -a -um adj foul, filthy, horrible, ugly, disgusting, repulsive; disgraceful, vile

foed·us -ĕris n treaty, charter, league; compact, agreement; law; **aequo foedere** on equal terms, mutually; **foedere certo** by fixed law; **foedere pacto** by fixed agreement

foen- = faen-

foet·ĕŏ -ēre vi to stink

foetĭd·us -a -um adj stinking

foet·or -ōris m stink, stench

foetu- = fētu-

folĭāt·us -a -um adj leafy; n nard oil

fol·ĭum -ĭī or **-ĭ** n leaf; **folium recitare Sibyllae** to tell the gospel truth

follĭcŭl·us -ī m small bag, sack; shell, skin; eggshell

foll·is -is m bag; punching bag; bellows; money bag; puffed-out cheeks

fōment·um -ī *n* bandage; mitigation, alleviation

fōm·es -itis *m* tinder

fon·s -tis *m* spring, fountain; spring water, water; stream; lake; source, origin, fountainhead

fontān·us -a -um *adj* spring

fonticul·us -ī *m* little spring, little fountain

for fārī fātus sum *vt & vi* to say, speak, utter

forābil·is -e *adj* vulnerable

forām·en -inis *n* hole, opening

forās *adv* out, outside; **foras dare** to publish (*writings*)

forc·eps -ipis *m* or *f* forceps, tongs

ford·a -ae *f* pregnant cow

fore = futur·us -a -um esse to be about to be

forem = essem

forens·is -e *adj* of the forum, in the forum; public, forensic

forf·ex -icis *f* scissors

for·is -is *f* door, gate; *f pl* double doors; opening, entrance; (fig) door

forīs *adv* outside, out of doors; abroad, in foreign countries; from outside, from abroad

form·a -ae *f* form, shape, figure; beauty; shape, image; mold, stamp; shoemaker's last; vision, apparition, phantom; species, form, nature, sort, kind; outline, design, sketch, plan

formāment·um -ī *n* shape

formāt·or -ōris *m* fashioner

formātūr·a -ae *f* fashioning, shaping

Formī·ae -ārum *f pl* town in S. Latium

formīc·a -ae *f* ant

formīcīn·us -a -um *adj* ant-like

formīdābil·is -e *adj* terrifying

formīd·ō -āre *vt* to fear, dread; *vi* to be frightened

formīd·ō -inis *f* fear, dread, awe, terror; scarecrow; threats

formīdolōsē *adv* dreadfully, terribly

formīdolōs·us -a -um *adj* dreadful, terrifying, terrible; afraid, terrified

form·ō -āre *vt* to form, shape, mold, build; to make, produce, invent; to imagine; to regulate, direct

formōsē *adv* beautifully, gracefully

formōsit·ās -ātis *f* beauty

formōs·us -a -um *adj* shapely, beautiful, handsome

formul·a -ae *f* nice shape, beauty; form, formula, draft; contract, agreement; rule, regulation; (law) regular method, formula, rule; (phil) principle

fornācāl·is -e *adj* of an oven

fornācul·a -ae *f* small oven

forn·ax -ācis *f* oven, furnace, kiln; forge

fornicāt·us -a -um *adj* arched

forn·ix -icis *m* arch, vault; arcade; brothel

fornus see **furnus**

for·ō -āre *vt* to bore, pierce

fors *adv* perhaps, chances are, there is a chance, possibly

for·s -tis *f* chance, luck, fortune, accident; **forte** by chance, accidentally, by accident; as it happens, as it happened; perhaps

forsan, forsit, or **forsitan** *adv* perhaps

fortasse or **fortassis** *adv* perhaps

forte see **fors**

forticul·us -a -um *adj* quite bold, rather brave

fort·is -e *adj* strong, mighty, powerful; brave, courageous, valiant, resolute, steadfast, firm

fortiter *adv* strongly, vigorously, firmly, bravely, boldly

fortitūd·ō -inis *f* strength; bravery, courage, resolution

fortuitō *adv* by chance, accidentally, casually

fortuīt·us -a -um *adj* accidental, fortuitous, casual

fortūn·a -ae *f* chance, luck, fate, fortune; good luck, prosperity; bad luck, misfortune; lot, circumstances, state, rank, position; property, goods, fortune

fortūnātē *adv* fortunately, prosperously

fortūnāt·us -a -um *adj* fortunate, lucky, prosperous, happy; rich, well-off

fortūn·ō -āre *vt* to make happy, make prosperous, bless

forul·ī -ōrum *m pl* bookcase

for·um -ī *n* shopping center, market, marketplace; market town; trade, commerce; forum, civic center; court; public life, public affairs; jurisdiction; **cedere foro** to go bankrupt; **extra suum forum** beyond his jurisdiction; **forum agere** to hold court; **forum attingere** to enter public life; **in foro versari** to be engaged in commerce

For·um Appiī (*genit*: **For·ī Appiī**) *n* town in Latium on the Via Appia

For·um Aurēliī (*genit*: **For·ī Aurēliī**) *n* town N. of Rome on the Via Aurelia

For·um Jūliī (*genit*: **For·ī Jūliī**) *n* town in S. Gaul, colony of the eighth legion

for·us -ī *m* gangway; tier of seats; tier of a beehive

foss·a -ae *f* ditch, trench; **fossam deprimere** to dig a deep trench

fossi·ō -ōnis *f* digging

foss·or -ōris *m* digger; lout, clown

fossūr·a -ae *f* digging

fossus *pp* of **fodio**

fōtus *pp* of **foveo**

fov·e·a -ae *f* small pit; (fig) pitfall

foveō fovēre fōvī fōtum *vt* to warm, keep warm; to fondle, caress; to love, cherish; to support, encourage; to pamper

fract·us -a -um *pp* of **frango**; *adj* interrupted, irregular; weak, feeble

frāg·a -ōrum *n pl* strawberries

fragil·is -e *adj* fragile, brittle;

crackling; weak, frail; unstable, fickle

fragilit·ās -ātis *f* weakness, frailty

fraglō see fragro

fragm·en -inis *n* fragment; *n pl* debris, ruins, wreckage

fragment·um -ī *n* fragment, remnant

frag·or -ōris *m* crash, noise, uproar, din; applause; clap of thunder

fragōs·us -a -um *adj* broken, uneven, rough; crashing, roaring

fragr·ō or **fraglō -āre** *vi* to smell sweet, be fragrant; to reek

framē·a -ae *f* German spear

frangō frangěre frēgī fractum *vt* to break in pieces, smash to pieces, shatter; to grind, crush; (fig) to break down, overcome, crush, dishearten, humble, weaken, soften, move, touch; **diem mero frangere** to break up the day with wine

frāt·er -ris *m* brother; cousin; friend, comrade

frātercūl·us -ī *m* little brother

frāternē *adv* like a brother

frāternit·ās -ātis *f* brotherhood

frātern·us -a -um *adj* brotherly; brother's; fraternal

frātricīd·a -ae *m* murderer of a brother, a fratricide

fraudāti·ō -ōnis *f* swindling

fraudāt·or -ōris *m* swindler

fraud·ō -āre *vt* to swindle, cheat, defraud; to embezzle; (with *abl*) to defraud (*someone*) of, cheat (*someone*) of

fraudulenti·a -ae *f* tendency to swindle, deceitfulness

fraudulent·us -a -um *adj* fraudulent; deceitful, treacherous

frau·s -dis *f* fraud, deception, trickery; error, delusion; crime, offense; harm, damage; deceiver, fraud, cheat; **sine fraude** without harm

fraxinē·us or **fraxin·us -a -um** *adj* of ash wood, ashen

fraxin·us -ī *f* ash tree; spear (*made of ash wood*)

Fregell·ae -ārum *f pl* ancient Volscan city on the Liris River, in Latium, made a Roman colony in 328 B.C.

fremebund·us -a -um *adj* roaring

fremit·us -ūs *m* roaring, growling, snorting; din, noise

frem·ō -ěre -ǔī -ǐtum *vt* to grumble at, complain loudly of; to demand angrily; *vi* to roar, growl, snort, howl, grumble, murmur; to resound

frem·or -ōris *m* roaring, grumbling, murmuring

frend·ō -ěre -ǔī *vi* to gnash the teeth; **dentibus frendere** to gnash the teeth

frēnī see frenum

frēn·ō -āre *vt* to bridle, curb; (fig) to curb, control

frēn·um -ī *n* or **frēn·a -ōrum** *n pl* or **frēn·ī -ōrum** *m pl* bridle, bit; (fig) curb, control, restraint

frequ·ens -entis *adj* crowded, in crowds, numerous, filled; frequent, repeated, usual, common; (may be rendered adverbially) often, repeatedly

frequentāti·ō -ōnis *f* piling up

frequenter *adv* frequently, often; in great numbers

frequenti·a -ae *f* crowd, throng; crowded assembly, large attendance

frequent·ō -āre *vt* to visit often, frequent, resort to; to do often, repeat; to crowd, people, stock; to attend (*e.g., games*) in large numbers

fretens·is -e *adj* **fretense mare** Strait of Messina

fret·um -ī *n* strait, channel; sea, waters; (fig) seething flood

frēt·us -a -um *adj* confident; (with *dat* or *abl*) supported by, relying on, depending on

fret·us -ūs *m* strait

fric·ō -āre -ǔī -tum *vt* to rub, rub down

frictus *pp* of frigo

frigefact·ō -āre *vt* to make cold or cool

frig·ĕō -ēre *vi* to be cold, be chilly; to freeze; (fig) to be numbed, be lifeless, be dull; (fig) to get a cool reception, be snubbed, get a cold shoulder; (fig) to fall flat

frigesc·ō -ěre *vi* to become cold, become chilled; to become lifeless

frigidāri·us -a -um *adj* cooling

frigidē *adv* feebly

frigidǔl·us -a -um *adj* rather cold; rather faint

frigid·us -a -um *adj* cold, cool; numbed, dull, lifeless, indifferent, unimpassioned, feeble; flat, insipid, trivial; *f* cold water

frigō frigěre frixī frictum *vt* to fry, roast

frig·us -ōris *n* cold, coldness, chill, coolness; frost; cold of winter, winter; coldness of death, death; chill, fever; cold shudder, chill; cold region; cold reception; coolness, indifference; slowness, inactivity; *n pl* cold spell, cold season

frigutt·iō -īre *vi* to stutter

fri·ō -āre *vt* to crumble

fritill·us -ī *m* dice box

frīvŏl·us -a -um *adj* frivolous, trifling, worthless, sorry, pitiful; *n pl* trifles

frondāt·or -ōris *m* pruner

frond·ĕō -ēre *vi* to have leaves; to become green

frondesc·ō -ěre *vi* to get leaves

frondě·us -a -um *adj* leafy, covered with leaves

frondif·er -ěra -ěrum *adj* leafy

frondōs·us -a -um *adj* full of leaves, leafy

fron·s -dis *f* foliage; leafy bough, green bough; chaplet, garland

fron·s -tis *f* forehead, brow; front end, front; countenance, face, look; face, façade; van, vanguard; exterior, appearance; outer end of a scroll; sense of shame; **a fronte** in front; **frontem contrahere** to knit the brow, frown; **frontem ferire** to hit oneself on the head (*in self-annoyance*); **frontem remittere** to smooth the brow, to cheer up; **in fronte** (in measuring land) in breadth, frontage; **salvā fronte** without shame; **tenuis frons** low forehead

frontāl·ia -ium *n pl* frontlet (*ornament for forehead of a horse*)

front·ō -ōnis *m* one with a large forehead

frūctuāri·us -a -um *adj* productive; subject to land tax

frūctuōs·us -a -um *adj* fruitful, productive

frūctus *pp of* **fruor**

frūct·us -ūs *m* produce, fruit; proceeds, profit, income, return, revenue; enjoyment, satisfaction; benefit, reward, results, consequence

frūgāl·is -e *adj* frugal; honest; worthy

frūgālit·ās -ātis *f* frugality, economy; temperance; honesty; worth

frūgāliter *adv* frugally, economically; temperately

frūgēs see **frux**

frūgī (indecl) *adj* frugal; temperate; honest, worthy; useful, proper

frūgif·er -era -erum *adj* fruitful, productive, fertile; profitable

frūgifer·ens -entis *adj* fruitful

frūgilēg·us -a -um *adj* (of ants) food-gathering

frūgipār·us -a -um *adj* fruitful

fruitus *pp of* **fruor**

frūmentāri·us -a -um *adj* of grain, grain; grain-producing; of provisions; **res frumentaria** (mil) supplies, quartermaster corps; *m* grain dealer

frūmentāti·ō -ōnis *f* (mil) foraging

frūmentāt·or -ōris *m* grain merchant; (mil) forager

frūment·or -ārī -ātus sum *vi* (mil) to forage

frūment·um -ī *n* grain; wheat; *n pl* grain fields, crops

frūn·iscor -iscī -ītus sum *vt* to enjoy

fruor frui frūctus sum or **fruitus sum** *vt* to enjoy; *vi* (with *abl*) **a** to enjoy, delight in; **b** to enjoy the company of; **c** (law) to have the use and enjoyment of

frustillātim *adv* in bits

frustrā *adv* in vain, uselessly, for nothing; without reason, groundlessly; **frustra discedere** to go away disappointed; **frustra esse** to be mistaken; **frustra habere** to have (*someone*) confused or baffled

frustrām·en -inis *n* deception

frustrāti·ō -ōnis *f* deception; frustration

frustrāt·us -ūs *m* deception; **frustratui habere** (coll) to take for a sucker

frustr·or -ārī -ātus sum or **frustr·ō -āre** *vt* to deceive, trick; to

disappoint; to frustrate

frustulent·us -a -um *adj* crumby, full of crumbs

frust·um -ī *n* crumb, bit, scrap; **frustum pueri** (coll) whipper-snapper

frut·ex -icis *m* shrub, bush; (coll) blockhead

fruticēt·um -ī *n* thicket, shrubbery

frutic·ō -āre or **frutic·or -ārī -ātus sum** *vi* to sprout; to become bushy; (fig) (of the hair) to become bushy

fruticōs·us -a -um *adj* bushy, overgrown with bushes

frux frūgis *f* or **frūg·ēs -um** *f pl* fruit, produce, grain, vegetables; barley meal (*for sacrifice*); fruits, benefit, result; **se ad frugem bonam recipere** to turn over a new leaf; **expers frugis** worthless

fūcāt·us -a -um *adj* dyed, colored, painted; artificial, spurious

fūc·ō -āre *vt* to dye red, redden, paint red; to disguise, falsify

fūcōs·us -a -um *adj* painted, colored; spurious, phoney

fūc·us -ī *m* red paint; rouge; drone; bee glue; disguise, pretense, deceit

fue or **fu** *interj* phui!

fug·a -ae *f* flight, escape; avoidance; exile; speed, swift passage; disappearance; (with *genit*) avoidance of, escape from; **fugae sese mandare, fugam capere, fugam capessere, fugam facere, se in fugam conferre, se in fugam conicere**, or **sese in fugam dare** to flee, take flight; **in fugam conferre, in fugam conicere, in fugam dare**, or **in fugam impellere** to put to flight

fugācius *adv* more cautiously, with one eye on flight

fug·ax -ācis *adj* apt to flee, fleeing; shy, timid; swift; passing, transitory; (with *genit*) shy of, shunning, avoiding, steering clear of, averse to

fugi·ens -entis *adj* fleeing, retreating; (with *genit*) avoiding, averse to

fugiō fugere fūgī fugitum *vt* to escape, escape from, run away from, shun, avoid; to leave (*esp. one's country*); to be averse to, dislike; to escape the notice of, escape, be unknown to; **fuge** (with *inf*) do not; **fugit me scribere** I forgot to write; *vi* to flee, escape, run away; to go into exile; to speed, hasten; to vanish, disappear; to pass away, perish

fugit·ans -antis *adj* fleeing; (with *genit*) averse to

fugitīv·us -a -um *adj & m* runaway, fugitive

fugit·ō -āre *vt* to run away from

fugit·or -ōris *m* deserter

fug·ō -āre *vt* to put to flight, drive away, chase away; to exile, banish; to avert

fulcim·en -inis *n* support, prop, pillar

fulciŏ fulcīre fulsī fultum vt to prop up, support; to secure, sustain

fulcr·um -ī n bed post; couch, bed

fulgĕŏ fulgēre fulsī or fulg·ō -ĕre vi to gleam, flash, blaze, shine, glare; to shine, be conspicuous, be illustrious

fulgid·us -a -um adj flashing, shining

fulgō see fulgeo

fulg·or -ōris m flash of lightning, lightning; brightness; thing struck by lightning

fulgurāl·is -e adj of lightning; librī fulgurales books on lightning

fulgurāt·or -ōris m interpreter of lightning

fulgurīt·us -a -um adj struck by lightning

fulgŭr·ō -āre vi to lighten, send lightning; v impers it is lightning

fulic·a -ae or ful·ix -icis f coot (waterfowl)

fūlīg·ō -inis f soot; black paint

fulix see fulica

full·ō -ōnis m fuller

fullōnic·a -ae f fuller's craft, fulling

fullōni·us -a -um adj fuller's

fulm·en -inis n thunderbolt, lightning bolt; (fig) bolt, bolt out of the blue

fulment·a -ae f heel

fulmine·us -a -um adj of lightning, lightning; shine, sparkling, flashing

fulmin·ō -āre vi to lighten; (fig) to flash

fultŭr·a -ae f support, prop

fultus pp of fulcio

fulv·us -a -um adj yellow, yellowish brown, reddish yellow, tawny; blond

fūmĕ·us -a -um adj smoky

fūmid·us -a -um adj smoking, smoky

fūmif·er -ĕra -ĕrum adj smoking

fūmific·ō -āre vi to smoke; to burn incense

fūmific·us -a -um adj smoking, steaming

fūm·ō -āre vi to smoke, fume, steam, reek

fūmōs·us -a -um adj smoked, smoky

fūm·us -ī m smoke, steam, fume

fūnāl·e -is n rope; torch; chandelier, candelabrum

fūnambŭl·us -ī m tightrope walker

functi·ō -ōnis f performance

functus pp of fungor

fund·a -ae f sling; sling stone; dragnet

fundām·en -inis n foundation

fundāment·um -ī n foundation; (fig) basis, ground, beginning; a fundamentis utterly, completely; fundamenta agere, jacere, or locare to lay the foundations

fundāt·or -ōris m founder

fundāt·us -a -um adj well-founded, established

fundit·ō -āre vt to sling, shoot with a sling; (fig) to sling (e.g., words) around

fundīt·or -ōris m slinger

fundītus adv from the bottom, utterly, entirely

fund·ō -āre vt to found, build, establish; to secure to the ground, make fast

fundō fundĕre fūdī fūsum vt to pour, pour out; to melt (metals); to cast (in metal); to pour in streams, shower, hurl; (mil) to pour in (troops); (mil) to rout; to pour out, empty; to spread, extend, diffuse; to bring forth, bear, yield in abundance; to throw to the ground, bring down; to give up, lose, waste; to utter, pour out (words)

fund·us -ī m bottom; farm, estate; (law) sanctioner, authority

fūnēbr·is -e adj funeral; deadly, murderous

fūnerāt·us -a -um adj done in, killed

fūnerĕ·us -a -um adj funeral; deadly, fatal

fūnĕr·ō -āre vt to bury; prope funeratus almost sent to my (his, etc.) grave

fūnest·ō -āre vt to defile with murder, desecrate

fūnest·us -a -um adj deadly, fatal, calamitous; sad, dismal, mournful; annales funesti obituary column

fungīn·us -a -um adj of a mushroom

fungor fungī functus sum vi (with abl) a to perform, execute, discharge, do; b to busy oneself with, be engaged in; c to finish, complete; morte fungi to suffer death, die

fung·us -ī m mushroom, fungus; candle snuff; (fig) clown

fūnicŭl·us -ī m cord

fūn·is -is m rope, cable, cord; rigging; funem ducere (fig) to command; funem reducere (fig) to change one's mind; funem sequi (fig) to serve, follow

fūn·us -ĕris n funeral rites, funeral, burial; corpse; death, murder; havoc; ruin, destruction; sub funus on the brink of the grave; n pl shades of the dead

fūr fūris m or f thief; (fig) rogue, rascal

fūrācissimē adv quite like a thief

fūr·ax -ācis adj thievish

furc·a -ae f fork; fork-shaped prop (for supporting vines, bleachers, etc.); wooden yoke (put around slave's neck as punishment)

furcif·er -ĕrī m rogue, rascal

furcill·a -ae f little fork

furcill·ō -āre vt to support, prop up

furcŭl·a -ae f fork-shaped prop; f pl narrow pass, defile

Furcŭl·ae Caudīn·ae (genit: Furcŭl·ārum Caudīn·ārum) f pl Caudine Forks (mountain pass near Caudium, in Samnium, where the Roman army was trapped in 321 B.C. by the Samnites and made to pass under the yoke)

furenter *adv* furiously

furf·ur -ŭris *m* chaff; bran

Furi·a -ae *f* Fury (*one of the three goddesses of frenzy and vengeance, who were named Megaera, Tisiphone, and Alecto*)

furi·a -ae *f* frenzy, madness; rage; remorse; madman

furiāl·is -e *adj* of the Furies; frenzied, frantic, furious; infuriated

furiāliter *adv* frantically

furibund·us -a -um *adj* frenzied, frantic, mad; inspired

furīn·us -a -um *adj* of thieves

furi·ō -āre *vt* to drive mad, infuriate

furiōsē *adv* in a rage, in a frenzy

furiōs·us -a -um *adj* frenzied, frantic, mad, furious; maddening

furn·us or **forn·us -ī** *m* oven; bakery

fur·ō -ĕre *vi* to be crazy, be out of one's mind, rage, rave

fūr·or -ārī -ātus sum *vt* to steal, pilfer; to pillage; to plagiarize; to obtain by fraud; to withdraw in secret; to impersonate

fur·or -ōris *m* madness, rage, fury, passion; furor, excitement; prophetic frenzy, inspiration; passionate love

furtific·us -a -um *adj* thievish

furtim *adv* secretly, by stealth, clandestinely

furtīvē *adv* secretly, stealthily

furtīv·us -a -um *adj* stolen; secret, hidden, furtive

furt·um -ī *n* theft, robbery; trick, stratagem; secret action, intrigue; secret love; *n pl* intrigues; secret love affair; stolen goods

fūruncŭl·us -ī *m* petty thief

furv·us -a -um *adj* black, dark, gloomy, eerie

fuscīn·a -ae *f* trident

fusc·ō -āre *vt* to blacken

fusc·us -a -um *adj* dark, swarthy; low, muffled, indistinct (*sound*)

fūsē *adv* widely; in great detail

fūsil·is -e *adj* molten, liquid

fūsi·ō -ōnis *f* outpouring, effusion

fust·is -is *m* club, stick, cudgel; beating to death (*as a military punishment*)

fustitūdin·us -a -um *adj* (coll) whip-happy (*jail*)

fustuār·ium -iī or **-ī** *n* beating to death (*as a military punishment*)

fūs·us -a -um *pp* of **fundo**; *adj* spread out; broad, wide; diffuse (*style*)

fūs·us -ī *m* spindle

futtil·is or **fūtil·is -e** *adj* brittle; futile, worthless, untrustworthy

futtilit·ās or **fūtilit·ās -ātis** *f* futility, worthlessness

fut·ŭō -ŭĕre -ŭī -ŭtum *vt* to have sexual intercourse with (*a woman*)

futūr·us -a -um *fut p* of **sum**; *adj* & *n* future

G

Gabī·ī -ōrum *m pl* ancient town in Latium

Gad·ēs -ium *f pl* Cadiz (*town in S. Spain*)

gaes·um -ī *n* Gallic spear

Gaetūl·ī -ōrum *m pl* a people in N.W. Africa along the Sahara Desert

Gā·ius -ī *m* Roman praenomen (*the names of Gaius and Gaia were formally given to the bridegroom and bride at the wedding ceremony*)

Galăt·ae -ārum *m pl* Galatians (*a people of central Asia Minor*)

Galati·a -ae *f* Galatia (*country in central Asia Minor*)

Galb·a -ae *m* Servius Sulpicius Galba, the Roman emperor from June, 68 A.D., to January, 69 A.D. (5 B.C.-69 A.D.)

galbanĕ·us -a -um *adj* of galbanum

galban·um -ī *n* galbanum (*resinous sap of a Syrian plant*)

galbin·us -a -um *adj* chartreuse; (fig) effeminate; *n pl* pale green clothes

galĕ·a -ae *f* helmet

galeāt·us -a -um *adj* helmeted

galēricŭl·um -ī *n* cap

galērīt·us -a -um *adj* wearing a farmer's cap, countryish

galēr·um -ī *n* or **galēr·us -ī** *m* cap; (fig) wig

gall·a -ae *f* gallnut

Gall·ī -ōrum *m pl* Gauls (*inhabitants of modern France and N. Italy*)

Galli·a -ae *f* Gaul

Gallic·us -a -um *adj* Gallic

gallīn·a -ae *f* chicken, hen; (as term of endearment) chick

gallīnācĕ·us or **gallīnācī·us -a -um** *adj* poultry

gallīnār·ius -iī or **-ī** *m* poultry farmer

Gallograec·ī -ōrum *m pl* Galatians (*Celts who migrated from Gaul to Asia Minor in the 3rd cent. B.C.*)

Gall·us -a -um *adj* Gallic; *m* Gaul; priest of Cybele; C. Cornelius Gallus, lyric poet and friend of Virgil (69-27 B.C.)

gall·us -ī *m* rooster, cock

gănĕ·a -ae *f* or **gănĕ·um -ī** *n* brothel, dive; cheap restaurant

gănĕ·ō -ōnis *m* glutton

gănĕum see **ganea**

Gangarid·ae -ārum *m pl* an Indian people on the Ganges

Gang·ēs -is *m* Ganges River

gann·ĭō -īre *vi* to snarl, growl

gannīt·us -ūs *m* snarling, growling

Ganymēd·ēs -is *m* Ganymede (*handsome youth carried off to Olympus by the eagle of Jupiter to become the cupbearer of the gods*)

Garamant·es -um *m pl* tribe in N. Africa

Gargaphĭ·ē -ēs *f* valley in Boeotia sacred to Diana

Gargān·us -ī *m* mountain in S.E. Italy

garr·ĭō -īre *vt* to chatter, prattle, talk; nugas garrīre to talk nonsense; *vi* to chatter, chat; (of frogs) to croak

garrŭlĭt·ās -ātis *f* talkativeness; chattering

garrŭl·us -a -um *adj* talkative, babbling, garrulous

gar·um -ī *n* fish sauce

gaud·ens -entis *adj* cheerful

gaudĕō gaudēre gāvīsus sum *vt* to rejoice at; gaudium gaudēre to feel joy; *vi* to rejoice, be glad, feel pleased; (with *abl*) to delight in; in sē gaudēre or in sinu gaudēre to be secretly glad

gaud·ium -ī or -ī *n* joy, gladness, delight; sensual pleasure, enjoyment; joy, cause of joy; mala mentis gaudia gloating

gaul·us -ī *m* bucket

gausăp·e -is or gausăp·um -ī *n* felt; (fig) shaggy beard

gāvīsus *pp* of gaudeo

gaz·a -ae *f* royal treasure; treasure, riches

gelĭdē *adv* coldly, indifferently

gelĭd·us -a -um *adj* cold, icy, frosty; icy cold, stiff, numbed; *f* cold water

gel·ō -āre *vt* & *vi* to freeze

Gelōn·ī -ōrum *m pl* Scythian tribe

gel·u -ūs *n* or gel·um -ī *n* or gel·us -ūs *m* coldness, cold, frost, ice; chill, coldness (*of death, old age, fear*)

gemebund·us -a -um *adj* sighing, groaning

gemellĭpăr·a -ae *f* mother of twins

gemell·us -a -um *adj* & *m* twin

gemĭnātĭ·ō -ōnis *f* doubling; compounding

gemĭn·ō -āre *vt* to double; to join, unite, pair; to repeat, reproduce

gemĭn·us -a -um *adj* twin; double, twofold, two, both; similar; *m pl* twins

gemĭt·us -ūs *m* sigh, groan

gemm·a -ae *f* bud; gem, jewel; jeweled goblet; signet ring, signet; eye of a peacock's tail; literary gem

gemmāt·us -a -um *adj* set with jewels, jeweled

gemmĕ·us -a -um *adj* set with jewels, jeweled; brilliant, glittering, sparkling

gemmĭf·er -ĕra -ĕrum *adj* gem-producing

gemm·ō -āre *vi* to sprout, bud; to sparkle

gem·ō -ĕre -ŭī -ĭtum *vt* to sigh over, lament; *vi* to sigh, groan, moan; to creak

Gemōnĭ·ae -ārum *f pl* steps on the Capitoline slope from which criminals were thrown

gen·a -ae *f* or gen·ae -ārum *f pl* cheek; cheekbone; eye socket; eye

geneālŏg·us -ī *m* genealogist

gen·er -ĕrī *m* son-in-law; daughter's boyfriend or fiancé

generāl·is -e *adj* of a species, generic; general, universal

generālĭter *adv* in general, generally

generasc·ō -ĕre *vi* to be generated

generātim *adv* by species, by classes; in general, generally

generāt·or -ōris *m* producer, breeder

gener·ō -āre *vt* to beget, procreate, produce, engender

generōsĭus *adv* more nobly

generōs·us -a -um *adj* of good stock, highborn, noble; noble, noble-minded

genĕs·is -is *f* birth, creation; horoscope

genesta see genista ..

genetĭv·us -a -um *adj* inborn, innate; (gram) genitive; *m* genitive case

genētr·ix -īcis *f* mother, ancestress

geniāl·is -e *adj* nuptial, bridal; genial; joyous, festive, merry

geniālĭter *adv* merrily

genĭcŭlāt·us -a -um *adj* knotted, having knots, jointed

genist·a or genest·a -ae *f* broom plant; broom

genitābĭl·is -e *adj* productive

genitāl·is -e *adj* generative, productive; of birth; dies genitālis birthday

genitālĭter *adv* fruitfully

genitīvus see genetivus

genit·or -ōris *m* father, creator

genitrix see genetrix

genitus *pp* of gigno

gen·ius -ĭī or -ī *m* guardian spirit; taste, appetite, natural inclination; talent, genius

gen·s -tis *f* clan; stock; tribe; folk, nation, people; species, breed; descendant, offspring; *f pl* foreign nations; longe gentium abīre to be far, far away; minime gentium by no means; ubi gentium where in the world, where on earth

gentĭc·us -a -um *adj* tribal; national

gentĭlĭcĭ·us -a -um *adj* family

gentīl·is -e *adj* family, hereditary; tribal; national; *m* clansman, kinsman

gentīlĭt·ās -ātis *f* clan relationship

gen·ū -ūs *n* knee; genibus minor kneeling; genibus nixus on one's knees; genuum junctura knee joint

genuāl·ia -ĭum *n pl* garters

genuīn·us -a -um *adj* innate, natural; of the cheek; jaw, of the jaw; *m pl* back teeth

gen·us -ĕris n race, descent, lineage, breed, stock, family; noble birth; tribe; nation, people; descendant, offspring, posterity; kind, sort, species, class; rank, order, division; fashion, way, style; matter, respect; genus; sex; gender; **aliquid id genus** (acc of description instead of genit of quality) something of that sort; **in omni genere** in every respect

geŏgraphĭ·a -ae f geography

geŏmĕtr·ēs -ae m geometer, mathematician

geŏmetrĭ·a -ae f geometry

geŏmetrĭc·us -a -um adj geometrical; n pl geometry

geŏrgĭc·us -a -um adj agricultural; n pl Georgics (poems on farming by Virgil)

ger·ens -entis adj (with genit) managing (e.g., a business)

germān·a -ae f full sister, real sister

germānē adv sincerely

Germān·ī -ōrum m pl Germans

Germānĭ·a -ae f Germany

Germānĭc·us -a -um adj Germanic; m cognomen of Tiberius' nephew and adoptive son (15 B.C.-19 A.D.)

germānĭt·ās -ātis f brotherhood, sisterhood (relationship between brothers and sisters of the same parents); relationship between colonies of the same mother-city

germān·us -a -um adj having the same parents; brotherly; sisterly; genuine, real, true; m full brother, own brother; f see germana

germ·en -ĭnis n sprout, bud, shoot, offspring; embryo

germĭn·ō -āre vt to put forth, grow (hair, wings, etc.); vi to sprout

gerō gerĕre gessī gestum vt to bear, carry, wear, have, hold; to bring; to display; exhibit, assume; to bear, produce; to carry on, manage, govern, regulate, administer; to carry out, transact, do, accomplish; **bellum gerere** to fight, carry on war; **dum ea geruntur** while that was going on; **gerere morem** (with dat) to gratify, please, humor; **personam gerere** (with genit) to play the part of; **rem gerere** to run a business, conduct an affair; **se gerere** to behave; **se gerere** (with pro + abl) to claim to be for; **se medium gerere** to remain neutral

ger·ō -ōnis m porter

gerr·ae -ārum f pl trifles, nonsense

gerr·ō -ōnis m (coll) loafer

gerŭlĭfĭgŭl·us -ī m accomplice; (with genit) accomplice in

gerŭl·us -ī m porter

Gēry·ŏn -ŏnis or **Gēry̆ŏn·ēs -ae** m mythical three-headed king of Spain who was slain by Hercules

gestām·en -ĭnis n that which is worn or carried; load; vehicle, litter; n pl ornaments; accouterments; arms

gestātĭ·ō -ōnis f drive (place where one drives)

gestāt·or -ōris m bearer, carrier

gestĭ·ō -ōnis f performance

gestĭ·ō -īre -īvī or **-ĭī -ītum** vi to be delighted, be thrilled, be excited; to be eager; (with inf) to be itching to, long to

gestĭt·ō -āre vt to be in the habit of carrying or wearing

gest·ō -āre vt to bear, wear, carry; to carry about, blab, tell; to cherish; **gestari** to ride, drive, sail (esp. for pleasure)

gest·or -ōris m tattler

gestus pp of gero; adj **res gestae** accomplishments, exploits

gest·us -ūs m gesture; gesticulation; posture, bearing, attitude

Get·ae -ārum m pl Thracian tribe of the lower Danube

gibb·us -ī m hump

Gigant·es -um m pl Giants (race of gigantic size, sprung from Earth as the blood of Uranus fell upon her. They tried to storm heaven but were repelled by the gods with the aid of Hercules and placed under various volcanoes)

gignō gignĕre genŭī genĭtum vt to beget, bear, produce; to cause, occasion, create, begin

gilv·us -a -um adj pale-yellow; **equus gilvus** palomino

gingīv·a -ae f gum (of the mouth)

glab·er -ra -rum adj hairless, bald, smooth; m young slave, favorite slave

glacĭāl·is -e adj icy, frozen

glacĭ·ēs -ēī f ice; f pl ice fields

glacĭ·ō -āre vt to turn into ice, freeze

gladĭāt·or -ōris m gladiator; m pl gladiatorial combat, gladiatorial show; **gladiatores dare** or **gladiatores edere** to stage a gladiatorial show

gladĭātōrĭ·us -a -um adj gladiatorial; n gladiator's pay

gladĭātūr·a -ae f gladiatorial profession

gladĭ·us -ĭī or **-ī** m sword; murder, death; **gladium educere** or **gladium stringere** to draw the sword; **gladium recondere** to sheathe the sword

glaeb·a -ae f lump of earth, clod; soil, land; lump, piece

glaebŭl·a -ae f small lump; bit of land, small farm

glaesum see glesum

glandĭf·er -ĕra -ĕrum adj acorn-producing

glandĭōnĭd·a -ae f choice morsel

gland·ĭum -ĭī or **-ī** n choice cut (of meat)

glan·s -dis f mast; nut; acorn; chestnut; bullet

glārĕ·a -ae f gravel

glāreōs·us -a -um *adj* full of gravel, gravelly

glaucōm·a -ătis *n* cataract; **glaucomam ob oculos objicere** (with *dat*) to throw dust into the eyes of

glauc·us -a -um *adj* grey-green, greyish; bright, sparkling

Glauc·us -ī *m* leader of the Lycians in the Trojan War; fisherman of Anthedon, in Euboea, who was changed into a sea deity

glēba see **glaeba**

glēs·um or **glaes·um -ī** *n* amber

glī·s -ris *m* dormouse

glīsc·ō -ĕre *vi* to grow, swell up, spread, blaze up; to grow, increase

globōs·us -a -um *adj* spherical

glob·us -ī *m* ball, sphere, globe; crowd, throng, gathering; clique

glomerăm·en -ĭnis *n* ball, globe

glomĕr·ō -āre *vt* to form into a ball, gather up, roll up; to collect, gather together, assemble

glom·us -ĕris *n* ball of yarn

glōri·a -ae *f* glory, fame; glorious deed; thirst for glory, ambition; pride, boasting, bragging

glōriāti·ō -ōnis *f* boasting, bragging

glōriŏl·a -ae *f* bit of glory

glōri·or -ārī -ātus sum *vt* (only with *neut pron* as object) to boast about, e.g., **haec gloriari** to boast about this; **idem gloriari** to make the same boast; *vi* to boast, brag; (with *abl* or with **de** or **in** + *abl*) to take pride in, boast about; (with **adversus** + *acc*) to boast or brag to (*someone*)

glōriōsē *adv* gloriously; boastfully, pompously

glōriōs·us -a -um *adj* glorious, famous; boastful

glossēm·a -ătis *n* word to be glossed

glūt·en -ĭnis *n* glue

glūtināt·or -ōris *m* bookbinder

glūtin·ō -āre *vt* to glue together

glutt·iō or **glūt·iō -īre** *vt* to gulp down

glutt·ō -ōnis *m* glutton

Gnae·us or **Gnē·us -ī** *m* Roman praenomen

gnār·us -a -um or **gnărŭr·is -e** *adj* skillful, expert; known; (with *genit*) familiar with, versed in, expert in

gnātus see **natus**

gnāv- = **nav-**

gnōbilis see **nobilis**

Gnōsi·a -ae or **Gnōsi·as -ădis** or **Gnōs·is -ĭdis** *f* Ariadne (*daughter of King Minos*)

gnoscō see **nosco**

Gnoss·us or **Gnōs·us -ī** *f* Cnossos (*ancient capital of Crete and residence of Minos*)

gnōtus see **nosco**

gōb·ius or **cōb·ius -ĭī** or **-ī** or **gōbi·ō -ōnis** *m* goby (*small fish*)

Gorgi·as -ae *m* famous orator and sophist of Leontini, in Sicily (*c.* 480-390 B.C.)

Gorg·ō -ōnis *f* Gorgon (*a daughter*

of Phorcys and Ceto); *f pl* Gorgons (*Stheno, Medusa, and Euryale*)

Gorgonē·us -a -um *adj* Gorgonian; **Gorgoneus equus** Pegasus; **Gorgoneus lacus** fountain Hippocrene on Mount Helicon

grabāt·us -ī *m* cot

Gracch·us -ī *m* Tiberius Sempronius Gracchus (*social reformer and tribune in* 133 B.C.); Gaius Sempronius Gracchus (*younger brother of Tiberius and tribune in* 123 B.C.)

gracĭl·is -e or **gracĭl·us -a -um** *adj* slim, slender; thin, skinny; poor; slight, insignificant; plain, simple (*style*)

gracĭlĭt·ās -ātis *f* slenderness; thinness, leanness, meagerness

grācŭl·us or **graccŭl·us -ī** *m* jackdaw

gradātim *adv* step by step, gradually, little by little

gradāti·ō -ōnis *f* climax

gradĭor gradī gressus sum *vi* to go, walk, step

Grădīv·us or **Grădīv·us -ī** *m* epithet of Mars

grad·us -ūs *m* step, pace, walk, gait; step, degree, grade, stage; approach, advance, progress; status, rank; station, position; step, rung, stair; footing; **concito gradu** on the double; **de gradu dejicere** (fig) to throw off balance; **gradum celerare** or **gradum corripere** to pick up the pace, speed up the pace; **gradum conferre** (mil) to come to close quarters; **gradūs ferre** (mil) to charge; **pleno gradu** on the double; **suspenso gradu** on tiptoe

Graecē *adv* Greek, in Greek; **Graece loqui** to speak Greek; **Graece scire** to know Greek

Graeci·a -ae *f* Greece; **Magna Graecia** southern Italy

graeciss·ō -āre *vi* to ape the Greeks

graec·or -ārī -ātus sum *vi* to go Greek, act like a Greek

Graecŭl·us -a -um *adj* (in contemptuous sense) Greek through and through, hundred-percent Greek; *mf* Greekling, dirty little Greek

Graec·us -a -um *adj* & *mf* Greek; *n* Greek, Greek language

Grā·iī or **Grā·ī -ōrum** *m pl* Greeks

Grāiŭgĕn·a -ae *m* Greek, Greek by birth

grall·ae -ārum *f pl* stilts

grallāt·or -ōris *m* stilt walker

grām·en -ĭnis *n* grass; meadow, pasture; plant, herb

grāmĭnĕ·us -a -um *adj* grassy, of grass; of bamboo

grammatĭc·us -a -um *adj* grammatical, of grammar; *m* teacher of literature and language; philologist; *f & n pl* grammar; philology

grānāri·a -ōrum *n pl* granary

grandaev·us -a -um *adj* old, aged

grandesc·ō -ĕre *vi* to grow, grow big

grandicŭl·us -a -um *adj* rather large; pretty tall

grandíf·er -ĕra -ĕrum *adj* productive

grandilŏqu·us -ī *m* braggart

grandĭn·at -āre *v impers* it is hailing

grand·ĭō -īre *vt* to enlarge, increase

grand·is -e *adj* full-grown, grown up, tall; large, great; aged; important, powerful, strong; grand, lofty, dignified (*style*); loud, strong (*voice*); heavy (*debt*); dignified (*speaker*)

grandit·ās -ātis *f* grandeur

grand·ō -ĭnis *f* hail

graníf·er -ĕra -ĕrum *adj* (of ants) grain-carrying

grān·um -ī *n* grain, seed

graphĭcē *adv* masterfully

graphĭc·us -a -um *adj* masterful

graph·ĭum -ĭī or **-ī** *n* stilus

grassāt·or -ōris *m* vagabond, tramp; bully; prowler

grass·or -ārī -ātus sum *vi* to walk about, prowl around; to hang around, loiter; to go, move, proceed; (with **adversus** or **in** + *acc*) to attack, waylay

grātē *adv* willingly, with pleasure; gratefully

grātēs (*genit* not in use) *f pl* thanks, gratitude; **grates agere** (with *dat*) to thank, give thanks to; **grates habere** (with *dat*) to feel grateful to

grātĭ·a -ae *f* grace, charm, pleasantness, loveliness; influence, prestige; love, friendship; service, favor, kindness; thanks, gratitude, acknowledgment; cause, reason, motive; **cum gratia** (with *genit*) to the satisfaction of; with the approval of; **eā gratiā ut** for the reason that; **exempli gratiā** for example; **gratiā** (with *genit*) for the sake of, on account of; **gratiam facere** (with *dat* of person and *genit* of thing) to pardon (*someone*) for (a *fault*); **gratias agere** (with *dat*) to thank, give thanks to; **gratias habere** (with *dat*) to feel grateful to; **in gratiam** (with *genit*) in order to win the favor of, in order to please; **in gratiam habere** to regard (*something*) as a favor; **meā gratiā** for my sake; **quā gratiā** why

Grātĭ·ae -ārum *f pl* Graces (*Aglaia, Euphrosyne, and Thalia, daughters of Jupiter by Eurynome*)

grātĭficātĭ·ō -ōnis *f* kindness

grātĭfic·or -ārī -ātus sum *vt* to give up, surrender, sacrifice; *vi* (with *dat*) **a** to do (*someone*) a favor; **b** to gratify, please

grātĭis *adv* gratis, free, for nothing, gratuitously

grātĭōs·us -a -um *adj* popular, influential; obliging

grātis *adv* gratis, free, for nothing, gratuitously

grāt·or -ārī -ātus sum *vi* to rejoice; to express gratitude; (with *dat*) to congratulate; **invicem inter se gratari** to congratulate one another

grātuītō *adv* gratuitously, gratis, for nothing; for no particular reason

grātuīt·us -a -um *adj* gratuitous, free, spontaneous; voluntary; unprovoked

grātŭlābund·us -a -um *adj* congratulating

grātŭlātĭ·ō -ōnis *f* congratulation; rejoicing, joy; public thanksgiving

grātŭlāt·or -ōris *m* congratulator, well-wisher

grātŭl·or -ārī -ātus sum *vi* to be glad, rejoice, manifest joy; (with *dat*) **a** to congratulate; **b** to render thanks to

grāt·us -a -um *adj* pleasing, pleasant, agreeable, welcome; thankful, grateful; deserving thanks, earning gratitude; *n* favor; **gratum facere** (with *dat*) to do (*someone*) a favor

gravanter *adv* reluctantly

gravātē *adv* with difficulty; unwillingly, grudgingly

gravātim *adv* with difficulty; unwillingly

gravēdinōs·us -a -um *adj* prone to catch colds

gravēd·ō -ĭnis *f* cold, head cold

gravesc·ō -ĕre *vi* to grow heavy; (fig) to become worse

gravidit·ās -ātis *f* pregnancy

gravid·ō -āre *vt* to impregnate

gravid·us -a -um *adj* loaded, filled, full; pregnant; (with *abl*) teeming with

grav·is -e *adj* heavy, weighty; burdensome; troublesome, oppressive, painful, harsh, hard, severe, unpleasant; unwholesome, indigestible; important, influential, venerable, grave, serious; pregnant; hostile; low, deep, bass; flat (*note*); harsh, bitter, offensive (*smell or taste*); impressive (*speech*); stormy (*weather*); oppressive (*heat*)

gravit·ās -ātis *f* weight; severity, harshness, seriousness; importance; dignity, influence; pregnancy; violence, vehemence

graviter *adv* heavily, ponderously; hard, violently, vehemently; severely, harshly, unpleasantly, disagreeably; sadly, sorrowfully; with dignity, with propriety, with authority; (to feel) deeply; (to smell) offensive, strong; (to speak) impressively; **graviter ferre** to take (*something*) hard

grav·ō -āre *vt* to weigh down, load, load down; to burden, be oppressive to; to aggravate; to increase

grav·or -ārī -ātus sum *vt* to feel annoyed at, object to, refuse, decline; to bear with reluctance, regard as a burden; *vi* to feel annoyed, be vexed

gregāl·is -e *adj* of the herd or flock; common; **sagulum gregale** uniform of a private; *m pl* comrades, companions

gregārī·us -a -um *adj* common; (mil) of the same rank; **miles gregarius** private

gregātim *adv* in flocks, in herds, in crowds

grem·ium -iī or **-ī** *n* lap, bosom; womb

gressus *pp* of **gradior**

gress·us -ūs *m* step; course, way

gre·x -gis *m* flock, herd; swarm; company, group, crowd, troop, set, clique, gang; theatrical cast

gruis see **grus**

grunn·iō or **grund·iō -īre -īvī** or **-iī -itum** *vi* to grunt

grunnīt·us -ūs *m* grunt, grunting

grū·s or **gru·is -is** *m* or *f* crane

grȳ (indecl) *n* scrap, crumb

grȳps grȳpis *m* griffin

gubernācŭl·um or **gubernācl·um -ī** *n* rudder, tiller, helm; *n pl* (fig) helm

gubernātī·ō -ōnis *f* navigation

gubernāt·or -ōris *m* navigator, pilot; governor

gubernātr·ix -īcis *f* directress

gubern·ō -āre *vt* to navigate, pilot; to direct, govern

gul·a -ae *f* gullet, throat; palate, appetite, gluttony

gulōs·us -a -um *adj* appetizing, dainty

gurg·es -itis *m* abyss, gulf, whirl-pool; waters, flood, depths, sea; spendthrift

gurgūli·ō -ōnis *m* gullet, windpipe

gurgust·ium -iī or **-ī** *n* dark hovel; (fig) hole in the wall

gustātōr·ium -iī or **-ī** *n* appetizer

gustāt·us -ūs *m* sense of taste; flavor, taste

gust·ō -āre *vt* to taste; (fig) to enjoy; to overhear; *vi* to have a snack

gust·us -ūs *m* tasting; appetizer

gutt·a -ae *f* drop; spot, speck

guttātim *adv* drop by drop

guttŭl·a -ae *f* tiny drop

gutt·ur -ŭris *n* gullet, throat, neck; *n pl* throat, neck

gŭt·us or **gutt·us -ī** *m* cruet, flask

Gy·ās -ae *m* hundred-armed giant

Gȳg·ēs -is or **-ae** *m* king of Lydia (716-678 B.C.)

gymnasiarch·us -ī *m* manager of a gymnasium

gymnas·ium -iī or **-ī** *n* gymnasium

gymnastic·us -a -um *adj* gymnastic

gymnic·us -a -um *adj* gymnastic

gymnosophist·ae -ārum *m pl* Hindu Stoics

gynaecē·um or **gynaecī·um -ī** *n* women's apartments

gypsāt·us -a -um *adj* covered with plaster

gyps·um -ī *n* gypsum, plaster

gȳr·us -ī *m* circle, cycle, ring, orbit, course

H

ha, hahae, hahahae *interj* expression of joy, satisfaction, or laughter

habēn·a -ae *f* strap; *f pl* reins; (fig) reins, control; **habenae rerum** reins of the state; **habenas adducere, dare, effundere,** or **immittere** (with *dat*) to give free rein to

hab·eō -ēre -ŭī -itum *vt* to have, hold, keep; to retain, detain; to contain; to possess, own; to wear; to treat, handle, use; to hold, conduct (*meeting*); to deliver (*speech*); to occupy, inhabit; to pronounce, utter (*words*); to hold, manage, govern, wield; to hold, think, consider, believe; to occupy, engage, busy; to occasion, produce, render; to know, be informed of, be acquainted with; to take, accept, endure, bear; **in animo habere** to have on one's mind; **in animo habere** (with *inf*) to intend to; **pro certo habere** to regard as certain; **secum** or **sibi habere** to keep (*something*) to oneself, keep secret; **se habere** (with *adv*) to be,feel (*well, etc.*); *vi* **bene habet** it is well, all is well; **sic habet** that's how it is

habĭl·is -e *adj* handy; suitable, convenient; active, nimble; skillful

habĭlĭt·ās -ātis *f* aptitude

habĭtābĭl·is -e *adj* habitable, fit to live in

habĭtātī·ō -ōnis *f* dwelling, house

habĭtāt·or -ōris *m* inhabitant, tenant

habĭt·ō -āre *vt* to inhabit; *vi* to dwell, live, stay, reside; (with **in** + *abl*) **a** to live in, reside at; **b** to be always in (*a certain place*); **c** (fig) to dwell upon

habĭtūd·ō -ĭnis *f* condition, appearance

habĭt·us -a -um *adj* well-kept, fat, stout

habĭt·us -ūs *m* condition (*of the body*); character, quality; style, style of dress, attire; disposition, state of feeling; habit

hāc *adv* this way, in this way

hactēnus *adv* to this place, thus far; up till now, hitherto, so far; to this extent, so far, so much

Hadrĭ·a -ae *f* city in Picenum, the birthplace of Hadrian; city in the country of the Veneti, on the coast of the sea named after it; *m* Adriatic Sea

Hadrián·us -ī *m* Hadrian (*Roman emperor,* 117-138 A.D.)

haec hōrum (*neut pl* of **hoc**) *adj & pron* these

haec hūjus (older form; **haece**; *genit:* **hujusce**) (*fem* of **hic**) *adj* this; the present, the actual; the latter; (occasionally) the former; **haec** . . . **haec** one . . . another; *pron* this one, she; the latter; (occasionally) the former; **haec** . . . **haec** one . . . another one; **haecine** (**haec** with *interrog* enclitic **-ne**) is this . . .?

haece see **haec**

haecine see **haec**

Haed·ī -ōrum *m pl* pair of stars in the constellation Auriga

haedíll·a -ae *f* little kid

haedill·us -ī *m* (term of endearment) little kid or goat

haedīn·us -a -um *adj* kid's, goat's

haedúl·us -ī *m* little kid, little goat

haed·us -ī *m* young goat, kid

Haemoni·a -ae *f* Thessaly

Haem·us or **Haem·os -ī** *m* mountain range in Thrace

haerēō haerēre haesī haesum *vi* to cling, stick; to hang around, linger, stay, remain fixed, remain in place; to be rooted to the spot, come to a standstill, stop, to be embarrassed, be at a loss, hesitate, be in doubt; (with *dat* or *abl* or with **in** + *abl*) **a** to cling to, stick to, adhere to, be attached to; **b** to loiter in, hang around in, waste time in (*a place*) or at (*an activity*); **c** to adhere to, stick by (*an opinion, purpose*); **d** to gaze upon; **e** to keep close to; **in terga, in tergis,** or **tergis hostium haerere** to pursue the enemy closely

haeresc·ō -ēre *vi* to adhere

haerēs·is -is *f* sect, school of thought

haesitābund·us -a -um *adj* hesitating, faltering

haesitanti·a -ae *f* stammering

haesitáti·ō -ōnis *f* hesitation, indecision; stammering

haesitāt·or -ōris *m* hesitator

haesit·ō -āre *vi* to get stuck; to stammer; to hesitate, be undecided, be at a loss

hahae hahahae *interj* expression of joy, satisfaction, or laughter

halagŏra -ae *f* salt market

hāl·ans -antis *adj* fragrant

hāl·ēc -ēcis *n* fish sauce

haliaeēt·os -ī *m* sea eagle, osprey

hālit·us -ūs *m* breath; steam, vapor

hall·ex -ĭcis *m* big toe

hallūcin·or or **hālūcīn·or -ārī -ātus sum** *vi* to daydream, have hallucinations, talk wildly

hāl·ō -āre *vt* to exhale; *vi* to exhale; to be fragrant

halophant·a -ae *f* scoundrel

hālūcinor see **hallucinor**

ham·a or **am·a -ae** *f* bucket, pail

Hamādrý·as -ādis *f* wood nymph

hāmātĭl·is -e *adj* with hooks

hāmāt·us -a -um *adj* hooked, hook-shaped

Hamīlc·ar -āris *m* famous Carthaginian general in the First Punic War, surnamed Barca, and father of Hannibal (*d.* 228 B.C.)

hāmiōt·a -ae *m* angler

hāmŭl·us -ī *m* small hook

hām·us -ī *m* hook, fishhook

Hannĭb·al -ălis *m* son of Hamilcar Barca and famous general in the Second Punic War (246-172 B.C.)

har·a -ae *f* pen, coop, stye

harēn·a -ae *f* sand; seashore, beach; arena; *f pl* desert

harēnōs·us -a -um *adj* sandy

hariŏl·or -ārī -ātus sum *vi* to foretell the future; to talk gibberish

hariŏl·us -ī *m* or **hariŏl·a -ae** *f* soothsayer

harmoni·a -ae *f* harmony

harpăg·ō -āre *vt* to steal

harpăg·ō -ōnis *m* hook, harpoon, grappling hook; greedy person

Harpalýc·ē -ēs *f* daughter of a Thracian king, brought up as a warrior

harp·ē -ēs *f* scimitar

Harpýi·ae -ārum *f pl* Harpies (*mythical monsters, half woman, half bird*)

harundīf·er -ěra -ěrum *adj* reed-bearing

harundiné·us -a -um *adj* made of reed

harundinōs·us -a -um *adj* overgrown with reeds

harund·ō -ĭnis *f* reed, cane; fishing rod; pen; shepherd's pipe; arrow shaft, arrow; fowler's rod; weaver's comb; hobbyhorse (*toy*)

harusp·ex -ĭcis *m* soothsayer who foretold the future from the inspection of the vital organs of animals; prophet

haruspĭc·a -ae *f* soothsayer (*female*)

haruspĭcín·us -a -um *adj* of divination; *f* art of divination

haruspĭc·ium -iī or **-ī** *n* divination

Hasdrŭb·al or **Asdrŭb·al -ălis** *m* brother of Hannibal (*d.* 207 B.C.); son-in-law of Hamilcar Barca (*d.* 221 B.C.)

hast·a -ae *f* spear; **sub hasta vendere** to sell at auction, auction off

hastāt·us -a -um *adj* armed with a spear; *m pl* soldiers in first line of a Roman battle formation

hastīl·e -is *n* shaft; spear, javelin

hau or **au** *interj* cry of pain or grief

haud or **haut** or **hau** *adv* not, hardly, not at all, by no means

hauddum *adv* not yet

haudquāquam *adv* not at all, by no means

hauriō haurīre hausī haustum *vt* to draw, draw up, draw out; to drain, drink up; to spill, shed; to swallow, devour, consume, exhaust; to derive; (fig) to drink in, seize upon, imbibe

haustr·um -ī *n* scoop, bucket

haustus *pp* of **haurio**

haust·us -ūs *m* drawing (*of water*); drinking, swallowing; drink, draught; handful; stream (*of blood*)

haut see **haud**

havĕō see **aveo**

hebdŏm·as -ădis *f* week

Hĕb·ē -ēs *f* goddess of youth, daughter of Juno, and cupbearer of the gods

hebĕn·us -ī *f* ebony

heb·ĕō -ēre *vi* to be blunt, be dull; (*fig*) to be inactive, be sluggish

heb·es -ĕtis *adj* blunt, dull; faint, dim; dull, obtuse, stupid

hebesc·ō -ēre *vi* to grow blunt, grow dull; to become faint or dim; to lose vigor

hebĕt·ō -āre *vt* to blunt, dull, dim

Hebr·us -ī *m* principal river in Thrace

Hecăt·ē -ēs *f* goddess of magic and witchcraft and often identified with Diana

hecatomb·ē -ēs *f* hecatomb

Hect·or -ŏris *m* son of Priam and Hecuba, husband of Andromache, and bravest Trojan warrior in fighting the Greeks

Hecŭb·a -ae or **Hecŭb·ē -ēs** *f* wife of Priam who, after the destruction of Troy, became a captive of the Greeks and was eventually changed into a dog

heder·a -ae *f* ivy

hederĭg·er -ĕra -ĕrum *adj* wearing ivy

hederōs·us -a -um *adj* overgrown with ivy

hĕdўchr·um -ī *n* perfume

hei hēia see **ei, ēia**

Helĕn·a -ae or **Helĕn·ē -ēs** *f* Helen (*wife of Menelaus, sister of Clytemnestra, Castor, and Pollux, who was abducted by Paris*)

Helĕn·us -ī *m* prophetic son of Priam and Hecuba

Hēliăd·es -um *f pl* daughters of Helios and sisters of Phaëthon, who were changed into poplars and whose tears were changed to amber

Helĭc·ē -ēs *f* Big Bear (*constellation*)

Helĭc·ōn -ōnis *m* mountain in Boeotia sacred to the Muses and to Apollo

Helĭcōniăd·es or **Helĭcōnĭd·es -um** *f pl* Muses

Hell·as -ădis *f* Greece

Hell·ē -ēs *f* daughter of Athamas and Nephele who, while riding the golden-fleeced ram, fell into the Hellespont and drowned

hellĕbor- = ellebor-

Hellespont·us -ī *m* Dardanelles

hellŭ·ō -ōnis *m* glutton, squanderer

hellŭ·or -ārī -ātus sum *vi* to be a glutton

hel·ops or **el·ops** or **ell·ops -ŏpis** *m* highly-prized fish (*perhaps the sturgeon*)

helvell·a -ae *f* delicious herb

Helvĕtĭ·ī -ōrum *m pl* people of Gallia Lugdunensis (*modern Switzerland*)

helv·us -a -um *adj* light-bay

hem *interj* (expression of surprise) well!

hēmerodrŏm·us -ī *m* courier

hēmicill·us -ī *m* mule

hēmicycl·ium -iī or **-ī** *n* semicircle of seats

hēmin·a -ae *f* half of a sextarius (*half a pint*)

hendecasyllăb·ī -ōrum *m pl* hendecasyllabics (*verses with eleven syllables*)

hēpatāri·us -a -um *adj* of the liver

heptēr·is -is *f* galley with seven banks of oars

hera see **era**

Hēr·a -ae *f* Greek goddess identified with Juno

Hēraclīt·us -ī *m* early Greek philosopher of Ephesus who believed that fire was the primary element of all matter (*fl* 513 B.C.)

herb·a -ae *f* blade, stalk; herb, plant; grass, lawn; weed

herbesc·ō -ēre *vi* to sprout

herbĕ·us -a -um *adj* grass-green

herbĭd·us -a -um *adj* grassy

herbĭf·er -ĕra -ĕrum *adj* grassy, grass-producing; made of herbs

herbōs·us -a -um *adj* grassy; made with herbs

herbŭl·a -ae *f* little herb

hercisc·ō -ēre *vi* to divide an inheritance

herct·um or **erct·um -ī** *n* inheritance

Herculānĕ·um -ī *n* town on the seacoast of Campania which was destroyed with Pompeii in an eruption of Vesuvius in 79 A.D.

Hercŭl·ēs -is or **-ī** *m* son of Jupiter and Alcmena, husband of Deianira, and after his death and deification, husband of Hebe

herculēs or **hercŭle** or **hercle** *interj* by Hercules!

here *adv* yesterday

hērēditāri·us -a -um *adj* of or about an inheritance; inherited, hereditary

hērēdĭt·ās -ātis *f* inheritance

hērēd·ium -iī or **-ī** *n* inherited estate

hēr·ēs -ēdis *m* heir; (*fig*) heir, successor; *f* heiress

herī or **here** *adv* yesterday

herif- herīl- = erif- eril-

Hermăphrodīt·us -ī *m* son of Hermes and Aphrodite who combined with the nymph Salmacis to become one person

Herm·ēs or **Herm·a -ae** *m* Greek god identified with Mercury

Hermĭŏn·ē -ēs or **Hermĭŏn·a -ae** *f* daughter of Helen and Menelaus and wife of Orestes

Hērodŏt·us -ī *m* father of Greek history, born at Halicarnassus on coast of Asia Minor (484-425 B.C.)

hērŏĭc·us -a -um *adj* heroic, epic

hērŏĭn·a -ae *f* demigoddess

hērŏ·ĭs -ĭdis *f* demigoddess

hēr·ōs -ōĭs *m* demigod, hero (*rarely used of men born of human parents*)

hērŏ·us -a -um *adj* heroic, epic

herus see erus

Hēsĭŏd·us -ī *m* Hesiod (*early Greek poet, born in Boeotia, 8th cent. B.C.*)

Hēsĭŏn·ē -ēs or Hēsĭŏn·a -ae *f* daughter of Laomedon, king of Troy, whom Hercules rescued from a sea monster

Hespĕr·us or Hespĕr·os -ī *m* evening star

hestern·us -a -um *adj* yesterday's

hetaīrĭ·a -ae *f* secret society

hetaīrĭc·ē -ēs *f* Macedonian mounted guard

heu! *interj* (expression of pain or dismay) oh!, ah!

heus! *interj* (to draw attention) say there!, hey!

hexamĕt·er -rī *m* hexameter verse

hexēr·ĭs -ĭs *f* ship with six banks of oars

hĭāt·us -ūs *m* opening; open or gaping mouth; mouthing, bluster; basin (*of fountain*); chasm; (*gram*) hiatus

Hībēr·us -um *m pl* Spaniards

hībern·a -ōrum *n pl* winter quarters

hībernācŭl·a -ōrum *n pl* winter bivouac; winter residence

hībern·ō -āre *vi* to spend the winter; to stay in winter quarters; (*fig*) to hibernate

hībern·us -a -um *adj* winter, in winter, wintry

hibīsc·um -ī *n* hibiscus

hībrĭd·a or hybrĭd·a -ae *m* or *f* hybrid, mongrel, half-breed

hīc (or hic) hūjus (*older form:* hīce hūjusce) *adj* this; the present, the actual; the latter; (*occasionally the former*); hic . . . hic one . . . another; *pron* this one, he; this man, myself, your's truly (*i.e., the speaker or writer*); the latter; (*occasionally*) the former; (*in court*) the defendant, my defendant; hic . . . hic one . . . another; hicine (hic with *interrog* enclitic -ne) is this . . . ?

hīc *adv* here, in this place; at this point; in this affair, in this particular, herein

hīce see hīc

hicine see hīc

hiemāl·ĭs -e *adj* winter, wintry; stormy

hiĕm·ō -āre *vi* to spend the winter, pass the winter; to be wintry, be cold, be stormy

hiem·s or hiem·ps -ĭs *f* winter; cold; storm

Hiĕr·ō -ōnĭs *m* ruler of Syracuse and patron of philosophers and poets (?-466 B.C.); friend of the Romans in the First Punic War (306?-215 B.C.)

Hierosolÿm·a ōrum *m pl* Jerusalem

hiĕt·ō -āre *vi* to keep yawing

hilāre *adv* cheerfully, merrily, gaily

hilăr·ĭs -e or hilăr·us -a -um *adj* cheerful, merry, gay

hilarĭt·ās -ātĭs *f* cheerfulness, gaiety

hilarĭtūd·ō -ĭnĭs *f* cheerfulness

hilăr·ō -āre *vt* to cheer up

hilarŭl·us -a -um *adj* merry little

hilărus see hilaris

hill·ae -ārum *f pl* smoked sausage

Hīlŏt·ae or Īlŏt·ae -ārum *m pl* Helots (*slaves of the Spartans*)

hīl·um -ī *n* something, trifle

hinc *adv* from here, from this place; on this side, here; for this reason; from this source; after this, henceforth, from now on

hinn·ĭō -īre *vi* to whinny, neigh

hinnīt·us -ūs *m* neighing

hinnŭl·us -ī *m* fawn

hĭ·ō -āre *vt* to sing; *vi* to open, be open; to gape; to yawn; to make eyes (*in surprise or greedy longing*)

hippagōg·ī -ōrum *f pl* ships for transporting horses and cavalry

Hipparch·us -ī *m* son of Pisistratus, the tyrant of Athens, and was slain by Harmodius and Aristogiton in 514 B.C.

Hippĭ·ās -ae *m* son of Pisistratus, the tyrant of Athens, and tyrant of Athens himself, 527-510 B.C.

hippocentaur·us -ī *m* centaur

Hippocrăt·ēs -is *m* famous physician, founder of scientific medicine (*c.* 460-380 B.C.)

Hippocrēn·ē -ēs *f* spring on Mt. Helicon, sacred to the Muses and produced when the hoof of Pegasus hit the spot

Hippŏdăm·ē -ēs or Hippŏdamē·a or Hippŏdamī·a -ae *f* daughter of Oenamaus, the king of Elis, and wife of Pelops; daughter of Adrastus and wife of Pirithous

hippodrŏm·os -ī *m* racetrack

Hippŏlÿt·ē -ēs or Hippŏlÿt·a -ae *f* Amazonian wife of Theseus; wife of Acastus, king of Magnesia

Hippŏlÿt·us -ī *m* son of Theseus and Hippolyte

hippomăn·es -ĭs *n* membrane of the head of a new-born foal; discharge of a mare in heat

Hippŏmăn·ēs -ae *m* son of Megareus who competed with Atalanta in a race and won her as his bride

Hippōn·ax -actĭs *m* Greek satirist (*fl* 540 B.C.)

hippotoxŏt·ae -ārum *m pl* mounted archers

hippūr·us -ī *m* goldfish

hīr·a -ae *f* empty gut

hircīn·us or hirquīn·us -a -um *adj* goat, of a goat

hircōs·us -a -um *adj* smelling like a goat

hirc·us -ī *m* goat

hirnĕ·a -ae f jug

hirsūt·us -a -um adj hairy, shaggy, bristly; prickly; rude

Hirt·ius -iī or -ī m Aulus Hirtius (consul in 43 B.C. and author of the eighth book of Caesar's Memoirs on the Gallic War)

hirt·us -a -um adj hairy, shaggy; uncouth

hirūd·ō -inis f bloodsucker, leech

hirundinīn·us -a -um adj swallow's

hirund·ō -inis f swallow

hisc·ō -ĕre vt to murmur, utter; vi to open, gape, yawn; to open the mouth

Hispān·ī -ōrum m pl Spaniards

Hispān·i·a -ae f Spain

Hispāniens·is -e adj Spanish

hispĭd·us -a -um adj hairy, shaggy, rough

Hist·er or Ist·er -rī m lower Danube

histori·a -ae f history; account, story; theme (of a story)

historic·us -a -um adj historical; m historian

histric·us -a -um adj theatrical

histri·ō -ōnis m actor

histriōnāl·is -e adj theatrical; histrionic

histriōni·a -ae f dramatics, art of acting

hiulcē adv with frequent hiatus

hiulc·ō -āre vt to split open

hiulc·us -a -um adj split, split open; open, gaping; with hiatus

hōc hūjus (older form: hōce; genit: hūjusce) (neut of hic) adj this; the present, the actual; the latter; (occasionally) the former; pron this one, it; the latter; (occasionally) the former; (with genit) this amount of, this degree of, so much; hoc erat quod this was the reason why; hoc est that is, I mean, namely; hocine (hoc with interrog enclitic -ne) is this . . . ?; hoc facilius all the more easily

hōce see hoc

hōcine see hoc

hodiē adv today; now, nowadays; still, to the present; at once, immediately; hodie mane this morning; numquam hodie (coll) never at all, never in the world

hodiern·us -a -um adj today's; hodiernus dies this day, today

holit·or -ōris m grocer

holitōri·us -a -um adj vegetable

hol·us -ĕris n vegetables

Hōmēr·us -ī m Homer

homicīd·a -ae m or f murderer, killer

homicīd·ium -iī or -ī n murder, manslaughter

hom·ō -inis m or f human being, man, person, mortal; mankind, human race; fellow; fellow creature; (coll) this one; m pl persons, people; infantry; bodies, corpses; members (of the senate); inter homi-

nes esse to be alive; to see the world

homull·us -ī or homucĭ·ō -ōnis or homuncŭl·us -ī m poor man, poor creature

honest·a -ae f lady

honestāment·um -ī n ornament

honest·ās -ātis f good reputation, respectability; sense of honor, respect; beauty, grace; honesty, integrity, uprightness; decency; f pl respectable persons, decent people

honestē adv honorably, respectably, decently, virtuously

honest·ō -āre vt to honor, dignify, embellish, grace

honest·us -a -um adj honored, respected; honorable, decent, respectable, virtuous; handsome; m gentleman; n virtue, good

hon·or or hon·ōs -ōris m honor, esteem; position, office, post; mark of honor, reward, acknowledgment; offering, rites (to the gods or the dead); beauty, grace, charm; glory, fame, reputation; honoris causā out of respect, with all respect

honōrābil·is -e adj honorable

honōrāri·us -a -um adj honored, respected, highly esteemed; honorary, conferring honor

honōrātē adv with honor, honorably

honōrāt·us -a -um adj honored, respected; in high office; honorable, respectable; honoratum habere to hold in honor

honōrificē adv honorably, respectfully

honōrific·us -a -um adj honorable, complimentary

honōr·ō -āre vt to honor, respect; to embellish, decorate

honōr·us -a -um adj honorable, complimentary

honōs see honor

hoplomāch·us -ī m gladiator

hōr·a -ae f hour; time; season; in diem et horam continually; in horam vivere to live from hand to mouth; quota hora est? what time is it?; f pl clock; in horas from hour to hour, every hour

Hōr·a -ae f wife of Quirinus (i.e., of deified Romulus), called Hersilia before her death

Hōr·ae -ārum f pl Hours (daughters of Jupiter and Themis and goddesses who kept watch at the gates of heaven)

hōrae·us -a -um adj pickled

Horāt·ius -iī or -ī m Quintus Horatius Flaccus (65-8 B.C.); Horatius Cocles (defender of the bridge across the Tiber in the war with Porsenna)

hordĕ·um -ī n barley

hori·a -ae f fishing boat

horiŏl·a -ae f small fishing boat

hornō adv this year, during this year

hornōtīn·us -a -um adj this year's

horn·us -a -um adj this year's

hōrolog·ium -iī or **-ī** n clock; water clock; sundial

horrend·us -a -um adj horrendous, horrible, terrible; awesome

horr·ens -entis adj bristling, bristly, shaggy

horr·eō -ēre -uī vt to dread; to shudder at, shrink from; to be amazed at; vi to stand on end, stand up straight; to get gooseflesh; to shiver, tremble, quake, shake; to look frightful, be rough

horr·escō -escĕre -uī vt to dread, become terrified at; vi to stand on end; (of the sea) to become rough; to begin to shake or shiver; to start (in fear)

horr·eum -ī n barn, shed; silo, granary; wine cellar; beehive

horribil·is -e adj horrible, terrifying; amazing

horridē adv roughly, rudely, sternly

horridŭl·us -a -um adj rather shaggy; somewhat shabby; somewhat unsophisticated (style)

horrid·us -a -um adj bristling, bristly, shaggy, prickly; rude, uncouth, rough, rugged, wild; disheveled; blunt, unpolished, course (manner); frightful, frightened, awful

horrif·er -ĕra -ĕrum adj causing shudders; freezing, chilling; terrifying

horrificē adv awfully

horrific·ō -āre vt to make rough, ruffle; to terrify, appall

horrific·us -a -um adj frightful, terrifying

horrisŏn·us -a -um adj frightening (sound), frightening to hear

horr·or -ōris m bristling; shivering, shuddering, quaking; dread, horror; awe, reverence; chill; thrill

horsum adv this way, here

hortām·en -ĭnis n injunction; encouragement

hortāment·um -ī n encouragement

hortātĭ·ō -ōnis f exhortation, encouragement

hortāt·or -ōris m backer, supporter, rooter, instigator

hortāt·us -ūs m encouragement, cheering, cheer

Hortens·ius -iī or **-ī** m Quintus Hortensius (famous orator and friendly competitor of Cicero, 114-50 B.C.)

hort·or -ārī -ātus sum vt to encourage, cheer, incite, instigate; to give a pep talk to (soldiers)

hortŭl·us -ī m little garden, garden plot

hort·us -ī m garden; m pl park

hosp·es -ĭtis m host, entertainer; guest, visitor; friend; stranger, foreigner

hospĭt·a -ae f hostess; guest, visitor; friend; stranger, foreigner

hospitāl·is -e adj host's; guest's; hospitable

hospitālĭt·ās -ātis f hospitality

hospitālĭter adv hospitably, as a guest

hospit·ium -iī or **-ī** n hospitality, friendship; welcome; guest room; lodging; inn

hosti·a -ae f victim, sacrifice

hostiāt·us -a -um adj bringing offerings

hostic·us -a -um adj hostile; foreign, strange; n enemy territory

hostil·is -e adj enemy's, enemy, hostile

hostīlĭter adv hostilely, like an enemy

Hostīl·ius -iī or **-ī** m Tullus Hostilius (third king of Rome)

hostīment·um -ī n compensation, recompense

host·iō -īre vi to return like for like

host·is -is m or f enemy

hūc adv here, to this place; to this, to this point, so far; to such a pitch; for this purpose; **hūc atque illūc** here and there, in different directions; **hucine?** (hūc + interrog enclitic) so far?

huī interj (expressing surprise or admiration) wow!

hūjusmŏdī or **hūjuscemŏdī** adj of this sort, such

hūmānō or **hūmānĭter** adv like a man; politely, gently, with compassion

hūmānĭt·ās -ātis f human nature; mankind; kindness, compassion; courtesy; culture, refinement, civilization

hūmānĭtus adv humanly; humanely, kindly, compassionately

hūmān·us -a -um adj of man, human; humane, kind, compassionate; courteous; cultured, refined, civilized, well educated

hūmātĭ·ō -ōnis f burial

hūme- = ume-

humī adv on or in the ground

hūmid- = umid-

humil·is -e adj low, low-lying, low-growing; shallow; stunted; low, common, colloquial; lowly, humble, poor, obscure, insignificant; base, mean, small-minded, cheap

humilĭt·ās -ātis f lowness; lowliness, insignificance; smallness of mind, meanness, cheapness

humilĭter adv low, deeply; meanly, abjectly

hum·ō -āre vt to bury

hum·us -ī f ground, earth; land, region, country

hyacinthĭn·us -a -um adj of the hyacinth; crimson

hyacinth·us or **hyacinth·os -ī** m hyacinth

Hyacinth·us or **Hyacinth·os -ī** m Spartan youth, who was accidently killed by his friend Apollo and from whose blood flowers of the same name sprang

Hyăd·es -um f Hyads (group of seven stars in the head of the constellation Taurus whose rising with the sun was accompanied by rainy weather)

hyaen·a -ae f hyena

hyăl·us -ī m glass

Hybl·a -ae or Hybl·ē -ēs f Sicilian mountain, famous for its honey

hybrĭd·a -ae m or f hybrid, mongrel, half-breed

Hydasp·ēs -is m tributary of the Indus River

Hȳdr·a -ae f Hydra (seven-headed dragon killed by Hercules); Hydra or Anguis (constellation); fifty-headed monster at the gates of the lower world

hydraulĭc·us -a -um adj hydraulic

hydraul·us -ī water organ

hydrĭ·a -ae f jug, urn

Hydrochŏ·us -ī m Aquarius (constellation)

hydrōpĭc·us -a -um adj dropsical

hydr·ops -ōpis m dropsy

hydr·us or hydr·os -ī m serpent

Hyl·ās -ae m youthful companion of Hercules who was carried off by the nymphs as he was drawing water

Hyll·us or Hūl·us -ī m son of Hercules and husband of Iole

Hym·ēn -ĕnis or Hymenae·us or

Hymenae·os -ī m Hymen (god of marriage); wedding ceremony; wedding; wedding song

Hymett·us or Hymett·os -ī m mountain in E. Attica, famous for its honey

Hypăn·is -is m river in Sarmatia (modern Bug)

hyperbăt·on -ī n (rhet) transposition of words

hyperbŏl·ē -ēs f hyperbole

Hyperborĕ·ī -ōrum m pl legendary people in the land of the midnight sun

Hyperī·ōn -ŏnis m son of Titan and Earth, father of the Sun

Hypermestr·a -ae or Hypermestr·ē -ēs f the only one of the fifty daughters of Danaus who did not kill her husband on her wedding night

hypocaust·um or hypocaust·on -ī n sweat bath

hypodidascăl·us -ī m instructor

hypomnēm·a -ătis n memorandum, note

Hypsipȳl·ē -ēs f queen of Lemnos at the time of the Argonauts

Hyrcăn·ī -ōrum m pl a people on the Caspian Sea

I

ia- = ja-

Iacch·us -ī m Bacchus; wine

iambē·us -a -um adj iambic

iamb·us -ī m iamb; iambic poem, iambic poetry

ianthĭn·a -ōrum n pl violet-colored garments

Iapĕt·us -ī m Titan, father of Prometheus, Epimetheus, and Atlas

Iāpȳd·es -um m pl Illyrian tribe

Iāp·yx -ȳgis m son of Daedalus that ruled in S. Italy; wind that blew from Apulia to Greece

Ias·ĭus -ĭī or -ī m son of Jupiter and Electra and brother of Dardanus

Iās·ōn -ŏnis m Jason (son of Aeson, leader of the Argonauts, and husband of Medea and afterwards of Creusa)

iasp·is -ĭdis f jasper

Iber· = Hiber-

ibi or ibī adv there, in that place; then, on that occasion; therein

ibīdem adv in the same place, just there; at that very moment; at the same time; in the same matter

Ib·is -is or -ĭdis f ibis (bird sacred to the Egyptians)

Icăr·us -ī m son of Daedalus, who, on his flight from Crete with his father, fell into the sea; father of Penelope

ichneum·ōn -ŏnis m ichneumon

(Egyptian rat that eats crocodile eggs)

ĭcŏ ĭcĕre ĭcī ictum vt to hit, strike, shoot

ĭc·ōn -ŏnis f image

icterĭc·us -a -um adj jaundiced

ict·is -ĭdis f weasel

ictus pp of ĭcŏ

ict·us -ūs m stroke, blow, hit; cut, sting, bite, wound; range; stress, beat; **sub ictum** within range

id adv for that reason, therefore

id ejus (neut of is) adj this, that, the said, the aforesaid; pron it; a thing, the thing; **ad id** for that purpose; **aliquid id genus** something of that sort, something like that; **cum eo ... ut** on condition that, with the stipulation that; **eo plus** the more; **ex eo** from that time on; as a result of that, consequently; **id consili** some sort of plan, some plan; **id quod a** thing which, the thing which; **id temporis** at that time; of that age; **in id** to that end; **in eo esse** to depend on it; **in eo esse ... ut** to be so far gone that, to get to the point where

Id·a -ae or Id·ē -ēs f mountain near Troy; mountain in Crete where Jupiter was brought up

Idal·ĭum -ĭī or -ī n city in Cyprus dear to Venus

idcircō *adv* on that account, for that reason, therefore

idem eādem idem *adj* the same, the very same, exactly this; (often equivalent to a mere connective) also, likewise; *pron* the same one

identidem *adv* again and again, continually, habitually; now and then, at intervals

ideō *adv* therefore

idiōt·a -ae *m* uneducated person, ignorant person, layman

idōl·on -ī *n* apparition, ghost

idōnēē *adv* suitably

idōne·us -a -um *adj* suitable, fit, proper; (with *dat* or with **ad** or **in** + *acc*) fit for, capable of, suited for, convenient for, sufficient for

id·ūs -uum *f pl* Ides (*fifteenth day of March, May, July, and October, and thirteenth of the other months; interest, debts, and tuition were often paid on the Ides*)

ie- = je-

iens euntis *pres p* of **eo**

igitur *adv* then, therefore, accordingly; (resumptive after parenthetical matter) as I was saying; (in summing up) so then, in short

ignār·us -a -um *adj* ignorant, unaware, inexperienced; unsuspecting; senseless; unknown, strange, unfamiliar; (with *genit*) unaware of, unfamiliar with

ignāvē *adv* listlessly, lazily

ignāvi·a -ae *f* listlessness, laziness; cowardice

ignāviter *adv* listlessly

ignāv·us -a -um *adj* listless, lazy, idle, inactive; relaxing; cowardly, bastardly; unproductive (*field, etc.*)

ignesc·ō -ēre *vi* to catch fire, become inflamed, burn; (fig) to flare up

ignē·us -a -um *adj* of fire, on fire, fiery; red-hot, fiery

ignicul·us -ī *m* small fire, little flame, spark

ignif·er -ēra -ērum *adj* fiery

ignigen·a -ae *m* son of fire (*epithet of Bacchus*)

ignip·ēs -ēdis *adj* fiery-footed

ignipōt·ens -entis *adj* lord of fire (*epithet of Vulcan*)

ign·is -is *m* fire; conflagration; watch fire, signal fire; torch; lightning, bolt of lightning; funeral pyre; star; brightness, glow, brilliancy, splendor; (fig) fire, rage, fury, love, passion; flame, sweetheart; agent of destruction, fanatic; *m pl* love poems

ignōbil·is -e *adj* insignificant, obscure, unknown, undistinguished; low-born, ignoble

ignōbilit·ās -ātis *f* obscurity; humble birth

ignōmini·a -ea *f* ignominy, dishonor, disgrace; **ignominiā afficere** to dishonor, disgrace; **ignominia senatūs** public censure imposed by the senate

ignōminiōs·us -a -um *adj* disgraced, degraded; disgraceful, shameful, ignominious; *m* infamous person

ignōrābil·is -e *adj* unknown

ignōranti·a -ae *f* ignorance

ignōrāti·ō -ōnis *f* ignorance

ignōr·ō -āre *vt* to not know, be ignorant of, be unfamiliar with; to mistake, misunderstand; to ignore, disregard, take no notice of

ignōsc·ens -entis *adj* forgiving

ig·nōscō -nōscēre -nōvī -nōtum *vt* (with *dat* of person and *acc* of the offense) to pardon, forgive, excuse (*someone a fault*); *vi* (with *dat*) to pardon, forgive, excuse

ignōt·us -a -um *adj* unknown, unfamiliar, strange; inglorious; unnoticed; low-born, ignoble; vulgar; ignorant

īl·ex -icis *f* holm oak

Īli·a -ae *f* Rhea Silvia (*mother of Romulus and Remus*)

īl·ia -ium *n pl* guts, intestines; groin, belly

Īliac·us -a -um *adj* Trojan

Īli·as -ādis *f* Iliad; Trojan woman

ilicet *adv* (ancient form for adjourning an assembly) let us go; all is lost, kaput; at once, immediately, instantly

ilicō *adv* on the spot, right then and there; immediately

īlign·us or **īlignē·us -a -um** *adj* of holm oak, oak

Īl·ios -iī or **-ī** *f* Troy

Īlithȳi·a -ae *f* goddess who aided women in childbirth

Īl·ium -iī or **-ī** or **Īli·on -ī** *n* Troy

Īli·us -a -um *adj* Trojan

illa *adv* that way

ill·a -ius *adj fem* that; that famous; *pron* that one; she

illabefact·us -a -um *adj* unbroken, uninterrupted

il·lābor -lābī -lapsus sum *vi* to flow; to sink, fall; fall in, cave in; to slip; (with *dat* or with **ad** or **in** + *acc*) to flow into, enter into, penetrate

illabōr·ō -āre *vi* (with *dat*) to work at, work on

illāc *adv* that way

illacessīt·us -a -um *adj* unprovoked

illacrimābil·is -e *adj* unlamented, unwept; inexorable

illacrim·ō -āre or **illacrim·or -ārī -ātus sum** *vi* (with *dat*) to cry over

ill·aec (*acc:* -anc; *abl:* -āc) *adj fem* that; *pron* she

illaes·us -a -um *adj* unhurt, unharmed

illaetābil·is -e *adj* sad, melancholy

illapsus *pp* of **illabor**

illaqu·ō -āre *vt* to trap

illātus *pp* of **infero**

illaudāt·us -a -um *adj* without fame, obscure; detestable

ill·e -ius *adj masc* that; that famous; the former; **ille aut ille** this or that, such and such; *pron* that one; he; the former one

illecēbr·a -ae *f* attraction, allurement

illecēbrōs·us -a -um *adj* alluring, seductive

illect·us -a -um *adj* unread

illect·us -ūs *m* allurement

illepidē *adv* inelegantly, rudely, impolitely

illepid·us -a -um *adj* inelegant, impolite, churlish

ill·ex -icis *m* or *f* lure, decoy

ill·ex -ēgis *adj* lawless

illibāt·us -a -um *adj* undiminished, unimpaired

illiberāl·is -e *adj* ungenerous, stingy

illiberālit·ās -ātis *f* stinginess

ill·īc (*acc:* **-ūnc;** *abl:* **-ōc**) *adj masc* that; *pron* he

illīc *adv* there, yonder, in that place; in that matter, therein

il·liciō -licěre -lexī -lectum *vt* to allure, attract, seduce, mislead, lead astray

illicitāt·or -ōris *m* fake bidder (*one who bids at an auction to make others bid higher*)

illicit·us -a -um *adj* unlawful

il·līdō -līděre -līsī -līsum *vt* to smash to pieces, crush; (with *dat* or with **ad** or **in** + *acc*) to smash (*something*) against

illig·ō -āre *vt* to attach, connect; to tie, bind; to oblige; to impede, hamper

illim *adv* from there

illim·is -e *adj* unmuddied, clear

illinc *adv* from there; on that side; **hinc illinc** from one side to another

il·līnō -liněre -lēvī -lītum *vt* to cover; to smear; (with *dat*) to smear or spread (*something*) on

illiquefact·us -a -um *adj* melted

illīsus *pp* of **illīdo**

illiterāt·us -a -um *adj* uneducated, illiterate

illītus *pp* of **illino**

illō or **illōc** *adv* there, to that place; to that point

illōt·us -a -um *adj* unwashed, dirty

illūc *adv* to that place, in that direction; to that person, to him, to her; to that matter; to that point

ill·ūc (*acc:* **-ūc;** *abl:* **-ōc**) *adj neut* that; *pron* it

illuc·ĕō -ēre *vt* to shine on; *vi* to shine

il·lucescō -lucescěre -luxī *vi* to grow light, dawn, to begin to shine

ill·ud -ius *adj neut* that; the former; *pron* it

il·lūdō -lūděre -lūsī -lūsum *vt* to make fun of, ridicule; to waste, abuse; *vi* (with *dat*) to play around with, do mischief to

illūmināte *adv* clearly

illūmin·ō -āre *vt* to light up, make bright, illuminate; to illustrate

illūsi·ō -ōnis *f* irony

illustr·is -e *adj* bright, clear, bril-

liant; plain, distinct, evident; distinguished, famous, illustrious, noble

illustr·ō -āre *vt* to light up, illuminate; to make clear, clear up, explain, illustrate; to adorn, embellish; to make famous

illūsus *pp* of **illudo**

illuvi·ēs -ēi *f* inundation; offscouring, filth, dirt

Illyric·us -a -um *adj* Illyrian; *n* Illyria

Illyri·us -a -um *adj & m* Illyrian; *f* Illyria (*country on the E. coast of the Adriatic Sea*)

Īl·us -ī *m* son of Tros, father of Laomedon, and founder of Ilium; Ascanius

imāgināri·us -a -um *adj* imaginary

imāginātiōn·ēs -um *f pl* imaginings

imāgin·or -ārī -ātus sum *vt* to imagine

imāg·ō -inis *f* image, likeness, picture, bust; bust of ancestor; ghost, vision; echo; appearance, semblance, shadow; mental picture, image, conception, thought, idea; figure of speech, simile, metaphor

imbēcillit·ās -ātis *f* weakness, feebleness; helplessness

imbēcillius *adv* more weakly, more faintly

imbēcill·us -a -um *adj* weak, feeble; helpless

imbell·is -e *adj* anti-war, pacifistic; peaceful; unfit for war, soft, cowardly; peaceful, quiet

imb·er -ris *m* rain, shower, rain storm; rain cloud; water; stream of tears; shower (*of gold, spears, etc.*)

imberb·is -e or **imberb·us -a -um** *adj* beardless

im·bibō -biběre -bibī *vt* to imbibe, drink in; to resolve on; **animō imbibere** to conceive, form (*e.g., an opinion*)

imbr·ex -icis *f* tile

imbric·us -a -um *adj* rainy

imbrif·er -ěra -ěrum *adj* rainy

im·buō -buěre -buī -būtum *vt* to wet, soak, saturate; to stain, taint, infect, imbue, fill, steep; to instruct, train, educate

imitābil·is -e *adj* imitable

imitām·en -inis *n* imitation; *n pl* likeness, image

imitāti·ō -ōnis *f* imitation; pretense

imitāt·or -ōris *m* or **imitātr·ix -icis** *f* imitator

imitāt·us -a -um *adj* fictitious, copied

imit·or -ārī -ātus sum *vt* to imitate, copy, portray; to ape

immad·escō -escěre -uī *vi* to become wet

immānē *adv* savagely

immān·is -e *adj* huge, enormous, monstrous; inhuman, savage, monstrous

immānit·ās -ātis *f* vastness, enormity; savageness, cruelty, monstrousness, barbarity

immansuēt·us **-a** **-um** *adj* wild, savage

immātūrit·ās **-ātis** *f* overanxiousness

immātūr·us **-a** **-um** *adj* immature, unripe, premature

immedicābil·is **-e** *adj* incurable

immĕm·or **-ŏris** *adj* forgetful, forgetting; negligent

immemorābil·is **-e** *adj* not worth mentioning; untold

immemorāt·a **-ōrum** *n pl* novelties

immensit·ās **-ātis** *f* immensity; *f pl* immense stretches

immens·us **-a** **-um** *adj* immense, unending; *n* infinite space, infinity

immĕr·ens **-entis** *adj* undeserving, innocent

im·mergō **-mergĕre** **-mersī** **-mersum** *vt* to immerse, dip, plunge; (with **in** + *acc*) to dip (*something*) into; **se immergere** (with **in** + *acc*) **a** to plunge into; **b** to insinuate oneself into

immeritō *adv* undeservedly, innocently

immerit·us **-a** **-um** *adj* undeserving, innocent; undeserved, unmerited; **immeritō meo** through no fault of mine

immersābil·is **-e** *adj* unsinkable

immersus *pp* of **immergo**

immētāt·us **-a** **-um** *adj* unmeasured

immigr·ō **-āre** *vi* to immigrate; (with **in** + *acc*) **a** to move into; **b** (*fig*) to invade

immin·ĕō **-ēre** *vi* to project, stick out; to be near, be imminent, be near at hand; to threaten, menace; (with *dat*) **a** to jut out over; **b** to look out over, overlook (*a view*); **c** to hover over, loom over, threaten; (with *dat* or **in** + *acc*) to be intent on, be eager for

immin·ŭō **-ŭĕre** **-ŭī** **-ūtum** *vt* to lessen, curtail; to weaken, impair; to infringe upon, encroach upon, violate, subvert, destroy

imminūti·ō **-ōnis** *f* lessening; mutilation; understatement

im·miscĕō **-miscēre** **-miscŭī** **-mixtum** *vt* to mix in, intermix, blend; (*fig*) to mix up, confound; **immisceri** or **se immiscere** (with *dat*) **a** to join, join in with, mingle with, get lost in (*e.g., a crowd*); **b** to blend with, disappear in (*o.g., night, cloud, etc.*); **manūs manibus immiscere** (of boxers) to mix it up

immiserābil·is **-e** *adj* unpitied

immisericordĭter *adv* unmercifully

immisericor·s **-dis** *adj* merciless, pitiless

immissi·ō **-ōnis** *f* letting grow, letting alone

immissus *pp* of **immitto**

immit·is **-e** *adj* unripe, sour, green; rude, harsh, stern, severe; pitiless, inexorable

im·mittō **-mittĕre** **-mīsī** **-missum** *vt* to insert; to let in, let go in, admit; let go of, let drop; to let go, let fly, launch; to set on, incite, egg on; **immitti** or **se immittere** (with *dat* or **in** + *acc*) **a** to plunge or dive into; **b** to rush against, attack; **in terram immittere** to ground

immixtus *pp* of **immisceo**

immo or **immō** *adv* (in contradiction or correction of preceding words) no, on the contrary, or rather; (in confirmation of preceding words) quite so, yes indeed; **immo vero** yes and in fact

immōbil·is **-e** *adj* motionless, unshaken; immovable; clumsy

immoderātē *adv* without limit; immoderately, extravagantly

immoderāti·ō **-ōnis** *f* lack of moderation, excess

immoderāt·us **-a** **-um** *adj* unmeasured, limitless; immoderate, uncontrolled, excessive

immodestē *adv* immoderately, shamelessly

immodesti·a **-ae** *f* excesses; insubordination

immodest·us **-a** **-um** *adj* immoderate, uncontrolled

immodicē *adv* excessively

immodic·us **-a** **-um** *adj* huge, enormous; immoderate, excessive; (with *genit* or *abl*) given to, excessive in

immodulāt·us **-a** **-um** *adj* unrhythmical

immolāti·ō **-ōnis** *f* sacrifice

immolāt·or **-ōris** *m* sacrificer

immolīt·us **-a** **-um** *adj* constructed, erected; *n pl* buildings

immol·ō or **inmol·ō** **-āre** *vt* to immolate, sacrifice, offer

im·morior **-mŏrī** **-mortŭus sum** *vi* (with *dat*) to die in, die upon; (*fig*) to get sick over

immŏr·or **-ārī** **-ātus sum** *vi* (with *dat*) to dwell upon

immors·us **-a** **-um** *adj* bitten into; excited

immortāl·is **-e** *adj* immortal

immortālit·ās **-ātis** *f* immortality

immortālĭter *adv* infinitely

immortŭus *pp* of **immorior**

immōt·us **-a** **-um** *adj* unmoved, immovable; unshaken, undisturbed, steadfast

immūg·ĭō **-īre** **-īvī** or **-ĭī** **-ītum** *vi* to bellow, roar

immulg·ĕō **-ēre** *vt* to milk

immunditi·a **-ae** *f* dirtiness, filth

immund·us **-a** **-um** *adj* dirty, filthy, foul

immūn·ĭō **-īre** **-īvī** *vt* to reinforce, fortify

immūn·is **-e** *adj* without duty or office; tax-exempt, free, exempt; pure, innocent; (with *abl* or **ab** + *abl*) free from, exempt from; (with *genit*) free of, free from, devoid of, without

immūnit·ās -ātis f immunity, exemption, exemption from taxes

immūnit·us -a -um adj unfortified, undefended; unpaved (street)

immurmŭr·ō -āre vi to grumble; (with dat) (of the wind) to whisper among

immūtābil·is -e adj immutable, unchangeable

immūtābilit·ās -ātis f immutability

immūtātĭ·ō -ōnis f exchange, substitution; metonymy

immūtāt·us -a -um adj unchanged

immūt·ō -āre vt to change, alter; to substitute

impācāt·us -a -um adj restless; aggressive

impactus pp of **impingo**

impall·escō -escĕre -ŭī vi (with abl) to turn pale at

im·pār -ăris adj uneven, odd (numbers); uneven (in size or length); not matching, unlike (in color or appearance); unequal; unfair; ill-matched; uneven, crooked; (with dat) not a match for, inferior to, unable to cope with

imparāt·us -a -um adj unprepared

imparĭter adv unequally

impast·us -a -um adj unfed, hungry

impatĭ·ens -entis adj impatient; (with genit) unable to stand, endure, tolerate

impatĭenter adv impatiently; intolerably

impatientĭ·a -ae f impatience; (with genit) inability to stand or endure

impavĭdē adv fearlessly

impavĭd·us -a -um adj fearless, dauntless

impedīment·um -ī n impediment, hindrance; difficulty; n pl baggage, luggage; mule train

imped·ĭō -īre -īvī or **-ĭī -ītum** vt to entangle; to hamper, hinder; to entwine, encircle; to clasp, embrace; to block up (road); to hinder, prevent; to embarrass; **impedīre** (with **ne, quīn,** or **quōmĭnus**) to prevent (someone) from

impedītĭ·ō -ōnis f obstacle, obstruction

impedīt·us -a -um adj hampered; obstructed, blocked; difficult, intricate; impassable; busy, occupied

im·pellō -pellĕre -pŭlī -pulsum vt to strike against, strike, reach; to push, drive, drive forward, impel, propel; to urge, persuade, stimulate, induce; to force, compel; to put to rout; to swell (sails)

impend·ĕō -ēre vi to be near, be at hand, be imminent, threaten; (with dat) to hang over; (with dat or in + acc) to hover or loom over, threaten

impendĭōs·us -a -um adj extravagant

impend·ĭum -ī or **-ī** n expense, cost, outlay; interest (paid out); loss

im·pendō -pendĕre -pendī -pen-sum vt to weigh out, pay out; to expend, devote, apply, employ; (with in + acc) a to spend (money) on; b to expend (effort) on, pay (attention) to

impenetrābil·is -e adj impenetrable

impens·a -ae f expense, cost, outlay; waste; contribution; **meis impensis** at my expense

impensē adv at a high cost, expensively; with great effort

impens·us -a -um pp of **impendo**; adj high, costly, expensive; strong, vehement, earnest; n high price

imper·ans -antis m master, ruler, conqueror

imperāt·or -ōris m commander, general; commander in chief; emperor; director, master, ruler, leader

imperātorĭ·us -a -um adj of a general, general's; imperial

imperātr·ix -īcis f controller, mistress

imperāt·um -ī n command, order

impercept·us -a -um adj unperceived, unknown

impercuss·us -a -um adj noiseless

imperdīt·us -a -um adj unscathed

imperfect·us -a -um adj unfinished, imperfect

imperfoss·us -a -um adj unpierced, not stabbed

imperĭōs·us -a -um adj imperial; magisterial; tyrannical, overbearing, domineering, imperious

imperītē adv unskillfully, clumsily, ignorantly

imperītĭ·a -ae f inexperience, awkwardness, ignorance

imperĭt·ō -āre vt & vi to command, rule, govern

imperīt·us -a -um adj inexperienced, unfamiliar, ignorant, unskilled; (with genit) inexperienced in, unacquainted with, ignorant of

imperĭum -ī or **-ī** n command, order; right to command; exercise of authority; military commission, supreme command; mastery, sovereignty; realm, empire, dominion, supremacy, authority; public office, magistracy; term of office

imperjūrāt·us -a -um adj sacrosanct, inviolable

impermiss·us -a -um adj forbidden, unlawful

imper·ō -āre vt to requisition, give orders for, order, demand; (with acc of thing demanded and dat of source demanded from) to demand (e.g., hostages) from; vi to be in command, rule, be master; (with dat) to give orders to, order, command, govern, master

imperterrĭt·us -a -um adj undaunted, unterrified

impert·ĭō -īre vt (with dat) to impart, communicate, bestow, assign, direct (something) to, share (something) with; (with acc of person and abl of thing) to present (someone) with

imperturbāt·us -a -um *adj* unperturbed, unruffled

impervi·us -a -um *adj* impassable; (with *dat*) impervious to

impetibil·is -e *adj* intolerable

impĕt·ō -ĕre *vt* to make for; to attack

impetrābil·is -e *adj* obtainable; successful

impetrātī·ō -ōnis *f* obtaining, procurement

impetr·ĭō -īre *vt* to try to obtain through favorable omens

impĕtr·ō -āre *vt* to obtain, procure (*by asking*); to achieve, accomplish, bring to pass

impĕt·us -ūs *m* attack, assault; rush; impetus, impetuosity, vehemence, vigor, violence, fury, force; impulse, passion

impex·us -a -um *adj* uncombed; unpolished

impiē *adv* wickedly

impiĕt·ās -ātis *f* impiety, irreverence; disloyalty; treason

impig·er -ra -rum *adj* diligent, active, energetic

impigrē *adv* energetically, actively, quickly

impigrit·ās -ātis *f* energy, activity

im·pingō -pingĕre -pēgī -pactum *vt* (with *dat* or **in** + *acc*) **a** to fasten to; **b** to pin against, force against, dash against; **c** to press or force (*something*) on; **d** to fling at

impĭ·ō -āre *vt* to make irreverent

impĭ·us -a -um *adj* impious, irreverent; disobedient, undutiful; disloyal, unpatriotic; wicked, unscrupulous, shameless

implācābil·is -e *adj* implacable, unappeasable

implācāt·us -a -um *adj* unappeased, unsatisfied

implācĭd·us -a -um *adj* fierce, savage

impl·ĕō -ēre -ēvī -ētum *vt* to fill up; to satisfy; to fatten; to impregnate, make pregnant; to enrich; to cover with writing, fill up (*a book*); to discharge, fulfill, execute, implement; to complete, finish, end; to spend (*time*)

implex·us -a -um *adj* enfolded, entwined; involved

implicātī·ō -ōnis *f* entanglement; incorporation; embarrassment

implicāt·us -a -um *adj* entangled, involved, complicated, confused

implicisc·or -ī *vi* to become confused

implicītē *adv* intricately

implicītus *pp* of **implico**; *adj* confused, confounded; **implicītus morbo** disabled by sickness, sick

implic·ō -āre -āvī -ātum or **-āre -ŭī -ĭtum** *vt* to entangle, involve, enfold, envelop; to embrace, clasp, grasp; to connect, unite, join; to involve, implicate, engage; to embarrass; **se dextrae implicāre** to embrace, shake hands

implōrātī·ō -ōnis *f* begging, imploring

implōr·ō -āre *vt* to implore, appeal to, call upon for aid; (with double *acc*) to beg (*someone*) for; (with **ab** + *abl*) to ask for (*something*) from

implūm·is -e *adj* without feathers, unfledged

impl·ŭō -ŭĕre -ŭī -ūtum *vi* (with *dat*) to rain on

impluviāt·us -a -um *adj* shaped like an impluvium, square

impluv·ĭum -ĭī or **-ī** *n* skylight, impluvium (*opening in the roof of the atrium of the Roman house to get rid of smoke and let in light*); built-in basin in the atrium to catch the rain water; uncovered space in the atrium

impolītē *adv* simply, without fancy words

impolīt·us -a -um *adj* unpolished, rough; unrefined, inelegant; unfinished

impollūt·us -a -um *adj* unsullied

im·pōnō -pōnĕre -posŭī -positum or **-postum** *vt* to impose; to establish, introduce; to place, set; to inflict, impose, dictate; to assign; to apply, give; to impose, assess, exact; to put (*someone*) in charge; (with *dat*, with **in** | *acc*, **in** + *abl*, or **supra** | *acc*) to place, put, set, lay (*someone or something*) on or in; (with *dat*) **a** to impose (*taxes, etc.*) upon; **b** to put (*someone*) in charge of; *vi* (with *dat*) to impose upon, trick, cheat

import·ō -āre *vt* to bring in, import; to introduce

importūnĭt·ās -ātis *f* importunity, rudeness, insolence; unfitness

importūn·us -a -um *adj* inconvenient, unsuitable; troublesome, annoying; lacking consideration for others, rude, ruthless, churlish; stormy; ill-omened

importŭōs·us -a -um *adj* without a harbor

imp·os -ŏtis *adj* without control; (with *genit*) without control of

impositus *pp* of **impono**

impossibil·is -e *adj* impossible

impostus *pp* of **impono**

impŏt·ens -entis *adj* impotent, powerless; having no control of oneself, wild, uncontrollable, impetuous, violent

impotenter *adv* impotently, weakly

impotentĭ·a -ae *f* weakness, helplessness; lack of self-control, violence, fury, passion

impraesentĭārum *adv* for the present, under present circumstances

imprans·us -a -um *adj* without breakfast, fasting

imprecātī·ō -ōnis *f* imprecation, curse

imprĕc·or -ārī -ātus sum *vt* to call down (*a curse*); to invoke

impressĭ·ō -ōnis *f* pressure; assault, attack, charge; rhythmical beat;

emphasis; impression (*on the mind*)

impressus *pp* of **imprimo**

imprīmīs or **in prīmīs** *adv* in the first place, chiefly, especially

im·prīmō ·prīmere ·pressī ·pressum *vt* to press down; to impress, imprint, stamp; (fig) to impress, engrave, mark

improbāti·ō ·ōnis *f* disapprobation, blame

impróbē *adv* badly, wickedly, wrongfully; recklessly; persistently

improbit·ās ·ātis *f* wickedness, depravity; roguishness

impró·ō ·āre *vt* disapprove, condemn, blame, reject

improbul·us ·a ·um *adj* naughty

impró·us ·a ·um *adj* below standard, poor, inferior, bad, shameless; rebellious, unruly; restless, indomitable, self-willed; cruel, merciless; persistent

imprócēr·us ·a ·um *adj* undersized

imprōdict·us ·a ·um *adj* not postponed

imprompt·us ·a ·um *adj* slow

improperāt·us ·a ·um *adj* slow, deliberate

improprī·us ·a ·um *adj* unsuitable

improsp·er ·era ·erum *adj* unfortunate

improspērē *adv* unfortunately

impróvidē *adv* without foresight, thoughtlessly

impróvid·us ·a ·um *adj* not foreseeing, not anticipating; (with *genit*) indifferent to

imprōvis·us ·a ·um *adj* unexpected; **de imprōvisō, ex imprōvisō** or **imprōvisō** unexpectedly; *n pl* emergencies

imprūd·ēns ·entis *adj* not foreseeing, not anticipating, unsuspecting, off one's guard; inconsiderate; (with *genit*) unaware of, ignorant of, heedless of, not experienced in

imprūdenter *adv* without foresight, thoughtlessly, inconsiderately, imprudently

imprūdenti·a ·ae *f* thoughtlessness; ignorance, imprudence

impūb·ēs ·ēris or **·is** *adj* youthful, young; innocent, chaste, celibate, virgin

impūd·ēns ·entis *adj* shameless

impudenter *adv* shamelessly

impudenti·a ·ae *f* shamelessness

impudīciti·a ·ae *f* immodesty, lewdness, shamelessness

impudic·us ·a ·um *adj* immodest, lewd, shameless

impugnāti·ō ·ōnis *f* assault, attack

impugn·ō ·āre *vt* to assault, attack; (fig) to impugn

impulsi·ō ·ōnis *f* pressure; impulse

impuls·or ·ōris *m* instigator

impulsus *pp* of **impello**

impuls·us ·ūs *m* push, pressure, impulse, shock; instigation, incitement

impūne or **inpūne** *adv* with impunity, unpunished, scot-free; safely,

unscathed

impūnīt·ās ·ātis *f* impunity

impūnītē *adv* with impunity

impūnīt·us ·a ·um *adj* unpunished; unrestrained

impūrē *adv* impurely

impūrit·ās ·ātis *f* impurity

impūr·us ·a ·um *adj* impure, unclean, filthy; (morally) impure, filthy, vile

imputāt·us ·a ·um *adj* unpruned, untrimmed

imput·ō ·āre *vt* to charge to someone's account, enter in an account; (with *dat*) to charge to, ascribe to, give credit for (*something*) to, put the blame for (*something*) on

īmul·us ·a ·um *adj* cute little

īm·us ·a ·um *adj* deepest, lowest; last; the bottom of, the foot of, the tip of; *n* bottom, depth; **ab imo** utterly; **ab imo ad summum** from top to bottom; **ex imo** utterly, completely; *n pl* lower world

in *prep* (with *abl*) in, on, upon, among, at; before; under; during, within, in, at, in the course of, on the point of, in case of, in relation to; subject to, affected by, engaged in, involved in; (with *acc*) into, up to, towards; till, to, for; in relation to, about, respecting, against; for, with a view to, according to, after

inaccess·us ·a ·um *adj* inaccessible

inac·escō ·escere ·uī *vi* to turn sour

Īnachīd·ēs ·ae *m* descendant of Inachus; Perseus; Epaphus

Īnách·is ·idis *f* female descendant of Inachus (*esp. Io*)

Īnách·us or **Īnách·os ·ī** *m* first king or Argos and father of Io

inadsc- = **inasc-**

inadt- = **inatt-**

inadust·us ·a ·um *adj* unburned

inaedific·ō ·āre *vt* to build on, build as an addition, erect, construct; to wall up, barricade; (with **in** + *abl*) to build (*something*) on top of

inaequābil·is ·e *adj* uneven

inaequābiliter *adv* unevenly, unequally

inaequāl·is ·e *adj* uneven, unequal; unlike, changeable, inconstant

inaequālit·ās ·ātis *f* unevenness

inaequāliter *adv* unevenly

inaequāt·us ·a ·um *adj* unequal

inaequ·ō ·āre *vt* to level off

inaestimābil·is ·e *adj* inestimable; invaluable; valueless

inaestu·ō ·āre *vi* **bilis inaestuat** anger flares up

inaffectāt·us ·a ·um *adj* unaffected, natural

inamābil·is ·e *adj* hateful, revolting

inamāresc·ō ·ēre *vi* to become bitter

inambitiōs·us ·um *adj* unambitious

inambulāti·ō ·ōnis *f* walking about, strutting about

inambŭl·ō -āre *vi* to walk up and down

inamoen·us -a -um *adj* unpleasant

ināni·ae -ārum *f pl* emptiness

inānilogist·a -ae *m* chatterbox

ināniment·um -ī *n* empty space

inanĭm·us -a -um *adj* inanimate

inān·e -is *n* empty space, vacuum; emptiness; worthlessness

inān·is -e *adj* empty, void; deserted, abandoned, unoccupied; hollow; worthless, idle; lifeless, unsubstantial; penniless, poor; unprofitable; groundless, unfounded

inānit·ās -ātis *f* empty space, emptiness; uselessness, worthlessness

inānĭter *adv* uselessly, vainly

inarāt·us -a -um *adj* untilled, fallow

in·ardescō -ardescĕre -arsī *vi* to catch fire, burn, glow

inăresc·ō -ĕre *vi* to become dry, dry up

inascens·us -a -um *adj* not climbed

inassuēt·us -a -um *adj* unaccustomed

inattenuāt·us -a -um *adj* undiminished; unappeased

inaud·ax -ācis *adj* timid, cowed

inaud·ĭō -īre -īvī or **-iī -ītum** *vt* to hear, learn

inandīt·us -a -um *adj* unheard-of, unusual; without a hearing in court

inaugurātō *adv* after taking the auspices

inaugŭr·ō -āre *vt* to inaugurate, consecrate, install; *vi* to take the auspices

inaurāt·us -a -um *adj* gilded, gilt

inaur·ēs -ium *f pl* earrings

inaur·ō -āre *vt* to goldplate, gild; to line the pockets of (*someone*) with gold, to make rich

inauspicātō *adv* without consulting the auspices

inauspicāt·us -a -um *adj* undertaken without auspices; unlucky

inaus·us -a -um *adj* unattempted

inb- = imb-

inbĭt·ō -ĕre *vt* enter

incaedŭ·us -a -um *adj* uncut

incal·escō -escĕre -ŭī *vi* to grow warm or hot; to get excited

incalfac·ĭō -ĕre *vt* to warm, heat

incallĭdē *adv* unskillfully

incallĭd·us -a -um *adj* unskillful; stupid, simple, clumsy

incand·escō -escĕre -ŭī *vi* to become white; to get white-hot

incān·escō -escĕre -ŭī *vi* to get grey

incantāt·us -a -um *adj* enchanted

incān·us -a -um *adj* grown grey

incassum *adv* in vain

incastīgāt·us -a -um *adj* unscolded, unpunished

incautē *adv* incautiously, recklessly

incaut·us -a -um *adj* incautious, inconsiderate, thoughtless, reckless; unforeseen, unexpected; unguarded

in·cēdō -cēdĕre -cessī -cessum *vi* to go, step, move, walk, stalk; to proceed, go forward; to come along, happen, occur, appear, arrive; to advance, go on

incelebrāt·us -a -um *adj* unheralded

incēnāt·us -a -um *adj* supperless

incendiār·ĭus -iī or **-ī** *m* agitator

incend·ĭum -iī or **-ī** *n* fire; heat

in·cendō -cendĕre -cendī -censum *vt* to light, set on fire, burn; to light up, make bright; (*fig*) to inflame, fire, excite, enrage

incēn·is -e *adj* dinnerless, without dinner

incensi·ō -ōnis *f* burning

incensus *pp of* **incendo**

incens·us -a -um *adj* not registered (*with the censor*)

inceptĭ·ō -ōnis *f* beginning; undertaking

incept·ō -āre *vt* to begin; to undertake

incept·or -ōris *m* beginner, originator

incept·us -a -um *pp of* **incipio**; *n* beginning; undertaking, attempt, enterprise; subject, theme

in·cernō -cernĕre -crēvī -crētum *vt* to sift

incēr·ō -āre *vt* to wax, cover with wax

incertō *adv* not for certain

incert·ō -āre *vt* to render doubtful, make uncertain

incert·us -a -um *adj* uncertain, vague, obscure; doubtful, dubious; unsure, hesitant; *n* uncertainty, insecurity; contingency; **in incertum** for an indefinite time

incess·ō -ĕre -īvī *vt* to fall upon, assault, reproach, accuse, attack; (*fig*) to attack

incess·us -ūs *m* walk, gait, pace; tread, trampling; invasion, attack

incostē *adv* impurely, sinfully; indecently

incest·ō -āre *vt* to pollute, defile; to violate (*a girl*)

incest·us -a -um *adj* polluted, defiled, unclean, impure, sinful; lewd, unchaste, incestuous

incest·us -ūs *m* indecency, incest

in·cĭdō -cĭdĕre -cĭdī -cāsum *vi* to happen, occur; (with **in** or **ad** + *acc*) to fall into, fall upon; (with **in** + *acc*) **a** to come upon unexpectedly, fall in with; **b** to attack; (with *dat* or **in** + *acc*) **a** to occur to (*mentally*); **b** to fall on (*a certain day*); **c** to befall; **d** to agree with

in·cīdō -cīdĕre -cīdī -cīsum *vt* to carve, engrave, inscribe; to cut, sever; (*fig*) to cut into, cut short, put an end to, break off, interrupt

incīl·e -is *n* ditch, trench

in·cingō -cingĕre -cinxī -cinctum *vt* to drape; to wreathe; to invest, surround

incīn·ō -ĕre *vt* to sing; to play

incipessō *see* **incipisso**

in·cipĭō -cipĕre -cēpī -ceptum *vt & vi* to begin, start

incipiss·ō -ĕre vt to begin

incisē or **incisim** adv in short phrases

incīsi·ō -ōnis f or **incīs·um -ī** n clause

incīsus pp of incido

incitāment·um -ī n incitement, incentive

incitāti·ō -ōnis f inciting, rousing; speed

incitātius adv rather impetuously

incitāt·us -a -um adj rapid, speedy; **equo incitato** at full gallop

incit·ō -āre vt to incite, urge on, spur on, drive on; to stimulate; to inspire; to stir up, arouse; to increase, augment; **currentem incitare** (fig) to spur a willing horse; **se incitare** to rush

incit·us -a -um adj rapid, swift, immovable; **ad incita redigere** to bring to a standstill

inclāmit·ō -āre vt to cry out against, abuse

inclām·ō -āre vt to shout at, scold, chide; vi to yell

inclār·escō -escĕre -ŭī vi to become famous

inclēm·ens -entis adj inclement, harsh, unmerciful

inclēmenter adv harshly, severely

inclēmenti·a -ae f harshness, severity, rigor

inclīnāti·ō -ōnis f leaning; inclination, tendency, bias; change; inflection

inclīnāt·us -a -um adj inclined, prone; sinking; low, deep

inclīn·ō -āre vt to bend, turn, to turn back, drive back, repulse; (fig) to divert, shift (e.g., blame); to change, alter; **inclinari** (mil) to fall back, give way; **inclinari** or **se inclinare** to lean, bend, turn; to change (esp. for the worse); vi to bend, turn, lean, dip, sink, (mil) to fall back, give way; (fig) to change, deteriorate; (fig) to change for the better

inclit·us -a -um adj famous

in·clūdō -clūdĕre -clūsī -clūsum vt to shut in, confine, lock up; to include, insert; to block, obstruct, shut off, stop up; (fig) to include, embrace, comprehend; to restrain, control; to close, end (e.g., day)

inclūsi·ō -ōnis f locking up, confinement

inclŭt·us or **inclĭt·us -a -um** adj famous

incoct·us -a -um pp of incoquo; adj uncooked, raw

incōgitābil·is -e adj thoughtless, inconsiderate

incōgit·ans -antis adj unthinking, thoughtless

incōgitanti·a -ae f thoughtlessness

incōgitāt·us -a -um adj thoughtless, inconsiderate

incōgit·ō -āre vt to think up

incognit·us -a -um adj not investigated; unknown, unrecognized, unidentified; unparalleled

incohāt·us -a -um adj unfinished

incoh·ō -āre vt to begin, start

incŏl·a -ae m & f inhabitant, resident

incŏl·ō -ĕre -ŭī vt to live in, inhabit, occupy; vi to live, reside

incolŭm·is -e adj unharmed, safe and sound, unscathed, alive; (with abl) safe from

incolumit·ās -ātis f safety

incomitāt·us -a -um adj unaccompanied

incommendāt·us -a -um adj unprotected

incommŏdē adv at the wrong time; inconveniently; unfortunately

incommodestio·us -a -um adj (coll) ill-timed, inconvenient

incommodit·ās -ātis f inconvenience; unsuitableness; disadvantage

incommŏd·ō -āre vi (with dat) to be inconvenient to, to be annoying to, to inconvenience

incommŏd·us -a -um adj inconvenient, annoying; n inconvenience; trouble, setback, disaster

incommūtābil·is -e adj unchangeable

incomparābil·is -e adj unequaled, incomparable

incompert·us -a -um adj unknown, forgotten

incompositē adv in disorder

incomposĭt·us -a -um adj disordered, confused, unstudied, uncouth, irregular

incomprehensibil·is -e adj incomprehensible

incompt·us -a -um adj unkempt, messy; primitive, rude (discourse)

inconcess·us -a -um adj forbidden, unlawful

inconcili·ō -āre vt to deceive, trick, to rob, fleece

inconcinn·us -a -um adj clumsy, awkward; absurd

inconcuss·us -a -um adj unshaken

inconditē adv confusedly

incondĭt·us -a -um adj unorganized, disorderly, confused, irregular; rough, undeveloped (style); raw (jokes)

inconsīderātē adv thoughtlessly

inconsīderāt·us -a -um adj thoughtless

inconsōlābil·is -e adj incurable

inconst·ans -antis adj inconsistent, fickle, shifty

inconstanter adv inconsistently

inconstanti·a -ae f inconsistency, fickleness

inconsultē adv indiscreetly

inconsult·us -a -um adj indiscreet, ill-advised, imprudent; not consulted

inconsult·us -ūs m **inconsultu meo** without consulting me

inconsumpt·us -a -um adj unconsumed

incontāmĭnāt·us -a -um adj untainted

incontent·us -a -um *adj* loose, untuned (*string*)

incontin·ens -entis *adj* incontinent

incontinenter *adv* without self-control, incontinently

incontinenti·a -ae *f* lack of self-control

inconveni·ens -entis *adj* unsuitable, dissimilar

in·cŏquŏ -cŏquĕre -coxī -coctum *vt* to boil, cook; to dye

incorrect·us -a -um *adj* uncorrected, unrevised

incorruptē *adv* justly, fairly

incorrupt·us -a -um *adj* untainted; uncorrupted, unspoiled; genuine, pure

incrēbr·escō or incrēb·escō -escĕre -ŭī *vi* to grow, rise, increase, spread

incrēdibil·is -e *adj* incredible

incrēdibiliter *adv* incredibly

incrēdŭl·us -a -um *adj* incredulous

increment·um -ī *n* growth, increase; increment, addition; addition to the family, offspring

increpitŏ -āre *vt* to scold, rebuke

inorep·ŏ -āre -ŭī (or -āvī) -itum (or -ātum) *vt* to cause to make noise; to rattle; (*of Jupiter*) to thunder at; to scold, rebuke; *vi* to make a noise, to rustle, rattle, clatter, clash; to speak angrily

incr·escō -escĕre -ēvī *vi* to grow, increase; (*with dat or abl*) to grow in or upon

incrētus *pp* of incerno

incruentāt·us -a -um *adj* unbloodied

incruent·us -a -um *adj* bloodless, without bloodshed

incrust·ŏ -āre *vt* to cover with a coat, encrust

incŭb·ŏ -āre -ŭī -itum *vi* (with *dat*) a to lie in or upon; b to lean on; c to brood over; d to watch jealously over

inculc·ŏ -āre *vt* to impress, inculcate; (*with dat*) to force (*something*) upon

inculpāt·us -a -um *adj* blameless

incultē *adv* uncouthly, roughly

incult·us -a -um *adj* untilled, uncultivated; neglected, slovenly; rough, uneducated, uncivilized; *n pl* desert, wilderness

incult·us -ūs *m* neglect; dirt, squalor

in·cumbō -cumbĕre -cubŭī -cubĭtum *vi* (with *dat or in + acc*) a to lean on or against; b to lie down on (a *couch, bed*); c to bend to (the *oars*); d to light on, fall on; e (*fig*) to press upon, burden, oppress, weigh down; f to apply onself to, take pains with, pay attention to; (with *ad or in + acc*) to be inclined towards, lean towards

incūnābŭl·a -ōrum *n pl* baby clothes, swaddling clothes; (*fig*) cra-

dle, infancy, birthplace, source, origin

incūrāt·us -a -um *adj* neglected; uncured

incūri·a -ae *f* carelessness, negligence

incūriōsē *adv* carelessly

incūriōs·us -a -um *adj* careless, unconcerned, indifferent; neglected

in·currō -currĕre -currī or -cucurrī -cursum *vt* to attack; *vi* (with *dat or in + acc*) a to run into, rush at, charge, attack, invade; b to extend to; c to meet, run into; d to fall on, coincide with

incursi·ŏ -ōnis *f* incursion, invasion, raid; assault, attack, collision

incurs·ŏ -āre *vt* to assault, attack; to invade; *vi* (with *dat or in + acc*) a to assault, attack; b to run into, bump against; c to strike, meet (*e.g., the eyes*); d to affect, touch, move

incurs·us -ūs *m* assault, attack; invasion; impulse

incurv·ŏ -āre *vt* to bend, curve

incurv·us -a -um *adj* bent, crooked

inc·ūs -ūdis *f* anvil

incūsātiŏ -ōnis *f* accusation

incūs·ŏ -āre *vt* to blame, find fault with, accuse

incuss·us -ūs *m* shock

incussus *pp* of incutio

incustōdīt·us -a -um *adj* unguarded; unconcealed; imprudent

incūs·us -a -um *adj* forged; lapis incussus indented millstone

in·cutiō -cutĕre -cussī -cussum *vt* to throw; to produce; (with *dat or in + acc*) to strike (*something*) on or against; (with *dat*) a to strike into, instill in; b to throw at, to fling upon; metum incutere (with *dat*) to inspire fear in, strike fear in; scipionem in caput alicujus incutere to beat someone over the head with a stick

indāgātiŏ -ōnis *f* investigation, search

indāgāt·or -ōris *m* or indāgātr·ix -ĭcis *f* investigator

indāg·ŏ -āre *vt* to track down, hunt; (*fig*) to track down, investigate, explore

indāg·ŏ -ĭnis *f* dragnet; indagine agĕre to ferret out

indaudiŏ see inaudio

inde *adv* from there; from that source, therefrom; from that time on, after that, thereafter; then; from that cause

indēbit·us -a -um *adj* not owed, not due

indēc·ens -entis *adj* unbecoming, improper, indecent

indecenter *adv* improperly, indecently

indec·ĕŏ -ēre *vt* to be improper for

indēclīnāt·us -a -um *adj* unchanged, constant

indēc·or -ōris or indecŏr·is -e *adj* disgraceful, dishonorable, cowardly

indecōrē adv indecently, improperly

indecŏr·ō -āre vt to disgrace

indecōr·us -a -um adj unsightly, improper, disgraceful

indēfens·us -a -um adj undefended

indēfess·us -a -um adj tireless; not tired

indēflēt·us -a -um adj unwept

indēject·us -a -um adj undemolished

indēlēbil·is -e adj indestructible, indelible

indēlībāt·us -a -um adj undiminished

indemnāt·us -a -um adj unconvicted

indēplōrāt·us -a -um adj unwept

indēprens·us -a -um adj undetected

indeptus pp of **indipiscor**

indēsert·us -a -um adj unforsaken

indēspect·us -a -um adj unfathomable

indēstrict·us -a -um adj unscathed

indētons·us -a -um adj unshorn

indēvītāt·us -a -um adj unerring (e.g., arrow)

ind·ex -ĭcis m index, sign, mark, indication, proof; title (of book); informer, spy; index finger

Indĭ·a -ae f India

indicātĭ·ō -ōnis f value; price

indic·ens -entis adj not speaking; **me indicente** without a word from me

indic·ium -ĭī or **-ī** n information, disclosure; evidence; indication, proof, permission to give evidence; reward for giving evidence

indic·ō -āre vt to point out; to reveal, disclose, make known; to betray, inform against, accuse; to put a price on; vi to give evidence

in·dīcō -dīcere -dīxī -dīctum vt to proclaim, announce, publish; to summon, convoke; to impose (a fine); **bellum indicere** to declare war; **diem indicere** to set a date

indict·us -a -um adj unsaid; **causā indictā** without a hearing

Indīc·us -a -um adj Indian; m Indian; n indigo

indīdem adv from the same place; from the same source, from the same thing

indiffĕr·ens -entis adj (morally) indifferent; unconcerned, indifferent

indigĕn·a -ae adj masc & fem native

indig·ens -entis adj indigent; (with genit) in need of

indigentĭ·a -ae f indigence, want, need; craving

indig·ĕō -ēre -ŭī vi (with genit or abl) to need, be in need of, require; (with genit) to crave, desire

indig·es -ĕtis adj indigenous, native; m native god; national hero

indigest·us -a -um adj unarranged, confused

indignābund·us -a -um adj indignant, highly indignant

indign·ans -antis adj indignant; impatient, reluctant

indignātĭ·ō -ōnis f indignation, displeasure; provocation; occasion for indignation; f pl expressions of indignation

indignē adv unworthily, undeservedly; indignantly

indignit·ās -ātis f unworthiness; indignation; indignity, shameful treatment; enormity, shamefulness

indign·or -ārī -ātus sum vt to be indignant at, displeased at, angry at, offended at

indign·us -a -um adj unworthy, undeserving; undeserved; (with abl) a unworthy of; b not deserving; c not worth; (with genit) unworthy of, undeserving of; **indignum!** shame!

indĭg·us -a -um adj (with genit or abl) in need of, needing

indīlĭg·ens -entis adj careless

indīligenter adv carelessly

indīligentĭ·a -ae f carelessness

ind·ipiscor -ipiscī -eptus sum or **indipisc·ō -ĕre** vt to obtain, get; to attain, reach

indīrept·us -a -um adj unplundered

indiscrēt·us -a -um adj closely connected; indiscriminate, undistinguishable; confused

indisertē adv without eloquence

indisert·us -a -um adj not eloquent; at a loss for words

indisposit·us -a -um adj confused, disorderly

indissolūbil·is -e adj imperishable, indestructible

indistinct·us -a -um adj indistinct, obscure; confused

inditus pp of **indo**

indivĭdŭ·us -a -um adj indivisible; inseparable; n atom, indivisible particle

in·dō -dĕre -dĭdī -dĭtum vt to put, place; to introduce; to impart, give; (with **in** + acc) to put or place (something) into or on, insert in

indocĭl·is -e adj difficult to teach, slow to learn; hard to learn; untaught

indoctē adv unskillfully

indoct·us -a -um adj untaught, untrained, unschooled; illiterate, ignorant

indolentĭ·a -ae f freedom from pain, insensibility

indŏl·ēs -is f inborn quality, natural quality; nature, character, disposition; natural ability, talent, genius

indol·escō -escĕre -ŭī vi to feel sorry; to feel resentment

indomābil·is -e adj untameable

indomit·us -a -um adj untamed, wild; (fig) wild, unmanageable

indorm·ĭō -īre -īvī or **-ĭī -ītum** vi to fall asleep; to grow careless; (with dat or abl or with **in** + abl) a to fall asleep at or on; b to fall asleep over; c to become careless about

indōtāt·us -a -um adj without dowry; poor; without funeral rites or funeral honors; **ars indotata** unadorned style; **corpora indotata** bodies that have not been accorded the usual honors paid to the dead

indubitābil·is -e *adj* indubitable

indubitāt·us -a -um *adj* undoubted

indubit·ō -āre *vi* (with *dat*) to begin to distrust, begin to doubt

indubi·us -a -um *adj* undoubted, certain

indūci·ae -ārum *f pl* armistice, truce

in·dūcō -dūcere -duxī -ductum *vt* to lead or bring in; to bring in, introduce; to induce, persuade, seduce, move; to overlay, drape, wrap, cover, put on, clothe; to strike out, erase; to repeal, cancel; to present, exhibit; to mislead, delude; (with **in** + *acc*) **a** to lead to, lead into, lead against; **b** to bring into, introduce into; **c** (fig) to introduce (*e.g., a new custom*) into; **d** to enter into (*account books*), charge to (*someone's account*); (with *dat* or **super** + *acc*) to put (*item of apparel*) on, spread over, wrap around, draw over; **animum inducere** or **in animum inducere** to make up one's mind, convince oneself, be convinced, conclude, suppose, imagine

inductī·ō -ōnis *f* bringing in, introduction, admission; resolution, determination; intention; induction, generalization; **animi inductio** inclination; **erroris inductio** deception

induct·or -ōris *m* (referring to a whip) persuader

induct·us -ūs *m* persuasion, inducement

indūcŭl·a -ae *f* skirt, petticoat

indulg·ens -entis *adj* indulgent, lenient; (with *dat* or **in** + *acc*) lenient toward, kind toward

indulgenter *adv* indulgently, leniently, kindly

indulgentǐ·a -ae *f* indulgence, leniency, kindness

in·dulgeō -dulgēre -dulsī *vt* (with *dat*) to grant, concede (*something*) to; **veniam indulgere** (with *dat*) to make allowances for; *vi* (with *dat*) **a** to be lenient toward, be kind to, be tender to; **b** to yield to, give way to; **c** to indulge in, be addicted to; **sibi indulgere** to be self-indulgent, take liberties

ind·ŭō -ŭere -ŭī -ūtum *vt* to put on (*e.g., a tunic*); to cover, wrap, clothe, array, envelop; to engage in; to assume, put on; to assume the part of; to involve, entangle; (with *dat*) to put (*e.g., a tunic*) on (*someone*)

indup- = **imp-**

indūr·escō -escĕre -ŭī *vi* to become hard, harden

indūr·ō -āre *vt* to harden

Ind·us -a -um *adj* Indian; *m* Indian; Ethiopian; mahout

industrǐ·a -ae *f* industry, diligence;

industriā or **de** or **ex industria** or **ob industriam** on purpose

industriē *adv* industriously, diligently

industrǐ·us -a -um *adj* industrious, diligent, painstaking

indūti·ae or **indūci·ae -ārum** *f pl* armistice, truce

indūtus *pp* of **induo**; *adj* (with *acc* or *abl*) dressed in, wearing

indūt·us -ūs *m* wearing; clothing

indŭvǐ·ae -ārum *f pl* clothes

inebrǐ·ō -āre *vt* to make drunk; (fig) to fill (*e.g., ear with gossip*)

inedǐ·a -ae *f* fasting; starvation

inedīt·us -a -um *adj* not made known, unknown, unpublished

inelēg·ans -antis *adj* inelegant, undistinguished

ineleganter *adv* without distinction

ineluctābil·is -e *adj* inescapable

inemor·ǐor -ī *vi* (with *dat*) to die in or at

inempt·us -a -um *adj* unpurchased; without ransom

inenarrābil·is -e *adj* indescribable

inenarrābiliter *adv* indescribably

inenōdābil·is -e *adj* inexplicable

in·ĕō -īre -ǐī -itum *vt* to enter; to enter upon, undertake, form; to begin, engage in; **consilium inire** to form a plan; **consilium inire ut, qua,** or **quemadmodum** to plan how to (*do something*); **inire numerum** (with *genit*) to go into an enumeration of, enumerate; **inire rationem** (with *genit*) to form an estimate of; **inire rationem ut, qua,** or **quemadmodum** to consider, find out, or figure out how to (*do something*); **viam inire** to begin a trip; to find a way, devise a means

ineptē *adv* foolishly, absurdly, inappropriately, pointlessly

ineptǐ·a -ae *f* foolishness; *f pl* nonsense; trifles

inept·ǐō -īre *vi* to be absurd, make a fool of oneself

inept·us -a -um *adj* foolish, silly; inept, awkward, absurd; unsuitable, out of place; tactless, tasteless

inerm·is -e or **inerm·us -a -um** *adj* unarmed, defenseless; undefended; toothless (*gums*); harmless

inerr·ans -antis *adj* not wandering, fixed

inerr·ō -āre *vi* to wander about

iner·s -tis *adj* unskillful, incompetent; inactive, sluggish; weak, soft, helpless; stagnant, motionless; ineffective, dull, insipid; numbing (*cold*); expressionless (*eyes*); uneventful, leisurely (*time*)

inertǐ·a -ae *f* lack of skill, ignorance, rudeness; inactivity, laziness

inerudīt·us -a -um *adj* uneducated; crude, inconsiderate

inesc·ō -āre *vt* to bait; (fig) to bait, trap, deceive

inevect·us -a -um *adj* mounted

inēvītābil·is -e *adj* inevitable, inescapable

inexcīt·us -a -um *adj* unexcited, calm

inexcūsābil·is -e *adj* without excuse; admitting no excuse

inexercitāt·us -a -um *adj* untrained

inexhaust·us -a -um *adj* unexhausted, not wasted; inexhaustible

inexōrābil·is -e *adj* inexorable, relentless; unswerving, strict

inexperrect·us -a -um *adj* unawakened

inexpert·us -a -um *adj* untried, untested; novel; (with *abl*. or with **in** or **adversus** + *acc*) inexperienced in, unaccustomed to

inexpiābil·is -e *adj* inexpiable, not to be atoned for; irreconcilable, implacable

inexplēbil·is -e *adj* insatiable

inexplēt·us -a -um *adj* unsatisfied, unfilled

inexplicābil·is -e *adj* inextricable; inexplicable; impassable (*road*); involved, unending (*war*)

inexplōrātō *adv* without reconnoitering

inexplōrāt·us -a -um *adj* unexplored; unfamiliar

inexpugnābil·is -e *adj* impregnable, unassailable; invincible

inexspectāt·us -a -um *adj* unexpected

inexstinct·us -a -um *adj* unextinguished; insatiable

inexsuperābil·is -e *adj* insuperable, insurmountable

inextrīcābil·is -e *adj* inextricable

īnfābrē *adv* unskillfully

īnfabricāt·us -a -um *adj* unshaped, untrimmed

īnfacētē *adv* witlessly

īnfacētī·ae -ārum *f pl* coarse jokes

īnfacēt·us -a -um *adj* not witty, not funny, dull, stupid

īnfācund·us -a -um *adj* ineloquent

īnfāmi·a -ae *f* bad reputation, bad name; disrepute, disgrace, scandal; embarrassment

īnfām·is -e *adj* infamous, notorious, disreputable, disgraceful

īnfām·ō -āre *vt* to defame, dishonor, disgrace

īnfand·us -a -um *adj* unspeakable, shocking

īnf·āns -antis *adj* speechless, unable to speak; baby, infant, young; childish, silly; (fig) incapable of speaking, tongue-tied; *m* or *f* infant

īnfanti·a -ae *f* infancy; childishness; inability to speak; lack of eloquence

īnfar- = īnfer-

īnfatu·ō -āre *vt* to make a fool of

īnfaust·us -a -um *adj* ill-omened, unpropitious; unfortunate

īnfect·or -ōris *m* dyer

īnfect·us -a -um *pp* of **īnficiō**; *adj* not made, not done, undone, unfinished, unachieved; unfeasible; impossible

īnfēcundit·ās -ātis *f* unfruitfulness

īnfēcund·us -a -um *adj* unfruitful

īnfēlīcit·ās -ātis *f* bad luck, misfortune

īnfēlīciter *adv* unhappily; unluckily, unsuccessfully

īnfēlīc·ō -āre *vt* to make unhappy

īnfēl·īx -īcis *adj* unfruitful; unhappy, unfortunate; causing misfortune, ruinous; ill-omened; pessimistic

īnfēnsē *adv* hostilely, aggressively

īnfēns·ō -āre *vt* to antagonize; to make dangerous; *vi* to be hostile

īnfēns·us -a -um *adj* hostile, antagonistic; dangerous; (with *dat* or **in** + *acc*) a hostile to, antagonistic toward; b dangerous to

in·ferciō or īnfarciō -fercīre -fersī -fersum or -fertum *vt* to stuff, cram

īnfer·a -ōrum *n pl* lower world

īnfer·ī -ōrum *m pl* the dead; the world below

īnferi·ae -ārum *f pl* rites and offerings to the dead

īnferi·or -us *adj* lower, farther down; (fig) inferior, lower; subsequent, later

īnferius *adv* lower, too low

īnfernē *adv* below, beneath

īnfern·us -a -um *adj* lower; infernal, of the lower world

īnfer·ō īnferre intulī illātum *vt* to bring in, introduce, carry in; to import; to bring forward, adduce, produce, make, occasion, incite, cause; to offer, render, sacrifice; to bury, inter; **arma, bellum, gradum, pedem,** or **signa inferre** to make an attack, make an advance, begin hostilities; **arma, bellum, pedem,** or **signa inferre** (with *dat* or with **in** or **contra** + *acc*) to attack, advance against, invade; **conversa signa inferre** (with *dat*) to turn around and attack; **ignem inferre** (with *dat*) to set fire to; **sē inferre** to go, march, rush, charge, plunge; **sē in periculum inferre** to expose oneself to danger; *vi* to infer, conclude

īnfer·us -a -um *adj* lower; southern

in·fervescō -fervescere -ferbuī *vi* to simmer, boil

īnfestē *adv* hostilely, violently, outrageously

īnfest·ō -āre *vt* to annoy; to infest; to attack

īnfest·us -a -um *adj* infested, molested, disturbed, unsafe; hostile, aggressive; dangerous; threatening

īnficēt- = īnfacēt-

in·ficiō -ficere -fēcī -fectum *vt* to dip, dye, tint; to infect; to stain; to corrupt, spoil; to imbue, instruct; (fig) to poison, infect

īnfidēl·is -e *adj* unfaithful, untrue, disloyal

īnfidēlit·ās -ātis *f* infidelity, unfaithfulness, disloyalty

īnfidēliter *adv* disloyally

infĭd·us -a -um *adj* untrustworthy, treacherous

in·fīgō -fīgĕre -fixī -fixum *vt* to drive in, nail, thrust; to imprint, fix, impress; (with *dat*) **a** to drive into, thrust into; **b** to impale on; **c** to imprint on or in

infĭmātis see **infumatis**

infĭm·us or **infĭm·us -a -um** (*superl* of **infĕrus**) *adj* lowest, last; lowest, worst, humblest; **ab infĭmo colle** at the foot of the hill; **infĭmum mare** the botton of the sea; **n** bottom

in·findō -findĕre -fīdī -fissum *vt* (with *dat*) to cut (*e.g., furrows*) into

infinĭt·ās -ātis *f* endlessness, infinity

infinĭtē *adv* without bounds, without end, infinitely; without exception

infinĭtĭ·ō -ōnis *f* boundlessness, infinity

infinĭt·us -a -um *adj* unlimited, boundless; without end, endless, infinite; countless; indefinite

infirmātĭ·ō -ōnis *f* invalidation; refutation

infirmē *adv* weakly, faintly, feebly

infirmĭt·ās -ātis *f* weakness, feebleness; infirmity, sickness; inconstancy

infirm·ō -āre *vt* to weaken, enfeeble; to refute, disprove; to annul

infirm·us -a -um *adj* weak, faint, feeble; infirm, sick; trivial; inconstant

infissus *pp* of **infindo**

infit *v defect* he, she, it begins

initĭ·ae -ārum *f pl* denial; **initĭas ire** (with *acc*) to deny

initĭāl·is -e *adj* negative

initĭātĭ·ō -ōnis *f* denial

initĭāt·or -ōris *m* repudiator

initĭ·or -ārī -ātus sum *vt* to deny, repudiate, contradict, disown

infixus *pp* of **infigo**

inflammātĭ·ō -ōnis *f* setting on fire; **inflammationem inferre** (with *dat*) to set on fire

inflamm·ō -āre *vt* to set on fire, kindle, light up; (fig) to inflame, excite

inflātĭ·ō -ōnis *f* swelling up; **habet inflationem faba** beans cause gas

inflātus *adv* too pompously

inflāt·us -a -um *adj* blown up, swollen, inflated; haughty; turgid (*style*)

inflāt·us -ūs *m* puff, blast; inspiration

in·flectō -flectĕre -flexī -flexum *vt* to bend, curve, bow, turn aside; to change; to influence; to inflect

inflĕt·us -a -um *adj* unwept

inflexibĭl·is -e *adj* inflexible

inflexĭ·ō -ōnis *f* bending

inflexus *pp* of **inflecto**

inflex·us -ūs *m* curve

in·flīgō -flīgĕre -flixī -flictum *vt* to strike, smash, dash, swing; to inflict (*wound*); to bring (*e.g., disgrace*)

inflĭ·ō -āre *vt* to blow (*horn*), play (*flute*); to inspire; to inflate, puff up, fill

in·fluō -fluĕre -fluxī *vi* (with **in +** *acc*) **a** to flow into; **b** (fig) to spill over into, stream into, pour into

in·fodĭō -fodĕre -fōdī -fossum *vt* to dig; to bury

informātĭ·ō -ōnis *f* sketch; idea

inform·is -e *adj* unformed, shapeless; ugly, hideous

inform·ō -āre *vt* to form, shape

infŏr·ō -āre *vt* to bring into court

infortūnāt·us -a -um *adj* unfortunate

infortūn·ĭum -iī or **-ī** *n* misfortune, calamity; punishment

infossus *pp* of **infodio**

infrā *adv* below, underneath; down south, down the coast; *prep* (with *acc*) below, beneath, under; later than

infractĭ·ō -ōnis *f* weakening; **animi infractio** discouragement

infract·us -a -um *pp* of **infringo**; *adj* broken, weakened, exhausted; **infractos animos gerere** to feel down and out

infragĭl·is -e *adj* unbreakable, strong

infrĕm·ō -ĕre -ŭī *vi* to growl, bellow, roar; to rage

infrenat·us -a -um *adj* unbridled

infrend·ĕō -ēre or **infrend·ō -ĕre** *vi* **dentibus infrendere** to gnash the teeth

infrēn·is -e or **infrēn·us -a -um** *adj* unbridled

infrēn·ō -āre *vt* to put a bridle on; to harness; (fig) to curb

infrēnus see **infrenis**

infrĕqu·ens -entis *adj* uncrowded, not numerous; poorly attended; thinly populated; inconstant, irregular

infrequentĭ·a -ae *f* small number, scantiness; poor attendance; emptiness

in·fringō -fringĕre -frēgī -fractum *vt* to break, break in; to impair, affect, subdue, weaken, break down

infr·ons -ondis *adj* leafless

infructuōs·us -a -um *adj* unfruitful; pointless

infūcāt·us -a -um *adj* painted over, varnished; hidden

infūl·a -ae *f* bandage; fillet; mark of distinction, badge of honor

infumāt·is or **infimāt·is -is** *m* one of the lowest (*in rank*)

infimus see **infimus**

in·fundō -fundĕre -fūdī -fūsum *vt* to pour in, pour on, pour out; (with *dat* or **in +** *acc*) **a** to pour into, pour upon; **b** to administer to; **infundi** or **se infundere** (with *dat*) to lay on, spread out on

infusc·ō -āre *vt* to darken, obscure; to stain, corrupt, sully

infūsus *pp* of **infundo**; *adj* diffused, permeating; fallen (*snow*); crowded

ingemin·ō -āre vt to redouble; to repeat, reiterate; vi to redouble

ingem·iscō or **ingem·escō -iscĕre -ŭī** vi to groan, heave a sigh; (with dat or in + abl) to groan over, sigh over

ingĕm·ō -ĕre -ŭī vt to groan over, sigh over; vi (with dat) to sigh over

ingenĕr·ō -āre vt to engender, generate, produce, create

ingeniāt·us -a -um adj naturally endowed, talented

ingeniōsē adv ingeniously

ingeniōs·us -a -um adj ingenious, clever, talented; (with dat or ad + acc) naturally suited to

ingenĭt·us -a -um adj inborn, natural

ingen·ium -iī or **-ī n** innate or natural quality; nature, temperament, character, bent, inclination; natural ability, talent, genius; clever person, genius

ing·ens -entis adj huge, vast; great, mighty, powerful

ingenŭē adv liberally; frankly

ingenŭit·ās -ātis f noble birth; noble character; frankness

ingenŭ·us -a -um adj native, indigenous; natural; free-born; like a freeman, noble; frank

in·gĕrō -gerĕre -gessī -gestum vt to carry in, throw in, heap; to hurl, shoot (weapon); to pour out (angry words), heap (abuse)

inglōri·us -a -um adj inglorious, without glory, inconspicuous

ingluvi·ēs -ēī f crop, maw; gluttony

ingrātē adv unpleasantly; unwillingly; ungratefully

ingrātific·us -a -um adj ungrateful

ingrātiīs or **ingrātīs** adv without thanks; unwillingly

ingrāt·us -a -um adj unpleasant, unwelcome; ungrateful; receiving no thanks, unappreciated; thankless

ingraves·cō -ĕre vi to grow heavier; to become pregnant; to grow worse; to become more serious; to become weary; to become dearer (in price); to become more important

in·gredior -grĕdī -gressus sum vt to enter; to undertake; to begin; to walk in, follow (footsteps); vi to go in, enter; to go, walk, walk along; to begin, commence; to begin to speak; (with in + acc) a to go in, enter; b to enter upon, begin, take up, undertake; **in rem publicam ingredī** to enter politics, enter public life

ingressi·ō -ōnis f entering; walking; gait, pace; beginning

ingress·us -ūs m entering; (mil) inroad; walking; gait; beginning

ingru·ō -ĕre -ī vi to come, come on, rush on; (of war) to break out; (of rain) to pour down; (with dat or in + acc) to fall upon, attack

ingu·en -inis n groin; swelling, tumor; n pl private parts

ingurgĭt·ō -āre vt to gorge, stuff; **se ingurgitāre** to stuff oneself; **se ingurgitāre** (with in + acc) to steep oneself in, devote oneself to

ingustāt·us -a -um adj untasted

inhabĭl·is -e adj clumsy, unhandy; (with dat or ad + acc) unfit for

inhabitābĭl·is -e adj uninhabitable

inhabĭt·ō -āre vt inhabit

in·haerĕō -haerēre -haesī -haesum vi to stick, cling; (fig) to cling, adhere; to be inherent; (with dat, with ad + acc, or with in + abl) a to cling to; b to be closely connected with; c to gaze upon

in·haerescō -haerescĕre -haesī vi to stick fast, take hold

inhāl·ō -āre vt (with dat) to breathe (e.g., bad breath) on (someone)

inhib·ĕō -ēre -ŭī -ĭtum vt to hold back, curb, check, control; to use, practice, perform; to apply, inflict; **retro navem inhibēre** to back up the ship; vi to row backwards, backwater

inhibiti·ō -ōnis f backing up

inhĭ·ō -āre vt to gape at; to covet; vi to stand open-mouthed, be amazed

inhonestē adv dishonorably, disgracefully; dishonestly

inhonest·ō -āre vt to dishonor, disgrace

inhonest·us -a -um adj dishonorable, disgraceful, shameful, inglorious; indecent; ugly, degrading

inhonōrāt·us -a -um adj unhonored, disregarded, unrewarded

inhonōr·us -a -um adj defaced

inhorr·ĕō -ēre -ŭī vi to stand on end, bristle

inhorr·escō -escĕre -ŭī vi to stand on end, bristle; to vibrate; to shiver, tremble, shudder

inhospitāl·is -e adj inhospitable, unfriendly

inhospitālĭt·ās -ātis f inhospitality

inhospĭt·us -a -um adj inhospitable

inhūmānē adv inhumanly, savagely

inhūmānĭt·ās -ātis f inhumanity; barbarity; churlishness; extreme stinginess

inhūmānĭter adv impolitely

inhūmān·us -a -um adj inhuman, savage; brutal; crude, impolite

inhumāt·us -a -um adj unburied

inĭbī or **inĭbī** adv there, in that place; near at hand

inimīc·a -ae f (personal) enemy (female)

inimīcē adv hostilely, in an unfriendly way

inimīcĭti·a -ae f unfriendliness, enmity; f pl feuds

inimīc·ō -āre vt to make into enemies, set at odds

inimīc·us -a -um adj unfriendly, hostile; harmful; m (personal) enemy; **inimicissimus suus** his bitterest enemy

inīquē adv unequally, unevenly; unfairly

inīquĭt·ās -ātis f unevenness; inequality; disadvantage; unfairness

iniqu·us -a -um *adj* uneven, unequal; not level, sloping; unfair; adverse, harmful; dangerous, unfavorable; prejudiced; excessive; impatient, discontented; **iniquo animo** impatiently, unwillingly; *m* enemy, foe

initi·ō -āre *vt* to initiate, begin; to initiate (*into mysteries*)

init·ium -iī *or* **-ī** *n* entrance; beginning; *n pl* elements; first principles; sacred rites, sacred mysteries

initus *pp* of **ineo**

init·us -ūs *m* entrance; beginning

in·jiciō -jicĕre -jēcī -jectum *vt* to throw, inject; to impose, apply; to inspire, infuse; to cause, occasion; to furnish (*a cause*); to bring up, mention (*a name*); (with *dat* or **in** + *acc*) to throw or fling into, on or over; (with *dat* or **in** + *acc*) **a** to throw oneself into, rush into, expose oneself to; **b** to fling oneself down on; **c** (*of the mind*) to turn itself to, concentrate on, reflect on; **manum injicere** (with *dat*) to lay hands on, take possession of

injūcundit·ās -ātis *f* unpleasantness

injūcundius *adv* rather unpleasantly

injūcund·us -a -um *adj* unpleasant

injūdicāt·us -a -um *adj* undecided

in·jungō -jungĕre -junxī -junctum *vt* to join, attach, fasten; to inflict, impose; (with *dat*) **a** to join, attach, fasten to; **b** to inflict on, impose (*e.g., taxes, obligations*) on

injūrāt·us -a -um *adj* not under oath

injūri·a -ae *f* injury, wrong, outrage, injustice; insult, affront; harshness, severity; revenge; damage, harm; ill-gotten goods; **injuriā** unjustly, undeservedly, innocently; **per injuriam** unjustly, outrageously

injūriōsē *adv* unjustly, wrongfully

injūriōs·us -a -um *adj* unjust, wrongful; harmful

injūri·us -a -um *adj* unjust, wrong

injūr·us -a -um *adj* wrongful

injussū (*abl only*) *m* without orders; **injussu meo** without my orders

injuss·us -a -um *adj* unasked, unbidden, voluntary

injustē *adv* unjustly

injustiti·a -ae *f* injustice

injust·us -a -um *adj* unjust

inl- = **ill-**

inm- = **imm-**

innābil·is -e *adj* unswimmable

in·nascor -nascī -nātus sum *vi* (with *dat*) to be born in, grow in or on; (with **in** + *abl*) (fig) to originate in

innāt·ō -āre *vt* to swim; *vi* (with *dat*) to swim around in, float on; (with **in** + *acc*) to swim into

innāt·us -a -um *pp* of **innascor**; *adj* inborn, natural

innāvigābil·is -e *adj* unnavigable

in·nectō -nectĕre -nexuī -nexum *vt* to entwine; to tie, fasten together; to join, attach, connect; (fig) to devise, invent, plan

in·nītor -nītī -nixus sum *or* **-nīsus sum** *vi* (with *abl*) to lean on, rest on, be supported by

inn·ō -āre *vt* to swim; to sail, sail over; *vi* (with *abl*) **a** to swim in, float on; **b** to sail on; **c** (of the sea) to wash against (*a shore*)

innŏc·ens -entis *adj* harmless; guiltless, innocent; upright; unselfish; (with *genit*) innocent of

innocenter *adv* blamelessly

innocenti·a -ae *f* innocence; integrity; unselfishness

innocuē *adv* harmlessly; innocently

innocu·us -a -um *adj* harmless, innocuous; innocent; unharmed

innōt·escō -escĕre -uī *vi* to become known; to become notorious

innŏv·ō -āre *vt* to renew, restore; **se innovare** (with **ad** + *acc*) to return to

innox·us -a -um *adj* harmless; safe; innocent; unhurt; (with *genit*) innocent of

innūbil·us -a -um *adj* cloudless

innūb·a -ae (*fem* only) *adj* unmarried

in·nūbō -nūbĕre -nupsī *vi* (with *dat*) to marry into

innumerābil·is -e *adj* innumerable

innumerābilit·ās -ātis *f* countless number

innumerābiliter *adv* innumerably

innumerāl·is -e *adj* innumerable

innumĕr·us -a -um *adj* countless

in·nūō -nuĕre -nuī -nūtum *vi* to give a nod; (with *dat*) to nod to

innupt·a -ae (*fem* only) *adj* unmarried; *f* unmarried girl, maiden

innutr·iō -īre -īvī *or* **-iī -ītum** *vt* (with *dat*) to bring up in

In·ō -ūs *f* daughter of Cadmus and Harmonia, wife of Athamas, mother of Learchus and Melicerta, and stepmother of Phrixus and Helle; pursued by mad Athamas, she and Melicerta hurled themselves into the sea, whereupon they were changed into sea deities

inoblīt·us -a -um *adj* unforgetful

inobrŭt·us -a -um *adj* not overwhelmed

inobservābil·is -e *adj* unnoticed

inobservanti·a -ae *f* inattention

inobservāt·us -a -um *adj* unobserved

inoccidŭ·us -a -um *adj* never setting

inodōr·us -a -um *adj* odorless

inoffens·us -a -um *adj* unobstructed, uninterrupted, unhindered

inofficiōs·us -a -um *adj* irresponsible; not obliging

inŏl·ens -entis *adj* odorless

inol·escō -escĕre -ēvī *vi* to become inveterate; (with *dat*) to grow on or in

inōmināt·us -a -um *adj* ill-omened, inauspicious

inopī·a -ae *f* lack, want, need, poverty; scarcity; barrenness (*of style*); helplessness

inopīn·ans -antis *adj* unsuspecting, taken by surprise

inopīnanter *adv* unexpectedly

inopīnātō *adv* unexpectedly, by surprise

inopīnāt·us -a -um *adj* not expected, unexpected, unsuspected, surprising; *n* surprise; **ex inopinato** by surprise

inopīn·us -a -um *adj* unexpected

inopiōs·us -a -um *adj* (with *genit*) in need of

in·ops -ōpis *adj* without means or resources; poor, needy, destitute; helpless, weak, forlorn; bald (*style*); poor (*expression*); pitiful, wretched, contemptible; (with *genit*) destitute of, stripped of, without; (with *abl*) lacking in, deficient in, poor in

inōrāt·us -a -um *adj* not presented; **re inorata** without presenting one's case

inordināt·us -a -um *adj* disordered

inornāt·us -a -um *adj* unadorned; plain (*style*); unheralded

inp- = imp-

inpendiōs·us -a -um *adj* extravagant

inperc·ō -ēre *vi* (with *dat*) to spare

inpluviāt·us -a -um *adj* square, shaped like an impluvium

inpūrāt·us -a -um *adj* (morally) defiled

inpūritī·ae -ārum *f pl* (moral) impurity

inquam *v defect* say; after one or more words of direct quotation, e.g., **Desilite, inquit, milites et . . .** "Jump down, fellow soldiers", he says, "and . . ."; in emphatic repetition, e.g., **tuas, tuas inquam suspiciones . . .** your suspicions, yes I say yours . . . ; **inquit** it is said, one says

inqui·ēs -ētis *adj* restless

inquiēt·ō -āre *vt* to disquiet, disturb

inquiēt·us -a -um *adj* restless, unsettled

inquilīn·us -ī *m* tenant, inhabitant

inquinātē *adv* filthily·

inquināt·us -a -um *adj* filthy, foul

inquīn·ō -āre *vt* to mess up, defile, contaminate

in·quīrō -quīrēre -quīsīvī -quīsitum *vt* to search for, inquire into, examine, pry into; *vi* to hold an investigation; to hold a preliminary hearing

inquīsitī·ō -ōnis *f* search, inquiry, investigation; preliminary hearing; (with *genit*) search for, inquiry into, investigation of

inquīsīt·or -ōris *m* inspector, examiner; spy; (law) investigator

inquīsīt·us -a -um *pp* of **inquiro**; *adj* not investigated

inquit see **inquam**

inr- = irr-

insalūbr·is -e *adj* unhealthy

insalūtāt·us -a -um *adj* ungreeted

insānābil·is -e *adj* incurable

insānē *adv* crazily, madly

insānī·a -ae *f* insanity, madness, frenzy; rapture; mania; excess; inspiration

insān·iō -īre -īvī or -iī -ītum *vi* to be crazy, be mad, be insane; to be absurd, be wild

insānit·ās -ātis *f* unsoundness, disease

insān·us -a -um *adj* insane, mad, crazy; absurd, foolish; excessive, extravagant; monstrous, outrageous; inspired; maddening

insatiābil·is -e *adj* insatiable; that cannot cloy, uncloying

insatiābiliter *adv* insatiably

insatiēt·ās -ātis *f* insatiety

insaturābil·is -e *adj* insatiable

insaturābiliter *adv* insatiably

in·scendō -scendēre -scendī -scensum *vt* & *vi* to climb up, mount

inscensi·ō -ōnis *f* mounting; **in navem inscensio** boarding a ship

inscensus *pp* of **inscendo**

insci·ens -entis *adj* unaware; silly, stupid

inscienter *adv* ignorantly, inadvertently

inscientī·a -ae *f* ignorance; inexperience; foolishness; awkwardness

inscīt·us -a -um *adj* ignorant, clumsy, stupid

insci·us -a -um *adj* ignorant, unaware

in·scrībō -scrībēre -scrīpsī -scrīptum *vt* to inscribe; to ascribe; to title (*a book*); to assign, attribute, appropriate; to advertise; to address (*a letter*); (with *dat* or **in** + *abl*) to write (*something*) on or in

inscriptī·ō -ōnis *f* inscribing

inscript·us -a -um *pp* of **inscribo**; *adj* unwritten

in·sculpō -sculpēre -sculpsī -sculptum *vt* to cut, carve, engrave; (with *abl* or **in** + *abl*) to cut, carve, or engrave upon

insectātī·ō -ōnis *f* hot pursuit

insectāt·or -ōris *m* persecutor

insect·or -ārī -ātus sum or insect·ō -āre *vt* to pursue, attack; to attack with words, criticize

insect·us -a -um *adj* indented, notched

insecūtus *pp* of **insequor**

insēdābiliter *adv* incessantly

insen·escō -escēre -uī *vi* (with *dat*) to grow old amidst, grow old over

insensil·is -e *adj* imperceptible

insepult·us -a -um *adj* unburied

insēqu·ens -entis *adj* next, following, succeeding

in·sēquor -sēquī -secūtus sum *vt* to follow, follow after; to succeed, to follow up; to attack; to prosecute; to pass, overtake; to reproach;

to strive after; *vi* to follow, come next

in·sĕrō -serĕre -sēvī -sĭtum *vt* to graft; (fig) to implant

in·sĕrō -serĕre -serŭī -sertum *vt* to insert; to introduce; to involve; to join, enroll, associate; to mingle, blend; to let in

insert·ō -āre *vt* to insert

inserv·ĭō -īre -īvī or **-ĭī -ītum** *vt* to serve, obey; *vi* to be a slave, be a subject; (with *dat*) to serve, be subservient to, be devoted to

insessus *pp* of **insido**

insībĭl·ō -āre *vi* (of the wind) to whistle, hiss

in·sīdĕō -sīdĕre -sēdī -sessum *vt* to hold, occupy; *vi* to sit down; to settle down; to be deep-seated; (with *abl* or *in* + *abl*) a to sit on; b to settle down on or in; c (fig) to be fixed in, stamped in

insidĭ·ae -ārum *f pl* ambush; plot, trap; **insidias dare, comparare, collocare, parare,** or **struere** (with *dat*) to lay a trap for

insidĭāt·or -ōris *m* soldier in ambush; (fig) plotter, subversive

insidĭ·or -ārī -ātus sum *vi* to lie in wait; (with *dat*) a to lie in wait for; b (fig) to plot against; c (fig) to watch for (*an opportunity*)

insidĭōsē *adv* insidiously, by underhand means

insidĭōs·us -a -um *adj* insidious, treacherous, tricky

in·sīdō -sīdĕre -sēdī -sessum *vt* to occupy, keep possession of, possess; *vi* (with *dat*) to settle in or on; (with *in* + *abl*) (fig) to become fixed in

insign·e -is *n* insignia, mark, token; (mil) decoration, medal; standard; coat of arms; signal; honor, distinction; brilliant passage, gem; *n pl* insignia, regalia, uniform, attire, accouterments

insign·ĭō -īre -īvī or **-ĭī -ītum** *vt* to make conspicuous, distinguish

insign·is -e *adj* conspicuous, distinguished; prominent, eminent, extraordinary, singular

insignītē *adv* extraordinarily, notably

insignĭter *adv* remarkably

insignīt·us -a -um *adj* marked, conspicuous, clear, glaring; distinguished, striking, notable

insĭlĭ·a -ĭum *n pl* treadle (*of a loom*)

insĭl·ĭō -īre -ŭī or **-īvī** *vt* to jump up on, mount; *vi* (with *dat*) to jump on; (with *in* + *acc*) a to jump into or on; b to jump on, mount, climb aboard

insimulātĭ·ō -ōnis *f* charge, accusation

insimŭl·ō -āre *vt* to accuse, accuse falsely, allege

insincēr·us -a -um *adj* mixed, spoiled, not pure

insinuātĭ·ō -ōnis *f* winning sympathy

insinŭ·ō -āre *vt* to bring in secretly, sneak in; **se insinuare** (with **inter** + *acc*) to wriggle in between, work one's way between or among; **se insinuare in familiaritatem** (with *genit*) to ingratiate oneself with

insipĭ·ens -entis *adj* foolish

insipĭenter *adv* foolishly

insipĭentĭ·a -ae *f* foolishness

in·sistō -sistĕre -stĭtī *vt* to stand on, trample on; to set about, keep at (*a task, etc.*); to follow, chase after, pursue; **iter insistere** or **viam insistere** to enter upon a course, pursue a course; *vi* to stand, stop, come to a standstill; to pause; (with *dat*) a to tread on the heels of, pursue closely; b to press on with; c (fig) to dwell upon; (with *dat* or *in* + *acc*) to set foot on or in, step on, tread on, stand on; (with *dat* or *in* + *abl*) to persist in; (with *ad* or *in* + *acc*) to keep at, keep after, keep the pressure on, pursue vigorously

insitĭ·ō -ōnis *f* grafting; grafting time

insitīv·us -a -um *adj* grafted; (fig) spurious

insĭt·or -ōris *m* grafter

insĭt·us -a -um *pp* of **insero**; *adj* inborn, innate; incorporated

insociābĭl·is -e *adj* incompatible

insōlābĭlĭter *adv* unconsolably

insŏl·ens -entis *adj* unaccustomed, unusual; immoderate, excessive; extravagant; insolent; (with *genit* or *in* + *abl*) unaccustomed to, inexperienced in; **in aliena re insolens** free with someone else's money

insŏlenter *adv* unusually; excessively; insolently

insŏlentĭ·a -ae *f* unusualness, strangeness, novelty; inexperience; affectation; insolence, arrogance

insŏlesc·ō -ĕre *vi* to become strange; to become insolent; to become elated

insŏlĭd·us -a -um *adj* soft

insŏlĭt·us -a -um *adj* unaccustomed, inexperienced; unusual, strange, uncommon; *n* the unusual

insomnĭ·a -ae *f* insomnia, sleeplessness

insomn·is -e *adj* sleepless

insomn·ĭum -ĭī or **-ī** *n* nightmare; dream

insŏn·ō -āre -ŭī *vi* to make noise; to sound, resound, roar; **calamis insonare** to make music with a reed pipe; **flagello insonare** to crack the whip; **pennis insonare** to flap the wings

ins·ons -ontis *adj* innocent; harmless

insōpīt·us -a -um *adj* sleepless

insŏp·or -ōris *adj* sleepless

inspect·ō -āre *vt* to look at, view, observe

inspectus *pp* of **inspicio**

inspēr·ans -antis *adj* not expecting

inspērāt·us -a -um *adj* unhoped for, unexpected, unforeseen; unwelcome; **ex insperato** unexpectedly

in·spergō -spergĕre -spersī -spersum *vt* to sprinkle

in·spiciō -spicĕre -spexī -spectum *vt* to inspect, look into, examine, consider; to inspect, review; to look at, consult (*books*)

inspīc·ō -āre *vt* to make pointed; to sharpen

inspīr·ō -āre *vt* to inspire, infuse, enkindle; *vi* (with *dat*) to blow on, breathe on

inspoliāt·us -a -um *adj* undespoiled

insput·ō -āre *vt* to spit on

instābil·is -e *adj* unstable, unsteady; (fig) unsteady, changeable

inst·ans -antis *adj* present; immediate, threatening, urgent

instanter *adv* vehemently

instanti·a -ae *f* presence; vehemence

instar (indecl) *n* image, likeness, appearance, resemblance; (with *genit*) like, equal to, as large as, worth, as good as

instaurāti·ō -ōnis *f* renewal, repetition

instaurātīv·us -a -um *adj* begun anew, repeated

instaur·ō -āre *vt* to set up; to renew, repeat, start all over again (*esp. games and celebrations*); to repay, requite

in·sternō -sternĕre -strāvī -strātum *vt* to cover

instīgāt·or -ōris *m* or **instīgātr·ix -īcis** *f* instigator, ringleader

instīg·ō -āre *vt* to instigate, goad on, stimulate, incite

instill·ō -āre *vt* (with *dat*) to pour (*something*) on, instill (*something*) in

instimulāt·or -ōris *m* instigator

instimul·ō -āre *vt* to stimulate, urge on

instinct·or -ōris *m* instigator

instinct·us -a -um *adj* incited, inspired

instinct·us -ūs *m* inspiration, impulse

instipul·or -ārī -ātus sum *vi* to bargain

instīt·a -ae *f* border, flounce; (fig) lady

instīti·ō -ōnis *f* standing still

instīt·or -ōris *m* salesman, huckster, hawker

instit·uō -uĕre -uī -ūtum *vt* to set, fix, plant; to set up, erect, establish; to arrange; to build, make, construct; to prepare, make ready; to provide, furnish; to institute, organize, set up; to appoint, designate; to undertake, begin; to decide, determine; to control, direct, govern; to teach, train, instruct, educate

institūti·ō -ōnis *f* arrangement; custom; instruction, education; *f pl* principles of education

institūt·um -ī *n* practice, custom,

usage; precedent; principle; decree, regulation, stipulation, terms; purpose, intention; **ex instituto** according to custom

in·stō -stāre -stitī *vt* to follow, pursue; to work hard at; to menace, threaten; *vi* to be at hand, approach, be impending; to insist; (with *dat* or **in** + *abl*) to stand on or in; (with *dat*) a to be close to; b to be on the heels of, pursue closely; c to harass

instrātus *pp* of **insterno**

instrēnu·us -a -um *adj* lethargic

instrēp·ō -āre -ŭī -ĭtum *vi* to creak, rattle

instructi·ō -ōnis *f* construction; array

instructius *adv* with better preparation

instruct·or -ōris *m* supervisor

instruct·us -a -um *pp* of **instruo**; *adj* provided, equipped, furnished; prepared, arranged; instructed, versed

instruct·us -ūs *m* equipment; stock-in-trade (*of an orator*)

instrūment·um -ī *n* instrument, tool, utensil; equipment; dress, outfit; repertory, stock-in-trade; means, supply, provisions; document

in·struō -struĕre -struxī -structum *vt* to build up, construct; to furnish, prepare, provide, fit out; to instruct; (mil) to deploy

insuās·um -ī *n* dark-orange color

insuāv·is -e *adj* unpleasant, disagreeable

insūd·ō -āre *vi* (with *dat*) to sweat on, drip sweat on

insuēfact·us -a -um *adj* accustomed

in·suescō -suescĕre -suēvī -suētum *vt* to accustom, familiarize; *vi* (with *dat*, with **ad** + *acc*, or with *inf*) to get used to

insuēt·us -a -um *adj* unusual; (with *genit* or *dat*, with **ad** + *acc*, or with *inf*) unused to

insŭl·a -ae *f* island; apartment building

insulān·us -ī *m* islander

insulsē *adv* in poor taste; insipidly, absurdly

insulsit·ās -ātis *f* lack of taste; silliness, absurdity

insuls·us -a -um *adj* unsalted, without taste; coarse, tasteless, insipid; silly, absurd; bungling; *f pl* silly creatures (*i.e., women*)

insult·ō -āre *vt* to insult, scoff at, taunt; (of votaries) to dance about in; *vi* to jump, gambol, prance; to gloat; (with *abl*) a to jump in, cavort in, gambol on, jump upon; b to gloat over; (with *dat* or **in** + *acc*) to scoff at, gloat over

insultūr·a -ae *f* jumping in

insum inesse infŭī *vi* to be there; (with *dat* or **in** + *abl*) a to be in, be on; b to be implied in, be contained in, be in, belong to

in·sūmō -sūmĕre -sumpsī -sumptum *vt* to spend, devote, waste; (with *dat* or **in** + *acc*) to devote to, apply to; (with *abl* or **in** + *abl*) to expend on; **operam insumere** (with *dat*) to devote effort to, waste effort on

in·sŭō -sŭĕre -sŭī -sūtum *vt* to sew up; (wth *dat*) **a** to sew up in; **b** to embroider (*something*) on

insŭper *adv* above, overhead, on the top; from above; moreover, besides, in addition; *prep* (with *acc*) above, over, over and above; (with *abl*) in addition to, besides

insŭperābĭl·is -e *adj* insurmountable; unconquerable

in·surgō -surgĕre -surrexī -surrectum *vi* to rise, stand up; to rise, stand high, tower; to rise, increase, grow, grow intense; to rise to power; (with *dat*) **a** to rise up against; **b** to strain at (*e.g.*, *oars*)

insusurr·ō -āre *vt* (with *dat*) to whisper (*something*) to; **insusurrare in aurem** (with *genit*) to whisper into the ear of; **sibi cantilenam insusurrare** to hum a tune to oneself; *vi* to whisper; (of *wind*) to blow gently

intāb·escō -escĕre -ŭī *vi* to melt away gradually, dissolve gradually; (fig) to waste away, pine away

intactĭl·is -e *adj* intangible

intact·us -a -um *adj* untouched; uninjured; intact; unpolluted; untried; unmarried; virgin, chaste

intact·us -ūs *m* intangibility

intāmĭnāt·us -a -um *adj* unsullied

intect·us -a -um *pp* of **intego**; *adj* uncovered; naked; open, frank

integell·us -a -um *adj* fairly pure or chaste; in fair condition

intĕg·er -ra -rum *adj* whole, complete, intact, unimpaired; unhurt, unwounded; healthy, sound, fresh; new, fresh; pure, chaste; untouched, unaffected; unbiased, unprejudiced; unattempted; unsubdued, unconquered; unbroken (*horse*); not worn, unused; inexperienced, ignorant; virtuous, honest, blameless, irreproachable; healthy, sane; **ab integro** or **de integro** anew, all over again; **in integrum restituere** to restore to a former condition; to pardon; **integrum alicui esse** (with *inf*) to be in someone's power to

in·tĕgō -tegĕre -texī -tectum *vt* to cover up; to protect

integrasc·ō -ĕre *vi* to break out fresh, start all over again

integrātĭ·ō -ōnis *f* renewal, new beginning

intĕgrē *adv* wholly, entirely; honestly; correctly

integrĭt·ās -ātis *f* soundness; integrity; innocence; purity, chastity; correctness

intĕgr·ō -āre *vt* to make whole; to heal, repair; to renew, begin again;

to refresh

integument·um -ī *n* covering; lid; protection

intellectus *pp* of **intellego**

intellect·us -ūs *m* perception; comprehension, understanding; intellect

intellĕg·ens -entis *adj* intelligent; (with *genit*) appreciative of; (with **in** + *abl*) versed in

intellegenter *adv* intelligently

intellegentĭ·a -ae *f* intelligence; understanding, knowledge; perception, judgment, discrimination, taste, skill; concept, notion; (with *genit*) knowledge or understanding of; (with **in** + *abl*) judgment in

intel·lĕgō -legĕre -lexi -lectum *vt* to understand, perceive, discern, comprehend, gather; to realize, recognize; to have an accurate knowledge of, be an expert in; *vi* **intellego** (in answers) I understand, I get it

intemerāt·us -a -um *adj* undefiled; pure; pure, undiluted

intemper·ans -antis *adj* intemperate, without restraint; profligate; excessive

intemperanter *adv* intemperately

intemperantĭ·a -ae *f* intemperance, lack of self-control; extravagance, excess

intemperātē *adv* intemperately

intemperāt·us -a -um *adj* excessive

intemperārĭ·ae -ārum *f pl* wild outbursts, wildness

intemperĭ·ēs -ēī *f* wildness, excess; outrageous conduct, excesses; **intemperies aquarum** heavy rain; **intemperies caeli** stormy weather

intempestīvē *adv* at a bad time, inopportunely

intempestīv·us -a -um *adj* untimely, unseasonable; poorly timed

intempest·us -a -um *adj* unseasonable; dark, dismal; unhealthy; **nox intempesta** dead of night

intemptāt·us or **intentāt·us -a -um** *adj* unattempted

in·tendō -tendĕre -tendī -tentum or **-tensum** *vt* to stretch, stretch out, extend, spread out; to stretch, bend (*e.g.*, *bow*); to aim, direct, shoot (*weapon*); to increase, magnify, intensify; to intend; to urge, incite; to aim at, intend; to assert, maintain; to aim, turn, direct; to raise (*voice*); to stretch (*truth*); to direct, turn, focus (*mind, attention*); to pitch (*tent*)

intentātus see **intemptatus**

intentē *adv* intently, attentively

intentĭ·ō -ōnis *f* stretching, straining, tension; attention; effort, exertion; accusation

intent·ō -āre *vt* to stretch out; to aim, direct; to threaten

intent·us -a -um *pp* of **intendo**; *adj* taut, tense; intent, attentive; eager, waiting, tense; strict (*discipline*); vigorous, tense, nervous (*speech*)

intent·us -ūs *m* stretching out, extending (*of the palms*)

intep·ĕō -ēre -uī *vi* to be lukewarm

intep·escō -pescĕre -uī *vi* to grow warm, be warmed

inter *prep* (with *acc*) between, among, amidst; during, within, in the course of; in spite of; (in classifying) among, in, with; **inter se** each other, one another, mutual, mutually

interaestŭ·ō -āre *vi* to retch

interāment·a -ōrum *n pl* framework of a ship

Interamn·a -ae *f* town in Latium, on the Liris; town in Umbria, birthplace of Tacitus

interapt·us -a -um *adj* joined together

interāresc·ō -ĕre *vi* to dry up

interātim *adv* meanwhile

interbĭb·ō -ĕre *vt* to drink up

interbĭt·ō -ĕre *vi* to come to nothing

intercalār·is -e *adj* intercalary, inserted

intercalārĭ·us -a -um *adj* intercalary, inserted

interoŭl·ō -āre *vt* to intercalate, insert

intercapēd·ō -ĭnis *f* interruption, break, pause

inter·cēdō -cēdĕre -cessī -cessum *vi* to come or go in between; (of time) to intervene, pass, occur; to act as an intermediary; to intercede; (of tribunes) to exercise the veto; (with *dat*) **a** to veto, protest against; **b** to interfere with, obstruct, hinder

interceptĭ·ō -ōnis *f* interception

intercept·or -ōris *m* embezzler

interceptus *pp of* **intercipio**

intercessĭ·ō -ōnis *f* intercession, mediation; (tribune's) veto

intercess·or -ōris *m* intercessor, mediator; interferer, obstructor; tribune exercising the veto

inter·cĭdō -cĭdĕre -cĭdī *vi* to fall short, miss the mark; to happen in the meantime; to drop out, be lost

inter·cĭdō -cĭdĕre -cĭdī -cīsum *vt* to cut through, sever, cut down

intercĭn·ō -ĕre *vt* to interrupt with song or music

inter·cipĭō -cĭpĕre -cēpī -ceptum *vt* to intercept; to cut off (*the enemy*); to interrupt, cut off, preclude; to appropriate, misappropriate; to receive by mistake (*e.g., poison*)

intercīsē *adv* piecemeal

intercīsus *pp of* **intercido**

inter·clūdō -clūdĕre -clūsī -clūsum *vt* to shut off, shut out, cut off; to stop, block up; to hinder, prevent; to blockade, shut in; to cut off, intercept, separate, divide

interclūsĭ·ō -ōnis *f* stopping; parenthesis; **animae interclusio** shortwindedness

interclūsus *pp of* **intercludo**

intercolumn·ium -iī or **-ī** *n* space between columns, intercolumniation

inter·currō -currĕre -cucurrī -cursum *vi* to intervene, mediate; to mingle; to rush in

intercurs·ō -āre *vi* to crisscross; to infiltrate; **inter se intercursare** to crisscross each other

intercurs·us -ūs *m* intervention

interc·us -ūtis *adj* between the skin and flesh; **aqua intercus** dropsy

inter·dīcō -dīcĕre -dīxī -dictum *vt* to forbid, prohibit; *vi* to make a provisional decree; **aquā et igni interdicere** (with *dat*) to outlaw, banish

interdictĭ·ō -ōnis *f* prohibiting; **aquae et igni interdictio** banishment

interdict·um -ī *n* prohibition; contraband; provisional decree (*of a praetor*)

interdictus *pp of* **interdico**

interdĭū or **interdĭūs** *adv* by day, in the daytime

interd·ō -āre *vt* to give intermittently; to distribute

interduct·us -ūs *m* punctuation

interdum *adv* sometimes, now and then, occasionally; meanwhile

interdŭ·ō -āre *vt* floccum **interduo** or **nihil interduo** I don't give a hoot

intereā *adv* meanwhile, in the interim; meanwhile, anyhow, nevertheless

interemptus *pp of* **interimo**

inter·ĕō -īre -iī -itum *vi* to be done for, be finished, perish, be lost; to become extinct

interequĭt·ō -āre *vt* to ride between (*e.g., the ranks or columns*); *vi* to ride in between

interfātĭ·ō -ōnis *f* interruption

interfectĭ·ō -ōnis *f* killing

interfect·or -ōris *m* or **interfec·trīx -īcis** *f* killer

inter·ficĭō -ficĕre -fēcī -fectum *vt* to destroy; to kill

inter·fīō -fĭĕrī *vi* to pass away, be destroyed

inter·flŭō -fluĕre -flūxī *vt* to flow between; *vi* to flow in between

inter·fodĭō -fodĕre -fōdī -fossum *vi* to pierce

interf·or -ārī -ātus sum *vt & vi* to interrupt

interfug·ĭō -ĕre *vi* to scatter

interfulg·ĕō -ēre *vi* (with *abl*) to shine amidst or among

interfūs·us -a -um *adj* spread here and there; (with *acc*) flowing between

interĭbī *adv* in the meantime

interim *adv* meanwhile; for the moment; sometimes; however, anyhow

inter·ĭmō -ĭmĕre -ēmī -emptum *vt* to do away with, abolish; to kill

inter·ĭor -ĭus *adj* inner, interior; inner side of; secret, private; deeper, more profound; more intimate, more personal, more confidential

interitĭ·ō -ōnis *f* ruin, destruction

interĭt·us -ūs *m* ruin; death

interius *adv* on the inside, in the middle; too short; (to listen) closely

interjac·ĕō -ēre *vi* (with *dat*) to lie between

interjaciō see **interjicio**

interjectī·ō -ōnis *f* interjection; parenthesis

interject·us -a -um *pp* of **interjicio**; *adj* (with *dat* or **inter** + *acc*) set or lying between

interject·us -ūs *m* interposition; interval

inter·jiciō -jicĕre -jēcī -jectum *vt* to interpose; (with *dat* or **inter** + *acc*) to throw or set (*something*) between; **b** to intermingle (*something*) with, intermix (*something*) with

inter·jungō -jungĕre -junxī -junctum *vt* to join together; to clasp

inter·lābor -lābī -lapsus *vi* to glide or flow in between

inter·lĕgō -legĕre -lēgī -lectum *vt* to pick or pluck here and there

inter·līnō -linĕre -lēvī -litum *vt* to smear; to alter by erasing

inter·lŏquor -lŏquī -locūtus sum *vi* to interrupt; (with *dat*) to interrupt (*someone*)

inter·lūcĕō -lūcēre -luxī *vi* to shine through; to lighten now and then; to be transparent; to be plainly visible

interlūni·a -ōrum *n pl* new moon

interlŭ·ō -ĕre *vt* to flow between, wash

intermenstru·us -a -um *adj* of the new moon; *n* new moon

intermināt·us -a -um *adj* endless

intermīn·or -ārī -ātus sum *vt* (with *dat*) to threaten (*someone*) with (*something*); *vi* to threaten

inter·miscĕō -miscēre -miscuī -mixtum *vt* to intermingle

intermissi·ō -ōnis *f* interruption

inter·mittō -mittĕre -mīsī -missum *vt* to interrupt, break off, suspend, omit, neglect; to leave gaps in, leave unoccupied, leave undefended; to allow (*time*) to pass; *vi* to pause, stop

intermixtus *pp* of **intermisceo**

inter·morior -mŏrī -mortŭus sum *vi* to die suddenly; to faint

intermortu·us -a -um *adj* dead; unconscious; (fig) half-dead, moribund

intermundi·a -ōrum *n pl* outer space

intermūrāl·is -e *adj* intermural, between two walls

internāt·us -a -um *adj* (with *dat*) growing among or between

internecīn·us -a -um *adj* internecine, exterminating, of extermination

internecī·ō -ōnis *f* massacre, extermination

internecīv·us -a -um *adj* exterminating; **bellum internecivum** war of extermination

internĕc·ō -āre *vt* to kill off, exterminate

internect·ō -ĕre *vt* to intertwine

internit·ĕō -ēre *vi* to shine out

internōd·ium -iī or **-ī** *n* space between two joints

inter·nöscō -noscĕre -nōvī -nōtum *vt* to distinguish, recognize; (with **ab** + *abl*) to distinguish (*one thing*) from (*another*)

internunti·ō -āre *vi* to exchange messages

internunt·ius -iī or **-ī** *m* or **internunti·a -ae** *f* messenger, courier, mediator, go-between

intern·us -a -um *adj* internal; civil, domestic

in·tĕrō -terĕre -trīvī -trītum *vt* to rub in, mash together

interpellātī·ō -ōnis *f* interruption

interpellāt·or -ōris *m* interrupter, disturber

interpell·ō -āre *vt* to interrupt, break in on; to disturb, obstruct, hinder; to raise as an objection

interpŏl·is -e *adj* patched up

interpŏl·ō -āre *vt* to polish, dress up; to interpolate, falsify

inter·pōnō -pōnĕre -posuī -positum *vt* to insert, interpose, intersperse; to introduce, insert; to introduce, admit (*a person*); to let (*time*) pass or elapse; to alter, falsify (*writings*); to allege, use as pretext; **operam** or **studium interponere** to apply effort; **se interponere** (with *dat* or **in** + *acc*) to interfere with, meddle with, get mixed up with

interpositī·ō -ōnis *f* insertion; introduction; parenthesis

interpositus *pp* of **interpono**

interposit·us -ūs *m* interposition

interpr·es -ĕtis *m* & *f* mediator, negotiator; middleman, broker; interpreter; expounder; translator

interpretātī·ō -ōnis *f* interpretation, explanation; meaning; translation

interprĕt·or -ārī -ātus sum *vt* to interpret, put a construction on, construe; to understand, infer, conclude; to decide, determine; to translate

inter·primō -primĕre -pressī -pressum *vt* to squeeze

interpunct·a -ōrum *n pl* pauses, punctuation

interpunctī·ō -ōnis *f* punctuation

interpunct·us -a -um *adj* well-divided

inter·quiescō -quiescĕre -quiēvī *vi* to rest awhile; to pause awhile

interregn·um -ī *n* interregnum (*time between death of one king and election of another or similar interval between consuls*)

inter·rex -rēgis *m* interrex, regent

interrit·us -a -um *adj* undaunted

interrogātī·ō -ōnis *f* question; interrogation, cross-examination; syllogism

interrogāt·um -ī *n* question.

interrŏg·ō -āre *vt* to ask, question; to interrogate, cross-examine; to indict, sue

inter·rumpō -rumpĕre -rūpī -ruptum *vt* to break apart, break in half, break up, smash; to divide, scatter; to interrupt, break off

interruptē *adv* with interruptions

interruptus *pp* of **interrumpo**

inter·saepiō -saepīre -saepsī -saeptum *vt* to fence off, enclose; to stop up, close, cut off

inter·scindō -scindĕre -scīdī -scissum *vt* to tear apart, tear down; to cut off, separate

inter·scrībō -scrībĕre -scripsī -scriptum *vt* to write (*something*) in between

inter·sĕrō -serĕre -seruī *vt* to interpose; to allege as an excuse

interspīrātī·ō -ōnis *f* breathing pause, correct breathing (*in delivering a speech*)

interstinct·us -a -um *adj* blotchy

inter·stinguō -stinguĕre — -stinctum *vt* to spot, blotch; to extinguish

interstring·ō -ĕre *vt* to strangle

inter·sum -esse -fuī *vi* to be present, assist, take part; to differ; to be of interest; (with *dat*) to be present at, attend, take part in; (with in + *abl*) to be present at; *v impers* there is a difference; it makes a difference; it is of importance; it is of interest; (with inter + *acc*) there is a difference between; (with in + *abl*) there is a difference among; (with *genit* or with *fem* of possessive pronouns meā, tuā, nostrā, *etc.*) it make a difference to, it is of importance to, it concerns (*me, you, us, etc.*); (with *genit* of value, e.g. magni, permagni, tanti, or with *adv* multum, plurimum, maxime) it makes a (*great, very great, such a great*) difference, it is of (*great, very great, such great*) importance, it is of (*great, very great, such great*) concern; ne minimum quidem interest there is not the slightest difference; nihil omnino interest there is no difference whatever

intertext·us -a -um *adj* interwoven

inter·trāhō -trahĕre -traxī *vt* (with *dat*) to take (*something*) away from

intertrīment·um -ī *n* wear and tear; loss, wastage

interturbātī·ō -ōnis *f* confusion, turmoil

interturb·ō -āre *vt* to confuse

intervall·um -ī *n* interval, space, distance; interval of time, spell, pause, intermission; contrast, difference

inter·vellō -vellĕre -vulsī -vulsum *vt* to pluck here and there

inter·veniō -venīre -vēnī -ventum *vt* to interfere with; *vi* to happen along; to intervene, intrude; to happen, occur; (with *dat*) to interfere with, interrupt, put a stop to, come in the way of, oppose, prevent

intervent·or -ōris *m* intruder, untimely visitor

intervent·us -ūs *m* intervention, intrusion; mediation

inter·vertō or **inter·vortō -vertĕre -vertī -versum** *vt* to divert, embezzle; (with *acc* of person and *abl* of thing) to rob or cheat (*someone*) of

inter·vīsō -vīsĕre -vīsī -vīsum *vt* to visit from time to time; to look after

intervolit·ō -āre *vi* to flit about

intervom·ō -ĕre -uī -itum *vt* (with inter + *acc*) to throw up amongst

intervulsus *pp* of **intervello**

intestābil·is -e *adj* infamous, notorious; wicked

intestātō *adv* intestate

intestāt·us -a -um *adj* intestate; unconvicted by witnesses.

intestāt·us -a -um *adj* castrated

intestīn·us -a -um *adj* internal; *n* & *n pl* intestines

in·texō -texĕre -texuī -textum *vt* to interweave, interlace; to weave; to embroider; to surround, envelop

intīb·um -ī *n* endive

intimē *adv* intimately, cordially

intim·us or **intum·us -a -um** *adj* innermost; deepest, most profound; most secret, most intimate; *m* intimate friend

in·tingō or **in·tinguō -tingĕre -tinxī -tinctum** *vt* to dip, soak

intolerābil·is -e *adj* intolerable; irresistible

intoleran·dus -a -um *adj* intolerable

intolĕr·ans -antis *adj* intolerable, insufferable; (with *genit*) unable to stand, unable to put up with

intoleranter *adv* intolerably, immoderately, excessively

intoleranti·a -ae *f* unbearableness, insolence

intŏn·ō -āre -uī -ātus *vt* to thunder out; *vi* to thunder

intons·us -a -um *adj* unshorn, untrimmed; long-haired; rude

in·torqueō -torquēre -torsī -tortum *vt* to twist, turn, roll; (with circum + *acc*) to wrap (*something*) around; (with *dat* or in + *acc*) to aim, cast, throw (*a weapon*) at

intort·us -a -um *adj* twisted; tangled; (fig) crooked

intrā *adv* on the inside, inside, within; inward; *prep* (with *acc*) inside, within; during, within, in the course of, in less than; less than, fewer than, within the limits of

intrābil·is -e *adj* inaccessible

intractābil·is -e *adj* intractable, unmanageable; formidable, dangerous

intractāt·us -a -um *adj* untamed, wild; unbroken (*horse*); unattempted

intrem·iscō -iscĕre -ŭī *vi* to begin to shake or tremble

intrĕm·ō -ĕre -ŭī *vi* to shake, tremble, shiver

intrepĭdē *adv* calmly, intrepidly

intrepĭd·us -a -um *adj* calm, intrepid, not nervous

intrīc·ō -āre *vt* to entangle, involve

intrinsĕcus *adv* on the inside

intrīt·us -a -um *adj* not worn away; (fig) not worn out

intrō *adv* inwards, inside, in

intr·ō -āre *vt & vi* to enter; to penetrate

intrō·dūcō -dūcĕre -duxī -ductum *vt* to introduce

intrōductī·ō -ōnis *f* introduction

intro·ĕō -īre -ĭī -ĭtum *vt & vi* to enter

intrō·fĕrō -ferre -tŭlī -lātum *vt* to carry in

intrō·grĕdĭor -grĕdī -gressus sum *vi* to step inside

introĭt·us -ūs *m* entrance; beginning, prelude

intrōlātus *pp* of introfero

intrō·mittō -mittĕre -mīsī -missum *vt* to let in, admit

introrsum or **introrsus** *adv* inwards, towards the inside; (fig) inwardly, inside

intrō·rumpō -rumpĕre -rūpī -ruptum *vi* to break in, enter by force

introspect·ō -āre *vt* to look in on

intrō·spicĭō -spicĕre -spexī -spectum *vt* to look into, look at; (fig) to inspect, examine, observe; *vi* (with **in** + *acc*) to look into; (fig) to look into, inspect, examine

intūb·um -ī *n* endive

in·tŭeor -tŭerī -tŭitus sum *vt* to look at, gaze upon; to contemplate, consider; to look up to, have regard for, admire; to keep an eye on

intum·escō -escĕre -ŭī *vi* to swell up, rise; (of voice) to grow louder; (of river) to rise; to become angry; to get a big head, swell with pride

intumulāt·us -a -um *adj* unburied

in·tŭor -tŭī *vt* to look at, gaze at; to consider

inturbĭd·us -a -um *adj* undisturbed, quiet

intus *adv* inside, within; at home, in; to the inside; from within

intūt·us -a -um *adj* unguarded; unsafe

inŭl·a -ae *f* elecampane (*plant*)

inult·us -a -um *adj* unavenged; unpunished, without being punished

inumbr·ō -āre *vt* to shade; to cover

inundātī·ō -ōnis *f* inundation

inund·ō -āre *vt* to flood, inundate; *vi* to overflow; **sanguine inundare** to run red with blood

in·ungō -ungĕre -unxī -unctum *vt* to anoint

inurbānē *adv* impolitely, rudely; without wit

inurbān·us -a -um *adj* impolite, rude, rustic

in·urgĕō -urgĕre -ursī *vi* to butt

in·ūrō -ūrĕre -ussī -ustum *vt* to burn in, brand, imprint; (with *dat*) **a** to brand upon, imprint upon, affix to; **b** to inflict upon

inūsĭtātē *adv* unusually, strangely

inūsĭtāt·us -a -um *adj* unusual, strange, uncommon, extraordinary

inustus *pp* of inuro

inūtil·is -e *adj* useless, unprofitable; impractical; injurious, harmful

inūtilĭt·ās -ātis *f* uselessness; harmfulness

inūtilĭter *adv* uselessly, unprofitably

in·vādō -vādĕre -vāsī -vāsum *vt* to come or go into, enter; to enter upon, undertake, attempt; to invade, attack, assault, rush upon; (fig) to seize, take possession of; *vi* to come or go in; to invade; (with **in** + *acc*) **a** to assail, attack, invade; **b** to seize, get possession of, usurp

inval·escō -escĕre -ŭī *vi* to grow stronger

invalĭd·us -a -um *adj* weak, feeble, impotent; inadequate, unsuitable

invāsus *pp* of invado

invectĭ·ō -ōnis *f* importing, importation; arrival by boat

in·vĕhō -vehĕre -vexī -vectum *vt* to carry in, bring in (*by cart, horse, boat, etc.*); (with *dat*) to bring (*e.g. evils*) upon; **invehi** (with *acc* or **in** + *acc*) **a** to ride into, sail into; **b** to attack; **c** to inveigh against, attack (*with words*); **invehi equo** to ride a horse; **invehi nave** to sail; **se invehere** (with *acc* or **in** + *acc*) to rush against, attack

invendibĭl·is -e *adj* unsalable

in·vĕnĭō -venīre -vēnī -ventum *vt* to come upon, find, come across, discover; to find out, invent, devise; to learn, ascertain; to acquire, get, reach, earn

inventĭ·ō -ōnis *f* inventiveness; inventing, invention

invent·or -ōris *m* or **inventr·ix -īcis** *f* inventor, author, discoverer

invent·us -a -um *pp* of invenio; *n* invention, discovery

invenust·us -a -um *adj* having no sex appeal; homely, unattractive; unlucky in love

inverēcund·us -a -um *adj* disrespectful, immodest, shameless

inverg·ō -ĕre *vt* to pour upon

inversĭ·ō -ōnis *f* inversion (*of words*); irony; allegory

invers·us -a -um *adj* turned upside down; turned inside out

in·vertō -vertĕre -vertī -versum *vt* to invert, turn upside down, upset, reverse, turn inside out; to transpose, reverse; to pervert, abuse, misrepresent; to use ironically

invesperasc·it -ĕre *v impers* evening is approaching, twilight is falling

investīgātĭ·ō -ōnis *f* investigation

investigāt·or -ōris m investigator, researcher

investīg·ō -āre vt to track, trace, search after; to investigate, search into, search after

inveter·ascō -ascĕre -āvī vi to begin to grow old, grow old; to become fixed, become established; to become rooted, grow inveterate; to become obsolete

inveterātī·ō -ōnis f chronic illness

inveterāt·us -a -um adj inveterate, long-standing

invicem or **in vicem** adv in turn, taking turns, one after another, alternately; mutually, each other

invict·us -a -um adj unconquered; invincible

invĭd·ens -entis adj envious, jealous

invidenti·a -ae f enviousness, jealousy

ĭn·vidĕō -vidēre -vīdī -vīsum vt to cast an evil eye on; to envy, begrudge; vi (with dat) to envy, begrudge; (with dat of person and abl of cause or in + abl) to begrudge (someone something), envy (someone because of something)

invidĭ·a -ae f envy, jealousy; unpopularity; invidiae esse (with dat) to be a cause of envy to; invidiam habere to be unpopular, be hated

invidiōsē adv spitefully

invidiōs·us -a -um adj envious, spiteful; envied; causing envy

invĭd·us -a -um adj envious, jealous; (with dat) hostile to, unfavorable to

invigĭl·ō -āre vi to be alert, be on one's toes; (with dat) to be on the lookout for, keep an eye on, pay attention to, watch over; (with pro + abl) to watch over

inviolābĭl·is -e adj inviolable; invulnerable, indestructible

inviolātē adv inviolately

inviolāt·us -a -um adj inviolate, unhurt; inviolable

invisitāt·us -a -um adj rarely seen; not seen before, unknown, strange

in·vīsō -vīsĕre -vīsī -vīsum vt to visit, get to see; to look into, inspect; to look after; to get sight of

invīs·us -a -um pp of invideo; adj unseen; hateful, detested; hostile

invītāment·um -ī n attraction, allurement, inducement

invītātĭ·ō -ōnis f invitation; challenge

invītāt·us -ūs m invitation

invītē adv unwillingly, against one's wish

invīt·ō -āre vt to invite; to entertain; to summon, challenge; to ask, request; to allure, attract; to encourage, court

invīt·us -a -um adj reluctant, unwilling, against one's will; invitā Minervā against one's better judgment, against the grain

invĭ·us -a -um adj without a road, trackless, impassable; n pl rough terrain

invocātĭ·ō -ōnis f invocation

invocāt·us -a -um adj unbidden

invŏc·ō -āre vt to invoke, call upon, appeal to

involāt·us -ūs m flight

involgō see invulgo

involĭt·ō -āre vi (with dat) (of long hair) to float over, trail over

invŏl·ō -āre vt to swoop down upon, pounce upon; vi to swoop down; (with in + acc) to swoop down upon, pounce upon

involūcr·e -is n smock

involūcr·um -ī n wrapper, cover, case, envelope; (fig) cover-up, front

involūt·us -a -um adj complicated

in·volvō -volvĕre -volvī -volūtum vt to wrap up, involve, envelop; to cover completely, overwhelm; (with dat or in + acc) to pile (something) on; se involvere (with dat) (fig) to get all wrapped up in

involvŏl·us -ī m caterpillar

invulg·ō -āre vi to give evidence

invulnerāt·us -a -um adj unwounded

iō interj ho!

io- = **jo-**

Ī·ō -ūs or **Ī·ōn -ōnis** f Io (daughter of Argive King Inachus, changed by Jupiter into a heifer, and driven by Juno in this form over the world under the surveillance of hundred-eyed Argus)

Iocast·a -ae or **Iocast·ē -ēs** f wife of Laius and mother as well as wife of Oedipus

Iolā·us -ī m son of Iphicles and companion of Hercules

Iŏl·ē -ēs f daughter of Eurytus, the king of Oechalia, who fell in love with Hercules

Iōn see Io

Iōn·es -um m pl Ionians (Greek inhabitants of the W. coast of Asia Minor)

Iōnĭ·cus -a -um adj Ionic; n pl Ionic dance

Iōnĭ·us -a -um adj Ionian; f Ionia (coastal district of Asia Minor); n Ionian Sea (off the W. Coast of Greece)

Iōt·a (indecl) n iota (ninth letter of the Greek alphabet)

Iphianass·a -ae f Iphigenia

Iphigenĭ·a -ae f daughter of Agamemnon and Clytemnestra, who was to have been sacrificed at Aulis but was saved by Diana and conveyed to the Tauric Chersonese, where she became priestess of Diana

Iphĭt·us -ī m Argonaut, son of Eurytus and Antiope

ips·a -īus or **-īus** adj self, very, just, mere, precisely; in person; by herself, alone; of herself, of her own accord; *pron* she herself; mistress of the house

ips·e (or **ips·us**) **-īus** (or **-īus**) *adj* self, very, just, mere, precisely; in person; by himself, alone; of himself, of his own accord; *pron* he himself; master; host

ips·um -īus or **-īus** *adj* self, very, just, mere, precisely; by itself, alone; of itself, spontaneously; **nunc ipsum** just now; **tunc ipsum** just then; *pron* it itself, that itself; **ipsum quod . . .** the very fact that . . .

ipsus see **ipse**

īr·a -ae *f* ire, wrath, resentment

īrācundē *adv* angrily; passionately

īrācundi·a -ae *f* quick temper; anger, wrath, violence, passion; resentment

īrācund·us -a -um *adj* hot-tempered, quick-tempered, irritable; angry; resentful

īrasc·or -ī *vi* to get angry, fly into a rage; (with *dat*) to get angry at

īrātē *adv* angrily

īrāt·us -a -um *adj* angry, irate, enraged; (with *dat*) angry at

īr·is -idis *f* goddess of the rainbow and messenger of the gods

īrōni·a -ae *f* irony

irrās·us -a -um *adj* unshaven

irrātiōnāl·is -e *adj* irrational

ir·raucescō -raucescĕre -rausī *vi* to become hoarse

irredivīv·us -a -um *adj* irreparable

irrēd·ux -ūcis *adj* one-way (*road*)

irrelīgāt·us -a -um *adj* not tied

irreligiōsē *adv* impiously

irreligiōs·us -a -um *adj* impious, irreligious

irremeābil·is -e *adj* not to be traversed; one-way

irreparābil·is -e *adj* irretrievable

irrepert·us -a -um *adj* undiscovered, not found

ir·repō -repĕre -repsī -reptum *vi* to creep in; (fig) to sneak in; (with **ad** or **in** + *acc*) to creep toward or into; (fig) to sneak up on

irreprehens·us -a -um *adj* blameless

irrequiēt·us -a -um *adj* restless

irresect·us -a -um *adj* untrimmed

irresolūt·us -a -um *adj* not loosened, still tied

irrēt·iō -īre -īvī or **-iī -ītum** *vt* to trap

irretort·us -a -um *adj* not turned back

irrevĕr·ens -entis *adj* irreverent, disrespectful

irreverenter *adv* irreverently, disrespectfully

irreverenti·a -ae *f* irreverence, disrespect

irrevocābil·is -e *adj* irrevocable; implacable, relentless

irrevocāt·us -a -um *adj* not called back, not asked back

ir·rīdeō -rīdēre -rīsī -rīsum *vt* to

ridicule, laugh at, mock; *vi* to laugh, joke; (with *dat*) to laugh at

irrīdiculē *adv* with no sense of humor

irrigāti·ō -ōnis *f* irrigation

irrig·ō -āre *vt* to irrigate, water; to inundate; (fig) to diffuse; (fig) to flood, steep, soak

irrigŭ·us -a -um *adj* wet, soaked, well-watered; refreshing

irrīsi·ō -ōnis *f* ridicule, mockery

irrīs·or -ōris *m* reviler, mocker

irrīsus *pp* of **irrīdeō**

irrīs·us -ūs *m* mockery, derision; laughing stock, object of derision

irritābil·is -e *adj* easily excited, easily enraged, irritable, sensitive

irrītām·en -inis *n* incentive; provocation

irrītāment·um -ī *n* incentive; provocation

irrītāti·ō -ōnis *f* incitement; irritation, provocation; stimulant

irrīt·ō -āre *vt* to incite, excite, provoke, enrage

irrit·us -a -um *adj* invalid, null and void; futile, pointless, useless; unsuccessful (*person*)

irrogāti·ō -ōnis *f* imposing (*e.g., of a fine*)

irrŏg·ō -āre *vt* to impose, inflict; to object to (*proposals*)

irror·ō -āre *vt* to wet, moisten, sprinkle

irruct·ō -āre *vi* to belch

ir·rumpō -rumpĕre -rūpī -ruptum *vt* to rush into, break down; *vi* to rush in; (with *dat* or **in** + *acc*) a to rush into, rush through; **b** (fig) to intrude upon

ir·ruō -ruĕre -ruī *vi* to rush in, force one's way in; to make a slip (*in speaking*); (with **in** + *acc*) to rush into, rush on, invade, attack; **inruere in odium** (with *genit*) to incur the anger of

irrupti·ō -ōnis *f* invasion

irrupt·us -a -um *pp* of **irrumpo**; *adj* unbroken

Īr·us -ī *m* beggar in the palace of Ulysses in Ithaca

is ejus *adj* this, that, the said, the aforesaid; *pron* he; **is qui** he who, the person who, the one who

Īs·is -is or **-idis** *f* Egyptian goddess

Ismari·us -a -um *adj* of Mt. Ismarus in Thrace; Thracian

Īsocrāt·ēs -is *m* famous orator and teacher of rhetoric at Athens (436-338 B.C.)

ista see **iste**

istāc *adv* that way

istactĕnus *adv* thus far

istaec see **istic**

ist·e -a -ud *adj* that of yours; this, that, the very, that particular; such, of such a kind; that terrible, that despicable; *pron* that one; (in court) your client

Isthm·us or **Isthm·os -ī** *m* Isthmus of Corinth

ist·ic -aec -oc or **-uc** *adj* that, that of yours; *pron* the one, that one

istic *adv* there, in that place; here-in; on this occasion

istinc *adv* from there, from where you are

istiusmŏdī or **istimŏdī** or **istĭus modī** or **istī modī** *adj* that kind of, such

istŏ *adv* where you are; therefore; in that matter

istōc *adv* there, to where you are, yonder

istorsum *adv* in that direction

istūc *adv* there, to that place, to where you are, that way; **istuc veniam** I'll come to that matter

istūcĭne see **istic**

istud see **iste**

ita *adv* thus, so, in this way; (of natural consequence) thus, accordingly, therefore, under these circumstances; (in affirmation) yes, true, exactly; (in questions) really?, truly?; **ita . . . ut** (in comparisons) just as, although . . . nevertheless; (as correlatives) both . . . and, both . . . as well as; (in restriction) on condition that, in sofar as, on the assumption that; (of degree) to such a degree . . . that, so much . . . that, so . . . that; **non ita** not very, not especially; **quid ita?** how so?, what do you mean?

Ītăli·a -ae *f* Italy

Ītălic·us -a -um *adj* Italian

Ītăl·is -ĭdis *adj* Italian; *f pl* Italian women

Ītali·us -a -um *adj* Italian; *f* see **Italia**

Ītăl·us -a -um *adj* Italian

ităque *conj* and so, and thus, accordingly, therefore, consequently

item *adv* likewise, besides, moreover, also

it·er -ĭnĕris *n* journey, trip, march, walk; day's march, day's journey; route; right of way; passage (*of voice, etc.*); method, course, way, road; **ex itinere** or **in itinere** en route; **iter flectere** to change course; **iter terrestre** overland route; **maximis itineribus** by marching at top speed

iterātĭ·ō -ōnis *f* repetition

itĕr·ō -āre *vt* to repeat, renew; to plow again

itĕrum *adv* again, a second time; **iterum atque iterum** repeatedly, again and again

Ithăc·a -ae or **Ithăc·ē -ēs** *f* island off the W. coast of Greece in the Ionian Sea and home of Odysseus

itĭdem *adv* in the same way

itĭ·ō -ōnis *f* going, walking

it·ō -āre *vi* to go

it·us -ūs *m* going; going away, departure

It·ys -ўos *m* son of Tereus and Procne, who was killed by Procne and served up as food to Tereus

iu- = ju-

Ixī·ōn -ōnis *m* son of Antion or of Jupiter, king of the Laipthae in Thessaly, and father of Pirithous; he was allowed into heaven by Jupiter after killing his father-in-law, but for trying to seduce Juno, was tied to a wheel and sent flying into Tartarus

J

jac·ĕō -ēre -ŭī *vi* to lie, lie down; to lie ill, be sick; to lie dead, to have fallen; to lie in ruins; to hang loose; to lie idle, rest; to lie, be situated; to lie flat, lie low; to feel low, be despondent; to lie prostrate, be powerless; to fall, fail, be refuted; to be low in someone's pinion; to linger, stay

jacĭō jacēre jēcī jactum *vt* to lay, build, establish, set, found, construct; to throw, cast, fling; to emit, produce; to sow, scatter; to throw away; to mention, utter, declare, intimate

jact·ans -antis *adj* boasting, bragging, showing off

jactanter *adv* boastfully

jactanti·a -ae *f* boasting, showing off

jactātĭ·ō -ōnis *f* tossing to and fro; swaying; shaking; writhing; boasting, bragging, showing off; gesticulation; **jactatio animi** agitation; **jactatio maritima** seasickness

jactāt·us -ūs *m* tossing, waving

jactĭt·ō -āre *vt* to display, show off

jact·ō -āre *vt* to throw, hurl; to toss about, shake; to throw away, throw out, throw overboard; to disturb, disquiet, stir up; to consider, discuss; to throw out, mention; to brag about, show off; **jactari** to toss, rock; (of money) to fluctuate in value; **se jactare** to boast, show off, throw one's weight around

jactūr·a -ae *f* throwing away, throwing overboard; loss, sacrifice

jactus *pp* of **jacio**

jact·us -ūs *m* toss, throw, cast

jaculābĭl·is -e *adj* missile

jaculāt·or -ōris *m* thrower, shooter; light-armed soldier; spearman

jaculāt·rix -īcis *f* huntress

jacŭl·or -ārī -ātus sum *vt* to throw; to shoot at; (fig) to aim at, strive after

jacŭl·us -a -um *adj* throwing, casting; *n* dart, javelin; casting net

jājūn- = jejun-

jam _adv_ (present) now, already;
(past) already, by then; (future)
very soon, right away; (in transition) now, next, moreover; (for emphasis) actually, precisely, quite;
(in a conclusion) then surely; **jam
dūdum** long ago, long since; **jam
inde** immediately; **jam jam** even
now, at every moment; **jam . . .
jam** at one time . . . at another;
jam nunc even now; **jam prīdem**
long since; **jam tum** even then,
even at that time

Jānicul·um -ī _n_ Roman hill on the
right bank of the Tiber

jānit·or -ōris _m_ doorman

jānītr·ix -īcis _f_ portress

jānu·a -ae _f_ door, house door; entrance; (fig) entrance, approach

Jānuāri·us -a -um _adj & m_ January

jān·us -ī _m_ covered passage, arcade

Jān·us -ī _m_ Janus (old Italian deity,
represented as having two faces);
temple of Janus (at the bottom of
the Argīlētum in the Forum)

jec·ur -ōris _n_ liver; (as the seat of
emotions) anger, lust

jecuscul·um -ī _n_ little liver

jējūnē _adv_ (fig) drily

jējūniōs·ior or **jājūniōs·ior -ius**
adj fasting, hungry

jējūnit·ās or **jājūnit·ās -ātis** _f_
fasting; dryness (of style)

jējūn·ium -ī or **-ī** _n_ fasting, fast;
hunger; leanness

jējūn·us or **jājūn·us -a -um** _adj_
fasting; hungry; poor (land); thin;
insignificant, paltry, contemptible,
low; dry (style)

jentācul·um -ī _n_ breakfast

joc·or -ārī -ātus sum or **joc·ō -āre**
_vt_ to say in jest; _vi_ to joke, crack a
joke, be joking

jocōsē _adv_ humorously, as a joke,
jokingly

jocōs·us -a -um _adj_ humorous, funny, clowning

joculār·is -e _adj_ humorous, funny

joculāri·us -a -um _adj_ ludicrous

joculāt·or -ōris _m_ joker

jocul·or -ārī -ātus sum _vi_ to joke

jocul·us -ī _m_ joke

joc·us -ī (_pl:_ **joc·ī -ōrum** _m_ or **joc·a
-ōrum** _n_) _m_ joke; laughingstock;
child's play; **joco remoto** all joking aside; **per jocum** as a joke,
jokingly

jub·a -ae _f_ mane; crest

jub·ar -āris _n_ radiance, brightness;
sunshine

jubāt·us -a -um _adj_ crested

jubeō jubēre jussī jussum _vt_ to
order; (pol) to order, decree, enact,
ratify; to designate, appoint, assign; (med) to prescribe; **jube frā-
trem tuum salvere** (in letters)
best regards to your brother

jūcundē _adv_ pleasantly, delightfully,
agreeably

jūcundit·ās -ātis _f_ pleasantness,
delight, enjoyment, agreeableness;
_f pl_ favors

jūcund·us -a -um _adj_ pleasant, delightful, agreeable

Jūdae·us -a -um _adj_ Jewish; _m_
Jew; _f_ Jewess; Judaea, Palestine

jūd·ex -icis _m_ judge; juror; arbitrator; umpire; critic, scholar; **judex
morum** censor; **me judice** in my
judgment

jūdicāti·ō -ōnis _f_ judicial investigation; (fig) judgment, opinion

jūdicāt·us -a -um _adj_ decided, determined; _m_ condemned person; _n_
decision, precedent; fine; **judicatum facere** to carry out a decision; **judicatum solvere** to pay
a fine

jūdicāt·us -ūs _m_ judgeship

jūdiciāl·is -e _adj_ judicial, forensic

jūdiciāri·us -a -um _adj_ judiciary

jūdic·ium -ī or **-ī** _n_ trial, court,
court of justice; sentence; jurisdiction; opinion, decision; faculty of
judging, judgment, good judgment,
taste, tact, discretion

jūdic·ō -āre _vt_ to judge; to examine;
to sentence, condemn; to form an
opinion of; to conclude; to declare,
proclaim; (with _dat_ of person and
acc of the offense) to convict (someone) of; (with _genit_) to find (someone) guilty of; (with _dat_ of person
and _genit_ of the offense) to convict
(someone) of

jugāl·is -e _adj_ yoked together; nuptial

jugāti·ō -ōnis _f_ tying up

jūgěr·um -ī _n_ jugerum (land measure: about two thirds of an acre)

jūg·is -e _adj_ continual, perennial,
inexhaustible

jugl·ans -andis _f_ walnut tree

jugōs·us -a -um _adj_ hilly

Jugul·ae -ārum _f pl_ Orion's belt
(three stars in the constellation
Orion)

jugul·ō -āre _vt_ to cut the throat of,
kill, murder; to destroy; to silence

jugul·um -ī _n_ or **jugul·us -ī** _m_
throat

jug·um -ī _n_ yoke, collar; pair, team;
(mil) yoke (consisting of a spear
laid crosswise on two upright spears,
under which the conquered had to
pass); crossbar (of a loom); thwart
(of a boat); common bond, union;
wedlock; pair, couple; mountain
ridge; _n pl_ heights

Jugurth·a -ae _m_ king of Numidia
(160-104 B.C.)

Jūli·a -ae _f_ aunt of Julius Caesar
and wife of Marius; daughter of
Julius Caesar and wife of Pompey
(d. 54 B.C.); daughter of Augustus
by Scribonia (39 B.C.-14 A.D.)

Jūli·us -a -um _adj_ Julian; of July;
_m_ Roman praenomen; July

jūment·um -ī _n_ beast of burden,
horse, mule

junce·us -a -um _adj_ of reeds; slim,
slender

juncōs·us -a -um _adj_ overgrown
with reeds

juncti·ō -ōnis _f_ joining

junctūr·a -ae *f* joining, uniting, joint, juncture; connection, relationship; combination

junct·us -a -um *pp* of jungo; *adj* connected, associated, united, attached

juno·us -ī *m* reed

jungō jungēre junxī junctum *vt* to join, join together, unite, connect; to yoke, harness; to couple, pair, mate; to bridge (*a river*); to bring together, unite, associate, ally; to add; to compose (*poems*); to combine (*words*)

jūni·or -ōris *adj* younger

jūnipěr·us -ī *f* juniper

Jūni·us -a -um *adj* June, of June; *m* Roman praenomen; June

jūn·ix -īcis *f* heifer

Jūn·ō -ōnis *f* daughter of Saturn and wife and sister of Jupiter

Juppiter (or Jupiter or Diespiter) Jovis *m* son of Saturn, brother and husband of Juno, and chief god of the Romans

jūrāt·or -ōris *m* judge; assistant censor

jūreconsult·us -ī *m* legal expert, lawyer

jūrejūr·ō -āre *vi* to swear

jūreperītus see jurisperitus

jurg·ium -iī or -ī *n* quarrel; *n pl* reproaches

jurg·ō -āre *vi* to quarrel

jūridiciāl·is -e *adj* juridical

jūrisconsult·us or jūreconsult·us -ī *m* legal expert, lawyer

jūrisdictī·ō -ōnis *f* administration of justice; jurisdiction

jūrisperīt·us or jūreperīt·us -ī *m* legal expert, lawyer

jūr·ō -āre *vt* to swear; to swear by, attest, call to witness; to swear to, attest; *vi* to swear, take an oath; to conspire; (with in + *acc*) to swear allegiance to, swear to observe, vow obedience to; in haec verba jurare to swear according to the prescribed form; to conspire against; jurare calumniam to swear that the accusation is not false

jū·s -ris *n* juice, broth, gravy, soup; law (*as established by society and custom rather than statute law*); right, justice; law court, court of justice; legal right, authority, permission, prerogative; jurisdiction; in jus ire to go to court; jure by right, rightfully, in justice; jus dicere to sit as judge, hold court; jus

gentium international law; jus publicum common right; summum jus strict letter of the law

jūs jūrand·um (*genit:* jūr·is jūrand·ī) *n* oath

jussū (*abl* only) *m* by order; meo jussu by my order

juss·us -a -um *pp* of jubeo; *n* order, command, bidding

justē *adv* justly, rightly

justificus -a -um *adj* just-dealing

justiti·a -ae *f* justice, fairness

justit·ium -iī or -ī *n* suspension of legal business; (*fig*) standstill

just·us -a -um *adj* just, fair; justified, well-founded; formal; in due order, according to protocol, regular; *n* justice; due measure; plus quam justo more than due measure, too much; *n pl* rights; formalities; ceremonies, due ceremony; funeral rites, obsequies

Jūturn·a -ae *f* nymph, sister of Turnus, the king of the Rutuli

jūtus *pp* of juvo

juvenāl·is -e *adj* youthful; juvenile

Juvenāl·is -is *m* Juvenal (*D. Junius Juvenalis, Roman satirist in the time of Domitian and Trajan, c. 62-142 A.D.*)

juvenc·us -a -um *adj* young; *m* bullock; young man; *f* heifer; girl

juven·escō -escēre -uī *vi* to grow up; to get young again

juvenīl·is -e *adj* youthful; juvenile; cheerful

juvenīlĭter *adv* youthfully, boyishly

juvĕn·is -e *adj* young; *m* young man (*between the ages of twenty and forty-five*); warrior; *f* young lady

juvĕn·or -ārī -ātus sum *vi* to act like a kid

juvent·a -ae *f* youth

juvent·ās -ātis *f* youth, prime of life, manhood; (collectively) young people, youth

juvent·us -ūtis *f* youth, prime of life, manhood; (collectively) young people, youth

juvō juvāre jūvī jūtum *vt* to help; to please, delight; juvat (with *inf*) it helps to; juvat me it delights me, I am glad

juxtā *adv* nearby, in close proximity; alike, in like manner, equally; (with ac, atque, et, quam, or cum) as well as, just the same as; *prep* (with *acc*) close to, near to, next to; next to, immediately after; near, bordering upon; next door to

juxtim *adv* near; equally

K

Kalend·ae or Calend·ae -ārum *f pl* Kalends (*first day of the Roman month*); tristes Kalendae gloomy Kalends (*because interest was due on the Kalends*)

Kalendār·ium -iī or -ī *n* account book

Karthāginiens·is -e *adj* Carthaginian

Karthāg·ō -ĭnis *f* Carthage (*city of N. Africa*)

L

labasc·ō -ĕre vi to waver; to give in, yield

lābēcŭl·a -ae f blemish, spot, stain (e.g., on someone's reputation)

labe·faciō -facĕre -fēcī -factum vt to cause to totter, to shake, to weaken; (fig) to weaken, ruin, destroy

labefact·ō -āre vt to shake; (fig) to weaken, ruin, destroy

labell·um -ī n lip

lābell·um -ī n small basin

lāb·ēs -is f fall, falling down; stroke, blow, ruin, destruction; blemish, spot, defect; disgrace, discredit

labi·a -ae f lip

Labiēn·us -ī m Caesar's officer who defected to Pompey

labiōs·us -a -um adj thick-lipped

lab·ium -ī or -ī n lip

lab·ō -āre vi to totter, wobble; to waver, hesitate, be undecided; to fall to pieces, go to ruin

lābor lābī lapsus sum vi to glide, slide, slip; to slip, fall, sink; to slip away, disappear, escape; (of time) to slip by, pass, elapse; (fig) to fade

lab·or or lab·ōs -ōris m effort; trouble, distress, suffering; work, task

labōrif·er -ĕra -ĕrum adj struggling

labōriōs·us -a -um adj full of troubles, troublesome; energetic, industrious

labōr·ō -āre vt to work out, make, produce; vi to work; to suffer, be troubled; to be in danger; (with inf) to try to

labōs see labor

labr·um -ī n lip, edge

lābr·um -ī n basin, tub, bathtub

labrusc·a -ae f wild vine

labrusc·um -ī n wild grape

labyrinthē·us -a -um adj labyrinthine

labyrinth·us -ī m labyrinth

lac lactis n milk; milk of plants

Lacaen·a -ae f Spartan woman

Lacedaem·ōn -ŏnis f Sparta

Lacedaemŏni·us -a -um adj Spartan

lac·er -ĕra -ĕrum adj mangled, torn, lacerated, mutilated; lacerating, tearing

lacerāti·ō -ōnis f tearing, laceration, mangling

lacern·a -ae f coat, topcoat, overcoat

lacernāt·us -a -um adj wearing an overcoat

lacĕr·ō -āre vt to lacerate, tear, mangle; to slander, abuse; to waste, squander, destroy; to wreck (ship)

lacert·us -a -um adj muscular, brawny; m lizard; upper arm, muscle; m pl muscles, strength, brawn; f lizard

lacess·ō -ĕre -īvī or -iī -ītum vt to provoke, exasperate; to challenge; to move, arouse

Lachĕs·ēs -is f one of the three Fates

lacini·a -ae f flap (of a garment)

Lacīn·ium -iī or -ī n promontory in Bruttium with a temple to Juno

Lac·ō or Lac·ōn -ōnis m Spartan; Spartan dog

Lacōni·a -ae f district of the Peloponnesus of which Sparta was the chief city

Lacōnic·us -a -um adj Spartan; n sweat bath

lacrĭm·a or lacrŭm·a -ae f tear; gumdrop (plant)

lacrimābĭl·is -e adj worthy of tears, deplorable

lacrimābund·us -a -um adj tearful, about to break into tears

lacrĭm·ō or lacrŭm·ō -āre vt to cry for, shed tears over; (of trees) to drip; vi to cry, shed tears

lacrimōs·us -a -um adj crying, tearful; causing tears, bringing tears to the eyes

lacrimŭl·a -ae f teardrop, little tear; (fig) crocodile tear

lacrum- = lacrim-

lact·ans -antis adj milk-giving

lactāri·us -a -um adj milky

lactāti·ō -ōnis f allurement

lact·ens -entis adj suckling; milky, juicy, tender; full of milk; m suckling

lacteŏl·us -a -um adj milk-white

lact·ēs -ium f pl intestines; laxae lactes empty stomach

lactesc·ō -ĕre vi to turn to milk

lactĕ·us -a -um adj milky, full of milk, milk-colored, milk-white

lact·ō -āre vt to cajole, wheedle

lactūc·a -ae f lettuce

lacūn·a -ae f ditch, hole, pit; pond, pool; (fig) hole, gap

lacūn·ar -āris n paneled ceiling

lacūn·ō -āre vt to panel

lacūnōs·us -a -um adj sunken

lac·us -ūs m vat; tank, pool, reservoir, cistern; lake

laedō laedĕre laesī laesum vt to knock, strike; to hurt, rub open; to wound; to break (promise, pledge); to offend, outrage, violate; (with ad + acc) to smash (something) against

laen·a -ae f lined coat

Lāërt·ēs -ae m father of Ulysses

Lāërtĭåd·ēs -ae m Ulysses

laesi·ō -ōnis f attack, provocation

Laestrỹg·ōn -ōnis m Laestrygonian (one of the mythical race of cannibals in Italy, founders of Formiae)

laes·us pp of laedo

laetābĭl·is -e adj cheerful, glad

laet·ans -antis adj joyful, glad

laetāti·ō -ōnis f rejoicing, joy

laetē adv joyfully, gladly

laetific·ans -antis *adj* joyous

laetific·ō -āre *vt* to gladden, cheer up; **laetificari** to rejoice

laetific·us -a -um *adj* joyful, cheerful

laetiti·a -ae *f* joyfulness, gladness, exuberance

laet·or -ārī -ātus sum *vi* to rejoice, be glad

laet·us -a -um *adj* rejoicing, glad, cheerful; happy, fortunate, auspicious; fertile, rich, smiling (*grain*); sleek, fat (*cattle*); bright, cheerful (*appearance*); cheering, welcome (*news*)

laevē *adv* awkwardly

laev·us -a -um *adj* left, on the left side; awkward, stupid; ill-omened; lucky, propitious; *f* left hand, left side; *n* the left; *n pl* the area on the left

lagān·um -ī *n* pancake

lagē·os -ī *f* Greek vine

lagoen·a or **lagōn·a -ae** *f* jug

lagō·is -idis *f* grouse

lagunncul·a -ae *f* flask

Laïad·ēs -ae *m* son of Laius (*Oedipus*)

Laï·us -ī *m* Laius (*father of Oedipus*)

lall·ō -āre *vi* to sing a lullaby

lām·a -ae *f* swamp, bog

lambĕr·ō -āre *vt* to tear to pieces

lamb·ō -ĕre -ī *vt* to lick, lap; (of a river) to wash, flow by; (of ivy) to cling to

lāment·a -ōrum *n pl* wailing, moaning, lamentation

lāmentābil·is -e *adj* pitiable; doleful; mournful, sorrowful

lāmentāri·us -a -um *adj* sorrowful, pitiful

lāmentātī·ō -ōnis *f* lamentation

lāment·or -ārī -ātus sum *vt* to cry over, lament; *vi* to wail, cry

lamī·a -ae *f* witch, sorceress

lāmin·a or **lammin·a** or **lamn·a -ae** *f* plate, leaf (*of metal or wood*); blade; coin; peel, shell

lamp·as -ādis *f* torch; brightness; day; meteor; light

Lam·us -ī *m* mythical king of the Laestrygonians; son of Hercules and Omphale

lān·a -ae *f* wool; working in wool, spinning, **lana aurea** golden fleece; **lanam trahere** to card wool; **lanas ducere** to spin wool; **rixari de lana caprina** to argue over nothing

lānār·ius -iī or **-ī** *m* wool worker

lānāt·us -a -um *adj* woolly; *f pl* sheep

lancĕ·a -ae *f* lance, spear

lancīn·ō -āre *vt* to squander, waste

lānĕ·us -a -um *adj* woolen; soft

langue·faciō -facĕre -fēcī -factum *vt* to make tired

langu·ens -entis *adj* languid, drooping, listless

langu·ĕō -ēre *vi* to be tired, be weary, to be weak, feeble (*from disease*); (fig) to be dull, languid, listless; to be without energy

langu·escō -escĕre -uī *vi* to become weak, grow faint; (fig) to become listless; to decline, decrease; to relax

languidē *adv* weakly, faintly, without energy

languidŭl·us -a -um *adj* languid; withered, faded

languĭd·us -a -um *adj* weak, faint, languid, sluggish; listless; enervating

langu·or -ōris *m* weakness, faintness, languor; dullness, listlessness, sluggishness

laniāt·ŭs -ūs *m* mangling; *f pl* mental anguish

laniēn·a -ae *f* butcher shop

lānific·ium -iī or **-ī** *n* weaving

lānific·us -a -um *adj* spinning, weaving, of spinning, of weaving

lānĭg·er -ĕra -ĕrum *adj* fleecy; *m* sheep (*ram*); *f* sheep (*ewe*)

lani·ō -āre *vt* to tear to pieces, mangle

lanist·a -ae *m* gladiator trainer, fencing master; (*in derision*) ringleader

lānit·ium -iī or **-ī** *n* wool

lan·ius -iī or **-ī** *m* butcher; (*in derision*) executioner, butcher

lantern·a -ae *f* lantern

lanternār·ius -iī or **-ī** *m* guide

lānŭg·ō -ĭnis *f* down (*of plants, cheeks, etc.*)

Lānuv·ium -iī or **-ī** *n* town in Latium on the Appian Way

lan·x -cis *f* dish, platter; scale

Lāocŏ·ōn -ontis *m* son of Priam and priest of Apollo, who, with his two sons, was killed by two serpents from the sea

Lāomĕd·ōn -ontis *m* king of Troy and father of Priam and Ganymede

Lāomedontĕ·us or **Lāomedontĭ·us -a -um** *adj* Trojan

Lāomedontĭăd·ēs -ae *m* son of Laomedon; Priam; *m pl* Trojans

lapăth·um -ī *n* or **lapăth·us -ī** *f* sorrel (*plant*)

lapicīd·a -ae *m* stonecutter, quarry worker

lapicīdīn·ae -ārum *f pl* stone quarry

lapidāri·us -a -um *adj* stone; **latomiae lapidariae** stone quarries

lapidātĭ·ō -ōnis *f* throwing stones

lapidăt·or -ōris *m* stone thrower

lapidĕ·us -a -um *adj* of stones, stone, stony; **lapideus sum** (fig) I am petrified

lapid·ō -āre *vt* to throw stones at; *v impers* it is raining stones, it is hailing stones

lapidōs·us -a -um *adj* full of stones, stony; hard as stone; gritty (*bread*)

lapill·us -ī *m* pebble; precious stone, gem, jewel; *m pl* small stones (*esp. for mosaics*)

lap·is -ĭdis *m* stone; milestone; platform; boundary stone, landmark; tombstone; precious stone, gem, pearl, jewel, stone statue; marble table; **lapides loqui** to speak harsh words

Lapith·ae -ārum *m pl* mountain tribe in Thessaly that fought the centaurs at the marriage of their king Pirithous

lapp·a -ae *f* burr

lapsi·ō -ōnis *f* sliding, slipping; (fig) tendency

laps·ō -āre *vi* to keep slipping, stumble

laps·us -a -um *pp* of **labor; adj** fallen

laps·us -ūs *m* falling, fall, sliding, slipping, gliding, flow, flight; blunder, error, fault, slip

laqueār·ia -ium *n pl* paneled ceiling

laqueāt·us -a -um *adj* paneled, having a paneled ceiling

laquĕ·us -ī *m* noose; snare; (fig) snare, trap; *m pl* (fig) subtleties

Lār Laris *m* tutelary deity, household god; hearth, home; *m pl* hearth, home, house, household, family

lard·um -ī *n* lard, fat

Larentī·a -ae *f* wife of Faustulus who reared Romulus and Remus

largē *adv* liberally, generously

largific·us -a -um *adj* bountiful

largiflu·us -a -um *adj* gushing

largilŏqu·us -a -um *adj* talkative

larg·ior -īrī -ītus sum *vt* to give generously, bestow freely; to lavish; to bestow, confer; to grant, concede; *vi* to give bribes, bribe

largit·ās -ātis *f* generosity, bounty

largītī·ō -ōnis *f* generosity; bribery

largīt·or -ōris *m* generous donor; spendthrift; briber

larg·us -a -um *adj* abundant, plentiful, large, much; generous, liberal, bountiful, profuse

lārid·um -ī *n* lard, bacon fat

Lāriss·a -ae *f* town in Thessaly on the Peneus River

Lār·ius -iī or **-ī** *m* Lake Como

lar·ix -icis *f* larch tree

larv·a -ae *f* mask; ghost

larvāt·us -a -um *adj* bewitched

lasăn·um -ī *n* chamber pot

lasarpīcīf·er -ēra -ĕrum *adj* producing asafetida (*used as an antispasmodic*)

lascivī·a -ae *f* playfulness; petulence; lewdness

lascīvībund·us -a -um *adj* petulant, roguish

lascīv·iō -īre -iī -ītum *vi* to frolic, be frisky; to run riot, run wild

lascīv·us -a -um *adj* playful, frisky; brash, impudent, petulant; licentious, lustful; luxuriant (*growth*)

lāserpīc·ium -iī or **-ī** *n* silphium (*plant which yielded asafetida*)

lassitūd·ō -inis *f* physical weariness, lassitude

lass·ō -āre *vt* to fatigue, exhaust

lassŭl·us -a -um *adj* somewhat tired

lass·us -a -um *adj* tired, weary, fatigued, exhausted

lātē *adv* widely, extensively; pro-

fusely; **lātē longeque** far and wide

latēbr·a -ae *f* hiding place, hideaway, hideout; (fig) loophole

latebrĭcŏl·a -ae *m* or *f* person who hangs around dives or brothels

latebrōsē *adv* secretly

latebrōs·us -a -um *adj* full of holes; hidden, secret; porous

lat·ens -entis *adj* hidden, secret

latenter *adv* in secret

lat·ĕō -ēre -uī *vi* to lie hidden, lie concealed, lurk; to keep out of sight, sulk; to live a retired life, remain in obscurity, remain unknown, escape notice; to be in safety; to avoid a summons, lie low; to be obscure

lat·er -ĕris *m* brick, tile; **laterem lavare** to waste effort

laterām·en -inis *n* earthenware

latercŭl·us -ī *m* small brick; tile; biscuit

laterici·us -a -um *adj* brick, made of brick; *n* brickwork

lātern·a -ae *f* lantern

latesc·ō -ĕre *vi* to hide

lat·ex -icis *m* liquid, fluid; water; spring; wine; oil

latibŭl·um -ī *n* hiding place, hideout, lair, den; (fig) refuge

lāticlāvi·us -a -um *adj* having a broad crimson stripe (*distinctive mark of senators, military tribunes of the equestrian order, and of sons of distinguished familias*)

Latīnē *adv* Latin, in Latin; in proper Latin; in plain Latin; **Latīnē loqui** to speak Latin; to speak correct Latin; **Latīnē reddere** to translate into Latin; **Latīnē scire** to understand Latin

Latīnit·ās -ātis *f* pure Latin, Latinity; Latin rights and privileges

Latīn·us -a -um *adj* Latin; possessing Latin rights and privileges; *m* Latinus (*king of the Laurentians, who gave his daughter Lavinia in marriage to Aeneas*); *n* Latin language; **in Latīnum convertere** to translate into Latin

lātī·ō -ōnis *f* bringing, rendering; proposing

latit·ō -āre *vi* to keep hiding oneself; to be concealed, hide, lurk; to lie low (*in order to avoid a summons*)

lātitūd·ō -inis *f* breadth, width; size, extent; broad pronunciation; richness of expression

lātius *adv* of late

Lati·us -a -um *adj* of Latium, Latin, Roman; *n* Latium (*district in W. central Italy, in which Rome was situated*); **jus Lati** or **Latium** Latin political rights and privileges

Lātō·is -idis *f* Diana

lātom- = lautom-

Lātōn·a -ae *f* daughter of the Titan Coeus and Phoebe, and mother of Apollo and Diana

Lātōnigĕn·a -ae *m* or *f* child of Latona; *m pl* children of Latona, i.e., Apollo and Diana

Lătōnĭ·us -a -um *adj* of Latona; *f* Diana

lāt·or -ōris *m* bringer, bearer; proposer (*of a law*)

Lătō·us -ī *m* Apollo

lātrāt·or -ōris *m* barker; dog

lātrāt·us -ūs *m* barking

lātrīn·a -ae *f* wash room, toilet

lātr·ō -āre *vt* to bark at, snarl at; to clamor for; *vi* to bark; (fig) to rant

latr·ō -ōnis *m* mercenary; freebooter; brigand, bandit; (in chess) pawn

latrōcĭn·ĭum -ĭī or -ĭ *n* military service (*as a mercenary*); freebooting; brigandage, banditry, vandalism, piracy, robbery, highway robbery; villany, outrage; band of robbers

latrōcĭn·or -ārī -ātus sum *vi* to serve as a mercenary, be a mercenary soldier; to be a bandit, be a highwayman, be a pirate

latruncŭl·us -ī *m* small-time bandit

lātumĭ·ae -ārum *f pl* stone quarry; prison

lātus *pp* of fero

lāt·us -a -um *adj* wide, broad; extensive; widespread; broad (*pronunciation*); diffuse (*style*)

lat·us -ĕris *n* side, flank; body, person; lungs; lateral surface; coast; (mil) flank, wing; a latere (mil) on the flank; a latere (with *genit*) a at the side of, in the company of; b from among the friends of; aperto latere (mil) on the exposed flank; latere tecto scot free; latus dare to expose oneself; latus tegere (with *genit*) to walk by the side of, to escort (*someone*)

lātuscŭl·um -ī *n* small side

laudābĭl·is -e *adj* laudable, praiseworthy

laudābĭlĭter *adv* laudably

laudātĭ·ō -ōnis *f* commendation; eulogy, panegyric, funeral oration; (in court) testimony by a character witness

laudāt·or -ōris *m* praiser; eulogist, panegyrist; (law) character witness

laudāt·us -a -um *adj* praiseworthy, commendable, excellent

laud·ō -āre *vt* to praise, commend; to name, quote, cite; to pronounce a funeral oration over

laurĕ·a -ae *f* laurel tree; laurel, laurel branch, laurel crown, bay wreath; triumph

laureāt·us -a -um *adj* laureate, laureled, crowned with laurel; litterae laureatae communiqué announcing victory

Laurent·ēs -ĭum *m pl* Laurentians (*people of Lanuvium*)

Laurentĭn·us or Laurentĭ·us -a -um *adj* Laurentian

laureŏl·a -ae *f* little laurel crown; triumph

laurĕ·us -a -um *adj* laurel, of laurel; *f* see laurea

lauricŏm·us -a -um *adj* laurel-covered (*mountain*)

laurĭf·er -ĕra -ĕrum *adj* crowned with laurel

laurĭg·er -ĕra -ĕrum *adj* wearing laurel

laur·us -ī *f* laurel tree, bay tree; triumph, victory

laus laudis *f* praise, commendation; fame, glory; approval, praiseworthy deed; merit, worth

Laus·us -ī *m* son of Numitor and brother of Rhea Silvia; son of Mezentius, killed by Aeneas

lautē *adv* sumptuously, splendidly; excellently

lautĭ·a -ōrum *n pl* state banquet (*given to foreign ambassadors and official guests*)

lautitĭ·a -ae *f* luxury, high living

lautumĭ·ae or lātomĭ·ae or lātumĭ·ae -ārum *f pl* stone quarry; prison

laut·us -a -um *adj* expensive, elegant, fine; well-heeled; refined, fashionable

lavăbr·um -ī *n* bath

lavātĭ·o -ōnis *f* washing, bathing, bath; bathing kit

Lāvīnĭ·us -a -um *adj* Lavinian, of Lavinium; *n* town in Latium founded by Aeneas; *f* wife of Aeneas

lavō lavāre (or lavĕre) lāvī lautum (or lavātum or lōtum) *vt* to wash, bathe; to wet, drench; to wash away; lavi to wash, wash oneself, bathe; *vi* to wash, wash oneself, bathe

laxāment·um -ī *n* relaxation, respite, letup, mitigation

laxāt·us -a -um *adj* loose, extended (*e.g., ranks*)

laxē *adv* loosely, widely; freely

laxĭt·ās -ātis *f* roominess, extent

lax·ō -āre *vt* to extend, widen, expand, open; to open, undo, release; to relax, slacken; to mitigate; (fig) to release, relieve; *vi* (of price) to go down

lax·us -a -um *adj* roomy, wide; loose, slack; prolonged, extended (*time*); (fig) relaxed, easygoing, free; low (*price*)

le·a -ae *f* lioness

leaen·a -ae *f* lioness

Lēand·er -rī *m* youth of Abydos who swam across the Hellespont every night to his lover Hero of Sestos

Learch·us -ī *m* son of Athamas and Ino, killed by his mad father

leb·ēs -ētis *m* pan, cauldron, basin

lectĭc·a -ae *f* litter; sofa, couch

lectĭcār·ĭus -ĭī or -ĭ *m* litter bearer

lectĭcŭl·a -ae *f* small litter; small bier

lectĭ·ō -ōnis *f* selection; reading, reading aloud; perusal; lectio senātūs revision of the senate roll (*by the censor*)

lectisternĭāt·or -ōris *m* slave who arranged the seating at table

lestistern·ĭum -ĭī or -ĭ *n* ritual feast (*at which images of the gods were placed on couches at the table*)

lectit·ō -āre vt to read and reread; to like to read

lectiuncul·a -ae f light reading

lect·or -ōris m reader (esp. slave who read aloud to his master)

lectūl·us -ī m cot; small couch, settee; humble bier

lect·us -ī or **-ūs** m bed, couch; bier

lect·us -a -um pp of **lego**; adj select, choice, special, elite

Lēd·a -ae or **Lēd·ē -ēs** f Tyndarus's wife, whom Jupiter visited in the form of a swan and who bore Helen, Clytemnestra, Castor, and Pollux

lēgātī·ō -ōnis f embassy, mission, legation; members of an embassy, work or report of work of a mission; nominal staff appointment; command of a legion; **legatio libera** junket (all-expenses-paid trip, a privilege granted to senators, nominally in an official capacity, to visit the provinces to transact private business)

lēgāt·um -ī n bequest, legacy

lēgāt·us -ī m deputy, representative; ambassador, envoy; adjutant (of a consul, proconsul, or praetor); commander of a legion

lēgif·er -ěra -ěrum adj law-giving

legi·ō -ōnis f legion (divided into 10 cohorts and numbering between 4,200 and 6,000 men); army

legiōnāri·us -a -um adj legionary

lēgirup·a -ae or **lēgirup·iō -ōnis** m lawbreaker

lēgitimē adv legitimately, lawfully; properly

lēgitim·us -a -um adj legitimate, lawful; regular, right, just, proper; n pl legal formalities

legiuncul·a -ae f under-manned legion

lēg·ō -āre vt to commission; to send on a public mission, despatch; to delegate, deputize; to bequeath, will; (fig) to entrust

lěgō lěgěre lěgī lectum vt to gather, collect, pick; to pick out, choose; to pick one's way through, cross; to sail by, coast along; to read, peruse; to recite, read out loud; to pick up, steal; to pick up (news, rumor); **fila legere** to wind up the thread of life; **senatum legere** to read off the senate roll

lēgulē·ius -iī or **-ī** pettifogger

legum·en -inis n leguminous plant; vegetable; pulse; bean

lemb·us -ī m cutter, yacht (built for speed), speedboat

lemm·a -ătis n theme, subject matter; epigram

Lemnicŏl·a -ae m inhabitant of Lemnos, i.e., Vulcan

lemniscāt·us -a -um adj heavily decorated (with combat ribbons)

lemnisc·us -ī m ribbon which hung down from a victor's wreath

Lemni·us -a -um adj Lemnian; m Lemnian; Vulcan

Lemn·os or **Lemn·us -ī** f large island in the Aegean

Lemŭr·ēs -um m pl ghosts

Lemŭri·a -ōrum n pl night festival to drive ghosts from the house

lēn·a -ae f procuress, madame; seductress

Lēnae·us -a -um adj Lenaean, Bacchic; m Bacchus

lēnē adv gently

lēnīm·en -inis n consolation, comfort, compensation, reward

lēnīment·um -ī n alleviation

lēn·iō -īre -īvī or **-iī -ītum** vt to soften, alleviate, soothe, calm; vi to calm down

lēn·is -e adj soft, gentle, mild, smooth, calm; gradual (slope); (fig) gentle, mild, kind

lēnit·ās -ātis f softness, gentleness, mildness, smoothness; (fig) gentleness, mildness, tenderness, clemency

lēniter adv softly, gently, mildly; (fig) mildly, quietly, calmly; (of style) smoothly; halfheartedly

lēnitūd·ō -inis f softness, mildness, gentleness, smoothness

lēn·ō -ōnis m pander, procurer, pimp; seducer

lēnōcin·ium -iī or **-ī** n pandering, pimping; allurement, attraction; bawdy or gaudy clothes; flattery

lēnōcin·or -ārī -ātus sum vi to be a pimp; (with dat) to play up to, humor, pander to; **b** to stimulate, promote

lēnōni·us -a -um adj pimp's

lens -tis f lentil

lentē adv slowly; indifferently, halfheartedly; calmly, leisurely, deliberately

lent·escō -ěre vi to get sticky, soften; (fig) to soften, weaken; (with ad + acc) to stick to

lentiscif·er -ěra -ěrum adj (of a region) producing mastic trees

lentisc·us -ī f mastic tree; toothpick (made of mastic wood)

lentitūd·ō -inis f slowness; insensibility, apathy, dullness

lent·ō -āre vt to bend

lentŭl·us -a -um adj somewhat slow

lent·us -a -um adj sticky, clinging; pliant, limber; slow, sluggish; lingering; irresponsive, reluctant, indifferent, backward; slow-moving; tedious; drawling; at rest, at leisure, lazy; calm, unconcerned

lēnŭl·us -ī m little pimp

lēnuncŭl·us -ī m little pimp; small sailboat, skiff

le·ō -ōnis m Lion

Le·ō -ōnis m Lion (constellation)

Leōnid·ās -ae m king of Sparta (487-480 B.C.), who fell at Thermopylae in 480 B.C. after a gallant stand

leōnīn·us -a -um adj lion's, of a lion

Leontīn·ī -ōrum m pl town in E. Sicily

lep·as -ădis f limpet

lepidē adv pleasantly, charmingly,

neatly; (as affirmative answer) yes, indeed; (of approval) bravo!

lepĭd·us -a -um *adj* pleasant, charming, neat; effeminate

lep·ōs or **lep·or** -ōris *m* pleasantness, charm, attractiveness

lep·us -ŏris *m* hare

Lep·us -ŏris *m* Hare (*constellation*)

lepuscŭl·us -ī *m* little hare

Lern·a -ae or **Lern·ē** -ēs *f* marsh near Argos, where Hercules slew the Hydra

Lernae·us -a -um *adj* Lernaean

Lesbĭ·us -a -um *adj* Lesbian; *f* pseudonym for the girl friend of the poet Catullus; *n* Lesbian wine

Lesb·os or **Lesb·us** -ī *f* large island in the N. Aegean, the birthplace of the lyric poets Alcaeus and Sappho

less·us (only *acc:* **lessum** in use) *m* wailing

lētāl·is -e *adj* lethal, fatal, mortal

Lēthae·us -a -um *adj* of Lethe; infernal; causing drowsiness

lēthargĭc·us -ī *m* lazy fellow

lētharg·us -ī *m* lethargy

Lēth·ē -ēs *f* Lethe (*river of oblivion in the lower world*); forgetfulness

lētĭf·er -ĕra -ĕrum *adj* deadly, fatal; **locus letifer** mortal spot

lēt·ō -āre *vt* to kill

lēt·um -ī *n* death; ruin, destruction; **leto dare** to put to death

Leuc·as -ādis *f* island off W. Greece

leucasp·is -ĭdis *adj* armed with a white shield

Leucipp·us -ī *m* philosopher, teacher of Democritus, and one of the founders of Atomism (5th *cent.* B.C.)

Leucothĕ·a -ae or **Leucothē** -ēs *f* name of Ino, daughter of Cadmus, after she was changed into a sea deity

Leuctr·a -ōrum *n pl* small town in Boeotia where Epaminondas defeated the Spartans in 371 B.C.

levām·en -ĭnis *n* alleviation, comfort, consolation

levāment·um -ī *n* alleviation, comfort, consolation

levātĭ·ō -ōnis *f* lightening; relief, comfort; lessening

levĭcŭl·us -a -um *adj* somewhat vain

levĭdens·is -e *adj* poor, inferior

levĭfĭd·us -a -um *adj* untrustworthy

lĕv·is -e *adj* light, not heavy; lightarmed; lightly dressed; light, easily digested; thin, poor (*soil*); light, nimble; flitting; slight, small; unimportant, trivial; unfounded (*rumor*); easy, simple; mild; gentle, easygoing; capricious, unreliable, fickle

lēv·is -e *adj* smooth; slippery; smooth, hairless, beardless; delicate, tender; effeminate; smooth (*style*)

levisomn·us -a -um *adj* light-sleeping

levit·ās -ātis *f* lightness; mobility, nimbleness; levity, frivolity; (*fig*) shallowness

lēvĭt·as -ātis *f* smoothness; (*fig*) smoothness, fluency

levĭter *adv* lightly; slightly, a little, somewhat; easily, without difficulty; nimbly

lĕv·ō -āre *vt* to lift up, raise; to lighten, relieve, ease; to console, comfort; to lessen, weaken; to release, free; to take away; to avert

lēv·ō -āre *vt* to make smooth, polish; to soothe

lēv·or -ōris *m* smoothness

lex lēgis *f* motion, bill; law, statute; rule, regulation, principle, precept; condition, stipulation; **eā lege ut** with the stipulation that, on condition that; **lege** or **legibus** legally; **lege agere** to proceed legally; **legem abrogare** to repeal a law; **legem ferre** to propose a bill; **legem derogare** to amend a bill or law; **legem jubere** to sanction a law; **legem perferre** to pass a law; **sine legibus** without restraint, without control

lībām·en -ĭnis *n* libation; firstfruits

lībāment·um -ī *n* libation; firstfruits

lībātĭ·ō -ōnis *f* libation

lībell·a -ae *f* small silver coin, ace; small sum; level (*instrument*); **ad libellam** to a tee, exactly; **heres ex libella** sole heir

libell·us -ī *m* small book, pamphlet; notebook; journal, diary; program; handbill, advertisement; petition; answer to a petition; letter; written accusation, indictment, libel; satirical verse

lib·ens or **lub·ens** -entis *adj* willing, ready, glad; merry, cheerful

libenter or **lubenter** *adv* willingly, gladly, with pleasure

lib·er -rī *m* bark of a tree; book; work, treatise; catalog, list, register; letter, rescript

līb·er -ĕra -ĕrum *adj* free; open, unoccupied; unrestricted; unprejudiced; outspoken, frank; uncontrolled, unrestricted; (not slave) free; (of states or municipalities) independent, autonomous; exempt; free of charge; (with *abl* or **ab** + *abl*) free from, exempt from; (with *genit*) free of; *m pl* see **liberi**

Līb·er -ĕrī *m* Italian fertility god, later identified with Bacchus; wine

Lībĕr·a -ae *f* Proserpina; Ariadne, the wife of Bacchus

Līberāl·ia -ium *n pl* festival of Liber, held on March 17th, at which young men received the toga virilis

līberāl·is -e *adj* relating to freedom, relating to civil status, of free citizens; worthy of a freeman, honorable, gentleman's; courteous; liberal, generous; handsome

līberālĭt·ās -ātis *f* courtesy, politeness; liberality, generosity; grant, gift

līberālĭter *adv* like a freeman, nobly; liberally (*e.g., educated*); courteously; liberally, generously

liberāti·ō -ōnis f liberation, delivery, freeing, release; acquittal

liberāt·or -ōris m liberator

libērē adv freely; frankly, outspokenly; ungrudgingly; like a freeman, liberally

liber·ī -ōrum m pl children

liber·ō -āre vt to set free, free, release; to acquit, discharge; to cancel, get rid of (e.g., debts); to exempt; to manumit, set free; (with abl or with ab or ex + abl) to free or release from, acquit of; **fidem liberare** to keep one's promise; **nomina liberare** to cancel debts; **se aere alieno liberare** to pay up a debt

libert·a -ae f freedwoman, ex-slave

libert·ās -ātis f liberty, freedom; status of a freeman; political freedom; freedom of speech, freedom of thought; frankness

libertīn·us -a -um adj & mf ex-slave; m freedman; f freedwoman

libert·us -ī m freedman, ex-slave

lib·et (or **lub·et**) **-ēre -uit** (or **libitum est**) v impers (with dat) it pleases, is pleasant, is agreeable to, is nice for (someone); (with inf) it is nice, pleasant to (do something); **sī lubet** if you please; **ut lubet** as you please

libīdin·or -ārī -ātus sum vi to gratify lust

libīdinōsē adv willfully; arbitrarily

libīdinōs·us -a -um adj willful; arbitrary; lustful, sensual

libīd·ō or **lubīd·ō -inis** f desire, longing, inclination, pleasure; will, willfulness, arbitrariness, caprice, fancy; lust, rut, heat; **ex libidine** arbitrarily

libīt·a -ōrum n pl will, pleasure, liking

Libitīn·a -ae f burial goddess; implements for burial; grave, death

līb·ō -āre vt to taste, sip; to pour as a libation, offer, consecrate; to touch lightly, barely touch, graze; to spill, waste; to extract, collect, compile

lībr·a -ae f balance, scales; plummet, level; pound (of twelve ounces)

lībrāment·um -ī n weight; balance, ballast; plane surface; gravity

lībrāri·a -ae f forelady (who weighed out wool for slaves to spin)

lībrāriōl·us -ī m copyist, scribe

lībrāri·us -a -um adj book, of books; **taberna libraria** bookstore; m copyist, scribe; n bookcase

lībrāt·us -a -um adj poised; hurled; powerful

lībrīl·is -e adj one-pound, weighing a pound

lībrit·or -ōris m artilleryman

lībr·ō -āre vt to balance; to poise, level, hurl, launch; to sway

līb·um -ī n cake; birthday cake

Liburni·a -ae f district of Illyria between Istria and Dalmatia

Liburn·us -a -um adj & mf Liburnian; f Liburnian galley

Libÿ·a -ae or **Libÿ·ē -ēs** f Libya (Africa)

Libÿ·es -um m pl Libyans

Libÿc·us or **Libyss·us** or **Libystīn·us** or **Libÿ·us -a -um** or **Libyst·is -idis** adj Libyan; (in general) African

lic·ens -entis adj free, bold

licenter adv freely, boldly, without restraint, licentiously

licenti·a -ae f license, liberty, freedom; lawlessness, licentiousness

lic·eō -ēre vi to cost; to be for sale

lic·eor -ērī -itus sum vt to bid on, bid for, make an offer for; vi to bid, make a bid

lic·et -ēre -uit or **-itum est** v impers it is permitted or lawful; (with dat & inf) it is all right for (someone) to; **licet** (to express assent) yes, all right

licet conj granted that, even if, although

Lich·ās -ae m companion of Hercules

lich·ēn -ēnis m ringworm

licitāti·ō -ōnis f bidding (at auction); haggling

licit·or -ārī -ātus sum vt to bid for

licit·us -a -um adj permissible, lawful

līc·ium -iī or **-ī** n thread

līct·or -ōris m lictor (attendant and bodyguard of a magistrate, of whom twenty-four attended a dictator, twelve a consul, and six a praetor)

li·ēn -ēnis m spleen

liēnōs·us -a -um adj splenetic

ligām·en -inis n bandage

ligāment·um -ī n bandage

lignār·ius -iī or **-ī** m carpenter

lignāti·ō -ōnis f gathering of lumber

lignāt·or -ōris m woodcutter, lumberjack

ligneōl·us -a -um adj wooden

ligne·us -a -um adj wooden

lign·or -ārī -ātus sum vi to gather wood

lign·um -ī n wood; timber, firewood, log, plank; writing tablet; tree; **in silvam ligna ferre** to carry coals to Newcastle

lig·ō -āre vt to tie, tie up, bandage; to close (a deal)

lig·ō -ōnis m mattock, hoe; farming

ligul·a -ae f shoe strap

Lig·ur or **Lig·us -uris** m or f Ligurian

Liguri·a -ae f Liguria (district along the N.W. coast of Italy)

ligūr·iō or **ligurr·iō -īre -īvī** or **-iī -ītum** vt to lick, pick at; to eat daintily; (fig) to prey on; (fig) to be dying for

ligūrīti·ō -ōnis f daintiness

Ligus see **Ligur**

Ligusc·us or **Ligustīc·us** or **Ligustīn·us -a -um** adj Ligurian

ligustr·um -ī n privet

lil·ium -ii or -i n lily; (mil) trench lined with sharp stakes

lim·a -ae f file; (fig) polishing, revision

limātius adv in a more polished manner

limātul·us -a -um adj (fig) rather sharp (judgment)

limāt·us -a -um adj (fig) polished, refined

lim·ax -ācis m or f snail

limolāri·us -a -um adj **textores limbolarii** tassel makers, hemmers

limb·us -i m fringe, hem, tassel

lim·en -inis n lintel, threshold; doorway, entrance; threshold, outset, beginning; starting gate (at racetrack); house, home

lim·es -itis m country trail; path; road along a boundary; boundary, frontier; channel, course, way; zodiac

lim·ō -āre vt to file; (fig) to polish, refine; to file down, take away from, lessen; to get down to (the truth)

limōs·us -a -um adj muddy; mud, growing in mud

limpid·us -a -um adj limpid, clear

limtul·us -a -um adj squinting

lim·us -a -um adj squinting; sidelong, askance; m mud; dirt, grime; ceremonial apron (worn by priests at sacrifice)

līne·a -ae f line, string, thread; fishing line; plumb line; outline; boundary line, limit; **ad līneam or rectā līneā** in a straight line, vertically; horizontally; **extrēmā līneā amāre** to love at a distance; **līneas trānsīre** to go out of bounds

līneāment·um -i n line; characteristic, feature; outline

līnē·ō -āre vt to make straight, make perpendicular

līnē·us -a -um adj flaxen, linen

lingō lingěre linxi linctum vt to lick up, lap up

lingu·a -ae f tongue; speech, language, dialect; (of animals) note, song, bark; tongue of land; eloquence; **lingua promptus** insolent; **utraque lingua** Greek and Latin

lingul·a -ae f tongue of land

linguāc·a -ae m or f gossip, chatterbox

linig·er -ěra -ěrum adj wearing linen

linō liněre lēvi or līvi litum vt to smear; to erase; to cover, overlay; (fig) to mess up

linquō linquěre liqui vt to leave, forsake, depart from; to leave or let alone; to leave in a pinch; **linqui animo or linqui** to faint; **linquitur** (with ut) it remains to (do something)

linteāt·us -a -um adj canvas

lintě·ō -ōnis m linen weaver

linteōl·um -i n small linen cloth

lint·er -ris f skiff; tub, vat

lintě·us -a -um adj linen; n linen,

linen cloth; canvas, sail; kerchief

lintricŭl·us -i m small boat

lin·um -i n flax; linen; thread, rope, line; fishing line; net

Lin·us -i m son of Apollo and instructor of Orpheus and Hercules

Lipăr·a -ae or **Lipăr·ē** -ēs f island off the N. coast of Sicily; f pl the Aeolian islands

Liparae·us -a -um or **Liparens·is** -e adj of Lipara

lipp·iō -īre -īvi or -ii -ītum vi to have sore eyes; (of eyes) to burn, ache

lippitūd·ō -inis f running eyes, inflammation of the eyes

lipp·us -a -um adj with sore eyes, sore-eyed; burning (eyes); (fig) blind

lique·faciō -facěre -fēci -factum (passive: **lique·fiō** -fiěri -factus sum) vt to melt; dissolve; to decompose; to waste, weaken

liqu·ens -entis adj clear, limpid; flowing, gliding; liquid, fluid

liquěō liquěre licŭi vi to be liquid; v impers it is clear, is apparent, is evident; **liquet mihi** (with inf) I am free to; **non liquet** (law) it is not clear (legal formula used by a hung jury)

liquescō liquescěre licŭi vi to melt; to decompose; to grow soft, grow effeminate; (fig) to melt away; to become clear

liquidē adv clearly; (fig) clearly, plainly

liquidiuscŭl·us -a -um adj somewhat softer

liquidō adv clearly, plainly, certainly

liquid·us -a -um adj liquid, fluid, flowing; clear, transparent; pure (pleasure); clear (voice); calm (mind); clear, evident, certain; n liquid, water; clearness, certainty

liqu·ō -āre vt to melt, dissolve; to strain, filter

liqu·or -i vi to flow; to melt, dissolve; (fig) to melt away, waste away

liqu·or -ōris m fluidity; liquid, fluid; sea

Līr·is -is m river between Campania and Latium

līs lītis f lawsuit, litigation; matter of dispute; quarrel, wrangling; charge, accusation; **lītem intenděre or lītem inferre** (with dat) to sue (someone); **lītem aestimāre** to assess damages; **līs capitis** criminal charge

litāti·ō -ōnis f success in sacrificing, efficacious sacrifice

litātō adv with favorable omens

litěra see **littera**

litic·en -inis m clarion player

lītigāt·or -ōris m litigant

lītigiōs·us -a -um adj quarrelsome, litigious; contested, disputed

lītig·ium -ii or -i n quarrel, dispute

lītig·ō -āre vi to quarrel, squabble; to go to court

lit·ō -āre vt to offer duly or acceptably; *vi* to offer acceptable sacrifice; to receive a good omen; (with *dat*) to propitiate, satisfy, appease

litorāl·is -e *adj* shore, of the shore

litorē·us -a -um *adj* seashore, at or along the seashore

littĕr·a or **lītĕr·a -ae** *f* letter (*of the alphabet*); handwriting; *f pl* epistle, letter, dispatch; edict, ordinance; literature, books, literary works; learning, liberal education, scholarship; records, accounts; **littera salutaris** (*i.e.*, A = absolvo) vote of acquittal; **littera tristis** (*i.e.*, C = condemno) vote of guilty; **litteras discere** to learn to read and write; **litteras scire** to know how to read and write

litterārĭ·us -a -um *adj* of reading and writing; **ludus litterarius** elementary school

litterātē *adv* legibly, in a clear handwriting; literally; learnedly

litterāt·or -ōris *m* elementary-school teacher; grammarian, philologist

litterātūr·a -ae *f* alphabet

litterāt·us -a -um *adj* marked with letters, engraved; learned, scholarly; liberally educated; devoted to literature

litterŭl·a -ae *f* small letter, note; slight literary endeavors

litūr·a -ae *f* erasure; erased passage; correction, emendation; blot, smear; wrinkle

litus *pp* of lino

līt·us -ŏris *n* seashore, beach, coast; river bank; **in litus harenas fundere** to carry coals to Newcastle; **litus arare** to waste effort

litŭ·us -ī *m* cavalry trumpet, clarion; (*fig*) signal; augur's wand (*crooked staff carried by an augur*); **lituus meae profectionis** signal for my departure

līv·ens -entis *adj* black-and-blue, livid

līv·ĕō -ēre *vi* to be black and blue, be livid; to be envious; (with *dat*) to be jealous of

līvescō -ĕre *vi* to turn black and blue

Līvĭ·a -ae *f* second wife of Augustus (58 B.C.-29 A.D.)

līvĭdŭl·us -a -um *adj* inclined to be jealous, somewhat envious

līvĭd·us -a -um *adj* leaden (*in color*); blue; black and blue; jealous, envious, spiteful

Līv·ĭus -iī *m* T. Livius Patavinus or Livy (*famous historian*, 59 B.C.-17 A.D.)

līv·or -ōris *m* leaden color; bluish color; black-and-blue mark; jealousy, envy, spite

lix·a -ae *m* camp follower

locātĭ·ō -ōnis *f* arrangement, placement; renting out, contract, lease

locāt·um -ī *n* lease, contract

locĭt·ō -āre *vt* to lease out

loc·ō -āre *vt* to place, put, set, lay; to establish, constitute, lay, set; to give in marriage, marry off; to let, rent out; to contract for; to invest

locŭl·us -ī *m* little place, spot; pocket

locuplēs -ētis *adj* rich; reliable, responsible

locuplēt·ō -āre *vt* to make rich, enrich

loc·us -ī (*pl:* loc·ī -ōrum *m*; loc·a -ōrum *n*) *m* place, site, spot, locality, district; place, seat; period, period of time; opportunity, room, occasion; situation, position, category; rank, degree, birth; passage in a book; topic, subject, point, division; (mil) position, post, station; **adhuc locorum** till now; **ad id locorum** till then; **ex aequo loco dicere** to speak in the senate; to hold a conversation; **ex or de loco superiore dicere** to speak from the rostrum; **ex loco inferiore dicere** to speak before a judge, speak in court; **inde loci** since then; **in eo loci** in such a condition; **interea loci** meanwhile; **loci communes** general topics; public places, parks; **loco** (with *genit*) instead of; **loco** or **in loco** at the right time; **loco cedere** to give way, yield; **postea loci** afterwards; **post id locorum** afterwards; **ubicumque loci** whenever

lōcust·a -ae *f* locust

Lōcust·a -ae *f* woman notorious as poisoner in the time of Claudius and Nero

locūtĭ·ō -ōnis *f* speech; way of speaking, pronunciation

locūtus *pp* of loquor

lōd·ix -īcis *f* blanket

logic·us -a -um *adj* logical; *n pl* logic

log·os or **log·us -ī** *m* word; witticism; *m pl* mere words, empty talk

lōlīgō see lolligo

lol·ium -iī or **-iī** *n* darnel

lollīg·ō or **lōlīg·ō -ĭnis** *f* cuttlefish

lolligunŏul·a -ae *f* small cuttlefish

lōment·um -ī *n* face cream

Londin·ium -iī or **-iī** *n* London

longaev·us -a -um *adj* aged

longē *adv* far, far off, long way off; away, distant; out of reach, of no avail; long, for a long period; (to speak) at greater length; (with comparatives) far, by far, much; **longe lateque** far and wide, everywhere

longinquit·ās -ātis *f* length, extent; remoteness, distance; length, duration

longinqu·us -a -um *adj* long, extensive; far off, distant, remote; from afar, foreign; long, prolonged, continued, tedious; **ex** or **e longinquo** from far away

longĭter *adv* far

longitūd·ō -ĭnis *f* length; **in longitudinem** lengthwise

longiuscŭl·us -a -um *adj* pretty long

longur·ius -iī or **-ī** *m* long pole

long·us -a -um *adj* long; spacious; long, protracted, drawn-out; tedious; **longa navis** battleship; **longum esse** (with *inf*) to be tedious to; *n* length; **in longum** for a long while; **ne longum faciam** in short

loquācĭt·ās -ātis *f* talkativeness

loquācĭter *adv* long-windedly; at length, in detail

loquācŭl·us -a -um *adj* rather talkative

loqu·ax -ācis *adj* talkative, loquacious

loquell·a -ae *f* speech, language

loquĭt·or -ārī -ātus *vi* to chatter away

loquor loquī locūtus sum *vt* to say; to talk of, speak about; to tell, tell of, mention; (fig) to declare, show, indicate; *vi* to speak; to rustle, murmur

lōrār·ius -iī or **-ī** *m* flogger, slave driver

lōrāt·us -a -um *adj* tied with thongs

lōrĕ·us -a -um *adj* striped

lōrĭc·a -ae *f* breastplate; parapet; **libros mutare lorĭcis** to exchange books for arms

lōrĭcāt·us -a -um *adj* wearing a breastplate

lōrĭp·ēs -ēdis *adj* bowlegged

lōr·um -ī *n* strip of leather, thong, strap; whip, scourge; leather badge; *n pl* reins

lōt·os or **lōt·us -ī** *f* lotus; flute (*of lotus wood*)

lōtus *pp* of **lavo**

lub- = lib-

lŭbentĭ·a -ae *f* pleasure

lūbrĭc·ō -āre *vt* to oil, grease, make smooth

lūbrĭc·us -a -um *adj* slippery; smooth; slimy; gliding; deceitful, tricky; precarious; *n* precarious situation, critical period

Lūc·a bōs (*genit:* **Lūc·ae bovis**) *f* elephant

Lūcānĭ·a -ae *f* district in S.W. Italy

Lūcānĭc·us -a -um *adj* Lucanian; *f* Lucanian sausage

Lūcān·us -a -um *adj* Lucanian; *m* Lucanian; Lucan (*M. Annaeus Lucanus, epic poet, 39-65 A.D.*)

lūc·ar -āris *n* forest tax

lŭcell·um -ī *n* slight profit

lūcĕō lūcēre luxī *vi* to shine, be light, glow, glitter, be clear; (fig) to be clear, be apparent, be conspicuous; *v impers* it is light, day is dawning

Lūcĕr·ēs -um *m pl* one of the three original Roman tribes

lucern·ae -ae *f* lamp; (fig) midnight oil

lūcescō or **lūciscō lūcescĕre luxī** *vi* to begin to shine; *v impers* it is getting light

lūcĭdē *adv* clearly, distinctly

lūcĭd·us -a -um *adj* shining, bright, clear; lucid, clear

lūcĭf·er -ĕra -ĕrum *adj* shiny

Lūcĭf·er -ĕrī *m* morning star; planet Venus; son of Aurora and Cephalus; day

lūcĭfŭg·us -a -um *adj* light-shunning

Lūcĭl·ius -iī or **-ī** *m* C. Lucilius (*first Roman satiric poet, c. 180-102 B.C.*)

Lucin·a -ae *f* goddess of childbirth; childbirth

lūciscō see **lucesco**

Lucrētĭ·a -ae *f* daughter of Spurius Lucretius and wife of Collatinus, who, having been raped by Sextus Tarquinius, committed suicide in 509 B.C.

Lucrēt·ius -iī or **-ī** *m* Spurius Lucretius (*father of Lucretia and consul in 509 B.C.*); Titus Lucretius Carus (*philosophical poet, 94?-55? B.C.*)

lucrĭfĭcābĭl·is -e or **lucrĭfĭc·us -a -um** *adj* profitable

lucrĭfŭg·a -ae *m* or *f* person not out for gain, disinterested person

Lucrīn·us -a -um *adj* Lucrine; *m* Lake Lucrine (*small lake near Baiae, famous for its oysters*)

lucrĭpĕt·a -ae *m* profiteer

lucr·or -ārī -ātus sum *vt* to gain, win, get

lucrōs·us -a -um *adj* profitable

lucr·um -ī *n* profit, gain; wealth; greed, love of gain; **lucri facere** to gain; **lucri fieri** to be gained; **lucro esse** (with *dat*) to be advantageous for (*someone*); **ponere in lucro** or **in lucris** to regard as gain

luctām·en -ĭnis *n* wrestling; struggle, effort

luct·ans -antis *adj* reluctant

luctātĭ·ō -ōnis *f* wrestling; struggle, contest

luctāt·or -ōris *m* wrestler

luctĭfĭc·us -a -um *adj* causing sorrow, doleful, woeful

luctĭsŏn·us -a -um *adj* sad-sounding

luct·or -ārī -ātus sum or **luct·ō -āre** *vi* to wrestle; (with *inf*) to struggle to

luctuōsĭus *adv* more pitifully

luctuōs·us -a -um *adj* causing sorrow, sorrowful; sad, feeling sad

luct·us -ūs *m* sorrow, mourning, grief, distress; signs of sorrow, mourning clothes; source of grief, affliction

lūcubrātĭ·ō -ōnis *f* moonlighting, working by lamp light; evening gossip; nighttime writing

lūcŭbr·ō -āre *vt* to compose at night; *vi* to moonlight, burn the midnight oil

lūculentē *adv* splendidly, well; (to beat) soundly

lūculenter *adv* brilliantly, smartly, very well

lūculent·us -a -um *adj* bright, brilliant; (fig) brilliant, smart, excellent; considerable (*wealth*); sound (*beating*); trustworthy (*sources*)

Lūcull·us -ī *m* Lucius Licinius Lucullus (*Roman general and politician,* 117-56 B.C.)

Lucūm·ō or **Lucm·ō -ōnis** *m* Etruscan prince, Etruscan priest

lūc·us -ī *m* sacred grove; woods

lūdi·a -ae *f* actress; gladiator (*female*)

lūdibr·ium -ī or **-ī** *n* derision; subject of derision, butt of ridicule; (fig) plaything, sucker; **ludibrio esse** (with *dat*) to be made a fool of by (*someone*), be taken in by (*someone*); **ludibrio habere** to take for a sucker, make fun of

lūdibund·us -a -um *adj* playful, playing around; without effort, without danger

lūdic·er -ra -rum *adj* for sport, in sport; **ludicra exercitatio** sports; athletics; **ludicrum praemium** sports award; **ludicra res** drama; *n* sport, game; toy; show, public game; stage play

lūdificābil·is -e *adj* used in mockery

lūdificāti·ō -ōnis *f* ridiculing, mocking; fooling, tricking

lūdificāt·or -ōris *m* mocker

lūdificāt·us -ūs *m* mockery

lūdific·ō -āre or **lūdific·or -ārī -ātus sum** *vt* to make a fool of, fool, take for a sucker; to fool, trick, baffle

lūdi·ō -ōnis or **lūd·ius -ī** or **-ī** *m* actor

lūdō lūdēre lūsī lūsum *vt* to play; to spend in play; to amuse oneself with, do for amusement, practice as a pastime; to imitate, mimic, mock, do a takeoff on, ridicule; to deceive, delude; *vi* to play; to frisk, frolic; to play around, make love; **aleā ludere** to shoot craps; **pilā ludere** to play ball, play tennis

lūd·us -ī *m* play, game, sport, pastime, diversion; school; mere child's play; joke, fun; playing around, fooling around, lovemaking; public show, public game; **amoto ludo** all joking aside; **in ludum ire** to go to school; **per ludum** as a joke, for fun; *m pl* public games, public exhibition; games, tricks; **ludos facere** or **ludos reddere** (with *dat*) to play tricks on, make fun of

luell·a -ae *f* expiation, atonement

lu·ēs -is *f* infection, contagion, plague, pestilence; calamity

Lugdūnens·is -e *adj* of Lyons

Lugdūn·um -ī *n* Lyons (*town in E. Gaul*)

lūgeō lugēre luxī *vt* to mourn, lament, deplore; *vi* to mourn, be in mourning; to be in mourning clothes

lūgubr·ia -ium *n pl* mourning clothes

lūgŭbr·is -e *adj* mourning; doleful; disastrous

lumbifrag·ium -ī or **-ī** *n* physical wreck

lumbric·us -ī *m* worm; (as term of reproach) worm

lumb·us -ī *m* loin; *m pl* loins; genital organs

lūm·en -ĭnis *n* light; lamp, torch; brightness, sheen, gleam; daylight; light of the eye, eye; light of life, life; window, window light; distinguished person, luminary, celebrity; glory, pride

lūminār·e -is *n* window

lūminōs·us -a -um *adj* luminous; (fig) bright, conspicuous

lūn·a -ae *f* moon; month; night; crescent (*worn as ornament by senators on their shoes*); **luna laborans** moon in eclipse, eclipse of the moon; **luna minor** waning moon

lūnār·is -e *adj* lunar, of the moon

lūnāt·us -a -um *adj* crescent-shaped

lūn·ō -āre *vt* to make crescentshaped, to shape like a crescent

lūnŭl·a -ae *f* little crescent (*ornament worn by women*)

lu·ō -ĕre -ī *vt* to wash; to cleanse, purge; to set free, let go; to pay (*debt of penalty*); to suffer, undergo; to atone for, expiate; to satisfy, appease; to avert by expiation or punishment

lup·a -ae *f* she-wolf; flirt, prostitute

lupān·ar -āris *n* brothel

lupāt·us -a -um *adj* jagged (*like wolf's teeth*); *m pl* or *n pl* jagged bit

Luperc·al -ālis *n* shrine on the Palatine hill sacred to Pan

Lupercāl·ia -ium *n pl* festival of Lycaean Pan, celebrated in February

Luperc·us -ī *m* Pan

lupill·us -ī *m* small lupine (*plant*)

lupin·us -a -um *adj* lupine, wolf's; *m & n* lupine, wolf's-bane (*plant*); stage money

lup·us -ī *m* wolf; (fish) pike; jagged bit; grapnel

lurc·ō -ōnis *m* glutton

lūrid·us -a -um *adj* pale-yellow, wan, ghastly, lurid; making pale

lūr·or -ōris *m* sallowness

luscini·a -ae *f* nightingale

lusciniŏl·a -ae *f* little nightingale

luscin·ius -ī or **-ī** *m* nightingale

lusciōs·us or **luscitiōs·us -a -um** *adj* purblind, partly blind

lusc·us -a -um *adj* one-eyed

lūsi·ō -ōnis *f* play, game

Lūsitān·ī -ōrum *m pl* Lusitanians

Lūsitāni·a -ae *f* Lusitania (*modern Portugal and W. part of Spain*)

lūsit·ō -āre *vi* to like to play

lūs·or -ōris *m* player, gambler; humorous writer; joker

lustrāl·is -e *adj* lustral, propitiatory; quinquennial

lustrāti·ō -ōnis *f* purification, lustration; wandering

lustr·ō -āre *vt* to purify; to travel

over, traverse; to check, examine;
to go around, encircle; to survey;
(mil) to review (troops); to light up,
make bright, illuminate; to scan
(with the eyes); to consider, review

lustr·or -ārī -ātus sum vi to frequent brothels

lustr·um -ī n haunt, den, lair; wilderness; brothel; sensuality; purificatory sacrifice, lustration; lustrum, period of five years; period of years; **ingens lustrum** one hundred years, century

lūsus pp of ludo

lūs·us -ūs m play, game, sport, amusement; playing around (amorously)

lūteŏl·us -a -um adj yellowish

lūte·us -a -um adj of mud, of clay; muddy; dirty, grimy; (fig) dirty; mud-colored; golden-yellow, yellow, orange

lutit·ō -āre vt to splatter with mud; (fig) to throw mud at

lut·ō -āre vt to make dirty

lutulent·us -a -um adj muddy, filthy; (fig) filthy; turbid (style)

lut·um -ī n mud, mire; clay; yellow

lux lūcis f light; light of day, daylight; light of day, life; public view, publicity; the public, the world; light of hope, encouragement; glory; elucidation; **luce** or **luci** by daylight, in the daytime; **lux aestiva** summer; **lux brumalis** winter

lux·ō -āre vt to put out of joint, dislocate

lux·or -ārī -ātus sum vi to live riotously, have a ball

luxurĭ·a -ae or **luxurĭ·ēs -ēī** f luxurience; luxury, extravagance, excess

luxurĭ·ō -āre or **luxurĭ·or -ārī -ātus sum** vi to grow luxuriantly; to luxuriate; (of the body) to swell up; (of animals) to be frisky; to run riot, lead a wild life

luxurĭōsē adv luxuriously, voluptuously

luxurĭōs·us -a -um adj luxuriant; exuberant; extravagant, voluptuous

lux·us -ūs m extravagance, excess, luxury; splendor, pomp, magnificence

Lyae·us -a -um adj Bacchic; m Bac-

chus; wine

Lycae·us -a -um adj Lycaean (esp. applied to Pan); m mountain in Arcadia where Jupiter and Pan were worshiped

Lycā·ōn -ŏnis m king of Arcadia, the father of Callisto, who was changed into a wolf

Lycāŏn·is -ĭdis f Callisto, who was changed into the Great Bear

Lycē·um or **Lycī·um -ī** n Aristotle's school at Athens

Lycĭ·us -a -um adj & m Lycian; f country in S.W. Asia Minor

lychnūch·us -ī m lamp stand; chandelier

lychn·us -ī m lamp

Lyctĭ·us -a -um adj Cretan

Lycurg·us -ī m Thracian king who prohibited the worship of Bacchus and was punished with madness and death; Spartan lawgiver (date unknown); Athenian orator and friend of Demosthenes (390-324 B.C.)

Lyc·us or **Lyc·os -ī** m husband of Antiope, who divorced her to marry Dirce

Lȳdĭ·us -a -um adj & m Lydian; Etruscan; f country of Asia Minor, whose capital was Sardis

Lȳd·us -a -um adj & m Lydian; Etruscan

lymph·a -ae f water, spring water; water nymph

lymphātĭc·us -a -um adj crazy, frantic; n craziness

lymphāt·us -a -um adj crazy, mad

Lyncē·us -a -um adj sharp-eyed; m Argonaut, famous for keen vision; son of Egyptus and Hypermnestra

lyn·x -cis m or f lynx

lyr·a -ae f lyre; lyric poetry, lyric

Lyr·a -ae f Lyra (constellation)

lyrĭc·us -a -um adj lyric; of the lyre; m pl lyric poets; n pl lyric poems

lyrist·ēs -ae m lyrist

Lyrnēs·is or **Lyrnēs·is -ĭdis** f Briseis

Lyrnēs·us -ī f town in the Troad, the birthplace of Briseis

Lysĭ·ās -ae m Athenian orator in the time of Socrates (c. 450-370 B.C.)

M

Macăr·eus -ĕī or **-ĕos** m son of Aeolus, who lived in incest with his sister Canace

Macĕd·ō -ŏnis m Macedonian

Macedonĭc·us -a -um adj Macedonian

Macedonĭ·us -a -um adj Macedonian; f Macedonia (country lying between Thessaly and Thrace)

macell·um -ī n butcher shop, meat market

mac·ĕō -ēre vi to be lean, be skinny

mac·er -ĕra -ĕrum adj lean; skinny; thin, poor (soil)

Mac·er -rī m C. Licinius Macer (Roman historian and orator who was impeached by Cicero and committed suicide in 66 B.C.); C. Licinius Macer Calvus (*son of the former, and distinguished orator and poet, 82-46 B.C.*)

mācerī·a -ae *f* brick or stone wall; garden wall

mācer·ō -āre *vt* to knead, soften, make tender; to weaken, waste; to distress, vex, torment

macesc·ō -ere *vi* to grow thin

machaer·a -ae *f* sword

machaerophŏr·us -ī *m* soldier armed with sword

Machā·ōn -ŏnis *m* famous physician of the Greeks in the Trojan War and son of Aesculapius

Machāonĭus -a -um *adj* surgical

māchĭn·a -ae *f* machine, engine; crane; pulley, windlass, winch; (fig) scheme, stratagem

māchināment·um -ī *n* machine, engine, contrivance

māchinātĭ·ō -ōnis *f* mechanism; machine; trick

māchināt·or -ōris *m* engineer, machinist; (fig) contriver

māchĭn·or -ārī -ātus sum *vt* to engineer, design, contrive; to scheme, plot

macĭ·ēs -ēī *f* leanness, thinness; barrenness; poverty (*of style*)

macilent·us -a -um *adj* skinny

macresc·ō -ere *vi* to grow thin, get skinny

macritūd·ō -ĭnis *f* leanness, skinniness

macrocoll·um -ī *n* large-size sheet of paper

mactābĭl·is -e *adj* deadly

mactāt·us -ūs *m* sacrifice

mactē *interj* well done!; good luck!

mact·ō -āre *vt* to magnify, glorify, honor; to sacrifice; to slaughter, put to death; to destroy, ruin, overthrow; to trouble, afflict

mact·us -a -um *adj* glorified, honored, adored; **macte virtute** (**esto**) (*congratulatory exclamation*) good luck!; well done!

macŭl·a -ae *f* spot, stain, blemish; mesh (*of a net*); (fig) stigma, blemish, disgrace, defect

macŭl·ō -āre *vt* to spot; to stain; to defile, pollute; to dishonor

maculōs·us -a -um *adj* spotted; stained

made·faciō -facĕre -fēcī -factum (*passive*: **made·fīō -fĭerī -factus sum**) *vt* to wet, moisten, drench, soak, steep

mad·ens -entis *adj* wet, moist; flowing (*hair*); melting (*snow*); reeking (*with blood*)

mad·ĕō -ēre -uī *vi* to be wet, be moist, be soaked, be drenched; to drip; to flow; to be soused; to be full, overflow

mad·escō -escĕre -uī *vi* to become wet, become moist

madĭdē *adv* drunkenly

madĭd·us -a -um *adj* wet, moist, drenched; dyed, steeped; drunk

mad·or -ōris *m* moisture

madŭls·a -ae *m* souse, drunkard

Maeand·er or **Maeandr·os** or **Maeandr·us -ī** *m* river in Asia Minor, famous for its winding course; winding; winding border; devious course

Maecēn·ās -ātis *m* C. Cilnius Maecenas (*adviser to Augustus and friend of Virgil and Horace, d. 8 B.C.*)

maen·a -ae *f* sprat (*fish*)

Maenăl·is -ĭdis *adj* **Maenalis ursa** Callisto (*who was changed into the Great Bear*)

Maenăl·us or **Maenăl·os -ī** *m* or **Maenăl·a -ōrum** *n pl* Mt. Maenalus (*mountain range in Arcadia, sacred to Pan*)

Maen·as -ădis *f* Bacchante

Maenĭ·us -a -um *adj* Maenian; **Maenia Columna** pillar in the forum at which thieves, slaves, and debtors were tried and flogged

Maeŏn·es -um *m pl* Maeonians (*ancient name of the Lydians*)

Maeonĭd·ēs -ae *m* native of Maeonia; Homer; Etrurian

Maeŏn·is -ĭdis *f* Maeonian woman (*esp. Arachne or Omphale*)

Maeonĭ·us -a -um *adj* Lydians; Homeric; Etruscan; *f* Maeonia, Lydia; Etruria

Maeōt·ae -ārum *m pl* Scythian tribe on Lake Maeotis on the N.E. coast of the Black Sea

Maeōt·is -ĭdis *adj* Maeotic; Scythian; **Maeotis lacus** Sea of Azov

maer·ĕō -ēre *vi* to mourn

maer·or -ōris *m* mourning, sadness

maestĭter *adv* like a mourner

maestitĭ·a -ae *f* sadness, gloom, melancholy

maestitūd·ō -ĭnis *f* sadness

maest·us -a -um *adj* mourning, sad, gloomy

Maev·ĭus -ĭī or **-ī** *m* poetaster often ridiculed by Virgil and Horace

māgāl·ĭa -ĭum *n pl* huts

mage see **magis**

magĭc·us -a -um *adj* magic; **artes magicae** magic

magis or **mage** *adv* more, in a higher degree, rather; **eo magis** all the more, the more; **magis magisque** more and more; **magis . . . quam** or **magis . . . atque** rather . . . than; **non magis . . . quam** not so much . . . as

magist·er -rī *m* chief, master, director; teacher; adviser, guardian; ringleader, author; captain, pilot; (in apposition with another noun) expert; **magister morum** censor; **magister sacrorum** chief priest

magister·ĭum -ĭī or **-ī** *n* directorship, presidency; **magisterium morum** censorship

magistr·a -ae *f* directress, mistress, instructress

magistrāt·us -ūs *m* magisterial office, magistracy; magistrate, official; body of magistrates; military command

magnanimit·ās -ātis *f* magnanimity; bravery

magnanim·us -a -um *adj* magnanimous; brave

Magn·ēs -ētis *adj* & *m* Magnesian; *f* city in Caria, near the Meander; city in Lydia near Mt. Sipylus; district in Thessaly on the Aegean Sea

magnidic·us -a -um *adj* talking big

magnificē *adv* magnificently, splendidly; pompously

magnificenti·a -ae *f* magnificence, grandeur, splendor; pompousness

magnific·ō -āre *vt* to think much of

magnific·us -a -um *adj* grand, great, splendid, august; rich, costly, magnificent; pompous

magniloquenti·a -ae *f* lofty style; pompous language

magnilŏqu·us -a -um *adj* sublime; bragging

magnitūd·ō -inis *f* greatness, magnitude, size; large quantity, large number; vastness, extent

magnopĕre or **magnō opĕre** *adv* greatly, very much, particularly; strongly, earnestly, heartily, urgently

magn·us -a -um (*comp:* **major**; *superl:* **maximus**) *adj* big, large, great; long (*time*); high (*price*); important, momentous; significant; impressive; high, powerful (*in rank*); loud (*voice*); heavy (*rain*); advanced (*age*); noble (*character*); proud, boastful; *n* great thing; great value; **magni (pretii) aestimare** or **magni habere** to value highly, have a high regard for; **magno emere** to buy at a high price; **magno vendere** to sell at a high price; **vir magno jam natu** aged man, man advanced in years

mag·us -a -um *adj* magic; **artes magae** magic; *m* learned man (*among the Persians*); magician

Māi·us -a -um *adj* & *m* May; *f* daughter of Atlas and Pleione, and mother of Mercury by Jupiter

mājāl·is -is *m* castrated hog; (as term of abuse) swine

mājest·ās -ātis *f* majesty, dignity, grandeur; high treason; sovereign power, sovereignty; authority

māj·or -us (*comp* of **magnus**) *adj* bigger, larger, greater; **annos natu major quadraginta** forty years older; **in majus ferre** to exaggerate; **majoris (pretii)** at a higher price; more highly; **major natu** elder, older

mājōr·ēs -um *m pl* ancestors, forefathers

mājuscŭl·us -a -um *adj* somewhat greater; a little older

māl·a -ae *f* cheekbone, upper jaw; *f pl* cheek; (fig) jaws (*e.g., of death*)

malaci·a -ae *f* calm at sea, dead calm

malaciss·ō -āre *vt* to soften, soften up

malăc·us -a -um *adj* soft; luxurious

male *adv* badly, wrongly; wickedly, cruelly, maliciously; unfortunately, unsuccessfully, awkwardly; excessively, extremely, very much; (with adjectives having a good sense) not, scarcely, not at all; (with adjectives having a bad sense) very much; terribly; **male audīre** to be ill spoken of; **male dicere** (with *dat*) to say nasty things to, abuse; **male emere** to buy at a high price; **male facere** (with *dat*) to treat badly or cruelly; **male habere** to harass; **male metuere** to be terribly afraid of; **male vendere** to sell at a loss; **male vivere** to be a failure in life

maledic·ax -ācis *adj* abusive, foul-mouthed

maledicē *adv* abusively, slanderously

maledīc·ens -entis *adj* abusive, foul-mouthed

male-dīcō -dīcĕre -dīxī -dictum *vi* (with *dat*) **a** to speak ill of, abuse, slander; **b** to say nasty things to

maledictī·ō -ōnis *f* abusive language, abuse

maledictĭt·ō -āre *vi* (with *dat*) to keep saying nasty things to

maledict·um -ī *n* curse; abuse

maledĭc·us -a -um *adj* abusive, scurrilous, foul-mouthed

malefact·or -ōris *m* malefactor

malefact·um or **malfact·um -ī** *n* wrong, injury

maleficē *adv* mischievously

maleficenti·a -ae *f* harm, wrong, mischief

malefic·ium -iī or **-ī** *n* evil deed, crime, offense; harm, injury, wrong, mischief; **maleficium admittere** or **committere** to commit an offense or crime

malefĭc·us -a -um *adj* wicked, vicious, criminal; *m* mischief-maker

malesuād·us -a -um *adj* seductive, tempting

malevŏl·ens -entis *adj* spiteful

malevolenti·a -ae *f* spitefulness, malice, meanness

malevŏl·us -a -um *adj* spiteful, malicious, mean; *mf* enemy; jealous person

malĭf·er -ĕra -ĕrum *adj* apple-growing

malignē *adv* spitefully, jealously, meanly; stingily, grudgingly

malignit·ās -ātis *f* spite, malice, jealousy, meanness; stinginess

malign·us -a -um *adj* spiteful, malicious, jealous, mean; stingy; (fig) stingy, unproductive (*soil*); scanty (*light*)

maliti·a -ae *f* malice, ill-will, bad behavior; *f pl* devilish tricks

malitiōsē *adv* craftily, wickedly

malitiōs·us -a -um *adj* crafty, wicked, malicious, devilish

mallĕŏl·us -ī *m* small hammer, small mallet; fiery arrow

mallĕ·us -ī *m* hammer, mallet; pole-ax (*for slaughtering animals*)

mālō or **māvŏlō malle mālŭī** *vt* to prefer; *vi* (with *dat*) to incline toward, be more favorably disposed to

malobăthr·um -ī *n* malobathrum oil, betel juice

māl·um -ī *n* apple; **aureum malum** quince; **felix malum** lemon; **malum Punicum** or **malum granatum** pomegranate

mal·um -ī *n* evil, ill; harm; punishment; disaster; hardship

mālus -ī *m* mast (*of ship*); pole; *f* apple tree

mal·us -a -um *adj* bad; ill, evil; ugly; unpatriotic; adverse, unsuccessful; unlucky; **i in malam rem** go to hell!; *n see* **malum**

malv·a -ae *f* mallow

Mām·ers -ertis *m* Mars

Māmertĭn·ī -ōrum *m pl* (*mercenaries of Agathocles who after his death seized Messana, c. 282 B.C., and precipitated the First Punic War*)

mamill·a -ae *f* breast, teat

mamm·a -ae *f* breast (*of a woman*); dug

mammeāt·us -a -um *adj* large-breasted, full-bosomed

mānābĭl·is -e *adj* penetrating (*cold*)

manc·eps -ĭpis *m* purchaser; contractor

mancĭp·ium or **mancŭp·ium -iī** or **-ī** *n* formal purchase; possession, right of ownership; slave; **mancipio accipere** to take possession of; **mancipio dare** to turn over possession of; **res mancipi** possessions basic to running a farm (*e.g., land, slaves, livestock, farm implements*); **res nec mancipi** possessions other than those needed to run a farm

mancĭp·ō or **mancŭp·ō -āre** *vt* to sell, transfer

manc·us -a -um *adj* crippled, maimed; (*fig*) defective, imperfect

mandāt·um -ī *n* command, order, commission; *n pl* instructions

mandāt·us -ūs *m* command, order

mand·ō -āre *vt* to commit, entrust; to command, order, enjoin, commission

mandō mandĕre mandī mansum *vt* to chew; to champ; to eat, devour; **humum mandere** to bite the dust (*said of those who fall in battle*)

mandr·a -ae *f* stable, stall; drove of cattle; checkerboard

manduc·us -ī *m* mask representing a glutton

māne (indecl) *n* morning; *adv* early in the morning; **bene mane** very early; **cras mane** tomorrow morning; **heri mane** yesterday morning; **hodie mane** this morning; **postridie ejus diei mane** the following morning

manĕō manēre mansī mansum *vt*

to wait for, await; *vi* to stay, remain; to stop off, pass the night; to last, endure, continue, persist; **in condicione manere** to stick by an agreement; **in sententia manere** to stick to an opinion

mān·ēs -ĭum *m pl* souls of the dead; ghosts; lower world; last remains (*of the body*), ashes

mang·ō -ōnis *m* pushy salesman; slave dealer

manic·ae -ārum *f pl* handcuffs; grappling hook; long sleeves; gloves

manicāt·us -a -um *adj* long-sleeved

manicŭl·a -ae *f* little hand

manifestē *adv* plainly, distinctly

manifestō *adv* manifestly, evidently, plainly

manifest·ō -āre *vt* to reveal, betray

manifest·us -a -um *adj* manifest, plain, clear, distinct; exposed, brought to light, detected, caught; (with *genit*) convicted of, caught in; (with *inf*) known to

manipl- = **manipul-**

manipulār·is -e *adj* of a maniple or company; **miles manipularis** private

manipulār·is -is *m* private; soldier of the same company; comrade

manipulātim *adv* by companies

manipŭl·us or **manĭpl·us -ī** *m* handful (*esp. of hay*); (coll) gang; (mil) maniple, company (*three of which constituted a cohort*)

Manl·ius -iī or **-ī** *m* M. Manlius Capitolinus (*consul in 392 B.C., who, in 389 B.C., saved the Capitoline from the invading Gauls*); T. Manlius Torquatus (*consul in 340 B.C., famous for his military discipline*)

mannŭl·us -ī *m* pony

mann·us -ī *m* small Gallic horse

mān·ō -āre *vi* to drip, trickle, flow; to stream; (fig) to spread, emanate

mansĭ·ō -ōnis *f* stopover

mansĭt·ō -āre *vi* to stay on

mansuē·faciō -facĕre -fēcī -factum (*passive*): **mansuē·fīō -fĭĕrī -factus sum**) *vt* to tame; (fig) to tame, pacify, civilize

mansu·ēs -is or **-ētis** *adj* tame, mild

mansu·escō -escĕre -ēvī -ētum *vt* to tame; *vi* to grow tame, become tame; (fig) to grow gentle, grow mild

mansuētē *adv* gently, mildly

mansuētūd·ō -ĭnis *f* mildness, gentleness

mansuēt·us -a -um *adj* tame; mild, gentle

mansus *pp of* **mando** and **maneo**

mantēl·e -is *n* napkin, towel

mantell·um or **mantēl·um -ī** *n* mantle

mantĭc·a -ae *f* knapsack

mantĭcĭn·or -ārī -ātus sum *vi* to predict, prophesy

mant·ō -āre *vt* to wait for; *vi* to stay, remain, wait

Mant·ō -ūs *f* prophetic daughter of Tiresias

Mantŭ·a -ae *f* birthplace of Virgil, in N. Italy

manuāl·is -e *adj* that can be held in hand, hand-sized (*e.g., rocks*)

manubĭ·ae -ārum *f pl* money derived from the sale of booty

manubĭārĭ·us -a -um *adj* (coll) bringing in the loot

manūbr·ium -iī or **-ī** *n* handle; hilt

manufestārĭ·us -a -um *adj* plain, obvious

manulĕ·a -ae *f* long sleeve

manuleār·ius -iī or **-ī** *m* sleeve maker

manuleāt·us -a -um *adj* long-sleeved

manūmissĭ·ō -ōnis *f* manumission, freeing of a slave

manŭ·mittō or **manū·mittō -mittēre -mīsī -missum** *vt* to manumit, emancipate, set free (*a slave*)

manupretĭum -iī or **-ī** *n* workman's pay, wages; (fig) pay, reward

man·us -ūs *f* hand; band, company; gang; force, violence, close combat; finishing touch; handwriting; work; workmanship; elephant's trunk; grappling irons; power; (law) power of the husband over his wife; **ad manum habere** to have at hand, have in readiness; **ad manum venire** to come within reach; **e manu** at a distance, from a distance; **in manibus esse** to be in everyone's hands, be well known; to be near, be at hand; to be present; **in manu esse** (with *genit*) to be in the power of, be under the jurisdiction of; **in manu esse** (with *dat*) to be obvious to; **inter manus** under one's hands, with one's care; in one's hands, in one's arms; **manibus pedibusque** (fig) with might and main; **manu** by hand, artificially; (mil) by force of arms; **manu tenere** to know for sure; **manum committere, conserere,** or **conferre** to begin to fight; **manum dare** to lend a hand; **manum injicere** (with *dat*) to lay hands on, arrest; **manus dare** or **manus dedere** to give oneself up, surrender; **per manus** by hand; by force, by main force; from hand to hand, from mouth to mouth, from father to son; **plenā manu** generously; **prae manibus** or **prae manu** at hand, in readiness; **sub manu** or **sub manum** at hand, near; immediately

mapāl·ĭa -ĭum *n pl* African huts; African village, kraal

mapp·a -ae *f* napkin; flag (*used in starting races at the racetrack*)

Marăth·ōn -ōnis *f* site, in E. Attica, of victory by Miltiades over the Persians (490 B.C.)

Marcell·us -ī *m* Roman cognomen in the gens Claudia; M. Claudius Marcellus (*nephew of Augustus, whose premature death is referred to in the Aeneid*, 43-23 B.C.)

marc·ĕō -ēre *vi* to wither, droop, shrivel; to be weak, be feeble, be decrepit, be run-down; to slack off

marcesc·ō -ēre *vi* to begin to wither, begin to droop; to become weak, become run-down; to become lazy

marcĭd·us -a -um *adj* withered, drooping; groggy

Marc·ius -iī or **-ī** *m* Ancus Marcius (*fourth king of Rome*)

marcŭl·us -ī *m* small hammer

mar·e -is *n* sea; seawater, saltwater; **mare inferum** Tyrrhenian Sea; **mare nostrum** Mediterranean Sea; **mare superum** Adriatic Sea

Mareŏt·a -ae *f* town and lake near Alexandria in Egypt

Mareōtic·us -a -um *adj* Mareotic; Egyptian

margarĭt·a -ae *f* or **margarīt·um -ī** *n* pearl

margĭn·ō -āre *vt* to furnish with a border; to curb (*a street*)

marg·ō -ĭnis *f* margin, edge, border; frontier

Marĭăn·ī -ōrum *m pl* partisans of Marius

Marĭc·a -ae *f* nymph of Minturnae, mother of Latinus

marīn·us -a -um *adj* sea, of the sea, marine

marisc·a -ae *f* fig; **tumidae mariscae** the piles

marĭt·a -ae *f* wife, married woman

marĭtāl·is -e *adj* marital, nuptial, matrimonial

marĭtĭmus or **marĭtŭm·us -a -um** *adj* sea, of the sea; seafaring, maritime; (fig) changeable (*like the sea*); **ora maritima** seacoast; *n pl* seacoast

marĭt·ō -āre *vt* to marry; to train (*a vine to a tree*)

marĭt·us -a -um *adj* matrimonial nuptial; *m* husband, married man; lover; *f* see **marita**

Mar·ius -iī or **-ī** *m* C. Marius (*conqueror of Jugurtha and of the Cimbri and Teutons, and seven times consul*, 157-86 B.C.)

marm·or -ŏris *n* marble; marble statue, marble monument; smooth surface of the sea

marmorĕ·us -a -um *adj* marble, made of marble; marble-like

Mar·ō -ōnis *m* cognomen of Virgil

marr·a -ae *f* hoe, weeding hook

Mar·s -tis *m* god of war and father of Romulus and Remus; battle, war; engagement; planet; **aequo Marte** on an equal footing; **suo Marte** by one's own exertions, independently

Mars·ī -ōrum *m pl* Marsians (*a people of S. central Italy, regarded as tough warriors*)

marsupp·ium -iī or **-ī** *n* pouch, purse

Marsў·ās or **Marsў·a -ae** *m* satyr who challenged Apollo with the flute and was flayed alive upon his defeat; statue in the Roman forum of Marsyas

Martiāl·is -is *m* M. Valerius Martialis (*commonly called Martial and famous for his epigrams, c.* 40-120 A.D.)

Marticŏl·a -ae *m* worshiper of Mars

Marti·us -a -um *adj* Martian, of Mars; sacred to Mars; descended from Mars; March; *m* March, month of March

mās maris *adj* male, masculine; manly, masculine, brave; *m* male

masculīn·us -a -um *adj* male, masculine

mascŭl·us -a -um *adj* male, masculine; manly, vigorous; *m* male

mass·a -ae *f* mass, lump; (coll) chunk of money

Massic·us -a -um *adj* Massic; *m* Mt. Massicus (*between Latium and Campania, famous for its wine*); *n* Massic (*wine*)

Massili·a -ae *f* Greek colony on S. coast of Gaul (*modern Marseilles*)

Massȳl·ī -ōrum *m pl* tribe of E. Numidia

mastigī·a ae *m* rascal

mastrūc·a -ae *f* sheepskin; (as term of abuse) ninny

mastrūcāt·us -a -um *adj* clothed in sheepskin

matär·a -ae or **matăr·is -is** *f* Celtic javelin

matell·a -ae *f* chamber pot

matellī·ō -ōnis *m* pot

māt·er -ris *f* mother; matron; **mater familias** lady of the house; (of animals) dam; cause, origin, source

mātercŭl·a -ae *f* a little mother, poor mother

māt·erfamiliās -risfamiliās *f* lady of the house, mistress of the household

māteri·a -ae or **māterī·ēs -ēī** *f* matter, stuff, material; lumber, wood, timber; fuel; subject, subject matter, theme, topic; cause, source, occasion, opportunity; capacity, natural ability, disposition

māteriār·ius -iī or **-ī** *m* timber merchant

māteriāt·us -a -um *adj* built with lumber; **male materiatus** built with poor lumber

māteriēs see **materia**

māteri·or -ārī -ātus sum *vi* to fetch or gather wood

mātern·us -a -um *adj* maternal, mother's, of a mother

mātertĕr·a -ae *f* aunt, mother's sister

mathēmatic·us -ī *m* mathematician; astrologer

Matīn·us -ī *m* mountain in Apulia, near Horace's birthplace

mātricīd·a -ae *m* matricide, mother's murderer

mātricīd·ium -iī or **-ī** *n* matricide, murder of one's mother

mātrimōn·ium -iī or **-ī** *n* matrimony, marriage; **in matrimonium ire** to enter matrimony, get married; **in matrimonium aliquam ducere** to marry some girl

mātrim·us -a -um *adj* having a mother still living

mātrōn·a -ae *f* married woman, matron, wife; woman of quality, lady

Mātrōnāl·ia -ium *n pl* festival celebrated by matrons on March 1 in honor of Mars

mātrōnāl·is -e *adj* matronly, womanly, wifely

matt·a -ae *f* straw mat

matŭl·a -ae *f* pot; chamber pot

mātūrātē *adv* in good time

mātūrē *adv* at the right time; in time; betimes, in good time, promptly, quickly; prematurely

mātūr·escō -escĕre -ŭī *vi* to get ripe, ripen, mature

mātūrit·ās -ātis *f* ripeness, maturity; (fig) maturity, height, perfection

mātūr·ō -āre *vt* to ripen, bring to maturity; to accelerate, speed up; (with *inf*) to be too quick in doing; *vi* to hasten

mātūr·us -a -um *adj* ripe, mature, full-grown; opportune, at the right time; early, coming early (*e.g., winter*); advanced in years; marriageable; mellow (*with age*)

Mātūt·a -ae *f* goddess of the dawn

mātūtīn·us -a -um *adj* morning, early; **tempora matutina** morning hours

Mauritāni·a -ae *f* country of N.W. Africa

Maur·us -a -um *adj* Moorish; African

Maurūsi·us -a -um *adj* Moorish, Mauretanian

Māvor·s -tis *m* Mars

Māvorti·us -a -um *adj* Martian, of Mars

maxill·a -ae *f* jaw

maximē or **maxŭmē** *adv* very, most, especially, particularly; just, precisely, exactly; (in sequences) in the first place, first of all; (in affirmations) by all means; certainly, yes; **immo maxime** certainly not; **nuper maxime** just recently; **quam maxime** as much as possible; **tum cum maxime** at the precise moment when; **tum maxime** just then, precisely at that time; **ut maxime . . . ita maxime** the more . . . so much the more

maximit·ās -ātis *f* magnitude

maximus or **maxŭmus** (*superl* of **magnus**) see **magnus**

mazonŏm·us -ī *m* large dish

meāmet = meā, *abl fem sing* of **meus**, strengthened by **-met**

meapte = mea, *nom fem sing* of **meus**, strengthened by **-pte**

meāt·us -ūs *m* motion, movement; course, channel

mecastor *interj* by Castor!

mēd = me

mēcum = cum me

medd·ix or **med·ix -īcis** *m* magistrate (*among the Oscans*); **meddix tuticus** senior magistrate (*among the Oscans*)

Mēdē·a -ae *f* daughter of Aeetes, the king of Colchis, and wife of Jason, famous for her magic

Mēdē·is -idis *adj* magic

med·ens -entis *m* physician

med·eor -ērī *vt* to heal; *vi* (with *dat*) to heal, cure, be good for, remedy

Mēd·ī -ōrum *m pl* Medes; Persians; Parthians

Mēdi·a -ae *f* Asian country between Armenia, Parthia, Hyrcania, and Assyria

mediastin·us -ī *m* servant, drudge

mēdic·a -ae *f* alfalfa

medicābil·is -e *adj* curable

medicām·en -inis *n* medicine, remedy, drug, antidote; tincture; cosmetic; (fig) cure, remedy

medicāment·um -ī *n* medication, medicine; potion; (fig) relief, antidote; (rhet) embellishment

medicāt·us -ūs *m* magic charm

medicīn·a -ae *f* medicine, medical science; medicine, remedy; doctor's office; (with *genit*) (fig) cure for, remedy for

medic·ō -āre *vt* to medicate, cure; to dye

medic·or -ārī -ātus sum *vt* to cure; *vi* (with *dat*) to heal, cure

medic·us -a -um *adj* medical; healing; *m* doctor, surgeon

Mēdic·us -a -um *adj* Median, of the Medes

mediē *adv* moderately

mediēt·ās -ātis *f* mean

medimn·um -ī *n* or **medimn·us -ī** *m* bushel, medimnus (*containing six modii*)

mediōcr·is -e *adj* medium, average, ordinary; mediocre; narrow, small

mediocrit·ās -ātis *f* mean; moderation; mediocrity; *f pl* moderate passions

mediocriter *adv* moderately, fairly; not particularly, not very, not much; calmly

Mediōlān·um -ī *n* Milan

medioxim·us -a -um *adj* (coll) in the middle

meditāment·um -ī *n* practice, drill

meditātē *adv* purposely

meditātī·ō -ōnis *f* reflection, contemplation; practice; rehearsal; (with *genit*) reflection on, contemplation of

meditāt·us -a -um *adj* premeditated

mediterrāne·us -a -um *adj* inland

medit·or -ārī -ātus sum *vt* to think over, reflect on; to practice; to plan, design

medi·us -a -um *adj* middle, central, the middle of, in the middle; intervening (*time*); middling, ordinary, common; undecided, neutral, ambiguous; meddling; **in mediā insulā** in the middle of the island; **media pars** half, one half; *m* mediator; *n* middle, center; commu-

nity, common good; public, publicity; **e medio abire** to disappear; **in medio relinquere** to leave undecided, leave hanging in the air; **in medium** into the center; on behalf of the public; for the common good; **in medium proferre** to publish

medius fidius *interj* by Heaven!

med·ix -icis *m* magistrate (*among the Oscans*); **medix tuticus** senior magistrate

medull·a -ae *f* marrow; middle, center

medullitus *adv* (fig) with all one's heart

Medūs·a -ae *f* one of the three Gorgons, the daughter of Phorcys, whose eyes turned everything they looked upon into stone

Medūsae·us -a -um *adj* Medusan; **equus Medusaeus** Pegasus

Megaer·a -ae *f* one of the three Furies

Megalēns·ia or **Megalēs·ia -ium** *n pl* festival of Cybele, celebrated on the 4th of April

Megăr·a -ae *f* or **Megăr·a -ōrum** *n pl* town near Athens

Megarē·us or **Megaric·us -a -um** *adj* Megarean

megistān·es -um *m pl* grandees

mehercle or **mehercule** or **mehercŭles** *interj* by Hercules!

mēi·ō -ĕre *vi* to urinate

mel mellis *n* honey; **meum mel** (as term of endearment) my honey!; *n pl* drops of honey

melancholic·us -a -um *adj* melancholy

melandrў·um -ī *n* piece of salted tuna

Melanth·ius -iī or **-ī** *m* goatherd of Ulysses

melcŭl·um -ī *n* (*term of endearment*) little honey

Meleăg·er or **Meleăg·ros -rī** *m* son of King Oeneus of Calydon and participant in the famous Calydonian boar hunt

Meleagrīd·es -um *f pl* sisters of Meleager, who were changed into birds

Melicert·a or **Melicert·ēs -ae** *m* son of Ino and Athamas, who was changed into a sea god, called by the Greeks Palaemon and by the Romans Portunus

melic·us -a -um *adj* musical; lyric

melilōt·os -ī *m* clover

melimēl·a -ōrum *n pl* honey apples

melīn·a -ae *f* mead

mēlīn·a -ae *f* leather wallet

Mēlin·um -ī *n* pigment; Melian white

mel·ior -ius (*comp of* **bonus**) *adj* better

melisphyll·um -ī *n* balm

Melīt·a or **Melīt·ē -ēs** *f* Malta

Melitens·is -e *adj* Maltese

melius (*comp of* **bene**) *adv* better

meliuscŭlē *adv* pretty well

meliuscŭl·us -a -um *adj* a little better

mell·a -ae *f* mead

mellicŭl·us -a -um *adj* sweet as honey

mellif·er -ĕra -ĕrum *adj* honey-producing

mellific·ō -āre *vi* to make honey

mellill·a -ae *f* (term of endearment) little honey

mellīn·a -ae *f* sweetness, delight

mellīn·a -ae *f* leather wallet

mellīt·us -a -um *adj* honeyed, sweetened with honey; sweet as honey

mel·os -ī (Greek *pl*: **mel·e**) *n* tune, melody, song

Melpomĕn·ē -ēs *f* Muse of tragic poetry

membrān·a -ae *f* membrane, skin; slough; parchment; film

membrānŭl·a -ae *f* small piece of parchment

membrātim *adv* limb by limb; piecemeal, singly; in short sentences

membr·um -ī *n* limb, member; part, division; clause

mēmet *pron* (emphatic form of **me**) me

memin·ī -isse *vt* to remember; *vi* (with *genit*) to be mindful of, remember

Memn·ōn -ŏnis *m* son of Tithonus and Aurora, king of the Ethiopians, and ally of the Trojans, who was killed by Achilles

Memnŏnĭd·es -um *f pl* birds that rose from the pyre of Memnon

Memnŏnĭ·us -a -um *adj* Memnonian; Oriental, Moorish, black

mem·or -ŏris *adj* mindful, remembering; having a good memory; reminding; (with *genit*) mindful of, remembering

memorābĭl·is -e *adj* memorable, remarkable

memorand·us -a -um *adj* worth mentioning, notable

memorāt·us -ūs *m* mention

memorĭ·a -ae *f* memory; remembrance; period of recollection, recollection, time, lifetime; a memory, past event, history; historical account; **memoriae prodere** to hand down to posterity; **paulo supra hanc memoriam** not long ago; **post hominum memoriam** within the memory of man; **superiore memoriā** in earlier times

memorĭŏl·a -ae *f* weak memory

memorĭter *adv* from memory, by heart; accurately, correctly

memŏr·ō -āre *vt* to mention, bring up, relate; to name, call; *vi* (with **de** + *abl*) to speak of

Memph·is -is or -idos *f* city in central Egypt

Memphītĭc·us -a -um *adj* Egyptian

Menand·er or Menand·ros -rī *m* Greek comic playwright, the most important representative of the Attic New Comedy (342-291 B.C.)

Menandrē·us -a -um *adj* of Menander

mend·a -ae *f* fault, blemish

mendācilŏqui·or -us *adj* more false, more mendacious

mendāc·ium -iī or -ī *n* lie

mendāciuncŭl·um *n* white lie, fib

mend·ax -ācis *adj* mendacious, given to lying, false; *m* liar

mendīcābŭl·um -ī *n* beggary

mendīcĭt·ās -ātis *f* beggary

mendīc·ō -āre or mendīc·or -ārī -ātus sum *vt* to beg, beg for; *vi* to beg, go begging

mendīcŭl·us -a -um *adj* beggarly

mendīc·us -a -um *adj* needy, poor, poverty-stricken; (fig) poor, sorry, paltry; *m* beggar

mendōsē *adv* faultily, carelessly

mendōs·us -a -um *adj* full of physical defects; full of faults, faulty, incorrect, erroneous; blundering

mend·um -ī *n* defect, fault; blunder

Menelā·us -ī *m* son of Atreus, brother of Agamemnon, and husband of Helen

Menen·ĭus -iī or ī *m* Menenius Agrippa (*patriotic Roman who told the plebs the fable of the belly and the limbs during the secession of the plebs in 494 B.C.*)

Monoec·eus -ĕī or -ĕos *m* son of Theban king Creon, who hurled himself off the city walls to save the city

Menoetĭăd·es -ae *m* Patroclus

Menoet·ĭus -iī or -ī *m* father of Patroclus

men·s -tis *f* mind, intellect; understanding, reason; thought, opinion, intention, plan; courage, boldness; passion, impulse; **addere mentem** to give courage; **captus mente** crazy; **demittere mentem** to lose heart; **in mentem venire** to come to mind; **mentis suae esse** to be in one's right mind

mens·a -ae *f* table; meal, course, dinner; guests at table; counter; bank; sacrificial table, altar; **mensa secunda** dessert

mensār·ĭus -iī or -ī *m* banker; treasurer, treasury-board member

mensĭ·ō -ōnis *f* measure, measuring; quantity (*of a syllable*)

mens·is -is *m* month; **primo mense** at the beginning of the month

mens·or -ōris *m* surveyor

menstruāl·is -e *adj* for a month

menstru·us -a -um *adj* monthly; lasting for a month; *n* rations for a month; month's term of office

mensŭl·a -ae *f* little table

mensūr·a -ae *f* measuring, measurement; standard of measure; amount, size, proportion, capacity, extent, limit, degree

mens·us *pp* of **metior**

ment·a or menth·a -ae *f* mint

menti·ens -entis *m* sophism, fallacy

mentĭ·ō -ōnis *f* mention; **mentio-**

nem facere (with *genit* or **de** + *abl*) to make mention of; **mentiones serere** (with **ad** + *acc*) to throw hints to

ment·ior -īrī -ītus sum *vt* to invent, fabricate; to feign, imitate, fake; *vi* to lie; to act deceitfully

Ment·or -ōris *m* friend of Ulysses; famous artist in metalwork; ornamental cup

ment·um -ī *n* chin

mē·ō -āre *vi* to go, pass

mephīt·is -is *f* malaria

mepte *pron* (emphatic form of **mē**) me, me myself

merācul·us or **merācl·us -a -um** *adj* pretty pure, rather pure

merāc·us -a -um *adj* pure, unmixed, undiluted, straight

mercābil·is -e *adj* buyable

mercāt·or -ōris *m* merchant, trader, dealer, wholesale dealer

mercātōri·us -a -um *adj* merchant, trading; **navis mercatoria** merchant ship

mercātūr·a -ae *f* trading, trade, commerce; purchase; *f pl* goods

mercāt·us -ūs *m* trade, traffic; market, marketplace; fair

mercēdŭl·a -ae *f* poor pay; low rent, low income

mercēnāri·us -a -um *adj* hired, paid, mercenary; *m* common laborer, servant

merc·ēs -ēdis *f* pay, wages, salary; bribe; reward, recompense; cost; injury, detriment; stipulation, condition, retribution, punishment; rent, income, interest

mercimōn·ium -iī or **-ī** *n* merchandise

mer·cor -ārī -ātus sum *vt* to deal in, trade in, purchase

Mercurial·is -e *adj* of Mercury; *m pl* corporation of merchants in Rome

Mercur·ius -iī or **-ī** *m* Mercury (*son of Jupiter and Maia, messenger of the gods, patron of commerce, diplomacy, lying, gambling, and conductor of departed souls to the world below*); Mercury (*planet*)

merd·a -ae *f* droppings, excrement

merend·a -ae *f* lunch, snack

mer·eō -ēre -uī -itum or **mer·eor -ērī -itus sum** *vt* to deserve, merit, be entitled to; to win, earn, acquire, merit; *vi* to serve; to serve in the army; (with **de** + *abl*) to serve, render service to, do a favor for; **bene de re publica merere** or **mereri** to serve one's country well; **de te merui** I have done you a favor, I have treated you well; **equo merere** to serve in the cavalry

meretrīci·us -a -um *adj* prostitute's

meretrīcŭl·a -ae *f* cute little wench

meretr·īx -īcis *f* prostitute, harlot, wench, strumpet

merg·ae -ārum *f pl* pitchfork

merg·es -itis *f* sheaf

mergō mergĕre mersī mersum *vt* to dip, plunge, sink; to engulf, swallow up; to swamp, overwhelm, bury, drown; **mergi** to sink, drown; to go bankrupt

merg·us -ī *m* diver (*bird*)

meridiān·us -a -um *adj* midday, noon; southern, southerly

merīdiātĭ·ō -ōnis *f* siesta

merīdi·ēs -ēī *m* midday, noon; south; **spectare ad meridiem** to face south

merīdi·ō -āre *vi* to take a siesta

Mēriŏn·ēs -ae *m* charioteer of Idomeneus

merĭtō *adv* deservedly, rightly

merit·ō -āre *vt* to earn regularly

meritōr·ius -a -um *adj* rented, hired; *n pl* rented apartment

merit·us -a -um *adj* deserved, just, right, proper, deserving; guilty; *n* service, favor, kindness; blame, fault, offense; merit, worth

merobīb·us -a -um *adj* drinking unmixed wine

Merŏp·ē -ēs *f* one of the Pleiades, the daughter of Atlas and Pleione

Mer·ops -ŏpis *m* king of Ethiopia, husband of Clymene, and reputed father of Phaethon

mer·ops -ŏpis *f* bee eater (*bird*)

mers·ō -āre *vt* to keep dipping or plunging, to immerse; (fig) to engulf; **mersari** (with *dat*) to plunge into

mersus *pp* of **mergo**

merŭl·a -ae *f* blackbird

mer·us -a -um *adj* pure, unmixed, undiluted, unadulterated; (fig) undiluted; (fig) nothing but, mere; *n* wine

mer·x -cis *f* merchandise, wares; **mala merx** (fig) bad lot

Messalīn·a -ae *f* wife of the Emperor Claudius; wife of Nero

Messān·a -ae *f* town in N.E. Sicily

Messāpi·us -a -um *adj* Apulian; *f* town and district in S.E. Italy, named after the mythical founder Messapus

mess·is -is *f* harvest; harvest time; **adhuc tua messis in herba est** (fig) don't count your chickens before they are hatched

mess·or -ōris *m* reaper, mower

messōr·ius -a -um *adj* reaper's

messus *pp* of **meto**

mēt·a -ae *f* marker for measuring the distance at a racetrack; (fig) goal, end; (fig) turning point, critical moment

metall·um -ī *n* metal; *n pl* mine

metamorphōs·is -is *f* transformation

metaphŏr·a -ae *f* metaphor

mētāt·or -ōris *m* planner; **metator urbis** city planner

Metaur·us -ī *m* small river in Umbria, at the banks of which Hasdrubal was defeated in 207 B.C.

Metell·us -ī *m* Roman surname; Q.
Caecilius Metellus Numidicus (*commander of the Roman forces against Jugurtha from 109 B.C. until replaced by Marius in 107 B.C.*)

Methymn·a -ae *f* town on the island of Lesbos

mētior mētīrī mensus sum *vt* to measure; to traverse, travel; to judge, estimate; (with *dat*) to measure (*something*) out to, distribute (*something*) among; (with *abl*) to judge (*someone*) by the standard of

metō metěre messū̆ī messum *vt* to reap, mow, gather, collect, harvest; (fig) to mow down (*e.g.*, *with the sword*)

mēt·or -ārī -ātus sum *vt* to measure off; to lay out (*e.g.*, *a camp*)

metrēt·a -ae *f* liquid measure (*about nine gallons*)

metuculōs·us -a -um *adj* fearful; scary

metŭ·ens -entis *adj* afraid, apprehensive, anxious

metŭ·ō -ěre -ī *vt* to fear, be afraid of; *vi* to be afraid, be apprehensive

met·us -ūs *m* fear, anxiety, apprehension

me·us -a -um *adj* my; *pron* mine; meā interest it is of importance to me; **meum est** (with *inf*) it is my duty to; **meus est** (coll) I've got him

Mezent·ius -iī or **-ī** *m* Etruscan tyrant of Caere, slain by Aeneas

mī = mihi

mic·a -ae *f* crumb, morsel

Micips·a -ae *m* son of Masinissa and king of Numidia (148-118 B.C.); *m pl* (fig) Numidians, Africans

mic·ō -āre *vi* to vibrate, quiver, twinkle, sparkle, flash

mictur·iō -īre *vi* to have to urinate

Mid·ās -ae *m* king of Phrygia, at whose touch everything turned to gold (*8th cent. B.C.*)

migrātī·ō -ōnis *f* moving, changing residence; metaphorical use

migrāt·us -ūs *m* transporting

migr·ō -āre *vt* to transport; (fig) to transgress, violate; *vi* to move, change residence, depart, migrate; (fig) to go away, change, turn

mīl·es -itis *m* soldier; infantryman; private; army

Mīlēsi·us -a -um *adj* Milesian, of Miletus

Mīlēt·us -ī *f* Miletus (*town on the W. coast of Asia Minor*)

mīl·ia -ium *n pl* thousands; see **mille**

mīliār·ium -iī or **-ī** *n* milestone

mīlitār·is -e *adj* military

mīlitāriter *adv* in a military manner, like a soldier

mīlitāri·us -a -um *adj* soldierly, military

mīlitī·a -ae *f* army; war; the military; military discipline; **militiae** in war, on the battlefield, in the army; **militiae domique** abroad

and at home, on the war front and on the home front

mīlit·ō -āre *vt* to carry on (*war*); *vi* to serve as a soldier, be in the service

mil·ium -iī or **-ī** *n* millet

mille (indecl) *adj* thousand; *n* thousand; **mille homines** a thousand men; **milia** *n pl* thousands; **duo milia passuum** two miles

millēsim·us or **millensim·us -a -um** *adj* thousandth

milliār·ium -iī or **-ī** *n* milestone

milliens or **milliēs** *adv* a thousand times; innumerable times

Mil·ō -ōnis *m* T. Annius Milo (*friend of Cicero and enemy of Clodius, defended by Cicero on a charge of having murdered Clodius in 52 B.C.*)

Miltiăd·ēs -is *m* Athenian general victorious at Marathon (490 B.C.)

miluīn·us -a -um *adj* rapacious

milŭ·us or **milŭ·os -ī** *m* kite (*bird of prey*); gurnard (*fish*)

Milŭ·us -ī *m* Kite (*constellation*)

mim·a -ae *f* actress

Mīmallōn·is -idis *f* Bacchante

Mim·ās -antis *m* one of the giants

mīmicē *adv* like a mime actor

mīmic·us -a -um *adj* suitable for the mimo, farcical

Mimnerm·us -ī *m* Greek elegiac poet of Colophon (*fl. 560 B.C.*)

mīmŭl·a -ae *f* miserable little actress

mīm·us -ī *m* mime, farce; actor of a mime; (fig) farce

min·a -ae *f* Greek coin (*about 100 denarii*)

mināci·ae -ārum *f pl* menaces, threats

mināciter *adv* threateningly

min·ae -ārum *f pl* menaces, threats; projecting points of a wall

minanter *adv* threateningly

minātī·ō -ōnis *f* threatening

min·ax -ācis *adj* threatening, menacing; projecting, jutting out

min·eō -ēre *vi* to project, jut out

Minerv·a -ae *f* goddess of wisdom and of the arts and sciences, identified with Pallas Athene; (fig) skill, genius; spinning and weaving; **invitā Minervā** against one's better judgment

mingō mingěre minxī mictum *vi* to urinate

miniān·us -a -um *adj* vermilion

miniātŭl·us -a -um *adj* reddish

minimē or **minŭmē** *adv* least of all, least, very little; by no means, certainly not, not in the least; **minŭme gentium** (coll) by no means

minim·us or **minŭm·us -a -um** (*superl* of **parvus**) *adj* smallest, least, very small; slightest, very insignificant; youngest; shortest (*time*); **minimus natu** youngest; *n* the least, minimum; lowest price; **minimo emere** to buy at a very low price; **minimo provocare** to provoke for the least thing or on the flimsiest pretext

mini·ō -āre vt to color red, paint red

minist·er -rī m servant, attendant, helper; agent, tool, instrument

minister·ium -iī or **-ī** n office, ministry, service, occupation, work, employment; retinue

ministr·a -ae f servant, attendant, helper; waitress; handmaid

ministrāt·or -ōris m or **ministrātr·ix -īcis** f assistant, helper

ministr·ō -āre vt to serve, wait on; to tend; to execute, carry out (*orders*); (with *dat*) to hand out (*something*) to; (with *abl*) to supply (*someone or something*) with

minitābund·us -a -um adj threatening

minit·ō -āre or **minit·or -ārī -ātus sum** vt to make threats of (*e.g.*, *war*); (with *acc* of thing and *dat* of person) to threaten to bring (*e.g.*, *evil*, *death*) upon, hold (*something*) threateningly over (*someone*); vi to make threats; (with *dat* of person threatened and *abl* of means) to threaten (*somone*) with

min·ium -iī or **-ī** n vermilion; red lead

Minō·is -idis f Ariadne

Minō·us or **Minō·us -a -um** adj of Minos, Cretan

min·or -ārī -ātus sum vt to threaten; to promise boastfully; (with *dat* of person and *acc* of thing) to threaten (*someone*) with (*something*), to hold (*something*) over (*someone*) as a threat; vi to jut out, project; to be menacing, make threats; (with *dat*) to threaten, make threats to

min·or -us (*comp* of *parvus*) adj smaller, less; less, shorter (*time*); younger; inferior, less important; (with *abl*) a (of time) too short for; b inferior to; c unworthy of; (with *inf*) unfit to, incapable of; dimidio minor quam half as small as; minores facere filios quam to think less of the sons than of; minor natu younger; m pl descendants, posterity; n less, smaller amount; minoris emere to buy at a lower price; minus praedae less booty

Min·ōs -ōis or **-ōnis** m son of Zeus and Europa, king of Crete, and, after his death, judge in the lower world; grandson of the former, likewise king of Crete, husband of Pasiphaë, and father of Ariadne and Phaedra

Minōtaur·us -ī m monstrous offspring of Pasiphaë, half man and half bull, and kept in the labyrinth

minūmē see minime

minūmus see minimus

min·uō -uěre -uī -ūtum vt to diminish, lessen, reduce; to weaken, lower; to modify (*plans*); to settle (*controversies*); to limit, restrict (*authority*); to offend against, try to cheapen (*e.g.*, *the majesty of the*

Roman *people*); vi to diminish, abate, ebb; **minuente aestu** at ebbtide

minus adv less; not; by no means, not at all

minuscul·us -a -um adj rather small, smallish

minūt·al -ālis n hamburger, hash

minūtātim adv piecemeal; bit by bit

minūtē adv in a small-minded way

minūtul·us -a -um adj tiny

minūt·us -a -um adj small, minute; petty, narrow-minded

Miny·ae -ārum m pl Argonauts, the companions of Jason

Miny·ās -ae m mythical king of Thessaly

mirābil·is -e adj wonderful, marvelous, amazing, extraordinary

mirābiliter adv wonderfully, amazingly

mirābund·us -a -um adj full of amazement, astonished

mirācul·um -ī n wonder, marvel; surprise, amazement

mirand·us -a -um adj fantastic

mirāti·ō -ōnis f admiration, wonder

mirāt·or -ōris m admirer

mirātr·ix -īcis adj fem admiring

mirē adv wonderfully, uncommonly, strangely; **mire quam** it is strange how, strangely

mirificē adv wonderfully

mirific·us -a -um adj causing wonder, wonderful

mirimōdis adv in a strange way

mirmill·ō -ōnis m gladiator (*who fought with Gallic arms*)

mir·or -ārī -ātus sum vt to be amazed at, be surprised at; to look at with wonder, admire

mir·us -a -um adj amazing, surprising, astonishing; wonderful; **mirum est** (with *acc & inf*) it is surprising that; **mirum quam** or **mirum quantum** it is amazing how, it is amazing to what extent

miscellāne·a -ōrum n pl hash

miscēō miscēre miscūī mixtum vt to mix, blend, mingle; to combine, associate, share; to mix up, confuse, turn upside down; to mix, prepare, brew

misell·us -a -um adj poor little

Misēn·um -ī n promontory and town near the bay of Naples

mis·er -ěra -ěrum adj poor; wretched, miserable, unhappy; sorry, worthless

miserābil·is -e adj miserable, pitiable; piteous

miserābiliter adv pitiably; piteously

miserand·us -a -um adj pitiful, deplorable

miserāti·ō -ōnis f pity, compassion, sympathy; appeal for sympathy

miserē adv wretchedly, miserably, unhappily; pitifully; desperately

miser·eō -ēre -uī -itum or **miser·eor -ērī -itus sum** vi (with *genit*) to pity, feel sorry for, sympathize with; v impers (with *acc* of person who feels pity and *genit* of object of pity), e.g., **miseret** or **miseretur me aliorum** I feel sorry for the others

miseresc·ō -ěre *vi* to feel pity, feel sympathetic; (with *genit*) to pity, feel sorry for; *v impers* (with *acc* of person who feels pity and *genit* of object of pity), e.g., **me miserescit tui** I feel sorry for you, I pity you

miseri·a -ae *f* poverty; misery, unhappiness, distress, trouble

misericordi·a -ae *f* pity, sympathy, compassion; mercy

misericor·s -dis *adj* sympathetic, merciful

miseriter *adv* sadly

miser·or -ārī -ātus sum *vt* to deplore; to pity; *vi* to feel pity

missicŭl·ō -āre *vt* to keep sending

missil·is -e *adj* missile, flying; *n pl* missiles

missi·ō -ōnis *f* release, liberation; sending off, despatching; military discharge; dismissal from office; cessation, end; **sine missione** without letup, to the death

missĭt·ō -āre *vt* to keep sending

missus *pp* of **mitto**

miss·us -ūs *m* letting go, throwing, hurling; sending

mītesc·ō -ěre *vi* to grow mild, grow mellow, become ripe; (fig) to get soft; (fig) to become gentle, become tame

Mithr·ās -ae *m* Mithra (*sun-god of the Persians*)

Mithridāt·ēs -is *m* Mithridates the Great (*king of Pontus from 120 B.C. to 63 B.C.*)

Mithridātē·us or **Mithridātĭc·us -a -um** *adj* Mithridatic

mītigātĭ·ō -ōnis *f* mitigation, soothing

mītig·ō -āre *vt* to mellow, ripen; to soften; to calm down, appease, pacify

mīt·is -e *adj* mellow, ripe, soft; calm, placid; mild, gentle

mitr·a -ae *f* miter, turban

mittō mittěre mīsī missum *vt* to send; let fly, throw, fling, launch; to emit, shed; to let out, utter; to let go of, drop; to free, release, discharge, dismiss; to pass over in silence, omit; to send for, invite; to pass up, forego; to dedicate (*a book*); to yield, produce, export; to dismiss, forget; **sanguinem mittere** to bleed; **sanguinem provinciae mittere** (fig) to bleed a province dry

mitŭl·us -ī *m* limpet

mixtim *adv* promiscuously

mixtūr·a -ae *f* mixing, blending

Mnēmosÿn·ē -ēs *f* mother of the Muses

mnēmosÿn·on -ī *n* souvenir

mōbĭl·is -e *adj* mobile, moveable, portable, nimble, active; shifty, changing; impressionable, excitable

mōbĭlĭt·ās -ātis *f* mobility; agility, quickness; shiftiness

mōbĭlĭter *adv* quickly, rapidly

mōbĭlĭt·ō -āre *vt* to impart motion to, endow with motion

moderābĭl·is -e *adj* moderate

moderām·en -ĭnis *n* control

moderanter *adv* under control

moderātē *adv* with moderation

moderātim *adv* gradually

moderātĭ·ō -ōnis *f* controlling, control, regulation, guidance; moderation, self-control; rules, regulation

moderāt·or -ōris *m* or **moderātr·īx -īcis** *f* controller, director, guide

moderāt·us -a -um *adj* controlled, well regulated, orderly, restrained

moděr·ō -āre or **moděr·or -ārī -ātus sum** *vt* to control, direct, guide; *vi* (with *dat*) a to moderate, restrain, put restraint upon; b to allay, mitigate

modestē *adv* with moderation, discreetly; modestly

modesti·a -ae *f* moderation, restraint; discretion; modesty, sense of shame, sense of honor, dignity; propriety; mildness (*of weather*)

modest·us -a -um *adj* moderate, restrained; modest, discreet; orderly, obedient

modiāl·is -e *adj* containing a modius or peck

modicē *adv* moderately, with restraint; in an orderly manner; only slightly

modĭc·us -a -um *adj* moderate; small; modest, unassuming; ordinary, puny, trifling

modĭficāt·us -a -um *adj* regulated (*in length*)

mod·ĭus -ĭī or **-ī** *m* modius, peck (*one sixth of a medimnus*); measure; **plēno modiō** in full measure

modo *adv* only, merely, simply, solely; (of time) just now, just recently, lately; presently, in a moment; **modo . . . deinde** (or **tum** or **postea** or **interdum**) first . . . then, at one time . . . next time; **modo . . . modo** now . . . now, sometimes . . . sometimes, at one moment . . . at another; **non modo . . . sed etiam** or **verum etiam** not only . . . but also; *conj* if only, provided that

modulātē *adv* according to measure, in time; melodiously

modulāt·or -ōris *m* director, musician

modŭl·or -ārī -ātus sum *vt* to regulate the time of, measure rhythmically; to modulate; to sing; to play

modŭl·us -ī *m* small measure, small stature

mod·us -ī *m* standard of measurement, measure; time, rhythm; size; limit, boundary; rule, regulation; way, manner, mode; **ad modum** (with *genit*) or **in modum** (with *genit*) or **modo** (with *genit*) in the manner of, according to the style of, like; **ejus modi homo** that kind of man; **hujus modi homo** this kind of man

moech·a -ae f adultress

moechiss·ō -āre vt to ravish, rape

moech·or -ārī -ātus sum vi to have an affair, commit adultery

moech·us -ī m adulterer

moen·ia -ium n pl town walls, ramparts, fortifications; fortified town; castle, stronghold; defenses

moeniō see **munio**

moerus see **murus**

Moes·ī -ōrum m pl a people on the lower Danube

mol·a -ae f millstone; mill; flour; f pl mill

molār·is -is m millstone; molar (tooth)

mōl·ēs -is f mass, bulk, pile; massive structure, dam, mole, pier; mass (of people, etc.); burden, effort, trouble; calamity; might, greatness

molestē adv with annoyance; with difficulty, with trouble; **moleste ferre** to be annoyed at, be disgruntled at, just about stand

molesti·a -ae f annoyance, trouble; worry; affectation (in style)

molest·us -a -um adj annoying, troublesome, distressing; labored, affected (style)

mōlīm·en -inis n great exertion, great effort; attempt; undertaking

mōliment·um -ī n great exertion, great effort

mōl·ior -īrī -ītus sum vt to do with great effort, strain at, exert oneself over; to wield, heave, hurl; to work hard at; to build, erect; to rouse; to displace; to undertake, attempt; to perform; to cause, occasion; vi to exert oneself, struggle, take great pains

mōlīti·ō -ōnis f building, erection; demolition

mōlīt·or -ōris m builder

molītus pp of **molo**

molītus pp of **molior**

mollesc·ō -ēre vi to become soft; to become gentle; to become effeminate

mollicul·us -a -um adj tender, dainty

moll·iō -īre -īvī or **-iī -ītum** vt to make soft, soften; (fig) to soften, mitigate; to demoralize

mollip·ēs -ēdis adj soft-footed

moll·is -e adj soft; springy; flexible; flabby; mild, calm; easy; gentle (slope); sensitive, impressionable; tender, touching; weak, effeminate; amatory (verses); complaint; changeable, untrustworthy

molliter adv softly; gently, smoothly; effeminately; voluptuously; patiently, with fortitude

mollīti·a -ae or **mollīti·ēs -ēī** f softness; flexibility; tenderness; sensitivity; weakness, irresolution; effeminacy, voluptuousness

mollitūd·ō -inis f softness; flexibility; susceptibility

mol·ō -ēre -uī -itum vt to grind

Moloss·us -a -um adj Molossian; m Molossian hound; m pl Molassians (a people of Epirus)

mōl·y -yos n magic herb

mōm·en -inis n movement, motion; momentum

mōment·um -ī n movement, motion; alteration; turn, critical time; moment; impulse; momentum; influence, importance; motive

Mōn·a -ae f Isle of Man

monēdul·a -ae f jackdaw

mon·eō -ēre -uī -itum vt to call to mind, remind, advise, point out; to warn; to foretell; to teach, instruct, inform

monēr·is -is f galley

Monēt·a -ae f Juno Moneta, in whose temple on the Capitoline Hill money was kept; coin, money; stamp or die (for money)

monētāl·is -e adj of the mint; m (coll) money man

monīl·e -is n necklace

monim- = **monum-**

monit·a -ōrum n pl warnings; prophecies

moniti·ō -ōnis f reminder

monit·or -ōris m reminder, counselor; teacher

monit·us -ūs m reminder, warning

monogramm·us -a -um adj sketchy, shadowy

monopod·ium -iī or **-ī** n table with a single central leg

monotrōp·us -a -um adj single, alone

mon·s -tis m mountain, mountain range; mass, heap; hill; **montis auri polliceri** to make wild promises; **summus mons** mountain top

monstrāti·ō -ōnis f pointing out

monstrāt·or -ōris m displayer; inventor

monstr·ō -āre vt to show, to point out, exhibit, make known, advise, teach; to appoint, institute, ordain; to advise, urge

monstr·um -ī n sign, portent, wonder; warning; monster, monstrosity; miracle, marvel

monstruōsē adv unnaturally

monstruōs·us -a -um adj unnatural, strange, monstrous

montān·us -a -um adj mountain, of a mountain; mountainous; m pl mountaineers; n pl mountainous regions

monticol·a -ae m mountaineer, highlander

montivāg·us -a -um adj wandering over the mountains

montōs·us or **montuōs·us -a -um** adj mountainous

monument·um -ī n reminder; monument, memorial; record (written or oral); token of identification

Mopsopi·us -a -um adj Athenian; f Attica, Athens

mor·a -ae f delay; pause; spell, period of time; stop-off; division of the Spartan army consisting of from three to seven hundred men

mōrāl·is -e adj moral

morāt·or -ōris m obstructionist; (in court) lawyer who spoke only to gain time

mōrāt·us -a -um adj -mannered; -natured; in character; **bene morātus** well-mannered; **male morātus** ill-mannered, rude

morbĭd·us -a -um adj sickly; causing sickness, unwholesome

morbōs·us -a -um adj debauched

morb·us -ī m sickness, disease; fault, vice; distress; **in morbum cadere** or **in morbum incidere** to fall sick

mordācĭus adv more bitingly; (fig) more radically

mord·ax -ācis adj biting, snapping; (fig) sharp, stinging, caustic, snarling; pungent (taste)

mordĕō mordēre momordī morsum vt to bite; to eat, devour; to bite, grip, (of cold) to nip; (of words) to cut, hurt; (of a river) to bite its way through

mordĭc·ēs -um m pl bites

mordĭcus adv by biting, with the teeth; (fig) tightly, doggedly

mŏrē adv foolishly

morēt·um -ī n salad

morĭbund·us -a -um adj dying, at the point of death; mortal; deadly

mōrĭgĕr·ō -āre or **mōrĭgĕr·or -ārī -ātus sum** vi (with dat) to humor, pamper, yield to, comply with

mōrĭgĕr·us -a -um adj obedient, obsequious

morĭor morī mortŭus sum vi to die; (fig) to die out, wither, decay, pass away

morm·yr -ȳris f Pontic fish

mōrŏlŏg·us -a -um adj speaking nonsense, foolish

mor·or -ārī -ātus sum vt to delay, detain; to entertain, hold the attention of; to hinder, prevent; **nihil morarī** (with acc) a to disregard, care nothing for, not value; b to have nothing against, have nothing to say against; vi to delay, linger, tarry, loiter; to stay, remain, wait; **quid moror?** or **quid multis morer?** why should I drag out the point?, to make a long story short

mōrōsē adv morosely, crabbily

mōrōsĭt·ās -ātis f moroseness, peevishness, crabbiness

mōrōs·us -a -um adj morose, peevish, crabby; fastidious, particular; (fig) stubborn (disease)

Morph·eus -ĕos m god of dreams

mors mortis f death; destruction; corpse; **mortem obīre** to meet death; **mortis poena** death penalty; **sibi mortem consciscere** to commit suicide

mors·a -ōrum n pl bits, little pieces

morsiuncŭl·a -ae f peck, kiss

morsus pp of mordeo

mors·us -ūs m bite; pungency; grip; corrosion; gnawing pain; sting, vicious attack

mortāl·is -e adj mortal, subject to death; human, mortal; transient; man-made; m mortal, human being

mortālĭt·ās -ātis f mortality; mortals, mankind

morticīn·us -a -um adj dead; corpse-like, rotting

mortĭf·er or **mortĭf·ĕrus -ĕra -ĕrum** adj lethal, deadly

mortĭfĕrē adv mortally

mortuāl·ĭa -ĭum n pl dirges

mortŭ·us -a -um pp of morior; adj dead, deceased; withered, decayed; scared to death; m corpse

mōrŭl·us -a -um adj dark, black

mōr·um -ī n blackberry, mulberry

mōr·us -ī f mulberry tree

mōr·us -a -um adj foolish; mf fool

mōs mōris m caprice, mood; nature, manner; custom, usage, practice; fashion, style; rule, regulation, law; **de more** or **ex more** according to custom; **morem gerere** (with dat) to humor (someone); m pl morals, character, behavior; customs; laws

Mōs·ēs or **Mŏys·ēs -is** m Moses

mōtĭ·ō -ōnis f motion

mōt·ō -āre vt to keep moving, keep shifting

mōtus pp of moveo

mōt·us -ūs m motion, movement; gesture; dancing; change (e.g., of fortune); impulse, inspiration; emotion, passion; rebellion, riot; **motus animi** emotion; **motus terrae** earthquake

mov·ens -entis adj movable; **res moventes** personal property; n pl motives

movĕō movēre mōvī mōtum vt to move; to stir, shake, disturb; to dislodge (the enemy); to eject, expel; to degrade; to remove, take away; to plow; to cause, occasion, promote; to begin; to undertake; to trouble, torment; to move, influence, affect; to dissuade; to exert, exercise; to turn over in the mind, ponder; **se ex loco movere** to budge from the spot; **se movere** to dance; vi to move

mox adv soon, presently; hereafter; next, then, later on

Mŏys·ēs -is m Moses

mūcĭd·us -a -um adj sniveling, driveling; moldy, musty

Mūc·ĭus -ĭī or **-ī** m Roman family name

mūcr·ō -ōnis m sharp point, sharp edge; sword; edge, boundary; keenness

mūc·us -ī m nasal mucus

mūgĭent·ēs -ĭum m pl oxen

mūgĭl or **mūgĭl·is -is** m mullet

mūgĭn·or -ārī -ātus sum vi to dillydally

mŭg•ĭŏ -īre -īvī or -ĭī -ītum *vi* to bellow, low; to rumble, roar

mūgīt•us -ūs *m* bellowing, lowing; rumbling, roaring

mūl•a -ae *f* mule

mulcĕŏ mulcēre mulsī mulsum *vt* to stroke, pet; to stir gently; to soothe, alleviate; to appease; to flatter, delight

Mulcĭb•er -ērī or -ĕris *m* Vulcan; fire

mulc•ō -āre *vt* to beat, cudgel; to mistreat, injure

mulctr•a -ae *f* milk pail

muctrār•ĭum -ĭī or -ī or **muctr•um** -ī *n* milk pail

mulgĕŏ mulgēre mulsī mulsum or **mulctum** *vt* to milk

muliĕbr•is -e *adj* woman's, womanly, feminine; womanish, effeminate

muliebrĭter *adv* like a woman; effeminately

mŭlĭ•er -ĕris *f* woman; wife

muliĕrār•ĭus -a -um *adj* woman's; *m* woman chaser, wolf

muliercŭl•a -ae *f* little woman; little hussy

mulierōsĭt•ās -ātis *f* weakness for women

mulierōs•us -a -um *adj* womancrazy

mūlīn•us -a -um *adj* mulish

mūl•ĭō -ōnis *m* mule driver

mūlĭōnĭ•us -a -um *adj* mule driver's

mullŭl•us -ī *m* little mullet

mull•us -ī *m* mullet

muls•us -a -um *pp* of **mulceo;** *adj* honeyed, sweet as honey; *f* (term of endearment) honey; *n* mead (*wine mixed with honey*)

mult•a -ae *f* fine; penalty; loss of money; **multam certare** to contest a fine; **multam committere** to incur a fine; **multam dicere** (with *dat* of person and *acc* of the fine) to fine (*someone a certain amount*); **multam subire** to incur a fine, be fined

multa *adv* much, very, greatly, earnestly

mult•a -ōrum *n pl* many things; much; **ne multa** in short, to be brief

multangŭl•us -a -um *adj* manyangled

multātĭcĭ•us -a -um *adj* fine, of a fine; **multaticia pecunia** fine

multātĭ•ō -ōnis *f* fine, penalty

multēsĭm•us -a -um *adj* trifling, negligible

mult•ī -ōrum *m pl* many men, many; multitude, mass, common people

multĭbĭb•us -a -um *adj* heavydrinking

multĭcāv•us -a -um *adj* porous

multĭcĭ•a -ōrum *n pl* diaphanous garments

multĭfārĭam *adv* in many places

multĭfĭd•us -a -um *adj* divided into many parts; (of a river) having many tributaries; **dens multĭfĭda** comb

multĭform•is -e *adj* multiform, manifold

multĭfŏr•us -a -um *adj* many-holed; (flute) having many stops

multĭgenĕr•is -e or **multĭgĕn•us** -a -um *adj* of many kinds, various, complex

multĭjŭg•is -e or **multĭjŭg•us** -a -um *adj* yoked together; (fig) various, complex

multĭlŏqu•ax -ācis *adj* talkative

multĭlŏqu•ĭum -ĭī or -ī *n* talkativeness

multĭlŏqu•us -a -um *adj* talkative

multĭmŏdīs *adv* in many ways

multĭpl•ex -ĭcis *adj* with many folds; winding, labyrinthine, serpentine; manifold; many; (in implied comparisons) many times as great, far greater; varied, complicated; changeable, versatile, many-sided; sly, cunning; *n* manifold return

multĭplĭcābĭl•is -e *adj* manifold, many

multĭplĭcĭter *adv* in various ways

multĭplĭc•ō -āre *vt* to multiply, increase, enlarge

multĭpŏt•ens -entis *adj* mighty, powerful

multĭtūd•ō -ĭnis *f* great number, multitude, crowd, throng; rabble, common people

multĭvŏl•us -a -um *adj* passionate

multō *adv* (with comparatives) much, far, by far, a great deal; **multo aliter ac** far otherwise than, much different from; **multo ante** long before; **multo post** long after; **non multo secus fieri** to turn out just about the same

mult•ō -āre *vt* to punish, fine

mult•us -a -um (*comp:* **plures;** *superl:* **plurimus**) *adj* many a, much, great; abundant, considerable, extensive; tedious, long-winded; full, numerous, thick, loud, heavy, constant; **ad multum diem** till late in the day; **multā nocte** late at night; **multo die** late in the day; (with plural nouns) many; *m pl* see **multi;** *n* much; **multi** of great value, highly; **multi facere** to think highly of, make much of, think much of; **multum est** it is of great importance; **multum temporis** a great deal of time, much time; *n pl* see **multa**

multum *adv* much, greatly, very, often, frequently, far; (with comparatives) much, far; **multum valere** to have considerable influence

mūl•us -ī *m* mule

Mulvĭ•us -a -um *adj* Mulvian; **Mulvius pons** Mulvian bridge (*across the Tiber, above Rome, on the Via Flaminia*)

Mumm•ĭus -ĭī or -ī *m* L. Mummius Achaicus (*conqueror of Corinth, 146 B.C.*)

mundān•us -ī *m* world citizen

mundē or mundĭter adv neatly, cleanly

mundĭti·a -ae or mundĭti·ēs -ēī f neatness, cleanness; elegance; politeness

mundŭl·us -a -um adj trim, neat, sharp

mund·us -a -um adj neat, clean, nice; fine, smart, sharp, elegant; choice (words); m neat person; world, universe, heavens; earth, mankind; beauty aids

mūnerigerŭl·us -ī m bearer of presents

mūner·ō -āre or mūner·or -ārī -ātus sum vt to reward, honor, present; (with acc of thing and dat of person) to present to

mūni·a -ōrum n pl official duties or functions

mūnic·eps -ĭpis m or f citizen of a municipality; fellow citizen, fellow countryman

mūnicipāl·is -e adj municipal; (as term of contempt) provincial, country

mūnicip·ĭum -ĭī or -ī n municipality, town (whose people were Roman citizens, but otherwise autonomous)

mūnificē adv generously

mūnificentĭ·a -ae f generosity

mūnific·ō -āre vt to treat generously

mūnific·us -a -um adj generous; splendid

mūnīm·en -ĭnis f defense

mūnīment·um -ī n defense, protection, fortification, rampart; (fig) shelter, defense

mūn·ĭō or moen·ĭō -īre -īvī or -ĭī -ītum vt to wall, defend with a wall, fortify, strengthen, defend, protect, guard, secure; to build (road); (fig) to guard, shelter, protect, support

mūn·is -e adj obliging

mūnītĭ·ō -ōnis f building, fortifying, defending; fortification, rampart, trenches, lines; mūnitio flūminum bridging of rivers; mūnitio viae road construction

mūnīt·ō -āre vt to open up (a road)

mūnīt·or -ōris m builder, engineer

mūnīt·us -a -um adj fortified; (fig) protected, safe

mūn·us or moen·us -ĕris n service, function, duty; gift; service, favor, kindness; duty; tribute; public entertainment, gladiatorial show, extravaganza; tribute (to the dead), rite, sacrifice; public office

mūnuscŭl·um -ī n small present

mūraen·a -ae f moray (eel-like fish)

mūrāl·is -e adj wall; wall-destroying; wall-defending; corona mūralis mural crown (award for being the first to scale the enemy walls)

mūr·ex -ĭcis m murex, mollusk (yielding purple dye); purple dye, purple; jagged rock; spiked trap (as defense against cavalry attack)

murĭ·a -ae f brine

muriātĭc·um -ī n pickled fish

mūricīd·us -ī m mouse killer; (fig) coward

murmill·ō -ōnis m gladiator with Gallic arms, who fought against a retarius

murm·ur -ŭris n murmur, murmuring; buzz, hum; roar, crash; growling, grumbling; rumbling; hubbub

murmurill·um -ī n low murmur

murmŭr·ō -āre vi to murmur; to mutter, grumble; to rumble, roar

murr·a or murrh·a or myrrh·a -ae f myrrh tree; myrrh

murrĕ·us or myrrhĕ·us -a -um adj made of myrrh; perfumed with myrrh; myrrh-colored, yellowish

murrĭn·us or myrrhĭn·us -a -um adj of myrrh; f drink flavored with myrrh; n pl vases

murt- = myrt-

mūr·us -ī m wall, city wall; dam, dike; rim (of dish or pot); (fig) wall, protection

mūs mūris m or f mouse, rat

Mūs·a -ae f Muse (patron goddess of poetry, song, dance, literature, astronomy, etc.); poem, song; talent, genius, taste; f pl studies

Mūsae·us -ī m mythical pre-Homeric bard and musician in the time of Orpheus

musc·a -ae f fly

muscār·ĭum -ĭī or -ī n fly swatter

muscipŭl·a -ae f or muscipŭl·um -ī n mousetrap

muscōs·us -a -um adj mossy

muscŭl·us -ī m little mouse; muscle; (mil) mantelet

musc·us -ī m moss

Mūse·us or Mūsae·us -a -um adj of the Muses, musical, poetic

mūsĭc·a -ae or mūsĭc·ē -ēs f or mūsĭc·a -ōrum n pl music, art of music (including poetry)

mūsĭcē adv pleasantly

mūsĭc·us -a -um adj musical; poetic; cultural; m musician

mussĭt·ō -āre vt to bear in silence; vi to be silent; to mutter, grumble

muss·ō -āre vt to bear in silence, bear silently; to brood over; vi to mutter, murmur; (of bees) to hum; to hesitate

mustāc·us -ī m or mustācĕ·um -ī n cake, wedding cake

mustēl·a or mustēl·a -ae f weasel

mustēlĭn·us or mustēlĭn·us -a -um adj of a weasel

must·um -ī n fresh grape juice, unfermented wine, must; vintage

mūtābĭl·is -e adj changeable; fickle

mūtābĭlĭt·ās -ātis f mutability; fickleness

mūtātĭ·ō -ōnis f mutation, change, alteration; exchange, interchange

mutĭl·ō -āre vt to cut off, lop off, crop; to mutilate; to reduce, shorten, lessen; to rob

mutĭl·us -a -um adj maimed, mutilated; defective

Mutīn·a -ae f town of N. central Italy, S. of the Po, which played a role in the civil war after the death of Julius Caesar

mūtĭō see **muttio**

mūtītĭō see **muttitio**

mūt·ō -āre vt to move, shift, change, alter; to exchange, interchange, barter, sell; to modify, transform, vary; to change for the better; to change for the worse; (with abl or pro + abl) to exchange or substitute (something or someone) for; vi to change

mūt·ō -ōnis m penis

mutt·ĭō or mūt·ĭō -īre -īvī -ītum vi to mutter, mumble

muttītĭ·ō or mūtītĭ·ō -ōnis f muttering, mumbling

mūtuātĭ·ō -ōnis f borrowing

mūtŭē adv mutually; in return

mūtuĭt·ō -āre vt to wish to borrow

mūtŭō adv mutually, in return

mūtŭ·or -ārī -ātus sum vt to borrow; to derive, obtain, get

mūt·us -a -um adj mute, speechless; silent, still; n pl brutes

mūtŭ·us -a -um adj mutual, reciprocal, interchangeable; borrowed, lent; n reciprocity; loan; **mutuum dare** (with cum + abl) to lend to (someone); **mutuas pecunias sumere** (with ab + abl) to borrow money from (someone); **mutuum argentum rogare** to ask for a loan of cash

Mycēn·ae -ārum f pl or **Mycēn·ē -ēs** f Mycene (city of Agamemnon in Argolis)

Mycēnae·us -a -um or **Mycēnens·is -e** adj Mycenean

Mycēn·is -ĭdis f Mycenaean girl (Iphigenia)

Mygdŏn·es -um m pl a people of Thrace, some of whom later migrated to Phrygia

Mygdonĭ·us -a -um adj Phrygian

myopăr·ō -ōnis m pirate ship

myrĭc·a -ae or **myrĭc·ē -ēs** f tamarisk

Myrmĭdŏn·es -um m pl Myrmidons (people of Thessaly whom Achilles led in battle)

Myr·ōn -ōnis m famous Greek sculptor, whose most famous work is the Discus Thrower, 5th cent. B.C.

myropōl·a -ae m perfumer

myropōl·ium -iī or **-ī** n perfume shop

myrrh- = murr-

myrtēt·um or **murtēt·um -ī** n myrtle grove

myrtĕ·us or **murtĕ·us -a -um** adj myrtle; crowned with myrtle

Myrtŏ·um mar·e (genit: **Myrtŏ·ī mar·is**) n sea between the Peloponnesus and the Cyclades

myrt·um -ī n myrtle berry

myrt·us -ūs or **-ī** f myrtle

Mўsĭ·us -a -um adj Mysian; f Mysia (country in N.W. Asia Minor)

myst·a or **myst·ēs -ae** m priest of the mysteries of Ceres; an initiate

mystagōg·us -ī m initiator

mystēr·ĭum -iī or **-ī** n secret religion, secret service, secret rite or worship, divine mystery; secret; **mysteria facere** to hold service; **mysteria Romana** festival of Bona Dea

myst·ēs -ae m priest of the mysteries of Ceres

mystĭc·us -a -um adj mystic

Mytilēn·ae -ārum f pl or **Mytilēn·ē -ēs** f capital of the island of Lesbos

N

Nabatae·us -a -um adj Nabataean; Arabian, Eastern, Oriental; m pl Nabataeans; f Nabataea (ancient Arab kingdom S.E. of Palestine)

nablĭum -iī or **-ī** n Phoenician harp (an instrument of ten or twelve strings, played with both hands)

nactus pp of **nanciscor**

Naevĭān·us -a -um adj of Naevius

Naev·ĭus -iī or **-ī** m Cn. Naevius (early Roman dramatic and epic poet, c. 270-200 B.C.)

naev·us -ī m body mole

Nāĭ·as -ădis or **Nā·is -ĭdis** or **-ĭdos** f Naiad, water nymph

nam conj for; for instance; (transitional) now, but now, on the other hand

namque conj for, for in fact, for no doubt, for surely

nanciscor nanciscī nanctus sum

or **nactus sum** vt to get by accident (esp. by good luck), obtain, chance upon, find

nān·us -ī m dwarf, midget

Napae·ae -ārum f pl dell nymphs

nāp·us -ī m turnip

Narb·ō -ōnis m town in S. Gaul, from which the province of Narbonese Gaul took its name

Narbōnens·is -e adj Narbonese

narciss·us -ī m narcissus

Narciss·us -ī m son of Cephisus and the nymph Liriope, who was changed into a flower of the same name; powerful freedman of Claudius

nard·um -ī n or **nard·us -ī** f nard, spikenard (fragrant ointment)

nār·is -is f nostril; f pl nostrils, nose; **acutae nares** keen perception; **homo naris obesae** dimwit;

naribus ducere to smell; **naribus uti** (with **ad** + acc) to turn up the nose at

narrābil·is -e adj to be told

narrāti·ō -ōnis f narration, narrative

narrātiuncul·a -ae f short story

narrāt·or -ōris m narrator, historian

narrāt·um -ī n account, statement, narrative

narrāt·us -ūs m narration, narrative

narr·ō -āre vt to tell, relate, narrate, recount; to describe; vi to speak, tell; **bene narrare** (with **de** + abl) to tell good news about (someone); **male narrare** (with **de** + abl) to tell bad news about (someone); **tibi narro** I'm telling you, I assure you

narthēc·ium -iī or **-ī** n medicine chest

narus see **gnarus**

Nārycī·us -a -um adj of Naryx (city of the Opuntian Locrians and birthplace of Ajax Oileus)

nascor nascī nātus sum or **gnātus sum** vi to be born; to rise, begin, originate, be produced, spring forth, proceed, grow, be found; **post homines natos** since the beginning of the world

Nās·ō -ōnis m Publius Ovidius Naso (Roman poet, born in Sulmo, in central Italy, 43 B.C.-c. 17 A.D.)

nass·a -ae f wicker trap (for catching fish); (fig) trap

nassitern·a -ae f large water jug

nasturc·ium -iī or **-ī** n garden cress

nās·us -ī m or **nās·um -ī** n nose; sense of smell; sagacity; anger; scorn; nozzle, spout

nāsūtē adv sarcastically

nāsūt·us -a -um adj big-nosed; satirical, sarcastic

nāt·a or **gnāt·a -ae** f daughter

nātālici·us -a -um adj birthday, natal; n pl birthday party

nātāl·is -e adj of birth, natal; m birthday; m pl birth, origin, lineage

nat·ans -antis m or f fish

natāti·ō -ōnis f swimming

natāt·or -ōris m swimmer

nat·ēs -ium f pl buttocks, rear, rear end

nāti·ō -ōnis f race, stock; tribe, nation, people; (in contemptuous sense) breed, set

nat·is -is f buttock, rump; f pl see **nates**

nātīv·us -a -um adj born; inborn, innate, original; produced by nature, natural; primitive (words)

nat·ō -āre vi to swim, float; to flow; to swim, overflow, be flooded; (of the eyes) to be glassy; (of birds) to fly, glide; to waver, fluctuate, be uncertain; to hover, move to and fro

nātr·ix -īcis f water snake

nātūr·a -ae f blood relationship,

natural affinity, birth; nature, natural constitution, quality, property; nature, natural disposition, character; physical nature, world, universe; order of the world, course of things; element, substance; reproductive organs

nātūrāl·is -e adj natural; by birth, one's own (e.g., father, son); produced by nature; according to nature

nātūrāliter adv naturally, by nature

nāt·us or **gnāt·us -a -um** pp of **nascor**; adj born, made, destined, fit; (with dat or with **ad** or **in** or **propter** + acc) born for, made for, naturally suited to; (with **annos**) at the age of . . . . . . years old, e.g., **annos viginti natus** at the age of twenty, twenty years old; **non amplius novem annos natus** no more than nine years old; **pro** or **e re nata** under the existing circumstances, as matters stand; m son; m pl children; f see **nata**

nauarch·us -ī m captain of a ship, skipper

nauclēric·us -a -um adj ship owner's, skipper's

nauclēr·us -ī m ship owner, skipper

nauc·um -ī n trifle; (mostly in genitive of value with a negative) **non nauci esse** to be of no value, be good for nothing; **non nauci facere** or **non nauci habere** to regard as worthless, regard as good for nothing

naufrag·ium -iī or **-ī** n shipwreck; wreck, ruin, destruction; wreckage; **naufragium facere** to be shipwrecked

naufrag·us -a -um adj shipwrecked, wrecked, of the shipwrecked; causing shipwreck, dangerous to shipping; (fig) ruined; m shipwrecked person

naul·um -ī n fare

naumachi·a -ae f simulated sea engagement (staged as an exercise or for amusement)

nause·a -ae f seasickness; vomiting, nausea

nauseō·ō -āre vt to make (someone) throw up; (fig) to belch forth, throw up, utter; vi to be seasick; to vomit; to feel squeamish, feel disgust; to cause disgust

nauseōl·a -ae f slight squeamishness

Nausicā·a -ae f daughter of Alcinous, king of the Phaeacians

naut·a or **nāvit·a -ae** m sailor, seaman, mariner; captain

nautē·a -ae f nausea; bilge water; stinking liquid

nautic·us -a -um adj nautical, sailors'; m pl sailors, seamen

nāvāl·is -e adj naval, of ships, of a ship; **castra navalia** camp for the protection of ships; **forma navalis** shape of a ship; n tackle, rigging; n pl dock, dockyard, shipyard; rigging

năvicŭl·a -ae _f_ small ship

năviculāri·us -a -um _adj_ of a small ship; _m_ skipper; ship owner; _f_ shipping business

năvifrăg·us -a -um _adj_ dangerous, treacherous, causing shipwreck

năvigābil·is -e _adj_ navigable

năvigāti·ō -ōnis _f_ sailing, navigation, voyage

năvig·er -ěra -ěrum _adj_ navigable

năvig·ium -iī _or_ -ī _n_ ship

năvig·ō -āre _vt_ to sail across, navigate; _vi_ to sail, put to sea; (fig) to swim

năv·is -is _f_ ship; **navem appellere** _or_ **navem terrae applicare** to land a ship; **navem deducere** to launch a ship; **navem solvere** to set sail; **navem subducere** to beach a ship; **navis aperta** ship without a deck; **navis longa** battleship; **navis mercatoria** merchant vessel; **navis oneraria** transport, cargo ship; **navis praetoria** flagship; **navis tecta** ship with a deck

năvit·a -ae _m_ sailor, seaman; captain

năvit·ās -ātis _f_ energy, zeal

năviter _adv_ energetically, zealously, actively, busily; utterly, completely

năv·ō -āre _vt_ to do or perform energetically, conduct or prosecute with vigor; **operam navare** to act energetically; **operam navare** (with _dat_) to render assistance to

năv·us _or_ **gnāv·us -a -um** _adj_ energetic, busy

Max·os -ī _f_ largest island of the Cyclades, famous for its wine and as the place where Theseus abandoned Ariadne

nē _interj_ (always with a personal or demonstrative pronoun) indeed, certainly, surely; _adv_ not; **ne ... quidem** (to negate emphatically the words placed between) not even; (in negative commands) not; **ne time-te** do not fear; _conj_ that not, lest; (after verbs and nouns denoting fear) lest, that

-ne enclitic (introducing a question and added to the first important word of a clause)

nebŭl·a -ae _f_ mist, fog, vapor; cloud; smoke; darkness, obscurity

nebŭl·ō -ōnis _m_ loafer, good-for-nothing

nebulōs·us -a -um _adj_ foggy

nec _or_ **neque** _adv_ not; _conj_ nor, and not; **nec ... et** not only not ... but also; **nec ... nec** _or_ **neque ... neque** neither ... nor; **nec non** (introducing an emphatic affirmative) and certainly, and besides

necdum _or_ **neque dum** _conj_ and not yet, nor yet

necessāriē _or_ **necessāriō** _adv_ necessarily, of necessity

necessāri·us -a -um _adj_ necessary, indispensable, needful, requisite; necessary, inevitable; pressing, urgent; connected by blood or friend-

ship, related, closely connected; _mf_ relative, kinsman; friend; _n pl_ necessities

necesse (indecl) _adj_ necessary; unavoidable, inevitable; requisite; **necesse esse** to be necessary; **necesse habere** to regard as necessary, regard as inevitable

necessit·ās -ātis _f_ necessity, inevitableness, compulsion, urgency; requirement; privation, want; relationship, friendship, connection

necessitūd·ō -inis _f_ necessity, need, want, distress; relationship, bond, connection, relationship, friendship; _f pl_ ties of friendship; relatives, friends, personal connections

necessum (indecl) _adj_ necessary, requisite; inevitable

necne _adv_ or not

necnōn _adv_ also, besides, moreover

nec·ō -āre _vt_ to kill, murder, slay, destroy

necopīn·ans -antis _adj_ unaware

necopīnātō _adv_ unexpectedly, by surprise

necopīnāt·us -a -um _adj_ unexpected

necopīn·us -a -um _adj_ unexpected; unsuspecting, careless, off guard

nect·ar -ăris _n_ nectar (_drink of the gods_); nectar (_as term for honey, milk, wine, poetry, sweetness, etc._)

nectarě·us -a -um _adj_ of nectar, sweet or delicious as nectar

nectō nectěre nexŭī _or_ **nexī nexum** _vt_ to tie, connect, fasten together, join; to weave; to clasp; to imprison, fetter; to devise, contrive; (fig) to attach, affix

nēcŭbi _conj_ lest anywhere, so that nowhere

nēcunde _conj_ lest from anywhere

nēdum _adv_ (after an expressed or implied negative) much less, still less; (after an affirmative) not to say, much more

nefand·us -a -um _adj_ unspeakable, impious, abominable

nefāriē _adv_ impiously, abominably

nefāri·us -a -um _adj_ impious, abominable, criminal; _n_ crime, criminal act

nefās (indecl) _n_ crime, wrong, wickedness, act contrary to divine law, sin; criminal, monster; **per omne fas ac nefas** by hook or by crook

nefast·us -a -um _adj_ forbidden, unlawful; impious, irreligious; criminal; unlucky, inauspicious; _n_ crime, outrage

negāti·ō -ōnis _f_ denial

negit·ō -āre _vt_ to deny, refuse, turn down

neglecti·ō -ōnis _f_ neglect

neglectus _pp_ of **neglego**

neglect·us -ūs _m_ neglect

neglěg·ens -entis _adj_ negligent, careless, indifferent

neglegenter _adv_ carelessly

neglegenti·a -ae _f_ negligence, carelessness, neglect

neg·lěgō -legěre -lexī -lectum _vt_

to be unconcerned about; to neglect, disregard, overlook; to slight, despise

neg·ō -āre vt to deny, refuse, decline; vi to say no; to refuse

negōtiāl·is -e adj business

negōti·ans -antis m business man

negōtiāti·ō -ōnis f banking, banking business

negōtiāt·or -ōris m business man; banker; salesman, dealer

negōtiŏl·um -ī n minor matter

negōti·or -ārī -ātus sum vi to do business, do banking; to trade

negōtiōs·us -a -um adj business; busy

negōt·ium -iī or **-ī** n business, occupation, employment; matter, thing, affair; situation; trouble; banking, money lending; trade, commerce; **negotium suum** private affairs; **quid negoti est?** what's the matter?; **quid negoti tibi est?** what business is it of yours?

Nēl·eus -ĕī or **-ĕos** m son of Neptune and the nymph Tyro, king of Pylos, and father of Nestor

Nēmae·us -a -um adj Nemean

Nemĕ·a -ae or **Nemĕ·ē -ēs** f town in Argolis, where Hercules slew the Nemean lion and founded the Nemean games

Nemĕ·a -ōrum n pl Nemean games (held every two years at Nemea)

Nemĕs·is -is or **-ios** f goddess of vengeance

nēm·ō -inis m or f no one, nobody; **nemo quisquam** nobody at all; **nemo unus** no single person, no one by himself; **non nemo** someone, many a one

nemorāl·is -e adj sylvan

nemorens·is -e adj of a grove; of Diana's grove

nemoricult·ix -icis f denizen of the forest

nemorivǎg·us -a -um adj roaming the woods

nemorōs·us -a -um adj wooded; covered with foliage

nempe adv (in confirmation or in sarcasm) certainly, to be sure, of course, naturally; (in questions) do you mean?

nem·us -ōris n grove; sacred grove; plantation

nēni·a or **naeni·a -ae** f funeral dirge; doleful song; incantation; ditty

neō nēre nēvī nētum vt to spin; to weave

Neoptolĕm·us -ī m Pyrrhus, the son of Achilles

nep·a -ae f scorpion; crab

Nephelē·is -idos f Helle (daughter of Nephele and Athamas)

nep·ōs -ōtis m grandson; nephew; descendant; spendthrift

Nep·ōs -ōtis m Cornelius Nepos (Roman biographer and friend of Cicero, c. 100- c. 25 B.C.)

nepōtǔl·us -ī m little grandson

nept·is -is f granddaughter

Neptūnǐ·us -a -um adj of Neptune

Neptūn·us -ī m Neptune (god of the sea and brother of Jupiter)

nēquam (indecl) adj worthless, bad, good for nothing

nēquāquam adv by no means, not at all

neque see nec

nequēdum see necdum

nequ·eō -īre -īvī or **-ǐī -ǐtum** vi to be unable; (with inf) to be unable to, not to be able to, be incapable of; **nequit** (with quin) it is impossible to

nēquǐ·or -us adj (comp of nequam) worse, more worthless

nēquiquam or **nēquicquam** adv pointlessly, for nothing, to no purpose; without good reason; with impunity

nēquissim·us -a -um adj (superl of nequam) worst, most worthless

nēquiter adv worthlessly, wretchedly, miserably, vilely, wrongly

nēquiti·a -ae or **nēquiti·ēs -ēī** f worthlessness, vileness, wickedness

Nērē·is -idis f sea nymph, Nereid (daughter of Nereus, of whom there were 50)

Nēr·eus -ĕī or **-ĕos** m son of Oceanus and Tethys, husband of Doris and father of the Nereids; sea

Nērin·ē -ēs f daughter of Nereus

Nēritǐ·us -a -um adj of Neritos; **Neritius dux** Ulysses

Nērit·os or **Nērit·us -ī** m island near Ithaca

Nēr·ō -ōnis m Nero Claudius Caesar (Roman emperor 38-68 A.D.; reigned 54-68 A.D.)

Nērōniān·us -a -um adj Nero's, Neronian

Nerv·a -ae m M. Cocceius Nerva (Roman emperor 30-98 A.D., reigned 96-98 A.D.)

nervōsē adv strongly, vigorously

nervōs·us -a -um adj sinewy, brawny, strong

nervǔl·us -ī m a little vigor

nerv·us -ī m sinew, tendon, muscle; string, wire; bowstring; thong, strap; penis; leather covering of a shield; prison; power, vigor, strength, nerve, force, energy

nesc·iō -īre -īvī or **-ǐī -ǐtum** vt not to know, be ignorant of, be unacquainted with; (with inf) a not to know how to; b to be unable to; **nescio modo** somehow or other; **nescio quando** sometime or other; **nescio quid** something or other; **nescio quis** someone or other

nesci·us -a -um adj unaware, not knowing, ignorant; unknown; (with genit or de + abl) ignorant of, unaware of; (with inf) not knowing how to, unable to, incapable of; (with acc & inf) unaware that, not knowing that

Ness·us -ī m centaur who was slain by Hercules with a poisoned arrow for trying to molest his wife

Nest·or -ŏris m son of Neleus, king

of Pylos, and wise counselor of the Greeks at Troy

neu see **neve**

neut·er -ra -rum *adj* neither (*of two*); neuter; of neither sex; *pron* neither one (*of two*)

neutiquam or **ne utiquam** *adv* on no account, in no way

neutrō *adv* to neither side

neutrŭbi *adv* in neither the one place nor the other

nēve or **neu** *conj* or not, and not; **neve . . . neve** or **neu . . . neu** neither . . . nor

nex necis *f* death, murder, slaughter

nexil·is -e *adj* tied up, bound together

nex·um -ī *n* slavery for debt; voluntary servitude for debt

nex·us -a -um *pp* of **necto**; *m* free person who has pledged his person as security for a debt

nex·us -ūs *m* grip; bond; enslavement for debt

nī *adv* not; **quid nī?** why not?; *conj* (in prohibition or negative purpose) that not; (in negative condition) if not, unless

nīcētēr·ium -iī or **-ī** *n* prize

nic·ō -ēre -ī *vi* to beckon

nict·ō -āre *vi* to wink; (with *dat*) to wink at

nīdāment·um -ī *n* material for a nest

nīd·or -ōris *m* steam, vapor, smell

nīdŭl·us -ī *m* little nest

nīd·us -ī *m* nest; (fig) home; *m pl* nestlings, brood

nig·er -ra -rum *adj* black; swarthy, dark; dismal; unlucky, ill-omened; black, bad (*character*); malicious

nigr·ans -antis *adj* black, dusky

nigr·escō -escēre -ŭī *vi* to grow black, grow dark

nigr·ō -āre *vi* to be black

nigr·or -ōris *m* blackness, darkness

nihil or **nīl** (indecl) *n* nothing; (with *genit*) no, not a bit of; **nihil boni** no good, not a bit of good; **nil est** it is pointless, it's no good

nihil or **nīl** *adv* not, not at all, in no respect

nihilōmĭnus *adv* nonetheless, nevertheless, just the same; no less

nihil·um or **nīl·um -ī** *n* nothing; **de nihilo** for nothing, for no reason; **nihil est quod, cur,** or **quam ob rem** there is no reason why; **nihili esse** to be worthless, be of no value; **nihili facere** or **nihili pandere** to consider as worthless; **nihilo minus** nonetheless, nevertheless; **nihil quicquam** nothing whatever, nothing at all; **pro nihilo putare** to regard as worthless

nīl see **nihil**

Nīliăc·us -a -um *adj* Nile, of the Nile, Egyptian

Nīligĕn·a -ae *masc & fem adj* born on the Nile, Egyptian

Nīlum see **nihilum**

Nīl·us -ī *m* Nile River; god of the Nile

nimbāt·us -a -um *adj* light, frivolous

nimbif·er -ĕra -ĕrum *adj* stormy

nimbōs·us -a -um *adj* stormy, rainy

nimb·us -ī *m* cloud; storm cloud, black rain cloud; rainstorm, heavy shower, pouring rain; (fig) storm

nimiō *adv* far, much; **nimio plus** far more, much more

nimīrum *adv* no doubt, certainly, surely; (ironically) doubtless, of course

nimis *adv* very, very much, too much; **non nimis** not particularly

nimium *adv* too, too much; very, very much; **nimium quam** or **nimium quantum** very much indeed, ever so much, very; **nimium quam es barbarus** you are as barbarous as can be; **non nimium** not particularly, not very much

nimi·us -a -um *adj* very much, very great; too great, excessive; *n* excess, abundance

ningit (or **ninguit**) **ningĕre ninguit** (or **ninxit**) *v impers* it is snowing

ningu·ēs -ium *f pl* snowflakes, snow

Nin·us -ī *m* son of Belus, the first king of Assyria, husband of Semiramis, and builder of Nineveh; Nineveh

Nĭŏb·a -ae or **Nĭŏb·ē -ēs** *f* daughter of Tantalus and wife of Amphion, who was turned into a weeping mountain after Apollo and Diana had slain her seven sons and seven daughters

Nīr·eus -ĕī or **-ĕos** *m* handsomest Greek at Troy

Nīsē·is -ĭdis *f* Scylla (*daughter of Nisus*)

nisi *conj* unless, if not; except, but

nīsus *pp* of **nitor**

nīs·us or **nix·us -ūs** *m* pressure, effort; labor pain (*of childbirth*); soaring, flight; posture; **nisu immotus eodem immobile** in the same posture

Nīs·us -ī *m* king of Megara, father of Scylla, who betrayed her country by cutting off his purple lock of hair; friend of Euryalus in the Aeneid

nĭtēdŭl·a -ae *f* dormouse

nit·ens -entis *adj* shining, bright; brilliant; beautiful, glowing with beauty, glamorous; sleek (*cattle*); greasy

nit·ĕō -ēre -ŭī *vi* to shine, gleam, glisten; to be glamorous; to glow with health; (of animals) to be sleek; to be greasy; to be flashy

nit·escō -escĕre -ŭī *vi* to become shiny, become bright; to begin to glow (*with health or beauty*); to grow sleek

nitĭdē *adv* brightly

nitidiuscŭlē *adv* somewhat more sprucely

nitidiuscŭl·us -a -um *adj* a little more shiny

nitid·us -a -um *adj* shining, bright; glowing (*with health or beauty*); shiny, greasy; glamorous, flashy; smart, spruce, handsome; cultivated, refined; sleek (*cattle*)

nit·or -ōris *m* brightness, sheen; luster; glamour, beauty, healthy glow; elegance (*of style*); dignity (*of character*)

nītor nītī nixus sum (usually in the literal sense) or **nīsus sum** (usually in the figurative sense) *vi* to make an effort, struggle, strain, strive; to be in labor; to push forward, advance, climb, fly; to contend, insist; (with *abl* or **in** + *acc*) to lean on, support oneself on; (with *abl* or **in** + *abl*) (fig) to depend on, rely on, trust to; (with **ad** + *acc*) to aspire to; (with *inf*) to try to, endeavor, to struggle to

nitr·um -ī *n* soda; soap, cleanser

nivāl·is -e *adj* snowy; covered with snow; cold, wintry; (fig) cold, chilly

nivě·us -a -um *adj* of snow, snowy, snow; covered with snow; snow-white

nivōs·us -a -um *adj* snowy

nix nivis *f* snow; *f pl* (fig) grey hair

nix·or -ārī -ātus sum *vi* to struggle hard; (with *abl*) to lean upon, rest on

nixus *vp* of **nitor**

nix·us -ūs see **nisus**

nō nāre *vi* to swim, float; to sail; to fly; (of eyes) to be glazed

nōbil·is -e *adj* known; noted; notable, famous; notorious; noble; thorough-bred (*horse*); fine, excellent; *m pl* notables, nobles

nōbilit·ās -ātis *f* fame, renown; noble birth; the nobility; excellence

nōbilit·ō -āre *vt* to make famous; to make notorious

noc·ens -entis *adj* harmful; guilty criminal

noc·ěō -ēre -uī -ītum *vi* (with *dat*) to harm, injure

nocīv·us -a -um *adj* harmful, injurious

noctif·er -ěrī *m* evening star

noctilūc·a -ae *f* moon

noctivāg·us -a -um *adj* night-wandering

noctū *adv* by night, at night

noctu·a -ae *f* owl

noctuābund·us -a -um *adj* traveling by night

noctuīn·us -a -um *adj* of owls

nocturn·us -a -um *adj* nocturnal, of night, at night, by night, night

noctuvigil·us -a -um *adj* awake at night

nocŭ·us -a -um *adj* harmful, injurious

nōd·ō -āre *vt* to tie in a knot, knot, tie

nōdōs·us -a -um *adj* knotty

nōd·us -ī *m* knot; knob, knot (*in wood*); girdle; bond, tie; obligation; knotty point, difficulty, crisis

nōlō nolle nōlŭī *vt* (with *inf*) to be unwilling to, wish not to, refuse to; *vi* to be unwilling

nom·as -ădis *m* or *f* nomad; Numidian

nōm·en -ĭnis *n* name; gentile name (*e.g., Julius, as distinct from the praenomen*); race, stock; title; noun; bond, claim, debt; debtor; name, fame, reputation; title, pretext, pretense, excuse, account, reason, responsibility, authority, sake, behalf; mere name (*as opposed to reality*); **aetatis nomine** on the pretext of age, on account of age; **eo nomine** on that account; **nomen dare** or **nomen profiteri** to enlist (*in the army*); **nomen deferre** (with *genit*) to bring an accusation against, accuse (*someone*); **nomen dissolvere** or **nomen expedire** or **nomen solvere** to liquidate an account, pay a debt; **nomina sua exigere** to collect one's debt

nōmenclāt·or -ōris *m* name caller (*slave who accompanied his master and identified those whom they met, esp. during a political campaign*)

nōminātim *adv* by name, expressly

nōminātĭ·ō -ōnis *f* nomination for office

nōminātīv·us -a -um *adj & m* nominative

nōmināt·us -a -um *adj* renowned

nōminit·ō -āre *vt* to usually call

nōmin·ō -āre *vt* to name, call by name; to mention by name; to make famous; to nominate for an office; to denounce, arraign

nomism·a -ătis *n* coin

nōn *adv* not; no; by no means

Nōn·ae -ārum *f pl* Nones (*fifth day in all months, except March, May, July, and October, in which they occurred on the seventh*)

nōnāgensim·us or **nōnāgēsim·us -a -um** *adj* ninetieth

nōnāgiens or **nōnāgiēs** *adv* ninety times

nōnāgintā (indecl) *adj* ninety

nōnān·us -a -um *adj* of the ninth legion; *m* soldier of the ninth legion

nōnāri·a -ae *f* prostitute

nondum *adv* not yet

nongent·ī -ae -a *adj* nine hundred

nonne *adv* is it not?; (in indirect questions) whether not; **nonne vides?** don't you see?, you see, don't you?; **quaeritur nonne ire statim velis** the question is whether you do not wish to go at once

nonnull·us -a -um *adj* some, many a; **nonnulli** some, some people

nonnunquam *adv* sometimes

nonnusquam *adv* in some places

nōn·us -a -um *adj* ninth; *f* ninth hour

nōn·us decĭm·us -a -um *adj* nineteenth

Noric·us -a -um *adj* of Noricum; *n* region between the Danube and the Alps

norm·a -ae *f* square (*carpenter's tool*); (fig) rule, standard

nōs *pron* we; us

noscit·ō -āre *vt* to examine closely, observe; to recognize, know

noscō noscĕre nōvī nōtum or **gnoscō — gnōvī gnōtum** *vt* to get to know, become acquainted with, recognize, learn; to examine, inquire into; to approve of; **novisse** to have become acquainted with, (*and therefore*) to know

nosmet *pron* (emphatic form of **nōs**) we ourselves; us

noster·ra -rum *adj* our, our own; *pron* ours; **noster** our friend; **nostri** our men, our soldiers, our side

nostr·ās -ātis *adj* native, of our country

not·a -ae *f* note, mark, sign; letter, character; note, short letter; punctuation mark; brand (*of wine*); marginal note, critical mark; tattoo marks, brand; distinctive mark, distinctive quality; stamp (*on coin*); brand, stigma; nickname; black mark (*against one's name*); reproach, disgrace; nod, sign, beck; *f pl* letters of the alphabet; shorthand notes; memoranda

notābil·is -e *adj* notable, noteworthy, memorable; notorious

notābiliter *adv* notably, remarkably; perceptibly

notār·ius -iī or **-ī** *m* stenographer; secretary

notāti·ō -ōnis *f* notation, mark; black mark (*of a censor*); choice; observation; etymology

notāt·us -a -um *adj* noted, distinguished

nōt·escō -escĕre -uī *vi* to become known

noth·us -a -um *adj* bastard, illegitimate; mongrel; not genuine, phoney

nōti·ō -ōnis *f* acquaintance; (*law*) investigation; (*fig*) notion, idea

nōtiti·a -ae or **nōtiti·ēs -ēī** *f* acquaintance; fame; notion, conception

not·ō -āre *vt* to mark; to mark out; to note, mark, observe; to write down; to record; to take down in shorthand; to mark critically; to brand; to indicate, denote; to brand, reproach

not·us or **not·os -ī** *m* south wind; wind

nōt·us -a -um *pp* of **nosco**; *adj* known, well known; notorious; familiar, customary; *m pl* acquaintances

novācul·a -ae *f* razor

novāl·is -is *f* or **novāl·e -is** *n* field plowed for the first time, reclaimed land; cultivated field; fallow land; crops

novātr·ix -īcis *f* renovator, renewer (*female*)

novē *adv* newly, in an unusual manner

novell·us -a -um *adj* new, fresh, young, newly acquired

novem (indecl) *adj* nine

Novemb·er or **Novemb·ris -re** *adj* & *m* November

novendĕcim or **novemdĕcim** (indecl) *adj* nineteen

novendiāl·is or **novemdiāl·e -e** *adj* nine-day; occurring on the ninth day

novensil·ēs -ium *m pl* new gods (*introduced from abroad*)

novēn·ī -ae -a *adj* in groups of nine, nine each, nine

noverc·a -ae *f* stepmother

novercāl·is -e *adj* stepmother's, of a stepmother, like a stepmother

novici·us -a -um *adj* new, brand new

noviens or **noviēs** *adv* nine times

novissimē *adv* very recently, of late

novissim·us -a -um *adj* latest, last, most recent; **novissimum agmen** (mil) the rear; **novissima verba** parting words; *m pl* (mil) rear guard

novit·ās -ātis *f* newness, novelty; rareness, strangeness, unusualness; novelty of high rank, recently acquired rank

nov·ō -āre *vt* to make new, renovate, renew; to repair, fix; to refresh; to change, alter; to invent, coin (*words*); **res novare** to bring about a revolution

nov·us -a -um *adj* new, young, fresh, novel; strange, unusual, unheard-of; recent, modern; new, unused; inexperienced; renewed, revived; **homo novus** self-made man (*first man of a family to reach a curule office*); **res novae** political innovations, revolution; *n* news

nox noctis *f* night; night activity; sleep; death; darkness, blindness; mental darkness, ignorance; gloom; **ad multam noctem** till late at night; **nocte** or **de nocte** at night, by night; **noctem et diem** night and day; **sub noctem** at nightfall

nox·a -ae *f* harm, injury; offense, fault, guilt, responsibility; punishment

noxi·us -a -um *adj* harmful, noxious; guilty; (with *genit* or *abl*) guilty of; *f* harm, damage, injury; blame, guilt; fault, offense; **in noxia esse** to be at fault

nūbĕcul·a -ae *f* little cloud; gloomy expression

nūb·ēs -is *f* or **nūb·is -is** *m* cloud; gloom; veil

nūbif·er -ĕra -ĕrum *adj* cloudy; cloud-capped (*mountain*); cloud-bringing (*wind*)

nūbigĕn·a -ae *adj masc* or *fem* born of clouds

nūbil·is -e *adj* marriageable

nūbil·us -a -um *adj* cloudy; cloud-bringing (*wind*); troubled; dark, gloomy, melancholy

nūbō nūbĕre nupsī nuptum *vi* (of women) to marry; (with *dat*) to marry (*a man*), be married to (*a man*)

nucifrangĭbŭl·um -ī *n* (colloquially of teeth) nutcracker

nuclĕ·us -ī *m* nut; kernel, stone (*of fruit*)

nudius *adv* it is now the . . . day since, e.g., **nudius tertius dedi ad te epistolam** it is now the third day since I mailed you a letter; ago, e.g., **nudius tertius decimus** twelve days ago

nūd·ō -āre *vt* to strip, bare; to lay bare, uncover; (mil) to leave undefended; (with *abl*) to divest of

nūd·us -a -um *adj* nude, naked; lightly clothed; bare, empty; defenseless; poor, needy; bare, mere, simple, sole, only; (with *genit* or *abl* or with ab + *abl*) bare of, without, stripped of, destitute of, deprived of

nūg·ae -ārum *f pl* trifles, nonsense; good-for-nothing, a nobody

nūgāt·or -ōris *m* joker; fibber, babbler, braggart

nūgātōrĭ·us -a -um *adj* worthless, useless, nonsensical

nūg·ax -ācis *adj* nonsensical

nūgivend·us -ī *m* dealer in women's apparel

nūg·or -ārī -ātus sum *vi* to talk nonsense; (with *dat*) to trick, cheat

null·us -a -um *adj* no; (coll) not, not at all; non-existent, of no account; *pron* none

num *adv* (of time, used only with **etiam**) now, e.g., **etiam num** now, even now, still; *interrog particle* (expecting negative answer) surely not, really, actually, e.g., **num ista est nostra culpa?** is that really our fault?, that isn't our fault, is it?; *conj* (in indirect questions) whether

Num·a -ae *m* Numa Pompilius (*second king of Rome*)

numcŭbi *adv* ever?, at any time?

numell·a -ae *f* shackle

nūm·en -ĭnis *n* nod; will, consent; divine will; divine power, divinity; deity, godhead

numerābĭl·is -e *adj* easily counted, few in number

numerāt·us -ī *n* ready cash

numĕrō *adv* at the right time, just now; too soon

numĕr·ō -āre *vt* to number, count; to pay out (*money*); to consider; to enumerate, mention; to relate, recount; to reckon as one's own, possess, own

numerōsē *adv* rhythmically

numerōs·us -a -um *adj* numerous; rhythmical

numĕr·us -ī *m* member; (mil) division, troop; mere cipher; class, category; rank, position; estimation, regard; rhythm, meter, verse; quantity, measure; portion (*of work*), part, function; **aliquo numero esse** to be of some account; **in numero haberi** (with *genit*) to be regarded as, be ranked among; **nul-**

lo numero esse to be of no account; *m pl* mathematics, astronomy

Numĭd·a -ae *m* Numidian

Numĭdĭ·a -ae *f* Numidia (*a country of N. Africa*)

Numĭdĭc·us -a -um *adj* Numidian

Numĭt·or -ōris *m* king of Alba, brother of Amulius, father of Ilia, and grandfather of Romulus and Remus

nummārĭ·us -a -um *adj* financial; mercenary

nummāt·us -a -um *adj* rich; **bene nummatus** well-off, well-to-do

nummulārĭ·us -ĭī or **-ī** *m* banker

nummŭl·ī -ōrum *m pl* petty cash

numm·us -ī *m* coin, cash, money; sesterce (*small silver coin, worth about a nickel*); small sum, trifle, mere nothing; **in nummis habere** to have in ready cash

numquam or **nunquam** *adv* never; **non numquam** sometimes

numquid *adv* (to introduce direct question): **numquid meministi?** do you remember?; (to introduce indirect question): whether

nunc *adv* now; nowadays, today; now, in view of this, but as matters now stand; **nunc . . . nunc** at one time . . . at another, once . . . once

nuncŭpātĭ·ō -ōnis *f* name, appellation; public pronouncing (*of vows*)

nuncŭp·ō -āre *vt* to name, call; to take or make (*a vow*) publicly; to proclaim publicly

nundĭn·ae -ārum *f pl* market day; marketplace, market town; trade, sale

nundĭnāl·is -e *adj* market

nundĭnātĭ·ō -ōnis *f* trading, bargaining, buying and selling

nundĭn·or -ārī -ātus sum *vt* to buy; *vi* to hold a market, attend a market; to trade; to gather in large numbers

nundĭn·um -ī *n* market time; **trinum nundinum** period of three market times, i.e., seventeen days

nunq- = numq-

nuntĭātĭ·ō -ōnis *f* announcement (*by an augur*)

nuntĭ·ō -āre *vt* to announce, declare, report, relate

nuntĭ·us -a -um *adj* bringing news; *m* messenger, courier; news, message; order, injunction; **nuntium remittere** (with *dat*) to send a letter of divorce to, to divorce (*a wife*); *n pl* message, news

nūper *adv* recently

nūpĕr·us -a -um *adj* recent

nupt·a -ae *f* bride, wife

nuptĭ·ae -ārum *f pl* marriage, wedding

nuptĭāl·is -e *adj* nuptial, wedding

nur·us -ūs *f* daughter-in-law; young lady, young married woman

nusquam *adv* nowhere; on no occasion; for nothing, to nothing; **nus-**

quam alibi nowhere else; **nusquam esse** to not exist; **nusquam gentium** nowhere in the world

nūt·ō -āre vi to keep nodding; to sway to and fro, totter; to hesitate, waver

nūtrīcāt·us -ūs m nursing (of babies)

nūtrīc·ius -iī or **-ī** m tutor

nūtrīc·ō -āre or **nūtrīc·or -ārī -ātus sum** vt to nurse, suckle; to rear, bring up

nūtrīcŭl·a -e f nurse

nūtrīm·en -inis n nourishment

nūtrīment·um -ī n nutriment, nourishment, support; fuel (for fire)

nūtr·iō -īre -īvī or **-iī -ītum** vt to nurse, suckle, nourish, feed; to rear, bring up, support, maintain, foster; to take care of, attend to; to cherish, cultivate

nūtr·īx -īcis f nurse; f pl breasts

nūt·us -ūs m nod; hint, intimation; will, pleasure, command; gravity

nux nucis f nut; nut tree, almond tree; **nuces relinquere** (fig) to put away childish things

Nyctē·is -ĭdis f Antiope (wife of Lycus, the king of Thebes, and mother of Amphion and Zethus)

Nyct·eus -ĕī or **-ĕos** m father of Antiope

nymph·a -ae or **nymph·ē -ēs** f bride; nymph (demi-goddesses who inhabit fountains, rivers, sea, woods, and mountains); water

Nȳs·a -ae f mythical birthplace of Bacchus

Nȳsae·us or **Nȳsï·us -a -um** adj of Nysa, Nysaean

Nȳs·eus -ĕī or **-ĕos** m Bacchus

Nȳsĭgĕn·a -ae m native of Nysa

O

ō interj oh!

Oax·ēs or **Oax·is -is** m river in Crete

ob prep (with acc) before, in front of; on account of, because of; for the sake of, in the interest of; in return for, instead of; in proportion to, balanced against; **ob rem** to the purpose, usefully, profitably; **quam ob rem** wherefore, accordingly

obaerāt·us -a -um adj deeply in debt; m debtor

obambŭl·ō -āre vt to prowl all over, prowl about (e.g., the city); vi to walk about, wander, prowl about; (with dat) to prowl about near; (with **ante** + acc) to wander around in front of

obarm·ō -āre vt to arm

obăr·ō -āre vt to plow up, plow over

obbrūtescō -ĕre vi to grow dull

obc- = occ-

ob·dō -dĕre -dĭdī -dĭtum vt to close, lock; to expose

obdorm·iō -īre -īvī or **-iī -ītum** vi to fall asleep

obdorm·iscō -iscĕre -īvī — vi to fall asleep

ob·dūcō -dūcĕre -duxī -ductum vt to put on (clothes); to cover, veil, surround, envelop; to hide; to swallow; to pass (time); to bring forward as a candidate; to run or dig (ditch); (with dat of thing protected) to draw or place (something) over; (with dat or **ad** + acc) to pit (someone or something) against

obductī·ō -ōnis f veiling

obduct·ō -āre vt to introduce as a rival

obdūr·escō -escĕre -ŭī vi to grow hard, harden; to become insensitive

obdūr·ō -āre vi to persist, stick it out

ob·ĕō -īre -īvī or **-iī -ītum** vt to go to meet; to travel, travel to, travel over, wander through, traverse, encircle, visit; to run over, review, enumerate (in a speech); to undertake, engage in; **diem edictī obīre** to meet one's death; vi to go; to pass away, die; to fade, disappear; (of heavenly bodies) to go down, set

obequĭt·ō -āre vi to ride up; (with dat) to ride up to

oberr·ō -āre vi to ramble about, wander around; (with abl) **a** to wander about, wander among; **b** to make a mistake on or at

obēs·us -a -um adj fat, plump; swollen; crude, coarse

ob·ex -ĭcis m or f bar, bolt; barrier; obstacle, hindrance

obf- = off-

obg- = ogg-

ob·haerescō -haerescĕre -haesī vi to get stuck

obīr·ascor -ascī -ātus sum vi (with dat) to get angry at

obĭter adv on the way, as one goes along; (fig) in passing, incidentally

obĭtus pp of obeo

obĭt·us -ūs m approach, visit; death, passing, ruin, downfall; setting (of heavenly bodies)

objac·ĕō -ēre -ŭī vi (with dat) to lie before, lie at

objectātĭ·ō -ōnis f reproach

object·ō -āre vt to oppose; to expose, endanger; to throw in the way; to cause (delay); (with dat) **a** to expose to, abandon to; **b** to impute, throw up (faults) to, bring a charge of (e.g., madness) against, fling (charges, abuse) at; (with dat & acc & inf) to throw a hint to (someone) that

object·us -a -um adj lying in the

way, lying in front; (with *dat*) a opposite; b exposed to; *n pl* charges, accusations

object·us -ūs *m* interposition; obstacle, hindrance; protection; (with *genit*) protection afforded by

ob·jiciō -jicĕre -jēcī -jectum *vt* to cast, hurl; to present, offer, expose; to hold up as an example; to set up as a defense, use as a defense; (with *dat*) a to cast before, throw to, offer to, expose to, set up as a defense against; b to throw up (*faults, weaknesses, etc.*) to; c to bring upon, inflict on, inspire in; objici (with *dat*) to happen to, befall, occur to; se objicere (with *dat*) to expose oneself to

objurgāti·ō -ōnis *f* scolding, rebuke

objurgāt·or -ōris *m* critic

objurgātōri·us -a -um *adj* scolding, reproachful

objurgit·ō -āre *vt* to keep on scolding

objurg·ō -āre *vt* to scold, rebuke, blame, reprimand; to chastise, correct; to deter

oblangu·escō -escĕre -ŭī *vi* to taper off

oblātrātr·ix -īcis *f* nagging woman, nag

oblātus *pp* of offero

oblectām·en -inis *n* delight

oblectāment·um -ī *n* delight, amusement, pastime

oblectāti·ō -ōnis *f* delight, amusement; attraction; (with *genit*) diversion from

oblect·ō -āre *vt* to attract, delight, amuse, divert; to spend (*time*) pleasantly; se oblectare to amuse oneself, enjoy oneself

ob·līdō -līdĕre -līsī -līsum *vt* to crush; to squeeze together, strangle

obligāti·ō -ōnis *f* binding, pledging, obligation

obligāt·us -a -um *adj* obliged, under obligation; (with *dat*) (vow) made to

oblig·ō -āre *vt* to tie up, bandage; to bind, oblige, put under obligation, make liable; to hamper, tie down; to embarrass; to mortgage; fidem obligare to pledge one's word; obligari (with *abl*) a to be guilty of; b to be obliged to, compelled to

oblim·ō -āre *vt* to cover with mud; to dissipate, squander

ob·līnō -linĕre -lēvī -litum *vt* to smear; (fig) to smear, defile; (fig) to overload

oblīquē *adv* sideways; (fig) indirectly

obliqu·ō -āre *vt* to turn aside, twist, shift, slant

obliqu·us -a -um *adj* slanting, crosswise; from the side; indirect; sly; envious; downhill (*road*); obliquus oculus disapproving look, envious look; *n* side; ab obliquo from the side; per obliquum across

oblīsus *pp* of oblido

oblit·escō -escĕre -ŭī *vi* to hide

oblittĕr·ō -āre *vt* to erase; to cancel; (fig) to blot out; nomina oblitterare to cancel debts

oblītus *pp* of oblino

oblītus *pp* of obliviscor

oblivi·ō -ōnis *f* oblivion; forgetting; forgetfulness

obliviōs·us -a -um *adj* forgetful, oblivious; (wine) causing forgetfulness

ob·līviscor -līviscī -lītus sum *vt* to forget; *vi* to forget; (with *genit*) to forget, neglect, disregard, be indifferent to

oblīv·ium -iī or -ī *n* forgetfulness, oblivion

oblocūt·or -ōris *m* contradictor

oblong·us -a -um *adj* oblong

ob·lōquor -lōquī -locūtus sum *vt* (with *dat*) a to interrupt; b to answer (*in argument*), contradict; c to speak against, abuse, rail at; d to accompany (*in music*), sing to

oblnct·or -ārī -ātus sum *vi* (with *dat*) to struggle with, fight against, struggle against

oblūd·ō -ĕre *vt* to play jokes on

obmōl·ior -īrī -ītus sum *vt* to make a barricade of

obmurmŭr·ō -āre *vi* (with *dat*) to roar in answer to

obmūt·escō -escĕre -ŭī *vi* to become silent, hush up; to cease

obnāt·us -a -um *adj* growing on (*e.g., the bank of a river*)

ob·nitor -nītī -nixus sum *vi* to strain, struggle, put on the pressure; (with *dat*) a to press against, lean against; b to resist, oppose

obnixē *adv* with all one's might, obstinately

obnix·us -a -um *pp* of obnitor; *adj* steadfast, firm, resolute

obnoxiē *adv* guiltily; timidly

obnoxiōsius *adv* more slavishly

obnoxiōs·us -a -um *adj* submissive

obnoxi·us -a -um *adj* liable, addicted, guilty; submissive, servile, obedient; weak, timid; obliged, under obligation, indebted; answerable, responsible; liable, subject, exposed; obnoxium est (with *inf*) it is dangerous to

ob·nūbō -nūbĕre -nupsī -nuptum *vt* to veil, cover

obnuntiāti·ō -ōnis *f* announcement (of omens)

obnunti·ō -āre *vi* to make an announcement; to make an announcement that the omens are adverse; to announce bad news

oboedi·ens -entis *adj* obedient; (with *dat* or *ad* + *acc*) obedient to

oboedienter *adv* obediently

oboedienti·a -ae *f* obedience

oboed·iō -īre -īvī or -iī -ītum *vi* (with *dat*) to give ear to, listen to, obey

obol·ĕō -ēre -ŭī *vt* to smell of; *vi* to smell

ob·orior -orīrī -ortus sum vi to rise, appear

obp- = opp-

ob·rēpō -rēpere -repsī -reptum vt to creep up on, sneak up on; vi to creep up; (with dat) a to creep up on, sneak up on, take by surprise; b to trick, cheat; (with in + acc) to steal over; obrepere ad honores to worm one's way into high positions

obrept·ō -āre vi to sneak up

obrēt·iō -īre -īvī or -iī -ītum vt to entangle

obrig·escō -escere -uī vi to stiffen; to freeze

obrōd·ō -ēre vt to gnaw at

obrōg·ō -āre vi (with dat) to supersede (a law)

ob·ruō -ruere -ruī -rūtum vt to cover up, cover, hide, bury; to overwhelm, overthrow; to sink, cover with water, swamp, overflow; to overpower, surpass, obscure, eclipse; vi to fall to ruin

obruss·a -ae f test, proof

obsaep·iō -īre -sī -tum vt to fence in; to block (road); (fig) to close, block

obsatūr·ō -āre vt to sate, cloy; istius obsaturari to have enough of him

obscaen- = obscen-

obscaev·ō -āre vi to give a bad omen

obscēnē adv obscenely

obscēnit·ās -ātis f obscenity

obscēn·us -a -um adj dirty, filthy; indecent, obscene; ominous

obscūrāti·ō -ōnis f obscuring, darkening; disappearance

obscūrē adv indistinctly; secretly, imperceptibly

obscūrit·ās -ātis f obscurity

obscūr·ō -āre vt to obscure, darken; to cover, hide; to veil (words); (of love) to blind; to hide, suppress

obscūr·us -a -um adj obscure, dark, shady; obscure, lowly, mean; dim, indistinct, unintelligible; secret; reserved; vague, uncertain; gloomy; n the dark, darkness; obscurity

obsecrāti·ō -ōnis f entreaty; public appeal to the gods

obsecr·ō -āre vt to entreat, appeal to, implore

obsecund·ō -āre vi (with dat) to comply with, humor

obsecūtus pp of obsequor

obsēp- = obsaep-

obsēqu·ens -entis adj compliant, obedient; indulgent, gracious (gods); (with dat) obedient to

obsequenter adv compliantly, obsequiously

obsequenti·a -ae f obsequiousness

obsequiōs·us -a -um adj obsequious

obsequ·ium -iī or -ī n compliance, indulgence; obedience, allegiance

ob·sequor -sequī -secūtus sum vi (with dat) to comply with, yield to, give into, gratify, humor

obser·ō -āre vt to bolt, bar, lock up

ob·serō -serere -sēvī -situm vt to sow or plant thickly; to fill, cover

observ·ans -antis adj attentive, respectful; (with genit) respectful of, attentive to, careful about

observanti·a -ae f regard, respect; (with genit or in + acc) regard for, respect for

observāti·ō -ōnis f observation; caution, care

observāt·or -ōris m observer

observit·ō -āre vt to watch carefully, note carefully

observ·ō -āre vt to watch, watch out for, take careful note of; to guard; to observe, keep, obey, comply with; to pay attention to, pay respect to

obs·es -idis m or f hostage; guarantee

obsessi·ō -ōnis f blockade

obsess·or -ōris m frequenter, regular visitor; blockader

ob·sideō -sidēre -sēdī -sessum vt to sit near or at, remain by or near; to frequent; (mil) to besiege, invest, blockade; to block, choke; to occupy, fill; to look out for, watch closely; to keep guard over

obsidiāl·is -e adj for breaking a blockade; corona obsidialis decoration for breaking a blockade

obsidi·ō -ōnis f blockade, siege; imminent danger

obsid·ium -iī or -ī n blockade, siege; imminent danger, great peril; status of hostage

ob·sīdō -sīdere -sēdī -sessum vt to besiege, invest, beset, blockade; to take possession of, occupy

obsignāt·or -ōris m sealer; witness; obsignator testamenti witness to a will

obsign·ō -āre vt to seal, seal up: to sign and seal; (fig) to stamp, impress

ob·sistō -sistere -stitī -stitum vi (with dat) to stand in the way of, block, resist, oppose, disapprove of, forbid

obsitus pp of obsero (to sow)

obsolē·fiō -fierī -factus sum vi to wear out, become spoiled; to become worthless

obsol·escō -escere -ēvī -ētum vi to wear out, go out of style, become obsolete, get shabby, lose value

obsolētius adv rather shabbily

obsolēt·us -a -um adj out of date, old, obsolete, worn out; shabby, threadbare; low, mean, poor

obsōnāt·or -ōris m shopper

obsōnāt·us -ūs m shopping

obsōn·ium -iī or -ī n shopping items, food

obsōn·ō -āre or obsōn·or -ārī -ātus sum vt to shop for; famem obsonare to work up an appetite; vi to go shopping; to provide food; (with de + abl) to provide a feast for

obsōn·ō -āre vi (with dat) to drown out

obsorb·eō -ēre -uī vt to gulp down

obstant·ia -ium *n pl* obstacles, obstructions

obstētr·ix -īcis *f* midwife

obstinātē *adv* resolutely, with determination; obstinately, stubbornly

obstināti·ō -ōnis *f* resolution, determination; obstinacy, stubbornness

obstināt·us -a -um *adj* resolute, determined, fixed; obstinate, stubborn

obstin·ō -āre *vt* to be resolved on, resolve, determine; (with *inf*) to resolve to, determine to; *vi* to be determined, be resolved; (with **ad** + *acc*) to be set on

obstipescō see **obstupesco**

obstīp·us -a -um *adj* bent, bent to one side; bent forwards, bowed; **capite obstīpo stare** to stand with head bowed

ob·stō -stāre -stētī *vi* to stand in the way, be in the way, raise opposition; (with *dat*) to stand in the way of, oppose, object to, resist, hinder, obstruct; (with **ne, quin, quōminus,** or **cur nōn**) to prevent (*someone*) from

obstrep·ō -ere -uī -itum *vt* to fill with noise, drown out; *vi* to make a racket, make noise; **a** (with *dat*) to shout at, drown out with shouts, interrupt with shouts; **b** (*of the sea*) to resound against

ob·stringō -stringere -strinxī -strictum *vt* to shut in, confine, tie up; (fig) to tie up, involve, put under obligation, oblige; **fidem obstringere** (with *dat*) to pledge one's word to; **obstringi** or **se obstringere** (with *abl*) to get involved in, be guilty of

obstructi·ō -ōnis *f* obstruction

obstructus *pp* of **obstruo**

obs·trūdō or **ob·trūdō -trūdere -trūsī -trūsum** *vt* to gulp down; (with *dat*) to force (*something*) upon, thrust (*something*) upon

ob·struō -struere -struxī -structum *vt* to pile up, block up, stop up; (with *dat*) to block or close (e.g., *the road*) against

obstrūsus *pp* of **obstrudo**

obstupe·faciō -facere -fēcī -factum *vt* to astound, astonish, paralyze, stupefy

obstup·escō or **obstip·escō -escēre -uī** *vi* to be astounded, be struck dumb, be paralyzed

obstupid·us -a -um *adj* stupefied

ob·sum -esse -fuī *vi* (with *dat*) to be opposed to, be against; to be prejudicial to, harm; **nihil obest dicere** there is no harm in saying

ob·suō -suere -suī -sūtum *vt* to sew on; to sew up

obsurd·escō -escēre -uī *vi* to become deaf; (fig) to turn a deaf ear

ob·tegō -tegere -texī -tectum *vt* to cover up; to protect; (fig) to conceal, keep secret; **animus sui obtegens** secretive mind

obtemperāti·ō -ōnis *f* compliance, obedience

obtemper·ō -āre *vi* (with *dat*) to comply with, submit to, obey

ob·tendō -tendere -tendī -tentum *vt* to spread, stretch out; to offer as an excuse; to envelop, conceal; **obtendī** (with *dat*) to lie opposite; **obtentā nocte** under cover of darkness

obtentus *pp* of **obtineo**

obtent·us -ūs *m* screen, cover; pretext, pretense

ob·terō -terere -trīvī -trītum *vt* to trample on, trample down, crush; (fig) to trample on, crush, degrade, destroy

obtestāti·ō -ōnis *f* adjuring, adjuration; solemn entreaty, supplication

obtest·or -ārī -ātum sum *vt* to call as witness; to make an appeal to, implore, entreat

obtex·ō -ere -uī *vt* to cover, veil

obtic·ĕō -ēre *vi* to be silent

obtic·escō -escēre -uī *vi* to fall silent, be dumbstruck

ob·tineō -tinēre -tinuī -tentum *vt* to get hold of; to hold on to, keep, maintain, preserve, uphold; to assert, maintain; to obtain, gain, acquire; *vi* to continue

ob·tingō -tingere -tigī *vi* to happen, occur; (with *dat*) to happen to, befall, occur to

obtorp·escō -escēre -uī *vi* to become numb, become stiff, become insensible

ob·torquĕō -torquēre -torsī -tortum *vt* to twist

obtrectāti·ō -ōnis *f* detraction, disparagement

obtrectāt·or -ōris *m* detractor, disparager

obtrect·ō -āre *vt* to treat spitefully, mistreat, disparage; to carp at; *vi* (with *dat*) to detract from, disparage, belittle

obtrītus *pp* of **obtero**

obtrūdō see **obstrudo**

obtrunc·ō -āre *vt* to cut off, cut down; (in battle) to cut down, kill

ob·tuĕor -tuērī -tuitus sum *vt* to gaze at, gaze upon; to see clearly

ob·tundō -tundere -tudī -tūsum or **-tunsum** *vt* to beat, beat on, thump on; to blunt; (fig) to pound away at, stun, deafen, annoy, molest, importune

obturb·ō -āre *vt* to throw into disorder; (fig) to disturb, confuse, distract

obturgesc·ō -ere *vi* to begin to swell up

obtur·ō -āre *vt* to block up, stop up, plug up; **aures obturare** to refuse to listen

obtūsus or **obtunsus** *pp* of **obtundo**; *adj* blunt, dull; (fig) dulled, blurred

obtūt·us -ūs *m* stare, gaze

obumbr·ō -āre *vt* to overshadow, shade; to darken, obscure; to cover, screen

obunc·us -a -um *adj* hooked

obust·us -a -um *adj* singed; hardened in the fire; nipped (*by cold*)

obvāg·iō -īre *vi* to whimper

obvall·ō -āre *vt* to fortify

ob·veniō -venīre -vēnī -ventum *vi* to come up, happen, occur; (with *dat*) to fall to the lot of, be alloted to

obvers·or -ārī -ātus sum *vi* to make an appearance, show oneself; (fig) hover

obvers·us -a -um *adj* (with ad + *acc*) a turned toward, facing; b inclined to; (with *dat*) engaged in; *m pl* opponents

ob·vertō or **ob·vortō -vertēre -vertī -versum** *vt* (with *dat* or ad + *acc*) to turn (*something*) towards or in the direction of; (with **in** + *acc*) to turn (*e.g., the soldiers*) to face (*e.g., the enemy*); **obvertī** (with **ad** + *acc*) to turn toward

obviam or **ob viam** *adv* (with *dat*) a to meet, in order to meet, in the way of; b (fig) opposed to; **effundi obviam** (with *dat*) to pour out to meet, go out in great numbers to meet; **obviam esse** (with *dat*) a to meet; b to oppose, resist; **obviam īre** (with *dat*) or **obviam procedere** (with *dat*) to go to meet; **obviam obsistere** (with *dat*) to stand in the way of (*someone*); **obviam prodire** or **obviam proficisci** or **obviam progredī** (with *dat*) to go out to meet; **obviam venire** (with *dat*) to go to meet, come to meet

obvigilāt·um -ī *n* vigilance

obvi·us -a -um *adj* in the way; exposed, open; accessible (*person*); ready, at hand; (with *dat*) a to meet, so as to meet; b opposed to; c exposed or open to; **obvius esse** (with *dat*) to meet, encounter; **obvius venire** (with *dat*) to come to meet

ob·volvō -volvēre -volvī -volūtum *vt* to wrap up, cover up

occaec·ō -āre *vt* to blind, make blind; to darken, obscure; to hide; to numb

occall·escō -escēre -uī *vi* to become thick-skinned; (fig) to become callous

occan·ō -ēre -uī *vi* to sound the charge

occāsi·ō -ōnis *f* occasion, opportunity, good time, chance; pretext; (mil) surprise, raid; **occasionem amittere** to lose the opportunity; **occasionem arripere** to seize the opportunity; **per occasionem** at the right time

occāsiuncŭl·a -ae *f* nice little opportunity

occās·us -ūs *m* setting; sunset, west; (fig) downfall, ruin, death

occāti·ō -ōnis *f* harrowing

occāt·or -ōris *m* harrower

oc·cēdō -cēdēre -cessī -cessum *vi* to go up; **obviam occedere** (with *dat*) to go to meet

occent·ō -āre *vt* to serenade; to satirize in verse

occept·ō -āre *vt* to begin

occid·ens -entis *m* the setting sun; west

occidi·ō -ōnis *f* massacre, annihilation; **occidione occidere** to massacre, annihilate, wipe out

oc·cidō -cidēre -cidī -cāsum *vt* to knock down; to cut down, slay, kill; to murder; to ruin; to pester to death; **se occidere** to commit suicide

oc·cidō -cidēre -cidī -cāsum *vi* to fall, fall down; (of the sun) to go down, set; to fall, be slain, perish; (of hope, etc.) to fade, die; (fig) to be ruined, be lost; **occidi!** I'm finished!

occidŭ·us -a -um *adj* setting; western; (fig) sinking, fading, dying

occili·ō -āre *vt* to smash

oc·cinō -cinēre -cecinī or **-cinuī** *vi* to sound ominous

oc·cipiō -cipēre -cēpī -ceptum *vt & vi* to begin

occipit·ium -iī or **-ī** or **occip·ut -itis** *n* back of the head

occisi·ō -ōnis *f* massacre; **occisionem facere** to cause a massacre

occis·or -ōris *m* killer, murderer

occisus *pp* of **occīdō**

oc·clāmit·ō -āre *vt* to shout at; *vi* to cry out, bawl

oc·clūdō -clūdēre -clūsī -clūsum *vt* to close up, shut up, lock up; to check, control

occ·ō -āre *vt* to harrow

occŭb·ō -āre *vi* to lie; to rest

occulc·ō -āre *vt* to trample down

occŭl·ō -ēre -uī -tum *vt* to cover; to cover up, hide

occultāti·ō -ōnis *f* concealment, hiding

occultāt·or -ōris *m* hideout

occultē *adv* secretly, in concealment

occult·ō -āre *vt* to hide

occult·us -a -um *adj* hidden, secret; reserved (*person*); *n* concealment; secret; **ex occulto** from a place of concealment; secretly

oc·cumbō -cumbēre -cubŭī -cubitum *vt* to fall to, meet; **mortem occumbere** to meet death; *vi* to sink down in death, fall dying; **certae morti occumbere** to meet certain death; **morti occumbere** to fall prey to death; **occumbere** (with **per** + *acc*) to die at the hands of

occupāti·ō -ōnis *f* occupation (*e.g., of a town*); occupation, employment, business; business engagement, task; job; involvement, concern

occupāt·us -a -um *adj* occupied, busied, engaged, involved

occŭp·ō -āre *vt* to occupy, seize; to win, gain; to attack, strike down; to outstrip, overtake; to fill, take up; to invest, loan, lend; (with *inf*) to be the first to

oc·currō -currēre -currī or **-cu-**

curri -cursum *vi* to run up; (with *dat*) **a** to run up to, run to meet, meet; **b** to rush against, attack; **c** to resist, oppose, counteract; **d** to meet, answer, reply to, object to; **e** to relieve, remedy; **f** to occur to, suggest itself to, present itself to; **g** (fig) to run into, run up against, get involved in

occursāti·ō -ōnis *f* hustle and bustle; excited welcome; officiousness

occurs·ō -āre *vt* to run to meet; *vi* (with *dat*) **a** to run to meet, go or come to meet, meet; **b** to go to meet (*the enemy*), attack, charge, oppose; **c** (of thoughts) to occur to

occurs·us -ūs *m* meeting; (with *genit*) running into (*someone or something*)

Ōceanit·is -ĭdis *f* ocean nymph

Ōcean·us -ī *m* ocean; Oceanus (*son of Caelus and Terra, husband of Tethys, and father of rivers and of ocean nymphs*)

ocell·us -ī *m* eye; gem; darling

ōcĭm·um -ī *n* basil

ōcĭ·or -us *adj* swifter, quicker

ōcĭus *adv* more swiftly, more quickly; sooner; more easily; immediately, on the spot; (with *abl*) rather than; **ocius serius** sooner or later; **quam ocissime** as quickly as possible

ocrĕ·a -ae *f* greave, shin guard

ocreāt·us -a -um *adj* wearing shin guards

Octāvi·a -ae *f* sister of Augustus, wife of C. Marcellus, and later of M. Antony (64-11 B.C.); daughter of Claudius and wife of Nero (*murdered in 62 A.D.*)

Octāv·ĭus -ĭī or -ī *m* C. Octavius (*Emperor Augustus, who, upon adoption by Julius Caesar, became C. Julius Caesar Octavianus*, 63 B.C.-14 A.D.)

octāvum *adv* for the eighth time

octāv·us -a -um *adj* eighth; **octava pars** one eighth; *f* eighth hour of the day (*i.e.*, 2 *p.m.*); *n* **cum octavo efficere** to produce eightfold

octāv·us decĭm·us -a -um *adj* eighteenth

octiens or octiēs *adv* eight times

octingentēsĭm·us or octingentēnsĭm·us -a -um *adj* eight hundredth

octingent·ī -ae -a *adj* eight hundred

octĭp·ēs -ĕdis *adj* eight-footed

octō (indecl) *adj* eight

Octōb·er -ris *adj & m* October

octōdĕcim (indecl) *adj* eighteen

octōgēnāri·us -a -um *adj & m* octogenarian

octōgēn·ī -ae -a *adj* eighty each

octōgēsĭm·us or octōgēnsĭm·us -a -um *adj* eightieth

octōgiēs or octōgiens *adv* eighty times

octōgintā (indecl) *adj* eighty

octōjŭg·is -e *adj* eight-team

octōn·ī -ae -a *adj* eight at a time, eight each

octōphŏr·os -on *adj* carried by eight carriers; *n* eight-man litter

octuplicāt·us -a -um *adj* eightfold

octŭpl·us -a -um *adj* eightfold; *n* eightfold fine

octuss·is *m* sum of eight aces

oculāt·us -a -um *adj* having eyes; exposed to view, conspicuous; **oculata testis** eyewitness

oculē·us -a -um *adj* many-eyed

oculissĭm·us -a -um *adj* dearest

ocultus *adv* like one's own eyes, dearly

ocŭl·us -ī *m* eye; eye, bud (*in plants*) sight, vision; mind's eye; apple of the eye; **aequis oculis** contentedly; altero oculo captus blind in one eye; ante oculos in full view; (fig) obvious; ante oculos ponere to imagine; ex oculis abire to go out of sight, disappear; in oculis in view, in public, in the limelight; in oculis ferre or gestare to hold dear, value; oculos adjicere (with ad + *acc*) to eye; to covet; oculos dejicere (with ab + *abl*) to take one's eyes off; (fig) to lose sight of; oculos pascere (with *abl*) to feast one's eyes on; sub oculis (with *genit*) in the presence of, under the very nose of

ōd·ī -isse *vt* to have taken a dislike to, dislike, hate, be disgusted at

ōdiōsē *adv* hatefully; unpleasantly

ōdiōsĭc·us -a -um *adj* odious, unpleasant, annoying

ōdiōs·us -a -um *adj* odious, unpleasant, annoying

ōd·ium -ĭī or -ī *n* dislike, hatred, aversion; object of hatred, nuisance; dissatisfaction, disgust; offensive conduct, insolence; **odio esse** (with *dat*) to be hateful to, be disliked by, he hated by; *n pl* feelings of hatred

ŏd·or or ŏd·ōs -ōris *m* odor, smell, scent; stench, stink; pleasant smell, fragrance, perfume; inkling, suggestion, hint; *m pl* perfume

odōrāti·ō -ōnis *f* smell, smelling

odōrāt·us -a -um *adj* fragrant, scented

odōrāt·us -ūs *m* smell, smelling; sense of smell

odōrĭf·er -ĕra -ĕrum *adj* fragrant

odōr·ō -āre *vt* to make fragrant

odōr·or -ārī -ātus sum *vt* to sniff at, scent; to aspire to, aim at; to be sniffing after, search for, investigate; to get a smattering of

odōr·us -a -um *adj* smelly, fragrant; keen-scented

odōs see odor

Odrysi·us -a -um *adj & m* Thracian

Odyssē·a or Odyssī·a -ae *f* the Odyssey

Oeăg·er -rī *m* king of Thrace and father of Orpheus

Oeagri·us -a -um *adj* Thracian

Oebalid·ēs -ae *m* male descendant of Oebalus; *m pl* Castor and Pollux

Oebali·us -a -um adj Spartan; Tarentine; Sabine; f Tarentum (Spartan colony in S. Italy)

Oebăl·us -ī m king of Sparta, father of Tyndareus, and grandfather of Helen and Clytemnestra

Oedĭp·us -ŏdis or **-ī** m Oedipus

Oen·eus -ĕī or **-ĕos** m king of Calydon, husband of Althaea, and father of Meleager and Deianira

Oenĭd·ēs -ae m descendant of Oeneus; Meleager; Diomedes (son of Tydeus)

Oenomā·us -ī m king of Pisa in the Peloponnesus and father of Hippodamia

oenophŏr·um -ī n wine-bottle basket

Oenopi·a -ae f ancient name of Aegina (island between Attica and Argolis)

oenopōl·ĭum -iī or **-ī** n wine shop, tavern

Oenōtri·us -a -um adj Oenotrian, Italian; f ancient name of S.E. Italy; Italy

oestr·us -ī m horsefly, gadfly; fancy, inspiration

oesўp·um -ī n lanolin

Oet·a -ae or **Oet·ē -ēs** f Mt. Oete (mountain in S. Thessaly, on which Hercules died)

Oetae·us -a -um adj Oetean; m Hercules

ofell·a -ae f bit, morsel

off·a -ae f pellet, lump, dumpling; swelling; shapeless mass

offātim adv in bits, in little lumps

offectus pp of **officio**

of·fendō -fendĕre -fendī -fensum vt to bump, bump against, stub, strike, hit; to hit upon, come upon, meet with, bump into, stumble upon, find; to offend, shock, vex, disgust; to hurt (feelings); to injure (reputation); **nihil offendere** to suffer no damage, receive no injury; vi to make a blunder, make a mistake, blunder; to give offense, be offensive; to fail, take a loss, be defeated, come to grief; to run aground; (with dat or **in** + abl) to hit against, bump against; (with dat) to give offense to; (with **in** + acc) to take offense at; **terrae offendere** to run aground

offens·a -ae f offense, affront, injury; displeasure, resentment, hatred; crime; **offensā** (with genit) out of hatred for

offensĭ·ō -ōnis f stubbing; tripping; stumbling; dislike, displeasure, hatred, digust, aversion; discredit, bad reputation, mishap, failure, disaster, accident, defeat; f pl offensive acts; feelings of displeasure

offensiuncŭl·a -ae f slight displeasure; minor setback; disappointment

offens·ō -āre vt & vi to bump

offens·us -a -um pp of **offendo**; adj offensive, odious; offended, displeased, annoyed

offens·us -ūs m bump; shock; offense

offerō offerre obtŭlī oblātum vt to offer, bring forward, present, show; to cause, occasion; to confer, bestow, inflict; **se offerre** (with dat) a to meet; encounter; b to expose oneself to

offerument·a -ae f (said humorously of a blow or welt) present

officin·a or **opificin·a -ae** f shop, workshop, factory, office

of·ficiō -ficĕre -fēcī -fectum vi (with dat) to get in the way of, interfere with, oppose, obstruct, be detrimental to, hinder

officiōsē adv obligingly, courteously

officiōs·us -a -um adj ready to serve, obliging; dutiful, obligatory

offic·ĭum -iī or **-ī** n service, favor, kindness, courtesy; obligation, duty, function, office, part; social obligation, social call, social visit; ceremony, ceremonial observance, attendance; official duty; employment, business, job; sense of duty, conscience; allegiance

of·figō -figĕre -fixī -fixum vt to fasten down, nail down, drive in

offirmāt·us -a -um adj determined, resolute

offirm·ō -āre vt se **offirmare** to steel oneself, be determined; vi to be determined

offlect·ō -ĕre vt to turn (something) around

offrēnāt·us -a -um adj curbed

offūci·a -ae f cosmetic; (fig) trick

of·fulgeō -fulgēre -fulsī -fulsum vi (with dat) to shine on

of·fundō -fundĕre -fūdī -fūsum vt to pour out; to cover, fill; to eclipse; **offundi** (with dat) to pour out over, spread over

oggan·ĭō -īre -īvī or **-iī -ītum** vt & vi to growl

og·gerō -gerĕre vt to bring, offer, give

Ŏgўg·ēs -is or **Ŏgўg·us -ī** m mythical king of Thebes, in whose reign the Deluge occurred

Ŏgўgi·us -a -um adj Theban

oh interj oh!

ŏhē or **ōhē** interj whoa!

oi interj (express complaint) oh no!

Oïl·eus -ĕī or **-ĕos** m king of Locris and father of Ajax the archer

olĕ·a -ae f olive; olive tree

oleāgĭn·us -a -um adj olive, of an olive tree

oleāri·us -a -um adj oil, of oil; m oil merchant

oleast·er -rī m oleaster, wild olive tree

ŏlenĭ·us -a -um adj of Olenus (town in Achaia and Aetolia); Achaian, Aetolian

ol·ens -entis adj smelling; fragrant; smelly, stinking; musty

ol·eō -ēre -ĕī vt to smell of, smell like; (fig) to betray; vi to smell; (with abl) to smell of

olĕ·um -ī n olive oil, oil; (fig) palaestra; **oleum addere camino** (fig) to pour oil on the fire; **oleum**

et operam perdere to waste time and effort

ol·faciō -facĕre -fēcī -factum *vt* to smell

olfact·ō -āre *vt* to sniff at

olīd·us -a -um *adj* smelly

ōlim *adv* once, once upon a time; at the time; for a good while; someday, in the future, hereafter; now and then, at times; ever, at any time

olit- = holit-

olīv·a -ae *f* olive; olive tree; olive wreath; olive branch; olive staff

olīvēt·um -ī *n* olive grove

olivíf·er -ĕra -ĕrum *adj* olive-producing, olive-growing

olīv·um -ī *n* oil; ointment; (fig) palaestra

oll·a -ae *f* pot, jar

olle or ollus = ille

ol·or -ōris *m* swan

olōrīn·us -a -um *adj* swan, of a swan

olus see holus

Olympi·a -ae *f* Olympia (*region in Elis, in the Peloponnesus, where the Olympian games were held*)

Olympi·a -ōrum *n pl* Olympian games

Olympiāc·us -a -um *adj* Olympian

Olympi·as -ădis *f* Olympiad (*period of four years between Olympian games, starting in the year 776 B.C., according to which the Greeks reckoned time*); wife of Philip V of Macedon and mother of Alexander the Great

Olympic·us or Olympi·us -a -um *adj* Olympian

Olympionīc·ēs -ae *m* Olympic victor

Olymp·us -ī *m* Mt. Olympus (*mountain on the boundary of Macedonia and Thessaly, regarded as the home of the gods or heaven*)

omās·um -ī *n* tripe; (fig) paunch, belly

ōm·en -inis *n* omen, sign, token, foreboding; solemn assurance

ōment·um -ī *n* fat; bowels

ōmināt·or -ōris *m* diviner

ōmin·or -ārī -ātus sum *vt* to forebode, predict, prophesy

ōminōs·us -a -um *adj* ominous

omiss·us -a -um *adj* remiss, negligent

omittō omittĕre omīsī omissum *vt* to let go, let fall, let go of; to give up, abandon; to omit, pass over, say nothing of; to overlook, disregard

omníf·er -ĕra -ĕrum *adj* all-sustaining

omnigĕn·us -a -um *adj* of every kind

omnimŏdīs or omnimŏdō *adv* by all means, wholly

omnīnō *adv* altogether, entirely, wholly; (with numerals) in all; (in generalizations) in general; (in concessions) no doubt, to be sure, yes, by all means, certainly; haud om-

nīnō or nōn omnīnō not quite, not entirely; absolutely not, not at all; not expressly; omnīnō nemo no one at all

omnipār·ens -entis *adj* all-producing (*earth*)

omnipŏt·ens -entis *adj* almighty

omn·is -e *adj* all, every; every kind of, every sort of; the whole; *m pl* all, all men, everybody; *n* the universe; *n pl* all things, everything, all nature, all the world

omnitū·ens -entis *adj* all-seeing

omnivăg·us -a -um *adj* roving everywhere

omnivŏl·us -a -um *adj* all-craving

Omphăl·ē -ēs *f* Lydian queen whom Hercules had to serve

onăg·er or onagr·us -ī *m* wild ass

onăg·os -ī *m* ass driver

Onchesmīt·ēs -ae *m* wind blowing from Onchesmus (*harbor in Epirus*)

onerāri·us -a -um *adj* carrying freight; jumenta oneraria beasts of burden; oneraria or navis oneraria freighter, transport

oner·ō -āre *vt* to load, load down, burden; (fig) to overload, oppress; (fig) to pile on, aggravate

onerōs·us -a -um *adj* onerous, burdensome, oppressive, heavy

on·us -ĕris *n* load, burden; freight; cargo; burden, difficulty; trouble; tax expense; foetus, embryo; oneri esse (with *dat*) to be a burden to

onust·us -a -um *adj* loaded, burdened; filled, full

on·yx -ўchis *m* or *f* onyx; onyx box

opācit·ās -ātis *f* shade, darkness

opāc·ō -āre *vt* to shade

opāc·us -a -um *adj* shady; dark, obscure; *n pl* per opaca locorum through shady places

opell·a -ae *f* light work

opĕr·a -ae *f* effort, pains, exertion, work, labor; care, attention; service, assistance; leisure, spare time; laborer, workman, artisan; operae esse or operae pretium esse to be worthwhile; operam dare to take pains, exert oneself, be busied, pay attention, give attention; operam funeri dare to attend a funeral; operam sermoni dare to listen to a conversation; operam tonsori dare to see a barber, get a haircut; operā meā (tuā, etc.) through my (*your, etc.*) agency, thanks to me (*you, etc.*)

operāri·us -a -um *adj* working; *m* working man, workman, laborer; *f* working woman

opercŭl·um -ī *n* lid, cover

operīment·um -ī *n* lid, cover

oper·iō -īre -ŭī -tum *vt* to cover, cover up; to shut, close; to hide; to overwhelm

opĕr·or -ārī -ātus sum *vi* to work, work hard, take pains; (with *dat*) a to work hard at, be busied with, be engaged in; b to perform (*religious services*); c to attend; d to worship

operōsē *adv* with great effort, at great pains

operōs·us -a -um *adj* active, busy, painstaking; troublesome, difficult, elaborate; efficacious, powerful (*drugs*)

opert·us -a -um *pp* of **operio**; *adj* closed; hidden; secret; *n* secret; secret place; **in operto** inside, in secret; *n pl* depths; veiled oracles

opēs see **ops**

ophīt·ēs -ae *m* serpentine (*type of marble*)

Ophiūsi·us -a -um *adj* Cyprian; *f* old name of Cyprus

ophthalmī·ās -ae *m* a fish

opīc·us -a -um *adj* boorish

opīf·er -ĕra -ĕrum *adj* helpful

opīf·ex -icis *m* maker, framer, creator; craftsman, mechanic

opificīn·a -ae *f* workshop

ōpīli·ō -ōnis *m* shepherd

opīmē *adv* richly, splendidly

opīmit·ās -ātis *f* abundance

opīm·us -a -um *adj* fat, plump; fertile, fruitful; rich, enriched; abundant, copious, plentiful; sumptuous, splendid; lucrative; noble; **spolia opima** armor stripped from one general by another on the field of battle

opīnābil·is -e *adj* conjectural, imaginary

opīnāti·ō -ōnis *f* mere opinion, conjecture, supposition, hunch

opīnāt·or -ōris *m* guesser

opīnāt·us -a -um *adj* supposed, imagined

opīnāt·us -ūs *m* supposition

opīni·ō -ōnis *f* opinion, conjecture, supposition, guess, belief, expectation; general impression, estimation; rumor; reputation, bad reputation; **amplius opinione** beyond expectation, beyond all hopes; **celerius opinione** sooner than expected; **hac opinione ut** under the impression that; **in opinione esse** (with *acc & inf*) to be of the opinion that; **praebere opinionem timoris** to convey the impression of fear; **praeter opinionem** contrary to expectation, sooner than expected; **ut opinio mea est** as I suppose

opīniōs·us -a -um *adj* opinionated

opīn·ō -āre or **opīn·or -ārī -ātus sum** *vt* to suppose, imagine, conjecture; *vi* (parenthetical) to suppose, imagine

opīpărē *adv* splendidly, sumptuously

opīpăr·us -a -um *adj* splendid, sumptuous, ritzy

opisthōgrăph·us -a -um *adj* written on the back

opitŭl·or -ārī -ātus sum *vi* (with *dat*) to bring help to, assist

oport·e -ēre -uit *v impers* it is right, it is proper; **me ire oportet** I ought to go, should go

op·pangō -pangĕre -pēgī -pactum *vt* to affix, imprint

oppect·ō -ĕre *vt* to comb off; (coll) to pluck, pick, eat

oppēd·ō -ĕre *vi* (with *dat*) **a** to break wind at; **b** (fig) to deride, mock

opper·ior -īrī -tus sum *vt* to wait for, await; (with *num*) to wait and see whether; *vi* to wait

oppĕt·ō -ĕre -īvī or **-iī -ītum** *vt* to go to meet; **mortem oppetere** to go to meet death, perish, die; *vi* to perish, die

oppidān·us -a -um *adj* of a town, in a town; (disparagingly) provincial; *m pl* townsfolk, townspeople

oppidō *adv* absolutely, quite, completely; (as affirmative answer) exactly

oppidŭl·um -ī *n* small town

oppid·um -ī *n* town

oppignĕr·ō -āre *vt* to pledge

oppīl·ō -āre *vt* to shut up, shut off

op·plĕō -plēre -plēvī -plētum *vt* to fill up, choke up

op·pōnō -pōnĕre -posŭī -positum *vt* to put, place, station; to oppose; to expose, lay bare, open; to wager, mortgage; to bring forward, present, adduce, allege; to reply, respond, object; to compare

opportūnē *adv* opportunely, at the right time

opportūnit·ās -ātis *f* suitableness, fitness, convenience; opportunity, right time; advantage

opportūn·us -a -um *adj* suitable, fit, convenient; advantageous, useful; exposed; **tempore opportunissimo** in the nick of time; *n pl* exposed parts

oppositi·ō -ōnis *f* opposition

opposit·us -a -um *pp* of **oppono**; *adj* opposite; (with *dat*) opposite, across from

opposit·us -ūs *m* opposing, opposition

oppressi·ō -ōnis *f* force, violence; violent seizure; suppression, overthrow

oppressiuncŭl·a -ae *f* slight pressure

oppressus *pp* of **opprimo**

oppress·us -ūs *m* pressure

op·primō -primĕre -pressī -pressum *vt* to press down, weigh down; to pressure, put pressure on; to close, shut; to overwhelm; to put down, suppress, quell; to sink (*a ship*); to subvert, overthrow, crush, subdue, overpower; to conceal, suppress; to seize, catch, surprise

opprobrāment·um -ī *n* disgrace, scandal

opprobr·ium -iī or **-ī** *n* disgrace, scandal, reproach; cause of disgrace; taunt, abuse, abusive word

opprobr·ō -āre *vt* to taunt

oppugnāti·ō -ōnis *f* assault; (fig) attack, assault, accusation

oppugnāt·or -ōris *m* assailant, attacker

oppugn·ō -āre *vt* to assault, assail, attack, storm; (fig) to attack, assail

ops opis *f* power, might; help, aid; influence, weight; **opem ferre** (with *dat*) to bring help to, help; *f pl* wealth, resources, means; military or political resources

Ops Opis *f* goddess of abundance, sister and wife of Saturn, and identified with Earth

ops- = obs-

optābil·is -e *adj* desirable

optātī·ō -ōnis *f* wishing, wish

optātō *adv* according to one's wish

optāt·us -a -um *adj* longed-for, desired, welcome; *n* wish, desire

optigō see **obtego**

optim·ās -ātis *m* aristocrat; *m pl* aristocracy, aristocratic party

optimē or **optumē** (*superl* of **bene**) *adv* very well, thoroughly, best; most opportunely, just in time

optim·us or **optum·us -a -um** (*superl* of **bonus**) *adj* very good, best; excellent

optī·ō -ōnis *m* helper, assistant; (mil) adjutant

optīv·us -a -um *adj* chosen

opt·ō -āre *vt* to choose, select; to wish for, desire

optum- = optim-

opūl·ens -entis *adj* opulent, rich

opulens or **opulenter** *adv* richly, splendidly

opulenti·a -ae *f* opulence, wealth; resources; power

opulentit·ās -ātis *f* opulence; power

opulent·ō -āre *vt* to make rich, enrich

opulent·us -a -um *adj* opulent, rich, wealthy; powerful; sumptuous

op·us -ĕris *n* work; product of work, structure, building; literary work, composition, book; work of art, workmanship; deed, achievement; (mil) offensive works, siege works; (mil) defensive works, fortifications; **magnō opere** greatly; **quantō opere** how much, how greatly; **tantō opere** so much, so greatly; **opus est** (with *inf*) it is useful or beneficial to; **opus est** (with *dat* of person in need and *abl* of person or thing needed) to need, e.g., **vōbis duce opus est** you need a leader

opuscŭl·um -ī *n* little work, minor work

ōr·a -ae *f* boundary, border, edge; coastline, coast; region, district; cable, hawser; (fig) people of the coast, people of the region; **ora maritima** seacoast

ōrācŭl·um or **ōrācl·um -ī** *n* oracle; prophesy

ōrāri·us -a -um *adj* coasting; **navis oraria** coaster, coasting vessel

ōrāt·a -ōrum *n pl* prayers, requests

ōrātī·ō -ōnis *f* faculty of speech; speech, language; style of speech, manner of speaking, style, expression; oration, speech; theme, subject; prose; eloquence; imperial rescript; **orationem habere** to give a speech

ōrātiuncŭl·a -ae *f* short speech, insignificant speech

ōrāt·or -ōris *m* orator, speaker; spokesman; suppliant

ōrātōriē *adv* oratorically

ōrātōri·us -a -um *adj* orator's, oratorical

ōrātr·ix -īcis *f* suppliant (*female*)

ōrāt·us -ūs *m* request

orb·a -ae *f* orphan; widow

orbāt·or -ōris *m* murderer (*of someone's children or parents*)

Orbil·ius -iī or **-ī** *m* Horace's teacher in Venusia

orb·is -is *m* circle; disk, ring, orbit; quoit; hoop; wheel; round shield; eye socket, eye; globe, earth, world, universe; region, territory, country; circuit, round; rotation; cycle, period; (rhet) balance; zodiac; **orbis lacteus** Milky Way; **orbis terrae** or **terrarum** earth, world, universe

orbit·a -ae *f* rut, wheel track; (fig) rut, routine

orbit·ās -ātis *f* childlessness, widowhood, orphanhood

orbitōs·us -a -um *adj* full of ruts

orb·ō -āre *vt* to bereave of parents, father, mother, children, husband, or wife; to strip, rob, deprive, make destitute

orb·us -a -um *adj* bereaved, bereft; destitute; orphaned; fatherless; childless; widowed; (with *genit* or *abl* or with **ab** + *abl*) bereft of, deprived of, without; *m* orphan; *f* see **orba**

orc·a -ae *f* vat, barrel

Orcăd·es -um *f pl* islands N. of Scotland (*modern* Orkneys)

orch·as -ădis *f* olive

orchestr·a -ae *f* senatorial seats (*in the theater*); (fig) senate

Orc·us -ī *m* lower world; Pluto (*king of the lower world*); death

orde- = horde-

ordināri·us -a -um *adj* ordinary, usual, regular

ordinātim *adv* in order, in good order, in succession; regularly, properly

ordinātī·ō -ōnis *f* orderly arrangement; orderly government

ordināt·us -a -um *adj* regular; appointed

ordin·ō -āre *vt* to set in order, arrange, regulate; to govern, rule; to record chronologically

ordior ordīrī orsus sum *vt* to begin, undertake; to describe; *vi* to begin, begin to speak

ord·ō -inis *m* line, row, series; row of seats (*in a theater*); order, methodical arrangement; (pol) rank, order, class; (mil) line, file (*of soldiers*), company, century, command of a company or century; *m pl* officers of a company; promotions; **amplissimus ordo** senatorial order; **ex ordine** in succession, without a break; **extra ordinem** extraordinarily, especially, uncommonly; **ordine, in ordine,** or **per ordinem** in order, in sequence, in detail, with regularity, regularly

Orē·as -ădis *f* Oread, mountain nymph

Orest·ēs -is or **-ae** *m* son of Agamemnon and Clytemnestra who avenged his father's death by killing his mother

orex·is -is *f* longing, appetite

organic·us -ī *m* organist

orgăn·um -ī *n* instrument, implement; musical instrument, organ

orgi·a -ōrum *n pl* Bacchic revels; orgies

orichalc·um -ī *n* copper ore; brass

ōricill·a -ae *f* lobe

ori·ens -entis *m* rising sun, morning sun; morning; day; land of the rising sun, Orient, the East

orīg·ō -ĭnis *f* origin, source, beginning, start; birth, lineage, descent; race, stock, family; founder, progenitor

Orī·ōn or **Orī·ōn -ōnis** or **-ōnis** *m* mythical hunter, turned into a constellation

orĭor orīrī ortus sum *vi* to rise, get up; to become visible, appear; to be born, originate, be descended; to proceed, begin, start

Ōrīthyī·a -ae *f* daughter of Erechtheus and mother of Calais and Zetes by Boreas

oriund·us -a -um *adj* descended, sprung, born

ornāment·um -ī *n* equipment, trappings, apparatus; ornament, adornment, decoration; trinket, jewel; (fig) distinction; rhetorical ornament; pride and joy

ornātē *adv* ornately, elegantly

ornātr·ix -īcis *f* hairdresser (female)

ornātŭl·us -a -um *adj* fancy

ornātŭl·us -a -um *adj* equipped, fitted out, furnished, dressed, harnessed; adorned, decorated, embellished; handsome; illustrious, excellent

ornāt·us -ūs *m* equipment; attire, apparel, outfit; furniture; decoration, ornament; world, universe

orn·ō -āre *vt* to equip, fit out, furnish, dress; to set off, decorate, adorn; to honor, praise, commend

orn·us -ī *f* mountain ash

ōr·ō -āre *vt* to beg, entreat, implore, plead with; to ask for; to plead (*a case*); (with double *acc*) to ask (*someone*) for; *vi* to plead, beg, pray; (with **cum** + *abl*) to plead or argue with

Oront·ēs -is or **-ae** *m* chief river of Syria; companion of Aeneas

Oront·ēus -a -um *adj* Syrian

Orph·eus -ĕī or **-ĕos** *m* son of Oeagrus and Calliope, husband of Eurydice, and famous musician and poet

Orphē·us or **Orphic·us -a -um** *adj* Orphic

ors·us -a -um *pp* of **ordior;** *n pl* beginnings; utterance, words; attempt

ors·us -ūs *m* beginning; attempt, undertaking

ortus *pp* of **orior**

ort·us -ūs *m* rising; the East; birth, origin; source

Ortygĭ·a -ae or **Ortygĭ·ē -ēs** *f* Delos; island in the port of Syracuse

or·yx -ȳgis *m* gazelle

oryz·a -ae *f* rice

os ossis *n* bone; marrow, innermost parts; *n pl* skeleton

ōs ōris *n* mouth; beak; voice, speech, expression; lip, face, countenance, look; sight, presence (*of a person*); impudence; mask, mouth, opening, orifice, front; **habere aliquid in ore** to be talking about something continually; **in ore omnium esse** to be on the lips of everyone, be talked about

osc·en -inis *m* bird of augury (*e.g., crow, raven, owl*)

oscill·um -ī *n* small mask

oscĭt·ans -antis *adj* yawning; (fig) indifferent, bored

oscĭt·ō -āre or **oscĭt·or -ārī -ātus sum** *vi* to gape; to yawn

osculātĭ·ō -ōnis *f* kissing

oscŭl·or -ārī -ātus sum *vt* to kiss; (fig) to make a fuss over

oscŭl·um -ī *n* little mouth; kiss; **breve osculum** peck

Osc·us -a -um *adj* Oscan; *m pl* Oscans (*ancient people of Campania and Samnium*)

Osīr·is -is or **-īdis** *m* Egyptian god, the husband of Isis

ōs·or -ōris *m* hater

Oss·a -ae *f* mountain in N.E. Thessaly

osse·us -a -um *adj* bony

ossifrăg·a -ae *f* osprey

ostendō ostendĕre ostendī ostentum *vt* to stretch out, stretch forth; to expose; to show, exhibit, display, present; to reveal, disclose; to declare, make known

ostentātĭ·ō -ōnis *f* display; ostentation, showing off; mere show, pretense

ostentāt·or -ōris *m* show-off

ostent·ō -āre *vt* to show, exhibit; to show off, display, parade, boast of; to declare, point out, set forth

ostent·um -ī *n* portent, prodigy

ostent·us -ūs *m* display, show; **ostentui** for appearances, in pretense

Osti·a -ae *f* or **Osti·a -ōrum** *n pl* Ostia (*port and town at the mouth of the Tiber*)

ostiār·ium -ĭī or **-ī** *n* tax on doors

ostiātim *adv* from door to door

ost·ium -ĭī or **-ī** *n* door; entrance, mouth

ostrĕ·a -ae *f* or **ostrĕ·um -ī** *n* oyster

ostreāt·us -a -um *adj* covered with oyster shells; (fig) black and blue

ostreōs·us -a -um *adj* abounding in oysters

ostrif·er -ĕra -ĕrum *adj* oyster-growing

ostrīn·us -a -um *adj* purple

ostr·um -ī *n* purple; purple dress, purple covering

ōsus *pp* of **odi**

Oth·ō -ōnis *m* L. Roscius Otho (*author of the law in 67 B.C. reserving fourteen rows in the theaters for the equestrian order*); M. Salvius Otho (*Roman emperor in 69 A.D.*)

Othr·ys -ўos *m* mountain in S. Thessaly

ōtiŏl·um -ī *n* bit of leisure

ōti·or -ārī -ātus sum *vi* to take it easy

ōtiōsē *adv* at leisure; leisurely, without haste; calmly, fearlessly

ōtiōs·us -a -um *adj* at leisure, relaxing; free from official obligations; quiet, calm; unconcerned, in-different, neutral; passionless; *m* private person (*not holding public office*); *m pl* civilians, non-combatants

ōt·ium -iī or **-ī** *n* leisure, free time, relaxation; freedom from public affairs, retirement; peace, quiet; ease, idleness, inactivity

Ovid·ius -iī or **-ī** *m* P. Ovidius Naso or Ovid (*Latin poet, born at Sulmo, 43 B.C.-17 A.D.*)

ovīl·e -is *n* sheepfold; voting enclosures in the Campus Martius

ovīl·is -e *adj* sheep, of sheep

ovill·us -a -um *adj* sheep, of sheep

ov·is -is *f* sheep; wool; simpleton

ov·ō -āre *vi* to rejoice; to hold a celebration; to celebrate a minor triumph

ōv·um -ī *n* egg; *n pl* wooden balls used to mark the laps at the racetrack

P

pābulātī·ō -ōnis *f* foraging

pābulāt·or -ōris *m* forager

pābŭl·or -ārī -ātus sum *vi* to forage; (coll) to make a living

pābŭl·um -ī *n* food, fodder; pasturage, grass; (fig) nourishment

pācāl·is -e *adj* of peace

pācāt·us -a -um *adj* peaceful, quiet, calm; *n* friendly country

Pachўn·um -ī *n* S.E. point of Sicily

pācif·er -ĕra -ĕrum *adj* peace-bringing, peaceful

pācificātī·ō -ōnis *f* pacification

pācificāt·or -ōris *m* peacemaker

pācificātōri·us -a -um *adj* peace-making

pācific·ō -āre *vt* to pacify, appease; *vi* to make peace, conclude peace

pācific·us -a -um *adj* peace-making; peaceable

pacīsc·or pacīscī pactus sum *vt* to bargain for, agree upon; to stipulate; to barter; to betroth; *vi* to come to an agreement, agree, make a bargain, make a contract; (with *inf*) to agree to, pledge oneself to

pac·ō -āre *vt* to pacify, soothe, subdue

pact·a -ae *f* fiancee; bride

pactī·ō -ōnis *f* pact, contract, agreement, treaty; stipulation; collusion

Pactŏl·us -ī *m* river in Lydia famous for its gold

pact·or -ōris *m* contractor, negotiator, party (*in a contract*)

pact·us -a -um *pp* of **paciscor** and of **pango**; *n* pact, contract, agreement; way, manner; **aliquo pacto** somehow; **hoc pacto** in this way; **in pacto manere** to stick to the agreement; **quo pacto** how, in what way

Pācuv·ius -iī or **-ī** *m* Roman tragic poet, native of Brundisium, and nephew of Ennius (*c. 220-130 B.C.*)

Pad·us -ī *m* Po River (*in N. Italy*)

pae·ān -ānis *m* epithet of Apollo as the god of healing; paean, hymn of praise, victory song

paedagōg·ium -iī or **-ī** *n* training school for pages

paedagōg·us -ī *m* slave in charge of school children; (fig) guide, leader

paedic·ō -āre *vt* to have abnormal relations with (*young boys*)

paed·or -ōris *m* filth

pael·ex -icis *f* concubine, mistress

paelicāt·us -ūs *m* concubinage

Paelign·ī -ōrum *m pl* a people of central Italy

paenē *adv* almost, nearly

paeninsŭl·a -ae *f* peninsula

paenitend·us -a -um *adj* regrettable

paenitenti·a -ae *f* repentance, regret

paenit·ĕō -ēre -ŭī *vt* to cause to regret; to displease; *vi* (with *genit*) to regret; *v impers* (with *acc* of person), e.g., **me paenitet** I am sorry; (with *acc* of person and *genit* of thing), e.g., **me paenitet consili** I regret the plan, I am dissatisfied with the plan; (with *acc* of person and *inf* or *quod*), e.g., **eos paenitet animum tuum offendisse** or **eos paenitet quod animum tuum offenderint** they regret having offended your feelings

paenŭl·a -ae *f* traveling coat; raincoat

paenulāt·us -a -um *adj* wearing a traveling coat

pae·ōn -ōnis *m* metrical foot containing one long and three short syllables

paeonĭ‧us **-a** **-um** adj healing, medicinal

Faest‧um **-ī** n town in Lucania in S. Italy

paetŭl‧us **-a** **-um** adj slightly squint-eyed

paet‧us **-a** **-um** adj squinting, squint-eyed; leering

pāgān‧us **-a** **-um** adj of a village, rustic; ignorant, untaught; m villager, peasant; (as term of contempt) yokel

Pagăs‧a **-ae** f or **Pagăs‧ae** **-ārum** f pl town on the coast of Thessaly, from which the Argonauts sailed

Pagasae‧us **-a** **-um** adj Pagasaean; m Jason

pāgātim adv by villages, in every village

pāgell‧a **-ae** f small page

pāgĭn‧a **-ae** f page (of book)

pāginŭl‧a **-ae** f small page

pāg‧us **-ī** m village; canton, province; country people, villagers

pāl‧a **-ae** f spade

palaestr‧a **-ae** f palaestra, wrestling school, gymnasium; school of rhetoric; rhetorical training; school; wrestling; exercise; brothel

palaestrĭcē adv as at the palaestra

palaestrĭc‧us **-a** **-um** adj of the palaestra, gymnastic; f gymnastics

palaestrīt‧a **-ae** m professional wrestler; director of a palaestra

palam adv openly, publicly, plainly; **palam esse** to be public, be well known; **palam facere** to make public, disclose; prep (with abl) before, in the presence of, face to face with

Palātīn‧us **-a** **-um** adj Palatine; imperial

Palāt‧ium **-iī** or **-ī** n Palatine Hill (residential area of distinguished Romans and several Roman emperors); palace

palāt‧um **-ī** n or **palāt‧us** **-ī** m palate; taste; literary taste

palĕ‧a **-ae** f chaff

paleār‧ia **-ium** n pl dewlap

Pal‧ēs **-is** f Italic goddess of shepherds and flocks

Palĭc‧ī **-ōrum** m pl twin sons of Jupiter and the nymph Thalia

Palīl‧is **-e** adj of Pales; n pl festival of Pales celebrated on April 21st

palimpsest‧us **-ī** m palimpsest

Palinūr‧us **-ī** m pilot of Aeneas who fell overboard and drowned; promontory named after him

paliūr‧us **-ī** m Christ's thorn (plant)

pall‧a **-ae** f ladies' long robe; outer garment, mantle; tragic actor's costume

Palladĭ‧us **-a** **-um** adj of Pallas; n statue of Pallas, Palladium

Pall‧as **-ădis** or **-ădos** f Athene; olive oil, olive tree; Palladium (Trojan statue of Pallas)

pall‧ens **-entis** adj pale, sallow;

grey-green, yellow-green, chartreuse, yellowish, sickly-looking

pall‧ĕō **-ēre** **-uī** vi to be pale, look pale; to be yellow, look yellow; to change color, fade; (with dat) to grow pale over, worry about

pall‧escō **-escĕre** **-uī** vt to turn pale at; vi to turn pale; to turn yellow; to fade

palliāt‧us **-a** **-um** adj wearing a Greek cloak; **fabula palliata** Latin play with Greek setting and characters

pallĭdŭl‧us **-a** **-um** adj somewhat pale

pallĭd‧us **-a** **-um** adj pale, sallow; grey-green, yellow-green, chartreuse

palliolātim adv in a mantle

palliolāt‧us **-a** **-um** adj wearing a short mantle, wearing a hood

palliŏl‧um **-ī** n short cloak; cape, hood

pall‧ium **-iī** or **-ī** n coverlet, cover; Greek cloak

pall‧or **-ōris** m paleness, pallor; **pallorem ducere** to turn pale

pallŭl‧a **-ae** f short cloak

palm‧a **-ae** f palm of the hand, hand; palm tree, date; palm branch, palm wreath; palm of victory, prize, victory, honor, distinction; blade of an oar

palmār‧is **-e** adj excellent, deserving the palm or prize

palmārĭ‧us **-a** **-um** adj prize-winning, excellent; n masterpiece

palmāt‧us **-a** **-um** adj embroidered with palm branches; **tunica palmata** palm-embroidered tunic (worn by a general)

palm‧es **-itis** m vine sprout, vine branch; branch, bough

palmēt‧um **-ī** n palm grove

palmĭf‧er **-ĕra** **-ĕrum** adj palm-growing, full of palm trees

palmōs‧us **-a** **-um** adj full of palm trees

palmŭl‧a **-ae** f oar blade

pāl‧or **-ārī** **-ātus sum** vi to roam about, wander aimlessly

palpātĭ‧ō **-ōnis** f stroking; f pl flattering

palpāt‧or **-ōris** m flatterer

palpĕbr‧a **-ae** f eyelid

palpĭt‧ō **-āre** vi to throb, palpitate, quiver

palp‧ō **-āre** or **palp‧or** **-ārī** **-ātus sum** vt to stroke, pat; to wheedle, coax; to flatter; vi (with dat) a to coax; b to flatter

palp‧us **-ī** m palm of the hand; coaxing

palūdāment‧um **-ī** n military coat; general's coat

palūdāt‧us **-a** **-um** adj wearing a general's coat

palūdōs‧us **-a** **-um** adj swampy, marshy

palumb‧ēs **-is** m or f pigeon, dove

pāl‧us **-ī** m stake, post; wooden post used in sword practice

pal·us -ūdis f swamp, marsh; sedge

palust·er -ris -re adj swampy, marshy, in the swamps

pampinē·us -a -um adj of vine tendrils, made of vine leaves; **odor pampineus** bouquet of wines

pampin·us -ī m vine shoot, tendril; vine leaf; tendril (of any plant)

Pān Pānos m Pan (Greek god of flocks, shepherds, and woods, often identified with Faunus)

panacē·a -ae f or **panāc·es -is** n panacea

Panaetōlic·us -a -um adj Pan-Aetolian

pānār·ium -iī or **-ī** n bread basket

Panchāi·a -ae f region in Arabia famous for its frankincense

panchrest·us or **panchrist·us -a -um** adj good for everything, universally useful

pancraticē adv (coll) fine, splendidly; **pancratice valere** to get along splendidly

pancrat·ium or **pancrat·ion -iī** or **-ī** n contest which included both boxing and wrestling

Pandar·us -ī m famous Lycian archer in the Trojan army; companion of Aeneas, killed by Turnus

pandicul·or -ārī -ātus sum vi to stretch oneself

Pandī·on -ōnis m king of Athens and father of Procne and Philomela

Pandīoni·us -a -um adj of Pandion

pandō pandēre pandī pansum or **passum** vt to spread out, extend, expand, unfold; to open, lay open, throw open; to reveal, make known, publish

pand·us -a -um adj crooked, bent, curved

pangō pangěre panxī or **pepěgī -pactum** vt to fasten, fix, drive in; to fix, settle, agree upon, determine; to write, compose, celebrate, record; to promise in marriage; **indutias pangere** (with **cum** + abl) to conclude an armistice with

pānicě·us -a -um adj made of bread; **milites panicei** (coll) Breadville brigade

pānicul·a -ae f tuft

pānic·um -ī n millet

pān·is -is m bread, loaf; **panis cibarius** coarse bread; **panis secundus** stale bread

Pāniscus -ī m little Pan

pannīcul·us -ī m rag

Pannoni·us -a -um adj Pannonian; f Pannonia (country on the Danube)

pannōs·us -a -um adj tattered, ragged; shriveled, wrinkled, sadlooking

pannūce·us or **pannūci·us -a -um** adj ragged; shriveled, wrinkled

pann·us -ī m patch; rag

Panŏp·ē -ēs or **Panopē·a -ae** f a sea nymph

pans·a -ae masc & fem adj flatfooted, splayfooted

pansus pp of pando

panthēr·a -ae f panther

Panthoīd·ēs -ae m Euphorbus (Trojan warrior)

Panth·us -ī m priest of Apollo at Troy and father of Euphorbus

pantic·ēs -um m pl bowels; sausages

papae interj great!, wonderful!

pāp·as -ae or **-ātis** m tutor

papāv·er -ěris n poppy

papāvorē·us -a -um adj of poppies

Paphi·ē -ēs f Venus

Paphi·us -a -um adj Paphian, of Paphos

Paph·os -ī f town in Cyprus sacred to Venus

pāpiliō -ōnis m butterfly

papill·a -ae f nipple, teat; breast

papp·ō -āre vi to eat baby food, eat pap

papp·us -ī m hairy seed (of certain plants)

papūl·a -ae f pimple

papyrif·er -ěra -ěrum adj papyrus-producing

papýr·us -ī m & f or **papýr·um -ī** n papyrus; paper; garment (made of papyrus)

pār paris adj equal, like, on a par, equally matched, well matched; suitable, adequate, of equal size; (with **dat** or **cum** + abl) equal to, comparable to, similar to, as large as; (with limiting abl, **ad** + acc, or **in** + abl) equal, similar, alike in; **par est** it is right, it is proper; **par proelium** indecisive battle; **ut par est** (used parenthetically) as is only right; m companion, comrade; equal; mate, spouse; **pares cum paribus facillime congregantur** birds of a feather flock together; n pair, couple; the like; **par pari** like for like, tit for tat

parābil·is -e adj available

parasīt·a -ae f parasite (female)

parasītast·er -rī m poor parasite

parasītāti·ō -ōnis f sponging

parasītic·us -a -um adj parasitical

parasīt·or -ārī -ātus sum vi to sponge, freeload, be a parasite

parasīt·us -ī m parasite, sponger, freeloader

parātē adv with preparation; carefully; readily, promptly

parāti·ō -ōnis f preparing, procuring, acquisition

paratragoed·ō -āre vi to talk in a tragic style, be melodramatic

parāt·us -a -um adj prepared, ready; well prepared, furnished, equipped; learned, well versed, skilled; (with **dat** or **ad** + acc) a ready for; b equipped to; (with inf) prepared to, ready to; (with abl or **in** + abl) versed in, experienced in

parāt·us -ūs m preparation, provision, equipment, outfit; clothing, apparel

Parc·a -ae f goddess of Fate, Fate

parcē adv sparingly, thriftily; moderately, with restraint; stingily; rarely, seldom

parceprōm·us -ī *m* stingy person

parcō *parcĕre* **pepercī parsum** *vt* to spare, use sparingly; *vi* to be sparing, economize; (with *dat*) **a** to spare, use carefully; **b** to show mercy to; **c** to abstain from, refrain from; **d** to refuse (*help*); (with *inf*) to cease, stop (*e.g., doing, talking*)

parc·us -a -um *adj* thrifty, economical, frugal; niggardly, stingy; moderate, conservative; slight, little, scanty, paltry (*thing given*)

pard·us -ī *m* panther

par·ens -entis *adj* obedient; *m* parent, father; ancestor, grandparent; founder, inventor; *m pl* subjects; ancestors; *f* parent, mother

parentāl·is -e *adj* parental; **dies parentalis** memorial day; *n pl* festival in honor of dead ancestors and relatives

parent·ō -āre *vi* to hold memorial service in honor of dead parents or relatives; (with *dat*) **a** to offer sacrifice to (*the dead*); **b** to avenge (*a dead person*) with the death of another person; **c** to appease, satisfy

pār·eō -ēre -uī *vi* to appear, be visible, be evident, be at hand; (with *dat*) **a** to obey, be obedient to, comply with, be subject to, be subservient to; **b** to yield to, gratify, satisfy (*pleasures, etc.*); **c** to fulfill (*promises*)

pari·ēs -ĕtis *m* wall (*esp. partition in a house or building*)

parietīn·ae -ārum *f pl* tumbleddown walls; ruins; (fig) ruins

Parīl·ia -ium *n pl* festival of Pales (*celebrated on April 21st*)

paril·is -e *adj* equal, like; **aetas parilis** same age, like age

pariō *parĕre* **pepĕrī partum** *vt* to bear, bring forth, give birth to; (of *animals*) to lay, spawn, produce; (fig) to produce, create, devise, cause, effect, accomplish, acquire, obtain

Par·is -ĭdis *m* son of Priam and Hecuba, also called Alexandros; famous pantomime actor in the reign of Nero; famous pantomime actor in the reign of Domitian, the freedman of Domitia

parĭter *adv* equally, in like manner, as well, alike; at the same time, simultaneously, together, at once; **parĭter ac** (or **atque**), **parĭter ut** as well as; **parĭter ac si** just as if; **parĭter** (with **cum** + *abl*) together with, at the same time as

parit·ō -āre *vt* (with *inf*) to get ready to

Parī·us -a -um *adj & mf* Parian

parm·a -ae *f* small round shield; shield

parmāt·us -a -um *adj* armed with a shield, light-armed

parmŭl·a -ae *f* small shield

Parnās·is -ĭdis or **Parnāsi·us -a -um** *adj* of Parnassus, Parnassian

Parnās·us or **Parnās·os -ī** *m* mountain in Phocis, in central

Greece, sacred to Apollo and the Muses, on whose slopes Delphi was located

par·ō -āre *vt* to prepare, make ready, provide, furnish; to get, procure, acquire, gather, purchase; **se parare** to prepare oneself, get ready; *vi* to get ready, make preparations, make arrangements; (with *dat* or **ad** + *acc*) to get ready for

parŏch·a -ae *f* room and board (*required of provincials for traveling Roman officials*)

parŏch·us -ī *m* official host (*local official who provided accommodations for traveling Roman dignitaries*); host

parops·is -ĭdis *f* dish, dessert dish

Par·os or **Par·us -ī** *f* island of the Cyclades, famous for its white marble

parr·a -ae *f* owl

Parrhās·is -ĭdis *f* Arcadian woman; Callisto

Parrhāsi·us -a -um *adj* Arcadian; **Parrhasia virgo** Callisto; *f* district in Arcadia

parricīd·a -ae *m* or *f* parricide (*murder of a parent or close relative*); assassin of a high magistrate; murderer, assassin; traitor, outlaw, criminal

parricīd·ium -iī or **-ī** *n* parricide (*murderer of a parent or close relative*); murder, assassination; treason, high treason

par·s -tis *f* part, portion, share, section, fraction; side, direction, region; part, function, duty; part of body, member (*esp. genital organs*); *f pl* part, role, character; political party; **ab omni parte** in all respects; **ex altera parte** on the other hand; **ex magna parte** to a great extent; **ex parte** partly; **in eam partem** in that direction; in that sense; in such a manner; **in pejorem partem rapere** to put a worse construction on; **in utramque partem** in both directions; **major pars populi** the majority; **maximam partem** for the most part; **minor pars populi** the minority; **omnibus partibus** in all respects; **pars ... pars**, **pars ... alii** some . . . others; **parte** in part, partly; **pro mea parte** to the best of my abilities; **tres partes** three fourths

parsimōni·a -ae *f* parsimony

parsus *pp* of **parco**

parthenic·ō -ēs *f* parthenium (*plant*)

Parthenopae·us -ī *m* son of Meleager and Atalanta and one of the Seven who fought against Thebes

Parthenŏp·ē -ēs *f* one of the Sirens, after whom Naples was originally named

Parthi·a -ae *f* Parthia (*country located S.E. of the Caspian*)

Parthĭc·us -a -um *adj* Parthian

Parth·us -a -um *adj & m* Parthian

partic·eps -ipis adj (with genit) sharing in, taking part in; m partner, confederate

particip·ō -āre vt to make (someone) a partner; to share (something)

particul·a -ae f bit, particle, grain

partim adv partly, in part, to some extent; for the most part, mostly; (with genit or **ex** + abl) some of; **partim . . . partim** some . . . others

parti·ō -ōnis f bringing forth, producing

part·iō -īre -īvī or **-iī -ītum** or **part·ior -īrī -ītus sum** vt to share, distribute, apportion, divide

partītē adv with proper divisions, methodically

partīti·ō -ōnis f division, distribution, sharing; division of a speech

partītūd·ō -inis f bearing (of young)

partur·iō -īre -īvī or **-iī** vt to teem with; to be ready to produce; to bring forth, yield; (fig) to brood over; vi to be in labor

partus pp of **pario**; adj acquired; n acquisition, gain, store

part·us -ūs m birth; young, offspring; (fig) beginnings

parum adv a little, too little, insufficiently; **parum est** it is not enough, it does not suffice; **parum habere** to regard as unsatisfactory; **satis eloquentiae sapientiae parum** enough eloquence but too little wisdom

parumper adv for a little while, a moment; **operire parumper** wait a moment

parvit·ās -ātis f smallness

parvūl·us or **parvōl·us -a -um** adj tiny; slight, petty; young; n childhood, infancy; **ab parvulis** from childhood, from infancy

parv·us -a -um (comp **minor**; superl **minimus**) adj small, little, puny; short; young; brief, short (time); small, insignificant, unimportant; low, cheap (price); n a little, trifle; childhood, infancy; **a parvis** or **a parvo** from childhood, from infancy; **parvi esse** to be of little importance; **parvi facere, aestimare, habere,** or **dūcere** to think little of, care little for; **parvi refert** it makes little difference, it matters little

pascēōl·us -ī m money bag

pascō pascēre pāvī pastum vt to feed, pasture, keep, raise (animals); to cultivate, cherish; to feed (flames, passions); to pile up (debts); to grow (beard); to lay waste, ravage (fields); to feast, gratify (the eyes); to cherish (hope)

pascor pascī pastus sum vi to graze, browse, be fed; (with abl) a to graze on; b (fig) to feed on, feast on, thrive on

pascu·us -a -um adj grazing, pasture; n pasture

Pāsiphā·ē -ēs or **Pāsiphǎ·a -ae** f daughter of Helios, sister of Circe, husband of Minos, and mother of Androgeos, Ariadne, Phaedra, and the Minotaur

pass·er -ĕris m sparrow; plaice, flounder; **passer marīnus** ostrich

passercŭl·us -ī m little sparrow

passim adv here and there, all over, at random; without order, indiscriminately, promiscuously

passus pp of **pando** and of **patior**; adj spread out, extended, open; disheveled; dried, dry; n wine made from dried grapes, raisin wine

pass·us -ūs m step, pace; footstep, track; **mille passūs** mile; **tria milia passuum** three miles

pastill·us -ī m lozenge

pasti·ō -ōnis f pasture, grazing

past·or -ōris m shepherd

pastōrāl·is -e adj shepherd's, pastoral

pastōrici·us or **pastōri·us -a -um** adj shepherd's, pastoral

pastus pp of **pasco**

past·us -ūs m pasture, fodder, food; (fig) food

patagiār·ius -iī or **-ī** m fringe maker

patagiāt·us -a -um adj (tunic) with fringes

Patăr·a -ae f town in Lycia with an oracle of Apollo

Patăr·eus -ĕi or **-ĕos** m Apollo

Patavīn·us -a -um adj of Patavium

Patav·ium -iī or **-ī** n city in N. Italy, the birthplace of Livy (modern Padua)

pate·faciō -facĕre -fēcī -factus (passive; **pate·fiō -fĭĕrī**) vt to throw open; to open up, make accessible; to bring to light

patefacti·ō -ōnis f disclosure

patell·a -ae f pan, dish, plate

pat·ens -entis adj open, accessible; extensive; exposed; evident

patentius adv more openly, more clearly

pat·ĕō -ēre -ŭī vi to stand open, be open; to be accessible; to be exposed; to open, stretch out, extend; to be clear, be plain, be well known; to be accessible, be attainable, be free; (of the mind) to be open, be receptive

pat·er -ris m father; **pater cenae** host; **pater familiās** head of the household, head of the family; m pl forefathers; senators

patĕr·a -ae f flat dish (used esp. in making libations)

pat·erfamiliās -risfamiliās m head of the household, head of the family

patern·us -a -um adj father's, paternal; ancestral; of a native country, native

pat·escō -escĕre -ŭī vi to be opened, be open; to stretch out, extend; to be disclosed, be divulged, become evident

pathic·us -a -um adj lustful

patibil·is -e adj tolerable, endurable; sensitive

patibulāt·us -a -um *adj* gibbeted; wearing a yoke

patibul·um -ī *n* fork-shaped yoke (*tied around the neck of a criminal*); fork-shaped gibbet

pati·ens -entis *adj* hardy, tough; hard; stubborn, unyielding, patient, tolerant; (*with genit or* ad + *acc*) able to endure, inured to, able to take; **amnis patiens navium** navigable river

patienter *adv* patiently

patienti·a -ae *f* patience, endurance; resignation, forbearance; submissiveness; sexual submission

patin·a -ae *f* dish, pan

patināri·us -a -um *adj* of pans; in a pan; **strues patinaria** pile of dishes

patior pātī passus sum *vt* to experience, undergo, suffer; to put up with, allow; to submit to sexually; **aequo animo pati** to suffer patiently; **aegre pati** to resent, be displeased with

patrāt·or -ōris *m* perpetrator

patrāt·us *adj masc* **pater patratus** plenipotentiary

patri·a -ae *f* native land, native city, home

patricē *adv* paternally

patrici·us -a -um *adj* of patrician status, patrician; *m pl* patricians, patrician class

patrimōn·ium -iī *or* **-ī** *n* patrimony, inheritance

patrim·us -a -um *adj* having a father living

patriss·ō -āre *vi* to take after one's father

patrīt·us -a -um *adj* father's, inherited from one's father

patri·us -a -um *adj* father's, of a father, fatherly, paternal; ancestral, traditional, heriditary; native; *f see* **patria**

patr·ō -āre *vt* to bring about, effect, achieve, accomplish, perform, finish, conclude; **bellum patrare** to bring the war to an end; **jus jurandum patrare** to take an oath (*confirming a treaty*); **pacem patrare** to conclude a peace

patrōcin·ium -iī *or* **-ī** *n* patronage, protection, legal defense, legal representation

patrōcin·or -ārī -ātus sum *vi* to be a patron, afford protection; (*with dat*) to serve (*someone*) as patron, protect, defend

Patrocl·us -ī *m* son of Menoetius and friend of Achilles, who wearing the armor of Achilles, was killed by Hector

patrōn·a -ae *f* legal protectress, patroness; advocate; defender, safeguard

patrōn·us -ī *m* legal protector, patron; advocate (*in court*); defender

patruēl·is -e *adj* of or descended from a father's brother, cousin's; *m* cousin

patru·us -a -um *adj* uncle's; *m* (paternal) uncle

patul·us -a -um *adj* open, standing open; spreading, spread out, broad

pauciloqu·ium -iī *or* **-ī** *n* reticence

paucit·ās -ātis *f* paucity, scarcity, small number

pauculi·ī -ae -a *adj* just a few, very few; *n pl* few words

pauc·us -a -um *adj* few, little; *pron masc pl* few, a few; the select few, elite; **inter paucos (paucas)** *or* **in paucis** especially; *pron neut pl* a few things, a few words; **paucis** in a few words, briefly

paulātim *adv* little by little, gradually, by degrees; a few at a time

paulisper *adv* for a little while

paulō *adv* (*as abl of degree of difference in expressions of comparison*) by a little, a little, somewhat; **paulo antea** a little before; **paulo post** a little later

paulŭlō *adv* somewhat, a little; cheaply, at a low price

paulŭlum *adv* somewhat, a little

paulŭl·us -a -um *adj* very little; *n* a bit; **paululum pecuniae** a bit of money

paulum *adv* a little, to some extent, to some degree

paul·us -a -um *adj* small, little; *n* bit, trifle; **post paulum** after a bit, after a while

Paul·us -ī *m* L. Aemilius Paulus (*conqueror of Macedonia through the victory at Pydna in 168 B.C.*)

paup·er -ĕris *adj* poor; scanty, meager; (*with genit*) poor in; *m* poor man, pauper

paupercŭl·us -a -um *adj* poor

pauperi·ēs -ēī *f* poverty

pauper·ō -āre *vt* to impoverish; (*with abl*) to rob (*someone*) of

paupert·ās -ātis *f* poverty

paus·a -ae *f* pause, stop, end

pausi·a -ae *f* plump olive

pauxillātim *adv* bit by bit, little by little

pauxillisper *adv* by degrees

pauxillŭlum *adv* a little, a bit

pauxillŭl·us -a -um *adj* very little, tiny; *n* bit

pauxillum *adv* a little, a bit

pauxill·us -a -um *adj* very little, tiny; *n* small amount

pavefact·us -a -um *adj* frightened, scared

pavĕō pavēre pāvī *vt* to be scared of; *vi* to be terrified, tremble, or shiver with fear

pavesc·ō -ĕre *vt* to get scared of; *vi* to begin to be alarmed

pavidē *adv* in panic

pavid·us -a -um *adj* panicky, alarmed, shivering or trembling with fear, startled; with beating heart, nervous; causing alarm

paviment·ō -āre *vt* to pave

paviment·um -ī *n* pavement; floor

pav·iō -īre -īvī *or* **-iī -itum** *vt* to strike, beat

pavit·ō -āre *vt* to be panicky over; *vi* to quake with fear, be scared to death; to shiver (*with fever*)

pāv·ō -ōnis *m* peacock

pav·or -ōris *m* panic, terror, dismay, quaking, shivering; **pavorem injicere** (*with dat*) to throw the fear of the Lord into, to terrify

pax pācis *f* peace; peace treaty, reconciliation, compact, agreement; harmony, tranquility; favor, pardon (*from the gods*); **pace tua** with your permission, with your leave

pecc·ans -antis *m* offender, sinner

peccāt·um -ī *n* fault, mistake, slip, transgression, sin

pecc·ō -āre *vi* to make a mistake, commit a fault, sin

pecorōs·us -a -um *adj* rich in cattle

pect·en -inis *m* comb; plectrum (*for strumming a lyre*); scallop (*sea food*)

pectō pectĕre pexī pexum *vt* to comb; to card (*wool*); (coll) to clobber (*with stick or fist*)

pect·us -ōris *n* breast; heart, feeling; soul, conscience, mind, understanding; character, person

pecū (*genit not in use*) *n* flock; *n pl* cattle; pastures

pecuāri·us -a -um *adj* of sheep, of cattle; **res pecuaria** livestock; *m* cattle man, cattle breeder, rancher; *f* livestock; *n pl* herds of cattle, herds of sheep

peculāt·or -ōris *m* embezzler

peculāt·us -ūs *m* embezzlement

peculiār·is -e *adj* one's own, as one's own private property; special

peculiāt·us -a -um *adj* rich, well off

pecūli·ō -āre *vt* to give away for good

pecūliōs·us -a -um *adj* owning private property

pecūl·ium -iī *or* **-ī** *n* small savings (*esp. accumulated by slaves*); private property

pecūni·a -ae *f* money; **pecunia praesens** ready cash

pecūniāri·us -a -um *adj* pecuniary, financial, money

pecūniōs·us -a -um *adj* rich, wealthy, loaded with money; profitable, bringing in money

pec·us -ōris *n* cattle, herd, flock; sheep; head of cattle; **pecus equinum** stud; (as term of scorn) cattle

pec·us -ūdis *f* head of cattle; beast; sheep; domestic animal; land animal (*as opposed to birds*); (as term of abuse) brute, beast, swine

pedāl·is -e *adj* one-foot-long

pedār·ius -iī *or* **-ī** *m* inferior senator (*who let others step all over him*)

ped·es -itis *m* infantryman; pedestrian; infantry

pedest·er -ris -re *adj* infantry; pedestrian; on land, by land; written in prose; prosaic, plain

pedetemptim *adv* by feeling one's

way, step by step, slowly, cautiously

pedic·a -ae *f* foot chain; trap, snare

pedīculōs·us -a -um *adj* lousy

ped·is -is *m or f* louse

pedisĕqu·a -ae *f* attendant, handmaid

pedisĕqu·us -ī *m* footman, page, lackey

peditastell·us -ī *m* poor infantryman

pedit·us -ūs *m* infantry

pēdit·um -ī *n* wind, gas

pēdō pēdĕre pepēdī *vi* to break wind

ped·um -ī *n* shepherd's hook

Pēgasē·ō *or* **Pēgasei·us -a -um** *adj* of Pegasus, Pegasean

Pēgasid·es -um *f pl* Muses

Pēgas·us -ī *m* winged horse which sprang from the blood of Medusa and whose hoof, as it hit Mt. Helicon, caused Hippocrene, a fountain dear to the Muses, to flow

pēgm·a -ătis *n* bookcase; scaffolding

pējerātiuncŭl·a -ae *f* petty oath

pējerāt·us *or* **pējurāt·us -a -um** *adj* offended by false oaths; **jus pejeratum** false oath

pējĕr·ō *or* **perjūr·ō -āre** *vt* to swear falsely by; *vi* to swear a false oath; (coll) to lie

pejerōs·us -a -um *adj* perjured

pēj·or -us (*comp of malus*) *adj* worse

pējus (*comp of male*) *adv* worse

pelagi·us -a -um *adj* of the sea

pelăg·us -ī *n* sea, open sea

pēlăm·is -ĭdis *or* **pēlăm·ys -ȳdis** *f* young tuna fish

Pelasg·ī -ōrum *m pl* aborigines of Greece

Pēl·eus -ĕī *or* **-ĕos** *m* king of Thessaly, son of Aeacus, husband of Thetis, and father of Achilles

Peli·ās -ae *m* king of Iolcos in Thessaly and uncle of Jason

Pēlīd·ēs -ae *m* descendant of Peleus; Achilles; Neoptolemus

Pēli·on -ī *n* mountain in E. Thessaly

Pēli·us *or* **Pēliăc·us -a -um** *adj* of Mt. Pelion

Pell·a -ae *or* **Pell·ē -ēs** *f* city of Macedonia and birthplace of Alexander the Great

pellăci·a -ae *f* charm, allurement

Pellae·us -a -um *adj* of or from Apella; **Pellaeus juvenis** Alexander

pell·ax -ācis *adj* seductive, alluring

pellecti·ō -ōnis *f* perusal

pel·liciō -licĕre -lexī -lectum *vt* to allure, entice, coax, wheedle

pellicŭl·a -ae *f* small hide, skin, fleece

pelli·ō -ōnis *m* furrier

pell·is -is *f* skin, hide; leather; felt; tent; shield cover; **detrahere pellem** to expose one's true character

pellīt·us -a -um *adj* clothed in skins, wearing leather coat

pellō pellĕre pepūli pulsum *vt* to push, beat, strike, knock, hurl; to drive out or away, expel, banish; to repel, drive back, rout; to play or strum (*lyre, etc.*); to affect, impress, move, strike; to stamp (*the earth*)

pelluc- = **perl-**

Pelopeï·as -ădis or **Pelopë·is -ĭdis** *adj* Peloponnesian

Pelopeï·us or **Pelopë·us -a -um** *adj* Pelopian; Mycenaean; Phrygian

Pelopĭd·ae -ārum *m pl* descendants of Pelops

Peloponnens·is -e *adj* Peloponnesian

Peloponnēsiǎc·us or **Peloponnēsǐ·us -a -um** *adj* Peloponnesian

Peloponnēs·us -ī *f* the Peloponnesus (*modern Morea*)

Pel·ops -ŏpis *m* son of Tantalus, father of Atreus and Thyestes, and grandfather of Agamemnon and Menelaus

pelōr·is -ĭdis *f* large shellfish

Pelōr·us or **Pelōr·os -ī** *m* N.E. promontory of Sicily

pelt·a -ae *f* small leather shield

peltast·ēs or **peltast·a -ae** *m* soldier armed with a small leather shield

peltāt·us -a -um *adj* armed with a small leather shield

Pēlūs·ium -ĭī or **-ī** *n* city on the E. mouth of the Nile

pelv·is -is *f* bucket, basin

penāri·us -a -um *adj* food, supply, storage

Penāt·ēs -ium *m pl* Penates, household gods; hearth, home, house; cells (*of bees*)

penātĭg·er -ĕra -ĕrum *adj* carrying the household gods

pendĕō pendēre pependī *vi* to hang, hang down, be suspended; to hang loose; to hang down, be flabby, be weak; to depend, be dependent; to be in suspense, be uncertain, hesitate; to hang around, loiter; to hang in the air, be suspended, hover, float, overhang; (with *abl* or with **ab, dē** or **ex** + *abl*) **a** to hang down from, hang by; **b** to depend on, be dependent upon; **c** to hang on to, be devoted to; (with **in** + *abl*) to be poised on, hover in, hover over

pendō pendĕre pependī pensum *vt* to weigh, weigh out; to pay, pay out; to weigh, ponder, consider, value, esteem; to pay (*penalty*); **floccī pendere** to think little of; **magnī pendere** to think much of, value highly; *vi* to weigh, have weight

pendŭl·us -a -um *adj* hanging, hanging down; doubtful, uncertain

Pēnē·is -ĭdis or **Pēnēï·us -a -um** *adj* of Peneus

Pēnelŏp·a -ae or **Pēnelŏp·ē -ēs** *f* daughter of Icarius and Periboea and wife of Ulysses

penes *prep* (with *acc* of person only) in the possession of, in the power of, belonging to, resting with; at the house of, with; **penes se esse** to be in one's senses

penetrābil·is -e *adj* penetrating, piercing; penetrable

penetrāl·is -e *adj* penetrating, piercing; inner, internal, interior; *n pl* the interior, center; inner chambers; sanctuary; the interior, hinterlands

penětr·ō -āre *vt & vi* to penetrate, enter

Pēnē·us -a -um *adj* of Peneus, of the Peneus River; *m* Peneus River (*largest river in Thessaly*); river god, the father of Cyrene and Daphne

pēnicill·us -ī *m* paint brush, pencil

pēnicŭl·us -ī *m* brush; sponge

pēn·is -is *m* tail; penis; lechery

penĭtē *adv* inwardly

penĭtus *adv* internally, inside, deep within, deeply; from within; thoroughly, completely, through and through; heartily

penĭt·us -a -um *adj* inner, inward

penn·a -ae *f* feather; wing; flight

pennāt·us -a -um *adj* feathered

pennĭg·er -ĕra -ĕrum *adj* winged, feathered

pennĭpŏt·ens -entis *adj* winged, able to fly

pennŭl·a -ae *f* little wing

pensil·is -e *adj* hanging; **uva pensilis** grape hung out to dry

pensĭ·ō -ōnis *f* payment, instalment

pensĭt·ō -āre *vt* to pay; to weigh, ponder, consider; *vi* to be taxable

pens·ō -āre *vt* to weigh out; to weigh, ponder, consider, examine; to compare, contrast; to pay, atone for; to repay, compensate, requite

pens·um -ī *n* work quota; duty, task; consideration, scruple; **pensī esse** to be of value, be of importance; **pensī habere** to value, consider of importance

pensus *pp* of **pendo**

pentēr·is -is *f* galley, quinquereme

Penthesilē·a -ae *f* Amazon, warrior queen who was killed by Achilles at Troy

Penth·eus -ĕī or **-ĕos** *m* king of Thebes, son of Echion and Agave, grandson of Cadmus, and opponent of the Bacchic cult

pen·um -ī *n* supplies, provisions, food

pēnūri·a -ae *f* want, need, dearth

pen·us -ūs or **-ī** *m* or **pen·us -ŏris** *n* supplies, provisions, food

pepl·um -ī *n* or **pepl·us -ī** *m* robe for the statue of Athena

per *prep* (with *acc*) (of space) through, throughout, all over, along; (of time) through, during, for, in the course of, at, at the time of; (of agency) through, by, by means of, at the hands of; (of means or manner) through, by, under pretense of; for the sake of, with a view to; (in oath) by

pēr·a -ae *f* wallet

perabsurd·us -a -um *adj* completely absurd

peraccommodāt·us -a -um *adj* very convenient

perăc·er -ris -re *adj* very sharp

peracerb·us -a -um *adj* very harsh, very sour

perac·escō -escĕre -ŭi *vi* to become completely sour

peractĭ·ō -ōnis *f* conclusion, last act (*of a play*)

peractus *pp* of perago

peracūtē *adv* very acutely

peracūt·us -a -um *adj* very sharp; very clear (*voice, intellect*)

peradulesc·ens -entis *adj* very young

peradulescentŭl·us -ī *m* very young man

peraequē *adv* quite evenly, uniformly

peragĭt·ō -āre *vt* to harass

per·agō -agĕre -ēgī -actum *vt* to carry through to the end, complete, accomplish; to pierce; to travel through; to harass, disturb, trouble; to describe, relate, go over; to work over, till, cultivate; to deliver (*speech*); (*law*) to prosecute to a conviction

peragrātĭ·ō -ōnis *f* traveling

per·agr·ō -āre *vt* to travel through, travel, traverse; *vi* (*fig*) to spread, penetrate

peralt·us -a -um *adj* very high

per·ăm·ans -antis *adj* (with *genit*) very fond of

peramantēr *adv* very lovingly

perambŭl·ō -āre *vt* to travel, traverse, walk through

peramoen·us -a -um *adj* very pleasant, very charming

perampl·us -a -um *adj* very large, very spacious

perangustē *adv* very narrowly

perangust·us -a -um *adj* very narrow

perantīqu·us -a -um *adj* very ancient, very old

perapposit·us -a -um *adj* very suitable

perardŭ·us -a -um *adj* very difficult

perargūt·us -a -um *adj* very clear; very sharp, very witty

perarmāt·us -a -um *adj* heavily armed

per·ărō -āre *vt* to plow through; to furrow; to write on (*a wax tablet*); to write

pĕrātim *adv* bag by bag

perattentē *adv* very attentively

perattent·us -a -um *adj* very attentive

peraudiend·us -a -um *adj* that must be heard to the end

perbacch·or -ārī -ātus sum *vt* to carouse through (*e.g., many days*)

perbeāt·us -a -um *adj* very happy

perbellē *adv* very prettily

perbĕne *adv* very well

perbenevŏl·us -a -um *adj* very friendly

perbenignē *adv* very kindly

perbĭb·ō -ĕre -ī *vt* to drink up, drink in, imbibe

perbĭt·ō -ĕre *vi* to go to ruin

perbland·us -a -um *adj* very attractive, very charming

perbŏn·us -a -um *adj* very good, excellent

perbrĕv·is -e *adj* very short, very brief; **perbrevi** or **perbrevi tempore** in a very short time

perbrevitēr *adv* very briefly

perc·a -ae *f* perch

percalefact·us -a -um *adj* warmed through and through

percal·escō -escĕre -ŭi *vi* to become quite hot

percall·escō -escĕre -ŭi *vt* to become thoroughly versed in; *vi* to become very hardened

percār·us -a -um *adj* very dear, very costly; very dear, much loved

percaut·us -a -um *adj* very cautious

percelĕbr·or -ārī -ātus sum *vi* to be quite famous

percĕl·er -ĕris *adj* very quick

perceleritēr *adv* very quickly

per·cellō -cellĕre -cŭlī -culsum *vt* to knock down, beat down, overthrow; to scare to death; to overthrow, ruin; to send scurrying; to hit hard

percens·ĕō -ēre -ŭī *vt* to count up; to review, survey; to travel through, traverse

perceptĭ·ō -ōnis *f* harvesting; comprehension; *f pl* concepts

percept·us -a -um *pp* of percipio; *n* precept, rule, doctrine

per·cīdō -cīdĕre -cīdī -cīsum *vt* to smash to pieces

perci·ĕō -ēre or **perc·ĭō -īre -īvī** or **-iī -ītum** *vt* to stir up, excite

per·cipĭō -cipĕre -cēpī -ceptum *vt* to get a good hold of; to catch; to occupy, seize; to gather in, harvest, reap; (of the senses) to take in, perceive, feel; (of feelings) to get hold of, get the better of; to learn, know, comprehend, understand, perceive

percĭt·us -a -um *pp* of percieo; *adj* aroused, provoked; impetuous, excitable

percoctus *pp* of percoquo

percōl·ō -āre *vt* to strain, filter

per·cŏlō -colĕre -colŭī -cultum *vt* to reverence, revere, worship; to beautify; to crown, complete

percōm·is -e *adj* very courteous

percommŏdē *adv* very conveniently, very well, very suitably

percommŏd·us -a -um *adj* very convenient, very suitable

percontātĭ·ō -ōnis *f* thorough investigation

percontāt·or -ōris *m* inquisitive fellow

percont·or -ārī -ātus sum *vt* to question, investigate, interrogate; (with double *acc*) to ask (*someone something*)

percontŭm·ax -ācis *adj* very stubborn

per·cŏquō -coquĕre -coxī -coctum *vt* to cook through and through, cook thoroughly; to heat thoroughly; to ripen; to scorch, blacken

percrēb·escō or **percrēbr·escō -escĕre -ŭī** *vi* to become prevalent, be spread abroad

percrĕp·ō -āre -ŭī -ĭtum *vi* to resound, ring

percruci·or -ārī -ātus sum *vi* to torment oneself

perculsus *pp* of **percello**

percult·us -a -um *pp* of **percolo**; *adj* decked out; (coll) dolled up (*woman*)

percupĭd·us -a -um *adj* (with *genit*) very fond of

percup·ĭō -ĕre *vt* (with *inf*) to be eager to, desire very much to, be dying to

percūriōs·us -a -um *adj* very curious

percūr·ō -āre *vt* to heal completely

per·currō -currĕre -cucurrī or **currī -cursum** *vt* to run through, run along, run over, pass over, speed over; (fig) to scan briefly, look over; (in a speech) to treat in succession, go over, run over; (of feelings) to run through, penetrate, pierce; *vi* to run fast, hurry along; (with *ad* + *acc*) to dash to (*e.g.*, *the Forum*); (with *per* + *acc*) **a** to run through or across, travel through; **b** (fig) to run through, mention quickly, treat in succession

percursātĭ·ō -ōnis *f* traveling; **percursatio Italiae** traveling through Italy

percursĭ·ō -ōnis *f* quick survey

percurs·ō -āre *vi* to roam about, range about

percussĭ·ō -ōnis *f* hitting, striking; snapping (*of fingers*); (mus) beat, time

percuss·or -ōris *m* assailant; assassin

percussus *pp* of **percutio**

percuss·us -ūs *m* beating, striking

per·cutĭō -cutĕre -cussī -cussum *vt* to beat or hit hard; to pierce, transfix, run through; to shoot, kill; to shock, impress, move, astound; to cut through; to dig (*ditch*); to coin, stamp (*money*); to cheat, trick

perdecŏr·us -a -um *adj* very pretty

perdēlīr·us -a -um *adj* very silly, quite mad

perdeps·ō -ĕre -ŭī *vt* to knead thoroughly; (fig) to seduce

perdiffĭcĭl·is -e *adj* very difficult

perdiffĭcĭlĭter *adv* with great difficulty

perdign·us -a -um *adj* (with *abl*) quite worthy of

perdilĭg·ens -entis *adj* very diligent, very conscientious

perdilĭgenter *adv* very diligently, very conscientiously

per·discō -discĕre -dĭdĭcī *vt* to learn thoroughly, learn by heart

perdisertē *adv* very eloquently

perdītē *adv* recklessly, desperately

perdĭt·or -ōris *m* destroyer

perdĭt·us -a -um *adj* ruined, lost; profligate, degenerate, infamous, reckless, incorrigible, hopeless

perdiū *adv* for a very long time

perdiūturn·us -a -um *adj* longlasting, protracted

perdīv·es -ĭtis *adj* very rich

perd·ix -īcis *m* partridge

per·dō -dĕre -dĭdī -dĭtum *vt* to wreck, ruin, destroy; to waste, squander; to lose

perdoc·ĕō -ēre -ŭī -tum *vt* to teach thoroughly

perdoctē *adv* very skillfully

perdoct·us -a -um *pp* of **perdoceo**; *adj* very learned, very skillful

perdol·escō -escĕre -ŭī *vi* to become resentful

perdŏm·ō -āre -ŭī -ĭtum *vt* to tame completely, subdue, subjugate

perdormisc·ō -ĕre *vi* to sleep on, keep on sleeping

per·dūcō -dūcĕre -duxī -ductum *vt* to lead, guide; to cover, spread; to prolong, drag out; to induce; to seduce; (with *ad* + *acc*) **a** to lead, bring, guide, escort to; **b** to build, run (*wall, ditch, road, etc.*) to; **c** to prolong, protract, drag out, continue (*something*) **to** or **till**; **d** to win over to, convince of

perduct·ō *vt* to lead, conduct

perduct·or -ōris *m* guide; pimp

perdūdum *adv* long long ago

perduellĭ·ō -ōnis *f* treason, high treason

perduell·is -is *m* enemy

perdūr·ō -āre *vi* to hold out, last, endure

per·ĕdō -esse -ēdī -ēsum *vt* to eat up, devour

peregrē *adv* abroad, away from home; from abroad; **peregre abire** or **peregre exire** to go abroad

peregrīnābund·us -a -um *adj* traveling around

peregrīnātĭ·ō -ōnis *f* living abroad, travel, touring; roaming, ranging (*said of animals*)

peregrīnāt·or -ōris *m* traveler, wanderer

peregrīnĭt·ās -ātis *f* foreign manners, strange ways

peregrīn·or -ārī -ātus sum *vi* to live abroad, travel abroad, travel around; (fig) to be a stranger

peregrīn·us -a -um *adj* foreign, strange, alien, exotic; (fig) strange, inexperienced; **amores peregrīnī** love affairs with foreign women; **praetor peregrinus** praetor who tried cases involving foreigners and Roman citizens; **terror peregrinus** fear of a foreign enemy; *mf* foreigner, alien

perēlĕg·ans -antis *adj* very elegant

perēleganter *adv* very elegantly

perēlŏqu·ens -entis *adv* very eloquent

peremn·ia -ium n pl auspices taken before crossing a river

peremptus pp of **perimo**

perendiē adv the day after tomorrow

perendin·us -a -um adj dies perendinus the day after tomorrow; m the day after tomorrow

perenn·is -e adj perennial, continual, everlasting

perenniserv·os -ī m slave for life

perennit·ās -ātis f continuance, perpetuity

perenn·ō -āre vi to last

pērenticid·a -ae m (coll) crook

per·eō -īre -iī -itum vi to pass away, pass on, die; to go to waste, perish, be destroyed; to be lost, be ruined, be undone; to be desperately in love, pine away; (of snow) to melt away; (of iron) to rust away; perii! I'm ruined!, I'm finished!, I'm washed up!

perequit·ō -āre vt to ride up through; vi to ride around

pererr·ō -āre vt to roam around, wander through; to survey, look (someone) over

pererudīt·us -a -um adj very learned

peresus pp of **peredo**

perexcels·us -a -um adj very high, exalted

perexiguē adv very sparingly

perexigu·us -a -um adj tiny; insignificant; very short (day)

perfacētē adv very wittily

perfacēt·us -a -um adj very witty, very sharp

perfacile adv very easily, very readily

perfacil·is -ē adj very easy; very courteous

perfamiliār·is -e adj very close, intimate; m very close friend

perfectē adv completely, perfectly

perfecti·ō -ōnis f completion; perfection

perfect·or -ōris m perfecter; dicendi perfector stylist

perfect·us -a -um pp of **perficio**; adj complete, finished, perfect, excellent

per·ferō -ferre -tulī -lātum vt to carry through; to endure to the end, bear with patience, put up with; to pass (a law); to bring, announce, report (news)

per·ficiō -ficere -fēcī -fectum vt to complete, finish, accomplish, carry out, perform, execute, bring to an end; to bring to completion, finish, perfect; to bring about, cause

perfic·us -a -um adj perfecting; natura perfica nature which perfects

perfidēl·is -e adj very faithful, very trusty

perfidi·a -ae f perfidy, treachery

perfidiōsē adv treacherously

perfidiōs·us -a -um adj treacherous, faithless

perfid·us -a -um adj treacherous, untrustworthy, dishonest, sneaky; m sneak

per·figō -figere -fixī -fixum vt to pierce

perflābil·is -e adj airy; invisible (gods)

perflāgitiōs·us -a -um adj utterly disgraceful

perfl·ō -āre vt to blow through, blow across

perfluctū·ō -āre vt to surge through

per·fodiō -fodere -fōdī -fossum vt to dig through; to pierce

perfor·ō -āre vt to bore through, pierce; to make by boring

perfortiter adv very bravely

perfoss·or -ōris m perfossor parietum burglar

perfossus pp of **perfodio**

perfractus pp of **perfringo**

perfrem·ō -ere -uī vi to snort loud

perfrēqu·ens -entis adj very crowded, over-crowded

perfric·ō -āre -uī -ātum or **-tum** vt to rub well, rub all over; os perfricare to rub away blushes, put on a bold front

perfrīgefac·iō -ere vt (fig) to send a chill over, make shudder

per·frigescō -frigescere -frixī vi to catch a bad cold

perfrigid·us -a -um adj very cold, ice-cold

per·fringō -fringere -frēgī -fractum vt to break through; to break to pieces, batter in, smash; (fig) to break (laws, etc.), break up (conspiracy)

per·fruor -fruī -fructus sum vi (with abl) to experience to the full, fully enjoy, be delighted by, perform gladly

perfug·a -ae m military deserter; political turncoat

per·fugiō -fugere -fūgī vi (with ad or in + acc) a to flee to for refuge; b to desert to; c (fig) to have recourse to, find comfort in

perfuncti·ō -ōnis f performance, performing, discharge

perfunctus pp of **perfungor**

per·fundō -fundere -fūdī -fūsum vt to drench, bathe; to sprinkle; to dye; (fig) to fill, flood, steep, inspire

per·fungor -fungī -functus sum vt to enjoy; vi (with abl) a to perform, discharge, fulfill; b to go through, endure, undergo; c to get rid of; d to be finished with, be done with; e to enjoy

perfur·ō -ere vi to rage wildly, rage on

perfūsus pp of **perfundo**

Pergam·a -ōrum n pl or **Pergam·us -ī** f citadel of Troy, Troy

Pergamē·us -a -um adj Trojan; m pl Trojans

Pergam·um -ī n Troy; Pergamum (city in Mysia, the capital of the Attalid kingdom, famous for its library)

pergaud·ĕō -ēre vi to be very glad

per·gō -gĕre -rexī -rectum vt to go on uninterruptedly with, continue; (with inf) to continue to; vi to go straight on, continue, proceed; (with ad + acc) to pass on to, proceed to (esp. in speaking)

pergraec·or -ārī -ātus sum vi to go completely Greek, have a ball

pergrand·is -e adj very large, huge; **pergrandis natu** very old

pergraphic·us -a -um adj very cunning

pergrāt·us -a -um adj very pleasant; n distinct pleasure

pergrav·is -e adj very heavy; very important; very impressive

pergraviter adv very seriously

pergŭl·a -ae f veranda, balcony; school; brothel

Perg·us -ī m lake in Sicily, near Henna, where Pluto carried off Proserpina

perhib·ĕō -ēre -uī -itum vt to hold, assert, maintain; to call, name; to adduce, cite

perhīlum adv very little

perhonōrificē adv very respectfully, with all due respect

perhonōrific·us -a -um adj very honorable, very complimentary; very respectful

perhorr·escō -escĕre -uī vt to begin to shudder at; to develop a terror of; vi to begin to quake, begin to tremble violently

perhorrid·us -a -um adj horrible, dreadful

perhūmāniter adv very kindly

perhūmān·us -a -um adj very courteous

Pericl·ēs -is or **-ī** m Athenian statesman, son of Xanthippus and political leader of Athens during the city's most flourishing period (c. 495-429 B.C.)

periclitātī·ō -ōnis f test, experiment

periclit·or -ārī -ātus sum vt to test, put to the test, try; to jeopardize; to risk; vi to be in danger, be in jeopardy; to run a risk; (with abl) to be in danger of losing (e.g., life, reputation); **capite periclitārī** to be in danger of losing one's life, risk one's life

periculōsē adv dangerously

periculōs·us -a -um adj dangerous, perilous, risky

pericŭl·um or **pericl·um -ī** n danger, peril, risk; trial, attempt, experiment, test; literary venture; (law) trial, case, lawsuit, legal record, writ, sentence

peridōnĕ·us -a -um adj very suitable; (with dat or ad + acc) well adapted to, well suited to

perillustr·is -e adj very clear; very illustrious, very distinguished

perimbēcill·us -a -um adj very weak, very feeble

per·imō -imĕre -ēmī -emptum vt

to take away completely; to destroy; to slay, kill

perimpedīt·us -a -um adj rough (terrain), full of obstacles

perincommŏdē adv very inconveniently

perincommŏd·us -a -um adj very inconvenient

perinde adv in the same manner, equally, just as, quite as; (with atque, ac, ut, or quam) just as, exactly as; (with ac si, quasi, tamquam, or quam si) just as if

perindulg·ens -entis adj very tender; (with ad + acc) very tender toward

perinfirm·us -a -um adj very weak

peringeniōs·us -a -um adj very clever

periniqu·us -a -um adj very unfair; very upset, very annoyed, very impatient, very reluctant; **periniquo animo patī** or **ferre** to be quite upset at, be quite annoyed at, be very reluctant about

perinsign·is -e adj very remarkable

perinvīt·us -a -um adj very unwilling

period·us -ī f sentence, rhetorical period

peripatētic·us -a -um adj peripatetic, Aristotelian; m pl peripatetics, Aristotelians

peripetasmăt·a -um n pl curtains, drapes

perīrāt·us -a -um adv very angry; (with dat) very angry with

periscēl·is -idis f anklet

periström·a -ătis n carpet

peristyl·ium -iī or **-ī** n peristyle (open court surrounded by a colonnade)

peristyl·um -ī n colonnade around a building, peristyle

perītē adv skillfully, expertly

perīti·a -ae f experience, practical knowledge, skill; (with genit) experience in, familiarity with, knowledge of

perīt·us -a -um adj experienced, skillful, expert, familiar; (with genit or abl, with in + abl, or with ad + acc) experienced in, skillful in, expert in or at, familiar with; (with inf) skilled in, expert at, e.g., **perītus cantāre** skilled in singing, expert at singing

perjūcundē adv very pleasantly

perjūcund·us -a -um adj very pleasant

perjūr·ium -iī or **-ī** n perjury, false oath

perjūrō see **pejero**

perjūr·us or **pejĕr·us -a -um** adj perjured, oath-breaking; lying, dishonest

per·lābor -lābī -lapsus sum vi to glide along, skim across or over; (with per + acc) to slip through; (with ad + acc) to come, move, glide, or slip toward; (with in + acc) to glide into, slip into

perlaet·us -a -um *adv* very glad, most joyful

perlapsus *pp* of **perlabor**

perlātē *adv* very extensively

perlat·ĕŏ -ēre -ŭī *vi* to be completely hidden

perlātus *pp* of **perfero**

perlecti·ō -ōnis *f* thorough perusal

per·lĕgō -legĕre -lēgī -lectum *vt* to scan, survey thoroughly; to read through

perlepidē *adv* very nicely

perlĕv·is -e *adj* very light, very slight

perleviter *adv* very lightly, very slightly

perlib·ens or **perlub·ens** -entis *adj* very willing

perlibenter or **perlubenter** *adv* very gladly

perlīberāl·is -e *adj* very genteel

perlib·et or **perlub·et** -ēre *v impers* (with *inf*) I should very much like to

perliciō see **pellicio**

perlīt·ō -āre *vi* to sacrifice with favorable omens

perlongē *adv* a long way off, very far

perlonginqu·us -a -um *adj* very long; very tedious

perlub- = **perlib-**

per·lūcĕō or **pel·lūcĕō** -lūcēre -luxī *vi* to shine clearly, be bright; to be clearly visible; to be transparent; to be clear, be intelligible

perlūcidŭl·us -a -um *adj* somewhat transparent

perlūcid·us or **pellūcid·us** -a -um *adj* very bright; transparent

perluctuōs·us -a -um *adj* very sad

per·lŭō -luĕre -lŭī -lūtum *vt* to wash thoroughly, wash off, bathe

perlustr·ō -āre *vt* to traverse; to scan, survey, review

permadefac·iō -ĕre *vt* to soak through and through, drench

permagn·us -a -um *adj* very great; very important; *n* great thing; **permagno** at a very high price, very dearly; **permagnum aestimare** (with *inf*) to think it quite something to

permānanter *adv* by flowing through

permānasc·ō -ĕre *vi* (of a report) to begin to spread

per·manĕō -manēre -mansī -mansum *vi* to last, continue, hold out, remain, persist, endure

permān·ō -āre *vt* to seep through, penetrate; *vi* to penetrate; (with **ad** or **in** + *acc*) **a** to seep through to, seep into, penetrate; **b** (fig) to reach, extend to, penetrate

permansi·ō -ōnis *f* persistence, continuance

permarīn·us -a -um *adj* sea-going

permātūr·escō -escĕre -ŭī *vi* to become fully ripe

permediōcr·is -e *adj* completely normal

permeditāt·us -a -um *adj* well rehearsed, well trained

permensus *pp* of **permetior**

permě·ō -āre *vt* to go through, cross over, cross; *vi* (with **in** + *acc*) to penetrate; (with **per** + *acc*) to penetrate, permeate

Permess·us -ī *m* river in Boeotia sacred to Apollo and the Muses

per·mētior -mētīrī -mensus sum *vt* to measure out, measure; to traverse, travel, travel over

per·mingō -mingĕre -minxī *vt* to soak with urine; to pollute

permīr·us -a -um *adj* very surprising, truly amazing

per·miscĕō -miscēre -miscŭī -mixtum *vt* to mix together, intermingle; (fig) to mix together, mix up, confuse

permissi·ō -ōnis *f* unconditional surrender; permission

permiss·us -a -um *pp* of **permitto**; *n* permission

permiss·us -ūs *m* permission, leave

permitiāl·is -e *adj* destructive, deadly

permiti·ēs -ēī *f* wasting away; ruin, decay

per·mittō -mittĕre -mīsī -missum *vt* to let through, let go through; to throw, hurl; to give up, surrender, to concede, relinquish; to let loose, let go; to let, permit, allow, grant; (with *dat*) to give up to, surrender (*something*) to, entrust (*something*) to, grant (*something*) to; (with **in** + *acc*) to send flying at, hurl or throw at

permixtē or **permixtim** *adv* confusedly, promiscuously

permixti·ō -ōnis *f* mixture; confusion, bedlam

permixt·us -a -um *pp* of **permisceo**; *adj* confused, promiscuous

permodest·us -a -um *adj* very modest, very moderate

permolest·ē *adv* with much trouble; **permolesta ferre** to be quite annoyed at

permolest·us -a -um *adj* very troublesome, very annoying

permōl·ō -ĕre *vt* to grind up; **alienas uxores permolere** (fig) to seduce other men's wives

permōti·ō -ōnis *f* excitement; **animi permotio** or **mentis permotio** excitement, deep emotion

per·movĕō -movēre -mōvī -mōtum *vt* to stir up, churn up (*the sea*); to move deeply, make a deep impression upon; to excite, agitate, rouse; to influence, induce, prevail on

per·mulcĕō -mulcēre -mulsī -mulsum *vt* to stroke, pet, caress; to soothe, charm; to delight, flatter; to appease, tame, mitigate, allay

permultō *adv* (with comparatives) by far, far, much

permult·us -a -um *adj* very much; **per-multum** *adv* very often; before; **permultum interest** it makes a world of difference

permult·us -a -um *adj* very much, very many; *n* a lot, much

permūn·iō -īre -īvī or -iī -ītum *vt* to fortify thoroughly; to finish fortifying

permūtāti·ō -ōnis *f* permutation, complete change; change, alteration; crisis, revolution; exchange, barter; substitution

permūt·ō -āre *vt* to change completely, alter completely; to exchange, interchange

pern·a -ae *f* ham

pernecessāri·us -a -um *adj* very necessary; very closely related; *m* close friend; close relative

pernecesse (indecl) *adj* very necessary, indispensable

pernĕg·ō -āre *vt* to deny flatly; to turn down flat

per·nĕō -nēre -nēvī -nētum *vt* (of the Fates) to spin out

perniciābil·is -e *adj* ruinous

pernici·ēs -ēī *f* ruin, destruction, disaster, calamity; pest, curse

perniciōsē *adv* perniciously, ruinously

perniciōs·us -a -um *adj* pernicious, ruinous

pernicit·ās -ātis *f* agility, nimbleness, swiftness

perniciter *adv* nimbly, swiftly

pernig·er -ra -rum *adj* jet black

pernimi·us -a -um *adj* much too much

pern·ix -īcis *adj* agile, nimble, active, swift

pernōbil·is -e *adj* famous, illustrious

pernoct·ō -āre *vi* to spend the night

per·noscō -noscĕre -nōvī -nōtum *vt* to examine thoroughly; to become fully acquainted with, get an accurate knowledge of

pernōt·escō -escĕre -uī *vi* to become generally known

pern·ox -octis *adj* all-night; luna pernox full moon

pernumĕr·ō -āre *vt* to count up

pēr·ō -ōnis *m* clodhopper, brogue (*worn by peasants and soldiers*)

perobscūr·us -a -um *adj* very obscure

perodiōs·us -a -um *adj* very annoying

perofficiōsē *adv* with devotion, with attention

perol·eō -ēre *vi* to have a strong odor

pērōnāt·us -a -um *adj* wearing clodhoppers

peropportūnē *adv* very opportunely, very conveniently

peropportūn·us -a -um *adj* very opportune, very convenient, well timed

peroptātō *adv* very much to one's wish

perōpus (indecl) *n* great need; **peropus est** it is absolutely essential

perōrāti·ō -ōnis *f* peroration, conclusion of a speech

perōrnāt·us -a -um *adj* very flowery (*style*)

perorn·ō -āre *vt* to enhance the prestige of (*e.g., the senate*)

perōr·ō -āre *vt* to plead (*a case*) all by oneself; to wind up, conclude (*a speech, case*), rest (*a case*); *vi* to give the summation

perōs·us -a -um *adj* hating, detesting

perpāc·ō -āre *vt* to silence completely; to pacify thoroughly

perparcē *adv* very stingily

perparvŭl·us -a -um *adj* tiny

perparv·us -a -um *adj* very small

perpast·us -a -um *adj* well fed

perpauc·ī -ae -a *adj* very few; *n pl* very few words; **perpauca dicere** to speak very briefly

perpaucŭl·ī -ae -a *adj* very few

perpaulum *adv* somewhat, slightly

perpaul·um -ī *n* small bit

perpaup·er -ĕris *adj* very poor

perpauxill·um -ī *n* little bit

perpavefac·iō -ĕre *vt* to frighten the daylight out of

per·pellō -pellĕre -pulsī -pulsum *vt* to push hard; to urge strongly, force

perpendicŭl·um -ī *n* plumb line, plummet; ad perpendiculum perpendicularly

per·pendō -pendĕre -pendī -pensum *vt* to weigh carefully, consider; to value, judge

perpĕram *adv* incorrectly, falsely

perp·es -ĕtis *adj* continuous, uninterrupted

perpessi·ō -ōnis *f* suffering, endurance

per·petior -pĕtī -pessus sum *vt* to endure, put up with, stand; to allow, permit

perpetr·ō -āre *vt* to accomplish, go through with, carry out, achieve, perform; to perpetrate, commit

perpetuit·ās -ātis *f* perpetuity

perpetuō *adv* constantly, without interruption, forever

perpetu·ō -āre *vt* to perpetuate

perpetu·us -a -um *adj* perpetual, continuous, uninterrupted; general, universal; whole, entire; **quaestiones perpetuae** standing courts; permanent committee; *n* in perpetuum without a break, continuously; for all time, forever

perplac·eō -ēre -uī *vi* (with *dat*) to please immensely

perplexābil·is -e *adj* obscure, perplexing

perplexābiliter *adv* perplexingly

perplexē or **perplexim** *adv* confusedly, unintelligibly

perplex·or -ārī -ātus sum *vi* to cause confusion

perplex·us -a -um *adj* intricate, confused; ambiguous, obscure; *n* ambiguity, confusion

perplicāt·us -a -um *adj* entangled

perplŭ·ō -ĕre *vt* (fig) to rain, pour; *vi* (of roof, etc.) to leak, let the rain in

perpol·iō -īre -īvī or **-iī -ītum** *vt* to polish well, bring to a high polish; (fig) to polish up, perfect

perpolīt·us -a -um *adj* polished, refined

perpopŭl·or -ārī -ātus sum *vt* to ravage, devastate

perpōtāti·ō -ōnis *f* heavy drinking; drinking party

perpōt·ō -āre *vt* to drink off; *vi* to drink heavily, drink constantly

per·prīmō -prīmĕre -pressī *vt* to press hard, squeeze hard; to lie on

perpropinqu·us -a -um *adj* very near

perprūrisc·ō -ĕre *vi* to begin to itch all over

perpugn·ax -ācis *adj* very belligerent

perpulch·er -ra -rum *adj* very beautiful, very handsome

perpulsus *pp* of **perpello**

perpurg·ō -āre *vt* to cleanse thoroughly, clean up; (fig) to clear up, explain

perpusill·us -a -um *adj* puny

perpŭt·ō -āre *vt* to prune back hard; to clear up, explain in detail

porquam *adv* very, extremely

per·quīrō -quīrĕre -quīsīvī -quīsītum *vt* to search carefully for; to examine carefully

perquīsītius *adv* more accurately, more critically

perquīsīt·or -ōris *m* enthusiast; **auctionum perquīsitor** auction enthusiast

perrārō *adv* very rarely, very seldom

perrār·us -a -um *adj* very rare, quite uncommon

perrecondīt·us -a -um *adj* recondite, abstruse

perrectus *pp* of **pergo**

per·rēpō -rēpĕre -repsī -reptum *vt* to crawl over, crawl along

perrept·ō -āre *vt* to creep through, sneak through; *vi* to creep around

perrīdiculē *adv* most absurdly

perrīdicŭl·us -a -um *adj* utterly absurd

perrogāti·ō -ōnis *f* passage (*of a law*)

perrŏg·ō -āre *vt* to ask in succession; to poll (*opinions*); **sententias perrogare** to have roll call (*in the senate*)

per·rumpō -rumpĕre -rūpī -ruptum *vt* to break through, force one's way through; to break in two, shatter, smash; to offend against, violate; *vi* to break through, make a breakthrough

Pers·a or **Pers·ēs -ae** *m* Persian

persaepe *adv* very often

persalsē *adv* very wittily

persals·us -a -um *adj* very witty

persalūtāti·ō -ōnis *f* round of greetings, greeting all in turn

persalūt·ō -āre *vt* to salute one after another

persanctē *adv* very solemnly

persapi·ens -entis *adj* very wise

persapienter *adv* very wisely

perscienter *adv* very wisely, very discreetly

per·scindō -scindĕre -scĭdī -scissum *vt* to tear to pieces; to scatter (*e.g., clouds*)

perscīt·us -a -um *adj* very clever, very smart

per·scrībō -scrībĕre -scripsī -scriptum *vt* to write out; to describe fully, give in detail; to record, register; to enter (*into an account book*); to make over by writing; to pay by check

perscripti·ō -ōnis *f* entry, official record; check, payment by check

perscript·or -ōris *m* bookkeeper, accountant

perscriptus *pp* of **perscribo**

perscrūt·ō -āre or **perscrūt·or -ārī -ātus sum** *vt* to search or examine thoroughly, scrutinize

per·sĕcō -secāre -secŭī -sectum *vt* to dissect, cut into pieces; (fig) to cut through, cut out, eliminate

persect·or -ārī -ātus sum *vt* to follow eagerly, investigate

persecūti·ō -ōnis *f* prosecution, suing, lawsuit

persecūtus *pp* of **persequor**

per·sedĕō or **per·sidĕō -sēdī -sessum** *vt* to remain seated

persegn·is -e *adj* very slow-moving, dull, tedious

per·sentiō -sentīre -sensī -sensum *vt* to perceive clearly; to feel deeply

persentisc·ō -ĕre *vt* to detect; to feel deeply

Persephŏn·ē -ēs *f* daughter of Demeter and queen of the lower world, called Proserpina by the Romans

persĕqu·ens -entis *adj* pursuing; (with *genit*) given to the practice of

per·sĕquor -sĕquī -secūtus sum *vt* to follow persistently, follow up; to be in hot pursuit of, be on the heels of; to chase after, catch up to; to follow verbatim; to imitate, copy; to prosecute; to take vengeance on; to follow out, execute, perform; to describe, explain

Pers·ēs -ae or **Pers·eus -ĕī** *m* last king of Macedonia, conquered by Aemilius Paulus at Pydna (169 B.C.)

Pers·eus -ĕī or **-ĕos** *m* son of Jupiter and Danae, who killed Medusa and slew the sea monster who was about to devour Andromeda

Persē·us or **Persēi·us -a -um** *adj* of Perseus

persevēr·ans -antis *adj* persevering, persistent, relentless

persevēranter *adv* persistently, relentlessly

persevēranti·a -ae *f* perseverance, persistence

persevēr·ō -āre *vt* to persist in; *vi* to persist

persevēr·us -a -um *adj* very strict

Persi·a -ae or **Pers·is -ĭdis** *f* Persia

Persic·us -a -um *adj* Persian; (fig) luxurious, soft; **of Perses** (*king of Macedonia*); *m pl* Persians; *f* peach tree; *n* peach; *n pl* Persian history

per·sīdō -sīdĕre -sēdī -sessum *vi* to sink down, penetrate

persign·ō -āre *vt* to record in detail

persimil·is -e *adj* very similar; (with *genit* or *dat*) very similar to, very much like

persimpl·ex -ĭcis *adj* very plain, very simple

Pers·is -ĭdis *adj* Persian; *f* Persia; Persian woman

Pers·ius -iī or **-ī** *m* A. Persius Flaccus (*famous satirist in the reign of Nero, 34-62 A.D.*)

persoll·a -ae *f* little mask; (as term of abuse) you ugly little thing!

persōl·us -a -um *adj* completely alone

per·solvō -solvĕre -solvī -solūtum *vt* to solve, explain; to pay up; to pay (*a penalty*); to fulfill (*a vow*); to render (*thanks*); to offer (*sacrifice*); **poenas persolvere** (with *dat*) to suffer at the hands of

persōn·a -ae *f* mask; part, character; mask, pretense; personality, person, character

persōnāt·us -a -um *adj* wearing a mask, masked; under false pretenses; **pater personatus** father on the stage

persōn·ō -āre *vt* to make resound, make ring; to shout; **aurem persōnare** to make the ear ring; *vi* to resound, reecho; **cithārā persōnare** to play the zither loudly

perspectē *adv* intelligently

perspect·ō -āre *vt* to look all around

perspect·us -a -um *pp* of perspicio; *adj* well known, clear, evident

perspĭcŭl·or -ārī -ātus sum *vt* to examine thoroughly, explore thoroughly

persperg·ō -ĕre *vt* to sprinkle

perspic·ax -ācis *adj* sharp-sighted; keen, penetrating, perspicacious

perspĭcientĭ·a -ae *f* clear perception

per·spĭciō -spĭcĕre -spexī -spectum *vt* to see through; to look closely at, examine, inspect, observe

perspicŭē *adv* clearly

perspĭcŭĭt·ās -ātis *f* clarity

perspĭcŭ·us -a -um *adj* clear, transparent; clear, evident, perspicuous

per·sternō -sternĕre -strāvī -strātum *vt* to pave

perstĭmŭl·ō -āre *vt* to stimulate violently

per·stō -stāre -stĭtī -stātum *vi* to stand firm, hold one's ground; to keep standing; to remain unchanged, last; to be firm, persevere, persist, hold out

perstrātus *pp* of persterno

perstrĕp·ō -ĕre -ŭī -ĭtum *vi* to make a loud noise, make a lot of noise

per·stringō -stringĕre -strinxī -strictum *vt* to tie, tie up; to blunt, deaden (*the senses*), dazzle (*the eyes*), deafen (*the ears*); to touch lightly, graze, graze against; to glance over, touch lightly on; to belittle, slight

perstudiōsē *adv* enthusiastically

perstudiōs·us -a -um *adj* very eager, enthusiastic; (with *genit*) fond of, enthusiastic about

per·suādeō -suādēre -suāsī -suāsum *vi* (with *dat*) to persuade, convince; **sibi persuasum habere** to convince oneself, be convinced

persuāsĭ·ō -ōnis *f* convincing

persuastr·ix -ĭcis *f* seductress

persuāsus -ūs *m* persuasion

persuās·us -ūs *m* persuasion

persubtīl·is -e *adj* very subtle, very ingenious

persult·ō -āre *vt* to gambol about, prance about; to scour (*woods*); *vi* to gambol, prance, run around

per·taedet -taedēre -taesum est *v impers* (with *acc* of person = subject in English and *genit* of thing = object in English) to be weary of, be sick and tired of, be bored with, e.g., **me negotiī pertaedet** I am sick and tired of this business

per·tĕgō -tĕgĕre -texī -tectum *vt* to cover, cover up

pertempt·ō -āre *vt* to test thoroughly; to sound (*someone*) out; to consider well; (fig) to pervade, fill, overwhelm; **gaudia pertemptant pectus** joy fills (*their*) hearts

per·tendō -tendĕre -tendī -tensum or **-tentum** *vt* to press on with, continue, carry out; *vi* to press on, continue, persevere, persist, keep going

pertĕnŭ·is -e *adj* very thin, very slight, very small, very fine

p.

pertin·ĕō -ēre -ŭī *vi* to reach, extend; (with **per** + *acc*) to pervade, reach; (with **ad** + *acc*) a to extend to, reach; b to pertain to, relate to, concern; c to apply to, be applicable to, suit, be suitable to; d to tend toward, be conducive to; e to belong to; **quod pertinet** (with **ad** + *acc*) as regards, as far as concerns

perting·ō -ēre *vi* to extend

pertolĕr·ō -āre *vt* to put up with, endure to the end

pertorqu·ĕō -ēre *vt* to twist, distort

pertractātē *adv* systematically

pertractāti·ō -ōnis *f* handling, treatment

pertract·ō -āre *vt* to handle, fondle; (fig) to handle carefully, treat systematically; to influence

per·trăhō -trahĕre -traxī -tractum *vt* to drag; to allure, lead on, decoy

pertrect- = pertract-

pertrist·is -e *adj* very sad, very gloomy

pertumultuōsē *adv* very excitedly, hysterically

per·tundō -tundĕre -tŭdī -tūsum *vt* to punch a hole through, perforate

perturbātē *adv* confusedly, in confusion

perturbāti·ō -ōnis *f* confusion, disorder; political disturbance, revolution; mental disturbance; disturbing emotion

perturbātr·ix -īcis *f* disturbing element

perturbāt·us -a -um *adj* disturbed, troubled; excited, alarmed; embarrassed

perturb·is -e *adj* downright shameful

perturb·ō -āre *vt* to throw into confusion, confuse, disturb; to embarrass; to upset, alarm

pertūs·us -a -um *pp* of **pertundo**; *adj* perforated; tattered (*clothes*)

per·ungō -ungĕre -unxī -unctum *vt* to oil well, anoint thoroughly

perurbān·us -a -um *adj* very urbane, very sophisticated; *m* sophisticate

per·ūrō -ūrĕre -ussī -ustum *vt* to burn up; to consume; to inflame, rub sore; to scorch; (of cold) to nip, bite; (fig) to fire, inflame

Perusi·a -ae *f* town in Etruria

perustus *pp* of **peruro**

perūtil·is -e *adj* very useful, very practical

per·vādō -vādĕre -vāsī -vāsum *vt* to pass through, go through; to spread throughout, pervade; to penetrate, reach; *vi* to spread, penetrate; (with **ad** or **in** + *acc*) to go as far as, spread to, reach, arrive at, penetrate; (with **per** + *acc*) to spread through or over

pervagāt·us -a -um *adj* widespread,

prevalent, well known; general, common

pervăg·or -ārī -ātus sum *vt* to spread through or over, pervade; *vi* to wander all over, range about; (with **ad** + *acc*) to spread to, extend to, be known as far as

pervăg·us -a -um *adj* wandering about

pervariē *adv* in various versions

pervast·ō -āre *vt* to devastate

pervāsus *pp* of **pervado**

per·vĕhō -vehĕre -vexī -vectum *vt* to bring, carry, convey; to bring (*e.g., supplies*) through; **pervehi** to ride, drive, sail; to reach; **in portum pervehi** to sail into port, reach port

per·vellō -vellĕre -vellī *vt* to pull hard; to pinch hard; to excite, arouse; (fig) to tear apart (*with words*), disparage

per·vĕniō -venīre -vēnī -ventum *vi* to come to, reach; *vi* to come up, arrive; (with **ad** or **in** + *acc*) a to arrive at, reach; b (fig) to attain to

pervĕn·or -ārī -ātus sum *vt* to search through (*e.g., all the city*)

perversē or **pervorsē** *adv* wrongly, perversely

perversĭt·ās -ātis *f* perversity, distortion

pervers·us or **pervors·us -a -um** *adj* turned the wrong way, awry, crooked; cross-eyed; (fig) crooked, wrong, perverse; spiteful, malicious

per·vertō or **per·vortō -vertĕre -vertī -versum** *vt* to overturn, upset, knock down; (fig) to abuse, misuse, undo, destroy, pervert

pervespĕrī *adv* late in the evening

pervestigāti·ō -ōnis *f* thorough search, examining, investigation

pervestig·ō -āre *vt* to track down, hunt down; (fig) to trace, detect

pervĕt·us -ĕris *adj* very old, ancient

pervetust·us -a -um *adj* outdated, antiquated

perviam *adv* **perviam facere** to make accessible

pervicāci·a -ae *f* persistence; stubbornness

pervicācius *adv* more obstinately, more stubbornly

pervic·ax -ācis *adj* persistent, determined; headstrong, stubborn, obstinate

pervictus *pp* of **pervinco**

per·vidĕō -vidēre -vīdī -vīsum *vt* to look over, overlook, survey; to see through; to examine, investigate; to realize

pervig·ĕō -ēre -ŭī *vi* to continue to thrive

pervig·il (*genit:* **-ĭlis**) *adj* wide awake, ever watchful

pervigilāti·ō -ōnis *f* religious vigil

pervigil·ĭum -ĭī or **-ī** *n* all-night vigil

pervigil·ō -āre *vt* to spend or pass (*nights, days*) without sleep; *vi* to stay awake all night, keep an all-night vigil

pervil·is -e adj very cheap

per·vincō -vincĕre -vīcī -victum vt to defeat completely, completely overcome, completely get the better of; to outdo, surpass, exceed; to outbid; to convince; to prove; vi to win, succeed; to carry a point; (with **ut**) to succeed in, bring it about that; **non pervicit ut referrent consules** he did not succeed in having the consuls make a formal proposal

pervisus pp of **pervideo**

pervi·us -a -um adj crossable, passable, accessible; n passage, thoroughfare

per·vīvō -vīvĕre -vixī vi to live on; **pervivere usque ad summam aetatem** to live on to a ripe old age

pervulgō see **pervulgo**

pervolit·ō -āre vt & vi to fly about, flit about

pervŏl·ō -āre vt to fly through or about, flit about; to dart through, pass quickly over; vi to fly about, flit about; (with **in +** acc) to fly through to, arrive at, reach

per·vŏlō -velle -voluī vt to want badly, wish very much; (with inf) to wish very much to; (with acc & inf) to eagerly wish (someone) to

pervolūt·ō -āre vt to turn over often, read through (books)

per·volvō -volvĕre -volvī -volūtum vt to roll (someone) over; to keep reading, read through (books); **pervolvi** to be busy, be engaged

pervor- see **perver-**

pervulgāt·us or **pervolgāt·us -a -um** adj widely known, very common

pervulg·ō or **pervolg·ō -āre** vt to make known, make public, publicize; to frequent; **se pervulgare** to prostitute oneself, become a prostitute

pēs pedis m foot; foot (measure); foot, meter (in verse); leg (of table, couch, etc.); sail rope, sheet; **ad pedes descendere** to dismount (in order to fight on foot); **aequis pedibus labi** to sail on an even keel; **ante pedes** in plain view; **pede dextro, felice, or secundo** auspiciously; **pedem conferre** to come to close quarters; **pedem ferre** to come; to go; **pedem ponere** (with **in +** abl) to set foot on; **pedem referre** to go back, retreat; **pedibus** on foot; **pedibus claudere** to set to verse, put in meter; **pedibus ire in sententiam** (with genit) to vote in favor of the proposal of; **pedibus itur in sententiam** the proposal is put to a vote, a vote is taken on the proposal; **pedibus merere or pedibus mereri** to serve in the infantry; **pedibus vincere** to win a foot-race; **pugna ad pedes** infantry

battle; **se in pedes conjicere** to take to one's heels; **servus a pedibus** footman; **sub pedibus** under one's sway

pessĭmē (superl of **male**) adv very badly, most wretchedly

pessĭm·us -a -um (superl of **malus**) adj worst; m scoundrel

pessŭl·us -ī m bolt (of a door)

pessum adv down, to the ground, to the bottom; **pessum dare** to send to the bottom, sink, drown, ruin, destroy; **pessum ire** to go down, sink, go to ruin

pestĭf·er -ĕra -ĕrum adj pestilential; destructive, pernicious; m trouble maker

pestĭfĕrē adv balefully

pestĭl·ens -entis adj pestilential, unhealthful; (fig) destructive, pernicious

pestilentĭ·a -ae f unhealthful atmosphere, unhealthful climate; pestilence, plague; destruction, death

pestilĭt·ās -ātis f pestilence, plague

pest·is -is f contagious disease, plague; destruction, death; trouble maker, anarchist, subversive

petasāt·us -a -um adj wearing a hat; (fig) ready to travel

petasĭ·ō or **petăs·ō -ōnis** m ham

petasuncŭl·us -ī m little ham

petăs·us -ī m hat

petaur·um -ī n springboard

petess·ō or **petiss·ō -ĕre** vt to be eager for, pursue; **pugnam petessere** to be spoiling for a fight

petĭtĭ·ō -ōnis f attack, blow, thrust, aim; petition, request, application; candidacy, political campaign; claim, suit, suing; right to sue; **petitioni se dare** to become a candidate

petīt·or -ōris m applicant; political candidate; plaintiff

petitur·ĭō -īre vi to be eager for office

petīt·us -a -um pp of **peto**; n request, desire

petīt·us -ūs m (with genit) heading for

pet·ō -ĕre -īvī or **-iī -ītum** vt to make for, head for; to attack; to strive for, aim at; to demand, require, exact; to claim, sue for; to beg, desire, entreat; to look for, go in search of, search for; to run after, chase, court (girls); to fetch, bring, obtain, draw; to run for (office); to refer to, relate to

petorrĭt·um -ī n open four-wheeled carriage

petr·a -ae f rock, crag

petr·ō -ōnis m yokel

Petrōn·ĭus -ĭī or **-ī** m Petronius Arbiter (author and master of ceremonies at the court of Nero)

petŭl·ans -antis adj pert, impudent, smart-alecky, petulant, forward

petŭlanter adv pertly, impudently, petulantly

petulanti·a -ae *f* pertness, impudence, forwardness; carelessness

petulc·us -a -um *adj* butting, apt to butt

pex·us -a -um *pp* of **pecto**; *adj* combed; new, still having the nap on

Phaeāc·es -um *m pl* Phaeacians (*people described in the Odyssey as living on a utopian island*)

Phaeācĭ·us -a -um *adj* Phaeacian; *f* Phaeacia

Phaeāc·us -a -um *adj* Phaeacian

Phaedr·a -ae *f* daughter of Minos and Pasiphae and wife of Theseus

Phaedr·us -ī *m* pupil of Socrates; freedman of Augustus and famous writer of Latin fables

Phaest·um -ī *n* town in Crete

Phaëth·ōn -ontis *m* son of Helios and Clymene who was killed trying to drive his father's chariot

Phaëthontĕ·us -a -um *adj* of Phaethon

Phaëthontiăd·es -um *f pl* sisters of Phaethon

phalang·ae -ārum *f pl* wooden rollers

phalangīt·ae -ārum *m pl* soldiers belonging to a Macedonian phalanx

phal·anx -angis *f* phalanx, battalion (*compact body of heavy-armed men in battle array first developed by the Macedonians*)

phalārĭc·a or **falārĭc·a -ae** *f* firebrand, fiery missile (*shot by a catapult or thrown by hand*)

phalēr·ae -ārum *f pl* military medals; medallions (*worn by horses on forehead and chest*)

phalerāt·us -a -um *adj* wearing medals, decorated; ornamental

Phalērĭc·us -a -um *adj* of Phaleron

Phalēr·um -ī *n* Athenian harbor

pharetr·a -ae *f* quiver

pharetrāt·us -a -um *adj* wearing a quiver

pharmaceutrī·a -ae *f* witch, sorceress

pharmacopōl·a -ae *m* druggist; quack

Pharsālĭc·us -a -um *adj* of Pharsalus

Pharsālĭ·us -a -um *adj* Pharsalian; *f* district of Pharsalia

Pharsāl·os or **Pharsāl·us -ī** *f* town in Thessaly near which Caesar defeated Pompey (48 B.C.)

Phar·os or **Phar·us -ī** *m* or *f* island in the harbor at Alexandria famous for its lighthouse; lighthouse

phasēl·us -ī *m* or *f* kidney bean; pinnace (*light boat*); yacht

Phāsĭăc·us -a -um *adj* Colchian

Phāsĭān·a -ae *f* pheasant (*female*)

Phāsĭān·us -ī *m* pheasant

Phāsĭ·as -ădis *adj* Colchian

Phās·is -ĭdis or **-ĭdos** *m* river in Colchis

phasm·a -ătis *n* ghost

Pher·ae -ārum *f pl* city in Thessaly, the home of Admetus

Pherae·us -a -um *adj* of Pherae

phiăl·a -ae *f* saucer

Phīdĭ·ās -ae *m* famous Greek sculptor and friend of Pericles (*fl* 440 B.C.)

philēm·a -ătis *n* kiss

Philēm·ōn -ōnis *m* pious rustic who was changed into an oak tree while his wife Baucis was changed into a linden tree

Philipp·ī -ōrum *m pl* city in Macedonia where Octavian and Antony defeated Brutus and Cassius (42 B.C.)

Philippĭc·ae -ārum *f pl* series of vitriolic speeches directed at Antony by Cicero

Philipp·us -ī *m* name of several kings of Macedon (*esp. Philip II, son of Amyntas, and father of Alexander the Great, c.* 382-336 B.C.)

philitĭ·a or **phiditĭ·a -ōrum** *n pl* communal meals at Sparta

Phil·ō or **Phil·ōn -ōnis** *m* Academic philosopher and teacher of Cicero

Philoctēt·ēs -ae *m* Greek warrior and famous archer who was abandoned by the Greek army on the island of Lemnos

philologĭ·a -ae *f* love of study, study of literature

philolŏg·us -a -um *adj* learned, scholarly

Philomēl·a -ae *f* daughter of Pandion and sister of Procne, who was changed into a nightingale

philosophē *adv* philosophically

philosophĭ·a -ae *f* philosophy

philosŏph·or -ārī *vi* to pursue philosophy

philosŏph·us -a -um *adj* philosophical; *mf* philosopher

phitr·um -ī *n* love potion

philўr·a -ae *f* inner bark of the lime tree; linden tree

phīm·us -ī *m* dice box

Phīn·eus -ĕī or **-ĕos** *m* king of Salmydessus in Thrace, whom the Argonauts rescued from the torments which the Harpies visited upon him

Phlegĕth·ōn -ontis *m* river of fire in the lower world

Phlegethont·is -ĭdis *adj* of Phlegethon

Phlegў·ās -ae *m* king of the Lapiths and father of Ixion

Phlī·ūs -untis *f* city in N.E. Peloponnesus

phōc·a -ae or **phōc·ē -ēs** *f* seal

Phōcāĭc·us or **Phōcē·us** or **Phōcĭ·us -a -um** *adj* & *mf* Phocian

Phōc·is -ĭdis *f* a country of Greece W. of Boeotia

Phoeb·as -ădis *f* prophetess, priestess of Apollo

Phoeb·ē -ēs *f* moon goddess, the sister of Phoebus; night

Phoebigĕn·a -ae *m* son of Phoebus (*i.e., Aesculapius*)

Phoeb·us -ī *m* Apollo as sun god; sun

Phoenīc·ē -ēs *f* Phoenicia

Phoenīc·es -um *m pl* Phoenicians

phoenīcoptēr·us -ī *m* flamingo

Phoeniss·a -ae *f* Phoenician woman (*esp. Dido*)

phoen·ix -īcis *m* phoenix (*famous Arabian bird which was said to live 500 years and from whose ashes a young phoenix would be born*)

Phoen·ix -īcis *m* son of Amyntor and companion of Achilles

Phorc·is -īdos *f* female descendant of Phorcus; Medusa

Phorc·us -ī *m* son of Neptune and father of Medusa and the other Gorgons

Phorcȳn·is -idis or **-idos** *f* Medusa

Phraāt·ēs or **Phrahāt·ēs -ae** *m* king of Parthia

phrenēs·is -is *f* frenzy, delirium

phrenētic·us -a -um *adj* frenetic, frantic, delirious

Phrix·us -ī *m* son of Athamas and Nephele and brother of Helle, with whom he fled to Colchis mounted on the ram with the golden fleece

Phryg·es -um *m pl* Phrygians (*a people of Asia Minor*)

phrygĭ·ō -ōnis *m* embroiderer

Phrygĭ·us -a -um *adj & mf* Phrygian; Trojan; *f* Phrygia (*a country of Asia Minor*)

Phthi·a -ae *f* home of Achilles in Thessaly

Phthiōt·a or **Phthiōt·ēs -ae** *m* native of Phthia

phthis·is -is *f* consumption, tuberculosis

phy *interj* bah!

phylǎc·a -ae *f* jail

phylacist·a -ae *m* jailer; overanxious creditor

phylarch·us -ī *m* tribal chief

physĭc·a -ae or **physĭc·ē -ēs** *f* physics

physĭc·us -a -um *adj* natural, physical, belonging to natural philosophy or physics; *m* natural philosopher, physicist, scientist; *n pl* physics

physiognōm·ōn -ŏnis *m* physiognomist

physiologĭ·a -ae *f* natural philosophy, natural science

piābĭl·is -e *adj* expiable

piācŭlār·is -e *adj* expiatory, atoning; *n pl* expiatory sacrifices

piācŭl·um -ī *n* propitiatory sacrifice; victim; atonement, expiation; remedy; crime, sacrilege; punishment

piām·en -inis *n* atonement

pīc·a -ae *f* magpie

picāri·a -ae *f* place where pitch is made

picě·a -ae *f* pine tree

Pic·ens -entis *adj* Picene, of Picenum

Picēn·us -a -um *adj & m* Picene; *n* district of Central Italy on the Adriatic coast

picě·us -a -um *adj* made of pitch; pitch-black

pict·or -ōris *m* painter

Pict·or -ōris *m* Q. Fabius Pictor (*earliest Roman historian, who wrote a history of Rome in Greek, fl 225 B.C.*)

pictūr·a -ae *f* painting, art of painting; a painting, picture; embroidery

pictūrāt·us -a -um *adj* painted; embroidered

pict·us -a -um *pp of* **pingo**; *adj* decorated, colored; tattooed; ornate (*style*); false, unreal

pīc·us -ī *m* woodpecker; griffin (*fabulous bird*)

Pīc·us -ī *m* son of Saturn and grandfather of Latinus, who was changed by Circe into a woodpecker

piē *adv* dutifully, affectionately

Pierĭ·a -ae *f* district in Macedonia

Piēr·is -idis or **-idos** *f* daughter of Pieros; Muse; *f pl* the nine Muses

Pierĭ·us -a -um *adj* Pierian; poetic; musical; *f see* **Pieria**; *f pl* Muses

Piēr·os or **Piēr·us -ī** *m* father of the nine Muses

piět·ās -ātis *f* responsibility, sense of responsibility, sense of duty; devotion, piety; kindness, tenderness; loyalty, patriotism

pig·er -ra -rum *adj* reluctant, unwilling; apathetic, slow, lazy; numbing (*cold*); slow-moving, tedious, dull (*war, etc.*); backward, slow, dull (*person*)

pig·et -ēre -ŭit or **-itum est** *v impers* it irks, pains, annoys, makes regretful; (with *genit* of cause of feeling), e.g., **piget stultitiae meae** I am irked by my foolishness; (with *inf*), e.g., **illa me composuisse** piget I repent having written those verses

pigmentār·ius -iī or **-ī** *m* paint dealer

pigment·um -ī *n* pigment, paint, color; coloring, color (*of style*)

pignerāt·or -ōris *m* mortgagee

pignĕr·ō -āre *vt* to pledge, mortgage, pawn; (fig) to pledge

pignĕr·or -ārī -ātus sum *vt* to take as pledge, accept in good faith; to claim to

pign·us -ŏris or **-ŏris** *n* pledge, security, guarantee; hostage; mortgage; income from mortgages; wager, stake; (fig) pledge, assurance, proof; *n pl* children

pigrē *adv* slowly, sluggishly

pigritĭ·a -ae or **pigritĭ·ēs -ēī** *f* sluggishness, laziness

pigr·ō -āre or **pigr·or -ārī -ātus sum** *vi* to be slow, be sluggish, be lazy

pīl·a -ae *f* a mortar; pillar; pier

pĭl·a -ae *f* ball; ball game; ballot (*used by jury*); **mea pila est** the ball is mine, I've won; **pilā ludere** to play ball

pīlān·us -ī *m* soldier in the third rank in battle

pīlāt·us -a -um *adj* armed with javelin

pilent·um -ī *n* ladies' carriage

pilleāt·us -a -um *adj* wearing a felt skullcap (*as a symbol of free status*)

pilleŏl·us -ī *m* skullcap

pillĕ·um -ī *n* or **pille·us -ī** *m* felt cap or hat (*worn by Romans at festivals, esp. at the Saturnalia, and given to a slave when freed as a symbol of his freedom*); freedom, liberty

pilōs·us -a -um *adj* hairy

pīl·um -ī *n* javelin

pīl·us -ī *m* maniple or company of the triarii, company of veteran reserves; **primi pili centuriō** chief centurion of a legion (*centurion of the first century of the triarii*); **primus pilus** chief centurion of the triarii and therefore of the legion

pil·us -ī *m* hair; (fig) whit; **non pili facere** to care not a whit for

Pimpl·a -ae *f* town in Pieria sacred to the Muses

Pimplē·a -ae or **Pimplē·is -ĭdis** *f* Muse

Pindaric·us -a -um *adj* Pindaric

Pindăr·us -ī *m* Pindar (*famous lyric poet from Thebes in Boeotia*, 518-438 B.C.)

Pind·us -ī *m* mountain range separating Thessaly from Epirus

pīnēt·um -ī *n* pine forest

pīne·us -a -um *adj* pine, of pine

pingō pingĕre pinxī pictum *vt* to draw, paint; to embroider; to depict, represent, portray; to stain, color; to decorate; to color, embellish (*style*)

pingu·e -is *n* fat, grease

pinguescō -ĕre *vi* to get fat; to become fertile

pingu·is -e *adj* fat; oily, greasy; juicy; rich, fertile; thick, dense; stupid, dull; quiet, comfortable

pīnif·er -ĕra -ĕrum *adj* pine-producing, pine-covered

pīnig·er -ĕra -ĕrum *adj* pine-producing, pine-covered

pinn·a -ae *f* feather; wing; flight; fin; feathered arrow; pinnacle, battlement

pinnāt·us -a -um *adj* feathered, winged

pinnig·er -ĕra -ĕrum *adj* winged; having fins, finny

pinnip·ēs -ĕdis *adj* wing-footed

pinnirăp·us -ī *m* crest-snatcher (*gladiator who tried to get his opponent's helmet crest*)

pinnŭl·a -ae *f* little wing

pīnotēr·ēs -ae *m* hermit crab

pins·ō -ĕre -ī (or **-ŭī**) **-um** (or **-ĭtum**) *vt* to pound

pīn·us -ūs or **-ī** *f* pine tree, fir tree; pine forest; ship; torch; wreath of pine

pĭ·ō -āre *vt* to appease by sacrifice, propitiate; to honor with religious rites, worship; to purify with religious rites; to atone for, expiate; to avert

pip·er -ĕris *n* pepper

pīpĭl·ō -āre *vi* to chirp

pīpŭl·um -ī *n* or **pīpŭl·us -ī** *m* shrieking, yelling

Pīrae·eus or **Pīrae·us -ī** *m* or **Pīrae·a -ōrum** *n pl* principal harbor of Athens

pīrāt·a -ae *m* pirate

pīrātĭc·us -a -um *adj* pirate; *f* piracy; **pīrātĭcam facere** to practice piracy

Pīrēn·ē -ēs *f* fountain on the citadel of Corinth near which Bellerophon caught Pegasus

Pīrithŏ·us -ī *m* son of Ixion and king of the Lapiths

pir·um -ī *n* pear

pir·us -ī *f* pear tree

Pīs·a -ae *f* of **Pīs·ae -ārum** *f pl* Pisa (*city in Elis on the Alpheus River near which the Olympic games were held*)

Pīs·ae -ārum *f pl* Pisa (*ancient city of N. Etruria*)

Pīsae·us -a -um *adj* of Pisa; *f* Hippodamia

piscārĭ·us -a -um *adj* fish, of fishing or fish; **forum piscārium** fish market

piscāt·or -ōris *m* fisherman; fishmonger

piscātōrĭ·us -a -um *adj* fishing; fish

piscāt·us -ūs *m* fishing; fish; (fig) good haul

piscicŭl·us -ī *m* little fish

piscīn·a -ae *f* fish pond; swimming pool

piscinār·ius -ĭī or **-ī** *m* person fond of swimming pools or fish ponds

pisc·is -is *m* fish

Pisc·is -is *m* Piscis (*constellation*)

pisc·or -ārī -ātus sum *vi* to fish

piscōs·us -a -um *adj* full of fish

pisculent·us -a -um *adj* well stocked with fish

Pīsistratĭd·ae -ārum *m pl* sons of Pisistratus (*i.e., Hippias and Hipparchus*)

Pīsistrăt·us -ī *m* enlightened tyrant of Athens (560-527 B.C.)

pistill·um -ī *n* pestle

pist·or -ōris *m* miller; baker

pistrill·a -ae *f* little mill

pistrīn·um -ī *n* flour mill; bakery; drudgery

pistr·is -is or **pistr·ix -īcis** *f* sea monster (*of any kind*); whale, shark; swift ship

pithēc·ium -ĭī or **-ī** *n* little ape

Pitth·eus -ĕī or **-ĕos** *m* king of Troezen and father of Aethra, the mother of Theseus

pītuīt·a -ae *f* phlegm; rheum; head cold

pītuītōs·us -a -um *adj* full of phlegm, phlegmatic

pi·us -a -um *adj* conscientious; godfearing, godly, holy; fatherly, motherly, brotherly, sisterly; affectionate; patriotic; good; sacred, holy (*objects connected with religion*)

pix picis *f* pitch; *f pl* chunks of pitch

plācābĭl·is -e *adj* easily appeased; pacifying, appeasing

plācābĭlit·ās -ātis *f* readiness to forgive, conciliatory disposition

plăcăm·en -ĭnis n means of appeasing, peace offering

plăcăment·um -ī n means of appeasing, peace offering

plăcātē adv calmly, quietly

plăcātĭ·ō -ōnis f pacifying, propitiating

plăcăt·us -a -um adj calm, quiet; appeased, reconciled

plac·ens -entis adj pleasing

plăcent·a -ae f cake

plăc·ĕō -ēre -ŭī -ĭtum vi (with dat) to please, satisfy, give pleasure to, be acceptable to; sibi placere to be satisfied with oneself, pride oneself; v impers it seems right, seems proper; it is settled, is agreed; it is resolved, is decided; eis placitum est ut considerent they decided to consider; senatui placuit the senate decreed

plăcĭdē adv calmly, placidly, gently, quietly

plăcĭd·us -a -um adj calm, placid, gentle, quiet

plăcĭt·ō -āre vi to be very pleasing

plăcĭt·us -a -um adj pleasing, acceptable; agreed upon; n principle, belief, tenet; ultra placitum laudare to praise excessively

plāc·ō -āre vt to calm, quiet; to appease; to reconcile

plāg·a -ae f blow; wound; (fig) blow

plāg·a -ae f region, tract, zone; hunting net; mesh of a net; curtain; (fig) trap

plagiăr·ĭus -ĭī or -ī n plunderer; kidnapper; plagiarist

plāgĭg·er -ĕra -ĕrum adj covered with welts

plāgĭgerŭl·us -a -um adj covered with welts

plāgĭpătĭd·a -ae m whipping boy

plāgōs·us -a -um adj quick to use the rod

plăgŭl·a -ae f curtain

plăgūsĭ·a -ae f a fish

planctus pp of plango

planct·us -ūs m beating

plānē adv clearly, distinctly; legibly; completely, entirely, quite; certainly, to be sure

plangō plangĕre planxī planctum vt to strike, beat; to beat (breast, head as sigh of grief); to lament, bewail; vi to wail, lament; (fig) to wring the hands

plang·or -ōris m striking, beating; beating of the breast; wailing

plānĭlŏqu·os -a -om adj speaking clearly

plānĭp·ēs -ĕdis m ballet dancer

plānĭt·ās -ātis f distinctness

plānĭtĭ·ēs -ēī or plānĭtĭ·a -ae f flat surface, level ground, plain

plant·a -ae f sprout, shoot; young plant, slip; sole (of the foot)

plantār·ĭa -ĭum n pl slips; young trees; hair

plān·us -a -um adj flat, level, even; plain, clear; n level ground, plain

plăn·us -ī m tramp; imposter, cheat

plasm·a -ătis n phoney accent

Platae·ae -ārum f pl Plataea (town in Boeotia near which the Greeks defeated the Persians in 479 B.C.)

platălĕ·a -ae f waterfowl, spoonbill

plătăn·us -ī or -ūs f plane tree

plătĕ·a or plătē·a -ae f street

Plat·ō or Plat·ōn -ōnis m Plato (famous Greek philosopher, 429-348 B.C.)

Platōnĭc·us -a -um adj Platonic; m pl Platonists

plaudō plaudĕre plausī plausum vt to slap, clap, beat; vi to flap, beat, clap; (with dat) to applaud, approve of; alis plaudere to flap the wings; manibus plaudere to clap the hands

plausĭbĭl·is -e adj deserving applause

plaus·or -ōris m applauder

plaustr·um -ī n wagon, cart

Plaustr·um -ī n the Great Bear (constellation)

plausus pp of plaudo

plaus·us -ūs m clapping, flapping; clapping of the hands; applause

Plaut·us -ī m T. Maccius Plautus (famous Roman writer of comedies, born at Sarsina in Umbria, c. 254-184 B.C.)

plēbēcŭl·a -ae f rabble

plēbēĭ·us or plēbēj·us -a -um adj plebeian, of the common people; common, low, vulgar

plēbĭcŏl·a -ae m democrat; demagogue

plēbĭscīt·um -ī n decree of the commons

pleb·s -is or plēb·ēs -ēī or -ī f plebeians, common people; the masses, proletariat

plectĭl·is -e adj plaited

plectō plectĕre plexī or plexŭī plexum vt to plait, braid

plect·ō -ĕre vt to punish

Plēĭ·as -ădis f pl Pleiad; f pl Pleiades (seven daughters of Atlas and Pleione, who were placed among the stars)

Plēĭŏn·ē -ēs f daughter of Oceanus and Tethys, wife of Atlas, and mother of the Pleiades

plēnē adv fully, completely

plēn·us -a -um adj full; stout, plump; pregnant; filled, satisfied; full, packed; full, strong, loud (voice); full-length, unabridged, uncontracted; abundant, plentiful; advanced, mature (years); complete, finished

plērumque adv generally, mostly; often, frequently

plēr·usque -ăque -umque adj a very great part of, the greater part of, most; very many, a good many; n the greatest part

plex·us -a -um pp of plecto; adj plaited

plĭcātr·ix -īcis f woman who folds clothes, folder

plic·ō -āre -āvī or -ŭī -ātum or -ĭtum *vt* to fold, wind, coil up

Plīn·ius -iī or -ī *m* C. Plinius Secundus (*author of a work on natural history, who perished in the eruption of Vesuvius in 79 A.D.*); C. Plinius Caecilius (*his nephew, author of Letters and a Panegyric to Trajan, 62 A.D.-c. 114 A.D.*)

plōrābil·is -e *adj* deplorable

plōrāt·or -ōris *m* mourner

plōrāt·us -ūs *m* wailing, wail

plōr·ō -āre *vt* to cry over; *vi* to cry aloud, wail

plostell·um -ī *n* cart

ploxem·um -ī *n* wagon frame

pluit pluĕre pluit *vt* it is raining (*stones, blood, etc.*); *vi* it is raining; (*with abl*) it is raining (*stones, etc.*)

plūm·a -ae *f* down, soft feather; (collectively) feathers, down

plūmātil·e -is *n* dress embroidered with feathers

plūmāt·us -a -um *adj* covered with feathers

plumbē·us -a -um *adj* lead, of lead; leaden, oppressive (*weather*); dull, stupid

plumb·um -ī *n* lead; bullet; pipe; ruler (*for drawing lines*); plumbum album tin

plūmě·us -a -um *adj* downy, filled with down; like feathers

plūmip·ēs -ēdis *adj* with feathered feet

plūmōs·us -a -um *adj* downy, feathered

plūrimum *adv* very much, especially, commonly, generally, most

plūrim·us -a -um (*superl of multus*) *adj* many & most; very much; very many; very great, very intense; plurimam salutem dare to send warmest greetings; *n* a great deal; plurimi facere to think very highly of, think a great deal of; quam plurimum as much as possible

plūs *adv* more; multō plūs much more; paulō plūs a little more

plūs plūris (*comp of multus*) *adj* more; *n* more; too much; et, quod plus est, Rōmanī estis and what is more, you are Romans; plus animi more courage; plus nimiō much too much; plus plusque more and more; ūnō virō plus habēre to have one man too much; plūris esse (*genit* of value) to be of more value, of a higher price, worth more, be higher, be dearer; *n pl* more words; quid plūra? why should I say more?, in short

plūscul·us -a -um *adj* a little more, somewhat more; *n* a little more; plusculum negoti a little more business

plutě·us -ī *m* or plutě·um -ī *n* (mil) movable mantlet or shed used to protect soldiers in siege work; parapet; couch, dining couch; book shelf; book case; board, slab

Plūt·ō or Plūt·ōn -ōnis *m* king of the lower world, husband of Proserpina, and brother of Jupiter and Neptune

pluvi·a -ae *f* rain

pluviāl·is -e *adj* rain, of rain, rainy; fungi pluviales mushrooms brought out by the rain

pluvi·us -a -um *adj* rain, of rain, rainy; pluvia aqua rain water; pluvius arcus rainbow; *f* see pluvia

pōcill·um -ī *n* small drinking cup

pōcŭl·um -ī *n* drinking cup; drink, draught; poculum ducere or exhaurire to drain a cup

podāgr·a -ae *f* arthritis

podagrōs·us -a -um *adj* arthritic

pōd·ex -icis *m* anus, rectum

pod·ium -iī or -ī *n* balcony; box seat (*for the emperor*)

Poeantiăd·ēs -ae *m* Philoctetes

Poe·ās -antis *m* father of Philoctetes

poēm·a -ătis *n* poem

poēmat·ium -iī or -ī *n* short poem

poen·a -ae *f* compensation, recompense, retribution, satisfaction, penalty, fine, punishment; hardship, loss, pain; (in games) penalty; poenam or poenas dare, dependere, pendere, persolvere, reddere, solvere, suscipere, or sufferre to pay the penalty, make restitution, give satisfaction; poenam or poenas capere, persequi, petere, repetere, or reposcere to exact a penalty, demand satisfaction; poena mortis capital punishment, death penalty

poeniō see puniō

Poen·us -a -um *adj* & *m* Carthaginian

poēs·is -is *f* art of poetry; poetry, poems

poēt·a -ae *m* maker, contriver; poet

poētic·a -ae or poētic·ē -ēs *f* art of poetry; poetics

poēticē *adv* poetically

poētic·us -a -um *adj* poetic, poetical; *f* see poetica

poētr·ia -ae *f* poetess

poētr·is -idis or -idos *f* poetess

pol *interj* by Pollux!; Lord!

polent·a -ae *f* pearl barley

polentāri·us -a -um *adj* caused by eating barley

pol·iō -īre -īvī or -iī -ītum *vt* to polish, smooth; (fig) to polish, improve, perfect

polītē *adv* in a polished manner, with taste, smoothly, elegantly

polītic·us -a -um *adj* political

polīt·us -a -um *adj* polished, smooth; (fig) polished, smooth, smooth-spoken, smooth-mannered, refined, cultivated

poll·en -inis *n* or poll·is -inis *m* or *f* flour

poll·ens -entis *adj* strong, powerful, thriving, able

pollenti·a -ae *f* might, power

pŏll·ĕŏ -ēre vi to be strong, be powerful; to be capable, be able; (of medicines) to be powerful, be efficacious; to have influence; **in re publica plurimum pollere** to have tremendous influence in politics

poll·ex -ĭcis m thumb; big toe

pollic·ĕor -ērī -ĭtus sum vt to promise

pollicĭtātĭ·ŏ -ōnis f promise

pollicĭt·or -ārī -ātus sum vt to keep promising

pollicĭt·us -a -um pp of polliceor; n promise

pollinārĭ·us -a -um adj flour, for flour

pollinct·or -ōris m embalmer

pol·lingŏ -lingĕre -linxī -linctum vt to lay out, embalm

Pollĭ·ŏ -ōnis m C. Asinius Pollio (distinguished orator, poet, historian, patron of literature, and statesman, 76 B.C.-4 A.D.)

poll·is -ĭnis m or f flour

pol·lūcĕŏ -lūcēre -luxī -luctum vt to offer, offer up as sacrifice; to serve (meal); to entertain

pollūcĭbilĭter adv sumptuously, in grand style

pollŭctŭr·a -ae f sumptuous dinner

pollŭct·us -a -um pp of polluceo; n offering, sacrificial meal

pol·lŭŏ -luĕre -luī -lūtum vt to pollute, defile, soil, mess up; to defile, violate

Poll·ux or **Poll·ūcēs -ūcis** m son of Tyndareus and Leda, twin brother of Castor, and famous boxer

pol·us -ī m end of an axis, pole; North Pole; **polus australis** South Pole

Polyb·ĭus -ī or **-ī** m Greek historian and friend of Scipio Aemilianus (c. 203-120 B.C.)

Polydăm·ās -antis m son of Panthus and friend of Hector

Polydōr·us -ī m son of Priam and Hecuba, murdered by Polymestor the king of Thrace

Polyhymnĭ·a -ae f one of the nine Muses

Polymest·or -ōris m king of the Thracian Chersonese, husband of Ilione the daughter of Priam

Polynĭc·ēs -is m son of Oedipus and Jocasta and brother of Eteocles

Polyphēm·us -ī m son of Neptune and one of the Cyclops of Sicily

pŏlyp·us -ī m polyp (sea animal; tumor)

Polyxĕn·a -ae f daughter of Priam whom Pyrrhus, the son of Achilles, sacrificed at his father's tomb

pōmārĭ·us -a -um adj fruit, of fruit trees; m fruit vendor; n orchard

pōmerĭdĭān·us -a -um adj afternoon

pōmēr·ium or **pōmoer·ium -ĭī** or **-ī** n space kept free of buildings inside and outside a city wall

pōmĭf·er -ĕra -ĕrum adj fruit-bearing

pōmōs·us -a -um adj loaded with fruit

pomp·a -ae f solemn or religious procession; retinue; pomp, ostentation

Pompēĭ·us or **Pompēj·us -ī** m Pompey the Great (Roman general and statesman, 106-48 B.C.)

Pompējān·us -a -um adj Pompeian; m pl inhabitants of Pompeii; soldiers or followers of Pompey

Pompēj·ī -ōrum m pl city south of Naples, destroyed by the eruption of Vesuvius in 79 A.D.

Pompil·ĭus -ĭī or **-ī** m Numa Pompilius (second king of Rome and traditional founder of Roman state religion)

Pomptīn·us -a -um adj Pomptine; **Pomptinae paludes** Pomptine Marshes in Latium

pōm·um -ī n fruit; fruit tree

pōm·us -ī f fruit; fruit tree

pondĕr·ŏ -āre vt to weigh; to consider, ponder

ponderōs·us -a -um adj weighty, heavy; full of meaning

pondŏ adv in weight

pondŏ (indecl) n pound, pounds; **auri quinque pondo** five pounds of gold

pond·us -ĕris n weight; mass; burden; importance; stability of character; n pl balance, equilibrium

pōne adv behind, after, back; prep (with acc) behind

pōnŏ pōnĕre posŭī positum or **postum** vt to put, place, put down, set down, set, fix, deposit; to lay aside, lay down; to lay out, spend; to stake; to place, station, post; to set up, erect, build, found; to regard, consider; to cite, assert; to suppose, assume; to lay out for burial; to smooth, calm; to arrange, smooth (hair); vi to abate, calm down

pons pontis m bridge; gangway; drawbridge; deck

pontĭcŭl·us -ī m small bridge

pontĭf·ex -ĭcis m pontiff, pontifex, priest (one of a board of fifteen); **pontifex maximus** chief pontiff

pontĭfĭcāl·is -e adj pontifical

pontĭfĭcāt·us -ūs m pontificate

pontĭfĭc·us -a -um adj pontifical

pont·ŏ -ōnis m ferry

pont·us -ī m sea; sea water

Pont·us -ī m Euxine or Black Sea; region around the Black Sea; kingdom of Mithridates between Bithynia and Armenia, subsequently a Roman province

pop·a -ae m priest's assistant (attendant who slew the victim)

popăn·um -ī n sacrificial cake

popell·us -ī m rabble, mob

popīn·a -ae f restaurant; food sold at a restaurant

popīn·ŏ -ōnis m diner at a restaurant

popl·es -ĭtis m hollow of the knee;

knee; **duplicato poplite** on bended knee; **contento poplite** with a stiff knee

Pōplicŏla see **Publicola**

poppysm·a -ătis n clicking with the tongue (*as sign of approval*)

populābil·is -e *adj* destructible

populābund·us -a -um *adj* ravaging, laying waste

populār·ēs -ium m pl people's party, democrats

populār·ia -ium n pl general-admission seats

populār·is -e *adj* of the people, by the people, for the people, people's, popular; approved by the people, popular; favoring the people, democratic; demagogic; of the same country, native; common, coarse

populār·is -is m or f fellow countryman; party member; fellow member, associate; (*with genit*) partner or associate in

populārit·ās -ātis f fellow citizenship; popularity

populāriter *adv* like the people; like a demagogue; **populariter loqui** to use slang

populātī·ō -ōnis f ravaging, devastation

populāt·or -ōris m ravager, destroyer

populāt·us -ūs m devastation

pōpulē·us -a -um *adj* of poplars, poplar

pōpulif·er -ěra -ěrum *adj* filled with poplar trees

pōpuln·us -a -um *adj* of poplars, poplar

popŭl·ō -āre or **popŭl·or -ārī -ātus sum** vt to ravage, devastate, lay waste; (fig) to pillage, ruin, destroy, spoil

popŭl·us -ī m people (*as a political community*), nation; people, crowd, public; citizens (*as opposed to soldiers*), civilians; region, district

pōpŭl·us -ī f poplar tree

porc·a -ae f sow

porcella -ae f little sow

porcell·us -ī m little hog

porcīnār·ius -iī or **-ī** m pork seller

porcīn·us -a -um *adj* hog's, pig's; f pork

Porc·ius -iī or **-ī** m M. Porcius Cato the Censor (235-149 B.C.); M. Porcius Cato Uticensis (95-46 B.C.)

porcŭl·a or **porculēn·a -ae** f little sow

porcŭl·us -ī m little pig

porc·us -ī m pig, hog

porgō see **porrigo**

Porphyrĭ·ōn -ōnis m a Giant

porrect·a -ōrum n pl offering; **inter caesa et porrecta** (fig) at the eleventh hour

porrectĭ·ō -ōnis f extending, stretching out

porrect·us -a -um pp of **porrigo**; *adj* stretched out, extended, extensive, long; protracted (*delay*); laid out, dead; (fig) wide-spread

porric·ĭō -ěre vt to offer up, make an offering of

por·rigō or **porg·ō -rigěre -rexī -rectum** vt to reach out, stretch out, extend; to offer, present, hand; to lengthen (*a syllable*); **se porrigere** to extend

porrig·ō -ĭnis f dandruff

porrō *adv* forwards, farther on, on; far off, at a distance; long ago; in the future, hereafter; again, in turn; next, furthermore, moreover, on the other hand

porr·um -ī n leek; chive

Porsenn·a or **Porsēn·a** or **Porsinn·a -ae** m king of Clusium in Etruria who sided with Tarquin in a war against Rome

port·a -ae f city gate; gate; entrance; outlet; camp gate (*of which there were always four*)

portātĭ·ō -ōnis f carrying, conveyance

por·tendō -tenděre -tendī -tentum vt to indicate, foretell, portend, predict

portentific·us -a -um *adj* monstrous, abnormal

portentōs·us -a -um *adj* monstrous, abnormal, unnatural, portentous

portent·um -ī n portent, omen, sign; monstrosity, monster; fantasy, farfetched fiction; (as term of contempt) monster, demon

portentus pp of **portendo**

porthm·eus -ěī or **-ěos** m ferryman (*i.e., Charon, who piloted the ferry across the Styx*)

porticŭl·a -ae f small portico

portic·us -ūs f colonnade, portico; (mil) gallery (*formed by placing vineae end to end*); Stoicism

portĭ·ō -ōnis f portion, share; ratio, portion; instalment, payment; **pro portione** proportionally, relatively

portiscŭl·us -ī m gavel

portĭt·or -ōris m customs officer; ferryman, boatman

port·ō -āre vt to carry; to bring

portōr·ĭum -ĭī or **-ī** n port duty, customs duty; tax (*on peddlers*)

portŭl·a -ae f small gate

Portūn·us -ī m tutelary deity of harbors

portuōs·us -a -um *adj* having good harbors

port·us -ūs m port, harbor; haven, refuge; mouth of a river

posc·a -ae f sour drink

poscō poscěre poposcī vt to ask, request, beg, demand; (of things) to require, demand, need, call for, make necessary; (with ab + abl) to ask for (*something*) from, demand (*something*) of; (with double acc) to demand (*something*) of, ask (*someone*) for

Posīdōn·ius -iī or **-ī** m Stoic philosopher at Rhodes, teacher of Cicero

positĭ·ō -ōnis f putting, placing, setting; position, posture; situation

posĭt·or -ōris m builder

posĭtūr·a -ae f posture; formation

posĭt·us -a -um pp of pono; adj situated, located

posĭt·us -ūs m position; arrangement

possessī·ō -ōnis f possession; getting possession, occupation; possession, estate

possessiuncŭl·a -ae f small estate

possess·or -ōris m possessor, occupant; (law) defendant

possibĭl·is -e adj possible

pos·sĭdĕō -sĭdēre -sēdī -sessum vt to possess, occupy; to have, own; to dwell in, live in; (fig) to take hold of

pos·sīdo -sīdĕre -sēdī -sessum vt to take possession of, occupy, seize

possum posse potŭī vi to be able; multum (plus, plurimum) posse to have much (more, very great) influence; non possum quin exclamem I can't help exclaiming; quantum or ut fieri potest as far as is possible

post adv (of place) behind, back, backwards; (of time) later, afterwards; (of order) next; aliquanto post somewhat later; multis post annis many years later; prep (with acc) (of place) behind; (of time) after, since

postĕā adv afterwards, after this, after that, hereafter, thereafter

posteāquam conj after

posterī·or -us adj later, next, following; latter, posterior; inferior, worse; hind

posterĭt·ās -ātis f the future, afterages, posterity, later generations; offspring (of animals); in posteritatem in the future

posterĭus adv later, at a later date

poster·us -a -um adj following, ensuing, next, subsequent, future; m pl future generations, posterity, descendants; n future time; next day; consequence; in posterum till the next day; for the future

post·fĕrō -ferre vt to put after; to esteem less; to sacrifice

postgenĭt·us -a -um adj born later; m pl later generations

posthabĕ·ēō -ēre -ŭī -ĭtum vt to consider of secondary importance; to slight, neglect; (with dat) to think (something) less important than

posthāc adv hereafter, in the future

posthinc or post hinc adv from here, from this place, next

posthōc or post hōc adv after this, afterwards

postĭbĭ adv afterwards, then

postĭcŭl·um -ī n small building in the rear

postĭc·us -a -um adj hind, back, rear; n back door

postĭdĕā adv afterwards, after that

postĭlēn·a -ae f crupper; buttocks

postillā adv afterwards

post·is -is m door post; door; m pl double doors

postlīmĭn·ĭum -ĭī or -ī n right to return home and resume one's former rank and privileges, right of recovery; postlīminĭō by the right of recovery

postmerīdĭān·us -a -um adj afternoon

postmŏdō or postmŏdum adv after a bit, a little later, afterwards

postpart·or -ōris m successor, heir

post·pōnō -pōnĕre -posŭī -posĭtum or -postum vt to consider of secondary importance; to neglect, disregard; (with dat) to consider (something) of less importance than, set (something) aside in favor of

postprincipĭ·a -ōrum n pl sequel

postpŭt·ō -āre vt to consider of secondary importance; (with prae + abl) to consider (something) less important than

postquam conj after, when

postrēmō adv at last, finally; primo ... deinde ... postremo first ... then ... finally

postrēmum adv for the last time, last of all

postrēm·us -a -um (superl of posterus) adj last, last in line, rear; lowest, worst

postrīdĭē adv on the day after, on the following day; postridie mane the next morning; prep (with genit), e.g., postridie ejus diei on the day after that; (with acc), e.g., postridie ludos on the day after the games

postrīdŭō adv on the day after

postscaen·ĭum -ĭī or -ī n backstage

post·scrībō -scrībĕre -scrīpsī scrīptum vt (with dat) to add (e.g., a name) to; Tiberi nomen suo postscribere to add the name of Tiberius to his own name

postŭlāt·a -ōrum n pl demands, claims, requests

postŭlātĭ·ō -ōnis f demand, request, desire; complaint; (law) application for permission to present a claim

postŭlāt·us -ūs m claim, suit

postŭl·ō -āre vt to demand, claim; to arraign, prosecute; to apply for (a writ from the praetor to prosecute)

postŭm·us -a -um adj last, latest-born

postus pp of pono

pōtātĭ·ō -ōnis f drinking, drinking party

pōtāt·or -ōris m drinker

pot·ens -entis adj capable; mighty, powerful, strong; efficacious, potent; fit, capable, equal; influential; (with genit) a capable of, equal to, fit for; b having power over; c presiding over; d having obtained (one's wish); e having carried out (an order)

potentāt·us -ūs *m* political power, rule, dominion

potenter *adv* powerfully, mightily, effectually, vigorously; according to one's ability

potentï·a -ae *f* force, power; political power (*esp. unconstitutional power*)

potēr·ium -iī or **-ī** *n* goblet

potest·ās -ātis *f* power, ability, capacity; efficacy, force; public authority, rule, power, sway, dominion, sovereignty, empire, rule; magisterial power, magistracy, office; possibility, opportunity, permission; person in office, magistrate, ruler; property, quality

potin or **potin'** = **potisne** can you?, are you able?

pōtï·ō -ōnis *f* drinking; drink, draught; magic potion

pot·ior -īrī -ītus sum *vt* to acquire, get possession of; *vi* (with *genit* or *abl*) to acquire, get possession of, become master of, get hold of, get

pot·ior -us (*comp of* **potis**) *adj* better, preferable, superior; more important

potis or **pote** (indecl) *adj* able, capable; possible

potissimum *adv* chiefly, especially, eminently

potissim·us -a -um *adj* chief, principal, most important

potius *adv* rather, more, by preference; **potius quam** more than, rather than

pōt·ō -āre *vt* to drink; to absorb

pōt·or -ōris *m* drinker

pōtr·ix -īcis *f* drinker (*female*)

pōtulent·us -a -um *adj* drinkable; *n pl* drinks

pōt·us -a -um *adj* drunk

pōt·us -ūs *m* drink

prae *adv* before, in front; in preference; *prep* (with *abl*) before, in front of; compared with, in comparison with; in view of; because of; by reason of, on account of, through; **prae manu** at hand; **prae se** publicly, openly, plainly; **prae se ferre** to display, manifest, exhibit, profess

praeacū·ō -ēre *vt* to sharpen to a point

praeacūt·us -a -um *adj* pointed

praealt·us -a -um *adj* very high; very deep

praeb·ĕō -ēre -uī -ītum *vt* to hold out, offer, present; to supply, give; to exhibit, represent, show; to give up, yield, surrender; to cause, occasion; to permit, allow; **se praebere** to show oneself, behave

praebib·ō -ēre -ī *vt* (with *dat*) to drink (*e.g., a toast*) to

praebit·or -ōris *m* supplier

praecalid·us -a -um *adj* very warm, hot

praecantr·ix -īcis *f* witch, enchantress

praecān·us -a -um *adj* prematurely grey

prae·cavĕō -cavēre -cāvī -cautum *vt* to guard against, try to avoid; *vi* to take precautions, be on one's guard; (with *dat*) to look out for, look after; (with *abl*) to guard against, be on one's guard against

prae·cēdō -cēdĕre -cessī -cessum *vt* to precede, go out before, lead; to surpass, excel; *vi* to excel, be superior; (with *dat*) to excel, be superior to

praecell·ens -entis *adj* superior, excellent, preeminent

praecell·ō -ĕre *vt* to surpass, outdo; *vi* to distinguish oneself, excel; (with *dat*) to rule over

praecels·us -a -um *adj* towering

praecenti·ō -ōnis *f* musical prelude (*before a sacrifice*)

praecent·ō -āre *vi* (with *dat*) to sing to

praecentus *pp of* **praecino**

praec·eps -ipitis *adj* headfirst; downhill, steep, precipitous; sinking (*sun*); swift, rushing, violent; hasty, rash, inconsiderate; dangerous; *n* edge of a cliff, cliff, precipice; danger, critical situation

praeceps *adv* headfirst

praeceptï·ō -ōnis *f* preconception; precept, rule; priority

praecept·or -ōris *m* or **praeceptr·ix -īcis** *f* teacher, preceptor

praecept·um -ī *n* rule, maxim; order, command, direction

prae·cerpō -cerpĕre -cerpsī -cerptum *vt* to pick or gather before time; (with *dat*) (fig) to snatch away from

prae·cīdō -cīdĕre -cīdī -cīsum *vt* to lop off, cut short; to cut, cut through; to damage, mutilate; to break off, finish abruptly, end suddenly (*a speech, etc.*); to end, destroy (*hopes, etc.*); to refuse, decline

prae·cingō -cingĕre -cinxī -cinctum *vt* to gird; to surround, ring; to dress; **ense cingi** to wear a sword; **male cinctus** improperly dressed; **recte cinctus** properly dressed

prae·cinō -cinĕre -cinuī -centum *vt* to predict; (with *dat*) to predict (*something*) to; *vi* to make predictions; (with *dat*) to sing or play before or at (*e.g., dinner, sacrifice*)

prae·cipïō -cipĕre -cēpī -ceptum *vt* to take or receive in advance; to grasp beforehand, anticipate; to teach, instruct, direct, warn; to prescribe; **animo praecipere** or **cogitatione praecipere** to imagine beforehand, reckon on, anticipate, expect; **oculis praecipere** to see beforehand, get a preview of; **opinione praecipere** to suspect in advance; **pecuniam mutuam praecipere** to get an advance loan

praecipitanter *adv* at a high speed

praecipit·ō -āre *vt* to throw down

head first; to hasten, hurry, precipitate; **se praecipitare** to throw oneself down, throw oneself down headfirst, jump down, dive; to sink; *vi* to rush headfirst, rush at top speed, fall thoughtlessly; to fall, sink; to be ruined

praecipŭē *adv* especially, chiefly

praecipŭ·us -a -um *adj* special, peculiar, particular; chief, principal; distinguished, excellent, extraordinary; *n* excellence, superiority; *n pl* outstanding or important elements; **praecipua rerum** highlights

praecisē *adv* briefly, concisely; absolutely

praecis·us -a -um *pp* of **praecido**; *adj* abrupt, precipitous; rugged, rough; brief, abrupt (*speech*)

praeclārē *adv* very clearly; excellently; (to express agreement) very good, splendid

praeclār·us -a -um *adj* very clear; very nice; splendid, noble, distinguished, excellent; famous, distinguished; notorious

prae·clūdō -clūdĕre -clūsī -clūsum *vt* to shut, shut off, obstruct; to hinder, stop, impede; **portas consuli praecludere** to shut the gates on the consul, shut the gates in the consul's face; **vocem praecludere alicui** to shut someone up, to hush someone up

praec·ō -ōnis *m* crier, herald; auctioneer; (fig) pangyrist

precōgĭt·ō -āre *vt* to premeditate

praecognĭt·us -a -um *adj* known beforehand, foreseen

prae·cōlō -colĕre — -cultum *vt* to cultivate prematurely; (fig) to embrace prematurely

praecomposĭt·us -a -um *adj* arranged beforehand; studied, self-conscious

praecōnĭ·us -a -um *adj* of a public crier, of an auctioneer; *n* crier's office; proclamation, announcement; praising, praise

praecon·sūmō -sūmĕre -sumpsī -sumptum *vt* to spend or use up beforehand

praecontrect·ō -āre *vt* to consider in advance

praecordĭ·a -ōrum *n pl* diaphragm, midriff; insides, stomach; breast, heart

praecor·rumpō -rumpĕre -rūpī -ruptum *vt* to bribe in advance

praec·ox -ōcis *adj* premature, hasty, rash

praecurrent·ĭa -ĭum *n pl* antecedents

prae·currō -currĕre -cucurrī or **-currī -cursum** *vt* to precede, anticipate; to outdo, surpass; *vi* to run out ahead, take the lead; (with **ante** + *acc*) to run out ahead of; (with *dat*) to outdo

praecursĭ·ō -ōnis *f* previous occurrence; (mil) skirmish; (rhet) warm-up (*of the audience*)

praecurs·or -ōris *m* forerunner; spy; (mil) scout; advance guard

praecursōrĭ·us -a -um *adj* sent in advance

prae·cutĭō -cutĕre -cussī -cussum *vt* to wave, brandish in front

praed·a -ae *f* booty, spoils, plunder; prey; **praedae esse** (with *dat*) to fall prey to

praedābund·us -a -um *adj* pillaging, plundering

praedamn·ō -āre *vt* to condemn beforehand; **spem praedamnare** to give up hope too soon

praedatĭ·ō -ōnis *f* pillaging, plunder

praedāt·or -ōris *m* marauder, looter, vandal; hunter; greedy man

praedātōrĭ·us -a -um *adj* marauding, looting; graspy, greedy

praedēlass·ō -āre *vt* to tire out, weaken beforehand

praedestin·ō -āre *vt* to predetermine

praediāt·or -ōris *m* real-estate agent

praediātōrĭ·us -a -um *adj* real-estate; **jus praediatorium** mortgage law

praedicābĭl·is -e *adj* praiseworthy, laudable

praedicātĭ·ō -ōnis *f* announcement, publication; praising

praedicāt·or -ōris *m* appreciator; eulogist

praedic·ō -āre *vt* to announce, proclaim; to report; to assert; to praise

prae·dīcō -dīcĕre -dīxī -dictum *vt* to mention beforehand or earlier; to prearrange; to predict; to order, command beforehand

praedictĭ·ō -ōnis *f* prediction

praedict·um -ī *n* prediction, prophecy; command, order; **velut ex praedicto** as if by prearrangement

praediŏl·um -ī *n* small estate, small farm

praedisc·ō -ĕre *vt* to learn beforehand, find out in advance

praedisposĭt·us -a -um *adj* previously arranged

praedĭt·us -a -um *adj* endowed, gifted, provided, furnished; (with *abl*) endowed with, provided with, furnished with

praed·ĭum -ĭī or **-ī** *n* estate, farm; **praedia urbana** city lots

praedĭv·es -ĭtis *adj* very rich

praedīvīn·ō -āre *vt* to know in advance, have a presentiment of

praed·ō -ōnis *m* marauder, looter, robber, pirate

praedoct·us -a -um *adj* instructed beforehand

praed·or -ārī -ātus sum *vt* to raid, plunder, loot, rob; (fig) to rob, ravish; **amores alicujus praedari** to steal away someone's sweetheart; *vi* to plunder, loot, make a raid; (with **ex** + *abl*) to prey on, profit by, take advantage of, e.g., **ex al-**

terius inscientiā praedari to prey on someone else's ignorance

prae-dūcō -dūcēre -duxī -ductum vt to run or construct (*trench, wall*) out in front (*for defensive purposes*)

praedulc·is -e adj very sweet; (fig) very satisfying (*honor, reward*)

praedūr·us -a -um adj very tough (*skin*); tough, brawny

praeēmin·ēō -ēre vt to surpass, excel; vi to project forward, stick out

prae·eō -īre -īvī or **-iī -itum** vt to lead, precede; to read out, dictate, lead (*prayers*); vi to go out ahead, take the lead; (with *dat*) to walk in front of

praefāti·ō -ōnis f preface, introduction; formula

praefātus pp of **praefor**

praefectūr·a -ae f supervision, superintendence; prefectship, office of prefect, superintendency; government of a district; prefecture (*Italian city governed by a Roman prefect*); territory of a prefecture, district

praofect·us -ī m prefect, supervisor, superintendent; commander; governor; (with *genit* or *dat*) supervisor of, commander of, prefect or governor of

prae·ferō -ferre -tūlī -lātum vt to hold out, carry in front; to prefer; to anticipate; to display, reveal, betray; to offer, present; to offer as a model; **praeferri** to ride past, ride by, march past, outflank; **praeferri** or **se praeferri** (with *dat*) to surpass

praefer·ox -ōcis adj very belligerent, very defiant

praeferrāt·us -a -um adj iron-tipped; (coll) chained (*slave*)

praefervid·us -a -um adj boiling; (fig) boiling; **ira praefervida** boiling anger

praefestin·ō -āre vt to hurry past; (with *inf*) to be in a hurry to

praefic·a -ae f hired mourner (*female*)

prae·ficiō -ficere -fēcī -fectum vt to put (*someone*) in charge; (with double *acc*) to appoint (*someone*) as; (with *dat*) to put (*someone*) in charge of, set (*someone*) over, appoint (*someone*) to command

praefīd·ens -entis adj too trustful, overconfident; (with *dat*) too trustful of; **homines sibi praefidentes** overconfident men

prae·figō -figēre -fixī -fixum vt to fix, fasten, set up in front, fasten on the end; to tip, point; to transfix; **capistris praefigere** to muzzle; **cuspidibus praefixus** pointed; **ferro praefixus** iron-tipped

praefin·iō -īre -īvī or **-iī -itum** vt to determine in advance; to prescribe, appoint; to limit

praefinītō adv in the prescribed manner

praefiscīnē or **praefiscīnī** adv meaning no offense

praefiōr·ō -āre vt to deflower, deprive of its bloom; (fig) to tarnish, spoil

praefiu·ō -ēre vt & vi to flow by

praefōc·ō -āre vt to choke, choke up, strangle

prae·fodiō -fodere -fōdī vt to bury beforehand; to dig in front of; **portas praefodire** to dig trenches in front of the gates

prae·for -fārī -fātus sum vt to say beforehand, utter in advance, preface; to address in prayer beforehand; to foretell; to invoke; vi to pray beforehand; (with *dat*) to pray before

praefractē adv obstinately

praefract·us -a -um pp of **praefringo**; resolute, determined; abrupt

praefrigid·us -a -um adj very cold, freezing

prae·fringō -fringēre -frēgī -fractum vt to break off at the tip or end, break to pieces, smash

prae·fulciō -fulcīre -fulsī -fultum vt to prop up, support in front; (with *dat*) to use (*someone*) as a prop or support for; **illud praefulci ut** make sure that

prae·fulgeō -fulgēre -fulsī vi to shine forth, glitter, sparkle

praegelid·us -a -um adj very cold

praegest·iō -īre vi to be very eager

praegn·ans -antis or **praegn·ās -ātis** adj pregnant; (with *abl*) full of, swollen with

praegracil·is -e adj very lean or slender

praegrand·is -e adj huge, very great; very powerful

praegrav·is -e adj very heavy; very fat; oppressive; very tiresome

praegrav·ō -āre vt to weigh down; to outweigh; (fig) to burden

prae·gredior -gredī -gressus sum vt to go in advance of, go ahead of; to go by, go past; vi to walk out in front; (with *dat*) to precede, lead

praegressi·ō -ōnis f procession; (fig) precedence

praegustāt·or -ōris m taster, sampler

praegust·ō -āre vt to taste beforehand, get a sample of

praehib·eō -ēre vt to offer, furnish, supply; to utter, speak (*words*); **praehibere operam** (with *dat*) to offer to help

praejac·eō -ēre vt to lie before, be located in front of; vi (with *dat*) to lie before

praejūdicāt·us -a -um adj decided beforehand; prejudiced; **n** prejudged matter; prejudice; **id pro praejudicato ferre** to take it as a foregone conclusion

praejūdic·ium -iī or **-ī** n preliminary hearing; prejudgment; precedent, example

praejūdic·ō -āre vt to decide beforehand, prejudge

prae·jŭvō -jŭvāre -jūvī vt to help in advance

prae·lābor -lābī -lapsus sum vt & vi to glide along, glide by, float by

praelamb·ō -ĕre vt to pretaste

praelarg·us -a -um adj very ample

praelātus pp of **praefero**

prae·lēgō -legĕre -lēgī -lectum vt to sail past

praelĭg·ō -āre vt to tie up; (with dat) to tie (something) to

praelong·us -a -um adj very long

prae·lŏquor -lŏquī -locūtus sum vt to make (a speech) before someone else; to present (a case) first; to say by way of preface; vi to speak first

prae·lūcĕō -lūcēre -luxī vi (with dat) a to throw light on; b to outshine, outdo, surpass

praelūsĭ·ō -ōnis f prelude

praelustr·is -e adj magnificent

praemandāt·a -ōrum n pl warrant for arrest

praemand·ō -āre vt to order in advance

praemātūrē adv too soon, prematurely

praemātūr·us -a -um adj premature

praemedicāt·us -a -um adj protected by charms

praemeditātĭ·ō -ōnis f premeditation, prior consideration

praemedit·or -ārī -ātus sum vt to think over beforehand; to practice, practice on (a musical instrument)

praemerc·or -ārī -ātus sum vt to buy in advance

praemetŭ·ens -entis adj apprehensive

praemetuenter adv anxiously

praemetŭ·ō -ĕre vt to fear beforehand; vi (with dat) to be apprehensive about

prae·mittō -mittĕre -mīsī -missum vt to send out ahead, send in advance; vi to send word

praem·ĭum -ī or **-ĭ** n prize, reward, recompense; exploit (worthy of reward); gift, bribe

praemolestĭ·a -ae f apprehension, presentiment of trouble

praemōl·ĭor -īrī vt to prepare beforehand

praemon·ĕō -ēre -ŭī -ĭtum vt to forewarn; to warn of; to foreshadow, presage, predict

praemonĭt·us -ūs m forewarning, premonition

praemonstrāt·or -ōris m director, guide

praemonstr·ō -āre vt to point out the way to, guide, direct; to predict

prae·mordĕō -mordēre -mordī or **morsī -morsum** vt to bite the tip off of; (fig) to crib, pilfer

prae·morior -mŏrī -mortŭus sum vi to die too soon, die prematurely

praemūn·ĭō -īre -īvī -ītum vt to fortify, protect, secure

praemūnītĭ·ō -ōnis f (rhet) preparation, conditioning (of the minds of the hearers)

praenarr·ō -āre vt to relate beforehand

praenăt·ō -āre vt to float past, flow by

Praenest·e -is n or f ancient town in Latium (modern Palestrina)

Praenestīn·us -a -um adj & m Praenestine

praenĭt·ĕō -ēre -ŭī vi (with dat) a to outshine; b to appear more attractive to

praenōm·en -ĭnis n first name

praenosc·ō -ĕre vt to find out beforehand, foreknow

praenōtĭ·ō -ōnis f innate idea, preconception

praenūbĭl·us -a -um adj heavily clouded; dark, gloomy

praenuntĭ·a -ae f harbinger, foreteller, omen

praenuntĭ·ō -āre vt to foretell

praenuntĭ·us -a -um adj foreboding; m forecaster, harbinger, omen

praeoccupātĭ·ō -ōnis f seizing beforehand, advance occupation

praeoccŭp·ō -āre vt to occupy before another; to preoccupy; to anticipate, prevent

praeŏl·it -ĕre v impers there is a smell is emitted, there is a strong smell; **praeolit mihi quod tu velis** I scent your wishes before you express them

praeopt·ō -āre vt to prefer

praepand·ō -ĕre vt to spread, extend

praeparātĭ·ō -ōnis f preparation

praeparāt·us -a -um adj prepared, supplied, furnished, ready; n stores; **ex ante preparato** from the stores; (fig) by previous arrangement

praepăr·ō -āre vt to get ready, prepare, prepare for; to gather together

praepedīment·um -ī n impediment, hindrance

praeped·ĭō -īre -īvī or **-ĭī -ītum** vt to shackle, chain; to hinder, obstruct, hamper; to embarrass

praepend·ĕō -ēre vi to hang down in front

praep·es -ĕtis adj nimble, fast; winged; of good omen, favorable; m or f bird of good omen; bird, large bird

praepilāt·us -a -um adj tipped with a ball; **missile prapilatum** blunted missile

praepingu·is -e adj very fat; very fertile

praepoll·ĕō -ēre vi to be powerful; to be superior; (with dat) to surpass in power

praepondĕr·ō -āre vt to outweigh; to regard as superior

prae·pōnō -pōnĕre -posŭī -posi-

tum vt (with dat) a to place, set, put (something) in front of or before; b to entrust (someone) with, put (someone) in command of, in charge of; c to prefer (someone or something) to

praeport·ō -āre vt to carry before oneself

praepositi·ō -ōnis f preference; prefixing

praeposit·us -a -um pp of **praepōnō**; adj preferred, preferable; m prefect, commander; n that which is desirable, a desirable good

prae·possum -posse -potuī vi to get the upper hand, have the better of it

praepostĕrē adv in reversed order, out of order

praepostĕr·us -a -um adj inverted, in reverse order; absurd, preposterous

praepot·ens -entis adj very powerful; (with genit) in full control of, fully controlling

praeproperanter or **praepropĕrē** adv very quickly

praepropĕr·us -a -um adj very quick; overhasty, sudden

praeput·ium -iī or **-ī** n foreskin

praequam conj in comparison to; nihil hoc est, praequam alios sumptus facit this is nothing in comparison to the other expenses that he runs up

praequest·us -a -um adj complaining beforehand; multa praequestus having first raised many complaints

praeradi·ō -āre vt to outshine

praerapid·us -a -um adj very swift

praereptus pp of **praeripio**

praerig·escō -escĕre -uī vi to become very stiff

prae·ripiō -ripĕre -ripuī -reptum vt to snatch away, carry off; to anticipate, forestall; to count on too soon, presume upon; (with dat) to snatch from, steal from

prae·rōdō -rōdĕre -rōsī -rōsum vt to bite the ends of, nibble at; digitos praerodere to bite the fingernails

praerogātīv·us -a -um adj asked before others; voting first, privileged; f first tribe or century to vote; vote of the first tribe or century; previous election; sure sign, omen

praerōsus pp of **praerodo**

prae·rumpō -rumpĕre -rūpī -ruptum vt to break off, tear away (something) in front

praerupt·us -a -um adj broken off, broken up; broken up, rough (terrain); steep; hasty, impetuous

praes praedis m bondsman, surety; collateral

praesaep- = **praesep-**

praesāg·iō -īre -īvī or **praesāg·ior -īrī** vt to have forebodings of, feel beforehand; to cause

praesāgītǐ·ō -ōnis f presentiment, strange feeling, foreboding, prophetic power

praesāg·ium -iī or **-ī** n presentiment, presage, prediction

praesāg·us -a -um adj divining, prophetic

praesc·iō -īre -īvī vt to know beforehand

praesciscō·ō -ĕre vt to find out or learn beforehand

praesci·us -a -um adj prescient; (with genit) foreseeing; praescius venturi foreseeing the future

prae·scrībō -scrībĕre -scrīpsī -scriptum vt to prefix in writing; to describe beforehand; to determine in advance, prescribe, ordain; to dictate; to outline, map out; to put forward as an excuse

praescripti·ō -ōnis f heading, title; preface; pretext; rule, law; limit, restriction

praescript·um -ī n regulation, rule, proviso

praesĕc·ō -āre -uī -tum vt to cut off, cut out, cut short

praesegmīn·a -um n pl clippings

praes·ens -entis adj present, in person, at hand; existing, contemporary; prompt, immediate, impending; efficacious, powerful, effective; influential; resolute; propitious; sermo praesens a face-to-face talk; in praesens time; ad praesens or in praesens for the present

praesensi·ō -ōnis f presentiment; preconception

praesensus pp of **praesentio**

praesentāri·us -a -um adj ready, at hand

praesenti·a -ae f presence; efficacy, effect; animi praesentia presence of mind; in praesentia at the present time, just now, for the present

praesent·ia -ium n pl present circumstances, present state of affairs

prae·sentiō -sentīre -sensī -sensum vt to feel beforehand, to realize in advance, have strange feelings about, divine

praesēp·e or **praesaep·e -is** n or **praesēp·is** or **praesēp·es -is** f stall, stable; crib, manger; room, lodgings; tavern; hovel; beehive

praesēp·iō or **praesaep·iō -īre -sī -tum** vt to fence in, barricade

praesertim adv especially, particularly, principally; praesertim cum especially because

praeserv·iō -īre vi (with dat) to serve as a slave to

praes·es -idis m guard, guardian, protector, defender; president, superintendent; captain, pilot; f guardian, protectress

praesid·ens -entis m president, ruler

prae·sideō -sidēre -sēdī vt to guard, protect, defend; to command, be in command of; vi to be in charge, be in command; (with *dat*) **a** to watch over, guard, protect; **b** to preside over, direct, manage, command

praesidiāri·us -a -um *adj* on garrison duty

praesid·ium -iī or **-ī** *n* protection, defense; help, assistance; guard, garrison; convoy, escort; garrison post, defensive position

praesignific·ō -āre *vt* to indicate in advance, foretoken

praesign·is -e *adj* outstanding

praesŏn·ō -āre -uī *vi* to sound beforehand

praesparg·ō -ĕre *vt* to strew, scatter

praestābil·is -e *adj* excellent, outstanding

praest·ans -antis *adj* outstanding, eminent, exceptional

praestanti·a -ae *f* excellence, superiority, preeminence

praestern·ō -ĕre *vt* to strew

praest·es -itis *adj* guardian, protecting, presiding

praestigi·ae -ārum *f pl* sleight of hand, juggling, tricks, illusion, deception

praestigiāt·or -ōris *m* or **praestigiātr·ix -īcis** *f* juggler, magician; imposter

praestīn·ō -āre *vt* to buy, shop for

prae·stituō -stituĕre -stituī -stitūtum *vt* to fix or set up beforehand, prescribe

praestitus *pp* of **praesto**

praestō *adv* at hand, ready, present; **praesto esse** (with *dat*) **a** to be on hand for, attend, serve, be helpful to, aid; **b** to be in the way of, resist, oppose

prae·stō -stāre -stitī -stitum *vt* to excel, be superior to; to show, exhibit, give evidence of, display; to answer for, be responsible for, take upon oneself; to perform, discharge, fulfill; to keep, maintain, retain; **fidem praestare** to keep one's word; **impetūs populi praestare** to be responsible for popular outbreaks; **nihil praestare** to be answerable for nothing; **officia praestare** to perform duties; **se praestare** to show oneself, behave; **socios salvos praestare** to keep the allies safe; **terga hosti praestare** to show one's back to the enemy, retreat; **virtutem praestare** to display courage; *vi* to stand out, be outstanding, be preeminent, be superior; *v impers* it is preferable, it is better

praestŏl·or -ārī -ātus sum *vt* to wait for, expect; *vi* (with *dat*) to wait for

prae·stringō -stringĕre -strinxī -strictum *vt* to draw together, squeeze; to blunt (*an edge*); to dazzle (*the eyes*); to dazzle, baffle, confuse

prae·struō -struĕre -struxī -structum *vt* to build up, block up,

block, stop up; to build up (*e.g., confidence*) beforehand

praes·ul -ūlis *m* or *f* public dancer

praesult·ō -āre *vi* (with *dat*) to jump around in front of

prae·sum -esse -fuī *vi* to preside, be in charge, be in command; (with *dat*) **a** to preside over, be in charge of, be in command of; **b** to protect; (with **in** + *abl*) to be governor in

prae·sūmō -sūmĕre -sumpsī -sumptum *vt* to take in advance; to anticipate, take for granted, presume

praesumptǐ·ō -ōnis *f* anticipation

praesūt·us -a -um *adj* sewed up; covered

praetĕg·ō -ĕre *vt* to protect

praetempt·ō -āre *vt* to try out in advance, test in advance; to grope for

prae·tendō -tendĕre -tendī -tentum *vt* to hold or stretch in front of oneself; to present; to offer as an excuse, give as pretext, allege, pretend; (with *dat*) to hold or draw (*e.g., a toga*) in front of (*e.g., the eyes*); **praetendi** (*of places*) to lie to the front or opposite; **praetendi** (with *dat*) to lie or be situated opposite or over against

praetentō see **praetempto**

praetentus *pp* of **praetendo**

praetep·escō -escĕre -uī *vi* (of *love*) to glow

praeter *conj* besides, other than; *prep* (with *acc*) (of place) past, by, along, before, in front of; (in comparison) above, beyond, more than; against, contrary to, aside from; besides, apart from, except; besides, in addition to

praeterāg·ō -ĕre *vt* (with double *acc*) to drive (*e.g., a horse*) past (*a place*)

praeterbīt·ō -ĕre *vt* & *vi* to go by or past

praetereā *adv* besides, moreover; hereafter, thereafter

praeter·eō -īre -īvī or **-iī -itum** *vt* to go past, pass by; to skip, pass over in silence, neglect; to escape the notice of; to go beyond; to surpass

praeterequǐt·ans -antis *adj* riding by

praeter·ferō -ferre -tulī -lātum *vt* (with double *acc*) to carry or take (*someone*) past (*something*); **praeterferri** to move or sweep by (*a place*)

praeterflǔ·ō -ĕre *vt* & *vi* to flow by

praeter·gredior -gredī -gressus sum *vt* to march by, go past; to surpass

praeterhāc *adv* in addition

praeterit·us -a -um *pp* of **praetereo**; *adj* past, past and gone, bygone; *n pl* bygone events, the past

praeter·lābor -lābī -lapsus sum *vt* to glide by; *vi* to glide by, slip away

praeterlātus *pp* of **praeterfero**

praetermĕ·ŏ -āre vt & vi to go past or by

praetermissī·ŏ -ōnis f leaving out, omission; passing over, neglecting; (with genit) omission of, neglecting of

praeter·mittŏ -mittĕre -mīsī -missum vt to let pass, let go by; to leave undone; to pass over, omit, disregard, overlook, neglect

praetĕr·ŏ -ĕre vt to wear down in front

praeterquam adv besides, other than; **praeterquam quod** apart from the fact that

praetervectī·ŏ -ōnis f passing by

praeter·vĕhor -vĕhī -vectus sum vt & vi to ride by; to sail by; to march or go by

praetervŏl·ŏ -āre vt & vi to fly by; (of opportunity) to slip by; to escape

praetex·ŏ -ĕre -uī -tum vt to border, edge, fringe; to adorn in front; (fig) to cloak, conceal, disguise; to allege as a pretext

praetextāt·us -a -um adj wearing the toga praetexta (crimson-bordered toga); underage, juvenile, mores praetextati loose morals

praetext·us -a -um pp of **praetexo**; adj bordered; wearing the crimson-bordered toga; **fabula praetexta** Roman tragic drama; f toga praetexta (crimson-bordered toga which was worn by higher magistrates and by freeborn boys); tragedy; **praetextas docere** to put on tragedies; n pretext, pretense, excuse

praetext·us -ūs m outward show, splendor; pretense, pretext

praetim·ĕŏ -ēre vi to be apprehensive

praetinct·us -a -um adj previously dipped

praet·or -ōris m praetor (judicial magistrate, accompanied by six lictors); commander; (during the early years of the republic) chief magistrate, chief executive; (in Italian municipalities) chief magistrate; **praetor peregrinus** praetor who had jurisdiction over cases involving foreigners; **praetor urbanus** or **praetor urbis** praetor who had jurisdiction over cases involving Roman citizens

praetōriān·us -a -um adj praetorian, belonging to the emperor's bodyguard; m pl praetorian guard, soldiers of the praetorian guard

praetōricī·us -a -um adj received from the praetor (at public games)

praetōri·us -a -um adj of the commander in chief, of the commander or general; praetor's, of the praetor; propraetor's; **cohors praetoria** general's bodyguard; **comitia praetoria** praetorian elections; **navis praetoria** flagship; **porta praetoria** camp gate nearest the general's tent; **turba praetoria**

crowd around the praetor; n general's quarters, headquarters; official residence of the governor in a province; council of war; emperor's bodyguard; palace, mansion

praetorqu·ĕŏ -ēre vt to twist beforehand; to strangle first

praetrepĭd·ans -antis adj very nervous

praetrepĭd·us -a -um adj very nervous, trembling

praetrunc·ŏ -āre vt to cut off, cut short

praetūr·a -ae f praetorship; **praeturā se abdicare** to resign the praetorship

praeumbr·ans -antis adj casting a shadow; (fig) overshadowing

praeust·us -a -um adj burnt at the tip; hardened by fire at the point; frost-bitten

praeut conj as compared with, when compared with

praeval·ĕŏ -ēre -uī vi to be stronger, have more power; to have greater influence; to have the upper hand

praevalĭd·us -a -um adj of superior strength, unusually strong, unusually powerful, imposing; too strong

praevāricātī·ŏ -ōnis f collusion

praevāricāt·or -ōris m phoney accuser, prosecutor in collusion, prevaricator

praevāric·or -ārī -ātus sum vi to make a sham defense or prosecution; (with dat) to favor because of collusion

prae·vĕhor -vĕhī -vectus sum vt (of a river) to flow past; vi to ride in front, ride by; to sail by

prae·venio -venire -vēnī -ventum vt to come before, precede, get the jump on, anticipate; to prevent; vi to come before, precede

praeverr·ŏ -ĕre vt to sweep before

praevert·ŏ -ĕre -ī or **prae·vertor -vertī** vt to go before, precede, outrun, outstrip; to turn to first, attend to first; to prefer; to come before, anticipate, prevent; to preoccupy; (with dat or prae + abl) to prefer (someone or something) to; vi (with dat or ad + acc) to go to first, turn to first, attend to first

prae·vidĕŏ -vidēre -vīdī -vīsum vt to foresee

praeviti·ŏ -āre vt to taint or pollute beforehand

praevi·us -a -um adj going before, leading the way

praevŏl·ŏ -āre vi to fly out in front

pragmatic·us -a -um adj experienced; m lawyer, attorney

prandĕŏ prandēre prandī pransum vt to eat for breakfast, eat for lunch; vi to have breakfast, have lunch

prand·ium -iī or **-ī** n breakfast, lunch

pransĭt·ŏ -āre vt to usually eat for lunch

prans·or -ōris m guest at lunch

prans·us -a -um pp of **prandeo**; adj having had breakfast, after eating; well fed; **pransus potus** having been wined and dined

prasin·us -a -um adj green; **factio prasina** the Greens (one of the stables of horses at the racetrack in Rome)

prātens·is -e adj meadow, growing in the meadow

prātŭl·um -ī n small meadow

prāt·um -ī n meadow; (fig) plain (of the sea); n pl meadow grass

prāvē adv crookedly; improperly, wrongly, badly, poorly; **prave facti versus** poorly written verses

prāvĭt·ās -ātis f crookedness, distortion; impropriety, irregularity; perverseness, depravity

prāv·us -a -um adj crooked, distorted, deformed; irregular, improper, wrong, bad; perverse, vicious

Praxitěl·ēs -is m famous Greek Athenian sculptor (4th cent. B.C.)

precāriō adv upon request

precāri·us -a -um adj obtained by prayer; dependent on another's will, uncertain, precarious

precātĭ·ō -ōnis f prayer; **precationes facere** to say prayers

precāt·or -ōris m intercessor, suppliant

preces = pl of **prex**

precĭ·ae -ārum f pl grapevine

prec·or -ārī -ātus sum vt to entreat, supplicate, pray to; to pray for; to wish for; (with double acc) to pray to (someone) for; (with acc of thing and abl of person) to request (something) from; (with **pro** + abl) to entreat (e.g., the gods) on behalf of; (with **ut** or **ne**) to pray that, pray that not; **longum Augusto diem precari** to wish Augustus long life; vi to pray; (with **ad** + acc) to pray to, e.g., **di ad quos precantur** the gods to whom they pray; **male precari** to curse, utter curses

pre·hendō -hendĕre -hendī -hensum or **prendō prendĕre prendī prensum** vt to take hold of, grasp, seize; to detain; to arrest; to occupy; to catch, surprise; to reach, arrive at; to grasp, understand

prēl·um -ī n wine press, oil press; clothes press

premō premĕre pressī pressum vt to press, squeeze; to lie down on; to hug (shore); to suppress, hide; to cover, crown; to press hard, bear down on; to chase, attack; to weigh down, load; to press together, close; to curb, stop; to depress, lower; to mark, impress; to prune; to pressure, urge, importune; to degrade, humble, disparage; to abridge; to subjugate

prensātĭ·ō -ōnis f campaigning (for office)

prens·ō or **prehens·ō -āre** vt to take hold of, clutch at, grab; to stop, detain; vi to campaign, be a candidate

prensus pp of **prendo**

pressē adv distinctly, with articulation; concisely; accurately; simply

pressĭ·ō -ōnis f fulcrum; leverage

press·ō -āre vt to press

press·us -a -um pp of **premo**; adj closed, shut tight; suppressed; slow; lowered, low, subdued; concise, precise, accurate; articulate

press·us -ūs m pressing, pressure; expression (of the face)

prest·ēr -ēris m waterspout

pretĭōsē adv at great cost, expensively

pretĭōs·us -a -um adj previous, valuable; expensive; extravagant

pret·ĭum -ĭī or **-ī** n price; value, worth; reward, return, recompense; bribe; pay, wages; **in pretio esse** to be prized; to be held in high esteem; **in pretio habere** to prize, hold in high esteem; **pretium curae esse** to be worth the trouble; **pretium habere** to have value, be worth something; **pretium facere** to set a price; **pretium operae esse** to be worth the effort, be worthwhile

prex precis f prayer, request; curse, imprecation; intercession

Priamē·is -idis f daughter of Priam

Priamēĭ·us -a -um adj Priam's, of Priam

Priamĭd·ēs -ae m son of Priam

Priam·us -ī m Priam (son of Laomedon, husband of Hecuba, father of Hector, Paris, etc., king of Troy at the time of its fall)

prīdem adv long ago, long, since; **haud ita pridem** not so long ago; not long before; **quam pridem** how long ago

prīdĭē adv the day before, the previous day

prīm·a -ōrum n pl first part, beginning; first principles or elements; **cum primus** among the first, especially; **in primis** above all, chiefly, particularly, especially, principally

prīm·ae -ārum f pl lead, first rank, highest place, highest importance; **primas dare** (with dat) to attach supreme importance to

prīmaev·us -a -um adj young, youthful

prīmān·ī -ōrum m pl soldiers of the first legion

prīmāri·us -a -um adj first in rank; first-rate

prīmĭgĕn·us -a -um adj original

prīmĭpīl·us -ī m first-ranking centurion of a legion

prīmĭtĭ·ae -ārum f pl firstfruits

prīmĭtus adv originally, at first; for the first time

prīmō adv first, in the first place; at first, at the beginning

prīmordĭ·um -ĭī or **-ī** n origin, beginning; commencement; beginning of a new reign

prīmōr·ēs -um *m pl* chiefs, nobles, leaders; (mil) front line

prīmōr·is -e *adj* first, foremost, extreme, tip of; first, principal; **digitulī primōrēs** fingertips; **prīmōrī in aciē** all the way up front

prīmūlum *adv* first of all, at first

prīmūl·us -a -um *adj* very first

prīmum *adv* first, in the first place, before all else; at first; for the first time; **cum prīmum, ubī prīmum, ut prīmum** as soon as; **prīmum dum** in the first place; **quam prīmum** as soon as possible

prīm·us -a -um *adj* first, foremost; principal; eminent, distinguished; earliest; **prīmās partēs agere** to play the lead role; **prīmīs digitīs** with or at the fingertips; **prīmō annō** at the beginning of the year or season; **prīmus in prōvinciam introiit** he was the first to enter the province; **prīmus quisque** the very first, the first possible; *f pl* see **prīmae;** *n* beginning, front; **ā prīmō** from the first, from the beginning; **in prīmō** in the beginning; (mil) at the head of the column; *n pl* see **prīma**

prīnc·eps -ipis *adj* first, in front; foremost, chief; *m* leader, chief; emperor; (mil) maniple, company; captain, company commander, centurion; captaincy, centurionship; *m pl* soldiers of the second line (*between the hastati and triarii*), second line

prīncipāl·is -e *adj* first, foremost; original, primitive; chief, principal; of the emperor; **via prīncipālis** (mil) main street of a camp; **porta prīncipālis** (mil) main gate of a camp

prīncipāt·us -ūs *m* first place; post of commander in chief; principate, rule, sovereignty; origin, beginning

prīncipi·a -ōrum *n pl* first principles; foundations; front line, frontline troops; headquarters

prīncipiāl·is -e *adj* initial

prīncipi·um -iī or **-ī** *n* start, commencement, origin; beginner, originator; first to vote; right to vote first; **ā prīncipiō** or **prīncipiō** at the beginning, at first

pri·or -us *adj* previous, preceding, prior, former; first; better, superior, preferable

priōr·ēs -um *m pl* forefathers, ancestors, ancients; *f pl* (only *acc*) lead, preference

priscē *adv* in the old-fashioned style

prisc·us -a -um *adj* old, ancient; old-time, old-fashioned; former, previous

pristin·us -a -um *adj* former, earlier; pristine, primitive, original; preceding, previous, yesterday's; *n* former condition; **in pristinum restituere** to restore to its former condition

pristis see **pistrix**

prius *adv* earlier, before, previously,

sooner, first; sooner, rather

priusquam *conj* before

prīvātim *adv* privately, in private, in a private capacity, as a private citizen; at home

prīvāti·ō -ōnis *f* removal

prīvātō *adv* at home

prīvāt·us -a -um *adj* private; personal, individual, peculiar; isolated, withdrawn; ordinary (*language*); *m* private citizen, civilian; *n* privacy, retirement; private property, private land; **ex prīvātō** out of one's own pocket; **in prīvātō** in private; **in prīvātum** for private use

prīvign·a -ae *f* stepdaughter

prīvign·us -ī *m* stepson; *m pl* stepchildren

prīvilēg·ium -iī or **-ī** *n* special bill directed against an individual; special bill in favor of an individual

prīv·ō -āre *vt* to deprive, rob, strip; to free, release

prīv·us -a -um *adj* every, each single; own, private; (with *genit*) deprived of

prō *adv* (with **quam** or **ut**) just as, according as; *prep* (with *abl*) before, in front of, in, on, in the presence of; for, in behalf of, in favor of, in the service of, on the side of; instead of, in place of, for; in return for, in exchange for, for; just as, as, the same as, for; in proportion to, according to, in comparison with, by virtue of; **prō eō** just the same; **prō eō atque** or **ac** just as, the same as; **prō eō quod** in view of the fact that; **prō sē quisque** each one for himself, individually; **prō ut** or **prō eō quantum** as, in proportion as; *interj* oh!; **prō dī immortālēs!** Oh, heavens above!

proāgor·us -ī *m* chief magistrate in some provincial towns

proavi·a -ae *f* great-grandmother

proavīt·us -a -um *adj* great-grandfather's, ancestral

proav·us -ī *m* great-grandfather; ancestor, forefather

probābil·is -e *adj* worthy of approval, commendable, acceptable, pleasing, agreeable; probable, plausible, credible, likely

probābilit·ās -ātis *f* probability, plausibility

probābiliter *adv* probably

probāti·ō -ōnis *f* approval, approbation, assent; test, trial; proof

probāt·or -ōris *m* approver, supporter, backer

probāt·us -a -um *adj* approved, acceptable; tried, tested, good; esteemed

probē *adv* well, properly, correctly; well, thoroughly, very, very much

probit·ās -ātis *f* probity, honesty, worth, goodness

prob·ō -āre *vt* to approve, commend, esteem; to make good, represent as good, make acceptable; to pronounce judgment on; to pronounce approval of; to make credible, prove, show, demonstrate; to test, try, inspect; probare pro (with *abl*) to pass (*someone*) off for; probari pro (with *abl*) to pass for, be taken for

probriperlecebr·ae -ārum *f pl* temptations

probrōs·us -a -um *adj* scandalous, shameful, abusive

probr·um -ī *n* abuse, invective, reproach; shameful act, vile deed; lewdness, indecency; shame, disgrace; charge of disgraceful conduct

prob·us -a -um *adj* good, honest, upright, virtuous, decent; (coll) real, proper, downright

Proc·a or Proc·ās -ae *m* king of Alba and father of Numitor and Amulius

procācit·ās -ātis *f* brashness

procācĭter *adv* brashly

proc·ax -ācis *adj* brash

prō·cēdō -cēdĕre -cessī -cessum *vi* to proceed, go forward, advance; to make progress, advance; to come out (*in public*), show oneself, appear; to come forth, arise; (of time) to pass, elapse; to turn out, result, succeed; to continue

procell·a -ae *f* violent wind, squall, hurricane, storm; (fig) violence, commotion, storm; (mil) charge, sudden attack

procell·ō -ĕre *vt* to throw down; se procellere in mensam to lie down at the table

procellōs·us -a -um *adj* gusty

proc·er -ĕris *m* chief, noble, prince, leader

procērit·ās -ātis *f* height, tallness; length; *f pl* the different heights

procērĭus *adv* farther, to a greater extent, more

procēr·us -a -um *adj* tall; long; palmae procerae upraised palms

processiō·ō -ōnis *f* advance

processus *pp* of procedo

process·us -ūs *m* advance, progress

Prochȳt·a -ae or Prochȳt·ē -ēs *f* small island off the Campanian coast

prō·cĭdō -cĭdĕre -cĭdī *vi* to fall forwards, fall over, fall down, fall prostrate

prōcinctū (*abl* only) *m* in procinctu under arms, ready for combat

prōclāmāt·or -ōris *m* loudmouth

prōclām·ō -āre *vi* to yell

prōclīn·ō -āre *vt* to bend forward, bend; res proclinata critical situation, crisis

prōclīv·e -is *n* slope, descent; in proclivi esse to be easy

prōclīve *adv* downward, downhill; rapidly

prōclīv·is -e or prōclīv·us -a -um *adj* sloping forward; downhill; easy; inclined, disposed, subject, ready, willing

prōclīvĭt·ās -ātis *f* proclivity, tendency, predisposition

prōclīvus see proclivis

Procn·ē or Progn·ē -ēs *f* daughter of Pandion, sister of Philomela, wife of Tereus, and mother of Itys, who was changed into a swallow; swallow

proc·ō -āre *vt* to require, demand

prōcons·ul -ŭlis *m* vice-consul, proconsul; governor of a province; military commander

prōconsulār·is -e *adj* proconsular

prōconsulāt·us -ūs *m* proconsulship, proconsulate

prōcrastināti·ō -ōnis *f* procrastination

prōcrastin·ō -āre *vt* to postpone, put off from day to day

prōcreāti·ō -ōnis *f* procreation, breeding

prōcreāt·or -ōris *m* procreator, sire, parent, father

prōcreātr·ix -īcis *f* mother

prōcre·ō -āre *vt* to procreate, beget, produce

prōcresc·ō -ĕre *vi* to spring forth, be produced; to continue to grow, grow up

Procr·is -is or -ĭdis *f* wife of Cephalus who mistook her for a wild beast and shot her

Procrust·ēs -ae *m* notorious robber in Attica who stretched his victims to the length of his bed or mutilated them if they were too tall

prōcŭb·ō -āre *vi* to lie stretched out

prō·cūdō -cūdĕre -cūdī -cūsum *vt* to forge, fashion; to bring forth, produce

procul *adv* at a distance, in the distance, far; from a distance, from far; haud procul afuit quin legatos violarent they came close to outraging the ambassadors

prōculc·ō -āre *vt* to trample upon, trample down

prō·cumbō -cumbĕre -cubŭī -cubitum *vi* to fall down, sink down; to lean forward, bend over, be broken down; to extend, spread; (fig) to go to ruin

prōcūrāti·ō -ōnis *f* management, administration, superintendence; expiation, expiatory sacrifice

prōcūrāt·or -ōris *m* procurator, manager, administrator, superintendent, agent, deputy; governor of a province

prōcūrātr·ix -īcis *f* governess, protectress

prōcūr·ō -āre *vt* to manage, administer; to take care of, attend to; to avert by sacrifice; to expiate; *vi* to serve as procurator

prō·currō -currĕre -cucurrī or -currī -cursum *vi* to run out ahead, dash forward; to jut out, project

prōcursāti·ō -ōnis *f* sally, charge

prōcursātōr·ēs -um *m pl* skirmishers

prōcurs·ō -āre vi to keep charging out, continue to skirmish

prōcurs·us -ūs m sally, charge, onset

prōcurv·us -a -um adj curving forwards; curving, winding (shore)

proc·us -ī m noble; gigolo; **impudentes proci** shameless candidates

Procȳ·ōn -ōnis m Lesser Dog Star, Sirius

prōdactus pp of **prodigo**

prōdeambul·ō -āre vi to go out for a walk

prōd·eō -īre -iī -itum vi to go out, come out, go forth, come forth; (of a cliff) to project; (of plants) to come out, appear; to appear in public; to go ahead, advance, proceed

prō·dīcō -dīcere -dīxī -dictum vt to put off, defer, postpone; **diem prodicere** to adjourn a case to a later date

prōdictāt·or -ōris m vice-dictator

prōdigē adv lavishly

prōdigenti·a -ae f profusion, extravagance; openhandedness

prōdigiāliter adv to a fantastic degree

prōdigiōs·us -a -um adj prodigious; freakish

prōdig·ium -iī or **-ī** n portent; unnatural crime, monstrous crime; monster, freak

prōd·igō -igere -ēgī -actum vt to squander, waste

prōdig·us -a -um adj wasteful; lavish, openhanded; (with genit) free with; **animae prodigus** free with or careless with one's life; **herbae prodigus** locus spot with luxuriant growth of grass

prōditi·ō -ōnis f betrayal, treason; **proditionem agere** (with dat) to commit treason against, betray

prōdit·or -ōris m betrayer, traitor

prō·dō -dere -didī -ditum vt to bring out, bring forth, produce; to reveal, disclose; to record, relate, report, hand down, transmit; to proclaim, appoint, elect; to give up, surrender; to forsake, betray; to prolong, protract; (fig) to display, exhibit

prōdoc·eō -ēre vt to preach publicly

prodrom·us -ī m forerunner, advance messenger

prō·dūcō -dūcere -dūxī -ductum vt to bring out, bring forth; to produce; to promote, advance; to bring to light, reveal; to bring into the world, produce, raise, bring up; to educate; to drag out, protract, stretch out, lengthen; to lead on, induce; to put off, adjourn; to put (a slave) up for sale; to produce (on the stage), perform; to bring to court

prōductē adv long; **producte litteram dicere** to lengthen the letter or vowel

prōducti·ō -ōnis f lengthening

prōduct·ō -āre vt to drag out, delay

prōduct·us -a -um pp of **produco**; adj lengthened, prolonged, long

proēgmen·on -ī n preference

proeliār·is -e adj battle, of battle

proeliāt·or -ōris m combatant

proeli·or -ārī -ātus sum vi to battle, fight

proel·ium -iī or **-ī** n battle, combat, fight; n pl fighting men, warriors

Proet·us -ī m king of Tiryns

prōfān·ō -āre vt to profane, desecrate

prōfān·us -a -um adj unconsecrated, ordinary, common; impious, wicked; ill-omened

profātus pp of **profor**

profecti·ō -ōnis f setting out, departure; source (of money)

profectō adv really, actually

profectus pp of **proficiscor**

profectus pp of **proficio**

prōfect·us -ūs m progress, advance, success; increase, profit

prō·ferō -ferre -tulī -lātum vt to bring forward, advance, bring out; to extend, enlarge; to put off, postpone, defer; to produce, discover, invent; to make known, reveal, publish; to mention, cite, quote; **pedem proferre** to advance; **signa proferre** to march forward

profess·ae -ārum f pl professional prostitutes, professionals

professi·ō -ōnis f public acknowledgment, profession, declaration; registration (at which property, etc., was declared); profession, business

profess·or -ōris m professor, teacher

professōri·us -a -um adj professorial; professional, expert

professus pp of **profiteor**

profest·us -a -um adj non-holiday, ordinary; **dies profestus** working day

prō·ficiō -ficere -fēcī -fectum vi to make progress, make headway, advance, have success, succeed; to be useful, do good, help, be conducive; **nihil proficere** to do no good

pro·ficiscor -ficiscī -fectus sum vi to set out, start, go, depart; to originate, proceed, arise

pro·fiteor -fitērī -fessus sum vt to declare publicly, acknowledge, confess, profess; to offer freely, promise, volunteer; to follow as a profession, practice (e.g., law); to make a declaration of, register (property, etc.) before a public official; **indicium profiteri** to volunteer evidence, testify freely; **nomen profiteri** to put one's name in as a candidate, announce oneself as a candidate; **se adjutorem profiteri** (with ad + acc) to volunteer to help (someone); **se amicum profiteri** to avow oneself a friend, profess to be a friend; vi to make a confession, make an admission; to be a professor, be a teacher

prōflīgāt·or -ōris m big spender

prōflīgāt·us -a -um adj profligate, dissolute

prōflīg·ō -āre vt to knock to the ground, knock down; to defeat, conquer; to bring to an end, do away with, finish off; to ruin, crush; to debase, degrade

prōflō -āre vt to breathe out

prōflū·ens -entis adj flowing along; fluent (speech); f running water

prōfluenter adv easily, effortlessly

prōfluenti·a -ae f fluency

prō·flŭō -flŭĕre -flūxī vi to flow out; to flow along; (fig) to proceed

prōflŭv·ĭum -ĭī or -ĭ n flow

prof·or -ārī -ātus sum vt to say, declare; vi to speak out

prō·fugĭō -fugĕre -fūgī vt to run away from, escape from; vi to run away, escape; (with ad + acc) to take refuge with, take refuge at the house of

prōfŭg·us -a -um adj fugitive; banished, exile; nomadic; m fugitive, refugee

prō·fundō -fundĕre -fūdī -fūsum vt to pour, pour out; to shed; to utter; to give vent to; to spend freely, waste, squander; se profundere (of things) to come pouring out; (of persons) to come pouring out, come charging out, break out

prōfund·us -a -um adj deep; boundless, vast; dense (forest, cloud); high (heaven); infernal; (fig) bottomless, boundless; n depth; the deep, deep sea; (fig) abyss

prōfūsē adv in disorder, helter-skelter, haphazardly; extravagantly

prōfūsĭ·ō -ōnis f profusion

prōfūs·us -a -um pp of profundō; adj extravagant, lavish, profuse; excessive, expensive

prōgĕn·er -ĕrī m granddaughter's husband

prōgenĕr·ō -āre vt to beget, produce

prōgenĭ·ēs -ēī f line, lineage; progeny, descendants, offspring, posterity

prōgenĭt·or -ōris m progenitor, founder, ancestor

prō·gignō -gignĕre -genŭī -genĭtum vt to beget, produce

prōgnārĭter adv precisely, exactly

prōgnāt·us -a -um adj born, descended; (with abl or with ab or ex + abl) born of, descended from; m child; grandson

Prognē see Procne

prognostic·on or prognostic·um -ī n sign of the future, prognostic

prō·gredĭor -grĕdī -gressus sum vi to go forward, march forward, proceed, advance; to go on, make headway, make progress; to go forth, go out

prōgressĭ·ō -ōnis f progress, advancement; increase, growth; (rhet) climax

prōgressus pp of prōgredior

prōgress·us -ūs m progress, advance; march (of time or events)

prōh interj oh!, O!

prohib·ĕō -ēre -ŭī -ĭtum vt to hold back, check, hinder, prevent, avert, keep off; to prohibit, forbid; to keep away; to defend, protect

prohibitĭ·ō -ōnis f prohibition

proinde or proīn adv consequently, accordingly; proinde atque (or ac), proinde ut, or proinde quam just as, exactly as; proinde atque sī (or ac sī), proinde quasī just as if

prōjectīcĭ·us -a -um adj exposed (child)

prōjectĭ·ō -ōnis f stretching out; projectio bracchii stretching out of the arm

prōject·ō -āre vt to accuse, blame

prōject·us -a -um pp of projicio; adj jutting out, projecting; prostrate, stretched out; inclined; prone; abject, contemptible; downcast

prōject·us -ūs m projection, extension

prō·jicĭō -jicĕre -jēcī -jectum vt to throw down, throw out, throw; to throw away, abandon, forsake; to hold out, extend; to throw out, banish, exile; to neglect, desert; to blurt out; to throw away, give up, sacrifice; to put off, delay; to throw overboard; se projicere ad pedes (with genit) to throw oneself at the feet of, fall prostrate before; se projicere ex nave to jump overboard; se projicere in forum to rush into the forum

prō·lābor -lābī -lapsus sum vi to glide forward, slip or move forward; to fall forwards, fall on one's face; to slip out; (of words) to slip out, escape; to be led on, led astray (by greed, fear, etc.); (fig) to fail, go to ruin, collapse

prōlapsĭ·ō -ōnis f falling, collapse

prōlapsus pp of prōlabor

prōlātĭ·ō -ōnis f expansion, extension (of territory); adducing, mentioning (of precedents); delay, postponement

prōlāt·ō -āre vt to extend; to put off, delay

prōlātus pp of prōferō

prōl·ēs -is f offspring, progeny, children, descendants; race, stock; child; young man

prōlētārĭ·us -ĭī or -ĭ m proletarian; m pl proletariat

prō·licĭō -licĕre -lixī vt to entice, bring out, incite

prōlixē adv freely, wildly; readily, cheerfully, freely

prōlix·us -a -um adj long, freely growing, wild (beard, hair, etc.); obliging, ready and unwilling; favorable (circumstances)

prōlocūtus pp of prōloquor

prōlŏg·us -ī m prologue (of a play); actor who gives the prologue

prō·lŏquor -lŏquī -locūtus sum vt & vi to speak out

prōlŭb·ĭum -ĭī or **-ī** n desire, inclination, yen

prō·lūdō -lūděre -lūsī -lūsum vi to practice; (of boxers) to spar, shadowbox

prō·lŭō -lŭěre -lŭī -lūtum vt to wash out, flush, wash off, wash away; to wet, drench

prōlūsĭ·ō -ōnis f sparring, shadowboxing

prōlūtus pp of **proluo**

prōlŭvĭ·ēs -ēī f flood; refuse, sewage

prōmer·ĕō -ēre -ŭī -ĭtum or **prōmer·ĕor -ērī -ĭtus sum** vt to deserve, merit, earn; vi to be deserving; (with de + abl) to deserve the gratitude of; **bene de multis promerere** or **promereri** to deserve the full gratitude of many people

prōmerit·um -ī n reward, due; merit; guilt

Promēth·ĕus -ĕī or **-ĕos** m son of Iapetus and Clymene, brother of Epimetheus, and father of Deucalion, who by teaching men the use of fire, incurred the wrath of Jupiter

Promēthē·us -a -um adj Promethean, of Prometheus

Promēthid·ēs -ae m son of Prometheus, Deucalion (who, with his wife Pyrrha, was the sole survivor of the Deluge)

prōmin·ens -entis adj projecting, prominent; n headland

prōmin·ĕō -ēre -ŭī vi to jut out, hang forward, bend forward, extend; (with in + acc) to reach down to

prōmiscam or **prōmiscē** adv in common, without distinction, indiscriminately

prōmiscŭē adv indiscriminately, promiscuously

prōmiscŭ·us or **prōmisc·us -a -um** adj promiscuous, haphazard, indiscriminate, in common, open to all; common, ordinary

prōmissĭ·ō -ōnis f promise

prōmiss·or -ōris m promiser, fourflusher

prōmiss·us -a -um adj allowed to grow, long, hanging down; n promise

prō·mittō -mittěre -mīsī -missum vt to let (e.g., the hair) grow; to promise; to give promise of, give hope of; vi to promise to go; **ad cenam promittere** to promise to go to dinner, make a dinner engagement

prōmō prōměre prompsī promptum vt to bring out, draw out; to produce (arguments); to bring to light, reveal; to bring out, express (feelings, ideas, emotions)

prōmontōr·ĭum -ĭī or **-ī** n promontory

prōmōt·a -ōrum n pl second choice

(things preferred next after absolute good)

prō·mŏvĕō -mŏvēre -mōvī -mōtum vt to move (something) forward, cause to advance; to enlarge, extend; to effect, accomplish; to promote (to higher office); to bring to light, reveal; to put off, postpone; **nihil promovere** to accomplish nothing, do no good, make no progress

promptē adv readily, quickly; easily; frankly

prompt·ō -āre vt to give out, distribute

promptŭ (only abl) m **in promptu** in readiness, ready, at hand; public, visible, manifest; **in promptu gerere, habere,** or **ponere** to display

promptŭārĭ·us -a -um adj of a storehouse, storage; **cella promptuaria** (coll) jail

prompt·us -a -um pp of **promo**; adj prompt, ready; easy; brought to light, evident; bold, enterprising; (with dat or with ad or in + acc) a ready or prepared for, set for; b inclined to, disposed to; (with in + abl) quick at, prompt at; (with adversus + acc) ready for, prepared against; (with inf) ready to, quick to

prōmulgātĭ·ō -ōnis f promulgation, publication

prōmulg·ō -āre vt to promulgate, publish

prōmuls·is -ĭdis f hors d'oeuvres

prōmuntŭr·ĭum -ĭī or **-ī** n promontory

prōm·us -ī m butler

prōmūtŭ·us -a -um adj on credit, advanced, given in advance

prōnē adv downwards

prōnĕp·ōs -ōtis m great-grandson

prōnept·is -is f great-granddaughter

prōnŏe·a -ae f providence

prōnŭb·a -ae f patroness of marriage

prōnuntĭātĭ·ō -ōnis f proclamation, declaration; announcement (of the jury's verdict); delivery (of a speech); proposition (in logic)

prōnuntĭāt·or -ōris m narrator

prōnuntĭāt·um -ī n proposition (in logic)

prōnuntĭ·ō -āre vt to proclaim, announce; to utter, pronounce, express (opinion, judgment); to hold out, promise, offer; to recite, deliver, narrate, relate; (in the senate) to formulate, announce, put to a vote

prōnŭr·us -ūs f grandson's wife

prōn·us -a -um adj leaning, inclined, bending, stooping, bent over, bent forwards; swift, rushing, dashing, moving swiftly along; sloping, steep (hill, road); sinking, setting (sun, etc.); downhill; easy; inclined, disposed, prone; n downward tendency, gravity; n pl slopes

procoemi·or -ārī *vi* to make an introduction or preface

procoem·ium -iī or **-ī** *n* preface; prelude; (fig) prelude (*e.g., to a fight*)

propāgātī·ō -ōnis *f* propagation; extension, prolongation; **nominis propagatio** perpetuation of the name

propāg·ō -āre *vt* to propagate (*race*); to extend (*territory*); to prolong (*life*)

prōpalam *adv* openly, publicly

prōpatul·us -a -um *adj* open; *n* open space; **in propatulo habere** to display

prope *adv* near, nearby; (of time) near, at hand; (of degree) nearly, almost, practically, just about; (with **ab** + *abl*) close by, near to; **prope est cum** the time has come when; *prep* (with *acc*) near, near to; **prope diem** very soon, presently

prō·pellō -pellĕre -pŭlī -pulsum *vt* to drive forward, push forward; to drive away, drive out

propemŏdo or **propemŏdum** *adv* nearly, practically, almost

prō·pendĕō -pendĕre -pendī -pensum *vi* to hang down; to preponderate; (with **in** + *acc*) to be inclined to, to be favorably disposed to

propensē *adv* readily, willingly

propensi·ō -ōnis *f* propensity, inclination, tendency

propens·us -a -um *pp* of **propendeo;** *adj* important; coming near, approaching; inclined, disposed, ready, willing; **propenso animo** with a ready mind, willingly; **propensus in alteram partem** inclined toward the other point of view

properanter *adv* quickly, hastily

properanti·a -ae *f* haste

properātī·ō -ōnis *f* haste

properātō *adv* quickly, speedily

properāt·us -a -um *adj* hurried, quick, speedy; *n* haste, speed; **properato opus est** speed is required

properē *adv* quickly, in haste, hastily

properip·ēs -ĕdis *adj* quick-moving

proper·ō -āre *vt* to speed up, accelerate; to prepare hastily, do in haste; *vi* to be quick; to go or move quickly

Propert·ius -iī or **-ī** *m* Sextus Propertius (*Latin elegiac poet, c. 50-15 B.C.*)

proper·us -a -um *adj* quick, speedy

prōpex·us -a -um *adj* combed forward

prōpīnātī·ō -ōnis *f* toast

propīn·ō or **prōpīn·ō -āre** *vt* to drink (*e.g., a cup of wine*) as a toast; to drink a toast to, toast; (with *dat*) **a** to drink (*e.g., a cup of wine*) as a toast to; **b** to pass on (*a cup*) as a toast

propinqu·a -ae *f* relative (*female*)

propinquē *adv* near, near at hand

propinquit·ās -ātis *f* proximity, nearness, vicinity; (fig) relationship, affinity; friendship

propinqu·ō -āre *vt* to bring on; to accelerate, hasten; *vi* to draw near, approach; (with *dat*) to draw near to, approach

propinqu·us -a -um *adj* near, neighboring; (of time) near, at hand; related; *m* relative; *f* see **propinqua;** *n* neighborhood, vicinity

propi·or -us *adj* nearer, closer; later, more recent; more closely related, more like, more nearly resembling, more intimate, closer; of more concern, of greater import; (with *dat*) **a** nearer to, closer to; **b** closer to in resemblance, more like; (with *acc* or with **ab** + *abl*) closer to

propiŏr·a -um *n pl* closer side (*e.g., of a river*); more recent events

propitī·ō -āre *vt* to propitiate, appease

propitī·us -a -um *adj* propitious, well-disposed, favorable

propnigē·um -ī *n* room where the bath was heated

propōl·a -ae *m* retailer

propollŭ·ō -ĕre *vt* to pollute further

prō·pōnō -pōnĕre -posuī -positum *vt* to put or place forward, expose to view, display; to propose; to imagine; to offer, propose; to say, report, relate, publish; to threaten; to denounce; to design, determine, intend

Propont·is -ĭdis or **-ĭdos** *f* Sea of Marmora

prōporrō *adv* furthermore; wholly, completely

prōportī·ō -ōnis *f* proportion, symmetry; analogy

prōpositī·ō -ōnis *f* proposition; intention, purpose; theme; basic assumption (*in logic*)

prōposit·us -a -um *pp* of **propono;** *adj* exposed, open; accessible; impending, at hand; *n* intention, design, purpose, resolution; main point, theme; first premise (*in logic*)

prōpraet·or -ōris *m* propraetor (*expraetor who was made governor of a province*)

propriē *adv* in the strict sense; strictly for oneself, personally; peculiarly, especially

propriēt·ās -ātis *f* property, peculiarity, quality

propritim *adv* specifically, properly

propri·us -a -um *adj* own; very own; special, peculiar, individual, particular, personal; lasting, permanent

propter *adv* near, near at hand

propter *prep* (with *acc*) near, close to, next to; on account of, because of, for the sake of; through, by means of

propterĕā *adv* for that reason, therefore, on that account; **propterea quod** for the very reason that

prōpudiōs·us -a -um *adj* shameful, disgraceful

prōpud·ium -iī or **-ī** *n* shameful act; (said of a person) disgrace

prōpugnācŭl·um -ī *n* rampart, battlement; defense; (fig) safeguard

prōpugnātĭ·ō -ōnis *f* defense, vindication

prōpugnāt·or -ōris *m* defender, champion

prōpugn·ō -āre *vt* to defend; *vi* to come out and fight; to fight a defensive action, repel an assault; (fig) to put up a defense

prōpulsātĭ·ō -ōnis *f* repulse

prōpuls·ō -āre *vt* to drive back, repel, repulse; (fig) to ward off, repel

prōpulsus *pp* of **propello**

Propylae·a -ōrum *n pl* entrance to the Athenian Acropolis

prōquam *conj* according as

prōr·a -ae *f* prow; (fig) ship; **mihi prora et puppis est** my intention from first to last is

prō·rēpō -rēpĕre -repsī *vi* to creep ahead, crawl out

prōrēt·a -ae *m* look-out at the prow

prōrē·us -ī *m* look-out at the prow

prō·ripiō -ripĕre -ripŭī -reptum *vt* to drag forth, drag out; to rush; **se proripere** to rush, dash

prōrogātĭ·ō -ōnis *f* extension, prolongation (*of a term of office*); postponement

prōrog·ō -āre *vt* to prolong, extend; to put off, postpone

prorsum *adv* forwards; (with a negative) absolutely, at all, e.g., **prorsum nihil** absolutely nothing, nothing at all

prorsus *adv* forward; by all means, certainly; in short, in a word; (with a negative) absolutely, at all, e.g., **nullo prorsus modo assentior** I don't agree in any way at all

prō·rumpō -rumpĕre -rūpī -ruptum *vt* to make (*something*) break forth, fling forth; **prorumpi** to burst forth; *vi* to break out, rush out, make an attack

prō·ruō -ruĕre -ruī -rūtum *vt* to overthrow, demolish; *vi* to rush forth; to tumble

prōrupt·us -a -um *pp* of **prorumpo**; *adj* unrestrained

prōsāpĭ·a -ae *f* stock, race, line

proscaen·ĭum -ĭī or **-ī** *n* front part of a stage; *n pl* stage; theater

prō·scindō -scindĕre -scīdī -scissum *vt* to plow up, break up; (fig) to criticize harshly, satirize, cut to pieces

prō·scrībō -scrībĕre -scripsī -scriptum *vt* to publish in writing; to proclaim, announce; to advertise (*for sale, etc.*); to confiscate (*property*); to punish with confiscation of property, deprive of property; to proscribe, outlaw

proscriptĭ·ō -ōnis *f* advertisement; proscription, notice of confiscation, notice of outlawry

proscriptur·ĭō -īre *vi* to be anxious to hold a proscription

proscript·us -a -um *pp* of **proscribo**; *m* proscribed person, outlaw

prōsěc·ō -āre -ŭī -tum *vt* to cut off (*esp. parts of a sacrificial victim*)

prōsecūtus *pp* of **prosequor**

prōsēd·a -ae *f* prostitute

prōsēmĭn·ō -āre *vt* to sow, scatter about, plant; to propagate, raise (*family*)

prō·sentĭō -sentīre -sensī *vt* to sense or realize beforehand

prō·sĕquor -sĕquī -secūtus sum *vt* to escort, attend; to pursue (*enemy*); to chase, follow; to pursue, go on with, continue (*a topic*); to describe in detail; to follow, imitate; to attend, honor

Proserpin·a -ae *f* daughter of Ceres and wife of Pluto

prōserp·ō -ĕre *vi* to creep or crawl forwards, creep along

proseuch·a -ae *f* synagogue

prōsil·ĭō -īre -ŭī *vi* to jump forward, jump up; to jump to one's feet; (of blood) to spurt; (of sparks) to shoot out; to rush, dash

prōsōc·er -ĕrī *m* wife's grandfather

prospect·ō -āre *vt* to view, look out at, gaze upon; (of places) to look towards, command a view of, to look for, hope for, expect, await

prospectus *pp* of **prospicio**

prospect·us -ūs *m* distant view; sight, view; faculty of sight; sight (*thing seen*)

prospecŭl·or -ārī -ātus sum *vt* to look out for, watch for; *vi* to look around, reconnoiter

prosp·er see **prosperus**

prospĕrē *adv* favorably, luckily, as desired, successfully

prosperit·as -ātis *f* success, good fortune, prosperity; **prosperitas valetudinis** good health

prospĕr·ō -āre *vt* to cause to succeed, make happy, make fortunate

prosp·ĕrus or **prosp·er -ĕra -ĕrum** *adj* successful, fortunate, lucky, favorable, prosperous

prospicientĭ·a -ae *f* foresight, precaution

prō·spiciō -spicĕre -spexī -spectum *vt* to see far off, see in the distance; to spot; to command a view of; to watch for; to look out for, provide for; to foresee; *vi* to look forward; to look into the distance, have a distant view, have a view; to be on the lookout, exercise foresight; (with **in** + *acc*) to command a view of, overlook; **ex superioribus in urbem prospicere** to have a view of the city from a vantage point; **parum prospiciunt oculi** the eyes are nearsighted

prō·sternō -sternĕre -strāvī -strātum *vt* to throw to the ground, throw down, knock down; to wreck, ruin, overthrow, subvert; to debase; **se prosternere** to debase oneself; **se prosternere ad**

pedes (with *genit*) to throw oneself at the feet of, fall down before

prostibil·is -is *f* prostitute

prostibŭl·um -ī *n* prostitute

prostit·ŭō -ŭĕre -ŭī -ūtum *vt* to expose for sale; to prostitute

pro·stō -stāre -stĭtī *vi* to project; (of wares) to be set out for sale; to prostitute oneself, be a prostitute

prostrātus *pp* of **prosterno**

prōsubig·ō -ĕre *vt* to dig up, root up

prō·sum -desse -fŭī *vi* to be useful, be of use, do good, be profitable; **multum prodesse** to do a lot of good

Prōtagŏr·ās -ae *m* Greek sophist, contemporary of Socrates, born at Abdera (*c.* 485-415 B.C.)

prō·tĕgō -tegĕre -texī -tectum *vt* to cover in front, cover, cover up; to cover with a roof; to shelter, protect; (fig) to cover, defend, protect

prōtĕl·ō -āre *vt* to chase away, drive off

prōtĕl·um -ī *n* team of oxen; (fig) row, series

prō·tendō -tendĕre -tendī -tentum *vt* to stretch forth, stretch out, extend

prōtent·us -a -um *adj* extended

prōtĕnus see **protinus**

prō·tĕrō -terĕre -trīvī -trītum *vt* to wear down, rub out; to trample down, trample under foot; (fig) to trample upon, rub out, crush

prōterr·ĕō -ēre -ŭī -ĭtum *vt* to scare away

protervē *adv* boldly, brashly, impudently, brazenly

protervit·ŏ -ātis *f* brashness, brazenness

proterv·us -a -um *adj* bold, brash, brazen, impudent

Prōtesilā·us -ī *m* first Greek casualty in the Trojan War

Prōt·eus -ĕī or **-ĕos** *m* god of the sea with power to assume various forms

prothȳmē *adv* willingly, readily

prothymi·a -ae *f* willingness, readiness

prōtĭnam *adv* immediately

prōtĭnus or **prōtĕnus** *adv* straight on, forward, farther on; continuously, right on, without pause; immediately, at once, on the spot

prōtŏll·ō -ĕre *vt* to stretch out (*hand*); to put off, postpone

prōtopraxi·a -ae *f* priority (*among creditors in receiving payment*)

prō·trăhō -trahĕre -traxī -tractum *vt* to drag forward, drag out; to produce; to reveal, expose, disclose, bring to light

prōtrītus *pp* of **protero**

prō·trūdō -trūdĕre -trūsī -trūsum *vt* to push forwards, push out; to push off, postpone

prōturb·ō -āre *vt* to drive ahead, drive on, drive away, repel; to knock down

prout *conj* as, just as

prōvect·us -a -um *adj* advanced; **aetate provectus** advanced in years; **nox provecta erat** the night had been far advanced

prō·vĕhō -vehĕre -vexī -vectum *vt* to carry forwards; to transport, convey; to lead, lead on; to promote, advance, raise; **provehi** to ride, drive, move, or sail ahead

prō·vĕnĭō -venīre -vēnī -ventum *vi* to go on, proceed; to succeed; to come out, appear; to come out, grow, be produced; to come about, happen

prōvent·us -ūs *m* result, outcome; success; yield, produce; harvest

prōverb·ĭum -ĭī or **-ī** *n* proverb

prōvid·ens -entis *adj* prudent

prōvidenter *adv* prudently, with foresight

prōvidenti·a -ae *f* foresight, foreknowledge; precaution; **providentia deorum** providence

prō·vidĕō -vidēre -vīdī -vīsum *vt* to see in the distance; to see coming; to foresee; to provide for; to provide against, guard against, avert, avoid; to look after, look out for, care for; to prepare, make ready

prōvid·us -a -um *adj* foreseeing; prudent, cautious; provident; (with *genit*) providing

prōvincĭ·a -ae *f* sphere of administration; sphere of jurisdiction; office, duty, charge; public office, commission, command, administration; sphere of action; province

prōvincĭāl·is -e *adj* provincial, of a province, in a province; **bellum provinciale** war in a province; **molestia provincialis** annoyance of administering a province; *m* provincial

prōvīsĭ·ō -ōnis *f* foresight; precaution; (with *genit*) precaution against

prōvīsō *adv* with forethought

prōvīs·ō -ĕre *vt* to go out to see; to be on the lookout for

prōvīs·or -ōris *m* lookout (*person*); provider

prōvīsū (only *abl*) *m* by looking forward; (with objective *genit*) **a** by foreseeing (*e.g., danger*); **b** by providing, providing for

prōvīsus *pp* of **provideo**

prō·vīvō -vīvĕre -vixī *vi* to live on

prōvocātĭ·ō -ōnis *f* appeal (*to a higher court*); challenge

prōvocāt·or -ōris *m* challenger; type of gladiator

prōvŏc·ō -āre *vt* to challenge; to provoke; to exasperate; to stir, stimulate; **bellum provocare** to provoke a war; **beneficio provocatus** touched or stirred by an act of kindness; **in aleam provocare** to challenge to a game of dice; **provocare maledictis** to provoke or exasperate with nasty remarks

prōvŏl·ō -āre *vi* to fly out, rush out, dash out

prō·volvō -volvĕre -volvī -volū-
tum vt to roll forward, roll along;
to roll over, overturn; to humble,
ruin; se provolvere to prostrate
oneself, fall down, grovel, humble
oneself

prōvŏm·ō -ĕre vt to vomit, throw
up

proximē or proxŭmē adv (of place)
nearest, next; (of time) most recently, just recently; (with acc)
close to, next to, at the side of, very
much like, closely resembling; (with
dat) (of place) next to; proxime
atque almost as much as, nearly
the same as; proximē Pompeium
sedebam I was sitting next to
Pompey; quam proxime (with
dat or acc) as close as possible to

proximit·ās -ātis f proximity, vicinity; resemblance, similarity; close
relationship

proximō adv very recently, just recently

proxim·us or proxŭm·us -a -um
adj nearest, next; next, following,
ensuing; previous, most recent, latest, last; closely related; adjoining;
most direct (route); m close relative,
next of kin; n neighborhood; next
door, next-door neighbor

prūd·ens -entis adj foreseeing, fore-
knowing; conscious, aware; skilled,
skillful, experienced, versed; prudent, discreet, sensible, intelligent;
(with genit or abl or with in + abl)
aware of, conscious of, familiar
with, skilled in, experienced in

prūdenter adv prudently, cautiously;
skillfully

prūdenti·a -ae f foreseeing; prudence, discretion, good sense; prudentia juris publici knowledge of
or experience in public law

prūïn·a -ae f frost; winter

prūïnōs·us -a -um adj frosty

prūn·a -ae f live coal

prūniti·us -a -um adj of plum-tree
wood

prūn·um -ī n plum

prūn·us -ī f plum tree

prūrīg·ō -inis f itching, itch; yen

prūr·iō -īre vi to itch; to have an
itch; (with in + acc) to be itching
for

prytanē·um -ī n state dining hall
(where the Prytanes dined)

prytăn·is -is m prytane (member of
the executive body in some Greek
states)

psall·ō -ĕre -ī vi to play the lyre or
lute

psaltēr·ium -iī or -ī n stringed instrument, lute

psaltri·a -ae f lutist, musician (female)

psēc·as -ădis f female slave who
perfumed her lady's hair

psēphism·a -ătis n plebiscite of the
Greek assembly

pseudocăt·ō -ōnis m a make-believe
Cato

pseudomĕn·os or pseudomĕn·us -ī
m fallacious syllogism

pseudothȳr·um -ī n back door

psittăc·us -ī m parrot

Psych·ē -ēs f maiden loved by Cupid
and made immortal by Jupiter

psychomantī·um or psychoman-
tē·um -ī n place where people attempted to communicate with the
dead

-pte enclitic (added to pronouns) self,
own

ptisanăr·ium -iī or -ī n gruel

Ptolemae·us -ī m Ptolemy (name
of a series of Egyptian kings descended from Lagus, a general of
Alexander the Great)

pūb·ens -entis adj mature; juicy
(plant)

pūber see pubes

pūbert·ās -ātis f puberty; manhood,
virility; sign of maturity, beard

pūb·ēs or pūb·er -ĕris adj grown
up, adult; downy, covered with
down; m pl grown-ups, adults, men;
pūb·ēs -is f pubic hair; groin;
youth, young men, grown-up males;
throng, people; bullocks

pūb·escō -escĕre -uī vi to reach the
age of puberty, arrive at maturity;
(of plants) to grow up, ripen; (of
meadows, etc.) to be clothed, covered (e.g., with flowers)

pūblicān·us -a -um adj of public
revenues; m revenue agent

pūblicātī·ō -ōnis f confiscation

pūblicē adv publicly, officially, in behalf of the state, for the state;
at public expense; generally, universally; publice dicere to speak
officially

pūblicĭtus adv at public expense, at
the expense of the state; publicly

pūblic·ō -āre vt to confiscate; to
throw open to the general public;
to prostitute

Pūblicŏl·a or Pōplicŏl·a -ae m Publius Valerius Publicola (fl 509 B.C.)

pūblic·us -a -um adj of the people,
public, common; of the state, state,
federal, national; common, ordinary, vulgar; common, general,
public; causa publica affair of national importance; (law) federal
case (i.e., criminal case); res publica state, government, politics,
public life, country; m public official; n public, publicity; public
property, national treasury, federal
revenue; de publico at public expense; in publico in public, publicly; in publicum prodire to go
out in public; in publicum redigere to hand over to the national
treasury

pudend·us -a -um adj shameful,
scandalous

pud·ens -entis adj modest, bashful

pudenter adv modestly, bashfully

pud·eō -ēre -uī or puditum est vt
to make ashamed; v impers (with
acc of person and genit or abl of

cause of feeling), e.g., **me tui pu-det** I am ashamed of you

pudibund·us -a -um *adj* modest, bashful

pudīcē *adv* chastely, modestly, virtuously

pudīcitī·a -ae *f* chastity, modesty, purity

pudīc·us -a -um *adj* chaste, modest, virtuous, pure

pud·or -ōris *m* shame, decency, modesty, sense of shame; sense of honor, propriety; cause for shame, shame, disgrace; blush

puell·a -ae *f* girl; girl friend, sweetheart; young wife

puellār·is -e *adj* young girl's, girlish, youthful

puellārīter *adv* girlishly

puellŭl·a -ae *f* little girl; little sweetheart

puell·us -ī *m* little boy, lad

pŭ·er -ĕrī *m* boy, lad, young man; servant, slave, page; bachelor; **a puerīs** or **a puerō** from boyhood, from childhood; **ex puerīs excedere** to outgrow childhood

puerīl·is -e *adj* boyish, childish, youthful, puerile

puerīlĭter *adv* like a child, childishly

pueritī·a or **puertī·a -ae** *f* childhood, boyhood

puerper·ĭum -iī or **-ī** *n* childbirth, lying-in, giving birth

puerper·us -a -um *adj* helping childbirth, easing labor pains; *f* woman in labor

puertī·a see **pueritīa**

puerŭl·us -ī *m* little boy, little slave

pūg·a or **pȳg·a -ae** *f* rump, rear, buttocks

pug·īl -īlis *m* boxer

pugilātī·ō -ōnis *f* boxing

pugilāt·us -ūs *m* boxing

pugilĭcē *adv* like a boxer

pugillār·is -e *adj* hand-size; *m pl* & *n pl* notebook

pugillātōrĭ·us -a -um *adj* boxing, punching; **follis pugillatorius** punching bag

pugĭ·ō -ōnis *m* dagger

pugincŭl·us -ī *m* small dagger

pugn·a -ae *f* fist fight, brawl; fight, combat, battle

pugnācĭt·ās -ātis *f* pugnacity, aggressiveness

pugnācĭter *adv* pugnaciously, doggedly

pugnācŭl·um -ī *n* fortress

pugnant·ēs -ĭum *m pl* fighters, warriors

pugnant·ĭa -ĭum *n pl* contradictions, inconsistencies

pugnāt·or -ōris *m* fighter, combatant

pugn·āx -ācis *adj* pugnacious, scrappy, aggressive; quarrelsome; dogged, obstinate

pugnĕ·us -a -um *adj* of the fist; **mergae pugneae** punches

pugn·ō -āre *vt* to fight; *vi* to fight; to contend, dispute; (with *dat* or

cum + *abl*) **a** to fight, fight against, struggle with, oppose; **b** to contradict

pugn·us -ī *m* fist

pulchell·us -a -um *adj* cute little

pulch·er -ra -rum *adj* beautiful, fair, handsome

pulchrē *adv* beautifully; (as exclamation of applause) fine!; **pulchre mihi est** I am fine

pulchritūd·ō -ĭnis *f* beauty; excellence, attractiveness

pūlē·ĭum or **pūleg·ĭum -iī** or **-ī** *n* pennyroyal, mint; (fig) fragrance, pleasantness

pūl·ex -ĭcis *m* flea

pullār·ĭus -iī or **-ī** *m* keeper of the sacred chickens

pullāt·us -a -um *adj* wearing black, in black, in mourning

pullŭl·ō -āre *vi* to sprout; (of animals) to produce young

pull·us -a -um *adj* dark-grey, dark, blackish; mourning; **toga pulla** mourning toga; *n* dark-grey garment

pull·us -ī *m* young (of animals), foal, offspring, chick, chicken

pulmentār·ĭum -iī or **-ī** *n* relish, appetizer

pulment·um -ī *n* relish; food, rations

pulm·ō -ōnis *f* lung

pulmōnĕ·us -a -um *adj* of the lungs, pulmonary

pulp·a -ae *f* meat, flesh

pulpāment·um -ī *n* meat; game

pulpĭt·um -ī *n* platform; stage

puls pultis *f* pulse, porridge, mush

pulsātī·ō -ōnis *f* knock

puls·ō -āre *vt* to batter, keep hitting; to knock at; to strum (*lyre*); to beat on, strike against; (fig) to jolt, disquiet; *vi* to throb

pulsus *pp* of **pello**

puls·us -ūs *m* push, pushing; beat, beating, striking, stamping, blow, stroke; trample; (fig) impression, influence

pultātī·ō -ōnis *f* knocking (*at the door*)

pultiphagōnĭd·ēs -ae *m* porridge eater

pultiphăg·us -ī *m* porridge eater

pult·ō -āre *vt* to knock at

pulverĕ·us -a -um *adj* dust, of dust; dusty; fine as dust; raising dust

pulverulent·us -a -um *adj* dusty; raising dust; covered with dust

pulvill·us -ī *m* small cushion

pulvīn·ar -āris *n* cushioned couch, couch; sacred couch for the images of the gods; seat of honor; shrine, temple

pulvīnār·ĭum -iī or **-ī** *n* cushioned seat of a god; dry dock

pulvīn·us -ī *m* pillow, cushion; seat of honor

pulv·is -ĕris *m* dust, powder; scene of action, arena, field; effort, work

pulviscŭl·us -ī *m* fine dust, fine powder

pūm·ex -ĭcis m pùmice stone; porous stone, lava

pùmicĕ·us -a -um adj pumice, lava

pùmic·ō -āre vt to smooth or polish with pumice stone

pùmill·ō -ōnis m or f midget, dwarf, pygmy

punctim adv with the point, with the pointed end

punct·um -ī n prick, puncture; point, mathematical point; point, spot; vote, ballot; clause, phrase, moment; **puncto temporis eodem** at the same instant; **punctum temporis** moment, instant, point of time

pungō pungĕre pupŭgī punctum vt to prick, puncture, dent; to sting, bite; to cause (a wound); to stab; (fig) to sting, annoy, trouble, disturb

Pūnicān·a -a -um adj Punic, Carthaginian, in the Carthaginian style

Pūnicē adv Punic, in the Punic language

pùnicĕ·us -a -um adj reddish, red, crimson, pink

Pūnic·us -a -um adj Punic, Carthaginian; red, crimson, reddish, pink; n pomegranate

pūn·iō -īre -īvī or **-ĭī -ītum** or **pūn·ior -īrī -ītus sum** vt to punish, chastise; to avenge, revenge

punīt·or -ōris m avenger

pūp·a -ae f doll, puppet; girl, lass

pūpill·a -ae f orphan girl, ward; minor; pupil (of the eye)

pūpillār·is -e adj of an orphan, belonging to an orphan

pūpill·us -ī m orphan boy, orphan, ward

pupp·is -is f stern; ship; (coll) back; a puppi astern

pūpŭl·a -ae f pupil; eye

pūpŭl·us -ī m little boy

pūrē adv clearly, brightly; plainly, simply; purely, chastely

purgām·en -ĭnis n dirt, filth; means of expiation, purification

purgāment·a -ōrum n pl offscourings, refuse, dirt, filth, garbage; (term of abuse) trash, dregs, garbage

purgātĭ·ō -ōnis f cleansing, cleaning, cleanup; apology, justification

purgāt·us -a -um adj cleansed, clean, pure

purg·ō -āre vt to clean, cleanse, clear, clear away, remove; to clear of a charge, exculpate, excuse, justify; to refute; to cleanse, purify ritually; to purge (the body)

pūrific·ō -āre vt to purify

pūriter adv purely, cleanly; **vitam puriter agere** to lead a clean life

purpŭr·a -ae f purple, deep-red, dark-red; purple or deep-red cloth or garment; royal-purple robe; royalty; consular dignity, imperial dignity

purpurāt·us -a -um adj wearing royal purple; m courtier

purpurĕ·us -a -um adj deep-red, crimson, pink, violet, royal-purple (and various shades, as applied to roses, poppies, lips, flesh, blood, wine, dawn, hair)

purpurissāt·us -a -um adj rouged

purpuriss·um -ī m rouge; red dye

pūr·us -a -um adj pure, clear, clean; cleared, cleansed; cleansing, purifying; pure, chaste; plain, naked, unadorned, natural; plain (toga), without crimson border; pure, accurate, faultless (style); (law) unconditional, absolute; subject to no religious claims; n clear sky

pūs pūris n pus; (fig) venom, malice

pusill·us -a -um adj petty, puny; n bit, trifle

pūsĭ·ō -ōnis m little boy

pustŭl·a -ae f pimple; blister

pustulāt·us or **pusulāt·us -a -um** adj refined, purified

putām·en -ĭnis n clipping, peeling, shell, husk

putātĭ·ō -ōnis f pruning

putāt·or -ōris m pruner

putĕ·al -ālis n low wall (around a well or sacred spot), stone enclosure; **puteal Libonis** stone enclosure in the Roman Forum near which much business was transacted

puteāl·is -e adj well, of a well

pūt·ĕō -ēre vi to stink; to be rotten, be putrid

Puteolān·us -a -um adj of Puteoli

Puteŏl·ī -ōrum m pl commercial city on the coast of Campania (modern Pozzuolo)

put·er or **put·ris -e** adj putrid, rotting; crumbling; flabby

pūt·escō -escĕre -ŭī vi to become rotten

putĕ·us -ī m well; pit; dungeon

pūtĭdē adv disgustingly, disagreeably

pūtĭdiuscŭl·us -a -um adj rather tedious

pūtĭd·us -a -um adj stinking, rotten; affected, unnatural (style)

putĭll·us -a -um adj tiny

put·ō -āre vt to trim, prune; to think, ponder, consider, judge, suppose, imagine; to reckon, estimate, value; to believe in, recognize (gods); to clear up, settle (accounts); **magni putare** to think highly of; **pro certo putare** to regard as certain; in vi to think, imagine, suppose

pūt·or -ōris m stench

putre·faciō -facĕre -fēcī -factum vt to make rotten, rot; to cause to crumble, soften

putresc·ō -ĕre vi to become rotten, get moldy

putrĭd·us -a -um adj rotten; flabby

putris see puter

pūt·us -a -um adj pure, bright, perfectly pure; splendid; unmixed; unmitigated; m boy

pyct·a or **pyct·ēs -ae** m boxer

Pydn·a -ae f city in Macedonia near which Aemilius Paulus defeated

Perseus, the Macedonian king (169 B.C.)

pȳg·a -ae *f* rump, rear, buttocks

Pygmali·ōn -ōnis *m* son of Belus the king of Cyprus and brother of Dido; king of Cyprus who fell in love with a statue

Pylăd·ēs -ae *m* son of Strophius and friend of Orestes

Pyl·ae -ārum *f pl* Thermopylae (*narrow pass in E. Thessaly*)

Pyl·us -a -um *adj* of Pylos

Pyl·os -ī *f* Pylos (*home of Nestor in S.E. Peloponnesus*)

pyr·a -ae *f* pyre

pyrăm·is -idis *f* pyramid; cone

Pyrăm·us -ī *m* neighbor and boy friend of Thisbe

Pyrēnae·us -a -um *adj* of the Pyrenees

Pyrēn·ē -ēs *f* the Pyrenees Mountains

pyrĕthr·on or **pyrĕthr·um -ī** *n* Spanish camomile (*plant*)

pyrōp·us -ī *m* bronze

Pyrrh·a -ae or **Pyrrh·ē -ēs** *f* daughter of Epimetheus, wife of Deucalion, and survivor of the Deluge

Pyrrh·ō -ōnis *m* philosopher of Elis, contemporary of Aristotle, and founder of the philosophical school of Skepticism (*c.* 360-270 B.C.)

Pyrrh·us -ī *m* son of Achilles and founder of Epirus (*also called Neoptolemus*); king of Epirus who invaded Italy to assist the Tarentines against the Romans in 280 B.C. (319-272 B.C.)

Pȳthagŏr·ās -ae *m* Greek philosopher and mathematician (*6th cent.* B.C.)

Pȳthagorē·us or **Pȳthagoric·us -a -um** *adj* Pythagorean

Pȳthi·us -a -um *adj* Pythian, Delphic; *m* Apollo; *f* Pythia (*priestess of Apollo at Delphi*); *n pl* Pythian games (*held in honor of Apollo every four years*)

Pȳth·ō -ūs *f* Delphi

Pȳth·ōn -ōnis *m* dragon slain by Apollo near Delphi

pȳtism·a -ătis *n* spit, squirt of wine

pȳtiss·ō -āre *vt* to spit, spit out (*wine*)

pyx·is -idis *f* powder box, cosmetic box

Q

quā *adv* where, in what direction, by what way; to what extent, as far as; whereby, how, by what means; in any way, to any degree; **qua ... qua** partly ... partly, both ... and

quācumque *adv* wherever, by whatever way, in whatever way; by whatever means, howsoever

quādam tenus *adv* to a certain point, only so far and no farther

quadr·a -ae *f* square table, dining table; square crust; square morsel, square bit (*of cheese, etc.*)

quādrāgēsĭm·ī -ae -a *adj* forty each

quadrāgēsĭm·us or **quadrāgēnsĭm·us -a -um** *adj* fortieth; *f* one fortieth; 2½ percent tax

quadrāgiēs or **quadrāgiēns** *adv* forty times

quadrāgintā (indecl) *adj* forty

quadr·ans -antis *m* fourth part, a fourth, a quarter; cent (*smallest coin, worth one sixth of an ace*); quarter of a pound; quarter pint (*quarter of a sextarius*); **quadrante lavatum īre** take a bath for one cent (*usual price of a bath*)

quadrant·al -ālis *n* five-gallon jar

quadrantāri·us -a -um *adj* quarter; **mulier quadrantaria** two-bit wench (*woman who sold herself for a pittance*); **tabulae quadrantariae** record of debts reduced to a fourth

quadrāt·us -a -um *adj* squared, square; *n* square

quadrīdŭ·um -ī *n* four-day period, four days

quadrienn·ium -iī or **-ī** *n* four-year period, four years

quadrifāriam *adv* in four parts

quadrifĭd·us -a -um *adj* split into four parts

quadrig·ae -ārum *f pl* four-horse team; four-horse chariot

quadrigār·ius -iī or **-ī** *m* chariot racer

quadrigāt·us -a -um *adj* stamped with a four-horse chariot

quadrigŭl·ae -ārum *f pl* little four-horse team

quadrijŭg·is -e *adj* four-horse-team

quadrijŭg·us -a -um *adj* four-horse-team; *m pl* four-horse team

quadrilĭbr·is -e *adj* four-pound

quadrimŭl·us -a -um *adj* only four years old

quadrīm·us -a -um *adj* four-year-old

quadringēnāri·us -a -um *adj* consisting of four hundred men each

quadringēn·ī -ae -a *adj* four hundred each

quadringentēsĭm·us -a -um *adj* four-hundredth

quadringentiēs *adv* four hundred times

quadripertīt·us -a -um *adj* four-fold

quadrirēm·is -e *adj* having four banks of oars; *f* quadrireme

quadriv·ium -iī or **-ī** *n* crossroads

quadr·ō -āre vt to make square; to complete; to round out, give rhythmic finish to (a speech); vi to make a square; to be exact; (of accounts) to agree, come out right, tally; (with dat or in + acc) to suit, fit, seem proper to

quadr·um -ī n square; **in quadrum redigere sententias** to balance sentences

quadrupĕd·ans -antis adj galloping; m pl horses

quadrŭp·ēs -ēdis adj four-footed; on all fours; mf quadruped

quadruplātŏr -ōris m informer (who received one fourth of the forfeiture); corrupt judge

quadrŭpl·ex -icis adj quadruple, fourfold

quadruplic·ō -āre vt to quadruple, increase fourfold

quadrŭpl·or -ārī -ātus sum vi to be an informer

quadrŭpl·us -a -um adj quadruple, fourfold; n four times the amount

quaerit·ō -āre vt to keep looking for; to keep asking

quaerō quaerĕre quaesīvī quaesītum vt to look for, search for; to try to get; to get, obtain; to try to gain, earn, acquire; to miss, lack; to require, demand, call for; to ask, interrogate; to examine, investigate; to plan, devise, aim at; (with inf) to try to, wish to; (with ab or de or ex + abl) to ask (something) of or from (someone); vi to hold an examination; (with de + abl) to ask about, inquire about; **si quaeris** or **si quaerimus** (coll) to tell the truth

quaesīti·ō -ōnis f questioning under torture

quaesīt·or -ōris m judge (praetor or other official who presided over a criminal trial)

quaesīt·us -a -um pp of quaero; adj select, special; far-fetched, artificial, affected; n question; n pl gains, earnings, acquisitions, store

quaes·ō -ĕre vt to beg, ask; **quaeso** (usually parenthetical) please

quaestiŏcŭl·us -ī m slight profit

quaesti·ō -ōnis f inquiry, investigation, questioning, examination; judicial investigation, criminal trial; court of inquiry, court; questioning under torture, third degree; question, subject of investigation, case; court record; (with **de** + abl of the nature of the charge) court investigating a charge of (e.g., forgery, etc.); **in quaestione versare** to be under investigation; **quaestio extraordinaria** investigation by a special board; **quaestio inter sicarios** murder trial, court investigating a murder; **quaestio perpetua** standing court; **quaestioni praeesse** to preside over a case, be judge at a trial; **servos in quaestionem dare** or **ferre** to hand over slaves for questioning under torture

quaestiuncŭl·a -ae f minor or trifling question

quaest·or -ōris m quaestor; financial officer; treasury official; public prosecutor of criminal offenses

quaestōri·us -a -um adj quaestor's, of a quaestor; m ex-quaestor; n quaestor's tent in a camp; quaestor's residence in a province

quaestuōs·us -a -um adj profitable, lucrative, productive; acquiring wealth; eager to make a profit, acquisitive; enriched, wealthy

quaestūr·a -ae f quaestorship; quaestor's safe, public funds

quaest·us -ūs m gain, profit; acquisition; way of making money, job, occupation, business, trade; (fig) profit, gain, benefit, advantage; **ad quaestum** for profit, to make a profit; **quaestui rem publicam habere** to use public office for personal profit; **quaestum facere** to make money

quālĭbet or **quālŭbet** adv anywhere, everywhere; in any way, as you please

quāl·is -e adj what sort of, what kind of; of such a kind, such as, as; (with quotations and citations) as, as for example; **in hoc bello, quale** in this war, the likes of which; **qualis erat!** what a man he was!

quāl·iscumque -ecumque adj of whatever kind; of any kind whatever, any at all; **homines, qualescumque sunt** men, no matter what kind they are

quāl·islĭbet -elĭbet adj of whatever kind, of whatever sort

quālĭt·ās -ātis f quality, nature, property

quālĭter adv as, just as

quāl·us -ī m wicker basket, straw basket

quam adv (in questions and exclamations) to what extent, how, how much; (in comparisons) as, than; (with superlatives) as . . . as possible, e.g., **quam celerrime** as fast as possible; **quam plurimo vendere** to sell at the highest price possible; **quam primum** as soon as possible; (after verbs implying preference) rather than

quamdiū or **quam diū** adv how long; conj as long as, until

quamlĭbet or **quamlŭbet** adv as much as you please

quamōbrem or **quam ob rem** adv for what reason, why; for which reason, wherefore, why

quamquam conj though, although

quamvīs adv (with adj or adv) however; ever so; conj although

quānam adv by what route, by what way

quandō adv (in questions) when, at what time; (indefinite, after **si, ne,**

num) ever, at any time; *conj* when; because, since

quandōcumque or **quandōcunque** *adv* at some time or other, some day; *conj* whenever; as often as, no matter when

quandōque *adv* at some time, at one time or other, some day; *conj* whenever; as often as; since

quandōquīdem *conj* in as much as, whereas, seeing that

quantill·us -a -um *adj* how much, how little

quantit·ās -ātis *f* quantity

quantō *adv* by how much, how much; **quanto ante** how much earlier; **quanto ... tanto** the ... the

quantopēre *adv* how much, how greatly; with how great effort, how carefully

quantulum *adv* how little; **quantulum interest utrum** how little difference it makes whether

quantul·us -a -um *adj* how great, how much, how little, how small, how insignificant

quantul·uscumque -acumque -umcumque *adj* however small, however unimportant

quantum *adv* as much as, so much as, as great an extent; how much, how far, to what extent; (with comparatives) the more, the greater; **quantum in me fuit** as much as I could, to the best of my ability; **quantum maximā voce potuit** at the top of his voice; **quantum potest** as much (*or fast, quickly, soon, long, etc.*) as possible

quantumcumque *adv* as much as

quantumlībet *adv* however much

quantumvīs *adv* however; **quantumvīs rusticus** however unsophisticated, although unsophisticated

quant·us -a -um *adj* how great, how much; **quantus quantus** however great, however much; *pron neut* what amount; (with *genit*) how much; **in quantum** to whatever extent, as far as; **quantī** (*genit* of price) at what price, how much, how dearly, how high; **quanto** (*abl* of price) at what price, for how much; **quantum frumentī** how much grain

quant·uscumque -acumque -umcumque *adj* however great; of whatever size; however small, however trifling, however unimportant

quant·uslibet -alibet -umlibet *adj* however great; ever so great

quant·usvīs -āvīs -umvīs *adj* however great

quāpropter *adv* wherefore, why

quāquā *adv* by whatever route, whatever way

quāquam *adv* by any way

quārē or **quā rē** *adv* by what means, how; from what cause, why; whereby; wherefore

quartadecumān·ī -ōrum *m pl* sol-

diers of the fourteenth legion

quartān·us -a -um *adj* occurring every fourth day; *f* quartan fever; *m pl* soldiers of the fourteenth legion

quartār·ius -iī or **-ī** *m* quarter pint

quartō *adv* for the fourth time

quartum *adv* for the fourth time

quart·us -a -um *adj* fourth

quart·us decim·us -a -um *adj* fourteenth

quasi *conj* as if, just as if, as though

quasi *adv* as it were, so to speak; about, nearly, almost

quasill·um -ī *n* or **quasill·us -ī** *m* small basket

quassāti·ō -ōnis *f* shaking

quass·ō -āre *vt* to keep shaking, keep tossing, keep waving; to batter, shatter, smash to pieces; (fig) to shake, weaken

quass·us -a -um *pp* of quatio; *adj* shattered, broken; **vox quassa** weak voice

quate·faciō -facere -fēcī -factum *vt* to shake; (fig) to weaken

quātēnus *adv* how far, to what point; as far as; till when, how long; to what extent; **est quatenus** there is an extent to which; *conj* as far as; insofar as, inasmuch as, seeing that, since, as

quater *adv* four times

quater deciens or **quater deciēs** *adv* fourteen times

quatern·ī -ae -a *adj* four together, four in a group, four each

quatiō quatēre — quassum *vt* to shake, cause to tremble, cause to vibrate; to brandish, wave about; to beat, strike, drive; to batter, crush; (fig) to touch, move, affect; (fig) to plague, harass

quattŭor (indecl) *adj* four

quattuordēcim (indecl) *adj* fourteen

quattuorvirāt·us -ūs *m* membership on the board of four

quattuorvir·ī -ōrum *m pl* board of four officials (*executive board of municipalities and colonies*)

-que *conj* and

quemadmōdum or **quem ad modum** *adv* in what way, how; *conj* just as, as

qu·eō -īre -īvī or **-iī -ītum** *vi* to be able; (with *inf*) to be able to

quercēt·um -ī *n* oak forest

quercĕ·us -a -um *adj* oak, of oak

querc·us -ūs *f* oak tree; oak-leaf crown (*awarded to a soldier who saved citizen in battle*); acorns

querell·a or **querēl·a -ae** *f* complaint

queribund·us -a -um *adj* complaining; **vox queribunda** whining voice

querimōni·a -ae *f* complaint, grievance; elegy

querĭt·or -ārī -ātus sum *vi* to keep complaining

quern·us -a -um *adj* oak, of oak

queror querī questus sum *vt* to

complain of, complain about; to lament; *vi* to complain; (of birds) to sing, warble, sing sadly, coo mournfully

querquētulān·us -a -um *adj* oak, covered with oak trees

querūl·us -a -um *adj* complaining, full of complaints, querulous; plaintive; warbling, cooing

questus *pp* of queror

quest·us -ūs *m* complaint; plaintive note (*of the nightingale*)

quī quae quod *adj* (interrog) which, what, what kind of; (indefinite) any; *pron* (rel) who, that; (indef, after **sī, nisi, num, ne**) anyone

quī *adv* how; why; at what price; whereby; in some way, somehow

quia *conj* because

quiānam *adv* why

quicquam cūjusquam *pron* anything

quicque cūjusque *pron* each, each one

quidquid (*genit* not in use) *pron* whatever

quīcum (old *abl* + **cum**) *pron* with whom, with which

quīcumque quaecumque quodcumque or **quīcunque quaecunque quodcunque** *pron* (rel) whoever, whosoever, everyone who, whatever, whatsoever, everything that, all that; (indef) any whatsoever, any possible, every possible

quid *adv* why

quid cūjus *pron* (interrog) what; (indef, after **sī, nisi, num, or ne**) anything

quīdam quaedam quiddam *pron* a certain one, a certain person, a certain thing

quīdam quaedam quoddam *adj* a certain; (to soften an expression) a kind of, what one might call

quidem *adv* (emphasizing the word that is placed before it) indeed, in fact; (qualifying or limiting) at least, at any rate; (concessive) it is true; of course; all right; (exemplifying) for example; **ne ... quidem** (emphasizing the intervening word) not even, e.g., **ne tu quidem** not even you

quidnam cūjusnam *pron* (interrog) what

quidnam *adv* why, why in the world

quidnī *adv* why not

quidpiam cūjuspiam *pron* anything, something

quidquid (*genit* not in use; *abl:* **quōquō**) *pron* whatever, whatsoever, everything which; **per quidquid deorum** by all the gods

quidquid *adv* to whatever extent, the further

qui·ēs -ētis *f* quiet, peace, rest; calm, lull; neutrality; sleep; dream; sleep of death, death

qui·ēscō -ēscere -ēvī -ētum *vt* to stand by and watch, quietly allow; *vi* to rest, keep quiet, be inactive;

to rest, sleep, be asleep; to lie still, be still, be undisturbed; to pause, make a pause; to be calm, be unruffled; to be neutral, keep neutral; (with *inf*) to cease to, stop; (with **ab** + *abl*) to be free from

quiētē *adv* quietly, calmly

quiēt·us -a -um *adj* at rest, resting, free from exertion, inactive; quiet, peaceful, undisturbed; neutral; calm, quiet; still, silent; idle; *n pl* period of peace

quīlibet quaelibet quidlibet *pron* anyone, any you wish, no matter who, anything, anything you wish, not matter what, everything

quīlibet quaelibet quodlibet *adj* any, any at all, any you wish

quīn *adv* (interrog) why not; (corroborative) in fact, as a matter of fact; *conj* so that not, without; **facere non possum, quīn ad te mittam librum** I can't help sending you the book; **nūllō modō introīre possem, quīn vidērent mē** I just couldn't walk in without their seeing me; (after verbs of preventing, opposing) from: **mīlitēs aegrē sunt retentī quīn oppidum oppugnārent** the soldiers could hardly be kept from assaulting the town; (after verbs of hesitation, doubt, suspicion): **nōn dubitō quīn** I do not doubt that; (esp. representing a nominative of a relative pronoun with a negative) that ... not, without: **nēmo aspicere potest quīn dīcat** no one can look on without saying; **nēmo est quīn velit** there is no one who does not prefer

quīnam quaenam quodnam *adj* which, what, just which, just what

Quīnct- = Quīnt-

quīnc·unx -uncis *m* five twelfths; five percent (*interest*); the figure five (*as arranged on dice or cards*)

quīndeciēns or **quīndeciēs** *adv* fifteen times

quīndecim (indecl) *adj* fifteen

quīndecimprīm·ī -ōrum *m pl* executive board of fifteen (*magistrates of a municipality*)

quīndecimvirāl·is -e *adj* of the board of fifteen

quīndecimvir·ī -ōrum *m pl* board of fifteen; **quīndecimvirī Sibyllīnī** board of fifteen in charge of the Sibylline Books

quīngēnārī·us -a -um *adj* of five hundred each, consisting of five hundred men

quīngēn·ī -ae -a *adj* five hundred each

quīngentēsim·us -a -um *adj* five-hundredth

quīngent·ī -ae -a *adj* five hundred

quīngentiēns or **quīngentiēs** *adv* five hundred times

quīn·ī -ae -a *adj* five each; **quīnī dēnī** fifteen each; **quīnī vīcēnī** twenty-five each

quīnquāgēn·ī -ae -a *adj* fifty each

quinquāgēsim·us -a -um *adj* fiftieth; *f* two-percent tax

quinquāginta (indecl) *adj* fifty

Quinquātr·ūs -ŭum *f pl* or **Quinquātr·ia -ium** *n pl* festival in honor of Minerva (*celebrated from March 19th to 23rd*)

quinque (indecl) *adj* five

quinquennāl·is -e *adj* quinquennial, occurring every five years; five-year, lasting five years

quinquenn·is -e *adj* five years old, of five years

quinquenn·ium -ii or **-i** *n* five-year period, five years

quinquepartīt·us -a -um *adj* fivefold, divided into five parts

quinqueprīm·ī -ōrum *m pl* fiveman board of magistrates

quinquerēm·is -e *adj* having five banks of oars; *f* quinquereme

quinquě·vir -virī *m* member of a five-man board

quinquevirāt·us -ūs *m* membership on a board of five

quinquevir·ī -ōrum *m pl* five-man board (*created at various times to serve various purposes*)

quinquiens or **quinquiēs** *adv* five times

quinquiplic·ō -āre *vt* to multiply by five

quintadecimān·ī -ōrum *m pl* soldiers of the fifteenth legion

quintān·us -a -um *adj* of the fifth; *m pl* members of the fifth legion; *f* camp street running between the fifth and sixth maniple (*used as the market street of the camp*)

Quintiliān·us or **Quinctiliān·us -ī** *m* M. Fabius Quintilianus (*Quintilian, famous orator and rhetoric teacher, c. 35-c. 95 A.D.*)

Quintīl·is or **Quinctīl·is -e** *adj & m* July

quintō or **quintum** *adv* for the fifth time

quint·us -a -um *adj* fifth

Quint·us -ī *m* Roman first name

quint·us decim·us -a -um *adj* fifteenth

quippe *adv* of course, naturally, obviously, by all means; *conj* since, for; **quippe qui** since he (*is, was, will be one who*), inasmuch as he; **multa Caesar questus est quippe qui vidisset** Caesar complained a lot since he had seen

quippiam = quidpiam

quippinī *adv* why not?; of course, to be sure

Quirīnāl·ia -ium *n pl* festival in honor of Romulus (*celebrated on the 17th of February*)

Quirīnāl·is -e *adj* of Quirinus; **collis Quirinalis** Quirinal Hill (*one of the seven hills of Rome*)

Quirīn·us -a -um *adj* of Quirinus; *m* Quirinus (*epithet applied to Romulus after his deification, to Janus, to Augustus, and to Antony*)

Quir·īs -ītis *m* Roman citizen; inhabitant of Cures (*Sabine town*)

quirītāti·ō -ōnis *f* shrieking, shrieking

quirītāt·us -ūs *m* scream, shriek

Quirītēs = *pl* of Quiris

quirīt·ō -āre *vi* to scream, shriek

quis cūjus *pron* (interrog) who, which one; (indef) anyone

quīs = quibus

quisnam quaenam (see **quidnam**) *pron* (interrog) who

quispiam cūjuspiam *pron* someone

quispiam quaepiam quodpiam *adj* any

quisquam cūjusquam *pron* anyone, anybody, any person

quisque cūjusque *pron* each, each one, everybody, every one; **doctissimus quisque** every one of great learning, all the most learned; **optimus quisque** all the best ones

quisque quaeque quodque *adj* each

quisquili·ae -ārum *f pl* refuse, trash, junk, rubbish, odds and ends

quisquis (*genit* not in use; *abl:* **quoquo**) *pron* whoever, whosoever, every one who; every one, each

quīvīs quaevīs quidvīs *pron* anyone, anyone you please, anyone at all; **quivis unus** any one person

quīvīs quaevīs quodvīs *adj* any, any you please, any at all

quō *adv* (interrog) where, to what place; what for, to what purpose; (after **si, nisi,** or **ne**) to any place, anywhere; **quo . . . eo** the . . . the; **quo magis . . . eo magis** the more . . . the more; *conj* where, to which place; whereby, wherefore; (replacing **ut** when the clause contains a comparative) in order that, so that

quoad *adv* how far; how long; *conj* as long as; as far as; until

quōcircā *adv* for which reason, wherefore, therefore, that's the reason why

quōcumque *adv* to whatever place, wherever

quod *conj* because; as for the fact that; for the fact that; insofar as; as far as; **quod si** or **quodsi** but if

quōdammodō or **quōdam modo** *adv* in a way

quoi = cui

quōjus = cujus

quōlibet *adv* anywhere you please

quom see **cum**

quōminus *conj* that not; (after verbs of hindering) from, e.g., **deterrere aliquem quominus habeat** to keep someone from having

quōmodo *adv* (interrog) in what way, how; (rel) just as, as

quōmodocumque *adv* in whatever way, however

quōmodōnam *adv* in just what way, how then

quōnam *adv* where, where to; to what purpose, to what end

quondam *adv* once, at one time, formerly; at times, sometimes, once in a while; some day, one day (*in the future*)

quŏnĭam *conj* because, seeing that, now that

quŏpĭam *adv* to any place, anywhere

quŏque *adv* too, also

quŏquō *adv* to whatever place, wherever

quŏquŏmŏdŏ *adv* in whatever way, however

quŏquŏversum or **quŏquŏversus** *adv* in every direction, every way

quorsum or **quorsus** *adv* in what direction, where to; to what end, why

quot (indecl) *adj* (interrog) how many; (correlative) as many; **quot Kalendis** every first of the month; **quot mensibus** every month

quotannis *adv* every year

quotcumque (indecl) *adj* however many

quotēn-ī -ae -a *adj* how many each

quotīdĭē *adv* daily

quotiens or **quotiēs** *adv* (interrog) how many times; (correlative) as often as

quotienscumque or **quotienscun-que** *adv* however often, as often as

quotquot (indecl) *adj* however many, no matter how many

quotŭm-us -a -um *adj* which in number, which in order

quot-us -a -um *adj* which, what; what a small, what a trifling; **quota hora est?** what time is it?; **quota pars** what part; **quot erit iste liber qui . . .** which will be the book which . . .; **quotus quisque philosophorum invenitur** how rarely is one of the philosophers found, how few philosophers are found

quot-uscumque -acumque -um-cumque *adj* just what, just which; **quotacumque pars** just what part

quōusque *adv* how far, how long

quōvīs *adv* to any place whatsoever, anywhere; **quovis gentium** anywhere in the world

quum see **cum** *conj*

R

rabĭdē *adv* rabidly, madly, furiously

rabĭd-us -a -um *adj* rabid, mad, furious, raving, uncontrolled

rabĭ-ēs (genit not in use) *f* rage, madness; (fig) rage, anger, fury, wild passion, eagerness

rabĭōsē *adv* furiously, ravingly

rabĭōsŭl-us -a -um *adj* half-crazy

rabĭōs-us -a -um *adj* rabid, mad, raving, crazy

rabŭl-a -ae *m* ranting lawyer

racēmĭf-er -ĕra -ĕrum *adj* clustered; covered with grape clusters

racēm-us -ī *m* cluster, bunch (esp. of grapes); (fig) wine

radĭ-ans -antis *adj* shining, beaming, radiant

radĭāt-us -a -um *adj* spoked; having rays, radiant

rādīcĭtus *adv* by the roots, root and all; completely

rādīcŭl-a -ae *f* small root

radĭ-ō -āre or **radĭ-or -ārī -ātus sum** *vt* to radiate; *vi* to radiate, shine, gleam

radĭōs-us -a -um *adj* radiant

rad-ĭus -ĭī or **-ī** *m* stake; stick; spoke; ray, beam; shuttle; radius; measuring rod; elongated olive

rād-ix -īcis *f* root; radish; foot (of hill or mountain); base, foundation; basis, origin

rādō rādĕre rāsī rāsum *vt* to scrape, scratch; to shave; to scratch out, erase; to graze, touch in passing; to strip off; (of the wind) to lash

raed-a -ae *f* four-wheeled carriage, coach

raedār-ĭus -ĭī or **-ī** *m* coach driver

Raetĭ-a -a -um *adj* Raetian; *f* Raetia (Alpine country between Germany and Italy)

Raet-us -a -um *adj* & *m* Raetian

rall-us -a -um *adj* thin, threadbare

rāmāl-ĭa -ĭum *n pl* brushwood, undergrowth

rāment-um -ī *n* or **rament-a -ae** *f* chip, shaving

rāme-us -a -um *adj* of branches, of boughs

rām-ex -ĭcis *m* hernia, rupture; blood vessel of the lung

Ramn-ēs or **Ramnens-ēs -ĭum** *m pl* one of the three original Roman tribes; (fig) blue bloods

rāmōs-us -a -um *adj* branchy, branching; branch-like

rāmŭl-us -ī *m* twig

rām-us -ī *m* branch, bough; branch (of an antler); stick, club

rān-a -ae *f* frog; **rana marina** frog fish

rancĕ-ns -entis *adj* putrid, stinking

rancidŭl-us -a -um *adj* rank, stinking; disgusting

rancĭd-us -a -um *adj* rancid, rank, stinking; disgusting

rānuncŭl-us -ī *m* little frog, tadpole

rapācĭd-a -ae *m* son of a thief

rapācĭt-as -ātis *f* rapacity, greediness

rap-ax -ācis *adj* rapacious, grasping, grabby, greedy for plunder; insatiable

raphăn-us -ī *m* radish

rapĭdē *adv* rapidly; (to burn) fiercely

rapĭdĭt-as -ātis *f* rapidity, velocity, swiftness, rush

rapĭd-us -a -um *adj* tearing away,

seizing; fierce, consuming, white-hot (*fire*); rapid, swift, rushing, hurrying, impetuous

rapin·a -ae *f* rapine, pillage; prey, booty

rapiō rapere rapuī raptum *vt* to seize and carry off, to snatch, tear, pluck; to drag off; to hurry, drive, cause to rush; to carry off by force, rob, ravish, ravage, lay waste; to lead on hurriedly; **flammam rapere** to catch fire; **in jus rapere** to drag off to court, hale before a court; **se rapere** to hurry, dash, take off

raptim *adv* hurriedly, speedily, suddenly

rapti·ō -ōnis *f* abduction, ravishing, rape

rapt·ō -āre *vt* to seize and carry off, drag away; to drag along; to plunder; to hale, arraign

rapt·or -ōris *m* plunderer, robber; rapist

rapt·us -a -um *pp* of **rapiō**; *n* plunder, loot

rapt·us -ūs *m* snatching away; looting, robbery; rape, abduction

rāpul·um -ī *n* little turnip

rāp·um -ī *n* turnip

rārē *adv* rarely, seldom

rārē·faciō -facere -fēcī -factum *vt* to rarefy, thin out

rāresc·ō -ere *vi* to grow thin, lose density, become rarefied; to grow wider, widen out, open up; to become fewer; to disappear, die away

rārit·ās -ātis *f* looseness of texture; thinness; small number

rārō *adv* rarely, seldom

rār·us -a -um *adj* wide apart, of loose texture, thin; far apart, scattered far apart; scarce, sparse; few; (mil) in open rank; uncommon, rare, unusual

rāsil·is -e *adj* shaved smooth, scraped, polished

rastr·um -ī *n* rake; mattock

rāsus *pp* of **rado**

rati·ō -ōnis *f* calculation, computation, reckoning, account; matter, affair, business, transaction; consideration, respect, regard; grounds; scheme, system, method, procedure; theory, doctrine; science; relation, connection, reference; fashion, way, style; reasoning, reason, judgment, understanding; reasonableness, order, law; rule; view, opinion; **propter rationem** (with *genit*) out of regard for; **ratio aeraria** rate of exchange; **ratio atque usus** theory and practice; **ratio constat** the accounts tally; **rationem conferre, referre,** or **deferre** (with *genit*) to render or give an account of, account for; **rationem ducere** to make a calculation, reckon; **rationem habere** (with *cum* + *abl*) to have to do with; **rationem inire** to calculate, make a calculation

ratiōcināti·ō -ōnis *f* (rhet) exercise of the reasoning powers, reasoning; syllogism

ratiōcinātīv·us -a -um *adj* syllogistic

ratiōcināt·or -ōris *m* accountant

ratiōcin·or -ārī -ātus sum *vt* & *vi* to calculate, reckon; to reason, argue, conclude, infer

rat·is -is *f* raft; boat; *f pl* pontoons

ratiuncul·a -ae *f* small account; trifling reason; petty syllogism

rat·us -a -um *pp* of **reor**; *adj* reckoned, calculated; fixed, established, settled, certain, sure, approved; **pro rata parte** or **pro rata** in proportion, proportionately; **ratum facere** or **ratum efficere** to confirm, ratify, approve; **ratum habere** or **ducere** to consider valid, regard as certain or sure

raucisōn·us -a -um *adj* hoarse

rauc·us -a -um *adj* raucous, hoarse; screaming, strident; scraping; deep, deep-voiced

raud·us or **rūd·us -ĕris** *n* copper coin

rauduscul·um or **rūduscul·um -ī** *n* bit of money

rāv·iō -īre *vi* to talk oneself hoarse

rāv·is -is *f* hoarseness

rāv·us -a -um *adj* greyish

re·a -ae *f* defendant, guilty woman

reapse *adv* in fact, actually, really

Reāt·e -is *n* Sabine town

Reātin·us -a -um *adj* & *m* Reatine

rebellāti·ō -ōnis *f* rebellion

rebellātr·ix -īcis *f* rebel; **Germania rebellatrix** rebel Germany

rebell·iō -ōnis *f* rebellion

rebell·is -e *adj* rebellious; *m pl* rebels

rebell·ium -iī or **-ī** *n* rebellion

rebell·ō -āre *vi* to rebel

rebit·ō -ere *vi* to go back

rebo·ō -āre *vt* to make reecho; *vi* to reecho, bellow back

recalcitr·ō -āre *vi* to kick back

recal·ĕō -ēre *vi* to be warmed; (of a river) to run warm (*e.g., with blood*)

recal·escō -escĕre -uī *vi* to grow warm again

recal·faciō -facĕre -fēcī *vt* to make warm again, warm up again

recalv·us -a -um *adj* bald in front, with receding hairline

recand·escō -escĕre -uī *vi* to grow white; to grow hot, glow; (with *dat*) to grow white, grow hot, glow in response to

recant·ō -āre *vt* to recant; to charm back, charm away; *vi* to reecho

re·cēdō -cēdĕre -cessī -cessum *vi* to go back, go away, withdraw, recede, give ground, fall back; to depart; to vanish, disappear; to stand back, be distant

recell·ō -ere *vi* to spring back, recoil

rec·ens -entis *adj* recent, fresh, young; newly arrived, just arrived; modern; fresh, rested; *n pl* recent events

recens *adv* just, recently, lately, newly

recens·ĕō -ēre -ŭī -um *vt* to count, enumerate, number, survey; to review, hold a review of (*the army*); (of a censor) to revise the roll of, review, enroll; to recount, go over again, retell

recensĭ·ō -ōnis *f* revision

recensus *pp* of **recenseo**

recens·us -ūs *m* review

receptācŭl·um -ī *n* receptacle, container; reservoir; place of refuge, shelter; hiding place

receptĭ·ō -ōnis *f* reception

recept·ō -āre *vt* to take back; to welcome frequently into the home, entertain; to tug at; **se receptare** to beat a hasty retreat

recept·or -ōris *m* or **recept·rīx -īcis** *f* shelterer; concealer

recept·us -a -um *pp* of **recipio**; *n* obligation

recept·us -ūs *m* taking back, recantation; (mil) retreat; way of escape; refuge, place of retreat; return; (**signum**) **receptui canere** to sound retreat

recessim *adv* backwards

recess·us -ūs *m* retreat, withdrawal; departure; secluded spot, retreat; inner room, central chamber; recess; background

recharmid·ō -āre *vi* to stop being a Charmides (*character in Roman comedy*)

recidīv·us -a -um *adj* recurring, returning; rebuilt

re·cīdō -cīdĕre -cīdī -cīsum *vt* to cut back, cut away, cut off, cut down; to abridge, cut short

re·cĭdō -cĭdĕre -cĭdī -cāsum or **rec·cĭdō -cĭdĕre** *vi* to fall back; to jump back, recoil; to suffer a relapse; (fig) to fall back, fall, sink, relapse; to turn out, result; (with **ad** or **in** + *acc*) to pass to, be handed over to

re·cĭngō -cĭngĕre — -cĭnctum *vt* to loosen, undo, take off

recĭn·ō -āre *vt* to repeat, reecho; *vi* to sound a warning

reciper· = recuper·

re·cĭpĭō -cĭpĕre -cēpī -ceptum *vt* to keep back, keep in reserve; to take back, withdraw, bring back, carry back, retake, recover, regain; to take in, accept, receive, welcome; to gain, collect, take in, make (*money*); to take up, assume, undertake; to guarantee, pledge; (mil) to retake, reoccupy, recapture, seize, take, occupy; **ad se** or **in se recipere** to take upon oneself, take responsibility for, promise, guarantee; **se recipere** to get hold of oneself again, regain self-composure, recover, come to again; to retreat, escape; **se recipere** (with **ad** or **in** + *acc*) to retreat to, escape to, find refuge in

reciprŏc·ō -āre *vt* to move back and forth; to turn back; to back (*e.g., a ship*) about, reverse the direction of; to reverse, convert (*a proposition*); *vi* (of the tide) to ebb and flow, rise and fall

reciprŏc·us -a -um *adj* ebbing and flowing, going backwards and forwards

recīsus *pp* of **recīdo**

recitātĭ·ō -ōnis *f* reading aloud, recitation

recitāt·or -ōris *m* reader, reciter

recĭt·ō -āre *vt* to read out, read aloud, recite; to name in writing, appoint, constitute; **senatum recitare** to have roll call in the senate

reclāmātĭ·ō -ōnis *f* cry of disapproval

reclāmĭt·ō -āre *vi* to voice disapproval

reclām·ō -āre *vt* to protest; *vi* to raise a protest, voice disapproval, shout objections; to reverberate; (with *dat*) to express disapproval to, contradict

reclīn·is -e *adj* reclining, leaning back

reclīn·ō -āre *vt* to bend back, lean back, rest; (with **ab** + *abl*) to distract (*someone*) from; **se reclinare** to lean

re·clūdō -clūdĕre -clūsī -clūsum *vt* to open; to lay open, disclose; to draw (*sword*); to break up (*the soil*)

recoctus *pp* of **recoquo**

recōgĭt·ō -āre *vi* (with **de** + *abl*) to think again about, reconsider, reflect on

recognitĭ·ō -ōnis *f* reinvestigation

reco·gnoscō -gnoscĕre -gnōvī -gnĭtum *vt* to call to mind again, review; to recognize; to look over, examine, inspect, investigate; to certify, authorize

recol·lĭgō -lĭgĕre -lēgī -lectum *vt* to gather again, gather up, collect; **te recolligе** get hold of yourself, pluck up your courage

re·cŏlō -cŏlĕre -cŏluī -cultum *vt* to till again; to honor again; to recall to mind, think over, consider; to cultivate once more, practice again, resume

recommĭnisc·or -ī *vt* to call to mind again, recall

recomposĭt·us -a -um *adj* rearranged

reconcĭliātĭ·ō -ōnis *f* winning back again, reestablishment, restoration; reconciling, reconciliation

reconcĭl·ō -āre *vt* to bring back, regain, recover; to restore, reestablish; to win over again, conciliate; to bring together again, reconcile

reconcinn·ō -āre *vt* to set right again, repair

recondĭt·us -a -um *adj* hidden, concealed; recondite, abstruse, profound; reserved (*person*)

recon·dō -dĕre -dĭdī -dĭtum *vt* to put back again, put away, hoard; to hide, conceal; to plunge (*sword*); to close (*eyes*) again; to store up (*in the mind*)

reconfl·ō -āre *vt* to blow up again, rekindle

re·cŏquŏ -coquĕre -coxī -coctum *vt* to cook, boil, or bake again; to recast, remold

recordātĭ·ō -ōnis *f* recollection, remembrance

record·or -ārī -ātus sum *vt* to recall, recollect, remember

recrĕ·ō -āre *vt* to recreate, restore, renew; (fig) to revive, refresh

recrēp·ō -āre *vt & vi* to reecho

re·crescŏ -crescĕre -crēvī *vi* to grow again; to be renewed

recrūd·escō -escĕre -ŭī *vi* to become raw again; (of a wound) to open up again; (of a revolt) to break out again

rectā *adv* by a direct route, right on, directly

rectē *adv* in a straight line; rightly, correctly, suitably, properly, well; quite; (in answers) well, right, quite well; fine

rectĭ·ō -ōnis *f* direction, controlling

rect·or -ōris *m* guide, controller, leader, ruler, master, pilot

rect·us -a -um *pp* of **rego**; *adj* in a straight line, straight, direct; correct, right, proper, appropriate; just, upright, conscientious, virtuous; *n* right; uprightness, rectitude, virtue

recŭb·ō -āre *vi* to lie on one's back, lie down, rest

rēcŭl·a -ae *f* little thing

recultus *pp* of **recolo**

re·cumbŏ -cumbĕre -cubŭī *vi* to lie down again, lie down; to recline (*esp. at table*); to sink down (*e.g., in a swamp*); to fall; (of fog) to settle down

recuperātĭ·ō -ōnis *f* recovery

recuperāt·or or **reciperāt·or -ōris** *m* recoverer, regainer; (law) arbiter (*member of a bench of from three to five men who expedited cases needing speedy decisions*)

recuperātōrĭ·us or **reciperātōrĭ·us -a -um** *adj* of the special court for summary civil suits

recuper·ō or **reciper·ō -āre** *vt* to regain, recover, get back; to win over again

recŭr·ō -āre *vt* to restore, refresh, restore to health

re·currŏ -currĕre -currī *vi* to run back, hurry back; to return, recur, come back

recurs·ō -āre *vi* to keep running back; to keep recurring

recurs·us -ūs *m* return; retreat

recurv·ō -āre *vt* to curve, bend back

recurv·us -a -um *adj* curving, curved, bent, crooked

recusātĭ·ō -ōnis *f* refusal; (law) objection, protest; counterplea

recūs·ō -āre *vt* to raise objections to, reject, refuse; (with *inf*) to be

reluctant to, refuse to; *vi* to raise an objection, object; to make a rebuttal

recuss·us -a -um *adj* reverberating

recutīt·us -a -um *adj* with the foreskin cut back, circumcised; Jewish

redactus *pp* of **redigo**

redambŭl·ō -āre *vi* to walk back

redăm·ō -āre *vt* to love in return

redargu·ō -ĕre -ī *vt* to disprove, contradict, refute

redauspic·ō -āre *vi* to take the return auspices; (coll) to return

red·dŏ -dĕre -didī -ditum *vt* to give back, return, restore, replace; to repay; to repeat, recite (*words*); to translate; to render, make; to give as due, pay, deliver; to reflect, reproduce, imitate; **se reddere** to return, come back

redemptĭ·ō -ōnis *f* ransoming; bribing; revenue collection

redempt·ō -āre *vt* to ransom, repeatedly

redempt·or -ōris *m* contractor; revenue agent

redemptūr·a -ae *f* revenue collection

redemptus *pp* of **redimo**

red·eŏ -īre -iī -ĭtum *vi* to go or come back, return; (of a speaker) to return (*to the main theme*); (with **ad** + *acc*) a return to, revert to; **b** to fall back on, have recourse to, be reduced to; **c** (of power, inheritances, etc.) to revert to, devolve upon; **ad se redire** to come to again, regain consciousness; to control oneself

redhāl·ō -āre *vt* to exhale

redhib·eŏ -ēre — -ĭtum *vt* to take back

red·igŏ -igĕre -ēgī -actum *vt* to drive back, lead back, bring back; to call in, collect, raise (*money, revenues*); to reduce, diminish (*numbers*); to force, compel, subdue, reduce; (with double *acc*) to render, make; (with **in** or **sub** + *acc*) to bring under the power of; **ad vanum et irritum redigere** to make meaningless; **in memoriam redigere** to remember, recall; **in provinciam redigere** to reduce to the rank of a province

redimicŭl·um -ī *n* band, chaplet, fillet; chain, fetter

redim·ĭŏ -īre -iī -ĭtum *vt* to crown, wreathe

red·imŏ -imĕre -ēmī -emptum *vt* to buy back; to ransom, redeem; to buy off, rescue by payment, rescue, release, set free; to buy up; to buy off, ward off, avert; to pay for, compensate for, atone for; to get by contract, collect under contract

redintĕgr·ō -āre *vt* to make whole again, restore, refresh; (mil) to bring to full strength

redipisc·or -ī *vt* to get back

reditĭ·ō -ōnis *f* return

redit·us -ūs m return; revenue, proceeds, returns; (of heavenly bodies) revolution, orbit; (fig) restoration

redivia see **reduvia**

redivīv·us -a -um adj second-hand (building materials)

redol·eō -ēre -uī vt to smell of; vi to smell, be redolent

redomit·us -a -um adj retamed, broken in again

redōn·ō -āre vt to restore, give back again; to give up, abandon

redorm·iō -īre vi to go to sleep again

re·dūcō -dūcĕre -duxī -ductum vt to draw back; to lead back, bring back; to escort (official as mark of honor to his home); to remarry (after a separation); to restore to normal; to withdraw (troops); **in gratiam reducere** to restore to favor

reductĭ·ō -ōnis f restoration

reduct·or -ōris m restorer

reduct·us -a -um pp of **reduco**; remote, secluded, aloof, removed

redunc·us -a -um adj bent backwards, curved backwards

redundantĭ·a -ae f excess; redundancy

redund·ō -āre vi to overflow; to be too numerous, be too large; to be soaked (e.g., with blood); (with abl) to abound in; (with de or ex + abl) to stream from, overflow with

reduvĭ·a or **redivĭ·a -ae** f hangnail, loose fingernail

red·ux -ūcis adj guiding back, rescuing; brought back, restored

refectus pp of **reficio**

refell·ō -ĕre -ī vt to refute, disprove

re·ferciō -fercīre -fersī -fertum vt to stuff, cram, choke, crowd

refer·ĭō -īre vt to strike back, hit back

refĕrō referre rettŭlī relātum vt to bring back, carry back; to give back, return, restore, pay back, repay; to bring back, return, echo (a sound); to renew, revive, repeat; to bring back, direct, focus, turn (mind, attention); to present again, represent; to say in turn, answer, reply; to announce, report, relate, tell; to note down, enter, register, record; to reckon, consider, regard; to refer, attribute, ascribe; to bring up, spit out, vomit; **gradum referre** to go back, retreat; **gratiam** or **gratias referre** to return thanks, show gratitude; **in rationibus referendis** in accounting; **pedem referre** to go back, retreat, withdraw, retire; **pedes fertque refertque** he walks up and down; **rationes referre ad aerarium** to make an accounting to the treasury; **se referre** to go back, return; **vestigia referre** to retrace footsteps, return; vi to make a motion, make a proposal; **ad senatum referre** (with de + abl) to bring before the senate the matter of, make a proposal to the senate about; v impers it is of importance, it is of consequence; **meā** (**tuā, nostrā**) **refert** it is of importance, of consequence, of advantage to me (you, us); **non refert utrum** it makes no difference whether; **parvi refert** (with inf) it is of little importance, of little advantage to; **quid refert?** what's the difference?

refert·us -a -um pp of **refercio**; adj stuffed, packed, crammed; crowded

referv·eō -ēre vi to boil over, bubble over

refervesc·ō -ēre vi to begin to boil or bubble

re·ficiō -ficĕre -fēcī -fectum vt to rebuild, repair, restore; to revive (hope, etc.); to refresh, invigorate; to get (e.g., money) back again; to reappoint, reelect

re·fīgō -fīgĕre -fīxī -fīxum vt to unfasten, undo; to take down (pictures, posters, etc.); to annul (laws)

refing·ō -ĕre vt to refashion

refixus pp of **refigo**

reflāgit·ō -āre vt to demand again, ask back

reflāt·us -ūs m head wind

re·nectō -flectĕre -flexī -flexum vt to bend back or backwards, turn around, turn away; (fig) to turn back, bring back, change

refl·ō -āre vt to breathe out again; vi to blow in the wrong direction

reflu·ō -ĕre vi to flow back, run back; to overflow

reflu·us -a -um adj ebbing, receding

refocill·ō -āre vt to rewarm; to revive

reformāt·or -ōris m reformer

reformīdāti·ō -ōnis f dread

reformīd·ō -āre vt to dread, stand in awe of; to shrink from, shun

reform·ō -āre vt to reshape, remold, transform

re·fovĕō -fovēre -fōvī -fōtum vt to warm again; to restore, revive, refresh

refractārĭōl·us -a -um adj a bit refractory, somewhat stubborn

refractus pp of **refringo**

refrāg·or -ārī -ātus sum vi (with dat) to oppose, resist, thwart

refrēn·ō -āre vt to curb, restrain, keep down, control

refric·ō -āre -uī -ātum vt to rub open, scratch open; to irritate, reopen, inflame (a wound); (fig) to irritate, exasperate; (fig) to renew; vi to break out again

refrigerāti·ō -ōnis f coolness

refrigĕr·ō -āre vt to cool off, cool, chill; to refresh; to weary, exhaust; **refrigerari** to grow cool, grow weary

re·frigescō -frigescĕre -frixī vi to grow cool, become cool; (fig) to lose force, flag, abate, fail, grow dull, grow stale, fall flat

re·fringō -fringĕre -frēgī -fractum vt to break open, break down; to tear off (clothes); (fig) to break, check, destroy, put an end to

re·fugiō -fugĕre -fūgī vt to run away from; to avoid; vi to run away, escape; to disappear

refug·ium -iī or **-ī** n place of refuge; recourse

refúg·us -a -um adj receding, vanishing; m fugitive

re·fulgeō -fulgĕre -fulsī vi to gleam, reflect, reflect light, glitter

re·fundō -fundĕre -fūdī -fūsum vt to pour back, pour out; **refundi** to flow back, overflow

refūtāti·ō -ōnis f refutation

refūtāt·us -ūs m refutation

refūt·ō -āre vt to repress, suppress; to refute, disprove

rēgāl·is -e adj kingly, regal; king's, of a king, royal

rēgāliter adv royally, in royal style, splendidly; despotically

regel·ō -āre vt to cool off; to thaw

re·gerō -gerĕre -gessī -gestum vt to carry back, throw back; (fig) to throw back (remarks)

rēgi·a -ae f palace, castle, court; fortress, residence; (in camp) king's tent; royal family, king and courtiers, court; regia (originally the palace of King Numa on the Sacred Way in the Roman Forum and later the residence of the Pontifex Maximus)

rēgiē adv royally; despotically

Rēgiens·is -e or **Rēgīn·us -a -um** adj of Regium; m pl inhabitants of Regium

rēgific·us -a -um adj royal, kingly, magnificent

regign·ō -ĕre vt to reproduce

Rēgillān·us -a -um or **Rēgillens·is -e** adj of or at Lake Regillus

rēgill·us -a -um adj royal, magnificent

Rēgill·us -ī m lake in Latium famous for the victory over the Latins won by the Romans under the dictator Postumius (496 B.C.)

regim·en -inis n steering, controlling; rudder; government, rule, command, guidance; director, ruler, governor

rēgin·a -ae f queen; princess; noble woman, lady

regi·ō -ōnis f straight line, line, direction; boundary, boundary line; region, area, quarter, neighborhood; ward (of Rome); district, province (of a country); department, sphere; **ab recta regiōne** in a straight line; **dē recta regiōne deflectere** to veer off from a straight path; **e regiōne** in a straight line, directly; **e regiōne** (with genit) in the opposite direction to, exactly opposite; **rectā regiōne** by a direct route

regiōnātim adv by wards, by districts

Rēg·ium or **Rhēg·ium -iī** or **-ī** n city on the toe of Italy; town in Cisalpine Gaul

rēgi·us -a -um adj king's, kingly, royal, regal; like a king, worthy of a king, magnificent; m pl the king's troops; f see regia

reglūtin·ō -āre vt to unglue

regnāt·or -ōris m ruler, sovereign

regnātr·ix -īcis adj fem imperial

regn·ō -āre vi to be king, reign; to be supreme, hold sway; to domineer; (with genit) to be king of; (with in + acc) to rule over; **regnari** to be ruled by a king, be under a king

regn·um -ī n monarchy, royal power, kingship; absolute power, despotism, power; supremacy, control, direction, sovereignty; realm, kingdom; domain, estate

regō regĕre rexī rectum vt to keep in a straight line; keep in a proper course; to guide, conduct; to govern, rule, command; to manage, direct; **regĕre finīs** (law) to mark out the limits

re·gredior -grĕdī -gressus sum vi to step or go back; to come back, return; to march back, retreat

regress·us -ūs m return; retreat

rēgul·a -ae f ruler (for measuring); straight stick; straight board; rule, standard, example, model, principle

rēgul·us -ī m petty king, prince, chieftain; prince

Rēgul·us -ī m M. Atilius Regulus (Roman general who was taken prisoner by the Carthaginians in the First Punic War, refused to let himself be ransomed, and was killed in 250 B.C.)

regust·ō -āre vt to taste again; (fig) to delve again into (e.g., literature)

re·iciō -icĕre -jēcī -jectum vt to throw back, fling back; to throw over one's shoulders or behind one; to beat back, repel, repulse; to reject, refuse, disdain, scorn; (of judges) to challenge, overrule; to refer, direct, assign; to postpone; **rem reicere** (with ad + acc) to turn over or refer the matter to (someone for consideration or decision); **potestas reiciendi** (law) right to challenge

rējectāne·us -a -um adj to be rejected

rējecti·ō -ōnis f rejection; (law) challenging; **rejectio judicum** challenging of the members of the jury

rēiect·ō -āre vt to throw back

rējectus pp of reicio

re·lābor -lābī -lapsus sum vi to slide or glide back; to sink down (upon a couch); (of rivers) to flow back; to sail back; (fig) to return

relangu·escō -escĕre -ī vi to faint; to be relaxed, relax; to weaken

relāti·ō -ōnis f report (made by a

magistrate to the senate or emperor); repetition, reiteration; **relatio criminis** (law) answering to a
charge

relāt·or -ōris m proposer of a motion

relātus pp of **refero**

relāt·us -ūs m official report; narration, recital, listing; **relatus car-
minum** recital of poems

relaxātī·ō -ōnis f relaxation, easing;
mitigation

relax·ō -āre vt to stretch out, widen,
open; to loosen, open; to release, set
free; to ease, ease the tensions of,
relieve, cheer up; to alleviate, mitigate

relectus pp of **relego**

relēgātī·ō -ōnis f banishment, sending into retirement

relēg·ō -āre vt to send away, remove,
send into retirement, retire; to banish; to put aside, reject; to refer

re·lĕgō -legĕre -lēgī -lectum vt to
collect again, gather up, gather together, to travel over, sail over
again; to go over, review (in
thought, in a speech); to reread

relentesc·ō -ĕre vi to slack off, cool
off

relĕv·ō -āre vt to lighten; to lift up
or raise again; (fig) to relieve, free,
lighten, soothe, alleviate

relictī·ō -ōnis f abandonment

relictus pp of **relinquo**

relicūus see **reliquus**

religātī·ō -ōnis f tying back, tying
up

religi·ō -ōnis f religious scruple,
conscientiousness, sense of right;
misgivings; reverence, awe; religion; superstition; sanctity, holiness; religion, sect, cult, mode of
worship; object of veneration, sacred object, sacred place; divine
service, worship, religious observation

religiōsē adv scrupulously, conscientiously, carefully, exactly; reverently, piously, religiously

religiōs·us -a -um adj scrupulous,
conscientious, exact, precise, accurate; religious, reverent, pious, devout; superstitious; sacred, holy,
consecrated; subject to religious
claims, under religious liability

relig·ō -āre vt to bind back, tie up;
to moor (a ship); to unbind, untie,
loosen; (fig) to bind

re·linō -linĕre -lēvī — vt to unseal, open

re·linquō -linquĕre -līquī -lictum
vt to leave behind, not take along;
to leave behind, bequeath; to permit to remain, let remain; to leave
alive; to forsake, abandon, desert,
leave in a lurch; to give up, abandon, relinquish, resign; to leave unmentioned; **locum integrum relinquere** to leave the place untouched

reliqui·ae -ārum f pl remains, rem-
nants

reliqu·us or **relicū·us -a -um** adj
remaining, left over, left; remaining, subsequent, future (time); outstanding (debt); m pl the others; n
remainder, rest, residue; **in reliquum** in the future, for the future;
nihil reliqui facere to leave
nothing undone, omit nothing, leave
no stone unturned; **reliqui omnes**
all the rest; **reliquum est** (with
inf or ut) it only remains to; **reliquum aliquem facere** to leave
someone behind; to spare someone;
reliquum aliquid facere or **aliquid reliqui facere** to leave something remaining, leave something
behind, neglect something

rellig- = **relig-**

relliq- = **reliq-**

re·lūcĕō -lūcēre -luxī vi to reflect
light, gleam, shine out, blaze

re·lūcescō -lūcescĕre -luxī vi to
grow bright again, clear

reluct·or -ārī -ātus sum vi to fight
back, put up a struggle, resist; to
be reluctant

re·manĕō -manēre -mansī vi to
stay behind; to remain, continue (in
a certain state)

remān·ō -āre vi to flow back

remansi·ō -ōnis f staying behind,
stay

remedi·um -iī or **-ī** n remedy, cure,
antidote, medicine

remensus pp of **remetior**

remĕ·ō -āre vt to retrace, relive; vi
to go or come back, return

re·mētior -mētīrī -mensus sum
vt to remeasure; to retrace, go back
over

rēm·ex -igis m rower, crew member,
oarsman

Rēm·ī -ōrum m pl a people of Gaul
(near modern Rheims)

rēmigātī·ō -ōnis f rowing

rēmig·ium -iī or **-ī** n rowing; oars;
oarsmen, rowers

rēmig·ō -āre vi to row

remigr·ō -āre vi to move back, go
back, return

reminisc·or -ī vt to call to mind, remember; vi to remember; (with
genit) to be mindful of, conscious of,
remember

re·misceō -miscēre — -mixtum
vt to mix up, intermingle; **veris
falsa remiscere** to intermingle
lies with truth

remissē adv mildly, gently

remissi·ō -ōnis f release; easing,
letting down, lowering; relaxing (of
muscles); relaxation, recreation;
mildness, gentleness, submissiveness; abatement, diminishing; remission (of debts)

remiss·us -a -um adj relaxed, loose,
slack; mild, gentle; negligent, remiss; easy-going, indulgent, yielding; gay, merry, light; low, cheap
(price)

re·mittō -mittĕre -mīsī -missum
vt to send back; to release; to slack-
en, loosen; to emit, produce, let out,

yield, send forth, give off; to send back, return, restore; to give up, reject, resign, concede; to relax, relieve (*the mind*); to pardon; to remit, remove (*penalty*); (with *inf*) to stop (*doing something*); *vi* (of wind, rain, etc.) to slack off, abate

remixtus *pp* of **remisceo**

remōl·ior -īrī -ītus sum *vt* to push or move back or away, heave back

remollesc·ō -ēre *vi* to get soft again, soften; to weaken

remŏr·a -ae *f* hindrance, delay

remorāmin·a -um *n pl* hindrances, delays

re·mordĕō -mordēre — -morsum *vt* to bite back; to attack in return; to disturb, annoy, worry, torture

remŏr·or -ārī -ātus sum *vt* to delay, hinder, hold back, detain; *vi* to loiter, delay, linger, stay behind

remōtē *adv* at a distance, far away

remōtĭ·ō -ōnis *f* removal

remōt·us -a -um *adj* removed, out of the way, far off, remote, distant; (fig) remote, apart, separate, clear, free; dead; (with ab + *abl*) removed from, separate from, apart from, clear of, free from

re·movĕō -movēre -mōvī -mōtum *vt* to move back, withdraw, put away, remove; to shroud, veil; (fig) put out of sight, set aside, abolish; to subtract

remūg·ĭō -īre *vi* to bellow back; to resound, reecho

re·mulcĕō -mulcēre -mulsī *vt* to stroke, smooth back; **caudam remulcere** to put the tail between the legs (*in fear*)

remulc·um -ī *n* tow rope, tow line

remūnerātĭ·ō -ōnis *f* remuneration, reward, recompense, repayment

remūnĕr·or -ārī -ātus sum *vt* to repay, reward

remurmŭr·ō -āre *vi* to murmur back in reply

rēm·us -ī *m* oar; (fig) wing; **remi corporis** hands and feet (*of a swimmer*)

Rem·us -ī *m* brother of Romulus

renarr·ō -āre *vt* to tell over again, recount

re·nascor -nascī -nātus sum *vi* to be born again; to rise again, spring up again, be restored; to reappear; to recur

renāvĭg·ō -āre *vi* to sail back

ren·ĕō -ēre *vt* to unravel, undo

rēn·ēs -um *m pl* kidneys

renīd·ens -entis *adj* beaming, glad

renīd·ĕō -ēre *vi* to reflect, reflect light, glitter, shine; to smile, grin all over; to beam with joy

renīdesc·ō -ĕre *vi* to begin to reflect light, begin to glitter

renīt·or -ī *vi* to put up a struggle, fight back, resist

ren·ō -āre *vi* to swim back, float back

rēn·ō or **rhēn·ō -ōnis** *m* fur

renōd·ō -āre *vt* to tie back in a knot; to untie

renovām·en -ĭnis *n* renewal, new condition

renovātĭ·ō -ōnis *f* renovation, renewal; revision; compound interest

renŏv·ō -āre *vt* to make new again; to renovate, repair, restore; to plow up (*a fallow field*); to reopen (*wounds*); to revive (*old customs, etc.*); to start (*battles*) all over again; to refresh (*the memory*); to repeat, keep repeating, reaffirm; **faenus renovare in singulos annos** to compound the interest on a yearly basis

renŭmĕr·ō -āre *vt* to count over again, recount; to pay back, repay

renuntĭātĭ·ō -ōnis *f* formal or official report, announcement

renuntĭ·ō -āre *vt* to report; to announce; to retract (*promise, etc.*); to renounce, call off, reject; (with double *acc*) to announce or declare elected as; (with *acc & inf*) to bring back word that

renunt·ĭus -ĭī or **-ī** *m* bringer of news, reporter

re·nŭō -nŭĕre -nŭī *vt* to nod refusal to, deny, refuse, turn down, decline, say not to, reject; *vi* to shake the head in refusal, refuse, say no; (with *dat*) to say no to, deny (*a charge*)

renūt·ō -āre *vt* to refuse emphatically

reor rērī ratus sum *vt* to think, deem; (with *acc & inf*) to think that; (with *acc & adj* as objective complement) to regard (*something*) as; *vi* to think, suppose

repāgŭl·a -ōrum *n pl* bolts, bars; (fig) restraints, regulations, rules, limits

repand·us -a -um *adj* curved backwards, concave; (*shoes*) with turned-up toes

reparābĭl·is -e *adj* capable of being repaired, reparable, retrievable

reparc·ō -ēre *vi* (with *dat*) to be sparing with, take it easy with

repăr·ō -āre *vt* to get again, acquire again; to recover, retrieve, make good; to restore, renew, repair; to recruit (*a new army*); **vīna merce reparare** to get wine in exchange for wares, barter for wine

repastinātĭ·ō -ōnis *f* digging up again

re·pectō -pectĕre — -pexum *vt* to comb back; to comb again, recomb

repellō repellĕre reppŭlī repulsum *vt* to drive back, push back, repel, repulse; to reject; to remove; to refute

re·pendō -pendĕre -pendī -pensum *vt* to repay, pay back; to ransom, redeem; (fig) to repay in kind, requite, recompense, reward; to compensate for; to balance, balance out; **magna rependere** to pay back in full

rep·ens -entis *adj* sudden, unexpected, unlooked-for, hasty

repensus *pp* of **rependo**

repentē *adv* suddenly, unexpectedly, all of a sudden

repentīnō *adv* suddenly, unexpectedly

repentīn·us -a -um *adj* sudden, unexpected, unlooked-for; hasty, impetuous

reperc·ō -ēre *vi* (with *dat*) **a** to be sparing with; **b** to refrain from

repercussus *pp* of **repercutiō**

repercuss·us -ūs *m* rebounding, reflected, reflecting; echoed, echoing

repercuss·us -ūs *m* rebounding, reverberation, echo, repercussion

reper·cutiō -cutere -cussī -cussum *vt* to make (*something*) rebound, reverberate, or reflect

reperiō reperīre repperī repertum *vt* to find, find again, discover; to get, procure, obtain, win; to find out, ascertain, learn, realize; to invent, devise

repert·or -ōris *m* discoverer, inventor, author

repert·us -a -um *pp* of **reperio;** *n pl* discoveries, inventions

repetītī·ō -ōnis *f* repetition; (rhet) anaphora, repetition

repetīt·or -ōris *m* claimant

repet·ō -ere -īvī or **-iī -ītum** *vt* to head back to, try to reach again, return to; to aim at again; to fetch back; to attack again; to prosecute again; to demand anew; to demand back, claim, demand in compensation, retake; to trace back, retrace; to trace in thought, think over, recall, recollect; to trace back (*in speech*); to repeat, undertake again, resume, renew; **lex de pecuniis** (or **rebus**) **repetundis** law on extortion, extortion law; **pecuniam repetere** to sue for the recovery of money; **res repetere** to sue for the recovery of property; **reus pecuniarum repetundarum** guilty of extortion

repetund·ae -ārum *f pl* extortion; money extorted; **repetundarum arguī** to be charged with extortion; **repetundarum teneri** to be held on an extortion charge

repexus *pp* of **repecto**

repl·eō -plēre -plēvī -plētum *vt* to refill, fill up, replenish; to fill to overflowing; to make up for, replace, compensate for; to recruit, bring (*an army*) to full strength

replēt·us -a -um *adj* filled, full; well provided

replicātī·ō -ōnis *f* folding back, rolling back, rolling up; reflex action

replic·ō -āre *vt* to fold back, unfold, turn back

rēp·ō -ere -sī *vi* to creep, crawl

re·pōnō -pōnere -posuī -positum or **repostum** *vt* to put back, set back, lay (*e.g., the head*) back; to replace; to restore; to substitute; to lay out, stretch out (*the body*); to lay aside, store, keep, preserve; to lay aside, put away; to renew, repeat; to place, class; to replay, requite;

in **sceptra reponere** to reinstate in power; **membra reponere** (with *abl* or **in** + *abl*) to stretch out on (*e.g., a bed*); **se in cubitum reponere** to rest on one's elbow, prop oneself up on one's elbow; **spem reponere** (with **in** + *abl*) to put one's hope in or on, count on

report·ō -āre *vt* to bring back; to report; to carry off, gain, obtain; **victoriam reportare** to win a victory

reposc·ō -ere *vt* to demand back; to ask for, claim, require, demand

reposit·us -a -um *pp* of **repono;** *adj* distant, remote

repost·or -ōris *m* restorer

repostus *pp* of **repono**

repōtī·a -ōrum *n pl* second round of drinks

praesentātī·ō -ōnis *f* vivid presentation; cash payment

praesent·ō -āre *vt* to present again, show, exhibit, display, depict; to pay in cash; to do immediately, accomplish instantly, do on the spot; to rush, speed up (*e.g., plans*); to anticipate; to apply (*medicines*) immediately

repreh·endō or **repr·endō -endere -endī -ensum** *vt* to hold back; to restrain, check; to blame, find fault with, rebuke, criticize; (law) to prosecute, convict, condemn; to refute

reprehensi·ō -ōnis *f* checking, check; interruption (*of a speech*); blame, rebuke, criticism; refutation

reprehens·ō -āre *vt* to hold back continually; to detain from time to time

reprehens·or -ōris *m* critic

repress·or -ōris *m* restrainer

re·primō -primere -pressī -pressum *vt* to hold back, keep back; to restrain, limit, confine, curb, repress, suppress; **se reprimere** to control oneself; **se reprimere** (with **ab** + *abl*) to refrain from

reprōmissi·ō -ōnis *f* return promise

reprō·mittō -mittere -misī -missum *vt* to promise in return

rept·ō -āre *vi* to creep or crawl around

repudiātī·ō -ōnis *f* repudiation; refusal, rejection

repudi·ō -āre *vt* to repudiate, scorn; to refuse, reject; to jilt; to divorce

repudiōs·us -a -um *adj* objectionable, offensive

repud·ium -iī or **-ī** *n* repudiation, separation, divorce; **repudium renuntiare** or **repudium remittere** (with *dat*) to send a letter of divorce to, divorce

repuerasc·ō -ere *vi* to become a child again; to behave childishly

repugn·ans -antis *n* contradiction

repugnanter *adv* reluctantly

repugnantl·a -ae *f* incompatibility

repugn·ō -āre *vi* to fight back; (with *dat*) **a** to oppose, offer opposition to, fight against, be against; **b** to disagree with, be inconsistent with, be incompatible with; (with **contra** + *acc*) to fight against

repuls·a -ae *f* defeat at the polls; rebuff, cold shoulder; **repulsa consulatūs** defeat in running for the consulship; **repulsam ferre** to lose an election

repuls·ans -antis *adj* throbbing; re-echoing

repulsus *pp* of **repello**

repuls·us -ūs *m* reverberation, echo

repung·ō -ĕre *vt* to goad again

repurg·ō -āre *vt* to clean or clear again; to purge away, remove

reputāti·ō -ōnis *f* reconsideration, review

reput·ō -āre *vt* to count back, calculate; to think over, reflect upon, reconsider

requi·ēs -ētis *f* rest, relief; relaxation, recreation

requi·escō -escĕre -ēvī -ētum *vt* to put to rest, quiet down, calm down; *vi* to rest, take a rest, come to rest, stop, end; to rest, relax; to find rest, be consoled, find relief; to rest, lie quietly, sleep; (of the dead) to rest, sleep

requiēt·us -a -um *adj* rested up, refreshed

requirit·ō -āre *vt* to keep asking for, be on a constant lookout for

re·quīrō -quīrĕre -quīsīvī or **-quīsīī -quīsītum** *vt* to look for, search for, hunt for; to look around for, miss; to ask; to ask for, demand, require; (with **ab** or **dē** + *abl*) to ask or demand (*something*) from or of

rēs reī or **rēī** *f* thing, matter, affair, object, business, circumstance, event, occurrence, deed, condition, case; reality, truth, fact; property, possessions, estate, effects; benefit, advantage, interest, profit; business affair, transaction; cause, reason, motive, ground; (law) case, suit; (mil) operation, campaign, battle; state, government, politics; historical event; theme, topic, subject matter; **ab re** contrary to interests, disadvantageous, useless; **contra rem pūblicam** unconstitutional(ly), contrary to public interests; **eā re** therefore, for that reason; **ex re** according to the circumstances, according to the situation; **ex re istius** for his good; **ex re pūblicā** constitutionally, for the common good, in the public interest; **ex tuā re** to your advantage; **in re** in fact, in reality; **in rem** for the good; useful, advantageous; **ob eam rem** for that reason; **ob rem** to the purpose; **prō rē** according to circumstances; **rē** in fact, in practice, in reality, in truth, actually, really; **rem gerere** to conduct a military operation; **rērum potīrī** to get control of the government; **rērum scrīptor** historian, annalist; **rēs est mihi tēcum** I have some busi-

ness with you; **rēs sit mihi cum hīs** let me handle them; **rēs frūmentāria** foraging; grain situation, grain supply; **rēs gestae** exploits, achievements, military achievements; **rēs jūdiciāria** administration of justice, department of justice; **rēs novae** revolution; **rēs pecuāria et rūstica** livestock; **rēs Persicae** Persian history, Parthian history; **rēs rūstica** agriculture; **rēs pūblica** state, government, politics, public life, commonwealth, country; **rēs secundae** prosperous times, prosperity; **rēs uxōria** marriage; dowry; **summa rērum** world, universe

resācr·ō -āre *vt* to ask again for; to free from a curse

resaev·iō -īre *vi* to go wild again

resalūt·ō -āre *vt* to greet in return

resān·escō -escĕre -ŭī *vi* to heal up again

re·sarciō -sarcīre — -sartum *vt* to patch up, repair; to make good (*a loss*)

re·scindō -scindĕre -scīdī -scissum *vt* to tear off; to cut down; to tear open; to rescind, repeal, abrogate; (fig) to tear open, expose

re·scīscō -scīscĕre -scīvī or **-scīī -scītum** *vt* to find out, learn, ascertain

re·scrībō -scrībĕre -scrīpsī -scrīptum *vt* to write back in reply; to rewrite, revise; to enlist, enroll; to repay, pay back; *vi* to write a reply

rescrīpt·um -ī *n* imperial rescript

resēc·ō -āre -ŭī -tum *vt* to cut back, cut short; to reap; (fig) to trim, curtail; **ad vīvum resecāre** to cut to the quick

resēcr·ō or **resācr·ō -āre** *vt* to ask again for; to free from a curse

resectus *pp* of **reseco**

resecūtus *pp* of **resequor**

resēmin·ō -āre *vt* to reproduce

re·sĕquor -sĕquī -secūtus sum *vt* to reply to, answer

reser·ō -āre *vt* to unlock, unbar, open; to disclose; to open, begin (*a year*)

reserv·ō -āre *vt* to reserve, hold back; to spare; to hold on to

res·es -idis *adj* remaining, left; lazy, idle, inactive; slow, sluggish; calm

re·sīdĕō -sīdĕre -sēdī *vi* to remain seated; to stay behind, be left, remain; to tarry, linger; to stay, reside

re·sīdō -sīdĕre -sēdī *vi* to sit down, settle back; to sink down, sink, settle, subside; to calm down

residŭ·us -a -um *adj* remaining, left; in arrears, outstanding (*money*); *n* the remainder, rest

resign·ō -āre *vt* to unseal, open; to disclose, reveal; to give up, resign; to annul, cancel; to destroy (*confidence*)

resil·iō -īre -ŭī *vi* to spring back,

jump back; to recoil; to contract; to shrink back

resim·us -a -um adj turned up, snub

resin·a -ae f resin

resināt·us -a -um adj resined, rubbed with resin

resip·iō -ēre vt to taste of, have the flavor of

resip·iscō -iscĕre -īvī or **-iī** or **-uī** vi to come to one's senses

resist·ens -entis adj firm, tough

re·sistō -sistĕre -stitī vi to stand still, stop, pause; to stay, stay behind, remain, continue; to resist, put up resistance; to rise again; (with dat) **a** to be opposed to, resist; **b** to reply to

re·solvō -solvĕre -solvī -solūtum vt to untie, unfasten, undo; to open; to dissolve, melt, thaw; to relax (the body); stretch out (the limbs); to unravel; to cancel; to dispel; to unnerve, enervate; to release, set free

resonābil·is -e adj resounding, answering (echo)

reson·ō -āre vt to repeat, reecho, to resound with, make ring; vi to resound, ring, reecho; (with dat or ad + acc) to resound in answer to

reson·us -a -um adj resounding, reechoing

resorb·eō -ēre vt to suck in, swallow again

respect·ō -āre vt to look back on; to keep an eye on, care for; to have regard for; to gaze at, look at; vi to look back; to look around

respectus pp of **respicio**

respect·us -ūs m backward glance, looking back; looking around; refuge, asylum; regard, respect, consideration; **respectum habere** (with dat or ad + acc) to have respect for

re·spergō -spergĕre -spersī spersum vt to sprinkle, splash, spray; to defile

respersi·ō -ōnis f sprinkling, splashing

respersus pp of **respergo**

re·spiciō -spicĕre -spexī -spectum vt to look back at, see behind oneself; to look back for, look around for; to look back upon (the past, etc.); to look at, gaze at, look upon, regard, contemplate, consider; to notice; to look after, take care of, see to; to respect; vi to look back; to look around; (with ad + acc) to look at, gaze at

respirām·en -inis n windpipe

respirāti·ō -ōnis f respiration, breathing; exhalation; letup, rest, pause (to catch one's breath), breathing space

respirāt·us -ūs m respiration

respir·ō -āre vt to breathe, breathe out, exhale; vi to breathe, take a breath; to catch one's breath, breathe again, recover (from fright, etc.); (of combat, passions, etc.) to slack off, die down, subside; a con-

tinuis cladibus respirare to catch one's breathe again after continuous fighting; **ab metu respirare** to breathe again after a shock

resplend·eō -ēre vi to glitter

re·spondĕō -spondēre -spondī -sponsum vt to answer; to say in reply; ficta respondere to make up answers; multa respondere to give a lengthly reply; **par pari respondere** to answer tit for tat; **verbum verbo respondere** to answer word for word; vi to answer, respond, reply; to echo; (law) to answer (to bail), appeal (in court); (of lawyers) to give an opinion, give legal advice; (of priests, oracles) to give a response; (with dat) **a** to answer, reply to; **b** to match, balance, correspond to, be equal to, resemble, measure up to; **amori amore respondere** to return love for love

responsi·ō -ōnis f response, answer, reply; refutation; **sibi ipsi responsio** a reply to one's own arguments

responsit·ō -āre vi to give professional advice

respons·ō -āre vt to answer, reply; to reecho; (with dat) **a** to answer to, agree with; **b** to resist, defy; **c** to answer back to (in disobedience or defiance)

respons·or -ōris m answerer

respons·us -a -um pp of **respondeo**; n answer, response, reply; professional advice, oracular response; **responsum auferre** or **ferre** (with ab + abl) to receive an answer from; **responsum referre** to deliver an answer

rēspūblica reīpūblicae f state, government, politics, public life, commonwealth, country

respu·ō -ĕre -ī vt to spit out, cast out, eject, expel; to reject, refuse, dislike, spurn

restagn·ō -āre vi to form pools; to run over, overflow; to be inundated

restaur·ō -āre vt to restore, rebuild

resticŭl·a -ae f thin rope, cord

restincti·ō -ōnis f quenching

re·stinguō -stinguĕre -stinxī -stinctum vt to quench, extinguish, put out; to snuff out, extinguish, exterminate, destroy

resti·ō -ōnis m rope maker; (coll) roper (person who whipped with ropes)

restipulāti·ō -ōnis f counterclaim

restipŭl·or -ārī -ātus sum vt to stipulate in return

rest·is -is f rope

restit·ō -āre vi to stay behind, lag behind, hold back, hang back

restitr·ix -īcis f stay-behind (female)

re·stituō -stituĕre -stituī -stitūtum vt to set up again; to restore, rebuild, reconstruct; to renew, reestablish, revive; to bring back, restore, reinstate; to give back, return, replace; to restore, repair, remedy; to reenact (*a law*); to reverse, revoke, make void, undo, cancel; to make good, compensate for, repair

restitūti•ō -ōnis *f* restoration; reinstatement, pardon; recall (*from exile*)

restitūt•or -ōris *m* restorer, rebuilder

restitūtus *pp of* **restituo**

re•stō -stāre -stitī *vi* to stand firm, stand one's ground, resist; to stay behind, stay in reserve; to be left, be left over; *v impers* (with *inf* or **ut**) it remains to (*do something*)

restrictē *adv* sparingly; exactly, precisely

restrict•us -a -um *adj* tied back, tight; stingy; moderate; strict, stern

re•stringō -stringĕre -strinxī -strictum *vt* to draw back tightly, tie back, tighten; (of dogs) to show (*the teeth*); (fig) to restrain

resūd•ō -āre *vt & vi* to sweat

result•ō -āre *vi* to rebound; to reverberate, resound

re•sūmō -sūmĕre -sūmpsī -sūmptum *vt* to take up again, resume; to recover (*strength*)

resupīn•ō -āre *vt* to throw (*someone*) on his back, throw over, throw down; (coll) to knock for a loop; to break down (*doors*)

resupīn•us -a -um *adj* bent back, thrown back; supine, lying on the back; leaning backward; proud, haughty (*gait*)

re•surgō -surgĕre -surrexī -surrectum *vi* to rise again, appear again

resuscit•ō -āre *vt* to resuscitate, revive, renew

retardāti•ō -ōnis *f* retarding, delaying

retard•ō -āre *vt* to slow down, retard, hold back, delay, keep back, check, hinder

rēt•e -is *n* net; (fig) trap

re•tegō -tegĕre -texī -tectum *vt* to uncover; to open

retempt•ō -are *vt* to attempt again, try again, test again

re•tendō -tendĕre -tendī -tentum or **-tensum** *vt* to release from tension, unbend, relax

retenti•ō -ōnis *f* holding back, slowing down; withholding (*of assent*)

retent•ō -āre *vt* to hold back, hold tight; to attempt again, try again, test again

retentus *pp of* **retendo** and **retineo**

re•texō -texĕre -texuī -textum *vt* to unravel; to cancel, annul, reverse, undo; to weave anew; to renew, repeat; to correct, revise; to take back, retract (*words*)

rētiār•ius -iī or **-ī** *m* gladiator who tried to entangle his opponent in a net

reticenti•a -ae *f* reticence, silence; (rhet) abrupt pause; **poena reticentiae** punishment for suppressing the truth

retic•ĕō -ēre *vt* to be silent about, suppress, keep secret; *vi* to be silent, keep silence; (with *dat*) to make no answer to

rēticŭl•um -ī *n* small net; hair net; network bag, reticule (*for protecting bottles*); racket (*for playing ball*)

retinācŭl•a -ōrum *n pl* cable, rope, hawser, tether

retin•ens -entis *adj* (with *genit*) clinging to

retinenti•a -ae *f* recollection, retention

re•tinĕō -tinēre -tinuī -tentum *vt* to hold back, keep back; to restrain; to keep, retain; to hold in reserve; to keep, preserve, maintain, uphold; to hold, engross (*attention*); to detain, delay

retinn•iō -īre *vi* to ring again, ring out

retŏn•ō -āre *vi* to resound

re•torquĕō -torquēre -torsī -tortum *vt* to twist or bend back; to hurl back (*weapons*); **mentem retorquere** to change the mind; **oculos retorquere** (with **ad +** *acc*) to look back wistfully at

retorrĭd•us -a -um *adj* parched, dried out, withered; wily, old, shrewd

retortus *pp of* **retorqueo**

retractāti•ō -ōnis *f* rehandling, retreatment; hesitation

retract•ō or **retrect•ō -āre** *vt* to rehandle, take in hand again, undertake once more, take up once more; to reexamine, review; to revise; *vi* to refuse, decline; to be reluctant

retract•us -a -um *adj* withdrawn, distant, remote

re•trāhō -trahĕre -traxī -tractum *vt* to draw back, withdraw, drag back; to bring to light again, make known again; (fig) to drag away, divert, remove, turn

retrectō see **retracto**

retrib•uō -uĕre -uī -ūtum *vt* to give back, restore, repay

retrō *adv* backwards, back, to the rear; behind, on the rear; in the past, formerly, back, past; in return, on the contrary, on the other hand

retrorsum or **retrorsus** *adv* back, backwards, behind; in reversed order

re•trūdō -trūdĕre — -trūsum *vt* to push back; to hide, conceal

retundō retundĕre retūdī (or rettūdī) retunsum (or retūsum) *vt* to pound back; to dull, blunt; (fig) to deaden, weaken, repress, restrain

retuns•us or **retūs•us -a -um** *adj* blunt, dull; (fig) dull

re•us -ī *m* defendant, plaintiff, the accused; convict, criminal, culprit

reval·escō -escĕre -ŭī *vi* to regain one's strength, recover; to become valid again

re·vehō -vehĕre -vexī -vectum *vt* to carry back, bring back; **revehi** to ride or drive back, sail back; (fig) to go back (*e.g., to an earlier period*)

re·vellō -vellĕre -vellī -vulsum *vt* to pull out, pull back, tear off, tear out; to tear up (*the ground*), dig up; (fig) to abolish, remove

revēl·ō -āre *vt* to unveil, uncover

re·veniō -venīre -vēnī -ventum *vi* to come again, come back, return

rēvērā *adv* in fact, actually

rēverbĕr·ō -āre *vt* to beat back, repel

reverend·us -a -um *adj* venerable, awe-inspiring

revĕr·ens -entis *adj* reverent, respectful

reverenter *adv* respectfully

reverenti·a -ae *f* awe, respect, reverence

rever·eor -ērī -itus sum *vt* to revere, respect, stand in awe of

reversi·ō or **revorsi·ō -ōnis** *f* turning back (*before reaching one's destination*); recurrence (*of fever, etc.*)

revert·ō -ĕre -ī or **re·vertor** (or **re·vortor**) **-vertī -versus sum** *vi* to turn back, turn around, come back, return; (in speaking) to return, revert, recur

revictus *pp of* **revinco**

revid·ĕō -ēre *vt* to go back to see, revisit

re·vinciō -vincīre -vinxī -vinctum *vt* to tie back, tie behind, tie up

re·vincō -vincĕre -vīcī -victum *vt* to conquer, crush, repress; to refute, disprove, convict

revinctus *pp of* **revinco**

revir·escō -escĕre -ŭī *vi* to grow green again, become green again; to grow young again; to grow again, grow strong again, revive

revīs·ō -ĕre *vt* to go to see again, revisit; to look back to see; *vi* to come or go back; (with **ad** + *acc*) **a** to look at again, look back at; **b** to return to, revisit

re·vīvīscō or **re·vīvescō -vīvescĕre -vixī** *vi* to come back to life, be restored to life, revive; (fig) to revive, recover, gain strength

revocābil·is -e *adj* revocable, capable of being recalled

revocām·en -inis *n* recall

revocāti·ō -ōnis *f* calling back, calling away, recall; revoking, retracting (*of a word*)

revoc·ō -āre *vt* to call back, recall; to recall, call off, withdraw (*troops*); to call back (*an actor, singer*) for an encore; to bring back to life, revive; (law) to arraign again; to recover, regain (*strength, etc.*); to resume (*career, studies*); to revoke, retract;

to check, control; to cancel; (with **ad** + *acc*) to refer, apply, subject, submit (*someone or something*) to

revōl·ō -āre *vi* to fly back

revolsus *see* **revulsus**

revolūbil·is -e *adj* able to be rolled back; **non revolubilis** irrevocable (*fate*)

re·volvō -volvĕre -volvī -volūtum *vt* to roll back, unroll, unwind; to retravel (*a road*); to unroll, read over, read again (*a book*); to reexperience; to go over, think over; **revolvī** to revolve, come around again, recur, return

revŏm·ō -ĕre -ŭī *vt* to vomit forth again, disgorge

revor- = **rever-**

revorr·ō -ĕre *vt* to sweep back, scatter again

revulsus *pp of* **revello**

rex rēgis *m* king; (with bad connotations during the republican period) tyrant, dictator; patron; rich man; leader, king (*in children's game*); queen bee

Rhadamanth·us -ī *m* son of Jupiter, brother of Minos, and one of the three judges in the lower world

Rhaet·ī -ōrum *m pl* people of Raetia

Rhaeti·a -ae *f* Alpine country between Germany and Italy

rhapsōdi·a -ae *f* Homeric lay, selection from Homer

Rhe·a -ae *f* Cybele

Rhe·a Silvi·a -ae *f* daughter of Numitor and mother of Romulus and Remus

rhēd- = **raed-**

Rhēg·ium -iī or **-ī** *n* town on the toe of Italy

rhēn·ō -ōnis *m* fur

Rhēnān·us -a -um *adj* Rhenish

Rhēn·us -ī *m* Rhine

Rhēs·us -ī *m* Thracian king who fought as an ally of Troy

rhēt·or -ŏris *m* rhetorician, teacher of rhetoric; orator

rhētoric·a -ae or **rhētoric·ē -ēs** *f* rhetoric

rhētoric·a -ōrum *n pl* treatise on rhetoric

rhētoricē *adv* rhetorically, in an oratorical manner

rhētoric·us -a -um *adj* rhetorician's, rhetorical; **doctōres rhetorici** rhetoric professors; **libri rhetorici** rhetoric textbooks

rhīnocĕr·ōs -ōtis *m* rhinoceros; vessel made of a rhinoceros's tusk

rhō (*indecl*) *n* seventeenth letter of the Greek alphabet

Rhodān·us -ī *m* Rhone

Rhodiens·is -e or **Rhodi·us -a -um** *adj* Rhodian, of Rhodes; *m pl* Rhodians

Rhodŏp·ē -ēs *f* mountain range in Thrace

Rhodopēi·us -a -um *adj* Thracian

Rhod·os or **Rhod·us -ī** *f* Rhodes (*island off the coast of Asia Minor*)

Rhoetē·us -a -um *adj* Trojan;

Rhoeteus ductor Aeneas; *m* promontory on the Dardanelles near Troy; sea near the promontory of Rhoeteum

rhomb·us -ī *m* magic wheel; turbot (*fish*)

rhomphae·a -ae *f* long javelin

rhythmic·us -a -um *adj* rhythmical; *m* teacher of prose rhythm

rhythm·os or **rhythm·us -ī** *m* rhythm, symmetry

rīc·a -ae *f* veil (*worn by Roman women at sacrifices*)

rīcin·ium -iī or **-ī** *n* short mantle with a cowl

rict·um -ī *n* snout; wide-open mouth

rict·us -ūs *m* snout; wide-open mouth; **risū rictum dīducere** to break into a grin; *m pl* jaws, gaping jaws

rīdĕō rīdēre rīsī rīsum *vt* to laugh at, ridicule; to smile upon; *vi* to smile, laugh; (*with* *dat* or *ad* + *acc*) to smile to

rīdibund·us -a -um *adj* laughing

rīdiculāri·us -a -um *adj* laughable, funny; *n pl* jokes

rīdiculē *adv* jokingly, humorously; ridiculously, absurdly

rīdiculōs·us -a -um *adj* funny, amusing; ridiculous

rīdicul·us -a -um *adj* funny, amusing, laughable; ridiculous, silly; *m* joker, clown; *n* joke

rig·ens -entis *adj* stiff, rigid, unbending

rig·ĕō -ēre *vi* to be still, be numb, stiffen; to be rigid, stand on end, stand erect; to stand stiff, rise

rig·escō -escĕre -uī *vi* to grow stiff, become numbed, stiffen, harden; to stand on end

rigidē *adv* rigorously, severely

rigid·us -a -um *adj* rigid, stiff, hard, inflexible; stern, rigid, severe; rough, rude

rig·ō -āre *vt* to wet, moisten, water; to conduct, convey (*water*)

rig·or -ōris *m* stiffness; numbness, cold; hardness; sternness, severity

rigŭ·us -a -um *adj* irrigating, watering; irrigated, watered

rīm·a -ae *f* crack; **rīmas agere** to be cracked

rīm·or -ārī -ātus sum *vt* to lay open, tear open; to pry into, search, tear at, examine; to ransack; **naribus rimari** to sniff at

rīmōs·us -a -um *adj* full of cracks, leaky

ringor ringī rictus sum *vi* to open the mouth wide, to show the teeth; to snarl; (fig) to be snappy, snarl

rīp·a -ae *f* bank, shore

rīpŭl·a -ae *f* river bank

rīsc·us -ī *m* chest, trunk

rīsiōn·ēs -um *f pl* laughs

rīs·or -ōris *m* scoffer, teaser

rīs·us -ūs *m* laugh, smile, laughter; laughingstock; **risum continere** to keep back a laugh, keep from laughing; **risum movere** (*with* *dat*

of person) to make (*someone*) laugh; **rīsūs captāre** to try to make people laugh, try to get laughs

rīte *adv* according to religious usage; duly, justly, rightly, fitly; in the usual way, customarily

rīt·us -ūs *m* ceremony, rite; custom, habit, way, manner, style; **rītū** (*with genit*) in the manner of, like; **pecudum ritū** like cattle

rīvāl·is -is *m* one who uses the same stream, neighbor; one who uses the same mistress, rival

rīvālit·ās -ātis *f* rivalry in love

rīvŭl·us or **rīvŏl·us -ī** *m* brook, rivulet

rīv·us -ī *m* brook, stream

rix·a -ae *f* brawl, fight; quarrel, squabble

rix·or -ārī -ātus sum *vi* to brawl, come to blows, fight; to quarrel, squabble

rōbiginōs·us or **rūbiginōs·us -a -um** *adj* rusty; envious

rōbīg·ō -inis *f* rust; blight, mildew; film (*on teeth*), tartar

rōborĕ·us -a -um *adj* oak, of oak

rōbŏr·ō -āre *vt* to make strong, strengthen

rōb·ur or **rōb·us -ŏris** *n* hard wood; oak; prison (*at Rome, also called Tullianum*); objects made of hard wood: lance, club, bench; physical strength, power, vigor, toughness; vigor, strength, power, quality (*of mind*); best part, flower, choice, cream, élite; stronghold

rōbust·us -a -um *adj* hardwood; oak; robust, strong, firm, tough (*body*); firm, vigorous, solid (*character*)

rōd·ō rōdĕre rōsī rōsum *vt* to gnaw, gnaw at; to rust, corrode; to say nasty things about, slander, run down

rogāl·is -e *adj* of a pyre

rogāti·ō -ōnis *f* proposal, referendum, bill, resolution; request; (rhet) question; **rogationem ferre** to introduce a bill; **rogationem perferre** to pass a bill; **rogationem suadere** to back, push, speak in favor of a bill; **rogationi intercedere** to veto a bill

rogātiuncŭl·a -ae *f* inconsequential bill; little question

rogāt·or -ōris *m* proposer (*of a bill to the people*); poll clerk (*who collected and counted votes*); beggar

rogāt·us -ūs *m* request

rogitāti·ō -ōnis *f* proposal

rogit·ō -āre *vt* to keep asking, keep asking for

rog·ō -āre *vt* to ask, ask for, beg, request, solicit, question; to invite; to nominate for election; to bring forward for approval, introduce, propose (*bill or resolution*); (with double *acc*) to ask (*someone for something*), ask (*someone something*); **legem rogare** to introduce a bill; **milites sacramento rogare** to swear in soldiers; **senatorem sententiam rogare** to ask a senator for his opinion, ask a senator how he votes; **sententias rogare** to call the roll (*in the senate*); **populum rogare** to ask the people about a bill, to propose or introduce a bill; **primus sententiam rogari** to have the honor of being the first (*senator*) to be asked his view, be the first to vote

rog·us -ī *m* funeral pile, pyre; (*fig*) grave, destruction

Rōm·a -ae *f* Rome

Rōmān·us -a -um *adj* Roman; *m pl* Romans

Rōmulē·us -a -um *adj* of Romulus

Rōmulid·ae -ārum *m pl* descendants of Romulus, Romans

Rōmul·us -a -um *adj* of Romulus; *m* Romulus (*son of Rhea Silvia and Mars, twin brother of Remus, and founder as well as first king of Rome*)

rōrāri·ī -ōrum *m pl* skirmishers (*light-armed Roman troops who usually initiated an attack and then withdrew*)

rōrid·us -a -um *adj* dewy

rōrif·er -ĕra -ĕrum *adj* dew-bringing, dewy

rōr·ō -āre *vt* to drip, trickle, pour drop by drop; to moisten; *vi* to drop dew, scatter dew

rōs rōris *m* dew; moisture; water; teardrop; **rōs Arabus** perfume; **rōs marinus** or **rōs maris** rosemary; **rōres pluviī** rain drops; **rōres sanguineī** drops of blood

rōs·a -ae *f* rose; rose bush; rose bed; wreath of roses

rosār·ium -iī or **-ī** *n* rose garden

roscid·us -a -um *adj* dewy; moistened, sprayed

Rosc·ius -iī or **-ī** *m* L. Roscius Otho (*friend of Cicero, whose law in 67 B.C. reserved fourteen rows of seats in the theater for members of equestrian order*); Q. Roscius (*famous Roman actor and friend of Cicero, d. 62 B.C.*); Sextus Roscius (*of Ameria, defended by Cicero in a patricide trial in 80 B.C.*)

rosēt·um -ī *n* rose bed, rose garden

rose·us -a -um *adj* rosy, rose-colored; of roses

rosmarīn·um -ī *n* rosemary (*spice*)

rostrāt·us -a -um *adj* beaked; (ship) having a pointed bow; **columna rostrata** column adorned with the beaks of conquered vessels to commemorate a naval victory; **corona rostrata** navy medal (*awarded to the first man to board the enemy's ship*)

rostr·um -ī *n* bill, beak; snout, muzzle; curved bow (*of a ship*); *n pl* speaker's stand in the Roman Forum (*so called because it was adorned with the beaks of ships taken from the battle of Antium, 338 B.C.*)

rōsus *pp* of **rodo**

rot·a -ae *f* wheel; potter's wheel; torture wheel; disk; chariot, car

rot·ō -āre *vt* to turn, whirl about; **rotārī** to roll around; to revolve

rotŭl·a -ae *f* little wheel

rotundē *adv* smoothly, elegantly

rotund·ō -āre *vt* to make round, round off; to round out, complete

rotund·us -a -um *adj* rolling, revolving; round, circular, spherical; rounded, perfect; well-turned, smooth, polished, balanced (*style*)

rube·faciō -facĕre -fēcī -factum *vt* to make red, redden

rubell·us -a -um *adj* reddish

rub·ens -entis *adj* red; blushing

rub·ĕō -ēre *vi* to be red, be ruddy; to be bloody; to blush

rub·er -ra -rum *adj* red; ruddy

rub·escō -escĕre -ŭī *vi* to grow red, redden; to blush

rubēt·a -ae *f* toad

rubēt·a -ōrum *n pl* bramble bush

rubĕ·us -a -um *adj* bramble, of brambles

Rubic·ō -ōnis *m* small stream marking the boundary between Italy and Cisalpine Gaul

rubicundŭl·us -a -um *adj* reddish

rubicund·us -a -um *adj* red; ruddy

rubĭd·us -a -um *adj* reddish, red

rūbig- = robig-

rub·or -ōris *m* redness; blush; bashfulness, sense of shame; shame, disgrace

rubric·a -ae *f* red clay; red ochre; red chalk; rubric, law

rub·us -ī *m* bramble bush; blackberry bush; blackberry

ruct·ō -āre or **ruct·or -ārī -ātus sum** *vt & vi* to belch

ruct·us -ūs *m* belch, belching

rud·ens -entis *m* rope; *m pl* rigging

Rudi·ae -ārum *f pl* town in Calabria in S. Italy (*birthplace of Ennius*)

rudiār·ius -iī or **-ī** *m* retired gladiator

rudiment·um -ī *n* first attempt, beginning, commencement; **rudimentum adulescentiae ponere** to pass the novitiate; **rudimentum militare** basic training

Rudīn·us -a -um *adj* of Rudiae

rud·is -e *adj* in the natural state; raw, undeveloped, rough, wild, unformed; inexperienced, unskilled, ignorant, awkward, uncultured, uncivilized; (with *genit* or *abl*, with **ad** + *acc*, or with **in** + *abl*) inexperienced in, ignorant of, awkward at

rud·is -is f stick, rod; practice sword

rud·ō -ĕre -īvī -ītum *vi* to roar, bellow, bray; to creak

rūd·us -ĕris *n* crushed stone; rubble; rubbish; piece of brass or copper

rūfŭl·us -a -um *adj* reddish

Rūfŭl·ī -ōrum *m pl* military tribunes appointed by a general (*as opposed to military tribunes elected by the people*)

rūf·us -a -um *adj* red, reddish

rūg·a -ae *f* wrinkle

rūg·ō -āre *vi* to become wrinkled, become creased

rūgōs·us -a -um *adj* wrinkled, shriveled; corrugated

ruīn·a -ae *f* tumbling down, falling down, fall; collapse; debris, ruins; crash; catastrophe, disaster, destruction, defeat; wrecker, destroyer; **ruīnam dare** or **trahere** to fall with a crash

ruīnōs·us -a -um *adj* going to ruin, ruinous, ruined, tumbling, fallen

rum·ex -ǐcis *f* sorrel

rūmǐfǐc·ō -āre *vt* to report

Rūmǐn·a -ae *f* Roman goddess who was worshiped near the fig tree under which the she-wolf had suckled Romulus and Remus

Rūmǐnāl·is -e *adj* **fīcus Rūmǐnālis** fig tree of Romulus and Remus

rūmǐnātǐ·ō -ōnis *f* chewing of the cud; (fig) rumination

rūmǐn·ō -āre *vt* to chew again; *vi* to chew the cud

rūm·or -ōris *m* shouting, cheering, noise; rumor, hearsay; popular opinion, current opinion; reputation, fame; notoriety; calumny; **adverso rumore esse** to be in bad repute, be unpopular

rumpǐ·a -ae *f* long javelin

rumpō rumpěre rūpī ruptum *vt* to break, break down, break open; to burst, burst through; to tear, split; to force, make (*e.g.*, *a path*) by force; to break in on, interrupt, cut short; to break (*a law, treaty*); to break out in, utter (*complaints, etc.*)

rūmuscŭl·ī -ōrum *m pl* gossip

rūn·a -ae *f* dart

runc·ō -āre *vt* to weed, weed out

ru·ō -ěre -ī -tum *vt* to throw down, hurl to the ground; to level (*e.g.*, *sand dunes*); to destroy, overthrow, lay waste; to throw up, upturn, churn up; *vi* to fall hard, fall in ruins, totter; to run, dash, rush on, hurry; (of rain) to come pouring down; (of the sun) to set rapidly

rūp·ēs -is *f* cliff

rupt·or -ōris *m* breaker, violator

ruptus *pp* of rumpo

rūricŏl·a -ae *m* or *f* rustic, peasant, farmer; *m* ox

rūrigěn·a -ae *m* rustic, peasant, farmer

rūr·ō -āre *vi* to live in the country

rursus or rursum or rūsum *adv* back, backwards; on the contrary, on the other hand, in turn; again, back again, once more; **rursus rursusque** again and again

rūs rūris *n* the country, countryside, lands, fields; farm, estate; **rure redire** to return from the country; **ruri** or **rure vitam ageere** to live in the country; **rus ire** to go into the country; *n pl* countryside

rusc·um -ī *n* or **rusc·us -ī** *f* broom (*of twigs*)

russ·us -a -um *adj* red, russet

rusticān·us -a -um *adj* rustic, country, rural

rusticātǐ·ō -ōnis *f* country life

rusticē *adv* like a farmer; plainly, simply; unsophisticatedly, boorishly

rusticǐt·ās -ātis *f* simple country ways, rusticity; boorishness, coarseness

rustic·or -ārī -ātus sum *vi* to live in the country

rusticǔl·us -a -um *adj* somewhat coarse; *m* peasant

rustǐc·us -a -um *adj* of or in the country, country, rural; plain, simple, unspoiled, unsophisticated; coarse, boorish, rude; *m* farmer, peasant; *f* country girl

rūsum see rursus

rūt·a -ae *f* rue (*bitter herb*); bitterness, unpleasantness

rūt·a -ōrum *n pl* minerals; **ruta caesa** or **ruta et caesa** (law) everything mined or cut down on an estate, timber and minerals

rutǐl·ō -āre *vt* to make red, color red, dye red; *vi* to glow red

rutǐl·us -a -um *adj* red, reddish yellow; strawberry-blond

rutr·um -ī *n* spade

rutŭl·a -ae *f* a bit of rue

Rutŭl·ī -ōrum *m pl* ancient people of Latium whose capital was Ardea

rutus *pp* of ruo

S

Sab·a -ae *f* town in Arabia Felix, famous for its incense

Sabae·us -a -um *adj* Sabaean

Sabāz·ǐus -ǐī or -ī *m* Bacchus; *n pl* festival in honor of Bacchus

sabbǎt·a -ōrum *n pl* Sabbath

sabbatārǐ·ī -ōrum *m pl* Sabbath-keepers, Jews

Sabell·us -a -um *adj* Sabellian, Sabine; *m* Sabine (*i.e.*, *Horace*)

Sabīn·us -a -um *adj* & *mf* Sabine; *n* Sabine wine; Horace's Sabine estate

Sabrīn·a -ae *f* Severn River

saburr·a -ae *f* sand, ballast

saburr·ō -āre *vt* to ballast; (coll) to gorge with food

Sac·ae -ārum *m pl* Scythian tribe

saccipēr·ǐum -ǐī or -ī *n* purse pocket

sacc·ō -āre *vt* to filter, strain

saccŭl·us -ī *m* little bag; purse

sacc·us -ī *m* sack, bag; wallet; filter, strainer

sacell·um -ī *n* chapel

sac·er -ra -rum *adj* sacred, holy, consecrated; devoted to a deity for destruction, accursed; detestable; criminal, infamous; *n* see **sacrum**

sacerd·ōs -ōtis *m* priest; *f* priestess

sacerdōtāl·is -e *adj* sacerdotal

sacerdōt·ium -iī or **-ī** *n* priesthood

sacrāment·um -ī *n* guarantee, deposit (*sum of money which each of the parties to a law suit deposited and which was forfeited by the loser*); civil law suit; dispute; oath; voluntary oath of recruits; military oath; **eum obligare militiae sacramento** to swear him in; **jus-tis sacramentis contendere** to argue on equal terms; **omnes sacramento adigere** or **rogare** to swear in everyone; **sacramentum dicere** to sign up, swear in; **sacramentum dicere** (with *dat*) to swear allegiance to (*a general or emperor*)

sacrār·ium -iī or **-ī** *n* sacristy; shrine, chapel

sacrāt·us -a -um *adj* hallowed, consecrated, holy, sacred

sacrif·er -ĕra -ĕrum *adj* carrying sacred objects

sacrificāl·is -e *adj* sacrificial

sacrificāti·ō -ōnis *f* sacrifice, sacrificing

sacrific·ium -iī or **-ī** *n* sacrifice

sacrific·ō or **sacrufic·ō -āre** *vt & vi* to sacrifice

sacrificŭl·us -ī *m* sacrificing priest

sacrific·us -a -um *adj* sacrificial

sacrileg·ium -iī or **-ī** *n* sacrilege; temple robbing

sacrilĕg·us -a -um *adj* sacrilegious; profane, impious, wicked; *m* temple robber; wicked person; *f* impious woman

sacr·ō -āre *vt* to consecrate; to dedicate; to set apart, devote, give; to doom, curse; to hallow, declare inviolable; to hold sacred, worship; to immortalize

sacrōsanct·us -a -um *adj* sacred, inviolable, sacrosanct

sacruficō see **sacrificō**

sacr·um -ī *n* holy object, sacred vessel; holy place, temple, sanctuary; religious rite, act of worship, religious service, sacrifice; victim; *n pl* worship, religion; secret, mystery; **sacra facere** to sacrifice

saeclum see **saeculum**

saeculār·is or **sēculār·is -e** *adj* centennial

saecŭl·um or **sēcŭl·um** or **saecl·um -ī** *n* generation, lifetime; century; spirit of the age, fashion

saepe *adv* often

saepenumĕrō or **saepe numĕrō** *adv* very often, again and again, oftentimes

saep·ēs or **sēp·ēs -is** *f* hedge, fence, enclosure

saepiment·um or **sēpiment·um -ī** *n* hedge, fence, enclosure

saep·iō or **sēp·iō -īre -sī -tum** *vt* to fence in, hedge in, enclose; to surround, encircle; to guard, fortify, protect, strengthen

saept·um or **sept·um -ī** *n* fence, wall, enclosure; stake; sheepfold; voting booth; *n pl* enclosure; voting booths, polls

saet·a -ae or **sēt·a -ae** *f* stiff hair, bristle

saetig·er -ĕra -ĕrum *adj* bristly; *m* boar

saetōs·us -a -um *adj* bristly, hairy

saevē *adv* fiercely, savagely

saevidic·us -a -um *adj* spoken in anger, savage

saev·iō -īre -iī -ītum *vi* to be fierce, be savage, be furious; (*of persons*) to be brutal, be violent

saeviter *adv* savagely, ferociously, cruelly

saeviti·a -ae *f* rage, fierceness; brutality, savageness, barbarity (*of persons*)

saev·us -a -um *adj* raging, fierce, furious, cruel; brutal, savage, barbarous (*persons*)

sāg·a -ae *f* fortune-teller (*female*)

sagācit·ās -ātis *f* keenness; sagacity, keenness of perception, shrewdness

sagāciter *adv* keenly; shrewdly, accurately, acutely, sagaciously

sagāt·us -a -um *adj* wearing a military coat

sag·ax -ācis *adj* keen, sharp, acute; intellectually quick, sharp, shrewd; prophetic

sagīn·a -ae *f* stuffing, cramming, fattening up; food, rations; rich food; fattened animal; fatness (*from overeating*)

sagīn·ō -āre *vt* to fatten

sāg·iō -īre *vi* to perceive quickly, catch on quickly

sagitt·a -ae *f* arrow

Sagitt·a -ae *f* Sagitta (*constellation*)

sagittāri·us -a -um *adj* of or for an arrow; *m* archer, bowman

Sagittār·ius -iī or **-ī** *m* Sagittarius (*constellation*)

sagittif·er -ĕra -ĕrum *adj* arrow-bearing

Sagittipŏt·ens -entis *m* Sagittarius (*constellation*)

sagitt·ō -āre *vt* to shoot (*arrows*); *vi* to shoot arrows

sagm·en -inis *n* tuft of sacred herbs (*plucked in the Capitol by the consul or praetor and worn by the fetiales as a sign of inviolability*)

sagŭl·um -ī *n* short military coat (*esp. that of general officers*)

sag·um -ī *n* coarse mantle; military uniform; **ad sagum ire** or **sagum sumere** to get into uniform; **in sagis esse** to be in uniform, be in the armed forces

Saguntin·us -a -um *adj & m* Saguntine

Sagunt·um -ī *m* Saguntum (*city on the E. coast of Spain which Hannibal attacked and which thereby brought on the First Punic War*)

sāl salis *m* salt; salt water, sea water, sea; seasoning, flavor; good taste, elegance; pungency (*of words*), wit, humor; sarcasm; *m pl* witticisms, jokes, sarcastic remarks

salāc·ō -ōnis *m* braggart, show-off

salamandr·a -ae *f* salamander

Salaminī·us -a -um *adj* of Salamis; *m pl* people of Salamis

Salăm·īs -īnis *f* island in the Saronic gulf near Athens; city in Cyprus founded by Teucer

salapūt·ium -iī or **-ī** *n* midget

Salāri·a -ae *f* Via Salaria (*from the Porta Collina to the Sabine district*)

salāri·us -a -um *adj* salt, of salt; annona salaria revenue from salt mines; *m* salt-fish dealer; *n* salary, allowance; a meal

sal·ax -ācis *adj* lustful; salacious, provocative

salĕbr·a -ae *f* jolting; rut; harshness, roughness (*of speech*)

Saliār·is -e *adj* Salian, of the Salii; sumptuous

Saliăt·us -ūs *m* office of Salius, Salian priesthood

salict·um -ī *n* willow grove

salient·ēs -ium *f pl* springs, fountains

salign·us -a -um *adj* willow, of willow

Sali·ī -ōrum *m pl* college of twelve priests dedicated to Mars who went in solemn procession through Rome on the Kalends of March

salill·um -ī *n* small salt cellar

salīn·ae -ārum *f pl* salt pits, salt works; **salīnae Rōmānae** salt works at Ostia (*a state monopoly*)

salīn·um -ī *n* salt cellar

sal·iō -īre -uī or **-iī -tum** *vi* to jump, leap, bound, hop

Salisubsul·ī -ōrum *m pl* dancing priests of Mars

saliunc·a -ae *f* wild nard (*aromatic plant*)

salīv·a -ae *f* saliva; taste, flavor

salīv·ō -āre -ōis *f* willow tree

Sallust·ius -iī or **-ī** *m* Sallust (*C. Sallustius Crispus, a Roman historian, 86-35 B.C.*)

Salmăc·is -idis *f* fountain in Caria which made all who drank from it soft and effeminate

Salmōn·eus -eos *m* son of Aeolus and brother of Sisyphus who imitated lightning and was thrown by Jupiter into Tartarus

Salmōn·is -idis *f* Tyro (*daughter of Salmoneus*)

salsāment·um -ī *n* salted or pickled fish; brine

salsē *adv* facetiously, humorously

Salsipŏt·ens -entis *adj* ruling the sea

sals·us -a -um *adj* salted; briny, salty; facetious, humorous, sharp, witty; *n pl* salty food; witty remarks, satirical writings

saltāti·ō -ōnis *f* dancing, dance

saltăt·or -ōris *m* dancer

saltātōri·us -a -um *adj* dance, for dancing

saltātr·ix -īcis *f* dancing girl, dancer

saltăt·us -ūs *m* dance, religious dance

saltem *adv* at least, in any event, anyhow; **nōn saltem** not even

salt·ō -āre *vt & vi* to dance

saltuōs·us -a -um *adj* wooded, covered with forest

salt·us -ūs *m* wooded pasture, forest; upland; jungle; ravine; valley, glen; (coll) female organ; leap, leaping; **saltum dare** to leap

salūb·er (or **salūb·ris**) **-re** *adj* healthful, healthy, wholesome; (with *dat* or with ad + *acc*) healthful for, good for, beneficial to

salūbrit·ās -ātis *f* healthiness, wholesomeness; health, soundness

salūbriter *adv* healthfully; healthily; beneficially

sal·um -ī *n* seas, high seas

sal·ūs -ūtis *f* health; welfare; prosperity, safety; greeting, good wish, best regards; **salūtem dīcere** (abbreviated **s. d.**) to say hello, send greetings; (at the end of a letter) to say good-bye; **salūtem magnam dīcere** to send warm greetings; (at the end of a letter) to say good-bye; **salūtem plūrimam dīcere** (abbreviated **s.p.d.**) to send warmest greetings; (at the end of a letter) to give best regards

salūtār·is -e *adj* salutary, healthful, wholesome; beneficial, advantageous, useful; **ars salūtāris** art of healing; **salūtāris littera** vote of acquittal

salūtāriter *adv* beneficially, profitably, advantageously

salūtāti·ō -ōnis *f* greeting, salutation; formal morning reception or morning call at the house of an important person; callers; **ubi salūtātiō dēfluxit** when the morning callers have dispersed

salūtāt·or -ōris *m* or **salūtātr·ix -īcis** *f* morning caller

salūtif·er -era -erum *adj* health-giving

salūtigerul·us -a -um *adj* bringing greetings

salūt·ō -āre *vt* to greet, wish well, salute; to send greetings to; to visit, pay respects to, pay a morning call on; to pay reverence to (*gods*); to greet, welcome; (with double *acc*) to salute as, hail as, e.g., **aliquem imperātōrem salūtāre** to hail someone as a victorious general

salvē *adv* well; in good health; **satine salve?** (coll) everything O.K.?

salv·eō -ēre *vi* to be well, be in good

health; to be getting along well; **salve, salvete,** or **salveto!** hello!, good morning!, good day!; goodbye!; **te salvere jubeo** I bid you good day

salv·us or **salv·os -a -um** or **-om** *adj* well, sound, safe, unharmed, unscathed; living, alive; (with substantive in an *abl* absolute) without violation of, without breaking, e.g., **salvā lege** without breaking the law; **salvos sum** (coll) I'm all right, I'm O.K.

sambūc·a -ae *f* triangular stringed instrument, harp

sambūcin·a -ae *f* harpist (female)

sambūcistri·a -ae *f* harpist (female)

Sam·ē -ēs *f* ancient name of the island of Cephallenia

Sami·us -a -um *adj* of Samos; **Juno Samia** Juno worshiped at Samos; **vir Samius** Pythagoras

Samn·īs -ītis *adj* Samnite; *m* Samnite gladiator; *m pl* Samnites

Samn·ium -iī or **-ī** *n* district of central Italy

Sam·os or **Sam·us -ī** *f* island off the W. coast of Asia Minor, famous for temple to Juno and as the birthplace of Pythagoras

Samothrāc·ēs -um *m pl* Samothracians

Samothrāci·us -a -um *adj* Samothracian; *f* Samothrace (island in the N. Aegean)

sānābil·is -e *adj* curable

sānāti·ō -ōnis *f* healing, curing

sanciō sancīre sanxī sanctum *vt* to consecrate, hallow, make inviolable; to ratify; to condemn; (with *abl*) to forbid under penalty of

sanctē *adv* solemnly, reverently, religiously, conscientiously, purely

sanctimōni·a -ae *f* sanctity, sacredness; chastity

sancti·ō -ōnis *f* consecration, confirmation, sanctioning; penalty clause (that part of the law that provided for penalties against those breaking that law), sanction

sanctit·ās -ātis *f* sanctity, sacredness, inviolability; integrity, purity, chastity, holiness

sanctitūd·ō -inis *f* sanctity, sacredness

sanct·or -ōris *m* enactor (of laws)

sanct·us -a -um *adj* consecrated, hallowed, sacred, inviolable; venerable, august, divine; pure, holy, chaste, virtuous

sandaligerūl·ae -ārum *f pl* maids who brought their mistress's slippers

sandal·ium -iī or **-ī** *n* slipper, sandal

sandapil·a -ae *f* cheap coffin (for people of the lower classes)

sand·yx -ȳcis *f* vermilion

sānē *adv* reasonably, sanely, sensibly; certainly, doubtless, truly, very; (ironically) of course, naturally;

(with negatives) really, at all; (in concessions) to be sure, however; (in answers) yes, of course, to be sure; (with imperatives) then; (with **quam**) how very

sanguen see **sanguis**

sanguin·ans -antis *adj* bleeding; (fig) bloodthirsty, savage

sanguinārí·us -a -um *adj* bloodthirsty, savage

sanguiné·us -a -um *adj* bloody, bloodstained; bloodred

sanguinolent·us -a -um *adj* bloody, bloodstained; bloodred; sanguinary

sangu·is or **sangu·is -inis** *m* or **sangu·en -inis** *n* blood; blood, consanguinity, descent, family; descendant, offspring; slaughter, murder, bloodshed; forcefulness, life, vigor (of a speech); life, strength; **pugnatum plurimo sanguine** fought out in a real massacre; **sanguinem dare** to bleed; **sanguinem effundere** or **profundere** to bleed heavily; **sanguinem haurire** to shed (someone else's) blood; **sanguinem mittere** (of a physician) to let blood, bleed

saniēs (genit not found) *f* blood (from a wound); gore; foam, froth, slaver; venom

sānit·ās -ātis *f* health, sanity; common sense, discretion; solidity, healthy foundation (for victory, etc.); soundness, propriety (of style)

sann·a -ae *f* mocking grimace, face

sanni·ō -ōnis *m* one who makes faces, clown

sān·ō -āre *vt* to cure, heal; to correct, repair; to allay, quiet, relieve

Sanquāl·is -e *adj* of Sangus (Sabine deity); **Sanqualis avis** osprey (bird)

sān·us -a -um *adj* sound, hale, healthy; sane, rational, sensible; sober; (with **ab** + *abl*) free from (faults, vices)

sap·a -ae *f* new wine

sāperd·a -ae *m* a fish (from the Black Sea)

sapi·ens -entis *adj* wise, sensible, judicious, discreet; *m* sensible person; sage, philosopher; man of discriminating taste, connoisseur

sapienter *adv* wisely, sensibly, prudently

sapienti·a -ae *f* good taste, common sense, prudence, wisdom; science; philosophy

sap·iō -ĕre -īvī or **-iī** *vt* to have the flavor of, taste of; to have the smell of, smell like; to have knowledge of, understand; *vi* to have a sense of taste; to have sense, be sensible, be discreet, be wise; **sero sapiunt** they are wise too late

sāp·ō -ōnis *m* soap

sap·or -ōris *m* taste, flavor; delicacy, dainty; elegance, refinement, sense of taste

Sapph·ō -ūs *f* celebrated Greek lyric poetess of Lesbos

sarcin·a -ae *f* package, bundle, pack; burden (*of the womb*); sorrow, trouble; *f pl* luggage, gear

sarcinári·us -a -um *adj* pack, of luggage; **jumenta sarcinaria** pack animals

sarcinát·or -óris *m* patcher, botcher

sarcinát·us -a -um *adj* loaded down, burdened

sarcinúl·ae -árum *f pl* small bundles, little trousseau

sarció sarcíre sarsí sartum *vt* to patch, fix, repair

sarcophág·us -í *m* sarcophagus, tomb

sarcúl·um -í *n* light hoe, garden hoe

Sard·és or **Sard·is -ium** *f pl* Sardis (*capital of Lydia*)

Sardián·us -a -um *adj* Sardian

Sardíni·a -ae *f* Sardinia

Sardiniens·is -e *adj* Sardinian

Sardis see **Sardes**

sardón·yx -ýchis *m* sardonyx (*precious stone*)

Sardó·us or **Sard·us -a -um** *adj* & *m* Sardianian

sarg·us -í *m* bream (*fish*)

sar·ió or **sarr·ió -íre -íví** or **-úí** *vt* to hoe, weed

saris·a -ae *f* long Macedonian lance

sarisophór·os -í *m* Macedonian lancer

sarit·or or **sart·or -óris** *m* hoer, weeder

Sarmát·ae -árum *m pl* Sarmatians (*barbarous people of S.E. Russia*)

Sarmáti·a -ae *f* Sarmatia

Sarmátic·us -a -um *adj* Sarmatian

sarm·en -ínis or **sarment·um -í** *n* brushwood; *n pl* twigs, fagots

Sarpéd·on -ónis *m* king of Lycia who was killed by Patroclus at Troy

Sarr·a -ae *f* Tyre

sarrác·um or **serrác·um -í** *n* cart

Sarrán·us -a -um *adj* Tyrian

sarrió see **sario**

sartág·ó -ínis *f* frying pan

sartor see **saritor**

sart·us -a -um *pp* of **sarcio**; *adj* (*occurring only with* **tectus**) in good repair; **aedem Castoris sartam tectam tradere** to hand over the temple of Castor in good repair; *n pl* repairs; **sarta tecta exigere** to complete the repairs

sat (indecl) *adj* enough, sufficient, adequate; *n* enough; **sat agere** (with *genit*) to have enough of, have the hands full with

sat *adv* sufficiently, quite; **sat scio** I am quite sure

sat·a -ae *f* daughter

sat·a -órum *n pl* crops

satág·ó -ére *vi* to have trouble enough, have one's hands full

satell·es -itis *m* or *f* attendant, follower; partisan; accomplice

sati·ás -átis *f* sufficiency; overabundance, satiety, satisfied desire

satiét·ás -atis *f* sufficiency, adequacy; satiety, weariness, disgust

satin' or **satine** *adv* quite, really

sati·ó -áre *vt* to satisfy, appease; to fill, glut; to saturate; to cloy

sati·ó -ónis *f* sowing, planting; *f pl* sown fields

satis (indecl) *adj* enough, sufficient, adequate; *n* enough; (law) satisfaction, security, guarantee; **satis accipere** to accept a guarantee; **satis dare** (with *dat*) to give a guarantee to; **satis facere** (with *dat*) to satisfy; to pay (*a creditor*); to make amends to (*by word or deed*), apologize to; **satis facere** (with *dat* of person and *acc* & *inf*) to satisfy (*someone*) with proof that, demonstrate sufficiently to (*someone*) that; **satis superque dictum est** more than enough has been said

satis *adv* enough, sufficiently, adequately, fully; **satis bene** pretty well

satisdati·ó -ónis *f* putting up bail, giving a guarantee

satisfacti·ó -ónis *f* amends, satisfaction, apology

satius (*comp of* **satis**) *adj* **satius est** (with *inf*) it is better or preferable

sat·or -óris *m* sower, planter; father; promoter, author

satrapé·a or **satrapí·a -ae** *f* satrapy (*office or province of a satrap*)

satráp·és -is *m* satrap (*governor of a province of the Persian empire*)

sat·ur -úra -úrum *adj* full, well fed, stuffed; plump; rich, fertile; rich, deep (*colors*); *f* mixture, hotchpotch; medley; satire, satirical poem; **per saturam** at random, pell-mell

saturei·a -órum *n pl* savory (*aromatic herb used as seasoning*)

saturit·ás -átis *f* satiety; plenty, overabundance

Sáturnáli·a -órum *n pl* festival in honor of Saturn, beginning on the 17th of December and lasting several days

Saturni·a -ae *f* Juno (*daughter of Saturn*)

Saturnin·us -í *m* L. Appuleius Saturninus (*demagogic tribune in 103 B.C. and 100 B.C.*)

Sáturni·us -a -um *adj* Saturnian; **Saturnius numerus** Saturnian meter (*archaic Latin meter based on stress accent*); *m* Jupiter; Pluto

Sáturn·us -í *m* Saturn (*Italic god of agriculture, equated with the Greek god Cronos, ruler of the Golden Age, and father of Jupiter, Neptune, Juno, and Pluto*)

satur·ó -áre *vt* to fill, satisfy, glut, cloy, saturate; to satisfy, content

sat·us -a -um *pp* of **sero**; *m* son; *f* see **sata**; *n pl* see **sata**

sat·us -ús *m* sowing, planting; begetting; race, stock; seed (*of knowledge*)

satyrisc·us -í *m* little satyr

satyr·us -ī m satyr; satyr play (*Greek drama in which satyrs often formed the chorus*)

sauciātī·ō -ōnis f wounding

sauci·ō -āre vt to wound

sauci·us -a -um adj wounded; (fig) smitten, offended, hurt; melted (*snow*)

Sauromāt·ae -ārum m pl Sarmatians (*barbaric tribe of S. Russia*)

sāviātī·ō or **suāviātī·ō -ōnis** f kissing

sāviōl·um or **suāviōl·um -ī** n little kiss

sāvi·or -ārī -ātus sum vt to kiss

sāv·ium or **suāv·ium -iī** or **-ī** n puckered lips; kiss

saxātil·is -e adj rock, living among rocks; m saxatile (*fish*)

saxēt·um -ī n rocky place

saxē·us -a -um adj rocky, stony; **umbra saxea** shade of the rocks

saxific·us -a -um adj petrifying, changing objects into stone

saxōs·us -a -um adj rocky, stony

saxul·um -ī n small rock, little crag

sax·um -ī n bolder, rock; Tarpeian Cliff (*W. side of the Capitoline Hill*)

scabellum see **scabillum**

scab·er -ra -rum adj itchy; rough, scurfy

scab·iēs (*genit not found*) f itch; roughness, scurf; (fig) itch

scabill·um or **scabell·um -ī** n stool, footstool; castanet tied to the foot

scabiōs·us -a -um adj itchy, mangy; moldy

scab·ō -ĕre -ī vt to scratch

Scae·a port·a -ae f Scaean gate (*W. gate of Troy*)

scaen·a or **scēn·a -ae** f stage setting, stage; scene; (fig) public view, publicity; pretense, pretext; **tibi scenae serviendum est** you must keep yourself in the limelight

scaenāl·is or **scēnāl·is -e** adj theatrical, scenic

scaenic·us or **scēnic·us -a -um** adj of the stage, theatrical, scenic; m actor

Scaevŏl·a -ae m C. Mucius Scaevola (*Roman hero who infiltrated into Porsenna's camp to kill Porsenna, and, on being discovered, burned off his own right hand*)

scaev·us -a -um adj left, on the left; perverse; f sign or omen appearing on the left

scāl·ae -ārum f pl ladder, flight of steps, stairs

scalm·us -ī m oarlock; oar; boat

scalpell·um -ī n scalpel

scalp·ō -ĕre -sī -tum vt to carve; to scratch; to tickle

scalpr·um -ī n chisel; knife; penknife

scalpurr·iō -īre vi to scratch

Scamand·er -rī m river at Troy, also called Xanthus

scammōnĕ·a -ae f scammony (*plant*)

scamn·um -ī n bench, stool; throne

scandō scandĕre scandī scansum vt & vi to climb, mount, ascend

scandŭl·a -ae f shingle (*for roof*)

scaph·a -ae f light boat, skiff

scaph·ium -iī or **-ī** n boat-shaped drinking cup; chamber pot

scapŭl·ae -ārum f pl shoulder blades; shoulders, back

scāp·us -ī m shaft; yarn beam (*of a loom*)

scarif·ō -āre vt to scratch open

scar·us -ī m scar (*fish*)

scatēbr·a -ae f bubbling, gushing, jet

scat·ĕō -ēre or **scat·ō -ĕre** vi to bubble up, gush out, jet; to teem

scatūrigin·ēs or **scaturrigin·ēs -um** f pl springs

scaturr·iō -īre vi to bubble, gush; to bubble over with enthusiasm

scaur·us -a -um adj clubfooted

scaz·ōn -ōntis m scazon (*iambic trimeter with a spondee or trochee in the last foot*)

scelerātē adv criminally, wickedly

scelerāt·us -a -um adj profaned, desecrated; outlawed; criminal, wicked, infamous; m villain, criminal

scelĕr·ō -āre vt to pollute, desecrate

scelerōs·us -a -um adj full of wickedness, vicious

scel·us -ĕris n wicked deed, crime, wickedness; calamity; scoundrel, criminal

scēn- = **scaen-**

sceptrif·er -ĕra -ĕrum adj sceptered

sceptr·um -ī n scepter; kingship, dominion, authority; kingdom

sceptŭch·us -ī m scepter-bearer (*high officer of state in the East*)

sched·a or **scid·a -ae** f sheet, page

schēm·a -ae f figure, form, style; figure of speech

Schoenē·is -ĭdis f Atalanta

Schoenē·us -a -um adj of Schoeneus; f Atalanta

Schoen·eus -ĕī m king of Boeotia and father of Atalanta

schoenobāt·ēs -ae m ropewalker

schol·a -ae f learned debate, dissertation, lecture; school; sect, followers

scholastic·us -a -um adj school, scholastic; m rhetoric teacher, rhetorician

scida see **scheda**

sci·ens -entis adj having knowledge; having full knowledge, with one's eyes open; (with genit) having knowledge of, familiar or acquainted with, expert in; (with inf) knowing how to

scienter adv wisely, expertly

scienti·a -ae f knowledge, skill

scīlicet adv of course, evidently, certainly; (ironically) naturally, of course, to be sure; (as an explanatory particle) namely, that is to say, in other words

scill·a or **squill·a -ae** *f* shrimp

scīn = scisne, i.e., **scis + ne**

scindō scindĕre scidī scissum *vt* to cut, split, tear apart or open; to divide, separate; to interrupt

scindŭla see **scandula**

scintill·a -ae *f* spark

scintill·ō -āre *vi* to sparkle, flash

scintillŭl·a -ae *f* little spark

sciō scīre scīvī or **scii scītum** *vt* to know; to realize, understand; to have skill in; (with *inf*) to know how to

Scīpiăd·ēs -ae *m* a Scipio, one of the Scipio family

Scīpi·ō -ōnis *m* famous family in the gens Cornelia; P. Cornelius Scipio Africanus Major (*conqueror of the Carthaginians in the Second Punic War*, 236-184 B.C.); P. Cornelius Scipio Aemilianus Africanus Minor (*conqueror of the Carthaginians in the Third Punic War*, c. 185-132 B.C.)

scirpĕ·us or **sirpĕ·us -a -um** *adj* wicker, of wicker; *f* wickerwork

scirpicŭl·a -ae *f* wicker basket

scirpicŭl·us -ī *m* wicker basket

scirp·us or **sirp·us -ī** *m* bulrush

sciscĭt·ō -āre or **sciscĭt·or -ārī -ātus sum** *vt* to ask, question, interrogate; to consult; (with *acc* of thing asked about and **ex** or **ab + abl** of person) to ask (*something*) of (*someone*), check on (*something*) with (*someone*); *vi* (with **de + abl**) to ask about

sciscō sciscĕre scīvī scītum *vt* (pol) to approve, adopt, enact, decree; to learn, ascertain

sciss·us -a -um *pp* of **scindo**; *adj* split, rent; furrowed (*cheeks*); shrill, harsh (*voice*)

scītāment·a -ōrum *n pl* dainties, delicacies

scītē *adv* expertly

scīt·or -ārī -ātus sum *vt* to ask; to consult (*oracle*); (with *acc* of thing and **ab** or **ex + abl**) to ask (*something*) of (*someone*); *vi* (with **de + abl**) to ask or inquire about

scītŭl·us -a -um *adj* neat, trim, smart

scīt·um -ī *n* statute, decree

scīt·us -a -um *adj* experienced, skillful; suitable, proper; judicious, sensible, witty (*words*); smart, sharp (*appearance*); (with *genit*) skilled in, expert at

scīt·us -ūs *m* decree, enactment

sciūr·us -ī *m* squirrel

scob·is -is *f* sawdust, scrapings, filings

scomb·er -rī *m* mackerel

scōp·ae -ārum *f pl* twigs, shoots; broom

Scop·ās -ae *m* famous Greek sculptor of Paros (*4th cent*. B.C.)

scopulōs·us -a -um *adj* rocky, craggy

scopŭl·us -ī *m* rock, cliff, crag; promontory

scorpi·ō -ōnis or **scorp·ius** or **scorp·ios -iī** or **-ī** *m* scorpion; (mil) artillery piece, catapult

Scorpi·ō -ōnis *m* Scorpion (*sign of the zodiac*)

scortāt·or -ōris *m* fornicator, lecher

scortĕ·us -a -um *adj* leather, of leather

scort·or -ārī -ātus sum *vi* to associate with prostitutes

scort·um -ī *n* prostitute; sex fiend

screāt·or -ōris *m* one who clears his throat noisily, hawker

screāt·us -ūs *m* clearing the throat, hawking

scre·ō -āre *vi* to clear the throat, hawk, hem

scrīb·a -ae *m* clerk, secretary

scriblīt·a -ae *f* tart

scrībō scrībĕre scrīpsī scrīptum *vt* to write, draw; to write down; to write out, compose, produce; to enlist (*soldiers*); (with double *acc*) to appoint (*someone*) as

scrīn·ium -iī or **-ī** *n* bookcase, letter case, portfolio

scrīpti·ō -ōnis *f* writing, composition, authorship; wording, text

scrīptĭt·ō -āre *vt* to keep writing, write regularly

scrīpt·or -ōris *m* writer; scribe, secretary; composer, author; **rerum scriptor** historian

scrīptŭl·a -ōrum *n pl* lines on a game board

scrīptūr·a -ae *f* writing; composing; a writing, written work; tax paid on public pastures; testamentary provision

scrīpt·us -a -um *pp* of **scribo**; *n* written composition, treatise, work, book; literal meaning, letter; **orationem de scripto dicere** to read off a speech; **scriptum legis** or **scriptum** written ordinance, law

scrīpŭl·um or **scrŭpŭl·um -ī** *n* small weight, smallest measure of weight, scruple (*one twenty fourth of an uncia*)

scrob·is -is *m* ditch, trench; grave

scrōf·a -ae *f* breeding sow

scrōfĭpasc·us -ī *m* swine keeper, pig breeder

scrŭpĕ·us -a -um *adj* stony, rugged, jagged, rough

scrŭpōs·us -a -um *adj* full of sharp stones, rugged, jagged, rough

scrŭpŭlōsē *adv* precisely, carefully

scrŭpŭlōs·us -a -um *adj* rough, rugged, jagged; precise, careful

scrŭpŭlum see **scripulum**

scrŭpŭl·us -ī *m* small sharp pebble; uneasy feeling, scruple

scrŭp·us -ī *m* rough or sharp stone; uneasiness

scrūt·a -ōrum *n pl* trash, junk

scrūtāt·or -ōris *m* examiner

scrūt·or -ārī -ātus sum *vt* to scrutinize, examine

sculp·ō -ĕre -sī -tum *vt* to carve, chisel, engrave

sculpōnĕ·ae -ārum f pl clogs

sculptĭl·is -e adj carved, engraved

sculpt·or -ōris m sculptor

sculptūr·a -ae f carving; sculpture

sculptus pp of **sculpo**

scurr·a -ae m jester, comedian; man-about-town

scurrĭl·is -e adj scurrilous

scurrīlĭt·ās -ātis f scurrility

scurrīlĭter adv jeeringly

scurr·or -ārī -ātus sum vi to clown around

scūtāl·e -is n thong of a sling

scūtăr·ĭus -ĭī or **-ī** m shield maker

scūtāt·us -a -um adj carrying a shield; m pl troops armed with shields

scutell·a -ae f saucer, shallow bowl

scutĭc·a -ae f whip

scūtĭgerŭl·us -ī m shield bearer

scutr·a -ae f pan, flat dish

scutŭl·a or **scytāl·a** or **scytāl·ē -ae** f platter; eye patch; wooden cylinder; secret letter

scutulāt·us -a -um adj diamond-shaped; n pl checkered clothing

scūtŭl·um -ī n small shield

scūt·um -ī n oblong shield; (fig) shield, defense, protection

Scyll·a -ae f dangerous rock on the Italian side of Straits of Messina, said to have been the daughter of Phorcus and transformed by Circe into a sea monster with howling dogs about her midriff; daughter of Nisus who betrayed her father by cutting off his purple lock of hair

Scyllae·us -a -um adj Scyllan

scymn·us -ī m cub, whelp

scyph·us -ī m goblet, cup

Scyr·os or **Scyr·us -ī** f island off Euboea

scytăl·a see **scutula**

scytălē see **scutula**

Scyth·a or **Scyth·ēs -ae** m Scythian; m pl Scythians (general name for the nomadic tribes of the section of Europe and Asia beyond the Black Sea)

Scythĭ·a -ae f Scythia

Scythĭc·us -a -um adj Scythian

Scyth·is -ĭdis f Scythian woman

sē or **sēsē** (genit: **suī**; dat: **sibī** or **sibi**; abl **sē** or **sēsē**) pron acc (reflex) himself, herself, itself, themselves; one another; **ad sē** or **apud sē** at home; **apud sē** in one's senses; **inter sē** one another, mutually

sēb·um -ī n tallow, grease

sē·cēdō -cēdĕre -cessī -cessum vi to go apart, go aside, withdraw; to rebel

sē·cernō -cernĕre -crēvī -crētum vt to separate; to dissociate; to distinguish; to reject, set aside

sēcessĭ·ō -ōnis f withdrawal; secession

sēcess·us -ūs m retirement, retreat; isolated spot

sē·clūdō -clūdĕre -clūsī -clūsum

vt to shut off, shut up; to seclude, bar; to hide

sec·ō -āre -ŭī -tum vt to cut, cut off, reap, carve; (in surgery) to cut out, excise, cut off, amputate; to scratch, tear, wound, injure; to cut through, traverse; to cut short, settle, decide; to follow, chase

sēcordĭa see **socordia**

sēcrētĭ·ō -ōnis f dividing, separating

sēcrētō adv separately, apart; secretly; in private

sēcrēt·us -a -um pp of **secerno**; separate; isolated, solitary; secret; (with genit or abl) deprived of, in need of; n secret, mystery; private conversation or interview; isolated place, solitude

sect·a -ae f path; way, method, course; school of thought; political party

sectārĭ·us -a -um adj gelded; leading

sectāt·or -ōris m follower, adherent

sectĭl·is -e adj cut, divided

sectĭ·ō -ōnis f cutting; auctioning off of confiscated property; right to confiscated property; confiscated property

sect·or -ōris m cutter; buyer at a sale of confiscated property, speculator in confiscated estates

sect·or -ārī -ātus sum vt to keep following, follow eagerly, run after, keep trailing after; to chase, hunt

sectūr·a -ae f digging, excavation; f pl diggings, mines

sectus pp of **seco**

sēcubĭt·us -ūs m sleeping alone

sēcŭb·ō -āre -ŭī vi to lie alone, sleep by oneself; to live alone

sēcul- = saecul-

secund·a -ōrum n pl success, good fortune

secund·ae -ārum f pl secondary role (in a play); second fiddle

secundān·ī -ōrum m pl soldiers of the second legion

secundārĭ·us -a -um adj secondary, second-rate, inferior

secundō adv secondly

secund·ō -āre vt to favor, further, back, support

secundum adv after, behind; prep (with acc) (of space) beside, by, along; (of time) immediately after, after; (in rank) next to, after; (of agreement) according to, in compliance with; in favor of, to the advantage of

secund·us -a -um adj following; next, second (in time); backing, favorable, supporting; next, second (in rank); secondary, subordinate, inferior, second-string; **anno secundo** the next year; **a mensi fine secunda dies** the second-last day of the month; **in secundam aquam** with the current; **secunda mensa** dessert; **secundo flumine** downstream, with the current; **se-**

cundo lumine on the following
day; secundo mari with the tide;
secundo populo with the backing
of the people; secundus panis inferior bread, stale bread; secundus
ventus tail wind, fair wind; f pl
see secundae; n pl see secunda

sēcūrē adv securely, safely

sēcūricŭl·a -ae f hatchet

sēcūrĭf·er -ĕra -ĕrum adj carrying
an ax, ax-carrying

sēcūrĭg·er -ĕra -ĕrum adj ax-carrying

sēcūr·is -is f ax, hatchet; blow, mortal blow; power of life and death;
supreme authority, sovereignty

sēcūrĭt·ās -ātis f freedom from
care, unconcern, composure; freedom from danger, security, safety;
false sense of security; carelessness

sēcūr·us -a -um adj carefree; secure, safe; cheerful; careless; offhand

secus (indecl) n sex; secus mulie-
bre females; secus viriles males

secus adv otherwise, differently;
non secus ac or non secus
quam not otherwise than, just as,
exactly as; si secus accidet if it
turns out otherwise (than expected),
if it turns out badly

secūt·or -ōris m gladiator (who
fought against an opponent who
had a net)

secūtus pp of sequor

sed or set conj but; but also; but in
fact

sēdātē adv sedately, calmly

sēdātĭ·ō -ōnis f calming

sēdāt·us -a -um adj calm, composed

sēdĕcim (indecl) adj sixteen

sēdēcŭl·a -ae f little seat, low stool

sedentārĭ·us -a -um adj sedentary

sēdĕō sedēre sēdī sessum vi to sit,
remain sitting; (of magistrates,
esp. judges) to sit, preside, hold
court, be a judge; (of an army) to
remain encamped; to keep the field;
to settle down in blockade; to be
idle, be inactive; (of clothes) to fit;
(of places) to be low-lying; to sink,
settle; to be firm, be fixed, be established; to stick fast, be stuck; to be
determined, be firmly resolved

sēd·ēs -is f seat, chair, throne; residence, home; last home, burial
place; base, foundation, bottom

sedīl·e -is n seat, chair, bench, stool;
n pl seats in the theater; rowers'
benches

sēdĭtĭ·ō -ōnis f sedition, insurrection, mutiny; dissension, quarrel,
disagreement; warring (of elements, etc.)

sēdĭtĭōsē adv seditiously

sēdĭtĭōs·us -a -um adj seditious,
mutinous; quarrelsome; troubled,
disturbed

sēd·ō -āre vt to calm, settle, still,
allay

sē·dūcō -dūcĕre -dūxī -ductum
vt to lead aside, draw aside, lead

away, carry off; to put aside; to
separate, divide

sēductĭ·ō -ōnis f taking sides, siding

sēduct·us -a -um pp of seduco;
distant, remote

sēdŭlĭt·ās -ātis f application, earnestness; officiousness

sēdŭlō adv diligently; intentionally,
on purpose

sēdŭl·us -a -um adj diligent, busy;
officious

seg·es -ĕtis f grain field; crop

Segest·a -ae f town in N.W. Sicily

Segestān·us -a -um adj of Segesta;
m pl people of Segesta; n territory
of Segesta

segmentāt·us -a -um adj trimmed
with a flounce

segment·um -ī n trimming, flounce;
brocade

segnĭp·ēs -ĕdis adj slow-footed

segn·is -e adj slow, inactive; sluggish, lazy

segnĭter adv slowly, lazily

segnĭtĭ·a -ae or segnĭtĭ·ēs (genit
not found) f slowness, inactivity,
laziness

sēgrĕg·ō -āre vt to segregate, separate

sējugāt·us -a -um adj separated

sējŭg·is -is m six-horse chariot

sējunctim adv separately

sējunctĭ·ō -ōnis f separation, division

sē·jungō -jungĕre -junxī -junc-
tum vt to separate, disunite, part,
sever; (fig) to sever, part, disconnect; to distinguish

sēlectĭ·ō -ōnis f selection

sēlectus pp of seligo

Seleuc·us -ī m name of a line of
kings of Syria

sēlibr·a -ae f half pound

sē·ligō -ligĕre -lēgī -lectum vt to
pick out, select, choose

sell·a -ae f chair, stool; sedan; magistrate's chair

sellārĭŏl·us -a -um adj (place) for
sitting or lounging

sellār·ĭus -ĭī or -ī m lecherer

sellisternĭ·a -ōrum n pl sacred ban-
quets in honor of goddesses

selltĭ·a -ae f stool; sedan

sellulār·ĭus -ĭī or -ī m mechanic

sēmanĭmis see semianimis

semel adv once, one time; but once,
once for all; first, the first time;
once, ever, at some time, at any time

Semĕl·ē -ēs or Semĕl·a -ae f
daughter of Cadmus and mother of
Bacchus by Jupiter

Semelēi·us -a -um adj of Semele

sēm·en -ĭnis n seed, germ; seedling,
young plant, shoot; offspring; race,
stock; (in physics) particle; instigator, cause

sēmenstris see semestris

sēmentĭf·er -ĕra -ĕrum adj seed-
bearing, fruitful

sēmentĭn·us -a -um adj of the sowing season

sēment·is -is *f* sowing, planting; young crops

sēmentīv·us -a -um *adj* at seed time, of the sowing season

sēmerm·is -e *adj* half-armed

sēmestr·is or **sēmenstr·is -e** *adj* for six months, half-yearly, semi-annual

sēmēs·us -a -um *adj* half-eaten

sēmet = emphatic form of **se**

sēmiadapert·us -a -um *adj* half-open

sēmianim·is -e or **sēmianim·us** or **sēmanim·us -a -um** *adj* half-dead

sēmiapert·us -a -um *adj* half-open

sēmib·ōs -ōvis *adj masc* half-ox; **semibos vir** Minotaur

sēmicăp·er -rī *adj masc* half-goat

sēmicremăt·us or **sēmicrēm·us -a -um** *adj* half-burned

sēmicubitāl·is -e *adj* half-cubit long

sēmidē·us -a -um *adj* semidivine; *m* demigod

sēmidoct·us -a -um *adj* half-educated

sēmierm·is -e or **sēmierm·us -a -um** *adj* half-armed

sēmiēs·us -a -um *adj* half-eaten

sēmifact·us -a -um *adj* half-finished

sēmif·er -ēra -ērum *adj* half-beast; half-savage; *m* centaur

sēmifult·us -a -um *adj* half-propped

sēmigermān·us -a -um *adj* half-German

sēmigrăv·is -e *adj* half-drunk

sēmigr·ŏ -āre *vi* to go away, depart

sēmihi·ans -antis *adj* half-open

sēmihŏm·ŏ -ĭnis *m* half man, half beast; subhuman

sēmihōr·a -ae *f* half hour

sēmilăc·er -ĕra -ĕrum *adj* half-mangled

sēmilaut·us -a -um *adj* half-washed

sēmilīb·er -ĕra -ĕrum *adj* half-free

sēmilix·a -ae *m* (term of reproach) sad sack

sēmimarīn·us -a -um *adj* semisubmerged (*in the sea*)

sēmim·ăs -ăris *adj* gelded, castrated; *m* hermaphrodite

sēmimortu·us -a -um *adj* half-dead

sēminār·ium -iī or **-ī** *n* nursery garden; (fig) breeding ground

sēminăt·or -ōris *m* originator, cause, source

sēminĕcis (*genit*; *nom* does not occur) *adj* half-killed, half-dead

sēmin·ĭum -iī or **-ī** *n* breeding; stock

sēmin·ŏ -āre *vt* to sow; to beget, procreate; to produce

sēminūd·us -a -um *adj* half-stripped; half-unarmed

sēmipăgăn·us -ī *m* little clown

sēmiplēn·us -a -um *adj* (garrison) at half strength

sēmiputāt·us -a -um *adj* half-pruned

Sēmīrăm·is -is or **-ĭdis** *f* famous queen of Assyria, the consort and successor of Ninus

Sēmīrami·us -a -um *adj* of Semiramis

sēmīrās·us -a -um *adj* half-shaven

sēmireduct·us -a -um *adj* bent back halfway

sēmirefect·us -a -um *adj* half-repaired

sēmirŭt·us -a -um *adj* half-ruined, half-demolished

sēm·is -issis *m* half; half an ace (*coin*); one half percent a month or six-percent per annum; **non semissis homo** man not worth a penny, worthless fellow

sēmisĕn·ex -is *m* elderly gent

sēmisepult·us -a -um *adj* half-buried

sēmisomn·is -e or **sēmisomn·us -a -um** *adj* half-asleep

sēmisupīn·us -a -um *adj* half-prone

sēmit·a -ae *f* path, lane

sēmitāl·is -a -um *adj* of byways

sēmitāri·us -a -um *adj* back-alley

sēmiustilăt·us or **sēmiustulăt·us -a -um** *adj* half-burned

sēmiv·ir -irī *adj* half-man, half-beast; unmanned; unmanly, effeminate; *m* half-man; eunuch

sēmivīv·us -a -um *adj* half-alive, half-dead

sēmŏd·ius -iī or **-ī** *m* half a peck

sēmōt·us -a -um *adj* remote, distant; *n pl* faraway places

sē-movĕŏ -movēre -mōvī -mōtum *vt* to move apart, separate, remove, put aside

semper *adv* always, ever; regularly, on each occasion

sempitern·us -a -um *adj* everlasting

Semprōnius see **Gracchus**

sēmunci·a -ae *f* half ounce (*one twenty-fourth of a Roman pound*); trifle

sēmunciāri·us -a -um *adj* half-ounce; **faenus semunciarium** interest at the rate of one twenty-fourth of the capital (*i.e., about five percent per annum*)

sēmust·us -a -um *adj* half-burned

senācŭl·um -ī *n* open-air meeting place of the senate in the Forum

sēnāriŏl·us -ī *m* trifling trimeter

sēnāri·us -a -um *adj* six-foot (*verse*); *m* iambic trimeter

senāt·or -ōris *m* senator

senātōri·us -a -um *adj* senatorial; in the senate; of a senator

senāt·us -ūs *m* senate; senate session; **senatūs consultum** decree of the senate

Senĕc·a -ae *m* L. Annaeus Seneca (*Stoic philosopher and instructor of Nero, 4 B.C.-65 A.D.*)

senect·us -a -um *adj* aged, old; *f* old age, senility

senect·ūs -ūtis *f* old age; old people

sen·eō -ēre vi to be old

sen·escō -escĕre -ŭi vi to grow old; to decline, become feeble, lose strength; to wane, draw to a close

sen·ex -is adj aged, old; m old man; f old woman

sēn·ī -ae -a adj six each, six in a group, six at a time; **sēnī dēni** sixteen each

senīl·is -e adj of old people, of an old man; aged; senile

sēni·ō -ōnis m a six (on dice)

seni·or -us (comp of **senex**) adj older, elder; more mature (years); m elderly person, an elder (over forty-five years of age)

sen·ium -ī or **-ī** n feebleness of age, decline, senility; decay; grief, trouble; gloom; crabbiness; old man

sens·a -ōrum n pl thoughts, sentiments, ideas

sensicul·us -ī m short sentence

sensif·er -ĕra -ĕrum adj producing sensation

sensil·is -e adj capable of sensation, sentient

sensim adv gropingly; tentatively; carefully, gradually, gently

sens·us -a -um pp of **sentio**; n pl see **sensa**

sens·us -ūs m sense faculty, capacity for feeling, sensation; feeling, emotion, sentiment; attitude, frame of mind, view; understanding, judgment, intelligence; meaning, intent, sense; sentence; **communes sensūs** commonplaces; universal human feelings

sententi·a -ae f opinion, view, judgment; purpose, intention; (law) sentence, verdict; (in the senate) motion, proposal, view; meaning, sense; sentence; maxim; **de sententia** (with genit) in accordance with the wishes of; **ex animi (mei) sententia** (in an oath) to the best of (my) knowledge and belief; **ex mea sententia** in my opinion, to my liking; **in sententiam alicujus pedibus ire** to vote in favor of someone's proposal; **sententia est** (with inf) I intend to; **sententiam dicere** (in the senate) to express a view; **sententiam pronuntiare** or **dicere** to pronounce or give the verdict

sententiŏl·a -ae f phrase; maxim

sententiōsē adv sententiously

sententiōs·us -a -um sententious, full of meaning

senticēt·um -ī n thorny bush

sentīn·a -ae f bilge water; cesspool; bilge; (fig) dregs, scum, rabble

sentiō sentīre sensī sensum vt to perceive with the senses, feel, hear, see, smell; to realize; to feel, observe, notice; to experience; to think, judge; vi (law) to vote, decide

sent·is -is m thorny bush, bramble, brier

sentisc·ō -ĕre vt to begin to realize;

to begin to observe, perceive

sent·us -a -um adj thorny; untidy (person)

seorsum or **seorsus** adv apart, separately; (with abl or ab + abl) apart from

sēparābil·is -e adj separable

sēparātim adv apart, separately

sēparāti·ō -ōnis f severing, separation

sēparātius adv less closely, more widely

sēparāt·us -a -um adj separate, distinct, different

sēpăr·ō -āre vt to separate, divide, part; to distinguish

sepelībil·is -e adj that may be buried

sepelĭō sepelīre sepelīvī or **sepeliī sepultum** vt to bury; (fig) to bury, overwhelm, ruin, destroy, suppress

sēpēs see **saepes**

sēpi·a -ae f cuttlefish

sēpimentum see **saepīmentum**

sēpiŏ see **saepio**

sēpiŏl·a -ae f little cuttlefish

sē·pōnō -pōnĕre -posŭī -positum vt to put aside; to separate, pick out, select; to assign, reserve; to remove, take away, exclude; to distinguish

sēposit·us -a -um adj remote, distant; select; distinct, private

seps sēpis m or f snake

sepse = emphatic sē

septem (indecl) adj seven

Septemb·er -ris adj & m September

septemdĕcim (indecl) adj seventeen

septemflŭ·us -a -um adj seven-mouthed (Nile)

septemgemin·us -a -um adj seven-fold

septempedāl·is -e adj seven-foot, seven-feet-high

septempl·ex -icis adj sevenfold

septemtriōnāl·ia -ium n pl northern regions, northern part

septemtriōnāl·is -e adj northern

septemtriōn·ēs or **septentriōn·ēs -um** m pl seven stars near the North Pole belonging to the Great Bear; the seven stars of the Little Bear; northern regions, the North; north wind

septemvirāl·is -e adj of the septemvirs, septemviral; m pl septemvirs

septemvirāt·us -ūs m septemvirate, office of the septemvirs

septemvir·ī -ōrum m pl septemvirs (board of seven officials)

septēnār·ius -iī or **-ī** m heptameter (verse of seven feet)

septendĕcim or **septemdĕcim** (indecl) adj seventeen

septēn·ī -ae -a adj seven each, seven in a group; **septeni dēni** seventeen each, seventeen in a group

septentr- = septemtr-

septiens or **septiēs** adv seven times

septimān·us -a -um *adj* of or on the seventh; *n pl* soldiers of the seventh legion

septimum *adv* for the seventh time

septim·us or **septum·us -a -um** *adj* seventh

septim·us decim·us -a -um *adj* seventeenth

septingentēsim·us -a -um *adj* seven hundredth

septingent·ī -ae -a *adj* seven hundred

septuāgēsim·us -a -um *adj* seventieth

septuāgintā (indecl) *adj* seventy

septuenn·is -e *adj* seven-year-old

septum see **saeptum**

septun·x -cis *m* seven ounces; seven twelfths

septus *pp* of **saepio**

sepulcrāl·is -e *adj* of a tomb, sepulchral, funeral

sepulcrēt·um -ī *n* grave, tomb

sepulcr·um -ī *n* grave, tomb

sepultūr·a -ae *f* burial

sepultus *pp* of **sepelio**

Sēquān·a -ae *m* Seine

sequ·ax -ācis *adj* following, pursuing; penetrating (*fumes*); eager

sequ·ens -entis *adj* next, following

sequest·er -ris (or **-ra**) **-re** *adj* intermediate; negotiating, mediating; **pace sequestrā** under the protection of a truce; *m* trustee; agent, mediator, go-between

sequius or **sētius** (*comp* of **secus**) *adv* less; worse, more unfavorably; **nihilo setius** or **nilo setius** nevertheless

sequor sequī secūtus sum *vt* to follow, escort, accompany, go with; to chase, pursue; to come after (*in time*); to go after, aim at; to head for (*a place*); *vi* to go after, follow, come next; (of words) to come naturally

ser·a -ae *f* bolt, bar (*of door*)

Serāp·is -is or **-idis** *m* Egyptian god of healing

serēnit·ās -ātis *f* fair weather; serenity; favorableness

serēn·ō -āre *vt* to make fair, clear up, brighten

serēn·us -a -um *adj* clear, bright, fair, cloudless; cheerful, serene; *n* clear sky, fair weather

Sēr·es -um *m pl* Chinese

seresc·ō -ēre *vi* to dry off

sēri·a -ae *f* large jar

sēri·a -ōrum *n pl* serious matters, serious business

Sēric·us -a -um *adj* Chinese; *n pl* silks

seri·ēs (*genit* not found) series, row, succession; train, sequence, order, connection; lineage

sēriō *adv* seriously, in all sincerity

sēri·us -a -um *adj* serious, earnest; *n* serious matter; seriousness, earnestness; *n pl* see **seria**

serm·ō -ōnis *m* conversation, talk; discussion, discourse; common talk;

rumor, gossip; language, diction; prose, everyday language

sermōcin·or -ārī -ātus sum *vi* to talk, converse

sermuncul·us -ī *m* small talk, chitchat

serō serĕre seruī sertum *vt* to join, connect; to entwine, wreathe; to compose, combine, contrive

serō serĕre -sēvī satum *vt* to sow, plant; (fig) to sow the seeds of

sērō *adv* late

serp·ens -entis *m* or *f* creeping thing, snake, serpent, dragon

Serp·ens -entis *m* Serpent, Draco (*constellation*)

serpentigen·a -ae *m* dragon offspring

serpentip·ēs -ĕdis *adj* dragonfooted

serperastr·a -ōrum *n pl* splints (*for straightening the crooked legs of children*); officer who keeps his soldiers in check

serpillum see **serpyllum**

serpō serpĕre serpsī serptum *vi* to creep, crawl; to move along slowly, spread slowly

serpyll·um or **serpill·um** or **serpull·um -ī** *n* wild thyme

serr·a -ae *f* saw

serrāt·us -a -um *adj* serrated, notched

serrul·a -ae *f* small saw

sert·a -ae *f* wreath

sert·a -ōrum *n pl* wreaths, festoons

Sertōr·ius -iī or **-ī** *m* general of Marius who held out in Spain against the partisans of Sulla until he was assassinated by Perperna (*c.* 122-72 B.C.)

sert·us -a -um *pp* of **sero** (to join); *f* see **serta**; *n pl* see **serta**

ser·um -ī *n* whey; serum

sēr·us -a -um *adj* late; too late; **anni sēri** ripe years; **ulmus sera** slow-growing elm; *n* late hour; **in serum rem trahere** to drag out the matter until late

serv·a -ae *f* slave (*female*)

servābil·is -e *adj* retrievable

serv·ans -antis *adj* keeping; (with *genit*) observant of

servāt·or -ōris *m* or **servātr·ix -īcis** *f* savior, preserver, deliverer

servil·is -e *adj* slave, servile

serviliter *adv* slavishly

serv·iō -īre -īvī or -iī -ītum *vi* to be a servant or slave; to be obedient; (of buildings, land) to be mortgaged; (with *dat*) **a** to be a slave to, be subservient to; **b** to serve; **c** to comply with, conform to, humor; **d** to be devoted to, work at; **e** to serve, be of use to

servit·ium -iī or **-ī** *n* slavery, servitude; slaves

servitūd·ō -inis *f* servitude, slavery

servit·ūs -ūtis *f* slavery; serfdom; slaves; property liability, easement

Serv·ius Tull·ius -iī or **-ī** *m* sixth king of Rome

serv·ō -āre vt to watch over, preserve, protect; to store, reserve; to keep, retain; to observe; to keep to, continue to dwell in

servŏl·a -ae f young slave girl

servŏlicŏl·a -ae f slave of a slave (female)

servŏl·us -ī m young slave

serv·us or serv·os -a -um adj slave, servant; mf slave, servant

sescēnār·is -e adj a year and a half old

sescēnāri·us -a -um adj six-hundred-man (cohort)

sescēn·ī -ae -a adj six hundred each, six hundred in a group

sescentēsim·us -a -um adj six hundredth

sescent·ī -ae -a adj six hundred

sescentiens or sescentiēs adv six hundred times

sēsē see se

sescunci·us -a -um adj inch and a half thick

sesěl·is -is f seseli (plant)

sesqui adv more by a half, one and a half times

sesqualt·er -ěra -ěrum adj one and a half

sesquihōr·a -ae f an hour and a half

sesquimod·ius -iī or -ī m peck and a half

sesquioctāv·us -a -um adj having a ratio of nine to eight

sesquiōp·us -ěris n day and a half's work

sesquipedāl·is -e adj foot and a half long or wide

sesquiplāg·a -ae f blow and a half

sesquipl·ex -ĭcis adj one and a half times as much

sesquiterti·us -a -um adj containing one and a third; having a ratio of four to three

sessĭbŭl·um -ī n chair, seat, easy chair

sessil·is -e adj for sitting on; (plants) growing close to the ground, low-growing

sessi·ō -ōnis f sitting; session; loafing

sessit·ō -āre vi to sit much, keep sitting, rest

sessiuncŭl·a -ae f small group, small circle

sess·or -ōris m spectator; resident

sestert·ium -iī or -ī n sesterce

sestert·ius -iī or -ī (genit pl: sestertium) (abbreviated HS) m sesterce (small silver coin, equal to one fourth of a denarius, i.e., about 8ç, and used as the ordinary Roman unit in accounting); centena milia sestertium 100,000 sesterces; deciens (i.e., deciens centena milia) sestertium 1,000,000 sesterces

Sest·os or Sest·us -ī f city on the Hellespont

sēt- = saet-

Sētĭ·a -ae f town in Latium famous for its wine

Sētīn·us -a -um adj Setine; n Setine wine

sētīus see sequius

seu conj or if; or; seu . . . seu whether . . . or

sevērē adv seriously; severely, austerely

sevērit·ās -ātis f severity, sternness, strictness

sevēritūd·ō -ĭnis f austerity

sevēr·us -a -um adj serious, grave; severe, strict, austere; ruthless, grim

sēvŏc·ō -āre vt to call aside, call away; to remove, withdraw, separate

sēv·um -ī n tallow, grease

sex (indecl) adj six

sexāgēnāri·us -a -um adj sixty-year-old

sexāgēn·ī -ae -a adj sixty each, sixty in a group

sexāgēsim·us -a -um adj sixtieth

sexāgiens or sexāgiēs adv sixty times

sexāgintā (indecl) adj sixty

sexangŭl·us -a -um adj hexagonal

sexcen- = sescen-

sexcēnāri·us -a -um adj six-hundred-man (cohort)

sexenn·is -e adj six-year-old, of six years; sexenni die in a six-year period

sexenn·ium -iī or -ī n six-year period, six years

sexiens or sexiēs adv six times

sexprīm·ī or sex prīm·ī -ōrum m pl six-member council (in provincial towns)

sextadecimān·ī -ōrum m pl soldiers of the sixteenth legion

sext·ans -antis m one sixth; small coin (one sixth of an ace); one sixth of a pint

sextār·ius -iī or -ī m pint

Sextil·is -e adj of or belonging to the sixth month of the old Roman year which was afterwards called August in honor of Augustus

sextŭl·a -ae f sixth of an ounce

sextum adv for the sixth time

sext·us -a -um adj sixth

sext·us decim·us -a -um adj sixteenth

sexungŭl·a -ae f six-clawed woman, rapacious woman

sex·us -ūs m sex

sī conj if, if only; quod sī but if; sī forte if perchance, in the hope that; sī minus if not

sibī see se

sībil·a -ōrum n pl hisses, hissing

sībil·ō -āre vt to hiss at; vi to hiss

sībil·us -a -um adj & m hissing

Sibyll·a or Sibull·a -ae f sibyl, prophetess

Sibyllīn·us -a -um adj sibylline

sīc adv thus, so, in this way; thus, as follows; in these circumstances; in such a way, to such a degree; (in assent) yes

Sicān·ī -ōrum *m pl* ancient people of Italy who migrated to Sicily

Sicāni·a -ae *f* Sicily

Sicān·is -idis *adj* Sicilian

Sicāni·us -a -um *adj* Sicilian; *f* see Sicania

Sicān·us -a -um *adj* Sicilian; *m pl* see Sicani

sicār·ius -iī or **-ī** *m* murderer, assassin; **inter sicarios accusare (defendere)** to prosecute (defend) on a murder charge

sicē *adv* firmly, solidly

siccit·ās -ātis *f* dryness; drought; firmness, solidity; dullness (*of style*)

sicc·ō -āre *vt* to dry, dry up, drain; to stanch, heal

siccocul·us -a -um *adj* dry-eyed

sicc·us -a -um *adj* dry; thirsty; sober; firm, solid (*body*); solid (*argument*); dry, insipid (*style*)

Sicil·a -ae *f* Sicily

sicilicissit·ō -āre *vi* to act like a Sicilian

sīcilicul·a -ae *f* sickle

Siciliens·is -e *adj* Sicilian

sīcine *adv* is this how . . . ?

sicŭbi *adv* if anywhere, wheresoever

sicŭl·a -ae *f* little dagger

Sicŭl·ī -ōrum *m pl* ancient Italian people who migrated to Sicily

sicunde *conj* if from some place, if from anywhere

sicut or **sicŭtī** *conj* as, just as; (in elliptical clauses) just as, like; (introducing a comparison) as it were, so to speak; (introducing an example) as, as for instance; (of condition) as, in the same condition as; as if, just as if; **sicut . . . ita although . . . yet**

Sicў·ōn -ōnis *f* town in the N. Peloponnesus

Sicyōni·us -a -um *adj* of Sicyon; *m pl* inhabitants of Sicyon

siderĕ·us -a -um *adj* starry; star-spangled; heavenly, divine

sīdō sīdĕre sīdī or **sēdī sessum** *vi* to sit down; to settle; (of birds) to alight, land; to sink; to settle down, subside; (of ships) to be grounded

Sīd·ōn -ōnis *f* city of Phoenicia

Sīdōn·is -idis *adj* Phoenician; *f* Dido; Europa

Sīdōni·us -a -um *adj* Sidonian, Phoenician; Theban; *m pl* Sidonians

sīd·us -ĕris *n* constellation; star, heavenly body; sky, heaven; light, glory, beauty, pride; season; climate, weather; (in astrology) star, destiny

Sigambr·ī -ōrum *m pl* powerful German tribe

Sigē·um -ī *n* promontory near Troy where Achilles was said to have been buried

Sigē·us -a -um *adj* Sigean

sigill·a -ōrum *n pl* figurines; seal (*on a seal ring*)

sigillāt·us -a -um *adj* adorned with little figures

signāt·or -ōris *m* sealer, signer; witness

signāt·us -a -um *adj* sealed, secured

signif·er -ĕra -ĕrum *adj* bearing the constellations, starry; *m* standard-bearer; chief, leader

signific·ans -antis *adj* clear, distinct, expressive

significanter *adv* clearly, graphically

significāti·ō -ōnis *f* signal, indication, sign, mark; expression of approval, applause; meaning, sense, signification; emphasis

signific·ō -āre *vt* to show, indicate, point out, express; to intimate; to notify, publish, make known; to portend; to mean, signify

sign·ō -āre *vt* to mark, stamp, impress, imprint; to seal, seal up; to coin; to point out, signify, indicate, express; to adorn, decorate; to distinguish, mark, note

sign·um -ī *n* sign, indication, proof; military standard, banner; password; cohort, maniple; omen, symptom; statue, picture; device on a seal, seal, signet; heavenly sign, constellation; **ab signis discedere** to break ranks, disband; **signa conferre** to engage in close combat; to concentrate troops; **signa constituere** to halt; **signa conversa ferre** to wheel around and attack; **signa ferre** to break camp; **signa movere** to advance; **signa movere in hostem** to advance against the enemy, attack the enemy; **signa proferre** to march forward, advance; **signa servare** to keep the order of battle; **signa sequi** to march in rank; **signa subsequi** to keep the order of battle; **signa transferre** to desert, join the other side; **signis collatis** in regular battle

sīlān·us -ī *m* jet of water

Sīlar·us -ī *m* river forming the boundary between Lucania and Campania

sil·ens -entis *adj* silent, calm, quiet; *mf pl* the dead

silent·ium -iī or **-ī** *n* silence; inactivity; **silentium facere** to obtain silence; to keep silence; **silentium significare** to call for silence

Sīlēn·us -ī *m* teacher and constant companion of Bacchus, usually drunk

sil·ĕō -ēre -uī *vt* to leave unmentioned, say nothing about; *vi* to be silent, be still; to keep silence; to be hushed; to rest, cease

sil·er -ĕris *n* willow

silesc·ō -ĕre *vi* to become silent, fall silent, become hushed

sil·ex -ĭcis *m* flint, flint stone; cliff, crag; hardheartedness

silicern·ium -iī or **-ī** *n* funeral feast; (coll) old fossil

silīg·ō -ĭnis *f* winter wheat; wheat flour

siliqu·a -ae *f* pod, husk; *f pl* pulse

sillyb·us -ī *m* label giving book's title

sil·ō -ōnis *m* (man) button nose, snub nose

silūr·us -ī *m* sheatfish

sil·us -a -um *adj* having a turned-up nose, snub-nosed

silv·a or silŭ·a -ae *f* woods, forest; shrubbery, bush, foliage, crop, growth; mass, abundance, quantity, material, supply

Silvān·us -ī *m* god of woods; *m pl* woodland gods

silvesc·ō -ēre *vi* (of a vine) to run wild

silvestr·is -e *adj* wooded, overgrown with woods; woodland, living in woods; wild, growing wild; rural, pastoral; *n pl* woodlands

silvicŏl·a -ae *m* or *f* denizen of the forest

silvicultr·ix -īcis *adj fem* living in the woods

silvifrāg·us -a -um *adj* forest-smashing (*wind*)

silvōs·us -a -um *adj* wooded, woody

sīmi·a -ae *f* ape

simil·is -e *adj* similar; (with *genit* or *dat*) resembling, like, similar to; homines inter se similes men resembling one another; veri similis probable; realistic; *n* comparison, parallel

similiter *adv* similarly; similiter atque or ac just as; similiter ut sī just as if

similitūd·ō -ĭnis *f* likeness, resemblance; imitation; analogy; comparison, simile; monotony; (with *genit*) similarity to; est homini cum deo similitudo there is a resemblance between a god and man

sīmiŏl·us -ī *m* monkey

simĭtū *adv* at the same time; (with cum + *abl*) together with

sīm·ĭus -iī or -ī *m* ape

Sīmŏ·īs -entis *m* river at Troy

Sīmōnĭd·ēs -is *m* famous lyric poet of Ceos (*fl* 500 B.C.); celebrated iambic poet of Amorgos (*7th cent.* B.C.)

simpl·ex -ĭcis *adj* single, simple, unmixed; plain, natural; frank; naive; in single file

simplicĭt·ās -ātis *f* simplicity; candor, frankness

simpliciter *adv* simply, plainly; candidly, frankly

simpl·us -a -um *adj* simple; *n* simple sum

simpŭl·um -ī *n* small ladle

simpuv·ĭum -iī or -ī *n* libation bowl

simul *adv* together, at the same time; likewise, also; (with *abl* or cum + *abl*) with, together with; simul atque or ac or et as soon as; simul . . . simul both . . . and; *conj* as soon as

simulācr·um -ī *n* image, likeness, representation; form, shape, phantom, ghost; conception; sign, emblem; mere shadow; portraiture, characterization

simulām·en -ĭnis *n* imitation, copy

simŭl·ans -antis *adj* imitating; (with *genit*) imitative of

simulātē *adv* insincerely, deceitfully

simulātĭ·ō -ōnis *f* faking, bluffing, bluff, pretense; simulatione (with *genit*) under the pretense of, under the guise of

simulāt·or -ōris *m* imitator; pretender, phoney

simŭl·ō -āre *vt* to imitate, copy, represent; to put on the appearance of, simulate

simult·ās -ātis *f* enmity, rivalry, feud, jealousy, grudge

sīmŭl·us -a -um *adj* rather snub-nosed

sīm·us -a -um *adj* snub-nosed, pug-nosed

sin *conj* if however, if on the other hand, but if

sināp·i -is *n* or sināp·is -is *f* mustard

sincērē *adv* sincerely, honestly, frankly

sincērĭt·ās -ātis *f* soundness, integrity

sincēr·us -a -um *adj* sound, whole, clean, untainted; real, genuine

sincĭp·ut -ĭtis or sincipitāment·um -ī *n* half a head; cheek, jowl (*of a hog*); brain

sind·ōn -ōnis *f* fine cotton or linen fabric, muslin

sine *prep* (with *abl*) without; flammā sine flameless

singillātim *adv* one by one, singly

singlāriter see singulāriter

singulār·is -e *adj* single, alone, one at a time; unique, unparalleled; *m pl* crack troops

singulāriter or singlāriter *adv* singly; particularly

singulāri·us -a -um *adj* single, separate

singulātim *adv* singly, individually

singŭl·ī -ae -a *adj* single, one at a time, individual; one each, one apiece; in singulos dies on each successive day; every day, daily; *m pl* individuals

singultim *adv* sobbingly, gaspingly; falteringly

singult·ĭō -īre *vi* to hiccup; to throb

singult·ō -āre *vt* to gasp out, spurt out; *vi* to sob, gasp; to gurgle

singult·us -ūs *m* sob, gasp; squirt (*of water, etc.*); death rattle

singŭl·us -a -um *adj* one by one, single; each one, one apiece

sinist·er -ra -rum *adj* left, on the left; (because in Roman augury the augur faced south, having the East on the left) favorable, auspicious, lucky; (because in Greek augury the augur faced north, having the East on his right) unfavorable, inauspicious, unlucky; wrong, perverse, improper; *m pl* soldiers on the left

flank; f left, left hand; left side; n
left side; **a sinistra** on the left

sinisterit·ās -ātis f awkwardness

sinistrē adv badly, wrongly, perversely

sinistrorsum or **sinistrorsus** adv to the left

sinō sinĕre sīvī or **sīī situm** vt to allow; **sine modo** only let, if only

Sin·ōn -ōnis m Greek soldier through whose treachery the Greeks were able to get the horse into Troy

Sinōp·a -ae or **Sinōp·ē -ēs** f Greek colony on the S. coast of the Euxine Sea

Sinuess·a -ae f city on the border between Latium and Campania

sin·um -ī n large drinking cup

sinu·ō -āre vt to wind, curve, arch

sinuōs·us -a -um adj winding, sinuous, serpentine

sin·us -ūs m curved or bent surface, indentation, curve, fold, hollow; fold of the toga about the breast; pocket, purse; breast, bosom, lap; bay, gulf, lagoon; winding coast; valley, hollow; heart (e.g., of a city), interior; intimacy; **in sinu meo est** he is dear to me

sīn·us -ī m large drinking cup

sipar·ium -lī or **-ī** n theater curtain; **post siparium** behind the scenes

siph·ō -ōnis m siphon; fire engine

siphuncul·us -ī m small pipe

Sipyl·us -ī m mountain in Lydia

siquandō or **sī quandō** conj if ever

siquidem conj if in fact

siremps or **sirempse = sī rem ipsam** adj the same, e.g., **sirempse legem** the same law

Sīr·ēn -ēnis f Siren (sea nymph who had the power of charming with her song)

Sīri·us -a -um adj of Sirius, of the Dog Star; m Sirius, Dog Star

sirp·e -is n silphium (plant)

sīr·us -ī m underground granary

sīs = sī vīs please, if you please

sistō sistĕre stitī statum vt to cause to stand, make stand, put, place, set; to set up (monument); to establish; to stop, check, arrest; to put an end to; to produce in court; **pedem sistere** or **gradum sistere** to halt, stop; **se sistere** to present oneself, appear, come; **sisti non potest** the crisis cannot be met, the case is hopeless; **vadimonium sistere** to answer bail, show up in court; vi to stand, rest; to stop, stay; to stand firm, last, endure; to show up in court; (with dat or **contra** + acc) to stand firm against

sistrāt·us -a -um adj with a tambourine

sistr·um -ī n rattle, tambourine

Sisyphid·ēs -ae m descendant of Sisyphus, i.e., Ulysses

Sīsyph·us -ī m son of Aeolus, king of Corinth, whose punishment in

Hades was to roll a rock repeatedly up a hill

sitell·a -ae f lottery urn

Sith·ōn -ōnis adj Thracian

Sithōn·is -idis or **Sīthonī·us -a -um** adj Thracian; m pl Thracians

siticulōs·us -a -um adj thirsty, dry

siti·ens -entis adj thirsting, thirsty; arid, parched; parching; (with genit) eager for

sitienter adv thirstily, eagerly

sit·iō -īre -īvī -ī vt to thirst for; vi to be thirsty

sit·is -is f thirst; (with genit) thirst for

sitit·or -ōris m thirsty person; **sititor aquae** thirster for water

sittybus see **sillybus**

sitŭl·a -ae f bucket

sit·us -a -um pp of **sino**; adj lying, situated; founded; (with **in** + abl) resting on, dependent on

sit·us -ūs m position, situation, site; structure; neglect; mustiness; dust, dirt; idleness, inactivity, lack of use

sīve conj or if; or; **sīve . . . sīve** whether . . . or

smaragd·us -ī m or f emerald

smar·is -idis f a small sea fish

smil·ax -ăcis f smilax, bindweed (plant)

Sminth·eus -ěī m epithet of Apollo

Smyrn·a -ae f town in Asia Minor

sobol- = subol-

sōbriē adv soberly, moderately; sensibly

sōbriet·ās -ātis f temperance (in drinking)

sōbrīn·a -ae f cousin (female, on the mother's side)

sōbrīn·us -ī m cousin (on the mother's side)

sōbri·us -a -um adj sober; temperate, continent; sensible, reasonable

soccŭl·us -ī m small or short sock

socc·us -ī m sock; slipper; low shoe worn by actors in comedies; comedy

soc·er or **soc·ĕrus -ĕrī** m father-in-law

soci·a -ae f associate, companion, ally, partner (female)

sociābil·is -e adj compatible, intimate

sociāl·is -e adj allied, confederate; nuptial, conjugal; companionable, sociable

sociāliter adv sociably, in comradeship

socienn·us -ī m comrade

societ·ās -ātis f companionship, fellowship; association, society, partnership, alliance, confederacy

soci·ō -āre vt to unite, associate; to share

sociofraud·us -ī m heel, double crosser

soci·us -a -um adj joint, allied, confederate; held in common, common; m associate, companion, ally, partner; f see **socia**

sōcordi·a or **sēcordi·a -ae** f silliness, stupidity; apathy, laziness

sŏcordĭus *adv* too apathetically

sŏc·ors -ordis *adj* silly, stupid; apathetic, lazy, inactive

Sŏcrăt·ēs -is *m* famous Athenian philosopher (469-399 B.C.)

Sŏcratic·ī -ōrum *m pl* Socratics, disciples of Socrates

socr·us -ūs *f* mother-in-law

sŏdālicĭ·us -a -um *adj* of companionship; *n* companionship, intimacy; society, secret society

sŏdāl·is -is *m or f* comrade, companion, fellow; member (*of a society, priestly college, etc.*); accomplice, conspirator; gallant

sŏdālit·ās -ātis *f* companionship, fellowship; society, club, association; secret society

sŏdālit- = sŏdālic-

sōdēs = sī audēs if you will, please

sōl sōlis *m* sun; sunlight, sunshine; day

sōlācĭŏl·um -ī *n* bit of comfort

sōlāc·ĭum -ī *or* **-ī** *n* comfort, relief

sōlām·en -ĭnis *n* comfort

sōlār·is -e *adj* sun; **lumen solare** sunlight, sunshine

sōlār·ĭum -ī *or* **-ī** *n* sundial; clock; sunny spot, balcony

sōlāt- = sōlac-

sōlāt·or -ōris *m* comforter

soldūr·ī -ōrum *m pl* retainers (*of a chieftain*)

soldus see **solidus**

sŏlĕ·a -ae *f* sole; sandal; fetter; sole (*flat fish*)

sŏleār·ĭus -ī *or* **-ī** *m* sandal maker

sŏleāt·us -a -um *adj* wearing sandals

sŏlĕō solēre solĭtus sum *vi* (with *inf*) to be in the habit of, usually, e.g., **solet cenare sero** he usually eats late; (with **cum** + *abl*) to have intercourse with

sŏlĭdē *adv* for certain; fully, wholly

sŏlĭdĭt·ās -ātis *f* solidity

sŏlĭd·ō -āre *vt* to make firm, make dense; to strengthen

sŏlĭd·us *or* **sŏldus -a -um** *adj* solid, firm, dense; whole, entire; genuine, real; trustworthy; firm, resolute; *n* entire sum, total; solid, solid body, mass, substance; solid earth

sōlĭferrĕ·um -ī *n* all-iron spear

sŏlĭstĭm·us -a -um *adj* perfect; **tripudium solistimum** perfectly auspicious omen

sōlĭtārĭ·us -a -um *adj* solitary, lonely

sōlĭtūd·ō -ĭnis *f* loneliness; deprivation; wilderness

sŏlĭt·us -a -um *adj* usual, customary, characteristic; *n* the usual, the customary; **formosior solito** more handsome than usual, unusually handsome; **magis solito** *or* **plus solito** more than usual

sŏl·ĭum -ī *or* **-ī** *n* seat, chair; throne; dominion, sway; bathtub; stone coffin, sarcophagus

sōlĭvăg·us -a -um *adj* roaming

alone; single, solitary

sollemn·is -e *adj* annual, periodic; religious, solemn; usual; *n* usage, practice; solemn rite, solemnity, ceremony, feast, sacrifice; festival, games (*in observance of Roman holy days*)

sollemnĭter *adv* solemnly, religiously

soll·ers -ertis *adj* skilled, skillful, expert, clever

sollerter *adv* skillfully, expertly, cleverly

sollertĭ·a -ae *f* skill, ingenuity, shrewdness; clever plan; (with *genit*) skill in

sollĭcĭtātĭ·ō -ōnis *f* vexation, anxiety; incitement, instigation

sollĭcĭtē *adv* anxiously, with solicitude; diligently

sollĭcĭt·ō -āre *vt* to shake, disturb; to disquiet, annoy, molest; to worry, make anxious; to provoke, tempt; to stir up, incite, incite to revolt

sollĭcĭtūd·ō -ĭnis *f* anxiety, uneasiness

sollĭcĭt·us -a -um *adj* stirred up, stormy (*sea*); tossed (*by the waves*); troubled, disturbed, disquieted, restless; anxious, solicitous, apprehensive, worried

sollif- = solif-

sollist- = solist-

soloecism·us -ī *m* grammatical mistake, solecism

Sol·ōn -ōnis *m* famous Athenian legislator (c. 640-c. 560 B.C.)

sōl·or -ārī -ātus sum *vt* to console, comfort; to relieve, mitigate (*fear, worry*)

sōlstĭtĭāl·is -e *adj* of the summer solstice; midsummer's; solar

sōlstĭt·ĭum -ī *or* **-ī** *n* summer solstice; midsummer, summer heat

sŏl·um -ī *n* bottom, ground, floor; soil, land, country; sole (*of foot or shoe*)

sōlum *adv* only, merely, barely; **non solum . . . sed etiam** not only . . . but also

sōl·us -a -um *adj* only, single, sole, alone; lonely, solitary

sŏlūtē *adv* loosely, freely, without hindrance; negligently; without vigor

sŏlūt·us -a -um *adj* loose, untied, unbandaged; negligent; free; fluent; unrhythmical; uncontrolled; exempt, free; unbiased; unbridled, loose

sŏlūtĭ·ō -ōnis *f* loosening; payment

sŏlvō solvĕre solvī *or* **solŭī solūtum** *vt* to loosen, untie; to free, release; to dissolve, break up; detach, disengage; to unlock, open; to melt, turn, change; to relax, smooth, soothe; to impair, weaken, destroy; to acquit, absolve; to accomplish, fulfill; to pay, pay off; to solve, explain; to suffer, undergo (*punishment*); to remove, get rid of (*feelings*); *vi* to weigh anchor, set sail

Sŏlўm·a -ōrum *n pl* Jerusalem

somniculōsē adv sleepily, drowsily

somniculōs-us -a -um adj sleepy, drowsy

somnif-er -ēra -ērum adj sleep-inducing, soporific; deadly (poison)

somni-ō -āre vt to dream of; to day-dream about, imagine; **somnium somniare** to have a dream

somn-ium -iī or **-ī** n dream; day-dreaming; nightmare

somn-us -ī m sleep; night; sleep of death; indolence

sonābil-is -e adj noisy

sonip-ēs -ĕdis adj loud-hoofed; m steed

sonit-us -ūs m sound, noise

sonivi-us -a -um adj noisy

son-ō -āre -uī -itum vt to speak, sound, express; to mean; to sound like; vi to sound, ring, resound, make a noise

son-or -ōris m sound, noise, clang

sonōr-us -a -um adj sonorous, loud, noisy, clanging

sons sontis adj guilty, criminal

sontic-us -a -um adj important

son-us -ī m sound, noise; tone (of style)

sophi-a -ae f wisdom

sophist-ēs -ae m sophist

Sophŏcl-ēs -is m famous Greek writer of tragedies (c. 495-406 B.C.)

Sophoclē-us -a -um adj Sophoclean, of Sophocles

soph-us -a -um adj wise; m wise man, sage

sōp-iō -īre -īvī or **-iī -ītum** vt to put to sleep; to stun, knock unconscious; (fig) to calm, still, settle, lull

sop-or -ōris m deep sleep; stupor; apathy, indifference; sleeping potion

soporāt-us -a -um adj stupefied; unconscious; buried in sleep; allayed (grief); soporific

soporif-er -ēra -ērum adj sleep-inducing

sopōr-us -a -um adj drowsy

Sōract-e -is n mountain in Etruria about twenty-six miles from Rome

sōrāc-um -ī n hamper

sorb-eō -ēre -uī vt to suck in, gulp down; to absorb; (fig) to swallow (e.g., hatred)

sorbill-ō -āre vt to sip

sorbilō adv drop by drop, bit by bit

sorbiti-ō -ōnis f drink, pleasant drink

sorb-um -ī n Juneberry, service-berry

sorb-us -ī f Juneberry tree, service-berry tree

sord-eō -ēre vi to be dirty, be shabby; to appear worthless

sord-ēs -is f dirt, filth; shabbiness, squalor; f pl shabby clothes, rags (often worn as a sign of mourning); mourning; meanness (of behavior); low rank, low condition, vileness; dregs, rabble; vulgarity

sord-escō -escēre -uī vi to become dirty, become soiled

sordidāt-us -a -um adj in dirty or shabby clothes (esp. as a sign of mourning)

sordidē adv vilely, meanly, vulgarly

sordidul-us -a -um adj rather soiled, rather shabby; (fig) low, mean

sordid-us -a -um adj dirty, filthy, shabby; soiled, stained; dressed in mourning clothes; low (rank); vile, vulgar (behavior)

sorditūd-ō -inis f dirt, filth

sōr-ex -icis m shrewmouse

sōricīn-us -a -um adj squealing like mice

sōrīt-ēs -ae m sorites (logical conclusion drawn from cumulative arguments)

sor-or -ōris f sister; cousin; companion, playmate; **sorores doctae** Muses; **sorores tres** three Fates; **sorores tristes** gloomy Fates

sorōricīd-a -ae f murderer of a sister

sorōri-us -a -um adj sister's, of a sister; sisterly; **stuprum sororium** incest with a sister

sors sortis f lot; casting of lots, decision by lot; prophecy; fate, destiny, lot in life; portion, share; sort, kind, class

sorsum see **seorsum**

sortilĕg-us -a -um adj prophetic; m soothsayer, fortune-teller

sorti-ō -īre or **sort-ior -īrī -ītus sum** vt to cast or draw lots for; to allot, assign by lot, appoint by lot; to obtain by lot; to choose, select; to share, divide; to receive, get by chance; vi to cast or draw lots

sortīti-ō -ōnis f drawing lots, determining by lots

sortītō adv by lot; by fate

sortīt-us -ūs m lottery

Sosi-ī -ōrum m pl the Sosii (two brothers famous as booksellers in Rome at the time of Horace)

sosp-es -itis adj safe and sound; auspicious, lucky

sospit-a -ae f preserver (epithet of Juno)

sospitāl-is -e adj beneficial

sospit-ō -āre vt to preserve, protect

sōt-ēr -ēris m savior, deliverer, protector

sōtēri-a -ōrum n pl party thrown for a person recovering from an illness

spād-ix -icis adj chestnut-brown

spad-ō -ōnis m eunuch

spargō spargĕre sparsī sparsum vt to scatter, sprinkle, strew; to scatter, disperse; to disseminate, broadcast; to spot, dapple

sparsi-ō -ōnis f sprinkling

spars-us -a -um pp of **spargo**; adj freckled, spotty

Spart-a -ae or **Spart-ē -ēs** f Sparta (capital of Laconia, also called Lacedaemon)

Spartāc-us -ī m Thracian gladiator who led a revolt of gladiators against Rome in 73-71 B.C.

Spartān·us -a -um adj Spartan

Spartiāt·ēs -ae m Spartan

Spartiātic·us or **Spartic·us -a -um** adj Spartan

spart·um -ī n Spanish broom (plant, used in making ropes, nets, etc.)

sparŭl·us -ī m bream (fish)

spar·us -ī m hunting spear

spath·a -ae f broad two-edged sword

spatĭ·or -ārī -ātus sum vi to walk, stroll, take a walk; to walk solemnly; to spread out

spatiōsē adv extensively; long, for a long time

spatiōs·us -a -um adj spacious; broad, large; prolonged

spat·ium -ĭī or **-ī** n room, space, extent; open space, public square; distance (between two points); walk, promenade (place); interval, period; time, opportunity; measure, quantity (in metrics); lap; race track

speci·ēs -ēī f sight, view; outward appearance, outline, shape; fine appearance, beauty; deceptive appearance, show, semblance, pretense, pretext; resemblance, likeness; display, splendor; vision, apparition; image, statue; idea, notion; reputation; species, sort; **in speciem** or **per speciem** as a pretext, for the sake of appearances

specill·um -ī n probe (surgical instrument)

specim·en -ĭnis n mark, sign, proof, example; model, ideal

speciō specēre spexī vt to look at, behold

speciōsē adv splendidly

speciōs·us -a -um adj handsome, good-looking, beautiful; plausible; specious

spectābil·is -e adj visible; remarkable

spectācŭl·um or **spectācl·um -ī** n sight, spectacle; public performance; stage play; theater

spectām·en -ĭnis n sign, proof

spectātĭ·ō -ōnis f observation, view; examining, testing

spectāt·or -ōris m observer; spectator; critic, judge

spectātr·ix -īcis f on-looker, observer; spectator

spectāt·us -a -um adj tried, tested, proved; esteemed

spectĭ·ō -ōnis f observing the auspices; right to take the auspices

spect·ō -āre vt to observe, watch; to face in the direction of; to consider; to bear in mind; to aim at, tend towards; to examine, test

spectr·um -ī n specter, apparition

specŭl·a -ae f look-out, watch tower; summit

specŭl·a -ae f bit of hope

speculābund·us -a -um adj on the look-out

speculār·is -e adj transparent; n pl windowpane, window

speculāt·or -ōris m spy; explorer

speculātōrĭ·us -a -um adj for spying, for reconnaissance; f reconnaissance ship

speculātr·ix -īcis f spy (female)

specŭl·or -ārī -ātus sum vt to reconnoiter, observe, watch for

specŭl·um -ī n mirror (made of polished metal)

spec·us -ūs m or n cave, cavern; artificial excavation, ditch, canal, channel, pit; hole, cavity (of a wound, etc.)

spēlae·um -ī n den, cave

spēlunc·a -ae f cave

spērābil·is -e adj possible (able to be hoped for)

spērāt·us -a -um adj hoped for, longed for, desired; f fiancee, bride-to-be

Sperchē·is -ĭdis adj of the Spercheos

Sperchē·os or **Sperchī·us -ī** m large river in S. Thessaly

spernō spernĕre sprēvī sprētum vt to remove; to scorn, reject

spēr·ō -āre vt to hope for, expect, look forward to; to trust, trust in; to anticipate, await with fear

spēs speī f hope, expectation; anticipation, apprehension (of evil); **praeter spem** beyond all expectation; unexpectedly

Speusipp·us -ī m nephew of Plato and his successor as head of the Academy (347-339 B.C.)

sphaer·a -ae f sphere, globe, ball

sphaeristēr·ium -ĭī or **-ī** n tennis court

Sphin·x -gis f sphinx

spīc·a -ae f point; ear (of grain); tuft, top, head (of plants)

spīcĕ·us -a -um adj made of ears of grain

spīcŭl·um -ī n point; sting; dart, arrow

spīc·um -ī n ear (of grain)

spīn·a -ae f thorn; thorn bush; prickle (of animals); backbone, spine; back; f pl subtleties

spīnēt·um -ī n thorn hedge, thorny thicket

spīnĕ·us -a -um adj made of thorns, thorn

spīnif·er -ĕra -ĕrum adj prickly

spīnōs·us -a -um adj thorny, prickly; (fig) stinging, irritating (worries); confused, obscure (style)

spint·ēr -ēris n elastic bracelet

spintrĭ·a -ae m male prostitute

spinturnīc·ium -ĭī or **-ī** n bird of ill omen

spīn·us -ī f blackthorn, sloe tree

spīr·a -ae f coil (of a serpent); chin strap

spīrābil·is -e adj good to breathe, life-giving (air)

spīrācŭl·um -ī n pore, vent; breathing space

spīrāment·um -ī n pore, vent; breathing space, pause, instant

spīrit·us -ūs m breathing, breath; breeze; air; breath of life, life; inspiration; spirit, character, courage; pride, arrogance; morale; **spiritum ducere** to take a breath, breathe

spīr·ŏ -āre *vt* to exhale, breathe out; to aspire to, aim at; *vi* to breathe; to be alive; to be favorable; to have poetic inspiration

spissāt·us -a -um *adj* condensed, concentrated

spissē *adv* thickly, closely, tightly; slowly

spissesc·ŏ -ĕre *vi* to condense, become thick

spissigrăd·us -a -um *adj* slow-paced

spiss·ŏ -āre *vt* to condense, concentrate

spiss·us -a -um *adj* thick, tight, dense; slow, late; difficult

splēn splēnis *m* spleen

splend·ĕŏ -ēre *vi* to be clear and bright, shine, gleam; to be illustrious, be glorious

splendesc·ŏ -ĕre *vi* to become clear and bright

splendid·us -a -um *adj* clear and bright, gleaming, glistening, sparkling; spotless, noble (*character*); splendid, magnificent; sumptuous; showy; illustrious

splend·or -ōris *m* brightness, brilliance; clearness; splendor, magnificence; noble

splēniāt·us -a -um *adj* wearing a patch

splēn·ium -iī or **-ī** *n* patch (*for the face*)

spoliātĭ·ŏ -ōnis *f* stripping, plundering; unjust deprivation (*of honor or dignity*); ousting (*from public office*)

spoliāt·or -ōris *m* or **spoliātr·ix -īcis** *f* despoiler, robber

spoliāt·us -a -um *adj* stripped, robbed

spoli·ŏ -āre *vt* to strip of clothes; to pillage, plunder, rob

spol·ium -iī or **-ī** *n* hide, skin; spoils, booty, loot

spond·a -ae *f* bed frame, sofa frame; bed, sofa

spondāl·ium or **spondaul·ium -iī** or **-ī** *n* ritual hymn accompanied by a flute

spondĕŏ spondēre spopondī sponsum *vt* to promise solemnly, pledge, vow; to promise in marriage; *vi* (law) to give a guarantee, put up bail; (with **pro** + *abl*) to vouch for

sponde·us -ī *m* spondee

spondȳl·us -ī *m* mussel

spongi·a -ae *f* sponge; coat of mail

spons·a -ae *f* fiancée

sponsāl·ia -ium *n* *pl* engagement; engagement party

sponsĭ·ŏ -ōnis *f* solemn promise, guarantee; bet; (law) agreement between two parties that the loser pay a certain sum to the other

spons·or -ōris *m* guarantor, surety

spons·us -a -um *pp* of **spondeo**; *m* fiancé, bridegroom; *f* see **sponsa**; *n* agreement, engagement

spons·us -ūs *m* contract

sponte (only *abl*) *f* (of persons, mostly with possessive *adj*) of one's own accord, voluntarily; by oneself, unaided; (of things) of itself, spontaneously; on its own account, for its own sake

sport·a -ae *f* plaited basket; sieve

sportell·a -ae *f* little basket, lunch basket

sportŭl·a -ae *f* little basket (*in which gifts of food were given by the patron to his clients*); dole, present (*of food or money*); gift

sprētĭ·ŏ -ōnis *f* scorn, contempt

sprēt·or -ōris *m* despiser

sprētus *pp* of **sperno**

spūm·a -ae *f* foam, froth; lather; scum

spūmāt·us -a -um *adj* covered with foam

spūmesc·ŏ -ĕre *vi* to grow foamy

spūmĕ·us -a -um *adj* foaming, frothing

spūmif·er -ĕra -ĕrum *adj* foaming

spūmig·er -ĕra -ĕrum *adj* foaming

spūm·ŏ -āre *vi* to foam, froth

spūmōs·us -a -um *adj* full of foam, foaming; bombastic (*poem*)

spŭŏ spuĕre spuī spūtum *vt* to spit, spit out; *vi* to spit

spurcāt·us -a -um *adj* foul, filthy

spurcē *adv* filthily; in filthy language

spurcidĭc·us -a -um *adj* foulmouthed, filthy, smutty, obscene

spurcĭfic·us -a -um *adj* smutty, obscene

spurcĭti·a -ae or **spurcĭti·ēs -ēī** *f* filth, smut

spurc·ŏ -āre *vt* to make filthy, foul up; to defile

spurc·us -a -um *adj* (morally) filthy, dirty

spūtātilic·us -a -um *adj* deserving to be spit at, contemptible, disgusting

spūtāt·or -ōris *m* spitter

spūt·ŏ -āre *vt* to spit, spit out; to avert by spitting

spūt·um -ī *n* spit

squāl·ĕŏ -ēre -uī *vi* to be rough, be scaly, be parched, be wrinkled; to be coated, be clotted, be stiff; to be covered with filth; to be covered with weeds, be overgrown; to wear mourning clothes, go in mourning

squālĭdē *adv* coarsely

squālĭd·us -a -um *adj* rough, scaly; stiff, coated with dirt, squalid; in mourning; rough, coarse (*speech*); cracked, parched (*land*)

squāl·or -ōris *m* squalor, dirtiness; desolation; filthy garments (*neglected as a sign of mourning*)

squal·us -ī *m* shark

squām·a -ae *f* scale; scale armor; fish

squāmĕ·us -a -um *adj* scaly

squāmif·er -ĕra -ĕrum *adj* scaly

squămig·er -ĕra -ĕrum *adj* scaly; *m pl* fish

squămōs·us -a -um *adj* covered with scales, scaly

squill·a or **scill·a -ae** *f* shrimp

st *interj* sh!

stabiliment·um -ī *n* support

stabil·iō -īre -īvī -ītum *vt* to stabilize; to establish

stabil·is -e *adj* stable, firm, steady; steadfast, unwavering, immutable

stabilit·ās -ātis *f* stability, firmness, steadiness, durability

stabiliter *adv* firmly

stabŭl·ō -āre *vt* to stable or house (*animals*); *vi* to have a stall

stabŭl·um -ī *n* stable, stall; lair; hut; brothel

stact·a -ae or **stact·ē -ēs** *f* myrrh oil

stad·ium -iī or **-ī** *n* furlong; race track

Stagīr·a -ōrum *n pl* town in Macedonia, the birthplace of Aristotle

Stagirīt·es -ae *m* Aristotle

stagn·ō -āre *vt* to overflow, inundate; *vi* to form a pool; to be inundated

stagn·um -ī *n* pool, swamp, lake, lagoon; straits; waters

stalagm·ium -iī or **-ī** *n* eardrop, earring (*with pendant*)

stām·en -inis *n* warp (*of a loom*); thread; string (*of an instrument*); fillet (*worn by priests*)

stāminĕ·us -a -um *adj* full of threads, consisting of threads, wrapped in threads

Stat·a -ae *f* surname of Vesta

statāri·us -a -um *adj* standing, stationary; steady, calm; *m pl* actors in a type of comedy; *f* quiet or refined comedy

statēr·a -ae *f* scales; **statera aurifiois** goldsmith's scales

staticŭl·us -ī *m* a dance

statim *adv* at once, immediately, on the spot

stati·ō -ōnis *f* standing still; station, post; position; residence; anchorage; *f pl* sentries

Stāt·ius -iī or **-ī** *m* P. Papinius Statius (*poet of the Silver Age of Latin literature*, *c.* 40-96 A.D.)

stativ·us -a -um *adj* stationary; *n pl* bivouac

stat·or -ōris *m* magistrate's attendant

Stat·or -ōris *m* Stayer (*epithet of Jupiter, who kept the Roman soldiers from retreating*)

statŭ·a -ae *f* statue

statŭm·en -inis *n* rib (*of a hull*)

stat·ŭō -ŭĕre -ŭī -ūtum *vt* to cause to stand, bring to a stop; to set up, erect; to establish (*precedent, etc.*); to set, fix, determine; to decide, settle; to decree; to strengthen, support; to appoint, create; to inflict, pass (*sentence, punishment*); to hold, think, consider; to fix (*a price*); to draw up, arrange (*a battle line*)

stat·us -a -um *pp* of **sisto**; *adj* fixed, set, appointed

stat·us -ūs *m* position, posture; position, situation, condition; social status, rank; form of government; (*mil*) position; **status rei publicae** type of government

statūt·us -a -um *adj* tall

steg·a -ae *f* deck

stell·a -ae *f* star; constellation; **stella comans** comet; **stella diurna** Lucifer; **stella errans** planet

stell·ans -antis *adj* starry

stellāt·us -a -um *adj* set with stars, starry; made into a star

stellif·er -ĕra -ĕrum *adj* star-bearing, starry

stellig·er -ĕra -ĕrum *adj* star-bearing, starry

stell·ō -ōnis *m* newt, lizard with spotted back

stemm·a -ătis *n* genealogical tree, pedigree; *n pl* antiquity, history

stercorē·us -a -um *adj* full of dung

stercŏr·ō -āre *vt* to manure, fertilize

sterc·us -ŏris *n* manure, dung

steril·is -e *adj* sterile, barren; causing barrenness, blighting; empty, bare; unprofitable; unrequited (*love*); wild (*trees*)

sterilit·ās -ātis *f* sterility, barrenness

stern·ax -ācis *adj* bucking (*horse*)

sternō sternĕre strāvī strātum *vt* to strew, spread; to pave (*roads, etc.*); to knock down, bring low, slay; to raze, level; to flatten, smooth; to calm, calm down; **sterni** to stretch out (*on the ground*)

sternūment·um -ī *n* sneezing, sneeze

sternū·ō -ĕre -ī *vt* to give (*e.g., an omen*) by sneezing; *vi* to sneeze; to sputter

Sterŏp·ē -ēs *f* one of the Pleiades

sterquilīni·um -iī or **-ī** or **sterquilīn·um -ī** *n* dung heap; (*term of abuse*) heap of dung

stert·ō -ĕre *vi* to snore

Stēsichŏr·us -ī *m* Greek lyric poet of Himera in Sicily (*c.* 640-*c.* 555 B.C.)

Sthenĕl·us -ī *m* king of Mycenae, son of Perseus, and father of Eurystheus; king of the Ligurians and father of Cycnus who was changed into a swan

stibad·ium -iī or **-ī** *n* semicircular seat

stigm·a -ătis *n* mark, brand; stigma (*of disgrace*)

stigmatī·ās -ae *m* branded slave

stigmōs·us -a -um *adj* branded

still·a -ae *f* drop; mere drop

still·ō -āre *vt & vi* to drip

stil·us -ī *m* stylus (*pointed instrument for writing*); writing, composition; style (*of writing or speaking*)

stimulāti·ō -ōnis *f* stimulation, incitement

stimulātr·ix -īcis f inciter (*female*)
stimulě·us -a -um *adj* of goads
stimǔlō -āre vt to goad, torment; to spur on, incite, excite
stimǔl·us -ī m or **stimǔl·um -ī** n goad, prick; (mil) pointed stake concealed below the ground; (fig) stimulus, incentive, spur
stingu·ō -ěre vt to quench, extinguish
stīpātī·ō -ōnis f crowd, throng
stīpāt·or -ōris m attendant; m pl retinue
stīpendārī·us -a -um *adj* liable to tax, tributary; m pl tributary peoples; mercenary troops
stīpend·ium -iī or **-ī** n tax, tribute, tariff; (mil) pay; military service; year's service, campaign; **emereri stipendia** to have served out one's term; **emeritis stipendiis** at the end of one's military service, at discharge; **merere stipendia** or **mereri stipendia** to serve, serve in the army
stīp·es -itis m log, trunk; branch, tree; blockhead
stīp·ō -āre vt to crowd, cram, pack; to crowd around, accompany in a group
stips stipis f gift, donation, alms
stipul·a -ae f stalk, blade; stubble; reed pipe
stipulātī·ō -ōnis f agreement, bargain; (law) formal promise
stipulātiuncǔl·a -ae f insignificant promise, slight stipulation
stipulāt·us -a -um *adj* promised
stipul·or -ārī -ātus sum vt to stipulate; vi to bargain; (law) to make a formal promise
stīri·a -ae f icicle
stirpitus *adv* by the roots
stirp·s or **stirp·ēs** or **stirp·is -is** f stock, stem, stalk, root; plant, shrub; race, lineage; offspring, descendant; character, nature; root, source, foundation, beginning, origin
stīv·a -ae f plow handle
stlattārī·us or **stlātārī·us -a -um** *adj* imported, costly
stlopp·us -ī m slap (*sound produced by slapping an inflated cheek*)
stō stāre stetī statum vi to stand, stand still, remain standing; to stand firm, hold one's ground; to stand upright; (of hair) to stand straight, stand on end; (of eyes) to remain fixed; (of battle) to continue; (of a ship) to be moored, ride at anchor; to be motionless; to be stuck; to depend, rest; to take sides, take part; (with abl of price) to come to, cost; (with abl or in + abl) to depend on, rest with; (with per + acc of person) to depend on, be due to, be the fault of, thanks to
Stōic·a -ōrum n pl Stoic philosophy
Stōicē *adv* like a Stoic
Stōic·us -a -um *adj* Stoic; m Stoic, Stoic philosopher; n pl see **Stoica**
stol·a -ae f dress (*long outer gar-*

ment worn by Roman women and reaching from the neck to the ankles); ceremonial gown (*worn by musicians*)
stolāt·us -a -um *adj* wearing a stola; (fig) proper for a lady, lady-like
stolidē *adv* stupidly
stolid·us -a -um *adj* dull, stupid, stolid, slow
stomǎch·or -ārī -ātus sum vi to be annoyed, fret, fume, glower
stomachōsius *adv* rather angrily
stomachōs·us -a -um *adj* irritable, resentful
stomǎch·us -ī m stomach; taste, appetite; irritation, anger, resentment; **stomachus bonus** good appetite; good humor, patience
storě·a or **stori·a -ae** f straw mat, rope mat
strab·ō -ōnis m squinter
strāg·ēs -is f heap, confused mass, pile of debris; havoc, massacre
strāgǔl·us -a -um *adj* covering, serving as a covering; n rug, carpet; bedspread; horse blanket
strām·en -inis n straw
strāment·um -ī n straw; covering, saddle cloth; **stramentum agreste** straw bed
strāmině·us -a -um *adj* straw, made of straw
strangǔl·ō -āre vt to choke, stifle
strangūri·a -ae f strangury
stratēgēm·a -ătis n stratagem; trick
stratēg·us -ī m commander, general; master of ceremonies
stratiōtic·us -a -um *adj* soldier-like, soldierly, military
strāt·us -a -um pp of **sterno**; n quilt, blanket; bed, couch; horse blanket, pack saddle; pavement
strēn·a -ae f good-luck omen
strēnuē *adv* briskly, quickly, actively, strenuously
strēnuit·ās -ātis f briskness, vigor, liveliness
strēnǔ·ō -āre vi to be brisk
strēnǔ·us -a -um *adj* brisk, vigorous, active; fast (*ship*); restless
strepit·ō -āre vi to be noisy, clatter, rustle
strepit·us -ūs m noise, din, racket; crash, bang, clank, rumble, rustle, creak, squeak; sound (*of musical instruments*)
strep·ō -ěre -ǔī -itum vt to shout; vi to make a noise (*of any kind*); to rattle, clatter, clang, rumble, rustle, creak, squeak; to roar; to hum, murmur; (of musical instruments) to sound, blare; (of places) to ring, resound, be filled
striāt·a -ae f scallop
strictim *adv* superficially, cursorily
strictūr·a -ae f mass of molten iron
strict·us -a -um pp of **stringo**; *adj* close, tight, narrow
strīd·ěō -ēre -ī or **strīd·ō -ěre -ī** vi to make a high-pitched noise; to hiss, whistle, whizz, shriek, scream; to grate, buzz, rattle

strīd·or -ōris *m* shrill sound, hiss, shriek, scream, whine; harsh noise, grating, rattle, buzz

strīdŭl·us -a -um *adj* shrill, strident, hissing, whistling, creaking

strigĭl·is -is *f* scraper

strig·ō -āre *vi* to stop, halt; to lose strength, give out

strigōs·us -a -um *adj* lean, thin; bald (*style*)

stringō stringĕre strinxī strictum *vt* to strip, clip; to draw (*sword*); to draw tight, tie tight; to press together, compress; to touch lightly, graze; to border on, touch (*places*); to affect, touch, move, pain, wound (*mind, good name, etc.*); to waste, consume

string·or -ōris *m* twinge, shock

strix strigis *f* owl, screech owl

stroph·a -ae *f* trick

Strophăd·es -um *f pl* island home of the Harpies

strophĭăr·ĭus -iī or **-ī** *m* brassiere maker

stroph·ĭum -iī or **-ī** *n* brassiere; head band, chaplet

Stroph·ĭus -iī or **-ī** *m* king of Phocis and father of Pylades

structĭl·is -e *adj* building, for building

struct·or -ōris *m* builder, mason, carpenter; carver (*at table*)

structūr·a -ae *f* construction; structure

structus *pp* of **struo**

stru·ēs -is *f* pile, heap

stru·ix -īcis *f* pile, heap

strūm·a -ae *f* tumor, swollen gland

strūmōs·us -a -um *adj* scrofulous

struō struĕre struxī structum *vt* to build, build up, erect; to arrange, deploy (*troops*); to arrange, regulate; to occasion, contrive, plot

strūthĕ·us -a -um *adj* sparrow's

strūthiocamēl·us -ī *m* ostrich

Strȳm·ōn -ōnis *m* river forming the border between Macedonia and Thrace

Strȳmonĭ·us -a -um *adj* Strymonian, Thracian

stud·ĕō -ēre -uī *vt* to desire, be eager for; *vi* to be eager; (with *dat*) **a** to be eager for, be keen on, be enthusiastic about, take pains with, busy oneself with, apply oneself to; **b** to study; **c** to be a partisan of

studiōsē *adv* eagerly, enthusiastically, diligently

studiōs·us -a -um *adj* eager, keen, enthusiastic; studious; (with *genit*) partial to (*a person or cause*); (with *genit* or *dat*) eager for, keen on, enthusiastic about, devoted to, fond of, desirous of; **litterarum studiosus** studious

stud·ĭum -iī or **-ī** *n* eagerness, keenness, enthusiasm; devotion (*to a person*); party spirit; study; (with *genit*) eagerness for, enthusiasm for

stultē *adv* foolishly

stutĭloquentĭ·a -ae *f* or **stultiloqu·ĭum -iī** or **-ī** *n* silly talk

stultilōqu·us -a -um *adj* talking foolishly

stultĭtĭ·a -ae *f* foolishness, silliness

stultĭvĭd·us -a -um *adj* foolish-looking

stult·us -a -um *adj* foolish, silly, stupid

stūp·a -ae *f* tow, coarse flax, hemp

stupe·facĭō -facĕre -fēcī -factum (passive: **stupe·fīō -fĭĕrī -factus sum**) *vt* to stupefy, stun, astonish, knock senseless

stup·ĕō -ēre -uī *vt* to be amazed at; *vi* to be knocked senseless, be stunned, be stupefied, be astounded, be amazed; to be stopped in one's tracks

stup·escō -escĕre -uī *vi* to become amazed, become bewildered

stūpĕ·us -a -um *adj* of tow, hempen

stupĭdĭt·ās -ātis *f* stupidity

stupĭd·us -a -um *adj* amazed, astounded; dull, stupid

stup·or -ōris *m* numbness, bewilderment, confusion; dullness, stupidity

stupp·a -ae *f* tow, coarse flax, hemp

stuppĕ·us -a -um *adj* of tow, hempen

stupr·ō -āre *vt* to ravish, rape; to defile

stupr·um -ī *n* immorality; rape; disgrace (*esp. from a sex crime*)

sturn·us -ī *m* starling

Stygĭāl·is -e *adj* Stygian

Stygĭ·us -a -um *adj* Stygian, infernal; deadly

Stymphalĭc·us or **Stymphalĭ·us -a -um** *adj* Stymphalian

Stymphăl·um -ī *n* or **Stymphăl·us -ī** *m* district in Arcadia famous for its vicious birds of prey which were killed by Hercules as one of his twelve labors

Sty·x -gis or **-gos** *f* chief river in the lower world; river in Arcadia

suādēl·a -ae *f* persuasion

suādĕō suādēre suāsī suāsum *vt* to recommend, propose, suggest; to urge, impel, induce; *vi* (with *dat*) to advise, urge, suggest to; to propose to; **sibi suadere** (with *acc & inf*) to satisfy oneself that

suās·ĭō -ōnis *f* recommendation; support, backing (*a proposal*); persuasive eloquence

suās·or -ōris *m* adviser; advocate, supporter

suās·um -ī *n* dye

suāsus *pp* of **suadeo**

suās·us -ūs *m* advice

suāvĕŏl·ens -entis *adj* fragrant

suāviātĭō see **saviatio**

suāvĭdĭc·us -a -um *adj* charming

suāvĭlŏqu·ens -entis *adj* charming

suāvĭloquentĭ·a -ae *f* charming manner of speech

suāvĭŏlum see **saviolum**

suāvĭor see **savior**

suāv·is -e *adj* charming, pleasant, agreeable, attractive

suāvit·ās -ātis f charm, pleasantness, sweetness, attractiveness

suāviter adv pleasantly, sweetly, charmingly, attractively

suāvitūd·ō -inis f (term of endearment) honey

suāvium see **savium**

sub prep (with abl) under, beneath, underneath, behind; at the foot of, close to, near (mountain, wall); during, in, within, at, by, in the time of, just before; during the reign of; (with acc) under, along under; up to (walls); approaching, about, just before, just after

subabsurdē adv a bit absurdly

subabsurd·us -a -um adj rather absurd

subaccūs·ō -āre vt to blame, find fault with

subacti·ō -ōnis f working (of the soil); development (of the mind)

subactus pp of **subigo**

subserāt·us -a -um adj (gold) having an inner layer of bronze

subagrest·is -e adj rather uncouth

subālār·is -e adj carried under the arms

subalb·us -a -um adj whitish

subamār·us -a -um adj somewhat bitter

subaquil·us -a -um adj somewhat dark, brownish

subarroganter adv rather arrogantly

subauscult·ō -āre vt to eavesdrop on; vi to eavesdrop

subbasilicān·us -ī m loafer (person who hangs around the basilicas)

subbib·ō -ěre -ī vt to drink a little

subbland·ior -īrī -ītus sum vi (with dat) to flirt with

subc- = succ-

subdifficil·is -e adj rather difficult

subdiffid·ō -ěre vi to be a little distrustful

subditīci·us -a -um adj substituted, phoney

subditīv·us -a -um adj substituted, phoney

subditus pp of **subdo**

subdiū adv by day

sub·dō -děre -didī -ditum vt to put under; to subdue; to substitute; to forge, make up; to spread (a rumor) falsely; (with dat) a to put or apply (something) to, add (something) to; b to subject (someone) to; **se aquis subdere** to plunge into the water

subdoc·ěō -ēre vt to instruct (as an assistant teacher)

subdōlē adv rather cunningly

subdōl·us -a -um adj underhand, sly, cunning

subdom·ō -āre vt to tame somewhat

subdubit·ō -āre vi to be rather undecided

sub·dūcō -dūcěre -duxī -ductum vt to draw up from below; to pull up, raise, to remove, take away, steal; to haul up, beach (a ship); to withdraw (troops); to balance (accounts)

subducti·ō -ōnis f drydocking, beaching; calculation, computation

sub·ēdō -esse -ēdī vt to eat away or wear away at the bottom; **scopulum unda subedit** water wears away the bottom of the cliff

sub·ěō -īre -īvī or -iī -itum vt to enter (a place), enter (the mind); to approach, attack; to undergo (dangers, punishment, etc.); to help, support; to climb; to slip under; to dodge (a blow); vi to come or go up, climb; to follow; to advance, press forward; (with ad or in + acc) a to come up against, attack; b to climb (a mountain); c to approach, enter

sūb·er -ěris n cork tree; cork

subf- = suff-

subg- = sugg-

subhorrid·us -a -um adj rather coarse, rather uncouth

sub·iciō -icěre -jēcī -jectum vt to throw up, fling up; to bring up; to bring up close, expose; to suggest; to add, append; to suborn; to substitute; to forge; (with dat or sub + acc) a to put, place (something) under; b to subject (someone) to (authority, danger, risk); c to classify (something) under; d to submit (something) to (one's judgment)

subigitātī·ō -ōnis f lewdness; intercourse

subigitātr·ix -īcis f loose woman

subigit·ō -āre vt to lie with

sub·igō -igěre -ēgī -actum vt to turn up, till, plow; to knead; to whet, sharpen; to rub down; to tame; to train, discipline (the mind); to conquer, subdue, subjugate, reduce; to force, impel, constrain; to incite; to row, propel (a boat)

subimpūd·ens -entis adj rather shameless

subinān·is -e adj rather empty, rather pointless

subinde adv immediately afterwards; from time to time

subinsuls·us -a -um adj rather insipid

subinvid·ěō -ēre vi (with dat) to envy (someone) a little

subinvīs·us -a -um adj rather disliked, rather unpopular

subinvīt·ō -āre vt to invite unenthusiastically

subīr·ascor -ascī -ātus sum vi to be annoyed; (with dat) to be peeved at

subitāri·us -a -um adj (mil) suddenly called up (to meet an emergency); built in a hurry

subitō adv suddenly, unexpectedly, at once; **subito dicere** to speak ex-tempore

subit·us -a -um adj coming on suddenly, sudden, unexpected; rash (*man*); emergency (*troops*); *n* emergency

subjac·ĕŏ -ēre -ŭī *vi* to lie nearby; (with *dat*) to lie under or close to; **monti subjacere** to lie at the foot of the mountain

subjectĭ·ō -ōnis *f* subjection; substitution; forgery

subjectissimē *adv* most humbly

subject·ō -āre *vt* to toss up

subject·or -ōris *m* forger

subject·us -a -um *pp* of **subicio**; *adj* (with *dat*) a located near, bordering on; b subject to; *m* subject (*conquered person*)

sub·jungō -jungĕre -junxī -junctum *vt* (with *dat*) a to yoke or harness to; b to join to, connect with, add to; c to make subject to

sub·lābor -lābī -lapsus sum *vi* to sink, fall down, collapse; to glide imperceptibly; to fall back, fail

sublātē *adv* loftily, in lofty tones

sublātĭ·ō -ōnis *f* elevation, raising

sublāt·us -a -um *pp* of **suffero** and of **tollo**; *adj* elated

sublect·ō -āre *vt* to coax, cajole

sub·lēgō -legĕre -lēgī -lectum *vt* to gather up, pick up; to pick up stealthily, steal, kidnap; to substitute; to overhear, pick up

sublest·us -a -um *adj* weak, trifling

sublevātĭ·ō -ōnis *f* alleviation, lightening

sublĕv·ō -āre *vt* to lift up, raise, support

sublĭc·a -ae *f* stake, pile (*esp. for a bridge*)

sublicĭ·us -a -um *adj* resting upon piles; **pons sublicius** wooden bridge across the Tiber, built by Ancus Marcius

sublīgācŭl·um -ī *n* short apron

sublĭg·ar -āris *n* apron

sublĭg·ō -āre *vt* (with *dat*) to tie or fasten (*e.g., a sword*) to or below

sublīmē *adv* aloft, on high

sublīmen *adv* upwards, on high

sublīm·is -e *adj* high, raised up, lifted high; lofty, elevated, exalted; raised high, borne aloft, through the sky; aspiring; eminent, distinguished

sublīm·us -a -um *adj* high, lofty

sublīmĭt·ās -ātis *f* loftiness, sublimity

sublingĭ·ō -ōnis *m* scullion

sub·lĭnō -linĕre -lēvī -lĭtum *vt* to smear secretly; **os sublinere** (with *dat*) to cheat (*someone*)

sublūc·ĕŏ -ēre *vi* to shine faintly, glimmer

sub·lŭō -luĕre — -lūtum *vt* to wash underneath; to flow at the foot of (*a mountain*)

sublustr·is -e *adj* dimly lighted, throwing some light, glimmering, flickering

subm- = *summ-*

sub·nascor -nascī -nātus sum *vi* (with *dat*) to grow up underneath

sub·nectō -nectĕre -nexŭī -nex- **um** *vt* to fasten, tie (*something*) underneath; to confine; (with *dat*) to fasten or tie (*something*) below (*something else*)

subnĕg·ō -āre *vt* to halfway refuse; (with *dat*) to halfway refuse (*something*) to (*someone*)

subnĭg·er -ra -rum *adj* blackish

subnĭmĭ·a -ae *f* robe

subnīs·us or **subnix·us -a -um** *adj* propped up, resting, leaning; (with *dat*) a propped up on, resting on, leaning on; b relying on, depending on, confiding in

subnŏt·ō -āre *vt* to note down, record, register; to observe secretly

subnŭb·a -ae *f* rival (*female*)

subnūbĭl·us -a -um *adj* somewhat cloudy, overcast

sub·ō -āre *vi* to be in heat

subobscēn·us -a -um *adj* somewhat obscene, shady

subobscūr·us -a -um *adj* rather obscure

subodiōs·us -a -um *adj* annoying

suboffend·ō -ēre *vi* to give some offense

subŏl·et -ēre *v impers* there is a faint smell; **mihi subolet** I have an inkling, I have a sneaking suspicion, I have a faint idea

subŏl·ēs -is *f* offspring

subolesc·ō -ēre *vi* to grow up instead

subor·ior -īrī *vi* to rise up in succession, arise, proceed

suborn·ō -āre *vt* to equip, supply, provide; to employ as a secret agent, incite secretly, suborn

subp- = *supp-*

subr- = *surr-*

sub·scrībō -scrībĕre -scripsī -scriptum *vt* to write underneath; to sign; to write down, record, register; *vi* to sign an accusation, act as prosecutor; (with *dat*) a to add (*something*) to, attach (*something*) in writing to; b to assent to, agree to; (with **in** + *acc*) to sign an accusation against, indict, accuse, prosecute

subscriptĭ·ō -ōnis *f* inscription underneath; signature; (law) subscription; recording (*of an offense by the censor*); record, register

subscript·or -ōris *m* signer or joint-signer (*of an accusation*)

subscriptus *pp* of **subscribo**

subsĕc·ūs -ūdis *f* tenon of a dovetail

subsecīvus see **subsicivus**

subsĕc·ō -āre -ŭī -tum *vt* to clip, trim, cut off

subsecūtus *pp* of **subsĕquor**

subsell·ĭum -ī or **-ĭ** *n* low seat or bench; seat or bench on a lower level; judge's seat, the bench; tribunal, court; seat in the senate, senator's seat; bleachers (*where the poor people sat*); **versatus in utrisque subsellis** experienced as judge and lawyer

sub·sentiō -sentīre -sensī vt to have some inkling of

sub·sequor -sequī -secūtus sum vt to follow close after, chase, pursue; to back up, support; to imitate; to adhere to, conform to; to come after, succeed (in time or order); vi to ensue

subserv·iō -īre vi (with dat) **a** to be subject to; **b** to accommodate oneself to, humor; **c** to support, aid

subsiciv·a -a -um adj left over; extra, spare (time); extra, overtime (work)

subsidiāri·us -a -um adj (mil) reserve; m pl reserves

subsid·ium -iī or **-ī** n aid, support; place of refuge, asylum; protection; (mil) reserves, triarii; military support, relief, aid; **subsidio esse** (with dat) to act as support to; **subsidiō mittere** to send in support

sub·sīdō -sīdēre -sēdī -sessum vt to lie in wait for; vi to sit down, crouch down, settle down; to sink, subside, settle; to establish oneself, settle down, establish residence, stay

subsignān·us -a -um adj special reserve (troops)

subsign·ō -āre vt to endorse, subscribe to (an opinion); to register, enter, record; to guarantee

subsil·iō -īre -iī vi to jump up

sub·sistō -sistere -stitī vt to hold out against; vi to stand up; to make a stand, take a firm stand; to come to a standstill, stop; to stay behind; (with dat) **a** to take a stand against, oppose, fight; **b** to meet (an expense)

subsort·ior -īrī -ītus sum vt to choose as a substitute by lot; vi to choose a substitute by lot; (in a passive sense) to be chosen as a substitute

subsortīti·ō -ōnis f substitution by lot

substanti·a -ae f substance, essence; means, wealth, property

sub·sternō -sternēre -strāvī -strātum vt to spread underneath; to cover; (with dat) to put at the disposal of, make subservient to; **rem publicam libidini suae substernere** to misuse high office to serve one's lust

substit·uō -uēre -uī -ūtum vt to submit, present; to substitute; (with dat or **in locum** with genit) to substitute for or in place of; **animo** or **oculis substituere** to imagine

subst·ō -āre vi to stand firm, hold out; (with dat) to stand up to

substrātus pp of **substerno**

substrict·us -a -um adj tight, narrow, small

sub·stringō -stringere -strinxī -strictum vt to tie up, draw up; to restrain, control; (with dat) to press (something) close to

substructi·ō -ōnis f substructure, foundation

sub·struō -struere -struxī -structum vt to lay (foundation); **vias glareā substruere** to lay a foundation of gravel on the roads

subsult·ō -āre vi to jump up, jump up and down

sub·sum -esse vi to be near, be at hand; (with dat) **a** to be below or beneath, be under; **b** to be concealed in; **c** to be subject to, subservient to

subsūt·us -a -um adj trimmed at the bottom

subtēm·en -inis n woof; thread, yarn

subter adv below, underneath; prep (with abl) beneath, below, underneath, under; (with acc) underneath, beneath; up to, close to, close beneath

subter·dūcō -dūcēre -duxī -ductum vt to withdraw secretly, lead away secretly

subter·fugiō -fugēre -fūgī vt to evade, avoid; vi to run away secretly, get off

subter·lābor -lābī vt to glide or flow under; vi to slip away, escape

sub·terō -terēre -trivī -trītum vt to wear away underneath

subterrāne·us -a -um adj subterranean, underground

subtex·ō -ēre -uī -tum vt to sew on; to veil, cover; (fig) to work up, compose; (with dat) **a** to sew onto; **b** to throw (a covering) over; **c** to work (something) into (a story or plot)

subtīl·is -e adj woven fine, of fine texture; delicate; subtle; discriminating, precise; plain, direct (style)

subtīlit·ās -ātis f fineness, minuteness; slenderness; exactness, precision; simplicity (of style)

subtīliter adv finely, delicately; accurately; plainly, simply

subtim·eō -ēre vt to be a bit afraid of

sub·trahō -trahere -traxī -tractum vt to drag up from beneath, drag out, draw off, withdraw, remove; to avert (the eyes); (with dat) to drag or draw (something) away from

subtrist·is -e adj rather sad

subtrītus pp of **subtero**

subturpicul·us -a -um adj somewhat disgraceful

subturp·is -e adj rather disgraceful

subtus adv below, underneath

subtūs·us -a -um adj somewhat bruised

subūcul·a -ae f man's undershirt

sūbul·a -ae f awl

subulc·us -ī m swineherd

Subūr·a -ae f rough, noisy district in Rome, N.E. of the Forum between the Esquiline and Quirinal

Subūrān·us -a -um adj of the Subura

suburbānit·ās -ātis f nearness to Rome

suburbān·us -a -um *adj* suburban, near Rome; *m* suburbanite; *n* suburban home

suburb·ium -iī or **-ī** *n* suburb

suburg·eō -ēre *vt* (with **ad** + *acc*) to keep or turn (*a ship*) close to

subvecti·ō -ōnis *f* transportation

subvect·ō -āre *vt* to bring up regularly

subvectus *pp* of **suveho**

subvect·us -ūs *m* bringing up, transportation

sub·vehō -vehĕre -vexī -vectum *vt* to carry or bring up, transport

sub·veniō -venīre -vēnī -ventum *vi* (with *dat*) to come up to aid, reinforce, relieve

subvent·ō -āre *vi* (with *dat*) to rush to the aid of

subver·eor -ērī *vi* to be a bit apprehensive

subvers·ō or **subvors·ō -āre** *vt* to ruin completely

subvers·or -ōris *m* subverter, repealer

sub·vertō or **sub·vortō -vertĕre -vertī -versum** *vt* to turn upside down, upset, overthrow, throw over, subvert

subvex·us -a -um *adj* sloping upward

subvŏl·ō -āre *vi* to fly up

subvolv·ō -ĕre *vt* to roll up

subvor- = subver-

subvulturi·us -a -um *adj* vulturelike

succāv·us -a -um *adj* hollow underneath

succēdānĕ·us or **succīdānĕ·us -a -um** *adj* substitute

suc·cēdō -cēdĕre -cessī -cessum *vt* to climb; to march on or against, advance to or as far as; *vi* to come up, climb; to come next, follow in succession; to turn out (*successfully*); (with **ad, in,** or **sub** + *acc*) to climb, climb up; (with *dat*) **a** to come next to, follow; **b** to succeed in (*an undertaking*); to yield, to submit to; **d** to relieve, take the place of (*e.g., tired troops*); **e** to enter, go below to (*e.g., a shelter; grave*); (with **in** or **ad** + *acc*) (*fig*) to reach, attain (*e.g., high honors*), receive by succession, enter upon (*an inheritance*)

suc·cendō -cendĕre -cendī -censum *vt* to set on fire, set fire to; to light (*a fire*); (*fig*) to inflame

succens·eō or **suscens·eō -ēre -ī** *vi* to be angry, be enraged; (with *dat*) to be enraged at

succensus *pp* of **succendo**

succenturiāt·us -a -um *adj* in reserve

succenturi·ō -āre *vt* to receive (*someone*) as a substitute into a century or company

succenturi·ō -ōnis *m* assistant centurion, substitute for a centurion

successi·ō -ōnis *f* succession

success·or -ōris *m* successor

success·us -ūs *m* approach, advance uphill; outcome, success

succīdānĕus see **succedaneus**

succīdi·a -ae *f* leg or side of meat; (*fig*) extra income

suc·cīdō -cīdĕre -cīdī -cīsum *vt* to cut down, cut off, mow down

suc·cīdō -cīdĕre -cīdī *vi* to sink, give way; to collapse, fail

succīd·us or **sūcid·us -a -um** *adj* juicy; (coll) fresh, plump (*girl*)

succīdŭ·us -a -um *adj* sinking, falling

suc·cingō -cingĕre -cinxī -cinctum *vt* to tuck up; to put on (*e.g., a sword*); to equip, arm, fit out

succingŭl·um -ī *n* belt

succin·ō -ĕre *vi* to chime in (*in conversation*)

succīsus *pp* of **succīdo**

succlāmāti·ō -ōnis *f* shouting in reply

succlām·ō -āre *vt* to shout out after, interrupt with shouts; (with *dat*) to shout out (*words*) at

succontumēliōsē *adv* rather insolently

suc·crescō -crescĕre -crēvī *vi* to grow up; to be replenished; (with *dat*) to attain to

succrisp·us -a -um *adj* rather curled

suc·cumbō -cumbĕre -cubŭī -cubĭtum *vi* to fall or sink back; to yield, succumb, submit

suc·currō -currĕre -currī -cursum *vi* (with *dat*) **a** to run up to; **b** to run to help; **c** to occur to, enter the mind of

succ·us or **sūc·us -ī** *m* sap, juice; taste, flavor

succuss·us -ūs *m* shaking, jolt

succust·ōs -ōdis *m* assistant guard

suc·cutiō -cutĕre -cussī -cussum *vt* to toss up

sūcidus see **succīdus**

sūcin·us -a -um *adj* & *n* amber

suctus *pp* of **sūgō**

sucŭl·a -ae *f* little pig; winch, windlass

sūcus see **succus**

sūdār·ium -iī or **-ī** *n* handkerchief, towel

sūdātōri·us -a -um *adj* sweat, for sweating; *n* sweat room

sūdātr·ix -īcis *adj* causing sweat

sud·is -is *f* stake, pile; pike (*weapon*); dorsal fin

sūd·ō -āre *vt* to sweat, exude; to soak with sweat; (*fig*) to sweat over; *vi* to sweat; to drip

sūd·or -ōris *m* sweat; moisture; hard work

sūductil·um -ī *n* sweat-maker (*i.e., whip*)

sūd·us -a -um *adj* dry; clear, cloudless (*weather*); *n* clear weather, bright sky

su·ĕō -ēre *vi* to be accustomed; (with *inf*) be accustomed or used to

su·escō -escĕre -ēvī -ētum *vt* to

accustom, familiarize; *vi* to become
used; (with *dat*) to get used to

Suess·a -ae *f* town in Latium

suēt·us *pp* of **suesco**; *adj* usual,
familiar

Suēv·ī -ōrum *m pl* a people of N.E.
Germany

sūf·es -ětis *m* chief magistrate at
Carthage

suffarcināt·us -a -um *adj* stuffed
full

suffarcīn·ō -āre *vt* to stuff full,
cram

suffectus *pp* of **sufficio**

sufferō sufferre sustulī sublātum
vt to suffer, bear, endure

suf·ficiō -ficěre -fēcī -fectum *vt*
to lay the foundation for; to dip,
tinge, dye; to appoint to a vacancy;
to yield, supply, afford; **consul
suffectus** substitute consul (*consul
appointed to complete an unexpired
term of another consul*); *vi* to suffice, be sufficient; (with *dat* or with
ad or **in** + *acc*) to suffice for, be
adequate to

suf·fīgō -fīgěre -fīxī -fīxum *vt* to
nail up, fasten

suffīm·en -inis *n* incense

suffīment·um -ī *n* incense

suffīxus *pp* of **suffīgo**

sufflām·en -inis *n* brake (*on a vehicle*)

sufflāt·us -a -um *adj* puffed up,
bloated; (fig) fuming (*with anger*)

suffl·ō -āre *vt* to blow up, inflate; *vi*
to blow, puff

suffōc·ō -āre *vt* to choke, strangle

suf·fodiō -foděre -fōdī -fossum
vt to stab, pierce; to dig under
(*walls*)

suffrāgātī·ō -ōnis *f* voting (*in someone's favor*), support

suffrāgāt·or -ōris *m* supporter (*at
the polls*), partisan

suffrāgātōri·us -a -um *adj* partisan

suffrāg·ium -iī or **-ī** *n* ballot, vote;
right to vote, franchise; decision,
judgment; applause, approbation;
suffragium ferre to cast a ballot; **suffragium ferre** (with **de** or
in + *abl*) to vote on

suffrāg·or -ārī -ātus sum *vi* to
cast a favorable vote; (with *dat*) to
vote in favor of, support, vote for;
fortūnā suffragante with luck
on our side

suffring·ō -ěre *vt* to break, smash

suf·fugiō -fugěre -fūgī *vt* to escape, avoid; *vi* (with **in** + *acc*) to
run to for cover

suffug·ium -iī or **-ī** *n* shelter, cover

suf·fulciō -fulcīre -fulsī -fultum
vt to prop up, underpin, support

suf·fundō -funděre -fūdī -fūsum
vt to pour in, fill; to suffuse, spread;
to tinge, color; to infuse; **virgi-
neum ore ruborem suffundere**
(with *dat*) to cause (*someone*) to
blush

suffūr·or -ārī *vt* to filch

suffusc·us -a -um *adj* darkish,
brownish

suffūsus *pp* of **suffundō**

sug·gěrō -gerěre -gessī -gestum
vt to supply, add; to prompt, suggest

suggest·um -ī *m* platform; stage

suggestus *pp* of **suggero**

suggest·us -ūs *m* platform; stage

suggrand·is -e *adj* rather huge

sug·gredior -grědī -gressus sum
vt & vi to approach

sūgillātiō -ōnis *f* bruise; affront

sūgill·ō -āre *vt* to beat black and
blue; to affront, insult

sūgō sūgěre suxī suctum *vt* to
suck

suī see **se**

suill·us -a -um *adj* of swine; **grex
suillus** herd of swine

sulc·ō -āre *vt* to furrow, plow; to
make a line in (*sand*)

sulc·us -ī *m* furrow; ditch, trench
(*for plants*); track (*of a wheel or
meteor*); wrinkle; plowing; wake (*of
ship*)

sulf·ur -ŭris *m* sulfur

Sull·a -ae *m* Sulla (*Cornelius Sulla
Felix, Roman general, dictator,
champion of the aristocratic party,
and political reformer, 138-78 B.C.*)

Sullān·ī -ōrum *m pl* partisans of
Sulla

sullāturiō -īre *vi* to wish to be a
Sulla

Sulm·ō -ōnis *m* town about ninety
miles east of Rome and birthplace
of Ovid

Sulmōnens·is -e *adj* of Sulmo

sulp·ur or **sulf·ur -ŭris** *n* sulfur

sulpurāt·us -a -um *adj* saturated
with sulfur; *n pl* matches

sulpure·us -a -um *adj* sulfurous

sultis = **si vultis** if you please,
please

sum esse fuī *vi* to be, exist; (with
genit of possession) to belong to,
pertain to, be characteristic of, be
the duty of; (with *genit* or *abl* of
quality) to be of, be possessed of,
have; (with *genit* or *abl* of value) to
be valued at, cost; (with *dat*) to belong to; (with **ab** + *abl*) to belong
to; (with **ad** + *acc*) to be designed
for; (with **ex** + *abl*) to consist of;
est (with *inf*) it is possible to, it is
permissible to; **est** (with **ut**) it is
possible that; **sunt quī** there are
those who, there are people who,
they are of the type that

sūm·en -inis *n* breast, teat, udder;
breeding sow

summ·a -ae *f* main thing; chief
point, gist, summary; sum, amount,
contents, substance; sum of money;
ad summam generally, on the
whole; in short; **summa rerum**
the world; supreme power; **summa
summarum** the whole universe

summān·ō -āre *vi* to drip a bit

Summān·us -ī *m* Roman god of
night lightning

summ·ās -ātis *adj* high-born, aristocratic, noble

summātim *adv* on the surface; generally, summarily

summāt·us -ūs *m* supremacy, supreme power

summē *adv* very, extremely

sum·mergō -mergĕre -mersī -mersum *vt* to sink, submerge, drown

summĕr·us -a -um *adj* pure, straight (*wine*)

sumministr·ō -āre *vt* to supply, furnish

summissē or **summissim** *adv* in a low voice, softly; modestly; humbly

summissi·ō -ōnis *f* lowering, dropping

summiss·us -a -um *adj* lowered, stooping; lowered, soft (*voice*); humble, unassuming; submissive; too submissive, abject

sum·mittō -mittĕre -mīsī -missum *vt* to let down, lower, sink, drop; to let (*hair*) grow long; to lower, reduce, moderate, relax, lessen; to bring down, humble; to rear, put forth, produce; to send secretly; to send as a reinforcement; to send as a substitute; **animum summittere** (with *dat*) to yield to; **se summittere** to bend down, stoop over; to condescend; **se summittere** (with *dat*) to yield to, give in to

summolestē *adv* with some annoyance

summolest·us -a -um *adj* rather annoying

summon·ĕō -ēre -ŭī *vt* to give (*someone*) a gentle reminder, remind privately

summopĕre *adv* with the greatest diligence, completely

summŏrōs·us -a -um *adj* rather crabby

sum·movĕō -movēre -mōvī -mōtum *vt* to move up, advance; to clear (*e.g., the court*); to remove; to expel, banish; (mil) to dislodge; (fig) to drive away, forget about (*e.g., worries*)

summ·us -a -um *adj* uppermost, highest; the top of, the surface of; last, latest, the end of; greatest, best, top, consummate; most distinguished; most important; *m* head of the table; *f* see **summa**; *n* top, surface, highest place, head of the table

summum *adv* at most; at latest; **uno aut summum altero proelio** in one or at most in two battles

sūmō sūmĕre sumpsī sumptum *vt* to take up; to put on, dress oneself in, wear; to exact, inflect (*penalty*); to take up, begin, enter upon; to eat, consume; to assume, suppose, take for granted; to cite, adduce, mention; to assume, appropriate; to select; to purchase, buy

sumpti·ō -ōnis *f* assumption

sumptuāri·us -a -um *adj* expense, relating to expenses, sumptuary, against extravagance

sumptuōsē *adv* sumptuously, expensively

sumptuōs·us -a -um *adj* costly, expensive; lavish, wasteful

sumptus *pp* of **sumo**

sumpt·us -ūs *m* cost, expense, charge; **sumptui esse** (with *dat*) to be costly to, be expensive to; **sumptum suum exercere** to earn one's keep; **sumptu tuo** at your expense, out of your pocket

Sūn·ium -iī or **-ī** *n* S.E. promontory of Attica

suō suĕre suī sūtum *vt* to sew, stitch, tack together

suōmet = emphatic form of **suo**

suopte = emphatic form of **suo**

suovetaurīl·ia -ium *n pl* sacrifice of a pig, sheep, and bull

supell·ex -ectīlis *f* furniture, household utensils; (fig) outfit, qualification

super *adv* on the top, above; besides, moreover; **super esse** to be left over; *prep* (with *abl*) above, over, upon, on; concerning, about; besides, in addition to; at, on (*time*); (with *acc*) over, above, upon; (with numbers) over, more than; besides, over and above

supĕr·a -ōrum *n pl* upper world, sky, Heaven; heavenly bodies

supĕrā *adv* above

superābil·is -e *adj* surmountable, climbable; conquerable

super·addō -addĕre — -addĭtum *vt* to add besides, add to boot

supĕr·ans -antis *adj* predominant

superast·ō -āre *vi* (with *dat*) to stand on

superāt·or -ōris *m* conqueror

superbē *adv* arrogantly, haughtily, snobbishly

superbi·a -ae *f* arrogance, haughtiness, snobbishness; (justifiable) pride

superbiloquenti·a -ae *f* haughty tone, arrogant speech

superb·ĭō -īre *vi* to be haughty; to be superb, be magnificent; (with *abl*) to take pride in

superb·us -a -um *adj* arrogant, haughty, snobbish; overbearing, tyrannical, despotic; fastidious, disdainful; superb, magnificent

supercil·ium -iī or **-ī** *n* eyebrow; frown, will (of *Jupiter*); summit, brow (*of a hill, etc.*); arrogance, superciliousness

superēmin·ĕō -ēre -ŭī *vt* to tower over, top

superficĭ·ēs -ēī *f* top, surface; (law) fixtures, improvements, buildings (*i.e., anything upon the property, but not the land itself*)

super·fĭō -fĭĕrī *vi* to be over and above; to be left over

superfix·us -a -um *adj* attached above

superflŭ·ens -entis *adj* superabundant, running over; (with *abl*) abounding in

superflŭ·ō -ĕre *vi* to overflow

super·fundō -fundĕre -fūdī -fūsum *vt* (with *abl*) to shower (*something*) with; (with *dat*) to pour (*something*) upon; **superfundi** or **se superfundere** to spread, spread out, extend; **fama superfudit se in Asiam** the report spread to Asia

super·gredior -grĕdī -gressus sum *vt* to walk or step over; to surpass

super·ī -ōrum *m pl* the gods above; men on earth; mortals; upper world

superimmin·ĕō -ēre *vt* to tower above

superimpend·ens -entis *adj* overhanging, towering overhead

superim·pōnō -pōnĕre -posŭī -positum *vt* to place on top, place overhead

superimposit·us -a -um *adj* superimposed

superincid·ens -entis *adj* falling from above

superincŭb·ans -antis *adj* lying above or on top

superin·cumbō -cumbĕre -cubŭī *vi* (with *dat*) to lay oneself down upon

superingĕr·ō -ĕre *vt* to pour down

superin·iciō -icĕre — -jectum *vt* to throw on top

superin·sternō -sternĕre -strāvī *vt* to cover

superi·or -us (*comp of* **supĕrus**) *adj* higher, upper; the upper part of; past, previous, preceding; older, elder, more advanced; victorious, conquering; superior, stronger; superior, greater; **de loco superiore dicere** to speak from the tribunal, handle a case in court; to speak from the rostra, deliver a formal address; **ex loco superiore pugnare** to fight from a vantage point

superin·jaciō -jacĕre -jēcī -jectum or **-jactum** *vt* to overspread, overwhelm; to overdo, exaggerate

superinjectus *pp of* **superinicio**

superlāti·ō -ōnis *f* exaggeration

superlāt·us -a -um *adj* exaggerated

supernē *adv* above, from above

supern·us -a -um *adj* upper; situated high up; supernal, celestial

supĕr·ō -āre *vt* to go over, pass over, rise above; to pass or go past, go beyond; to sail past, double; to outdo, surpass; to overcome, vanquish; *vi* to mount, ascend; to be superior, have the advantage; to be left over, survive; to be superfluous; to be abundant; (with *dat*) to pass over, pass above

superobrŭ·ō -ĕre *vt* to cover completely, smother

superpend·ens -entis *adj* towering overhead

super·pōnō -pōnĕre -posŭī -positum *vt* (with *dat*) to put or place (*something*) upon; (with **in** + *acc*) to put (*someone*) in charge of

superscand·ō -ĕre *vt* to step over, climb over

super·sedĕō -sedēre -sēdī -sessum *vi* (with *abl*) to refrain from, give up

superstagn·ō -āre *vi* (of a river) to overflow and form swamps

superst·es -itis *adj* standing by as a witness; surviving; posthumous; (with *genit* or *dat*) outliving, surviving; **superstes esse** to live on; **superstes esse** (with *genit* or *dat*) to outlive (*someone* or *something*)

superstiti·ō -ōnis *f* excessive fear; superstition

superstitiōsē *adv* superstitiously

superstitiōs·us -a -um *adj* superstitious; having magical powers

superst·ō -āre *vi* to be remaining, be left

superst·ō -āre *vt* to stand over; *vi* (with *dat*) to stand on, stand over

superstrāt·us -a -um *adj* spread over (*as a covering*)

super·strŭō -strŭĕre -struxī -structum *vt* to build on top

super·sum -esse -fŭī *vi* to be left over, still exist, survive; to abound; to be in excess, be superfluous; to be adequate, suffice; (with *dat*) to outlive, survive (*someone*)

supertĕg·ō -ĕre *vt* to cover, cover over

superurg·ens -entis *adj* putting on pressure, adding pressure

supĕr·us -a -um *adj* upper; of this world, of this life; northern; **ad auras superas redire** to return to the upper air, come back to life; **mare superum** Adriatic Sea; *m pl* see **superi**; *n pl* see **supera**

supervacānĕ·us -a -um *adj* superfluous

supervacŭ·us -a -um *adj* superfluous, needless

supervād·ō -ĕre *vt* to go over, climb over

super·vĕhor -vĕhī -vectus sum *vt* to sail, ride, or drive by or past

super·veniō -venīre -vēnī -ventum *vt* to come upon, come on top of; to overtake; to come over, close over, cover; to surprise; *vi* to arrive suddenly; (with *dat*) to come upon by surprise

supervent·us -ūs *m* sudden arrival, unexpected arrival

supervolit·ō -āre *vt* to hover over

supervol·ō -āre *vt* to fly over; *vi* to fly across

supīn·ō -āre *vt* to turn up, lay on its back; to turn over (*by plowing*)

supīn·us -a -um *adj* face-up; lying

upwards, turned upwards; sloping, sloping upwards; (streams) flowing upwards (*to their source*); on one's back; lazy, careless, indifferent

suppactus *pp* of **suppingo**

suppaenit·et -ēre *v impers* (with *acc* of person and *genit* of thing regretted), e.g., **illum furoris suppaenitet** he somewhat regrets the outburst

suppalp·or -ārī *vi* (with *dat*) to coax (*someone*) a little

supp·ār -āris *adj* nearly equal

supparasit·or -ārī -ātus sum *vi* (with *dat*) to flatter (*someone*) a little like a parasite

suppār·um -ī *n* or **suppār·us -ī** *m* linen dress; small sail

suppedităti·ō -ōnis *f* good supply, abundance

suppedit·ō -āre *vt* to supply, furnish; *vi* to stand by; to be at hand, be in stock, be available; (with *dat*) to be at hand for; (with **ad** or **in** + *acc*) to be adequate for, suffice for

suppēd·ō -ēre *vi* to break wind quietly

suppetl·ae -ārum *f pl* help, assistance

suppetl·or -ārī -ātus sum *vi* (with *dat*) to help, assist

suppĕt·ō -ĕre -īvī or **-iī -ītum** *vi* to be at hand, be in stock, be available; (with *dat*) **a** to be at hand for, be available to; **b** to be equal to, suffice for, be sufficient for; **c** to correspond to

suppīl·ō -āre *vt* to filch

sup·pingō -pingĕre — -pactum *vt* to fasten underneath

supplant·ō -āre *vt* to trip up

supplēment·um -ī *n* full complement; reinforcements

suppl·ĕō -ēre -ēvī -ētum *vt* to fill up; to make good (*losses, damage, etc.*); (mil) to bring to full strength

suppl·ex -icis *adj* kneeling, on one's knees, in entreaty; humble, submissive; *m* suppliant

supplicăti·ō -ōnis *f* public thanksgiving, day of prayer; thanksgiving for victory; day of humiliation

suppliciter *adv* suppliantly, humbly, submissively

supplic·ium -iī or **-ī** *n* kneeling down, bowing down, humble entreaty; public prayer, supplication; (because criminals were beheaded kneeling) execution, death penalty; punishment, torture; suffering, distress, pain

supplic·ō -āre *vi* (with *dat*) to go on one's knees, to entreat, beg

sup·plōdō -plōdĕre -plōsī *vt* to stamp (*the foot*)

supplōsi·ō -ōnis *f* stamping; **supplosio pedis** stamping of the foot

sup·pōnō -pōnĕre -posuī -positum *vt* (with *dat*) **a** to put, place, set (*something*) under; **b** to put (*something*) next to, add (*something*) to; **c** to substitute (*some-

thing*) for; **potentiam in gratiae locum supponere** to put power in place of influence, substitute power for influence

support·ō -āre *vt* to bring or carry up, transport

supposiţici·us -a -um *adj* spurious

suppositi·ō -ōnis *f* substitution

suppositus *pp* of **suppono**

suppostr·īx -īcis *f* unfair substituter (*female*)

suppressi·ō -ōnis *f* holding back (*of money*), embezzlement

sup·primō -primĕre -pressī -ressum *vt* to press down or under; to sink; to repress, stop; to suppress, keep secret

supprōm·us -ī *m* assistant butler

suppŭd·et -ēre *v impers* to cause (*someone*) a slight feeling of shame; (with *acc* of person and *genit* of cause), e.g., **eōrum me suppudet** I am a bit ashamed of them

suppūr·ō -āre *vi* to fester

supp·us -a -um *adj* (animals) facing the ground

supput·ō -āre *vt* to trim up; to count, compute

suprā *adv* on top, above; up above; earlier; beyond, more; **supra quam** more than; *prep* (with *acc*) over, above; beyond; (of time) before; (of amount) over, beyond; in charge of

suprascand·ō -ĕre *vt* to climb over

suprēmum *adv* for the last time

suprēm·us -a -um (*superl* of **superus**) *adj* highest, topmost; the top of; last, latest, final; greatest, supreme, extreme; closing, dying, final; **suprema manus** the finishing touches; **supremus mons** summit of the mountain, mountain top; *n* last moment; *n pl* moment of death; funeral rites, obsequies; testament

sūr·a -ae *f* calf of the leg

surcŭl·us -ī *m* shoot, sprout, twig; slip, graft

surdast·er -ra -rum *adj* somewhat deaf

surdit·ās -ātis *f* deafness

surd·us -a -um *adj* deaf; silent, noiseless; unheeding; dull, faint, indistinct

surēn·a -ae *f* grand vizier (*in the Parthian empire*)

surgō surgĕre surrexī surrectum *vi* to get up, rise, stand up; to get up (*from sleep*); to grow up, spring up

surp·ō -ĕre -uī *vt* to snatch, wrest; to pilfer

surrancĭd·us or **subrancĭd·us -a -um** *adj* somewhat rancid

surrauc·us or **subrauc·us -a -um** *adj* somewhat hoarse

surrectus *pp* of **surgo**

surrēmig·ō or **subrēmig·ō -āre** *vi* to row along

sur·rēpō or **sub·rēpō -rēpĕre -repsī -reptum** *vt* to creep under, crawl under; *vi* to creep up; (with *dat*) to creep up on, steal upon

surrepticĭ·us or **subreptĭcĭ·us -a -um** adj surreptitious; stolen

surreptus pp of **surrepo** and of **surripio**

sur·rīdĕŏ or **sub·rīdĕŏ -rīdēre -rīsī** vi to smile

surrīdĭcŭlē or **subrīdĭcŭlē** adv rather humorously

sur·rĭgŏ or **sub·rĭgŏ -rĭgĕre -rexī -rectum** vt to raise, lift up, erect

surring·or or **subring·or -ī** vi to grimace, make a face; to be somewhat annoyed

sur·rĭpĭŏ or **sub·rĭpĭŏ -rĭpĕre -rĭpŭī -reptum** vt to snatch secretly, pilfer; (with dat) to pilfer (something) from

surrŏg·ŏ -āre vt to propose as a substitute

surrostrān·ī or **subrostrān·ī -ōrum** m pl loafers around the rostra

surrub·ĕŏ or **subrub·ĕŏ -ēre** vi to blush slightly

surrūf·us or **subrūf·us -a -um** adj reddish

sur·rŭŏ or **sub·rŭŏ -ruĕre -rŭī -rŭtum** vt to undermine, dig under; to tear down, demolish; (fig) to wreck, stamp out, destroy

surrustĭc·us or **subrustĭc·us -a -um** adj rather unsophisticated

surrŭtus pp of **surruo**

sursum or **sursus** adv upwards, high up; **sursum deorsum** up and down, to and fro

sūs suis m pig, hog, boar; f sow

Sūs·a -ōrum n pl capital of Persia

suscensĕŏ see **succenseo**

susceptĭ·ŏ -ōnis f undertaking

sus·cĭpĭŏ -cĭpĕre -cēpī -ceptum vt to catch (something before it falls); to support; to pick up, resume (conversation); to bear (children); to accept, receive (under one's protection); to take up, undertake; to acknowledge, recognize (a child) as one's own

suscĭt·ŏ -āre vt to stir up; to erect, build; to awaken; to encourage; (fig) to stir up (rebellion, love, etc.)

suspect·ŏ -āre vt to gaze up at; to distrust, suspect

suspect·us -a -um pp of **suspicio**; adj suspected, mistrusted

suspect·us -ūs m respect, esteem

suspend·ĭum -ī or **-ī** n hanging; hanging oneself

sus·pendŏ -pendĕre -pendī -pensum vt to hang up, hang; to prop up, support; to keep in suspense; to check (temporarily); to interrupt; **suspendī** (with ex + abl) to depend on

suspens·us -a -um adj hanging, balanced; raised, poised; in suspense, uncertain, hesitant; (with ex + abl) dependent upon

suspĭc·ax -ācis adj suspicious; mistrusted, causing mistrust, suspicious

su·spĭcĭŏ -spĭcĕre -spexī -spec-

tum vt to look up at; to look up to, admire; to mistrust, suspect; vi to look up; (with in + acc) to look up at or into

suspĭcĭōsē adv suspiciously

suspĭcĭōs·us -a -um adj mistrustful, suspicious; suspicious-looking, suspicious; (with in + acc) suspicious of

suspĭc·ŏ -āre or **suspĭc·or -ārī -ātus sum** vt to mistrust, suspect; to suppose, believe, surmise

suspīrāt·us -ūs m deep breath, sigh

suspīr·ĭum -ī or **-ī** n deep breath, sigh; **suspirium ducere, repetere,** or **trahere** to draw a deep breath, sigh

suspīr·ŏ -āre vt to sigh for; vi to sigh, heave a sigh

susque deque adv up and down; **de Octavio susque deque est** it's all one (i.e., of no consequence) as far as Octavian is concerned

sustentācŭl·um -ī n prop, support

sustentātĭ·ŏ -ōnis f forbearance, patience

sustent·ŏ -āre vt to hold up, hold upright, support; to sustain (with food); to hold (enemy); to uphold (law); to delay; to postpone

sus·tinĕŏ -tinēre -tinŭī -tentum vt to hold up, support; to hold back, hold in, check; to uphold (law); to sustain, support (with food); to bear (trouble); to hold up, delay, put off

sustoll·ŏ -ĕre vt to lift up, raise; to destroy

susurrāt·or -ōris m mutterer, whisperer

susurr·ŏ -āre vt & vi to mutter, murmur, whisper

susurr·us -ī m low, gentle noise; murmur, whisper, buzz, hum

sūtēl·ae -ārum f pl patches; tricks

sūtĭl·is -e adj sewn together, fastened together

sūt·or -ōris m shoemaker

sūtōrĭ·us -a -um adj shoemaker's; m ex-shoemaker

sūtrīn·us -a -um adj shoemaker's; f shoemaker's shop; shoemaker's trade

sūtūr·a -ae f seam; suture

sūt·us -a -um pp of **suo**; n pl joints

su·us -a -um adj his, her, its, their, one's own; due, proper, peculiar; pron masc pl one's own people, one's own friends, one's own family; pron neut pl one's own property

Sybăr·is -is f town in S. Italy noted for its luxurious living

Sybarīt·a -ae m Sybarite

Sychae·us -ī m husband of Dido

sȳcophant·a -ae m sycophant; blackmailer; cheat; slanderer

sȳcophantĭ·a -ae f cunning, deceit

sȳcophantĭōsē adv deceitfully

sȳcophant·or -ārī -ātus sum vi to cheat; (with dat) to play a trick on

Syēn·ē -ēs f town in S. Egypt

syllăb·a -ae f syllable

syllabātim adv syllable by syllable

symbŏl·a -ae *f* contribution (*of money to a feast*); (coll) blows

symbŏl·us -ī *m* symbol, mark, token

symphōni·a -ae *f* agreement of sound, symphony, harmony

symphōniăc·us -a -um *adj* concert, musical; **puerī symphoniacī** choristers; *m pl* musicians

Symplēgăd·es -um *f pl* two islands in the Euxine which floated about and dashed against each other until they were fixed in place as the Argo sailed by them

symplegm·a -ătis *m* group (*of persons embracing or wrestling*)

synĕdr·us -ī *m* senator (*in Macedonia*)

syngrăph·a -ae *f* promissory note

syngrăph·us -ī *m* written contract; pass, passport

synŏd·ūs -ontis *m* bream (*fish*)

synthĕs·is -is *f* dinner service; suit of clothes; dinner clothes

Syph·ax -ācis *m* king of Numidia

at the time of the Second Punic War, siding with Carthage (*d.* 203 B.C.)

Syrācosi·us -a -um *adj* Syracusan; *m pl* Syracusans

Syrācūs·ae -ārum *f pl* Syracuse (*chief city in Sicily*)

Syrācūsan·us or **Syrācūsi·us -a -um** *adj* Syracusan

Syri·us -a -um *adj* Syrian; *m pl* Syrians; *f* Syria

Syr·us -a -um *adj* Syrian; *m pl* Syrians

Syr·inx -ingis *f* nymph who was pursued by Pan and changed into a reed

syrm·a -ae *f* robe with a train (*worn esp. by actors in tragedies*); tragedy

syrt·is -is *f* sand dune; quicksand

Syrt·is -is *f* Gulf of Sidra in N. Africa; Gulf of Cabes; *f pl* the Syrtes (*lakes and sand dunes of that area as representative of a wild, forbidding place*)

T

tabell·a -ae *f* small board; door sill; game board; writing tablet; ballot; picture, painting; votive tablet

tabellāri·us -a -um *adj* (law) regulating voting; *m* mailman, courier

tāb·ĕō -ēre *vi* to waste away; to melt away; to stream, run

tabern·a -ae *f* hut, hovel, cottage; booth, stall, shop; inn

tabernācŭl·um -ī *n* tent; **tabernaculum capere** to choose a place for a tent outside the city in which to take the auspices

tabernāri·ī -ōrum *m pl* shopkeepers

tāb·ĕs -is *f* melting, wasting, decay, dwindling, shrinking; decaying matter, rot; disease, pestilence

tāb·escō -escĕre -uī to begin to decay, begin to melt, melt gradually

tābidŭl·us -a -um *adj* wasting, consuming

tābid·us -a -um *adj* wasting, decaying, melting; corrupting, infectious

tābific·us -a -um *adj* melting, wasting; (fig) gnawing

tabŭl·a -ae *f* plank, board; writing tablet; advertisement; auction; picture, painting; map; votive tablet; *f pl* account books, records, register, lists

tabulār·ium -iī or **-ī** *n* archives, archives building

tabulāti·ō -ōnis *f* flooring, floor, story

tabulāt·us -a -um *adj* boarded; *n* floor, story; layer; row (*of trees*)

tāb·um -ī *n* putrid matter, decay, rot; disease, plague, pestilence

tac·ĕō -ēre -uī -itum *vt* to be silent

about, pass over in silence; *vi* to be silent, hold one's tongue; to be still, be noiseless

tacitē *adv* silently, secretly

taciturnit·ās -ātis *f* silence, taciturnity

taciturn·us -a -um *adj* silent, taciturn; noiseless, hushed, quiet

tacit·us -a -um *adj* silent, mute; unmentioned, secret; (law) assumed, implied, tacit; **per tacitum** in silence

Tacit·us -ī *m* C. Cornelius Tacitus (*Roman historian, c. 55-c. 115 A.D.*)

tactil·is -e *adj* tangible

tacti·ō -ōnis *f* touch, touching; feeling, sense of touch

tactus *pp* of **tango**

tact·us -ūs *m* touch; handling; influence, effect

taed·a -ae *f* pine wood, pitch pine; torch; wedding torch; wedding; pine board

taedet taedēre taedŭit or **taesum est** *v impers* it irks; (with *acc* of person and *genit* of the cause), e.g., **mē taedet stultitiae meae** my foolishness irks me, I am annoyed at my foolishness

taedif·er -ĕra -ĕrum *adj* torchbearing

taed·ium -iī or **-ī** *n* irksomeness, tediousness, weariness, boredom

taeni·a -ae *f* band, ribbon

Taenarid·es -ae *m* Spartan (*esp. Hyacinthus*)

Taenăr·is -idis *adj* Spartan

Taenăr·um or **Taenăr·on -ī** *n* or **Taenăr·us** or **Taenăr·os -ī** *m* or *f* most southerly point of the Peloponnesus (*thought to be the entrance to the lower world*); lower world, Hades

taet·er -ra -rum *adj* foul, revolting, offensive, shocking, loathsome; ugly, hideous; disgraceful; *n* offensiveness, repulsiveness

taetrē *adv* foully, hideously, shockingly

taetricus see **tetricus**

tag·ax -ācis *adj* light-fingered

tālār·is -e *adj* ankle-length; *n pl* angle-length clothes; sandals

tālār·ius -a -um *adj* of dice; **ludus talarius** game of dice

talāsiō or **talassiō** *interj* wedding cry

tāl·ea -ae *f* rod, bar, stake

talent·um -ī *n* talent (*Greek weight, varying from state to state, but equal to about fifty pounds*); sum of money (*consisting of sixty minae*)

tāli·ō -ōnis *f* (law) punishment in kind

tāl·is -e *adj* such, of such kind, of that kind; so great, so excellent, so distinguished

talp·a -ae *m* or *f* mole (*animal*)

Talthyb·ius -iī or **-ī** *m* herald of Agamemnon

tāl·us -ī *m* ankle, anklebone; heel, foot; die (*used in playing dice*)

tam *adv* to such an extent, to such a degree, so, so much; **tam . . . quam** the . . . the; **tam magis . . . quam magis** the more . . . the more

tamār·ix -īcis *f* tamarisk

tamdiū *adv* so long, how long; **tuamdiu quam** or **tuamdiu dum** as long as

tamen *adv* yet, nevertheless, still, all the same; in the same way

Tāmĕs·is -is or **Tāmĕs·a -ae** *m* Thames

tametsī *conj* even if, although

tamquam or **tanquam** *conj* as, just as, as much as; just as if; **tamquam si** just as if

Tanāgr·a -ae *f* town in Boeotia

Tanā·is -is *m* river of Sarmatia (*modern Don*)

Tanāqu·il -ilis *f* wife of the elder Tarquin

tandem *adv* at last, in the end, finally; (*expressing urgency or impatience*) now, tell me, please

tangō tangĕre tetigī tactum *vt* to touch; to handle, meddle with; to taste; to come to, reach; to border on; to hit, beat; to wash, anoint; to affect, gall, move to pity; to dupe; to touch upon, mention; to touch, be related to; to undertake

Tantalē·us -a -um *adj* of Tantalus

Tantalid·ēs -ae *m* descendant of Tantalus

Tantăl·is -idis *f* descendant of Tantalus (*female*)

Tantăl·us -ī *m* son of Jupiter and father of Pelops who was punished in the lower world with constant hunger and thirst

tantill·us -a -um *adj* so small, so little; *n* a bit

tantisper *adv* just so long (*and no longer*); just for the moment

tantopĕre or **tantō opĕre** *adv* so much, so greatly, to such a degree, so earnestly, so hard

tantŭlum *adv* so little, in the least

tantŭl·us -a -um *adj* so little, so small; *n* so little, such a trifle; **tantulo vendĕre** to sell for such a trifling amount

tantum *adv* so much, so greatly, to such a degree, so far, so long, so; only, just, but just, hardly, scarcely; **tantum modo** only

tantummŏdo *adv* only

tantundem *adv* just so much, just as far, to the same extent

tant·us -a -um *adj* of such size, so great; so much; so little; so important; *pron neut* so much; so little; so small an amount, so small a number; **tanti** of such value, worth so much, at so high a price; of little account, of such small importance; **tanto** (with comparatives) by so much, so much the; **tanto melior!** so much the better!, bravo!, excellent!; **tanto nequior!** so much the worse!

tant·usdem -ădem -undem *adj* so great, just as great, just as large

tapēt·a -ae *m* or **tapēt·a -ōrum** or **tapēt·ia -ium** *n pl* carpet; tapestry; coverlet

tardē *adv* slowly

tardesc·ō -ĕre *vi* to become slow; to falter

tardip·ēs -ĕdis *adj* limping

tardit·ās -ātis *f* tardiness, slowness; dullness, stupidity

tarditūd·ō -inis *f* tardiness, slowness

tardiuscŭl·us -a -um *adj* rather slow, slowish, dragging

tard·ō -āre *vt* to slow down, delay, hinder; *vi* to go slow, take it easy

tard·us -a -um *adj* tardy, slow; lingering; mentally slow, mentally retarded; deliberate; crippling

Tarentīn·us -a -um *adj* Tarentine; *m pl* Tarentines

Tarent·um -ī *n* town on S. coast of Italy, founded by the Spartans around 700 B.C.

tarm·es -itis *m* wood worm, borer

Tarpēī·us -a -um *adj* Tarpeian; **mons Tarpeius** Tarpeian cliff on the Capitoline Hill from which criminals were thrown; *f* Roman girl who treacherously opened the citadel to the Sabine attackers

tarpezīt·a or **trapezīt·a -ae** *m* banker

Tarquiniens·is -e *adj* of the town of Tarquinii

Tarquini·us -a -um *adj* Tarquinian; *m* Tarquinius Priscus (*fifth king of Rome and husband of Tanaquil*); Tarquinius Superbus (*seventh* *and last king of Rome*); *m pl* important Etrurian town

Tarracin·a -ae *f* or **Terracin·ae -ārum** *f pl* town in Latium

Tartar·a -ōrum *n pl* or **Tartar·us** or **Tartăr·os -ī** *m* Tartarus (*lower level of Hades reserved for criminals*)

Tartarĕ·us -a -um *adj* of Tartarus, infernal

tat or **tatae** *interj* exclamation of surprise

tat·a -ae *m* (coll) daddy

Tat·ius -iī or **-ī** *m* Titus Tatius (*king of the Sabines who later ruled jointly with Romulus until the latter had him killed*)

taurĕ·us -a -um *adj* bull's, of a bull; **terga taurea** bulls' hides; drums; *f* rawhide, whip

Taur·ī -ōrum *m pl* barbarous people living in the peninsula now called the Crimea

Tauric·us -a -um *adj* Tauric

taurif·er -ĕra -ĕrum *adj* bull-producing (*regions*)

tauriform·is -e *adj* bull-shaped

taurin·us -a -um *adj* bull's; made of bull's hide; bull-like

taur·us -ī *m* bull

Taur·us -ī *m* Taurus (*constellation*)

taxāti·ō -ōnis *f* rating, appraisal

taxill·us -ī *m* small die (*for playing dice*)

tax·ō -āre *vt* to appraise

tax·us -ī *f* yew, yew tree

Tāygĕt·ē -ēs *f* one of the Pleiades, the daughter of Atlas and Pleione

Tāygĕt·us -ī *m* mountain range in Laconia

tē *acc* & *abl* of **tu**

-te = suffix for **tu** and **te**

Teăn·um -ī *n* town in Campania; town in Apulia

techn·a or **techin·a -ae** *f* trick

Tecmess·a -ae *f* wife of Ajax the son of Telamon

tectē *adv* cautiously, guardedly

tect·or -ōris *m* plasterer

tectōriŏl·um -ī *n* bit of plaster work

tectōri·us -a -um *adj* roofing; plasterer's; painter's; *n* plaster, stucco; fresco painting; beauty preparation

tect·us -a -um *pp* of **tego**; *adj* concealed; secret; guarded (*words*); reserved, secretive (*person*); *n* roof; ceiling; canopy; cover, shelter; house

tēcum = **cum te**

Tegĕ·a -ae *f* town in Arcadia

Tegeae·us -a -um *adj* Tegean, Arcadian; *m* Pan; *f* Arcadian maiden (*i.e., Atalanta*)

Tegeāt·ae -ārum *m pl* Tegeans

teg·es -ĕtis *f* mat

tegill·um -ī *n* hood, cowl

tegim·en or **tegm·en** or **tegŭm·en -inis** *n* cover, covering; vault (*of heaven*)

tegiment·um or **tegment·um** or **tegument·um -ī** *n* cover, covering

tegō tegĕre texī tectum *vt* to cover; to protect, shelter, defend; to hide; to bury; **tegĕre latus** (with *genit*) to escort (*someone*)

tēgŭl·a -ae *f* tile; *f pl* roof tiles, tiled roof

tegŭmen see **tegimen**

tegumentum see **tegimentum**

tēl·a -ae *f* web; warp (*threads that run lengthwise in the loom*); yarn beam; loom; design, plan

Telăm·ōn -ōnis *m* son of Aeacus, brother of Peleus, king of Salamis, and father of Ajax and Teucer

Telamōniăd·ēs -ae *m* son of Telamon (*i.e., Ajax*)

Telamōn·ius -iī or **-ī** *m* Ajax

Tēlegŏn·us -ī *m* son of Ulysses and Circe

Tēlemăch·us -ī *m* son of Ulysses and Penelope

Tēlĕph·us -ī *m* king of Mysia, wounded by the spear of Achilles and later cured by its rust

tell·us -ūris *f* the earth; ground, earth; land, country

tēl·um -ī *n* missile, weapon; spear, javelin, dart; sword, dagger, ax; shaft

temerāri·us -a -um *adj* casual, accidental; rash, thoughtless

temĕrē *adv* by chance, without cause; at random; rashly, thoughtlessly; **non temere** not lightly; not easily; hardly ever; **nullus dies temere intercessit quo non scriberet** hardly a day ever passed without his writing

temerit·ās -ātis *f* chance, accident; rashness, thoughtlessness; *f pl* foolhardy acts

temĕr·ō -āre *vt* to darken, blacken; to violate, disgrace, defile

tēmēt·um -ī *n* alcohol, wine

temnō temnĕre tempsī temptum *vt* to slight, offend

tēm·ō -ōnis *m* pole, tongue (*of a carriage or plow*); wagon

Tempē (indecl) *n pl* scenic valley between Olympus and Ossa in Thessaly

temperāment·um -ī *n* moderation

tempĕr·ans -antis *adj* moderate, temperate

temperanter *adv* moderately

temperanti·a -ae *f* self-control, moderation

temperātē *adv* moderately, with due moderation

temperāti·ō -ōnis *f* blending, proportion, symmetry; temperament; organization, constitution; control

temperāt·or -ōris *m* controller

temperāt·us -a -um *adj* tempered; self-controlled, temperate

tempĕrī *adv* in time, on time; in due time, at the right time

temperi·ēs -ēī *f* blending, tempering; temperature, mild temperature

tempĕr·ō -āre *vt* to compound, combine, blend, temper; to regulate, moderate; to tune; to govern, control, rule; *vi* to be moderate, exercise restraint; (with *abl* or *ab* + *abl*) to abstain from

tempest·ās -ātis *f* time, period, season; stormy weather, storm, tempest

tempestīvē *adv* at the right time, seasonably

tempestīvit·ās -ātis *f* right time, timeliness

tempestīv·us -a -um *adj* timely, seasonable, fit; ripe, mature; in good time, early

templ·um -ī *n* space marked off in the sky or on the earth for observation of omens; open space, quarter; temple, shrine, sanctuary

temporāl·is -e *adj* temporary, transitory

temporāri·us -a -um *adj* temporary, changeable (*character*)

tempore or **temporī** *adv* in time, on time; in due time, at the right time

temptābund·us -a -um *adj* making constant attempts, trying

temptāment·um -ī *n* attempt, effort; temptation, trial

temptāmin·a -um *n pl* attempts, trials

temptātī·ō -ōnis *f* trial; attack (*of sickness*)

temptāt·or -ōris *m* assailant

tempt·ō or **tent·ō -āre** *vt* to test, feel, probe; to try, attempt; to attack; to try to influence, tamper with, tempt, try to induce; to urge, incite, sound out; to worry, distress, disquiet

temptus *pp* of **temno**

temp·us -ōris *n* temple (*of the head*); time, period, season; occasion, opportunity; right time, good time, proper period; times, condition, state, position; need, emergency; measure, quantity, cadence (*in metrics*); **ad tempus** punctually; at the right time, at the appointed time; for the time being, for the moment; for the occasion; **ante tempus** before time, too soon, prematurely; **ex tempore** on the spur of the moment; **id temporis** at that time; **in ipso tempore** in the nick of time; **in tempore** at the right moment, just in time; **in tempus** temporarily, for a time; **per tempus** just in time; **pro tempore** as time permits, according to circumstances; **tempori cedere** to yield to circumstances; **tempus in ultimum** to the last extremity

tēmulent·us -a -um *adj* intoxicated

tenācit·ās -ātis *f* tenacity; miserliness

tenāciter *adv* tightly, firmly

ten·ax -ācis *adj* holding tight, gripping, clinging; sticky; firm; obstinate; stingy; (with *genit*) clinging to, holding on to

tendicul·ae -ārum *f pl* little snare, little noose, little trap

tendō tendĕre tetendī tentum or **tēnsum** *vt* to stretch, stretch out, hold out, spread, strain; to head for (*a place*); to aim, shoot (*an arrow*); to bend (*a bow*); to tune (*an instrument*); to pitch (*a tent*); *vi* to pitch tents, be encamped; to travel, sail, move, march; to endeavor; to contend, fight; to exert oneself; (with *inf*) to try to, endeavor to; (with **ad** + *acc*) to tend toward, be inclined toward; **b** to move toward, travel to, aim for; (with **contra** + *acc*) to fight against

tenĕbr·ae -ārum *f pl* darkness; night; blindness; dark place, haunts; lower world; unconsciousness; death; obscurity, low station; ignorance

tenebricōs·us -a -um *adj* gloomy; darkened (*senses*); blind (*lust*)

tenebric·us -a -um *adj* dark, gloomy

tenebrōs·us -a -um *adj* dark, gloomy

Tenĕd·os or **Tenĕd·us -ī** *f* island off the coast of Troy

tenellŭl·us -a -um *adj* tender little, dainty little

tenell·us -a -um *adj* dainty

ten·eō -ēre -uī -tum *vt* to hold, hold tight, keep; to grasp, comprehend; to comprise; to possess, occupy, be master of; to hold back, restrain, repress; to hold, charm, amuse; to have control of, get the better of; to keep, detain; *vi* to hold out, last, keep on

ten·er -ĕra -ĕrum *adj* tender, soft, delicate; young, youthful; impressionable; weak; effeminate; voluptuous

tenerasc·ō -ĕre *vi* to grow weak

tenĕrē *adv* softly

tenerit·ās -ātis *f* weakness

tēnesm·os -ī *m* straining at stool

ten·or -ōris *m* uninterrupted course; **uno tenore** uninterruptedly

tēns·a -ae *f* car carrying images of the gods in procession

tēns·us -a -um *pp* of **tendō**; *adj* stretched, drawn tight, stretched out

tentīg·ō -inis *f* lust

tentō see **temptō**

tentōr·ium -iī or **-ī** *n* tent

tent·us -a -um *pp* of **tendō** and of **teneō**; *adj* stretched, drawn tight, stretched out

tenuicŭl·us -a -um *adj* poor, paltry

tenu·is -e *adj* thin, fine; delicate; precise; shallow (*groove, etc.*); slight, puny, poor, insignificant; plain, simple; small, narrow

tenuit·ās -ātis *f* thinness, fineness; leanness; simplicity; precision; poverty

tenuiter *adv* thinly; slightly; poorly, indifferently; exactly, minutely; superficially

tenu·ō -āre *vt* to make thin; to contract; to dissolve; to lessen, diminish, weaken

ten·us **-ōris** n trap, snare

tenus prep (with abl, always placed after the noun) as far as, up to, down to; **nomine tenus** or **verbo tenus** as far as the name goes, nominally, in name

Te·os or **Te·us** **-ī** f town on the coast of Asia Minor, the birthplace of Anacreon

tepe·faciō **-facĕre** **-fēcī** **-factum** vt to make warm, warm up

tep·ĕō **-ēre** **-uī** vi to be warm, be lukewarm; to glow with love; to be lukewarm, indifferent

tep·escō **-escĕre** **-uī** vi to grow warm; to grow lukewarm, grow indifferent

tepidius adv rather tepidly

tepid·us **-a** **-um** adj warm, lukewarm, tepid

tep·or **-ōris** m warmth; coolness; lack of heat (in the bath); lack of fire (in a speech)

ter adv three times, thrice

terdeciens or **terdeciēs** adv thirteen times

terebinth·us **-ī** f terebinth, turpentine tree

terēbr·a **-ae** f borer, drill

terēbr·ō **-āre** vt to bore, drill, bore out

terēd·ō **-ĭnis** f grub worm

Tēreīd·ēs **-ae** m Itys (son of Tereus)

Terent·ius **-ī** or **-ī** m Terence (M. Terentius Afer, Roman comic poet, c. 190-159 B.C.)

ter·es **-ĕtis** adj smooth, well-rounded; smooth and round, polished, shapely; round, cylindrical; (fig) smooth, elegant, fine

Tēr·eus **-ĕī** or **-ĕos** m king of Thrace, husband of Procne, and father of Itys

tergemin·us **-a** **-um** adj triple, threefold

tergĕō **tergēre** **tersī** **tersum** or **terg·ō** **-ĕre** vt to scour, wipe off, wipe dry, clean, cleanse

tergin·um **-ī** n rawhide; scourge

tergiversātĭ·ō **-ōnis** f refusal; evasion, subterfuge

tergivers·or **-ārī** **-ātus sum** vi to keep turning one's back; to be shifty, be evasive

tergō see **tergeo**

terg·um **-ī** or **terg·us** **-ŏris** n back; ridge; hide, leather; leather objects: bag, shield, drum; (mil) rear; **a tergo** in the rear, from behind; **in tergum** backward

term·es **-ĭtis** m branch

Termināl·ĭa **-ĭum** or **-iōrum** n pl festival of Terminus (the god of boundaries, celebrated on the 23rd of February)

terminātĭ·ō **-ōnis** f decision, determining; arrangement, ending (of a sentence)

termin·ō **-āre** vt to mark off with boundaries, bound, limit; to fix, determine, define; (rhet) to end, round out (a sentence)

termin·us **-ī** m boundary, limit

Termin·us **-ī** m god of boundaries

tern·ī **-ae** **-a** adj three in a group, three apiece, three each

terō terĕre trivī trītum vt to wear, rub, wear out, crush; to spend, waste; to smooth, grind, sharpen

Terpsichŏr·ē **-ēs** f Muse of dancing; poetry

terr·a **-ae** f the earth; land; earth, ground, soil; country, region, territory

terrāneŏl·a **-ae** f crested lark

terrēn·us **-a** **-um** adj earthly, terrestrial; earthen, made of earth; n land, ground

terr·ĕō **-ēre** **-uī** **-ĭtum** vt to frighten, scare, terrify; to deter

terrestr·is **-e** adj of the earth, on the earth; land, earth; **proelium terrestre** land battle

terrĕ·us **-a** **-um** adj sprung from the earth, earth-born

terribil·is **-e** adj terrible, frightful

terricŭl·a **-ōrum** n pl scarecrow

terrific·ō **-āre** vt to terrify

terrific·us **-a** **-um** adj terrifying, awe-inspiring, alarming

terrigēn·a **-ae** m or f earth-born creature

terrilŏqu·us **-a** **-um** adj ominous, alarming

territ·ō **-āre** vt to keep frightening; to intimidate

territōr·ĭum **-ĭī** or **-ī** n land around a town, territory, suburbs

terr·or **-ōris** m terror, alarm, dread, fright

ters·us **-a** **-um** pp of **tergeo**; adj clean, neat; neat, terse

tertiadecimān·ī **-ōrum** m pl soldiers of the thirteenth legion

tertiān·us **-a** **-um** adj recurring every second day, tertian; m pl soldiers of the third legion; f tertian fever

tertĭō adv in the third place, thirdly; the third time

tertĭum adv for the third time

terti·us **-a** **-um** adj third

terti·us decim·us **-a** **-um** adj thirteenth

terunc·ius **-ĭī** or **-ī** m three twelfths of an ace, quarter ace; **heres ex teruncio** heir to one fourth of the estate

tervenēfic·us **-ī** m (term of abuse) three-time killer

tesqu·a **-ōrum** n pl wilderness, wilds

tessell·a **-ae** f cubed mosaic stone

tessellāt·us **-a** **-um** adj tesselated

tessĕr·a **-ae** f cube; die; watchword, countersign; tally, token; ticket

tesserār·ius **-ĭī** or **-ī** m officer of the day

tesserŭl·a **-ae** f small cube; ticket

test·a **-ae** f brick, tile; jug, crock; potsherd; shell fish; shell

testāmentāri·us **-a** **-um** adj pertaining to a will or testament; *m* forger of a will

testāment·um -ī *n* will, testament

testāti·ō -ōnis *f* invoking as witness

testāt·us -a -um *adj* attested, public

testicŭl·us -ī *m* testicle

testificāti·ō -ōnis *f* giving evidence, testifying; proof, evidence

testific·or -ārī -ātus sum *vt* to give as evidence, attest; to vouch for; to bring to light; to call to witness

testimōn·ium -iī or -ī *n* testimony, deposition

test·is -is *m* or *f* witness; *m* testicle

test·or -ārī -ātus sum *vt* to give as evidence; to show, prove, vouch for; to call to witness, appeal to; *vi* to be a witness, testify; to make a will

testūdĭn·ĕ·us -a -um *adj* of a tortoise; made of tortoise shell

testūd·ō -ĭnis *f* tortoise; tortoise shell; lyre, lute; arch, vault; (mil) protective shed (*for besiegers*)

test·um -ī *n* earthenware lid; pot with a lid

tēte = emphatic form of **tē**

Tēth·ys -yos *f* wife of Oceanus and mother of the sea nymphs; sea

tetradrachm·um or **tetrachm·um** -ī *n* Greek silver coin (*worth four drachmas*)

tetrarch·ēs -ae *m* tetrarch (*ruler of one fourth of a country*); petty prince

tetrarch·i·a -ae *f* tetrarchy

tetric·us -a -um *adj* gloomy, sour, crabby

Teuc·er or **Teuc·rus** -rī *m* son of Telamon and brother of Ajax; son of Scamander of Crete, son-in-law of Dardanus, and later king of Troy

Teucr·i·a -ae *f* Troy

Teucr·us -a -um *adj* Teucrian, Trojan; *m pl* Trojans

Teutŏn·ēs -um or **Teutŏn·ī** -ōrum *m pl* Teutons

texō texĕre texŭī textum *vt* to weave; to plait; to build; to compose

textĭl·is -e *adj* woven; brocaded; *n* fabric

text·or -ōris *m* weaver

textrīn·um -ī *n* weaving

textr·ix -īcis *f* weaver (*female*)

textūr·a -ae *f* texture; web; fabric

text·us -a -um *pp* of **texo**; *n* woven cloth, fabric; web

text·us -ūs *m* texture

Thā·is -ĭdis *f* Athenian courtesan

thalăm·us -ī *m* woman's room; bedroom; marriage bed; marriage

thalassic·us -a -um *adj* sea-green

thalassĭn·us -a -um *adj* sea-green

Thal·ēs -is or -ētis *m* early Ionian philosopher of Miletus, regarded as one of the Seven Sages (*fl* 575 B.C.)

Thalī·a -ae *f* Muse of comedy; sea nymph

thall·us -ī *m* green bough, green stalk

Thaps·os or **Thaps·us** -ī *f* city in Africa where Caesar defeated the Pompeians (46 B.C.)

Thas·os or **Thas·us** -ī *f* island in the Aegean Sea, off the coast of Thrace

Thaumanti·as -ădis or **Thaumant·is** -ĭdis *f* Iris (*daughter of Thaumas*)

theātrāl·is -e *adj* theatrical

theātr·um -ī *n* theater

Thēb·ae -ārum *f pl* Thebes (*capital of Boeotia, founded by Cadmus*); Thebes (*city of Upper Egypt*)

Thēbae·us -a -um *adj & mf* Theban (*of Egypt*)

Thēbān·us -a -um *adj & mf* Theban (*of Boeotia*)

thēc·a -ae *f* case; envelope

Them·is -ĭdis *f* goddess of justice and of prophecy

Themistŏcl·ēs -is or -ī *m* Themistocles (*Athenian general and statesman, c. 528-459 B.C.*)

thensaurāri·us -a -um *adj* treasure, of treasure

thensaurus see **thesaurus**

Theocrit·us -ī *m* founder of Greek pastoral poetry, born at Syracuse (*3rd cent.* B.C.)

theolŏg·us -ī *m* theologian

therm·ae -ārum *f pl* hot springs, hot baths

thermopōl·ium -iī or -ī *n* hot-drink shop

thermopŏt·ō -āre *vt* to warm with a drink

Thermopyl·ae -ārum *f pl* famous pass in Thessaly between Mt. Oeta and the sea, defended by Leonidas and his four hundred Spartans (490 B.C.)

thermŭl·ae -ārum *f pl* little hot bath

Thersīt·ēs -ae *m* Greek soldier at Troy notorious for his ugliness

thēsaur·us or **thensaur·us** -ī *m* storehouse; store, treasure, hoard

Thēs·eus -ĕī or -ĕos *m* king of Athens, son of Aegeus and Aethra, and husband first of Ariadne and later of Phaedra

Thēsē·us -a -um *adj* of Theseus

Thēsĭd·ae -ārum *m pl* Athenians

Thēsĭd·ēs -ae *m* Hippolytus (*son of Theseus*)

Thespiăd·es -um *f pl* Muses

Thesp·is -is *m* traditional founder of Greek tragedy

Thespi·us -a -um *adj* Thespian; *f pl* town in Boeotia near Mt. Helicon

Thessali·a -ae *f* Thessaly (*most northerly district of Greece*)

Thessalic·us -a -um *adj* Thessalian

Thessăl·us -a -um *adj* Thessalian; *m pl* people of Thessaly, Thessalians

Thestorĭd·ēs -ae *m* Calchas (*famous Greek seer who joined the expedition to Troy*)

Thet·is -ĭdis or -ĭdos *f* sea nymph, daughter of Nereus and Doris, wife of Peleus, and mother of Achilles

thiăs·us -ī *m* Bacchic dance; Bacchic troop of dancers

Thisb·ē -ēs *f* girl in Babylon, loved by Pyramus

Tho·ās -antis *m* king of Tauris, slain by Orestes; king of Lemnos and father of Hypsipyle

thol·us -ī *m* rotunda

thōr·ax -ācis *m* breastplate

Thrāc·a -ae or **Thrāc·ē -ēs** *f* Thrace (*wild country to the N. of the Aegean*)

Thrāci·us -a -um *adj* Thracian; *f* Thrace

Thress·a or **Threiss·a -ae** *f* Thracian woman

Thr·ex -ēcis or **Thr·ax -ācis** *m* Thracian gladiator

thron·us -ī *m* throne

Thūcydĭd·ēs -is *m* Thucydides (*famous Greek historian of the Peloponnesian War, c. 456-c. 400 B.C.*)

thunn·us -ī *m* tuna fish

thūr- = tur-

Thūrĭ·ī -ōrum *m pl* city on the Tarentine Gulf in S. Italy

Thūrĭn·us -a -um *adj* & *m* Thurian

thūs thūris *n* incense, frankincense

Thybris see **Tiberis**

Thyĕn·ē -ēs *f* nymph who nursed Bacchus

Thyest·ēs -ae *m* son of Pelops, brother of Atreus, and father of Aegisthus

thymbr·a -ae *f* savory (*plant*)

thym·um -ī *n* thyme

Thȳnĭ·a -ae *f* Bithynia (*country in Asia Minor*)

Thȳnĭăc·us -a -um *adj* Bithynian

Thȳn·us -a -um *adj* & *m* Bithynian

thynn·us -ī *m* tuna fish

Thyōn·eus -ĕī *m* Bacchus

thyrs·us -ī *m* Bacchic wand twined with vine tendrils and ivy, and crowned with a fir cone

tiār·a -ae *f* or **tiār·ās -ae** *m* tiara

Tiberīn·is -ĭdis *adj* of the Tiber

Tiberīn·us -a -um *adj* of the Tiber; *m* river god of the Tiber

Tibĕr·is or **Tibr·is** or **Thybr·is -is** *m* Tiber River

Tibĕr·ius -iī or **-ī** *m* Tiberius (*Tiberius Claudius Nero Caesar, successor of Augustus, 42 B.C.-37 A.D., ruling from 14 A.D. to 37 A.D.*)

tībĭ·a -ae *f* shinbone, tibia; flute

tībĭc·en -ĭnis *m* flutist; prop; pillar

tībĭcĭn·a -ae *f* flutist (*female*)

Tibull·us -ī *m* Albius Tibullus (*Roman elegiac poet, c. 54-c. 19 B.C.*)

Tīb·ur -ŭris *n* town of Latium on the Anio (*modern Tivoli*)

Tīburt·ēs -um *m pl* Tiburtines

Tīburtīn·us or **Tīburn·us -a -um** *adj* Tiburtine

Tĭcīn·us -ī *m* tributary of the Po

Tigellīn·us -ī *m* notorious favorite of the emperor Nero

tigill·um -ī *n* beam, log

tignāri·us -a -um *adj* **faber tignarius** carpenter

tign·um -ī *n* trunk, log, beam, board

tigr·is -is or **-ĭdis** *f* tigress

Tigr·is -is or **-ĭdis** *m* large river of W. Asia which joins with the Euphrates

tĭlĭ·a -ae *f* lime tree

Tīmae·us -ī *m* Greek historian of Sicily (*c. 346-c. 250 B.C.*); Pythagorean philosopher of Locri in S. Italy after whom Plato named one of his dialogues (*5th cent. B.C.*)

Tīmāgĕn·ēs -is *m* brilliant rhetorician in the time of Augustus

timefact·us -a -um *adj* alarmed, frightened

tim·ĕō -ēre -ŭī *vt* to fear, be afraid of; *vi* to fear, be afraid

timĭdē *adv* timidly, fearfully

timĭdĭt·ās -ātis *f* timidity, fearfulness, cowardice

timĭd·us -a -um *adj* timid, fearful, cowardly; (*with genit*) fearful of, afraid of

tim·or -ōris *m* fear, alarm; dread; a terror

tinctĭl·is -e *adj* used for dipping

tinct·us -a -um *pp* of **tingo**

tinĕ·a -ae *f* moth; bookworm

tingō tingĕre tinxī tinctum *vt* to dip, soak; to dye, color; to tinge, imbue

tinnĭment·um -ī *n* ringing

tinn·iō -īre -īvī -iī -ĭtum *vt* & *vi* to ring

tinnīt·us -ūs *m* ring, ringing, tinkling, jingling

tinnŭl·us -a -um *adj* ringing, tinkling; shrill

tintinnābŭl·um -ī *n* bell, door bell, cattle bell

tintinnācŭl·us -a -um *adj* jingling; *m pl* chain gang

tintin·ō -āre *vi* to ring

tīn·us -ī *m* laurustinus (*shrub*)

Tiph·ys -yos *m* pilot of the Argo

tippŭl·a -ae *f* water spider

Tīresĭ·ās -ae *m* famous seer at Thebes at the time of Oedipus

Tīrīdāt·ēs -ae *m* king of Armenia

tīr·ō -ōnis *m* recruit; beginner

tīrōcĭn·ium -iī or **-ī** *n* first campaign; inexperience in military life; body of raw recruits; beginning, first try

tīruncŭl·us -ī *m* young beginner

Tīryn·s -this or **-thos** *f* town in Argolis where Hercules was raised

Tīrynthĭ·us -a -um *adj* Tirynthian

Tīsamĕn·us -ī *m* son of Orestes and king of Argos

Tīsiphŏn·ē -ēs *f* one of the three Furies who haunted murderers

Tīsiphonē·us -a -um *adj* guilty

Tītān -ānis of **Tītān·us -ī** *m* Titan; sun; *m pl* giant sons of Uranus and Ge who rebelled against Uranus and put Cronus on the throne

Tītānĭ·us -a -um *adj* of the Titans, Titanic; *f* Latona (*the mother of Apollo and Diana*); Pyrrha (*as descendant of Prometheus*); Circe (*as daughter of Sol*)

Tithōnǐ·us -a -um *adj* Tithonian; *f* Aurora

Tithōn·us -ī *m* son of Laomedon and husband of Aurora from whom he received the gift of immortality without eternal youth

Tĭt·iēs -ium *m pl* one of the three original tribes of Rome

tǐtillātǐ·ō -ōnis *f* tickling

tǐtill·ō -āre *vt* to tickle

tǐtǐvillǐt·ium -iī or **-ī** *n* trifle

tǐtubanter *adv* falteringly

tǐtubātǐ·ō -ōnis *f* staggering

tǐtŭb·ō -āre *vi* to stagger, reel, totter; to falter, waver (*in speech*)

tǐtŭl·us -ī *m* inscription; label; notice, advertisement; title of honor; renown; pretext

Tǐtў·os -ī *m* giant slain by Apollo for insulting Latona and thrown into Tartarus

Tǐtўr·us -ī *m* shepherd in Vergil's pastorals, sometimes identified with Virgil himself

Tlēpolēm·us -ī *m* son of Hercules

Tmōl·us or **Timōl·us -ī** *m* mountain in Lydia famous for its wines

tocull·ǒ -ōnis *m* banker

tǒf·us or **tǒph·us -ī** *m* tufa (*volcanic rock*)

tog·a -ae *f* outer garment of a Roman citizen; **toga candida** white toga (*worn by candidates for office*); **toga picta** brocaded toga (*worn by triumphant generals*); **toga praetexta** crimson-bordered toga (*worn by magistrates and freeborn children*); **toga pulla** dark-grey toga (*worn by mourners*); **toga pūra** or **virilis** or **libera** toga of manhood (*worn by young men from about the age of sixteen*)

togāt·us -a -um *adj* wearing a toga; *m* Roman citizen; civilian; humble client; *f* Roman drama (*treating of Roman themes*); prostitute

togŭl·a -ae *f* little toga

tolerābǐl·is -e *adj* tolerable; patient

tolerābǐlǐus *adv* more patiently, fairly patiently

tolēr·ans -antis *adj* tolerant; (with *genit*) tolerant of, enduring

toleranter *adv* patiently

tolerantǐ·a -ae *f* toleration, endurance

tolerātǐ·ō -ōnis *f* toleration, endurance

tolerāt·us -a -um *adj* tolerable, endurable

tolēr·ō -āre *vt* to tolerate, bear, endure; to support, maintain, sustain

tollēn·ō -ōnis *m* crane, lift, derrick

tollō tollěre sustŭlī sublātum *vt* to lift, raise; to have (*a child*); to acknowledge (*a child*); to raise, educate; to weigh (*anchor*); to take on, take on board; to remove; to do away with, destroy; to cancel, abolish, abrogate; to lift, steal; to uplift, cheer up, excite; to erect, build up; to waste (*time*); **amicum tollere** to cheer up a friend; **animos**

tollere to boost the morale; **deos tollere** to deny the existence of the gods; **hominem de medio tollere** to make away with or kill a man; **pecunias ex fano tollere** to steal money from a shrine; **signa tollere** to break camp

tolūtim *adv* at a trot

tomācŭl·um or **tomācl·um -ī** *n* sausage

tōment·um -ī *n* stuffing (*for pillows*)

Tom·ī -ōrum *m pl* or **Tom·is -is** *f* town in Moesia on the Black Sea to which Ovid was exiled

Tomīt·ae -ārum *m pl* people of Tomi

Tomītān·us -a -um *adj* of Tomi

Ton·ans -antis *m* Thunderer (*epithet of several gods, esp. Jupiter*)

tonděō tondēre totondī tonsum *vt* to clip, shear, shave; to prune; to reap, mow; to crop, browse on; (fig) to fleece, rob; **usque ad cutem tondere** to swindle, fleece

tonǐtrāl·is -e *adj* thunderous

tonǐtr·us -ūs *m* or **tonǐtrū·um -ī** *n* thunder; *m pl* or *n pl* claps of thunder

ton·ō -āre -ŭī -ǐtum *vt* to thunder out (*words*); *vi* to thunder

tons·a -ae *f* oar blade

tonsǐl·is -e *adj* clipped

tonsill·ae -ārum *f pl* tonsils

tonsǐt·ō -āre *vt* to shear regularly

tons·or -ōris *m* shearer, barber

tonsōrǐ·us -a -um *adj* shaving; barber's

tonstrǐcŭl·a -ae *f* little hairdresser, little barber (*female*)

tonstrīn·a -ae *f* barber shop

tonstr·ix -īcis *f* hairdresser, barber (*female*)

tonsūr·a -ae *f* clipping, shearing; **capillorum tonsura** haircut

tons·us -a -um *pp* of **tondeo**; *f* see **tonsa**

tons·us -ūs *m* haircut; hairdo

tǒph·us -ī *m* tufa (*volcanic rock*)

topiārǐ·us -a -um *adj* garden, landscape; *m* gardener, landscaper; *f* landscaping

topǐc·ē -ēs *f* resourcefulness in finding topics for speeches

tor·al -ālis *n* valance

torcŭl·ar -āris or **torcŭl·um -ī** *n* wine press, oil press

toreum·a -ātis *n* embossing, relief

torment·um -ī *n* windlass; catapult, artillery piece; shot; torture rack, torture; (fig) torture; *n pl* artillery

tormǐn·a -um *n pl* colic

tormǐnōs·us -a -um *adj* prone to colic

torn·ō -āre *vt* to form with a lathe, turn on a lathe

torn·us -ī *m* lathe; burin

torōs·us -a -um *adj* brawny, muscular

torpēd·ō -ǐnis *f* numbness, lethargy, listlessness; crampfish, torpedo (*fish*)

torp·ĕō -ēre -ŭī vi to be numb; to be stiff; to be stupefied; to be groggy

torp·escō -escĕre -ŭī vi to grow numb, grow listless

torpĭd·us -a -um adj groggy

torp·or -ōris m torpor, numbness; grogginess

torquāt·us -a -um adj wearing a necklace

Torquāt·us -ī m T. Manlius Torquatus (legendary Roman hero who is said to have slain a gigantic Gaul in single combat and to have worn the Gaul's necklace)

torquĕō torquēre torsī tortum vt to twist, turn, wind, wrench; to whirl, hurl, wind up and hurl; to rack; (fig) to torment

torqu·ēs or **torqu·is -is** m or f necklace; collar; festoon

torr·ens -entis adj burning, seething; rushing, roaring (stream); fiery (speech); m roaring stream, torrent

torrĕō torrēre torrŭī tostum vt to roast, bake, burn, scorch; to parch, dry up

torr·escō -escĕre -ŭī vi to become burned or parched

torrĭd·us -a -um adj baked, parched, dried up; frostbitten

torr·is -is m firebrand

tortē adv crookedly

tortĭl·is -e adj twisted, winding, spiral

tort·ō -āre vt to twist; **tortari** to writhe

tort·or -ōris m torturer, executioner

tortuōs·us -a -um adj full of turns, winding; (fig) tortuous, complicated

tort·us -a -um pp of **torqueo**; adj twisted, crooked; gnarled (oak); complicated

tort·us -ūs m twisting, twist, spiral; **tortūs dare** (of a serpent) to form loops

torŭl·us -ī m tuft (of hair)

tor·us -ī m knot; bulge; muscle; brawn; bed, couch; mattress; mound; boss; flowery expression

torvĭt·ās -ātis f grimness, wildness

torv·us -a -um adj grim, fierce, stern, savage

tostus pp of **torreo**

tot (indecl) adj so many, as many

totĭdem (indecl) adj just so many, just as many

totiens or **totiēs** adv so often, so many times

tōt·us -a -um adj the whole, all, entire; **totus in illis** wholly absorbed in those matters; n the whole matter, all; **ex toto** wholly, totally; **in toto** on the whole, in general; **in totum** wholly, totally

toxic·um -ī n poison

trabāl·is -e adj of or for beams; **clavus trabalis** spike; **telum trabale** beam-like shaft

trab·ĕa -ae f ceremonial robe (woven in stripes and worn by magistrates, augurs, etc.)

trabeāt·us -a -um adj wearing a ceremonial robe

trab·s -is f beam, plank; timber; tree; object made of beams: roof, shaft, table, battering ram

tractābĭl·is -e adj manageable; (weather) fit for navigation

tractātĭ·ō -ōnis f handling, management, treatment; discussion, treatment (of a subject)

tractāt·us -ūs m touching, handling, management

tractim adv little by little, slowly; at length, in a drawn-out manner

tract·ō -āre vt to drag around, haul, pull; to touch, handle; to manage, control, wield; to conduct, carry on, transact, practice; to discuss; **se tractare** to behave oneself, conduct oneself

tract·us -a -um pp of **traho**; adj flowing, fluent, continuous (discourse)

tract·us -ūs m dragging; drawing out, dragging out, extension (e.g., of a war); track, trail; tract, extent, distance; region, district

trādĭtĭ·ō -ōnis f handing over, surrender; transmission

trādĭt·or -ōris m betrayer, traitor

trādō trādĕre trādĭdī trādĭtum vt to hand over, surrender, deliver; to betray; to hand down, bequeath, transmit, pass on; to relate, recount; to teach; **se tradere** (with dat) a to surrender to; b to devote oneself to

trā·dūcō -dūcĕre -dūxī -ductum vt to lead across, bring over, transfer, to lead in parade, make a show of; to disgrace, degrade; to broadcast, proclaim; to pass, spend

trāductĭ·ō -ōnis f transfer, transference; course, passage (of time); metonymy

trāduct·or -ōris m conveyor

trāductus pp of **traduco**

trād·ux -ŭcis m vine branch

tragĭcē adv as in tragedy

tragicocōmoedĭ·a -ae f melodrama

tragic·us -a -um adj of tragedy, tragic; in the tragic style, grand, solemn; of a tragic nature, tragic, moving, terrible; **actor tragicus** tragedian; m tragic playwright

tragoedĭ·a -ae f tragedy

tragoed·us -ī m tragic actor, tragedian

trāgŭl·a -ae f javelin

trag·us -ī m body odor of the armpits; a fish (of unknown type)

trah·ax -ācis adj greedy

trah·ĕa -ae f sledge, drag

trahō trahĕre traxī tractum vt to draw, drag, trail; to draw out, pull out, extract; to lead, take along, be followed by; to contract, wrinkle; to inhale; to quaff; to take on, assume, acquire, get; to squander, dissipate; to spin, manufacture; to attract, allure, influence; to win over (to the other side); to refer, ascribe; to distract; to consider, ponder; to spin out, prolong, protract

Trājān·us -ī m Trajan (*M. Ulpius Trajanus, Roman emperor, 97-117 A.D.*)

trājectī·ō -ōnis f crossing, passage; transposition (*of words*); shift of meaning; exaggeration

trājectus pp of **trajicio**

trāject·us -ūs m crossing over, passage

trā·jiciō or **trans·iciō** or **trans·jiciō -jicĕre -jēcī -jectum** vt to have go across, cause to go across, transfer; to ship across, transport; to pass through, break through; to stab through, pierce; (*with double* acc) to bring (*e.g., troops*) across (*river, mountain*); (*with* **trans** + acc) to lead across; (*with* **in** + acc) to lead over into

trālāt- = translat-

Trall·ēs -ium f pl town in Lydia

trālŏqu·or -ī vt to talk over, enumerate, recount

trālūcĕō see **transluceo**

trām·a -ae f woof, web

trāmĕō = transmeo

trām·es -ĭtis m path, track, trail

trāmi- = transmi-

trānătō = transnato

trān·ō or **transn·ō -āre** vt to swim across; to pass through, permeate; vi to swim across; to pass through

tranquillē adv quietly, calmly

tranquillit·ās -ātis f tranquillity, stillness, calmness

tranquill·ō -āre vt to calm, quiet, tranquillize

tranquill·us -a -um adj calm, quiet, tranquil; n calm, calmness, peace, quiet, tranquillity; quiet sea

trans prep (*with* acc) across, over, beyond

transab·ĕō -īre -iī vt to go through, pierce

transact·or -ōris m manager

transactus pp of **transigo**

transad·igō -igĕre -ēgī -actum vt to pierce; to run (*someone*) through; (*with double* acc) to run (*e.g., a sword*) through (*someone*)

Transalpīn·us -a -um adj Transalpine, lying beyond the Alps

tran·scendō or **trans·scendō -scendĕre -scendī -scensum** vt to climb or step over, surmount; to overstep, transgress; vi to climb or step across

trans·cīdō -cīdĕre -cīdī vt to flog soundly

tran·scrībō or **trans·scrībō -scrībĕre -scrīpsī -scriptum** vt to transcribe, copy off; (*law*) to transfer, convey; to transfer, remove

trans·currō -currĕre -currī -cucurrī -cursum vt & vi to run or dash over; to run or dash through; to run or dash by or past

transcurs·us -ūs m running through, passage; cursory mention

transd- = trad-

transenn·a -ae f grating; lattice work, trellis work; lattice window; fowler's net

trans·ĕō -īre -iī -ītum vt to pass over, cross; to desert; to pass (*in a race*); to pass over, make no mention of; to treat cursorily; to overstep, pass beyond; to surpass; vi to go over, go across, pass over; to pass by, go by; to shift (*to another opinion, topic, etc.*); (*of time*) to pass, go by; to pass away; (*with* **ad** + acc) a to cross over to (*a place*); b to cross over to, desert to; (*with* **in** + acc) to change into, be transformed into; (*with* **per** + acc) to penetrate, permeate, pervade

trans·fĕrō -ferre -tŭlī -lātum (or **trālātum**) vt to carry or bring across; to transfer by writing, to copy; to shift, transfer; to transform; to postpone; to translate; to use (*words*) figuratively

trans·fīgō -fīgĕre -fīxī -fīxum vt to pierce, transfix; to run (*someone*) through

transfĭgūr·ō -āre vt to transform

transfīxus pp of **transfigo**

trans·fodiō -fodĕre -fōdī -fossum vt to run through, stab, pierce

transform·is -e adj transformed, changed in shape

transform·ō -āre vt to change in shape, transform

transfossus pp of **transfodio**

transfŭg·a -ae m or f deserter, turncoat

trans·fugiō -fugĕre -fūgī vi to desert

transfug·ium -iī or **-ī** n desertion

trans·fundō -fundĕre -fūdī -fūsum vt to transfuse; to pour; (*with* **in** + acc) to pour (*a liquid*) into; (*with* **ad** + acc) (fig) to shift (*affection, allegiance*) to (*another person*)

transfūsi·ō -ōnis f transmigration

transfūsus pp of **transfundo**

trans·gredior -grĕdī -gressus sum vt to cross, pass over; to exceed; vi to go across; to cross over (*to another party*)

transgressi·ō -ōnis f crossing, passage; transposition (*of words*)

transgressus pp of **transgredior**

transgress·us -ūs m crossing

transiciō see **trajicio**

transiect- = traject-

trans·igō -igĕre -ēgī -actum vt to pierce, run through; to finish, settle, transact, accomplish, perform, conclude; to pass, spend (*time*); vi to come to an agreement, reach an understanding

transil·iō or **transsil·iō -īre -uī** vt to jump over, jump across; to overstep, exceed; to skip, omit; vi to jump across

transit·ans -antis adj passing through

transitī·ō -ōnis f crossing, passage;

switching (*to another party*); contagion, infection; passageway

transitus *pp* of **transeo**

transit·us -ūs *m* crossing, passage; passing; traffic; crossing over, desertion; change, period of change, transition; fading (*of colors*); **in transitu** in passing

translātici·us or **trālātici·us** -a -um *adj* transmitted, traditional, customary; usual, common

translāti·ō or **trālāti·ō** -ōnis *f* transfer, shift; transporting; translation; metaphor, figure

translātiv·us -a -um *adj* transferable

translāt·or -ōris *m* middleman (*in a transfer*)

translātus *pp* of **transfero**

translēg·ō -ēre *vt* to read through

translūc·eō or **trālūc·eō** -ēre *vi* to be reflected; to shine through

transmarīn·us -a -um *adj* from beyond the seas, foreign, overseas

transmē·ō or **trāmē·ō** -āre *vi* to cross, pass

transmigr·ō -āre *vi* to move, migrate, emigrate

transmissi·ō -ōnis *f* crossing, passage

transmissus *pp* of **transmitto**

transmiss·us -ūs *m* passing over, crossing, passage

trans·mittō or **trā·mittō** -mittĕre **mīsī** -**missum** *vt* to send across; to transmit; to let pass; to hand over, entrust, commit; to pass over, leave unmentioned; to pass through, endure; (with **in** + *acc*) to send (*someone*) across to or into; (with **per** + *acc*) to let (*someone*) pass through; *vi* to cross over, cross, pass (*from one place to another*)

transmontān·ī -ōrum *m pl* people across the mountains

trans·moveō -**movēre** -**mōvī** -**mōtum** *vt* to move, transfer

transmūt·ō -āre *vt* to change, shift

transnat·ō or **trānat·ō** -āre *vt* to swim; *vi* to swim across

transnō see **trano**

Transpadān·us -a -um *adj* Transpadane, beyond or N. of the Po River

transpect·us -ūs *m* view, prospect

transpic·iō or **transspic·iō** -ĕre *vt* to look through

trans·pōnō -pōnĕre -posŭī -posĭtum *vt* to transfer

transport·ō -āre *vt* to transport

transposĭtus *pp* of **transpono**

Transrhēnān·us -a -um *adj* beyond the Rhine, E. of the Rhine

transs- = **trans-**

Transtiberīn·us -a -um *adj* across the Tiber

transtin·ĕō -ēre *vi* to pass through

transtr·um -ī *n* thwart

transult·ō -āre *vi* to jump across

transūt·us -a -um *adj* pierced through

transvectī·ō or **trāvectī·ō** -ōnis *f*

transportation, crossing

trans·vehō or **trā·vehō** -**vehĕre vexī** -**vectum** *vt* to transport; to carry, lead (*in a parade*); **trans·vehī** to ride by (*in a parade*); (of time) to elapse

transverbĕr·ō -āre *vt* to pierce through and through, transfix

transversa *adv* sideways; across one's course

transversāri·us -a -um *adj* transverse, lying crosswise

transvers·us or **trāvers·us** or **transvors·us** -a -um *adj* lying across, lying crosswise; inopportune; astray; in the wrong direction; *n* wrong direction, opposite direction; **de transverso** unexpectedly; **ex transverso** unexpectedly; sideways

transvolit·ō -āre *vt* to flit through, fly through

transvol·ō or **trāvol·ō** -āre *vt & vi* to fly over, fly across, fly by, zip by

transvorsus see **transversus**

trapēt·us -ī *m* oil press

trapezīt·a -ae *m* banker

Trapez·ūs -untis *f* city in Pontus on the Black Sea

Trasimenn·us or **Trasumenn·us** -ī *m* lake in Etruria where Hannibal defeated the Romans (217 B.C.)

trāv- = **transv-**

trecēn·ī -ae -a *adj* three hundred each

trecentēsĭm·us -a -um *adj* three hundredth

trecentiēs *adv* three hundred times

trechedipn·um -ī *n* light garment worn to dinner

tredĕcim (indecl) *adj* thirteen

tremebund·us -a -um *adj* trembling, shivering

treme·faciō -facĕre -fēcī -factum *vt* to shake, cause to shake

tremend·us -a -um *adj* terrible, frightful

trem·escō or **trem·iscō** -escĕre -ŭī *vt* to tremble at; *vi* to tremble

trem·ō -ĕre -ŭī *vt* to tremble at; *vi* to tremble, shiver, quake

trem·or -ōris *adj* trembling, shaking, shivering; dread

tremŭl·us -a -um *adj* trembling, quivering, tremulous, shivering

trepidanter *adv* tremblingly, nervously

trepidāti·ō -ōnis *f* nervousness, alarm

trepĭdē *adv* nervously, in alarm

trepĭd·ō -āre *vt* to start at, be jumpy or nervous at; *vi* to be nervous, be jumpy, be alarmed; (of a flame) to flicker; (of streams) to rush along

trepĭd·us -a -um *adj* nervous, jumpy, agitated, hurried, restless; bubbling; perilous, critical, alarming; **in re trepida** in a ticklish situation

trēs (or **trīs**) **tria** *adj* three; (denoting a small number) a couple of

tress·is -is *m* small coin: mere trifle

tresvirī (*genit*: **triumvirōrum**) *m pl* three-man board, triumvirs

Trēvĕr·ī -ōrum *m pl* people of E. Gaul

triangŭl·us -a -um *adj* triangular; *n* triangle

triāri·ī -ōrum *m pl* soldiers of the third rank in a battle line, reserves

tribuāri·us -a -um *adj* tribal

tribūl·is -is *m* fellow tribesman

tribŭl·um -ī *n* threshing sledge (*wooden platform with iron teeth underneath*)

tribŭl·us -ī *m* caltrop (*thistle*)

tribūn·al -ālis *n* raised platform; tribunal, judgment seat; (in camp) general's platform; cenotaph

tribūnāt·us -ūs *m* tribuneship, rank of tribune

tribūnici·us -a -um *adj* tribunician, tribune's; *m* ex-tribune

tribūn·us -ī *m* tribune; **tribunus aerarius** paymaster; **tribunus militaris** or **tribunus militum** military tribune (*six in each legion, serving under the legatus, and elected by the people or at times appointed by a commander*); **tribunus plebis** tribune of the people (*ten in number, serving the interests of the plebeians*)

trib·uō -uĕre -uī -ūtum *vt* to divide; to distribute, bestow, confer, assign; to give, present; to concede, grant, allow; to ascribe, impute; to devote, spend

trib·us -ūs *m* tribe (*originally three in number and eventually increased to thirty-five*)

tribūtāri·us -a -um *adj* subject to tribute; **tributariae tabellae** letters of credit

tribūtim *adv* by tribes

tribūti·ō -ōnis *f* distribution

tribūt·us -a -um *pp* of **tribuo**; *adj* arranged by tribes; *n* tribute, tax, contribution

tric·ae -ārum *f pl* tricks; nonsense

tricēn·ī -ae -a *adj* thirty each

tric·eps -ipitis *adj* three-headed

tricēsĭm·us -a -um *adj* thirtieth

trichĭl·a -ae *f* bower, arbor; summer home

triciēns or **triciēs** *adv* thirty times

triclīni·um -iī or -ī *n* dining couch (*running around three sides of a table*); dining room

tric·ō -ōnis *m* practical joker, trickster

tric·or -ārī -ātus sum *vi* to cause trouble; to pull tricks

tricorp·or -ŏris *adj* three-bodied

tricusp·is -ĭdis *adj* three-pronged

trid·ens -entis *adj* three-pronged; *m* trident

Trĭdentĭf·er or **Trĭdentĭg·er** -ĕrī *m* Trident Bearer (*epithet of Neptune*)

tridŭ·um -ī *n* three-day period, three days

trienn·ia -ĭum *n pl* triennial festi-

val, festival celebrated every three years

trienn·ium -iī or -ī *n* three-year period, three years

tri·ens -entis *m* one third; coin (*one third of an ace*); third of a pint

trientābŭl·um -ī *n* land given by the state as an equivalent for one third of the sum which the state owed

trientī·us -a -um *adj* sold for a third

triērarch·us -ī *m* captain of a trireme

triēr·is -is *f* trireme

trietēric·us -a -um *adj* triennial, recurring every three years; *n pl* festival of Bacchus

trietēr·is -ĭdis *f* three-year period; triennial festival

trifāriam *adv* in three places, on three sides

trifa·x -cis *adj* triple-throated

trifĭd·us -a -um *adj* three-forked; split into three parts

triform·is -e *adj* triple

trifĭl·is -e *adj* having three threads or hairs

tri·fūr -fūris *m* archthief

trifurcĭf·er -ĕrī *m* archvillain, hardened criminal

trigemĭn·us or **tergemĭn·us** -a -um *adj* threefold, triple; *m pl* triplets

trigintā (*indecl*) *adj* thirty

trig·ōn -ōnis *m* ball game

trilibr·is -e *adj* three-pound

trilingu·is -e *adj* triple-tongued

tril·ix -īcis *adj* three-ply, triplestranded

trimestr·is -e *adj* of three months

trimĕtr·us -ī *m* trimeter

trim·us -a -um *adj* three-year-old

Trīnacr·is -ĭdis *adj* Sicilian

Trīnacri·us -a -um *adj* Sicilian; *f* Sicily

trīn·ī -ae -a *adj* threefold, triple; three each

trinōd·is -e *adj* having three knots, triple-knotted

triōbŏl·us -ī *m* three-obol coin, halfdrachma piece

Triōn·ēs -um *m pl* Great Bear and Little Bear (*constellation*)

tripartītō *adv* in three parts, into three parts

tripartīt·us or **tripertīt·us** -a -um *adj* divided into three parts, threefold

tripectŏr·us -a -um *adj* triple-bodied, triple-breasted

tripedāl·is -e *adj* three-foot

tripertītus see **tripartītus**

trip·ēs -ĕdis *adj* three-legged

tripl·ex -ĭcis *adj* threefold, triple; *n* three times as much, threefold portion

tripl·us -a -um *adj* triple, threefold

Triptolĕm·us -a -um *m* son of Celeus the king of Eleusis, favorite of Ceres, inventor of agriculture, and one of the judges in the lower world

tripudi·ō -āre vi to dance (as a religious act); to do a war dance; to leap, dance, hop about

tripudium -iī or **-ī** n solemn religious dance; war dance; dance (in general); favorable omen (when the sacred chickens ate hungrily)

trip·us -ŏdis f tripod (three-footed vessel); oracle, Delphic oracle

triquĕtr·us -a -um adj triangular; Sicilian

trirēm·is -e adj having three banks of oars; f trireme

tris see **tres**

triscurri·a -ōrum n pl broad humor, fantastic nonsense

tristicŭl·us -a -um adj somewhat sad

tristific·us -a -um adj ominous; saddening

tristimōni·a -ae f sadness

trist·is -e adj sad, sorrowful, melancholy, glum, dispirited; bringing sorrow, saddening, dismal; gloomy, sullen; stern, harsh; disagreeable, offensive (odor); bitter (taste)

tristiti·a -ae f sadness, gloom, gloominess, melancholy; severity, sternness

tristiti·ēs -ēī f sadness, sorrow, melancholy

trisulc·us -a -um adj three-forked

tritāv·us -ī m great-great-great-grandfather

tritĭcĕ·us -a -um adj wheat, of wheat

tritĭc·um -ī n wheat

Trit·ōn -ōnis m son of Neptune who blows through a shell to calm the seas; lake in Africa where Minerva was said to be born

Tritōniăc·us -a -um adj Tritonian

Tritōn·is -idis or **-idos** f Minerva

Tritōni·us -a -um adj Tritonian; f Minerva

trīt·or -ōris m grinder

trītūr·a -ae f threshing

trīt·us -a -um pp of **tero**; adj worn, well-worn; beaten (path); experienced, expert; common, trite (language)

trīt·us -ūs m rubbing, friction

triumphāl·is -e adj triumphal; having had a triumph; n pl triumphal insignia (without the actual triumph)

triumph·ō -āre vt to triumph over, conquer completely, vanquish; vi to make a triumphal procession, celebrate a triumph, triumph

triumph·us or **triump·us -ī** m victory parade, triumph; victory, triumph; **triumphum agere** (with **dē** or **ex** + abl) to celebrate a triumph over

triumv·ir -irī m triumvir, commissioner; mayor (of a provincial town)

triumvirāl·is -e adj triumviral, of the triumvirs

triumvirāt·us -ūs m triumvirate, office of triumvir

triumvir·ī -ōrum m pl triumvirs, three commissioners, three-man commission (appointed at various times to serve various purposes); **triumvirī capitales** police commissioners, superintendents of prisons and executions

trivenēfic·a -ae f nasty old witch

Trivi·a -ae f Diana

triviāl·is -e adj of the crossroads; found everywhere, common, ordinary

triv·ium -iī or **-ī** n crossroads, intersection; public street, highway

trivi·us -a -um adj of or at the crossroads

Trō·as -ădis adj Trojan; f Troad, district of Troy; Trojan woman

trochae·us -ī m trochee; tribrach (metrical foot of three short syllables)

trochlĕ·a -ae f block and tackle

troch·us -ī m hoop

Trōi·a or **Trōj·a -ae** f Troy

Trōiăd·es -um f pl Trojan women

Trōïc·us -a -um adj Trojan

Trōïl·us -ī m son of Priam, killed by Achilles

Trōï·us -a -um adj Trojan; f see **Troia**

Trōjān·us -a -um adj Trojan; m pl Trojans

Trōjugĕn·a masc & fem adj Trojan-born, born at Troy, of Trojan descent, Trojan; m Trojan

tropae·um -ī n trophy, victory memorial; victory; mark, token, memorial, monument

Trōs Trōis m Tros (king of Phrygia after whom Troy was named)

trucīdāti·ō -ōnis f slaughter, massacre, butchery

trucīd·ō -āre vt to slaughter, massacre, cut down

truculentē or **truculenter** adv grimly, fiercely

truculenti·a -ae f savagery, ferocity; harshness; inclemency

truculent·us -a -um adj savage, grim, fierce, cruel

trud·is -is f pointed pole, pike

trūdō trūdĕre trūsī trūsum vt to push, thrust, drive, shove; to put forth (buds)

trull·a -ae f dipper, ladle, scoop; brazier; wash basin

trunc·ō -āre vt to lop off, mutilate, maim

trunc·us -a -um adj lopped; stripped (of branches and leaves), trimmed; maimed, mutilated; imperfect, undeveloped; m trunk, tree trunk; trunk, body (of human being); chunk of meat; blockhead

trūsĭt·ō -āre vt to keep pushing, keep shoving

trūsus pp of **trudo**

trutĭn·a -ae f balance, pair of scales; criterion

trutĭn·or -ārī -ātus sum vt to weigh, balance

trux trucis *adj* savage, grim, fierce, wild

trygōn·us -ī *m* stingray

tu *pron* you (*singular*)

tuātim *adv* in your manner, as is typical of you

tub·a -ae *f* bugle, war trumpet

tūb·er -ĕris *n* lump, bump, swelling; truffle (*food*)

tub·er -ĕris *f* apple tree; *m* apple

tubīc·en -ĭnis *m* bugler, trumpeter

tubilustr·ium -iī or **-ī** *n* festival of bugles or trumpets (*celebrated on March 23rd and May 23rd and including a ritual cleaning of the bugles or trumpets*)

taburcīn·or -ārī -ātus sum *vt* to devour, gobble up

tub·us -ī *m* tube, pipe

tuccēt·um or **tūcēt·um -ī** *n* sausage

tudĭt·ō -āre *vt* to keep hitting, keep beating

tuĕor or **tu·or tuērī tuĭtus sum** or **tūtus sum** *vt* to see, look at, gaze at, watch, observe; to look after, take care of, guard, defend, protect

tugur·ium -iī or **-ī** *n* hut, hovel, cottage

tuĭti·ō -ōnis *f* guarding, defense; **tuĭtio suī** self-defense

Tulliān·um -ī *n* state prison in Rome, reputedly built by Servius Tullius

Tullĭŏl·a -ae *f* little Tullia (*Cicero's daughter*)

Tull·ius -iī or **-ī** *m* Servius Tullius (*sixth king of Rome*)

tum *adv* then, at that time; next; moreover, besides; **cum . . . tum** both . . . and especially, not only . . . but also, if . . . then surely; **tum cum** at the point when, at the time when, just then when; **tum . . . tum** first . . . then, at one time . . . at another, now . . . now, both . . . and, partly . . . partly

tume·faciō -facĕre -fēcī -factum *vt* to make swell; (fig) to inflate

tum·ĕō -ēre -uī *vi* to be swollen, swell up, be inflated; (of business) to be in ferment, be cooking; (of language) to be bombastic; (of a person) to be excited, be in a dither, be in a rage; to be proud

tum·escō -escĕre -uī *vi* to begin to swell, begin to swell up; (of wars) to brew; to grow excited, become enraged, become inflated

tumĭd·us -a -um *adj* swollen, swelling; bloated; rising high; proud, inflated, puffed up; arrogant; incensed, enraged, exasperated; bombastic

tum·or -ōris *m* tumor, swelling; protuberance, bulging; elevation (*of the ground*); commotion, excitement, anger, rage; vanity, pride, arrogance

tumŭl·ō -āre *vt* to bury

tumulōs·us -a -um *adj* full of hills, hilly, rolling

tumultuārĭ·us -a -um *adj* hurried, confused, disorderly; (mil) emergency, drafted hurriedly to meet an emergency; **exercitus tumultuarius** emergency army; **pugna tumultuaria** irregular fight or battle (*i.e., not fought in regular battle formation*)

tumultuāti·ō -ōnis *f* confusion, hustle and bustle, panic

tumult·ō -āre or **tumultŭ·or -ārī -ātus sum** *vi* to make a disturbance; to be in uproar, be topsyturvy

tumultuōsē *adv* disorderly, in confusion

tumultuōs·us -a -um *adj* boisterous, uproarious, turbulent, panicky

tumult·us -ūs *m* commotion, uproar; insurrection, rebellion, civil war; confusion, agitation (*of the mind*); outbreak (*of crime*)

tumŭl·us -ī *m* mound; rising; ground swell; burial mound; **tumulus inanis** cenotaph

tūn = tūne (**tū & ne**)

tunc *adv* (of time past) then, at that time, on that occasion, just then; (of future time) then, at that time, in that event; (of succession in time) thereupon; (in conclusion) accordingly, consequently, in that case; **tunc . . . cum** then . . . when, just when, just at the time when; only when, whenever; **tunc demum** not until, then only, not till then; **tunc primum** then for the first time; **tunc quando** whenever; **tunc quoque** then too; **tunc vero** then to be sure, exactly then

tundō tundĕre tutŭdī tunsum or **tūsum** *vt* to beat, pound, hammer, thump; to buffet; to thresh; (fig) to harp on, keep at, importune

tunĭc·a -ae *f* tunic (*ordinary sleeved garment worn by both sexes*); skin, peel, husk, coating

tunicāt·us -a -um *adj* wearing a tunic; in shirt sleeves; coated, covered with skin

tunĭcŭl·a -ae *f* short tunic; thin skin or coating

tunsus *pp* of **tundo**

tuor see **tueor**

turb·a -ae *f* turmoil, disorder, uproar, commotion; brawl; crowd, disorderly crowd, mob, gang; multitude; common crowd, the masses; a large number

turbāment·a -ōrum *n pl* means of disturbance

turbātē *adv* in confusion, confusedly

turbāti·ō -ōnis *f* confusion, disorder

turbāt·or -ōris *m* ringleader, troublemaker, disturber

turbāt·us -a -um *adj* confused, disorderly; disturbed, annoyed

turbell·ae -ārum *f pl* stir, row; **turbellas facere** to cause a row

turben see **turbo** *m*

turbĭdē *adv* confusedly, in disorder

turbĭd·us -a -um *adj* wild, confused, boisterous; muddy, turbid;

troubled, perplexed; vehement; disheveled (*hair*); stormy (*sky, weather*)

turbinĕ·us -a -um *adj* cone-shaped

turb·ō -ĭnis *m* or **turb·en -ĭnis** *n* whirl, twirl, eddy; spinning, revolution; coil; spinning top; reel; spindle; wheel; tornado, whirlwind; wheel of fortune; (fig) whirlwind, storm

turb·ō -āre *vt* to throw into confusion, disturb, agitate; to break, disorganize (*in battle*), cause to break ranks; to confuse, confound; to muddy

turbulentē or **turbulenter** *adv* boisterously, tumultuously, confusedly

turbulent·us -a -um *adj* turbulent, wild, stormy; disturbed, confused; seditious, trouble-making

turd·a -ae *f* or **turd·us -ī** *m* thrush

tūrĕ·us -a -um *adj* of frankincense

turgĕō turgēre tursī *vi* to be swollen, be puffed up; to be bombastic

turgesc·ō -ĕre *vi* to begin to swell, begin to swell up; to begin to blow up (*in anger*)

turgidŭl·us -a -um *adj* poor swollen, swollen little (*eyes*)

turgid·us -a -um *adj* swollen, puffed up, inflated; turgid, bombastic

tūribŭl·um -ī *n* censer

tūricrĕm·us -a -um *adj* incense-burning

tūrif·er -ĕra -ĕrum *adj* incense-producing

tūrilĕg·us -a -um *adj* incense-gathering

turm·a -ae *f* troop, squadron (*of cavalry*); crowd, group

turmāl·is -e *adj* of a squadron; equestrian; *m pl* troopers

turmātim *adv* by troops, by squadrons, squadron by squadron

Turn·us -ī *m* king of the Rutuli, killed by Aeneas

turpicŭl·us -a -um *adj* ugly little; somewhat indecent

turpiñcāt·us -a -um *adj* corrupted, debased, degenerate

turpilucricupĭd·us -a -um *adj* (coll) eager to make a fast buck

turp·is -e *adj* ugly, deformed; foul, filthy, nasty; disgraceful, shameless; dirty, obscene, indecent

turpiter *adv* repulsively; disgracefully, scandalously, shamelessly

turpitūd·ō -ĭnis *f* ugliness, deformity; foulness; disgrace; moral turpitude

turp·ō -āre *vt* to make ugly, disfigure; to soil, dirty, defile, pollute

turrig·er -ĕra -ĕrum *adj* turreted; (Cybele) wearing a turreted crown (*representing the earth with its cities*)

turr·is -is *f* turret, tower; howdah (*on an elephant*); (fig) castle, mansion

turrīt·us -a -um *adj* turreted; fortified with turrets; crowned with turrets, adorned with a turret crown

turt·ur -ŭris *m* turtledove

tūs tūris *n* incense, frankincense

Tusculān·us -a -um or **Tusculens·is -e** *adj* Tusculan, of Tusculum; *m pl* Tusculans

Tuscŭl·us -a -um *adj* Tusculan; *n* Tusculum (*town in Latium near Alba Longa, about twelve miles from Rome*)

Tusc·us -a -um *adj* Etruscan

tussicŭl·a -ae *f* slight cough

tuss·iō -īre *vi* to cough, have a cough

tuss·is -is *f* cough

tūsus *pp* of **tundo**

tūtām·en -ĭnis or **tūtāment·um -ī** *n* means of defense, defense, protection

tūte = **tū** & **te** emphatic form of **tū**

tūtē *adv* safely

tūtēl·a or **tūtell·a -ae** *f* care, charge, patronage, protection, defense; guardianship; charge, thing protected; guardian, keeper, watcher

tūtēmet = **tū** & **te** & **met** emphatic form of **tū**

tūt·ō -āre or **tūt·or -ārī -ātus sum** *vt* to guard, protect, defend; to keep safe, watch, preserve; to ward off, avert; (with **ab** + *abl* or with **ad** or **adversus** + *acc*) to protect (*someone*) from, guard (*someone*) against

tūt·or -ōris *m* protector; guardian (*of minors, women, etc.*)

tūt·us -a -um *pp* of **tueor**; *adj* safe, secure; cautious, prudent; *n* safe place, safety, shelter, security; **ex tuto** from a safe place, in safety, safely

tūtō *adv* safely, in safety

tu·us -a -um *adj* your; right for you, proper for you; *pron* yours; **tuā interest** it is of importance to you; **tui** your friends, your people, your family; **tuum est** (with *inf*) it is your duty to, it is up to you to

tuxtax *adv* (word meant to imitate the sound of blows) whack, wham; **tuxtax meo tergo erit** (coll) it's going to go whack, wham, bang over my back

Tȳd·eus -ĕī or **-ĕos** *m* Tydeus (*son of Oeneus, one of the Seven against Thebes, and father of Diomedes*)

Tȳdīd·ēs -ae *m* Diomedes (*son of Tydeus*)

tympanotrīb·a -ae *m* timbrel player, drummer

tympăn·um or **typăn·um -ī** *n* timbrel, drum

Tyndar·ĕus -ĕī or **Tyndăr·us -ī** *m* king of Sparta, husband of Leda, father of Castor and Clytemnestra, and reputed father of Pollux and Helen

Tyndarid·ēs -ae *m* descendant of Tyndareus

Tyndar·is -ĭdis *f* descendant of Tyndareus (*female*)

Typhō·ĕus -ĕī or **ĕos** or **Typh·ōn -ōnis** *m* giant who was struck with lightning by Jupiter and buried under Mount Etna

typ·us -ī *m* figure, image (*on the wall*)

tyrannactŏn·us -ī *m* tyrannicide, assassin of a tyrant

tyrannicē *adv* tyrannically; arbitrarily, cruelly

tyrannicīd·a -ae *m* tyrannicide, assassin of a tyrant

tyrannic·us -a -um *adj* tyrannical; arbitrary, cruel

tyrann·is -ĭdis *f* tyranny, despotism

tyrianthĭn·a -ōrum *n pl* violet-colored clothes

Tyri·us -a -um *adj* Tyrian, Phoeni-cian; Carthaginian; Theban; crimson (*because of the famous dye produced at Tyre*); *m pl* Tyrians, Carthaginians

Tyr·ō -ūs *f* daughter of Salmoneus and mother of Pelias and Neleus by Poseidon

Tyr·os or **Tyr·us -ī** *f* Tyre (*famous commercial city of Phoenicia*)

tўrotarĭch·os -ī *m* dish of salted fish and cheese

Tyrrhēnĭ·a -ae *f* Etruria

Tyrrhēnĭc·us -a -um *adj* Etrurian, Etruscan

Tyrrhēn·us -a -um *adj* Etrurian, Etruscan; *m pl* Etruscans (*Pelasgian people who migrated to Italy perhaps from Lydia in Asia Minor and settled to the N. of the Tiber*)

Tyrtae·us -ī *m* Spartan poet (7th cent. B.C.)

U

ūb·er -ĕris *adj* rich, fruitful, fertile, plentiful, productive; rich, imaginative (*style*); (*fig*) fruitful, productive; *n* richness, fruitfulness, fertility; fertile soil, fruitful field; breast, teat; udder, dug

ūberius *adv* more fully, more copiously, more fruitfully

ūbert·as -ātis *f* richness, fertility, productiveness

ūbertim *adv* abundantly, copiously

ubī *adv* (*interrog*) where; **ubi gentium** (*coll*) where in the world; *conj* where, in which, whereby, with whom, by whom; when, whenever

ubicumque *adv* wherever, wheresoever; anywhere, everywhere

Ubi·ī -ōrum *m pl* German tribe on the lower Rhine

ubĭnam *adv* where; **ubĭnam gentium** (*coll*) where in the world

ubiquāque *adv* everywhere

ubĭque *adv* anywhere, everywhere

ubiubī *adv* wherever

ubīvis *adv* anywhere, everywhere, wherever you please; **ubīvis gentium** (*coll*) anywhere in the world

ūd·us -a -um *adj* wet, moist, damp, humid

ulcĕr·ō -āre *vt* to make sore; (*fig*) to wound

ulcerōs·us -a -um *adj* full of sores, ulcerous

ulcīscor ulcīscī ultus sum *vt* to avenge oneself on, take vengeance on, punish; to avenge, requite, repay

ulc·us -ĕris *n* sore, ulcer

ūlīg·ō -ĭnis *f* moisture, dampness

Ulix·ēs -is or **-ēī** or **-ei** *m* Ulysses (*king of Ithaca, son of Laertes, husband of Penelope, and father of Telemachus and Telegonus*)

ull·us -a -um *adj* any

ulmĕ·us -a -um *adj* elm, made of elm

ulmitrĭb·a -ae *m* (*coll*) slaphappy (*from being flogged with elm whips*)

ulm·us -ī *f* elm tree; *f pl* elm rods

uln·a -ae *f* elbow; arm; (*as measure of length*) ell

ulpĭc·um -ī *n* leek

ulterĭ·or -ūs *adj* farther, on the farther side, more remote; further, more, longer, in a higher degree; worse; *m pl* more remote people, those beyond; *n pl* things beyond

ultimum *adv* finally, for the last time

ultĭm·us -a -um *adj* farthest, most distant, extreme; earliest; latest, final, last; greatest; lowest; meanest; *n* last thing; end; **ad ultĭmum** to the end, to the extreme, in the highest degree, to the last degree, utterly; *n pl* extremes; the worst

ultĭ·ō -ōnis *f* vengeance, revenge

ult·or -ōris *m* avenger, punisher, revenger

ultrā *adv* beyond, farther, besides; *prep* (*with acc*) beyond, past; (*of number, measure, degree*) over, beyond, more than, over and above

ultr·ix īcis *adj* avenging

ultrō *adv* to the farther side, beyond; on the other side; besides, moreover, too; of one's own accord, without being asked; without being spoken to; **ultro tribŭta** expenditure incurred by the government for public works

ultus *pp* of **ulcīscor**

ulŭl·a -ae f screech owl

ululāt·us -ūs m crying, wailing (esp. of mourners); war cry

ulŭl·ō -āre vt to cry out to; vi to shriek, yell; (of places) to ring, resound

ulv·a -ae f sedge

umbell·a -ae f umbrella, parasol

umbilīc·us -ī m navel, belly button; midriff; middle, center; projecting end of dowels on which books were rolled; cockle, sea snail

umb·ō -ōnis m boss (of a shield); shield; elbow

umbr·a -ae f shade, shadow; phantom, shadow, ghost; mere shadow (of one's former self, etc.); shelter, cover; constant companion; grayling, umber (fish); rhetorica umbra rhetorician's school

umbrācŭl·um -ī n bower, arbor; school; umbrella, parasol

umbrātĭcŏl·a -ae m lounger, loafer (in the shade)

umbrătĭc·us -a -um adj too fond of the shade, lazy

umbrātĭl·is -e adj remaining in the shade, private, retired; academic

Umbri·a -ae f Umbria (district in central Italy)

umbrĭf·er -ĕra -ĕrum adj shady

umbr·ō -āre vt to shade, cover

umbrōs·us -a -um adj shady

ūmect·ō -āre vt to wet, moisten

ūmect·us -a -um adj moist, damp

ūm·ĕō -ēre vi to be moist, be damp, be wet

ūmĕr·us -ī m shoulder

ūmesc·ō -ĕre vi to become moist or wet

ūmidŭl·us -a -um adj dampish

ūmid·us -a -um adj moist, damp, wet; green (lumber); n wet place

ūm·or -ōris m moisture; liquid, fluid

umquam or unquam adv ever, at any time

ūnā adv together; ūnā venire to come along

ūnanim·ans -antis adj of one mind, of one accord

ūnanimĭt·ās -ātis f unanimity

ūnanĭmus -a -um adj unanimous; of one mind, of one heart, harmonious

ūnci·a -ae f a twelfth; ounce (one twelfth of a pound or libra)

unciāri·us -a -um adj containing a twelfth; faenus unciarium eight and one third percent interest per annum

ūnciātim adv little by little

unciōnāt·us -a -um adj hooked, barbed

ūnciŏl·a -ae f a mere twelfth

uncti·ō -ōnis f rubdown; (fig) wrestling

unctĭt·ō -āre vt to keep rubbing with oil, keep oiling

unctiuscŭl·us -a -um adj somewhat too unctuous

unct·or -ōris m anointer, rubdown man

unct·um -ī n sumptuous dinner; ointment

unctūr·a -ae f anointing

unct·us -a -um pp of ungo; adj greasy; resinous; sumptuous; n sumptuous dinner; ointment

unc·us -a -um adj hooked, crooked, barbed; m hook, clamp; grappling iron

und·a -ae f water; liquid; wave, billow; (fig) stream, tide, agitated mass

unde adv from where, whence; from whom; unde unde or undeunde from some place or other, somehow or other, by hook or by crook

undeciens or undeciēs adv eleven times

undĕcim (indecl) adj eleven

undecim·us -a -um adj eleventh

undecumque or undecunque adv from whatever place, from whatever source

undēn·ō -ae -a adj eleven in a group, eleven each, eleven

undēnōnāgintā (indecl) adj eighty-nine

undeoctōgintā (indecl) adj seventy-nine

undēquadrāgintā (indecl) adj thirty-nine

undēquinquāgensĭm·us or undēquinquāgēsĭm·us -a -um adj forty-ninth

undēquinquāgintā (indecl) adj forty-nine

undēsexāgintā (indecl) adj fifty-nine

undētrīcensĭm·us or undētrīcēsĭm·us -a -um adj twenty-ninth

undēvīcēsĭmān·ī -ōrum m pl soldiers of the nineteenth legion

undēvīcēsĭm·us -a -um adj nineteenth

undēvīgintī (indecl) adj nineteen

undĭque adv from all directions, on all sides, everywhere; in all respects, completely

undisŏn·us -a -um adj sea-roaring; undisoni dei gods of the roaring waves

und·ō -āre vi to move in waves, undulate; to billow; to overflow

undōs·us -a -um adj full of waves, billowy

ūnetvīcensĭm·us or ūnetvīcēsĭm·us -a -um adj twenty-first

ūnetvīcēsĭmān·ī -ōrum m pl soldiers of the twenty-first legion

ungō or unguō ungĕre unxī unctum vt to oil, grease, anoint

ungu·en -ĭnis n fat, grease, ointment

unguentār·ĭus -ĭī or -ī m perfumer

unguentāt·us -a -um adj anointed; perfumed, wearing perfume

unguent·um -ī n ointment; perfume

unguicŭl·us -ī m fingernail; toenail; a teneris unguiculis from earliest childhood

ungu·is -is m fingernail; toenail; claw, talon, hoof; ad unguen to a tee, complete, perfect; **de tenero ungui** from earliest childhood; **transversum unguem** a hair's breadth

ungul·a -ae *f* hoof, claw, talon; (fig) horse

unguo see **ungo**

ūnicē *adv* singularly, solely

ūnicŏl·or -ōris *adj* of one and the same color

ūnicorn·is -e *adj* one-horned

ūni·cus -a -um *adj* sole, only, single, singular, unique; uncommon, unparalleled, outstanding, unique

ūniform·is -e *adj* uniform

ūnigĕn·a -ae *masc & fem adj* only-begotten, only; of the same parentage

ūnimăn·us -a -um *adj* with one hand, one-handed

ūni·ō -ōnis *m* single large pearl

ūnīter *adv* jointly, conjointly

ūniversāl·is -e *adj* universal

ūniversē *adv* generally, in general

ūniversit·ās -ātis *f* aggregate, entirety, whole; whole world, universe

ūnivers·us -a -um *adj* all together, all taken collectively, whole, entire; *n* the whole; whole world, universe; **in universum** on the whole, in general

ūnŏcŭl·us -I *m* one-eyed person

ūnomammi·a -ae *f* (coll) single-breasted land (*country of the Amazons*)

unquam or **umquam** *adv* ever, at any time

ūn·us -a -um *adj* one; single, only, sole; one and the same; (indef) a, an, one, some; *pron* some one, a mere individual; **ad unum** to a man; **unus et alter** one or two; **unus quisque** every one individually, every single one

ūpili·ō or **ōpili·ō -ōnis** *m* shepherd

ūpŭp·a -ae *f* hoopoe; hoe, mattock

Ūrani·a -ae or **Ūrani·ē -ēs** *f* Muse of astronomy

urbānē *adv* politely, courteously; with sophistication; wittily, elegantly

urbānit·ās -ātis *f* living in the city, city life; refinement, politeness; sophistication; wit; raillery

urbān·us -a -um *adj* of the city, of the town, city, town; courteous; sophisticated; witty, facetious, humorous; forward, brash; *m* city man; city slicker

urbicăp·us -I *m* conqueror of cities

urbs urbis *f* city; the city of Rome, the capital

urcĕŏl·us -I *m* little pitcher, little pot

urcĕ·us -I *m* pitcher, water pot

ūrēd·ō -inis *f* blight (*of plants*)

urgĕō urgēre ursī *vt* to prod on, urge, urge forward; to pressure, put pressure on (*someone*); to crowd, hem in; to follow up, keep at, stick by; *vi* to be pressing, be urgent; to be insistent

ūrīn·a -ae *f* urine

ūrīnāt·or -ōris *m* diver

ūrīn·ō -āre or **ūrīn·or -ārī -ātus sum** *vi* to dive

urn·a -ae *f* pot, jar; water pot; voting urn; urn of fate; cinerary urn; money jar

ūrō ūrĕre ussī ustum *vt* to burn; to burn up, reduce to ashes, consume; to scorch, parch, dry up; to sting, pain; to nip, frostbite; to rub sore; to corrode; to annoy, gall, burn up, make angry; to inflame (*with love*), kindle, set on fire

urnŭl·a -ae *f* small urn

urs·a -ae *f* she-bear

Urs·a Major (*genit:* **Urs·ae Major·is**) *f* Great Bear (*constellation*)

Urs·a Minor (*genit:* **Urs·ae Minor·is**) *f* Little Bear (*constellation*)

ursīn·us -a -um *adj* bear, bear's

urs·us -I *m* bear

urtīc·a -ae *f* nettle; desire, itch

ūr·us -I *m* wild ox

Usipĕt·ēs -um *m pl* German tribe on the Rhine

ūsitātē *adv* in the usual way, as usual

ūsitāt·us -a -um *adj* usual, customary, familiar; **usitatum est** (*with inf*) it is customary to

uspiam *adv* anywhere, somewhere; in any matter

usquam *adv* anywhere, in any place; anywhere, to any place

usque *adv* all the way, right on, straight on; all the time, continuously; even, as much as; **usque** (*with* **ab** + *abl*) all the way from; **usque** (*with* **ad** + *acc*) all the way to; **usque quaque** every moment, continually; on all occasions, in everything

ust·or -ōris *m* cremator

ustŭl·ō -āre *vt* to burn a little, scorch, singe; to burn up

ustus *pp* of **uro**

ūsū·capiō -capĕre -cēpī -captum *vt* (law) to acquire possession of, acquire ownership of (*by long use, by prescription*)

ūsūcapti·ō -ōnis *f* (law) acquisition of ownership through long use or long possession

ūsūr·a -ae *f* use, enjoyment; interest (*on capital*)

ūsūrāri·us -a -um *adj* for use and enjoyment; paying interest

ūsūrpāti·ō -ōnis *f* use; (with *genit*) making use of, use of

ūsurp·ō -āre *vt* to make use of, use, employ, adopt, practice, exercise; (law) to take possession of, acquire; to seize wrongfully, usurp; to name, call, speak of; to adopt, assume; to perceive (*with the senses*), observe, experience

ūsus *pp* of **utor**

ūs·us -ūs *m* use, enjoyment; practice, employment; experience, skill; usage, custom; familiarity; usefulness, advantage, benefit; occasion, need, necessity; **ex usu esse** or **usui esse** (with *dat*) to be useful to, be beneficial to, be a good thing for; **si usus veniat** if the need should arise, if the opportunity should present itself; **usus adest** a good opportunity comes along; **usus est** (with *abl*) there is need of; **usus et fructus** use and enjoyment; **usu venit** it happens, it occurs

ususfructus (*genit:* **ususfructus**) *m* use and enjoyment

ut or **utī** *adv* how, in what way; *conj* (comparative) as; (adversative) although; (temporal) when, while; (purpose) in order that; (result) that; (concessive) granted that; (introducing examples) as, as for example; (after verbs of fearing) lest, that not; (introducing an explanation or reason) as, as being, inasmuch as; (introducing indirect commands) that

utcumque or **utcunque** *adv* however; whenever; one way or another

ūtensil·is -e *adj* useful; *n pl* utensils, materials

ut·er -ris *m* bag, skin, bottle

ut·er -ra -rum *adj* which (*of the two*); *pron* which one (*of the two*); one or the other

ut·ercumque -racumque -rumcumque *adj* whichever (*of the two*); *pron* whichever one (*of the two*)

ut·erlībet -ralībet -rumlībet *adj* whichever (*of the two*) you please; *pron* whichever one (*of the two*) you please, either one (*of the two*)

ut·erque -rāque -rumque *adj* each (*of the two*), both; **sermones utriusque linguae** conversations in both languages; *pron* each one (*of the two*), both; **uterque insaniunt** both are insane

ut·er·us -ī *m* or **ut·er·um -ī** *n* womb; belly, paunch (*of a man*)

ut·ervīs -rāvīs -rumvīs *adj* whichever (*of the two*) you please, either; *pron* whichever one (*of the two*) you please, either one

utī see **ut**

ūtibil·is -e *adj* useful, practical

Utic·a -ae *f* city in Africa, N.W. of Carthage, where the younger Cato committed suicide

Uticens·is -is *adj* of Utica, Utican

ūtil·is -e *adj* useful, profitable, expedient, practical; (with *dat* or **ad** + *acc*) fit for, useful for, practical in

ūtilit·ās -ātis *f* usefulness, advantage

ūtiliter *adv* usefully, profitably

utinam *conj* (introducing a wish) if only ,would that

utīque *adv* anyhow, at least, at any rate

ūtor ūtī ūsus sum *vi* (with *abl*) a to use, make use of; b to enjoy; c to practice, experience; d to enjoy the friendship or companionship of

utpote *conj* as, inasmuch as; **utpote qui** inasmuch as (*he is one*) who, inasmuch as he, because he

ūtrār·ius -iī or **-ī** *m* water carrier, water boy

utrimque or **utrinque** *adv* from or on both sides, on either side; **utrimque constitit fides** on both sides the word of honor held good, both parties kept their word

utrō *adv* to which of the two sides, in which direction

utrobīque *adv* on both sides, on either hand

utrōlībet *adv* to either side

utrōque *adv* to both places, in both directions

utrūbi or **utrūbī** *adv* at or on which of two sides

utrubīque *adv* on both sides, on either hand

utrum *conj* either; whether

utut or **ut ut** *adv* however, in whatever way

ūv·a -ae *f* grape; bunch or cluster of grapes; vine; cluster of bees

ūvesc·ō -ēre *vi* to become moist; (fig) to get drunk

ūvidul·us -a -um *adj* moist

ūvid·us -a -um *adj* wet, moist, damp, humid; drunken

ux·or -ōris *f* wife; mate (*of animals*)

uxorcul·a -ae *f* dear little wife

uxōr·ius -a -um *adj* of a wife, wifely; very fond of a wife; henpecked

▼

vac·ans -antis *adj* vacant, unoccupied; at leisure, unemployed; unengaged, single; (with *abl*) lacking, without; *n pl* unoccupied estates

vacāti·ō -ōnis *f* freedom, exemption (*from duty, service, etc.*); exemption from military service; payment for exemption from military service

vacc·a -ae *f* cow

vaccīn·ium -iī or **-ī** *n* hyacinth

vaccŭl·a -ae *f* heifer

vacē·fīō -fīŏrī -factus sum *vi* to become empty, be emptied

vacill·ō -āre *vi* to stagger, reel; to vacillate, waver; to be untrustworthy

vacīvē *adv* at leisure

vacīvit·ās -ātis *f* want, lack

vacīv·us or **vocīv·us -a -um** *adj* empty; free; (with *genit*) free of, void of, free from

vac·ō -āre *vi* to be empty, be vacant,

be unoccupied; to be free, be carefree; to be at leisure, have free time;
(with *abl* or *ab* + *abl*) to be free
from; (with *dat* or with *ad* or *in*
+ *acc*) to be free for, have time
for; *v impers* there is time, room,
leisure; (with *inf*) there is time to
or for

vacuāt·us -a -um *adj* empty

vacuē·faciō -facĕre -fēcī -factum
vt to empty, clear, free

vacuit·ās -ātis *f* freedom, exemption; vacancy (*in an office*)

vacu·ō -āre *vt* to empty, clear, free

vacu·us -a -um *adj* empty, clear,
free; vacant; worthless, useless; single, unmarried; widowed; at leisure;
carefree; (with *genit* or *abl* or with
ab + *abl*) free from, devoid of,
without; (with *dat*) free for

vadimōn·ium -iī or **-ī** *n* (law) promise (*to appear in court*), bail (*given
as a guarantee of one's appearance
in court*); **vadimōnium deserere**
to default, fail to show up in court;
vadimōnium differre to postpone
appearance in court, grant a continuance; **vadimōnium facere** to
put up bail; **vadimōnium sistere**
to appear in court

vād·ō -ĕre *vi* to go, make one's way,
advance

vad·or -ārī -ātus sum *vt* to put
(*someone*) under bail

vadōs·us -a -um *adj* shallow

vad·um -ī *n* shallow place, shallow,
shoal, ford; body of water, stream,
sea; bottom, depths

vae *interj* woe! (with *acc* or *dat*) woe
to

vaf·er -ra -rum *adj* sly, cunning;
subtle

vafrē *adv* slyly, cunningly

vagē *adv* far and wide

vāgin·a -ae *f* sheath, scabbard;
sheath (*of ear of grain*), hull, husk;
vagina

vāg·iō -īre -īvī -ī *vi* (esp. of an infant) to cry; (of swine) to squeal

vāgīt·us -ūs *m* cry; bleating

vāg·or -ōris *m* cry, wail (*of an infant*)

vag·or -ārī -ātus sum or **vag·ō
-āre** *vi* to wander, range, roam

vag·us -a -um *adj* wandering, ranging, roaming; unsteady, inconstant;
vague, uncertain

vah *interj* ah!, oh!

valdē *adv* greatly, intensely; (with
adj or *adv*) very; (as affirmative reply) yes, certainly; to be sure

valē *interj* good-bye

val·ens -entis *adj* strong, powerful;
healthy, hale, well

valenter *adv* strongly; energetically

valentul·us -a -um *adj* a strong
little

val·eō -ēre -uī *vi* to be strong, be
vigorous; to be powerful, be effective; to avail, prevail, succeed; to
be influential; to be valid; to be
strong enough, be adequate, be ca-

pable, be able; to be of value, be of
worth; to mean, signify; **tē valere
jubeo** I bid you farewell, good-by
to you; **vale** or **valete**! good-bye!;
vale dicere to say good-bye, take
leave

valesc·ō -ĕre *vi* to grow strong, acquire strength, thrive

valētūdinār·ium -iī or **-ī** *n* hospital

valētūd·ō -inis *f* state of health;
good health; ill health, illness

valg·us -a -um *adj* bowlegged

validē *adv* strongly, vehemently; (in
replies) of course, certainly, defin-
itely

valid·us -a -um *adj* strong, powerful, able; healthy, robust; fortified;
influential; efficacious

vallār·is -e *adj* (decoration) awarded
for scaling a rampart

vall·ēs or **vall·is -is** *f* valley

vall·ō -āre *vt* to fortify with a rampart, wall in; to protect, defend

vall·um -ī *n* rampart, palisade, en-
trenchment; protection

vall·us -ī *m* stake, pale; rampart
with palisades, stockade; tooth (*of a
comb*)

valv·ae -ārum *f pl* folding doors,
double doors

vanesc·ō -ĕre *vi* to vanish, fade, disappear

vānidic·us -a -um *adj* lying, boasting; *m* liar, boaster

vāniloquenti·a -ae *f* empty talk

vāniloquidōr·us -ī *m* liar

vānilōqu·us -a -um *adj* talking
nonsense; lying, boasting, bragging

vānit·ās -ātis *f* falsity, unreality,
deception, untruth; boasting, lying;
vanity, conceit; worthlessness, frivolity, fickleness

vānitūd·ō -inis *f* falsehood

vann·us -ī *f* fan, winnowing fan

vān·us -a -um *adj* empty, vacant;
groundless, pointless; hollow, unreal; lying, false; boastful, conceited, vain; *n* emptiness, uselessness, deceptive appearance

vapidē *adv* poorly, badly

vapid·us -a -um *adj* flat, vapid,
spoiled, bad; morally corrupt

vap·or -ōris *m* vapor, steam, smoke;
exhalation, warmth, heat

vapōrār·ium -iī or **-ī** *n* steam pipe

vapōr·ō -āre *vt* to steam, steam up;
to warm, heat; *vi* to steam, smoke

vapp·a -ae *f* sour wine; spoiled lad,
good-for-nothing

vāpulār·is -e *adj* in for a flogging

vāpul·ō -āre *vi* to get a beating; (of
savings, etc.) (fig) to take a beating

varianti·a -ae *f* diversity, variations

variāti·ō -ōnis *f* variation, difference

vāric·ō -āre *vt* to straddle

varicōs·us -a -um *adj* varicose

vāric·us -a -um *adj* with legs wide
apart

variē *adv* variously, in various ways,
differently

variĕt·ās -ātis f variety, difference, diversity; vicissitudes; inconstancy

vari·ō -āre vt to diversify, vary, change, make different; to variegate; vi to change color; to vary, differ, change; to differ in opinion; to waver

vari·us -a -um adj colored, variegated, spotted, striped; different, varying, various, changeable; versatile; inconstant, unsteady, untrustworthy

Var·ius -iī or **-ī** m epic and tragic poet and friend of Virgil and Horace (d. c. 12 B.C.)

var·ix -icis f varicose vein

Varr·ō -ōnis m M. Terentius Varro (*Roman antiquarian and philologist whose wide erudition earned him the title of the most learned of the Romans*, 116-27 B.C.)

vār·us -a -um adj knock-kneed; bent, crooked; opposed, contrary

vas vadis m bail, surety

vās vāsis or **vās·um -ī** (*pl:* **vās·a -ōrum**) n vessel, dish; utensil, implement; n pl equipment, gear; **vasa conclamare** (mil) to give the signal to pack the gear

vāsār·ium -iī or **-ī** n allowance for furnishings (*given to a provincial governor*)

vasculār·ius -iī or **-ī** m metal worker; goldsmith

vascul·um -ī n small vessel

vastāti·ō -ōnis f devastation, ravaging

vastāt·or -ōris m devastator, ravager

vastē adv vastly, widely; coarsely, harshly; violently

vastific·us -a -um adj devastating

vastit·ās -ātis f wasteland, desert; state of desolation, emptiness; devastation, destruction; vastness, immensity; (fig) destroyer

vastiti·ēs -ēī f ruin, destruction

vast·ō -āre vt to make empty, make desolate, vacate, empty; (mil) to lay waste, ravage, devastate, destroy

vast·us -a -um adj empty, deserted, desolate; ravaged, devastated; vast, enormous; uncouth, rude, uncultivated, clumsy

vāt·ēs -is m soothsayer, prophet; bard, poet; f prophetess; poetess

Vātīcān·us -a -um adj Vatican; **mons** or **collis Vaticanus** hill in Rome on the right bank of the Tiber

vāticināti·ō -ōnis f prophesying, prediction, soothsaying

vāticināt·or -ōris m prophet, soothsayer

vāticin·ium -iī or **-ī** n prediction, prophecy

vāticini·us -a -um adj prophetic

vāticin·or -ārī -ātus sum vt to foretell, prophesy; to keep harping on; vi to prophesy; to rant and rave, talk wildly

vatill·um -ī n brazier

-ve conj (enclitic) or; **-ve . . . -ve** either . . . or

vēcordi·a -ae f senselessness; insanity, madness

vēc·ors -ordis adj senseless; foolish; mad

vectīg·al -ālis n tax, toll, tariff; revenue, income (*of an individual*); honorarium (*given to a magistrate*)

vectīgāl·is -e adj tax, toll, tariff; paying tribute, subject to taxes, taxable, taxed; **pecunia vectigalis** tax money, tribute

vecti·ō -ōnis f conveyance, transporting

vect·is -is m crowbar, lever; bar, bolt (*on a door or gate*)

vect·ō -āre vt to carry around; **vectari** to keep riding around

vect·or -ōris m bearer, carrier; rider, passenger

vectōri·us -a -um adj transportation, of transportation; **navigia vectoria** transport ships, transports

vectūr·a -ae f transport, transportation, conveyance; freight costs; fare

vectus pp of **veho**

Vēdiōv·is or **Vējōv·is -is** m Anti-Jove (*Etruscan divinity of the lower world, identified with Apollo and with the Jupiter of the lower world*); Little Jove (*identified with the infant Jupiter*)

vegĕt·us -a -um adj lively, vigorous, vivacious

vēgrand·is -e adj not huge, small

vehĕm·ēns -entis adj vehement, violent, impetuous, ardent; great, tremendous; vigorous, active

vehementer or **vēmenter** adv vehemently, impetuously, violently, eagerly

vehementi·a -ae f vehemence

vehicŭl·um -ī n vehicle, carriage, cart; vessel, ship

vehō vehĕre vexī vectum vt to carry, convey, transport; **vehi** to ride, sail, be borne along

Vei·ēns -entis or **Veientān·us -a -um** adj of Veii

Vei·ī -ōrum m pl old Etrurian city about twelve miles from Rome, captured by Camillus (396 B.C.)

vel adv even, actually; perhaps; for instance; conj or, or perhaps; or rather; **vel . . . vel** either . . . or

Vēlābr·um -ī n low ground between the Capitoline and Palatine

vēlām·en -inis n drape, covering, veil; clothing, robe

vēlāment·um -ī n curtain, veil; n pl olive branches draped with woolen fillets

vēlār·ium -iī or **-ī** n awning (*over the open-air theater*)

vēlāt·ī -ōrum m pl (mil) reserves

vēl·es -itis m light-armed soldier, skirmisher

vēlif·er -ĕra -ĕrum adj sail, sailing;

carina velifera sail boat, sailing ship

velificāti·ō -ōnis f sailing

vēlific·ō -āre or vēlific·or -ārī -ātus sum vt to sail through; vi to sail; (with dat) (fig) to be under full sail toward, be hell-bent for (e.g., high office)

Velin·us -ī m river and lake in the Sabine territory

vēlitār·is -e adj of the light-armed troops

vēlitāti·ō -ōnis f skirmishing

vēlitēs = pl of veles

vēlit·or -ōris m skirmisher

vēlivōl·us -a -um adj sail-flying (ship); sail-covered (sea)

vellic·ō -āre vt to pluck, pinch, nip; to carp at, rail at

vellō vellĕre vellī (or vulsī) vul-sum (or volsum) vt to pluck, pull, tear at, tear away, tear out; to tear up, tear down, destroy

vell·us -ĕris n fleece; skin, pelt; wool; n pl fleecy clouds

vēl·ō -āre vt to veil, wrap, envelop, cover, cover up; to encircle, crown; to cover up, hide, conceal

vēlōcit·ās -ātis f speed, velocity

vēlōciter adv speedily, swiftly

vēl·ox -ōcis adj speedy, swift

vēl·um -ī n sail; veil, curtain, awning, covering; vela dare or vela facere to set sail; remis velisque with might and main

velut or velutī conj as, just as, even as; as for example; (to introduce a simile) as, as it were; (in elliptical clauses) like; velut or velut sī just as if, just as though, as if, as though

vēmens see vehemens

vēn·a -ae f vein, artery; vein of metal; water course; vein (in wood, stone, etc.); natural bent or disposition, genius; penis; strength; f pl (fig) heart, core

vēnābul·um -ī n hunting spear

Venāfrān·us -a -um adj of Venafrum

Venāfr·um -ī n town in S. central Italy

vēnālici·us -a -um adj for sale; m slave dealer; n pl merchandise, imports and exports

vēnāl·is -e adj for sale; open to bribes; mf slave offered for sale

vēnātic·us -a -um adj hunting

vēnāti·ō -ōnis f hunt, hunting; wild-beast show; game

vēnāt·or -ōris m hunter

vēnātōri·us -a -um adj hunter's

vēnātr·ix -īcis f huntress

vēnātūr·a -ae f hunting

vēnāt·us -ūs m hunting

vendibil·is -e adj salable; attractive, popular, acceptable, on sale

venditāti·ō -ōnis f boasting, showing off

venditi·ō -ōnis f sale

vendit·ō -āre vt to try to sell; to advertise; to give as a bribe; se

venditāre (with dat) to ingratiate oneself with

vendit·or -ōris m vendor, seller; recipient of a bribe

vend·ō -ĕre -idī -itum vt to put up for sale; to sell, vend; to sell (someone) out, betray; to advertise; to praise, recommend

venēfic·a -ae f poisoner; sorceress, witch; (term of abuse) hag, witch

venēfic·ium -iī or -ī n poisoning witchcraft, magic

venēfic·us -a -um adj poisoning, poisonous; magic; m poisoner; sorcerer, magician

venēnāt·us -a -um adj poisonous, venomous; filled with poison; magic; bewitched, enchanted; (fig) venomous, bitter

venēnif·er -ĕra -ĕrum adj poisonous, venomous

venēn·ō -āre vt to poison; (fig) to poison, injure by slander

venēn·um -ī n poison; drug, potion; magic charm; sorcery; ruin, destruction

vēn·eō -īre -iī -itum vi to go up for sale, be sold

venerābil·is -e adj venerable

venerābund·us -a -um adj reverent, reverential

venerand·us -a -um adj venerable

venerāti·ō -ōnis f veneration, reverence, great respect

venerāt·or -ōris m respecter, adorer; admirer

Venerĕ·us or Veneri·us -a -um adj of Venus; of sexual love, venereal; m Venus-throw (best throw in playing dice); m pl attendants in Venus's temple

vener·or -ārī -ātus sum vt to venerate, revere, worship, pray to; to implore, beg; to pray for

Venĕt·ī -ōrum m pl a people in N.E. Italy in the region around modern Venice

Veneti·a -ae f district of the Veneti

Venetic·us -a -um adj Venetian

Venĕt·us -a -um adj Venetian; bluish; m Venetian; a Blue (i.e., a member of one of the racing factions in Rome which were called Blues, Greens, etc.)

veni·a -ae f kindness, favor, goodwill; permission; pardon, forgiveness; veniam dare (with dat) to grant forgiveness to, do a favor to, grant permission to; veniam petere to ask for permission; veniā vestrā with your leave

veniō venīre vēnī ventum vi to come; (with in + acc) to come into, enter into (e.g., agreement, friendship); b to fall into (e.g., trouble, disgrace)

vēn·or -ārī -ātus sum vt & vi to hunt

vent·er -ris m stomach, belly; womb; embryo, unborn child; belly, protuberance; appetite, gluttony

ventil·ō -āre vt to fan, wave; to display, show off

venti·ō -ōnis f coming

ventit·ō -āre vi to keep coming, come regularly

ventōs·us -a -um adj windy, full of wind; of the wind; wind-like, swift as the wind; conceited; fickle

ventricul·us -ī m belly; ventricle (of the heart)

ventriōs·us -a -um adj pot-bellied

ventŭl·us -ī m breeze

vent·us -ī m wind

vēnŭcŭl·a -ae f grape (of the type well suited for preserving)

vēnum (genit not in use; dat: **vēnō**) n sale, that which is for sale; **venum** or **veno dare** to sell, sell as a slave; **venum** or **veno dari** to be sold; **venum** or **veno ire** to go up for sale, be sold

vēnum·dō or **vēnun·dō -dare -dēdī -dātum** vt to put up for sale, sell

ven·us -ĕris f beauty, charm; pleasure of love, sexual indulgence, mating; beloved, love

Ven·us -ĕris f Venus (goddess of love and beauty; planet); Venusthrow (highest throw of the dice)

Venusi·a -ae f town in Apulia, the birthplace of Horace

Venusīn·us -a -um adj of Venusia

venust·ās -ātis f beauty, charm, attraction

venustē adv prettily, charmingly

venustŭl·us -a -um adj cute, pretty, charming little

venust·us -a -um adj beautiful, charming, attractive

vēpallid·us -a -um adj very pale

veprēcŭl·a -ae f little brier bush

vepr·ēs -is m thorn bush, bramble bush

vēr vēris n spring, springtime; youth

vērātr·um -ī n hellebore

vēr·ax -ācis adj truthful

verbēn·a -ae f vervain; f pl sacred branches worn by heralds and priests

verb·er -ĕris n scourge, rod, whip; flogging, scourging; thong (of a sling and similar weapons); n pl strokes, flogging

verberābilissŭm·us -a -um adj altogether deserving of a flogging

verberāti·ō -ōnis f flogging

verberĕ·us -a -um adj deserving of a flogging

verber·ō -āre vt to scourge, flog, whip; to batter, beat

verbĕr·ō -ōnis m rascal

verbōsē adv verbosely

verbōs·us -a -um adj verbose, wordy

verb·um -ī n word; saying, expression; verb; proverb; mere talk, mere words; formula; **ad verbum** word for word, verbatim; **verba dare** (with dat) to cheat (someone); **verba facere** to speak, make a speech; **verbi causā** or **verbi gratiā** for instance; **verbo** orally; in a word, briefly; nominally, in name only; in theory; **verbum de verbo, verbum pro verbo, verbum verbo** word for word

Vercingetŏr·ix -īgis m famous leader of the Arverni in the Gallic War

vercŭl·um -ī n (term of endearment) sweet springtime

vērē adv really, truly

verēcundē adv bashfully, shyly, modestly

verēcundi·a -ae f bashfulness, shyness, modesty; respect, awe, reverence; sense of shame, feeling of disgrace, disgrace, shame

verēcund·or -ārī vi to be bashful, be shy, feel ashamed

verēcund·us -a -um adj bashful, shy, modest, reserved

verēd·us -ī m fast hunting horse

verend·us -a -um adj venerable; n pl the private parts

ver·eor -ērī -ĭtus sum vt to revere, have respect for, respect; to fear; vi to feel uneasy, be apprehensive, be afraid, be anxious; (with genit) to stand in awe of, be afraid of; (with dat) to be afraid for; (with **dē** + abl) to be apprehensive about; (with **ut**) to be afraid that not; (with **ne**) to be afraid that

verētr·um -ī n the private parts

Vergili·ae -ārum f pl Pleiads

Vergil·ius or **Virgil·ius -ī** or **-ī** m Virgil (P. Vergilius Maro, famous epic poet of the Augustan Age, 70-19 B.C.)

verg·ō -ĕre vt to turn, incline; vi to turn, incline; to decline; to lie, be situated; (with **ad** + acc) **a** to verge toward; **b** to face, face toward

vēridic·us -a -um adj truthful; truly spoken

vērisimil·is -e adj probable, likely; realistic

vērisimilitūd·ō -inis f probability, likelihood

vērit·ās -ātis f truth, truthfulness; the truth, the real facts; real life, reality; honesty, integrity; correctness (in etymology or grammar); **ex veritate** in accordance with the truth

vēriverb·ium -iī or **-ī** n truthfulness

vermiculāt·us -a -um adj inlaid with wavy lines, vermiculated

vermicŭl·us -ī m grub worm

vermin·a -um n pl stomach pains

verm·is -is m worm

vern·a -ae m or f slave (born in the master's house), home-born slave; native

vernācŭl·us -a -um adj of home-born slaves; native, domestic; m pl jesters

vernīl·is -e adj slavish, servile; pert, smart

vernīlit·ās -ātis f slavishness, subservience; pertness

vernīlĭter *adv* slavishly

vern·ō -āre *vi* to show signs of spring; to burgeon, break into bloom; to be young

vernŭl·a -ae *m* or *f* little home-born slave, young home-born slave; native

vern·us -a -um *adj* spring; **tempus vernum** springtime

vērō *adv* in truth, in fact; certainly, to be sure; even; however

Vērōn·a -ae *f* city in N. Italy, the birthplace of Catullus and of Pliny the Elder

Vērōnens·is -e *adj* Veronese

verp·a -ae *f* penis

verp·us -ī *m* circumcised man

verr·ēs -is *m* boar, pig

Verr·ēs -is *m* C. Cornelius Verres (*notorious for outrageous conduct in governing Sicily in* 73-70 B.C.)

verrīn·us -a -um *adj* of a boar, boar, hog, pork

verrō verrĕre verrī versum *vt* to pull, drag, drag away, carry off; to sweep, scour, brush; (of the wind) to whip across, sweep (*the land*)

verrūc·a -ae *f* wart (*on the body*); small failing, minor blemish

verrūcōs·us -a -um *adj* full of warts; (fig) faulty, full of blemishes

verrunc·ō -āre *vi* to turn out well

versābĭl·is -e *adj* shifting, movable

versābund·us -a -um *adj* revolving

versātĭl·is -e *adj* capable of turning, revolving, movable; versatile

versĭcŏl·or -ōris *adj* changing color, of various colors

versĭcŭl·us -ī *m* short line, single line (*of verse or prose*), versicle; *m pl* poor little verses

versĭfĭcāt·or -ōris *m* versifier

versĭpell·is -e *adj* changing appearance, of changed appearance; sly; *m* werwolf

vers·ō or **vors·ō -āre** *vt* to keep turning, twist, wind; to roll; to bend, shift; to move about, agitate; to disturb, harass; to handle; to consider

vers·or or **vors·or -ārī -ātus sum** *vi* to live, stay; (with **in** + *abl*) to be involved in, be engaged in, be busy with

versum or **vorsum** *adv* (usually after another *adv* of direction) back; **rusum vorsum** backward; **sursum versum** up and down

versūr·a or **vorsūr·a -ae** *f* rotation; loan (*of money to pay another debt*); **versuram facere** (with **ab** + *abl*) to get a loan from (*someone to pay another*); **versūrā solvere** to pay off (*another debt*) with borrowed money

versus *pp* of **verro** and of **verto**

vers·us or **vors·us -ūs** *m* turning; furrow; line, row; line, verse; line (*in writing*); turn, step (*in a dance*)

versus or **vorsus** *adv* (with **ad** + *acc*) towards, in the direction of; (with **in** + *acc*) into, in towards;

si **in urbem versus ventūrī erunt** if they intend to come into the city; **sursum versus** upwards

versūtē *adv* cunningly

versūtĭ·ae -ārum *f pl* cunning

versūtĭlŏqu·us -a -um *adj* smooth-speaking, sly

versūt·us or **vorsūt·us -a -um** *adj* clever, shrewd, ingenious; sly, crafty, cunning, deceitful

vert·ex or **vort·ex -ĭcis** *m* whirlpool, eddy, strong current; whirlwind, tornado; crown or top of the head; head; top, summit (*of mountain*); pole (*of the heavens*); **ex vertice** from above

vertĭcōs·us or **vortĭcōs·us -a -um** *adj* swirling, full of whirlpools

vertīg·ō -ĭnis *f* turning, whirling; dizziness

vert·ō or **vort·ō vertĕre vertī versum** *vt* to turn, turn around; to invert, tilt; to change, alter, transform; to overturn, overthrow, destroy; to ascribe, impute; to translate; **se vertere** or **verti** (with **in** + *acc*) to change into, change oneself into; **vertī** (with **in** + *abl*) **a** to be in (*a place or condition*); **b** to be engaged in, be involved in; *vi* to turn; to change; to turn out; (with **in** + *abl*) to center upon, depend upon

Vertumn·us -ī *m* god of the changing seasons

ver·ū -ūs *n* spit (*for roasting*); javelin, dart

verūĭn·a -ae *f* small javelin

vērum *adv* truly, yes; true but; but in fact; but yet, but even; yet, still; **verum tamen** or **verumtamen** nevertheless, but yet

vēr·us -a -um *adj* true, actual, genuine, real; fair, reasonable; *n* truth, the truth, reality; honor, duty, right; **verī similis** probable; realistic; **verī similitūdo** probability

verūt·um -ī *n* dart, javelin

verūt·us -a -um *adj* armed with a dart or a javelin

verv·ex -ēcis *m* wether, castrated hog; (term of abuse) muttonhead

vēsānĭ·a -ae *f* insanity, madness

vēsānĭ·ens -entis *adj* furious

vēsān·us -a -um *adj* insane, mad; furious, savage, raging

vesc·or -ī *vi* (with *abl*) to feed on, eat, feast on, enjoy

vesc·us -a -um *adj* nibbled off; little, feeble; corroding, consuming

vēsīc·a or **vensīc·a -ae** *f* bladder; bombast; objects made of bladder: purse, cap, football, lantern

vēsīcŭl·a -ae *f* little bladder; little bag

vesp·a -ae *f* wasp

Vespāsĭān·us -ī *m* Vespasian (*T. Flavius Vespasianus Sabinus, Roman emperor, 70-79 A.D., and father of Domitian and Titus*)

vesp·er -ĕris or **-ĕrī** *m* evening; supper; the West; **ad vesperum**

towards evening; **primo vespere** early in the evening; **sub vesperum** towards evening; **tam vesperi** so late in the evening; **vespere** or **vesperi** in the evening

vespĕr·a -ae f evening

vesperasc·ō -āre vi to become evening, grow towards evening; to get late

vespertīlī·ō -ōnis m bat

vespertīn·us -a -um adj evening, in the evening; eastern

vesperūg·ō -ĭnis f evening star

vespill·ō -ōnis m undertaker

Vest·a -ae f Roman goddess of the hearth

Vestāl·is -e adj Vestal, of Vesta, Vesta's; f Vestal, Vestal virgin

vest·er or **vost·er -ra -rum** adj (in addressing more than one person) your; pron yours; **voster** your master; your own stock or lineage

vestibŭl·um -ī n entrance, forecourt; beginning

vestīg·ĭum -ĭī or **-ī** n footstep, step; footprint, track; trace, vestige; moment, instant

vestīg·ō -āre vt to track, trace; to check, find out

vestīment·um -ī n garment, clothes

vest·iō -īre -īvī or **-ĭī -ītum** vt to dress, clothe; to adorn, deck, array, attire; (fig) to dress, clothe

vestiplĭc·a -ae f laundress

vest·is -is f garment, clothing; coverlet, tapestry; blanket; slough, skin (of a snake); **mutare vestem** to change one's clothes; to put on mourning clothes

vestispĭc·a -ae f wardrobe woman

vestīt·us -ūs m clothes, clothing, dress, apparel, attire; ornament (of speech); **mutare vestitum** to put on mourning clothes; **redire ad suum vestitum** to end the mourning period

vetĕr·a -um n pl tradition, antiquity

veterăn·us -a -um adj & m veteran

veter·ascō -ascĕre -āvī vi to grow old

veterāt·or -ōris m old hand, expert; sly old fox

veterātōrĭē adv cunningly, slyly

veterātōrĭ·us -a -um adj cunning, sly

vetĕr·ēs -um m pl the ancients; ancient authors

veterīn·us -a -um adj of burden; f pl & n pl beasts of burden

veternōs·us -a -um adj lethargic; sleepy, drowsy

vetern·us -ī m lethargy; old age; drowsiness; listlessness

vetĭt·um -ī n prohibition

vet·ō or **vot·ō -āre -ŭī** or **-āvī -ĭtum** vt to forbid, prohibit, oppose

vetŭl·us -a -um adj poor old

vet·us -ĕris adj old, aged; long-standing; m pl see **veteres**; n pl see **vetera**

vetust·ās -ātis f age; ancient times, antiquity; long duration, great age

vetust·us -a -um adj old, ancient; old-time, old-fashioned, good old (days, etc.); antiquated

vexām·en -ĭnis n shaking, quaking

vexātĭ·ō -ōnis f shaking, jolting, tossing; distress

vexāt·or -ōris m jostler; harasser; troublemaker

vexillār·ĭus -ĭī or **-ī** m standard-bearer, ensign; m pl special reserves

vexill·um -ī n standard, ensign, flag (esp. the red flag hoisted above the general's tent as a signal for battle); troops; **vexillum praeponere** to hoist the red flag (as a signal for battle)

vex·ō -āre vt to shake, toss; to vex, annoy; to harass (troops), attack

vi·a -ae f way, road, street, highway; march, journey; method; right way, right method; **inter vias** on the road

viāl·is -e adj highway

viāri·us -a -um adj for highway maintenance

viātĭcāt·us -a -um adj provided with traveling money

viātĭc·us -a -um adj for a trip, for traveling, travel; n travel allowance, provisions for the journey; (mil) soldiers' saving fund

viāt·or -ōris m traveler; passenger; (law) summoner

vīb·ix -īcis f weal, welt (from a blow)

vibr·ō -āre vt to brandish, shake, wave around; to hurl, fling; vi to vibrate, quiver; (of the tongue) to flick

vīburn·um -ī n wayfaring tree, guelder rose

vīcān·us -a -um adj village; m pl villagers

Vīc·a Pot·a (genit: **Vīc·ae Pot·ae**) f goddess of victory

vicāri·us -a -um adj substituted; m substitute, deputy, proxy; underslave (kept by another slave)

vīcātim adv from street to street; from village to village; in hamlets

vice prep (with genit) on account of; like, after the manner of

vicem adv in turn; prep (with genit) instead of, in place of; on account of; like, after the manner of

vīcēnāri·us -a -um adj of the number twenty

vīcēn·ī -ae -a adj twenty each, twenty in a group

vīcēsĭmān·ī -ōrum m pl soldiers of the twentieth legion

vīcēsĭmāri·us -a -um adj derived from the five-percent tax

vīcēsĭm·us -a -um adj twentieth; f five-percent tax

vicĭ·a -ae f vetch

vīcĭens or **vicĭēs** adv twenty times

vīcīnāl·is -e adj neighboring, nearby

vīcīnĭ·a -ae f neighborhood, nearness, proximity

vīcīnĭt·ās -ātis f neighborhood, proximity; the neighborhood (i.e., the neighbors)

vīcīn·us -a -um *adj* neighboring, nearby, near; *mf* neighbor; *n* neighborhood

vicis (*genit*; the *nom* does not occur; *acc*: **vicem**; *abl*: **vice**) *f* change, interchange, alteration, succession; return, recompense, retaliation; fortune, misfortune, condition, fate, changes of fate; duty, office, position; function, office; **in vicem** or **invicem** by turns, alternately, mutually; **in vicem** or **invicem** (with *genit*) instead of, in place of; **in vicīs** by turns, alternately, mutually

vicissim or **vicissātim** *adv* in turn, again

vicissitūd·ō -inis *f* change, interchange, alternation

victim·a -ae *f* victim; sacrifice

victimār·ius -iī or **-ī** *m* assistant at sacrifices

victit·ō -āre *vi* to live, subsist; (with *abl*) to live on, subsist on

vict·or -ōris *m* conqueror; (in apposition) **victor exercitus** victorious army

victōriāt·us -ī *m* silver coin stamped with the image of victory

Victōriŏl·a -ae *f* small statue of Victory

victr·ix -īcis *f* or *n* conqueror, victor

victus *pp* of **vinco**

vict·us -ūs *m* living, means of livelihood; way of life

vīcŭl·us -ī *m* hamlet

vīc·us -ī *m* village, hamlet; ward, quarter (*in a town or city*); street, alley (*running through the quarter*)

vidēlicet *adv* clearly, evidently; (in irony) of course, naturally; (in explanations) namely

viden = videsne? do you see?, do you get it?

vidĕŏ vidēre vīdī vīsum *vt* to see, look at; to know; to consider; to understand, realize; (with **ut**) to see to it that, take care that; **vidēri** to seem, appear, seem right, seem good

vidŭ·a -ae *f* widow; spinster

viduit·ās -ātis *f* bereavement; want, lack; widowhood

vidŭl·us -ī *m* leather travel bag, suitcase, knapsack

vidŭ·ō -āre *vt* to deprive, bereave; (with *genit* or *abl*) to deprive of, bereave of; **viduata** left a widow

vidŭ·us -a -um *adj* bereft, destitute; unmarried; (with *abl* or **ab** + *abl*) bereft of, destitute of, without; *f* see **vidua**

viēt·or -ōris *m* cooper

viēt·us -a -um *adj* shriveled

vig·eŏ -ēre -ŭī *vi* to thrive, be vigorous, flourish

vig·escō -escĕre -ŭī *vi* to become vigorous, gain strength, become lively

vigēsim·us -a -um *adj* twentieth

vig·il -ilis *adj* awake, wakeful; alert, on one's toes; *m* watchman,

guard, sentinel

vigil·āns -antis *adj* watchful, alert; disquieting (*worries*)

vigilanter *adv* vigilantly, alertly

vigilanti·a -ae *f* wakefulness; alertness

vigil·āx -ācis *adj* alert; sleep-disturbing, disquieting (*worries*)

vigili·a -ae *f* wakefulness, sleeplessness, insomnia; standing guard; guards, sentinels; vigil; vigilance, alertness

vigil·ō -āre *vt* to spend (*the night*) awake; to make, do, perform, write (*something*) while awake at night; *vi* to remain awake, stay awake; to be alert; (with *dat*) to be attentive to

vīgintī (indecl) *adj* twenty

vīgintivirāt·us -ūs *m* membership on a board of twenty

vīgintivir·ī -ōrum *m pl* twenty-man board or commission

vig·or -ōris *m* vigor, liveliness, energy

vīlic·a -ae *f* foreman's wife, manager's wife

vīlic·ō -āre *vi* to be a foreman, be a manager

vīlic·us -ī *m* foreman, manager (*of an estate*)

vīl·is -e *adj* cheap, inexpensive; cheap, mean, common, worthless

vīlit·ās -ātis *f* lowness of price, cheapness, low price; worthlessness

vīliter *adv* cheaply

vīll·a -ae *f* villa, country home, farm

vīllic- = vīlic-

vīllōs·us -a -um *adj* hairy, shaggy

vīllŭl·a -ae *f* small villa

vīll·um -ī *n* drop of wine

vīll·us -ī *m* hair, fleece; nap (*of cloth*)

vīm·en -inis *n* osier; basket

vīment·um -ī *n* osier

Vīmināl·is coll·is (*genit*: **Vīminālis coll·is**) *m* one of the seven hills of Rome

vīminĕ·us -a -um *adj* made of osiers

vīn or **vīn' = visne?** do you wish

vīnācĕ·us -a -um *adj* grape, of a grape; *m* a grape seed

Vīnāl·ia -ium *n pl* wine festival (*celebrated on the 23rd of April and on the 19th of August*)

vīnāri·us -a -um *adj* wine; *m* wine dealer, vintner; *n pl* wine flasks

vincibil·is -e *adj* easily won

vinciō vincīre vinxī vinctum *vt* to bind; to encircle, surround; to restrain; (rhet) to bind together, link together, arrange rhythmically

vincō vincĕre vīcī victum *vt* to conquer, vanquish; to get the better of, beat, defeat, outdo; to surpass, excel; to convince, refute, persuade; to prove, demonstrate; to outlast, outlive; *vi* to be victorious; to prevail, succeed

vinctus *pp* of **vincio**

vincŭl·um or **vincl·um -ī** *n* chain, fetter, cord, band; *n pl* prison

vindēmi·a -ae *f* vintage

vindēmiāt·or -ōris *m* vintager, grape gatherer

vindēmiŏl·a -ae *f* small vintage; minor sources of income

vind·ex -icis *adj* avenging; *m* (law) claimant; defender, protector, champion; deliverer, liberator; avenger, punisher

vindicāti·ō -ōnis *f* (law) claim; avenging, punishment

vindici·ae -ārum *f pl* legal claim; things or persons claimed; championship, protection; **vindicias dare, dicere,** or **decernere** to hand over the things or persons claimed

vindic·ō -āre *vt* to lay a legal claim to; to protect, defend; to appropriate; to demand; to demand unfairly; to claim as one's own; to avenge, punish; **in libertatem vindicare** to claim for freedom, set free, free, liberate, emancipate

vindict·a -ae *f* rod used in the ceremony of setting slaves free; defense, protection; vengeance, revenge, satisfaction

vīnē·a -ae *f* vineyard; vine; (mil) shed (*used to defend besiegers against the missiles of the enemy*)

vīnēt·um -ī *n* vineyard

vīnit·or -ōris *m* vinedresser

vinnūl·us -a -um *adj* charming, pleasant

vīnolenti·a -ae *f* wine drinking, intoxication

vīnolent·us -a -um *adj* intoxicated, drunk

vīnōs·us -a -um *adj* fond of wine

vīn·um -ī *n* wine

viŏl·a -ae *f* violet; violet color

violābil·is -e *adj* vulnerable

violār·ium -iī or **-ī** *n* bed of violets

violār·ius -iī or **-ī** *m* dyer of violet color

violāti·ō -ōnis *f* violation, profanation

violāt·or -ōris *m* violator, profaner, desecrator

viŏl·ens -entis *adj* violent, raging, impetuous

violenter *adv* violently, vehemently, impetuously

violenti·a -ae *f* violence, vehemence, impetuosity

violent·us -a -um *adj* violent, vehement, impetuous, boisterous

viŏl·ō -āre *vt* to do violence to, outrage, harm or injure by violence; to violate, break

vīpĕr·a -ae *f* viper; adder, snake

vīpĕr·us -a -um *adj* viper's, adder's, snake's

vīperīn·us -a -um *adj* of a viper or snake

vir virī *m* male person, man; real man; hero; husband; manhood, virility; (mil) infantryman

virāg·ō -inis *f* female warrior; heroine

virect·a -ōrum *n pl* green places; lawn

vir·ĕō -ēre -uī *vi* to be green; to be fresh, be vigorous, flourish

vīrēs = pl of vis

vir·escō -escĕre -uī *vt* to grow green

virg·a -ae *f* twig, sprout; graft; rod, switch (*for flogging*); walking stick, cane, staff; magic wand; wand; colored stripe in a garment; branch of a family tree

virgāt·or -ōris *m* flogger

virgāt·us -a -um *adj* made of twigs or osiers; striped

virgĕt·um -ī *n* osier thicket

virgĕ·us -a -um *adj* of twigs, of kindling wood

virgidēmi·a -ae *f* (coll) harvest of birch rods (*i.e., sound flogging*)

virgināl·is -e *adj* maiden's, girl's, girlish; *n* female organ

virgināri·us -a -um *adj* maiden's, girl's

virginĕ·us -a -um *adj* maidenly, virgin, of virgins

virginit·ās -ātis *f* virginity, girlhood

virg·ō -inis *f* virgin, maiden, girl, young woman; young married woman

Virg·ō -inis *f* Virgo (*constellation; aqueduct constructed by M. Vipsanius Agrippa*)

virgul·a -ae *f* little twig; wand; **virgula divina** divining rod

virgult·a -ōrum *n pl* thickets, brushwood; slips (*of trees*)

virguncŭl·a -ae *f* lass, young girl

virid·ans -antis *adj* growing green, green

viridār·ium -iī or **-ī** *n* garden; plantation

virid·is -e *adj* green; fresh, young; *n pl* greenery

viridit·ās -ātis *f* greenness; freshness

virid·or -ārī *vi* to become green

viril·is -e *adj* male, masculine; adult; manly; **pro virili parte** or **partione** to the best of one's ability; *n pl* manly or heroic deeds

virīlit·ās -ātis *f* manhood, virility

virīliter *adv* manfully

vīripŏt·ens -entis *adj* almighty

virītim *adv* individually, separately

vīrōs·us -a -um *adj* slimy; strong-smelling, fetid, stinking

virt·ūs -ūtis *f* manliness, manhood, virility; strength; valor, bravery, gallantry; gallant deeds; excellence, worth; virtue, moral perfection, good quality; *f pl* achievements

vīr·us -ī *n* slime; poison; pungency; saltiness

vīs (*genit* not in use) *f* power, strength, force; energy; hostile force, violence, attack, assault; amount, quantity; meaning (*of words*); **vīres** *f pl* strength, resources; (mil) troops; **per vim** forcibly, violently; **pro viribus** with all one's might

viscāt·us -a -um *adj* limed

viscĕr·a -um n pl viscera, internal organs; womb; heart, vitals, bowels; (fig) innermost part, bowels, heart, center; bosom friend, favorite

viscerāti·ō -ōnis f public distribution of meat

visc·ō -āre vt to make sticky

visc·um -ī n mistletoe; birdlime

visc·us -ĕris n organ (of the body); entrails

visi·ō -ōnis f appearance, apparition; notion, idea

visit·ō -āre vt to keep seeing; to visit, go to visit

vīs·ō -ĕre -ī -um vt to look at with attention, view; to come or go to look at; to find out; to visit

vīs·um -ī n sight, appearance

vīs·us -ūs m faculty of sight, sight; thing seen, sight, vision

vīt·a -ae f life, way of life; livelihood; course of life, career; biography

vītābil·is -e adj undesirable, deserving to be shunned

vītābund·us -a -um adj avoiding, evading

vītāl·is -e adj of life, vital; likely to live, staying alive; n means of life; n pl vital parts

vītālĭter adv vitally

vītātĭ·ō -ōnis f avoidance

Vitell·ius -iī or **-ī** m A. Vitellius (Roman emperor, 69 A.D.)

vitell·us -ī m little calf; yolk (of egg)

vīt·us -a -um adj of the vine

viticŭl·a -ae f little vine

vītif·er -ĕra -ĕrum adj vine-producing

vītigĕn·us -a -um adj produced from the vine

vitilēn·a -ae f procuress

viti·ō -āre vt to corrupt, spoil, violate, mar; to falsify

vitiōsē adv faultily, badly, corruptly

vitiōsĭt·ās -ātis f corrupt or bad condition

vitiōs·us -a -um adj faulty, defective, corrupt, bad; vicious

vīt·is -is f vine; vine branch; centurion's staff; centurionship

vītĭsāt·or -ōris m vine planter

vit·ium -iī or **-ī** n fault, defect, flaw; sin, offense, vice; flaw in the auspices

vīt·ō -āre vt to avoid, evade

vītor -ōris m basket maker

vitr·ĕus -a -um adj glass, of glass; glassy; n pl glassware

vitric·us -ī m stepfather

vitr·um -ī n glass

vitt·a -ae f headband, fillet

vittāt·us -a -um adj wearing a fillet

vitŭl·a -ae f heifer

vitulīn·us -a -um adj & f veal

vitŭl·or -ārī vi to celebrate, hold a celebration

vitŭl·us -ī m calf, young bull; foal; seal

vituperābĭl·is -e adj blameworthy

vituperātĭ·ō -ōnis f blaming, censuring; blame; scandalous conduct, blameworthiness

vituperāt·or -ōris m censurer

vitupĕr·ō -āre vt to spoil (omen), render void; to blame

vīvācĭt·ās -ātis f will to live

vīvār·ium -iī or **-ī** n game preserve; fish pond

vīvāt·us -a -um adj animated, lively

vīv·ax -ācis adj long-lived; longlasting, enduring; quick to learn

vīvescō or **vīvescō vīvescĕre vixī** vi to become alive, come to life; to grow lively, get full of life

vīvĭd·us -a -um adj teeming with life, full of life; true to life, vivid, realistic; quick, lively (mind)

vīvirad·ix -īcis f development of roots

vīviscō see vivesco

vīv·ō vīvĕre vixī victum vi to be alive, live; to be still alive, survive; to reside; (with abl or de + abl) to live on, subsist on

vīv·us -a -um adj alive, living; lively; fresh; natural (rock); speaking (voice); n (com) capital; **ad vivum resecare** to cut to the quick

vix adv with difficulty, hardly; scarcely

vixdum adv hardly then, scarcely yet

vocābŭl·um -ī n designation, name; noun

vōcāl·is -e adj having a voice, gifted with speech or song, singing, speaking; tuneful; f vowel

vocām·en -ĭnis f designation, name

vocātĭ·ō -ōnis f summons (to court); invitation (to dinner)

vocāt·or -ōris m inviter, host

vocāt·us -ūs m summons, call

vōciferātĭ·ō -ōnis f loud cry, yell

vōcifĕr·ō -āre or **vōcifĕr·or -ārī -ātus sum** vt & vi to shout, yell

vocit·ō -āre vt to usually call, name; to shout out again and again

voc·ō -āre vt to summon; to call, name; to call upon (the gods); to invite; (mil) to challenge; **in dubium vocare** to call in question; **in odium vocare** to bring into disfavor; **in periculum vocare** to lead into danger

vōcŭl·a -ae f small or weak voice; soft note, soft tone; whisper, gossip

volaem·um -ī n large pear

Volaterr·ae -ārum f pl old Etruscan town

Volaterrān·us -a -um adj of Volaterrae

volātic·us -a -um adj flying, winged; transitory, passing; inconstant

volātĭl·is -e adj flying, winged; rapid, swift; fleeting, transitory

volāt·us -ūs m flight

Volcānāl·ia -ium n pl festival of Vulcan (celebrated on the 23rd of August)

Volcān·us or **Vulcān·us -ī** m Vulcan (god of fire and son of Juno and Jupiter)

vol·ens -entis *adj* willing, permitting; willing, ready; favorable; *m* well-wisher

volg- = vulg-

volit·ans -antis *m* winged insect

volit·ō -āre *vi* to flit about, fly about, flutter; to move quickly; to hover, soar

volō velle voluī *vt* to wish, want; to propose, determine; to hold, maintain; to mean; to prefer; *vi* to be willing

volōn·ēs -um *m pl* volunteers (*slaves who enlisted after the battle of Cannae, 216 B.C.*)

volpēs see **vulpes**

Volsc·us -a -um *adj* Vulscan; *m pl* an ancient people in S. Latium

volsell·a -ae *f* tweezers

volsus *pp* of **vello**

volt = older form of **vult** he, she, it wishes

voltis = older form of **vultis** you wish

Volturn·a -ae *f* Etruscan goddess in whose temple the Etruscan states met

voltus see **vultus**

volūbil·is -e *adj* turning, spinning, revolving, swirling; voluble, rapid, fluent; changeable

volūbilit·ās -ātis *f* whirling motion; roundness; volubility, fluency; mutability

volūbiliter *adv* volubly, rapidly, fluently

volūc·er -ris -re *adj* flying, winged; rapid, speedy; *mf* bird; *f* insect

volūm·en -inis *n* roll, book; chapter, book; whirl, eddy; coil; fold

voluntāri·us -a -um *adj* voluntary; *m pl* volunteers

volunt·ās -ātis *f* will, wish, desire, purpose, aim; goodwill; last will, testament; attitude (*good or bad*); **ad voluntatem** (with *genit*) according to the wishes of; **de** or **ex voluntate** (with *genit*) at the desire of

volup *adv* to one's satisfaction, agreeably

voluptābil·is -e *adj* agreeable, pleasant

voluptāri·us -a -um *adj* pleasant, agreeable; voluptuous; *m* voluptary

volupt·ās -ātis *f* pleasure, enjoyment, delight; *f pl* sensual pleasures; games, sports, public performances

voluptuōs·us -a -um *adj* pleasant, agreeable

volūtābr·um -ī *n* wallow (*for swine*)

volūtābund·us -a -um *adj* wallowing about

volūtāti·ō -ōnis *f* rolling about, tossing about; wallowing; restlessness

volūt·ō -āre *vt* to roll about, turn over; to engross; to think over; **volutari** to wallow, luxuriate

volūtus *pp* of **volvo**

volv·a or **vulv·a -ae** *f* wrapper, cover; womb; sow's womb (*as a favorite dish*)

volvō volvēre volvī volūtum *vt* to roll, turn about, wind; (e.g., of a river) to roll (*rocks, etc.*) along; to breathe; to unroll, read (*books*); to pour out, utter fluently; to consider, weigh; (of time) to bring on, bring around; to form (*a circle*); to undergo (*troubles*); **volvī** to roll, tumble, revolve; *vi* to revolve; to roll on, elapse

vōm·er or **vōm·is -ĕris** *m* plowshare; penis

vomic·a -ae *f* sore, boil, abscess, ulcer; annoyance

vōmis see **vomer**

vomīti·ō -ōnis *f* vomiting

vom·ō -ĕre -uī -itum *vt & vi* to vomit, throw up

vorāg·ō -inis *f* deep hole, abyss, chasm, depth

vor·ax -ācis *adj* swallowing, devouring; greedy, ravenous

vor·ō -āre *vt* to swallow, devour; (fig) to devour (*by reading*)

vors- = vers-

vort- = vert-

vōs *pron* you; (reflex) yourselves

vosmet *pron* (emphatic form of **vōs**) you yourselves

voster see **vester**

vōtīv·us -a -um *adj* votive, promised in a vow

votō see **veto**

vōt·um -ī *n* solemn vow (*made to a deity*), vow; votive offering; wish, prayer

vovēō vovēre vōvī vōtum *vt* to vow, promise solemnly, pledge, devote (*to a deity*); to wish, wish for, desire

vox vōcis *f* voice; sound, tone, cry, call; word, utterance, saying, expression; proverb; language; accent

Vulcānus see **Volcanus**

vulgār·is or **volgār·is -e** *adj* common, general, usual

vulgāriter or **volgariter** *adv* in the common or usual way

vulgāt·or or **volgāt·or -ōris** *m* divulger

vulgāt·us or **volgāt·us -a -um** *adj* common, general; well known; notorious

vulgivāg·us or **volgivāg·us -a -um** *adj* roving; inconstant

vulg·ō or **volg·ō -āre** *vt* to spread, publish, broadcast; to divulge; to prostitute; to level, make common

vulgō or **volgō** *adv* generally, publicly, everywhere

vulg·us or **volg·us -ī** *n* masses, people, public; crowd, herd; rabble, populace

vulnerāti·ō or **volnerāti·ō -ōnis** *f* wounding, wound

vulner·ō or **volner·ō -āre** *vt* to wound; to damage

vulnific·us -a -um *adj* inflicting wounds

vuln·us or **voln·us -ĕris** *n* wound; blow, stroke; blow, disaster

vulpēcŭl·a or **volpēcŭl·a -ae** *f* little fox, sly little fox

vulp·ēs or **volp·ēs -is** *f* fox; craftiness, cunning

vuls·us or **vols·us -a -um** *pp* of **vello**; *adj* plucked, beardless, effeminate

vulticŭl·us or **volticŭl·us -ī** *m* mere look

vult·um -ī *n* face; looks, expression, features; look, appearance

vultuōs·us or **voltuōs·us -a -um** *adj* full of airs, affected

vult·ur or **volt·ur -ŭris** *m* vulture

Vult·ur or **Volt·ur -ŭris** *m* mountain in Apulia near Venusia

vulturĭn·us or **volturnĭn·us -a -um** *adj* of a vulture, vulture-like

vultur·ius or **voltur·ius -iī** or **-ī** *m* vulture

Vulturn·us or **Volturn·us -ī** *m* principal river of Campania (*modern Volturno*)

vult·us or **volt·us -ūs** *m* face; looks, expression, features; look, appearance

vulv·a or **volv·a -ae** *f* wrapper, cover; womb; sow's womb (*as a delicacy*)

X

Xanthipp·ē -ēs *f* wife of Socrates

Xanth·us -ī *m* river at Troy, identified with Scamander River

xen·ium -iī or **-ī** *n* gift, present

Xenophăn·ēs -is *m* early Greek philosopher (*c.* 565-470 B.C.)

Xenŏph·ōn -ontis *m* Greek historian and pupil of Socrates (*c.* 430-*c.* 354 B.C.)

xērampelĭn·ae -ārum *f pl* dark-colored clothes

Xerx·ēs -is *m* Persian king, defeated at Salamis (*c.* 519-465 B.C.)

xiphĭ·ās -ae *m* swordfish

xyst·us -ī *m* or **xyst·um -ī** *n* open colonnade or portico, walk, avenue

Z

Zacynth·us or **Zacynth·os -ī** *f* island off W. Greece

Zam·a -ae *f* town in Numidia where Scipio defeated Hannibal and brought the Second Punic War to an end

zāmi·a -ae *f* harm, damage, loss

Zancl·ē -ēs *f* old name of Messana in Sicily

Zēn·ō or **Zēn·ōn -ōnis** *m* founder of Stoic philosophy and a native of Citium in Cyprus (335-263 B.C.); Epicurean philosopher, the teacher of Cicero and Atticus

Zephўr·us -ī *m* zephyr; west wind; wind

Zēth·us -ī *m* son of Jupiter and Antiope and brother of Amphion

zmaragd·us -ī *f* emerald

zōdiăc·us -ī *m* zodiac

Zōĭl·us -ī *m* proverbially stern Alexandrine critic of Homer

zōn·a -ae *f* belt, sash, girdle (*worn by women*); money belt; zone

zōnārĭ·us -a -um *adj* of a belt or girdle; *m* belt maker, girdle maker

zōnŭl·a -ae *f* little girdle

zōthēc·a -ae *f* small room

zōthēcŭl·a -ae *f* small bedroom

A

a *indefinite article, unexpressed in Latin;* **twice — year** bis in anno

aback *adv* **taken —** stupefactus, attonitus, consternatus

abandon *vt* (de)relinquĕre, destituĕre, deserĕre, abjicĕre, omittĕre

abandoned *adj* derelictus, desertus; *(fig)* nefarius, perditus, flagitiosus

abandonment *s* derelictio, destitutio *f*

abase *vt* deprimĕre, comprimĕre, frangĕre, (de)minuĕre

abash *vt* perturbare, confundĕre, pudefacĕre, percellĕre

abashed *adj* pudendus, erubescens

abate *vt (to lower)* imminuĕre; *(to slacken)* laxare; *(the price)* remittĕre, detrahĕre; *vi (to lessen)* imminuĕre, decrescĕre; *(to decline)* cadĕre, decedĕre; *(of passion)* defervescĕre

abbess *s* abbatissa *f*

abbey *s* abbatia *f*

abbot *s* abbas *m*

abbreviate *vt* abbreviare, contrahĕre, imminuĕre

abbreviation *s* abbreviatio, contractio *f*, compendium *n*

abdicate *vt* abdicare; *vi* se abdicare

abdication *s* abdicatio *f*

abdomen *s* abdomen *n*

abduct *vt* abducĕre, rapĕre

abduction *s* raptio *f*, rapt·us -ūs *m*

aberration *s* error *m*; declinatio *f*

abet *vt* adjuvare, instigare; favēre *(with dat)*

abeyance *s* **to be in —** jacēre, intermitti

abhor *vt* abhorrēre ab *(with abl)*, detestari, odio habēre

abhorrence *s* detestatio *f*, odium *n*

abhorrent *adj* perosus; alienus, repugnans, abhorrens

abide *vt* tolerare, subire; *vi (to dwell)* habitare, manēre; **to — by** stare in *(with abl)*

abiding *adj* diuturnus, mansurus; constans, fidus

ability *s* facultas, potestas *f*; ingenium *n*; **to the best of one's —** summa ope; pro sua parte

abject *adj* abjectus, vilis; humilis; **—ly** abjecte; humiliter

abjure *vt* abjurare, ejurare

ablative *s* ablativus *m*

able *adj* potens; valens, capax, peritus; ingeniosus; **to be — to** posse, valēre, quire, sufficĕre

ablution *s* ablutio, lavatio *f*

ably *adv* experte; ingeniose

aboard *adv* in *or* super nave; **to go — a ship** navem conscendĕre

abode *s* domicilium *n*; sedes *f*; commoratio, mansio *f*

abolish *vt* abolēre; exstinguĕre, tollĕre, rescindĕre

abolition *s* abolitio, dissolutio *f*

abominable *adj* detestabilis, infandus, execrabilis; odiosus

abominably *adv* execrabiliter; odiose

abominate *vt* abominari, detestari

abomination *s* destestatio *f*

aborigines *s* aborigines, indigenae *m pl*

abortion *s* abortio *f*; abort·us -ūs *m*

abortive *adj* abortivus; *(fig)* irritus, frustratus

abound *vi* abundare, redundare, superesse; **to — in** abundare *(with abl)*

abounding *adj* abundans; copiosus, largus; creber

about *adv* circa, circiter; fere, ferme

about *prep (of place)* circa, circum *(with acc)*; *(of number)* circa, ad *(with acc)*; *(of time)* circa, sub *(with acc)*; *(of respect)* de *(with abl)*

above *adv* supra; insuper; **from —** desuper, superne

above *prep* supra, super *(with acc)*

abrasion *s* attrit·us -ūs *m*

abreast *adv* pariter; ex adverso

abridge *vt* contrahĕre; abbreviare; *(fig)* privare

abridgment *s* compendium *n*, epitome *f*

abroad *adv (in a foreign land)* peregre; *(of motion, out of doors)* foras; *(of rest, out of doors)* foris; **from —** extrinsecus; peregre; **to be** *or* **live abroad** peregrinari; patriā carēre; **to get —** *(fig)* divulgari

abrogate *vt* rescindĕre, abrogare, dissolvĕre

abrupt *adj* praeruptus; *(fig)* subitus, repentinus; *(of style)* abruptus; **—ly** abrupte; raptim

abruptness *s* declivitas, rapiditas, festinatio *f*

abscess *s* abscess·us -ūs *m*; suppuratio *f*; vomica *f*

absence *s* absentia *f*; **in my —** me absente

absent *adj* absens; **to be —** abesse

absent *vt* **to — oneself** se removēre, non comparēre

absentee *s* qui abest *m*; peregrinator *m*

absolute *adj* absolutus, summus, perfectus; *(unlimited)* infinitus; **—ly** absolute; prorsus; penitus, omnino

absolution *s* absolutio *f*; venia, indulgentia *f*

absolve *vt* veniam dare *(with dat)*; absolvĕre; dimittĕre; *(from punishment)* condonare

absorb *vt* absorbēre, combibēre; (*fig*) distringĕre, tenēre

absorbent *adj* bibulus; absorbens

abstain *vi* abstinēre, se abstinēre

abstinence *s* abstinentia *f*; continentia *f*; jejunium *n*

abstract *vt* abstrahĕre; separare, sejungĕre, excludĕre

abstract *adj* abstractus; mente perceptus

abstract *s* compendium *n*; epitome *f*; **in the —** in abstracto

abstracted *adj* abstractus; separatus; contractus; (*in mind*) parum attentus; **—ly** separatim; in abstracto

abstraction *s* separatio *f*; (*idea*) notio *f*

abstruse *adj* abstrusus; reconditus; obscurus, occultus; **—ly** abdite, occulte

absurd *adj* absurdus, insulsus; ridiculus; **—ly** inepte, absurde

absurdity *s* ineptia, insulsitas *f*

abundance *s* abundantia, copia *f*

abundant *adj* abundans; amplus; copiosus, plenus; uber; **to be —** abundare; **—ly** abundanter, copiose; cumulate; (*fruitfully*) feliciter

abuse *s* (*wrong use*) abus·us -ūs *m*; (*insult*) injuria *f*, convicium *n*; contumelia *f*; probra *n pl*, maledicta *n pl*

abuse *vt* (*misuse*) abuti (*with abl*); (*a woman*) stuprare; (*with words*) maledicĕre (*with dat*); lacerare

abusive *adj* contumeliosus; dicax, maledicus; injuriosus; **—ly** contumeliose; maledice, injuriose

abyss *s* profundum *n*, vorago *f*, gurges *m*; (*fig*) barathrum *n*

academic *adj* scholasticus; academicus

academy *s* Academia *f*; schola *f*, collegium *n*; societas *f*

accede *vi* accedĕre, assentire *or* assentiri

accelerate *vt* accelerare, festinare, maturare

acceleration *s* acceleratio *f*

accent *s* accent·us -ūs *m*; sonus *m*; vox *f*; (*mark*) apex *m*

accent *vt* (*in speaking*) acuĕre; (*in writing*) fastigare

accentuation *s* accent·us -ūs *m*

accept *vt* accipĕre; recipĕre

acceptable *adj* acceptus, aptus, gratus; probabilis; **to be —** placĕre

acceptably *adv* apte; grate

acceptance *s* acceptio *f*; approbatio *f*

access *s* adit·us -ūs, access·us -ūs *m*; **to have —** admitti

accessible *adj* (*of places*) patens; (*fig*) facilis, affabilis

accession *s* (*addition*) accessio *f*, cumulus *m*; (*to the throne*) regni principium *n*

accessory *adj* adjunctus; (*of crimes*) conscius

accessory *s* affinis, conscius *m*, par-

ticeps *m & f*

accident *s* cas·us -ūs *m*; calamitas *f*

accidental *adj* fortuitus; adventicius; **—ly** casu, forte, fortuito

acclaim *s* acclamatio *f*; clamor *m*

acclaim *vt* acclamare

acclamation *s* acclamatio *f*, clamor, consens·us -ūs, plaus·us -ūs *m*

accommodate *vt* accommodare, aptare; (*with lodgings*) hospitium parare (*with dat*)

accommodation *s* accommodatio *f*; (*convenience*) commoditas *f*; (*lodgings*) hospitium, deversorium *n*

accompaniment *s* concinentia *f*

accompany *vt* comitari; deducĕre; (*mus*) concinĕre (*with dat*)

accomplice *s* particeps, socius, conscius *m*; satelles *m*

accomplish *vt* efficĕre, perficĕre; peragĕre, implēre

accomplished *adj* completus; (*fig*) doctus, eruditus; (*eloquent*) disertus

accomplishment *s* exsecutio, peractio *f*; eruditio *f*

accord *s* consens·us -ūs *m*, concordia *f*; **of one's own —** sua sponte; ultro; **with one —** unanimiter

accord *vt* concedĕre, dare, praebēre; praestare; *vi* convenire; inter se congruĕre; inter se consentire

accordance *s* **in — with** ex, de (*with abl*); secundum (*with acc*); pro (*with abl*)

accordingly *adv* itaque; ita; pariter; sic

according to *prep* de, ex, pro (*with abl*); secundum (*with acc*)

accost *vt* appellare; compellare; alloqui, affari

account *s* (*financial*) ratio *f*; (*statement*) memoria *f*; (*esteem*) reputatio *f*; (*story*) narratio *f*; **of little —** parvi pretii; vilis; **of no —** nullius pretii; **on —** of ob, propter (*with acc*); causā (*with genit*); **on that —** propterea; ideo; **to call to —** rationem poscĕre; **to give an —** rationem reddĕre; **to take — of** rationem habēre (*with genit*)

account *vt* numerare; (*esteem*) aestimare, habēre, pendĕre; **to — for** rationem reddĕre (*with genit*)

accountable *adj* reus

accountant *s* calculator *m*; a rationibus (procurator) *m*

accredited *adj* aestimatus, honoratus

accretion *s* accessio *f*

accrue *vi* accrescĕre; advenire; cedĕre; (*advantage*) redundare

accumulate *vt* accumulare, coacervare; *vi* crescĕre, augēri

accumulation *s* cumulus, acervus, congest·us -ūs *m*; collectio *f*

accuracy *s* cura *f*; subtilitas *f*

accurate *adj* exactus; subtilis; diligens; **—ly** accurate, exacte; subtiliter; diligenter

accursed *adj* exsecratus; scelestus

accusation *s* accusatio *f*; (*charge*) crimen *n*; **to bring an — against** accusare

accusative *s* accusativus *m*

accuse *vt* accusare; criminari; (*to blame*) reprehendĕre; **to — falsely** calumniari, insimulare

accuser *s* accusator, delator *m*; (*in civil suit*) petitor *m*

accustom *vt* assuefacĕre; **to — one-self** assuefieri, consuescĕre; **to be accustomed to** solēre (*with inf*)

acerbity *s* acerbitas *f*; (*fig*) severitas *f*; rigor *m*

ache *s* dolor *m*

ache *vi* dolēre; **my head —s** caput mihi dolet

achieve *vt* patrare, conficĕre, perfi-cĕre; (*to win*) consequi

achievement *s* res gesta *f*; facinus *n*

acid *adj* acidus; vinosus

acid *s* acidum *n*

acknowledge *vt* agnoscĕre, recog-noscĕre; confitēri; (*a child*) tollĕre

acknowledgement *s* recognito *f*, confessio *f*; (*receipt for money*) apocha *f*

acme *s* fastigium *n*

acorn *s* glans *f*; balanus *f*

acoustics *s* acustica *n pl*; res audi-toria *f*

acquaint *vt* certiorem facĕre; **to — oneself with** noscĕre, cognoscĕre

acquaintance *s* familiaritas, notitia *f*; (*person*) familiaris *m & f*

acquainted *adj* notus; **— with** gnarus (*with genit*); peritus (*with genit or abl*); **to become — with** noscĕre, cognoscĕre, pernoscĕre

acquiesce *vi* acquiescĕre, assentire

acquiescence *s* assens·us -ūs *m*

acquire *vt* acquirĕre; adipisci, nan-cisci

acquisition *s* (*act of acquiring*) con-ciliatio *f*; quaest·us -ūs *m*; (*thing acquired*) quaesitum *n*

acquisitive *adj* quaestuosus

acquit *vt* absolvĕre, liberare; **to — oneself** se gerĕre

acquittal *s* absolutio *f*

acre *s* jugerum *n*; **— by —** jugera-tim

acrid *adj* acer, asper

acrimonious *adj* acerbus; asper, truculentus

acrimony *s* acrimonia *f*; acerbitas, amaritudo *f*; acor *m*

acrobat *s* funambulus *m*

across *adv* transversus

across *prep* trans (*with acc*)

act *s* (*deed, action*) factum, gestum *n*; (*decrees*) decretum *n*; (*in a play*) act·us -ūs *m*; **caught in the — deprehensus; in the very — in** flagranti

act *vt* (*role, part*) agĕre; *vi* agĕre, facĕre, gerĕre

acting *s* actio, gesticulatio *f*

action *s* actio *f*, act·us -ūs *m*; (*deed*) factum, facinus *n*; (*law*) actio *f*; (*mil*) pugna *f*, proelium *n*; (*of speaker*) gest·us -ūs *m*; **to bring an — against** actionem intendĕre (*with dat*)

active *adj* actuosus; activus; agilis; impiger, vegetus, strenuus, sedulus, navus; **—ly** impigre; strenue; (*gram*) active

activity *s* agilitas, mobilitas *f*; (*mo-tion*) mot·us -ūs *m*; (*energy*) in-dustria, sedulitas, gnavitas *f*

actor *s* histrio *m*; mimus *m*; (*in com-edy*) comoedus *m*; (*in tragedy*) tra-goedus *m*

actress *s* mima, scenica *f*

actual *adj* verus, ipse; **— re vera**

actuality *s* veritas *f*

acumen *s* acumen *n*; sagacitas *f*; in-genii acies *f*

acute *adj* acutus; acer; (*fig*) sagax, subtilis; **—ly** acute, acriter

acuteness *s* acies *f*; (*of the mind*) acumen, *n*, subtilitas *f*

adage *s* proverbium *n*

adamant *adj* obstinatus

adamant *s* adamas *m*

adapt *vt* accommodare, aptare

adaptation *s* accommodatio *f*

adapted *adj* aptus

add *vt* addĕre, apponĕre, adjungĕre; (*in speaking*) superdicĕre; (*in writ-ing*) subjungĕre; (*to reckon*) ad-scribĕre; **to — up** computare, sup-putare; **to be added** accedĕre

adder *s* coluber *m*, vipera *f*

addict *vt* **to be addicted** se addi-cĕre, se tradĕre, se dare

addition *s* additamentum *n*; adjectio, accessio *f*; appendix *f*; incremen-tum *n*; **in — praeterea, insuper; in — to** praeter (*with acc*)

additional *adj* novus, additilius, ad-junctus

address *s* alloquium *n*; allocutio, compellatio *f*; (*on letter*) forma di-rectionis, inscriptio *f*; (*speech*) con-tio, oratio *f*; (*adroitness*) dexteri-tas, comitas *f*

address *vt* (*to speak to*) alloqui, ag-gredi, compellare; (*letter*) inscri-bĕre

adduce *vt* (*witnesses*) producĕre; (*arguments*) afferre

adept *adj* peritus

adequacy *s* sufficientia *f*

adequate *adj* adaequatus, sufficiens, par; **to be — sufficĕre; —ly satis,** apte

adhere *vi* adhaerēre, cohaerēre; **to — to inhaerēre** (*with dat*); (*fig*) stare in (*with abl*)

adherence *s* adhaesio *f*

adherent *s* assectator, fautor, cliens *m*

adhesion *s* adhaesio *f*

adhesive *adj* tenax

adieu *interj* vale, valete; **to bid —** valedicĕre; valēre jubēre

adjacent *adj* confinis, conterminus; vicinus

adjective *s* adjectivum (nomen) *n*

adjectively *adv* adjective; ut ap-positum; pro apposito

adjoin *vt* adjungĕre; adjacēre (*with dat*); *vi* adjacēre

adjoining *adj* adjacens, confinis

adjourn *vt* comperendinare, differre, prorogare; *vi* deferri

adjournment *s* dilatio *f*

adjudge vt addicĕre, adjudicare

adjudicate vt addicĕre, decernĕre

adjudication s addictio, adjudicatio f; sententia f; arbitrium n

adjunct s adjunctum n, accessio, appendix f

adjuration s obtestatio f; obsecratio f

adjure vt adjurare; obtestari

adjust vt aptare, accommodare; (put in order) componĕre

adjustment s accommodatio, compositio f; (of a robe) structura f

adjutant s optio m

administer vt (to manage) administrare; (medicine, etc.) adhibēre; (oath) adigĕre; (justice) dispensare, reddĕre

administration s administratio, cura, procuratio f; jurisdictio f; magistrat·us -ūs m

administrative adj ad administrationem pertinens

administrator s administrator, procurator m

admirable adj admirabilis, mirabilis, admirandus; insignis, egregius

admiral s classis praefectus m

admiration s admiratio f

admire vt admirari; amare

admirer s admirator, mirator, laudator m; amator m

admiringly adv admirans

admissible adj accipiendus, aptus, aequus

admission s admissio, confessio f; adit·us -ūs, access·us -ūs m

admit vt admittĕre; recipĕre; (to recognize) asciscĕre; noscĕre; **it is admitted** constat

admittedly adv sane

admonish vt monēre, admonēre, commonēre; hortari

admonition s monitio, admonitio f; monitum n

adolescence s prima adulescentia f

adolescent adj adulescens, adulescens

adolescent s adulescentulus, adulescens m

adopt vt (a minor) adoptare; (an adult) arrogare; (a custom) asciscĕre; (a plan) capĕre, inire

adoption s adoptio, adoptatio f; (of an adult) arrogatio f; (of a custom) assumptio f; **by —** adoptivus

adoptive adj adoptivus

adorable adj adorandus, venerandus

adoration s adoratio f; cult·us -ūs m; (of kings) veneratio f

adore vt adorare, venerari; (fig) admirari, amare

adorn vt ornare, decorare, distinguĕre, illustrare; excolĕre, comare

adornment s exornatio f; ornat·us -ūs m; ornamentum n

Adriatic Sea s Hadria m or Adria m

adrift adv fluctuans; **to be —** fluctuare

adroit adj callidus, dexter, sollers, peritus; **—ly** callide, scite

adroitness s dexteritas, sollertia,

calliditas f

adulation s adulatio, assentatio f

adult adj adultus

adult s adultus homo, puber m

adulterate vt adulterare, vitiare, commiscēre

adulteration s adulteratio, commixtio f

adulterer s adulter m; moechus m

adulteress s adultera f; moecha f

adulterous adj stuprosus, adulterinus, incestus

adultery s adulterium, stuprum n; **to commit —** moechari; adulterare

advance vt promovēre; admovēre; (money) praerogare; (a cause) fovēre; (an opinion) exhibēre, praeferre; (to honors) provehēre; vi procedĕre, progredi, incedĕre; (mil) gradum or pedem inferre; signa proferre; (to progress) proficĕre

advance s progress·us -ūs m; (step) pass·us -ūs m; (attack) incursio f; impet·us -ūs m; (money) mutuae pecuniae f pl; **in —** maturius

advanced adj provectus; (of age) grandis

advance guard s primum agmen n

advancement s dignitatis accessio, promotio f; honos m

advantage s (benefit) commodum n, us·us -ūs m, bonum n; (profit) lucrum, emolumentum n; utilitas f, fruct·us -ūs m; **to be of —** prodesse; **to have an — over** praestare (with dat); superior esse (with dat); **to take — of** uti (with abl); (to deceive) decipĕre, fallĕre; **with —** faenerato

advantageous adj fructuosus, utilis; **—ly** utiliter; bene

advent s advent·us -ūs m

adventure s cas·us -ūs m; fors f; facinus n

adventurer s periclitator m; latro m; pirata m

adventurous adj audax

adverb s adverbium n

adverbial adj adverbialis; **—ly** adverbialiter

adversary s adversarius m, hostis m; adversatrix f

adverse adj adversus, infestus; asper; **—ly** male, contrarie, infeliciter

adversity s res adversae f pl; calamitas f

advertise vt communefacĕre; proscribĕre

advertisement s proscriptio f; libellus m; indicium n

advice s consilium n; **to ask — of** consulĕre; **to give —** suadēre (with dat)

advisable adj commodus, utilis

advise vt suadēre (with dat), censēre (with dat), monēre; **to — to the contrary** dissuadēre (with dat)

adviser s consultor m

advocate s (law) actor, causidicus m; (fig) patronus m; suasor m; auctor m

aedile s aedilis m

aegis s aegis f

aerial adj aërius, aethereus

affability s comitas, affabilitas, facilitas f

affable adj affabilis, comis, facilis

affably adv comiter

affair s negotium n; res f; (love) amores m pl

affect vt afficĕre; commovēre; jactare; ostentare; attingĕre

affectation s simulatio, affectatio f

affected adj simulatus, fictus; (in style) putidus; —ly putide

affection s amor m; benevolentia f; studium n

affectionate adj amans, benevolus; —ly amanter

affidavit s testimonium n

affiliate vt adoptare; attribuĕre

affinity s affinitas f; cognatio f

affirm vt affirmare, asseverare, testificari

affirmation s affirmatio f

affirmative adj affirmans; **I reply in the** — aio; —ly affirmative

affix vt affigĕre, annectĕre

afflict vt affligĕre, afflictare

affliction s afflictio, miseria f; res adversae f pl

affluence s abundantia, copia f; divitiae f pl

affluent adj affluens, abundans; dives; —ly abundanter

afford vt praebēre; (to yield) reddĕre, ferre; **I cannot** — res mihi non suppetit ad (with acc)

affront vt irritare; contumeliā afficĕre; offendĕre

affront s contumelia, injuria f

afield adv foris

afloat adj natans; fluctuans; **to be** — natare, fluctuare

afoot adv pedestris, pedibus; **to be** — geri

afraid adj timidus, pavidus; **to be** — timēre; **to make** — terrefacĕre

afresh adv de integro, iterum, de novo

after prep post (with acc); a, de, e, ex (with abl); (following immediately upon) sub (with acc); (in rank or degree) secundum (with acc); (in imitation of) ad (with acc); — all tamen; saltem; **a little** — paulo post; **the day** — postridie

after conj postquam

afternoon adj postmeridianus, pomeridianus

afternoon s pomeridianum n; **in the** — post meridiem

afterthought s posterior cogitatio f

afterwards adv post, postea; deinde, deinceps, dehinc

again adv iterum, rursus, denuo, rursum; deinde; (hereafter) posthac; (likewise, in turn) invicem, mutuo, vicissim; contra; — **and** — etiam atque etiam; identidem; **once** — denuo; **over** — de novo

against prep contra (with acc); adversus (with acc); (in a hostile manner) in (with acc); — **the current** adverso flumine; **to be** — adversari

age s (life) aetas f; (era) saeculum n, aetas f; **of the same** — aequaevus, aequalis; **old** — senectus f; **to be of** — sui juris esse; **twelve years of** — duodecim annos natus; **under** — impubis

age vi senescĕre; maturescĕre

aged adj aetate provectus; senilis; (things) antiquus

agency s actio f; (medium) opera f; (office) procuratio f; **through the** — of per (with acc)

agent s actor, auctor m; (in crime) minister m

aggravate vt aggravare; (pain) augēre; provocare; (a wound) ulcerare; **to become aggravated** ingravescēre

aggravating adj molestus

aggravation s exaggeratio f

aggregate adj aggregatus, totus

aggregate s summa f

aggregation s collatio f; aggregatum n

aggression s incursio f

aggressive adj hostilis, infensus; ferox

aggressor s qui bellum infert m; qui alterum prior lacessit m

aggrieve vt dolore afficĕre

aggrieved adj iratus

aghast adj attonitus, consternatus, stupefactus; **to stand** — obstupescĕre

agile adj agilis; pernix

agility s agilitas f; pernicitas f

agitate vt agitare; commovēre; perturbare

agitated adj tumultuosus; turbulentus; (fig) sollicitus

agitation s agitatio, commotio f; (of the sea) jactatio f; trepidatio f

agitator s concitator, turbator m

ago adv abhinc; **a short time** — haud ita pridem; dudum; **long** — iamdudum, iampridem, antiquitus; **some time** — pridem

agonize vt cruciare, excruciare; vi discruciari

agonizing adj crucians; horribilis

agony s dolor m; agonia f; cruciat·us -ūs m

agrarian adj agrarius

agree vi assentire, assentiri; convenire; (to make a bargain) pacisci; (of facts) constare, convenire; **to** — **with** assentiri (with dat), sentire cum (with abl)

agreeable adj gratus, acceptus; amabilis; congruens, conveniens; **very** — pergratus

agreeably adv grate, jucunde; suaviter

agreement s consens·us -ūs m; concordia f; (pact) pactio f, pactum n; (bargain) conditio f; (proportion) symmetria f; reconciliatio f

agricultural adj rusticus, agrestis

agriculture s agricultura f; res rustica f

agriculturist s agricola m

ah interj ah!, ejai, vahi, vae!

ahead *adv use verb with prefix* prae- *or* pro-

aid *s* auxilium, subsidium *n*

aid *vt* succurrĕre (*with dat*), subvenire (*with dat*), adjuvare

aide-de-camp *s* optio *m*

ail *vt* dolēre; *vi* aegrotare

ailing *adj* aegrotus, aeger

ailment *s* aegrotatio *f*; malum *n*; morbus *m*

aim *s* (*mark*) scopus *m*; (*fig*) finis *m*, propositum *n*

aim *vt* intendĕre, tendĕre; *vi* **to —at** affectare, spectare, petĕre, quaerĕre

aimless *adj* vanus, inanis; **—ly** sine ratione

air *s* aër *m*; caelum *n*; (*breeze*) aura *f*; (*attitude*) habit·us -ūs, gest·us -ūs *m*; (*tune*) modus *m*; **in the open —** sub divo *or* sub caelo; **to take the —** deambulare

air *vt* ventilare

airily *adv* hilare

airy *adj* aërius; apertus, patens; ventosus; (*fig*) hilaris

aisle *s* ala *f*

ajar *adj* semiapertus

akin *adj* cognatus, agnatus, consanguineus, propinquus

alabaster *s* alabaster *m*

alacrity *s* alacritas *f*

alarm *s* (*signal*) classicum *n*; (*sudden fright*) trepidatio *f*, pavor *m*; tumult·us -ūs *m*; **to give the —** increpare

alarm *vt* perterrefacĕre, consternĕre, perturbare

alarming *adj* formidolosus

alas *interj* eheu!, heu!

alchemist *s* alchemista *m*

alchemy *s* alchemistica *f*

alcohol *s* spirit·us -ūs vini *m*

alcoholic *adj* alcoolicus

alcove *s* zotheca *f*, cubiculum *n*

ale *s* cerevisia *f*

alert *adj* alacer, promptus, vegetus

alertness *s* alacritas *f*

alias *adv* aliter

alias *s* falsum nomen *n*

alibi *s* (law) absentia rei *f*; (*excuse*) species *f*

alien *adj* peregrinus

alien *s* peregrinus *m*; alienigena, advena *m*

alienate *vt* alienare, abalienare, avertĕre, avocare

alienation *s* abalienatio, alienatio *f*

alight *vi* descendĕre; (*from a horse*) desilire; (*of birds*) subsidĕre

alike *adj* aequus, par, similis

alike *adv* pariter, similiter, aeque

alimony *s* alimentum, alimonium *n*

alive *adj* vivus; (*fig*) alacer; **to be —** vivĕre; superesse

all *adj* omnis, cunctus, totus; integer; universus; **— over** undique, passim; **— the better** tanto melius; **— the more** eo plus

all *s* omnia *n pl*; **at —** omnino; **in — in** summa; **not at —** haudquaquam; **one's all** proprium *n*

allay *vt* sedare, lenire, mitigare; **to**

be allayed defervescĕre, temperari

allegation *s* affirmatio *f*; insimulatio *f*

allege *vt* affirmare, arguĕre; citare, allegare

allegiance *s* fides, fidelitas *f*; **to swear —** sacramentum dicĕre

allegorical *adj* allegoricus; **—ly** allegorice

allegorize *vi* allegorice scribĕre; allegorice explicare

allegory *s* allegoria *f*

alleviate *vt* levare, allevare, sublevare

alleviation *s* allevamentum *n*, levatio *f*

alley *s* angiport·us -ūs *m*

alliance *s* (*by blood*) consanguinitas *f*; (*by marriage*) affinitas *f*; (*of states*) foedus *n*; societas *f*

allied *adj* foederatus, socius; junctus, propinquus

alligator *s* crocodilus *m*

alliteration *s* alliteratio *f*

allocate *vt* impertire, assignare

allot *vt* distribuĕre, assignare

allotment *s* assignatio, portio *f*; assignatum *n*

allow *vt* concedĕre (*with dat*), permittĕre (*with dat*), sinĕre, pati; **it is allowed** licet; **to — for** indulgĕre (*with dat*); **to — of** admittĕre

allowable *adj* licitus

allowance *s* (*permission*) licentia, permissio *f*; (*concession*) venia, indulgentia *f*; (*portion*) portio *f*; salarium *n*; diaria *n pl*; cibaria *n pl*; demensum *n*; **to make — for** ignoscĕre (*with dat*), condonare

alloy *s* mixtura *f*

alloy *vt* miscēre, adulterare, diluĕre

allude *vi* **to —** attingĕre, designare, denotare, spectare

allure *vt* allicĕre, allectare, pellicĕre

allurement *s* illecebra, blanditia *f*; blandimentum *n*

alluring *adj* blandus; **—ly** blande

allusion *s* parodia *f*; indicium *n*, mentio *f*

allusive *adj* obliquus; **—ly** oblique

alluvial *adj* alluvius

ally *s* socius *m*, socia *f*

ally *vt* sociare

almanac *s* fasti *m pl*

almighty *adj* omnipotens

almond *s* amygdala *f*

almond tree *s* amygdalus *f*

almost *adv* fere, paene, prope, ferme

alms *s* stips *f*

aloft *adv* sublime

alone *adj* solus, unus, solitarius, unicus; **all —** persolus; **to leave —** deserĕre; **to let —** omittĕre, mittĕre

alone *adv* solum

along *adv* porro, protinus; **all —** jamdudum; **— with** una cum (*with abl*)

along *prep* per (*with acc*), praeter (*with acc*), secundum (*with acc*)

aloof *adv* procul; **to stand —** discedĕre, abstare

aloud *adv* magna voce; clare

alphabet s alphabetum n; prima elementa n pl

alphabetical adj litterarum ordine

Alpine adj alpinus

already adv jam

also adv etiam, quoque, et, idem, necnon

altar s ara f; altaria n pl

alter vt mutare, commutare; variare; vertĕre

alterable adj mutabilis

alteration s mutatio, commutatio f

altercation s altercatio f, jurgium n

alternate adj alternus; —ly invicem, per vices; alternis

alternate vt & vi alternare, variare

alternation s vicissitudo f

alternative adj alter

alternative s discrimen n, optio f; alternata conditio f

although conj etsi, etiamsi, tametsi, quamquam, licet, cum

altitude s altitudo f

altogether adv omnino; prorsus, plane

altruism s beneficentia f

always adv semper

amalgamate vt miscēre, conjungĕre

amalgamation s mixtio f

amass vt coacervare, cumulare

amateur s artium amator m; tiro m

amaze vt obstupefacĕre

amazed adj attonitus, stupefactus; to be — stupēre; obstupescĕre

amazement s stupor m; in — attonitus, stupefactus

amazing adj mirus, mirandus, mirabilis; —ly mirabiliter

Amazon s Amazon f

Amazonian adj amazonius, amazonicus

ambassador s legatus m

amber s sucinum n; electrum n

ambiguity s ambiguitas f, ambages f pl

ambiguous adj ambiguus, dubius, anceps; —ly ambigue

ambition s ambitio f; studium n

ambitious adj laudis or gloriae cupidus; studiosus; ambitiosus

amble vi ambulare

ambrosia s ambrosia f

ambush s insidiae f pl

ambush vt insidiari (with dat)

ameliorate vt meliorem or melius facĕre, corrigĕre

amenable adj docilis, obediens

amend vt emendare, corrigĕre; vi proficĕre

amendment s emendatio, correctio f

amends s compensatio, satisfactio f; to make — expiare, satisfacĕre, compensare

amenity s amoenitas f; (comfort) commodum n

amethyst s amethystus f

amiable adj amabilis, suavis

amiably adv amabiliter, suaviter

amicable adj amicus; pacatus; benevolus

amicably adv amice; pacate; benevole

amid prep inter (with acc)

amity s amicitia f

ammonia s ammoniaca f

ammunition s belli apparat-us -ūs m; missilium copia f

amnesty s venia, abolitio f

among prep inter (with acc); apud (with acc); ad (with acc); from — e, ex (with abl)

amorous adj amatorius; libidinosus, mulierosus; —ly amatorie; cum amore

amount s summa f, totum n

amount vi to — to crescĕre, exsurgĕre; (fig) esse

amour s amores m pl

amphitheater s amphitheatrum n

ample adj amplus; copiosus; satis

amplification s amplificatio, auctio, dilatatio f

amplify vt amplificare, dilatare

amply adv ample, abunde

amputate vt amputare, secare

amputation s amputatio, sectio f

amuck adv furiose; to run — delirare

amulet s amuletum n

amuse vt oblectare, delectare; to — oneself ludĕre

amusement s delectatio, oblectatio f; delectamentum n; ludibrium n

amusing adj ridiculus; festivus; facetus

an indefinite article, unexpressed in Latin

anachronism s temporum inversio f

analogous adj analogus

analogy s analogia, comparatio f

analysis s analysis f; explicatio f; separatio f

analytical adj analyticus; —ly per analysin

analyze vt in principia resolvĕre; (words) subtiliter enodare

anapest s anapaestus m

anapestic adj anapaesticus

anarchist s civis sediotiosus m

anarchy s anarchia f; rei publicae perturbatio f; licentia f

anathema s anathema n; exsecratio f

anatomical adj anatomicus

anatomy s anatomia, dissectio f

ancestor s proavus m; auctor m; —s majores, priores m pl

ancestral adj avitus; proavitus; patrius

ancestry s genus n; stirps f; origo f

anchor s ancora f; to lie at — in ancoris stare; to weigh — ancoram tollĕre or solvĕre

anchor vt in ancoris tenēre; vi ancoram jacĕre

anchorage s statio f

ancient adj antiquus, vetustus; priscus; pristinus; in — times antiquitus; the —s veteres m pl; barbati m pl

and conj et, ac, atque, -que

anecdote s fabella f

anemic adj exsanguis

anew adv denuo; ab integro

angel s angelus m

angelic *adj* angelicus; *(fig)* egregius, excellens
anger *s* ira *f*; bilis *f*
anger *vt* irritare, exacerbare
angle *s* angulus *m*
angle *vi* hamo piscari
angler *s* piscator *m*
angrily *adv* irate, iracunde
angry *adj* iratus, iracundus, indignans; **to be** — irasci, succensēre, stomachari; **to make** — irritare, exacerbare
anguish *s* angor *m*; dolor *m*; cruciat·us -ūs *m*
anguished *adj* animo fractus
angular *adj* angularis; angulosus
animal *s* animal *n*; *(wild beast)* bestia, fera *f*; *(domestic)* pecus *n*
animal *adj* animalis
animate *vt* animare; *(fig)* excitare
animated *adj* excitatus, vegetus
animation *s* animatio *f*; vigor, ardor, spirit·us -ūs *m*
animosity *s* acerbitas *f*; invidia *f*; odium *n*; inimicitia *f*
ankle *s* talus *m*
annalist *s* annalium scriptor *m*
annals *s* annales, fasti *m pl*
annex *s* appendix *f*
annex *vt* annectēre, adjungēre, addēre, supponēre
annexation *s* adjectio *f*
annihilate *vt* delēre, exstinguēre
annihilation *s* exstinctio *f*; internecio *f*
anniversary *adj* anniversarius; annuus
anniversary *s* festus dies anniversarius *m*
annotate *vt* annotare, commentari
annotation *s* annotatio, nota *f*
announce *vt* nuntiare; *(to report)* renuntiare; *(officially)* denuntiare, pronuntiare; *(laws, etc.)* proscribēre
announcement *s* denuntiatio, pronuntiatio *f*; *(news)* nuntius *m*
announcer *s* nuntius *m*
annoy *vt* incommodare, vexare, male habēre; **to be annoyed** stomachari, offensus esse
annoyance *s* vexatio, molestia *f*; dolor *m*
annoying *adj* molestus, odiosus
annual *adj* anniversarius, annuus; —ly quotannis
annuity *s* annua pecunia *f*; annuus redit·us -ūs *m*; *(law)* annuum *n*
annul *vt* rescindēre, tollēre, dissolvēre, abrogare
annulment *s* abolitio *f*; abrogatio *f*
anoint *vt* ung(u)ēre
anointing *s* unctio *f*
anomalous *adj* anomalus; enormis
anomaly *s* anomalia *f*; enormitas *f*
anonymous *adj* sine nomine; —ly sine nomine
another *adj* alius; —'s alienus; one after — alius ex alio; one — inter se; alius alium; **to — place** alio
answer *vt* respondēre *(with dat)*; *(by letter)* rescribēre *(with dat)*; *(to correspond to)* congruēre cum *(with abl)*; *vi* **to — for** rationēm reddēre

(with genit); **to — to the name of** vocari
answer *s* responsio *f*, responsum *n*; *(solution)* explicatio *f*
answerable *adj* reus; **to be — for** praestare
ant *s* formica *f*
antagonism *s* adversitas, inimicitia *f*
antagonist *s* adversarius *m*; adversatrix *f*; hostis *m*
antarctic *adj* antarcticus
antecedent *adj* antecedens; prior
antecedent *s* antecedens *n*
antechamber *s* atriolum *n*; antithalamus *m*
antedate *vt* diem vero antiquiorem ascribēre *(with dat)*
antelope *s* antilope *f*; dorcas *f*
antepenult *s* syllaba antepenultima *f*
anterior *adj* anterior, prior
anteroom *s* antithalamus *m*; vestibulum *n*
anthem *s* canticum sacrum *n*; hymnus elatior *m*
anthology *s* anthologia *f*; excerpta *n pl*
anticipate *vt* anticipare; *(to expect)* spectare; *(to forestall)* praevenire, praeoccupare; *(mentally)* pracsumēre
anticipation *s* anticipatio, praesumptio, anteoccupatio *f*
anticlimax *s* climax inversa *f*
antics *s* joca *n pl*; ineptiae *f pl*
antidote *s* antidotum *n*
antipathy *s* repugnantia, antipathia *f*; fastidium, odium *n*
antiquarian *adj* historicus
antiquarian *s* antiquitatis peritus *m*; antiquarius *m*
antiquated *adj* antiquatus, obsoletus
antique *adj* antiquus, vetus, priscus
antique *s* antiqui artificis opus *n*
antiquity *s* antiquitas, vetustas *f*
antithesis *s* contrarium *n*, contentio *f*
antler *s* cornu *n*
anvil *s* incus *f*
anxiety *s* anxietas, sollicitudo *f*
anxious *adj* anxius, sollicitus; trepidus; avidus; —ly anxie, sollicite; trepide; avide
any *adj* ullus; quivis, quilibet; aliquis; — longer diutius; — more amplius
anybody *pron* aliquis; quivis; quilibet; *(after si, nisi, num, ne)* quis; *(interrog)* ecquis, numquis; *(after negativa)* quisquam
anyhow *adv* quoquomodo
anyone *see* **anybody**
anything *pron* aliquid, quicquam, quidpiam, quodvis; *(after si, nisi, num, ne)* quid; *(interrog)* ecquid, numquid; *(after negative)* quicquam; **hardly** — nihil fere
anywhere *adv* ubilibet, alicubi, ubivis
apart *adv* seorsum, separatim; **to be** — distare; **to set** — seponēre; **to stand** — distare
apart from *prep* praeter *(with acc)*
apartment *s* conclave *n*; insula *f*

apathetic *adj* lentus, languidus

apathy *s* apathia, lentitudo *f*, languor *m*

ape *s* simius *m*, simia *f*

ape *vt* imitari

aperture *s* apertura *f*; foramen *n*

apex *s* cacumen *n*; fastigium *n*

aphorism *s* sententia *f*

apiary *s* alvearium *n*

apiece *adv* singuli

aplomb *s* confidentia *f*

apocalypse *s* apocalypsis *f*

apocryphal *adj* apocryphus, commenticius

apogee *s* apogaeum *n*

apologetic *adj* apologeticus; confitens

apologist *s* defensor *m*

apologize *vi* se excusare; veniam petēre

apology *s* excusatio, defensio *f*; (*written treatise*) apologia *f*, liber apologeticus *m*; **to make an —** for excusare

apoplectic *adj* apoplecticus

apoplexy *s* apoplexia *f*; apoplexis *f*

apostasy *s* apostasia *f*

apostate *s* apostata *m*

apostle *s* apostolus *m*

apostolic *adj* apostolicus

apostrophe *s* apostrophe *f*; (*gram*) apostrophus *f*

apostrophize *vt* abrupte compellare

apothecary *s* (*druggist*) medicamentarius *m*; (*drugstore*) medicina taberna *f*, pharmacopolium *n*

apotheosis *s* apotheosis *f*

appall *vt* exterrēre, percellēre

apparatus *s* apparat·us -ūs *m*

apparel *s* vestis *f*, vestit·us -ūs *m*; vestimenta *n pl*

apparel *vt* vestire; adornare

apparent *adj* manifestus, apertus, conspicuus; **to be —** apparēre; **—ly** manifeste, aperte, specie, per speciem

apparition *s* spectrum *n*; visum *n*; species *f*

appeal *vi* appellare; provocare; **to — to** (*a magistrate*) appellare; (*the people*) provocare ad (*with acc*); (*the gods*) obsecrare, invocare, testari

appeal *s* (*law*) appellatio *f*; (*entreaty*) obsecratio, testatio *f*; (*to the people*) provocatio *f*

appear *vi* apparēre, comparēre; se ostendēre; (*to seem*) vidēri; (*to arise*) exoriri, surgēre; **to begin to —** patescēre

appearance *s* (*becoming visible*) aspect·us -ūs *m*; (*outward show*) species *f*; (*likelihood*) similitudo *f*; (*vision*) visum *n*; **first —** exort·us -ūs *m*; **to all —s** probabilissime; **to make an —** prodire

appease *vt* placare, sedare; mitigare; (*fig*) expiare

appeasement *s* placatio *f*; (*of an enemy*) pacificatio *f*

appellation *s* nomen *n*

appendage *s* appendix, accessio, appendicula *f*

appendix *s* appendix *f*

appetite *s* appetit·us -ūs *m*, cupiditas *f*; **to have an —** esurire

applaud *vt* applaudēre; laudare

applause *s* plaus·us -ūs, applaus·us -ūs *m*; laus *f*

apple *s* malum, pomum *n*; **— of my eye** ocellus meus *m*

apple tree *s* malus *f*

appliance *s* instrumentum *n*, apparat·us -ūs *m*

applicable *adj* commodus, conveniens

applicant *s* petitor *m*

application *s* creatio *f*; adhibitio, appositio *f*; studium *n*, sedulitas, industria, diligentia *f*; (*med*) fomentum *n*

apply *vt* adhibēre, admovēre, apponēre; aptare, accommodare; (*fig*) applicare; *vi* **to — to** pertinēre ad (*with acc*); **to —** for petēre

appoint *vt* creare; facēre; designare; destinare; constituēre

appointment *s* creatio *f*; (*rendezvous*) constitutum *n*; (*order*) mandatum *n*; (*office*) magistrat·us -ūs *m*

apportion *vt* dividēre, distribuēre

apportionment *s* divisio, distributio *f*

apposition *s* appositio *f*

appraisal *s* aestimatio *f*

appraise *vt* aestimare

appraiser *s* aestimator *m*

appreciable *adj* aestimabilis, haud exiguus

appreciate *vt* aestimare

appreciation *s* aestimatio *f*

apprehend *vt* apprehendēre, comprehendēre, percipēre; (*to seize*) capēre; (*to take by surprise*) intercipēre; (*to fear*) timēre, metuēre

apprehension *s* comprehensio *f*; facultas, intelligentia *f*; suspicio *f*; (*seizing*) captura *f*; (*fear*) timor, met·us -ūs *m*

apprehensive *adj* timidus, sollicitus

apprentice *s* discipulus *m*; tiro *m*

apprenticeship *s* identura *f*; tirocinium *n*

apprize *vt* docēre

approach *vt* appropinquare (*with dat*), accedēre ad (*with acc*), adire; *vi* appropinquare, appetēre

approach *s* access·us -ūs, adit·us -ūs *m*; appropinquatio *f*; (*by sea*) appuls·us -ūs *m*

approachable *adj* (*person*) facilis, affabilis; (*place*) patens

approbation *s* approbatio, laus *f*

appropriate *adj* proprius, aptus, idoneus; **—ly** apte, congruenter

appropriate *vt* asciscēre, asserēre, vindicare; assumēre

appropriation *s* vindicatio *f*

approval *s* approbatio *f*

approve *vt* approbare, probare; (*law*) sciscēre; *vi* **to — of** probare

approved *adj* probatus, spectatus

approximate *adj* propinquus, proximus; **—ly** prope, propemodum; (*with numbers*) ad (*with acc*)

approximate *vt* appropinquare (*with dat*); accedēre ad (*with acc*)

approximation *s* appropinquatio *f*
apricot *s* malum armeniacum *n*
April *s* (mensis) Aprilis *m*
apron *s* praecinctorium *n*; operimentum *n*
apt *adj* aptus, idoneus; (*inclined, prone*) pronus, propensus; —**ly** apte
aptitude *s* habilitas *f*, ingenium *n*
aptness *s* convenientia, congruentia *f*; (*tendency*) proclivitas *f*
aquatic *adj* aquatilis, aquaticus
aqueduct *s* aquaeduct·us -ūs *m*, aquarum duct·us -ūs *m*
aquiline *adj* (*of the nose*) aduncus
arable *adj* arabilis, culturae idoneus; — **land** arvum *n*
arbiter *s* arbiter *m*
arbitrament *s* arbitrat·us -ūs *m*, arbitrium *n*
arbitrarily *adv* ad arbitrium; ad libidinem; libidinoso
arbitrary *adj* libidinosus; imperiosus, superbus
arbitrate *vt* & *vi* disceptare
arbitration *s* arbitrium *n*, dijudicatio *f*
arbitrator *s* arbiter *m*; disceptator *m*
arbor *s* umbraculum *n*, pergula *f*
arc *s* arc·us -ūs *m*
arcade *s* portic·us -ūs *f*
arch *s* arc·us -ūs, fornix *m*
arch *adj* astutus, callidus, vafer; nimius
arch *vt* arcuare, fornicare
archaeological *adj* archaeologiae (*genit*)
archaeologist *s* antiquitatis investigator *m*
archaeology *s* rerum antiquarum scientia *f*
archaism *s* locutio obsoleta *f*
archbishop *s* archiepiscopus *m*
archer *s* sagittarius *m*; (*constellation*) Arcitenens *m*
archery *s* ars sagittandi *f*
archetype *s* archetypum *n*
archipelago *s* insulis crebrum mare *n*
architect *s* architectus *m*
architectural *adj* architectonicus
architecture *s* architectura *f*
archives *s* tabulae *f pl*; tabularium *n*
arctic *adj* arcticus
ardent *adj* ardens, fervidus; —**ly** ardenter
ardor *s* ardor, fervor *m*
arduous *adj* arduus
area *s* regio *f*; area *f*; superficies *f*
arena *s* (h)arena *f*
argonaut *s* argonauta *m*
argue *vt* arguēre, probare; *vi* argumentari, disputare, disserēre
argument *s* (*discussion*) disputatio *f*; controversia *f*; (*theme*) argumentum, thema *n*, ratio *f*
argumentation *s* argumentatio *f*
argumentative *adj* ratiocinativus, litigiosus
aria *s* canticum *n*
arid *adj* aridus, siccus
aright *adv* recte
arise *vi* surgēre, exoriri, exsistēre;

to — **from** nasci ex (*with abl*)
aristocracy *s* (*class*) optimates, nobiles *m pl*; (*government*) optimatum dominat·us -ūs *m*
aristocrat *s* optimas *m*
aristocratic *adj* patricius, generosus
arithmetic *s* arithmetica *n pl*
ark *s* arca *f*
arm *s* bracchium *n*; (*of the sea*) sin·us -ūs *m*; fretum *n*; —**s** arma *n pl*; **by force of** —**s** vi et armis; **to be under** —**s** in armis esse; **to lay down** —**s** ab armis discedēre; arma dedēre; **to take up** —**s** armare; arma sumēre
arm *vt* armare; *vi* armari; **bellum parare**
armada *s* classis magna *f*
armament *s* belli apparat·us -ūs *m*; copiae *f pl*
armchair *s* anconibus fabrefacta sella *f*
armistice *s* indutiae *f pl*
armlet *s* bracchiolum *n*; (*bracelet*) bracchiale *n*
armor *s* armatura *f*, armat·us -ūs *m*; arma *n pl*
armorbearer *s* armiger *m*
armory *s* armamentarium *n*
armpit *s* ala *f*
army *s* exercit·us -ūs *m*; (*in battle*) acies *f*; (*on the march*) agmen *n*
aroma *s* aroma *n*; (*of wine*) flos *m*
aromatic *adj* armomaticus
around *adv* circum, circa; **all** — undique, passim
around *prep* circum (*with aco*)
arouse *vt* suscitare; (*fig*) erigēre; **to** — **oneself** expergisci
arraign *vt* accusare
arraignment *s* accusatio, actio *f*
arrange *vt* instruēre, struēre, ordinare, disponēre, componēre; (*to agree*) pacisci
arrangement *s* ordo *m*, collocatio *f*; dispositio *f*; pactum *n*
array *s* vestis *f*, vestit·us -ūs *m*; habit·us -ūs *m*; (*mil*) acies *f*
array *vt* vestire; adornare; instruēre
arrears *s* reliqua *n pl*; residuum *n*, residuae pecuniae *f pl*; **to be in** — relinqui
arrest *s* prehensio *f*
arrest *vt* (*to seize*) prehendēre, deprehendēre, arripēre; (*movement*) tardare, morari; (*attention*) in se convertēre
arrival *s* advent·us -ūs *m*; (*by sea*) appuls·us -ūs *m*
arrive *vi* pervenire, advenire; (*of a ship*) advehi, appelli
arrogance *s* arrogantia, superbia *f*
arrogant *adj* arrogans, superbus; —**ly** arroganter, insolenter, superbe
arrogate *vt* arrogare, assumēre
arrow *s* sagitta, arundo *f*
arsenal *s* armamentarium *n*; navalia *n pl*
arsenic *s* arsenicum *n*
arson *s* incendium dolo malo *n*
art *s* ars *f*; artificium *n*
artery *s* arteria *f*

artful *adj* artificialis; callidus, subtilis; —ly callide, eleganter

article *s* (*object*) res *f*; (*ware*) merx *f*; (*term*) condicio *f*; (*clause*) caput *n*; (*gram*) articulus *m*

articulate *adj* distinctus, dilucidus; —ly articulatim, distincte

articulate *vt* explanare, exprimēre; articulatim dicēre

articulation *s* commissura *f*; (*fig*) explanatio *f*

artifice *s* artificium *n*; ars *f*; dolum *n*

artificial *adj* artificiosus; factitius; —ly arte

artillery *s* tormenta *n pl*

artisan *s* faber *m*; artifex, opifex *m*

artist *s* artifex *m*

artistic *adj* artificiosus, elegans; —ally artificiose; affabre

as *conj* & *adv* ut; quam; (*of time*) dum, cum; ita ut; sicut, velut; — **far** — quoad, usque ad, quantum; — **if** quasi, perinde ac si; ita ut si; — **it were** seu, tamquam; — **long** — tamdiu, tantisper dum; — **many** — tot, totidem; quotquot, quodcumque; — **much** tantum; — **often** — toties quoties; — **soon** — cum primum, simul, simul ac, simul atque; — **well** — ut, tamquam; — **yet** adhuc; **not** — **yet** nondum, necdum

ascend *vt* & *vi* ascendēre

ascendency *s* auctoritas *f*

ascent *s* ascensio *f*; ascens·us -ūs *m*; acclivitas *f*

ascertain *vt* confirmare, comperire

ascetic *adj* asceticus

ascetic *s* asceta *m*

asceticism *s* duritia *f*

ascribe *vt* imputare, tribuēre, ascribēre

ash *s* cinis *m*; (*tree*) fraxinus *f*

ashamed *adj* pudibundus; **I am** — of pudet me (*with genit*)

ashen *adj* pallidus

ashore *adv* (*motion*) in litus; (*rest*) in litore

Asiatic *adj* Asiaticus

aside *adv* seorsum, oblique; **to call** — sevocare; **to lay** *or* **set** — ponēre, seponēre

aside from *prep* praeter (*with acc*)

asinine *adj* asininus

ask *vt* rogare, poscēre; interrogare; requirēre; *vi* **to** — **for** petēre

askance *adv* oblique

askew *adv* traverse

asleep *adj* dormiens; **to be** — dormire; **to fall** — obdormire, obdormiscēre

asp *s* aspis *f*

asparagus *s* asparagus *m*

aspect *s* aspect·us -ūs, prospect·us -ūs *m*; facies *f*

aspen *s* populus tremula *f*

asperity *s* acerbitas *f*

aspersion *s* opprobrium *n*, calumniatio *f*

asphalt *s* bitumen *n*

asphyxia *s* asphyxia *f*

aspirant *s* petitor *m*

aspiration *s* affectatio, spes *f*; (*pol*) ambitio *f*

aspire *vi* **to** — **to** affectare, spectare, petēre, anniti

aspiring to appetens; **aspiring to** appetens (*with genit*)

ass *s* asinus *m*; asina *f*; onager *m*; (*fig*) stultus *m*

assail *vt* appetēre; oppugnare, invehi

assailable *adj* expugnabilis

assailant *s* oppugnator *m*

assassin *s* sicarius *m*; percussor *m*

assassinate *vt* insidiis interficēre, occidēre

assassination *s* caedes *f*

assault *s* impet·us -ūs *m*; oppugnatio, vis *f*; **aggravated** — (*law*) vis *f*; **sexual** — stupratio *f*; **to take by** — expugnare

assault *vt* adoriri, oppugnare; manus inferre (*with dat*); aggredi; (*in speech*) invehi in (*with acc*)

assay *vt* (*metals*) spectare; tentare, conari

assay *s* (*of metals*) obrussa *f*; spectatio *f*

assemblage *s* congregatio *f*; coacervatio *f*

assemble *vt* congregare, convocare, contrahēre; *vi* convenire

assembly *s* coet·us -ūs *m*; convent·us -ūs *m*; (*pol*) comitia *n pl*; concilium *n*; (*of troops*) contio *f*; synodus *f*

assent *s* assens·us -ūs *m*

assent *vi* assentiri, annuēre

assert *vt* asserēre, affirmare, asseverare; (*to vindicate*) defendēre

assertion *s* affirmatio, asseveratio *f*; postulatio *f*

assess *vt* (*to tax*) censēre; (*to value*) aestimare

assessment *s* cens·us -ūs *m*; aestimatio *f*; vectigal, tributum *n*

assessor *s* (*judge*) consessor *m*; (*of taxes*) censor *m*

assets *s* bona *n pl*

assiduous *adj* assiduus; —ly assidue

assign *vt* attribuēre, tribuēre; (*land*) assignare; (*place*) indicare; (*time*) praestituēre; (*task*) delegare; (*to allege*) suggerēre, afferre

assignment *s* assignatio, attributio *f*; delegatio *f*

assimilate *vt* assimulare; (*food*) concoquēre; (*knowledge*) concipēre

assimilation *s* assimilatio, appropriatio *f*

assist *vt* adesse (*with dat*), succurrēre (*with dat*), juvare, adjuvare

assistance *s* auxilium *n*; opem (*no nominative*); **to be of** — **to** auxilio esse (*with dat*)

assistant *s* adjutor *m*, adjutrix *f*, administer *m*

associate *adj* socius; collegialis

associate *s* socius, sodalis, consors *m*

associate *vt* consociare, adsciscēre, conjungēre; *vi* **to** — **with** familiariter uti (*with abl*); se adjungēre (*with dat*)

association s societas f; communitas f; consociatio f; congregatio f

assort vt digerĕre, disponĕre; vi congruĕre

assortment s digestio, dispositio f; variae res f pl

assuage vt allevare, placare, lenire, mitigare

assume vt assumĕre, arrogare; induĕre; (office) inire

assuming adj arrogans

assumption s assumptio f; arrogantio f; (hypothesis) sumptio f

assurance s fiducia f; (guarantee) fides f; (boldness) confidentia, audacia f

assure vt confirmare, affirmare; promittĕre (with dat); adhortari; **to be assured** confidĕre

assuredly adv certo, profecto

asterisk s asteriscus m

asthmatic adj asthmaticus; **to be — suspirio laborare**

astonish vt obstupefacĕre; **to be astonished at** mirari

astonishingly adv admirabiliter

astonishment s admiratio f; stupor m

astound vt (ob)stupefacĕre

astray adj vagus; **to go — errare; to lead — seducĕre**

astride adj varicus

astrologer s astrologus m; Chaldaeus m; mathematicus m

astrological adj astrologicus

astrology s astrologia f; Chaldaeorum divinatio f

astronomer s astrologus m; astronomus m

astronomical adj astronomicus

astronomy s astrologia, astronomia f

astute adj callidus

asunder adv seorsum, separatim; use verb with prefix dis- or se-

asylum s asylum, perfugium n

at prep (of place) ad (with acc), apud (with acc), in (with abl), or locative case; (of time) in (with abl), ad (with acc), or abl case

atheism s deos esse negare (used as neuter noun)

atheist s atheos m

athlete s athleta m

athletic adj athleticus; lacertosus

atlas s orbis terrarum descriptio f

atmosphere s aër m; caelum n; inane n

atmospheric adj aëris (genit)

atom s atomus f; corpus individuum n; (fig) mica, particula f

atomic adj atomicus; **— theory** atomorum doctrina f

atone vi **to — for** piare, expiare

atonement s piaculum n; expiatio, compensatio f

atrocious adj atrox, dirus; nefarius, nefandus; immanis; **—ly** nefarie

atrocity s atrocitas f; atrox facinus n

atrophy s tabes, atrophia f

atrophy s tabescĕre, macrescĕre

attach vt annectĕre, adjungĕre; ap-

plicare; affigĕre; **to be attached to** adhaerēre (with dat)

attachment s adhaesio f; (emotional) amor m; vinculum n; studium n

attack s impet·us -ūs m; oppugnatio f; (of cavalry) incurs·us -ūs m; (of disease, etc.) tentatio f

attack vt adoriri, aggredi, oppugnare; (with words) invehi in (with acc), insequi; (of diseases) corripĕre, invadĕre, tentare

attacker s oppugnator, provocator m

attain vt adipisci, consequi; **to — to** pervenire ad (with acc)

attainable adj impetrabilis, obtinendus

attempt s conat·us -ūs m, inceptum n; (risk) ausum, periculum n; **first — tirocinium n**

attempt vt conari, niti, temptare, moliri

attend vt (to accompany) comitari; (to escort) deducĕre; (to be present at) adesse (with dat), interesse (with dat); vi **to — on** apparēre (with dat); frequentare, assectari; adesse (with dat); **to — to** animadvertĕre, procurare; (to comply with) obtemperare (with dat); invigilare

attendance s frequentia f; expectatio, adsectatio, cura, diligentia f; obsequium n; (retinue) comitat·us -ūs m

attendant adj adjunctus

attendant s comes m; assecla, apparitor m; famulus m, famula f

attention s animadversio f; animi attentio f; (to duty) cura, diligentia f; **to call — to indicare; to pay — to** operam dare (with dat), studēre (with dat)

attentive adj attentus; sedulus; officiosus; **—ly** attente, intento animo; sedulo; officiose

attenuate vt attenuare, extenuare

attenuation s extenuatio f

attest vt testari, testificari

attestation s testificatio f

attic s cenaculum n

Attic adj Atticus; (fig) subtilis, elegans

attire s ornat·us -ūs m; vestis f; habit·us -ūs m; vestit·us -ūs m

attire vt vestire; adornare

attitude s habit·us -ūs, stat·us -ūs m; (mental) ratio f

attorney s cognitor, procurator, advocatus, actor m

attorney general s advocatus fisci, procurator publicus m

attract vt trahĕre, attrahĕre; (fig) allicĕre

attraction s vis attractionis f; (fig) illecebra f, invitamentum n

attractive adj blandus, suavis, lepidus, venustus; **—ly** blande, suaviter, venuste, lepide

attractiveness s lepos m, venustas f

attribute s proprium, attributum n

attribute vt tribuĕre, attribuĕre; assignare, delegare

attrition s attrit·us -ūs m

attune *vt* modulari

auburn *adj* fulvus; aureus

auction *s* auctio *f*; (*public*) hasta *f*; to hold an — auctionem facĕre; to sell by — sub hasta vendĕre

auctioneer *s* praeco *m*

audacious *adj* audax; —ly audacter

audacity *s* audacia *f*

audible *adj* quod audiri potest

audibly *adv* clara voce

audience *s* auditores *m pl*; (*bystanders*) corona *f*

audit *s* rationum inspectio *f*

audit *vt* inspicĕre

auditory *adj* auditorius

Augean *adj* Augiae (*genit*)

auger *s* terebra *f*

augment *vt* augēre, ampliare; *vi* augēri, accrescĕre

augur *s* augur *m*

augur *vi* augurari

augury *s* augurium, auspicium *n*; auguratio *f*

august *adj* augustus; magnificus

August *s* (mensis) Sextilis, (mensis) Augustus *m*

Augustan *adj* Augustalis

aunt *s* (*on father's side*) amita *f*; (*on mother's side*) matertera *f*

auspices *s* auspicium *n*; to take — auspicari; without taking — inauspicato

auspicious *adj* auspicatus; faustus, felix; —ly auspicato; feliciter

austere *adj* austerus, severus; —ly austere, severe

austerity *s* austeritas, severitas *f*

authentic *adj* certus; verus; ratus; (*law*) authenticus; fide dignus; genuinus

authenticate *vt* recognoscĕre

authentication *s* auctoritas *f*; legibus confirmatio *f*

authenticity *s* auctoritas, fides *f*

author *s* auctor, scriptor *m*; (*inventor*) conditor *m*; (*of a crime*) caput *n*

authoress *s* auctor *f*

authoritative *adj* imperiosus; fidus; —ly praecise

authority *s* auctoritas, potestas *f*; (*leave*) licentia *f*; jus *n*; imperium *n*; magistrat·us ·ūs *m*; to have it on good — bono auctore habēre

authorization *s* auctoritate confirmatio *f*; licentia *f*

authorize *vt* potestatem *or* auctoritatem dare (*with dat*), mandare; (*law*) sancire

authorship *s* scriptoris munus *n*; auctoritas *f*

autobiography *s* de vita sua scriptus liber *m*

autocrat *s* dominus *m*

autograph *s* chirographum *n*

autograph *vt* manu propria scribĕre

automatic *adj* necessarius

automaton *s* automaton *n*

autumn *s* autumnus *m*

autumnal *adj* autumnalis

auxiliaries *s* (*mil*) auxilia *n pl*; auxiliarii *m pl*

auxiliary *adj* auxiliaris, auxiliarius

auxiliary *s* adjutor *m*

avail *vt* prodesse (*with dat*); to — oneself of uti (*with abl*); *vi* valēre esse

avail *s* to be of no — usui non esse

availability *s* utilitas *f*

available *adj* in promptu; utilis

avalanche *s* montis ruina *f*

avarice *s* avaritia *f*; sordes *f*

avaricious *adj* avarus, avidus; —ly avare

avenge *vt* vindicare, ulcisci

avenger *s* ultor *m*, vindex *m & f*

avenging *adj* ultrix, vindex

avenue *s* xystus *m*, xystum *n*

average *s* medium *n*; on the — fere

average *vi* fere esse

averse *adj* aversus; to be — to abhorrēre ab (*with abl*); —ly averse

aversion *s* odium, fastidium *n*; to have an — for fastidire

avert *vt* avertĕre, amovēre, abducĕre

aviary *s* aviarium *n*

avid *adj* avidus

avocation *s* officium *n*, negotia *n pl*

avoid *vt* vitare, fugĕre; (*a blow*) declinare

avoidable *adj* evitabilis

avoidance *s* vitatio *f*; declinatio *f*

avow *vt* asserĕre, profitēri

avowal *s* confessio *f*

avowedly *adv* palam, aperte, ex confesso

await *vt* exspectare

awake *adj* vigil, vigilans; to be — vigilare

awaken *vt* excitare, suscitare, expergefacĕre; *vi* expergisci

award *s* praemium *n*; (*decision*) arbitrium, judicium *n*

award *vt* tribuĕre; (*law*) adjudicare, addicĕre

aware *adj* gnarus, sciens; to be — of scire

away *adv* use verbs with prefix ab- *or* ab-; far — procul, longe; to be — abesse; to go — abire

awe *s* reverentia *f*; formido *f*, met·us ·ūs, terror *m*; to stand in — of verēri; venerari

awful *adj* formidulosus, dirus, terribilis; —ly terribiliter, formidulose

awhile *adv* paulisper, aliquamdiu, parumper

awkward *adj* ineptus; rusticus, rudis; inhabilis; (*fig*) molestus; —ly inepte; rustice; dure; inscite

awkwardness *s* ineptia *f*; imperitia, rusticitas *f*

awl *s* subula *f*

awning *s* velarium *n*; inductio *f*

awry *adj* obliquus; pravus

awry *adv* oblique; prave

ax *s* securis *f*

axiom *s* axioma, pronuntiatum *n*, sententia *f*

axis *s* axis *m*

axle *s* axis *m*

azure *adj* caeruleus

B

baa *s* balat·us -ūs *m*
baa *vi* balare
babble *s* garrulitas *f*
babble *vi* blaterare, garrire
babbler *s* blatero, garrulus *m*
babbling *adj* garrulus, loquax
babe *s* infans *m* & *f*
baboon *s* cynocephalus *m*
baby *s* infans *m* & *f*
babyish *adj* infantilis
bacchanal *s* bacchans *m*, baccha *f*
bacchanalian *adj* bacchanalis
Bacchic *adj* bacchicus
bachelor *s* caelebs *m*; (*degree*) baccalaureus *m*
back *s* tergum, dorsum *n*; aversum *n*; at one's — *a* tergo
back *adv* retro, retrorsum; *or use verbs with prefix* re- *or* retro-
back *vt* adjuvare, favēre (*with dat*), obsecundare (*with dat*), adesse (*with dat*); *vi* to — away from defugēre; to — up retrogradi
backboard *s* pluteus *m*
backbone *s* spina *f*
backdoor *s* posticum *n*
backer *s* adjutor, fautor *m*
background *s* recess·us -ūs *m*
backstairs *s* scalae posticae *f pl*
backward *adv* retro; retrorsum; rursus
backward *adj* (*reversed*) supinus; (*slow*) piger, tardus; (*late*) serus; to be — cunctari
backwardness *s* tarditas *f*; pigritia *f*
bacon *s* lardum *n*
bad *adj* malus, parvus, nequam; improbus; aegrotus; (*of weather*) adversus; to go — corrumpi; —ly male; prave; improbe
badge *s* insigne, signum *n*
badger *s* meles *f*
badger *vt* vexare, inquietare, sollicitare
badness *s* malitia, pravitas, nequitia, improbitas *f*
baffle *vt* decipēre, fallēre, eludēre
bag *s* saccus *m*; (*of leather*) uter *m*; (*of network*) reticulum *n*
baggage *s* sarcinae *f pl*; impedimenta *n pl*; scruta *n pl*
bail *s* vadimonium *n*; vas *m*; (*for debt*) praes *m*; to accept — for vadari; to put up — for spondēre pro (*with abl*), fidepromittēre
bailiff *s* (*sergeant of court of justice*) apparitor *m*; (*manager of estate*) villicus *m*
bailiwick *s* jurisdictio *f*
bait *s* esca *f*; (*fig*) incitamentum *n*, illecebra *f*
bait *vt* inescare; (*to tease*) lacessēre
bake *vt* torrēre, coquēre
baker *s* pistor *m*
bakery *s* pistrina *f*, pistrinum *n*
balance *s* libra, trutina, statera *f*; (*equipoise*) aequipondium *n*; (*in bookkeeping*) reliquum *n*; (*fig*) compensatio *f*

balance *vt* librare; compensare; (*accounts*) consolidare, dispungēre; *vi* constare; the account balances ratio constat
balance sheet *s* ratio accepti et expensi *f*
balcony *s* maenianum *n*; podium *n*
bald *adj* calvus, glaber; (*fig*) aridus; —ly (*in style*) jejune
baldness *s* calvitium *n*; (*of style*) ariditas, jejunitas *f*
bale *s* sarcina *f*, fascis *m*
bale *vt* (*e.g., hay*) involvēre; to — out exhaurire
baleful *adj* funestus; perniciosus, noxius
balk *s* (*of wood*) tignum *n*; (*fig*) frustratio *f*
balk *vt* frustrari, eludēre, decipēre
ball *s* globulus *m*; (*for playing*) pila *f*; to play — pilā ludēre
ballad *s* carmen *n*
ballast *s* saburra *f*
ballast *vt* saburrare
ballet *s* pantomimus *m*
ballet dancer *s* pantomimus *m*, pantomima *f*
ballot *s* tabella *f*; suffragium *n*
ballot box *s* cista, cistula *f*
balm *s* balsamum *n*; unguentum *n*; (*fig*) solatium *n*
balmy *adj* balsaminus; suavis, lenis
balsam *s* balsamum *n*
bamboo *s* arundo indica *f*
ban *s* edictum *n*; proscriptio *f*; interdictum *n*
ban *vt* interdicēre (*with dat*), vetare
banana *s* ariena *f*
band *s* vinculum, ligamentum *n*; (*for the head*) redimiculum *n*, infula *f*; (*troop*) caterva *f*, chorus *m*; grex *f*; man·us -ūs *f*; in —s turmatim
band *vi* to — together conjungi, consociari
bandage *s* fascia, ligatura *f*
bandage *vt* ligare, obligare
bandit *s* latro *m*
banditry *s* latrocinium *n*
bandy *vt* jactare; to — words altercari
bane *s* venenum *n*; virus *n*; (*fig*) pestis, pernicies *f*
baneful *adj* pestiferus, perniciosus, exitiosus
bang *s* crepit·us -ūs, sonit·us -ūs *m*
bang *vt* verberare; *vi* sonare, crepare
banish *vt* expellēre, pellēre, relegare, deportare; aquā et igni interdicēre (*with dat*)
banishment *s* (*act*) ejectio, relegatio *f*; interdictio aquae et ignis *f*; (*state*) exilium *n*
banister *s* epimedion *n*
bank *s* (*of a river*) ripa *f*; (*of earth*) agger *m*; (*com*) argentaria *f*, mensa publica *f*

banker s argentarius, mensarius m
banking s argentaria negotiatio f
bank note s tessera mensae publicae f
bankrupt s conturbator, decoctor m; to be or become — rationes conturbare; decoquère; to go — foro cedère
bankruptcy s rationum conturbatio f; (fig) naufragium patrimonii n
banner s vexillum n
banquet s convivium n, epulae f pl
banter s cavillatio f; jocus m
banter vi cavillari
bantering s cavillatio f
baptism s baptisma n, baptismus m
baptize vt baptizare
bar s vectis f; (of door) obex m; repagulum n; (fig) impedimentum n; (ingot) later m; (in court of justice) cancelli m pl, claustra n pl; (legal profession) forum n; (counter) abacus m; of the — forensis; to practice at the — causas agère
bar vt (door) obserare; (to keep away) obstare (with dat), prohibère, intercludère
barb s hamus m; aculeus m
barbarian adj barbarus
barbarian s barbarus m
barbaric adj barbaricus
barbarism s barbaria, barbaries f; feritas f; (of language) barbarismus m
barbarity s ferocia, saevitia, immanitas f
barbarous adj barbarus; ferus, immanis; —ly barbare; saeve
barbed adj hamatus
barber s tonsor m, tonstrix f
bard s vates m
bare adj nudus; merus; (of style) pressus; to lay — nudare, detegère
bare vt nudare, denudare, detegère, aperire
barefaced adj impudens; —ly impudenter
barefoot adj nudis pedibus; discalceatus
bareheaded adj nudo capite
barely adv vix, aegre
bargain s pactio f, pactum n; to strike a — pacisci
bargain vi pacisci
barge s linter f
bark s (of tree) cortex m & f, liber m; (of dog) latrat·us ·ūs m; (ship) navis, ratis f
bark vi latrare; to — at allatrare
barking s latrat·us ·ūs m
barley s hordeum n
barley adj hordeacus
barmaid s ministra cauponae f
barn s granarium, horreum n
barometer s barometrum n
barometric adj barometricus
baron s baro m
barracks s castra (stativa) n pl
barrel s cadus m, dolium n, cupa f
barren adj sterilis; macer; jejunus; (fig) angustus
barrenness s sterilitas f

barricade s munimentum n; claustrum n
barricade vt obsaepire, obstruère, oppilare
barrier s limes m; cancelli m pl; (fig) claustra n pl
barrister s advocatus m
barter s permutatio f; merx f
barter vt mutare, commutare; vi merces mutare, merces pacisci
base adj humilis, ignobilis, obscurus; inferior; servilis; infamis, vilis, turpis; —ly abjecte; turpiter
base s basis f; (mus) sonus gravis m; (fig) fundamentum n; (mil) castra n pl
baseless adj inanis, vanus, falsus
basement s fundamentum n, basis f; imum tabulatum n
baseness s humilitas f; turpitudo f
bashful adj erubescens; pudens; modestus; verecundus; —ly timide, verecunde; modeste
bashfulness s pudor m; rubor m; verecundia f
basic adj primus, principalis
basilica s basilica f
basin s (for washing) trulleum n, trulla f; (reservoir) labrum n
basis s fundamentum n
bask vi apricari
basket s corbis f, canistrum n; (for wool) quasillum n; cophinus m
bas-relief s caelamen n; toreuma n
bass s sonus gravissimus m
bast s tilia f
bastard adj spurius
bastard s nothus, spurius m
baste vt lardo perfundère
bastion s propugnaculum, castellum n
bat s (bird) vespertilio m; (club) clava f
batch s massa n; numerus m
bath s balneum n; (public) balnea n pl; (tub) alveus m, labrum n; lavatio f; cold — frigidarium n; hot — cal(i)darium n
bathe vt lavare; vi balneo uti, lavari, perlui
bathing s lavatio f; natatio f
bathtub s alveus m
batman s calo m
baton s virga f
battalion s cohors f
batter vt percutère, obtundère, diruère, verberare, quassare
battering ram s aries m
battle s proelium n, pugna f; acies f
battle vi pugnare, proeliari
battle array s acies f
battle-ax s bipennis f
battlement s pinna f
bauble s tricae f pl
bawd s lena f
bawdry s lenocinium n
bawl vi vociferari, clamitare
bawling s vociferatio f; indecorus clamor m
bay s (sea) sin·us ·ūs m; (tree) laurea, laurus f; at — interclusus
bay adj (light-colored) helvus; (dark-colored) spadix; (of bay) laureus

bay *vi* latrare
bayonet *s* pugio *f*
bayonet *vt* pugione fodĕre
bazaar *s* forum rerum venalium *n*
be *vi* esse; exsistĕre; (*condition*) se habēre; to — **absent** abesse; to — **against** adversari; to — **amongst** interesse (*with dat*); to — **for** (*to side with*) favēre (*with dat*), stare cum (*with abl*); to — **present** adesse
beach *s* litus *n*, acta *f*
beach *vt* subducĕre; *vi* vadis impingĕre
beacon *s* ignis in specula *m*; (*lighthouse*) pharus *m*
bead *s* pilula, sphaerula *f*
beagle *s* parvus canis venaticus *m*
beak *s* rostrum *n*
beaked *adj* rostratus
beaker *s* poculum *n*, cantharus *m*
beam *s* (*of wood*) tignum *n*, trabs *f*; (*of light*) radius *m*, jubar *n*; nitor *m*
beam *vi* radiare, refulgēre; (*of a person*) arridēre
beaming *adj* nitens, lucidus
bean *s* faba *f*; phaselus *m & f*
bear *vt* (*to carry*) portare, ferre; (*to endure*) ferre, pati, tolerare; (*to produce*) ferre; (*to beget*) parĕre; to — **away** auferre; to — **out** (*to confirm*) arguĕre; to — **witness** to testari; *vi* to — **down** on appropinquare; to — **upon** (*to refer to*) pertinēre ad (*with acc*); to — **up under** obsistĕre (*with dat*), sustinēre; to — **with** indulgēre (*with dat*)
bear *s* ursus *m*, ursa *f*
bearable *adj* tolerandus, tolerabilis
beard *s* barba *f*; (*of grain*) arista *f*
bearded *adj* barbatus; intonsus
beardless *adj* inberbis
bearer *s* (*porter*) bajulus *m*; (*of litter*) lecticarius *m*; (*of letter*) tabellarius *m*; (*of news*) nuntius *m*
bearing *s* (*posture*) gest·us -ūs *m*; (*direction*) regio *f*; to have a — **on** pertinēre ad (*with acc*)
beast *s* belua *f*; bestia *f*; (*wild*) fera *f*; (*domestic*) pecus *f*
beast of burden *s* jumentum *n*
beastly *adj* obscenus, foedus, spurcus
beat *vt* (*to punish*) verberare; (*to knock*) pulsare; (*to conquer*) superare, vincĕre; (*the body in grief*) plangĕre; to — **back** repellĕre; to — **down** demoliri; to — **in** perfringĕre; *vi* palpitare; to — **upon** (*of rain*) impluĕre; (*of waves*) illidĕre
beat *s* (*blow*) plaga *f*, ict·us -ūs *m*; (*of the heart*) palpitatio *f*; (*mus*) percussio *f*; (*patrol*) vigiles nocte ambulantes *m pl*
beaten *adj* victus; (*worn*) tritus
beating *s* verberatio *f*; ict·us -ūs *m*; verbera *n pl*; (*defeat*) repulsa *f*; clades *f*; (*of the heart*) palpitatio *f*
beautiful *adj* pulcher; (*shapely*) formosus; —ly pulchre, belle
beautify *vt* ornare, decorare

beauty *s* pulchritudo *f*; forma *f*; (*of places*) amoenitas *f*
beaver *s* castor, fiber *m*; (*of helmet*) buccula *f*
because *conj* quod, quia, quoniam; quippe qui
because of *prep* ob (*with acc*), propter (*with acc*), gratiā (*with genit*)
beck *s* nut·us -ūs *m*; at the — **and call** ad arbitrium
beckon *vt* nutare, annuĕre
become *vt* decēre; *vi* fieri
becoming *adj* decens; decorus; conveniens; —ly decenter; digne; honeste
bed *s* lectus *m*, cubile *n*; (*in a garden*) areola *f*; (*of a river*) alveus *m*; to go to — cubitum ire; to make the — lectum sternĕre
bedding *s* stragulum *n*
bedeck *vt* decorare, ornare
bedevil *vt* (*to enchant*) fascinare
bedfellow *s* tori socius *m*, tori socia *f*
bedlam *s* tumult·us -ūs *m*
bedpost *s* fulcrum *n*
bedraggled *adj* sordidus
bedridden *adj* to be — lecto tenēri
bedroom *s* cubiculum *n*
bedtime *s* hora somni *f*
bee *s* apis *f*
beef *s* bubula caro *f*
beehive *s* alveus *m*; alvearium *n*
beekeeper *s* apiarius *m*
beer *s* cerevisia *f*
beet *s* beta *f*
beetle *s* scarabaeus *m*
befall *vt* accidĕre (*with dat*); contingĕre (*with dat*); *vi* accidĕre, contingĕre, evenire
befit *vt* decēre, convenire in (*with acc*)
befitting *adj* decens; conveniens, idoneus; **it is —** decet
before *prep* ante (*with acc*); prae (*with abl*); pro (*with abl*); coram (*with abl*); apud (*with acc*); — **all things** imprimis; — **long** jamdudum; — **now** antehac
before *conj* antequam, priusquam
beforehand *adv* antea
befriend *vt* favēre (*with dat*), sublevare, adjuvare
beg *vt* petĕre, poscĕre, orare, obsecrare; *vi* mendicare
beget *vt* gignĕre, procreare, generare
beggar *s* mendicus *m*
begging *s* mendicitas *f*; to go — mendicare
begin *vt & vi* incipĕre, incohare, exordiri; to — **with** incipĕre ab (*with abl*)
beginner *s* auctor *m*; inceptor *m*; tiro *m*
beginning *s* inceptio *f*; initium *n*; exordium *n*; origo *f*; principium *n*; at the — **of winter** ineunte hieme
begone *interj* apage!
beguile *vt* fallĕre, fraudare
behalf *s* on — of pro (*with abl*)
behave *vi* se gerĕre; to — **towards**

uti (*with abl*); **well behaved** bene moratus

behavior *s* mores *m pl*

behead *vt* detruncare, obtruncare

beheading *s* decollatio *f*

behest *s* jussum *n*

behind *adv* pone, a tergo, post; **to be left** — relinqui

behind *prep* pone (*with acc*); post (*with acc*)

behold *vt* conspicěre; obtuēri

behold *interj* eccel, en!

being *s* ens *n*; natura *f*; essentia *f*; homo *m*

bejewelled *adj* gemmatus, gemmeus

belabor *vt* mulcare, verberare

belch *s* ruct·us -ūs *m*

belch *vi* ructare, eructare

belfry *s* campanile *n*

belie *vt* repugnare; (*to refute*) refutare, refellěre

belief *s* fides *f*; opinio, persuasio *f*

believe *vt* (*thing*) creděre; (*person*) creděre (*with dat*); (*to suppose*) existimare, opinari, putare, creděre, arbitrari; **to make** — simulare

believer *s* credens *m & f*; Christianus *m*

bell *s* (*large*) campana *f*; (*small*) tinnabulum *n*

belle *s* formosa puella *f*

belles lettres *s* litterae *f pl*

belligerent *adj* belliger, belligerans, bellans

bellow *vi* rugire, mugire

bellowing *s* mugit·us -ūs *m*

bellows *s* follis *m*

belly *s* venter *m*; abdomen *n*

bellyache *s* tormina *n pl*

belong *vi* **to** — to esse (*with genit*); inesse (*with dat*); pertinēre ad (*with acc*)

beloved *adj* dilectus, carus; **dearly** — carissimus

below *adj* inferus

below *adv* infra; subter

below *prep* infra (*with acc*); sub (*with abl or acc*)

belt *s* cingulum *n*; (*swordbelt*) balteus *m*; zona *f*

bemoan *vt* deplorare, lamentari

bemused *adj* attonitus

bench *s* scamnum, sedile, subsellium *n*; (*for rowers*) transtrum *n*

bend *vt* flectěre, curvare; inclinare; (*bow*) intenděre; (*to persuade*) intenděre; *vi* se inflectěre; **to** — **back** reflectěre; **to** — **down** *or* **over** se demittěre

bend *s* plica *f*; flex·us -ūs *m*; curvamen *n*; (*fig*) inclinatio *f*

bending *s* flexura, curvatura, inclinatio *f*

bending *adj* flexus; inclinans; acclivis; declivis; (*concave*) concavus

beneath *adv* subter

beneath *prep* sub (*with acc or abl*)

benediction *s* benedictio *f*

benefaction *s* beneficium *n*

benefactor *s* largitor *m*; patronus *m*

benefactress *s* patrona *f*

beneficence *s* beneficentia *f*

beneficent *adj* beneficus, benignus, liberalis; —**ly** benefice

beneficial *adj* utilis, commodus; salutaris; —**ly** utiliter

benefit *s* beneficium *n*, gratia *f*; fruct·us -ūs *m*; **to have the** — **of** frui (*with abl*)

benefit *vt* juvare; prodesse (*with dat*); *vi* proficěre; lucrari

benevolence *s* benevolentia *f*

benevolent *s* benevolus, beneficus; benignus, liberalis; —**ly** benevole

benign *adj* benignus; —**ly** benigne

bent *adj* curvus, flexus; (*of the mind*) attentus; — **backwards** recurvus; — **forwards** pronus; — **inwards** camur; sinuosus

bent *s* flex·us -ūs *m*, plica *f*; curvatura *f*; (*inclination*) ingenium *n*, inclinatio *f*

benumb *vt* torpore afficěre

bequeath *vt* legare

bequest *s* legatum *n*

bereave *vt* orbare; privare; spoliare

bereavement *s* orbitas *f*; damnum *n*

bereft *adj* orbus, orbatus, privatus

berry *s* bacca *f*; acinus *m*

berth *s* statio *f*; (*cabin*) diaeta *f*; **to give wide** — to devitare

beseech *vt* obsecrare, implorare, supplicare

beset *vt* circumdare, obsiděre, circumsedēre; urgēre

beside *prep* ad (*with acc*), apud (*with acc*), juxta (*with acc*); — **the point** nihil ad rem; **to be** — **oneself** delirare

besides *adv* praeterea, ultro, insuper

besides *prep* praeter (*with acc*)

besiege *vt* circumsedēre, obsiděre

besieging *s* obsessio, circumsessio *f*

besmirch *vt* maculare

best *adj* optimus, praestantissimus; **the** — **part** major pars *f*

best *s* flos *m*; **to do one's** — pro virili parte agěre; **to have the** — **of it** praevalēre, valēre; **to make the** — **of** aequo animo ferre; **to the** — **of one's ability** pro viribus

bestial *adj* bestialis; immanis

bestir *vt* **to** — **oneself** expergisci

bestow *vt* tribuěre, conferre; donare, largiri

bestower *s* largitor, dator *m*

bet *s* pignus, depositum *n*

bet *vt* deponěre; *vi* pignore contenděre

betide *vi* evenire, acciděre

betoken *vt* indicare, portenděre

betray *vt* traděre, proděre; (*feelings*) arguěre

betrayer *s* proditor, traditor *m*

betroth *vt* sponděre, desponděre

betrothal *s* sponsalia *n pl*; pactio nuptialis *f*

betrothed *adj* sponsus, pactus

better *adj* melior; potior, praestantior; superior; **it is** — praestat; **to get** — convalescěre; **to get the** — **of** superare, vincěre

better *adv* melius, potius; praestantius; rectius; satius

better *vt* meliorem facĕre; corrigĕre; to — oneself proficĕre
betters *s* superiores *m pl*
between *prep* inter (*with acc*); — whiles interim
betwixt *prep* inter (*with acc*)
bevel *vt* obliquare
beverage *s* potio *f*, pot·us -ūs *m*
bevy *s* grex *f*
bewail *vt* deplorare, ingemĕre, queri, lamentari
beware *vi* cavēre; to — of cavēre
bewilder *vt* perturbare, confundĕre
bewilderment *s* perturbatio *f*
bewitch *vt* fascinare; (*to charm*) demulcēre
beyond *adv* supra, ultra; ulterius
beyond *prep* ultra (*with acc*); (*motion*) trans (*with acc*); supra (*with acc*), extra (*with acc*); to go — excedĕre
bias *s* inclinatio *f*; praeponderatio *f*
bias *vt* inclinare
Bible *s* divina scriptura *f*, biblia *n pl*
Biblical *adj* biblicus
bibliography *s* bibliographia *f*
bicker *vi* jurgare, altercari
bickering *s* altercatio *f*
bid *vt* jubēre, mandare, rogare; (*to invite*) invitare; (*at auction*) licitari, licēri; to — farewell valedicĕre
bid *s* licitatio *f*; to make a — licēri
bidder *s* licitator *m*
bidding *s* jussum *n*; (*auction*) licitatio *f*
bide *vt* exspectare, manēre
biennial *adj* biennalis, bimus
bier *s* feretrum *n*, sandapila *f*
big *adj* ingens, vastus; grandis, amplus; — with child gravida; — with young praegnans; very — permagnus
bigamist *s* bimaritus *m*
bigamy *s* bigamia *f*
bigot *s* nimis obstinatus fautor *m*
bigoted *adj* nimis obstinatus
bigotry *s* contumacia *f*; nimia obstinatio *f*
bile *s* bilis *f*
bilge water *s* sentina *f*
bilious *adj* biliosus
bilk *vt* fraudare; frustrari
bill *s* (*of a bird*) rostrum *n*; (*proposed law*) rogatio *f*; lex *f*; plebiscitum *n*; (*com*) ratio debiti *f*; syngrapha *f*; (*notice*) libellus *m*; to introduce a — ferre, legem ferre; populum rogare; to pass a — legem perferre; to turn down a — antiquare
billet *s* hospitium *n*
billet *vt* per hospitia dispargĕre
billion *s* billio *m*
billow *s* fluct·us -ūs *m*
billowy *adj* fluctuosus, undabundus
bin *s* (*in wine cellar*) loculus *m*; (*for grain*) cista *f*, panarium *n*
bind *vt* ligare, nectĕre, stringĕre, vincire; (*by obligation*) obligare; (*books*) conglutinare; (*wounds*) obligare; to — fast devincire; to — together colligare; to — up alligare; (*med*) astringĕre

binding *adj* obligatorius; (*law*) ratus
binding *s* religatio *f*; compages *f*
biographer *s* vitae scriptor *m*
biography *s* vita *f*
biped *s* bipes *m*
birch *adj* betulinus
birch tree *s* betula *f*
bird *s* avis, volucris *f*
birdcage *s* cavea *f*
birdcall *s* fistula aucupatoria *f*
birdlime *s* viscum *n*
bird's nest *s* nidus *m*
birth *s* part·us -ūs *m*; ort·us -ūs *m*; (*race*) genus *n*
birthday *s* dies natalis *m*
birthday cake *s* libum *n*
birthplace *s* patria *f*
birthright *s* patrimonium *n*
biscuit *s* crustulum *n*
bisect *vt* dividĕre
bishop *s* episcopus *m*
bison *s* bison *m*; urus *m*
bit *s* (*for a horse*) frenum *n*; (*small amount*) pars *f*, fragmentum *n*; (*of food*) frustum *n*; — by — minutatim
bitch *s* canis *f*
bite *s* mors·us -ūs *m*; (*fig*) sarcasmus *m*
bite *vt* mordēre; (*as pepper, frost, etc.*) urĕre
biting *adj* mordax; (*fig*) asper; mordens
bitter *adj* amarus; (*fig*) acerbus; asper; gravis; —ly acerbe; aspere
bitterness *s* amaritas *f*; (*fig*) acerbitas *f*; asperitas *f*
bitters *s* absinthium *n*
bivouac *s* excubiae *f pl*
blab *s* garrulus *m*
blab *vi* garrire, deblaterare
black *adj* niger; ater; (*in looks*) trux; (*of character*) scelestus
black *s* nigrum *n*; (*negro*) Aethiops *m*; in — pullatus
black-and-blue *adj* lividus
blackberry *s* morum *n*
blackbird *s* merula *f*
black death *s* pestis *f*
blacken *vt* nigrare; denigrare
blackguard *s* nebulo *m*
blacklist *s* proscriptio *f*
black magic *s* magicae artes *f pl*
blackness *s* nigritia, nigrities *f*
blacksmith *s* ferrarius faber *m*
bladder *s* vesica *f*
blade *s* (*edge*) lamina *f*; (*of grass*) caulis *m*, herba *f*; (*of oar*) palma *f*
blamable *adj* culpabilis; reus
blame *vt* reprehendĕre, culpare, vituperare
blame *s* culpa *f*; reprehensio *f*
blameless *adj* integer, innoxius; irreprehensus; —ly integre, innocenter
blanch *vt* candefacĕre; *vi* exalbescĕre, pallescĕre
bland *adj* blandus
blandishment *s* blanditia *f*, blandimentum *n*; (*charm*) lenocinium *n*
blank *adj* vacuus, albus, purus; (*expression*) stolidus

blanket s lodix f; stragulum n

blare s strepit·us -ūs, clangor, stridor m

blare vi stridēre, canēre

blaspheme vi maledicēre, execrari; blasphemare

blasphemous adj maledicus, impius; blasphemus

blasphemy s maledicta n pl, impietas f; blasphemia, blasphematio f

blast s flat·us -ūs m, flamen n

blast vt discutēre, disjicēre; (crops) urēre, robigine afficēre

blaze s flamma f; fulgor m

blaze vi flagrare, ardēre; **to — up** exardescēre

bleach vt dealbare, candefacēre

bleak adj desertus; immitis

blear-eyed adj lippus; **to be — lippire

bleat vi balare

bleating s balat·us -ūs m

bleed vi sanguinem fundēre

bleeding adj crudus, sanguineus

bleeding s (bloodletting) sanguinis missio f; (flowing of blood) sanguinis profusio f

blemish s macula f, vitium n; labes f

blemish vt maculare, foedare

blend vt commiscēre, immiscēre

bless vt beare; (eccl) benedicēre; (consecrate) consecrare; (with success) secundare

blessed adj beatus; pius; fortunatus; (of emperors) divus

blessing s (thing) bonum, commodum n; (eccl) benedictio f

blight s robigo, uredo f

blight vt urēre; robigine afficēre; (fig) nocēre (with dat)

blind adj caecus; obscurus; (fig) ignarus; **—ly** (rashly) temere

blind vt caecare, occaecare; (fig) occaecare, fallēre

blindfold vt oculos obligare (with dat)

blindfolded adj obligatis oculis

blindness s caecitas f; (fig) temeritas f; stultitia f

blink vi connivēre

bliss s beatitudo f

blissful adj beatus; **—ly** beate

blister s pustula f

blister vt & vi pustulare

blithe adj hilaris, hilarus

bloated adj tumidus, turgidus

block s truncus, stipes m; (of stone) massa f; (of houses) insula f

block vt claudēre; (to impede) obstare (with dat); **to — up** obstruēre

blockade s obsidio f; **to raise a —** obsidionem solvēre

blockade vt obsidēre, claudēre

blockhead s caudex m

blood s sanguis m; (gore) cruor m, sanies f; (fig) (slaughter) caedes f; (lineage) genus n; **bad —** simultas f; **to staunch —** sanguinem supprimēre

bloodless adj exsanguis; (without bloodshed) incruentus

blood-red adj cruentus; sanguineus, sanguinolentus

bloodshed s caedes f

bloodshot adj cruore suffusus

bloodstained adj cruentus, cruentatus, sanguinolentus

bloodsucker s sanguisuga f; hirudo f

bloodthirsty adj sanguinarius; sanguinolentus

blood vessel s vena f

bloody adj cruentus

bloom s flos m

bloom vi florēre, florescēre; vigēre

blooming adj florens; floridus; nitidus

blossom s flos m

blot s macula, litura f; (fig) labes f, dedecus n

blot vt maculare; conspurcare; **to — out** delēre; (to erase) oblitterare

blotch s macula f; pustula f

blotched adj maculosus

blow s (stroke) plaga f, ict·us -ūs m; (with the fist) colaphus m; (fig) plaga f; calamitas f

blow vt (instrument) canēre; (breath) anhelare; **to — out** extinguēre; **to — the nose** emungēre; **to — up** inflare; vi flare; (of a flower) efflorescēre; **to — over** (of a storm) cadēre; (fig) abire

blowing s sufflatio f; flat·us -ūs m; (of the nose) emunctio f

blowup s scandalum n; (scolding) objurgatio f

blubber s adeps balaenarum m

blubber vi lacrimas effundēre

blue adj caeruleus

blueness s caeruleum n

blues s melancholia f

bluff s rupes f; promunturium n

bluff adj rusticus; declivis; ventosus

bluff vt fallēre, decipēre; vi ampullari, gloriari

blunder s (in writing) mendum n; error m, erratum n

blunder vi offendēre, errare

blunderer s homo ineptus m

blunt adj hebes; obtusus; (fig) inurbanus, rusticus; **—ly** plane, liberius

blunt vt hebetare, obtundēre, retundēre

bluntness s hebetudo f; (fig) candor m

blur s macula f

blur vt obscurare

blurt vt **to — out** inconsultum projicēre

blush s rubor m

blush vi erubescēre

bluster vi declamitare; fremēre, strepēre

bluster s jactatio, declamatio f; fremit·us -ūs m, strepit·us -ūs m

boar s aper m; verres m

board s (plank) tabula f; (table) mensa f; (food) vict·us -ūs m; (council, etc.) collegium n; consilium n; concilium n; (judicial) quaestio f; (for games) abacus, alveus m

board vt **to — a ship** navem conscendēre; **to — up** contabulare; vi **to — with** devertēre ad (with acc)

boarder s convictor, hospes m

boardinghouse s contubernium n

boast vi se jactare, gloriari

boast s jactantia, jactatio, gloriatio, vanitas f

boastful adj gloriosus; —ly gloriose

boasting s gloriatio f

boat s linter f; cymba f; scapha f; navicula f

boatman s nauta, lintrarius m

bode vt portendĕre, praesagire

bodiless adj incorporalis

bodily adj corporeus; corporalis; in persona

bodily adv corporaliter

body s corpus n; (corpse) cadaver n; truncus m; (person) homo m; (of troops) man·us -ūs, caterva f; (of cavalry) turma f; (of people) numerus m, multitudo f; (heavenly) astrum n

bodyguard s stipatores, satellites m pl; cohors praetoria f

bog s palus f

boil vt fervefacĕre, coquĕre; to — down decoquĕre; vi fervēre, effervescĕre; (fig) aestuare

boil s furunculus m, ulcus n

boiler s (vessel) ahenum, caldarium n; (kettle) lebes m

boisterous adj procellosus; violentus, turbidus; —ly turbide, turbulente

bold adj audax; impavidus; (rash) temerarius; (saucy) insolens, protervus, impudens; (language) liber; (stout) intrepidus; —ly audacter; temere; fortiter; insolenter

boldness s audacia, fidentia f; (in speech) libertas, impudentia f

bolster s pulvinar n; (of a bed) cervical n

bolster vt supportare, adjuvare; to — up suffulcire

bolt s (of a door) pessulus m; (of thunder) fulmen n; (pin) clavus m; (missile) sagitta f, telum n

bolt vt obserare, oppessulare, claudĕre, occludĕre

bomb s pyrobolus m

bombard vt tormentis verberare; (fig) lacessĕre

bombardment s tormentis verberatio f

bombast s ampulla f pl

bombastic adj inflatus, tumidus; to be — ampullari

bond s vinculum n; nodus m; copula, catena, jugum n; (document) syngrapha f

bondage s servitus f, servitium n; captivitas f

bondsman s servus m; verna m; addictus m

bone s os n; (of fish) spina f

boneless adj exos

bonfire s ignes festi m pl

bonnet s redimiculum n

bony adj osseus

book s liber m; volumen n; codex m;

bookcase s foruli m pl; librarium n; pegma n

bookish adj libris deditus

bookkeeper s calculator m; actuarius m

bookshelf s pluteus m

bookstore s bibliopolum n, libraria taberna f

bookworm s tinea f; (fig) librorum helluo m

boom s (of a ship) longurius m; (of a harbor) obex m & f, repagulum n

boom vi resonare

boon s bonum, donum n

boor s rusticus m

boorish adj agrestis, rusticus; —ly rustice

boost vt efferre

boot s calceus m; caliga f; (peasant's) pero m; (tragic) cothurnus m; to — insuper

boot vi prodesse; **what boots it?** cui bono?

booth s taberna f, tabernaculum n

booty s praeda f; spolia n pl

border s (edge) margo m & f; (seam) limbus m, fimbria f; (boundary) finis, terminus m

border vt tangĕre, attingĕre; circumjacēre; vi to — on adjacēre (with dat), attingĕre; imminēre (with dat)

bordering adj affinis, finitimus

bore vt terebrare, perforare; excavare; (fig) (to weary) obtundĕre, fatigare

bore s (tool) terebra f; (hole) foramen n; (fig) importunus, molestus m

borer s terebra f

born adj natus; genitus; to be — nasci; (fig) oriri

borough s municipium n

borrow vt mutuari; (fig) imitari

borrowed adj mutuatus, mutuus; alienus

borrowing s mutuatio f

bosom s (breast) pectus n; sin·us -ūs m; (of female) mammillae f pl; (fig) gremium n

Bosphorus s Bosporus m

boss s bulla f; (of a shield) umbo m; (of a book) umbilicus m

boss vt (to order about) dominari in (with acc)

botanical adj botanicus

botanist s herbarius m

botany s herbaria f

botch s bubo, carbunculus m; (bungling work) scruta n pl

botch vt male sarcire; male gerĕre

both adj ambo; uterque

both pron ambo; uterque

both conj . . . and et . . . et; cum . . . tum; vel . . . vel

bother vt vexare, sollicitare; molestus esse (with dat); vi to — about operam dare (with dat)

bother s negotium n; vexatio f; sollicitudo f

bottle s ampulla f; lagoena f

bottle vt in ampullas infundĕre

bottom s fundus m; (of a ship) carina f; (dregs) faex f, sedimentum n; (of a mountain) radix f; the — of imus; the — of the sea imum mare n

bottom adj imus, infimus

bottomless *adj* fundo carens, immensus; profundus

bough *s* ramus *m*

boulder *s* saxum *n*

bounce *vi* resilire, resultare

bound *adj* alligatus, obligatus, obstrictus; **it is — to happen** necesse est accidat; **to be — for** tendĕre ad (*with acc*)

bound *s* salt·us -us *m*; (*limit*) modus, terminus *m*; **to set —s** modum facĕre

bound *vt* finire, definire, terminare; *vi* (*to leap*) salire

boundary *s* finis, terminus *m*; (*fortified*) limes *m*

boundless *adj* infinitus, immensus; profundus

bountiful *adj* largus, benignus; **—ly** benigne, large

bounty *s* largitas, benignitas, liberalitas *f*; copia *f*

bouquet *s* corollarium *n*; (*of wine*) flos *m*

bow *s* arc·us -ūs *m*

bow *s* (*of a ship*) prora *f*; (*greeting*) summissio capitis *f*

bow *vt* flectĕre, inclinare; (*one's head*) demittĕre; *vi* flecti; (*fig*) **— to** (*to accede to*) obtemperare (*with dat*), obsequi

bowels *s* intestina, viscera *n pl*

bower *s* trichila *f*, umbraculum *n*

bowl *s* cratera, patera *f*; (*for cooking*) catina *f*

bowlegged *adj* valgus

bowman *s* sagittarius *m*

bowstring *s* nervus *m*

box *s* arca, cista *f*; scrinium *n*; (*for medicine*) pyxis *f*; (*tree*) buxus *f*

box *vt* includĕre; pugnis certare cum (*with abl*); **to — the ears of** alapam adhibēre (*with dat*)

boxer *s* pugil *m*

boxing glove *s* caest·us -ūs *m*

boxing match *s* pugilatio *f*

boy *s* puer, puerulus *m*

boyhood *s* pueritia *f*; aetas puerilis *f*

boyish *adj* puerilis; **—ly** pueriliter

brace *s* (*strap*) fascia *f*; (*couple*) par *n*; copula *f*; (*in architecture*) fibula *f*

brace *vt* ligare, alligare; (*to strengthen*) firmare

bracelet *s* armilla *f*

bracket *s* mutulus *m*; **—s** (*in writing*) unci *m pl*

brag *vi* se jactare, gloriari

braggart *s* jactator, salaco *m*

bragging *s* jactantia *f*

braid *s* limbus *m*; (*of hair*) cincinnus *m*

braid *vt* plectĕre, plicare

brain *s* cerebrum *n*; ingenium *n*

brainless *adj* stolidus, inconsultus, socors

brake *s* (*fern*) filix *f*; (*thicket*) dumetum *n*; (*on wheel*) sufflamen *n*

bramble *s* rubus *m*; (*thicket*) rubetum *n*; (*thorny bush*) sentis, vepris *m*

branch *s* (*of tree*) ramus *m*; (*of pedigree*) stemma *n*; (*division*) pars *f*

branch *vi* (*of trees*) germinare; **to**

— out ramos porrigĕre; (*fig*) dividi, scindi, diffundi

brand *s* (*mark*) stigma *n*, nota *f*; (*of fire*) fax *f*, torris *m*; (*type*) genus *n*

brand *vt* inurĕre, notare

branding iron *s* cauter *m*

brandish *vt* vibrare

brandy *s* aqua vitae *f*; vini spirit·us -ūs *m*; spirit·us -ūs gallicus *m*

brass *s* orichalcum, aes *n*

brat *s* infans *m & f*

brave *adj* fortis, animosus, strenuus; **—ly** fortiter, strenue

brave *vt* sustinēre

bravery *s* fortitudo *f*; virtus *f*

bravo *interj* eu!, euge!, benel, mactel

brawl *s* rixa *f*, jurgium *n*

brawl *vi* rixari, jurgare

brawler *s* rixator, rabula *m*

brawling *adj* contentiosus, jurgans

brawn *s* callum aprugnum *n*; (*muscle*) lacertus, torus *m*

brawny *adj* lacertosus, robustus

bray *vi* (*of asses*) rudĕre; (*of elephants*) barrire; (*to cry out*) emugire

braying *s* tritura *f*; barrit·us -ūs *m*; rugit·us -ūs *m*

brazen *adj* aënus; (*fig*) impudens

brazier *s* foculus *m*

breach *s* ruptura, ruina *f*; (*of treaty*) violatio *f*; dissidium *n*

bread *s* panis *m*; (*fig*) vict·us -ūs *m*

breadth *s* latitudo *f*

break *vt* frangĕre; rumpĕre; **to — apart** diffringĕre; **to — down** demoliri, destruĕre; **to — in** (*to tame*) domare, subigĕre; **to — in pieces** dirumpĕre; **to — off** abrumpĕre; (*friendship or action*) dirumpĕre; (*a meeting*) interrumpĕre; **to — open** effringĕre; **to — up** interrumpĕre, dissolvĕre; *vi* frangi; rumpi; (*of day*) illucescĕre; (*of strength*) deficĕre; **to — forth** erumpĕre; **to — into** irrumpĕre; invadĕre; **to — off** desinĕre; **to — out** erumpĕre; (*of trouble*) exardescĕre; (*of war*) exoriri; (*of fire*) grassari; **to — through** perrumpĕre; **to — up** dissolvi, dilabi; (*of a meeting*) dimitti; **to — with** dissidēre ab (*with abl*)

break *s* interruptio *f*, intervallum *n*; interstitium *n*

breakage *s* fractura *f*

breakdown *s* calamitas *f*; frustratio *f*; (*of health*) debilitas *f*; (*of a machine*) defect·us -ūs *m*

breaker *s* fluct·us -ūs *m*

breakfast *s* prandium *n*

breakfast *vi* prandēre

breakup *s* dissolutio *f*

breast *s* pectus *n*; (*of a woman*) mamma *f*; (*fig*) praecordia *n pl*; **to make a clean — of** confitēri

breastbone *s* sternum *n*; os pectorale *n*

breastplate *s* lorica *f*; thorax *m*

breath *s* spirit·us -ūs *m*, anima *f*; halit·us -ūs *m*; **— of air** aura *f*; **deep —** anhelit·us -ūs *m*; **to catch one's —** obstipescĕre; **to hold**

one's breath animam continēre;
to take one's — away exanimare;
to waste one's — operam perdēre

breathe vt ducēre; spirare; (to whisper) susurrare; to — out exspirare; vi spirare, respirare; to — upon inspirare (with dat)

breathing s respiratio f; halitus m; (gram) spiritus -ūs m

breathless adj exanimis, exanimus; exanimatus

breeches s bracae f pl

breed s genus n

breed vt parēre, gignēre; (to cause) producēre; (to engender) procreare, educare; (to raise) alēre; (horses) pascēre

breeder s (man) generator m; (stallion) admissarius m; (animal) matrix; (fig) nutrix f

breeding s fetura f; educatio f; good — urbanitas, humanitas f

breeze s aura f

breezy adj ventosus

brethren s fratres m pl

brevity s brevitas, breviloquentia f

brew vt coquēre; vi excitari, concitari

bribe s pretium n, merces f

bribe vt corrumpēre, largiri

briber s corruptor, largitor m

bribery s corruptio, corruptela, largitio f; ambitus -ūs m

brick s later m

brick adj latericius

bricklayer s laterum structor m

bridal adj nuptialis

bride s nupta f

bridegroom s maritus m

bridesmaid s pronuba f

bridge s pons m

bridge vt pontem imponēre (with dat)

bridle s frenum n

brief adj brevis, concisus; —ly breviter, paucis verbis

brief s diploma n; sententiola f; summarium n

brigade s (infantry) legio f; (cavalry) turma f

brigadier s tribunus militum m

brigand s latro, latrunculus m

bright adj clarus; lucidus, splendidus; nitidus, candidus; (flashing) fulgidus; (smart) argutus; —ly lucide, clare, splendide

brighten vt illustrare, illuminare; vi lucescēre; splendescēre; clarescēre; (of a person) in hilaritatem solvi

brightness s nitor, splendor, fulgor, candor m; (of the sky) serenitas f

brilliance s splendor m; fulgor m; (of style) nitor m, lumen n

brilliant adj splendidus; nitens; (fig) praeclarus, insignis, luculentus; —ly splendide, praeclare, luculenter

brim s ora, margo f, labrum n; to fill to the — explēre

brimful adj ad summum plenus

brimstone s sulfur n

brine s muria f, salsamentum n; (sea) salum n

bring vt ferre, afferre, inferre; (by

carriage, etc.) advehēre; **to —** about efficēre, perducēre; **to —** back referre, reducēre; reportare; (fig) revocare; (by force) redigēre; dejicēre; **to —** forth prodēre, depromēre; parēre; (to yield) ferre, efferre; **to —** forward proferre, efferre, agēre; **to —** in inferre; invehēre; inducēre; (as a farm, etc.) reddēre; **to —** off dissuadēre; **to —** on afferre; adducēre; (fig) objicēre; **to —** out efferre; producēre; excire; **to —** over perducēre, traducēre; (fig) perducēre, trahēre; conciliare; **to —** to adducēre; appellēre; (fig) persuadēre; **to —** together conferre; (to assemble) contrahēre; (fig) conciliare; **to —** pass efficēre; **to —** under subigēre; **to —** up subducēre; (children) educare; (to vomit) evomēre

brink s margo f; ora f; (fig) extremitas f

brisk adj alacer, agilis, vividus; laetus; **to be —** vigēre; **—ly** alacriter, agiliter

briskness s alacritas f, vigor m

bristle s seta f

bristle vi horrēre

bristly adj setiger, setosus; hirsutus; horridus

Britain s Britannia f

British adj Britannicus

brittle adj fragilis

broach vt in medium proferre

broad adj latus, largus, amplus; (fig) manifestus, apertus; **—ly** late

broadcast vt divulgare, disseminare

broaden vt dilatare

broadsword s gladius m

brocade s Attalica n pl

broccoli s brassica oleracea Botrytis f

brochure s libellus m

broil s rixa, turba f

broil vt torrēre

broken adj fractus; intermissus; dirutus; (fig) confectus; (of speech) refractus, infractus, corrupte pronuntiatus

brokenhearted adj abjectus, dejectus

broker s transactor, institor m

bronze s aes n

bronze adj aeneus, a(h)enus, aeratus

brooch s fibula f

brood s proles f; (chicks) pullities f

brood vi (as a hen) incubare; (fig) **to —** over agitare, meditari

brook vt ferre, tolerare

broom s genista f; scopae f pl

broth s jus n

brothel s lupanar n, ganea f

brother s frater m

brotherhood s germanitas, fraternitas f; (fig) sodalitium n

brother-in-law s levir m; sororis maritus m

brotherly adj fraternus

brow s supercilium n; frons f; (of a hill) dorsum n

browbeat vt terrēre, deprimēre, exagitare, objurgare

brown *adj* fulvus, fuscus, spadix; *(of skin)* adustus

browse *vi* depasci

bruise *vt* contundĕre, sugillare; infringĕre

bruise *s* contusio *f*, contusum *n*, sugillatio *f*

brunette *s* puella subfusca *f*

brunt *s* impet·us -ūs *m*; vehementia *f*

brush *s* scopula *f*; *(painter's)* penicillus *m*; *(bushy tail)* muscarium *f*; *(skirmish)* aggressio *f*

brush *vt* verrĕre, purgare; **to — aside** neglegĕre, spernĕre; **to — away** amovēre

brutal *adj* atrox, immanis, inhumanus; **—ly** atrociter, immaniter, inhumane

brutality *s* atrocitas, ferocitas, saevitia, immanitas *f*

brute *adj* brutus; stupidus

brute *s* belua, bestia *f*

brutish *adj* ferinus; stupidus

bubble *s* bulla *f*

bubble *vi* bullire; *(to gush up)* scatēre

bubbling *s* bullit·us -ūs *m*; scatebra *f*

buccaneer *s* pirata *m*

buck *s* cervus *m*; *(he-goat)* hircus *m*; *(male rabbit)* cuniculus *m*

bucket *s* hama, situla, fidelia *f*

buckle *vt* fibulā nectĕre; *vi* flectĕre

buckle *s* fibula *f*, spinther *n*

buckler *s* parma *f*

bucolic *adj* bucolicus, agrestis

bud *s* gemma *f*, germen *n*; *(of a flower)* flosculus *m*

bud *vi* gemmare, germinare

budding *s* germinatio *f*; emplastratio *f*

budge *vt* ciēre, movēre; *vi* movēri, cedĕre

budget *s* saccus *m*; publicae pecuniae ratio *f*

buffalo *s* urus *m*

buffet *s* *(sideboard)* abacus *m*; *(slap)* alapa *f*; *(fig)* plaga *f*

buffet *vt* jactare

buffoon *s* scurra *m*; sannio, balatro *m*; **to play the —** scurrari

bug *s* cimex *m & f*

bugle *s* buccina *f*

build *vt* aedificare; struĕre, condĕre; *(road)* munire; *(hopes)* ponĕre; **to — up** exstruĕre

builder *s* aedificator, structor *m*

building *s* *(act)* aedificatio *f*; exstructio *f*; *(structure)* aedificium *n*

bulb *s* bulbus *m*

bulge *vi* tumēre, tumescĕre; prominēre

bulk *s* amplitudo, magnitudo *f*; *(mass)* moles *f*; *(greater part)* major pars *f*

bulkiness *s* magnitudo *f*

bulky *adj* crassus; ingens; corpulentus; onerosus

bull *s* taurus *m*

bulldog *s* canis Molossus *m*

bullet *s* glans *f*

bulletin *s* libellus *m*

bullfrog *s* rana ocellata *f*

bullion *s* aurum infectum *n*; argentum infectum *n*; massa *f*

bully *s* salaco, thraso *m*

bully *vt* procaciter lacessĕre

bulwark *s* agger *m*; propugnaculum *n*; moenia *n pl*

bump *s* *(swelling)* tuber *n*; *(thump)* plaga *f*

bump *vt* pulsare, pellĕre; *vi* **to — against** offendĕre

bun *s* libum *n*, placenta *f*

bunch *s* fasciculus *m*; *(of grapes)* racemus *m*

bundle *s* fascis, fasciculus *m*; vesiculus *m*

bundle *vt* consarcinare

bungle *vt* inscite gerĕre; inscite agĕre; *vi* errare

bungler *s* homo rudis *m*

buoy *s* cortex *m*

buoy *vt* **to — up** attollĕre, sublevare

buoyancy *s* levitas *f*; *(fig)* hilaritas *f*

buoyant *adj* levis; *(fig)* hilaris

burden *s* onus *n*; *(fig)* scrupulus *m*

burden *vt* onerare; opprimĕre

burdensome *adj* onerosus, gravis, molestus

bureau *s* armarium, scrinium *n*

burglar *s* fur *m*

burglary *s* *(domūs)* effractura *f*

burial *s* *(act)* sepultura *f*; *(ceremony)* funus *n*

burial place *s* sepulturae locus *m*; sepulcrum *n*

burlesque *s* ridicula imitatio *f*

burly *adj* corpulentus

burn *vt* urĕre, cremare; *(to set on fire)* incendĕre; **to — down** deurĕre; **to — out** exurĕre; **to — up** amburĕre, comburĕre; *vi* flagrare; ardēre; **to — out** extingui; **to — up** conflagrare

burn *s* adustio *f*; combustum *n*

burning *s* ustio, adustio *f*; deflagratio *f*

burning *adj* ardens; fervens

burrow *s* cuniculus *m*

burrow *vi* defodĕre

bursar *s* dispensator *m*

burst *s* impet·us -ūs *m*; eruptio *f*; *(noise)* fragor *m*

burst *vt* rumpĕre, dirumpĕre; **to — open** effrangĕre; *vi* dirumpi; **to — forth** prorumpĕre; *(of tears)* prosilire; **to — in** irrumpĕre; **to — out** erumpĕre; **to — out laughing** cachinnum tollĕre

bury *vt* sepelire; *(to hide)* abdĕre, condĕre

bush *s* dumetum *n*, frutex *m*; *(of hair)* caesaries *f*

bushel *s* medimnus, modius *m*

bushy *adj* *(full of bushes)* dumosus; *(bush-like)* fruticosus

busily *adv* industrie, sedulo, impigre

business *s* negotium *n*; *(trade, calling)* ars *f*; *(employment)* occupatio *f*; *(matter)* res *f*; **to mind one's own —** negotium suum agĕre

businessman *s* negotiator *m*

buskin *s* cothurnus *m*

bust *s* imago *f*; effigies *f*

bustle *s* festinatio *f*; trepidatio *f*

bustle vi festinare; trepidare; **to —
about** discurrĕre

busy adj occupatus; negotiosus; operosus, impiger; (*meddling*) molestus

busybody s ardelio m

but prep praeter (*with acc*)

but adv modo, tantum

but conj sed; ast, at; atqui; ceterum;
vero, verum; autem; **— if** quodsi;
sin, sin autem; **— if not** sin aliter, sin minus

butcher s lanius m; (*fig*) carnifex m

butcher vt (*animals*) caedĕre; (*people*) trucidare

butcher shop s macellum n

butchery s caedes, trucidatio f

butler s promus m

butt s (*mark*) meta f; (*cask*) dolium
n; (*mound*) agger m; **— of ridicule** ludibrium n

butt vt arietare; vi **to — in** interpellare

butter s butyrum n

butter vt butyro inducĕre

buttercup s ranunculus tuberosus m

butterfly s papilio m

buttermilk s lactis serum n

buttock s clunis m & f

button s bulla f

button vt nectĕre, confibulare

buttress s anterides f pl; fulcrum n

buttress vt suffulcire

buxom adj alacer, hilaris, laetus

buy vt emĕre, mercari; **to — back**
or **off** redimĕre; **to — up** coemĕre

buyer s emptor m

buying s emptio f

buzz s bombus m; murmur n

buzz vi bombilare; (*in the ear*) insusurrare

buzzard s buteo m

by prep (*agency*) a, ab (*with abl*);
(*of place*) ad (*with acc*), apud (*with
acc*), juxta (*with acc*), prope (*with
acc*); (*along*) secundum (*with acc*);
(*past*) praeter (*with acc*); (*of time*)
ante (*with acc*); (*in oaths*) per (*with
acc*); **— and — mox; — means of**
per (*with acc*); **— oneself** solus

bygone adj praeteritus; priscus

bylaw s praescriptum n; regula f

bystander s arbiter m

byway s trames m, semita f, dever-
ticulum n

byword s adagium n

C

cabal s factio f; societas clandestina
f

cabbage s brassica f, caulis m

cabin s (*cottage*) tugurium n; (*on a
ship*) stega f

cabinet s armarium n; scrinium n;
cistula f; (*in government*) principis
consilium n

cable s funis, rudens m; (*anchor*) an-
corale n

cackle vi gracillare; (*fig*) deblaterare

cackle s glocitatio f; (*fig*) gerrae
f pl; clangor m

cacophony s dissonae voces f pl

cactus s cactus f

cadaver s cadaver n

cadence s numerus m

cadet s tiro m; discipulus militaris m

cage s cavea f, aviarium n; septum n

cage vt includĕre

cajole vt inescare, lactare, blandiri

cake s libum n, placenta f

calamitous adj calamitosus; funestus; exitiosus

calamity s calamitas f; clades f; malum n; res adversae f pl

calculate vt computare; (*fig*) aestimare, existimare

calculated adj aptus, accommodatus

calculation s computatio, ratio f;
(*fig*) ratiocinatio f

calculator s computator m; ratio-
cinator m

caldron s ahenum n, lebes m

calendar s fasti m pl; calendarium n

calends s Kalendae f pl

calf s vitulus m; (*of the leg*) sura f

caliber s (*fig*) ingenium n, indoles f

call vt vocare; (*to name*) appellare;
to — aside sevocare; **to — away**
avocare; (*fig*) devocare; **to — back**
revocare; **to — down** devocare; **to
— forth** evocare, provocare; (*fig*)
exciĕre, elicĕre; **to — in** advocare;
(*money*) cogĕre; **to — off** avocare,
revocare; **to — together** convocare; **to — to mind** recordari; **to
— to witness** testari; **to — up**
excitare, suscitare, elicĕre; vi **to —
on** or **upon** (*for help*) implorare;
(*to visit*) visĕre

call s vocatio f; clamor m; (*visit*) salutatio f; (*requisition*) postulatio f;
(*whistle*) fistula f

calling s (*profession*) ars f, artificium n

callous adj callosus; (*fig*) durus; expers sensūs; **to become — occal-
lescĕre; obdurescĕre

calm adj tranquillus, placidus, sedatus, quietus; (*mentally*) aequus;
—ly tranquille, aequo animo, placide

calm s tranquillitas f, tranquillum n

calm vt pacare, placare, sedare, mul-
cĕre; vi **to — down** defervescĕre

calmness s tranquillitas f; serenitas
f

calumny s maledictum n, obtrectatio
f, opprobria n pl

camel s camelus m

cameo s imago ectypa f

camouflage s dissimulatio f

camouflage vt dissimulare

camp *s* castra *n pl*; **summer** — aestiva *n pl*; **to strike** — castra movēre; **winter** — hiberna *n pl*

camp *adj* castrensis

camp *vi* castra ponēre

campaign *s* aestiva *n pl*; stipendium *n*; expeditio *f*

campaign *vi* stipendium merēre; expeditioni interesse

campaigner *s* veteranus *m*

camphor *s* camphora *f*

can *s* hirnea *f*

can *vi* posse; scire; **I — not** nequeo; nescio

canal *s* fossa navigabilis *f*

canary *s* fringilla Canaria *f*

cancel *vt* delēre, expungēre; abrogare, tollēre

cancellation *s* deletio, abolitio *f*

cancer *s* cancer *m*

cancerous *adj* cancerosus, canceraticus

candid *adj* candidus, apertus, liber, simplex; **—ly** candide

candidacy *s* petitio *f*

candidate *s* petitor *m*; candidatus *m*

candied *adj* saccharo conditus

candle *s* candela *f*; (*taper*) cera *f*

candlelight *s* lucerna *f*; **to study by** — lucubrare

candlestick *s* candelabrum *n*

candor *s* candor *m*, simplicitas, ingenuitas *f*

candy *s* saccharum crystallinum *n*

cane *s* baculus *m*; virga *f*; (*reed*) harundo *f*

cane *vt* baculo *or* virgā ferire; verberare

canine *adj* caninus

canister *s* canistrum *n*, pyxis *f*

canker *s* (*of plants*) rubigo, robigo *f*; (*fig*) serugo *f*

cannibal *s* anthropophagus *m*

cannon *s* tormentum *n*

cannon shot *s* tormenti ict·us -ūs *m*

canoe *s* linter *m*

canon *s* regula, norma *f*; canon *m*

canonical *adj* canonicus

canopy *s* canopeum *n*; aulaea *n pl*

cant *s* fucus *m*

cantata *s* carmen *n*

canteen *s* caupona castrensis *f*

canter *s* lenis atque quadrupedans grad·us -ūs *m*

canter *vi* leniter quadrupedare

canticle *s* canticum *n*

canto *s* liber *m*

canton *s* pagus *m*

canvas *s* linteum crassum *n*, carbasus *f*, carbasa *n pl*

canvass *s* (*legal*) ambitio *f*; (*illegal*) ambit·us -ūs *m*

canvass *vt* circumire, prensare; *vi* ambire

cap *s* pileus *m*; calyptra *f*; (*in rituals*) galerus *m*

capability *s* facultas, habilitas *f*

capable *adj* capax; idoneus, potens, doctus

capably *adv* bene, docte

capacity *s* capacitas, mensura *f*; mod·us *m*; ingenium *n*

cape *s* promontorium *n*; (*garment*)

humerale *n*, chlamys *f*

caper *vi* saltare, tripudire, assilire; (*of animals*) lascivire

caper *s* salt·us -ūs *m*, exsultatio *f*

capital *adj* praecipuus, princeps; (*law*) capitalis; (*of letters*) uncialis; (*outstanding*) insignis, eximius

capital *s* (*architecture*) capitulum *n*; (*chief city*) caput *n*; (*com*) sors *f*, caput *n*; faenus *n*

capitalist *s* faenerator *m*

capitol *s* capitolium *n*

capitulate *vi* ex pacto urbem tradēre; se dedēre

capitulation *s* deditio *f*

capon *s* capus, capo *m*

caprice *s* libido, inconstantia *f*

capricious *adj* levis, inconstans; ventosus, mobilis; **—ly** leviter, inconstanter, ex libidine

capricorn *s* capricornus *m*

capsize *vt* evertēre; *vi* everti

capsule *s* capsula *f*

captain *s* (*in infantry*) centurio *m*; (*in cavalry*) praefectus *m*; (*in navy*) navarchus *m*, (*in merchant marine*) magister *m*

caption *s* caput *n*

captious *adj* argutus, morosus; fallax; **—ly** captiose, morose

captivate *vt* captare, delenire, mulcēre

captive *adj* captivus

captive *s* captivus *m*

captivity *s* captivitas *f*

captor *s* captor *m*; expugnator *m*; victor *m*

capture *s* captura, comprehensio *f*

capture *vt* capēre, excipēre

car *s* carrus *m*

carat *s* unciae triens *m*

caravan *s* commeat·us -ūs, comitat·us -ūs *m*

carbon *s* carbonium *n*

carbuncle *s* carbunculus, furunculus *m*

carcass *s* cadaver *n*

card *s* charta *f*; (*ticket*) tessera *f*; (*for combing wool*) pecten *n*

card *vt* pectēre

cardboard *s* charta crassior *f*

cardinal *adj* principalis, praecipuus

cardinal *s* (*eccl*) cardinalis *m*

care *s* cura, sollicitudo *f*; (*diligence*) diligentia *f*; (*charge*) tutela, curatio, custodia *f*; **to take — of** curare

care *vi* curare; **to — for** (*to look after*) curare; (*to be fond of*) amare

career *s* curriculum *n*; decurs·us -ūs *m*; (*pol*) curs·us -ūs honorum *m*

carefree *adj* securus

careful *adj* (*attentive*) attentus, diligens; (*cautious*) cautus; (*of work*) accuratus; **—ly** diligenter; caute; accurate, exquisite

careless *adj* neglegens, incautus; (*loose*) dissolutus; **—ly** neglegenter; incuriose; (*loosely*) solute

carelessness *s* incuria, neglegentia *f*

caress *s* blanditiae *f pl*; complex·us -ūs *m*

caress *vt* blandiri, fovēre

cargo *s* onus *n*

caricature *s* imago in pejus detorta *f*

caricature *vt* in pejus fingĕre

carnage *s* caedes, strages *f*

carnal *adj* sensualis, carnalis

carnival *s* feriae *f pl*

carnivorous *adj* carnivorus

carol *s* cant·us -ūs *m*; carmen *n*; Christmas — hymnus de Christi natu *m*

carol *vi* cantare, cantillare

carouse *vi* comissari, perpotare, perbacchari

carp *s* cyprinus *m*

carp *vi* to — at carpĕre, mordēre, vellicare

carpenter *s* faber tignarius *m*

carpentry *s* ars fabrilis *f*

carpet *s* tapes *m*, tapeta *f*

carriage *s* (*act*) vectura *f*; (*vehicle*) vehiculum *n*; raeda *f*, petorritum *n*; (*bearing, posture*) habit·us -ūs, gest·us -ūs, incess·us -ūs *m*

carrier *s* portitor, vector, bajulus *m*; (*of letters*) tabularius *m*

carrion *s* caro morticina *f*

carrot *s* carota *f*; pastinaca *f*

carry *vt* portare, ferre; (*by vehicle*) vehĕre; gerĕre; (*law*) perferre; to — away auferre, evehĕre; (*fig*) rapĕre, to — back referre; revehĕre; to — in importare; invehĕre; to — off auferre; rapĕre; to — on promovēre; perducĕre; (*fig*) exercēre; gerĕre; to — out efferre, portare; evehĕre; (*fig*) exsequi; to — over transferre; to — round circumferre; to — through perferre; *vi* (*of sound*) audiri; to — on pergĕre; se gerĕre

cart *s* plaustrum *n*; curr·us -ūs *m*; curriculum *m*; to put the — before the horse praeposteris consiliis uti

cart *vt* plaustro vehĕre; to — away auferre

carve *vt* sculpĕre; caelare, incidĕre; (*at table*) secare

carver *s* caelator *m*; (*at table*) carptor *m*; (*knife*) cultellus *m*

carving *s* caelatura *f*

cascade *s* praeceps aquae laps·us -ūs *m*

case *s* (*law*) causa, actio *f*; (*matter*) res *f*; (*instance*) exemplum *n*; (*container*) involucrum *n*; theca *f*; capsula *f*; (*state*) stat·us -ūs *m*; conditio *f*; (*gram*) cas·us -ūs *m*; in — si; in that — ergo; since that is the — quae cum ita sint

cash *s* pecunia numerata *f*; nummi *m pl*; praesens pecunia *f*

cashier *s* dispensator *m*

cash payment *s* repraesentatio *f*

cask *s* cadus *m*, dolium *n*

casket *s* arcula *f*; pyxis *f*

cast *s* (*throw*) jact·us -ūs *m*; (*mold*) typus *m*; forma *f*

cast *vt* (*throw*) jacĕre; (*metal*) fundĕre; to — about circumjacĕre; to — away abjicĕre; dejicĕre; to — down dejicĕre; (*fig*) affligĕre; to — in in-

jicĕre; to — in one's teeth reprobrare; to — off (*the skin*) exuĕre; (*fig*) amovēre, ponĕre; repudiare; to — out ejicĕre, expellĕre; to — over trajicĕre; to — upon superinjicĕre; (*fig*) aspergĕre; conferre; *vi* to — off ancoram tollĕre

castaway *s* perditus *m*; ejectus *m*

caste *s* ordo *m*; to lose — degenerare

castigate *vt* castigare

castigation *s* castigatio *f*

castle *s* castellum *n*; arx *f*

castor oil *s* cicinum oleum *n*

castrate *vt* castrare

castration *s* castratio, castratura *f*

casual *adj* fortuitus; (*person*) neglegens; —ly fortuito, forte, casu

casualty *s* cas·us -ūs *m*; occisus *m*

cat *s* feles *f*

cataclysm *s* cataclysmos *m*

catacombs *s* puticuli *m pl*; catacumbae *f pl*

catalogue *s* catalogus *m*; index *m*

cataract *s* cataracta *f*, cataractes *m*; (*of the eye*) glaucoma *n*

catastrophe *s* calamitas *f*; ruina *f*; exit·us -ūs *n*

catch *vt* capĕre, captare; (*by surprise*) comprehendĕre; (*falling object*) suscipĕre; (*in a net*) illaquēre; (*with bait*) inescare; (*fire*) concipĕre; (*disease*) contrahĕre; *vi* to — at arripĕre; (*fig*) captare; to — up with consequi

catching *adj* contagiosus; (*fig*) gratus

categorical *adj* categoricus; —ly categorice, sine exceptione

category *s* categoria *f*; numerus *m*

cater *vi* obsonari; cibos suppeditare

caterer *s* obsonator *m*

caterpillar *s* eruca *f*

cathedral *s* ecclesia cathedralis *f*

catholic *adj* catholicus, generalis

cattle *s* pecus *n*

cauliflower *s* brassica oleracea botrytis *f*

cause *s* causa, res, materia *f*; (*pol*) partes *f pl*

cause *vt* facĕre, efficĕre; (*feelings*) exciēre, movēre

causeless *adj* sine causa; vanus

causeway *s* agger *m*

caustic *adj* causticus; (*fig*) mordax, acerbus

caution *s* cautio *f*; cura *f*; prudentia *f*; monitio *f*, monitum *n*

caution *vt* (ad)monēre

cautious *adj* cautus, consideratus; circumspectus; providus; —ly caute, prudenter; depetentim

cavalcade *s* pompa *f*

cavalier *s* eques *m*

cavalry *s* equitat·us -ūs *m*; equites *m pl*; copiae equestres *f pl*

cave *s* spec·us -ūs *m*; spelunca *f*; caverna *f*; antrum *n*

cavern *s* caverna *f*

cavernous *adj* cavernosus

caviar *s* ova acipenseris *n pl*

cavity *s* cavum *n*; caverna *f*

caw *vi* crocire, crocitare

cease *vi* desinĕre, desistĕre

ceaseless *adj* assiduus, perpetuus; **—ly** continenter, assidue, perpetuo

ceasing *s* cessatio, intermissio *f*

cedar *s* cedrus *f*

cedar *adj* cedreus, cedrinus

cede *vt* cedĕre, concedĕre

ceiling *s* laquear, lacunar *n*

celebrate *vt* celebrare; laudare, dicĕre

celebrated *adj* celeber; nobilis, notus, praeclarus

celebration *s* celebratio *f*; (*of rites*) sollemne *n*

celebrity *s* celebritas *f*; fama *f*; (*person*) vir illustris *m*

celery *s* heleoselinum *n*

celestial *adj* caelestis, divinus

celibacy *s* caelibat·us -ūs *m*, caelebs vita *f*

celibate *s* caelebs *m*

cell *s* cella *f*

cellar *s* cella *f*, cellarium *n*

cement *s* ferrumen *n*; caementum *f*; (*glue*) gluten *n*

cement *vt* conglutinare; ferruminare; *vi* coalescĕre

cemetery *s* sepulcretum *n*

censer *s* turibulum *n*

censor *s* censor *m*

censorship *s* censura *f*; magisterium morum *n*

censurable *adj* reprehensione dignus; culpandus

censure *s* vituperatio *f*

censure *vt* animadvertĕre, vituperare

census *s* cens·us -ūs *m*; civium enumeratio *f*

centaur *s* centaurus *m*

centenary *adj* centenarius

centenary *s* centesimus annus *m*

center *s* medium *n*; **in the — of the plain** in medio campo

center *vt* in centrum ponĕre; *vi* **to — on** niti (*with abl*)

central *adj* medius, centralis

centralize *vt* (*authority*) ad unum deferre

centurion *s* centurio *m*

century *s* (*pol*) centuria *f*; saeculum *f*

cereal *s* frumentum *n*

ceremonial *adj* caerimonialis, sollemnis; **—ly** sollemniter, rite

ceremonial *s* rit·us -ūs *m*

ceremonious *adj* sollemnis; (*person*) officiosus; **—ly** sollemniter; officiose

ceremony *s* caerimonia *f*, rit·us -ūs *m*; (*pomp*) apparat·us -ūs *m*

certain *adj* (*sure*) certus; (*indefinite*) quidam, nonnullus; **for —** certe, pro certo; **it is** — constat; **—ly** certe, profecto

certainty *s* certum *n*; (*belief*) fides *f*

certificate *s* testimonium *n*

certify *vt* recognoscĕre, confirmare

cessation *s* cessatio, intermissio *f*; **— of hostilities** indutiae *f pl*

chafe *vt* urĕre; (*with the hand*) fricare; (*to excoriate*) atterĕre; (*to vex*) irritare, succensĕre; *vi* stomachari

chaff *s* palea *f*; (*fig*) quisquiliae *f pl*

chagrin *s* dolor *m*; stomachus *m*

chain *s* catena *f*; (*necklace*) troques *m & f*; (*fig*) series *f*

chain *vt* catenis constringĕre; catenas injicĕre (*with dat*)

chair *s* sella, cathedra *f*

chairman *s* praeses *m*

chalice *s* calix *m*

chalk *s* creta *f*; calx *f*

chalk *vt* cretā notare; cretā illinĕre; **to — out** designare

chalky *adj* (*chalk-like*) cretaceus; (*full of chalk*) cretosus

challenge *s* provocatio *f*; (*law*) recusatio *f*

challenge *vt* provocare, lacessĕre; (*law*) rejicĕre; (*to reclaim*) arrogare

challenger *s* provocator *m*

chamber *s* cubiculum *n*, camera *f*, thalamus *m*; **pars** interior *f*

champ *vt & vi* mandĕre, mordĕre

champion *s* propugnator, defensor *m*; (*of a party*) antesignanus *m*

chance *s* (*accident*) cas·us -ūs, event·us -ūs *m*; fortuna *f*; (*fig*) alea *f*; (*probability*) spes *f*; **by —** casu, forte, fortuito

chance *vt* periclitari; *vi* accidĕre, contingĕre

chance *adj* fortuitus; inexpectatus

chancel *s* cancellus *m*

chancellor *s* cancellarius *m*

change *s* mutatio, commutatio, permutatio *f*; (*variety*) varietas *f*; (*pol*) res novae *f pl*; **small** — nummi *m pl*

change *vt* mutare, commutare, permutare; *vi* mutari, variare; (*of the moon*) renovari

changeable *adj* mutabilis; inconstans; (*of color*) versicolor

changeless *adj* immutabilis

changeling *s* subditus, suppositus *m*

channel *s* canalis *m*; (*of rivers*) alveus *m*; (*arm of the sea*) fretum *n*; (*in architecture*) stria *f*; (*fig*) cur·s·us -ūs *m*

channel *vt* sulcare, excavare; (*to guide*) ducĕre

chant *s* cant·us -ūs *m*

chant *vt* cantare

chaos *s* chaos *n*; (*fig*) confusio *f*

chaotic *adj* confusus; indigestus

chap *s* fissura *f*; (*person*) homo *m*

chap *vt* scindĕre, diffindĕre; *vi* scindi

chapel *s* aedicula *f*, sacellum *n*

chapter *s* caput *n*

char *vt* amburĕre

character *s* character *m*; mores *m pl*; (*inborn*) indoles, natura *f*; ingenium *n*; (*repute*) existimatio *f*; (*type*) genus *n*; (*letter*) littera *f*; (*in drama*) persona *f*

characteristic *adj* proprius; **—ally** proprie

characteristic *s* proprium *n*, proprietas *f*

characterize *vt* describĕre, notare, designare

charade *s* aenigma syllabicum *n*

charcoal *s* carbo *m*

charge s (*law*) crimen n; accusatio f; (*mil*) impet·us ·ūs, incurs·us ·ūs m; (*command*) mandatum n; (*trust*) cura, custodia f; (*office*) munus n; (*cost*) impensa f, sumpt·us ·ūs m; **to be in — of** praeesse (*with dat*); **to bring a — against** litem intendĕre (*with dat*); **to put in — of** praeficĕre (*with dat*)

charger s equus bellator m

chariot s curr·us ·ūs m; curriculum n; (*mil*) essedarium n

charioteer s auriga m

charitable adj benignus, beneficus; (*fig*) mitis

charitably adv benigne; miti animo

charity s caritas f; liberalitas f

charlatan s pharmacopola m; ostentator, jactator m

charm s incantamentum n; (*fig*) illecebra, gratia f; (*amulet*) amuletum n

charm vt incantare; (*to delight*) capĕre, captare, delectare; **to — away** recantare

charmer s fascinator m; (*thing*) deliciae f pl

charming adj suavis, lepidus, venustus; **—ly** lepide, suaviter, blande, venuste

chart s tabula f

charter s charta f, diploma n

charter vt conducĕre

chase s venatio f, venat·us ·ūs m

chase vt (*to hunt*) persequi, venari; (*to engrave*) caelare; **to — away** abigĕre, pellĕre

chasing s caelatura f

chasm s chasma n, hiat·us ·ūs m

chaste adj castus, pudicus; (*of language*) purus; **—ly** caste, pudice; pure

chasten vt purificare, castigare

chastise vt castigare

chastisement s castigatio, animadversio f

chastiser s castigator m

chastity s pudicitia, castitas f, pudor m

chat s familiaris sermo m; **to have a —** fabulari, garrire

chat vi fabulari, garrire, colloqui

chattel s bona n pl

chatter s clangor m; (*idle talk*) garrulitas f, loquacitas f; (*of the teeth*) crepit·us ·ūs m

chatter vi balbutire; (*to talk nonsense*) garrire, effutire; (*of teeth*) crepitare

cheap adj vilis; **— as dirt** pervilis; **—ly** bene, vili; viliter

cheapen vt pretium minuĕre (*with genit*)

cheapness s vilitas f

cheat vt decipĕre, fraudare

cheat s fraus f; dolus m; (*cheater*) fraudator m

check vt (*to restrain*) cohibēre, inhibēre; (*to stop*) retardare; (*to bridle*) refrenare; (*accounts*) dispungĕre; (*to verify*) comprobare

check s (*hindrance*) coercitio, suppressio f; impedimentum n; (*reprimand*) reprehensio f; (*bridle*) frenum n; (*disadvantage*) detrimentum n; (*admission ticket*) tessera f

checkered adj varius

cheek s gena f

cheekbone s maxilla f

cheer s (*shout*) clamor, plaus·us ·ūs m; hilaritas f

cheer vt hortari, hilarare, exhilarare; (*to console*) solari

cheerful adj hilaris, alacer, laetus; **—ly** hilare, laete; libenter

cheerfulness s hilaritas f

cheering s acclamatio f; plaus·us ·ūs m

cheerless adj maestus, tristis, illaetabilis

cheese s caseus m

chemical adj chemicus

chemical s chemicum n

chemise s indusium n

chemist s chemicus, chemiae peritus m

chemistry s chemia, chymia f

cherish vt (*to nourish*) alĕre; (*to treat tenderly*) fovēre; (*fig*) colĕre

cherry s cerasum n

cherry tree s cerasus f

chest s (*of the body*) pectus n; (*box*) cista, arca f; (*for clothes*) vestiarium n; scrinium n

chestnut s castanea f

chew vt mandĕre, manducare; **to — the cud** ruminare; (*fig*) meditari

chewing s manducatio, ruminatio f

chicanery s calumnia, praevaricatio f

chick s pullus m; (*term of endearment*) pulla f

chicken s gallina f

chicken-hearted adj timidus, ignavus

chicory s cichoreum n

chide vt objurgare; corripĕre

chief adj primus; praecipuus, summus; supremus; **—ly** praecipue, imprimis

chief s princeps, procer, dux, auctor m; caput n

chieftain s dux m

child s infans m & f; puer, filius m, puella, filia f; (*in the womb*) embryo m; **to bear a —** parturire; **with —** gravida

childbearing s part·us ·ūs m

childbirth s part·us ·ūs m; Lucinae labores m pl

childhood s infantia f; pueritia f; **from — a** puero or pueris; a primo tempore aetatis, a parvo

childish adj puerilis; **—ly** pueriliter

childless adj orbus

childlike adj puerilis

chill s frigusculum, frigus n

chill adj frigidulus

chill vt refrigerare

chilling adj algificus; frigidus, gelidus

chilly adj alsiosus; frigidulus

chime s sonus m

chime vi canĕre, sonare; **to — in** interpellare

chimera s chimaera f; figmentum n

chimney s caminus m

chin s mentum n

china s fictilia *n pl*

chink s rima *f*; (*sound*) tinnit·us -ūs *m*

chink *vi* tinnire

chip s segmen *n*, assula *f*; (*for lighting fire*) fomes *m*

chip *vt* ascio dedolare

chirp s (*of birds*) pipat·us -ūs *m*; (*of crickets*) stridor *m*

chirp *vi* (*of birds*) minurire, pipilare; (*of crickets*) stridēre

chisel s scalprum, caelum *n*

chisel *vt* scalpro caedēre, sculpēre; (*fig*) decipēre, fraudare

chivalrous *adj* magnanimus, nobilis

chivalry s equestris dignitas *f*; (*class*) equites *m pl*

chocolate s chocolatum *n*

choice s electio *f*, delect·us -ūs *m*; (*power of choosing*) optio *f*; (*diversity*) varietas *f*

choice *adj* electus, exquisitus

choir s chorus *m*

choke *vt* suffocare; strangulare; *vi* suffocari; strangulari

choking s suffocatio *f*; strangulatio *f*

choose *vt* eligēre, optare; to — to (*to prefer to*) malle (*with inf*)

choosing s electio *f*

chop s frustum *n*; (*of meat*) ofella *f*

chop *vt* concidēre; truncare; to — off detruncare; abscidēre; to — up minutatim concidēre

choral *adj* symphoniacus

chord s chorda *f*, nervus *m*

chorus s chorus *m*; symphonia *f*

Christ s Christus *m*

christen *vt* baptizare

Christendom s cuncti Christiani *m pl*

Christian *adj* Christianus

Christianity s Christianismus *m*

Christian name s praenomen in baptismo inditum *n*

Christmas s festum nativitatis Christi *n*

chronic *adj* diuturnus, perpetuus; inveteratus

chronicle s annales *m pl*; acta publica *n pl*

chronological *adj* in — order ordinem temporum respiciens

chronology s temporum ordo *m*, temporum ratio *f*

chubby *adj* crassus, pinguis

chuckle *vi* cachinnare

church s ecclesia *f*; templum *n*

churl s homo rusticus *m*

churlish *adj* agrestis, importunus; —ly rustice

cider s hydromelum *n*

cinder s cinis *m*, favilla *f*

cinnamon s cinnamomum *n*

cipher s (*code*) nota *f*; (*a nobody*) numerus *m*; (*zero*) nihil *n*

circle s circulus, orbis, gyrus *m*; (*around the moon*) halo *m*; **vicious** — circulus vitiosus *m*

circle *vt* circumdare, cingēre; *vi* circumire

circuit s circuit·us -ūs, circulus *m*; **to make a** — circumire

circuitous *adj* devius

circular *adj* orbicus, rotundus

circulate *vt* spargēre; (*news*) disseminare, divulgare; *vi* circulari

circulation s ambit·us -ūs *m*; (*of blood*) circulatio *f*

circumcise *vt* circumcidēre

circumcision s circumcisio *f*

circumference s peripheria *f*, ambit·us -ūs, circulus *m*

circumflex s circumflex·us -ūs *m*

circumlocution s circumlocutio, periphrasis *f*; ambages *f pl*

circumscribe *vt* finire, terminare, circumscribēre

circumspect *adj* prudens, cautus, providus

circumspection s cautio, prudentia *f*

circumstance s res, conditio *f*; tempus *n*; sit·us -ūs *m*; **under the** —s quae cum ita sint

circumstantial *adj* adventicius, fortuitus; enumeratus; (*of evidence*) conjecturalis; —ly subtiliter

circumvent *vt* circumvenire, fallēre, circumscribēre

circumvention s circumscriptio, fraus *f*

circus s circus *m*

cistern s cisterna *f*, lac·us -ūs *m*; puteus *m*

citadel s arx *f*

citation s citatio, prolatio *f*; (*law*) vocatio *f*

cite *vt* (*law*) citare, evocare; (*to quote*) proferre, memorare

citizen s civis *m & f*; (*of a municipality*) municeps *m*

citizen *adj* civicus

citizenship s civitas *f*

city *adj* urbanus; urbicus

city s urbs *f*

civic *adj* civilis, civicus

civil *adj* civilis; (*polite*) comis, urbanus; (*of war*) civilis, intestinus, domesticus

civilian s togatus *m*; privatus *m*

civility s urbanitas, comitas *f*

civilization s cult·us -ūs *m*; humanitas *f*

civilize *vt* excolēre; expolire

clad *adj* indutus, vestitus, amictus

claim s postulatio, vindicatio *f*, postulatum *n*

claim *vt* postulare, poscēre, vindicare, arrogare

claimant s petitor, vindicator *m*

clam s chama *f*

clamber *vi* scandēre, conscendēre

clammy *adj* umidus, viscidus, lentus

clamor s clamor *m*, vociferatio *f*

clamor *vi* exclamare, vociferari; — for flagitare

clamp s confibula *f*; uncus *m*

clamp *vt* constringēre

clan s gens *f*

clandestine *adj* clandestinus, furtivus; —ly clam, furtim

clang s clangor *m*

clang *vi* clangēre, strepēre

clank s strepit·us -ūs *m*

clank *vi* crepare

clap s (*of hand*) plaus·us -ūs m; (*of thunder*) fragor m

clap vi plaudĕre, applaudĕre

claptrap s apparat·us -ūs m

clarification s explicatio f, explanatio f

clarify vt deliquare, explanare, explicare

clarion s lituus m

clarity s claritas f; perspicuitas f

clash s concurs·us -ūs m; (*sound*) crepit·us -ūs m; (*fig*) dissonantia f

clash vi concurrĕre; increpare, increpitare; (*fig*) dissidēre, discrepare

clasp s fibula f; (*embrace*) amplex·us -ūs m

clasp vt (*to embrace*) amplecti, complecti; (*to grasp*) comprehendĕre

class s (*pol*) classis f, ordo m; (*kind*) genus n

class vt in classes distribuĕre; **to — as** in numero habēre

classical adj classicus

classics s scriptores classici m pl

classification s in classes distributio, in genera distributio f

classify vt describĕre, in classes distribuĕre, in genera distribuĕre

clatter s strepit·us -ūs, crepit·us -ūs m

clatter vi crepare, crepitare, strepĕre

clause s (*gram*) membrum, incisum n, articulus m, clausula f; (*law*) caput n

claw s unguis m

claw vt lacerare

clay s argilla, creta f; **made of —** fictilis

clean adj mundus, purus; (*fig*) purus, castus; **—ly** munde, pure

clean vt mundare, purgare

cleanliness s munditia f

cleanly adj mundus, nitidus

cleanse vt purgare, depurgare, abluĕre, detergēre

clear adj clarus; (*of weather*) serenus; (*bright*) lucidus; (*of liquids*) limpidus; (*transparent*) liquidus; (*of voice*) candidus, acutus, argutus; (*manifest*) conspicuus, manifestus; (*of space*) apertus, patens; (*of language*) dilucidus; (*of conscience*) rectus; (*of the mind*) sagax; **— of** expers (*with genit*) **it is —** apparet, liquet; **to keep — of** evitare; **—ly** clare; plane, aperte, haud dubie

clear vt purgare; (*to acquit*) absolvĕre; (*a doubt*) explanare; (*land, forests*) extricare; (*profit*) lucrari; **to — away** detergĕre, amovēre, tollĕre; **to — out** emundare; **to — up** enodare, explanare, explicare; vi **to — up** (*of weather*) disserenascĕre, disserenare

clearance s purgatio f; (*space*) intervallum n

clearness s claritas f; (*of sky*) serenitas f; (*of style*) perspicuitas f

cleavage s discidium n

cleave vt findĕre; vi **to — to** adhaerēre (*with dat*)

cleaver s dolabra f

cleft s rima, fissura f, hiat·us -ūs m

clemency s clementia f

clement adj clemens, mitis

clench vt comprimĕre

clerk s scriba m

clever adj sollers, ingeniosus, callidus, astutus, versutus; **—ly** sollerter, callide, ingeniose, astute

cleverness s dexteritas, sollertia, astutia f

click s crepit·us -ūs m

click vi crepitare

client s cliens m & f; consultor m

cliff s cautes f, scopulus m, rupes f

climate s caelum n

climax s gradatio f

climb vt & vi ascendĕre, conscendĕre, scandĕre

climb s ascens·us -ūs m

clinch vt confirmare

cling vi adhaerēre; **to — together** cohaerēre

clink s tinnit·us -ūs m

clink vi tinnire

clip s fibula f

clip vt tondēre, praecidĕre; (*words*) mutilare

clipping s tonsura f; **—s** resegmina n pl

cloak s pallium n; (*for travel*) paenula f; (*in rain*) lacerna f; (*mil*) sagum, paludamentum n

cloak vt dissimulare, praetendĕre, tegĕre

clock s horologium n; (*sundial*) solarium n

clod s glaeba f

clog s (*shoe*) sculponea f; (*fig*) impedimentum n

clog vt impedire

cloister s portic·us -ūs f; monasterium n

close adj (*dense*) densus, spissus; (*tight*) artus, angustus; (*shut*) occlusus, clausus; (*fast*) firmus; (*near*) propinquus; (*secret*) arcanus, obscurus; (*niggardly*) avarus, tenax, parcus; **at — quarters** comminus; **— together** confertus, refertus, densus, continuus; **to be — at hand** adesse, instare; **to keep —** to adhaerēre (*with dat*); **—ly** prope; (*attentively*) attente, exacte

close vt claudĕre, operire; (*to end*) finire, terminare; **to — a bargain** pacisci; vi coire; claudi, concludi, terminari; (*in a speech*) perorare

close s finis, terminus m, terminatio, conclusio f; **to bring to a —** finire; **to draw to a —** terminari

close adv prope, promime, juxta; **— to** prope (*with acc*), juxta (*with acc*)

closet s conclave n, cella f; (*for clothes*) vestiarium n

closing adj ultimus

closing s conclusio f, finis m

clot s (*of blood*) cruor, concretus sanguis m

clot vi concrescĕre

cloth s pannus m; (*linen*) linteum n

clothe vt vestire, induĕre; velare

clothes s vestit·us -ūs m, vestimenta n pl, vestis f

clothing s vestit·us -ūs m, vestimenta n pl, vestis f

cloud s nubes f

cloud vt nubibus velare; (fig) obscurare; vi nubilare

cloudiness s nubilum n

cloudless adj serenus, purus

cloudy adj nubilus; to grow — nubilare

clout s ict·us -ūs m; alapa f

cloven adj bisulcus, bifidus

clown s (boor) rusticus m; (buffoon, jester) scurra m

clown vi scurrari

clownish adj rusticus; scurrilis

cloy vt satiare, exsaturare

cloying adj putidus

club s (cudgel) clava f, fustis m; (society) sodalitas f, collegium n

club vt fuste dolare

cluck vi glocire; singultire

clue s indicium n

clump s massa f; (of trees) arbustum n, globus m

clumsily adv rustice, inscite, ineleganter, male, inepte

clumsiness s rusticitas, inscitia f

clumsy adj ineptus, inscitus, rusticus, agrestis; (of things) inhabilis

cluster s (of grapes, etc.) racemus m; (of flowers) corymbus m; (of people) corona f

cluster vi congregari; to — around stipare

clutch s unguis m; comprehensio f; from one's —es e manibus; in one's —es in sua potestate

clutch vt arripĕre, prehendĕre

coach s curr·us -ūs m, raeda f; (trainer) magister m

coagulate vt coagulare; vi concrescĕre

coagulation s coagulatio, concretio f

coal s carbo m

coalesce vi coalescĕre, coire

coalition s conjunctio, coitio, conspiratio f

coal mine s fodina carbonaria f

coarse adj (of material) crassus, rudis; (of manners) incultus, inurbanus, rusticus; —ly crasse; inurbane

coarseness s crassitudo f; rusticitas f

coast s ora f, litus n

coast vi praetervehi

coastal adj maritimus, litoralis

coat s tunica, toga f; (of fur) pellis f

coat vt illinĕre, inducĕre, obducĕre

coating s corium n

coat of arms s insignia n pl

coat of mail s lorica f; (skin) pellis f

coax vt cogĕre, mulcēre, blandiri

coaxing s blandimenta n pl, blanditiae f pl

coaxingly adv blande

cobbler s sutor m

cobweb s aranea f, araneum n

cock s gallus m

cockroach s blatta f

cocoa s faba Cacao f

cocoanut s nux palmae indicae f

cocoon s globulus m

coddle vt indulgēre (with dat)

code s notae f pl

codify vt digerĕre

coerce vt coercēre, refrenare, cogĕre

coercion s coercitio, vis f

coeval adj coaevus, aequalis

coexist vi simul existĕre

coffee s coffea Arabica f

coffer s arca, cista f

coffin s arca f, sarcophagus m

cog s dens m

cogency s vis f

cogent adj cogens, efficax, gravis

cognate adj cognatus

cognizance s cognitio f

cognizant adj conscius, gnarus

cohabit vi coire, consuescĕre

cohabitation s consuetudo f, convict·us -ūs m

coheir s coheres m & f

cohere vi cohaerēre; (fig) congruĕre

coherence s context·us -ūs m, convenientia f

coherent adj cohaerens, congruens; —ly constanter

cohesion s cohaerentia f

cohesive adj tenax

cohort s cohors f

coil s spira f

coil vt glomerare; vi glomerari

coin s nummus m

coin vt cudĕre, signare; (fig) fingĕre

coinage s res nummaria, moneta f

coincide vi congruĕre, convenire, concurrĕre; eodem tempore fieri

coincidence s concursatio f, concurs·us -ūs m; (fig) consens·us -ūs m; by — casu

coincidental adj fortuitus

cold adj frigidus, gelidus; to be — algēre, frigēre; to become — frigescĕre, algescĕre; —ly (fig) frigide, gelide, lente

cold s frigus n, algor m, gelu n; (sickness) gravedo f; to catch a — gravedinem contrahĕre; to have a — gravedine dolēre

coldness s frigus n, algor m

colic s tormina n pl

collapse s labes, ruina f

collapse vi collabi, concidĕre, in se corruĕre

collar s (of garment) collare n; (for dogs) millus m; jugum n

collar vt collo comprehendĕre

collarbone s jugulum n

collate vt conferre

collateral adj transversus; adjunctus, consentaneus

colleague s collega, consors m

collect vt conferre, colligĕre; (to assemble) convocare; (money) exigĕre; to — oneself mentem colligĕre; animum colligĕre; vi colligi, aggregari

collected adj praesens

collection s collectio, conquisitio, collecta, congeries f; (out of authors) collectanea n pl

collective adj communis, collectivus;
—**ly** una, simul, communiter
college s collegium n
collegiate adj collegialis, collegiarius
collide vi confligĕre, concurrĕre
collision s concursio, conflictio f,
concurs·us -ūs m
colloquial adj quotidianus
collusion s collusio, praevaricatio f,
dolus m
colon s colon n
colonel s legatus m
colonial adj colonicus
colonist s colonus m
colonize vt coloniam constituĕre in
(with abl)
colonnade s portic·us -ūs f
colony s colonia f
color s color m, pigmentum n; —**s**
vexillum n
color vt colorare; (to dye) tingĕre, inficĕre; (fig) obtegĕre; vi erubescĕre
colossal adj ingens, immanis
colossus s colossus m
colt s equulus, pullus equinus m
column s columna f; (mil) agmen n
comb s pecten m
comb vt pectĕre, comĕre
combat s pugna f, proelium, certamen n
combat vt pugnare cum (with abl), vi
pugnare, proeliari
combination s conjunctio, junctura
f; (of persons) conspiratio, conjuratio f
combine vt conjungĕre, miscĕre;
temperare; vi coire; conspirare
combustible adj igni obnoxius
combustion s concrematio, ustio f
come vi venire; (to arrive) pervenire;
(to happen) fieri; to — **about** evenire; to — **after** sequi; to —
again revenire; to — **along** procedĕre; to — **away** abscedĕre; to
— **back** revenire, redire; to — **before** praevenire; to — **by** praeterire; (to get) acquirĕre; to —
down descendĕre; (to fall down) de-
cidĕre; to — **forth** exire; (fig)
exoriri; to — **forward** procedĕre;
to — **in** introire; to — **near** appropinquare, accedĕre; to — **off**
recedĕre, discedĕre; to — **on** pergĕre; to — **out** (to be published)
edi, emitti; to — **over** supervenire;
(the face) obire; to — **round** (fig)
transgredi; to — **to** advenire; (to
come to one's senses) ad se redire;
to — **to pass** evenire, fieri; to —
together convenire, coire; to —
up subvenire; (to occur) accidĕre,
provenire; to — **upon** (to find) invenire; (to attack) ingruĕre
comedian s comoedus m; (playwright) comicus m
comedy s comoedia f
comely adj decens, venustus
comet s cometes m, stella crinita f
comfort s consolatio f, solatium n
comfort vt consolari, solari
comfortable adj commodus, amoenus
comfortably adv commode

comforter s consolator m
comfortless adj solatii expers, incommodus
comic adj comicus, facetus
comic s scurra m
comical adj comicus, ridiculus; —**ly**
comice, ridicule
coming adj venturus
coming s advent·us -ūs m
comma s comma n
command vt imperare (with dat), jubēre; (view) prospectare, despectare
command s (order) jussum, mandatum, praeceptum n, juss·us -ūs m;
(mil) imperium n; (jurisdiction)
provincia f; — **of language** copia dicendi f; to be in — of praeesse (with dat); to put someone
in — of aliquem praeficĕre (with
dat)
commander s dux, praefectus m
commander in chief s imperator m
commandment s mandatum n
commemorate vt celebrare
commemoration s celebratio f
commence vt incipĕre, inchoare
commencement s initium, exordium, principium n
commend vt approbare, laudare; (to
recommend) commendare; (to entrust) committĕre, mandare
commendable adj commendabilis,
probabilis, laudabilis
commendation s commendatio f
commensurate adj adaequans, conveniens
comment vi commentari; to — **on**
explicare, enarrare, interpretari
comment s sententia f, dictum n
commentary s commentarius m,
commentarium n
commentator s interpres m
commerce s commercium n, mer-
cat·us -ūs m, mercatura f; to engage in — negotiari
commercial adj negotialis
commiserate vi to — **with** miserēri
commiseration s misericordia f
commissariat s commeat·us -ūs m,
res frumentaria f
commissary s procurator, curator m
commission s mandatum n; (mil) legatio f
commission vt delegare, mandare
commissioner s delegatus m
commit vt (crime) admittĕre, patrare, perpetrare; (to entrust) committĕre; to — **to memory** ediscĕre
commitment s (obligation) munus,
officium n; (to jail) incarceratio f
committee s consilium n
commodity s res venalis, merx f
common adj communis, publicus;
(ordinary) vulgaris, quotidianus;
(well known) pervulgatus; (repeated)
creber; (inferior) mediocris; (gram)
promiscuus; —**ly** vulgo, fere, plerumque
commoner s plebeius m; —**s** plebs f
commonplace adj vulgaris, pervulgatus, tritus
commonwealth s respublica f

commotion s commotio, agitatio f, tumult·us -ūs m

commune vi confabulari

communicate vt communicare; (information) impertire, nuntiare; vi to — with communicare (with dat), agĕre cum (with abl)

communication s communicatio f; commercium n; (information) nuntius m

communicative adj affabilis, facilis

communion s communio, societas f

community s civitas f

commutation s mutatio, permutatio f

commute vt commutare

compact adj densus, spissus; (of style) pressus; —ly dense, spisse, confertim

compact s pactum, foedus n, pactio f

compact vt densare

companion s comes, socius, sodalis; (mil) contubernalis, commilito m

companionable adj affabilis, facilis

companionship s societas, sodalitas, consuetudo f; (mil) contubernium n

company s societas, consuetudo f; (gathering) convent·us -ūs m; (guests) convivium n; (com) societas f; (mil) manipulus m; (theatrical) grex f

comparable adj comparabilis

comparative adj comparatus, relativus; —ly comparate

comparative s grad·us -ūs comparativus m

compare vt comparare, conferre; compared with ad (with acc), adversus (with acc)

comparison s comparatio, collatio f; in — with prae (with abl), adversus (with acc)

compartment s loculus m, cella, pars f

compass s ambit·us -ūs m; (limits) fines m pl; (instrument) circinus m; (magnetic) ac·us -ūs magnetica f

compass vt circumvallare, cingĕre, circumdare; (to attain) consequi, patrare

compassion s misericordia f

compassionate adj misericors; —ly misericorditer

compatibility s congruentia, convenientia f

compatible adj congruus, conveniens

compatriot s civis, popularis m

compeer s par, aequalis m

compel vt cogĕre, compellĕre

compendium s summarium n

compensate vt compensare, renumerare; satisfacĕre (with dat)

compensation s compensatio f; poena f

compete vi contendĕre, petĕre, certare

competence s facultas f; (legal capacity) jus n

competent adj congruens, idoneus, peritus, capax; (of authorities) locuples; —ly satis, idonee

competition s contentio, aemulatio f, certamen n

competitor s petitor, rivalis, aemulus m

compilation s collectio f, collectanea n pl

compile vt colligĕre, componĕre

compiler s collector, scriptor m

complacency s amor sui m

complacent adj qui sibi placet

complain vi queri

complaint s querela, querimonia f; (law) crimen n; (med) morbus m

complaisance s comitas, accommodatio f, obsequium n

complaisant adj comis, officiosus; —ly comiter

complement s complementum, supplementum n

complete adj perfectus, integer, absolutus, plenus; —ly plane, prorsus, omnino, abolute, funditus

complete vt complēre; (to accomplish) perficĕre, conficĕre, peragĕre

completion s completio f; (accomplishment) perfectio f; (end) finis m

complex adj multiplex, implicatus, complicatus

complexion s color m

complexity s implicatio, multiplex natura f

compliance s obtemperatio f, obsequium n

compliant adj obsequens

complicate vt impedire

complicated adj impeditus, implicatus, complicatus, nodosus

complication s implicatio f

complicity s conscientia f

compliment s blandimentum n, verba honorifica n pl; to pay one's —s to salutare

compliment vt gratulari (with dat); laudare, blandiri

complimentary adj blandus, honorificus

comply vi to — with concedĕre (with dat), cedĕre (with dat), parēre (with dat), obsequi (with dat), morigerari (with dat)

component s pars f, elementum n

compose vt componĕre; (verses) condĕre, pangĕre; (to calm) sedare; (quarrel) componĕre; to — oneself tranquillari

composed adj tranquillus, quietus, placidus

composer s scriptor, auctor m

composite adj compositus, multiplex

composition s compositio, scriptura f; opus n

composure s tranquillitas f, animus aequus m

compound vt componĕre, miscēre; (words) jungĕre

compound adj compositus

compound s compositio f; (word) junctum verbum n

compound interest s anatocismus m

comprehend vt continēre, amplectari; (to understand) capĕre, percipĕre, comprehendĕre, intellegĕre

comprehensible adj perspicuus

comprehension s intellect·us -ūs m, intellegentia f

comprehensive *adj* plenus, capax;
—ly funditus, omnino
compress *vt* comprimĕre
compression *s* compressio *f*, compress·us -ūs *m*
comprise *vt* continēre
compromise *s* (*unilateral*) accommodatio *f*; (*bilateral*) compromissum *n*
compromise *vt* compromittĕre, implicare; *vi* pacisci
compulsion *s* compulsio, vis, necessitas *f*
compulsory *adj* necessarius, debitus
compunction *s* paenitentia, compunctio *f*
computation *s* ratio, computatio *f*
compute *vt* computare
comrade *s* socius, sodalis *m*; (*mil*) contubernalis *m*
conceal *vt* celare, occultare, abdĕre, dissimulare
concealment *s* occultatio, dissimulatio *f*; (*place*) latebrae *f pl*; **to be in —** latēre
concede *vt* concedĕre
conceit *s* (*haughtiness*) arrogantia, superbia *f*; (*idea*) notio *f*
conceited *adj* arrogans, superbiā tumens
conceive *vt* concipĕre, percipĕre, intellegĕre
concentrate *vt* in unum locum contrahĕre; *vi* **to — on** animum intendĕre in (*with acc*)
concentration *s* in unum locum contractio *f*; (*fig*) animi intentio *f*
conception *s* (*in womb*) concept·us -ūs *m*; (*idea*) imago, notio *f*
concern *s* (*affair*) res *f*, negotium *n*; (*importance*) momentum *n*; (*worry*) sollicitudo, cura *f*
concern *vt* pertinēre ad (*with acc*), attinēre ad (*with acc*); (*to worry*) sollicitare; **it — s me** meā interest, meā refert
concerned *adj* sollictus, anxius
concerning *prep* de (*with abl*)
concert *s* (*music*) concent·us -ūs *m*, symphonia *f*; **in —** uno animo, ex composito
concert *vt* (*plan*) inire
concession *s* concessio *f*; (*thing*) concessum *n*; **to make — s** concedĕre
conch *s* concha *f*
conciliate *vt* conciliare
conciliation *s* conciliatio *f*
concise *adj* brevis, concisus; (*style*) densus; —ly breviter, concise
conciseness *s* brevitas *f*
conclave *s* conclave, consilium *n*
conclude *vt* (*to end*) conficĕre, perficĕre, terminare, finire; (*to infer*) concludĕre, colligĕre
conclusion *s* (*end*) conclusio *f*; (*decision*) determinatio, sententia *f*; (*of speech*) peroratio *f*; (*of action*) exit·us -ūs *m*; (*inference*) conjectura *f*
conclusive *adj* certus, gravis
concoct *vt* concoquĕre; (*to contrive*) excogitare, conflare
concoction *s* pot·us -ūs *m*; (*fig*) ma-

chinatio *f*
concomitant *adj* adjunctus, conjunctus
concord *s* concordia, harmonia *f*; (*mus*) concent·us -ūs *m*
concordat *s* pactum *n*
concourse *s* concurs·us -ūs *m*, concursio *f*
concrete *adj* concretus
concrete *s* concretum *n*, concret·us -ūs *m*
concubinage *s* concubinat·us -ūs *m*
concubine *s* concubina *f*
concupiscence *s* libido *f*
concur *vi* congruĕre, consentire
concurrence *s* consens·us -ūs *m*, consensio *f*
concussion *s* concussio *f*
condemn *vt* damnare, condemnare; **to — to death** capitis damnare
condemnation *s* damnatio, condemnatio *f*
condensation *s* densatio, spissatio *f*
condense *vt* (con)densare, spissare; (*words*) premĕre
condescend *vi* dignari, descendĕre, concedĕre, se submittĕre
condescending *adj* comis; —ly comiter
condescension *s* comitas *f*
condition *s* (*state*) stat·us -ūs *m*, condicio, res *f*; (*stipulation*) condicio, lex *f*; **on — that** eā lege ut
condition *vt* formare, informare
conditional *adj* conditionalis; —ly (*law*) conditionaliter; **sub condicione**
condole *vi* **to — with** dolēre cum (*with abl*)
condone *vt* veniam dare (*with dat*), condonare
conducive *adj* utilis, accommodatus
conduct *s* mores *m pl*, vita *f*; (*management*) administratio *f*
conduct *vt* (*to lead*) adducĕre, deducĕre, perducĕre; (*to manage*) gerĕre, administrare
conductor *s* dux, ductor *m*
conduit *s* canalis, aqueduct·us -ūs *m*
cone *s* conus *m*
confection *s* conditura, cuppedo *f*
confectionery *s* cuppedia *n pl*, conditura *f*
confederacy *s* (*alliance*) foedus *n*, societas *f*
confederate *adj* foederatus
confederate *s* socius, conjuratus *m*
confederate *vi* foedus facĕre
confederation *s* societas *f*
confer *vt* conferre, tribuĕre; *vi* colloqui
conference *s* colloquium *n*
confess *vt* fatēri, confitēri; agnoscĕre, concedĕre
confessedly *adv* ex confesso; manifesto, aperte
confession *s* confessio *f*
confidant *s* familiaris *m & f*, conscius *m*, conscia *f*
confide *vt* committĕre, credĕre, mandare; *vi* **to — in** (con)fidĕre (*with dat*)
confidence *s* fides, confidentia, fiducia *f*; **to have — in** confidĕre (*with*

dat); **to inspire** — **in** fidem facĕre (*with dat*)

confident *adj* confidens, fidens; —**ly** confidenter

confidential *adj* fidus: (*secret*) arcanus

configuration *s* forma, figura *f*

confine *s* finis *m*

confine *vt* includĕre; (*to restrain*) coercēre, cohibēre; (*to limit*) circumscribĕre; **to be confined to** bed lecto tenēri

confinement *s* inclusio *f*; (*imprisonment*) incarceratio, custodia *f*; (*of women*) puerperium *n*

confirm *vt* confirmare; (*to prove*) comprobare; (*to ratify*) sancire

confirmation *s* confirmatio, affirmatio *f*

confiscate *vt* proscribĕre, publicare

confiscation *s* proscriptio, publicatio *f*

conflagration *s* incendium *n*

conflict *s* conflict·us -ūs *m*, contentio, pugna *f*, certamen *n*

conflict *vi* contendĕre; (*differ*) dissentire, discrepare

conflicting *adj* contrarius, adversus

confluence *s* confluens *m*

conform *vt* accommodare; *vi* obsequi, obtemperare

conformation *s* conformatio, figura, forma *f*

conformity *s* convenientia, congruentia *f*; **in** — **with** secundum (*with acc*)

confound *vt* confundĕre, permiscēre, perturbare; (*to frustrate*) frustrari

confounded *adj* miser, nefandus

confront *vt* obviam ire (*with dat*), se opponĕre (*with dat*)

confrontation *s* comparatio *f*

confuse *vt* confundĕre, perturbare, permiscēre

confused *adj* confusus, perplexus; —**ly** confuse, perplexe

confusion *s* confusio, perturbatio *f*; (*shame*) pudor *m*

congeal *vt* congelare, glaciare; *vi* consistĕre, concrescĕre

congenial *adj* consentaneus, concors

congenital *adj* nativus

congested *adj* refertus, densus; frequentissimus

congestion *s* congeries, frequentia *f*

congratulate *vt* gratulari (*with dat*)

congratulation *s* gratulatio *f*

congratulatory *adj* gratulans, gratulabundus

congregate *vt* congregare, colligĕre; *vi* congregari, convenire

congregation *s* coet·us -ūs *m*, auditores *m pl*

conical *adj* conicus

conjectural *adj* conjecturalis, opinabilis; —**ly** ex conjectura

conjecture *s* conjectura *f*

conjecture *vt* conjectare, conjicĕre

conjugal *adj* conjugalis

conjugate *vt* declinare

conjugation *s* conjugatio *f*

conjunction *s* unio *f*, concurs·us -ūs *m*; (*gram*) conjunctio *f*

conjure *vt* obtestari, incantare, fascinare; *vi* praestigiis úti

conjurer *s* magus, praestigiator *m*

conjuring *s* praestigiae *f pl*

connect *vt* connectĕre, jungĕre, copulare; (*in a series*) serĕre

connected *adj* conjunctus; continuus, continens; (*by marriage*) affinis; **to be closely connected with** inhaerēre (*with dat*); **to be connected with** contingĕre

connection *s* conjunctio, colligatio *f*, nex·us -ūs, context·us -ūs *m*; (*kin*) necessitudo *f*; (*by marriage*) affinitas *f*

connivance *s* indulgentia, dissimulatio *f*

connive *vi* connivēre

connoisseur *s* doctus, peritus, intellegens *m*

conquer *vt* vincĕre, superare; domare

conqueror *s* victor *m*, victrix *f*; domitor *m*

conquest *s* victoria *f*

consanguinity *s* consanguinitas *f*

conscience *s* conscientia *f*; guilty — mala conscientia; **to have no** — nullam religionem habēre

conscientious *adj* integer, pius, religiosus, diligens; —**ly** diligenter

conscious *adj* conscius, gnarus; —**ly** scienter

consciousness *s* conscientia *f*

conscript *s* tiro *m*

conscript *vt* conscribĕre

conscription *s* delect·us -ūs *m*

consecrate *vt* sacrare, consecrare, dedicare, devovēre

consecration *s* consecratio, dedicatio *f*

consecutive *adj* continuus; —**ly** deinceps, continenter

consent *vi* assentire, consentire

consent *s* consens·us -ūs *m*, consensio *f*; **without my** — me invito

consequence *s* consequentia, consecutio *f*, event·us -ūs, exit·us -ūs *m*; (*logical*) conclusio *f*; (*importance*) momentum *n*

consequent *adj* consequens, consectarius; —**ly** ergo, igitur, itaque

consequential *adj* consentaneus

conservation *s* conservatio *f*

conservative *adj* reipublicae status conservandi studiosus; — **party** optimates *m pl*

conserve *vt* conservare, servare

consider *vt* considerare, animo agitare, revolvĕre; (*to deem*) aestimare, ducĕre, habēre; (*to respect*) respicĕre

considerable *adj* aliquantus; (*of persons*) eximius, illustris; (*of size*) amplus

considerably *adv* aliquantum; multum; (*with comp*) multo, aliquanto

considerate *adj* prudens, humanus, benignus

consideration *s* consideratio, contemplatio, deliberatio *f*; (*regard*) respect·us -ūs *m*; (*ground, motive*)

ratio f; (*importance*) momentum n;
without — inconsulte, temere
considering *prep* pro (*with abl*)
consign *vt* committĕre, mandare,
consignare, tradĕre
consignment *s* consignatio f
consist *vi* consistĕre; **to — of** constare ex (*with abl*)
consistency *s* congruentia, constantia f
consistent *adj* constans; consentaneus; **—ly** constanter, congruenter
consolable *adj* consolabilis
consolation *s* consolatio f; (*thing*)
solacium n
console *vt* consolari
consolidate *vt* corroborare, firmare,
consolidare, stabilire; *vi* solidescĕre
consonant *adj* consonus, consentaneus
consonant *s* consonans littera f
consort *s* consors m & f; (*married*)
conjux *or* conjunx m & f
consort *vi* **to — with** familiariter
uti (*with abl*), se associare cum
(*with abl*)
conspicuous *adj* conspicuus; insignis, manifestus; **—ly** manifeste,
palam
conspiracy *s* conjuratio, conspiratio f
conspirator *s* conjuratus m
conspire *vi* conjurare, conspirare
constable *s* lictor m
constancy *s* constantia, firmitas,
perseverantia f
constant *adj* constans, firmus; perpetuus; fidelis; **—ly** constanter,
crebro
constellation *s* sidus, astrum n
consternation *s* consternatio, trepidatio f, pavor m; **to throw into**
— perterrēre
constituent *s* elector, suffragator m;
(*part*) elementum n
constitute *vt* constituĕre, creare
constitution *s* (*of body*) habit·us -ūs
m, constitutio f; (*pol*) civitatis stat-
t·us -ūs m, reipublicae leges f pl
constitutional *adj* legitimus; (*natural*) naturā insitus; **—ly** legitime
constrain *vt* cogĕre, compellĕre, detinēre
constraint *s* vis, coercitio, necessitas f
construct *vt* construĕre
construction *s* constructio, aedificatio f; figura, forma f; (*meaning*)
sens·us -ūs m, interpretatio f
constructor *s* structor, fabricator m
construe *vt* interpretari; (*gram*) construĕre
consul *s* consul m; **— elect** consul
designatus m
consular *adj* consularis
consulship *s* consulat·us -ūs m; **to
run for the —** consulatum petĕre;
during my — me consule
consult *vt* consulĕre, consultare; *vi*
deliberare
consultation *s* consultatio, deliberatio f
consume *vt* consumĕre, absumĕre;

(*food*) edĕre
consumer *s* consumptor m
consummate *adj* summus, perfectus
consummate *vt* consummare
consummation *s* consummatio f;
(*end*) finis m
consumption *s* consumptio f; (*disease*) tabes f
consumptive *adj* pulmonarius
contact *s* contact·us -ūs m, contagio
f; **to come in — with** contingĕre
contagion *s* contagium n, contagio f
contagious *adj* contagiosus, tabificus
contain *vt* continēre; (*to restrain*)
cohibēre
container *s* vas n
contaminate *vt* contaminare
contamination *s* contaminatio, labes f
contemplate *vt* contemplari, intuēri
contemplation *s* contemplatio, meditatio f
contemporaneous *adj* aequalis;
—ly simul
contemporary *s* aequalis, aequaevus
m
contempt *s* contemptio f, contempt·
us -ūs m
contemptible *adj* contemnendus,
abjectus, vilis
contemptibly *adv* contemptim, abjecte
contemptuous *adj* fastidiosus, superbus; **—ly** fastidiose
contend *vt* (*to aver*) affirmare, asseverare; *vi* contendĕre, certare; (*to
struggle*) luctari; (*to dispute*) verbis
certare; **to — against** repugnare,
adversari
contending *adj* aversus, contrarius
content *adj* contentus
content *vt* satisfacĕre (*with dat*), placēre (*with dat*), mulcēre
contented *adj* contentus; **—ly** aequo
animo, leniter
contention *s* contentio f; certamen
n; controversia f
contentious *adj* litigiosus; pugnax
contentment *s* aequus animus m
contents *s* quod inest, quae insunt;
(*of book*) argumentum n
contest *s* certamen n, contentio, certatio f
contest *vt* (*to dispute*) resistĕre (*with
dat*), repugnare (*with dat*); (*law*)
lege agĕre de (*with abl*)
contestant *s* petitor, aemulus m
context *s* context·us -ūs, sens·us
-ūs m
contiguous *adj* contiguus, conterminus, adjunctus
continence *s* continentia, abstinentia f
continent *adj* abstinens, continens;
—ly abstinenter, continenter
continent *s* continens f
continental *adj* in continenti positus; ad continentem pertinens
contingent *s* (*of troops*) numerus m,
man·us -ūs f
continual *adj* continuus; perpetuus,
assiduus; **—ly** assidue, semper

continuance s continuatio, perpetuitas, assiduitas f
continuation s continuatio f
continue vt continuare, producĕre; vi pergĕre; (to last) durare, persistĕre, perstare, (re)manēre
continuity s continuitas f; (of speech) perpetuitas f
continuous adj continuus, continens, perpetuus; **—ly** continenter
contortion s contortio, distortio f
contour s forma, figura f; lineamenta n pl
contraband adj interdictus, vetitus, illicitus
contract vt contrahĕre, astringĕre; (to shorten) deminuĕre; (sickness) contrahĕre; (to undertake) redimĕre; vi pacisci; (to shrink) contrahi
contract s pactum, conventum n; (pol) foedus n
contraction s contractio f; (of word) compendium n
contractor s redemptor, susceptor m
contradict vt contradicĕre (with dat), obloqui (with dat)
contradiction s contradictio f; (of things) repugnantia f
contradictory adj contrarius, repugnans
contrary adj (opposite) contrarius, diversus; (fig) aversus, repugnans; **— to** contra (with acc)
contrary s contrarium n, contraria pars f; **on the —** contra, e contrario
contrast s diversitas, dissimilitudo f
contrast vt comparare, opponĕre; vi discrepare
contribute vt contribuĕre, conferre; vi to **— towards** conferre ad (with acc)
contribution s contributio, collatio f; (money) stips f
contributory adj contribuens, adjunctus
contrite adj paenitens
contrition s paenitentia f
contrivance s inventio, machinatio f; (thing contrived) inventum, artificium n, machina f
contrive vt (to invent) fingĕre; excogitare, machinari, efficĕre
control s (restraint) continentia f; (power) potestas, moderatio, dictio f, imperium n; **to have — over** praeesse (with dat)
control vt moderari (with dat), continēre, regĕre, coercēre
controller s moderator m
controversial adj concertatorius
controversy s controversia, disceptatio, concertatio f
contusion s contusio f, contusum n
conundrum s aenigma n; (quibble) cavillum n
convalesce vi convalescĕre
convalescence s conditio convalescendi f
convalescent adj convalescens
convene vt convocare
convenience s commoditas, opportunitas, convenientia f; (thing) commodum n
convenient adj commodus, idoneus, opportunus; **—ly** commode, apte, opportune
convention s convent·us -ūs m; (custom) mos m
conventional adj usitatus, tralaticius, solitus
converge vi vergĕre, coire
conversant adj peritus, exercitatus; **to be — with** versari in (with abl)
conversation s colloquium n, sermo m
conversational adj in colloquio usitatus
converse vi colloqui
converse s contrarium n, convers·us -ūs m
conversely adv e contrario, e converso
conversion s conversio f
convert vt convertĕre, commutare; deducĕre
convert s neophytus, discipulus m
convertible adj commutabilis
convex adj convexus
convey vt portare, vehĕre, convehĕre; (property) abalienare; (fig) significare
conveyance s (act) advectio, vectura f; (vehicle) vehiculum n; (law) abalienatio, transcriptio f
convict s convictus, evictus, reus m
convict vt convincĕre
conviction s (law) damnatio f; (certainty) persuasio, fides f
convince vt persuadēre (with dat)
convivial adj hilaris, laetus
convocation s convocatio f
convoke vt convocare
convoy s praesidium n, deductor m
convoy vt deducĕre
convulse vt concutĕre, convellĕre
convulsion s convulsio f, spasmus m
convulsive adj spasticus
cook s coquus m, coqua f
cook vt & vi coquĕre
cool adj frigidulus; (fearless) sedatus, immotus, impavidus; (indifferent) lentus, frigidus; **—ly** frigide; sedate; lente
cool vt refrigerare; vi refrigerari; (fig) defervescĕre
coolness s frigus n; (fig) lentitudo, cautela f; animus aequus m
coop s (for chickens) cavea f
coop vt to **— up** includĕre
cooperate vi una agĕre; **to — with** adjuvare
cooperation s adjumentum n, consociatio, opera f
cope vi to **— with** certare cum (with abl); **able to — with** par (with dat)
copious adj copiosus, abundans; **—ly** copiose, abundanter
copper s aes, cuprum n
copper adj aēneus, cuprinus
copse s dumetum, fruticetum n
copy s exemplar n, imitatio, imago f
copy vt imitari; (writing) transcribĕre, exscribĕre

coquette s lupa, lasciva f
coquettish adj lascivus
coral adj coralinus
coral s coralium n
cord s funis, restis m
cordial adj benignus, comis; —ly benigne, comiter, ex animo
cordiality s comitas f
cordon s corona f
core s (of fruit) volva f; (fig) nucleus m
Corinthian adj Corinthiacus, Corinthius
cork s cortex m; (stopper) obturamentum n
corn s (grain) frumentum n; (on toes) callus m
corner s angulus m; (of house) versura f; (of street) compitum n
cornice s corona f
corollary s corollarium n
coronation s coronae impositio f
coronet s diadema n
corporal adj corporeus, corporalis
corporal s decurio m
corporate adj corporatus
corporation s collegium n; municipium n
corporeal adj corporeus
corps s legio f
corpse s cadaver n
corpulent adj corpulentus
corpuscle s corpusculum n
correct adj correctus, rectus, accuratus; —ly recte, bene
correct vt corrigère, emendare; (to punish) animadvertère, castigare
correction s correctio, emendatio f; (punishment) animadversio, castigatio f
correctness s puritas, accuratio f
correlation s reciprocitas, mutua ratio f
correspond vi congruère; (by letter) litteras mutuas scribère
correspondence s congruentia, convenientia f; epistolae f pl
correspondent s epistolarum scriptor m
corridor s portic·us -ūs f, andron, xystus m
corroborate vt confirmare
corrode vt erodère, edère
corrosion s rosio f
corrosive adj corrosivus; (fig) mordax
corrupt vt corrumpère, depravare; (a girl) stuprare
corrupt adj corruptus, putridus; (fig) pravus, impurus; venalis; —ly corrupte; inceste, turpiter
corrupter s corruptor m, corruptrix f, perditor m, perditrix f
corruption s corruptio, putredo f; (fig) depravatio, pravitas f
corselet s lorica f
corvette s celox f
cosily adv commode
cosmetic s medicamen n
cost s pretium n, impensa f; — of living anona f
cost vi (con)stare, venire
costliness adj caritas f

costly adj carus; (extravagant) sumptuosus, lautus
costume s habit·us -ūs, vestit·us -ūs m
cosy adj commodus, gratus
cot s lectulus m; (mil) grabatus m
cottage s casa f, tugurium n
cotton s xylinum n
cotton adj gossipinus
couch s cubile, pulvinar n; lectus m
cough s tussis f; to have a bad — male tussire
cough vi tussire
council s concilium n
councilor s consiliarius m
counsel s (advice) consilium n; (person) advocatus m
counsel vt consulère, monère
counselor s consiliarius, consiliator m
count s computatio, ratio f; (of indictment) caput n
count vt numerare, computare; (to regard as) ducère, habère; to — up enumerare; vi aestimari, haberi; to — upon confidère (with dat)
countenance s facies f, vult·us -ūs, aspect·us -ūs m; to put out of — confundère, perturbare
countenance vt favère (with dat), indulgère (with dat), adjuvare
counter s (of shop) abacus m; (in games) calculus m
counteract vt obsistère (with dat); (a sickness) medèri (with dat)
counteraction s oppositio f
counterfeit vt imitari, simulare, fingère, adulterare
counterfeit adj simulatus, spurius, ficticius, adulterinus
counterfeit s (money) nummus adulterinus m; simulatio, imitatio f
counterfeiter s imitator, falsarius m
countermand vt renuntiare
counterpart s res gemella f; par m, f & n
countersign vt contrascribère
countless adj innumerabilis, innumerus
country s terra, regio f; (territory) fines m pl; (not city) rus n; (native) patria f
country house s villa f
countryman s civis, popularis m
countryside s rus n, agri m pl
couple s par n; mariti m pl; a — of duo
couple vt copulare, unire; vi (of animals) coire
courage s virtus f, animus m, fortitudo f; to lose — animos dimittère; to take — bono animo esse
courageous adj fortis, animosus, acer; —ly fortiter, acriter
courier s cursor, nuntius, tabellarius m
course s (movement) curs·us -ūs m; (of life) ratio f; (of water) duct·us -ūs m; (route) iter n; (at table) ferculum n; (order) series f; (for racing) circus m, stadium n; in due — mox; in the — of inter (with acc); of — certe, scilicet
court s (law) forum, tribunal, judi-

cium n, judices m pl; (open area)
area f; (of house) atrium n; (palace)
aula f; (retinue) comitat·us -ūs m

court vt colĕre, ambire; (woman) petĕre; (danger) se offerre (with dat)

courteous adj comis, urbanus; **—ly** comiter, urbane

courtesan s meretrix f

courtesy s comitas, urbanitas f; (act) officium n

courtier s aulicus m

courtly adj aulicus; officiosus

court-martial s judicium castrense n

courtship s amor m, ambitio f

courtyard s aula f

cousin s consobrinus m, consobrina f, patruelis m & f

cove s sin·us -ūs m

covenant s pactum n, pactio f

covenant vi pacisci, stipulari

cover s tegmen, integumentum n; (lid) operculum n; (shelter) tectum n, (mil) praesidium n; (pretense) species f; **under — of** sub (with abl), sub specie (with genit)

cover vt tegĕre; (to hide) celare, velare; **to — up** obtegĕre

coverlet s lodix f

covet vt concupiscĕre, cupĕre, appetĕre

covetous adj avidus, appetens, cupidus; **—ly** avide, avare, appetenter

covey s grex m

cow vt domare

coward s homo or miles ignavus m

cowardice s ignavia f

cowardly adj ignavus

cower vi sudsidĕre

cowherd s bubulcus m

cowl s cucullus m

coy adj verecundus, pudens; **—ly** verecunde, pudenter

coyness s verecundia f, pudor m

cozily adv commode, jucunde

cozy adj commodus, jucundus

crab s cancer m

crabbed adj morosus, difficilis

crack s fissura, rima f; (noise) crepit·us -ūs m; **at — of dawn** prima luce

cracked adj rimosus; (fig) cerritus, delirus

cracker s crustulum n

crackle vi crepitare

crackling s crepit·us -ūs m

cradle s cunae f pl, cunabula n pl

craft s (cunning) astutia f, artes f pl, dolus m; (skill) ars f; (trade) ars f; (boat) scapha, cymba f, navigium n

craftily adv callide, astute; dolose

crafty adj astutus, callidus, subdolus

craftsman s artifex, faber m

craftsmanship s artificium n, man·us -ūs f

cram vt farcire; **to — together** constipare

cramp s spasmus m

cramp vt comprimĕre, coartare

crane s (bird) grus m & f; (machine) tolleno f; machina f

crank s (machine) uncus m; (person) morosus m

crash s fragor, strepit·us -ūs m, ruina f

crash vi strepĕre, frangorem dare

crater s crater m

crave vt efflagitare, appetĕre, concupiscĕre, desiderare

craven adj ignavus atque abjectus

craving s desiderium n, appetitio f

crawl vi repĕre, serpĕre

crayfish s commarus m

crayon s creta f

craze s libido f

craziness s imbecillitas, mens alienata f, furor m

crazy adj imbecillus, demens, cerritus; **to drive —** mentem alienare (with genit)

creak vi stridĕre, crepitare

creaking s stridor, crepit·us -ūs m

creaking adj stridulus

cream s flos lactis m; (fig) flos m

crease s plica, ruga f

crease vt corrugare, rugare

create vt creare; (fig) fingĕre

creation s (act) creatio f; (world) summa rerum f, mundus m; (fig) opus n

creative adj creatrix, effectrix

creator s creator, opifex, auctor m

creature s animal n; homo m; (lackey) minister m

credence s fides f; **to give — to** credĕre (with dat)

credentials s litterae commendaticiae f pl; testimonia n pl

credibility s fides, auctoritas f

credible adj credibilis; (of persons) locuples

credit s (authority) auctoritas f; (faith) fides f; (reputation) existimatio, fama f; (com) fides f; (recognition) laus f

credit vt credĕre (with dat); (com) acceptum referre (with dat)

creditable adj honorificus, honestus, laudabilis

creditor s creditor m

credulity s credulitas f

credulous adj credulus; **—ly** credens

creed s fides, religio f, dogma n

creek s aestuarium n; fluvius m

creep vi repĕre, serpĕre; (of flesh) horrēre

crescent s luna crescens f

crescent-shaped adj lunatus

crest s crista f

crested adj cristatus

crestfallen adj dejectus, demissus

crevice s rima, rimula f

crew s grex m; (of ship) remiges, nautae m pl

crib s (manger) praesepe n; (small bed) lectulus m

cricket s gryllus m, cicada f

crier s praeco m

crime s scelus, delictum, maleficium, flagitium n

Crimea s Tauris f

criminal adj criminosus, scelestus, flagitiosus; **—ly** nefarie, improbe; (law) criminaliter

criminal s reus, sceleratus m

crimp vt crispare

crimson *adj* coccineus

crimson *s* coccum *n*

cringe *vi* adulari, assentari

cringing *s* adulatio abjecta *f*

cripple *s* claudus *m*

cripple *vt* claudum facĕre, mutilare, debilitare; (*fig*) frangĕre

crippled *adj* mancus, claudus

crisis *s* discrimen *n*

crisp *adj* crispus, fragilis; (*fig*) alacer

criterion *s* norma *f*, indicium *n*, index *m*

critic *s* judex, censor, existimator *m*; (*literary*) criticus, grammaticus *m*

critical *adj* criticus, intellegens; (*careful*) accuratus; (*blaming*) fastidiosus, censorius; (*crucial*) anceps, periculosus; —ly accurate; periculose

criticism *s* ars critica *f*; censura, reprehensio *f*, judicium *n*

criticize *vt* judicare; carpĕre, reprehendĕre, agitare, castigare

croak *vi* coaxare; (*of raven*) crocitare, crocire; (*fig*) queritari

croaking *s* crecitatio *f*; (*fig*) querimonia *f*

croaking *adj* raucus

crock *s* olla *f*

crocodile *s* crocodilus *m*

crook *s* pedum *n*

crook *vt* curvare, flectĕre

crooked *adj* curvatus, flexus; (*fig*) pravus, dolosus; —ly prave

crop *s* (*of grain*) messis, seges *f*; (*of bird*) ingluvies *f*

crop *vt* abscidĕre, tondĕre; (*to harvest*) metĕre; (*to browse*) carpĕre

cross *s* crux *f*; (*figure*) quincunx *m*, decussis *f*; (*fig*) molestia *f*, cruciat·us -ūs *m*

cross *adj* transversus; (*contrary*) adversus; (*peevish*) acerbus, morosus

cross *vt* transire, transgredi; (*river*) trajicĕre; (*mountain*) transcendĕre; (*to thwart*) frustrari, adversari; to — out expungĕre, delĕre

cross-examination *s* percontatio, interrogatio *f*

cross-examine *vt* percontari, interrogare

crossing *s* transit·us -ūs, traject·us -ūs *m*; (*of roads*) bivium *n*; (*of three roads*) trivium *n*; (*of four roads*) quadrivium *n*

cross-roads *s* quadrivium *n*

crouch *vi* se submittĕre, subsidĕre

crow *s* (*bird*) cornix *f*; (*of cock*) cant·us -ūs *m*, gallicinium *n*

crow *vi* (*of cocks*) canĕre, cucurire; (*to boast*) jactare, gestire

crowbar *s* vectis *f*

crowd *s* turba, frequentia *f*, concurs·us -ūs *m*; in —s gregatim

crowd *vt* arctare, stipare, premĕre; *vi* frequentare; to — around stipare, circumfundi

crowded *adj* confertus, frequens, spissus

crowing *s* gallicinium *n*, cant·us -ūs *m*

crown *s* corona *f*, diadema *n*; (*top*) vertex *m*; (*fig*) apex *m*

crown *vt* coronare; (*with garlands, etc.*) cingĕre; (*fig*) cumulare

crucifix *s* imago Christi cruci affixi *f*

crucifixion *s* crucis supplicium *n*

crucify *vt* in cruce suffigĕre

crude *adj* crudus; rudis, incultus, informis; —ly imperfecte; inculte

cruel *adj* crudelis, atrox, saevus; —ly crudeliter, saeve, dure

cruelty *s* crudelitas, atrocitas, saevitia *f*

cruet *s* guttus *m*, acetabulum *n*

cruise *vi* circumvectari, navigare

cruise *s* navigatio *f*

crumb *s* mica *f*

crumble *vt* friare, putrefacĕre, comminuĕre, conterĕre; *vi* collabi, friari, corruĕre

crumbling *adj* puter, friabilis

crumple *vt* corrugare, duplicare

crunch *vt* dentibus frangĕre

crush *vt* contundĕre, conterĕre; (*fig*) opprimĕre, affligĕre

crush *s* contusio *f*; (*crowd*) turba, frequentia *f*

crust *s* crusta *f*, crustum *n*

crusty *adj* crustosus; (*fig*) cerebrosus, stomachosus

crutch *s* fulcrum *n*

cry *vt* clamare, clamitare; to — out exclamare, vociferari; *vi* (*to shout*) clamare, clamitare; (*to weep*) lacrimare, flĕre; (*of infant*) vagire; to — out exclamare; to — out against objurgare

cry *s* clamor *m*; (*of infant*) vagit·us -ūs *m*; (*weeping*) plorat·us -ūs *m*

crying *s* flet·us -ūs, plorat·us -ūs *m*

crypt *s* crypta *f*

crystal *adj* crystallinus, vitreus

crystal *s* crystallum *n*

crystal-clear *adj* pellucidus

cub *s* catulus *m*

cube *s* cubus *m*

cubic *adj* cubicus

cubit *s* cubitum *n*, ulna *f*

cuckoo *s* coccyx, cuculus *m*

cucumber *s* cucumis *m*

cud *s* ruma *f*, rumen *n*; to chew the — ruminare

cudgel *s* fustis *m*

cue *s* (*hint*) nut·us -ūs *m*, signum, indicium *n*

cuff *s* (*blow*) colaphus *m*; (*of sleeves*) extrema manica *f*

cull *vt* carpĕre, legĕre, decerpĕre

culminate *vi* ad summum fastigium venire

culpable *adj* culpandus, nocens

culprit *s* reus *m*, rea *f*

cultivate *vt* colĕre; (*the mind*) excolĕre; (*friends*) fovĕre

cultivation *s* cultura *f*, cult·us -ūs *m*

cultivator *s* cultor, colonus *m*

culture *s* cultura *f*, cult·us -ūs *m*

cumbersome *adj* onerosus, impediens

cunning *adj* sollers, callidus, doctus, peritus; (*in bad sense*) astutus

cunning *s* calliditas, peritia; astutia *f*

cup *s* poculum *n*, calix *m*; (*of flower*) calyx *m*

cupbearer *s* pocillator *m*

cupboard *s* armarium *n*

Cupid *s* Cupido, Amor *m*

cupidity *s* cupiditas *f*

cupola *s* tholus *m*; turricula rotunda *f*

cur *s* canis *m*; (*fig*) scelestus *m*

curable *adj* medicabilis, sanabilis

curative *adj* medicabilis

curator *s* curator *m*

curb *s* frenum *n*; (*fig*) coercitio *f*, frenum *n*

curb *vt* frenare, infrenare; (*fig*) coercēre, cohibēre

curdle *vt* coagulare; *vi* coagulare, concrescēre

cure *s* (*remedy*) remedium *n*; (*process*) sanatio *f*

cure *vt* medēri (*with dat*), sanare; (*to pickle*) salire

curiosity *s* curiositas *f*; (*thing*) miraculum *n*

curious *adj* curiosus; (*strange*) mirus, novus, insolitus; —ly curiose; mirabiliter, mirum in modum

curl *vt* (*hair*) crispare; torquēre; *vi* crispari; (*of smoke*) volvi

curl *s* (*natural*) cirrus *m*; (*artificial*) cincinnus *m*

curly *adj* crispus

currency *s* (*money*) moneta *f*; (*use*) us·us -ūs *m*

current *adj* vulgaris, usitatus; —ly vulgo

current *s* flumen *n*; (*of air*) afflat·us -ūs *m*, aura *f*; against the — adverso flumine; with the — secundo flumine

curse *s* exsecratio, maledictio *f*, maledictum *n*; (*fig*) pestis *f*

curse *vt* maledicĕre (*with dat*), exsecrari; *vi* exsecratione uti

cursed *adj* exsecrabilis

cursorily *adv* breviter, summatim

cursory *adj* levis, brevis

curt *adj* abruptus; —ly breviter

curtail *vt* minuĕre, coartare; decurtare

curtain *s* velum, aulaeum *n*

curvature *s* curvatura *f*

curve *s* curvamen *n*, flex·us -ūs *m*, curvatura *f*

curve *vt* incurvare, flectĕre, inflectĕre, arcuare

curved *adj* curvatus, curvus; (*as a sickle*) falcatus

cushion *s* pulvinar *n*; (*on a seat*) sedularia *n pl*

custard *s* artolaganus *m*

custody *s* custodia, tutela *f*; (*imprisonment*) carcer *m*; to keep in — custodire

custom *s* mos, us·us -ūs *m*, consuetudo *f*, institutum, praescriptum *n*; (*duty*) portorium, vectigal *n*

customary *adj* usitatus, consuetus, tralaticius

customer *s* emptor *m*

customs officer *s* portitor *m*

cut *vt* secare; (*to fell*) caedĕre; (*to mow*) succidĕre; to — apart intercidĕre, dissecare; to — away recidĕre, abscindĕre; (*to amputate*) amputare; to — down caedĕre; (*to kill*) occidĕre; to — in pieces concidĕre; to — off praecidĕre, abscindĕre; (*the head*) detruncare; (*to intercept*) intercludĕre, prohibĕre; (*to destroy*) exstinguĕre; to — open incidĕre; to — out exsecare; (*out of rock, etc.*) excidĕre; to — short intercidĕre; (*to abridge*) praecidĕre; (*fig*) (*to interrupt*) interpellare; to — up minutatim concidĕre; (*enemy*) trucidare

cutlass *s* ensis, gladius *m*

cutlery *s* cultri *m pl*

cutlet *s* offa *f*, frustum *n*

cutthroat *s* sicarius *m*

cutting *adj* (*sharp*) acutus; (*fig*) mordax

cutting *s* (*act*) sectio, consectio, exsectio *f*; (*thing*) segmen *n*

cuttlefish *s* loligo, sepia *f*

cycle *s* orbis *m*

cylinder *s* cylindrus *m*

cylindrical *adj* cylindratus

cymbal *s* cymbalum *n*

cynic *adj* cynicus

cynic *s* cynicus *m*

cynical *adj* mordax, difficilis; —ly mordaciter

cynicism *s* acerbitas *f*

cypress *s* cupressus *f*

D

dab *vt* illidĕre

dab *s* massula *f*

dabble *vi* to — in gustare

dactyl *s* dactylus *m*

dactylic *adj* dactylicus

daffodil *s* asphodelus, narcissus *m*

dagger *s* pugio *m*, sica *f*

daily *adj* diurnus, quotidianus *or* cottidianus

daily *adv* quotidie *or* cottidie, in dies

dainty *adj* (*of persons*) fastidiosus, mollis, elegans; (*of things*) delicatus, exquisitus

dairy *s* cella lactaria *f*

daisy *s* bellis *f*

dale *s* vallis *f*

dalliance *s* lus·us -ūs *m*, lascivia *f*

dally *vi* morari; (*to trifle*) nugari, ludificari

dam *s* moles *f*, agger *m*; (*of animals*) mater *f*

damage *s* damnum, incommodum, detrimentum *n*; (*injury*) injuria, noxa *f*

damage *vt* nocēre (*with dat*), laedĕre; (*reputation*) violare

dame *s* domina, hera, matrona *f*

damn *vt* damnare, exsecrari

damnable *adj* damnabilis, destestabilis

damnably *adv* damnabiliter, improbe

damnation *s* damnatio *f*

damp *adj* (h)umidus

dampen *vt* humectare; *(fig)* infringĕre, restinguĕre

dampness *s* uligo *f*

damsel *s* puella, virgo *f*

dance *s* saltat·us ‑ūs *m*, saltatio *f*

dance *vi* saltare

dancer *s* saltator *m*

dancing *s* saltatio *f*, saltat·us ‑ūs *m*

dandelion *s* taraxacum *n*

dandruff *s* porrigo *f*

dandy *s* homo bellus et lepidus *m*

danger *s* periculum *n*

dangerous *adj* periculosus; —ly periculose, graviter

dangle *vi* pendēre, dependēre

dangling *adj* pendulus

dank *adj* (h)umidus, uvidus, udus

dappled *adj* variatus, variegatus

dare *vt* provocare; *vi* audēre

daring *adj* audax; —ly audacter

daring *s* audacia, audentia *f*

dark *adj* obscurus, opacus; *(in color)* ater, fuscus; *(fig)* obscurus, ambiguus; atrox; —ly obscure

dark *s* tenebrae *f pl*; obscurum *n*, to keep in the — celare

darken *vt* obscurare, occaecare; *(of colors)* infuscare

darkness *s* obscuritas, opacitas *f*, tenebrae *f pl*

darling *adj* suavis, mellitus, carus, dilectus

darling *s* deliciae *f pl*, corculum *n*

darn *vt* resarcire

dart *s* jaculum, spiculum *n*

dart *vt* jaculari, jacēre; *vi* provolare, emicare, se conjicĕre

dash *vt (to splash)* aspergĕre; *(hopes)* frustrari, frangĕre; to — against illidĕre, incutĕre, offendĕre; to — off *(to write hurriedly)* scriptitare; to — to pieces discutĕre; to — to the ground prosternĕre; *vi (to rush)* ruĕre, ferri

dash *s* impet·us ‑ūs *m*; curs·us ‑ūs *m*; *(animation)* alacritas *f*; *(small amount)* admixtio *f*

dashing *adj* acer, alacer, fulgidus, splendidus

data *s* facta *n pl*

date *s (time)* dies *m & f*, tempus *n*; *(fruit)* palmula *f*; to become out of — exolescĕre; to — adhuc; out of — obsoletus

date *vt* diem ascribĕre *(with dat)*; *vi* to — from oriri ab *(with abl)*, originem trahĕre ab *(with abl)*

date palm *s* phoenix, palma *f*

dative *s* dativus *m*

daub *vt* oblinĕre, illinĕre

daughter *s* filia *f*

daughter-in-law *s* nurus *f*

daunt *vt* pavefacĕre, perterrēre

dauntless *adj* impavidus, intrepidus; —ly impavide, intrepide

dawdle *vi* morari, cessare

dawn *s* aurora, prima lux *f*, diluculum *n*; at — prima luce

dawn *vi* illucescĕre, dilucescĕre; *(fig)* to — on occurrĕre *(with dat)*

day *s* dies *m & f*; lux *f*, sol *m*; by — interdiu; — by — in dies; every — quotidie, cottidie; from — to — in dies; next — postridie; some — olim; the — after tomorrow perendie; the — before pridie

day *adj* diurnus, dialis

daybreak *s* lux prima *f*; before — antelucio

daylight *s* lux *f*, dies *m & f*

daystar *s* Lucifer, Phosphorus *m*

daytime *s* dies *m*, tempus diurnum *n*; in the — interdiu

daze *s* stupor *m*

daze *vt* obstupefacĕre

dazzle *vt* obcaecare, praestringĕre

dazzling *adj* fulgidus, splendidus

deacon *s* diaconus *m*

dead *adj* mortuus; defunctus; *(fig)* torpidus, segnis, iners

dead *s* manes *m pl*; — of night media nox *f*; — of winter summa hiems *f*

dead *adv* omnino, totaliter, prorsus

deaden *vt* hebetare, obtundĕre; *vi* hebetari, obtundi

deadly *adj* mortifer, letalis; *(fig)* capitalis, implacabilis

deaf *adj* surdus; to be — to non audire

deafen *vt* exsurdare, obtundĕre

deaf-mute *adj* surdus idemque mutus

deafness *s* surditas *f*

deal *s (quantity)* numerus *m*, copia *f*; *(com)* negotium *n*; a good — longer multo diutius; a good — of aliquantus

deal *vt* partiri, dividĕre, distribuĕre; *vi (com)* mercari, negotiari; to — with *(to treat of)* agĕre de *(with abl)*, tractare

dealer *s* mercator, negotiator, distributor *m*

dealing *s* negotiatio, mercatura *f*; *(doing)* facta *n pl*

dean *s* decanus *m*

dear *adj* carus, dulcis, gratus; *(costly)* carus, preciosus; —ly valde, ardenter; *(at high cost)* magni, magno

dear *interj (dismay)* hei!; *(surprise)* ahem!

dearness *s* caritas *f*

dearth *s* inopia, penuria, fames *f*

death *s* mors *f*, obit·us ‑ūs *m*; *(in violent form)* nex *f*

deathbed *s* on the — moriens, moribundus

deathless *adj* immortalis

deathlike *adj* cadaverosus, luridus

deathly *adj* pallidus

debase *vt* depravare, corrumpĕre; *(coinage)* adulterare; to — oneself se demittĕre, se prosternĕre

debasement *s* adulteratio *f*; ignominia *f*, dedecus *n*

debatable *adj* disputabilis, controversiosus, ambiguus

debate *vt* disputare, disceptare; *vi* argumentari, disserère

debate *s* disceptatio, controversia, altercatio *f*; (*law*) actio *f*

debater *s* disputator *m*

debauch *vt* stuprare, corrumpère, vitiare; *vi* (*to revel*) debacchari

debauchery *s* ganea *f*, stuprum *n*

debilitate *vt* debilitare

debit *s* expensum *n*

debit *vt* in expensum referre

debt *s* aes alienum *n*; (*fig*) debitum *n*; **to pay off a —** aes alienum persolvère; **to run up a —** aes alienum contrahère

debtor *s* debitor *m*

decade *s* decem anni *m pl*

decadence *s* occas·us -ūs *m*

decadent *adj* degener

decalogue *s* decalogus *m*

decamp *vi* (*mil*) castra movère; (*fig*) aufugère, discedère

decant *vt* diffundère

decanter *s* lagoena *f*

decapitate *vt* detruncare

decay *s* tabes, ruina *f*, laps·us -ūs *m*; (*fig*) defectio *f*

decay *vi* putrescère, tabescère, senescère

decease *s* mors *f*, obit·us -ūs *m*, decess·us -ūs *m*

deceased *adj* mortuus, defunctus

deceit *s* fraus *f*, dolus *m*

deceitful *adj* fallax, dolosus, fraudulentus; **—ly** fallaciter, dolose

deceive *vt* decipère, fallère, fraudare

December *s* (*mensis*) December *m*

decency *s* decorum *n*, honestas *f*

decent *adj* honestus, pudicus; **—ly** honeste, pudenter

deception *s* deceptio, fallacia, fraus *f*

deceptive *adj* fallax, fraudulentus, vanus, falsus

decide *vt & vi* (*dispute*) disceptare, dijudicare, decernère; **to — to** constituère (*with inf*), statuère (*with inf*); **the senate decided** placuit senatui; visum est senatui

decided *adj* firmus, constans; (*of things*) certus; **—ly** certe, plane

deciduous *adj* caducus

decimate *vt* decimare; (*fig*) depopulari

decipher *vt* explicare, expedire, enodare

decision *s* sententia *f*; judicium, arbitrium, decretum *n*; (*of senate*) auctoritas *f*

decisive *adj* certus, firmus; **—ly** praecise

deck *vt* exornare, ornare; (*table*) sternère

deck *s* pons *m*

declamatory *adj* declamatorius; (*fig*) inflatus

declaration *s* declaratio, professio, affirmatio *f*; (*of war*) denuntiatio *f*

declare *vt* declarare, affirmare, aperire, profitèri; (*war*) denuntiare, indicère; (*proclamation*) edicère; *vi* **to — for** favère (*with dat*)

declension *s* declinatio *f*

declinable *adj* declinabilis, casualis

---

declination *s* declinatio *f*; (*decay*) defectio *f*

decline *s* (*slope*) declive *n*; (*of strength*) defectio, diminutio *f*

decline *vt* (*to refuse*) recusare, renuère, abnuère; (*gram*) declinare, flectère; (*battle*) detrectare; *vi* vergère, inclinare; (*to decay, fail*) deficère, minui, decrescère; (*of prices*) laxare

decode *vt* enodare

decompose *vt* dissolvère, resolvère; *vi* tabescère, putescère, dissolvi

decomposition *s* dissolutio *f*

decorate *vt* ornare, decorare

decoration *s* ornatio *f*; (*ornament*) ornamentum *n*; (*distinction*) decus *n*

decorator *s* exornator *m*

decorous *adj* decorus, modestus, pudens; **—ly** decore, modeste, pudenter

decorum *s* decorum, honestum *n*, pudor *m*

decoy *s* illecebra *f*, illicium *n*

decoy *vt* allicère, inescare; (*fig*) illicère

decrease *s* deminutio, imminutio *f*

decrease *vt* (de)minuère, imminuère, extenuare; *vi* decrescère, (de)minui

decree *s* decretum, edictum *n*; (*of senate*) consultum *n*, auctoritas *f*; (*of assembly*) scitum *n*

decree *vt* decernère, edicère; (*of assembly*) jubère, sciscère; **the senate —s** senatui placet, senatui videtur

decrepit *adj* decrepitus, debilis

decry *vt* detrectare, obtrectare, vituperare

dedicate *vt* dedicare, consecrare, devovère

dedication *s* dedicatio, devotio *f*; (*of a book*) nuncupatio *f*

deduce *vt* deducère, concludère

deducible *adj* consectarius

deduct *vt* detrahère, subtrahère, demère

deduction *s* deductio, deminutio *f*; (*inference*) conclusio *f*, consequens *n*

deed *s* factum, facinus *n*; (*law*) syngrapha *f*, instrumentum *n*

deem *vt* judicare, existimare, ducère, habère

deep *adj* altus, profundus; (*of sounds*) gravis; (*of color*) satur; (*fig*) abstrusus, gravis; **—ly** alte, profunde; (*inwardly*) penitus; (*fig*) valde, graviter, vehementer

deep *s* profundum, altum *n*

deepen *vt* defodère; (*fig*) augère; *vi* altior fieri; (*fig*) crescère, densare

deer *s* cervus *m*, cerva *f*; (*fallow deer*) dama *f*

deface *vt* deformare, turpare, foedare

defaced *adj* deformis

defacement *s* deformitas *f*

defamation *s* calumnia *f*, opprobrium *n*

defamatory *adj* probrosus, contumeliosus

defame *vt* diffamare, infamare, calumniari

default s culpa f, delictum n, defect·us -ūs m

defeat s clades f; (at polls) repulsa f

defeat vt vincĕre, superare; (to baffle) frustrari

defect s vitium, mendum n; (lack) defect·us -ūs m

defect vi (to desert) deficĕre

defection s defectio f

defective adj vitiosus, imperfectus, mancus; (gram) defectivus

defend vt defendĕre, custodire, tuĕri; (in court) patrocinari

defendant s reus m, rea f

defender s defensor, propugnator m; (law) patronus m

defense s (act) defensio f; praesidium, munimentum n, tutela f; (law) patrocinium n; (speech) defensio f

defenseless adj inermis, infensus; defensoribus nudatus

defensible adj excusabilis, justus; inexpugnabilis

defensive adj defendens; — weapons arma n pl

defer vt differre; vi obsequi

deference s observantia, reverentia f, obsequium n; out of — reverenter

defiance s provocatio, ferocia f

defiant adj minax, insolens; —ly insolenter

deficiency s defectio, inopia, penuria f, defect·us -ūs m

deficient adj inops, mancus; to be — deficĕre, deesse

deficit s lacuna f

defile s fauces f pl

defile vt contaminare, inquinare; (fig) foedare

define vt (meaning) explicare; (limits) (de)finire, circumscribĕre, terminare

definite adj definitus, certus; —ly certe, certo, prorsus; definite

definition s definitio f

definitive adj definitivus; —ly definite, distincte

deflect vt deflectĕre, declinare; vi deflectĕre, errare

deflection s deflexio, declinatio f, flex·us -ūs m

deflower vt stuprare

deform vt deformare

deformed adj deformatus, deformis, distortus, pravus

deformity s deformitas, pravitas f

defraud vt fraudare, defraudare

defray vt praebēre, suppeditare

defunct adj defunctus, mortuus

defy vt provocare, contemnĕre, spernĕre

degeneracy s mores corrupti m pl

degenerate adj degener

degenerate vi degenerare

degradation s dedecus n, ignominia, infamia f

degrade vt dejicĕre, abdicare; ex loco movēre

degrading adj indignus

degree s grad·us -ūs, ordo m

deification s apotheosis f

deify vt divum habēre, inter deos referre, consecrare

deign vt dignari, curare

deism s deismus m

deity s numen n; deus m, dea f

dejected adj afflictus, demissus; —ly maeste

dejection s animi abjectio, maestitia f

delay s mora, cunctatio f

delay vt detinēre, tardare, remorari; vi morari, cunctari

delectable adj amoenus, jucundus

delegate s legatus m

delegate vt delegare, mandare, committĕre

delegation s delegatio, legatio f

delete vt delēre

deletion s litura f

deliberate adj deliberatus, consideratus, cautus, prudens; (speech) lentus; —ly deliberate, de industria; lente

deliberate vi deliberare, considerare, consulĕre

deliberation s deliberatio, consultatio f

delicacy s subtilitas, tenuitas f; elegantia f; (manner) lux·us -ūs m; (health) suavitas f; (food) cuppedia f

delicate adj (tender) delicatus, tener, mollis, exquisitus; (of texture) subtilis; (in taste) elegans, fastidiosus; (in health) infirmus; —ly delicate; eleganter; subtiliter

delicious adj suavis, dulcis

delight s delectatio f, gaudium n, voluptas f

delight vt delectare, oblectare; vi to — in delectari (with abl)

delightful adj suavis, jucundus; —ly suaviter, jucunde

delineate vt delineare, describĕre, adumbrare

delineation s designatio, descriptio f

delinquency s delictum n

delinquent s nocens m & f, noxius m

delirious adj delirus, phreneticus

delirium s delirium n, phrenesis f

deliver vt (to hand over) tradĕre, dare; (to free) liberare, eripĕre; (to surrender) prodĕre; (speech) habēre; (sentence) dicĕre; (message) referre; (blow) intendĕre; (child) obstetricari

deliverance s liberatio f

deliverer s liberator m; nuntius m

delivery s liberatio f; (of goods) traditio f; (of speech) actio, pronuntiatio f; (of child) part·us -ūs m

delude vt decipĕre, deludĕre

deluge s diluvium n, inundatio f

deluge vt inundare, obruĕre

delusion s delusio f, error m

demagogue s plebicola m

demand s postulatio, petitio f, postulatum n

demand vt postulare, flagitare, poscĕre; exigĕre

demarcation s confinium n

demean vt to — oneself se demittĕre

demeanor s gest·us -ūs m, mores m pl

demerit s culpa f, delictum n
demigod s heros m
demise s decess·us -ūs, obit·us -ūs m
democracy s civitas popularis f, liber populus m
democrat s homo popularis m
democratic adj popularis; **—ally** populi voluntate
demolish vt demoliri, disjicĕre, diruĕre, destruĕre
demolition s demolitio, destructio f
demon s daemon m
demonstrable adj demonstrabilis
demonstrably adv clare, manifeste
demonstrate vt (to show) monstrare, ostendĕre; (to prove) demonstrare
demonstration s demonstratio f
demonstrative adj demonstrativus; **—ly** demonstrative
demoralization s depravatio f
demoralize vt depravare, labefactare
demote vt loco movēre
demure adj taciturnus, modestus; **—ly** modeste, pudice
den s latibulum n
deniable adj infitiandus
denial s negatio, repudiatio f
denomination s nominatio f, nomen n; secta f
denote vt significare
denounce vt denuntiare, deferre
dense adj densus, spissus, confertus; **—ly** dense, crebro
density s densitas, crassitudo f; (crowd) frequentia f
dent s nota f
dentist s dentium medicus m
denude vt nudare, denudare
denunciation s denuntiatio, accusatio f
deny vt negare, abnegare; (to renounce) renuntiare
depart vi abire, discedĕre, proficisci; (to die) obire
departed adj mortuus, defunctus
department s pars, provincia f
departure s abit·us -ūs, discess·us -ūs, digress·us -ūs m; (deviation) digressio f; (death) obit·us -ūs m
depend vi to **—** on pendēre ex (with abl), niti (with abl); (to rely on) fidĕre (with dat or abl)
dependable adj fidus
dependence s clientela f; (reliance) fiducia f
dependency s provincia f
dependent adj subjectus, obediens, obnoxius
depict vt (de)pingĕre; describĕre, exprimĕre
deplete vt deminuĕre
depletion s deminutio f
deplorable adj miserabilis, flebilis, plorabilis
deplorably adv misere, pessime
deplore vt deplorare, deflēre
deploy vt (mil) explicare, expedire
deponent adj (gram) deponens
deportment s gest·us -ūs, habit·us -ūs m
depose vt (de)movēre

deposit vt deponĕre
deposit s depositum n, fiducia f
deposition s depositio f, testimonium n
depositor s depositor m
depot s (com) emporium n; (for military supplies) armamentarium n
deprave vt depravare
depravity s depravatio, turpitudo, pravitas f
deprecate vt deprecari
deprecation s deprecatio f
depreciate vt detrectare, obtrectare
depreciation s detrectatio, obrectatio f; (of price) vilitas f
depredation s spoliatio, direptio f
depress vt deprimĕre; (fig) infringĕre, affligĕre
depressed adj depressus, afflictus; (flat) planus; (hollow) cavus
depression s depressio, imminutio f; (fig) tristitia f
depressive adj tristis, affligens
deprivation s privatio, orbatio f; (state) inopia f
deprive vt privare, spoliare
depth s altitudo, profunditas f, profundum n; (bottom) fundus m
deputation s legatio f, legati m pl
deputy s legatus, vicarius m
derange vt (per)turbare, conturbare
deranged adj mente captus
derangement s perturbatio, confusio f; (of mind) mentis alienatio f
dereliction s derelictio, destitutio f
deride vt deridēre, irridēre
derision s ris·us -ūs m, irrisio f
derisive adj irridens
derivation s derivatio, origo f
derivative adj derivativus, derivatus
derive vt derivare, deducĕre; vi procedĕre, oriri
derogatory adj inhonestus, indignus
descend vi descendĕre, delabi; to **—** upon (to attack) irrumpĕre in (with acc)
descendant s progenies f; **—s** posteri m pl
descent s descens·us -ūs m; (slope) declivitas f, clivus m; (lineage) genus n
describe vt describĕre, perscribĕre; depingĕre; narrare
description s descriptio f; narratio f
desecrate vt profanare, polluĕre
desecration s profanatio, violatio f
desert s (wilderness) loca deserta n pl, solitudo f
desert s (merit) meritum n, dignitas f
desert vt deserĕre, relinquĕre; vi transfugĕre, deficĕre
deserter s desertor m; (mil) transfuga m
desertion s desertio, defectio f; transfugium n
deserve vt merēre, merēri
deserving adj meritus, dignus
design s (drawing) adumbratio f; (plan) consilium, propositum n
design vt designare; (to sketch) adumbrare; (fig) machinari

designate vt designare, nominare, appellare

designation s designatio f; vocabulum, nomen n, titulus m

designer s inventor, auctor, fabricator, machinator m

designing adj callidus

desirable adj optabilis, desiderabilis

desire s appetitio, cupiditas, cupido f; (request) rogat·us -ūs m

desire vt cupĕre, optare, expetĕre; (to request) orare, petĕre

desirous adj cupidus, appetens

desist vi desistĕre; (to cease) desinĕre

desk s scrinium, pulpitum n, mensa scriptoria f

desolate adj desolatus, solitarius; (of persons) afflictus

desolate vt devastare

desolation s vastatio f; (state) solitudo, vastitas f

despair s desperatio f

despair vi desperare

desperado s sicarius m

desperate adj desperatus; (dangerous) periculosus; —ly desperanter; to be —ly in love perdite amare

desperation s desperatio f

despicable adj abjectus, vilis, turpis

despise vt despicĕre, spernĕre, contemnĕre

despite prep contra (with acc)

despite s malevolentia f, odium n

despoil vt nudare, spoliare

despondency s animi abjectio f

despondent adj abjectus, demissus; —ly animo demisso

despot s dominus, tyrannus m

despotic adj tyrannicus; —ally tyrannice

despotism s dominatio f

dessert s secunda mensa f, bellaria n pl

destination s destinatio f, propositum n

destine vt destinare, designare

destiny s fatum n, sors f

destitute adj egens, inops, destitutus; — of expers (with genit)

destitution s inopia, mendicitas f

destroy vt destruĕre, subvertĕre, abolēre, delēre, vastare; to be destroyed interire

destroyer s deletor, vastator m

destruction s eversio, clades f, exitium n

destructive adj exitialis, perniciosus; —ly perniciose

desultory adj inconstans

detach vt sejungĕre, separare, amovēre

detached adj sejunctus; (of houses) solus

detachment s separatio f; (mil) man·us -ūs f; (aloofness) secess·us -ūs m

detail s singula n pl, singulae res f pl

detail vt enumerare

detain vt detinēre, retinēre, retardare

detect vt detegĕre, comperire, patefacĕre

detection s patefacio f, indicium n

detective s inquisitor m

detention s retentio f; (law) mora f

deter vt deterrēre, avertĕre

detergent s smegma n

deterioration s depravatio, corruptio f

determination s constantia, obstinatio f; (intention) propositum n

determine vt (to decide) statuĕre, constituĕre, discernĕre; (to fix) determinare, definire

determined adj certus; (resolute) firmus, obstinatus

detest vt abominari, detestari

detestable adj detestabilis, foedus

dethrone vt regno depellĕre

detonate vi crepare

detonation s fragor m

detour s circuit·us -ūs m

detour vi iter flectĕre, circumagi

detract vt detrahĕre; vi to — from detrectare, obtrectare

detraction s obtrectatio f

detractor s obtrectator m

detriment s detrimentum, damnum n

detrimental adj injuriosus, damnosus; to be — to detrimento esse (with dat)

devastate vt vastare, depopulari

devastation s (act) vastatio, populatio f; (state) vastitas f

develop vt evolvĕre, explicare; (person) alĕre; vi crescĕre; to — into evadĕre in (with acc)

development s explicatio f, progress·us -ūs m

deviate vi aberrare, degredi, decedĕre

deviation s aberratio, declinatio, digressio f

device s (contrivance) artificium n, machina f; (plan) consilium n; (emblem) insigne n

devil s diabolus, daemon m; go to the —! abi in malam crucem!

devilish adj diabolicus, daemonicus; (fig) nefandus

devious adj devius; vagus, erraticus

devise vt fingĕre, excogitare, concoquĕre

devoid adj inanis, vacuus, expers; to be — of carēre (with abl)

devolve vi to — upon obtingĕre, pervenire ad (with acc)

devote vt devovēre, consecrare; to — oneself to studēre (with dat), se dedĕre (with dat)

devoted adj deditus, studiosus; — to studiosus (with genit)

devotee s cultor m

devotion s devotio, addictio f, studium n

devour vt devorare; (fig) haurire

devout adj pius, religiosus; —ly pie, religiose

dew s ros m

dewdrop s gutta roscida f

dewy adj roscidus, roridus

dexterity s sollertia, calliditas f

dexterous adj sollers, callidus, habilis; —ly sollerter, callide, habiliter

diabolical adj nefarius, nefandus

diagnose vt dijudicare, discernĕre

diagnosis *s* judicium *n*
diagonal *adj* diagonalis; —**ly** in transversum
diagram *s* forma, descriptio *f*
dial *s* solarium *n*
dialect *s* dialectus *f*, sermo *m*
dialectic *adj* dialecticus
dialogue *s* sermo *m*, colloquium *n*; *(written discussion)* dialogus *m*
diameter *s* diametros *f*
diamond *s* adamas *m*
diaper *s* striatura *f*
diaphragm *s* praecordia *n pl*
diarrhea *s* alvi profluvium *n*
diary *s* diarium *n*, commentarii diurni *m pl*
diatribe *s* convicium *n*
dice *s* tali *m pl*; *(game)* alea *f*
dictate *vt* dictare, praescribēre
dictate *s* praescriptum, praeceptum, jussum *n*
dictation *s* dictatio *f*; dictatum *n*
dictator *s* dictator *m*
dictatorial *adj* imperiosus, dictatorius
dictatorship *s* dictatura *f*
diction *s* dictio, elocutio *f*
dictionary *s* lexicon *n*, thesaurus linguae *m*
didactic *adj* didascalicus
die *s* alea *f*
die *vi* mori, obire, perire; **to — off** demori; **to — out** emori
diet *s* *(food)* vict·us -ūs *m*; *(med)* diaeta *f*
diet *vi* secundum diaetam vivēre
dietary *adj* diaeteticus
differ *vi* differre, discrepare, distare; *(in opinion)* dissentire
difference *s* differentia, diversitas, dissimilitudo *f*; *(of opinion)* discrepantia, dissensio *f*
different *adj* diversus, dissimilis, dispar; alius; —**ly** diverse, aliter
difficult *adj* difficilis, arduus
difficulty *s* difficultas *f*, labor *m*, negotium *n*; **with —** aegre
diffidence *s* diffidentia, verecundia *f*
diffident *adj* diffidens, verecundus, modestus; —**ly** diffidenter
diffuse *adj* diffusus; *(fig)* verbosus; —**ly** effuse, latius
diffuse *vt* diffundēre
diffusion *s* diffusio *f*
dig *vt* fodēre
digest *s* summarium *n*
digest *vt* *(to arrange)* digerēre; *(food)* concoquēre
digestion *s* concoctio *f*
digestive *adj* pepticus
digging *s* fossio, fossura *f*
digit *s* numerus *m*
dignified *adj* gravis, augustus
dignify *vt* honestare, honorare
dignitary *s* vir amplissimus *m*
dignity *s* dignitas *f*, honor *m*
digress *vi* digredi, aberrare, abire
digression *s* digressio *f*, digress·us -ūs *m*
dike *s* agger *m*
dilapidated *adj* ruinosus, obsoletus
dilate *vt* dilatare; *vi* dilatari

dilatory *adj* cunctabundus, lentus, segnis
dilemma *s* dilemma *n*; nodus *m*, angustiae *f pl*
diligence *s* diligentia *f*
diligent *adj* diligens, sedulus; —**ly** diligenter, sedulo
dilute *vt* diluēre, miscēre
dilution *s* temperatio, mixtura *f*
dim *adj* hebes, obscurus; **to become —** hebescēre; —**ly** obscure, obtuse
dim *vt* hebetare, obscurare; *vi* hebescēre
dimension *s* dimensio, mensura *f*
diminish *vt* minuēre, deminuēre, extenuare; *vi* decrescēre, minui
diminutive *adj* exiguus, parvulus; *(gram)* deminutivus
diminutive *s* *(nomen)* deminutivum *n*
dimness *s* hebetudo, obscuritas, caligo *f*
dimple *s* lacuna *f*, gelasinus *m*
din *s* strepit·us -ūs, sonit·us -ūs, fragor *m*; **to make a —** strepere
dine *vi* cenare
diner *s* conviva *m*
dingy *adj* fuscus, squalidus
dining room *s* cenatio *f*, triclinium *n*
dinner *s* cena *f*
dinner party *s* convivium *n*
dint *s* ict·us -ūs *m*; **by — of** per *(with acc)*
dip *vt* immergēre, ting(u)ēre; *vi* mergi, tingi; *(to sink)* premi, declinare
dip *s* devexitas, declinatio *f*
diploma *s* diploma *n*
diplomacy *s* *(function)* officium legationis *m*; *(tact)* dexteritas *f*
diplomat *s* legatus *m*
diplomatic *adj* sagax, callidus, astutus
dire *adj* dirus
direct *adj* rectus, directus; —**ly** directe, rectā; *(immediately)* statim
direct *vt* dirigēre; *(to administer)* administrare; *(to rule)* gubernare; *(to order)* jubēre, imperare *(with dat)*; *(weapon)* intendēre; *(letter)* inscribēre; *(attention)* admovēre
direction *s* *(act)* directio *f*; *(quarter)* pars, regio *f*; *(management)* administratio *f*; *(instruction)* mandatum *n*; *(order)* praeceptum *n*
director *s* rector, magister, gubernator, curator *m*
directory *s* *(office of director)* curatio *f*, magisterium *n*; *(body of directors)* magistri, curatores *m pl*
dirge *s* nenia *f*
dirt *s* sordes *f*; *(mud)* lutum *n*, limus *m*
dirtiness *s* spurcitia *f*; *(fig)* obscenitas *f*
dirty *adj* spurcus, sordidus; *(fig)* obscenus
dirty *vt* foedare, spurcare
disability *s* impotentia *f*
disable *vt* debilitare, enervare
disabled *adj* inhabilis, debilis, mancus

disabuse *vt* errorem eripĕre (*with dat*)

disadvantage *s* incommodum, detrimentum *n*

disadvantageous *adj* incommodus, iniquus

disagree *vi* discrepare, dissidēre, dissentire

disagreeable *adj* injucundus, molestus, insuavis, gravis; (*of smells*) graveolens; (*of persons*) difficilis, morosus

disagreeably *adv* moleste, graviter, ingrate

disagreement *s* dissensio, discordia *f*, dissidium *n*

disappear *vi* vanescĕre, fugĕre, diffugĕre, abire, perire

disappearance *s* fuga *f*, exit·us ·ūs *m*

disappoint *vt* fallĕre, frustrari

disappointment *s* frustratio *f*; incommodum, malum *n*

disapproval *s* reprehensio, improbatio *f*

disapprove *vt* reprehendĕre, improbare

disarm *vt* exarmare

disarrange *vt* (per)turbare, confundĕre

disarray *s* perturbatio *f*

disaster *s* calamitas *f*, incommodum *n*

disastrous *adj* calamitosus, funestus, exitiosus; —**ly** calamitose

disavow *vt* diffitēri, infitiari

disavowal *s* infitiatio *f*

disband *vt* dimittĕre; *vi* dimitti

disbelief *s* diffidentia, incredulitas *f*

disbeliever *s* incredulus *m*

disburse *vt* erogare, expendĕre

disbursement *s* erogatio, solutio *f*

disc *s* orbis *m*

discard *vt* ponĕre, mittĕre; repudiare

discern *vt* discernĕre, distinguĕre

discernible *adj* dignoscendus

discerning *adj* perspicax, sagax, prudens

discernment *s* (*act*) perspicientia *f*; (*faculty*) discrimen, judicium *n*

discharge *vt* (*to unload*) exonerare; (*to dismiss*) dimittĕre; (*to perform*) perfungi (*with abl*); (*debt*) exsolvĕre; (*weapon*) immittĕre, jacĕre, jaculari; (*defendant*) absolvĕre

discharge *s* (*unloading*) exoneratio *f*; (*shooting*) emissio, conjectio *f*; (*dismissal*) missio *f*; (*payment*) solutio *f*; (*bodily*) defluxio *f*

disciple *s* discipulus *m*; (*fig*) sectator *m*

discipline *s* disciplina *f*

discipline *vt* assuefacĕre, coercēre

disclaim *vt* infitiari, diffitēri, negare

disclaimer *s* infitiatio *f*

disclose *vt* aperire, detegĕre, enuntiare

disclosure *s* patefactio *f*

discomfit *vt* fundĕre

discomfort *s* incommoda *n pl*, molestiae *f pl*

disconcerting *adj* molestus

disconnect *vt* sejungĕre, disjungĕre

disconsolate *adj* tristis, afflictus; —**ly** insolabiliter, triste

discontent *s* taedium *n*, molestia, offensio *f*

discontented *adj* parum contentus; —**ly** animo iniquo

discontinue *vt* intermittĕre; *vi* desinĕre, desistĕre

discord *s* discordia, dissensio *f*; (*mus*) dissonantia *f*

discordant *adj* discors, discrepans; (*mus*) dissonus

discount *vt* deducĕre; (*to disregard*) praetermittĕre

discount *s* (*com*) decessio *f*

discourage *vt* deterrēre, examinare; to be **discouraged** animum demittĕre

discouragement *s* animi abjectio *or* infractio *f*

discouraging *adj* adversus, incommodus

discourse *s* sermo *m*, colloquium *n*; (*written*) libellus *m*

discourse *vi* disserĕre, colloqui, verba facĕre

discourteous *adj* inurbanus; —**ly** inurbane

discourtesy *s* inurbanitas *f*

discover *vt* invenire, reperire; (*to find out*) explorare; (*to disclose*) patefacĕre

discoverable *adj* indagabilis, visibilis

discoverer *s* inventor, repertor *m*

discovery *s* inventio *f*; (*things discovered*) inventum *n*

discredit *s* dedecus *n*, ignominia *f*

discredit *vt* notare, infamare

discreet *adj* cautus, prudens; —**ly** consulto, prudenter

discrepancy *s* discrepantia *f*

discretion *s* pudentia, circumspectio *f*; (*tact*) judicium *n*

discretionary *adj* interminatus, liber

discriminate *vt* distinguĕre, dijudicare, discernĕre

discriminating *adj* sagax, discernens

discrimination *s* distinctio *f*; judicium, discrimen *n*

discuss *vt* agĕre, disputare, disserĕre

discussion *s* disputatio, disceptatio *f*

disdain *vt* fastidire, despicĕre, aspernari

disdain *s* fastidium *n*, despect·us ·ūs, contempt·us ·ūs *m*

disdainful *adj* fastidiosus, superciliosus; —**ly** fastidiose, contemptim

disease *s* morbus *m*, malum *n*

diseased *adj* aegrotus

disembark *vt* e navi exponĕre; *vi* e navi conscendĕre

disenchant *vt* errorem demĕre (*with dat*)

disengage *vt* expedire, eximĕre, avocare

disentangle *vt* expedire, extricare, explicare

disfavor *s* invidia *f*

disfigure vt deformare, turpare, mutilare

disfranchise vt civitatem adiměre (with dat)

disgorge vt revoměre, evoměre

disgrace s dedecus n, infamia f; (thing) flagitium n

disgrace vt dedecorare

disgraceful adj dedecorus, turpis, flagitiosus; —ly turpiter, flagitiose

disguise s (mask) persona f; simulatio f; (pretense) praetext·us -ūs m

disguise vt obtegěre; (fig) celare, dissimulare

disgust s (loathing) fastidium, taedium n, nausea f

disgust vt fastidium mověre (with dat); I am disgusted with me taedet (with genit), me piget (with genit)

disgusting adj taeter, foedus; —ly foede

dish s (flat) patina f; (large) lanx f; (course) ferculum n, dapes f pl

dishearten vt exanimare, percellěre; to be disheartened animum demittěre

disheveled adj passus, effusus

dishonest adj improbus, perfidus; —ly improbe, dolo malo

dishonesty s improbitas f, dolus malus m, fraus, perfidia f

dishonor s dedecus n, infamia, ignominia f

dishonor vt dedecorare

dishonorable adj inhonestus, turpis

disillusion vt errorem adiměre (with dat)

disinfect vt purgare

disinherit vt exheredare

disintegrate vi dilabi

disinter vt effoděre

disinterested adj integer; (of judge) severus; —ly integre, gratuito

disjoin vt segregare, disjungěre

disjointed adj incompositus; —ly incomposite

disk s orbis m

dislike s odium, fastidium n, aversatio f

dislike vt aversari, odisse, fastidire

dislocate vt extorquěre, luxare

dislocation s luxatura f

dislodge vt mověre, depellěre

disloyal adj perfidus; —ly perfide

disloyalty s infidelitas, perfidia f

dismal adj maestus, funestus, miser; —ly maeste, misere

dismantle vt diruěre, spoliare, nudare

dismay s pavor m, consternatio f

dismay vt terrěre, perterrefacěre, territare

dismember vt membratim dividěre, lacerare, discerpěre

dismemberment s mutilatio f

dismiss vt dimittěre; (fear) mittěre; (to discharge, to cashier) exauctorare

dismissal s missio, dimissio f

dismount vi ex equo desilire

disobedience s inobedientia, contumacia f

disobedient adj contumax

disobey vt non obedire (with dat), non parěre (with dat)

disorder s confusio f; (med) aegrotatio f; (of mind) perturbatio f; (pol) tumult·us -ūs m

disordered adj turbatus; (fig) dissolutus

disorderly adj inordinatus, incompositus, (per)turbatus; (insubordinate) turbulentus

disorganization s dissolutio f

disorganize vt conturbare, confunděre; to be disorganized dilabi

disown vt (statement) diffiteri, infitiari; (heir) abdicare; (thing) repudiare

disparage vt obtrectare, detrectare

disparagement s obtrectatio f

disparaging adj obtrectans

disparate adj dispar

disparity s inaequalitas, discrepantia f

dispassionate adj sedatus, tranquillus, frigidus; —ly sedate, frigide

dispatch vt mittěre, dimittěre, legare; (to finish) absolvěre, perficěre; (to kill) interficěre

dispel vt dispellěre; (worries) poněre

dispensary s medicamentaria taberna f

dispensation s distributio, partitio f; (exemption) immunitas, exemptio f

dispense vt distribuěre, dispertiri; (to release) solvěre; vi to — with indulgěre (with dat), omittěre, praetermittěre

dispenser s dispensator m

disperse vt spargěre, dispergěre, dissipare; vi dilabi, diffugěre

dispersion s dispersio, dissipatio f

dispirited adj abjectus, demissus, animo fractus

displace vt summověre; exauctorare

displacement s amotio f

display s (exhibit) ostent·us -ūs m; (ostentation) ostentatio, jactatio f

display vt ostenděre, ostentare, exhibēre

displease vt displicēre (with dat)

displeased adj offensus; to be — at aegre ferre

displeasing adj odiosus, ingratus

displeasure s offensa, offensio f

disposable adj in promptu

disposal s dispositio f; arbitrium n; at the — of penes (with acc)

dispose vt disponěre, ordinare; (to incline) parare, praeparare; vi to — of abalienare, venděre; (to get rid of) tollěre

disposed adj inclinatus; (in bad sense) pronus

disposition s (arrangement) dispositio f; (character) natura, mens f, ingenium n, animus m

dispossess vt ejicěre, detruděre, pellěre

disproportion s inaequalitas, inconcinnitas f

disproportionate adj inaequalis, impar, inconcinnus; **—ly** impariter, inaequaliter

disprove vt refutare, confutare, redarguēre

disputable adj disputabilis, ambiguus

dispute s (debate) disputatio f; (quarreling) altercatio, controversia f; **beyond — indisputabilis**

dispute vt & vi disputare, contendēre

disqualification s impedimentum n

disqualify vt inhabilem reddēre, impedire

disquiet vt inquietare, vexare

disregard s incuria, negligentia f

disregard vt negligĕre, omittēre

disreputable adj infamis

disrepute s infamia f

disrespect s negligentia, insolentia f

disrespectful adj irreverens, insolens; **—ly** insolenter, irreverenter

disrupt vt dirumpēre

disruption s dirumptio f; (fig) discidium n

dissatisfaction s molestia, offensio f

dissatisfied adj parum contentus

dissatisfy vt parum satisfacēre

dissect vt dissecare

dissection s incisio f

dissemble vt & vi dissimulare

disseminate vt disseminare, divulgare

dissension s dissensio f, dissidium n

dissent vi dissentire, dissidēre

dissent s dissensio f

dissertation s disputatio, dissertatio f

dissimilar adj dissimilis, dispar

dissimilarity s dissimilitudo f

dissipate vt dissipare, diffundēre; vi dissipari, diffundi

dissipation s dissipatio f

dissolute adj dissolutus, corruptus, perditus; **—ly** immoderate, prodige

dissolution s dissolutio f

dissolve vt dissolvēre; (to melt) liquefacĕre; (meeting) dimittēre; vi liquescēre; (to break up) dissolvi

dissonance s dissonantia f

dissonant adj dissonus

dissuade vt dissuadēre (with dat), dehortari

dissuasion s dissuasio f

distaff s colus f

distance s distantia f, intervallum n; (fig) frigus n; (long way) longinquitas f; **at a —** procul, longe

distant adj distans, disjunctus, longinquus; (fig) parum familiaris; **to be — abesse**

distaste s fastidium n

distasteful adj (of taste) teter; (fig) molestus, odiosus

distemper s morbus m

distend vt distendēre

distil vt & vi stillare, destillare

distillation s destillatio f

distinct adj (different) diversus, alius; (clear) distinctus; **—ly** clare, distincte, certe

distinction s distinctio, discrepantia f, discrimen n; (status) amplitudo f;

(honor) honos m; **there is no —** nil interest

distinctive adj proprius; **—ly** proprie

distinguish vt distinguēre, discernēre; **to — oneself** enitēre

distinguished adj insignis, clarus, notus, eximius

distort vt distorquēre; (fig) depravare

distortion s distortio f; (fig) depravatio f

distract vt distrahēre, avocare; (to madden) furiare

distracted adj amens, insanus; **—ly** amens, mente alienatus

distraction s (cause) invitamentum n; (state) negligentia f; **to — efflictim**

distress s afflictio, aegrimonia, aerumna f, dolor, labor m

distress vt afflictare, angēre

distressed adj anxius, afflictus, sollicitus

distressing adj tristis, gravis, acerbus

distribute vt distribuēre

distributer s distributor m

distribution s distributio f

district s regio f

distrust s diffidontia f

distrust vt diffidēre (with dat)

distrustful adj diffidens; **—ly** diffidenter

disturb vt perturbare; sollicitare, inquietare

disturbance s perturbatio f; confusio f; (pol) mot·us ·ūs, tumult·us ·ūs m

disturber s turbator, concitator m

disuse s desuetudo f

ditch s fossa f

ditty s cantilena f, canticum n

divan s lectulus m

dive vi mergi

diver s urinator m

diverge vi deflectēre, declinare, devertēre; (of views) discrepare

diverse adj alius, varius, diversus

diversification s variatio f

diversify vt variare

diversion s (recreation) oblectamentum n; (of thought) avocatio f; (of river, etc.) derivatio f

diversity s diversitas, varietas f

divert vt avertēre, divertēre; (attention) avocare; (to amuse) oblectare

divest vt exuēre, nudare, privare; **to — oneself of** exuēre, ponēre

divide vt dividēre, partiri, distribuēre; vi discedēre, se scindēre

divination s divinatio, vaticinatio f

divine adj divinus; **—ly** divine

divine s theologus m

divine vt divinare, augurari, vaticinari; (to guess) conjicēre

diviner s augur, haruspex m

divinity s divinitas f; (god) numen n; divus m, diva f

divisible adj dividuus, divisibilis

division s divisio, partitio f; (part) pars f; (mil) legio f; **— of opinion** dissensio f

divorce s divortium n
divorce vt repudiare, dimittĕre
divulge vt vulgare, palam facĕre, aperire, patefacĕre
dizziness s vertigo f
dizzy adj vertiginosus
do vt agĕre, facĕre, efficĕre; vi agĕre; **how do you —?** quid agis?; **to — away with** tollĕre, perdĕre
docile adj docilis, tractabilis
dock s navale n; (law) cancelli m pl
dock vt subducĕre
docket s lemniscus m
dockyard s navalia n pl
doctor s medicus m; (teacher) doctor m
doctor vt medicari, curare
doctorate s doctoris grad·us -ūs m
doctrine s doctrina f, dogma n
document s documentum, instrumentum n
dodge s dolus m
dodge vt eludĕre; vi tergiversari
doe s cerva f
dog s canis m & f
dogged adj pervicax, pertinax; **—ly** pertinaciter
doggedness s pervicacia f
doggerel s versus inepti m pl
dog kennel s canis cubile n
dogma s dogma, placitum, praeceptum n
dogmatic adj dogmaticus; arrogans; **—ally** arroganter
dogmatism s arrogantia doctrinae f
dog star s canicula f, Sirius m
doing s factum, facinus n
dole s sportula f; donatio f
dole vt **to — out** parce dare
doleful adj lugubris, maestus, flebilis; **—ly** maeste, flebiliter
doll s pupa f
dollar s thalerus m
dolphin s delphinus, delphin m
dolt s caudex, stipes m
domain s (estate) possessio f; (kingdom) regnum n
dome s tholus m
domestic adj domesticus, familiaris; intestinus
domestic s famulus, servus, verna m, famula, serva f
domesticate vt domare, assuefacĕre
domicile s domicilium n, dom·us -ūs f
dominant adj praevalens
domination s dominium n
domineer vi dominari
domineering adj imperiosus
dominion s imperium, regnum n
don vt induĕre
donation s donum n, stips f
donkey s asinus, asellus m
donor s donator m, donatrix f
doom s fatum, exitium n
doom vt damnare, condemnare
door s janua f, ostium n, fores f pl
doorkeeper s janitor m, janitrix f
doorpost s postis f
doorway s ostium n
Doric adj Doricus
dormant adj sopitus; (hidden) latens; **to lie —** jacēre

dormitory s cubiculum, dormitorium n
dorsal adj dorsualis
dose s potio f
dot s punctum n
dot vt punctum imponĕre (with dat)
dotage s senium n
dotard s senex delirus m
dote vi **to — upon** deamare, deperire
doting adj deamans, desipiens; **—ly** perdite amans
double adj duplex; (of pairs) geminus; (as much again) duplus; (meaning) ambiguus
double s duplum n; **to march on the —** currĕre
double vt duplicare; (cape) praetervehi; vi duplicari; (to run) currĕre
doubly adv bis, dupliciter
doubt s dubitatio f, dubium n; (distrust) suspicio f
doubt vt dubitare; suspicari
doubtful adj (of persons) dubius; (of things) incertus, ambiguus, anceps; **—ly** dubie; (hesitatingly) dubitanter
doubtless adv scilicet, haud dubie, sine dubio
dough s farina f
doughty adj strenuus, fortis
douse vt (to put out) exstinguĕre; (to drench) madefacĕre
dove s columba f
dowdy adj inconcinnus
down s pluma f; (of hair) lanugo f; (of plants) pappus m
down adv deorsum; **— from** de (with abl); **— to** usque ad (with acc)
down prep de (with abl)
down adj declivis; tristis; **ad inopiam redactus**
downcast adj (of eyes or head) dejectus, demissus; (fig) afflictus, maestus
downfall s occas·us -ūs m, ruina f
downhill adj declivis
downright adj directus, sincerus
downright adv prorsus, plane
downstream adv secundo flumine
downward adj declivis; pronus
downwards adv deorsum
downy adj plumeus; lanuginosus
dowry s dos f
doze vi dormitare
dozen s duodecim
drab adj cinereus
draft s (act of drawing) lineatio f; (drink) haust·us -ūs m; (of ship) immersio f; (first copy) exemplar n; (of air) aura f; (mil) dilect·us -ūs m; (money) syngrapha f; (of net) jact·us -ūs m
draft vt conscribĕre
draft horse s equus rhedarius m
drag vt trahĕre, rapĕre; vi trahi
drag s (fig) impedimentum n
dragnet s tragula f
dragon s draco, anguis m
drain s cloaca f
drain vt siccare; derivare; (to drink)

exhaurire, ebibĕre; (strength) exhaurire

drainage s derivatio, exsiccatio f; colluvies cloacarum f

draining s exsiccatio f

drake s anas m

drama s drama n, fabula f

dramatic adj dramaticus, scaenicus

dramatist s poeta scaenicus, scriptor fabularum m

dramatize vt ad scaenam componĕre

drape vt induĕre, amicire, velare

drapery s aulaeum n

drastic adj vehemens

draw vt (to pull) trahĕre, ducĕre; (picture) scribĕre, delineare; (sword) destringĕre; (bow) adducĕre; (inference) colligĕre; to — aside abducĕre, seducĕre; to — away avertĕre, distrahĕre; to — back retrahĕre; to — off detrahĕre, abducĕre; (wine) depromĕre; to — out extrahĕre; (sword, etc.) educĕre; (fig) elicĕre; to — together contrahĕre; to — up subducĕre; (troops) instruĕre, constituĕre; vi to — back pedem referre, cedĕre; (fig) recedĕre; to — near appropinquare; to — off cedĕre; to — up to (of ships) appetĕre

drawback s impedimentum, incommodum n, retardatio f

drawbridge s pons m

drawer s (sliding compartment) loculus m; (chest) armarium n

drawing s descriptio f; (art) graphice f

drawing room s exedra f

drawl vi lentius loqui

dray s plaustrum n

dread s terror, pavor m, formido f

dread adj terribilis, dirus

dread vt expavescĕre, formidare

dreadful adj terribilis, horribilis, atrox; —ly horrendum in modum, atrociter

dream s somnium n; in a — in somno

dream vt & vi somniare; (fig) dormitare

dreamer s (fig) nugator m

dreamy adj somniculosus

drearily adv triste, misere

dreariness s (place) solitudo, vastitas f; (mind) tristitia f

dreary adj (place) vastus, solus, incultus; (person) tristis, miser

dredge s everriculum n

dregs s faex f; (fig) sentina f

drench vt madefacĕre, perfundĕre

dress s habit·us -ūs, vestit·us -ūs m, vestis f, vestimenta n pl

dress vt vestire, induĕre; (to deck out) (ex)ornare; (wounds) curare; (to bind up) obligare; vi se induĕre

dressing s ornatio f; (of foods) coctio, coctura f; (med) fomentum n

dressing room s procoeton m

dribble vi stillare

drift s propositum n; (purpose) scopus m; (of sand) cumulus m; (of snow) vis f

drift vi ferri, fluitare

drill s (tool) terebra f; (mil) exercitatio f

drill vt (to bore) terebrare; (mil) exercēre; (pupil) instituĕre

drink vt bibĕre, potare; to — in absorbēre, haurire; to — up epotare; vi bibĕre, potare; to — to propinare (with dat)

drink s pot·us -ūs m, potio f

drinkable adj potabilis

drinker s potor, potator m; (drunkard) bibax m

drinking adj (given to drink) bibosus

drinking cup s poculum n

drip s stillicidium n

drip vi stillare

drive vt agĕre, pellĕre, impellĕre; (to force) compellĕre, cogĕre; (a nail, etc.) infigĕre; to — away abigĕre; (fig) depellĕre; (to dislodge) dejicĕre; to — back repellĕre; to — in (sheep, etc.) cogĕre; (fig) compellĕre; to — off abigĕre; to — on impellĕre; to — out expellĕre; to — out of one's senses infuriare; to — up subigĕre; vi (in carriage) vehi; to — off avehi; to — on praetervehi; to — past praetervehi

drive s (in carriage) vectio f; (energy) impigritas f

drivel s saliva f, sputum n; (nonsense) ineptiae, nugae f pl

drivel vi (fig) delirare

driver s agitator m; (of carriage) auriga m

drizzle vi leniter pluĕre

drizzle s lenis pluvia f

dromedary s dromas m

drone s (bee) fucus m; (person) nebulo m; (buzz) bombus m

drone vi fremĕre

droop vt demittĕre; vi languēre; (of flowers) languescĕre, tabescĕre

drooping adj languidus

drop s gutta, stilla f; (a little bit) paululum n; — by — guttatim

drop vt stillare; (to let slip) omittĕre; (to lay low) sternĕre; (hint) emittĕre; (anchor) jacĕre; (work) desistĕre ab (with abl); vi destillare; (to fall) cadĕre; to — behind cessare; to — off to sleep obdormire; to — out excidĕre

drought s siccitas, ariditas f

drove s grex m

drown vt immergĕre, demergĕre; (fig) opprimĕre; to — out obscurare; vi in aqua perire

drowsily adv somniculose

drowsy adj somniculosus, somnolentus; (fig) ignavus

drudge s (slave) mediastinus m; (fig) plagiger m

drudgery s opera servilis f

drug s medicamentum n

drug vt medicare

druggist s medicamentarius m

drugstore s taberna medicina, apotheca f

Druids s Druidae m pl
drum s typanum n
drum vi tympanum pulsare
drummer s tympanista m
drunk adj ebrius
drunkard s ebriosus, temulentus m
drunken adj ebrius, ebriosus
drunkenness s ebrietas, temulentia f
dry adj aridus, siccus; (thirsty) siti-
  culosus; (fig) jejunus; insulsus
dry vt siccare, desiccare, arefacĕre;
  (in the sun) insolare; vi arescĕre
dryad s dryas f
dryly adv (fig) insulse; (of jokes)
  facete
dryness s ariditas, siccitas f; (fig)
  aridum sermonis genus n
dual adj duplex
dub vt supernominare
dubious adj dubius; —ly dubie
duck s anas f
duck vt submergĕre, demergĕre; (an
  issue) evitare; vi (under water) uri-
  nari
duckling s anaticula f
due adj debitus, justus, meritus; to
  be — to fieri (with abl)
due adv rectā; **due east** rectā ad
  orientem
due s debitum n
duel s certamen n
duet s bicinium n
duke s dux m
dull adj hebes; (of mind) tardus, seg-
  nes, insulsus; (of style) frigidus
dull vt hebetare, obtundĕre; stupefacĕre
dullness s stupiditas, tarditas f
duly adv rite; recte
dumb adj mutus; to be — obmu-
  tescĕre
dumbfound vt obstupefacĕre
dumb show s mimus m
dumpling s farinae subactae globulus m
dumpy adj brevis atque obesus

dun adj fuscus, furvus
dun vt flagitare, exposcĕre
dunce s homo stupidus m
dung s stercus n, fimus m; (of birds)
  merda f
dungeon s carcer m, ergastulum n
dupe s homo credulus, homo stolidus m
dupe vt decipĕre
duplicate adj duplex
duplicate s duplicitas, fallacia f
duplicate vt duplicare
duplicity s duplicitas f
durability s firmitudo, stabilitas f
durable adj firmus, durabilis, stabilis
duration s spatium temporis n, diuturnitas, perpetuitas f
during prep per (with acc), inter
  (with acc)
dusk s crepusculum, obscurum n
dusky adj obscurus, tenebrosus; fuscus
dust s pulvis m
dust vt detergĕre
dusty adj pulverulentus, pulvereus
dutiful adj pius, officiosus; —ly pie,
  officiose
duty s (social or moral) officium n;
  (task) munus n; (tax) vectigal n; to
  be on — (mil) stationem agĕre
dwarf s nanus, pumilio m
dwarfish adj pumilus
dwell vi habitare, inhabitare; to —
  upon commorari in (with abl)
dweller s incola m & f, habitator m
dwelling place s domicilium n, sedes, habitatio f
dwindle vi decrescĕre, imminui
dye vt ting(u)ĕre, colorare, inficĕre,
  fucare
dye s tinctura f, color m
dying adj moriens, moribundus;
  (last) ultimus, extremus
dynamics s dynamica f
dynasty s dynastia, dom·us -ūs f
dysentery s dysenteria f

E

each adj & pron quisque; (of two)
  uterque; — other inter se, invicem
eager adj cupidus, avidus, acer, vehemens; —ly cupide, avide, acriter,
  vehementer
eagerness s aviditas, cupiditas, alacritas f, studium n
eagle s aquila f
ear s auris f; (of corn) spica f; to
  give — aurem praebēre
earache s aurium dolor m
earl s comes m
early adj (in morning) matutinus;
  (in season) maturus; (of early date)
  antiquus; (beginning) primus, novus
early adv (in morning) mane; (too
  soon) praemature; (quickly, soon)
  cito
earn vt lucrari, merēre or merēri,

consequi
earnest adj intentus, serius, impen-
  sus, vehemens; in — serio, sedulo,
  bona fide; —ly intente, impense,
  acriter, graviter
earnestness s assiduitas, gravitas f,
  ardor m
earnings s quaest·us -ūs m, lucrum n
earring s elenchus m
earth s terra, tellus f; (soil) solum n;
  (globe) orbis (terrarum) m
earthen adj terreus; fictilis
earthenware s fictilia n pl
earthly adj terrenus; terrestris; humanus
earthquake s terrae mot·us -ūs m
earthwork s opus terrenum n, agger m
earthy adj terrenus

ease s (*leisure*) otium n, quies f; (*grace*) lepor m, facilitas f; (*pleasure*) voluptas f; **at — otiosus, vacuus; securus**

ease vt levare, exonerare, expedire; (*fig*) lenire, mitigare

east adj orientalis

east s oriens m

Easter s pascha f, sollemnia paschalia n pl

eastern adj orientalis

eastward adv ad orientem

east wind s Eurus m

easy adj facilis; expeditus; (*manner*) facilis, affabilis; (*graceful*) lepidus

eat vi vesci (*with abl*), esse; (*fig*) rodĕre; **to — away** peredĕre; (*fig*) corrodĕre; **to — up** comesse, devorare, exesse

eating s es·us -ūs m

eaves s suggrundia n pl

eavesdropper s auceps, auricularius m

ebb s recess·us -ūs m; **to be at a low — jacēre**

ebb vi recedĕre; (*fig*) decrescĕre

eccentric adj insolens, inusitatus, abnormis

ecclesiastic adj ecclesiasticus

echo s echo, imago f

echo s repercutĕre, resonare; (*fig*) subsequi; vi resonare, resultare

eclipse s (*of sun or moon*) obscuratio solis or lunae f, defect·us -ūs m

eclipse vt obscurare, obumbrare

eclogue s ecloga f

economic adj economicus

economical adj frugi (*indecl*), parcus; **—ly** parce

economics s publicarum opum scientia f

economize vi parcēre

economy s parsimonia, frugalitas f; rei familiaris administratio f

ecstasy s ecstasis, insania f, furor m

eddy s vortex m

eddy vi volutari

edge s (*brink*) margo m & f; (*of knife, etc.*) acies f; (*of forest*) ora f

edge vt (*garment*) praetexĕre; (*to sharpen*) acuĕre; vi **to — closer** appropinquare

edged adj acutus

edging s limbus m

edible adj esculentus, edulis

edict s edictum, decretum n

edification s eruditio f

edify vt docēre

edit vt edĕre, recensēre

edition s editio f

editor s editor m

educate vt educare, erudire

education s educatio, eruditio f

educator s praeceptor, magister m

eel s anguilla f

efface vt delēre, obliterare, tollĕre

effect s effectum n, effect·us -ūs; (*show*) jactatio f; **—s** bona n pl; **in — re vera; without — irritus**

effect vt efficĕre, exsequi, facĕre

effective adj efficiens, efficax, valens; **—ly** valide, graviter

effectual adj efficax, valens, potens,

—ly efficaciter, potenter

effeminancy s mollities f

effeminate adj effeminatus, mollis, muliebris; **—ly** effeminate, muliebriter

effete adj effetus

efficacious adj efficax; **—ly** efficaciter

efficacy s efficacia, vis f

efficiency s virtus, peritia f

efficient adj efficiens, aptus, idoneus; efficax; **—ly** perite, bene

effigy s effigies f

effort s labor, conat·us -ūs, nis·us -ūs m, opera f; **to make an — eniti**

effrontery s audacia, impudentia f

effusion s effusio f

effusive adj officiosus

egg s ovum n; **to lay —s** ova parĕre

egotism s amor sui m

egotist s sui amator m

egotistical adj sibi soli consulens

egress s egress·us -ūs, exit·us -ūs m

eight adj octo; **— times** octies

eighteen adj duodeviginti, decem et octo

eighteenth adj decimus octavus, duodevicesimus

eighth adj octavus

eighth s octava pars f

eightieth adj octogesimus

eighty adj octoginta

either pron alteruter; uter; alter

either conj **— . . . or** aut . . . aut; vel . . . vel

ejaculate vt emittĕre

ejaculation s clamor m

eject vt ejicĕre

ejection s dejectio f

eke vt **to eke out a livelihood** victum aegre parare

elaborate adj elaboratus; **—ly** elaborate

elaborate vt elaborare

elaboration s nimia diligentia f

elapse vi praeterire, abire, labi

elastic adj resiliens; (*fig*) mobilis

elate vt inflare, superbum reddĕre; **to be elated** efferri

elation s gaudium n, laetitia f, animus elatus m

elbow s ulna f, cubitus m

elbow vt cubitis depulsare, cubitis trudĕre

elder adj major natu

elderly adj aetate provectior

eldest adj maximus natu

elect vt eligĕre, deligĕre, creare

elect adj designatus; (*elite*) lectus

election s electio f, delect·us -ūs m; (*pol*) comitia n pl

electioneering s ambitio f

elective adj suffragatorius

elector s suffragator m

electrical adj electricus

electricity s vis electrica f

electrify vt electricā vi afficĕre; (*fig*) percellĕre

elegance s elegantia f

elegant adj elegans, concinnus; **—ly** eleganter, cum elegantia

elegiac *adj* elegiacus; — **verse** elegi *m pl*

elegy *s* elegia *f*

element *s* elementum *n*; —**s** principia, initia *n pl*; (*fig*) rudimenta *n pl*

elementary *adj* elementarius

elephant *s* elephantus, elephas *m*

elevate *vt* levare, attollĕre; (*fig*) efferre, inflare

elevated *adj* editus

elevation *s* elatio *f*; (*height*) altitudo *f*; (*hill*) locus superior *m*

eleven *adj* undecim; — **times** undecies

eleventh *adj* undecimus

elf *s* larva *f*, numen pumilum *n*

elicit *vt* elicĕre

eligible *adj* eligibilis, idoneus

eliminate *vt* amovēre, tollĕre

elision *s* elisio *f*

elite *adj* lectus

elite *s* flos *m*, lecti *m pl*

elk *s* alces *f*

ellipsis *s* ellipsis *f*

elliptical *adj* ellipticus; —**ly** per defectionem

elm *s* ulmus *f*

elocution *s* pronuntiatio *f*

elongate *vt* producĕre

elope *vi* clam fugĕre, aufugĕre

elopement *s* fuga clandestina *f*

eloquence *s* eloquentia *f*; (*natural*) facundia *f*

eloquent *adj* eloquens, disertus; —**ly** diserte, eloquenter, graviter

else *adj* alius; no one — nemo alius; who — quis alius

else *adv* (*besides*) praeterea; (*otherwise*) aliter

elsewhere *adv* alibi; (*motion*) alio

elucidate *vt* illustrare, explicare

elucidation *s* explicatio *f*

elude *vt* eludĕre, frustrari, evitare

Elysian *adj* Elysius

Elysian fields *s* Elysii campi *m pl*

emaciate *vt* emaciare, macerare

emaciated *adj* macer, macilentus

emaciation *s* macies, tabes *f*

emanate *vi* emanare, oriri

emanation *s* emanatio, exhalatio *f*

emancipate *vt* emancipare, manumittĕre; (*fig*) liberare

emancipation *s* (*of slave*) manumissio *f*; (*of son*) emancipatio *f*; (*fig*) liberatio *f*

emasculate *vt* castrare, emasculare; (*fig*) enervare

embalm *vt* condire, pollingĕre

embalming *s* pollinctura *f*

embankment *s* agger *m*, moles *f*

embargo *s* retentio navium *f*, interdictum *n*; **to lay an — upon a ship** navem retinēre

embark *vt* imponĕre; *vi* conscendĕre; **to — upon** (*fig*) ingredi

embarkation *s* conscensio *f*

embarrass *vt* perturbare, confundĕre, impedire

embarrassing *adj* incommodus, difficilis

embarrassment *s* conturbatio, implicatio *f*; (*financial*) angustiae *f pl*

embassy *s* legatio *f*, legati *m pl*

embellish *vt* ornare, exornare

embellishment *s* ornamentum, decus *n*, exornatio *f*

embers *s* cinis *m*, favilla *f*

embezzle *vt* peculari

embezzlement *s* peculat·us -ūs *m*

embezzler *s* peculator *m*

embitter *vt* exacerbare

emblazon *vt* insignire

emblem *s* emblema, insigne, signum *n*

emblematic *adj* symbolicus

embody *vt* includĕre, repraesentare

emboss *vt* caelare

embrace *s* amplex·us -ūs, complex·us -ūs *m*

embrace *vt* amplecti, complecti; comprehendĕre

embroider *vt* acu pingĕre

embroidery *s* vestis picta *f*

embroil *vt* permiscĕre, implicare

embroilment *s* implicatio *f*

embryo *s* immaturus part·us -ūs *m*

emend *vt* emendare, corrigĕre

emendation *s* correctio, emendatio *f*

emerald *s* smaragdus *m*

emerge *vi* emergĕre; (*to arise*) exsistĕre

emergency *s* tempus, discrimen *n*, cas·us -ūs *m*

emigrant *s* emigrans *m*

emigrate *vi* emigrare

emigration *s* migratio *f*

eminence *s* praestantia, amplitudo *f*; (*rise of ground*) locus editus *m*

eminent *adj* eminens, egregius, praestans; —**ly** eximie, insigniter

emissary *s* emissarius, legatus *m*

emit *vt* emittĕre; exhalare

emotion *s* animi mot·us -ūs *m*, commotio *f*

emotional *adj* mobilis

emperor *s* imperator, princeps *m*

emphasis *s* energia, vis *f*, pondus *n*; impressio *f*

emphasize *vt* exprimĕre

emphatic *adj* emphaticus, gravis; —**ally** emphatice, graviter

empire *s* imperium, regnum *n*

empirical *adj* empiricus; —**ly** ex experimentis

empiricism *s* empirice *f*

employ *vt* uti (*with abl*), adhibēre, exercēre, occupare

employer *s* conductor, dominus *m*

employment *s* (*act*) us·us -ūs *m*; (*occupation*) quaest·us -ūs *m*; (*business*) negotium *n*

empower *vt* potestatem facĕre (*with dat*)

empress *s* imperatrix *f*

emptiness *s* inanitas *f*; (*fig*) vanitas *f*

empty *adj* vacuus, inanis; (*of street*) desertus; (*fig*) vanus

empty *vt* evacuare; exhaurire; *vi* (*of river*) influĕre

empyrean *s* aether *m*

emulate *vt* aemulari, imitari

emulation *s* aemulatio *f*

enable *vt* facultatem facĕre (*with dat*)

enact *vt* decernĕre, sancire

enactment *s* lex, sanctio *f*, decretum *n*

enamel *s* smaltum, vitrum metallicum *n*

enamel *adj* smaltinus

enamoured *adj* amans; **to be — of** amare, deamare

encamp *vi* castra ponĕre

encampment *s* castra *n pl*

encase *vt* includĕre

enchant *vt* fascinare; (*fig*) capĕre, captare, delectare

enchanter *s* incantator *m*

enchanting *adj* (*fig*) venustus, suavissimus

enchantment *s* incantamentum *n*; (*fig*) illecebrae *f pl*

enchantress *s* maga, cantatrix *f*; venefica *f*

encircle *vt* cingĕre, circumdare, circumplecti

enclose *vt* includĕre, saepire

enclosure *s* saeptum *n*

encompass *vt* complecti

encounter *s* (*meeting*) congress·us -ūs *m*; (*fight*) certamen *n*, pugna *f*

encounter *vt* congredi cum (*with abl*), obviam ire (*with dat*), occurrĕre (*with dat*); (*in battle*) concurrĕre cum (*with abl*)

encourage *vt* cohortari, confirmare; favēre (*with dat*)

encouragement *s* hortat·us -ūs *m*, confirmatio *f*, favor *m*

encroach *vi* invadĕre; **to — upon** usurpare, occupare, invadĕre

encroachment *s* usurpatio *f*

encumber *vt* impedire, onerare, praegravare

encumbrance *s* impedimentum, onus *n*

encyclopedia *s* encyclopaedia *f*

end *s* finis, terminus, exit·us -ūs *m*; (*aim*) propositum *n*; (*of a speech*) peroratio *f*; **in the — denique**; **to put an — to** finem imponĕre (*with dat*); **to what —?** quo?, quorsum?

end *vt* finire, terminare, conficĕre; *vi* desinĕre; (*of time*) exire; (*of events*) evadĕre

endanger *vt* periclitari

endear *vt* carum reddĕre, devincire

endearing *adj* carus, blandus

endearment *s* blanditiae *f pl*, blandimenta *n pl*

endeavor *s* conat·us -ūs, nis·us -ūs *m*

endeavor *vi* conari, eniti, laborare, contendĕre

ending *s* finis, exit·us -ūs *m*

endless *adj* infinitus; perpetuus; **—ly** sine fine, perpetuo

endorse *vt* ratum facĕre

endow *vt* dotare, donare, instruĕre

endowed *adj* praeditus

endowment *s* dotatio, dos *f*, donum *n*

endurable *adj* tolerabilis

endurance *s* tolerantia, patientia *f*; (*duration*) duratio *f*

endure *vt* tolerare, pati; *vi* durare; permanēre

enduring *adj* tolerans; durabilis

enemy *s* (*public*) hostis *m*; (*private*) inimicus, adversarius *m*

energetic *adj* impiger, acer, strenuus, navus; **—ally** acriter, impigre, strenuo

energy *s* vis, vehementia, efficacia *f*, impet·us -ūs *m*

enervate *vt* enervare, debilitare

enforce *vt* exsequi, cogĕre; (*arguments*) confirmare

enforcement *s* coactio, sanctio *f*

enfranchise *vt* (*slave*) manumittĕre; civitate donare

enfranchisement *s* (*of slave*) manumissio *f*; civitatis donatio *f*

engage *vt* (*to employ*) adhibēre; (*to reserve*) conducĕre; (*attention*) occupare; (*to involve*) implicare; (*enemy*) proelium facĕre cum (*with abl*); *vi* **to — in** suscipĕre, ingredi; **to engage in battle** proeliari, manum or manus conserĕre

engaged *adj* (*to marry*) sponsus; **to be — in** versari in (*with abl*)

engagement *s* (*to marry*) pactio nuptialis *f*; (*business*) negotium *n*, occupatio *f*; (*mil*) proelium *n*, pugna *f*; (*promise*) pactum *n*, pactio *f*, promissum *n*

engaging *adj* suavis, blandus, amabilis

engender *vt* ingenerare, gignĕre

engine *s* machina, machinatio *f*

engineer *s* machinator, faber *m*

engineering *s* machinalis scientia *f*; **civil — architectura *f***

England *s* Anglia, Britannia *f*

English *adj* Anglicus, Britannicus

Englishman *s* Anglus, Britannus, Britannicus *m*

engrave *vt* incidĕre, caelare, insculpĕre, scalpĕre

engraver *s* sculptor, caelator *m*

engraving *s* sculptura, caelatura *f*

engross *vt* occupare; **to be engrossed in** totus esse in (*with abl*)

enhance *vt* augēre, amplificare, ornare

enigma *s* aenigma *n*, ambages *f pl*

enigmatic *adj* ambiguus, obscurus; **—ally** ambigue

enjoin *vt* jubēre, injungĕre

enjoy *vt* frui (*with abl*); uti (*with abl*)

enjoyment *s* fruct·us -ūs *m*, voluptas *f*, gaudium *n*; possessio *f*

enlarge *vt* amplificare, augēre, dilatare; *vi* **to — upon** amplificare, prosequi

enlargement *s* amplificatio, dilatio *f*, auct·us -ūs *m*

enlighten *vt* illustrare, illuminare; erudire

enlightenment *s* eruditio, humanitas *f*

enlist *vt* (*support*) conciliare; (*mil*) conscribĕre; *vi* sacramentum dicĕre

enlistment *s* conscriptio *f*

enliven *vt* animare, incitare; exhilarare

enmity *s* inimicitia *f*, odium *n*

ennoble *vt* honestare

ennui *s* taedium *n*

enormity *s* immanitas *f*; atrocitas *f*

enormous adj ingens, enormis, immanis; **—ly** immensum, praeter modum

enough adj satis; **— trouble** satis laboris

enough adv satis; **more than —** satis superque

enrage vt infuriare, exasperare, incendĕre

enrapture vt rapĕre, captare

enrich vt locupletare, ditare

enroll vt adscribĕre, inscribĕre; vi nomen dare

enshrine vt consecrare, dedicare

enshroud vt involvĕre, amicire

ensign s (flag) vexillum n; (officer) signifer m

enslave vt in servitutem redigĕre

enslavement s servitus f

ensnare vt illaquĕre, irretire; (fig) illicĕre

ensue vi sequi, insequi

ensuing adj insequens, posterus, proximus

entail vt afferre, inferre

entangle vt illaquĕre, irretire, impedire, implicare

entanglement s implicatio f

enter vt intrare, inire, ingredi; introire in or ad (with acc); **to — politics** ad rem publicam accedĕre; vi intrare, inire, ingredi, introire; **to — upon** (to undertake) suscipĕre, ingredi

enterprise s (undertaking) inceptum, ausum n; (in bad sense) facinus n; (quality) animus alacer, animus promptus m

enterprising adj acer, promptus

entertain vt (guest) excipĕre, invitare, adhibĕre; (idea) admittĕre, habĕre; (to amuse) oblectare, delectare

entertainer s hospes m

entertainment s (amusement) oblectatio f, oblectamentum n; (cultural) acroama n; (by guest) hospitium n

enthrall vt captare

enthusiasm s studium n, fervor, furor, ardor m

enthusiastic adj fanaticus, ardens, fervidus; **—ally** fanatice, ardenter

entice vt allicĕre, elicĕre

enticement s illecebra f

enticing adj blandus

entire adj totus, integer, solidus; **—ly** omnino, plane, penitus

entirety s integritas, universitas f

entitle vt (to name) appellare, nominare; inscribĕre; (to give title to) potestatem dare (with dat)

entity s ens n, res f

entomologist s entomologicus m

entomology s entomologia f

entrails s viscera, exta, intestina n pl

entrance s adit·us -ūs, introit·us -ūs m; ostium n; (act) introit·us -ūs m, ingressio f

entrance vt rapĕre, consopire, capĕre

entrance hall s vestibulum n

entrap vt illaquĕre, inescare; capĕre

entreat vt obsecrare, orare, deprecari

entreaty s rogatio, obsecratio f, preces f pl

entrust vt credĕre, mandare, committĕre

entry s (act) introit·us -ūs m, ingressio f; (of house) vestibulum n; adit·us -ūs m; (in accounts) nomen n

entwine vt implicare, nectĕre

enumerate vt enumerare

enumeration s enumeratio, recensio f

enunciate vt enuntiare, pronuntiare, exprimĕre

enunciation s enuntiatio f

envelop vt involvĕre, amicire, implicare

envelope s involucrum n

enviable adj invidiosus

envious adj invidus, lividus

envoy s nuntius, legatus, orator m

envy s invidia f

envy vt invidēre (with dat)

ephemeral adj brevis; caducus

epic adj epicus, heroicus

epic s epos n

epicure s helluo, homo voluptarius m

Epicurean adj Epicureus

Epicurean s Epicureus m; (hedonist) voluptarius m

epidemic adj epidemus, contagiosus

epidemic s pestilentia f

epidermis s summa cutis, epidermis f

epigram s epigramma n

epilepsy s morbus comitialis m, epilepsia f

epilogue s epilogus m

epiphany s epiphania f

episode s embolium, eventum n, excurs·us -ūs m

epistle s epistola f

epistolary adj epistolaris

epitaph s epitaphium n, titulus m

epithet s epitheton n

epitome s epitome, epitoma f

epoch s epocha f, saeculum n

equal adj aequalis, aequus, par; **—ly** aeque, aequaliter, pariter

equal s par m, f & n

equal vt aequare, adaequare

equality s aequalitas f, aequum n

equalization s (act) aequatio, exaequatio f; (state) aequalitas f

equalize vt adaequare, exaequare

equanimity s aequus animus m

equation s aequatio f

equator s aequinoctialis circulus m

equatorial adj aequinoctialis

equestrian adj equestris

equestrian s eques m

equidistant adj **to be —** aequo intervallo inter se distare

equilibrium s aequilibrium n

equinox s aequinoctium n

equip vt armare, ornare, instruĕre

equipment s arma, instrumenta, armamenta n pl, armatura f, apparat·us -ūs m

equitable adj aequus, justus

equitably adv aeque, juste

equity s aequitas f, aequum n

equivalent *adj* aequus, par
equivocal *adj* ambiguus, anceps; —ly ambigue
equivocate *vi* tergiversari
era *s* tempus, saeculum *n*
eradicate *vt* eruĕre, exstirpare, eradicare
eradication *s* exstirpatio *f*
erase *vt* delēre, eradĕre
erasure *s* litura *f*
ere *conj* priusquam
ere *prep* ante (*with acc*); — long brevi, mox; — now ante hoc tempus
erect *adj* erectus, arrectus
erect *vt* (*to raise*) erigĕre; (*to build*) exstruĕre; (*statue*) ponĕre
erection *s* erectio, aedificatio, exstructio *f*
erotic *adj* amatorius, eroticus
err *vi* (ab)errare, peccare
errand *s* mandatum *n*
erratic *adj* inconstans
erroneous *adj* falsus, errore implicitus; —ly falso, perperam
error *s* error *m*; vitium *n*; delictum, peccatum *n*; (*in writing*) mendum *n*
erudite *adj* eruditus, doctus
erudition *s* eruditio *f*
erupt *vi* erumpĕre
eruption *s* eruptio *f*
escape *s* fuga *f*, effugium *n*
escape *vt* fugĕre, evitare; to — the notice of fallĕre; *vi* effugĕre, evadĕre, elabi; (*secretly*) subterfugĕre
escort *s* comitat·us -ūs *m*; (*protection*) praesidium *n*
escort *vt* comitari, deducĕre
especially *adv* praecipue, praesertim, maxime, in primis
essay *s* experimentum *n*, conat·us -ūs *m*; (*treatise*) libellus *m*
essay *vt* conari, tentare
essence *s* essentia, natura *f*
essential *adj* necessarius, proprius; —ly naturā, necessario
establish *vt* constituĕre, statuĕre; (*firmly*) stabilire, confirmare; (*to prove*) probare, arguĕre
establishment *s* (*act*) constitutio *f*; (*com*) negotium *n*
estate *s* (*state*) stat·us -ūs *m*, conditio *f*; (*property*) fundus *m*, praedium *n*; (*pol*) ordo *m*, dignitas *f*
esteem *s* aestimatio *f*, honor *m*
esteem *vt* aestimare, putare; (*to respect*) magni facĕre
estimable *adj* aestimandus
estimate *vt* aestimare, censēre
estimate *s* aestimatio *f*, judicium *n*
estimation *s* aestimatio, opinio, sententia *f*, judicium *n*
estimator *s* aestimator, calculator *m*
estrange *vt* abalienare
estrangement *s* alienatio *f*, discidium *n*
estuary *s* aestuarium *n*
eternal *adj* aeternus, sempiternus; —ly in aeternum, semper
eternity *s* aeternitas *f*
ether *s* aether *m*
ethereal *adj* aethereus
ethical *adj* moralis

ethics *s* mores *m pl*, ethice *f*; philosophia moralis *f*
etymology *s* etymologia, verborum notatio *f*
eulogize *vt* collaudare
eulogy *s* laudatio *f*, panegyricus *m*
eunuch *s* eunuchus *m*; (*in contempt*) spado *m*
euphony *s* euphonia *f*, sonus dulcis *m*
European *adj* Europaeus
Euxine *s* Euxinus pontus *m*
evacuate *vt* vacuare, vacuefacĕre; (*people*) deducĕre
evacuation *s* discessio *f*; (*of bowels*) egestio *f*
evade *vt* subterfugĕre, eludĕre, devitare
evaporate *vt* exhalare, evaporare; *vi* exhalari
evaporation *s* exhalatio *f*
evasion *s* effugium *n*, tergiversatio *f*
evasive *adj* ambiguus; —ly ambigue
eve *s* vesper *m*; (*of feast*) vigiliae *f pl*; on the — of sub (*with acc*)
even *adj* aequalis, aequus; (*level*) planus; (*of numbers*) par; —ly aequaliter
even *adv* et, etiam, vel; — if etsi, etiamsi; not — ne . . . quidem
evening *s* vesper *m*; in the — vespere, vesperi
evening *adj* vespertinus
evening star *s* Hesperus, Vesper *m*
evenness *s* aequalitas, aequabilitas *f*
event *s* cas·us -ūs *m*, factum *n*; (*outcome*) event·us -ūs, exit·us -ūs *m*; in any — saltem
eventful *adj* memorabilis
eventual *adj* ultimus; —ly aliquando, olim, denique
ever *adv* (*always*) semper; (*at any time*) umquam; (*after si, nisi, num, ne*) quando; for — in aeternum
evergreen *adj* sempervivus
everlasting *adj* sempiternus; —ly in aeternum
evermore *adv* semper, in aeternum
every *adj* quisque, omnis; — now and then interdum; — other day alternis diebus
everybody *pron* quisque, nemo non; omnes *m pl*
everyday *adj* quotidianus *or* cottidianus; usitatus
everything *pron* omnia *n pl*
everywhere *adv* ubique, ubivis
evict *vt* expellĕre, dejicĕre, detrudĕre
evidence *s* testimonium, indicium, argumentum *n*; (*witness*) testis *m & f*
evidence *vt* testari
evident *adj* apertus, manifestus; it is — apparet; —ly aperte, manifesto
evil *adj* malus, pravus, improbus
evil *s* malum *n*, improbitas *f*
evildoer *s* maleficus, malefactor *m*
evil-minded *adj* malevolus, malignus
evoke *vt* evocare, excitare, elicĕre
evolution *s* progress·us -ūs *m*, progressio *f*
evolve *vt* evolvĕre, explicare
exact *adj* exactus, subtilis, diligens;

—**ly** accurate, subtiliter, diligenter;
—**ly as** sic ut

exact vt exigĕre

exaction s exactio f

exactitude s diligentia f

exaggerate vt exaggerare, augēre,
in majus extollĕre

exaggeration s trajectio, superlatio f

exalt vt extollĕre, amplificare, evehĕre

exaltation s elatio f

examination s investigatio f; (in
school) probatio f; (of witnesses) interrogatio f

examine vt investigare, inquirĕre,
scrutari; (witnesses) interrogare

examiner s scrutator, investigator m

example s exemplum, exemplar, documentum n; **for** — exempli gratiā, verbi gratiā

exasperate vt exasperare, exacerbare, irritare

exasperation s ira f

excavate vt excavare, effodĕre

excavation s fossio, excavatio f, cavum n

exceed vt superare, excedĕre

exceedingly adv valde, magnopere

excel vt superare, praestare (with
dat); vi excellĕre

excellence s excellentia, praestantia f

Excellency s illustrissimus m

excellent adj praestans, egregius,
optimus; —**ly** egregie, optime

except vt excipĕre

except prep praeter (with acc); nisi
(followed by appropriate case); —
that nisi quod

exception s exceptio f; **with the** —
of praeter (with acc)

exceptional adj egregius, praestans,
singularis; —**ly** praeter modum

excess s excess·us -ūs m, intemperantia f

excessive adj immodicus, nimius;
—**ly** immodice, nimis

exchange s (barter) commutatio f;
(of money) collybus m

exchange vt mutare, permutare

excise vt excidĕre

excision s excisio f

excitable adj irritabilis, fervidus

excite vt excitare, stimulare; (to inflame) incendĕre

excitement s commotio f; perturbatio f; incitamentum n

exclaim vt exclamare; (as a group)
conclamare; (against) acclamare (with dat); declamitare in (with acc)

exclamation s exclamatio f, clamor m

exclude vt excludĕre, prohibēre

exclusion s exclusio f

exclusive adj proprius; — **of** praeter (with acc); —**ly** solum

excommunicate vt excommunicare

excommunication s excommunicatio f

excrement s excrementum, stercus n

excretion s excrementum n, excretio f

excruciating adj acerbissimus

exculpate vt (ex)purgare, excusare, absolvĕre

excursion s excursio f, iter n

excusable adj excusabilis

excuse vt excusare; ignoscĕre (with
dat), veniam dare (with dat)

excuse s excusatio f; (pretense) pretext·us -ūs m, species f

execute vt (to perform) exsequi, efficĕre; (to punish) necare, securi ferire

execution s effect·us -ūs m, effectio
f; (capital punishment) supplicium n

executioner s carnifex m

executive adj ad administrationem
pertinens

executive s administrator m

executor s curator testamenti m

exemplary adj egregius, eximius

exemplification s expositio f

exemplify vt explicare

exempt vt eximĕre, liberare

exempt adj exemptus, immunis, liber

exemption s exemptio, immunitas,
liberatio f

exercise s exercitatio f, us·us -ūs m;
(mil) exercitium n; (literary) thema n

exercise vt exercēre; uti (with abl)

exert vt adhibēre; **to** — **oneself**
viribus eniti

exertion s contentio f, nis·us -ūs m

exhalation s exhalatio f, vapor m

exhale vt exhalare, spargĕre; vi exspirare

exhaust vt exhaurire; (to tire) defatigare, conficĕre, debilitare

exhaustion s defatigatio, defectio
virium f

exhibit vt exhibēre, exponĕre, ostendĕre

exhibition s exhibitio, propositio f;
spectaculum n

exhilarate vt exhilarare

exhilaration s hilaritas f

exhort vt hortari

exhortation s hortatio f, hortamen n

exhume vt exhumare, eruĕre

exigency s necessitas f, angustiae
f pl

exile s (banishment) ex(s)ilium n;
(person) exsul, profugus m

exile vt relegare, in exilium pellĕre,
deportare

exist vi esse, exsistĕre; vivĕre

existence s existentia f; vita f

exit s exit·us -ūs m; ostium n

exonerate vt absolvĕre

exorbitant adj nimius, immodicus

exotic adj externus, peregrinus

expand vt expandĕre, extendĕre, dilatare; vi expandi, extendi, dilatari

expanse s spatium, expansum n

expansion s expansio f, spatium n

expatriate vt expellĕre

expect vt exspectare, sperare

expectancy s spes f

expectation s exspectatio, spes f

expectorate vt exspuĕre, exscreare

expediency s utilitas f

expedient adj utilis, commodus; —**ly**
apte, commode

expedient *s* modus *m*, ratio *f*
expedite *vt* expedire, maturare
expedition *s* (*mil*) expeditio *f*; (*speed*) celeritas *f*
expeditious *adj* celer, promptus; —ly celeriter, mature
expel *vt* expellĕre, ejicĕre
expend *vt* expendĕre, impendĕre
expenditure *s* sumpt·us -ūs *m*, impensa *f*
expense *s* impensa *f*, sumpt·us -ūs *m*
expensive *adj* carus, pretiosus; sumptuosus, lautus; —ly sumptuose
experience *s* experientia, peritia *f*, us·us -ūs *m*
experience *vt* experiri, cognoscĕre, pati
experienced *adj* peritus, expertus
experiment *s* experimentum *n*
experiment *vi* to — with experiri
experimental *adj* usu comparatus
expert *adj* sciens, peritus, callidus; —ly callide, scienter
expertness *s* calliditas, sollertia *f*
expiate *vt* expiare, luĕre
expiation *s* expiatio *f*; piaculum *n*
expiration *s* exspiratio *f*, finis, exit·us -ūs *m*
expire *vi* exspirare; (*of time*) exire
explain *vt* explanare, explicare, exponĕre
explanation *s* explanatio, explicatio, enodatio, interpretatio *f*
explicit *adj* apertus, expressus; —ly aperte, plane
explode *vt* displodĕre, discutĕre; *vi* displodi, dirumpi
exploit *s* res gesta *f*, factum, facinus *n*
exploit *vt* uti (*with abl*), abuti (*with abl*)
exploration *s* indagatio, investigatio *f*
explore *vt* explorare, scrutari, perscrutari
explorer *s* explorator *m*
explosion *s* fragor *m*
exponent *s* interpres *m*
export *vt* exportare, evehĕre
exporter *s* exportator *m*
exports *s* merces quae exportantur *f pl*
expose *vt* exponĕre; nudare, detegĕre, patefacĕre; (*to danger*) objicĕre, offerre
exposition *s* explicatio, expositio, interpretatio *f*; (*show*) spectaculum *n*
expostulation *s* expostulatio, querela *f*
exposure *s* (*of guilt*) deprehensio *f*; (*to cold*) expositio *f*
expound *vt* exponĕre, interpretari
express *adj* clarus, expressus; —ly plane
express *vt* exprimĕre, eloqui, dicĕre; significare
expression *s* vox *f*, verbum *n*; (*of face*) vult·us -ūs *m*
expressive *adj* significans; (*fig*) loquax; — of index (*with genit*)

expulsion *s* exactio, ejectio, expulsio *f*
expunge *vt* delēre, oblitterare
expurgate *vt* expurgare
exquisite *adj* exquisitus, elegans; —ly eleganter, exquisite
extant *adj* superstes, exsistens; to be — exstare
extempore *adv* ex tempore, subito
extemporize *vi* subito dicĕre, subita dicĕre
extend *vt* extendĕre, producĕre, propagare; *vi* extendĕre, porrigi
extension *s* extensio *f*; (*space*) spatium *n*; (*of boundaries*) prolatio *f*
extensive *adj* amplus, latus; —ly late
extent *s* spatium *n*; (*of a country*) tract·us -ūs *m*, fines *m pl*; to a great — magna ex parte; to some — aliqua ex parte; to this — hactenus
extenuate *vt* mitigare, minuĕre
extenuation *s* imminutio *f*
exterior *adj* externus, exterior
exterior *s* species *f*
exterminate *vt* exstirpare, exterminare, eradicare
extermination *s* exstirpatio *f*; internecio, occidio *f*
external *adj* externus, extraneus; —ly extrinsecus
extinct *adj* exstinctus, obsoletus; to become — obsolescĕre
extinction *s* exstinctio *f*, interit·us -ūs *m*
extinguish *vt* exstinguĕre, restinguĕre
extol *vt* laudibus efferre
extort *vt* extorquĕre, diripĕre, exprimĕre
extortion *s* res repetundae *f pl*
extortioner *s* exactor, extortor *m*
extra *adj* additus
extra *adv* insuper, praeterea
extract *vt* extrahĕre, excerpĕre; (*teeth, etc.*) evellĕre
extract *s* (*chemical*) expressio *f*; (*literary*) excerptum *n*; (*synopsis*) compendium *n*
extraction *s* (*act*) evulsio *f*; (*birth, orlyin*) stirps, origo *f*, genus *n*
extraneous *adj* extraneus, alienus, adventicius
extraordinarily *adv* mire, praeter solitum, extra modum
extraordinary *adj* extraordinarius, insolitus; (*outstanding*) eximius, mirus
extravagance *s* intemperantia *f*; sumpt·us -ūs *m*
extravagant *adj* immodicus, nimius; profusus, luxuriosus; (*spending*) prodigus; —ly immodice, absurde, prodige
extreme *adj* extremus, ultimus; —ly valde, summe
extreme *s* extremum, summum *n*
extremity *s* extremitas *f*, extremum *n*, finis *m*; (*distress*) miseria *f*
extricate *vt* expedire, extrahĕre, liberare

exuberance s ubertas, luxuria, redundantia f

exuberant adj uber, luxuriosus; **—ly** ubertim

exude vt exudare; vi emanare

exult vi exsultare, gestire

exultant adj laetabundus, laetus; **—ly** laete

exultation s laetitia f

eye s oculus m; (of needle) foramen n; (of plant) gemma f; **to keep one's —s on** oculos defigēre in (with abl)

eye vt aspicēre, intuēri

eyebrow s supercilium n

eyelash s palebrarum pilus m

eyelid s palpebra f

eyesight s acies, acies oculi f

eyewitness s arbiter m

F

fable s fabula, narratio commenticia f

fabric s fabrica f; (piece of cloth) textile n

fabricate vt fabricare, struēre; (fig) fingēre

fabrication s fabricatio f; (fig) mendacium n

fabulous adj fictus, commenticius; **—ly** ficte

face s facies f, os n, vult·us -ūs m; **— to —** coram

face vt aspicēre, intuēre; se opponēre (with dat), obviam ire (with dat); obire; vi spectare, vergēre; **to — about** (mil) signa convertēre

facet s pars f

facetious adj facetus; **—ly** facete

facilitate vt facilius reddēre

facility s facilitas f; opportunitas f

facing adj adversus, spectans

facsimile s imago f, exemplar n

fact s factum, verum n, res f; **as a matter of —** enimvero; **in — ve**-ro, re ipsa; enim, etenim; **the — that** quod

faction s factio f

factory s officina, fabrica f

faculty s facultas, vis f; (of university) ordo m

fade vi marcescēre, deflorescēre, pallescēre

fail vt (to disappoint) relinquēre, deserēre, deficēre; vi succumbēre, concidēre, cadēre; (com) decoquēre, foro cedēre

fail s **without —** certo, plane, omnino

failing s (deficiency) defect·us ūs m; (fault) culpa f, delictum, vitium n; (disappointment) frustratio f; (ceasing) remissio f

failure s defectio f, defect·us -ūs m; (fault) culpa f, delictum n

faint adj (weary) defessus; (drooping) languidus; (of sight, smell, etc.) hebes; (of sound) surdus; (of color) pallidus; (of courage) timidus; **—ly** languide; timide

faint vi collabi, intermori, (animo) linqui

fainthearted adj timidus, imbellis, ignavus

faintness s (of impression) levitas f; (of body) languor m

fair adj (in appearance) formosus,

pulcher; (of complexion) candidus; (of hair) flavus; (of weather) serenus; (of wind) secundus; (impartial) aequus; (of ability) mediocris; **— and square** sine fuco ac fallaciis; **—ly** aeque, juste; (moderately) mediocriter

fair s nundinae f pl

fairness s (of complexion) candor m; (justice) aequitas f

fairy s nympha f

faith s (trust) fides f; religio f; **to have — in** credēre (with dat), confidēre (with dat)

faithful adj fidelis, fidus; **—ly** fideliter

faithfulness s fidelitas, integritas f

faithless adj infidus, infidelis, perfidus; **—ly** perfide

falcon s falco m

fall s cas·us -ūs, laps·us -ūs m; (season) autumnus m

fall vi cadēre, concidēre, labi; (to die) occidēre; (to abate) decrescēre; (violently) corruēre; **to — apart** dilabi; **to — at** accidēre ad (with acc); **to — back** recidēre; (to retreat) pedem referre; **to — down** decidēre; concidēre; **to — forwards** procidēre, prolabi; **to — foul of** incurrēre; **to — in(to)** incidēre; **to — in with** (to meet) incidēre; (to agree) congruēre; **to — in love with** amare, adamare; **to — off** (fig) in deterius mutari; **to — out with** (to have a disagreement with) dissedēre; dissentire ab (with abl); **to — short of** non contingēre; **to — sick** in morbum incidēre; **to — to** (of inheritances, etc.) obvenire (with dat); **to — under** succumbēre; (to be reckoned) pertinēre; (to become subjected to) pati; **to — upon** incidēre ad (with acc); (to assail) incidēre in (with acc), ingruēre in (with acc)

fallacious adj fallax, captiosus; **—ly** fallaciter

fallacy s captio f

fallible adj errori obnoxius

fallow adj (of land) novalis; **to lie —** cessare

false adj falsus, fictus; **—ly** falso

falsehood s mendacium n

falsify vt supponēre, corrumpēre; (documents) vitiare, interlinēre

falter vi (to stammer) haesitare; (to totter) titubare

fame s fama f, nomen n

famed adj clarus, illustris

familiar adj familiaris, notus; intimus; —ly familiariter

familiarity s familiaritas, consuetudo f, us·us ·ūs m

familiarize vt assuefacĕre

family s familia, dom·us ·ūs, gens f, genus n

family adj familiaris; (of home) domesticus; (relating to race) gentilicus

famine s fames f

famished adj famelicus; fame confectus

famous adj clarus, celeber, inclitus; —ly praeclare, insigniter

fan s flabellum n; (admirer) fautor m; (winnowing) vannus f

fan vt ventilare; (fire) accendĕre; (fig) excitare, inflammare

fanatic adj fanaticus; —ly fanatice

fanaticism s furor religiosus m

fancied adj opinatus

fanciful adj (capricious) inconstans, levis; (imagined) commenticius

fancy s opinio, imaginatio f; (caprice) libido f; (liking) prolubium n; (faculty) phantasia f

fancy vt imaginari

fang s dens m

fantastic adj vanus; monstruosus

far adj longinquus, remotus

far adv procul, longe; as — as quantum, quatenus; tenus (with abl) by — longe, multo; — and near longe lateque; — be it from me to say equidem dicĕre nolim; — off procul; so — hactenus; thus — hactenus

farce s mimus m

farcical adj mimicus; —ly mimice

fare s (food) cibus, vict·us ·ūs m; (money) vectura f, portorium n

fare vi agĕre, se habēre

farewell interj vale!; salve!

farm s fundus m, praedium n

farm vt (to till) arare, colĕre; (taxes) redimĕre; to — out locare

farmer s agricola, colonus m; (of revenues) publicanus m

farming s agricultura f; res rustica f

farsighted adj providus

farther adj ulterior

farther adv longius, ulterius, ultra

farthermost adj remotissimus, ultimus

farthest adj ultimus, extremus

fasces n fasces m pl

fascinate vt fascinare

fascination s fascinatio f, fascinum n

fashion s (form) forma, figura f; (manner) mos, modus, rit·us ·ūs m; (custom) consuetudo f, us·us ·ūs m

fashion vt formare, fabricare, effingĕre

fashionable adj elegans, concinnus; it is — in usu est

fashionably adv ad morem; eleganter

fast adj (swift) celer; (firm) firmus, stabilis; (tight) astrictus; (shut) occlusus

fast adv celeriter; firmiter

fast s jejunium n

fast vi jejunare, cibo abstinēre

fasten vt affigĕre, astringĕre; to — down defigĕre; to — to annectĕre, impingĕre; to — together configĕre, colligare; vi to — upon arripĕre

fastening s colligatio f, vinculum n

fastidious adj fastidiosus, delicatus, elegans, morosus; —ly fastidiose, morose

fasting s jejunium n, abstinentia f

fat adj pinguis, obsesus; (productive) fertilis

fat s adeps m & f, lardum n

fatal adj fatalis; exitialis, funebris; —ly fataliter; funeste

fatality s fatum n; (misfortune) infortunium n

fate s fatum n, sors f

fated adj fatalis

Fates s Parcae f pl

father s pater m; — of the family paterfamilias m

fatherhood s paternitas f

father-in-law s socer m

fatherless adj orbus

fatherly adj paternus, patrius

fathom s ulna f

fathom vt exputare

fathomless adj profundissimus

fatigue s (de)fatigatio, lassitudo f

fatigue vt (de)fatigare, delassare

fatigued adj (de)fatigatus, (de)fessus

fatten vt saginare, farcire; vi pinguescĕre

fattening s saginatio f

fatty adj pinguis

fatuous adj fatuus, insulsus

fault s culpa f, delictum, vitium n, error m; (in writing) mendum n; to find — with vituperare, carpĕre, incusare

faultless adj integer, perfectus; (corrected) emendatus

faulty adj vitiosus; mendosus

faun s faunus m

favor s favor m, gratia f; (goodwill) benevolentia f; (good turn) beneficium n; (present) munus n

favor vt favēre (with dat), secundare

favorable adj prosperus, secundus; commodus, idoneus; benignus, propitius

favorably adv fauste, feliciter, benigne; opportune

favorite adj dilectus, gratus

favorite s deliciae f pl

favoritism s indulgentia f; iniquitas f

fawn s hinnuleus m

fawn vi to — on or upon adulari

fawning adj blandus, adulatorius; —ly blande, adulatorie

fawning s adulatio f

fear s timor, met·us ·ūs m, formido f

fear vt & vi timēre, metuĕre, verēri

fearful *adj* timidus, pavidus; *(terrible)* dirus, terribilis; **—ly** timide
fearless *adj* impavidus, intrepidus; **—ly** impavide, intrepide
feasibility *s* possibilitas *f*
feasible *adj* efficiendus, possibilis
feast *s* (*banquet*) convivium *n*, epulae *f pl*; (*holy day*) dies festus *m*
feast *vt* pascĕre; *vi* epulari, convivari
feat *s* facinus, factum *n*
feather *s* penna *f*; (*downy*) pluma *f*
feather *vt* to **— one's nest** opes accumulare
feathered *adj* pennatus; plumosus
feathery *adj* plumeus, plumosus
feature *s* lineamentum *n*; (*fig*) proprietas *f*, proprium *n*
February *s* (mensis) Februarius *m*
federal *adj* foederatus; rei publicae (*genit*)
federalize *vt* confoederare
federation *s* confoederatio *f*
fee *s* merces *f*
feeble *adj* infirmus, debilis; **to grow — languescĕre**
feebly *adv* infirme, languide
feed *vt* (*animals*) pascĕre; (*to nourish*) alĕre; (*fig*) (*of streams, etc.*) servire (*with dat*); *vi* pasci; **to — on** vesci (*with abl*)
feed *s* pabulum *n*
feel *vt* sentire; (*with hand*) tangĕre, tractare; **to — pain** dolore affici; **to — pity for** misereri (*with genit*); *vi* to **— happy** gaudēre; **to — sad** maestus esse
feel *s* tact·us -ūs *m*
feeling *s* (*touch*) tact·us -ūs *m*; (*sensibility*) sens·us -ūs *m*; (*emotion*) affect·us -ūs *m*; (*taste*) judicium *n*; (*pity*) miseratio *f*
feign *vt* fingĕre, dissimulare, mentiri
feint *s* simulatio *f*
felicitation *s* congratulatio *f*
felicitous *adj* felix; **—ly** feliciter
felicity *s* felicitas *f*
feline *adj* felin(e)us
fell *adj* atrox, saevus, crudelis
fell *vt* (*trees*) caedĕre; (*person*) sternĕre
fellow *s* socius, aequalis *m*
felon *s* scelestus, sceleratus *m*
felonious *adj* scelestus, sceleratus
felony *s* scelus *n*
felt *s* coacta *n pl*
female *adj* muliebris
female *s* femina *f*
feminine *adj* muliebris, femineus; (*gram*) femininus
fence *s* saepes *f*, saepimentum *n*
fence *vt* saepire; **to — off** intersaepire; *vi* batuĕre
fencing *s* ludus gladiatorius *m*
fend *vt* to **— off** arcēre; *vi* to **— for oneself** sibi providēre, sibi consulĕre
ferment *s* fermentum *n*; (*fig*) aest·us -ūs *m*
ferment *vt* fermentare; excitare; *vi* fermentari; (*fig*) fervēre
fermentation *s* fermentatio *f*
fern *s* filix *f*

ferocious *adj* ferox, truculentus, saevus, atrox; **—ly** truculente
ferocity *s* ferocitas, saevitia *f*
ferret *vt* to **— out** eruĕre
ferry *s* traject·us -ūs *m*
ferry *vt* trajicĕre, transvehĕre
ferryboat *s* scapha, cymba *f*
ferryman *s* portitor *m*
fertile *adj* fertilis, fecundus
fertility *s* fertilitas, ubertas *f*
fertilize *vt* fecundare
fervent *adj* fervidus, ardens; **—ly** ardenter, vehementer
fervid *adj* fervidus; **—ly** fervide
fervor *s* fervor, ardor *m*
fester *vi* suppurare, ulcerari
festival *s* dies festus *m*, sollemne *n*
festive *adj* festus
festivity *s* sollemnia *n pl*; (*gaiety*) festivitas *f*
fetch *vt* adducĕre, afferre, arcessĕre
fetid *adj* foetidus, graveolens
feud *s* simultas, inimicitia, lis *f*
fever *s* febris *f*; **to have a — febrire**
feverish *adj* febriculosus
few *adj* pauci; **a — aliquot; in a — words** paucis, breviter
fiasco *s* calamitas *f*
fiber *s* fibra *f*
fibrous *adj* fibratus
fickle *adj* inconstans, mobilis, instabilis
fiction *s* fictio *f*, commentum *n*; fabula *f*
fictitious *adj* fictus, commenticius; **—ly** ficte
fiddle *s* fides *f*
fiddle *vi* fide ludĕre
fiddler *s* fidicen *m*
fidelity *s* fidelitas, constantia *f*
fidget *vi* trepidare
fidgety *adj* inquietus
field *s* ager *m*; (*plowed*) arvum *n*; (*mil*) acies *f*, campus *m*; (*grassy*) pratum *n*; (*of grain*) seges *f*; (*sphere*) area *f*, locus, campus *m*
fieldpiece *s* tormentum *n*
fiend *s* inimicus *m*; diabolus *m*
fiendish *adj* diabolicus
fierce *adj* atrox, saevus, vehemens; **—ly** atrociter, saeve, vehementer
fierceness *s* atrocitas, saevitia, ferocitas *f*
fiery *adj* igneus; (*fig*) ardens, fervidus
fife *s* tibia *f*
fifteen *adj* quindecim; **— times** quindecies
fifteenth *adj* quintus decimus
fifth *adj* quintus; **for the — time** quintum, quinto
fifth *s* quinta pars *f*
fiftieth *adj* quinquagesimus
fifty *adj* quinquaginta
fig *s* ficus *f*
fight *s* pugna *f*, proelium *n*; (*struggle*) contentio, luctatio *f*
fight *vt* pugnare cum (*with abl*); **to — it out** decernĕre, depugnare; *vi* pugnare, dimicare; (*in battle*) proeliari; (*with sword*) digladiari; **to — hand to hand** cominus pugnare

figment s commentum n

figurative adj translatus, assumptus; —**ly** per translationem, tropice

figure s figura, forma, imago f; (of speech) tropus m, translatio f; (in art) signum n

figure vt figurare, formare; putare, opinari

figured adj sigillatus

filament s filum n, fibra f

filbert s nux avellana f

file s (tool) lima f; (for papers) scapus m; (row) ordo m, agmen n

file vt limare; (papers) in scapo condēre; vi to — off (mil) decurrēre

filial adj pius

filigree s diatreta n pl

filings s scobis f

fill vt complēre, implēre; (office) fungi (with abl); to — out implēre; to — up explēre, complēre, supplēre

fill s satietas f

fillip s talitrum n

filly s equula f

film s membranula f

filmy adj membranaceus; (fig) caliginosus

filter s colum n

filter vt percolare; vi percolari

filtering s percolatio f

filth s sordes, colluvies f, squalor m

filthiness s foeditas f, squalor m; (fig) obscenitas f

filthy adj sordidus, spurcus; (fig) obscenus

filtration s percolatio f

fin s pinna f

final adj ultimus, postremus, extremus; —**ly** denique, tandem; postremo

finance s (private) res familiaris f; (public) aerarium n, ratio aeraria f, vectigalia n pl

financial adj aerarius

find vt invenire, reperire; (to hit upon) offendēre; to — out comperire, cognoscēre

fine adj (thin) subtilis, tenuis; (of gold) purus; (handsome) bellus, elegans; (of weather) serenus; —**ly** subtiliter

fine s mul(c)ta f, damnum n

fine vt mul(c)tare

finery s ornat·us -ūs m

finesse s astutia f, argutiae f pl

finger s digitus m; (of glove) digitale n

finger vt tractare

finish vt conficēre, perficēre; (to put an end to) terminare; to — off conficēre; peragēre; vi desinēre

finish s finis m; (in art) perfectio f

finite adj finitus, circumscriptus

fire s ignis m; (conflagration) incendium n; (of artillery) conject·us -ūs m; (fig) fervor, ardor, impet·us -ūs m; by — and sword ferro ignique; to be on — flagrare; to catch — flammam concipēre; to set on — incendēre

fire vt accendēre, incendēre; (fig) in-

flammare; (missile) jaculari; (to dismiss) dimittēre

firefly s elater noctilucus m

fireplace s focus, caminus m

fireproof adj ignibus impervius

fireside s focus m

firewood s lignum n

firm adj firmus, solidus; constans; to be — perseverare; to stand — perstare; —**ly** firme, firmiter; solide; constanter

firm s societas f

firmament s firmamentum n

firmness s firmitas, constantia f

first adj primus; (of two) prior

first adv primum; at — primo; — of all imprimis

firstborn adj primogenitus

firstfruits s primitiae f pl

fiscal adj aerarius, fiscalis

fish s piscis m

fish vi piscari; (fig) expiscari

fisherman s piscator m

fishing s piscat·us -ūs m, piscatio f

fish market s forum piscarium n

fish pond s piscina f

fishy adj piscosus

fissure s fissura, rima f

fist s pugnus m

fit s (of anger, etc.) impet·us -ūs m; (med) access·us -ūs m, convulsio f; (whim) libido f; by —s and starts carptim

fit adj aptus, idoneus; habilis; (becoming) decens; (ready) paratus

fit vt accommodare; (to apply) applicare; (to furnish) instruēre; vi (fig) convenire

fitful adj mutabilis, inconstans

fitness s convenientia f; (of persons) habilitas f

fitting adj decens, idoneus; it is — convenit, decet

five adj quinque; — times quinquies

fix vt (to repair) reficēre; resarcire; (to fasten) figēre, firmare; (the eyes) intendēre; (time) dicēre; vi to — upon inhaerēre (with dat)

fixed adj firmus, fixus; certus; — on (intent upon) intentus (with dat)

fixture s affixum n

fizz vi sibilare

flabbiness s mollitia f

flabby adj flaccidus, flaccus; (drooping) marcidus

flaccid adj flaccidus

flag s vexillum n

flagrant adj impudens, apparens, nefarius

flail s pertica, tribula f

flake s squama f; (of snow) nix f

flaky adj squameus

flame s flamma f

flame vi flammare, flagrare; to — up scintillare; (fig) exardescēre

flank s (of animal) ilia n pl; (mil) lat·us n; on the — a latere

flank vt tegēre latus (with genit)

flap s (of dress) lacinia f

flap vt plaudēre (with abl); vi (to hang loosely) fluitare

flare s flamma f, fulgor m

flare vi flagrare, exardescēre

flash *s* fulgor *m*; (*of fire*) coruscatio *f*; (*of lightning*) fulmen *n*; — **of wit** sales *m pl*

flash *vi* fulgēre, coruscare, micare

flask *s* ampulla, laguncula *f*

flat *adj* (*level*) planus, aequus; (*not mountainous*) campester; (*on back*) supinus; (*on face*) pronus; (*insipid*) vapidus; (*fig*) frigidus, insulsus; **to fall** — (*fig*) frigēre

flatness *s* planities *f*

flatten *vt* complanare, planum reddēre

flatter *vt* adulari (*with dat*), blandiri (*with dat*), assentari (*with dat*)

flatterer *s* adulator, assentator *m*

flattering *adj* adulans, blandus, adulatorius

flattery *s* adulatio *f*, blanditiae *f pl*

flaunt *vt* jactare; *vi* tumēre, gloriari

flaunting *adj* lautus, gloriosus

flaunting *s* jactatio *f*

flavor *s* sapor, gustat·us -ūs *m*

flavor *vt* imbuēre, condire

flaw *s* (*defect*) vitium *n*; (*chink*) rimula *f*

flawless *adj* emendatus

flax *s* linum *n*

flaxen *adj* lineus

flay *vt* deglubare

flea *s* pulex *m*

fleck *s* macula *f*

fledged *adj* plumatus

flee *vi* fugēre; **to** — **away** aufugēre; **to** — **back** refugēre; **to** — **to** confugēre **ad** *or* **in** (*with acc*)

fleece *s* vellus *n*

fleece *vt* tondēre; (*fig*) spoliare

fleecy *adj* laniger

fleet *s* classis *f*

fleet *adj* celer; (*winged*) volucer; (*fig*) fugax

fleeting *adj* fugax; (*flowing*) fluxus

flesh *s* caro *f*; **in the** — vivus

fleshy *adj* carnosus

flexibility *s* flexibilitas *f*; (*fig*) mollitia *f*

flexible *adj* flexibilis, lentus; (*fig*) exorabilis

flicker *vi* coruscare

flickering *adj* tremulus

flight *s* (*flying*) volat·us -ūs *m*; (*escape*) fuga *f*, effugium *n*; (*covey*) grex *m*; (*of stairs*) scala *f*; **to put to** — fugare; **to take to** — aufugēre, terga vertēre

flighty *adj* levis

flimsy *adj* nimis subtilis, praetenuis; (*fig*) frivolus

flinch *vi* retrocedēre, tergiversari; (*to start*) absilire

fling *vt* jacēre, conjicēre; **to** — **away** abjicēre; **to** — **down** dejicēre; **to** — **off** rejicēre; **to** — **open** vehementer aperire

fling *s* jact·us -ūs *m*

flint *s* silex *m* & *f*

flinty *adj* siliceus

flippancy *s* petulantia *f*

flippant *adj* petulans; temere loquens; **—ly** temere ac leviter

flirt *s* lupus *m*, lupa *f*

flirt *vi* ludēre, lascivire

flirtation *s* amores *m pl*

flit *vi* volitare

float *s* (*raft*) rates *f*; (*on fishing line*) cortex *m*

float *vt* (*to launch*) demittēre; *vi* fluitare, (in)natare; (*in air*) volitare

flock *s* grex *m*; **in** —**s** gregatim

flock *vi* concurrēre, convenire, coire

floe *s* fragmentum glaciei *n*

flog *vt* verberare

flogging *s* verberatio *f*, verbera *n pl*

flood *s* (*deluge*) diluvies *f*; (*of river*) torrens *m*; (*tide*) access·us -ūs *m*; (*fig*) flumen *n*

floor *s* (*story of building*) tabulatum *n*; (*on the ground*) solum; (*paved*) pavimentum *n*

floor *vt* (*to throw down*) sternēre

flooring *s* contabulatio *f*

floral *adj* floreus

florid *adj* floridus

flotilla *s* classicula *f*

flounce *s* fimbria *f*

flounder *vi* volutari; (*in speech*) haesitare

flour *s* farina *f*; (*finest*) pollen *m*

flourish *vt* vibrare; (*to sound*) canēre; *vi* florēre, virēre; (*mus*) praeludēre

flourish *s* ornamentum *n*; (*of style*) calamistri *m pl*; (*mus*) praelusio *f*; (*of trumpet*) cant·us -ūs *m*

flout *vt* deridēre, contumeliis afficēre, aspernari

flow *vi* fluēre; (*of tide*) affluēre, accedēre

flow *s* fluxio *f*, laps·us -ūs *m*; (*of tide*) access·us -ūs *m*

flower *s* flos *m*; (*fig*) (*the best*) flos *m*; (*of army*) robur *n*; (*of age*) adulescentia *f*

flower *vi* florescēre

flowery *adj* floreus; floridus

fluctuate *vi* fluctuari; (*fig*) jactare

fluctuation *s* fluctuatio *f*; (*fig*) mutatio *f*

flue *s* cuniculus fornacis *m*

fluency *s* copia verborum, volubilitas linguae *f*

fluent *adj* volubilis; (*eloquent*) disertus; **—ly** volubiliter

fluid *adj* fluidus, liquidus

fluid *s* fluidum *n*, fluor *m*

fluke *s* (*of anchor*) dens *m*; (*luck*) fortuitum *n*

flurry *s* commotio *f*, tumult·us -ūs *m*

flurry *vt* perturbare, inquietare

flush *s* rubor *m*

flush *vi* erubescēre

fluster *vt* turbare, inquietare

flute *s* tibia *f*; (*in architecture*) stria *f*

flutist *s* tibicen *m*

flutter *s* volitatio *f*, tremor *m*; (*fig*) trepidatio *f*

flutter *vi* (*of the heart*) palpitare; (*of bird*) volitare; (*with alarm*) trepidare

flux *s* flux·us -ūs *m*; **to be in a state of** — fluēre

fly *s* musca *f*

fly *vi* volare; (*to flee*) fugēre; **to** — **apart** dissilire; **to** — **off** avolare;

to — open dissilire; to — out provolare; to — up subvolare

flying *adj* volatilis, volucer

foal *s* pullus *m*; (*of asses*) asellus *m*; (*of horses*) equulus *m*

foal *vi* parĕre

foam *s* spuma *f*

foam *vi* spumare; (*to boil*) exaestuare

foamy *adj* spumans; spumeus, spumosus

focus *vt* (*the mind*) intendĕre

fodder *s* pabulum *n*

fodder *vt* pabulum praebēre (*with dat*)

foe *s* (*public*) hostis *m*; (*private*) inimicus *m*

fog *s* caligo, nebula *f*

foggy *adj* caliginosus, nebulosus

foible *s* vitium *n*, error *m*

foil *s* (*for fencing*) rudis *f*; (*leaf of metal*) lamina *f*; (*very thin*) bractea *f*; (*contrast*) repulsa *f*

foil *vt* eludĕre; repellĕre

fold *s* sin·us -ūs *m*, plica *f*; (*wrinkle*) ruga *f*; (*for sheep*) ovile *n*; (*for cattle*) stabulum *n*

fold *vt* plicare, complicare

foliage *s* frons *f*, folia *n pl*

folio *s* liber maximae formae *m*

folk *s* homines *m pl*

follow *vt* sequi; (*close*) instare (*with dat*), assectari; (*a calling*) facĕre; (*instructions*) parēre (*with dat*); (*road*) pergĕre; (*to understand*) intellegĕre; to — out exsequi, prosequi; to — up subsequi

follower *s* sectator *m*; (*of teacher*) auditor *m*

following *adj* sequens; posterus, proximus

folly *s* stultitia, insipientia *f*

foment *vt* fovēre

fond *adj* amans, studiosus; ineptus; to be — of amare; —ly amanter; (*foolishly*) inepte

fondle *vt* mulcēre, fovēre

fondness *s* caritas *f*, studium *n*

food *s* cibus *m*

fool *s* stultus, fatuus *m*; to make a — of ludificare; to play the — ineptire

fool *vt* ludificari

foolhardy *adj* temerarius

foolish *adj* stultus, fatuus, ineptus, stolidus; —ly stulte, inepte

foot *s* pes *m*; (*of mountain*) radix *f*; (*of pillar*) basis *f*; on — pedester

football *s* pila pedalis *f*

footing *s* locus *m*; (*condition*) stat·us -ūs *m*

footprint *s* vestigium *n*

foot soldier *s* pedes *m*

footstool *s* scabellum, scamnum *n*

fop *s* bellus homo *m*

foppish *adj* nitidus, delicatus

for *prep* (*extent of time or space*) *render by acc*; (*price*) *render by genit or abl*; (*on behalf of*) pro (*with abl*); (*cause*) causā (*with genit*), ob (*with acc*), propter (*with acc*); (*after negatives*) prae (*with abl*); (*toward*) erga (*with acc*)

for *conj* nam; enim

forage *s* pabulum *n*

forage *vi* pabulari, frumentari

foray *s* incursio *f*

forbear *vi* parcĕre (*with dat*), desistĕre

forbearance *s* patientia, indulgentia *f*

forbid *vt* vetare, prohibēre, interdicĕre

forbidding *adj* insuavis, odiosus

force *s* vis *f*; (*law*) man·us -ūs *f*; (*mil*) copiae *f pl*, impet·us -ūs *m*; in — validus

force *vt* cogĕre, impellĕre; (*door, etc.*) rumpĕre; to — down detrudĕre; to — out extrudĕre, extorquēre

forced *adj* (*unnatural*) arcessitus, quaesitus

forced march *s* magnum *or* maximum iter *n*

forceps *s* forceps *m* & *f*

forcible *adj* per vim factus; (*of force*) validus; (*violent*) vehemens; (*weighty*) gravis

forcibly *adv* per vim, vi; violenter; graviter

ford *s* vadum *n*

ford *vt* vado transire

fore *adj* anterior, prior

forearm *s* bracchium *n*

forearm *vt* praemunire; to be forearmed praecavēre

forebode *vt* (*to foretell*) portendĕre; (*to be prescient of*) praesagire

foreboding *s* portentum, praesagium *n*; (*feeling*) praesensio *f*

foreboding *adj* praesagus

forecast *vt* providēre, prospicĕre; praedicĕre

forecast *s* praedictio *f*

forecastle *s* prora *f*

foredoom *vt* praedestinare

forefather *s* atavus *m*; —s majores *m pl*

forefinger *s* digitus index *m*

forego *vt* abdicare, dimittĕre

foregoing *adj* prior, proximus

forehead *s* frons *f*

foreign *adj* externus, alienus, peregrinus

foreigner *s* peregrinus, advena *m*

foreknowledge *s* providentia *f*

foreman *s* procurator, villicus *m*

foremost *adj* primus, princeps

forenoon *s* antemeridianum tempus *n*; in the — ante meridiem

forensic *adj* forensis

fore part *s* prior pars *f*

forerunner *s* praenuntius, antecursor *m*

foresee *vt* providēre, praevidēre, prospicĕre

foreseeing *adj* providus

foresight *s* providentia, prudentia *f*; (*precaution*) provisio *f*

forest *adj* silvestris

forest *s* silva *f*

forestall *vt* occupare, anticipare

foretell *vt* praedicĕre, vaticinari

forethought *s* providentia *f*

forewarn *vt* praemonēre

forewarning *s* praemonit·us -ūs *m*

forfeit *s* multa, poena *f*, damnum *n*

forfeit vt mul(c)tari (with abl), amittĕre, perdĕre

forfeiture s damnum n, amissio f

forge vt fabricari, excudĕre; (document) subjicĕre; (signature) imitari; **to — money** adulterinos nummos cudĕre

forge s furnus fabrilis m

forged adj falsus, adulterinus

forger s fabricator m; (of writings) falsarius m; (of money) qui adulterinos nummos cudit

forgery s falsum n

forget vt oblivisci (with genit)

forgetful adj immemor, obliviosus

forgetfulness s oblivio f

forgive vt ignoscĕre (with dat), veniam dare (with dat); condonare

forgiveness s venia f

forgiving adj clemens

fork s furca f; (of roads) bivium n

forked adj bifurcus, bicornis

forlorn adj destitutus, derelictus

form s forma, figura f; **in due — rite**

form vt formare, fingĕre; (to produce) efficĕre

formal adj justus; nimis accuratus; **—ly** frigide ac nimis accurate

formality s rit·us ·ūs m; **with due — rite**

formation s conformatio, forma, figura f; **in — (mil)** instructus

former adj prior; (immediately preceding) superior; antiquus, priscus; **the —** ille; **—ly** antehac, olim, quondam

formidable adj formidabilis

formidably adv formidolose

formless adj informis, rudis

formula s formula f, exemplar n

forsake vt deserĕre, derelinquĕre

forswear vt abjurare, repudiare

fort s castellum n

forth adv foras; (of time) inde; **and so —** et cetera

forthwith adv protinus, statim, extemplo

fortieth adj quadragesimus

fortification s munitio f, munimentum n

fortify vt munire

fortitude s fortitudo f

fortress s arx f, castellum n

fortuitous adj fortuitus; **—ly** fortuito

fortunate adj fortunatus, felix, prosperus; **—ly** feliciter

fortune s fortuna, felicitas f; (estate) opes f pl, res f, divitiae f pl; **to tell —s** hariolari

fortune-teller s fatidicus, sortilegus, astrologus m

forty adj quadraginta

forum s forum n

forward adv porro, prorsus, prorsum

forward adj (person) audax, protervus; anterior

forward vt (letter) perferre; (cause) adjuvare, promovēre

foster vt alĕre, fovēre, nutrire

foster brother s collacteus m

foster child s alumnus m, alumna f

foster father s altor, nutritor, educator m

foster mother s altrix, nutrix, educatrix f

foul adj (dirty) foedus, lutulentus, squalidus; (ugly) deformis; (of language) obscenus; (of weather) turbidus; **to fall — of** incurrĕre in (with acc), inruĕre in (with acc); **—ly** foede

foul vt foedare, inquinare

found vt condĕre, fundare, constituĕre, instituĕre

foundation s fundamentum n, substructio f

founder s conditor, fundator, auctor m

founder vi titubare, submergi

foundling s expositicius m, expositicia f

fountain s fons m

fountainhead s caput fontis n

four adj quattuor; **— each** quaterni; **— times** quater; **— years** quadriennium n; **on all —s** repens

fourfold adj quadruplex, quadruplus

fourscore adj octoginta

fourteen adj quattuordecim

fourteenth adj quartus decimus

fourth adj quartus; **—ly** quarto

fourth s quadrans n, quarta pars f; **three —s** tres partes f pl

fowl s avis, volucris f; (domestic) gallina f

fox s vulpes f; **an old — (fig)** veterator m

fraction s pars exigua f

fracture s fractura f

fracture vt frangĕre

fragile adj fragilis; (fig) caducus

fragility s fragilitas f

fragment s fragmentum n

fragrance s odor m

fragrant adj suaveolens, odorus; **—ly** suavi odore

frail adj fragilis; caducus, infirmus

frailty s fragilitas, debilitas f; (moral) error m

frame s (of buildings, etc.) compages f; (of body) figura f; (of bed) sponda f; (of mind) habit·us ·ūs m

frame vt fabricari; (to contrive) moliri; (a picture) in forma includĕre; (a document) componĕre

France s Gallia f

franchise s civitas f, suffragium n

frank adj candidus, sincerus, simplex; **—ly** candide, aperte

frankness s libertas, simplicitas, ingenuitas f

frantic adj amens, furiosus, furens; **—ally** furenter

fraternal adj fraternus; **—ly** fraterne

fraternity s fraternitas f; (association) sodalitas f

fratricide s (doer) fratricida m; (deed) fratris parricidium n

fraud s fraus f, dolus m; (person) dolus malus m

fraudulence s fraus f

fraudulent adj fraudulentus, dolosus; **—ly** fraudulenter, dolo malo

fraught adj plenus

fray s pugna f; (brawl) rixa f

freak s (whim) libido f; monstrum n

freckle s lentigo f

freckled adj lentiginosus

free adj liber; (disengaged) vacuus, otiosus; (generous) liberalis; (from duty) immunis; (unencumbered) expeditus; (in speech) liber, candidus; **—ly** libere; (of one's own accord) sponte, ultro; (frankly) aperte; (generously) large, copiose

free vt liberare; (slave) manumittĕre; (son) emancipare

freeborn adj ingenuus

freedman s libertus m

freedom s libertas f; (from duty) immunitas f

freehold s praedium liberum n

freeholder s dominus m

freeman s liber m

free will s voluntas f, liberum arbitrium n; **of one's own —** suā sponte, ultro, arbitrio suo

freeze vt congelare, glaciare; vi consistĕre, rigescĕre; **it is freezing** gelat

freezing adj gelidus

freight s onus n, vectura f

freight vt onerare

French adj Gallicus; **in — Gallice; the —** Galli m pl

Frenchman s Gallus m

frenzied adj furens, lymphatus

frenzy s furor m, insania f

frequency s crebritas, assiduitas f

frequent adj creber, frequens; **—ly** crebro, frequenter, saepe

frequent vt frequentare

frequenter s frequentator m

fresco s opus tectorium n

fresh adj (new) recens, novus; (cool) frigidulus; (not tired) integer; (forward) protervus; (green) viridis; **—ly** recenter

freshen vt recreare, renovare; vi (of wind) increbrescĕre

freshman s tiro m

freshman adj novicius

freshness s novitas, viriditas f

fret vi dolēre, angi

fretful adj morosus, stomachosus; **—ly** morose, stomachose

fretted adj laqueatus

friction s frictio f, attrit·us -ūs m

friend s amicus m, amica f, familiaris m & f; (of a thing) amator m

friendless adj amicorum inops, desertus

friendliness s benevolentia, comitas, affabilitas f

friendly adj amicus, benevolus, comis; **in a — manner** amice

friendship s amicitia f

frieze s zoophorus m

fright s pavor, terror m

frighten vt (per)terrēre; **to — away** absterrēre

frightful adj terribilis, terrificus; **—ly** foede

frigid adj frigidus; **—ly** frigide

frigidity s frigiditas f

frills s segmenta n pl; (rhet) calamistri m pl

fringe s fimbria f, cirrus m; (fig) limbus m

frisk vt scrutari; vi lascivire, exsilire

fritter vt **to — away** conterĕre, comminuĕre, dissipare

frivolity s levitas f, nugae f pl

frivolous adj levis, frivolus, inanis; **—ly** inaniter

fro adv **to and — huc illuc, ultro citroque**

frock s palla, stola f

frog s rana f

frolic s lascivia f, ludus m

frolic vi exsultare, hilarescĕre

from prep a or ab (with abl); de (with abl); e or ex (with abl); (cause) ob (with acc); **— above** desuper; **— abroad** peregre; **— day to day** de die in diem; **— time to time** interdum, passim; **— within** intus; **— without** extrinsecus

front s frons f; (mil) acies f, primum agmen n; (fig) impudentia f; **in — a fronte, adversus; in — of** pro (with abl)

front adj prior

frontier s limes m, confinia n pl

frost s gelu n, pruina f

frostbitten adj praeustus, adustus

frosty adj gelidus, glacialis

froth s spuma f

froth vi spumare, spumas agĕre

frothy adj spumeus, spumosus

frown s contractio frontis f

frown vi frontem contrahĕre or adducĕre

frozen adj conglaciatus, gelatus, gelu rigens

frugal adj parcus, frugi (indecl); **—ly** frugaliter, parce

frugality s parsimonia, frugalitas f

fruit s fruct·us -ūs m, frux f; (of tree) mala n pl; **—s of the earth** fruges f pl

fruitful adj fructuosus, fecundus, fertilis; **—ly** fecunde, feraciter

fruitfulness s fecunditas, fertilitas, ubertas f

fruitless adj sterilis; (fig) irritus; **—ly** frustra

fruit tree s pomus f

frustrate vt frustrari; (to baffle) decipĕre

frustration s frustratio f

fry s (dish of things fried) frixa f

fry vt frigĕre

frying pan s sartago f

fuel s fomes m, materia f

fugitive adj fugitivus

fugitive s profugus, transfuga, fugitivus m; (from abroad) extorris m

fulcrum s (of a lever) pressio f

fulfil vt explēre, exsequi, perficĕre

fulfilment s executio, peractio, perfectio f

full adj plenus; (filled up) expletus; (entire) integer, solidus; (satiated) satur; (of dress) fusus; **—ly** plene, funditus, penitus

full moon s plenilunium n

fumble vi haesitare
fume s fumus, vapor, halit·us -ūs m
fume vi irasci
fumigate vt fumigare, suffire
fumigation s suffit·us -ūs m
fun s jocus m, ludibrium n
function s munus, officium n
function vi munus implēre
functionary s magistrat·us -ūs m
fund s copia f, pecuniae f pl
fundamental adj fundamentalis, primus; —**ly** penitus, funditus
funeral s funus n, exsequiae f pl
funeral adj funebris
funereal adj funereus, lugubris
fungus s fungus m
funnel s infundibulum n
funny adj ridiculus, jocularis
fur s villi m pl, pellis m
furious adj furiosus, furens; —**ly** furiose, furenter
furl vt complicare; (sail) legēre
furlough s commeat·us -ūs m; on — in commeatu
furnace s fornax f
furnish vt suppeditare, ministrare, ornare, exornare, instruēre

furniture s supellex f
furrow s sulcus m
furry adj pelle insutus
further adj ulterior
further adv ultra, longius, ulterius
further vt promovēre, provehēre; (to aid) adjuvare
furtherance s progress·us -ūs m
furthermore adv insuper, porro, praeterea
furthest adj ultimus, extremus
furthest adv longissime
furtive adj furtivus; —**ly** furtim, furtive
fury s furor m
fuse vt fundēre; vi coalescēre
fusion s fusura f
fuss s strepit·us -ūs, tumult·us -ūs m
fuss vi sollicitari
fussy adj fastidiosus, importunus
futile adj futilis, inanis
futility s futilitas f
future adj futurus, posterus
future s futura n pl, posterum tempus n; in the — posthac
futurity s posteritas f

G

gab s garrulitas f
gab vi garrire
gable s fastigium n
gadfly s tabanus, oestrus m
gag s jocus m
gag vt os obstruēre (with dat)
gaiety s hilaritas f; nitor, splendor m
gaily adv hilare, festive
gain s quaest·us -ūs m, lucrum n
gain vt consequi, acquirēre, capēre; (profit) lucrari; (victory) reportare; (case) vincēre; to — possession of potiri (with abl)
gainful adj quaestuosus, lucrosus
gainsay vt contradicēre (with dat)
gait s incess·us -ūs m
gala s dies festus m
galaxy s orbis lacteus m
gale s ventus m
gall s fel n, bilis f
gall vt urēre
gallant adj fortis, animosus; (to ladies) officiosus; —**ly** fortiter
gallant s amator m
gallantry s virtus, fortitudo f; (to ladies) urbanitas f
galleon s navis oneraria f
gallery s portic·us -ūs f; (open) peristylium n; (for pictures) pinacotheca f
galley s navis longa, triremis f; (kitchen) culina f
Gallic adj Gallicus, Gallicanus
galling adj mordax
gallon s congius m
gallop s citatissimus curs·us -ūs m; at a — citato equo, admisso equo
gallop vi quadrupedare

gallows s patibulum n
gamble vt to — away ludēre, amittēre; vi aleā ludēre
gambler s aleator, lusor m
gambling s alea f
gambol s salt·us -ūs m
gambol vi lascivire, ludēre
game s ludus m; (with dice) alea f; (quarry) praeda f, ferae f pl; to make — of ludificari
gander s anser m
gang s grex m, caterva f
gangster s grassator m
gangway s forus m
gap s apertura, fissura, lacuna f, hiat·us -ūs m
gape vi hiare, dehiscēre
gaping adj hians, hiulcus, oscitans; (fig) stupidus
garb s vestit·us -ūs, habit·us -ūs m
garbage s quisquiliae f pl
garble vt vitiare, corrumpēre
garden s hortus m
gardener s hortulanus, olitor m
gardening s hortorum cult·us -ūs m
gargle vi gargarizare
gargling s gargarizatio f
garland s sertum n, corona f
garlic s alium n
garment s vestimentum n, vestit·us -ūs m
garner s horreum n
garnish vt decorare, ornare
garret s cenaculum n
garrison s praesidium n
garrison vt praesidio munire, praesidium collocare in (with abl), praesidium imponēre (with dat)

garrulity *s* garrulitas *f*

garrulous *adj* garrulus, loquax

garter *s* periscelis *f*

gas *s* spiritūs naturales *m pl*

gash *s* patens plaga *f*

gash *vt* caesim ferire

gasp *s* anhelit·us -ūs, singult·us -ūs *m*

gasp *vi* anhelare, singultare

gastric *adj* ad stomachum pertinens

gastronomy *s* gula *f*

gate *s* janua *f*, ostium *n*; (*of town*) porta *f*

gatekeeper *s* janitor *m*

gateway *s* porta *f*, postis *m*

gather *vt* (*to assemble*) congregare, colligĕre; (*fruit, etc.*) legĕre; (*to pluck*) decerpĕre, carpĕre; (*in logic*) concludĕre; (*to suspect*) suspicare; *vi* convenire, concurrĕre

gathering *s* convent·us -ūs *m*, congregatio *f*; collectio *f*

gaudily *adv* laute

gaudiness *s* lautitia *f*, ornat·us -ūs, nitor *m*

gaudy *adj* lautus, speciosus, splendidus

gauge *s* modulus *m*

gauge *vt* metiri

gaunt *adj* macer

gauntlet *s* manica *f*

gauze *s* coa *n. pl*

gawky *adj* ineptus, stolidus

gay *adj* laetus, hilaris, festivus

gaze *s* conspect·us -ūs *m*; (*fixed look*) obtut·us -ūs *m*

gaze *vi* intuēri; to — at intuēri, adspectare, contemplari

gazelle *s* dorcas *f*

gazette *s* acta diurna *n pl*

gazetteer *s* itinerarium *n*

gear *s* instrumenta *n pl*, apparat·us -ūs *m*

gelatin *s* glutinum *n*

gelding *s* (*horse*) canterius *m*

gem *s* gemma *f*

gender *s* genus *n*

genealogical *adj* genealogicus

genealogy *s* genealogia *f*

general *adj* generalis; vulgaris, publicus, universus; in — omnino; —ly plerumque, fere; generatim

general *s* dux, imperator *m*

generalize *vi* in summam loqui

generalship *s* duct·us -ūs *m*; (*skill*) consilium *n*

generate *vt* generare, gignĕre

generation *s* generatio *f*; (*age*) aetas *f*, saeculum *n*

generic *adj* generalis

generosity *s* liberalitas, largitas *f*

generous *adj* liberalis, largus; —ly large, liberaliter

genesis *s* origo *f*

genial *adj* comis, benignus; —ly comiter, benigne

geniality *s* comitas, benignitas *f*

genitals *s* genitalia *n pl*, veretrum *n*

genitive *s* genitivus *m*

genius *s* ingenium *n*, indoles *f*; vir ingeniosus *m*; of — ingeniosus

genteel *adj* elegans, urbanus; —ly eleganter

gentile *adj* gentilicus, gentilis

gentile *s* gentilis *m*

gentility *s* nobilitas, elegantia *f*

gentle *adj* lenis, mitis, clemens; (*gradual*) mollis; (*thing*) lenis

gentleman *s* vir honestus, homo liberalis *m*

gentleness *s* lenitas, clementia *f*; (*tameness*) mansuetudo *f*

gently *adv* leniter, clementer, placide; (*gradually*) sensim

gentry *s* optimates *m pl*

genuine *adj* sincerus, purus, verus; —ly sincere, vere

genus *s* genus *n*

geographer *s* geographus *m*

geographical *adj* geographicus

geography *s* geographia *f*

geological *adj* geologicus

geologist *s* geologus *m*

geology *s* geologia *f*

geometrical *adj* geometricus

geometry *s* geometria *f*

germ *s* germen *n*

German *adj* Germanus

germane *adj* affinis

Germanic *adj* Germanicus

Germany *s* Germania *f*

germinate *vi* germinare

germination *s* germinat·us -ūs *m*

gesticulate *vi* gestu agĕre, gestu uti

gesture *s* gest·us -ūs, mot·us -ūs *m*

get *vt* nancisci, adipisci, consequi, acquirĕre; (*by entreaty*) impetrare; to — back recuperare; to — down deprŏmĕre; to — hold of prehendĕre, occupare; to — out delēre, oblitterare; to — rid of amovēre, tollĕre; to — the better of superare; to — together colligĕre, cogĕre; congregare; *vi* (*to become*) fieri; (*to arrive at*) pervenire; to — abroad (*to spread*) palam fieri, emanare; to — along procedĕre; to — away aufugĕre; to — back revertĕre or reverti; to — down descendĕre; to — in pervenire; to — off aufugĕre, dimitti; to — on procedĕre, proficisci; (*to succeed*) bene succedĕre; to — out exire; (*e curru*) descendĕre; to — over transgredi; to — together congregari; to — up surgĕre; (*from sleep*) expergisci

ghastly *adj* luridus; (*shocking*) foedus

ghost *s* larva *f*, phantasma *n*; umbra *f*

ghostly *adj* spiritualis

giant *s* gigas *m*

gibberish *s* barbaricus sermo *m*

gibbet *s* furca *f*, patibulum *n*

gibe *s* sanna *f*

gibe *vt* illudĕre, subsannare

giblets *s* gigeria *n pl*, anseris trunculi *m pl*

giddiness *s* vertigo *f*

giddy *adj* vertiginosus; (*fig*) levis, inconsultus

gift *s* donum *n*; (*talent*) ingenium *n*

gifted *adj* (*endowed*) praeditus; ingeniosus

gig *s* (*carriage*) cisium *n*

gigantic *adj* ingens, immanis, praegrandis

giggle *vi* summissim cachinnare

gild *vt* inaurare

gilding *s* (*art*) auratura *f*; (*gilded work*) aurum inductum *n*

gill *s* branchia *f*

gilt *adj* auratus

gin *s* junipero infectus spirit·us ‑ūs *m*

ginger *s* zinziberi *n* (*indecl*)

gingerly *adv* pedetemptim

giraffe *s* camelopardalis *f*

gird *vt* cingēre; **to — oneself** cingi

girder *s* tignum *n*

girdle *s* cingulum *n*, zona *f*

girdle *vt* cingēre

girl *s* puella, virgo *f*

girlhood *s* puellaris aetas *f*

girlish *adj* puellaris, virginalis

girth *s* (*of horse*) cingula *f*; amplitudo *f*, ambit·us ‑ūs *m*

gist *s* cardo *m*

give *vt* dare, donare; (*to deliver*) tradēre; **to — away** donare; **to — back** reddēre; **to — forth** emittēre; **to — oneself up** to se addicēre (*with dat*); **to — out** edēre, emittēre; nuntiare, proclamare; distribuēre; **to — over** transferre; relinquere; **to — up** tradēre; (*to betray*) prodēre; (*to abandon*) dimittēre; *vi* **to — in** (*to yield*) cedēre; **to — way** (*mil*) pedem referre; (*to yield*) cedēre; (*to comply*) obsequi

giver *s* donator *m*

giving *s* datio, largitio *f*

glacial *adj* glacialis

glacier *s* moles conglaciata *f*

glad *adj* laetus, contentus; **to be — gaudēre; —ly** libenter

gladden *vt* laetificare

glade *s* salt·us ‑ūs *m*

gladiator *s* gladiator *m*

gladness *s* gaudium *n*, laetitia *f*

glamorous *adj* venustus, nitidus; **to be —** nitēre

glamour *s* venustas *f*, nitor *m*

glance *s* aspect·us ‑ūs *m*

glance *vi* aspicēre; **to — at** aspicēre; **to — off** stringēre

gland *s* glandula *f*

glare *s* fulgor *m*

glare *vi* fulgēre; torvis oculis aspicēre; **to — at** torvis oculis aspicēre *or* intuēri

glaring *adj* fulgens; manifestus

glass *s* vitrum *n*; (*for drinking*) calix vitreus *m*

glass *adj* vitreus

glassmaker *s* vitrarius *m*

glassware *s* vitrea *n pl*

glaze *vt* vitrum illinēre (*with dat*), polire

gleam *s* fulgor *m*, jubar *n*; (*fig*) aura *f*

gleam *vi* coruscare, micare, fulgēre

gleaming *adj* coruscus, renidens

glean *vt* colligēre, legēre

gleaning *s* spicilegium *n*

glee *s* laetitia, hilaritas *f*

gleeful *adj* laetus, hilaris; —ly laete, hilare

glen *s* vallis *f*

glib *adj* lubricus, volubilis; —ly volubiliter

glide *vi* labi

glimmer *s* lux dubia *f*; **— of hope** specula *f*

glimmer *vi* sublucēre

glimpse *s* aspect·us ‑ūs *m*; **to have a — of** despicēre

glisten *vi* nitēre

glitter *s* fulgor *m*

glitter *vi* fulgēre, micare, coruscare

gloat *vi* oculos pascēre; **to — over** inhiare (*with abl*), oculos pascēre (*with abl*)

globe *s* globus *m*; orbis terrarum *m*

globular *adj* globosus

globule *s* globulus *m*, pilula *f*

gloom *s* tenebrae *f pl*; (*fig*) tristitia *f*

gloomily *adv* maeste

gloomy *adj* tenebrosus, furvus; (*fig*) maestus, tristis

glorification *s* laudatio, glorificatio *f*

glorify *vt* celebrare, glorificare, extollēre

glorious *adj* gloriosus, illustris; —ly gloriose

glory *s* gloria, laus *f*

glory *vi* gloriari, se jactare

gloss *s* interpretatio *f*; (*sheen*) nitor *m*

gloss *vt* annotare; **to — over** extenuare, dissimulare

glossary *s* glossarium *n*

glossy *adj* nitidus, expolitus

glove *s* chirotheca *f*

glow *s* ardor, fervor, calor *m*

glow *vi* candēre, ardēre, calēre

glowing *adj* candens, fervens; (*fig*) fervidus

glue *s* gluten, glutinum *n*

glue *vt* glutinare

glum *adj* maestus, tristis

glut *s* satietas *f*

glut *vt* satiare, saturare

glutton *s* helluo, homo gulosus, ganeo *m*

gluttonous *adj* gulosus, edax; —ly gulose

gnarled *adj* nodosus

gnash *vt* **to — one's teeth** dentibus frendēre

gnat *s* culex *m*

gnaw *vt* & *vi* rodēre

gnawing *adj* mordax

go *vi* ire, incedēre, proficisci; **to — about** circumire, perambulare; (*fig*) aggredi; **to — abroad** peregrinari; **to — after** sequi, petēre; **to — aside** discedēre; **to — astray** aberrare, vagari; **to — away** abire; **to — back** reverti; **to — before** praeire, antecedēre; **to — between** intervenire; **to — beyond** egredi; (*fig*) excedēre; **to — by** praeterire; (*fig*) (*to follow*) sequi; **to — down** descendēre; (*of sun*) occidēre; **to — for** petēre; **to — forth** exire; **to — in** introire; **to — into** inire; **to — off** abire; (*as gun*) displodi; **to — on** (*to continue*) pergēre; (*to happen*)

fieri; (*to succeed, thrive*) succedère;
to — out exire; (*of fire*) extingui;
to — over transgredi; (*fig*) (*a subject*) percurrère: to — round circumire; to — through obire, pertendère; to — to adire, accedère;
to — towards petère; to — under subire; submergi; to — up ascendère; to let — dimittère; (*to let fall*) omittère

goad *s* pertica *f*, stimulus *m*
goad *vt* instigare; (*fig*) stimulare; (*to exasperate*) exasperare
goal *s* finis *m*; (*at racetrack*) calx *f*
goat *s* caper *m*, capra *f*
gobble *vt* devorare, deglutire
gobbler *s* helluo *m*
goblet *s* poculum *n*, scyphus *m*
goblin *s* larva *f*
god *s* deus, divus *m*
God *s* Deus *m*
goddess *s* dea, diva *f*
godhead *s* deitas *f*, numen *n*
godless *adj* atheus; improbus
godlike *adj* divinus
godliness *s* pietas *f*
gold *adj* aureus
gold *s* aurum *n*
golden *adj* aureus
goldfish *s* hippurus *m*
gold leaf *s* auri breactea *f*
gold mine *s* aurifodina *f*
goldsmith *s* aurifex *m*
good *adj* bonus, probus; (*beneficial*) salutaris; (*kindhearted*) benevolus; (*fit*) aptus, idoneus; — for nothing nequam (*indecl*); to do — prodesse; to make — compensare, restituère; to seem — videri
good *s* bonum *n*; (*profit*) commodum, lucrum *n*, utilitas *f*; to be — for prodesse (*with dat*); —s bona *n pl*, res *f*; (*for sale*) merx *f*
good *interj* bene!; euge!
good-by *interj* vale!; (*to more than one*) valete!; to say — valère jubère
goodly *adj* pulcher; (*quantity*) amplus; a — number of nonnulli
good-natured *adj* comis, benignus, facilis
goodness *s* bonitas *f*; (*moral*) probitas, virtus *f*; (*generosity*) benignitas *f*
goose *s* anser *m*
gooseberry *s* acinus grossulae *m*
gore *s* cruor *m*
gore *vt* cornu perforare, cornu ferire
gorge *s* fauces *f pl*; (*defile*) angustiae *f pl*
gorge *vt* to — oneself se ingurgitare
gorgeous *adj* splendidus, lautus; —ly splèndide, laute
gory *adj* cruentus, cruentatus
gospel *s* evangelium *n*
gossamer *s* aranea *f*
gossip *s* (*talk*) nugae, gerrae *f pl*; (*person*) garrulus *m*, garrula *f*, loquax *m & f*, lingulaca *f*
gossip *vi* garrire
gouge *vt* evellère, eruère
gourd *s* cucurbita *f*

gourmand *s* helluo, popino *m*
gout *s* morbus articularis *m*, arthritis *f*; (*in the legs*) podagra *f*; (*in hands*) chiragra *f*
govern *vt* imperare (*with dat*), regère, administrare, gubernare
governable *adj* tractabilis
governess *s* magistra, educatrix *f*
government *s* gubernatio, administratio, res publica *f*
governor *s* gubernator, moderator, praefectus *m*; (*of province*) proconsul, legatus *m*; procurator *m*
governorship *s* praefectura *f*
gown *s* (*of Roman citizen*) toga *f*; (*of women*) stola *f*
grace *s* gratia *f*; (*elegance, etc.*) venustas *f*, lepos *m*; (*pardon*) venia *f*; to say — gratias agère
grace *vt* exornare; honestare
graceful *adj* gratiosus, venustus, lepidus; —ly venuste, lepide
gracefulness *s* venustas *f*
graceless *adj* deformis, illepidus
Graces *s* Gratiae *f pl*
gracious *adj* benignus, misericors; —ly benigne, humane
gradation *s* grad·us -ūs *m*; (*in speech*) gradatio *f*
grade *s* grad·us -ūs *m*
gradient *s* proclivitas *f*
gradual *adj* lenis, mollis; per gradus; —ly gradatim, pedetentim
graduate *vt* gradibus distinguère; *vi* gradum suscipère
graduate *s* qui gradum academicum adeptus est
graft *s* surculus *m*; (*pol*) ambit·us -ūs *m*
graft *vt* inserère
grain *s* granum *n*; (*fig*) particula *f*; against the — (*fig*) Minervā invitā
grammar *s* grammatica *f*
grammarian *s* grammaticus *m*
grammatical *adj* grammaticus
granary *s* horreum *n*, granaria *n pl*
grand *adj* grandis
grandchild *s* nepos *m*, neptis *m & f*
granddaughter *s* neptis *f*
grandeur *s* magnificentia, majestas *f*
grandfather *s* avus *m*
grandiloquent *adj* magniloquus
grandmother *s* avia *f*
grandson *s* nepos *m*
granite *s* granites lapis *m*
grant *vt* concedère, permittère; (*to acknowledge*) fatèri; dare, praebère
grant *s* concessio *f*
grape *s* uva *f*, acinus *m*
grapevine *s* vitis *f*
graphic *adj* expressus, significans, manifestus; —ally expresse
grapple *vt* compleci; *vi* luctari
grasp *s* complex·us -ūs *m*, comprehensio *f*; pugillum *n*; (*power*) potestas *f*; (*of the hand*) man·us -ūs *f*
grasp *vt* prehendère, tenère, arripère;(*fig*) appetère, percipère, intellegère; *vi* to — at captare, appetère
grasping *adj* avidus, cupidus
grass *s* gramen *n*, herba *f*

grasshopper s grillus m

grassy adj graminosus, herbosus, herbidus

grate s clathri m pl; (hearth) caminus m

grate vt radĕre, conterĕre; vi stridĕre; to — upon offendĕre

grateful adj gratus, juncundus; —ly grate

gratification s gratificatio f; (pleasure, delight) voluptas, oblectatio f

gratify vt gratificari (with dat), morigerari (with dat)

gratifying adj gratus

grating s clathri, cancelli m pl; (sound) stridor m

gratis adv gratuito, gratis

gratitude s gratitudo f, gratus animus m

gratuitous adj gratuitus; —ly gratuito

gratuity s stips f, munus, praemium n

grave adj gravis, serius; (stern) severus; —ly graviter; severe

grave s sepulcrum n, tumulus m

gravedigger s tumulorum fossor m

gravel s glarea f

gravelly adj glareosus

gravestone s monumentum n

gravitate vi vergĕre

gravitation s ponderatio f

gravity s gravitas f, pondus n; (personal) severitas, dignitas f; momentum n

gravy s (broth) jus n; (juice) sucus m

gray adj canus; to become — canescĕre

gray-eyed adj caesius

gray-headed adj canus

grayish adj canescens

grayness s canities f

graze vt (cattle) pascĕre; (to touch lightly) perstringĕre, radĕre; vi pasci

grease s adeps m, pinguitudo, arvina f

grease vt ung(u)ĕre

greasy adj pinguis; unctus; (dirty) squalidus

great adj magnus; ingens, amplus, grandis; as — as tantus quantus; —ly magnopere, valde

great-grandfather s proavus m

greatness s magnitudo f

greaves s ocreae f pl

Grecian adj Graecus

greed s aviditas, avaritia f; voracitas f

greedily adv avide, cupide

greedy adj avarus, cupidus; vorax

Greek adj Graecus

Greek s Graecus m

green adj viridis; (fig) recens; (unripe) crudus, immaturus; to become — virescĕre

green s color viridis m; (lawn) locus herbidus m; —s olera n pl

greenhouse s viridarium hibernum n

greenish adj subviridis

greenness s viriditas f; (fig) cruditas, immaturitas f

greet vt salutem dicĕre (with dat), salutare

greeting s salutatio f

gregarious adj gregalis

grenade s pyrobolus m

greyhound s vertagus m

gridiron s craticula f

grief s maeror, dolor, luct·us -ūs m; to come to — perire

grievance s injuria, querimonia, querela f

grieve vt dolore afficĕre; vi maerĕre, dolĕre, lugĕre

grievous adj gravis, durus, atrox; —ly graviter, aegre

griffin s gryps m

grill vt torrēre

grim adj torvus, atrox, truculentus; —ly torve, truculente, atrociter

grimace s distortus vult·us -ūs m, oris depravatio f

grimace vi os ducĕre

grimy adj niger, squalidus

grin vi distorto vultu ridēre

grin s ris·us -ūs m

grind vt (grain) molĕre; (in mortar) contundĕre; (on whetstone) exacuĕre; to — the teeth dentibus frendĕre

grindstone s cos f

grip s pugillum n, comprehensio f

grip vt arripĕre, comprehendĕre

grisly adj horrendus, horridus

grist s farina f

gristle s cartilago f

gristly adj cartilagineus, cartilaginosus

grit s harena f

gritty adj harenosus, sabulosus

grizzly adj canus

groan s gemit·us -ūs m

groan vi gemĕre

groin s inguen n

groom s agaso, equiso m

groom vt curare

groove s canalis m, stria f

groove vt striare

grope vi praetentare

gropingly adv pedetentim

gross adj crassus, pinguis; turpis, foedus; nimius; —ly nimium, valde

grotesque adj distortus

grotto s antrum n

ground s solum n, terra, humus f; (reason) causa, ratio f; (place) locus m; on the — humi; to give — cedĕre

ground vt fundare; (to teach) instruĕre; (a ship) subducĕre

groundless adj vanus, falsus, fictus; —ly temere, de nihilo

group s corona, turba f, globus m

group vt disponĕre; vi to — around circulari, stipari

grouse s (bird) tetrao m

grove s lucus m, nemus n

grovel vi serpĕre, se prosternĕre

grow vt colĕre, serĕre; vi crescĕre, augĕri; (to become) fieri; to — out of (fig) oriri ex (with abl); to — up adolescĕre, pubescĕre

grower s cultor m

growl s fremit·us -ūs m

growl vi fremĕre

grown-up *adj* adultus; puber
growth *s* incrementum *n*, auct.us -ūs *m*
grub *s* vermiculus, lombricus *m*
grub *vi* effodĕre
grudge *s* odium *n*, invidia *f*; **to hold a — against** succensēre (*with dat*)
grudgingly *adv* invitus, aegre
gruesome *adj* taeter
gruff *adj* torvus, asper; **—ly** torve, aspere
gruffness *s* asperitas *f*
grumble *vi* murmurare, mussitare
grunt *s* grunnit.us -ūs *m*
grunt *vi* grunnire; (*fig*) fremĕre
guarantee *s* fides *f*; (*money*) sponsio *f*; (*person*) praes, vas, sponsor *m*; (*bail money*) vadimonium *n*
guarantor *s* sponsor *m*
guard *s* custodia, tutela *f*; (*mil*) praesidium *n*; (*person*) custos *m* & *f*; **to be on one's —** cavēre
guard *vt* custodire, defendĕre; *vi* **to — against** cavēre
guarded *adj* cautus, circumspectus; **—ly** caute
guardian *s* custos, praeses *m* & *f*, defensor *m*; (*of minor or orphan*) tutor *m*
guardianship *s* custodia, tutela, curatio *f*
guerdon *s* merces *f*
guess *s* conjectura *f*
guess *vt* & *vi* conjicĕre, divinare, opinari
guest *s* hospes *m*; advena *m*; (*at dinner*) conviva *m*
guidance *s* duct.us -ūs *m*, curatio, moderatio *f*
guide *s* dux, ductor *m*
guide *vt* ducĕre, regĕre; (*to control*) moderari
guidebook *s* itinerarium *n*
guild *s* collegium, corpus *n*, sodalitas *f*

guile *s* dolus *m*
guileful *adj* dolosus
guileless *adj* simplex, sincerus
guilt *s* culpa *f*, crimen, vitium *n*
guiltless *adj* innocens, insons
guilty *adj* sons, noxius, nocens, sceleratus
guinea hen *s* meleagris *f*
guise *s* species *f*
guitar *s* cithara Hispanica *f*; fides *f pl*; **to play the —** fidibus canēre
gulf *s* sin.us -ūs *m*; (*abyss*) abyssus *f*, gurges *m*
gull *s* larus marinus, mergus *m*
gullet *s* gula *f*, guttur *n*
gullible *adj* credulus
gulp *vt* absorbēre, glutire, haurire; *vi* singultare
gulp *s* haust.us -ūs, singult.us -ūs *m*
gum *s* (*of mouth*) gingiva *f*; gummi *n* (*indecl*)
gumption *s* alacritas *f*
gun *s* sclopetum *n*; tormentum *n*
gunner *s* tormentarius *m*
gurgle *vi* singultare; (*of stream*) murmurare
gurgling *s* singult.us -ūs *m*; (*of stream*) murmur *n*, murmuratio *f*
gush *vi* micare, scaturire
gush *s* scaturigines *f pl*
gust *s* impet.us -ūs *m*, flamen *n*
gusty *adj* ventosus, procellosus
gut *s* intestinum *n*
gut *vt* exenterare; (*fig*) diripĕre, amburĕre
gutted *adj* (*by fire*) ambustus
gutter *s* canalis *m*; (*rain gutter*) compluvium *n*; (*in fields or upon roofs*) colliciae *f pl*
guttural *adj* gutturalis
guzzle *vi* potare
guzzler *s* potor *m*
gymnasium *s* gymnasium *n*, palaestra *f*
gymnastic *adj* gymnicus
gymnastics *s* palaestra, palaestrica *f*

H

haberdasher *s* linteo *m*
habit *s* consuetudo *f*, mos *m*; (*dress*) habit.us -ūs, vestit.us -ūs *m*
habitation *s* habitatio, dom.us -ūs *f*
habitual *adj* usitatus, inveteratus; **—ly** de more, ex more
habituate *vt* insuescĕre, assuefacĕre
hack *vt* caedĕre; **to — to pieces** concidĕre
hack *s* (*horse*) caballus *m*
hackneyed *adj* tritus, pervulgatus
haddock *s* gadus morhua *m*
hag *f* an.us -ūs *f*
haggard *adj* macer; ferus
haggle *vi* cavillari, licitare
haggler *s* licitator *m*
hail *s* grando *f*
hail *vt* salutare, appellare

hail *vi* **it is hailing** grandinat
hail *interj* salve!; (*to several*) salvete!
hailstone *s* saxea grando *f*
hair *s* capillus, crinis *m*; (*single*) pilus *m*; (*of animals*) saeta *f*, villus *m*
hairoloth *s* cilicium *n*
hairdresser *s* concinnator, tonsor *m*
hairless *adj* (*of head*) calvus; (*of body*) glaber, depilis
hairpin *s* crinale *n*
hairy *adj* pilosus, crinitus; (*shaggy*) hirsutus
halberd *s* bipennis *f*
halcyon *s* alcedo, alcyon *f*
halcyon days *s* alcedonia *n pl*
hale *adj* robustus, validus
hale *vt* rapĕre, trahĕre
half *s* dimidia pars *f*, dimidium *n*

half *adj* dimidius, dimidiatus
half-hour *s* semihora *f*
half-moon *s* luna dimidiata *f*; *(shape)* lunula *f*
half-open *adj* semiapertus
half year *s* semestrium *n*
hall *s* atrium *n*; *(entrance)* vestibulum *n*
hallo *interj* heus!, ohe!
hallow *vt* consecrare
hallucination *s* error *m*, somnium *n*, alucinatio *f*
halo *s* corona *f*
halt *vt* sistĕre; *vi* consistĕre; *(fig)* haesitare; *(to limp)* claudicare
halt *s* pausa, mora *f*; **to come to a — consistĕre
halter *s* capistrum *n*
halting *adj* claudus
halve *vt* ex aequo dividĕre
ham *s* poples *m*; *(smoked, etc.)* perna *f*
hamlet *s* vicus, viculus *m*
hammer *s* malleus *m*
hammer *vt* tundĕre, cudĕre
hamper *s* corbis *f*
hamper *vt* impedire, implicare
hamstring *s* poplitis nervus *m*
hamstring *vt* poplitem succidĕre *(with dat)*
hand *s* man·us -ūs *f*; *(handwriting)* chirographum *n*; *(of dial)* gnomon *m*; **at — ad manum, praesto, prae manibus, prope; by — manu; — in — junctis manibus; — to — cominus; on the other — altera parte; on the right — a dextra; to have a — in interesse *(with dat)*; to take in — suscipĕre
hand *vt* tradĕre, porrigĕre; **to — down tradĕre, **to — over referre; *(to betray)* prodĕre, **to — round circumferre
handbill *s* libellus *m*
handbook *s* enchiridion *n*
handcuffs *s* manicae *f pl*
handful *s* manipulus *m*
handicraft *s* artificium *n*
handiwork *s* opus, opificium *n*
handkerchief *s* sudarium *n*
handle *s* manubrium *n*; *(of cup)* ansa, ansula *f*
handle *vt* tractare
handling *s* tractatio *f*
handsome *adj* pulcher, formosus; **—ly pulchre, *(liberally)* liberaliter
handsomeness *s* pulchritudo, forma, venustas *f*
handwriting *s* man·us -ūs *f*, chirographum *n*
handy *adj* *(of things)* habilis; *(of person)* sollers; *(at hand)* praesto
hang *vt* suspendĕre; *(by a line)* appendĕre; *(head)* demittĕre; *vi* pendĕre; **hanging down demissus; **hanging loose fluens; **to — down dependĕre; **to — on to haerēre *(with dat)*; **to — over imminēre *(with dat)*
hanging *adj* pensilis
hanging *s* *(execution)* suspendium, *n*; **—s aulaea *n pl*
hangman *s* carnifex *m*
haphazard *adj* fortuitus

happen *vi* accidĕre, fieri, evenire, contingĕre; **to — upon incidĕre in *(with acc)*
happily *adv* beate, feliciter
happiness *s* felicitas *f*
happy *adj* beatus, felix, fortunatus, faustus
harangue *s* contio *f*
harangue *vt & vi* contionari
harass *vt* vexare, inquietare, exagitare, fatigare
harassing *adj* molestus
harassment *s* vexatio *f*
harbinger *s* praenuntius, antecursor *m*
harbor *s* port·us -ūs *m*
harbor *vt* excipĕre
hard *adj* durus; *(difficult)* difficilis, arduus; *(severe)* acer, rigidus, asper; **to become — durescĕre
hard *adv* valde, sedulo, summa vi
harden *vt* durare; *(fig)* indurare; *vi* durescĕre; *(fig)* obdurescĕre
hardhearted *adj* durus, crudelis, inhumanus
hardihood *s* audacia *f*
hardiness *s* robur *n*
hardly *adv* vix, aegre; **— any nullus fere
hardness *s* duritia *f*; *(fig)* iniquitas, acerbitas *f*; *(difficulty)* difficultas *f*
hardship *s* labor *m*, difficultas, aerumna *f*
hardware *s* ferramenta *n pl*
hardy *adj* robustus, durus
hare *s* lepus *m*
harem *s* gynaeceum *n*
hark *interj* heus!
harken *vi* audire; **to — to auscultare *(with dat)*
harlot *s* meretrix *f*
harm *s* injuria *f*, damnum *n*; **to come to — detrimentum accipĕre
harm *vt* nocēre *(with dat)*, laedĕre
harmful *adj* noxius, nocivus, damnosus
harmless *adj* *(person)* innocens; *(thing)* innocuus; **—ly innocenter, incolumis
harmonious *adj* canorus, consonus; *(fig)* concors, consentiens; **—ly consonanter; *(fig)* concorditer, convenienter
harmonize *vt* componĕre; *vi* concinĕre; *(fig)* consentire
harmony *s* harmonia *f*, concent·us -ūs *m*; *(fig)* concordia *f*
harness *s* equi ornamenta *n pl*
harness *vt* ornare, insternĕre
harp *s* lyra *f*
harpist *s* psaltes *m*
harpoon *s* jaculum hamatum *n*
harpoon *vt* jaculo hamato transfigĕre
harpy *s* harpyia *f*
harrow *s* rastrum *n*, irpex *m*
harrow *vt* occare
harsh *adj* asper, raucus, discors, stridulus; *(in taste)* acer; *(fig)* durus, severus, inclemens; **—ly aspere, acerbe, severe
harshness *s* asperitas, acerbitas, severitas *f*

harvest *s* messis, seges *f*
harvest *vt* metĕre
hash *vt* comminuĕre
hash *s* minutal *n*
haste *s* festinatio, celeritas *f*; **in —**
  propere; **to make —** properare
hasten *vt* accelerare, properare,
  praecipitare; *vi* properare, festinare
hastily *adv* propere, raptim; *(without reflection)* temere, inconsulte
hastiness *s* celeritas, temeritas *f*
hasty *adj* properus, praeceps, temerarius, inconsultus
hat *s* pileus, galerus, petasus *m*
hatch *vt* *(fig)* coquĕre, machinari;
  (of chickens) ex ovis excludĕre
hatchet *s* ascia, securis, dolabra *f*
hate *s* odium *n*, invidia *f*
hate *vt* odisse
hateful *adj* odiosus, invisus; **to be —**
  to odio esse *(with dat)*; **—ly** odiose
hatred *s* odium *n*, invidia *f*
haughtily *adv* superbe, arroganter,
  insolenter
haughtiness *s* superbia, arrogantia
  f, fastidium *n*
haughty *adj* superbus, arrogans, insolens
haul *s* bolus *m*
haul *vt* trahĕre; **to — up** subducĕre
haunch *s* clunis, coxa *f*
haunt *vt* frequentare; *(fig)* agitare,
  inquietare
haunt *s* locus *m*; *(of animals)* lustra
  n pl, latebrae *f pl*
have *vt* habēre, possidēre, tenēre
haven *s* port·us -ūs *m*
havoc *s* strages *f*
hawk *s* accipiter *m* & *f*
hawk *vt* venditare
hawser *s* retinaculum *n*
hawthorn *s* crataegus oxyacantha *f*
hay *s* faenum *n*
hayloft *s* faenilia *n pl*
haystack *s* faeni meta *f*
hazard *s* periculum *n*
hazard *vt* periclitari
hazardous *adj* periculosus, anceps;
  —ly periculose
haze *s* nebula *f*
hazy *adj* caliginosus, nebulosus
he *pron* hic, is, ille; *(male)* mas *m*
head *s* caput *s*; *(mental faculty)* ingenium *n*; *(fig)* princeps; **— first**
  praeceps
head *adj* primus, principalis, capitalis
head *vt* praeesse *(with dat)*, ducĕre; *vi*
  to — for petĕre
headache *s* capitis dolor *m*
heading *s* caput *n*, titulus *m*
headland *s* promuntorium *n*
headless *adj* truncus
headlong *adv* praeceps
headquarters *s* praetorium *n*
headstrong *adj* pervicax, contumax
headway *s* profect·us -ūs *m*; **to**
  make — proficĕre
headwind *s* ventus adversus *m*
heady *adj* *(of drinks)* fervidus, vehemens
heal *vt* medēri *(with dat)*, sanare; *vi*
  sanescĕre; *(of wounds)* coalescĕre

healer *s* medicus *m*
healing *adj* salubris, salutaris
health *s* valetudo, salus *f*; **to be in**
  good — valēre; **to drink to the**
  — of propinare *(with dat)*
healthful *adj* salutaris, salubris
healthily *adv* salubriter
healthy *adj* sanus, integer; *(places)*
  salubris
heap *s* acervus, cumulus *m*, congeries
  f
heap *vt* acervare; **to — up** accumulare, exstruĕre
hear *vt* audire, exaudire; *(to learn)*
  certior fieri, accipĕre, cognoscĕre
hearing *s* *(act)* auditio *f*; *(sense)* auditus -ūs *m*; *(law)* cognitio *f*; **hard**
  of — surdaster
hearken *vi* auscultare
hearsay *s* fama *f*, rumor *m*
heart *s* cor *n*; *(fig)* pectus *n*; *(courage)*
  animus *m*; **to learn by —** ediscĕre
heartache *s* cura *f*, angor *m*
heartbreak *s* angor *m*
heartbroken *adj* aeger
hearth *s* focus *m*
heartily *adv* sincere, vehementer,
  valde
heartiness *s* studium *n*, alacritas *f*
heartless *adj* crudelis, inhumanus;
  —ly crudeliter, inhumane
heartlessness *s* inhumanitas *f*
hearty *adj* sincerus, vehemens, alacer
heat *s* calor, ardor *m*; *(fig)* fervor *m*
heat *vt* calefacĕre; *vi* calescĕre
heath *s* *(plant)* erice *f*; *(place)* loca
  inculta *n pl*
heathen *adj* paganus
heathen *s* paganus *m*
heather *s* erice *f*
heating *s* calefactio *f*
heave *vt* attollĕre, levare; **to — a**
  sigh gemitum ducĕre; *vi* tumēre,
  aestuare, fluctuare
heaven *s* caelum *n*; *(fig)* dii, superi
  m pl
heavenly *adj* caelestis, divinus
heavily *adv* graviter; *(slowly)* tarde
heaviness *s* gravitas *f*; *(slowness)*
  tarditas *f*
heavy *adj* gravis, ponderosus; *(fig)*
  tardus, segnis, iners; *(sad)* maestus
Hebraic *adj* Hebraicus
Hebrew *s* Hebraeus *m*; *(language)*
  Hebraea lingua *f*
hecatomb *s* hecatombe *f*
hectic *adj* fervidus, febriculosus
hedge *s* saepes *f*
hedge *vt* **to — in** saepire; **to — off**
  intersaepire; *vi* tergiversari
hedgehog *s* ericius *m*
heed *s* cura, opera *f*; **to take — ca**-
  vēre, curare
heed *vt* curare, observare, respicĕre;
  (to obey) parēre *(with dat)*
heedless *adj* incautus, temerarius;
  — of immemor *(with genit)*
heedlessness *s* neglegentia *f*
heel *s* calx *m* & *f*
heifer *s* bucula, juvenca *f*
height *s* altitudo *f*; *(of person)* pro-

ceritas *f*; (*top*) culmen *n*; (*fig*) fastigium *n*

heighten *vt* amplificare, exaggerare, augēre

heinous *adj* atrox, nefarius, foedus; **—ly** atrociter

heir *s* heres *m*; **sole** *or* **universal —** heres ex asse

heiress *s* heres *f*

heirloom *s* res hereditaria *f*

hell *s* Tartarus *m*, inferi *m pl*

Hellenic *adj* Hellenicus, Graecus

Hellenism *s* Hellenismus *m*

hellish *adj* infernus, diabolicus, nefarius

helm *s* gubernaculum *n*

helmet *s* cassis, galea *f*

helmsman *s* gubernator, rector *m*

help *s* auxilium, subsidium *n*

help *vt* adjuvare (*with acc*), auxiliari (*with dat*), succurrēre (*with dat*), opem ferre (*with dat*)

helper *s* adjutor *m*, adjutrix *f*

helpful *adj* utilis

helpless *adj* inops

helplessness *s* inopia *f*

hem *s* ora *f*, limbus *m*

hem *vt* (*to sew*) suēre; **to — in** circumsidēre, obsidēre

hem *interj* hem!, ehem!

hemisphere *s* hemisphaerium *n*

hemlock *s* cicuta *f*

hemp *s* cannabis *f*

hempen *adj* cannabinus

hen *s* gallina *f*

hence *adv* hinc; (*consequently*) igitur, ideo

henceforth *adv* posthac, dehinc

henpecked *adj* uxorius

her *pron* eam, illam, hanc

her *adj* ejus, illius, hujus; **— own** suus, proprius

herald *s* fetialis *m*; (*crier*) praeco *m*

herald *vt* nuntiare, praenuntiare

herb *s* herba *f*; **—s** herbae *f pl*, olus *n*

herd *s* grex *m*; armentum *n*; (*in contempt*) vulgus *n*

herd *vt* **to — together** congregare, cogēre; *vi* congregari

herdsman *s* pastor, armentarius *m*

here *adv* hic; **— and there** passim

hereafter *adv* posthac, in reliquum tempus

hereby *adv* ex hoc, ex hac re, hinc

hereditary *adj* hereditarius, patrius

heredity *s* genus *n*; **by — jure** hereditario, per successiones

herein *adv* in hoc, in hac re, hic

heresy *s* haeresis *f*

heretical *adj* haereticus; falsus, pravus

hereupon *adv* hic

herewith *adv* una cum hac re

heritage *s* hereditas *f*

hermaphrodite *s* androgynus, Hermaphroditus *m*

hermit *s* eremita *m*

hermitage *s* eremitae cella *f*

hernia *s* hernia *f*

hero *s* vir *m*; (*demigod*) heros *m*

heroic *adj* fortissimus, magnanimus, heroicus; **—ally** fortissime

heroine *s* virago *f*

heroism *s* virtus, fortitudo *f*

heron *s* ardea *f*

herring *s* harenga *f*

hers *pron* ejus, illius

herself *pron* (*refl*) se; (*intensive*) ipsa; **to —** sibi; **with —** secum

hesitant *adj* dubius, incertus; **—ly** cunctanter, dubitanter

hesitate *vi* dubitare, haesitare

hesitation *s* dubitatio, haesitatio, cunctatio *f*

Hesperian *adj* Hesperius

heterogeneous *adj* diversus

hew *vt* dolare, caedēre

hey *interj* ohe!

hiatus *s* hiat·us -ūs *m*

hiccup *s* singult·us -ūs *m*

hiccup *vi* singultare

hide *s* pellis *f*, corium *n*

hide *vt* abdēre, abscondēre, celare, occultare; (*to flog*) verberare; *vi* latēre, se abdēre

hideous *adj* foedus, perhorridus, turpis; **—ly** foede, turpiter

hideousness *s* foeditas *f*, horror *m*

hiding *s* occultatio *f*; (*whipping*) verberatio *f*

hiding place *s* latebra *f*

hierarchy *s* hierarchia *f*

high *adj* altus, excelsus, sublimis; (*tall*) procerus; (*of price*) pretiosus, carus; (*of ground*) editus; (*of rank*) amplus; **—ly** (*value*) magni; (*intensity*) vehementer, valde

high *adv* alte, sublimiter; **to aim —** magnas res appetĕre

highborn *adj* generosus, ingenuus, nobilis

high-flown *adj* inflatus, tumidus

highhanded *adj* insolens, superbus; **—ly** insolenter, superbe

highland *s* regio montuosa *f*

highlander *s* montanus *m*

high-minded *adj* (*noble*) magnanimus; (*arrogant*) arrogans, insolens

high priest *s* pontifex maximus *m*

highway *s* via *f*

highwayman *s* latro, grassator *m*

hilarity *s* hilaritas *f*

hill *s* collis, tumulus *m*; (*slope*) clivus *m*

hillock *s* tumulus *m*

hilly *adj* montuosus, clivosus

hilt *s* capulus *m*

him *pron* eum, hunc, illum; **of —** ejus, hujus, illius; **de eo, de hoc, de illo**

himself *pron* (*refl*) se; (*intensive*) ipse; **to —** sibi; **with —** secum

hind *s* cerva *f*

hind *adj* posterior

hinder *vt* obstare (*with dat*); impedire, morari

hindmost *adj* postremus, ultimus, novissimus

hindrance *s* impedimentum *n*

hinge *s* cardo *m*

hinge *vi* **to — on** (*fig*) niti (*with abl*)

hint *s* indicium *n*, significatio *f*

hint *vt & vi* significare, innuĕre, suggerĕre

hip *s* coxendix *f*

hippodrome *s* hippodromos *m*

hire *s* conductio, locatio *f*; *(wages)* merces *f*

hire *vt* conducĕre; **to — out** locare; *vi* **to — out** operam suam locare

hired *adj* conductus, conducticius, mercenarius

hireling *s* mercenarius *m*

his *adj* ejus, illius, hujus; **— own** suus, proprius

his *pron* ejus, illius, hujus

hiss *vt & vi* sibilare

hissing *s* sibilus *m*

historian *s* historicus, rerum gestarum scriptor *m*

historical *adj* historicus

history *s* historia, memoria rerum gestarum *f*; **ancient —** antiquitas *f*; **modern —** memoria recentioris aetatis *f*

histrionic *adj* histrionalis

hit *s* ict·us -ūs *m*, plaga *f*; **to be a — bene** succedĕre

hit *vt* icĕre, ferire, percutĕre; *vi* **to — upon** invenire

hitch *s* impedimentum *n*, mora *f*

hitch *vt* (ad)jungĕre

hither *adv* huc

hither *adj* citerior

hitherto *adv* *(of time)* adhuc; *(of place)* huc usque

hive *s* alvus *m*, alvearium *n*

hoard *s* acervus *m*

hoard *vt* coacervare, recondĕre

hoarder *s* accumulator *m*

hoarse *adj* raucus; **to get —** irraucescĕre; **—ly** raucā voce

hoary *adj* canus

hoax *s* fraus, ludificatio *f*

hoax *vt* fallĕre, decipĕre, ludificari

hobble *vi* claudicare

hobby *s* avocamentum *n*

hock *s* poples *m*

hoe *s* sarculum *m*

hoe *vt* sarculare; *(weeds)* pectĕre

hog *s* porcus, sus *m*

hoist *vt* sublevare, tollĕre

hold *vt* tenēre, possidēre, habēre; *(to contain)* capĕre; *(to think)* habēre, existimare, censēre; **to — back** retinēre; **to — forth** porrigĕre, extendĕre; *(to offer)* praebēre; **to — in** inhibēre, cohibēre; **to — off** abstinēre, arcēre; **to — up** *(to lift up)* attollĕre, sustinēre; *vi* **to — back** cunctari; **to — out** *(to last)* durare, permanēre

holder *s* possessor *m*; *(handle)* manubrium *n*

holding *s* possessio *f*

hole *s* foramen *n*; *(fig)* latebra *f*; *(of mice)* cavum *n*

holiday *s* dies festus *m*; **—s** feriae *f pl*

holiness *s* sanctitas *f*

hollow *adj* cavus; *(fig)* vanus, inanis

hollow *s* caverna *f*, cavum *n*; *(depression)* lacuna *f*

hollow *vt* **to — out** cavare, excavare

holly *s* ilex aquifolium *n*

holocaust *s* holocaustum *n*

holy *adj* sanctus

homage *s* obsequium *n*, cult·us -ūs *m*; **to pay —** to colere

home *s* domicilium *n*, dom·us -ūs *f*; **at —** domi; **from —** domo

home *adv* *(motion)* domum; *(place where)* domi

home *adj* domesticus

homeless *adj* tecto carens, profugus

homeliness *s* rusticitas *f*

homely *adj* rusticus, simplex

homemade *adj* domesticus, vernaculus, domi factus

homesickness *s* tecti sui desiderium *n*, nostalgia *f*

homestead *s* sedes *f*, fundus *m*

homeward *adv* domum

homicidal *adj* cruentus, sanguinolentus

homicide *s* *(person)* homicida *m*; *(deed)* homicidium *n*

homily *s* sermo, tractat·us -ūs *m*

homogeneous *adj* pari naturā praeditus

hone *vt* acuĕre

honest *adj* probus, sincerus; **—ly** probe, sincere

honesty *s* probitas, sinceritas *f*

honey *s* mel *n*

honeybee *s* apis mellifera *or* mellifica *f*

honeycomb *s* favus *m*

honeysuckle *s* clymenus *m*

honor *s* honos *m*; *(repute)* fama *f*; *(trust)* fides *f*; *(award)* decus *n*; *(official distinction)* dignitas *f*; **sense of —** pudor *m*

honor *vt* honorare; *(to respect)* colēre

honorable *adj* honestus

honorably *adv* honeste

honorary *adj* honorarius

hood *s* cucullus *m*

hoof *s* ungula *f*

hook *s* hamus, uncus *m*; **by — or by crook** quocumque modo

hook *vt* inuncare; confibulare; *(fig)* capĕre

hooked *adj* hamatus; *(crooked)* curvatus, aduncus

hoop *s* circulus *m*; *(toy)* trochus *m*; *(shout)* clamor *m*

hoop *vi* exclamare

hoot *vt* explodĕre; *vi* obstrepĕre; *(of owls)* canĕre

hop *s* salt·us -ūs *m*

hop *vi* salire, subsultare

hope *s* spes *f*

hope *vt* sperare; **to — for** exspectare

hopeful *adj* bonae spei; **—ly** magnā cum spe

hopeless *adj* exspes, desperatus; **—ly** desperanter

hopelessness *s* desperatio *f*

horde *s* turba, caterva *f*, grex *m*

horizon *s* orbis finiens *m*

horizontal *adj* libratus; **—ly** ad lībram

horn *s* cornu *n*; *(as trumpet)* buccina *f*

horned *adj* cornutus, corniger

hornet *s* crabo *m*

horoscope *s* horoscopus *m*

horrible *adj* horribilis, foedus; (*excessive*) immoderatus

horribly *adv* horribili modo, foede

horrid *adj* horridus, horrens; **—ly** horride

horrify *vt* horrificare, perterrēre

horror *s* horror *m*; (*deep hatred*) odium *n*

horse *s* equus *m*, equa *f*

horseback *s* on **—** in equo; ex equo; **to fight on —** ex equo pugnare; **to ride on —** in equo vehi

horsehair *s* pilus equinus *m*

horseman *s* eques *m*

horse race *s* curriculum equorum *n*, certatio equestris *f*

horseradish *s* armoracia *f*

horseshoe *s* solea *f*

horsewhip *s* flagellum *n*, scutica *f*

horsewhip *vt* verberare

horticultural *adj* ad hortorum cultum pertinens

horticulture *s* hortorum cult·us -ūs *m*

hose *s* (*stocking*) tibiale *n*; (*tube*) tubulus *m*

hosiery *s* feminalia *n pl*

hospitable *adj* hospitalis

hospitably *adv* hospitaliter

hospital *s* valetudinarium *n*

hospitality *s* hospitalitas *f*

host *s* (*entertainer*) hospes *m*; (*army*) copiae *f pl*, exercit·us -ūs *m*; (*crowd*) multitudo *f*; (*wafer*) hostia *f*

hostage *s* obses *m & f*

hostess *s* hospita *f*; (*at inn*) caupona *f*

hostile *adj* hostilis, infensus, inimicus; **in a — manner** hostiliter, infense

hot *adj* calidus *or* caldus; fervidus; (*boiling*) fervens; (*seething*) aestuosus; (*of spices*) acer; (*fig*) ardens; **to be —** calēre; **to become —** calescēre; **—ly** acriter, ardenter

hotel *s* hospitium *n*, caupona *f*

hound *s* catulus *m*

hound *vt* instare (*with dat*)

hour *s* hora *f*

hourglass *s* horarium *n*

hourly *adv* in horas

house *s* dom·us -ūs *f*, aedes *f pl*, tectum *n*; (*family*) dom·us -ūs, gens *f*; (*in country*) villa *f*; **at the — of** apud (*with acc*)

house *vt* domo excipēre; (*things*) condēre

housebreaker *s* fur, effractarius *m*

housebreaking *s* domūs effractura *f*

household *adj* familiaris, domesticus

household *s* familia, dom·us -ūs *f*

householder *s* paterfamilias *m*

household gods *s* Lares *m pl*; Penates *m pl*

housekeeper *s* promus *m*

housekeeping *s* rei familiaris cura *f*

housemaid *s* ancilla, vernacula *f*

housewife *s* materfamilias *f*

hovel *s* tugurium, gurgustium *n*

hover *vi* pendēre, volitare; **to — over** impendēre (*with dat*)

how *adv* quomodo, quo pacto, qui; (*to what degree*) quam; **— many** quot;

— much quantum; **— often** quotiens

however *adv* tamen, nihilominus, autem; quamvis, quamlibet; **— great** quantuscunque; **— many** quot; **— often** quotiescunque

howl *s* ululat·us -ūs *m*

howl *vi* ululare, fremēre

hub *s* axis *m*

huckster *s* propola, institor *m*

huddle *vi* congregari

huddle *s* corona *f*

huddled *adj* confertus

hue *s* color *m*

hue and cry *s* conclamatio *f*

huff *s* offensio *f*; **in a —** offensus

huff *vi* stomachari

hug *s* complex·us -ūs *m*

hug *vt* complecti, amplecti

huge *adj* ingens, immensus, vastus, immanis

hulk *s* alveus *m*; navis oneraria *f*

hull *s* alveus *m*

hum *s* murmur *n*, murmuratio *f*; (*of bees*) bombus *m*

hum *vi* murmurare; (*of bees*) bombilare

human *adj* humanus; **— feelings** humanitas *f*; **—ly humane**, humaniter, humanitus

human being *s* homo *m & f*

humane *adj* humanus, misericors; **—ly** humaniter, misericorditer, humanitus

humanity *s* humanitas *f*; homines *m pl*

humanize *vt* excolēre

humble *adj* (*obscure*) humilis, obscurus; (*modest*) summissus, modestus; **—ly** summisse

humble *vt* deprimēre, infringēre; **to — oneself** se summittēre

humid *adj* humidus

humidity *s* humor *m*

humiliate *vt* humiliare, deprimēre

humiliation *s* humiliatio *f*, dedecus *n*

humility *s* animus summissus *m*, modestia, humilitas *f*

humor *s* (*disposition*) ingenium *n*, natura *f*; (*whim*) libido *f*; **sense of —** facetiae *f pl*, festivitas *f*

humor *vt* obsequi (*with dat*), morigerari (*with dat*), indulgēre (*with dat*)

humorous *adj* facetus, ridiculus, jocularis; **—ly** facete

hump *s* gibber, gibbus *m*

humpbacked *adj* gibber

hunch *s* opinio *f*; **to have a —** opinari

hundred *adj* centum; **— times** centie(n)s

hundredfold *adj* centuplex

hundredfold *s* centuplum *n*

hundredth *adj* centesimus

hunger *s* fames *f*

hunger *vi* esurire

hungrily *adv* avide, voraciter, rabide; jejune

hungry *s* esuriens, jejunus; (*fig*) avide; **to be —** esurire

hunt *s* venatio *f*, venat·us -ūs *m*

hunt vt venari, indagare; vi to — for quaerĕre, exquirĕre

hunter s venator m; (horse) equus venaticus m

hunting s venatio f, venat·us -ūs m

hunting adj venaticus

huntress s venatrix f

huntsman s venator m

hurdle s crates f; (obstacle) obex m & f

hurl vt jacĕre, conjicĕre, jaculari

hurray interj io!, evax!

hurricane s procella f

hurriedly adv raptim, festinanter; (carelessly) negligenter

hurry vt rapĕre, accelerare, maturare; vi festinare, properare, maturare

hurry s festinatio f; in a — festinanter

hurt vt nocēre (with dat), laedĕre; (fig) offendĕre; vi dolēre

hurt s vulnus n; damnum n, injuria f

hurt adj saucius; (emotionally) saucius, offensus

husband s maritus, vir m

husbandry s agricultura, res rustica f

hush s silentium n

hush vt comprimĕre, pacare; (a secret) celare; vi tacēre

hush interj st!, tace!; (to several) tacete!

husk s folliculus m; (of beans, etc.) siliqua f; (of grain) gluma f

husky adj robustus; (of voice) raucus

hustle vt trudĕre, pulsare; vi festinare

hut s tugurium n, casa f

hyacinth s hyacinthus m

hydra s hydra f

hyena s hyaena f

hymen s Hymenaeus m

hymn s carmen n, hymnus m

hyperbole s superlatio f

hypercritical adj nimis severus

hyphen s hyphen n (indecl)

hypochondriac s melancholicus m

hypocrisy s simulatio, dissimulatio f

hypocrite s simulator, dissimulator m

hypocritical adj simulatus, fictus

hypothesis s hypothesis, sumptio, conjectura f

hypothetical adj hypotheticus, sumptus

hysteria s deliratio f

hysterical adj hystericus

I

I pron ego; — myself egomet, ego ipse

iambic adj iambeus

ice s glacies f

icicle s stiria f

icy adj glacialis

idea s notio, notitia, imago, conceptio f

ideal adj perfectus, summus, optimus; (as mere mental image) mente conceptus, idealis

ideal s exemplar n

identical adj idem

identify vt agnoscĕre

idiocy s fatuitas, animi imbecillitas f

idiom s proprietas linguae, consuetudo f

idiomatic adj proprius linguae

idiosyncrasy s proprium n

idiot s fatuus, excors m

idiotic adj fatuus, stultus, ineptus

idle adj otiosus, vacuus; (pointless) vanus, inanis; (lazy) ignavus, iners, deses; to be — cessare

idle vt to — away terĕre; vi cessare

idleness s otium n; ignavia, inertia, desidia f

idler s cessator, homo ignavus m

idle talk s nugae f pl

idly adv otiose; ignave, segniter; (in vain) vane, frustra

idol s simulacrum n; (eccl) idolum n; (person) deliciae f pl

idolater s simulacrorum cultor m

idolatrous adj idololatricus

idolatry s simulacrorum cult·us -ūs m

idolize vt venerari

idyl s idyllium n

if conj si; as — quasi, tamquam; and — quodsi; but — sin; quodsi; even — etiamsi; — not ni, nisi, si non; — only si modo, dummodo

igneous adj igneus

ignite vt accendĕre, incendĕre; vi exardescĕre, flammam concipĕre

ignoble adj ignobilis, obscurus; (base) turpis

ignobly adv turpiter

ignominious adj ignominiosus, turpis; —ly ignominiose, turpiter

ignominy s ignominia f

ignoramus s idiota m

ignorance s ignoratio, ignorantia f

ignorant adj ignarus, nescius; (unlearned) indoctus; to be — of ignorare, nescire; —ly inscienter, inscite, indocte

ignore vt praetermittĕre, neglegĕre

Iliad s Ilias f

ill adj aegrotus, aeger; (evil) malus; to be — aegrotare; to fall — in morbum incidĕre

ill adv male, prave

ill s malum n

ill-bred adj inurbanus, agrestis

illegal adj vetitus, illicitus; —ly contra leges, illicite

illegitimate adj haud legitimus; (of birth) spurius, nothus

illiberal adj illiberalis; —ly illiberaliter

illicit adj illicitus; —ly illicite

illiterate adj illitteratus, indoctus, ineruditus

illness s morbus m, aegritudo, aegrotatio, valetudo f

illogical adj absurdus; —ly absurde

ill-starred adj infelix

ill-tempered adj iracundus, stomachosus, difficilis

illuminate vt illustrare, illuminare

illumination s illuminatio f, lumina n pl

illusion s error m

illusive adj falsus, vanus

illusory adj fallax

illustrate vt illustrare; (fig) explanare

illustration s illustratio f; (fig) exemplum n

illustrative adj exemplaris

illustrious adj illustris, insignis, praeclarus; —ly praeclare

image s signum, simulacrum n; (likeness) effigies, imago f

imagery s figurae f pl

imaginary adj fictus, commenticius

imagination s cogitatio f

imaginative adj ingeniosus

imagine vt imaginari, fingĕre; (to suppose) opinari

imbecile adj (weak) imbecillus; (of mind) animo imbecillus, fatuus

imbecile s fatuus m

imbibe vt imbibĕre

imbue vt imbuĕre, tingĕre

imitate vt imitari

imitation s imitatio f; (copy) imago f

imitative adj ad imitandum aptus

imitator s imitator m, imitatrix f, aemulator m

immaculate adj integer, castus

immaterial adj incorporalis; (unimportant) nullius momenti

immeasurable adj immensus, infinitus

immeasurably adv infinito

immediate adj praesens, proximus; —ly statim, confestim, extemplo; —ly after sub (with acc)

immemorial adj antiquissimus; from time — ex omni memoria aetatum

immense adj immensus; —ly vehementer

immensity s immensitas f

immerge vt mergĕre, immergĕre

immersion s immersio f

imminent adj imminens, impendens

immobility s immobilitas f

immoderate adj immodicus; —ly immoderate, nimie

immodest adj immodestus, impudicus; —ly immodeste, inverecunde

immodesty s immodestia f

immolate vt immolare

immolation s immolatio f

immoral adj pravus, improbus, corruptus; —ly prave

immorality s mores mali m pl, turpitudo, improbitas f

immortal adj immortalis

immortality s immortalitas f

immortalize vt aeternare, ad deos evehĕre

immovable adj immobilis, immotus

immunity s immunitas, vacatio f

immure vt includĕre

immutability s immutabilitas f

immutable adj immutabilis

imp s larva f; (child) puer lascivus m

impair vt imminuĕre, atterĕre, debilitare

impale vt infigĕre

impart vt impertire, communicare

impartial adj aequus, aequabilis, severus; —ly severe

impartiality s aequitas, aequabilitas f

impassable adj insuperabilis, impervius

impassive adj impassibilis, frigidus, lentus

impatient adj impatiens, trepidus; —ly impatienter, aegre

impeach vt accusare

impeachment s accusatio f

impede vt obstare (with dat), impedire, retardare

impediment s impedimentum n; (in speech) haesitatio f

impel vt impellĕre

impenetrable adj impenetrabilis; (fig) occultus

impenitence s impaenitentia f

imperative adj necessarius; (gram) imperativus

imperceptible adj tenuissimus, obscurus

imperceptibly adv sensim

imperfect adj imperfectus, mancus, vitiosus; —ly imperfecte, vitiose

imperfection s vitium n, defect·us -ūs m

imperial adj imperatorius, regius; —ly regie

imperil vt in periculum adducĕre

imperishable adj perennis, aeternus, immortalis

impermeable adj impervius

impersonal adj impersonalis; —ly impersonaliter

impersonate vt sustinēre partes (with genit), imitari

impertinence s insolentia, protervitas f

impertinent adj (rude) insolens, protervus; (not to the point) ineptus, nihil ad rem; —ly insolenter, proterve; inepte

impervious adj impervius, impenetrabilis

impetuosity s impet·us -ūs m, vehementia, violentia f

impetuous adj vehemens, fervidus, violentus; —ly vehementer, fervide, violenter

impetus s impet·us -ūs m, vis f

impiety s impietas f

impinge vi incidĕre

impious adj impius, nefarius; —ly impie, nefarie

implacable adj implacabilis, inexorabilis, durus

implacably adv implacabiliter, dure

implant vt ingignĕre, inserĕre, ingenerare

implement s instrumentum n

implement *vt* exsequi

implicate *vt* implicare, impedire

implication *s* indicium *n*; **by — ta-**
cite

implicit *adj* tacitus, totus; **—ly** tacite, omnino

implore *vt* implorare, obsecrare

imply *vt* significare; **to be implied
in** inesse in (*with abl*)

impolite *adj* inurbanus; **—ly** inurbane

impoliteness *s* inurbanitas *f*

impolitic *adj* inconsultus

imponderable *adj* ponderis expers

import *vt* importare, invehĕre; (*to
mean*) significare, velle

import *s* significatio *f*; **—s** impor-
taticia *n pl*

importance *s* momentum *n*, gravitas *f*

important *adj* magnus, magni momenti, gravis

importunate *adj* importunus; **—ly**
importune

importune *vt* fatigare, efflagitare,
sollicitare

impose *vt* imponĕre; (*to enjoin*) injungĕre; **to — upon** abuti (*with
abl*)

imposition *s* (*tax*) vectigal, tributum *n*; (*excessive burden*) impor-
tunitas *f*

impossibility *s* impossibilitas *f*

impossible *adj* impossibilis

imposter *s* fraudator *m*

imposture *s* fraus *f*

impotence *s* imbecillitas, infirmitas *f*

impotent *adj* imbecillus, infirmus

impound *vt* publicare; (*animals*) includĕre

impoverish *vt* in egestatem redigĕre

impractical *adj* inutilis

imprecate *vt* imprecari, exsecrari

imprecation *s* exsecratio *f*, dirae
f pl

impregnable *adj* inexpugnabilis

impregnate *vt* imbuĕre, gravidam
facĕre

impregnation *s* fecundatio *f*

impress *vt* imprimĕre; (*person*) movēre; **to — something on** inculcare aliquid (*with dat*); (*e.g., someone's mind*) infigĕre aliquid (*with
dat*)

impression *s* impressio *f*; (*copy*)
exemplar *n*; (*mark*) vestigium *n*;
(*idea*) opinio, opinatio *f*; **to make
an — on** commovēre

impressive *adj* gravis; **—ly** graviter

imprint *s* impressio *f*

imprint *vt* imprimĕre, infigĕre

imprison *vt* in vincula conjicĕre

imprisonment *s* custodia *f*

improbable *adj* haud credibilis, parum verisimilis

impromptu *adv* ex tempore

improper *adj* indecorus; **—ly** indecore, perperam

impropriety *s* indecorum *n*

improve *vt* emendare, corrigĕre, excolĕre; *vi* melior fieri, proficĕre

improvement *s* emendatio, correctio *f*, profect·us -ūs *m*

improvident *adj* improvidus, imprudens; **—ly** improvide

improvise *vt* ex tempore dicĕre *or*
componĕre

imprudence *s* imprudentia *f*

imprudent *adj* imprudens, inconsultus, temerarius; **—ly** imprudenter,
inconsulte, temere

impugn *vt* impugnare, in dubium vocare

impulse *s* impuls·us -ūs *m*

impulsive *adj* vehemens, violentus;
—ly impulsu

impunity *s* impunitas *f*; **with —**
impune

impure *adj* impurus, obscenus, incestus; contaminatus; **—ly** impure,
obscene, inceste

impurity *s* impuritas, obscenitas,
impudicitia *f*

in *prep* in (*with abl*); (*in the writings
of*) apud (*with acc*); (*of time*) *render by abl*

in *adv* (*motion*) intro; (*rest*) intra,
intus

inability *s* impotentia *f*

inaccessible *adj* inaccessus

inaccuracy *s* neglegentia *f*

inaccurate *adj* neglegens, parum
accuratus, minime exactus; **—ly**
parum accurate

inactive *adj* iners, quietus, ignavus

inactivity *s* inertia, socordia, cessatio *f*

inadequate *adj* impar; **—ly** parum

inadmissible *adj* illicitus

inadvertence *s* imprudentia *f*

inadvertent *adj* imprudens; **—ly**
imprudenter

inalienable *adj* proprius

inane *adj* inanis

inanimate *adj* inanimus, inanimatus

inapplicable *adj* **to be —** non valēre

inappropriate *adj* haud idoneus, parum aptus; **—ly** parum apte

inarticulate *adj* indistinctus

inartistic *adj* durus

inasmuch as *conj* quandoquidem

inattentive *adj* haud attentus, neglegens; **—ly** neglegenter

inaudible *adj* **to be —** audiri non
posse

inaugurate *vt* inaugurare, consecrare

inauguration *s* inauguratio, consecratio *f*

inauspicious *adj* infaustus; **—ly**
malo omine

inborn *adj* ingenitus, innatus

incalculable *adj* inaestimabilis; (*fig*)
immensus, incredibilis

incantation *s* carmen, incantamentum *n*

incapable *adj* incapax, inhabilis; **to
be — of** non posse (*with inf*)

incapacitate *vt* debilitare

incarcerate *vt* in vincula conjicĕre

incarnate *adj* incarnatus

incarnation *s* incarnatio *f*

incautious *adj* incautus; **—ly** in-
caute

incendiary *adj* incendiarius

incense *s* tus *n*

incense *vt* ture fumigare; (*to anger*) irritare, exasperare

incentive *s* incitamentum *n*

incessant *adj* continuus, assiduus; —ly assidue

incest *s* incest·us -ūs *m*

incestuous *adj* incestus

inch *s* uncia *f*; — by — unciatim

incident *s* cas·us -ūs, event·us -ūs *m*

incidental *adj* fortuitus; —ly fortuito, casu, forte

incipient *adj* nascens, primus

incision *s* incis·us -ūs *m*, incisura *f*

incisive *adj* acer

incite *vt* incitare, stimulare

incitement *s* incitamentum *n*, incitatio *f*

incivility *s* rusticitas *f*

inclemency *s* inclementia *f*; (*of weather*) asperitas *f*

inclination *s* (*act*) inclinatio *f*; (*slope*) proclivitas *f*; (*propensity*) libido, inclinatio *f*

incline *vt* inclinare; *vi* propendēre

incline *s* acclivitas *f*

inclined *adj* inclinatus, propensus, pronus

include *vt* includēre, comprehendēre

inclusive *adj* comprehendens

incognito *adv* clam

incoherent *adj* interruptus; —ly interrupte

income *s* redit·us -ūs, fruct·us -ūs *m*, merces *f*

incomparable *adj* incomparabilis, singularis, unicus, eximius

incomparably *adv* eximie, unice

incompatibility *s* repugnantia, diversitas *f*

incompatible *adj* repugnans, discors

incompetence *s* jurisdictionis defect·us -ūs *m*; inscitia *f*

incompetent *adj* inscitus, inhabilis

incomplete *adj* imperfectus

incomprehensible *adj* haud comprehensibilis

inconceivable *adj* incredibilis

inconclusive *adj* anceps

incongruous *adj* inconveniens, male congruens; —ly parum apte

inconsiderable *adj* levis, exiguus

inconsiderate *adj* inconsultus

inconsistency *s* inconstantia, discrepantia *f*

inconsistent *adj* inconstans, absonus, contrarius; to be — with abhorrēre ab (*with abl*); —ly inconstanter

inconsolable *adj* inconsolabilis

inconstancy *s* inconstantia, levitas *f*

inconstant *adj* inconstans, levis

incontestable *adj* non contentendus

incontinence *s* incontinentia, impudicitia *f*

incontinent *adj* incontinens, intemperans, impudicus; —ly incontinenter

incontrovertible *adj* quod refutari non potest

inconvenience *s* incommodum *n*

inconvenience *vt* incommodare

inconvenient *adj* incommodus; —ly

incommode

incorporate *vt* concorporare, inserēre

incorporation *s* coagmentatio, cooptatio *f*

incorporeal *adj* incorporalis

incorrect *adj* mendosus, vitiosus, falsus; —ly mendose, falso, perperam

incorrigible *adj* incorrigibilis; (*fig*) perditus

incorrupt *adj* incorruptus, integer

incorruptibility *s* incorruptibilitas *f*, incorrupti mores *m pl*

incorruptible *adj* incorruptibilis, integer

increase *s* (*act*) accretio *f*; incrementum, additamentum *n*

increase *vt* augēre, ampliare; *vi* augēri, crescēre

incredible *adj* incredibilis

incredibly *adv* incredibiliter, ultra fidem

incredulity *s* incredulitas *f*

incredulous *adj* incredulus

increment *s* incrementum *n*

incriminate *vt* criminari

incubation *s* incubatio *f*

inculcate *vt* inculcare

inculcation *s* inculcatio *f*

incumbent *adj* it is — on oportet (*with acc*)

incur *vt* contrahēre, subire; (*guilt*) admittēre

incurable *adj* insanabilis

incursion *s* incursio *f*

indebted *adj* obaeratus; (*obliged*) obligatus, devinctus, obnoxius

indecency *s* indecorum *n*, obscenitas *f*

indecent *adj* indecorus, obscenus; —ly indecore, obscene

indecision *s* haesitatio, dubitatio *f*

indecisive *adj* anceps, dubius, incertus

indeclinable *adj* indeclinabilis

indeed *adv* vere, profecto, sane; (*concessive*) quidem; (*reply*) certe, vero; (*interr*) itane?, verone?

indefatigable *adj* indefatigabilis, indefessus

indefensible *adj* non excusandus; to be — defendi non posse; (*mil*) tenēri non posse

indefinite *adj* infinitus, incertus, anceps, obscurus; —ly indefinite

indelible *adj* indelebilis

indelicacy *s* indecorum *n*

indelicate *adj* putidus, indecorus

indemnify *vt* compensare; damnum restituēre (*with dat*)

indemnity *s* indemnitas *f*

independence *s* libertas *f*

independent *adj* sui potens, sui juris, liber; —ly libere, suo arbitrio

indescribable *adj* inenarrabilis; —ly inenarrabiliter

indestructible *adj* perennis, perpetuus

indeterminate *adj* indefinitus

index *s* index, elenchus *m*; (*of dial*) gnomon *m*

Indian *adj* Indicus

Indian *s* Indus *m*

indicate *vt* indicare, significare
indication *s* indicatio *f*, signum, indicium *n*
indicative *adj* indicativus
indict *vt* accusare; diem dicĕre (*with dat*)
indictment *s* libellus *m*, accusatio *f*
indifference *s* neglegentia, incuria, lentitudo *f*
indifferent *adj* (*apathetic*) remissus, neglegens, lentus; (*mediocre*) mediocris; —**ly** neglegenter, lente; (*without discrimination*) promiscue
indigenous *adj* indigena
indigent *adj* egens, inops
indigestible *adj* crudus
indigestion *s* cruditas *f*
indignant *adj* indignans, indignabundus, iratus; **to be** — indignari; —**ly** indignanter
indignation *s* indignatio *f*, dolor *m*
indignity *s* indignitas, contumelia *f*
indirect *adj* indirectus, obliquus; —**ly** indirecte, oblique
indiscreet *adj* inconsultus; —**ly** inconsulte, temere
indiscretion *s* immodestia *f*; (*act*) culpa *f*
indiscriminate *adj* promiscuus; —**ly** promiscue, sine discrimine
indispensable *adj* omnino necessarius
indisposed *adj* aversus; (*in health*) aegrotus; **to be** — aegrotare
indisputable *adj* manifestus, certus
indissoluble *adj* indissolubilis
indistinct *adj* indistinctus, parum clarus, obscurus; —**ly** indistincte
individual *adj* proprius, singularis, singuli; —**ly** singulatim
individual *s* homo *m* & *f*; —**s** singuli *m pl*
individuality *s* proprium ingenium *n*
indivisible *adj* indivisibilis, individuus
indolence *s* inertia, desidia *f*
indolent *adj* iners, ignavus; —**ly** ignave, segniter
indomitable *adj* indomitus
indorse *vt* ratum facĕre
indubitable *adj* indubitabilis
indubitably *adv* sine dubio
induce *vt* persuadĕre (*with dat*), inducĕre
inducement *s* incitamentum *n*, illecebra *f*
indulge *vt* indulgĕre (*with dat*), servire (*with dat*)
indulgence *s* indulgentia, venia *f*
indulgent *adj* indulgens, benignus; —**ly** indulgenter, benigne
industrious *adj* industrius, sedulus, strenuus; —**ly** industrie
industry *s* industria, assiduitas *f*
inebriated *adj* ebrius, madidus
ineffable *adj* ineffabilis
ineffective *adj* irritus, inutilis; **to be** — effectu carēre
ineffectual *adj* inefficax; —**ly** frustra, nequiquam
inefficiency *s* inutilitas *f*
inefficient *adj* inscitus, inhabilis
ineligible *adj* non eligibilis

inept *adj* ineptus
inequality *s* inaequalitas *f*
inert *adj* iners, segnis, socors
inertia *s* inertia *f*
inevitable *adj* necessarius
inexact *adj* haud accuratus; (*of persons*) indiligens
inexcusable *adj* inexcusabilis
inexhaustible *adj* inexhaustus
inexorable *adj* inexorabilis, durus
inexperience *s* imperitia, inscitia *f*
inexperienced *adj* imperitus, inexpertus
inexplicable *adj* inexplicabilis, inenodabilis
inexpressible *adj* inenarrabilis
inextricable *adj* inexplicabilis, inextricabilis
infallible *adj* certus, erroris expers
infamous *adj* infamis, turpis, flagitiosus; —**ly** flagitiose
infamy *s* infamia *f*, probrum *n*
infancy *s* infantia *f*
infant *adj* infans; puerilis
infant *s* infans *m* & *f*
infanticide *s* (*person*) infanticida *m*; (*deed*) infanticidium *n*
infantile *adj* infantilis
infantry *s* peditat·us -ūs *m*, pedites *m pl*
infatuate *vt* infatuare
infatuation *s* amentia, dementia *f*
infect *vt* inficĕre; (*fig*) contaminare
infection *s* contagium *n*, contagio *f*
infectious *adj* contagiosus
infer *vt* inferre, conjicĕre
inference *s* conjectura, conclusio *f*
inferior *adj* inferior, deterior, minor
infernal *adj* infernus
infertility *s* sterilitas *f*
infest *vt* infestare, frequentare
infidel *s* infidelis *m* & *f*
infidelity *s* infidelitas, perfidia *f*
infiltrate *vi* se insinuare
infinite *adj* infinitus, immensus; —**ly** infinite; (*very greatly*) infinito
infinitive *s* infinitivus modus *m*
infinity *s* infinitas, infinitio *f*
infirm *adj* infirmus, debilis
infirmary *s* valetudinarium *n*
infirmity *s* infirmitas, imbecillitas *f*
inflame *vt* inflammare, incendĕre, accendĕre
inflammable *adj* ad exardescendum facilis
inflammation *s* inflammatio *f*
inflammatory *adj* turbulentus, ardens
inflate *vt* inflare; **to be inflated** tumēre
inflation *s* inflatio *f*
inflect *vt* inflectĕre, curvare
inflection *s* flex·us -ūs *m*, declinatio *f*
inflexible *adj* rigidus; (*fig*) obstinatus, pertinax
inflexibly *adv* obstinate
inflict *vt* infligĕre, imponĕre
infliction *s* malum *n*, poena *f*
influence *s* gratia, auctoritas *f*, momentum *n*; **to have** — **on** valēre apud (*with acc*)
influence *vt* movēre, impellĕre
influential *adj* gravis, potens

influenza s catarrh·us -ūs m, grave-do f

influx s influxio f

inform vt (to teach) instruĕre; certiorem facĕre; vi to — against deferre de (with abl)

informant s index, delator m

information s informatio f, indicium n, nuntius m

informer s delator m

infraction s infractio f

infrequency s raritas f

infrequent adj rarus

infringe vt infringĕre, violare; vi to — upon occupare, usurpare

infringement s violatio, usurpatio f

infuriate vt efferare

infuse vt infundĕre; (fig) injicĕre

infusion s infusio f

ingenious adj sollers, callidus, ingeniosus; (of thing) artificiosus; —ly callide, artificiose

ingenuity s ars, sollertia f

ingenuous adj simplex

inglorious adj inglorius, inhonestus; —ly sine gloria, in honeste

ingrained adj insitus, inveteratus

ingratiate vt to — oneself with gratiam inire ab (with abl)

ingratitude s ingratus animus m

ingredient s pars f

inhabit vt incolĕre, habitare

inhabitable adj habitabilis

inhabitant s incola m & f

inhale vt haurire; vi spiritum ducĕre

inharmonious adj dissonus, absonus

inherent adj inhaerens, insitus; to be — in inesse (with dat)

inherit vt excipĕre

inheritance s hereditas, successio f, patrimonium n; to come into an — hereditatem adire

inheritor s heres m & f

inhospitable adj inhospitalis

inhospitably adv minime hospitaliter

inhospitality s inhospitalitas f

inhuman adj inhumanus; —ly inhumane

inhumanity s inhumanitas f

inimical adj inimicus

inimitable adj inimitabilis

iniquitous adj iniquus, improbus

iniquity s iniquitas, injustitia f

initial adj primus

initiate vt initiare, instituĕre

initiation s initiatio f

initiative s initium n

inject vt injicĕre, infundĕre, immittĕre

injection s injectio f

injudicious adj inconsultus; —ly inconsulte, temere

injunction s mandatum, imperatum n

injure vt nocēre (with dat), laedĕre

injurious adj noxius, damnosus, gravis; —ly male

injury s injuria f, damnum, detrimentum, malum n

injustice s injustitia f; (act) injuria f

ink s atramentum n

inkling s (hint) rumusculus m, obscura significatio f

inland adj mediterraneus

inlay vt inserĕre; (with mosaic) tessellare

inlet s sin·us -ūs m, aestuarium n

inmate s incola, inquilinus m

inmost adj intimus, imus

inn s caupona f, deversorium n

innate adj innatus, insitus

inner adj interior

innermost adj intimus, imus

innkeeper s caupo m

innocence s innocentia f; castitas f

innocent adj insons, innocens, integer, castus; —ly innocenter, integre, caste

innocuous adj innocuus; —ly innocue

innovation s novum n, res nova f

innovator s rerum novarum auctor m

innumerable adj innumerabilis

inoffensive adj innocens, innoxius

inopportune adj inopportunus; —ly parum in tempore

inordinate adj immoderatus; —ly immoderate

inquest s inquisitio f; (law) quaestio f; to hold an — quaerĕre

inquire vi inquirĕre, rogare; to — into investigare

inquiry s quaestio, investigatio f

inquisition s inquisitio f

inquisitive adj curiosus; —ly curiose

inquisitor s quaesitor m

inroad s incursio, irruptio f

insane adj insanus, vecors; —ly insane

insanity s insania, dementia f

insatiable adj insatiabilis, inexplebilis

inscribe vt inscribĕre, insculpĕre, incidĕre

inscription s inscriptio f, titulus m

inscrutable adj occultus, obscurus

insect s insectum n, bestiola f

insecure adj incertus, intutus, instabilis

insecurity s periculum n

insensible adj insensilis; (fig) durus

inseparable adj inseparabilis

insert vt inserĕre; (in writing) ascribĕre

insertion s insertio, interpositio f

inside adj interior

inside adv intrinsecus

inside s interior pars f, interiora n pl

inside prep intro (with acc)

insidious adj insidiosus, subdolus; —ly insidiose, subdole

insight s (knowledge) cognitio, intellegentia f; (intelligence) consilium, judicium n

insignia s insignia n pl

insignificance s exiguitas, levitas f

insignificant adj exiguus, levis, nullius momenti; (rank) humilis

insincere adj insincerus, simulatus, fucosus; —ly haud sincere, simulate

insincerity s simulatio, fallacia f

insinuate vt insinuare; (to hint) significare

insinuation s significatio f

insipid adj insulsus, hebes, frigidus; —ly insulse

insist vt flagitare, exposcère; vi instare; **to — on** urgère, postulare

insistence s pertinacia f

insolence s insolentia, arrogantia f

insolent adj insolens, arrogans; —ly insolenter

insoluble adj insolubilis; (fig) inexplicabilis

insolvent adj **to be —** solvendo non esse

inspect vt inspicère, introspicère, intuëri; (mil) recensëre

inspection s inspectio, cura f; (mil) recensio f

inspector s curator m

inspiration s (divine) afflat·us -ūs m; instinct·us -ūs m; (prophetic) furor m

inspire vt inspirare, incendère, injicère

instability s instabilitas f

install vt inaugurare, constituère

installation s inauguratio f

instalment s pensio, portio f

instance s exemplum n; **at my —** me auctore; **for —** exempli gratiā

instance vt memorare

instant adj instans, praesens; —ly extemplo, statim

instant s momentum n; **this — statim**, actutum

instantaneous adj praesens; —ly continuo

instead adv potius, magis

instead of prep pro (with abl), loco (with genit)

instigate vt instigare

instigation s incitatio f, stimulus m

instigator s instigator m, instigatrix f

instill vt instillare, imbuère, injicère

instinct s instinct·us -ūs m, natura f

instinctive adj naturalis; —ly instinctu

institute vt instituère, constituère, condère

institute s institutum n

institution s (act) institutio f; (thing instituted) institutum n

instruct vt (to teach) docère, instituère; (to order) praecipère (with dat), mandare

instruction s institutio, eruditio, doctrina f; —s mandata n pl

instructive adj ad docendum aptus

instructor s praeceptor, magister, doctor m, magistra f

instrument s instrumentum n; (mus) organum n; (law) tabula, syngrapha f

instrumental adj aptus, utilis

insubordinate adj seditiosus, male parens

insubordination s inobedientia, intemperantia f

insufferable adj intolerandus, intolerabilis

insufficiency s defect·us -ūs m, inopia f

insufficient adj impar, parum sufficiens; —ly haud satis

insular adj insulanus

insulate vt segregare

insult s probrum n, injuria, contumelia f

insult vt insultare; contumeliam imponère (with dat), contumeliā afficère

insultingly adv contumeliose

insure vt tutum praestare

insurgent adj rebellis

insurgent s rebellis m

insurmountable adj inexsuperabilis

insurrection s rebellio, seditio f

intact adj integer, intactus, incolumis

intangible adj intactilis

integral adj necessarius

integrity s integritas, innocentia, fides f

intellect s intellect·us -ūs, animus m, mens f, ingenium n

intellectual adj ingeniosus

intelligence s ingenium n, intellegentia f; (information) nuntius m

intelligent adj sapiens, argutus, prudens; —ly intelligenter, sapienter, prudenter

intelligible adj intelligibilis, perspicuus

intelligibly adv intelligibiliter, perspicue

intemperance s intemperantia f

intemperate adj immodicus, intemperatus; —ly intemperanter

intend vt (with inf) intendère, in animo habère; (with object) destinare

intended adj destinatus; (of future spouse) sponsus

intense adj acer, fervidus; (of heat) rapidus; (excessive) nimius; —ly vehementer, valde, nimium

intensify vt augère

intensity s vehmentia, vis f; (of winter, etc.) rigor m

intent adj intentus, attentus; **to be — on** animum intendère in (with acc); —ly intente

intention s propositum, consilium n; (meaning) significatio f

intentionally adv de industria

inter vt inhumare, sepelire

intercede vi intercedère, deprecari, se interponère

intercept vt excipère, intercipère, intercludère

intercession s deprecatio f; (of tribune) intercessio f

intercessor s deprecator m

interchange vt permutare, commutare

interchange s permutatio, vicissitudo f

intercourse s commercium n; (social) consuetudo f; (sexual) congress·us -ūs, coit·us -ūs m

interdict vt interdicère, prohibère

interdiction s interdictio f, interdictum n

interest s (attention) studium n; (advantage) utilitas f, us·us -ūs m, commodum *n*; (*money*) faenus *n*, usura *f*; **it is of — to me meā interest**, meā refert

interested *adj* — **in** studiosus (*with genit*), attentus (*with dat*)

interfere *vi* intercedĕre, intervenire, interpellare

interference *s* intercessio *f*, dissidium *n*, intervent·us -ūs *m*

interim *s* intervallum *n*; **in the —** interim, interea

interior *adj* interior

interior *s* interior pars *f*

interjection *s* interjectio *f*

interlinear *adj* interscriptus

interlude *s* embolium *n*

intermarriage *s* connubium *n*

intermarry *vi* matrimonio inter se conjungi

intermediary *s* internuntius *m*

intermediate *adj* medius

interment *s* sepultura, humatio *f*

interminable *adj* infinitus

intermission *s* intermissio, intercapedo *f*

intermittent *adj* intermittens, interruptus; **—ly** interdum, aliquando

internal *adj* intestinus, domesticus; **—ly** intus, interne; domi

international *adj* inter gentes

interpolate *vt* interpolare

interpolation *s* interpolatio *f*

interpret *vt* interpretari

interpretation *s* interpretatio *f*

interpreter *s* interpres *m*

interrogate *vt* interrogare, percontari

interrogation *s* interrogatio, percontatio *f*

interrogative *adj* interrogativus

interrupt *vt* interrumpĕre, interpellare

interruption *s* interruptio, interpellatio *f*

intersect *vt* intersecare

intersection *s* quadrivium *n*

intersperse *vt* inmiscēre

intertwine *vt* intertexēre

interval *s* intervallum, spatium *n*

intervene *vi* (*to be between*) interjacēre; (*to come between*) intercedĕre, intervenire

intervening *adj* medius

intervention *s* intercessio *f*, intervent·us -ūs *m*

interview *s* colloquium *n*, congress·us -ūs *m*

interview *vt* percontari

interweave *vt* intertexĕre, intexĕre

intestinal *adj* ad intestina pertinens

intestine *adj* intestinus *n*; (*pol*) domesticus, civicus

intestines *s* intestina *n pl*; (*of victim*) exta *n pl*

intimacy *s* familiaritas, consuetudo *f*

intimate *adj* familiaris; intimus; **—ly** familiariter; intime

intimate *vt* indicare, innuĕre, denuntiare

intimation *s* indicium *n*, denuntiatio *f*

intimidate *vt* minari (*with dat*), metum injicĕre (*with dat*), terrēre

intimidation *s* minae *f pl*

into *prep* in (*with acc*)

intolerable *adj* intolerabilis, intolerandus

intolerably *adv* intoleranter

intolerance *s* intolerantia *f*; superbia *f*

intolerant *adj* intolerans, impatiens

intonation *s* accent·us -ūs *m*

intone *vt* cantare

intoxicate *vt* ebrium reddĕre

intoxicated *adj* ebrius

intoxication *s* ebrietas *f*

intractable *adj* intractabilis, indocilis

intrepid *adj* intrepidus, impavidus; **—ly** intrepide

intricacy *s* perplexitas, implicatio *f*

intricate *adj* contortus, implicatus, perplexus; **—ly** contorte, perplexe

intrigue *s* conspiratio *f*, dolus *m*, artificia *n pl*

intrigue *vt* fascinare; *vi* machinari, dolis contendĕre

intrinsic *adj* innatus, verus; **—ally** vere, per se

introduce *vt* introducĕre, inducĕre

introduction *s* (*preface*) praefatio *f*, exordium, prooemium *n*; (*to person*) introductio *f*, adit·us -ūs *m*

intrude *vi* se interponĕre, se inculcare, intervenire

intruder *s* interpellator, advena *m*; homo molestus *m*

intrusion *s* interpellatio, usurpatio *f*

intuition *s* intuit·us -ūs *m*, cognitio *f*, acumen *n*

intuitive *adj* intuitivus; **—ly** mentis propriā vi ac naturā

inundate *vt* inundare

inundation *s* inundatio *f*, diluvium *n*

invade *vt* incurrĕre in (*with acc*), invadĕre

invader *s* invasor *m*

invalid *adj* infirmus, vitiosus; (*sick*) aeger, aegrotus

invalid *s* aegrotus *m*

invalidate *vt* irritum facĕre, rescindĕre

invaluable *adj* inaestimabilis

invariable *adj* constans, immutabilis

invariably *adv* semper

invasion *s* incursio, irruptio *f*

invective *s* convicium, probrum *n*

inveigh *vi* **to — against** invehi in (*with acc*), insectari

invent *vt* invenire, reperire; (*to contrive*) excogitare, fingĕre

invention *s* (*act*) inventio *f*; (*thing invented*) inventum *n*

inventive *adj* sollers, ingeniosus

inventor *s* inventor, auctor *m*

inventory *s* bonorum index *m*

inverse *adj* inversus, conversus; **—ly** inverso ordine

inversion *s* inversio, conversio *f*

invert *vt* invertĕre

invest *vt* (*money*) collocare, ponĕre; (*to besiege*) obsidēre

investigate *vt* investigare, indagare; (*law*) quaerĕre, cognoscĕre

investigation *s* investigatio *f*; (*law*) cognitio *f*

investigator s investigator, indaga-tor m; (law) quaesitor m

investment s (of money) collocatio f; (money invested) locata pecunia f; (mil) obsessio f

inveterate adj inveteratus

invigorate vt corroborare, recreare

invincible adj invictus, insuperabilis

inviolable adj inviolatus, sacrosanc-tus

inviolate adj inviolatus, intactus

invisible adj invisibilis, caecus

invitation s invitatio f

invite vt invitare, adhibēre

inviting adj suavis, gratus, blandus; —ly blande

invocation s invocatio, testatio f

invoice s libellus m

invoke vt vocare, invocare, obtestari

involuntarily adv invite, coacte

involuntary adj non voluntarius, coactus

involve vt implicare, involvēre; (to comprise) continēre

involved adj to be — illigari; to be — in debt aere alieno laborare

invulnerable adj invulnerabilis

inward adj interior; —ly intus, in-trinsecus

inwards adv introrsus

Ionian adj Ionicus

irascible adj iracundus

ire s ira f

Ireland s Hibernia f

iris s iris f

Irish adj Hibernicus

irk vt incommodare; **I am irked** taedet me, piget me

irksome adj molestus, odiosus

iron s ferrum n

iron adj ferreus

ironical adj ironicus, deridens; —ly per ironiam

irony s ironia, dissimulatio f

irradiate vt illustrare; vi effulgēre

irrational adj rationis expers, irra-tionalis, absurdus; —ly absurde

irreconcilable adj implacabilis; (in-compatible) repugnans, insociabilis

irrecoverable adj irreparabilis

irrefutable adj certus, invictus

irregular adj irregularis, abnormis; (disorderly) tumultuarius; (gram) anomalus; —ly irregulariter

irregularity s irregularitas f; (of conduct) luxuries, pravitas f; (gram) anomalia f

irrelevant adj non pertinens, alie-nus; **it is** — nil ad rem pertinet

irreligious adj impius

irremediable adj insanabilis

irreparable adj irreparabilis, irrevo-cabilis

irreproachable adj irreprehensus, integer

irresistible adj inexsuperabilis, in-victus

irresolute adj dubius, incertus ani-mi; (permanent characteristic) pa-rum firmus; —ly dubitanter

irresolution s dubitatio f; animus parum firmus m

irresponsibility s incuria f

irresponsible adj incuriosus

irretrievable adj irreparabilis, irre-vocabilis

irreverence s impietas f

irreverent adj impius, inverecundus; —ly impie

irrevocable adj irrevocabilis

irrigate vt irrigare

irrigation s irrigatio, inductio aquae f

irritability s iracundia f

irritable adj irritabilis, iracundus, difficilis

irritate vt irritare; (wound) inflam-mare

irritation s irritatio, iracundia f, stomachus m

island s insula f

islander s insulanus m

islet s parva insula f

isolate vt sejungēre, secernēre

issue s (result) event·us -ūs, exit·us -ūs m; (question) res f; (offspring) proles f; (of book) editio f; (of money) emissio f

issue vt (to distribute) distribuēre; (orders, etc.) edēre, proponēre, pro-mulgare; (money) erogare; (book) edēre; vi emanare, egredi; (to turn out, result) evenire, evadēre

isthmus s isthmus m

it pron id, hoc

itch s prurigo f, prurit·us -ūs m; (disease) scabies f

itch vi prurire; (fig) gestire

item s res f

itinerant adj circumforaneus, vagus

itinerary s itinerarium n

its pron ejus; — **own** suus

itself pron (refl) se, sese; (intensive) ipsum

ivory s ebur n

ivory adj eburneus

ivy s hedera f

J

jabber vi blaterare

jackass s asinus m; (fig) stultus m

jacket s tunica f

jaded adj defessus

jagged adj serratus; (of rocks) prae-ruptus

jail s carcer m

jailer s carcerarius m

jam s baccarum conditura f

jam vt frequentare, stipare; (to ob-struct) impedire, obstruēre

jamb s postis m

jangle vi crepitare

January s (mensis) Januarius m

jar s olla, amphora f, urceus, cadus m

jar vt vibrare; offendēre; vi discrepare

jargon s confusae voces f pl

jarring adj dissonus, discors

jaundice s morbus regius m

jaundiced adj ictericus, felle suffusus; (fig) lividus, morosus

jaunt s excursio f; **to take a —** excurrēre

javelin s pilum, jaculum n; **to hurl a —** jaculari

jaw s mala, maxilla f; **—s** (fig) fauces f pl

jawbone s maxilla f

jay s graculus m

jealous adj invidus, lividus; **to be — of** invidēre (with dat)

jealousy s invidia, aemulatio f

jeer s irrisio f, irris·us -ūs m

jeer vt deridēre, explodēre; vi **to — at** irridēre, alludēre

jelly s cylon, quilon n

jellyfish s pulmo, halipleumon m

jeopardize vt periclitari, in periculum adducēre

jeopardy s periculum n

jerk s verber, ict·us -ūs, impet·us -ūs m

jerk vt calcitrare, icēre

jerky adj (of style) salebrosus

jest s jocus m; **in —** joco, jocose

jest vi jocari, ludēre

jester s joculator m; (buffoon) scurra m

jestingly adv per jocum

Jesus s Jesus m

jet s scatebra f

jetty s moles f

Jew s Judaeus m

jewel s gemma f

jeweled adj gemmeus, gemmifer

jeweler s gemmarius m

jewelry s gemmae f pl

Jewish adj Judaicus

jig s tripudium n

jilt vt repudiare

jingle vi tinnire

jingle s tinnit·us -ūs m

job s negotiolum, opus n

jockey s agaso m

jocose adj jocosus; **—ly** jocose

jocular adj jocularis, facetus

jog vi **to — along** lente progredi

join vt (to connect) jungēre, conjungēre; (to come into the company of) se jungēre (with dat), se jungēre cum (with abl); vi conjungi, adjungi, cohaerēre; **to — in** particeps esse (with genit), interesse (with dat); **to — together** inter se conjungi

joint adj communis; **—ly** una, conjunctim, communiter

joint s (of body) articulus m, commissura f; (of plant) geniculum n; (of any structure) compages f

jointed adj geniculatus

joist s tignum n

joke s jocus m

joke vi jocari, ludēre

joker s joculator m

joking s jocus m; **all — aside** joco

remoto; **—ly** per jocum

jolly adj hilaris, festivus

jolt vt jactare, concutēre; (fig) percellēre; vi jactari

jolting s jactatio f

jostle vt pulsare, agitare, fodicare

jot s hilum n; **not a —** minime; **to care not a —** non flocci facēre

jot vt **to — down** notare, subscribēre

journal s ephemeris f, acta diurna n pl

journey s iter n

journey vi iter facēre; **to — abroad** peregrinari

journeyman s opifex m

Jove s Jupiter m

jovial adj hilaris

owl s bucca f

joy s gaudium n, laetitia f

joyful adj laetus; **—ly** laete, libenter

joyless adj illaetabilis

joyous adj hilaris, festivus

jubilant adj laetus, gaudio exsultans, gaudio triumphans

jubilation s exsultatio f

jubilee s dies anniversarius m, solemne n

Judaic adj Judaicus

Judaism s Judaismus m

judge s judex, quaesitor, arbiter m

judge vt judicare; (to think) existimare, censēre; (to value) aestimare; (to decide between) dijudicare

judgment s judicium, arbitrium n; (opinion) sententia f, judicium n; **to pass — on** statuēre de (with abl); **to pronounce —** jus dicēre

judgment seat s tribunal n

judicial adj judicialis, judicarius; **—ly** jure, lege

judicious adj sapiens, sagax, prudens; **—ly** sapienter, sagaciter, prudenter

jug s urceus m

juggle vi praestigias agēre

juggler s praestigiator m

juice s sucus, liquor m

juicy adj sucidus

July s (mensis) Quintilis or Julius m

jumble s congeries, confusio f

jumble vt confundēre, permiscēre

jump s salt·us -ūs m

jump vt transilire; vi salire; **to — at** (opportunity) captare; **to — for joy** exsultare

junction s conjunctio f

juncture s tempus n; **at this —** hic

June s (mensis) Junius m

jungle s salt·us -ūs m

junior adj junior, minor natu

juniper s juniperus m

jurisdiction s jurisdictio f

jurisprudence s jurisprudentia f

jurist s jurisconsultus m

juror s judex m

jury s judices m pl

just adj justus, aequus; (deserved) meritus; **—ly** juste; jure, merito

just adv (only) modo; (exactly) prorsus; (with adv) demum, denique; **— after** sub (with acc); **— as** aeque ac, perinde ac, sic ut, haud secus

ac; — **before** sub (with acc); — now modo; — **so** ita prorsus
justice s justitia, aequitas f; (just treatment) jus n; (person) praetor m
justifiable adj justus, legitimus, excusatus

justifiably adv jure
justification s purgatio, excusatio f
justify vt purgare, excusare, approbare
jut vi prominēre; **to — out** prominēre, eminēre, procurrēre
juvenile adj juvenilis, puerilis

K

kale s crambe f
keel s carina f
keen adj acer, sagax; **—ly** acute, acriter; sagaciter
keenness s (of scent) sagacitas f; (of sight) acies f; (of pain) acerbitas f; (enthusiasm) studium n
keep vt tenēre, habēre; (to preserve) servare; (to celebrate) agěre, celebrare; (to guard) custodire; (to obey) observare; (to support) alěre; (animals) pascěre; (to store) conděre; **to — apart** distinēre; **to — away** arcēre; **to — back** retinēre, cohibēre; (to conceal) celare; **to — company** comitari; **to — from** prohibēre; **to — in** cohibēre, claudēre; **to — off** arcēre, defendēre; **to — secret** celare; **to — together** continēre; **to — under** compescěre, supprimēre; **to — up** sustinēre; vi remanēre, durare; **to — away** abstinēre; **to — up with** subsequi
keep s custodia, cura f
keeper s custos m
keeping s tutela, custodia, cura f; **in — with** pro (with abl)
keepsake s monumentum, pignus n
keg s cadus m, testa f
ken s conspectus -ūs m
kennel s stabulum n
kernel s nucleus m; (fig) medulla f
kettle s lebes f
kettledrum s tympanum aeneum n
key s clavis f; (of a position) claustra n pl
keyhole s foramen n
kick vt calce ferire; vi calcitrare
kid s haedus m
kidnap vt surripěre
kidnapper s plagiarius m
kidney s ren m
kill vt interficěre, caeděre, occiděre, necare; (time) perděre
killer s interfector, necator m
kiln s fornax f
kin s cognati, consanguinei, necessarii m pl
kind adj amicus, benignus, benevolus; **—ly** benigne, clementer
kind s genus n; **what — of** qualis
kindhearted adj benignus
kindle vt incenděre, accenděre, inflammare
kindly adj benignus
kindness s benignitas, benevolentia f; (deed) beneficium, officium n
kindred adj consanguineus, cognatus

kindred s consanguinitas, cognatio f; cognati, propinqui m pl
king s rex m
kingdom s regnum n
kingfisher s alcedo f
kingly adj regius, regalis
kinsman s necessarius, cognatus, propinquus m
kinswoman s necessaria, cognata, propinqua f
kiss s osculum, basium n
kiss vt osculari
kissing s osculatio f
kitchen s culina f
kite s (bird) milvus m
kitten s catulus felinus m
knack s sollertia, calliditas f
knapsack s sarcina f
knave s nebulo, veterator m
knavish adj nefarius, improbus; (mischievous) malitiosus
knead vt subigěre
knee s genu n
kneel vi genibus niti
knell s campana funebris f
knife s culter m; (for surgery) scalprum n
knight s eques m
knighthood s equestris dignitas f
knightly adj equester
knit vt texěre; **to — the brow** frontem contrahěre
knob s tuber n, nodus m; (of door) bulla f
knock vt **to — down** dejicěre, sternēre; (fig) (at auction) addicěre; **to — in** impellěre, infigěre; **to — off** excutěre, deciděre; **to — out** excutěre; vi **to — about** (to ramble) vagari; **to — at** pulsare
knock s pulsatio f, pulsus -ūs m
knoll s tumulus m
knot s nodus m, geniculum n; (of people) corona f
knot vt nodare, nectēre
knotty adj nodosus; (fig) spinosus
know vt scire; (person) novisse; **not to — ignorare, nescire; **to — how to** scire (with inf)
knowing adj callidus, prudens; **—ly** sciens, de industria, consulto
knowledge s scientia, doctrina f; (of something) cognitio f; (skill) peritia f; (learning) eruditio f
known adj notus; (common) tritus; **to become —** enotescěre; **to make — divulgare, declarare
knuckle s articulus, condylus m
kowtow vi adulari

L

label *s* titulus *m*

labor *s* labor *m*; (*manual*) opera *f*; (*work done*) opus *n*; to be in — laborare utero; woman in — puerpera *f*

labor *vi* laborare, eniti; to — under laborare (*with abl*)

laboratory *s* officina *f*

labored *adj* affectatus

laborer *s* operarius *m*

labyrinth *s* labyrinthus *m*

labyrinthine *adj* labyrinthicus; (*fig*) inextricabilis

lace *s* opus reticulatum *n*

lace *vt* (*to tie*) nectĕre, astringĕre; (*to beat*) verberare

lacerate *vt* lacerare, laniare

laceration *s* laceratio *f*

lack *s* inopia *f*, defect·us -ūs *m*, defectio *f*

lack *vt* carēre (*with abl*), egēre (*with abl*)

lackey *s* pedisequus, servus a pedibus *m*

laconic *adj* brevis, astrictus; —ally breviter, paucis

lad *s* puer, adulescens *m*

ladder *s* scala *f*

ladle *s* ligula, spatha *f*, cochlear *n*

lady *s* domina, matrona *f*

lag *vi* cessare, morari, cunctari

lagoon *s* lacuna *f*, stagnum *n*

lair *s* cubile, latibulum *n*

laity *s* laici *m pl*

lake *s* lac·us -ūs *m*

lamb *s* agnus *m*, agna *f*; (*meat*) agnina *f*

lame *adj* claudus; to walk — claudicare; —ly (*fig*) inconcinne

lameness *s* clauditas *f*

lament *s* lamentum *n*, lamentatio *f*

lament *vt* lamentari, deplorare; *vi* flēre

lamentable *adj* lamentabilis, miserabilis

lamentably *adv* miserabiliter

lamentation *s* lamentatio *f*

lamp *s* lucerna *f*, lynchnus *m*

lampoon *s* satira *f*, libellus *m*

lampoon *vt* famosis carminibus lacessĕre

lance *s* lancea, hasta *f*

lance *vt* incidĕre

land *s* (*soil*) terra, tellus *f*; (*country*) regio *f*; (*estate*) fundus *m*, praedium *n*

land *vt* in terram exponĕre; *vi* egredi, appellĕre

landing place *s* egress·us -ūs *m*

landlord *s* (*of inn*) caupo *m*; (*of land*) dominus *m*

landmark *s* lapis, terminus *m*

landscape *s* regionis sit·us -ūs *m*

landslide *s* terrae laps·us -ūs *m*

land tax *s* vectigal *n*

lane *s* semita *f*

language *s* lingua *f*; (*style or manner of verbal expression*) oratio *f*, sermo *m*, verba *n pl*

languid *adj* languidus; —ly languide

languish *vi* languēre, languescĕre

languishing *adj* languidus, tabescens

languor *s* languor *m*

lanky *adj* prolixus, exilis

lantern *s* la(n)terna *f*

lap *s* sin·us -ūs *m*; (*fig*) gremium *n*; (*in racing*) spatium *n*

lap *vt* lambēre

lapse *s* laps·us -ūs *m*; (*error*) erratum, peccatum *n*, error *m*

lapse *vi* labi; (*of agreement*) irritus fieri; (*to err*) peccare

larceny *s* furtum *n*

lard *s* laridum, lardum *n*, adeps *m & f*

large *adj* magnus, amplus, grandis; to a — extent magna ex parte; —ly plerumque

largess *s* donativum *n*, largitio *f*; to give a — largiri

lark *s* alauda *f*

larynx *s* guttur *n*

lascivious *adj* lascivus, salax, libidinosus; —ly lascive, libidinose

lash *s* verber, flagellum *n*, scutica *f*; (*mark*) vibex *m*

lash *vt* (*to whip*) flagellare; (*to fasten*) alligare; (*fig*) castigare

lashing *s* verberatio *f*

lass *s* puella, virgo *f*

lassitude *s* lassitudo *f*

last *adj* postremus, ultimus; (*in line*) novissimus; (*preceding*) proximus; at — demum, tandem; for the — time postremo

last *vi* durare, perdurare

lasting *adj* diuturnus, perennis

lastly *adv* denique, postremo

latch *s* obex *m & f*

latch *vt* oppessulare

late *adj* serus, tardus; (*new*) recens; (*deceased*) demortuus; (*said of deceased emperor*) divus

late *adv* sero; too — sero, serius

lately *adv* modo, recens, nuper

latent *adj* latens, latitans, occultus

lateral *adj* lateralis

lather *s* spuma *f*

Latin *adj* Latinus; to speak — Latine loqui; to translate into — Latine reddĕre; to understand — Latine scire

Latinity *s* Latinitas *f*

latitude *s* latitudo *f*; (*liberty*) licentia *f*

latter *adj* posterior; the — hic

lattice *s* cancelli *m pl*

laudable *adj* laudabilis

laudably *adv* laudabiliter

laudatory *adj* laudativus, honorificus

laugh *s* ris·us -ūs *m*

laugh *vi* ridēre; to — at deridēre; to — with arridēre (*with dat*)

laughingstock *s* ludibrium *n*

laughter s ris·us -ūs m; (loud) cachinnus m, cachinnatio f

launch vt deducĕre; (to hurl) jaculari, contorquĕre; vi to — forth or out proficisci

laundress s lotrix f

laundry s lavatorium n

laureate adj laureatus

laurel adj laureus

laurel tree s laurus f

lava s liquefacta massa f

lavish adj prodigus; —ly prodige

lavish vt prodigĕre, profundĕre

lavishness s prodigalitas, profusio f

law s lex f; (right) jus n; (rule) norma f; (divine) fas n; to break the — leges violare; to pass a — legem perferre

law-abiding adj bene moratus

law court s judicium n; (building) basilica f

lawful adj legitimus, licitus, fas; —ly legitime, lege

lawless adj exlex, illegitimus; —ly illegitime, licenter

lawlessness s licentia f

lawn s pratulum n

lawsuit s lis, causa f

lawyer s jurisconsultus, causidicus m

lax adj remissus; (fig) neglegens; —ly remisse; neglegens

laxity s remissio f

lay vt ponĕre; (eggs) parĕre; (foundations) jacĕre; (hands) injicĕre; (plans) capĕre, inire; to — an ambush insidiari; to — aside ponĕre, amovĕre; to — before proponĕre; to — claim to arrogare, vindicare; to — down (office) resignare; (rules) statuĕre; to — down arms ab armis discedĕre; to — hold of prehendĕre, arripĕre; to — open patefacĕre; to — out (money) expendĕre; (plans) designare; to — up condĕre, reponĕre; to — waste vastare

lay s cantilena f

layer s (stratum) corium n; (of a plant) propago f

lazily adv ignave, pigre

laziness s segnities, pigritia f

lazy adv ignavus, piger, iners

lead s plumbum n

lead vt ducĕre; (life) agĕre; to — about circumducĕre; to — away abducĕre; to — off divertĕre; to — on conducĕre; vi to — up to tendĕre ad (with acc)

leaden adj plumbeus

leader s dux, ductor m; (fig) auctor m

leadership s duct·us -ūs m

leading adj princeps, primus, praecipuus

leaf s folium n; (of vine) pampinus m; (of paper) pagina, scheda f; (of metal) bractea f

leafless adj fronde nudatus

leafy adj frondosus, frondeus

league s foedus n, societas f

leak s rima f, hiat·us -ūs m

leak vi perfluĕre, rimas agĕre

leaky adj rimosus

lean adj macer, macilentus

lean vt inclinare; vi inclinare, niti; to — back se reclinare; to — on inniti in (with abl), incumbĕre (with dat)

leap s salt·us -ūs m

leap vi salire; to — for joy exsultare

leap year s bisextilis annus m

learn vt discĕre, cognoscĕre; (news) accipĕre, audire; to — by heart ediscĕre

learned adj eruditus, doctus; —ly docte

learning s (act) discĕre; (knowledge) eruditio f

lease s conductio, locatio f

lease vt conducĕre; to — out locare

leash s lorum n

least adj minimus

least adv minime; at — saltem; not in the — ne minimum quidem

leather s corium n; (tanned) aluta f

leather adj scorteus

leathery adj lentus

leave vt relinquĕre, deserĕre, destituĕre; (to entrust) mandare, tradĕre; (legacy) legare; to — behind relinquĕre; to — out omittĕre, praetermittĕre; vi (to depart) discedĕre, proficisci, abire; to — off desinĕre, desistĕre

leave s permissio f; — of absence commeat·us -ūs m; to ask — veniam petĕre; to obtain — impetrare; to take — of valĕre jubĕre; with your — pace tua

leaven s fermentum n

leaven vt fermentare

lecherous adj libidinosus, salax

lecture s lectio, praelectio, acroasis f

lecture vi (to reprove) objurgare; vi praelegĕre

lecturer s lector, praelector m

ledge s projectura f, limen, dorsum n

ledger s codex (accepti et expensi) m

leech s sanguisuga, hirudo f

leer vi limis oculis spectare

leering adj limus, lascivus

left adj laevus, sinister; on the — a sinistra; to the — ad sinistram, sinistrorsum

leftover adj reliquus

leftovers s reliquiae f pl

leg s crus n; (of table, etc.) pes m

legacy s legatum n

legal adj legalis, legitimus; judicialis; —ly legitime, lege

legalize vt sancire

legate s legatus m

legation s legatio f

legend s fabula f; (inscription) titulus m

legendary adj commenticius, fabulosus

legging s ocrea f

legible adj clarus

legion s legio f

legislate vi leges facĕre

legislation s leges f pl
legislator s legum lator m
legitimate adj legitimus; **—ly** legitime
leisure s otium n; **at —** otiosus, vacuus
leisure adj otiosus, vacuus; **—ly** otiose
leisurely adj lentus
lemon s pomum citreum n
lemonade s aqua limonata f
lend vt commodare; **to — money** pecuniam mutuam dare; (at interest) pecuniam faenerare or faenerari; **to — one's ear** aures praebēre
length s longitudo f; (of time) longinquitas, diuturnitas f; **at — tandem**
lengthen vt extendĕre, protrahĕre, producĕre
lengthwise adv in longitudinem
lengthy adj longus, prolixus
leniency s lenitas, clementia, mansuetudo f
lenient adj lenis, mitis, clemens; **—ly** leniter, clementer
lentil s lens f
leopard s leopardus, pardus m
leper s leprosus m
leprosy s leprae f pl
less adj minor
less adv minus
lessee s conductor m
lessen vt minuĕre; vi decrescĕre, minui
lesson s documentum n; **to give —s** in docĕre
lessor s locator m
lest conj ne
let vt (to allow) sinĕre, pati, permittĕre; (to lease) locare; **to — alone** omittĕre; **to — down** (to disappoint) deesse (with dat), destituĕre; **to — fall** a manibus mittĕre; **to — fly** emittĕre, contorquĕre; **to — go** (di)mittĕre; **to — in** admittĕre; **to — off** absolvĕre; **to — out** emittĕre; **to — pass** omittĕre; **to — slip** omittĕre
lethargic adj lethargicus
lethargy s lethargus m; (fig) veternus m
letter s (of alphabet) littera f; (epistle) litterae f pl, epistula f; **by — per** litteras; **to the — ad verbum**
letter carrier s tabellarius m
lettered adj litteratus
lettering s titulus m
lettuce s lactuca f
level adj planus, aequus
level s planities f; (tool) libra, libella f
level vt aequare, adaequare; (to the ground) solo aequare, sternĕre
lever s vectis m
levity s levitas f
levy s delect·us -ūs m
levy vt (troops) conscribĕre; (tax) exigĕre
lewd adj impudicus, incestus
lewdness s impudicitia f

liable adj obnoxius
liar s mendax m & f
libation s libatio f; **to pour a — libare**
libel s calumnia f
libel vt calumniari
libelous adj famosus, probrosus
liberal adj liberalis, munificus; (fig) ingenuus; **—ly** liberaliter
liberality s liberalitas, munificentia f
liberate vt liberare; (slave) manumittĕre
liberation s liberatio f
liberator s liberator m
libertine s homo dissolutus m
liberty s libertas f; licentia f; **at — liber**
librarian s librarius m
library s bibliotheca f
license s (permission) copia, potestas f; (freedom) licentia f
license vt potestatem dare (with dat)
licentious adj dissolutus, impudicus; **—ly** dissolute, impudice
lick vt lambĕre; (daintily) liqurrire
lictor s lictor m
lid s operculum, operimentum n
lie s mendacium n; **to give the — to** redarguĕre; **to tell a — mentiri**
lie vi (to tell a lie or lies) mentiri; (to be lying down) jacēre, cubare; (to be situated) situs esse; **to — down** jacēre; **to — in wait** insidiari; **to — on** or **upon** incubare (with dat), incumbĕre (with dat)
lieu s **in — of** loco (with genit), pro (with abl)
lieutenant s legatus, praefectus m
life s vita, anima f; (fig) vigor m, alacritas f
lifeblood s sanguis m
life history s vita f
lifeless adj inanimus, exanimis; (fig) exsanguis, frigidus; **—ly** (fig) frigide
lifetime s aetas f
lift vt tollĕre, attollĕre, sublevare; **to — up** attollĕre, efferre
ligament s ligamentum, ligamen n
ligature s ligatura f
light s lux f, lumen n; (lamp) lucerna f; **to bring to — in lucem** proferre; **to throw — on** lumen adhibēre (with dat)
light adj (bright) lucidus, fulgens; (in weight) levis; (of colors) candidus, dilutus; (easy) facilis; (nimble) agilis; **—ly** leviter
light vt accendĕre, incendĕre; (to illuminate) illuminare; vi flammam concipĕre; **to — on** or **upon** incidĕre (with dat), offendĕre; **to — up** (fig) hilaris fieri
lighten vt (to illumine) illustrare; (weight) allevare, exonerare; vi (in sky) fulgurare
lighthouse s pharus f
lightness s levitas, agilitas f
lightning s fulmen, fulgur n; **struck by — fulmine ictus, de caelo tactus**

like *adj* similis (*with dat*); (*equal*) par (*with dat*), aequus (*with dat*)

like *prep* instar (*with genit*); tamquam, ut, velut

like *vt* amare, diligĕre; **I — this** hoc mihi placet; **I — to do this** me juvat hoc facĕre

likelihood *s* verisimilitudo *f*

likely *adj* verisimilis, probabilis

likely *adv* probabiliter

liken *vt* comparare

likeness *s* similitudo *f*; (*portrait*) imago, effigies *f*

likewise *adv* pariter, similiter, item

liking *s* amor *m*; (*fancy*) libido *f*

lilac *s* syringa vulgaris *f*

lily *s* lilium *n*

lily of the valley *s* convallaria majalis *f*

limb *s* art·us ·ūs *m*, membrum *n*

limber *adj* flexilis

lime *s* calx *f*

limestone *s* calx *f*

lime tree *s* tilia *f*

limit *s* finis, terminus, modus *m*

limit *vt* terminare, finire, definire; (*to restrict*) circumscribĕre

limitation *s* determinatio *f*; (*exception*) exceptio *f*

limp *s* claudicatio *f*

limp *vi* claudicare

limp *adj* flaccidus, languidus

limpid *adj* limpidus

linden tree *s* tilia *f*

line *s* (*drawn*) linea *f*; (*row*) series *f*, ordo *m*; (*lineage*) stirps *f*, genus *n*; (*mil*) acies *f*; (*of poetry*) vers·us ·ūs *m*; (*cord*) funis *m*

line *vt* (*streets*) saepire

lineage *s* stirps *f*, genus *n*

lineal *adj* linearis; **—ly** rectā lineā

lineament *s* lineamentum *n*

linear *adj* linearis

linen *adj* linteus, lineus

linen *s* linteum, linum *n*

linger *vi* morari, cunctari, cessare

lingering *adj* cunctabundus, tardus; **—ly** cunctanter

lingering *s* cunctatio *f*

linguist *s* linguarum peritus *m*

liniment *s* unguentum *n*, linit·us ·ūs *m*

link *s* (*of chain*) anulus *m*; (*bond*) vinculum *n*, nex·us ·ūs *m*

link *vt* connectĕre, conjungĕre

linseed *s* lini semen *n*

lint *s* linamentum *n*

lintel *s* limen superum *n*

lion *s* leo *m*

lioness *s* lea, leaena *f*

lip *s* labrum *n*; (*edge*) ora *f*

liquefy *vt* liquefacĕre

liquid *adj* liquidus

liquid *s* liquidum *n*, liquor *m*; **to become —** liquescĕre

liquidate *vt* solvĕre, persolvĕre

liquor *s* liquor *m*

lisp *vi* balbutire

lisping *adj* blaesus

list *s* index *m*, tabula *f*; (*of ship*) inclinatio *f*

list *vt* enumerare; *vi* inclinare

listen *vi* auscultare, audire; **to — to** auscultare, audire

listless *adj* remissus, languidus; **—ly** languide

litany *s* litania *f*

literal *adj* litteralis; **—ly** ad litteram, ad verbum

literary *adj* (*person*) litteratus; **— style** scribendi genus *n*

literature *s* litterae *f pl*

litigant *s* litigator *m*

litigate *vi* litigare

litigation *s* lis *f*

litter *s* (*vehicle*) lectica *f*; (*of straw, etc.*) stramentum *n*; (*brood*) fet·us ·ūs, part·us ·ūs *m*

litter *vt* sternĕre

little *adj* parvus, exiguus

little *adv* parum, paulum; **a — paulum, aliquantulum; — by — paulatim**

little *s* paulum, aliquantulum *n*

live *vi* vivĕre, vitam agĕre; (*to reside*) habitare; **to — on** vesci (*with abl*)

live *adj* vivus; (*of colors*) vegetus

livelihood *s* vict·us ·ūs *m*

lively *adj* vivus, vividus, alacer; (*of colors*) vegetus

liver *s* jecur *n*

livid *adj* lividus; **to be — livĕre**

living *adj* vivus, vivens

living *s* (*livelihood, food*) vict·us ·ūs *m*

lizard *s* lacerta *f*

load *s* onus *n*

load *vt* onerare

loaf *s* panis *m*

loaf *vi* grassari

loafer *s* grassator *m*

loam *s* lutum *n*

loan *s* mutuum *n*, pecunia mutua *f*

loathe *vt* fastidire

loathing *s* fastidium *n*

loathsome *adj* foedus, taeter

lobby *s* vestibulum *n*

lobe *s* lobus *m*

lobster *s* astacus *m*

local *adj* indigena; loci (*genit*), regionis (*genit*)

locality *s* locus *m*, natura loci *f*

lock *s* (*of hair*) cinnus, floccus *m*; (*of door*) sera *f*

lock *vt* obserare, oppessulare; **to — in** includĕre; **to — out** exludĕre; **to — up** concludĕre

locker *s* loculamentum, armarium *n*

lockjaw *s* tetanus *m*

locust *s* locusta *f*

lodge *s* casa *f*

lodge *vt* (*complaint*) deferre; *vi* (*to stay*) deversari; (*to stick*) inhaerĕre

lodger *s* inquilinus *m*

lodging *s* hospitium, deversorium *n*

loft *s* tabulatum, cenaculum *n*

lofty *adj* (*ex*)celsus, sublimis; (*fig*) sublimis, superbus

log *s* tignum *n*, stipes *m*

logic *s* dialectica *n pl*

logical *adj* logicus, dialecticus; **—ly** dialectice, ex ratione

loin *s* lumbus *m*

loiter *vi* cessare, cunctari, grassari

loiterer *s* cessator, grassator *m*

loll vi recumbĕre
lone adj solus
loneliness s solitudo f
lonely adj solitarius; desolatus
long adj longus; (of time) diuturnus; (lengthened) productus
long adv diu; — after multo post; — ago jamdudum, jampridem; — before multo ante
long vi avēre; to — for desiderare
longevity s longaevitas f
longing s desiderium n
longing adj avidus; —ly avide
longitude s longitudo f
long-lived adj vivax
long-suffering adj patiens
long-winded adj longus
look s aspect·us -ūs, vult·us -ūs m; (appearance) facies, species f
look vi vidēre; (to seem) vidēri; to — about circumspicĕre; to — after curare; to — around circumspicĕre, respicĕre; to — at intuĕri, aspicĕre; to — back respicĕre; to — for quaerĕre; to — forward to exspectare; to — into inspicĕre, introspicĕre; (to examine) perscrutari; to — on intuĕri; to — out prospicĕre; to — out for quaerĕre; to — towards spectare; to — up suspicĕre; to — upon habĕre, aestimare
loom s tela f
loom vi in conspectum prodire
loop s sin·us -ūs m
loophole s fenestra f; (fig) effugium n
loose adj laxus, solutus, remissus; (morally) dissolutus; —ly laxe; dissolute
loosen vt solvĕre, laxare; vi solvi
loquacious adj loquax, garrulus
lord s dominus m
Lord s Dominus m
lord vi to — it over dominari in (with acc)
lordly adj imperiosus
lordship s dominatio f, imperium n
lore s doctrina f
lose vt amittĕre, perdĕre; to — one's way aberrare
loss s (act) amissio f; damnum, detrimentum n; (mil) repulsa f
lost adj perditus; to be — perire
lot s pars, portio, sors f; casting of —s sortitio f, sortit·us -ūs m; to draw —s for sortiri
lotion s lotio f
lottery s sortitio f
loud adj magnus; —ly magnā voce
lounge vi cessare, otiari
lounge s lectulus m
louse s pediculus m
lousy adj pediculosus; (fig) vilis
lout s rusticus m
loutish adj agrestis, rusticus
love s amor m; to fall in — amare, adamare
love vt amare, diligĕre
love affair s amores m pl
lovely adj venustus, amabilis
love potion s philtrum n
lover s amator, amans m

lovesick adj amore aeger
loving adj amans; —ly amanter
low adj humilis; (of price) vilis; (of birth) obscurus; (of voice) summissus; (vile) turpis; (downcast) abjectus
low adv humiliter; summissā voce
low vi mugire
lowborn adj obscurus, degener
lower vt demittĕre, deprimĕre; (price) imminuĕre; vi (of sky) obscurari
lower adj inferior; of the — world infernus; the — world inferi m pl
lowermost adj infimus
lowing s mugit·us -ūs m
lowlands s loca plana, campestria n pl, campi m pl
lowly adj humilis, obscurus
loyal adj fidelis, fidus; —ly fideliter
loyalty s fidelitas, fides f
lubricate vt unguĕre
lucid adj lucidus, clarus, perspicuus; (transparent) pellucidus
Lucifer s Lucifer m
luck s fortuna f; bad — fortuna f, infortunium n; good — fortuna f, felicitas f
luckily adv feliciter, fauste
luckless adj infelix
lucky adj felix, faustus
lucrative adj quaestuosus
lucre s lucrum n, quaest·us -ūs m
ludicrous adj ridiculus; —ly ridicule
luggage s sarcinae f pl, impedimenta n pl
lukewarm adj tepidus; (fig) segnis, frigidus; —ly (fig) segniter
lull s quies, intermissio f
lull vt sopire; (to calm, as a storm) sedare; (fig) demulcēre
lumber s scruta n pl
luminary s lumen n
luminous adj lucidus, illustris; (fig) dilucidus
lump s glaeba, massa, congeries f; (on body) tuber n
lump vt to — together coacervare
lumpy adj glaebosus, crassus
lunacy s alienatio mentis f
lunar adj lunaris
lunatic s insanus m
lunch s merenda f, prandium n
lunch vi prandĕre
luncheon s prandium n
lung s pulmo m
lunge s ict·us -ūs m, plaga f
lunge vi prosilire
lurch s impedimentum n; to leave in the — deserĕre, destituĕre
lurch vi titubare
lure s illecebra, esca f
lure vt illicĕre, inescare
lurk vi latēre, latitare
luscious adj suavis, praedulcis
lush adj luxuriosus
lust s libido f
lust vi concupiscĕre
luster s splendor, nitor m
lustful adj libidinosus, salax; —ly libidinose, lascive

lustily adv valide, strenue
lusty adj validus, robustus
lute s cithara f, fides f pl
luxuriance s luxuries, ubertas f
luxuriant adj luxuriosus; (fig) luxurians
luxuriate vi luxuriare, luxuriari
luxurious adj sumptuosus, lautus;
—**ly** sumptuose, laute

luxury s luxuria f, lux·us -ūs m
lye s lixivia f
lying adj mendax, fallax
lying s mendacium n
lymph s lympha f
lynx s lynx m & f
lyre s lyra f, fides f pl, barbitos m
lyric adj lyricus
lyric s carmen n

M

macaroni s collyra f
mace s fasces m pl
mace bearer s lictor m
macerate vt macerare
machination s dolus m
machine s machina f
machinery s machinamentum n, machinatio f
mackerel s scomber m
mad adj insanus, vesanus, demens, furiosus; **to be** — furēre, insanire; —**ly** insane, dementer
madam s domina f
madden vt mentem alienare (with dat); (fig) furiare
maddening adj furiosus
madman s homo furiosus m, demens m
madness s insania, dementia f, furor m
magazine s (journal) ephemeris f; (storehouse) horreum, armamentarium n
maggot s vermis, vermiculus m
magic s ars magica f
magic adj magicus
magically adv velut magica quadam arte
magician s magus m
magisterial adj ad magistratum pertinens
magistracy s magistrat·us -ūs m
magistrate s magistrat·us -ūs m
magnanimity s magnanimitas f
magnanimous adj magnanimus
magnet s magnes m
magnetic adj magneticus
magnetism s vis magnetica f
magnetize vt magnetica vi afficēre
magnificence s magnificentia f, splendor m
magnificent adj magnificus, splendidus; —**ly** magnifice, splendide
magnify vt amplificare, exaggerare
magnitude s magnitudo f
maid s ancilla f
maiden s virgo, puella f
maidenhood s virginitas f
maidenly adj puellaris, virginalis
mail s (letters) epistulae f pl; (armor) lorica f
maim vt mutilare
maimed adj mancus
main adj primus, praecipuus, princeps; — **point** caput n; —**ly** praecipue, maxime
main s (sea) altum n, pelagus m

mainland s continens f
maintain vt (to keep) tenēre; (to keep alive) nutrire, alĕre, sustentare; (to defend) tuēri, sustinēre; (to argue) affirmare
maintenance s (support) defensio, sustentatio f; (means of living) vict·us -ūs m, alimentum n
majestic adj augustus, imperatorius; —**ally** auguste
majesty s majestas, dignitas f
major adj major
major s (mil) tribunus militum m; (in logic) major praemissa f
majority s major pars f
make vt facĕre; (to form) fingĕre; (to render) reddĕre, facĕre; (to appoint) creare, facĕre, instituĕre; **to** — **amends** corrigĕre; **to** — **good** resarcire, reparare; **to** — **haste** accelerare, festinare; **to** — **much of** magni facĕre; **to** — **over** transferre; **to** — **ready** praeparare; **to** — **up** (story) fingĕre; (to compensate) resarcire; (one's mind) decernĕre; **to** — **way** cedĕre; vi **to** — **away with** tollĕre, amovēre; **to** — **for** petĕre
make s forma, figura, formatio f
maker s fabricator m; auctor m
maladministration s administratio mala f
malady s morbus m
male adj mas, masculinus
male s mas, masculus m
malediction s dirae f pl, exsecratio f
malefactor s homo maleficus, reus m
malevolence s malevolentia f
malevolent adj malevolus
malice s malevolentia, invidia f
malicious adj malevolus, invidiosus, malignus; —**ly** malevolo animo
malign vt obtrectare, vexare
malign adj malignus, invidiosus
malignant adj malevolus
malleable adj ductilis
mallet s malleus m
malpractice s delicta n pl
maltreat vt vexare, mulcare
man s (human being) homo m; (male human being) vir m
man vt (ship) complēre; (walls) praesidio firmare
manacle s manica f, compes m
manacle vt manicas injicĕre (with dat)
manage vt administrare, curare

manageable *adj* tractabilis
management *s* administratio, cura *f*
manager *s* curator *m*; *(steward)* procurator *m*; *(of estate)* villicus *m*
mandate *s* mandatum *n*
mandrake *s* mandragora *f*
mane *s* juba *f*
maneuver *s* *(mil)* decurs·us -ūs *m*, decursio *f*; *(trick)* dolus *m*, artificium *n*
maneuver *vi* *(mil)* decurrěre; *(fig)* machinari
mange *s* scabies *f*
manger *s* praesepe *n*
mangle *vt* lacerare, laniare
mangy *adj* scaber
manhood *s* pubertas *f*; virilitas, fortitudo *f*
mania *s* insania *f*
maniac *s* furiosus *m*
manifest *adj* manifestus, apertus; —ly manifeste, aperte
manifest *vt* declarare, ostenděre, aperire
manifestation *s* patefactio *f*
manifesto *s* edictum *n*
manifold *adj* multiplex, varius
manipulate *vt* tractare
manipulation *s* tractatio *f*
mankind *s* genus humanum *n*
manliness *s* virtus, fortitudo *f*
manly *adj* virilis
manner *s* modus *m*, ratio *f*; *(custom)* consuetudo *f*, mos *m*; **after the —** of ritu *(with genit)*, more *(with genit)*; **bad —s** rusticitas *f*; **good —s** urbanitas *f*
mannerism *s* affectatio *f*
mannerly *adj* urbanus
mannikin *s* homunculus, homuncio *m*
man-of-war *s* navis longa *f*
manor *s* praedium *n*, fundus *m*
man servant *s* servus, famulus *m*
mansion *s* dom·us -ūs, sedes *f*
manslaughter *s* homicidium *n*
mantle *s* penula, palla *f*
mantle *vt* celare, tegěre, dissimulare
manual *adj* manualis
manual *s* enchiridion *n*
manufacture *s* fabrica *f*
manufacture *vt* fabricari, fabrefacěre
manufacturer *s* fabricator, opifex *m*
manure *s* stercus *n*, fimus *m*
manure *vt* stercorare
manuscript *s* codex, liber *m*
many *adj* multi, plerique, complures; **a good —** nonnulli; **as — . . . as** quot . . . tot; **how —** quot; **— ways** multifariam; **so —** tot
many-colored *adj* multicolor
map *s* tabula geographica *f*
map *vt* **to — out** designare, describěre
maple *adj* acernus
maple tree *s* acer *n*
mar *vt* foedare, vitiare, corrumpěre
marauder *s* praedator, latro *m*
marauding *s* praedatio *f*, latrocinium *n*
marble *adj* marmoreus

marble *s* marmor *n*
March *s* (mensis) Martius *m*
march *s* iter *n*
march *vt* ducěre; *vi* iter facěre, inceděre, gradi; **to — on** signa proferre; **to — on a town** oppidum aggredi
mare *s* equa *f*
margin *s* margo *m & f*
marginal *adj* margini ascriptus
marigold *s* caltha *f*
marine *adj* marinus
marine *s* miles classicus, miles classiarius *m*
mariner *s* nauta *m*
maritime *adj* maritimus
mark *s* nota *f*, signum *n*; *(brand)* stigma *n*; *(impression)* vestigium *n*; *(target)* scopus *m*; *(of wound)* cicatrix *f*; *(fig)* indicium *n*
mark *vt* notare, signare; *(to observe)* animadvertěre; *(with pencil, etc.)* designare; **to — out** metari
marker *s* index *m*
market *s* macellum *n*, mercat·us -ūs *m*
marketable *adj* venalis
market day *s* nundinae *f pl*
marketing *s* emptio *f*
market place *s* forum *n*
market town *s* emporium *n*
marksman *s* jaculandi peritus *m*
marmalade *s* quilon ex aurantiis confectum *n*
marquee *s* tabernaculum *n*
marriage *s* matrimonium *n*, nuptiae *f pl*
marriageable *adj* nubilis
marriage contract *s* pactio nuptialis *f*
married *adj* *(of woman)* nupta; *(of man)* maritus
marrow *s* medulla *f*
marry *vt* *(said of man)* in matrimonium ducěre, uxorem ducěre *(with acc)*; *(said of woman)* nuběre *(with dat)*; **to get married** matrimonio *or* nuptiis conjungi
marsh *s* palus *f*
marshal *s* dux, imperator *m*
marshal *vt* disponěre
marshy *adj* paluster
mart *s* forum, emporium *n*
martial *adj* bellicosus, ferox, militaris
martyr *s* martyr *m & f*
martyrdom *s* martyrium *n*
marvel *s* res mira *f*, mirum *n*
marvel *vi* **to — at** mirari, admirari
marvelous *adj* mirus, mirabilis; **—ly** mire
masculine *adj* masculus, virilis; *(gram)* masculinus
mash *s* mixtura *f*; *(for cattle)* farrago *f*
mash *vt* commiscěre; *(to bruise)* contunděre
mask *s* persona, larva *f*; *(fig)* praetext·us -ūs *m*
mask *vt* *(fig)* dissimulare
mason *s* lapicida, caementarius *m*
masonry *s* opus caementicium *n*

mass s moles f; (of people) turba f; (eccl) missa f; **the —es** vulgus n
mass vt congerĕre, coacervare
massacre s caedes, trucidatio f
massacre vt trucidare
massive adj solidus, ingens
mast s (of ship) malus m; (for cattle) glans f, balanus m
master s dominus, herus m; (teacher) magister, praeceptor m; (controller) arbiter m; **to be — of** potens esse (with genit), compos esse (with genit); **not to be — of** impotens esse (with genit)
master vt superare, vincĕre; (to learn) perdiscĕre; (passion) continēre
masterly adj (artist) artificiosus; imperiosus
masterpiece s magnum opus n
mastery s dominatio f, imperium, arbitrium n
masticate vt mandĕre
mastiff s Molossus m
mat s teges, storea, matta f
match s (marriage) nuptiae f pl; (contest) certamen n; (an equal) par, compar m & f; **a — for** par (with dat); **not a — for** impar (with dat)
match vt adaequare, exaequare; vi quadrare
matchless adj incomparabilis
mate s socius, collega m; conju(n)x m & f
mate vi conjungi
material adj corporeus; (significant) haud levis, magni momenti; **—ly** magnopere
material s materia, materies f
maternal adj maternus
maternity s conditio matris f
mathematical adj mathematicus
mathematician s mathematicus m
mathematics s mathematica f, numeri m pl
matricide s (murder) matricidium n; (murderer) matricida m & f
matrimony s matrimonium n
matrix s forma f
matron s matrona f
matronly adj matronalis
matter s (substance) materia f; (affair) res f, negotium n; pus n; **no — nihil interest**
matter v impers **it does not —** nihil interest, nihil refert
matting s tegetes f pl
mattress s culcita f
mature adj maturus, adultus; **—ly** mature
mature vi maturescĕre
maturity s maturitas, aetas matura f
maudlin adj flebilis
maul vt mulcare, delaniare
mausoleum s mausoleum n
maw s ingluvies f
mawkish adj putidus; **—ly** putide
maxim s axioma, praeceptum n, sententia f
maximum adj quam maximus, quam plurimus
May s (mensis) Maius m

may vi posse; **I —** licet mihi
maybe adv forsitan
mayor s praefectus urbi m
maze s labyrinthus m
me pron me; **by — a me; to — mihi; with — mecum**
mead s (drink) mulsum n
meadow s pratum n
meager adj macer, exilis, jejunus; **—ly** exiliter, jejune
meagerness s macies f; (of soil) exilitas f; exigua copia f
meal s farina f; (food) cibus m; (dinner) epulae f pl
mean adj (middle) medius; (low) humilis; (cruel) crudelis, vilis
mean s medium n, mediocritas f
mean vt dicĕre, significare; (to intend) velle, cogitare, in animo habēre; (to refer to) significare, intellegĕre
meander vi sinuoso cursu labi
meaning s significatio, vis f, sens·us -ūs m
meanness s humilitas f; (cruelty) crudelitas f
means s (way, method) ratio, via f, consilium n; (wealth) opes f pl; **by all —** maxime, omnino; **by — of** render by abl or per (with acc); **by no —** nullo modo, haudquaquam
meanwhile adv interea, interim
measles s morbilli m pl
measurable adj mensurabilis
measure s mensura f, modus m; (course of action) ratio f, consilium n; (law) rogatio, lex f; **in some —** aliqua ex parte
measure vt metiri; (land) metari; **to — out** admetiri, dimetiri
measurement s mensura f
meat s caro f; (food) cibus m
mechanic s opifex, faber m
mechanical adj mechanicus, machinalis; **—ly** mechanica quadam arte
mechanics s mechanica ars, machinalis scientia f
mechanism s machinatio f
medal s insigne n
medallion s numisma sollemne n
meddle vi se interponĕre
meddler s ardelio m
mediate vi intercedĕre
mediation s intercessio f
mediator s intercessor, conciliator m
medical adj medicus, medicinalis
medicate vt medicare
medicinal adj medicus, salutaris
medicine s (science) medicina f; (remedy) medicamentum n
medieval adj medii aevi (genit, used as adj)
mediocre adj mediocris
mediocrity s mediocritas f
meditate vi meditari, cogitare
meditation s meditatio, cogitatio f
meditative adj cogitabundus
Mediterranean s mare internum or medium, mare nostrum n
medium s (middle) medium n; (expedient) modus m, ratio f; (agency) conciliator m

medium adj mediocris
medley s farrago f
meek adj mitis, demissus; —ly summisse
meekness s animus demissus m
meet adj aptus, idoneus; it is — convenit
meet vt obviam ire (with dat), occurrĕre (with dat); (fig) obire; vi convenire; to — with offendĕre, excipĕre
meeting s congressio f; (assembly) conventus-ūs m
melancholy s tristitia, maestitia f
melancholy adj tristis, maestus
mellow adj maturus, mitis; (from drinking) temulentus
mellow vt maturare, coquĕre; vi maturescĕre
melodious adj canorus; —ly canore, modulate
melody s melos n, modus m
melt vt liquefacĕre, dissolvĕre; vi liquescĕre, tabescĕre
member s membrum n; (fig) sodalis m
membrane s membrana f
memento s monumentum n
memoirs s commentarii m pl
memorable adj memorabilis, memoriā dignus
memorandum s nota f
memorial s monumentum n
memory s memoria f; from — ex memoria, memoriter; in the — of man post hominum memoriam; to commit to — ediscĕre, memoriae mandare
menace s minae f pl
menace vt minari, minitari; (of things) imminēre (with dat)
menacing adj minax; (only of persons) minitabundus
mend vt emendare, corrigĕre, restaurare, reparare; (clothes) sarcire; vi melior fieri
mendicant s mendicus m, mendica f
menial adj servilis, sordidus
menial s servus, famulus m
mental adj mente conceptus; —ly mente
mention s mentio, commemoratio f; to make — of mentionem facĕre (with genit)
mention vt commemorare, nominare; to not — silentio praeterire
mercantile adj mercatorius
mercenary adj mercenarius, venalis
mercenary s miles mercenarius m
merchandise s merces f pl
merchant s mercator, negotiator m
merciful adj misericors, clemens; —ly misericorditer, clementer
merciless adj immisericors, inclemens; —ly duriter, inhumane
mercurial adj vividus, acer, levis
Mercury s Mercurius m
mercury s argentum vivum n
mercy s misericordia f
mere adj merus; —ly tantummodo, solum, modo
meretricious adj meretricius, fucatus

merge vt confundĕre; vi confundi
meridian s meridianus circulus m; meridies m
merit s meritum n
merit vt merēre, merēri
meritorious adj laudabilis
mermaid s nympha f
merrily adv hilare, festive
merry adj hilaris, festivus
mesh s (of net) macula f
mess s (dirt) squalor m; (confusion) turba, rerum perturbatio f
messenger s nuntius m
metal adj metallicus, ferreus, aereus
metal s metallum n
metallurgy s metallurgia, scientia metallorum f
metamorphosis s transfiguratio f
metaphor s translatio f
metaphorical adj translatus; —ly per translationem
mete vt metiri
meteor s fax caelestis f
meteorology s prognostica n pl
meter s metrum n, numerus m
method s ratio f, modus m
methodical adj dispositus; (person) diligens; —ly ratione et viā
meticulous adj accuratus; —ly accurate
metonymy s immutatio f
metrical adj metricus, numerosus
metropolis s caput n
mettle s animus m, virtus, magnanimitas f
miasma s halitus-ūs m
microscope s microscopium n
mid adj medius
midday adj meridianus
midday s meridies m, meridianum tempus n
middle adj medius
middle s medium n; in the — of the road in media via
midget s pumilio m & f
midnight s media nox f
midrif s diaphragma n, praecordia n pl
midst s medium n; in the — of inter (with acc)
midsummer s summa aestas f
midway adv medius; he stood — between the lines stabat medius inter acies
midwife s obstetrix f
midwinter s bruma f
midwinter adj brumalis
mien s vultus-ūs m
might s vis, potestas, potentia f; with all one's — summa ope
might vi render by imperfect subjunctive
mightily adv valde, magnopere
mighty adj potens, validus
migrate vi migrare, abire
migration s peregrinatio f
migratory adj advena, migrans
mild adj mitis, lenis; (person) placidus, clemens; —ly leniter, clementer
mildew s robigo f, mucor, situs-ūs m
mildness s clementia, lenitas, mansuetudo f

mile *s* mille passuum, milliare *n*

milestone *s* milliarium *n*

militant *adj* ferox

military *adj* militaris

militia *s* milites *m pl*

milk *s* lac *n*

milk *vt* mulgēre

milky *adj* lacteus

Milky Way *s* orbis lacteus *m*, via lactea *f*

mill *s* mola *f*, pistrinum *n*

millennium *s* mille anni *m pl*

miller *s* molitor, pistor *m*

million *adj* decies centena milia (with *genit*)

millionaire *s* homo praedives *m*

millionth *s* pars una ex decies centenis milibus partium *f*

millstone *s* mola *f*

mime *s* mimus *m*

mimic *s* mimus *m*

mimic *vt* imitari

mimicry *s* imitatio *f*

mince *vt* concidēre; **not to — words** plane aperteque loqui

mind *s* mens *f*, animus *m*, ingenium *n*; (*opinion*) sens·us ·ūs *m*, sententia *f*; **to call to —** recordari; **to make up one's —** animum inducēre, statuēre, constituēre; **to show presence of —** praesenti animo uti

mind *vt* (*to look after*) curare; (*to regard*) respicĕre; (*to object to*) aegre ferre; **to — one's own business** suum negotium agĕre

mindful *adj* attentus, diligens; memor

mine *s* fodina *f*, metallum *n*; (*mil*) cuniculus *m*; (*fig*) thesaurus *m*

mine *vt* effodĕre

mine *pron* meus

miner *s* (*of metals*) metallicus *m*; fossor *m*

mineral *s* metallum *n*

mineral *adj* metallicus, fossilis

mineralogist *s* metallorum peritus *m*

mineralogy *s* metallorum scientia *f*

mingle *vt* commiscēre, confundĕre; *vi* commiscēri, se immiscēre

miniature *s* pictura minuta *f*

minimum *adj* quam minimus

minimum *s* minimum *n*

minion *s* cliens *m & f*

minister *s* minister, administer *m*

minister *vi* ministrare, servire

ministry *s* ministratio *f*, munus, officium *n*

minor *s* pupillus *m*, pupilla *f*

minor *adj* minor

minority *s* minor pars *f*

minstrel *s* fidicen *m*

mint *s* (*plant*) mentha *f*; (*for making money*) moneta *f*

mint *vt* cudĕre

minute *s* temporis momentum *n*

minute *adj* (*small*) minutus, exiguus, pusillus; (*exact*) accuratus, subtilis; **—ly** accurate, subtiliter

minx *s* puella procax *f*

miracle *s* miraculum, monstrum *n*

miraculous *adj* miraculosus; **—ly** divinitus

mirage *s* falsa species *f*

mire *s* lutum *n*

mirror *s* speculum *n*

mirth *s* hilaritas, laetitia *f*

mirthful *adj* hilaris

misadventure *s* infortunium *n*

misalliance *s* matrimonium impar *n*

misapply *vt* abuti (*with abl*)

misapprehend *vt* male intellegĕre

misapprehension *s* falsa conceptio *f*

misbehave *vi* indecore se gerĕre

misbehavior *s* morum pravitas *f*

misbelief *s* fides prava *f*

miscalculate *vi* errare

miscalculation *s* error *m*

miscarriage *s* abort·us ·ūs *m*; (*fig*) malus success·us ·ūs *m*

miscarry *vi* abortum facĕre; (*fig*) male succedĕre

miscellaneous *adj* promiscuus

miscellany *s* conjectanea, miscellanea *n pl*

mischance *s* infortunium *n*

mischief *s* incommodum, maleficium *n*; (*of children*) lascivia *f*

mischievous *adj* maleficus, noxius; (*playful*) lascivus

misconceive *vt* male intellegĕre

misconception *s* falsa conceptio, falsa opinio *f*

misconduct *s* delictum, peccatum *n*

misconstruction *s* sinistra interpretatio *f*

misconstrue *vt* male interpretari; perverse interpretari

misdeed *s* delictum, peccatum *n*

misdemeanor *s* levius delictum *n*

misdirect *vt* fallĕre

miser *s* avarus, sordidus *m*

miserable *adj* miser, infelix, aerumnosus

miserably *adv* misere

miserly *adj* avarus, sordidus

misery *s* miseria, aerumna *f*

misfortune *s* infortunium, incommodum *n*

misgiving *s* sollicitudo *f*

misgovern *vt* male regĕre

misguide *vt* seducĕre, fallĕre

misguided *adj* (*fig*) demens

mishap *s* incommodum *n*

misinform *vt* falsa docēre (*with acc*)

misinterpret *vt* male interpretari

misinterpretation *s* prava interpretatio *f*

misjudge *vt* male judicare

mislay *vt* amittĕre

mislead *vt* seducĕre, decipĕre

mismanage *vt* male gerĕre

mismanagement *s* mala administratio *f*

misnomer *s* falsum nomen *n*

misplace *vt* alieno loco ponĕre

misprint *s* erratum typographicum, mendum *n*

misquote *vt* falso citare, falso proferre

misquotation *s* falsa prolatio *f*

misrepresent *vt* calumniari

misrepresentation *s* calumnia *f*; falsa descriptio *f*

misrule s prava administratio f

miss s adulescentula, virgo f; error m

miss vt (to overlook) omittĕre, praetermittĕre; (one's aim) non ferire, non attingĕre; (to feel the want of) desiderare; (to fail to find) requirĕre; vi (to fall short) errare

misshapen adj pravus, deformis

missile s telum, missile, tormentum n

missing adj absens; **to be —** deesse

mission s legatio, missio f

misspell vt perperam scribĕre

misspend vt prodigĕre, perdĕre, dissipare

misstate vt parum accurate memorare

misstatement s falsum, mendacium n

mist s nebula, caligo f

mistake s error m, erratum n; (written) mendum n; **to make a —** errare, peccare

mistake vt habĕre pro (with abl)

mistaken adj falsus; **to be —** falli; **unless I am —** ni fallor

mistletoe s viscum n

mistress s domina, hera f; (sweetheart) amica f; (paramour) concubina f; (teacher) magistra f

mistrust s diffidentia, suspicio f

mistrust vt diffidĕre (with dat)

mistrustful adj diffidens; **—ly** diffidenter

misty adj nebulosus, caliginosus; (fig) obscurus

misunderstand vt perperam intellegĕre

misunderstanding s error m; (disagreement) offensio f, dissidium n

misuse vt abuti (with abl); (to revile) conviciari

misuse s abus·us -ūs m; (ill treatment) injuria f

mite s (bit) parvulus m; (coin) sextans m

miter s mitra f

mitigate vt mitigare, lenire

mitigation s mitigatio f

mix vt miscĕre; **to — in** admiscĕre; **to — up** commiscĕre; (fig) confundĕre

mixed adj promiscuus, confusus

mixture s mixtura, farrago f

moan vi gemĕre, ingemiscĕre

moan s gemit·us -ūs m

moat s fossa f

mob s turba f, vulgus n

mob vt conviciis insectari, stipare

mobile adj mobilis

mobility s mobilitas f

mock s irrisio, derisio f

mock vt ludĕre, ludificari, irridĕre

mock adj fictus, fucatus

mockery s irrisio f, irris·us -ūs m

mode s modus m, ratio f; (fashion) us·us -ūs m

model s exemplar, exemplum n

model vt formare, delineare, fingĕre

moderate adj moderatus, mediocris, modicus; **—ly** moderate, mediocriter, modice

moderate vt moderari, temperare, coercēre

moderation s moderatio, temperantia f, modus m

moderator s praeses m

modern adj recens, hodiernus, novus

modest adj (restrained) modestus, pudens, verecundus; (sight) modicus, mediocris; **—ly** pudenter, verecunde

modesty s modestia, pudicitia, verecundia f

modification s modificatio, mutatio f

modify vt (im)mutare

modulate vt (voice) flectĕre; modulari

modulation s flexio f, flex·us -ūs m

moist adj humidus, uvidus, madidus

moisten vt (h)umectare, rigare

moisture s humor m

molar s dens genuinus m

molasses s sacchari faex f

mold s (form) forma, matrix f; (mustiness) mucor m

mold vt formare, fingĕre; (to knead) subigĕre; vi mucescĕre

molder vi putrescĕre, dilabi

moldiness s mucor, sit·us -ūs m

moldy adj mucidus, situ corruptus

mole s (animal) talpa f; (sea wall) moles f, agger m; (on skin) naevus m

molecule s particula f

molehill s **to make a mountain out of a —** e rivo flumina magna facĕre

molest vt vexare, sollicitare

molt vi plumas ponĕre

molten adj liquefactus

moment s (of time) punctum temporis n; (importance) momentum n; **in a —** statim; **of great —** magni ponderis; **this —** ad tempus

momentarily adv statim, confestim

momentary adj brevis

momentous adj gravis, magni momenti (genit, used adjectively)

monarch s rex, princeps, dominus m

monarchical adj regius

monarchy s regnum n

monastery s monasterium n

monetary adj pecuniarius, argentarius, nummarius

money s pecunia f, nummi m pl; **for —** mercede

moneychanger s nummularius m

moneylender s faenerator m

mongrel s hybrida m

monitor s admonitor m

monk s monachus m

monkey s simia f

monogram s monogramma n

monologue s oratio f

monopolize vt monopolium exercēre in (with acc)

monopoly s monopolium n

monosyllabic adj monosyllabus

monosyllable s monosyllabum n

monotonous adj semper idem; (singsong) canorus

monotony s taedium n

monster s monstrum, portentum n, belua f

monstrosity s monstrum n

monstrous adj monstrosus, portentosus, prodigiosus; **—ly** monstrose

month *s* mensis *m*
monthly *adj* menstruus
monthly *adv* singulis mensibus
monument *s* monumentum *n*
monumental *adj* (*important*) gravis, magnus; (*huge*) ingens
mood *s* animi affect·us -ūs, habit·us -ūs *m*; (*gram*) modus *m*
moodiness *s* morositas *f*
moody *adj* morosus, maestus
moon *s* luna *f*
moonlight *s* lunae lumen *n*; by — per lunam
moonstruck *adj* lunaticus
Moor *s* Maurus *m*
moor *vt* religare, anchoris retinēre
moor *s* tesca *n pl*
mop *s* peniculus *m*
mop *vt* detergēre
mope *vi* maerēre
moral *adj* (*relating to morals*) moralis, ethicus; (*morally proper*) honestus; —ly moraliter; honeste
moral *s* (*of story*) documentum *n*
morale *s* animus *m*, animi *m pl*; —is low animus jacet, animi deficiunt
morality *s* boni mores *m pl*
moralize *vi* de moribus disserēre
morals *s* mores *m pl*
morass *s* palus *f*
morbid *adj* morbidus, morbosus
more *adj* plus (*with genit*); plures
more *adv* plus, magis, amplius; ultra; — and — magis magisque; — than plus quam; — than enough plus satis; no — non diutius
moreover *adv* praeterea, ultro, etenim vero
morning *s* mane *n* (*indecl*); tempus matutinum *n*; early in the — multo mane, bene mane, prima luce; in the — mane, matutino tempore; this — hodie mane
morning *adj* matutinus
morning star *s* Lucifer, phosphorus *m*
morose *adj* morosus; —ly morose
moroseness *s* morositas *f*
morsel *s* offa *f*, frustulum *n*
mortal *adj* mortalis; (*deadly*) mortifer, letalis; —ly letaliter
mortal *s* mortalis *m & f*, homo *m & f*
mortality *s* mortalitas *f*
mortar *s* mortarium *n*
mortgage *s* hypotheca *f*, pignus *n*
mortgage *vt* obligare
mortification *s* dolor *m*
mortify *vt* mortificare, coercēre; (*to vex*) offendēre
mosaic *s* tessellatum opus *n*
mosaic *adj* tesselatus
mosquito *s* culex *m*
moss *s* muscus *m*
mossy *adj* muscosus
most *adj* plurimus, maximus, plerusque; for the — part maximam partem
most *adv* maxime, plurimum
mostly *adv* plerumque, fere
mote *s* corpusculum *n*
moth *s* blatta *f*
mother *s* mater *f*

motherhood *s* matris conditio *f*
mother-in-law *s* socr·us -ūs *f*
motherless *adj* matre orbus
motherly *adj* maternus
motion *s* motio *f*, mot·us -ūs *m*; (*proposal of bill*) rogatio *f*; to make a — ferre; to set in — ciēre
motion *vi* significare, innuēre
motionless *adj* immotus, immobilis
motive *s* causa, ratio *f*, incitamentum *n*
motive *adj* movens, agens
motley *adj* varius, versicolor
mottled *adj* maculosus
motto *s* sententia *f*, praeceptum *n*
mound *s* tumulus, agger *m*, moles *f*
mount *s* mons *m*; (*horse*) equus *m*
mount *vt* scandēre, ascendēre, conscendēre; *vi* ascendēre, conscendēre, sublime ferri; subvolare
mountain *s* mons *m*
mountaineer *s* montanus *m*
mountainous *adj* montuosus, montanus
mounted *adj* (*on horseback*) inscensus
mourn *vt* lugēre, deflēre; *vi* lugēre, maerēre
mourner *s* plorator *m*
mournful *adj* lugubris, luctuosus, tristis, flebilis, maestus; —ly maeste, flebiliter
mourning *s* luct·us -ūs, maeror *m*; (*dress*) vestis lugubris *f*; in — pullatus, sorditatus; to go into — vestitum mutare
mouse *s* mus *m*
mousetrap *s* muscipulum *n*
mouth *s* os *n*; (*of beast*) faux *f*; (*of river*) ostium *n*; (*of bottle*) lura *f*
mouthful *s* buccella *f*
mouth piece *s* interpres *m*
movable *adj* mobilis
movables *s* res *f pl*, supellex *f*
move *vt* movēre; (*emotionally*) commovēre; (*to propose*) ferre; *vi* movēri, se movēre; (*to change residence*) migrare; to — on progredi
movement *s* mot·us -ūs *m*
moving *adj* flebilis, miserabilis
mow *vt* demetēre, secare
mower *s* faenisex *m & f*
mowing *s* faenisicium *n*
much *adj* multus; as — ... as tantus ... quantus; how — quantus; so — tantus; too — nimius; very — plurimus
much *adv* multum, valde; (*with comparatives*) multo; too — nimium; nimis; very — plurimum
muck *s* stercus *m*
mucous *adj* mucosus
mud *s* lutum *n*, limus *m*
muddle *vt* turbare; (*fig*) perturbare
muddle *s* confusio, turba *f*
muddy *adj* lutosus, lutulentus; (*troubled*) turbidus
muffle *vt* involvēre; to — up obvolvēre
muffled *adj* surdus
mug *s* poculum *n*
muggy *adj* humidus
mulberry *s* morum *n*

mulberry tree s morus f

mule s mulus m

muleteer s mulio m

mulish adj obstinatus

multifarious adj varius, multiplex

multiplication s multiplicatio f

multiply vt multiplicare; vi augēri, crescĕre

multitude s multitudo, turba f

multitudinous adj creberrimus

mumble vt opprimĕre; vi murmurare

munch vt manducare, mandĕre

mundane adj mundanus

municipal adj municipalis

municipality s municipium n

munificence s munificentia, largitas f

munificent adj munificus, liberalis; —ly munifice

munitions s belli apparat·us -ūs m

mural adj muralis

murder s caedes, nex f, homicidium n

murder vt necare, trucidare, obtruncare

murderer s homicida m & f, sicarius m

murderous adj (fig) sanguinarius, cruentus

murky adj caliginosus, tenebrosus

murmur s murmur n, fremit·us -ūs m

murmuring s admurmuratio f

muscle s musculus, lacertus, torus m

muscular adj lacertosus, robustus

Muse s Musa f

muse vi meditari, secum agitare

mushroom s fungus, boletus m

music s musica f; (of instruments and voices) cant·us -ūs, concent·us -ūs m

musical adj (of person) musicus; (of sound) canorus

musician s musicus m; (of stringed instrument) fidicen m; (of wind instrument) tibicen m

muslin s sidon f

must s mustum n

must vi I — go mihi eundum est, me oportet ire, debeo ire, necesse est (ut) eam

mustard s sinapi n

muster vt lustrare; (fig) cogĕre, convocare; to — up courage animum sumĕre; vi convenire, coire

muster s copiarum lustratio f, recens·us -ūs m

musty adj mucidus

mutable adj mutabilis

mute adj mutus

mutilate vt mutilare, truncare

mutilated adj mutilus, truncus

mutilation s mutilatio, laceratio f

mutineer s seditiosus m

mutinous adj seditiosus

mutiny s seditio f, mot·us -ūs m

mutiny vi tumultuari, seditionem facēre

mutter vi murmurare, mussitare

mutter s murmuratio f

mutton s ovilla f

mutual adj mutuus; —ly mutuo, inter se

muzzle s capistrum n

muzzle vt capistrare

my adj meus; — own proprius

myriad adj decem milia (with genit); (innumerable) sescenti

myrrh s myrrha, murrha f

myrtle s myrtus f

myself pron (reflexive) me; to — mihi; (intensive) ipse, egomet

mysterious adj arcanus, occultus; —ly arcane, occulte

mystery s mysterium, arcanum n; (fig) res occultissima f

mystical adj mysticus; —ly mystice

mystification s ambages f pl

mystify vt confundĕre, fallĕre

myth s mythos m, fabula f

mythical adj fabulosus

mythology s fabulae f pl, mythologia f

N

nab vt prehendĕre

nadir s fundus m

nag s caballus m

nag vt objurgitare

naiad s naias f

nail s clavus m; (of finger) unguis m

nail vt defigĕre

naive adj simplex; —ly simpliciter

naked adj nudus, apertus; —ly aperte

name s nomen n, appellatio f; (reputation) fama, celebritas f; (term) vocabulum n; by — nominatim

name vt nominare, appellare; (to appoint) dicĕre

nameless adj nominis expers

namely adv scilicet, videlicet

nap s brevis somnus m; (of cloth) villus m; to take a — meridiari, jacēre

nape s — of the neck cervix f

napkin s mappa f, mantele n

narcotic adj somnificus

narcotic s medicamentum somnificum n

nard s nardus f, nardum n

narrate vt narrare

narration s narratio, expositio f

narrative s fabula f

narrator s narrator m

narrow adj angustus; (fig) arctus; —ly vix, aegre

narrow vt coarctare; vi coarctari

narrow-minded adj animi angusti or parvi (genit, used adjectively)

narrowness s angustiae f pl

nasty adj (foul) foedus; (mean) amarus

natal *adj* natalis

nation *s* gens, natio *f*; (*as political body*) populus *m*; (*state*) res publica *f*

national *adj* publicus, civilis; rei publicae (*genit, used adjectively*)

nationality *s* civitas *f*

native *adj* indigena

native *s* indigena *m & f*

native land *s* patria *f*

native tongue *s* patrius sermo *m*

nativity *s* ort·us -ūs *m*

natural *adj* naturalis; (*innate*) nativus, innatus, insitus; (*fig*) sincerus, simplex; **—ly** naturā; (*unaffectedly*) simpliciter; (*of its own accord*) sponte

naturalization *s* civitatis donatio *f*

naturalize *vt* civitate donare

nature *s* natura, rerum natura *f*; (*character*) ingenium *n*, indoles *f*

naught *pron* nihil; **to set at —** parvi facĕre

naughty *adj* improbus, malus

nausea *s* nausea *f*; (*fig*) fastidium *n*

nauseate *vt* fastidium movēre (*with dat*); **to be nauseated** nauseare, fastidire

nautical *adj* nauticus

naval *adj* navalis, maritimus

nave *s* (*of church*) navis *f*

navel *s* umbilicus *m*

navigable *adj* navigabilis, navium patiens

navigate *vt* gubernare; *vi* navigare

navigation *s* navigatio *f*, res nauticae *f pl*

navigator *s* nauta, gubernator *m*

navy *s* classis *f*, copiae navales *f pl*

nay *adv* non ita

near *prep* prope (*with acc*), ad (*with acc*)

near *adj* propinquus, vicinus; (*of relation*) proximus; **— at hand** propinquus, in promptu

near *adv* prope, juxta

near *vt* appropinquare (*with dat*)

nearly *adv* prope, paene, fere, ferme

nearness *s* propinquitas *f*

nearsighted *adj* myops

neat *adj* mundus, nitidus, concinnus; **—ly** munde, concinne

neatness *s* munditia, concinnitas *f*

nebulous *adj* nebulosus

necessarily *adv* necessario

necessary *adj* necessarius; **it is —** opus est

necessitate *vt* cogĕre

necessity *s* necessitas *f*; (*want*) egestas, necessitudo *f*; (*thing*) res necessaria *f*

neck *s* collum *n*, cervix *f*

necklace *s* monile *n*, torques *m*

necktie *s* collare *n*

nectar *s* nectar *n*

need *s* (*necessity*) opus *n*, necessitas *f*; (*want*) inopia, egestas, penuria *f*; **there is —** of opus est (*with abl*)

need *vt* egēre (*with abl*), indigēre (*with abl*); (*to require*) requirĕre

needle *s* ac·us -ūs *f*

needless inutilis, minime necessarius, vanus; **—ly** sine causa

needy *adj* egens, indigens, inops

nefarious *adj* nefarius

negation *s* negatio *f*

negative *adj* negans, negativus; **—ly** negando

negative *s* negatio *f*; **to answer in the —** negare

neglect *vt* neglegĕre, omittĕre; deserĕre

neglect *s* neglegentia, incuria *f*, neglect·us -ūs *m*

neglectful *adj* neglegens

negligence *s* neglegentia, incuria *f*

negligent *adj* neglegens; **—ly** negleganter

negligible *adj* levis, tenuis

negotiable *adj* mercabilis

negotiate *vt* (*a deal*) agĕre; agĕre de (*with abl*); *vi* negotiari

negotiation *s* transactio, actio *f*, pactum *n*

negotiator *s* conciliator, orator *m*

Negro *s* Aethiops *m*

neigh *vi* hinnire

neigh *s* hinnit·us -ūs *m*

neighbor *s* vicinus, finitimus *m*

neighborhood *s* vicinia, vicinitas *f*; proximitas *f*

neighboring *adj* vicinus, finitimus

neighborly *adj* familiaris, comis, benignus

neither *pron* neuter

neither *conj* nec, neque, neve, neu; **neither . . . nor** neque . . . neque

neophyte *s* tiro *m*

nephew *s* fratris filius, sororis filius *m*

Nereid *s* Nereis *f*

nerve *s* nervus *m*; (*fig*) temeritas, audacia *f*

nervous *adj* trepidus; **—ly** trepide

nervousness *s* diffidentia, sollicitudo *f*

nest *s* nidus *m*

nest *vi* nidificare

nestle *vi* recubare

net *s* rete *n*

net *vt* irretire

netting *s* reticulum *n*

nettle *s* urtica *f*

nettle *vt* (*fig*) vexare

network *s* reticulum, opus reticulatum *n*

neuter *adj* neuter, neutralis

neutral *adj* medius, neuter

neutrality *s* nullam in partem propensio *f*

neutralize *vt* aequare

never *adv* nunquam

nevermore *adv* nunquam posthac

nevertheless *adv* nihilominus, attamen

new *s* novus, recens, integer; **—ly** nuper, modo

newcomer *s* advena *m & f*

news *s* fama *f*, rumor, nuntius *m*

newspaper *s* acta diurna *n pl*

next *adj* proximus; (*of time*) insequens; **— day** postridie

next *adv* dein, deinde, deinceps

nibble *vt* arrodĕre; (*fig*) carpĕre; *vi* rodĕre

nice *adj* (*dainty*) delicatus; (*choice*)

exquisitus; (*exact*) accuratus; (*fine*) bellus; (*effeminate*) mollis; (*amiable*) suavis; (*of weather*) serenus; —ly delicate, exquisite, belle; accurate

nicety *s* accuratio, subtilitas, elegantia *f*

niche *s* aedicula *f*

nick *s* incisura *f*; **in the very —of time** in ipso articulo temporis

nick *vt* incidĕre

nickname *s* agnomen *n*

niece *s* fratris filia, sororis filia *f*

niggardly *adj* parcus, avarus

nigh *adj* propinquus

night *s* nox *f*; **by —** nocte, noctu; **to spend the —** pernoctare

nightfall *s* primae tenebrae *f pl*; **at — sub noctem**

nightingale *s* luscinia *f*

nightly *adj* nocturnus

nightly *adv* noctu, de nocte

nightmare *s* incubus *m*

night watch *s* vigilia *f*; (*guard*) vigil *m*

nimble *adj* pernix, agilis

nine *adj* novem; **— times** noviens

nineteen *adj* undeviginti, decem et novem

nineteenth *adj* undevicesimus

ninetieth *adj* nonagesimus

ninety *adj* nonaginta

ninth *adj* nonus

nip *vt* vellicare; (*of frost*) urĕre; **to — off** desecare

nippers *s* forceps *m*

nipple *s* papilla *f*

no *adj* nullus; **— one** nemo *m*

no *adv* non, minime; **to say —** negare

nobility *s* nobilitas *f*; nobiles, optimates *m pl*; (*moral excellence*) honestas *f*

noble *adj* nobilis, generosus; (*morally*) ingenuus, honestus, liberalis

noble *s* optimas *m*

nobleman *s* vir nobilis *m*

nobly *adv* nobiliter, praeclare, generose

nobody *pron* nemo *m*

nocturnal *adj* nocturnus

nod *s* nut·us -ūs *m*

nod *vi* nutare; (*to doze*) dormitare; (*in assent*) annuĕre

noise *s* strepit·us -ūs *m*; (*high-pitched*) stridor *m*; (*loud*) fragor *m*; **to make —** strepĕre, strepitare, increpare

noise *vt* **to — abroad** promulgare, divulgare

noiseless *adj* tacitus; —ly tacite

noisily *adv* cum strepitu

noisome *adj* noxius, foedus, taeter

noisy *adj* clamosus

nomad *s* nomas *m & f*

nomadic *adj* vagus, vagabundus

nominal *adj* nominalis; —ly nomine, verbo

nominate *vt* nominare, designare

nomination *s* nominatio, designatio *f*; (*of heir*) nuncupatio *f*

nominative *adj* nominativus

nominee *s* nominatus, designatus *m*

none *pron* nemo *m*

nonentity *s* nihilum *n*

nones *s* Nonae *f pl*

nonplus *vt* (*to puzzle*) **ad incitas** redigĕre

nonsense *s* ineptiae, nugae *f pl*; **to talk —** absurde loqui, garrire

nonsense *interj* gerrae!

nonsensical *adj* ineptus, absurdus

nook *s* angulus *m*

noon *s* meridies *m*; **before —** ante meridiem

noonday *adj* meridianus

no one *pron* nemo *m*

noose *s* laqueus *m*

nor *conj* nec, neque, neve, neu

norm *s* norma *f*

normal *adj* solitus; —ly plerumque

north *s* septentriones *m pl*

north *adj* septentrionalis

northern *adj* septentrionalis

northern lights *s* aurora Borealis *f*

north pole *s* arctos *f*

northwards *adv* septentriones versus

north wind *s* aquilo *m*

nose *s* nas·us -ūs *m*, nares *f pl*; **to blow the —** emungĕre

nostril *s* naris *f*

not *adv* non, haud; **— at all** nullo modo, haudquaquam; **— even** ne ... quidem

notable *adj* notabilis, insignis, insignitus

notably *adv* insignite

notary *s* scriba *m*

notation *s* notatio *f*, signum *n*

notch *s* incisura *f*

notch *vt* incidĕre

note *s* (*mark*) nota *f*; (*comment*) adnotatio *f*; (*mus*) sonus *m*, vox *f*; (*com*) chirographum *n*; (*letter*) litterulae *f pl*

note *vt* notare; (*to notice*) animadvertĕre

notebook *s* commentarius *m*, tabulae *f pl*, pugillares *m pl*

noted *adj* insignis, insignitus, notus, praeclarus

noteworthy *adj* notabilis, memorabilis

nothing *pron* nihil, nil, nihilum; **for —** (*free*) gratis, gratuito; (*in vain*) frustra; **good for —** nequam; **but nihil nisi; to think — of** nihili facĕre

notice *s* (*act of noticing*) notatio, animadversio *f*; (*announcement*) denuntiatio *f*; (*sign*) proscriptio *f*, titulus, libellus *m*; **to escape —** latēre; **to escape the — of** fallēre; **to give — of** denuntiare

notice *vt* animadvertĕre, observare

noticeable *adj* insignis, conspicuus

noticeably *adv* insigniter

notification *s* denuntiatio, declaratio *f*

notify *vt* certiorem facĕre

notion *s* notio, suspicio *f*

notoriety *s* infamia *f*

notorious *adj* famosus, infamis, notus, manifestus; —ly manifeste

notwithstanding *adv* nihilominus

nought *pron* nihil; **to set at —** parvi facĕre

noun *s* nomen *n*

nourish *vt* alĕre, nutrire

nourishment *s* (*act*) alimentum *n*, cibus *m*

novel *adj* novus, inauditus

novel *s* fabula *f*

novelty *s* res nova *f*; novitas *f*

November *s* (*mensis*) November *m*

novice *s* tiro *m*

now *adv* nunc; (*past*) jam; **— and then** interdum, nonnunquam; **— ... —** modo ... modo

nowhere *adv* nusquam

noxious *adj* noxius

nozzle *s* ansa *f*

nude *adj* nudus

nudge *vt* fodicare

nudity *s* nudatio *f*

nugget *s* massa *f*

nuisance *s* incommodum *n*, molestia *f*

null *adj* irritus

nullify *vt* irritum facĕre

numb *adj* torpidus, torpens; **to become —** torpescĕre; **to be —** torpēre

numb *vt* torpefacĕre; (*fig*) obstupefacĕre

number *s* numerus *m*; **a — of** aliquot; **without —** innumerabilis

number *vt* numerare, enumerare, dinumerare

numberless *adj* innumerus, innumerabilis

numbness *s* torpor *m*; (*fig*) stupor *m*

numerical *adj* numeralis; **—ly** numero, ad numerum

numerous *adj* frequens, creber, multus

numismatics *s* doctrina nummorum *f*

nuptial *adj* nuptialis, conjugalis

nuptials *s* nuptiae *f pl*

nurse *s* nutrix *f*

nurse *vt* (*a baby*) nutrire; (*fig*) fovēre; (*the sick*) ancillari (*with dat*); curare

nursery *s* (*for children*) infantium cubiculum *n*; (*for plants*) plantarium, seminarium *n*

nurture *vt* nutrire, educare

nut *s* nux *f*; **a hard — to crack** (*fig*) quaestio nodosa *f*

nutriment *s* nutrimentum, alimentum *n*

nutrition *s* nutritio *f*, nutrimentum *n*

nutritious *adj* alibilis, salubris

nutshell *s* putamen *n*; **in a —** (*fig*) paucis verbis

nymph *s* nympha *f*

O

oaf *s* stultus, hebes *m*

oak *adj* querceus, quernus

oak *s* querc·us -ūs *f*; (*evergreen*) ilex *f*; (*timber*) robur *n*

oakum *s* stuppa *f*

oar *s* remus *m*; **to pull the —s** remos ducĕre

oarsman *s* remex *m*

oath *s* jusjurandum *n*; (*mil*) sacramentum *n*; **false —** perjurium *n*; **to take an —** jurare; (*mil*) sacramentum dicĕre

oats *s* avena *f*

obdurate *adj* obstinatus, pertinax; **—ly** obstinate, pertinaciter

obedience *s* obedientia *f*, obsequium *n*

obedient *adj* obediens, obsequens; **—ly** obedienter

obeisance *s* obsequium *n*, capitis summissio *f*; **to make — to** flectĕre ante (*with acc*); (*fig*) obsequi (*with dat*)

obelisk *s* obeliscus *m*

obese *adj* obesus

obesity *s* obesitas *f*

obey *vt* parēre (*with dat*), obedire (*with dat*), obtemperare (*with dat*), obsequi (*with dat*)

obituary *s* Libitinae index *m*

object *s* objectum *n*, res *f*; (*aim*) finis *m*, propositum *n*

object *vi* (*to feel annoyance*) gravari;

(*to make objections*) recusare; **to — to** aegre ferre

objection *s* objectio *f*; impedimentum *n*, mora *f*

objectionable *adj* injucundus, improbabilis

objective *s* finis *m*, propositum *n*

objective *adj* externus, objectivus, verus

oblation *s* donum *n*

obligation *s* debitum, officium *n*; **under —** noxius

obligatory *adj* necessarius, debitus

oblige *vt* (*to force*) cogĕre, impellĕre; (*to put under obligation*) obligare, obstringĕre; (*to do a favor for*) morigerari (*with dat*); **to be obliged to** debēre (*with inf*); (*to feel gratitude toward*) gratiam habēre (*with dat*)

obliging *adj* officiosus, comis, blandus; **—ly** officiose, comiter

oblique *adj* obliquus; **—ly** oblique

obliterate *vt* delēre, oblitterare

oblivion *s* oblivio *f*

oblivious *adj* obliviosus, immemor

oblong *adj* oblongus

obloquy *s* vituperatio *f*, maledictum *n*

obnoxious *adj* invisus, noxius

obscene *adj* obscenus; **—ly** obscene

obscenity *s* obscenitas *f*

obscure *adj* obscurus; **—ly** obscure

obscure *vt* obscurare

obscurity *s* obscuritas *f*, tenebrae *f pl*; (*of birth*) humilitas *f*

obsequies *s* exsequiae *f pl*

obsequious *adj* officiosus, morigerus, nimis obsequens

obsequiousness *s* obsequium *n*, assentatio *f*

observable *adj* notabilis

observance *s* observantia *f*; (*rite*) rit·us -ūs *m*

observant *adj* attentus; — **of** diligens (*with genit*)

observation *s* observatio, animadversio *f*; (*remark*) notatio *f*, dictum *n*

observe *vt* (*to watch*) observare, contemplari, animadvertĕre; (*to keep*) conservare, observare; (*to remark*) dicĕre

observer *s* spectator *m*

obsess *vt* occupare

obsession *s* studium *n*

obsolescent *adj* **to be** — obsolescĕre

obsolete *adj* obsoletus, antiquatus; **to become** — exolescĕre

obstacle *s* impedimentum *n*; (*barrier*) obex *m*

obstinacy *s* obstinatio *f*, animus obstinatus *m*

obstinate *adj* obstinatus, pertinax; —**ly** obstinate

obstreperous *adj* tumultuosus, clamosus

obstruct *vt* obstare (*with dat*), obstruĕre, impedire

obstruction *s* obstructio *f*, impedimentum *n*; (*pol*) intercessio *f*

obtain *vt* nancisci, adipisci, consequi; (*by entreaty*) impetrare; *vi* valēre

obtainable *adj* impetrabilis

obtrusive *adj* molestus, importunus

obtuse *adj* obtusus, hebes, stolidus

obviate *vt* praevertĕre

obvious *adj* apertus, manifestus, perspicuus; —**ly** aperte, manifesto

occasion *s* occasio *f*, locus *m*; (*reason*) causa *f*; (*time*) tempus *n*

occasion *vt* locum dare (*with dat*), movēre

occasionally *adv* interdum

occidental *adj* occidentalis

occult *adj* occultus, arcanus

occupant *s* possessor *m*

occupation *s* possessio *f*; (*engagement*) occupatio *f*; (*employment*) negotium *n*, quaest·us -ūs *m*

occupy *vt* occupare, tenēre; (*to possess*) possidēre; (*space*) complēre

occur *vi* accidĕre, evenire; (*to the mind*) occurrĕre, in mentem venire

occurrence *s* cas·us -ūs, event·us -ūs *m*

ocean *s* oceanus *m*, mare oceanum *n*

oceanic *adj* oceanus, oceanensis

October *s* (*mensis*) October *m*

ocular *adj* ocularis

oculist *s* ocularius medicus *m*

odd *adj* (*of number*) impar; (*quaint*) insolitus, novus; —**ly** mirum in modum

oddity *s* raritas *f*, ridiculum *n*

odds *s* **the** — **are against us** impares summus; **to be at** — **with** dissidēre ab (*with abl*)

odious *adj* odiosus, invisus

odium *s* invidia *f*

odor *s* odor *m*

odorous *adj* odoratus

Odyssey *s* Odyssea *f*

of *prep* (*possession*) rendered by genit; (*origin*) de (*with abl*), ex (*with abl*)

off *adv* procul; **far** — longe, procul; **well** — bene nummatus

off *prep* de (*with abl*)

offend *vt* offendĕre, laedĕre; *vi* **to** — **against** violare

offender *s* peccator, reus *m*

offense *s* (*fault*) offensa, culpa *f*; (*insult*) injuria *f*; (*displeasure*) offensio *f*

offensive *adj* injuriosus; (*odors, etc.*) odiosus, foedus, gravis; (*language*) malignus, contumeliosus; (*aggressive*) bellum inferens; —**ly** injuriose; odiose

offer *vt* offerre, donare, praebēre; (*violence*) adferre; (*help*) ferre

offer *s* conditio *f*

offhand *adj* incuriosus

offhand *adv* confestim, illico

office *s* (*place of work*) officina *f*; (*pol*) honos, magistrat·us -ūs *m*; (*duty*) munus, officium *n*

officer *s* magistrat·us -ūs *m*; (*mil*) praefectus *m*

official *adj* publicus

official *s* minister, magistrat·us -ūs *m*

officiate *vi* officio *or* munere fungi, interesse; (*of clergyman*) rem divinam facĕre

officious *adj* officiosus, molestus; —**ly** officiose, moleste

offing *s* **in the** — procul

offset *vt* compensare

offspring *s* proles, progenies *f*

often *adv* saepe; **very** — persaepe

ogre *s* larva *f*, monstrum *n*

oh *interj* oh!, ohe!

oil *s* oleum *n*

oil *vt* ung(u)ĕre

oily *adj* oleosus; (*like oil*) oleaceus

ointment *s* unguentum *n*

old *adj* (*aged*) senex; (*out of use*) obsoletus; (*worn*) exesus, tritus; (*ancient*) antiquus, priscus; **of** — olim, quondam; **to grow** — senescĕre

old age *s* senectus *f*

old-fashioned *adj* priscus, antiquus

old man *s* senex *m*

old woman *s* an·us -ūs *f*

oligarchy *s* optimates *m pl*

olive *s* olea *f*

olive grove *s* olivetum *n*

Olympiad *s* Olympias *f*

Olympic *adj* Olympicus

omelet *s* laganum de ovis confectum *n*

omen *s* omen, auspicium *n*

ominous *adj* infaustus; —**ly** malis ominibus

omission *s* praetermissio, neglegentia *f*

omit *vt* omittĕre, mittĕre, praetermittĕre

omnipotence *s* omnipotentia, infinita potentia *f*

omnipotent *adj* omnipotens

omnivorous *adj* omnivorus

on *prep* (*place*) in (*with abl*); (*time*) render by abl; (*about, concerning*) de (*with abl*); (*ranged with*) a(b) (*with abl*); (*depending, hanging on*) de (*with abl*); (*near*) ad (*with acc*)

on *adv* porro; (*continually*) usque; **and so** — et cetera, ac deinceps; **to go** — pergĕre

once *adv* (*one time*) semel; (*formerly*) olim, quondam; **at** — statim, illico, ex templo; **for** — aliquando; **— and for all** semel in perpetuum; **— more** iterum; **— upon a time** olim

one *adj* unus

one *pron* unus; unicus; (*a certain person or thing*) quidam; **it is all** — perinde est; **— after another** alternus; **— another** inter se, alius alium; **— by** — singulatim; **— or the other** alteruter; **— or two** unus et alter

one-eyed *adj* luscus

onerous *adj* onerosus, gravis

oneself *pron* (*refl*) se; **to** — sibi; **with** — secum; (*intensive*) ipse

one-sided *adj* inaequalis, iniquus, impar

onion *s* caepa *f*

only *adj* unicus, unus, solus

only *adv* solum, tantum, modo; **not** **— . . . but also** non solum . . . sed etiam

only-begotten *adj* unigenitus

onset *s* impet·us -ūs *m*

onslaught *s* incurs·us -ūs *m*

onward *adv* porro

ooze *vi* manare, (de)stillare

opaque *adj* densus, opacus

open *adj* (*not shut*) apertus, patens; (*evident*) manifestus; (*sincere*) candidus, ingenuus; (*public*) publicus, communis; (*of space*) apertus; (*of question, undecided*) integer; **in the** **— air** sub divo; **to lie** — patēre; **—ly** aperte, palam

open *vt* aperire, patefacĕre; (*to uncover*) retegĕre; (*letter*) resignare; (*book*) evolvĕre; (*to begin*) exordiri; (*with ceremony*) inaugurare; *vi* patescĕre, se pandĕre; (*to gape*) dehiscĕre; (*of wound*) recrudescĕre

open-handed *adj* liberalis, largus

open-hearted *adj* simplex, ingenuus

opening *s* (*act*) apertio *f*; (*aperture*) foramen *n*, hiat·us -ūs *m*; (*opportunity*) locus *m*, occasio *f*

open-minded *adj* docilis

operate *vt* agĕre, gerĕre; *vi* operari

operation *s* effectio *f*; (*business*) negotium *n*; (*med*) sectio *f*

operative *adj* efficax, activus

operator *s* opifex *m*

opiate *s* mendicamentum somnificum

opinion *s* opinio, sententia, mens *f*; (*esteem*) existimatio *f*; **public** —

fama *f*

opium *s* opion *n*

opponent *s* adversarius *m*

opportune *adj* opportunus, idoneus, commodus; **—ly** opportune, in tempore

opportunity *s* copia, occasio, opportunitas *f*

oppose *vt* opponĕre, objicĕre; *vi* repugnare, resistĕre, adversari

opposite *adj* adversus, contrarius, diversus

opposite *prep* contra (*with acc*)

opposite *adv* contra, ex adverso

opposition *s* oppositio, repugnantia, discrepantia *f*; (*obstacle*) impedimentum *n*; (*party*) adversa factio *f*

oppress *vt* opprimĕre, vexare, gravare, onerare

oppression *s* gravatio, injuria *f*

oppressive *adj* praegravis, acerbus, molestus; **to become** — ingravescĕre

oppressor *s* tyrannus *m*

opprobrious *adj* turpis, probrosus

opprobrium *s* dedecus, probrum *n*

optical *adj* opticus

option *s* optio *f*

opulence *s* opulentia *f*

opulent *adj* opulens, opulentus

or *conj* vel, aut, —ve; (*in questions*) an; **— else** aut, alioquin; **— not** annon; (*in indirect questions*) necne

oracle *s* oraculum *n*

oracular *adj* fatidicus

oral *adj* verbalis, verbo traditus; **—ly** voce, verbis

orange *s* malum aurantium *n*

oration *s* oratio *f*

orator *s* orator *m*

oratorical *adj* oratorius

oratory *s* ars oratoria, eloquentia, rhetorice *f*

orb *s* orbis, gyrus *m*

orbit *s* orbis *m*; (*in astronomy*) ambit·us -ūs *m*

orchard *s* pomarium *n*

orchestra *s* symphoniaci *m pl*

ordain *vt* (*to appoint*) edicĕre

ordeal *s* discrimen *n*, labor *m*

order *s* (*class, arrangement*) ordo *m*; (*command*) mandatum, jussum, imperatum *n*; (*fraternity*) collegium *n*; **by** — of jussu (*with genit*); **in** **— dispositus**; **in** — **that** ut; **in** — **that not** ne; **out of** — incompositus; **to put in** — ordinare, disponĕre

order *vt* (*to command*) imperare (*with dat*), jubēre; (*to demand*) imperare (*with acc*); (*to put in order*) ordinare, disponĕre, digerĕre

orderly *adj* compositus, ordinatus; (*well-behaved*) modestus

orderly *s* accensus *m*; (*mil*) tesserarius *m*

ordinal *adj* ordinalis

ordinance *s* edictum, rescriptum *n*

ordinarily *adv* fere, plerumque

ordinary *adj* usitatus, vulgaris, solitus, quottidianus

ordnance *s* tormenta *n pl*

ore *s* aes *n*

organ *s* (*of body*) membrum *n*; (*musical*) organum *n*

organic *adj* organicus

organism *s* compages *f*

organization *s* ordinatio *f*, structura *f*

organize *vt* ordinare, instituĕre

orgy *s* comissatio *f*

Orient *s* oriens *m*

oriental *adj* Asiaticus

orifice *s* foramen, os *n*

origin *s* origo *f*, principium *n*; (*birth*) genus *n*; (*source*) fons *m*

original *adj* pristinus, primitivus, primus; (*one's own*) proprius; (*new*) novus, inauditus; —ly primum, principio, initio

original *s* archetypum, exemplar *n*; (*writing*) autographum *n*

originality *s* proprietas ingenii *f*

originate *vt* instituĕre; *vi* oriri

originator *s* auctor *m*

ornament *s* ornamentum *n*, ornat·us ·ūs *m*

ornament *vt* ornare, decorare

ornamental *adj* decorus

ornate *adj* ornatus; —ly ornate

orphan *s* orbus *m*, orba *f*

orphaned *adj* orbatus

orphanage *s* orphanotrophium *n*

oscillate *vi* agitari; (*fig*) dubitare

oscillation *s* agitatio *f*; (*fig*) dubitatio *f*

ostensible *adj* simulatus, fictus

ostensibly *adv* specie, per speciem

ostentation *s* ostentatio, jactatio *f*

ostentatious *adj* ambitiosus, gloriosus, jactans; —ly ambitiose, jactanter

ostracism *s* ostracismus *m*

ostrich *s* struthiocamelus *m*

other *adj* (*different*) alius, diversus; (*remaining*) ceterus; every — day tertio quoque die; on the — hand contra, autem; the — alter

otherwise *adv* aliter

otter *s* lutra *f*

ought *vi* I — debeo, oportet me

ounce *s* uncia *f*

our *adj* noster

ours *pron* noster

ourselves *pron* (*reflex*) nos, nosmet; to — nobis; (*intensive*) nosmet ipsi

oust *vt* ejicĕre

out *adv* (*outside*) foris; (*motion*) foras; — of de (*with abl*), e(x) (*with abl*); (*on account of*) propter (*with acc*); — of the way devius

outbreak *s* eruptio *f*; (*fig*) seditio *f*

outburst *s* eruptio *f*

outcast *s* exsul, extorris, profugus *m*

outcome *s* event·us ·ūs *m*

outcry *s* clamor *m*, acclamatio *f*, convicium *n*

outdo *vt* superare

outdoors *adv* foris, sub divo

outer *adj* exterior

outermost *adj* extremus

outfit *s* apparat·us ·ūs *m*; (*costume*) vestimenta *n pl*

outflank *vt* circumire, circumvenire

outgrow *vt* excedĕre ex (*with abl*), staturā superare

outing *s* excursio *f*

outlandish *adj* externus, barbarus

outlast *vt* diutius durare (*with abl*)

outlaw *s* proscriptus *m*

outlaw *vt* aquā et igni interdicĕre (*with dat*), proscribĕre

outlay *s* sumpt·us ·ūs *m*, impensa *f*

outlet *s* exit·us ·ūs *m*

outline *vt* describĕre, adumbrare

outline *s* adumbratio *f*

outlive *vt* supervivĕre (*with dat*), superesse (*with dat*)

outlook *s* prospect·us ·ūs *m*

outlying *adj* externus; (*distant*) remotus

outnumber *vt* multitudine superare

outpost *s* statio *f*

outpouring *s* effusio *f*

output *s* fruct·us ·ūs *m*

outrage *s* injuria *f*, flagitium *n*

outrage *vt* flagitio afficĕre, violare

outrageous *adj* flagitiosus, atrox; (*excessive*) immodicus; —ly flagitiose; immodice

outright *adv* (*at once*) statim; (*completely*) prorsus, penitus

outrun *vt* praevertĕre, linquĕre

outset *s* initium, inceptum *n*

outshine *vt* praelucēre (*with dat*)

outside *s* pars exterior, superficies *f*; (*appearance*) species *f*; on the — extrinsecus

outside *adj* externus

outside *adv* foris, extra; (*motion*) foras; from — extrinsecus

outside *prep* extra (*with acc*)

outskirts *s* suburbium *n*, ager suburbanus *m*

outspoken *adj* candidus, liber

outspread *adj* patulus

outstanding *adj* praestans; (*of debts*) residùus

outstretched *adj* extentus, porrectus, passus

outstrip *vt* praevertĕre, cursu superare

outward *adj* externus

outward *adv* extra, extrinsecus

outweigh *vt* praevertĕre (*with dat*), praeponderare

outwit *vt* deludĕre, decipĕre

oval *adj* ovatus

ovation *s* plaus·us ·ūs *m*; (*triumph*) ovatio *f*

oven *s* furnus *m*, fornax *f*

over *prep* (*across*) super (*with acc*), trans (*with acc*), per (*with acc*); (*above*) super (*with abl*), supra (*with acc*); (*with numbers*) plus quam

over *adv* supra; (*excess*) nimis; all — ubique, passim; — and above insuper; — and — again iterum ac saepius, identidem

overall *adj* totus

overawe *vt* (de)terrēre

overbalance *vt* praeponderare

overbearing *adj* superbus, insolens

overboard *adv* ex nave; to jump — ex nave desilire

overburden *vt* nimis onerare

overcast *adj* obnubilus

overcharge vt plus aequo exigĕre ab (with abl)

overcoat s paenula, lacerna f

overdo vt exaggerare, in majus extollĕre

overdue adj (money) residuus

overestimate vt majoris aestimare

overflow s inundatio f

overflow vt inundare; vi abundare, redundare

overgrown adj obductus, obsitus; (too big) praegrandis

overhang vt impendĕre

overhaul vt reficĕre

overhead adv desuper, insuper

overhear vt excipĕre, auscultare

overjoyed adj to be — nimio gaudio exsultare

overladen adj praegravatus

overland adj per terram

overlay vt inducĕre, illinĕre

overload vt nimis onerare

overlook vt (not to notice) praetermittĕre; (to pardon) ignoscĕre (with dat); (a view) despectare

overlord s dominus m

overpower vt exsuperare, opprimĕre

overrate vt nimis aestimare

overreach vt circumvenire

overriding adj praecipuus

overripe adj praematurus

overrun vt (per) vagari; (fig) obsidēre

overseas adj transmarinus

oversee vt praeesse (with dat)

overseer s curator, praeses, custos m

overshadow vt obumbrare; (fig) obscurare

overshoot vt excedĕre, transgredi

oversight s incuria, neglegentia f, error m

oversleep vi diutius dormire

overspread vt obducĕre

overstate vt in majus extollĕre

overstep vt excedĕre, transgredi

overt adj apertus; —ly palam

overtake vt consequi

overtax vt (fig) abuti (with abl)

overthrow s eversio, ruina f, excidium n

overthrow vt subvertĕre, evertĕre, dejicĕre

overture s (mus) exordium n; (proposal) conditio f; to make —s to agĕre cum (with abl)

overturn vt evertĕre, subvertĕre

overweening adj superbus, insolens, arrogans

overwhelm vt obruĕre, opprimĕre

overwork vt to — oneself plus aequo laborare

owe vt debēre

owing to prep propter (with acc)

owl s bubo m, strix f

own adj proprius; one's — suus, proprius

own vt possidēre, tenēre; (to acknowledge) fatēri, confitēri

owner s dominus, possessor m

ownership s possessio f, mancipium, dominium n

ox s bos m

oyster s ostrea f

oyster shell s ostreae testa f

P

pace s (step) pass·us -ūs, grad·us -ūs m; (measure) pass·us -ūs m; (speed) velocitas f, grad·us -ūs m

pace vi incedĕre, gradi; to — up and down spatiari

pacific adj pacificus, tranquillus

pacification s pacificatio f

pacify vt pacare, placare, sedare

pack s (bundle) sarcina f, fasciculus m; (of animals) grex m; (of people) turba f, grex m

pack vt (items of luggage) colligĕre, componĕre; (to fill completely) frequentare, complēre; (to compress) stipare; vi vasa colligĕre

package s sarcina f, fasciculus m

packet s fasciculus m

pack horse s equus clitellarius m

packsaddle s clitellae f pl

pact s pactum n, pactio f; to make a — pacisci

pad s pulvinus, pulvillus m

pad vt suffarcinare

padding s fartura f

paddle s remus m

paddle vi remigare

paddock s saeptum n

pagan s paganus m

page s (of book) pagina, scheda f; puer m

pageant s pompa f, spectaculum n

pail s hama, situla f

pain s dolor m; (fig) angor m; to be in — dolēre; to take —s operam dare

pain vt dolore afficĕre, excruciare; vi dolēre

painful adj gravis, acerbus, molestus; —ly graviter, magno cum dolore

painless adj doloris expers

painstaking adj operosus

paint s pigmentum n; (for face) fucus m

paint vt pingĕre, depingĕre

paintbrush s penicillus m

painter s pictor m

painting s pictura f

pair s par n; (of oxen) jugum n

pair vt conjungĕre, componĕre

palace s regia f, palatium n

palatable adj jucundus, suavis, sapidus

palate s palatum n

palatial adj regius

pale *adj* pallidus; **to be —** pallēre; **to grow —** pallescĕre
pale *s* palus *m*
paling *s* saepes *f*
palisade *s* vallum *n*
pall *s* pallium *n*
pall *vt* satiare; *vi* vapescĕre
pallet *s* grabat·us -ūs *m*
palliative *s* lenimentum *n*
pallid *adj* pallidus
pallor *s* pallor *m*
palm *s* (*of hand*) palma *f*; (*tree*) palma *f*
palpable *adj* tractabilis; (*fig*) apertus, manifestus
palpitate *vi* palpitare
palsied *adj* paralyticus
palsy *s* paralysis *f*
paltry *adj* vilis, minutus
pamper *vt* indulgēre (*with dat*)
pamphlet *s* libellus *m*
pan *s* patina, patella *f*; (*for frying*) sartago *f*
pancake *s* laganum *n*
pander *s* leno *m*
pander *vi* lenocinari
panegyric *s* laudatio *f*
panel *s* (*of wall*) abacus *m*; (*of ceiling*) lacunar *n*; (*of jury*) decurio *m*; (*of door*) tympanum *n*
paneled *adj* laqueatus
pang *s* dolor *m*
panic *s* pavor *m*
panic-stricken *adj* pavidus
panoply *s* arma *n pl*
panorama *s* conspect·us -ūs *m*
pant *vi* palpitare, anhelare; **to — after** (*fig*) gestire
pantheism *s* pantheismus *m*
pantheist *s* pantheista *m*
pantheon *s* Pantheon *n*
panther *s* pantera *f*
panting *adj* anhelus
panting *s* anhelit·us -ūs *m*
pantomime *s* (*play and actor*) mimus *m*
pantry *s* cella penaria *f*
pap *s* papilla, mamilla *f*
paper *s* (*stationery*) charta *f*; (*newspaper*) acta diurna *n pl*; **—s** scripta *n pl*
paper *adj* chartaceus, charteus
papyrus *s* papyrus *f*
par *s* **to be on a — with** par esse (*with dat*)
parable *s* parabole *f*
parade *s* (*mil*) decurs·us -ūs *m*; pompa *f*; (*display*) apparat·us -ūs *m*, pompa *f*
parade *vt* (*fig*) ostentare, jactare; *vi* (*mil*) decurrĕre
paradise *s* paradisus *m*
paradox *s* oxymora verba *n pl*
paragon *s* specimen, exemplar *n*
paragraph *s* caput *n*
parallel *adj* parallelus; (*fig*) consimilis
parallel *vt* exaequare
paralysis *s* paralysis *f*; (*fig*) torpedo *f*
paralytic *adj* paralyticus
paralyze *vt* debilitare, enervare, percellĕre

paramount *adj* supremus
paramour *s* (*man*) moechus, adulter *m*; (*woman*) meretrix, pellex *f*
parapet *s* pluteus *m*
paraphernalia *s* apparat·us -ūs *m*
paraphrase *s* paraphrasis *f*
paraphrase *vt* vertĕre, interpretari
parasite *s* parasitus *m*
parasol *s* umbella *f*, umbraculum *n*
parcel *s* fasciculus *m*; (*plot of land*) agellus *m*
parcel *vt* **to — out** partire, dispertire
parch *vt* torrēre
parched *adj* torridus, aridus; **to be — arēre
parchment *s* membrana *f*
pardon *s* venia *f*
pardon *vt* ignoscĕre (*with dat*); (*an offense*) condonare
pardonable *adj* ignoscendus, condonandus
pare *vt* (*vegetables*) deglubĕre; (*the nails*) resecare
parent *s* parens *m & f*
parentage *s* genus *n*, stirps *f*
parental *adj* patrius
parenthesis *s* interpositio, interclusio *f*
parity *s* paritas, aequalitas *f*
park *s* horti *m pl*
parlance *s* sermo *m*
parley *s* colloquium *n*
parley *vi* colloqui
parliament *s* senat·us -ūs *m*
parliamentary *adj* senatorius
parlor *s* exedrium *n*
parody *s* ridicula imitatio *f*
parole *s* fides *f*
paroxysm *s* access·us -ūs *m*
parricide *s* (*murder*) parricidium *n*; (*murderer*) parricida *m & f*
parrot *s* psittacus *m*
parry *vt* avertĕre, defendĕre
parse *vt* flectĕre
parsimonious *adj* parcus; **—ly** parce
parsing *s* partium orationis flexio *f*
parsley *s* apium *n*
part *s* pars *f*; (*in play*) partes *f pl*; (*duty*) officium *n*; **for the most —** maximam partem; **in — partim; on the — of** ab (*with abl*); **to act the — of** sustinēre partes (*with genit*); **to take — in** interesse (*with dat*), particeps esse (*with genit*)
part *vt* separare, dividĕre; **to — company** discedĕre; *vi* discedĕre, abire; (*to go open*) dehiscĕre; **to — with** dimittĕre
partial *adj* iniquus; (*incomplete*) mancus; **to be — favēre (*with dat*); **—ly** aliqua ex parte
partiality *s* iniquitas *f*
participant *s* particeps *m & f*
participate *vi* interesse; **to — in** interesse (*with dat*), particeps esse (*with genit*)
participation *s* participatio, societas *f*
participle *s* participium *n*
particle *s* particula *f*

particular adj (own) proprius; (special) peculiaris, singularis, praecipuus; (fussy) fastidiosus; —**ly** praecipue, praesertim

particularize vt exsequi

particulars s singula n pl

parting s discess·us -ūs, digress·us -ūs m

partisan s fautor m

partition s partitio f; (between rooms) paries m; (enclosure) saeptum n

partly adv partim, ex parte

partner s socius m, socia f, particeps m & f; (in office) collega m; (in marriage) conju(n)x, consors m & f

partnership s consociatio, societas, consortio f

partridge s perdix m & f

party s (entertainment) convivium n; (pol) factio f, partes f pl; (detachment) man·us -ūs f; **to join a** — partes sequi

pass s angustiae f pl

pass vt (to go by) praeterire, transire, transgredi; (to exceed) excedĕre; (to approve) probare; (time) agĕre, degĕre; (a law) perferre; **to** — **around** circumferre, tradĕre; **to** — **down** tradĕre; **to** — **sentence** jus dicere; **to** — **the test** approbari; vi (of time) transire, abire, praeterire; **to come to** — evenire, fieri; **to let** — praetermittĕre, dimittĕre; **to** — **away** (to die) perire, abire; **to** — **for** habĕri, vidēri; **to** — **on** (to go forward) pergĕre; (to die) perire; **to** — **out** collabi, intermori; **to** — **over** transire

passable adj (of road) pervius; (fig) mediocris, tolerabilis

passably adv mediocriter, tolerabiliter

passage s (act) transit·us -ūs m; (by water) transmissio, trajectio f; (of book) locus m

passenger s viator m; (on ship) vector m

passer-by s praeteriens m

passing s obit·us -ūs m

passion s cupiditas, permotio f, fervor m; (anger) ira f; (lust) libido f

passionate adj fervidus, ardens; iracundus; —**ly** ardenter; iracunde

passive adj passivus; —**ly** passive

passport s diploma n

password s tessera f

past adj praeteritus; (immediately preceding) proximus, superior

past s tempus praeteritum n

past prep praeter (with acc), post (with acc)

paste s gluten n

paste vt agglutinare, conglutinare

pasteboard s charta crassa f

pastime s oblectamentum n, ludus m

pastoral adj pastoralis, bucolicus

pastoral s poema bucolicum n

pastry s crustum n

pasture s past·us -ūs m, pascuum n, pastio f

pasture vt pascĕre; vi (to graze)

pasci

pat adj idoneus

pat vt permulcēre, demulcēre

patch s assumentum n, pannus m

patch vt resarcire, assuĕre

patchwork s cento m

patent adj apertus, manifestus; —**ly** manifesto

patent s privilegium n

paternal adj paternus

paternity s paternitas f

path s semita f, trames, callis m; (fig) via f

pathetic adj maestus; —**ally** maeste

pathless adj invius

pathos s pathos n, dolor m

pathway s semita f, callis, trames m

patience s patientia f

patient adj patiens, tolerans; —**ly** patienter, aequo animo

patient s aegrotus m, aegrota f

patriarch s patriarcha m

patriarchal adj patriarchicus

patrician adj patricius

patrician s patricius m

patrimony s patrimonium n

patriot s amans patriae m

patriotic adj amans patriae

patriotism s amor patriae, amor in patriam m

patrol s excubiae f pl

patrol vt circumire; vt excubias agĕre

patron s patronus m

patronage s patrocinium, praesidium n

patroness s patrona f

patronize vt favēre (with dat), fovēre

patronymic s patronymicum nomen n

pattern s exemplar, exemplum, specimen n

paucity s paucitas f

paunch s ingluvies f

pauper s pauper m

pause s pausa, mora f; (mus) intermissio f, intervallum n

pause vi insistĕre, intermittĕre

pave vt sternere

pavement s pavimentum n, stratura f

pavilion s tentorium n

paving stone s saxum quadratum n

paw s ungula f, pes m

paw vt pedibus pulsare

pawn s pignus n

pawn vt pignerare

pawnbroker s pignerator m

pay s merces f; (mil) stipendium n

pay vt solvĕre; (in full) persolvĕre, pendĕre; (mil) stipendium numerare (with dat); **to** — **a compliment** to laudare; **to** — **for** solvĕre (with acc of thing and dat of person); **to** — **respects** to salutare; **to** — **the penalty** poenam dare, poenam luĕre; vi **it pays** operae pretium est, prodest, lucro est

payable adj solvendus

paymaster s dispensator m; (mil) tribunus aerarius m

payment s (act) solutio f; (sum of money) pensio f

pea s pisum, cicer n

peace s pax f; quies f, otium n

peaceful adj tranquillus, placidus, pacatus; —ly tranquille, placide, cum bona pace

peacemaker s pacificator m

peace offering s placamen, placamentum, piaculum n

peacetime s otium n

peach s malum Persicum n

peacock s pavo m

peak s (of mountain) cacumen n; vertex, apex m

peal s (of thunder) fragor m; (of bells) concent·us -ūs m

peal vi resonare

pear s pirum n

pearl s margarita f

pearly adj gemmeus

peasant s agricola, colonus m

peasantry s agricolae, agrestes m pl

pebble s lapillus, calculus m

peck s modius m

peck vt rostro impetěre, vellicare

peculation s peculat·us -ūs m

peculiar adj proprius, peculiaris, praecipuus, singularis; —ly praecipue

peculiarity s proprietas f

pecuniary adj pecuniarius

pedagogue s paedagogus m; (schoolmaster) magister m

pedant s scholasticus m

pedantic adj putidus, nimis diligens; —ally nimis diligenter

pedantry s eruditio insulsa f

peddle vt venditare, circumferre

peddler s venditor, institor m

pedestal s basis f

pedestrian adj pedester

pedestrian s pedes m

pedigree s stemma n, stirps f

pediment s fastigium n

peel s cortex m

peel vt decorticare, gluběre

peep s aspect·us -ūs, tuit·us -ūs m

peep vi inspicěre

peephole s conspicillum n

peer s par m; (of peerage) patricius m

peer vi to — at intueri

peerless adj unicus, incomparabilis

peevish adj stomachosus, morosus, difficilis; —ly stomachose, morose

peg s clavus, paxillus m

pelican s pelicanus, onocrotalus m

pellet s globulus m

pelt s pellis f

pelt vt (to hurl) jacěre; (to beat) verberare, petěre

pen s (to write with) calamus, stylus m; (enclosure) saeptum n; (for sheep) ovile n; (for pigs) suile n

pen vt scriběre, componěre; to — in includěre

penal adj poenalis

penalize vt poenā afficěre, mul(c)tare

penalty s poena, mul(c)ta f

penance s satisfactio f

pencil s stilus m, graphis f

pending adj suspensus; (law) sub judice

pending prep inter (with acc)

pendulum s libramentum n

penetrate vt penetrare

penetrating adj acer, perspicax

penetration s acies mentis f, acumen n

peninsula s paeninsula f

penitence s paenitentia f

penitent adj paenitens; —ly paenitenter

penitentiary s carcer m

penknife s scalpellum m

penmanship s man·us -ūs f

pennant s vexillum n

penniless adj inops

penny s quadrans m

pension s annua n pl

pensive adj meditabundus

penultimate s paenultima syllaba f

penurious adj parcus, sordidus

penury s egestas, inopia f

people s (nation) populus m; (common people) plebs f; — say dicunt

people vt frequentare

pepper s piper n

pepper vt pipere condire; (fig) (with blows) verberare

peppermint s mentha f

perceive vt percipěre, sentire, vidēre, intellegěre

percentage s portio f

perceptible adj percipiendus, manifestus

perceptibly adv sensim

perception s perceptio f, sens·us -ūs m

perch s (for birds) pertica f; (type of fish) perca f

perch vi insidēre

perchance adv forte

percolate vt percolare; vi permanare

percussion s ict·us -ūs, concuss·us -ūs m

perdition s interit·us -ūs m; exitium n

peremptory adj arrogans

perennial adj perennis

perfect adj perfectus, absolutus; (gram) praeteritus; —ly perfecte, absolute; (entirely) plane

perfect vt perficere, absolvěre

perfection s perfectio, absolutio f

perfidious adj perfidus, perfidiosus; —ly perfidiose

perfidy s perfidia f

perforate vt perforare, terebrare

perforation s foramen n

perform vt perficěre, peragěre; (duty) fungi (with abl); (to play) agěre

performance s perfunctio, executio f; (work) opus n; (of a play) actio f; (play, drama) fabula f

performer s actor m; (in play) histrio m

perfume s odor m, unguentum n

perfume vt odoribus imbuěre

perhaps adv forte, forsitan, fortasse

peril s periculum n

perilous adj periculosus; —ly periculose

period s (gram) periodus f; tempus, spatium n, aetas f; (rhet) circuit·us -ūs m

periodic adj certus; (style) periodicus; —ally certis temporibus

periphery s peripheria f, ambit·us -ūs m

periphrastic adj per periphrasin dictus

perish vi perire, interire

perishable adj fragilis, caducus, mortalis

peristyle s peristyl(i)um n

perjure vt to — oneself pejerare, perjurare

perjured adj perjurus

perjury s perjurium n; to commit — pejerare, perjurare

permanence s stabilitas, constantia f

permanent adj diuturnus, perpetuus, mansurus; —ly perpetuo

permeable adj pervius

permeate vt penetrare; vi permanare

permission s permissio, venia, potestas f

permit vt permittĕre (with dat), sinĕre

permutation s permutatio f

pernicious adj perniciosus; —ly perniciose

peroration s peroratio f

perpendicular adj perpendicularis, directus

perpendicular s linea perpendicularis f

perpetrate vt facĕre, perficĕre

perpetrator s auctor, reus m

perpetual adj perpetuus, perennis, sempiternus; —ly perpetuo

perpetuate vt perpetuare, continuare

perpetuity s perpetuitas f

perplex vt turbare, confundĕre

perplexing adj perplexus, ambiguus

perplexity s perturbatio, dubitatio f

persecute vt persequi, insequi, vexare

persecution s insectatio f

persecutor s insectator m

perseverance s perseverantia, constantia f

persevere vi perseverare, perstare, constare

persevering adj perseverans, constans, tenax; —ly perseverante, constanter

persist vi perstare, perseverare

persistence s permansio, pertinacia, perseverantia f

persistent adj pertinax; —ly pertinaciter

person s homo m & f, quidam m; (body) corpus n; in — ipse

personage s persona f

personal adj privatus, suus; (gram) personalis; —ly ipse, per se, coram

personality s persona, natura f, ingenium n

personification s prosopopoeia f

personify vt personā induĕre

personnel s membra n pl, socii m pl

perspective s scaenographia f

perspicacious adj perspicax

perspicacity s perspicacitas f

perspiration s sudatio f, sudor m

perspire vi sudare

persuade vt persuadēre (with dat)

persuasion s persuasio f

persuasive adj suasorius; —ly persuasibiliter

pert adj procax; —ly procaciter

pertain vi pertinēre, attinēre

pertinent adj appositus; to be — ad rem pertinēre; —ly apposite

perturb vt turbare, perturbare

perturbation s perturbatio f

perusal s perlectio f

peruse vt perlegere, evolvĕre

pervade vt invadĕre, permanare, perfundĕre

perverse adj perversus, pravus; —ly perverse

perversion s depravatio f

perversity s perversitas, pravitas f

pervert vt (words) detorquēre; depravare, corrumpĕre

pest s pestis f

pester vt vexare, infestare, sollicitare

pestilence s pestilentia f

pestle s pilum n

pet s corculum n, deliciae f pl

pet vt fovēre, in deliciis habēre

petal s floris folium n

petition s petitio f, preces f pl; (pol) libellus m

petition vt supplicare, orare

petitioner s supplex m

petrify vt in lapidem convertĕre; vi lapidescĕre

petticoat s subucula f

pettiness s animus angustus m

petty adj minutus, angustus, levis

petulance s petulantia, protervitas f

petulant adj protervus

phalanx s phalanx f

phantom s simulacrum, phantasma n, species f

pharmacy s ars medicamentaria f; (drugstore) taberna medicina, apotheca f

phase s (of moon) lunae facies f; (fig) vices f pl

pheasant s phasianus m, phasiana f

phenomenal adj singularis

phenomenon s res f; (remarkable event) portentum, prodigium n

philanthropic adj humanus

philanthropy s humanitas f

philologist s philologus, grammaticus m

philology s philologia f

philosopher s philosophus, sapiens m

philosophical adj philosophicus; —ly philosophice, sapienter; (calmly) aequo animo

philosophize vi philosophari

philosophy s philosophia, sapientia f; (theory) ratio f

philter s philtrum n

phlegm s pituita f, phelgma n

phlegmatic adj (fig) lentus

phosphorus s phosphorus m

phrase s locutio f; (gram) incisum n

phraseology s locutio, loquendi ratio f

physical adj physicus; (natural) corporis (genit, used adjectively); —ly naturā

physician *s* medicus *m*
physicist *s* physicus *m*
physics *s* physica *n pl*
physiognomy *s* oris habit·us -ūs *m*
physique *s* vires *f pl*
pick *vt* (*to choose*) eligĕre; (*to pluck*) carpĕre; (*to gather*) decerpĕre; **to — off** avellĕre; **to — out** eligĕre; **to — up** tollĕre
pick *s* (*tool*) dolabra *f*; (*best part*) flos *m*, lecti *m pl*
pickax *s* dolabra *f*
picked *adj* electus, delectus
picket *s* (*mil*) statio *f*
pickle *s* muria *f*
pickle *vt* in aceto condire, in muriā condire
pickled *adj* muriā conditus
picture *s* tabula picta, pictura *f*; (*fig*) descriptio *f*
picture *vt* (*to imagine*) fingĕre, ante oculos ponĕre
picture gallery *s* pinacotheca *f*
picturesque *adj* venustus, amoenus
pie *s* crustum *n*
piece *s* pars, portio *f*; (*of food*) frustum *n*; (*of cloth*) pannus *m*; (*broken off*) fragmentum *n*; (*coin*) nummus *m*; (*drama*) fabula *f*; **to fall to —s** dilabi; **to tear to —s** dilaniare, lacerare
piece *vt* resarcire; **to — together** fabricari, consuĕre
piecemeal *adv* frustatim, membratim
pier *s* moles *f*, agger *m*
pierce *vt* perforare; (*with sword, etc.*) transfigĕre, perfodĕre; (*fig*) pungĕre
piercing *adj* acutus, stridulus
piety *s* pietas, religio *f*
pig *s* porcus *m*, sus *m & f*
pigeon *s* columba *f*
pigment *s* pigmentum *n*
pigsty *s* hara *f*, suile *n*
pike *s* (*weapon*) hasta *f*; (*fish*) lupus *m*
pilaster *s* parasta, columella *f*
pile *s* (*heap*) acervus, cumulus *m*; (*for cremation*) rogus *m*; (*for building*) moles *f*; (*nap of cloth*) villus *m*
pile *vt* coacervare, congerĕre; **to — up** exstruĕre
pilgrim *s* peregrinator *m*
pilgrimage *s* peregrinatio *f*
pill *s* pilula *f*
pillage *s* vastatio, direptio, expilatio, rapina *f*
pillage *vt* vastare, diripĕre, depopulari, expilare, praedari
pillar *s* columna, pila *f*, columen *n*
pillow *s* pulvinus *m*, culcita *f*, cervical *n*
pillowcase *s* cervicalis integumentum *n*
pilot *s* gubernator *m*
pilot *vt* gubernare
pimp *s* leno *m*
pimple *s* pustula *f*
pimply *adj* pustulosus
pin *s* ac·us -ūs, acicula *f*; (*peg*) clavus *m*
pin *vt* acu figĕre; affigĕre
pincers *s* forceps *m & f*

pinch *vt* vellicare; (*as cold*) (*ad*)urēre; (*to squeeze*) coartare; (*of shoe*) urēre
pine *s* pinus *f*
pine *vi* **to — away** tabescĕre, languēre; **to — for** desiderare
pineapple *s* (*nux*) pinea *f*
pink *adj* rosaceus, rubicundus
pinnacle *s* fastigium *n*, summus grad·us -ūs *m*
pint *s* sextarius *m*
pioneer *s* praecursor *m*
pious *adj* pius; (*scrupulous*) religiosus; (*saintly*) sanctus; **—ly** pie, religiose, sancte
pipe *s* (*tube*) tubus *m*; (*mus*) fistula *f*
pipe *vt* fistulā canĕre
piper *s* tibicen *m*
piquant *s* salsus, facetus; **—ly** salse
pique *s* offensio *f*
pique *vt* offendĕre
piracy *s* latrocinium *n*
pirate *s* pirata, praedo *m*
piratical *adj* praedatorius
pit *s* fossa, fovea *f*, puteus *m*; (*in theater*) cavea *f*; (*quarry*) fodina *f*
pitch *s* pix *f*; (*sound*) sonus *m*; (*degree*) grad·us -ūs *m*, fastigium *n*; (*slope*) fastigium *n*; **to such a —** of eo (*with genit*)
pitch *vt* (*to fling*) conjicĕre; (*camp*) ponĕre; (*tent*) tendĕre
pitcher *s* urceus *m*
pitchfork *s* furca *f*
piteous *adj* miserabilis; **—ly** miserabiliter, misere
pitfall *s* fovea *f*
pith *s* medulla *f*
pithy *adj* (*fig*) sententiosus
pitiable *adj* miserandus
pitiful *adj* misericors; (*pitiable*) miserabilis, miserandus; **—ly** misere
pitiless *adj* immisericors, durus; **—ly** immisericorditer
pittance *s* (*allowance for food*) demensum *n*; (*trifling sum*) mercedula *f*
pity *s* misericordia, miseratio *f*
pity *vt* miserēri (*with genit*); **I — him** miseret me ejus
pivot *s* axis, paxillus *m*; (*fig*) cardo *m*
placard *s* titulus, libellus *m*
place *s* locus *m*; **in — of** pro (*with abl*), loco (*with genit*); **in the first —** primum, primo; **out of —** intempestivus; **to take —** fieri, accidĕre
place *vt* ponĕre, locare, collocare
placid *adj* placidus, tranquillus; **—ly** placide, tranquille
plagiarism *s* furtum litterarium *n*
plagiarist *s* fur litterarius *m*
plagiarize *vt* furari
plague *s* pestilentia *f*; (*fig*) pestis *f*
plague *vt* vexare, exagitare
plain *s* campus *m*, planities *f*; **of the —** campester
plain *adj* (*clear*) apertus, manifestus, perspicuus; (*unadorned*) inornatus, simplex; (*of one color*) unicolor; (*frank*) sincerus; (*homely*)

invenustus; —ly aperte, manifeste;
simpliciter; sincere

plaintiff s petitor m

plaintive adj querulus, flebilis; —ly
flebiliter

plan s consilium, propositum n;
(drawing) descriptio f; (layout) forma f

plan vt (to scheme) excogitare, meditari; (to intend to) in animo habēre
(with inf); (to draw) designare, describēre

plane s (tool) runcina f; (level surface) planities f

plane vt runcinare

planet s planeta, stella errans or
vaga f

plank s assis m, tabula f

plant s planta, herba f

plant vt serēre, conserēre; (feet) ponēre

plantation s plantarium n

planter s sator m

planting s sat·us -ūs m, consitura f

plaster s tectorium, gypsum n; (med)
emplastrum n

plaster vt gypsare, dealbare

plastic adj plasticus, ductilis

plate s (dish) patella f, catillus m;
(coating) lamina f; (silver) argentum n

plated adj bracteatus

platform s suggest·us -ūs m, suggestum n

platitude s trita sententia f

Platonic adj Platonis (genit, used
adjectively)

platter s patella, lanx f

plausible adj verisimilis

play s ludus m; (drama) fabula f

play vt ludēre; (instrument) canēre
(with abl); (game) ludēre (with abl)
(role) agēre; **to — a trick on** ludificari

player s (in game) lusor m; (on
stage) histrio, actor m; (on wind
instrument) tibicen m; (on string
instrument) fidicen m

playful adj lascivus, jocosus, ludibundus; (words) facetus; —ly per
ludum, per jocum

playmate s collusor m

plaything s ludibrium n

playwright s fabularum scriptor m

plea s (law) petitio, exceptio, defensio f; (excuse) excusatio f

plead vi (in court) causam agēre; (to
beg) obsecrare, implorare, orare; **to
— against** causam dicēre contra
(with acc); **to — for** defendēre

pleasant adj amoenus, gratus, jucundus, suavis; —ly jucunde, suaviter

pleasantry s jocosa dicacitas f, facetiae f pl

please vt placēre (with dat), delectare; **if you —** si placet; **please!**
obsecro! sis!, amabo! (colloquial)

pleasing adj gratus, jucundus

pleasurable adj jucundus

pleasure s voluptas f; **it is my —**
libet; **to derive —** voluptatem capēre

plebeian adj plebeius

plebeians s plebs f

pledge s pignus n; (proof) testimonium n

pledge vt (op)pignerare, obligare;
to — one's word fidem obligare

Pleiads s Pleiades f pl

plenary adj plenus, perfectus

plenipotentiary s legatus m

plentiful adj largus, affluens, uber;
—ly large, ubertim

plenty s copia, abundantia f

plethora s pletura f

pleurisy s pleuritis f

pliable adj flexibilis, tractabilis,
mansuetus

pliant adj lentus

plight s conditio f, stat·us -ūs m, discrimen n

plod vi assidue laborare

plodder s sedulus homo m

plodding adj laboriosus, assiduus,
sedulus

plot s (conspiracy) conjuratio f, insidiae f pl; (of drama) argumentum
n; (of ground) agellus m

plot vi conjurare, moliri

plow s aratrum n

plow vt arare; **to — up** exarare

plowing s aratio f

plowman s bubulcus, arator m

plowshare s vomer m

pluck s animus m

pluck vt carpēre; **to — off** avellēre,
decerpēre; **to — out** evellēre, eripēre; **to — up** eruēre; **to — up
courage** animo esse

plug s obturamentum n

plug vt obturare

plum s prunum n

plumage s plumae, pennae f pl

plumber s plumbarius m

plume s crista f

plummet s perpendiculum n

plump adj pinguis, obesus

plum tree s prunus f

plunder s (act) rapina f; (booty)
praeda f

plunder vt praedari

plunderer s praedator m

plundering s rapina, praedatio f

plundering adj praedatorius, praedabundus

plunge vt mergēre, submergēre;
(sword, etc.) condēre; vi immergi,
se mergēre

pluperfect s plus quam perfectum
tempus n

plural adj pluralis

plurality s multitudo f, numerus major m

plush adj lautus

ply vt exercēre, urgēre

poach vt (eggs) frigēre; vi illicita
venatione uti

poacher s fur m

pocket s sin·us -ūs, sacculus m

pocket vt in sacculis condēre

pocket book s pugillaria n pl

pockmark s cicatrix f

pod s siliqua f

poem s poema, carmen n

poet s poeta, vates m

poetess s poetria, poetris f

poetic adj poeticus; —ly poetice

poetics s ars poetica f

poetry s (art) poetice f; (poems) poemata, carmina n pl, poesis f

poignancy s acerbitas f

poignant adj acerbus, pungens

point s punctum n; (pointed end) acumen n, acies f; (of swords, etc.) mucro m; (fig) quaestio, res f, stat·us -ūs m, argumentum n; **beside the — ab re; from this — on posthac, hinc; — of view** sententia f; **to the — ad rem; up to this —** adhuc, hactenus

point vt (to sharpen) acuěre; **to — out** monstrare, indicare

pointed adj acutus; (fig) salsus; (stinging) aculeatus; —ly acute, aperte

pointer s index m & f

pointless adj (fig) insulsus, frigidus; —ly insulse

poise s (fig) urbanitas f

poise vt ponderare, pendēre, librare

poison s venenum, virus n

poison vt venenare, veneno necare; (fig) vitiare

poisoning s veneficium n

poisonous adj venenatus, venenosus

poke vt (to jab) cubito pulsare, fodicare; (fire) foděre

polar adj arcticus

polarity s polaritas f

pole s asser, contus m, pertica f; (of earth) polus m

polemic s controversiae f pl

pole star s stella polaris f

police s vigiles, custodes m pl

policeman s vigil m

policy s ratio f, consilium n

polish vt polire; **to — up** expolire

polish s nitor, levor m; (refined manners) urbanitas f; (literary) lima f

polite adj comis, urbanus; —ly comiter, urbane

politeness s urbanitas, comitas f

politic adj prudens, astutus

political adj civilis, publicus

politician s magistrat·us -ūs m

politics s res publica f; **to enter — ad rem publicam accedĕre**

poll s caput n; —s comitia n pl

poll vt suffragiis petěre

polling booth s saeptum n

poll tax s capitum exactio f

pollute vt polluěre, inquinare, contaminare

pollution s (act) contaminatio f; (filth) colluvio, impuritas f

polygamy s polygamia f

polysyllabic adj polysyllabus

polytheism s multorum deorum cult·us -ūs m

pomegranate s malum Punicum n

pommel vt pulsare, verberare

pomp s pompa f, apparat·us -ūs m

pomposity s magnificentia f

pompous adj magnificus, gloriosus; —ly magnifice, gloriose

pond s stagnum n

ponder vt in mente agitare, considerare, ponderare

ponderous adj ponderosus, praegravis

pontiff s pontifex m

pontifical adj pontificalis

pontificate s pontificat·us -ūs m

pontoon s ponto m

pony s mannulus, equulus m

pool s lacuna f, stagnum n

pool vt conferre

poor adj (needy) pauper, inops, egens; (inferior) tenuis, mediocris; (of soil) macer; (pitiable) miser; (meager) exilis; —ly parum, mediocriter, misere, tenuiter

pop s crepit·us -ūs m

pop vi crepare; **to — out** exsilire

poplar s populus f

poppy s papaver n

populace s vulgus n, plebs f

popular adj popularis; —ly populariter

popularity s populi favor m, populi studium n

populate vt frequentare

population s civium numerus, incolarum numerus m

populous adj frequens

porcelain s fictilia n pl

porch s vestibulum n, portic·us -ūs f

porcupine s hystrix f

pore s foramen n

pore vi **to — over** assidue considerare, scrutari

pork s porcina f

porous adj rarus

porpoise s porculus marinus m

porridge s puls f

port s port·us -ūs m

portal s porta f

portend vt praesagire, portenděre, significare

portent s monstrum, portentum, prodigium n

portentous adj monstruosus, prodigiosus

porter s janitor, ostiarius m; (carrier) bajulus m

portfolio s scrinium n

portico s portic·us -ūs f

portion s portio, pars f

portion vt partire

portly adj amplus, opimus

portrait s imago, effigies f

portray vt depingěre, expriměre

pose s stat·us -ūs, habit·us -ūs m

pose vi habitum or statum suměre

position s positio f, sit·us -ūs m; (of body) gest·us -ūs m; (office) honos m; (state) conditio f, stat·us -ūs m; (rank) amplitudo, dignitas f

positive adj certus; (gram) positivus; (fig) confidens; —ly praecise, certo

possess vt possiděre, tenēre

possession s possessio f; (estate) bona n pl; **in the — of** penes (with acc); **to gain — of** potiri (with abl), occupare

possessive adj quaestuosus, avarus; (gram) possessivus

possessor s possessor, dominus m

possibility s facultas f

possible adj **as quickly as** quam celerrime; **it is —** fieri potest; it is — for me to possum (with inf)

possibly adv fortasse

post s (stake) postis, cippus m; (station) statio, sedes stativa f; (position) munus n

post vt collocare, ponĕre, constituĕre; to — a letter tabellario litteras dare

postage s vectura (epistulae) f

postdate vt diem seriorem scribĕre (with dat)

poster s libellus m

posterior adj posterior

posterity s posteri, minores m pl, posteritas f

posthaste adv quam celerrime

posthumous adj postumus

postman s tabellarius m

postpone vt differre, prorogare

postscript s ascriptio f

posture s stat·us -ūs, habit·us -ūs, gest·us -ūs m

pot s olla f, ahenum n

potato s solanum tuberosum n

potentate s tyrannus m

potential adj futurus

potion s potio f

potter s figulus m

pottery s fictilia n pl

pouch s sacculus m, pera f

poultry s aves cohortales f pl

pounce vi to — on insilire (with dat or in + acc)

pound s libra f

pound vt contundĕre, conterĕre

pour vt fundĕre; to — in infundĕre; to — out effundĕre; vi fundi, fluĕre; to — down (of rain) ruĕre

pouring adj (of rain) effusus

pout vi stomachari

poverty s paupertas, pauperies f

powder s pulvis m

powder vt pulvere conspergĕre

power s vis, potestas f; (pol) imperium n; (mil) copiae f pl; (excessive) potentia f; (divine) numen n; to have great — multum posse, multum valēre

powerful adj validus, potens; (effectual) efficax; —ly valde

powerless adj invalidus, impotens; (vain) irritus; to be — nil valēre

practical adj utilis, habilis; —ly fere, paene

practice s us·us -ūs m, experientia, exercitatio f; (custom) mos m, consuetudo f

practice vt (to engage in) exercēre, tractare; (to rehearse) meditari

practitioner s exercitator m; (medical) medicus m

pragmatic adj pragmaticus

prairie s campus m

praise s laus f

praise vt laudare

praiseworthy adj laudabilis, laudandus

prance vi exsultare, subsultare; (of persons) jactare

prank s ludus m; (trick) jocus, dolus m

pray vt precari, orare; vi precari, orare; to — for petĕre, precari;

to — to adorare, supplicare

prayer s preces f pl

preach vt & vi praedicare

preamble s prooemium, exordium n

precarious adj precarius, periculosus, incertus; —ly precario

precaution s cautio, provisio f; to take — cavēre, praecavēre

precede vt praeire (with dat), antecedĕre

precedence s prior locus m; to take — over antecedĕre

precedent s exemplum n

preceding adj prior, superior

precept s praeceptum n

preceptor s praeceptor, magister m

precinct s termini, limites m pl, templum n; (ward) regio f

precious adj pretiosus, carus; — stone gemma f

precipice s praeceps n; down a — in praeceps

precipitate vt praecipitare

precipitous adj praeceps, praeruptus, declivis

precise adj certus, definitus; (exact) accuratus, exactus; —ly subtiliter, accurate

precision s accuratio, cura f

preclude vt praecludĕre, excludĕre

precocious adj praecox

preconceive vt praecipĕre, praesentire, preconceived idea praejudicium n

preconception s praeceptio, praejudicata opinio f

precursor s praenuntius m

predatory adj praedatorius, praedabundus

predecessor s antecessor, decessor m

predestine vt praedestinare

predicament s discrimen n, angustiae f pl

predicate vt praedicare

predicate s praedicatum n

predict vt praedicĕre, augurari

prediction s praedictio f, praedictum, vaticinium n

predilection s studium n

predispose vt inclinare

predisposition s inclinatio f

predominant adj praevalens

predominate vi praevalēre

preeminence s praestantia, excellentia f

preeminent adj praecipuus, praestans, excellens; —ly praecipue, excellenter

preexist vi antea exstare or esse

preface s praefatio f

prefatory adj to make a few — remarks pauca praefari

prefect s praefectus m

prefecture s praefectura f

prefer vt praeponĕre, anteponĕre; (charges) deferre; to — to (would rather) malle (with inf)

preferable adj potior, praestantior

preference s favor m; in — to potius quam; to give — to anteponĕre

preferment s honos m

prefix s syllaba praeposita f

prefix *vt* praefigĕre, praeponĕre

pregnancy *s* graviditas *f*

pregnant *adj* gravida; *(of language)* pressus

prejudge *vt* praejudicare

prejudice *s* praejudicata opinio *f*, praejudicium *n*

prejudice *vt* **to be prejudiced against** praejudicatam opinionem habēre in *(with acc)*, invidēre *(with dat)*; **to — the people against** studia hominum inclinare in *(with acc)*

prejudicial *adj* noxius

preliminary *adj* praevius; **to make a few — remarks** pauca praefari

prelude *s (mus)* prooemium *n*, praelusio *f*

prelude *vt* praeludĕre

premature *adj* praematurus, immaturus, praeproperus; **—ly** ante tempus

premeditate *vt* praemeditari

premier *s* princeps *m*

premise *s (major)* propositio *f*; *(minor)* assumptio *f*; **—s** fundus *m*, praedium *n*

premium *s* praemium *n*; **at a —** carus

premonition *s* monit·us -ūs *m*, monitum *n*

preoccupation *s* praeoccupatio *f*

preoccupy *vt* praeoccupare

preparation *s* comparatio, praeparatio *f*, apparat·us -ūs *m*; *(rehearsal)* meditatio *f*

prepare *vt* parare, comparare, apparare; *(to rehearse)* meditari; **to — to** parare *(with inf)*

preponderance *s* praestantia *f*

preposition *s* praepositio *f*

preposterous *adj* praeposterus; **—ly** praepostere, absurde

prerogative *s* jus *n*

presage *s* praesagium *n*

presage *vt* praesagire, portendĕre, significare

prescience *s* providentia *f*

prescient *adj* providus, sagax

prescribe *vt* praescribĕre, proponĕre

prescription *s* praescriptum *n*; *(of physician)* medicamenti formula *f*

presence *s* praesentia *f*; *(look)* aspect·us -ūs *m*; **in my —** me praesente; **in the — of** coram *(with abl)*

present *adj* praesens, hic; **for the — in praesens tempus; to be — adesse; —ly** mox, illico, statim

present *s* donum, munus *n*

present *vt* donare, offerre; introducĕre; *(in court)* sistĕre; *(to bring forward)* praebēre, offerre; **to — itself** *or* **oneself** occurrĕre, obvenire

presentation *s* donatio *f*; *(on stage)* fabula *f*

presentiment *s* praesagitio *f*, praesagium *n*

preservation *s* conservatio *f*

preserve *vt* conservare; *(fruits)* condire

preserver *s* conservator *m*

preside *vi* praesidēre, praeesse; **to — over** praesidēre *(with dat)*, praeesse *(with dat)*

presidency *s* praefectura *f*

president *s* praeses, praefectus *m*

press *s (for wine)* prelum *n*; *(of people)* turba *f*

press *vt* premĕre, comprimĕre; *(fig)* urgēre; **to — down** deprimĕre; *vi* **to — forward** anniti; **to — on** pergĕre, contendĕre

pressing *adj* gravis, urgens

pressure *s* pressio, pressura *f*, press·us -ūs *m*

pressure *vt* urgēre

prestige *s* auctoritas *f*

presumably *adv* sane

presume *vt* sumĕre, credĕre, conjicĕre; *(to take liberties)* sibi arrogare

presumption *s (conjecture)* conjectura *f*; *(arrogance)* arrogantia *f*

presumptuous *adj* arrogans, insolens, audax; **—ly** insolenter, arroganter

presuppose *vt* praesumĕre

pretend *vt* simulare, dissimulare, fingĕre

pretender *s* simulator, captator *m*

pretense *s* simulatio, species *f*; **under — of** per speciem *(with genit)*; **without —** sine fuco

pretension *s (claim)* postulatio *f*; *(display)* ostentatio *f*; **to make —s** to affectare

preterite *s* tempus praeteritum *n*

preternatural *adj* praeter naturam

pretext *s* species *f*, praetextum *n*; **under the — of** specie *(with genit)*, sub specie *(with genit)*, sub praetextu *(with genit)*

pretor *s* praetor *m*

pretorian *adj* praetorianus

pretorship *s* praetura *f*

prettily *adv* belle, concinne

pretty *adj* bellus, venustus, lepidus

pretty *adv* satis, admodum; **— well** mediocriter

prevail *vi (to be prevalent)* esse, obtinēre; *(to win)* vincĕre; **to — upon** persuadēre *(with dat)*

prevalent *adj (per)*vulgatus; **to become —** increbrescĕre

prevaricate *vi* tergiversari

prevarication *s* praevaricatio, tergiversatio *f*

prevaricator *s* praevaricator, mendax *m*

prevent *vt* impedire, prohibēre

prevention *s* anticipatio, impeditio *f*

preventive *adj* prohibens, anticipans

previous *adj* prior, superior; **—ly** antea, antehac

prey *s* praeda *f*

prey *vi* **to — on** praedari, rapĕre; *(fig)* vexare, consumĕre

price *s* pretium *n*; **at a high —** magni; **at a low —** parvi

priceless *adj* inaestimabilis

prick *vt* pungĕre; *(fig)* stimulare; **to — up the ears** aures arrigĕre

prickle *s* aculeus *m*

prickly *adj* spinosus

pride s superbia f; (source of pride) decus n

pride vt to — oneself on jactare

priest s sacerdos m; (of particular god) flamen m

priestess s sacerdos f

priesthood s (office) sacerdotium n; (collectively) sacerdotes m pl

priestly adj sacerdotalis

prig s homo fastidiosus m

prim adj (nimis) diligens

primarily adv praecipue

primary adj primus, principalis; (chief) praecipuus

prime s flos m; to be in one's — florēre, vigēre

prime adj primus, egregius, optimus, exquisitus

primeval adj pristinus, priscus

primitive adj priscus, antiquus, incultus

primordial adj priscus

primrose s primula vulgaris f

prince s regulus, regis filius m; (king) rex, princeps m

princely adj regius, regalis

princess s regia puella, regis filia f

principal adj principalis, praecipuus; —ly praecipue, maxime

principal s caput n, praeses, praefectus, princeps m; (money) caput n, sors f

principality s principat·us -ūs m

principle s principium n; (in philosophy) axioma n; (maxim) institutum n

print s nota impressa f; (of foot) vestigium n

print vt imprimēre

prior adj prior, potior

priority s primat·us -ūs m

prism s prisma n

prison s carcer m, vincula n pl

prisoner s reus m, rea f; (for debt) nex·us -ūs m

prisoner of war s captivus m

pristine adj pristinus

privacy s solitudo f, secretum n

private adj (secluded) secretus; (person) privatus; (home) domesticus; (one's own) proprius; (mil) gregarius; —ly clam, secreto; (in a private capacity) privatim

private s miles, miles gregarius m

privation s egestas, inopia f

privilege s privilegium n, immunitas f

privy adj privatus, secretus; — to conscius (with genit)

privy s forica, latrina f

prize s (reward) praemium n, palma f; (prey) praeda f

prize vt magni aestimare, magni facēre

prize fighter s pugil m

probability s veri similitudo, probabilitas f

probable adj verisimilis, probabilis

probably adv probabiliter

probation s probatio f

probe vt scrutari, inspicēre

probity s probitas, honestas f

problem s quaestio f; to have —s

laborare

problematical adj anceps, incertus

procedure s progress·us -ūs, modus m, ratio f

proceed vi (to go on) pergēre, procedēre, incedēre; to — against persequi; to — from oriri ex (with abl)

proceedings s acta n pl; (law) lis, actio f

proceeds s redit·us -ūs m

process s ratio f; (law) lis, actio f

proclaim vt promulgare, edicēre, pronuntiare, declarare

proclamation s pronuntiatio f, edictum n

proconsul s proconsul m

proconsular adj proconsularis

proconsulship s proconsulat·us -ūs m

procrastinate vi cunctari, procrastinare

procrastination s procrastinatio f

procreate vt procreare, generare

procreation s procreatio f

proctor s procurator m

procurable adj procurandus

procurator s procurator m

procure vt parare, acquirēre, nancisci, adipisci

procurement s comparatio f

procurer s leno m

prodigal adj prodigus

prodigal s ganeo m

prodigality s dissipatio, effusio f

prodigious adj prodigiosus, immanis, ingens

prodigy s prodigium, monstrum, portentum n; (fig) miraculum n

produce s fruct·us -ūs m; (of earth) fruges f pl; (in money) redit·us -ūs m

produce vt (to bring forward) proferre, producēre; (to bring into existence) parēre, procreare, gignēre; (to cause) efficēre, facēre; (to put on, as a play) docēre; (crops) ferre

product s (of earth) fruges f pl; opus n

production s productio f

productive adj ferax, fecundus, uber

productivity s feracitas, ubertas f

profanation s violatio f

profane adj profanus, impius; —ly impie

profane vt vilare, profanare, polluēre

profanity s impietas f, nefas n

profess vt profitēri

professed adj apertus, manifestus

profession s professio f

professional adj ad professionem pertinens; (expert) peritus

professor s doctor m

professorship s doctoris munus n

proffer vt offerre, promittēre, ponēre

proficiency s progress·us -ūs m, peritia f

proficient adj habilis, peritus

profile s facies obliqua f; (portrait) imago obliqua f

profit s quaest·us -ūs, redit·us -ūs m, lucrum n

profit vt prodesse (with dat); vi proficĕre; **to — by** uti (with abl), frui (with abl)

profitable adj fructuosus, quaestuosus, utilis; **to be —** prodesse

profitably adv utiliter

profitless adj inutilis, vanus

profligacy s nequitia f, perditi mores m pl

profligate adj perditus, flagitiosus, nequam (indecl)

profligate s nepos, ganeo m

profound adj altus, subtilis, abstrusus; **—ly** penitus

profundity s altitudo f

profuse adj profusus, effusus; **—ly** effuse

profusion s effusio, profusio, abundantia f

progeny s progenies, proles f

prognosticate vt praedicĕre

prognostication s praedictio f, praedictum n

program s libellus m

progress s progress·us -ūs m; **to make —** proficĕre

progress vi progredi

progression s progress·us -ūs m

progressive adj proficiens; **—ly** gradatim

prohibit vt interdicĕre (with dat), vetare

prohibition s interdictum n

project s propositum, consilium n

project vt projicĕre; vi prominēre, exstare; (of land) excurrĕre

projectile s missile n

projecting adj eminens, prominens

projection s projectura, eminentia f

proletarian adj proletarius

proletariat s plebs f

prolific adj fecundus

prolix adj longus, verbosus

prolixity s verbositas f

prologue s prologus m

prolong vt producĕre, prorogare, extendĕre

prolongation s proragatio, dilatio f

promenade s (walk) ambulatio f; (place) xystus m

promenade vi spatiari, ambulare

prominence s eminentia f

prominent adj prominens, insignis

promiscuous adj promiscuus; **—ly** promiscue, sine ullo discrimine

promise s promissio f, promissum n; **to break a —** fidem fallĕre; **to make a —** fidem dare

promise vt promittĕre, pollicēri; (in marriage) despondēre

promising adj bonā spe (abl used adjectively)

promissory note s chirographum n

promontory s promontorium n

promote vt (in rank) producĕre, provehĕre; (a cause, etc.) favēre (with dat), adjuvare

promoter s adjutor, fautor m

promotion s amplior grad·us -ūs m, dignitas f

prompt adj promptus, paratus; **—ly** statim, extemplo

prompt vt subjicĕre, suggerĕre; (to incite) impellĕre, commovēre

promulgate vt promulgare

promulgation s promulgatio f

prone adj pronus, propensus

prong s dens m

pronominal adj pronominalis

pronoun s pronomen n

pronounce vt (to declare) pronuntiare; (to articulate) enuntiare, eloqui; (sentence) dicĕre, pronuntiare

pronunciation s appellatio, elocutio, locutio f

proof s documentum, argumentum, indicium, signum n

proof adj tutus, securus; **— against** invictus ab (with abl), adversus (with acc)

prop s tibicen m, fulcrum n; (for vines) adminiculum n

prop vt fulcire, sustinēre

propaganda s divulgatio f

propagate vt propagare, vulgare, disseminare

propagation s propagatio f

propel vt impellĕre, propellĕre

propeller s impulsor m

propensity s propensio, inclinatio f

proper adj (becoming) decorus, decens; (suitable) aptus, idoneus: **it is —** decet; **—ly** decore; apte

property s (characteristic) proprium n, proprietas f; (things owned) res f, bona n pl, fortuna f; **private —** res familiaris f

prophecy s praedictum n, praedictio, vaticinatio f

prophesy vt vaticinari, praedicĕre

prophet s vates m & f, fatidicus m; (Biblical) propheta f

prophetess s vates, fatiloqua f

prophetic adj fatidicus, divinus, vaticinus; **—ally** divinitus

propitiate vt propitiare, placare

propitiation s propitiatio f, placamentum n

propitious adj felix, faustus; **—ly** fauste

proportion s ratio, proportio f; **in — pro rata parte**; **in — to** pro (with abl)

proportionately adv pro portione

proposal s propositio, conditio f; (of senate) rogatio f

propose vt ferre, rogare; **to — a toast to** propinare (with dat)

proposition s (offer) condicio f; (logic) propositio f, pronuntiatum n

propound vt proponĕre, exponĕre

proprietor s possessor, dominus m

propriety s decorum n, convenientia f

propulsion s propulsio f

prosaic adj aridus, jejunus

proscribe vt proscribĕre

proscription s proscriptio f

prose s prosa f

prosecute vt (to carry out) exsequi; (law) litem intendĕre (with dat), accusare

prosecution s exsecutio f; (law) accusatio f

prosecutor s accusator, actor m

prospect *s* prospect·us -ūs *m*; (*hope*) spes *f*

prospective *adj* futurus

prosper *vt* prosperare, secundare; *vi* prosperā fortunā uti, florēre, vigēre

prosperity *s* res secundae *f pl*

prosperous *adj* prosperus, secundus; —ly prospere, bene

prostitute *s* scortum *n*, meretrix *f*

prostitute *vt* prostituēre

prostrate *vt* sternēre, projicēre; (*fig*) affligēre

prostrate *adj* prostratus, projectus; (*fig*) afflictus, fractus; **to fall —** se projicēre

prostration *s* (*act*) prostratio *f*; (*state*) animus fractus *m*

protect *vt* tuēri, protegēre, defendēre, custodire

protection *s* praesidium *n*, tutela *f*

protector *s* defensor, patronus *m*

protest *s* obtestatio, denuntiatio *f*

protest *vt* affirmare; *vi* obtestari, reclamare; (*pol*) intercedēre

protestation *s* affirmatio *f*

prototype *s* exemplar *n*

protract *vt* protrahēre, differre

protrude *vt* protrudēre; *vi* prominēre

protuberance *s* tuber *n*, tumor, gibbus *m*

proud *adj* superbus, arrogans; **to be — superbire, —ly** superbe, arroganter

prove *vt* probare, confirmare, evincēre, arguēre; *vi* (*of person*) se praebēre, se praestare; (*of thing, event, etc.*) evadēre, fieri, exire

proverb *s* proverbium *n*

proverbial *adj* proverbialis, tritus, notus

provide *vt* (*to furnish*) suppeditare, (com)parare, praebēre; *vi* **to — for** providēre (*with dat*), consulēre (*with dat*); (*of laws*) jubēre

provided that *conj* dum, modo, dummodo, eā condicione ut

providence *s* providentia *f*

provident *adj* providus, cautus; —ly caute

providential *adj* divinus; —ly divinitus

province *s* provincia *f*

provincial *adj* provincialis; (*countrified*) inurbanus, rusticus; (*narrow*) angusti animi (*genit, used adjectively*)

provincialism *s* dialectos *f*

provision *s* (*stipulation*) condicio *f*; —s cibus, vict·us -ūs *m*, alimentum *n*; (*mil*) commeat·us -ūs *m*, res frumentaria *f*

provisional *adj* temporarius; —ly ad tempus

proviso *s* condicio *f*; **with the — that** eā lege ut

provocation *s* provocatio, offensio *f*

provoke *vt* provocare, irritare, stimulare

provoking *adj* molestus, odiosus

prow *s* prora *f*

prowess *s* virtus *f*

prowl *vi* vagari, grassari

prowler *s* praedator *m*

proximity *s* propinquitas *f*

proxy *s* vicarius *m*

prude *s* fastidiosa *f*

prudence *s* prudentia *f*

prudent *adj* prudens; —ly prudenter

prudish *adj* tetricus

prune *s* prunum conditum *n*

prune *vt* (am)putare, resecare, recidēre

pruning *s* putatio *f*

pry *vi* perscrutor; **to — into** investigare, explorare

prying *adj* curiosus

pseudonym *s* falsum nomen *n*

puberty *s* pubertas *f*

public *adj* publicus, communis; (*known*) vulgatus; —ly palam, aperte

public *s* homines *m pl*, vulgus *n*

publican *s* publicanus *m*

publication *s* publicatio, promulgatio *f*; (*of book*) editio *f*; (*book*) liber *m*

publicity *s* celebritas, lux *f*

publish *vt* publicare, divulgare, patefacēre; (*book*) edēre

publisher *s* editor *m*

pucker *vt* corrugare

pudding *s* placenta *f*

puddle *s* lacuna *f*, stagnum *n*

puerile *adj* puerilis

puerility *s* puerilitas *f*

puff *s* aura *f*, flamen *n*

puff *vt* inflare, sufflare; *vi* anhelare

puffy *adj* sufflatus, tumens

pugilist *s* pugil *m*

pugnacious *adj* pugnax

pull *vt* (*to drag*) trahēre, tractare; **to — apart** distrahēre; **to — away** avellēre; **to — down** detrahēre; (*buildings*) demoliri, destruēre, evertēre; **to — off** avellēre; **to — out** extrahēre; (*hair, etc.*) evellēre; *vi* **to — at** vellicare; **to — through** pervincēre; (*illness*) convalescēre

pull *s* (*act*) tract·us -ūs *m*; (*effort*) nis·us -ūs *m*; (*influence*) gratia *f*

pulley *s* trochlea *f*

pulmonary *adj* pulmoneus, pulmonaceus, pulmonarius

pulp *s* pulpa, caro *f*

pulpit *s* suggest·us -ūs *m*, rostra *n pl*

pulsate *vi* palpitare

pulse *s* puls·us -ūs *m*; (*plant*) legumen *n*; **to feel the — venas** temptare

pulverization *s* pulveratio *f*

pulverize *vt* pulverare, contundēre

pumice *s* pumex *m*

pump *s* antlia *f*

pump *vt* haurire, exantlare; **to — with questions** percontari

pumpkin *s* pepo, melopepo *m*

pun *s* verborum lus·us -ūs *m*, agnominatio *f*

punch *s* (*tool*) veruculum *n*; (*blow*) pugnus, ict·us -ūs *m*

punch *vt* pugnum ducēre (*with dat*)

punctilious *adj* scrupulosus, religiosus

punctual *adj* promptus, accuratus, diligens; —ly ad tempus, ad horam

punctuality *s* diligentia *f*
punctuate *vt* interpungĕre
punctuation *s* interpunctio *f*
punctuation mark *s* interpunctum *n*
puncture *s* punctio *f*, punctum *n*
pungent *adj* pungens, acutus; (*caustic, as speech*) mordax, aculeatus
Punic *adj* Punicus
punish *vt* punire
punishable *adj* puniendus, poenā dignus
punishment *s* (*act*) punitio, castigatio *f*; (*penalty*) poena *f*, supplicium *n*; **without —** impune
punster *s* argutator *m*
puny *adj* pusillus
pup *s* catulus *m*
pupil *s* pupillus, discipulus *m*, pupilla, discipula *f*; (*of eye*) pupilla, pupula *f*
puppet *s* pupa *f*
puppy *s* catulus *m*
purchase *s* (*act*) emptio *f*; (*merchandise*) merx *f*
purchase *vt* emĕre
purchase price *s* pretium *n*; (*of grain*) annona *f*
purchaser *s* emptor *m*
pure *adj* mundus, purus; (*unmixed*) merus; (*morally*) castus, integer; **—ly** pure, integre; (*quite*) omnino; (*solely*) solum
purgation *s* purgatio *f*
purge *vt* purgare, mundare
purge *s* purgatio *f*; (*pol*) proscriptio *f*
purification *s* purificatio, purgatio *f*
purify *vt* purgare; (*fig*) expiare
purity *s* puritas, munditia *f*; (*moral*) castitas, integritas *f*
purple *s* purpura *f*; **dressed in —** purpuratus
purple *adj* purpureus
purport *s* significatio, sententia, vis *f*
purport *vt* significare, spectare ad (*with acc*)
purpose *s* propositum, consilium *n*, animus *m*; (*end, aim*) finis *m*; (*wish*) mens *f*; **on —** consulto; **to good —** ad rem; **to no —** frustra, nequaquam; **to what —** quo, quorsum
purpose *vt* in animo habēre, velle
purposely *adv* consulto, de industria
purr *s* murmur *n*
purr *vi* mumurare

purring *s* murmuratio *f*
purse *s* crumena *f*, marsupium *n*
purse *vt* corrugare, contrahĕre
pursuance *s* continutatio *f*; **in — of** ex (*with abl*), secundum (*with acc*)
pursuant *adj* **— to** ex (*with abl*), secundum (*with acc*)
pursue *vt* (per)sequi, insequi, insectari; (*plan, course*) insistēre
pursuit *s* persecutio, insectatio *f*; (*occupation*) studium, artificium *n*, occupatio *f*
pus *s* pus *n*, sanies *f*
push *vt* trudĕre, urgēre, impellĕre; *vi* **to — on** contendĕre, iter facĕre
push *s* ict·us -ūs, puls·us -ūs, impuls·us -ūs *f*; (*fig*) conat·us -ūs *m*
pushing *adj* audax, confidens; (*energetic*) strenuus
pusillanimous *adj* timidus
put *vt* ponĕre, collocare; **to — an end to** finem facĕre (*with dat*); **to — aside** ponĕre; **to — away** seponĕre, abdĕre, amovēre; (*in safety*) recondĕre; **to — back** reponĕre; **to — down** deponĕre; (*to suppress*) supponĕre, sedare; (*in writing*) scribĕre; **to — in** inserĕre; **to — in order** ordinare; **to — off** (*to postpone*) differre; **to — on** imponĕre; (*clothes*) se induĕre (*with abl*); (*add*) addĕre; **to — out** ejicĕre, extrudĕre; (*fire*) extinguĕre; (*money*) ponĕre; **to — out of the way** demovēre; **to — together** componĕre, conferre; **to — up** erigĕre, statuĕre; **to — up for sale** proponĕre, venum dare; *vi* **to — in** (*of ships*) portum petĕre, appellĕre; **to — out to sea** solvĕre; **to — up with** tolerare
putrefaction *s* putredo *f*
putrefy *vi* putrescĕre, putrefieri
putrid *adj* puter *or* putris, putridus
puzzle *s* quaestio abstrusa *f*, nodus *m*, aenigma *n*
puzzle *vt* confundĕre, perturbare; **to be puzzled** haerēre, dubitare
puzzling *adj* perplexus, ambiguus
pygmy *s* nanus, pumilio, pumilus *m*
pyramid *s* pyramis *f*
pyre *s* rogus *m*
Pythagorean *adj* Pythagoraeus
Pythian *adj* Pythius

Q

quack *s* (*charlatan*) circulator, pharmacopola *m*
quack *vi* tetrinnire
quadrangle *s* area *f*
quadruped *s* quadrupes *m & f*
quadruple *adj* quadruplex, quadruplus
quadruple *vt* quadruplicare
quaestor *s* quaestor *m*
quaestorship *s* quaestura *f*

quaff *vt* ducĕre, haurire
quagmire *s* palus *f*
quail *s* coturnix *f*
quail *vi* pavēre
quaint *adj* rarus, insolitus, novus
quake *vi* tremĕre
qualification *s* (*endowment*) indoles *f*; (*limitation*) exceptio, condicio *f*
qualified *adj* (*suited*) aptus, idoneus, dignus; (*competent*) peritus, doctus

qualify *vt* aptum *or* idoneum reddĕre, instruĕre; (*to limit*) temperare, mitigare, extenuare

quality *s* proprietas, qualitas *f*; —**s** ingenium *n*, indoles *f*

qualm *s* fastidium *n*; — **of conscience** religio *f*, scrupulus *m*

quandry *s* confusio *f*, angustiae *f pl*

quantity *s* numerus *m*, multitudo, vis, copia *f*; (*in scansion*) quantitas, mensura *f*

quarrel *s* jurgium *n*; (*dispute*) altercatio, controversia *f*; (*violent*) rixa *f*

quarrel *vi* altercari, jurgare, rixari

quarrelsome *adj* jurgiosus, rixosus, pugnax

quarry *s* lapicidinae, lautumiae *f pl*; (*prey*) praeda *f*

quart *s* duo sextarii *m pl*

quarter *s* quarta pars *f*, quadrans *m*; (*side, direction*) pars, regio *f*; (*district*) regio *f*; **at close** —**s** comminus; —**s** (*dwelling*) tectum *n*, habitatio *f*; (*temporary abode*) hospitium *n*; (*mil*) castra, contubernia stativa *n pl*; (*of moon*) lunae phases *f pl*; **to give** — **to** parcĕre (*with dat*)

quarter *vt* in quattuor partes dividĕre; (*to receive in one's house*) hospitium praebēre (*with dat*)

quarterly *adj* trimestris

quarterly *adv* quadrifariam, tertio quoque mense

quartermaster *s* castrorum praefectus *m*

quash *vt* (*to subdue*) opprimĕre; (*law*) rescindĕre, abolēre

quatrain *s* tetrastichon *n*

queasy *adj* fastidiosus; **to feel** — nauseare

queen *s* regina *f*

queen bee *s* rex *m*

queer *adj* novus, insolitus, rarus, ineptus

quell *vt* opprimĕre, sedare, domare

quench *vt* exstinguĕre; **to** — **the thirst** sitim sedare

querulous *adj* querulus, queribundus

query *s* quaestio, interrogatio *f*

query *vt* dubitare; *vi* quaerĕre, quaeritare

quest *s* inquisitio *f*; **to be in** — **of** quarĕre, requirĕre; **to go in** — **of** investigare

question *s* interrogatio *f*; (*doubt*) dubitatio *f*, dubium *n*; (*matter*) res, causa *f*; **there is no** — **that** non

dubium est quin; **to ask a** — quaerĕre, rogare; **to call in** — dubitare; **without** — sine dubio, haud dubie

question *vt* interrogare, percontari; (*to doubt*) dubitare, in dubium vocare; (*to examine*) scrutari

questionable *adj* dubius, incertus

questioning *s* interrogatio, inquisitio *f*

questor *s* quaestor *m*

questorship *s* quaestura *f*

quibble *s* captio, argutiola *f*

quibble *vi* cavillari

quibbler *s* cavillator, sophista *m*

quibbling *s* cavillatio, captio *f*

quick *adj* (*swift*) celer, velox; (*nimble*) agilis; (*mentally*) sagax, astutus, acutus; (*with hands*) facilis; (*of wit*) argutus; —**ly** cito, velociter; (*with haste*) propere, festinanter

quicken *vt* accelerare; (*to enliven*) vivificare, animare; (*to rouse*) excitare

quicksand *s* syrtis *f*

quicksilver *s* argentum vivum *n*

quiet *adj* quietus, tranquillus, placidus; (*silent*) tacitus, taciturnus; **to keep** — quiescĕre; (*to refrain from talking*) silēre, tacēre; —**ly** quiete, tranquille; tacite, per silentium

quiet *s* quies, tranquillitas *f*; (*leisure*) otium *n*; (*silence*) silentium *n*

quiet *vt* tranquillare, pacare, sedare

quill *s* penna *f*, calamus *m*

quilt *s* culcita *f*

quince *s* cydonium *n*

quince tree *s* cydonia *f*

quintessence *s* vis, medulla *f*, flos *m*

quip *s* dictum *n*, facetiae *f pl*

quirk *s* cavillatio, proprium *n*

quit *vt* relinquĕre, deserĕre

quite *adv* omnino, penitus, prorsus, magnopere; **not** — minus, parum; (*not yet*) nondum

quiver *s* pharetra *f*; **wearing a** — pharetratus

quiver *vi* tremĕre, contremiscĕre, trepidare

quivering *s* tremor *m*, trepidatio *f*

Quixotic *adj* ridiculus

quoit *s* discus *m*

quota *s* portio, pars, rata pars *f*

quotation *s* (*act*) prolatio *f*; (*passage*) locus *m*

quote *vt* adducĕre, proferre, commemorare

R

rabbit *s* cuniculus *m*

rabble *s* plebecula, faex populi *f*; (*crowd*) turba *f*

rabid *adj* rabidus; —**ly** rabide

race *s* (*lineage*) genus *n*, stirps *f*; (*nation*) gens *f*; (*contest*) certamen *n*; curs·us -ūs *m*, curriculum *n*

race *vi* certare, cursu contendĕre

race horse *s* equus cursor *m*

racer *s* (*person*) cursor *m*; (*horse*) equus cursor *m*

racetrack *s* circus *m*, curriculum *n*

rack *s* (*shelf*) pluteus *m*; (*for punishment*) equuleus *m*, tormentum *n*

racket *s* (*noise*) strepit·us -ūs *m*

radiance *s* fulgor, splendor *m*

radiant *adj* radians, fulgidus, splendidus

radiate *vt* emittĕre; *vi* radiare, fulgēre, nitēre

radiation *s* radiatio *f*

radical *adj* insitus, innatus; (*thorough*) totus; —ly penitus, omnino

radical *s* rerum novarum cupidus *m*

radish *s* raphanus *m*

radius *s* radius *m*

raffle *s* alea *f*

raffle *vt* to — off aleā vendĕre

raft *s* ratis *f*

rafter *s* trabs *f*

rag *s* panniculus, pannus *m*

rage *s* furor *m*, rabies *f*

rage *vi* furĕre, saevire

ragged *adj* pannosus

raid *s* incursio, invasio *f*, latrocinium *n*

raider *s* praedator, latro *m*

raid *vt* praedari

rail *s* palus, asser transversus, longurius *m*

rail *vt* to — off consaepire; *vi* to — at insectari, conviciari

railing *s* (*fence*) saepimentum *n*; (*abuse*) convicium, maledictum *n*

raiment *s* vestis *f*, vestit·us -ūs *m*

rain *s* pluvia *f*, imber *m*

rain *vi* pluĕre; it is raining pluit

rainbow *s* pluvius arc·us -ūs *m*

rain cloud *s* imber *m*

rainy *adj* pluvius, pluvialis; pluviosus

raise *vt* tollĕre, elevare; (*to erect*) erigĕre; (*to build*) exstruĕre; (*money*) cogĕre; (*army*) conscribĕre; (*siege*) solvĕre; (*to stir up*) excitare; (*children*) educare; (*to promote*) provehĕre, producĕre; (*price*) augĕre; (*crops*) colĕre; (*beard*) demittĕre; to — up sublevare

raisin *s* astaphis *f*

rake *s* rastellus, irpex *m*; (*person*) nebulo, nepos *m*

rake *vt* radĕre; to — together corradĕre

rally *s* convent·us -ūs *m*, contio *f*

rally *vt* in aciem revocare; *vi* ex fuga convenire; (*from sickness*) convalescĕre

ram *s* aries *m*

ram *vt* fistucare, paviare; (*to cram*) infercire

ramble *s* vagatio *f*

ramble *vi* vagari, errare; to — on (*in speech*) garrire

rambling *adj* errans; (*fig*) vagus

ramification *s* ramus *m*

rampage *vi* saevire

rampant *adj* ferox

rampart *s* vallum, propugnaculum *n*

rancid *adj* rancidus

rancor *s* simultas *f*, dolor *m*

random *adj* fortuitus; at — temere

range *s* series *f*, ordo *m*; (*of mountains*) jugum *n*; (*reach*) jact·us -ūs *m*

range *vt* ordinare, disponĕre; *vi* pervagari

rank *s* series *f*, ordo, grad·us -ūs *m*, dignitas *f*

rank *vt* in numero habēre; *vi* in numero habēri

rank *adj* luxuriosus; (*extreme*) summus, maximus; (*of smell*) foetidus, gravis, graveolens

rankle *vi* suppurare, exulcerare

ransack *vt* diripĕre, spoliare; (*to search thoroughly*) exquirĕre

ransom *s* (*act*) redemptio *f*; pretium *n*

ransom *vt* redimere

rant *vi* ampullari; to — and rave debacchari

rap *s* (*slap*) alapa *f*; (*blow*) ict·us -ūs *m*; (*at door*) pulsatio *f*; (*with knuckles*) talitrum *n*

rap *vt* (*to criticize*) exagitare; *vi* to — at pulsare, ferire

rapacious *adj* rapax, avidus

rapacity *s* rapacitas, aviditas *f*

rape *s* stuprum *n*; (*act of carrying away*) rapt·us -ūs *m*

rape *vt* violare, per vim stuprare

rapid *adj* rapidus, celer, velox; —ly rapide, cito, velociter

rapidity *s* rapiditas, velocitas *f*

rapier *s* verutum *n*

rapine *s* rapina *f*

rapture *s* exsultatio *f*, animus exsultans *m*

rapturous *adj* mirificus

rare *adj* rarus, inusitatus; (*fig*) eximius, singularis; (*thin*) tenuis; —ly raro

rarefy *vt* extenuare, rarefacĕre

rarity *s* raritas, paucitas *f*; (*thing*) res rara, res singularis *f*

rascal *s* homo nequam, scelestus *m*

rascally *adj* scelestus, flagitiosus; nequam (*indecl*)

rash *adj* praeceps, temerarius; —ly temere, inconsulte

rash *s* eruptio pustulae *f*

rashness *s* temeritas *f*

raspberry *s* morum idaeum *n*

raspberry bush *s* rubus idaeus *m*

rat *s* sorex, mus *m*; (*person*) transfuga *m*

rate *s* proportio *f*; (*price*) pretium *n*; (*scale*) norma *f*; (*tax*) vectigal *n*; — of interest faenus *n*, usura *f*

rate *vt* aestimare

rather *adv* potius, prius, libentius; (*somewhat*) aliquantum, paulo, or render by comparative of adjective

ratification *s* sanctio *f*

ratify *vt* ratum facĕre, sancire

rating *s* aestimatio *f*

ratio *s* proportio *f*

ration *s* (*portion*) demensum *n*; (*mil*) cibaria *n pl*

ration *vt* demetiri

rational *adj* ratione praeditus, intellegens; —ly ratione, sapienter

rationalize *vi* ratiocinari

rattle *s* crepit·us -ūs, strepit·us -ūs *m*; (*toy*) crepitaculum *n*

rattle *vt* crepitare (*with abl*); *vi* increpare, crepitare; to — on inepte garrire

raucous *adj* raucus

ravage *vt* vastare, spoliare, populari

ravages *s* vastatio, direptio *f*

rave *vi* furĕre, saevire, bacchari

ravel *vt* involvĕre, implicare

raven *s* corvus *m*, cornix *f*

ravenous *adj* rapax, vorax; **—ly** voraciter

ravine *s* fauces *f pl*

raving *adj* furiosus, furens, insanus

ravish *vt* constuprare

raw *adj* crudus, incoctus; (*of person*) rudis, imperitus; (*of weather*) asper

rawboned *adj* strigosus

ray *s* radius *m*

raze *vt* solo aequare, excidĕre

razor *s* novacula *f*

reach *s* (*grasp, capacity*) capt·us -ūs *m*; (*of weapon*) ict·us -ūs, jact·us -ūs *m*; **out of my —** extra ictum meum

reach *vt* attingĕre; (*of space*) pertinĕre ad (*with acc*), extendi ad (*with acc*); (*to come up to*) assequi; (*to arrive at*) pervenire ad (*with acc*); (*to hand*) tradĕre

react *vi* affici; **to —** to ferre

read *vt* & *vi* legĕre; **to — aloud** recitare

readable *adj* lectu facilis

reader *s* lector *m*; (*lecturer*) praelector *m*

readily *adv* (*willingly*) libenter; (*easily*) facile

readiness *s* facilitas *f*; **in —** in promptu

ready *adj* paratus, promptus, expeditus; (*easy*) facilis; **— money** praesens pecunia *f*; **to be —** praesto esse

real *adj* verus, sincerus; **—ly** re vera; (*surely*) sane, certe

real estate *s* fundus *m*

realistic *adj* verisimilis

reality *s* veritas, res ipsa *f*, verum *n*

realization *s* effectio *f*; (*of ideas*) cognitio, comprehensio *f*

realize *vt* (*to understand*) intellegĕre, vidēre, comprehendĕre; (*to effect*) efficĕre, ad exitum perducĕre; (*to convert into money*) redigĕre

realm *s* regnum *n*

ream *s* (*of paper*) scapus *m*

reap *vt* metĕre, desecare; (*fig*) percipĕre, capĕre

reaper *s* messor *m*

reappear *vi* redire, revenire, resurgĕre

rear *vt* educare, alĕre; *vi* (*of horses*) arrectum se tollĕre

rear *s* tergum *n*; (*mil*) novissimum agmen *n*, novissima acies *f*; **on the — a tergo; to bring up the —** agmen cogĕre

rearing *s* educatio *f*

reascend *vt* & *vi* denuo ascendĕre

reason *s* (*faculty*) mens, ratio, intellegentia *f*; (*cause*) causa *f*; (*moderation*) modus *m*; **by — of** ob (*with acc*), propter (*with acc*), a(b) (*with abl*); **there is no — why** non est cur

reason *vi* ratiocinari; **to — with** disceptare cum (*with abl*)

reasonable *adj* (*fair*) aequus, justus; (*moderate*) modicus; (*judicious*) prudens

reasonably *adv* ratione, juste; modice

reasoning *s* ratiocinatio, ratio *f*; (*discussing*) disceptatio *f*

reassemble *vt* recolligĕre, cogĕre

reassert *vt* iterare

reassume *vt* resumĕre

reassure *vt* confirmare, redintegrare

rebel *s* rebellis *m*

rebel *vi* rebellare, desciscĕre, seditionem commovēre

rebellion *s* rebellio, seditio *f*, rebellium *n*

rebellious *adj* rebellis, seditiosus; (*disobedient*) contumax

rebound *s* result·us -ūs *m*

rebound *vi* resilire, resultare

rebuff *s* repulsa *f*

rebuff *vt* repellĕre, rejicĕre

rebuild *vt* reparare, reficĕre

rebuke *s* reprehensio *f*

rebuke *vt* reprehendĕre, vituperare

rebuttal *s* refutatio *f*

recall *s* revocatio *f*

recall *vt* revocare; **to — to mind** in memoriam redigĕre

recant *vt* retractare, revocare

recantation *s* recept·us -ūs *m*

recapitulate *vt* repetĕre, summatim colligĕre

recapitulation *s* repetitio, enumeratio *f*

recapture *s* recuperatio *f*

recapture *vt* recipĕre, recuperare

recede *vi* recedĕre, refugĕre

receipt *s* (*act*) acceptio *f*; (*note of acceptance*) apocha *f*; (*money*) acceptum *n*

receive *vt* accipĕre, capĕre, excipĕre

receiver *s* receptor *m*

recent *adj* recens; **—ly** nuper

receptacle *s* receptaculum *n*

reception *s* adit·us -ūs *m*, admissio *f*; (*of guest*) hospitium *n*

recess *s* (*place*) recess·us -ūs *m*; (*in wall*) adytum *n*, angulus *m*; (*intermission*) intermissio *f*; (*vacation*) feriae *f pl*

recipe *s* praescriptum, compositio *f*

recipient *s* acceptor *m*

reciprocal *adj* mutuus; **—ly** mutuo, vicissim, inter se

reciprocate *vt* reddĕre

reciprocity *s* reciprocatio *f*

recital *s* narratio, enumeratio, recitatio *f*

recitation *s* recitatio, lectio *f*

reckless *adj* temerarius; **—ly** temere

reckon *vt* numerare, computare, aestimare; *vi* **to — on** confidĕre (*with dat*)

reckoning *s* numeratio *f*; (*account to be given*) ratio *f*

reclaim *vt* reposcĕre, repetĕre

recline *vi* recubare, recumbĕre; (*at table*) accumbĕre

recluse *s* homo solitarius *m*

recognition *s* cognitio, agnitio *f*

recognize *vt* agnoscĕre, recognoscĕre; (*to acknowledge*) noscĕre; (*to admit*) fatēri

recoil *vi* resilire; **to — from** receděre ab (*with abl*), refugěre ab (*with abl*)

recoil *s* recessio *f*

recollect *vt* recordari

recollection *s* memoria, recordatio *f*

recommence *vt* redintegrare, renovare

recommend *vt* commendare

recommendation *s* commendatio, laudatio *f*; **letter of —** litterae commendaticiae *f pl*

recompense *s* remuneratio *f*

recompense *vt* remunerare; (*to indemnify*) compensare

reconcilable *adj* placabilis; (*of things*) conveniens

reconcile *vt* reconciliare, componěre; **to be reconciled** in gratiam restitui

reconciliation *s* reconciliatio *f*, in gratiam redit·us -ūs *m*

reconnoiter *vt* explorare

reconquer *vt* revincěre, recuperare

reconsider *vt* revolvěre, retractare

reconstruct *vt* restituěre, renovare

reconstruction *s* renovatio *f*

record *s* monumentum *n*, historia *f*; **—s** annales *m pl*, tabulae *f pl*

recorder *s* procurator ab actis *m*

recount *vt* referre, enarrare, commemorare

recoup *vt* recuperare

recourse *s* refugium *n*; **to have — to** (*for safety*) fugěre ad (*with acc*); (*to resort to*) descenděre ad (*with acc*)

recover *vt* recuperare, recipěre; *vi* (*from illness*) convalescěre; (*to come to one's senses*) ad se redire

recoverable *adj* reparabilis, recuperandus; (*of persons*) sanabilis

recovery *s* recuperatio, reparatio *f*; (*from illness*) recreatio *f*

recreate *vt* recreare

recreation *s* oblectatio, remissio *f*, lus·us -ūs *m*

recriminate *vi* invicem accusare

recrimination *s* mutua accusatio *f*

recruit *vt* (*mil*) conscriběre; (*strength*) reficěre

recruit *s* tiro *m*

recruiting *s* delect·us -ūs *m*

recruiting officer *s* conquisitor *m*

rectification *s* correctio *f*

rectify *vt* corrigěre, emendare

rectitude *s* probitas *f*

recumbent *adj* resupinus

recur *vi* recurrěre, redire

recurrence *s* redit·us -ūs *m*

recurrent *adj* assiduus

red *adj* ruber; (*ruddy*) rubicundus; **to be —** rubēre; **to grow —** rubescěre

redden *vt* rubefacěre, rutilare; *vi* rubescěre; (*to blush*) erubescěre

reddish *adj* subrufus, subruber, rubicundus

redeem *vt* rediměre, liberare

redeemer *s* liberator *m*

Redeemer *s* Redemptor *m*

redemption *s* redemptio *f*

redhead *s* rufus *m*

red-hot *adj* candens

redness *s* rubor *m*

redolence *s* fragrantia *f*

redolent *adj* fragrans, redolens; **to be —** redolēre

redouble *vt* ingeminare

redoubt *s* propugnaculum *n*

redoubtable *adj* formidolosus

redound *vi* redundare

redress *vt* restituěre

redress *s* satisfactio *f*; **to demand —** res repetěre

reduce *vt* minuěre, deminuěre; (*to a condition*) redigěre; (*mil*) vincěre, expugnare

reduction *s* deminutio *f*; (*mil*) expugnatio *f*

redundancy *s* redundantia *f*

redundant *adj* redundans, superfluus

reed *s* harundo *f*, calamus *m*

reef *s* scopulus *m*, saxa *n pl*

reek *s* fumus, vapor *m*

reek *vi* fumare; **to — of** olēre

reel *s* fusus *m*

reel *vi* (*to stagger*) titubare

reestablish *vt* restituěre

reestablishment *s* restitutio *f*

refer *vt* referre, remittěre; *vi* **to — to** perstringěre, attingěre

referee *s* arbiter *m*

reference *s* ratio *f*; (*in book*) locus *m*

refine *vt* purgare, excolěre, expolire; (*metals*) excoquěre

refined *adj* politus; (*fig*) elegans, urbanus, humanus

refinement *s* (*of liquids*) purgatio *f*; (*fig*) urbanitas, humanitas, elegantia *f*

reflect *vt* repercutěre, reverberare; (*fig*) afferre; *vi* **to — on** considerare, revolvěre

reflection *s* repercussio *f*, repercuss·us -ūs *m*; (*thing reflected*) imago *f*; (*fig*) consideratio, meditatio, cogitatio *f*; **without — inconsulte**

reflective *adj* cogitabundus

reflexive *adj* reciprocus

reform *vt* reficěre, refingěre; (*to amend*) corrigěre, emendare; *vi* se corrigěre

reform *s* correctio, emendatio *f*

reformation *s* correctio *f*

reformer *s* corrector, emendator *m*

refract *vt* refringěre

refraction *s* refractio *f*

refractory *adj* contumax, indocilis

refrain *s* vers·us -ūs intercalaris *m*

refrain *vi* **to — from** abstinēre ab (*with abl*), parcěre (*with dat*); **I — from speaking** abstineo quin dicam

refresh *vt* recreare, reficěre; (*the memory*) redintegrare

refreshing *adj* jucundus, dulcis

refreshment *s* (*food*) cibus *m*; (*drink*) pot·us -ūs *m*

refuge *s* refugium, perfugium, asylum *n*; **to take — with** confugěre in (*with acc*)

refugee *s* profugus *m*, ex(s)ul *m & f*

refulgence *s* fulgor *m*

refulgent *adj* fulgidus

refund *vt* refunděre, rependěre

refusal *s* recusatio, repulsa *f*
refuse *vt* recusare, negare; *(scornfully)* repudire, renuĕre
refutation *s* refutatio, confutatio *f*
refute *vt* refutare, refellĕre, redarguĕre
regain *vt* recipĕre, recuperare
regal *adj* regalis, regius; **—ly** regaliter
regale *vt* excipĕre
regalia *s* insignia regia *n pl*
regard *s* respect·us -ūs *m*, ratio *f*; *(care)* cura *f*; *(esteem)* gratia *f*
regard *vt (to look at)* respicĕre, intuĕri; *(to concern)* spectare ad *(with acc)*; *(to esteem)* aestimare; *(to consider)* habēre
regarding *prep* de *(with abl)*
regardless *adj* neglegens, incuriosus
regency *s* procuratio regni *f*, interregnum *n*
regenerate *vt* regenerare
regeneration *s* regeneratio *f*
regent *s* interrex *m*
regicide *s (murderer)* regis occisor *m*; *(murder)* caedes regis *f*
regime *s* administratio *f*
regimen *f* vict·us -ūs *m*
regiment *s* cohors, caterva *f*
region *s* regio, plaga *f*, tract·us -ūs *m*
register *s* tabulae *f pl*, catalogus *m*, album *n*
register *vt* in tabulas referre; *(emotion)* ostendĕre; *vi* profitĕri, nomen dare
registrar *s* tabularius, actuarius *m*
registration *s* perscriptio, in tabulas relatio *f*
registry *s* tabularium *n*
regret *s* indignatio, paenitentia *f*, dolor *m*
regret *vt* dolēre; **I —** paenitet me *(with genit)*, piget me *(with genit)*
regretful *adj* paenitens
regular *adj (common)* usitatus; *(proper)* justus, rectus; *(consistent)* constans, certus; **—ly** ordine, constanter; juste, recte
regularity *s* symmetria *f*; *(consistency)* constantia *f*
regulate *vt* ordinare, disponĕre, dirigĕre; *(to control)* moderari
regulation *s* ordinatio, temperatio, moderatio *f*; *(rule)* lex *f*, jussum *n*
rehabilitate *vt* restituĕre
rehearsal *s* meditatio *f*
rehearse *vt* meditari
reign *s* regnum *n*
reign *vi* regnare, dominari
reimburse *vt* rependĕre
reimbursement *s* pecuniae restitutio *f*
rein *s* habena *f*; **to give full — to** habenas immittĕre *(with dat)*; **to loosen the —s** frenos dare; **to tighten the —s** habenas adducĕre
reindeer *s* reno *m*
reinforce *vt* firmare, supplēre
reinforcement *s* supplementum, subsidium *n*; **—s** *(mil)* novae copiae *f pl*
reinstate *vt* restituĕre

reinstatement *s* restitutio *f*
reinvest *vt* iterum locare
reiterate *vt* iterare
reiteration *s* iteratio *f*
reject *vt* rejicĕre, repudiare, repellĕre, respuĕre
rejection *s* rejectio, repulsa *f*
rejoice *vi* gaudēre, exsultare
rejoin *vt* redire ad *(with acc)*; *vi* respondēre
rejoinder *s* responsum *n*
rekindle *vt* resuscitare
relapse *s* novus laps·us -ūs *m*
relate *vt* referre, memorare, narrare; *(to compare)* conferre; *vi* **to — to** pertinēre ad *(with acc)*
related *adj* propinquus, conjunctus; *(by blood)* consanguineus, cognatus; *(by marriage)* affinis
relation *s* narratio *f*; *(reference)* ratio *f*; *(relationship)* cognatio *f*; *(relative)* cognatus *m*, cognata *f*
relationship *s (by blood)* consanguinitas, cognatio *f*; *(by marriage)* affinitas *f*; *(connection)* necessitudo, vicinitas, conjunctio *f*
relative *adj* attinens; cum ceteris comparatus; **—ly** pro ratione, ex comparatione
relative *s* cognatus, propinquus *m*, cognata, propinqua *f*
relax *vt* remittĕre, laxare; *vi* languescĕre
relaxation *s* remissio, relaxatio, requies *f*
relaxing *adj* remissivus
release *s* liberatio, absolutio, missio *f*
release *vt (prisoner)* liberare; solvĕre, resolvĕre
relegate *vt* relegare
relent *vi* mitescĕre, mollescĕre, flecti
relentless *adj* immisericors, inexorabilis, atrox; **—ly** atrociter
relevant *adj* **to be —** ad rem attinēre
reliance *s* fiducia, fides *f*
reliant *adj* fretus
relic *s* reliquiae *f pl*
relief *s (alleviation)* levatio *f*, levamentum *n*; *(comfort)* solatium, lenimen *n*; *(help)* auxilium *n*; *(in sculpture)* toreuma *n*; *(of sentries)* mutatio *f*
relieve *vt* levare, allevare, mitigare; *(to aid)* succurrĕre *(with dat)*; *(a guard)* succedĕre *(with dat)*, excipĕre
religion *s* religio *f*, deorum cult·us -ūs *m*
religious *adj* religiosus, pius; **—ly** religiose
relinquish *vt* relinquĕre; *(office)* se abdicare ab *(with abl)*
relish *s (flavor)* sapor *m*; *(enthusiasm)* studium *n*; *(seasoning)* condimentum *n*
relish *vt* gustare
reluctance *s* aversatio *f*; **with —** invite
reluctant *adj* invitus; **—ly** invite
rely *vi* **to — on** confidĕre *(with dat)*, niti *(with abl)*
remain *vi* manēre, permanēre; *(of things)* restare

remainder *s* reliquum *n*
remains *s* reliquiae *f pl*
remark *vt* dicĕre
remark *s* dictum *n*
remarkable *adj* insignis, memorabilis, mirus, egregius
remarkably *adv* insignite, mire, egregie
remediable *adj* sanabilis
remedial *adj* medicabilis; emendatorius
remedy *s* remedium *n*; (*law*) regress·us ·ūs *m*
remedy *vt* medēri (*with dat*), sanare, corrigĕre
remember *vt* meminisse (*with genit*); reminisci (*with genit*); recordari
remembrance *s* memoria, commemoratio *f*
remind *vt* admonēre, commonefacĕre
reminder *s* admonitio *f*, admonitum *n*
reminisce *vi* meditari; **to — about** recordari
reminiscence *s* recordatio *f*
remiss *adj* neglegens
remission *s* venia, remissio *f*
remit *vt* remittĕre, condonare
remittance *s* remissio *f*
remnant *s* reliquum, residuum *n*; **—s** reliquiae *f pl*
remodel *vt* reformare, transfigurare
remonstrance *s* objurgatio *f*
remonstrate *vi* reclamare, reclamitare; **to — with** objurgare
remorse *s* paenitentia *f*
remorseless *adj* immisericors
remote *adj* remotus, longinquus, reconditus; **—ly** procul
remoteness *s* longinquitas, distantia *f*
removable *adj* mobilis
removal *s* amotio *f*; (*banishment*) amandatio *f*; (*change of residence*) migratio *f*
remove *vt* amovēre, tollĕre, auferre; *vi* migrare
remunerate *vt* remunerari
remuneration *s* remuneratio *f*
rend *vt* lacerare, scindĕre; (*to split*) findĕre
render *vt* reddĕre, tradĕre; (*to translate*) vertĕre; (*thanks*) referre
rendering *s* (*translation*) conversio *f*; (*interpretation*) interpretatio *f*
rendezvous *s* constitutum *n*
renegade *s* desertor, transfuga *m*
renew *vt* renovare, instaurare, redintegrare
renewal *s* renovatio, instauratio, repetitio *f*
renounce *vt* renuntiare, repudiare, abdicare; (*an office*) se abdicare (*with abl*)
renovate *vt* renovare, reficĕre
renovation *s* renovatio, reparatio *f*
renown *s* fama, gloria *f*
renowned *adj* praeclarus, insignis, celebris
rent *s* (*of lands*) vectigal *n*; (*of houses*) merces, pensio *f*; (*tear; fissure*) scissura *f*
rent *vt* (*to let out*) locare; (*to hire*) conducĕre

renunciation *s* repudiatio, cessio, abdicatio *f*
reopen *vt* iterum aperire
repair *vt* reparare, reficĕre, restituĕre; (*clothes*) resarcire
repair *s* refectio *f*; **in bad —** ruinosus
reparation *s* satisfactio *f*
repartee *s* sales *m pl*
repast *s* cena *f*
repay *vt* remunerari; (*money*) reponĕre, retribuĕre
repayment *s* solutio, remuneratio *f*
repeal *vt* abrogare, rescindĕre, tollĕre
repeal *s* abrogatio *f*
repeat *vt* iterare, repetĕre; (*ceremony*) instaurare
repeatedly *adv* iterum atque iterum, identidem
repel *vt* repellĕre; (*fig*) aspernari
repent *vi* **I — paenitet me**
repentance *s* paenitentia *f*
repentant *adj* paenitens
repercussion *s* repercuss·us ·ūs *m*
repetition *s* iteratio, repetitio *f*
repine *vi* conquĕri
replace *vt* reponĕre, restituĕre
replant *vt* reserĕre
replenish *vt* replēre
replete *adj* repletus, plenus
repletion *s* satietas *f*
reply *vi* respondēre
reply *s* responsum *n*
report *vt* referre, narrare, nuntiare; (*officially*) renuntiare
report *s* (*rumor*) fama *f*, rumor *m*; (*official*) renuntiatio *f*; (*noise*) fragor *m*
repose *vt* ponĕre, reponĕre; *vi* quiescĕre
repose *s* quies, requies *f*
repository *s* receptaculum *n*
reprehend *vt* reprehendĕre, vituperare
reprehensible *adj* culpā dignus, improbus
represent *vt* repraesentare, exprimĕre, describĕre, proponĕre; (*a character*) partes agĕre (*with genit*)
representation *s* (*act*) repraesentatio *f*; (*likeness*) imago *f*
representative *s* legatus, vicarius *m*
repress *vt* reprimĕre, coercēre, cohibēre
repression *s* coercitio, cohibitio *f*
reprieve *s* supplicii dilatio, mora, venia *f*; **to grant a — supplicium** differre, veniam dare
reprieve *vt* veniam dare (*with dat*)
reprimand *s* reprehensio *f*
reprimand *vt* reprehendĕre
reprint *vt* denuo imprimĕre
reprisal *s* ultio *f*; **to make —s on** ulcisci
reproach *s* exprobratio, vituperatio *f*, probrum *n*; (*cause for reproach*) opprobrium *n*
reproach *vt* opprobrare, vituperare, increpitare
reproachful *adj* objurgatorius, contumeliosus; **—ly** contumeliose
reprobate *s* perditus *m*

reproduce *vt* regenerare, propagare; (*likeness*) referre

reproduction *s* regeneratio, propagatio *f*; (*likeness*) effigies *f*

reproof *s* reprehensio, vituperatio, objuratio *f*

reprove *vt* reprehendĕre, objurgare

reptile *s* serpens, bestia serpens *f*

republic *s* civitas popularis, libera civitas *f*

republican *adj* popularis

repudiate *vt* repudiare

repudiation *s* repudiatio *f*

repugnance *s* fastidium *n*, aversatio *f*

repugnant *adj* aversus, repugnans, alienus

repulse *s* depulsio *f*; (*political defeat*) repulsa *f*

repulse *vt* repellĕre

repulsion *s* repulsio *f*

repulsive *adj* odiosus, foedus

reputable *adj* honestus

reputation *s* fama *f*, nomen *n*

repute *s* fama, opinio *f*, nomen *n*

request *s* petitio, rogatio *f*; **to obtain a —** impetrare

request *vt* rogare, petĕre

require *vt* postulare, poscĕre; (*to need*) egēre (*with abl*); (*to call for*) requirĕre

requirement *s* necessarium *n*

requisite *adj* necessarius

requisition *s* postulatio *f*, postulatum *n*

requital *s* retributio, merces *f*; (*return for a service*) gratia *f*

requite *vt* compensare, retribuĕre; (*for a favor*) remunerari

rescind *vt* rescindĕre, tollĕre

rescue *s* liberatio, salus *f*; **to come to the — of** subvenire (*with dat*)

rescue *vt* liberare, servare, eripĕre

research *s* investigatio *f*

resemblance *s* similitudo, imago *f*, instar *n* (*indecl*)

resemble *vt* similis esse (*with genit, esp. of persons, or with dat*)

resembling *adj* similis (*with genit, esp. of persons, or with dat*)

resent *vt* aegre ferre

resentful *adj* iracundus, indignans

resentment *s* indignatio *f*, dolor *m*

reservation *s* retentio *f*; (*mental*) exceptio *f*; (*proviso*) condicio *f*

reserve *s* (*restraint*) pudor *m*, taciturnitas *f*; (*stock*) copia *f*; (*mil*) subsidium *n*; **in — subsidiarius; without —** aperte

reserve *vt* servare, reservare, reponĕre

reserved *adj* (*of seat*) assignatus; (*of disposition*) taciturnus

reservoir *s* cisterna *f*, lac·us -ūs *m*

reset *vt* reponĕre

reside *vi* habitare, commorari; **to — in** inhabitare

residence *s* habitatio, sedes *f*, domicilium *n*

resident *s* incola *m & f*

residue *s* residuum *n*

resign *vt* cedĕre, remittĕre; se abdicare a(b) (*with abl*); **to — oneself** animum summittĕre (*with dat*); *vi* se abdicare

resignation *s* (*act*) abdicatio *f*; (*fig*) aequus animus *m*

resigned *adj* summissus; **to be — aequo animo esse; to be — to** aequo animo ferre

resilience *s* mollitia *f*

resilient *adj* resultans, mollis

resin *s* resina *f*

resist *vt* resistĕre (*with dat*), obstare (*with dat*), repugnare (*with dat*)

resistance *s* repugnantia *f*; **to offer to —** obsistĕre (*with dat*), repugnare (*with dat*)

resolute *adj* firmus, constans, fortis; **—ly** constanter, fortiter

resolution *s* (*determination*) constantia *f*; (*decision, decree*) decretum *n*; (*of senate*) consultum *n*

resolve *s* constantia *f*

resolve *vt* decernĕre, statuĕre, constituĕre; (*to reduce, convert*) resolvĕre, dissolvĕre

resonance *s* resonantia *f*

resonant *adj* resonus

resort *s* locus celeber *m*; (*refuge*) refugium *n*

resort *vi* **to — to** (*to frequent*) frequentare, celebrare; (*to have recourse to*) confugĕre ad (*with acc*)

resource *s* subsidium *n*; **—s** facultates, opes, copiae *f pl*

respect *s* (*regard*) respect·us -ūs *m*; (*reference*) ratio *f*; **in every — ex** omni parte

respect *vt* (re)verēri, observare

respectability *s* honestas *f*

respectable *adj* honestus, bonus

respectably *adv* honeste

respectful *adj* observans, reverens; **—ly** reverenter

respecting *prep* de (*with abl*)

respective *adj* proprius, suus; **—ly** mutuo

respiration *s* spirit·us -ūs *m*

respite *s* intermissio, cessatio, requies *f*

resplendence *s* nitor, splendor *m*

resplendent *adj* resplendens, splendidus; **—ly** splendide

respond *vi* respondēre

respondent *s* (*law*) reus *m*

response *s* responsum *n*

responsibility *s* cura *f*; **it is my —** est mihi curae

responsible *adj* obnoxius, reus

rest *s* quies, requies *f*; (*support*) fulcrum, statumen *n*; (*remainder*) reliqua pars *f*, reliquum *n*; **the — of the men** ceteri *m pl*

rest *vt* (*to lean*) reclinare; *vi* (re)quiescĕre; (*to pause*) cessare; **to — on** inniti in (*with abl*), niti (*with abl*)

restitution *s* restitutio *f*; (*restoration*) refectio *f*

restive *adj* (*balky, unruly*) contumax; (*impatient*) impatiens

restless *adj* inquietus, turbidus, tumultuosus; (*agitated*) sollicitus; **—ly** inquiete, turbulente

restoration *s* restauratio, refectio, renovatio *f*

restore *vt* restituĕre, reddĕre; (*to re-*

build) restaurare, reficĕre; (*to health*) recurare, recreare; to — to order in integrum reducĕre

restrain *vt* cohibēre, coercēre, continēre; (*to prevent*) impedire

restraint *s* temperantia, moderatio *f*

restrict *vt* cohibēre, restringĕre, circumscribĕre, (de)finire

restriction *s* modus, finis *m*, limitatio *f*

result *s* exit·us -ūs, event·us -ūs *m*; eventum *n*; **without** — nequiquam

result *vi* evenire, fieri, evadĕre

resume *vt* resumĕre, repetĕre

resumption *s* resumptio, continuatio *f*

resurrection *s* resurrectio *f*

resuscitate *vt* resuscitare

retail *vt* divendĕre

retailer *s* caupo, propola *m*

retain *vt* retinēre, obtinēre, conservare

retainer *s* (*adherent*) cliens, asectator, satelles *m*; (*fee*) arrabo *m*

retake *vt* recipĕre, recuperare

retaliate *vi* ulcisci

retaliation *s* ultio *f*

retard *vt* retardare

retch *vi* nauseare

retention *s* retentio, conservatio *f*

retentive *adj* tenax

reticence *s* taciturnitas *f*

reticent *adj* taciturnus

retinue *s* comit·us -ūs *m*

retire *vi* recedĕre, regredi; (*from office*) abire; (*for the night*) dormitum ire

retired *adj* (*of place*) remotus, solitarius; (*from work*) emeritus

retirement *s* (*act*) recess·us -ūs *m*, abdicatio *f*; (*state*) otium *n*, solitudo *f*

retiring *adj* modestus

retort *s* responsum *n*

retort *vt* respondēre

retrace *vt* repetĕre, iterare

retract *vt* revocare, recantare, renuntiare

retraction *s* retractatio *f*

retreat *vi* recedĕre, refugĕre, se recipĕre, pedem referre

retreat *s* (*act*) recess·us -ūs *m*, fuga *f*; (*place*) recess·us -ūs *m*, refugium *n*; (*mil*) recept·us -ūs *m*

retrench *vt* recidĕre

retrenchment *s* recisio *f*

retribution *s* compensatio, poena *f*

retrieve *vt* recuperare, recipĕre

retrogression *s* regress·us -ūs, retrogress·us -ūs *m*

retrospect *s* retrospect·us -ūs *m*; **in** — respicienti

retrospective *adj* respiciens; —**ly** retro

return *s* (*coming back*) redit·us -ūs *m*; (*repayment*) remuneratio *f*; (*income, profit*) fruct·us -ūs *m*

return *vt* (*to give back*) reddĕre, restituĕre, referre; *vi* (*to go back*) redire; (*to come back*) revenire, reverti

reunion *s* readunatio *f*, convivium *n*

reunite *vt* iterum conjungĕre; recon-

ciliare; *vi* reconciliari

reveal *vt* retegĕre, reclⁿudĕre, aperire; (*to unveil*) revelare

revel *s* comissatio, bacchatio *f*; —**s** orgia *n pl*

revel *vi* comissari, debacchari, luxuriare *or* luxuriari

revelation *s* patefactio, revelatio *f*

reveler *s* comissator *m*

revelry *s* comissatio *f*, orgia *n pl*

revenge *vt* ulcisci

revenge *s* ultio, vindicta *f*; **to take** — **on** se vindicare in (*with acc*)

revengeful *adj* ulciscendi cupidus

revenue *s* redit·us -ūs, fruct·us -ūs *m*, vectigal *n*

reverberate *vi* resonare

reverberation *s* repercuss·us -ūs *m*, resonantia *f*

revere *vt* reverēri, venerari

reverence *s* reverentia, veneratio, religio, pietas *f*

reverend *adj* reverendus

reverent *adj* reverens, pius, religiosus; —**ly** reverenter, religiose

reverential *adj* venerabundus

reverie *s* cogitatio, meditatio *f*

reversal *s* infirmatio *f*

reverse *s* contrarium *m*; (*change*) conversio, commutatio *f*; (*defeat*) clades *f*

reverse *vt* invertĕre, (com)mutare; (*decision*) rescindĕre, abrogare

revert *vi* redire, reverti

review *s* recognitio *f*; (*critique*) censura *f*; (*mil*) recensio, lustratio *f*

review *vt* recensēre, inspicĕre; (*mil*) recensēre, lustrare

reviewer *s* censor, editor *m*

revile *vt* maledicĕre (*with dat*), insectari

revise *vt* corrigĕre, recognoscĕre

revision *s* emendatio *f*; (*of literary work*) recensio, lima *f*

revisit *vt* revisĕre, revisitare

revival *s* redanimatio *f*; (*fig*) renovatio *f*

revive *vt* resuscitare; (*to renew*) renovare; (*to encourage*) animare, instigare, excitare; *vi* reviviscĕre

revocation *s* revocatio *f*

revoke *vt* revocare, renuntiare; (*a law*) rescindĕre

revolt *vt* offendĕre; *vi* rebellare, desciscĕre, deficĕre

revolt *s* rebellio, seditio, defectio *f*

revolting *adj* taeter, foedus

revolution *s* conversio *f*; (*change*) commutatio *f*; (*of planets*) ambit·us -ūs *m*; (*pol*) res novae *f pl*, mot·us -ūs *m*

revolutionary *adj* seditiosus, novarum rerum cupidus

revolutionize *vt* novare

revolve *vt* (*in mind*) meditari, volutare; *vi* revolvi, se (re)volvĕre

revulsion *s* taedium, fastidium *n*; **to cause** — fastidium movēre

reward *s* praemium *n*

reward *vt* remunerare, compensare

rewrite *vt* rescribĕre

rhapsody *s* rhapsodia *f*

rhetoric *s* rhetorica *n pl or f*

rhetorical *adj* rhetoricus, oratorius; to practice — declamare

rhetorician *s* rhetor *m*

rheumatism *s* dolor artuum *m*

rhinoceros *s* rhinoceros *m*

rhubarb *s* radix Pontica *f*

rhyme *s* homoeteleuton *n*

rhythm *s* numerus, rhythmus *m*

rhythmical *adj* numerosus

rib *s* costa *f*

ribald *adj* obscenus, spurcus

ribaldry *s* obscenitas *f*

ribbed *adj* costatus, striatus

ribbon *s* infula *f*

rice *s* oryza *f*

rich *s* dives, locuples; (*of soil*) fertilis, uber, opimus; (*food*) pinguis; (*costly*) pretiosus, lautus; —**ly** copiose, pretiose, laute

riches *s* divitiae, opes *f pl*

rickety *adj* instabilis

rid *vt* liberare; **to get** — **of** dimittĕre, deponĕre, exuĕre

riddle *s* aenigma *n*

ride *vi* **to** — **a horse** equo vehi; *vi* equitare; vehi; **to** — **away** *or* **off** avehi

ride *s* (*on horseback*) equitatio *f*; (*in carriage*) vectio *f*

rider *s* eques *m*; (*in carriage*) vector *m*; (*attached to documents*) adjectio *f*

ridge *s* jugum, dorsum *n*

ridicule *s* ridiculum, ludibrium *n*, irris·us -ūs *m*

ridicule *vt* irridēre; —**ly** ridicule

riding *s* equitatio *f*

rife *adj* frequens

riffraff *s* plebecula, faex populi *f*

rifle *vt* despoliare, diripĕre

rig *vt* adornare; (*ship*) armare, ornare

rigging *s* armamenta *n pl*, rudentes *m pl*

right *adj* rectus; (*just*) aequus, justus; (*opposed to left*) dexter; (*suitable*) idoneus, aptus; (*true*) verus, rectus; —**ly** recte, rite, juste, vere

right *s* (*hand*) dextra *f*; (*law*) jus, fas, aequum *n*; **on the** — **a dextra

right *vt* emendare, corrigĕre; (*to replace*) restituĕre; (*to avenge*) vindicare, ulcisci

righteous *adj* justus, pius; —**ly** juste, pie

righteousness *s* justitia, pietas, probitas *f*

rightful *adj* legitimus, justus; —**ly** juste

rigid *adj* rigidus; —**ly** rigide

rigidity *s* rigiditas *f*

rigor *s* severitas, duritia *f*

rigorous *adj* severus, asper; (*hardy*) durus

rill *s* rivulus *m*

rim *s* ora, margo *f*, labrum *n*

rind *s* crusta *f*

ring *s* anulus *m*; (*of people*) corona *f*; (*for fighting*) arena *f*; (*sound*) sonit·us -ūs *m*; (*of bells*) tinnit·us -ūs *m*

ring *vt* **to** — **a bell** tintinnabulum

tractare; *vi* tinnire, resonare

ringing *s* tinnit·us -ūs *m*

ringleader *s* auctor, dux *m*

rinse *vt* colluĕre, eluĕre

rinsing *s* colluvies *f*

riot *s* tumult·us -ūs, mot·us -ūs *m*; **to run** — luxuriari

riot *vi* seditionem movēre, tumultuari

rioter *s* seditiosus *m*

riotous *adj* seditiosus, tumultuosus; — **living** luxuria *f*

rip *vt* scindĕre; **to** — **apart** discindĕre, diffindĕre; (*fig*) discerpĕre

ripe *adj* mitis, maturus, tempestivus

ripen *vt* maturare; *vi* maturescĕre

ripple *s* flucticulus *m*

ripple *vi* trepidare

rise *vi* oriri, surgĕre; (*from sleep*) expergisci; (*to mount*) ascendĕre; (*to increase*) crescĕre; (*of rioters*) consurgĕre; (*of passion*) tumescĕre; **to** — **again** resurgĕre, reviviscĕre; **to** — **up** exsurgĕre

rise *s* (*ascent*) ascens·us -ūs *m*; (*origin*) origo *f*, ort·us -ūs *m*; (*increase*) incrementum *n*; (*slope*) clivus *m*; **to give** — **to** parĕre

rising *s* (*of sun*) ort·us -ūs *m*; (*insurrection*) mot·us -ūs, tumult·us -ūs *m*

risk *s* periculum *n*; **to run a** — periculum subire, periclitari

risk *vt* in periculum vocare, periclitari

rite *s* rit·us -ūs *m*

ritual *s* rit·us -ūs *m*, caeremonia *f*

rival *s* rivalis, aemulus, competitor *m*

rival *vt* aemulari

rivalry *s* aemulatio *f*, certamen *n*; (*in love*) rivalitas *f*

river *s* flumen *n*, amnis *m*

rivet *s* clavus *m*

rivet *vt* (*eyes, attention*) defigĕre

rivulet *s* rivus, rivulus *m*

road *s* via *f*, iter *n*; **on the** — **in itinere**; **to build a** — viam munire

roam *vi* errare, vagari

roar *s* fremit·us -ūs, rugit·us -ūs, strepit·us -ūs *m*

roar *vi* fremĕre, rudĕre, rugire

roast *vt* torrēre; (*in a pan*) frigĕre, assare, coquĕre

roast *adj* assus

roast *s* assum *n*

rob *vt* spoliare, compilare, latrocinari

robber *s* latro, fur *m*

robbery *s* latrocinium *n*, spoliatio *f*

robe *s* vestis, palla *f*

robe *vt* vestire

robin *s* sylvia rubecula, rubisca *f*

robust *adj* robustus, validus, lacertosus

rock *s* saxum *n*; (*cliff*) scopulus *m*, rupes *f*

rock *vt* jactare; **to** — **a cradle** cunas agitare; *vi* vibrare, vacillare

rocket *s* missile *n*

rocky *adj* saxosus, scopulosus

rod *s* virga, ferula *f*

roe *s* caprea *f*; (*of fish*) ova *n pl*

roebuck *s* capreolus *m*

rogue *s* nequam (homo), furcifer *m*

roguish *adj* malus, improbus

roll vt volvĕre, versare; vi volvi; (of tears) labi

roll s (book) volumen n; (of names) catalogus m, album n; (of bread) collyra f

roller s cylindrus m

Roman adj Romanus

Roman s Romanus, Quiris m

romance s fabula, narratio ficta f; (affair) amores m pl

romantic adj fabulosus, commenticius, amatorius

roof s tectum, fastigium n; (of mouth) palatum n

roof vt contegĕre, integĕre

room s (space) spatium n, locus m; (of house) conclave n

roomy adj laxus, spatiosus

roost s pertica f

roost vi cubitare, insidēre

root s radix f; (fig) fons m, origo f; to take — coalescĕre

root vt to become rooted (fig) inveterascĕre; to be rooted inhaerēre; to — out eradicare, exstirpare; vi radices agĕre; (fig) inveterascĕre

rope s funis m, restis f

rose s rosa f

roseate adj roseus

rosy adj roseus, rosaceus

rot vi putrescĕre, tabescĕre

rot s putredo, tabes, caries f

rotate vi volvi, se convertĕre

rotation s ambit·us -ūs m, conversio f; (succession) vicissitudo f; in — ordine

rote s by — memoriter

rotten adj putridus, tabidus, cariosus

rotunda s tholus m

rouge s fucus m

rough adj asper; (of character) agrestis, durus; (of weather) inclemens; (shaggy) hirsutus; —ly aspere, duriter

roughen vt asperare

roughness s asperitas f; (brutality) feritas f

round adj rotundus, globosus; —ly aperte, plane, praecise

round s orbis, circulus m; (series) ambit·us -ūs m

round vt (a corner) circumire, flectĕre; (a cape) superare; to — off concludĕre, complēre

rouse vt excitare, animare

rout s fuga f; (defeat) clades f; (crowd) turba f

rout vt fugare, fundĕre

route s via f, iter n

routine s consuetudo f, ordo, us·us -ūs m

rove vi vagari, errare

rover s ambulator m

row s series f, ordo m; (quarrel) rixa f

row vt remis propellĕre; vi remigare

rower s remex m

rowing s remigatio f, remigium n

royal adj regalis, regius; —ly regaliter, regie

royalty s regia potestas f, regnum n

rub vt fricare; to — away or off detergĕre

rub s fricatio f; (fig) difficultas f

rubbing s attrit·us -ūs, affrict·us -ūs m, fricatio, frictio f

rubbish s rudus n; (fig) quisquiliae f pl

rubble s rudus n

rubric s rubrica f

ruby s rubinus, carbunculus m

rudder s gubernaculum n

ruddy adj rubicundus, rubens, rutilus

rude adj rudis, rusticus, inurbanus; (impertinent) impudicus; —ly rustice, incondite

rudeness s rusticitas f, inhumanitas, insolentia f

rudiment s elementum, initium, rudimentum, principium n

rudimentary adj inchoatus, elementarius

rue vt I — me paenitet (with genit)

rueful adj maestus, luctuosus

ruffian s sicarius, grassator m

ruffle vt agitare, turbare; (to irritate) commovēre

ruffle s limbus m

rug s stragulum n

rugged adj asper, praeruptus

ruin s pernicies f, exitium n; ruina f; —s ruinae f pl

ruin vt perdĕre, corrumpĕre; (morally) depravare

ruination s vastatio f

ruinous adj damnosus, exitiosus

rule s (regulation) praeceptum n, lex f; (government) regimen, imperium n, dominatio f; (instrument) regula, norma f

rule vt regĕre, moderari; vi regĕre, dominari

ruler s (person) rector, dominus, rex m; (instrument) regula f

ruling s edictum n

rum s sicera f

rumble s murmur n

rumble vi murmurare, crepitare, mugire

rumbling s murmur n, mugit·us -ūs m

ruminate vi ruminare

rumination s ruminatio f

rummage vi to — through rimari

rumor s rumor m, fama f

rump s clunis f

rumple s (in garment) plica, ruga f

rumple vt corrugare

run vt (to manage) gerĕre, administrare; to — aground impingĕre; to — up (an account) augēre; vi currĕre; (to flow) fluĕre; to — about discurrĕre, cursare; to — after sequi, petĕre, sectari; to — aground offendĕre; to — away aufugĕre; to — away from defugĕre; to — down decurrĕre; (as water) defluĕre; to — for conquirĕre; to — foul of collidi; to — into (to meet) incidĕre in (with acc); to — off aufugĕre; (as water) defluĕre; to — on percurrĕre, continuare; to — out excurrĕre; (of time) exire; (of supplies) deficĕre; to — over (details) percurrĕre; (of fluids) superfluĕre; to — short deficĕre; to — through (to dissipate) dissipare; **to — together** concurrĕre; **to — up** accurrĕre; **to — up against** incurrĕre in (with acc)

runaway s transfuga m

runner s cursor m

running s curs·us -ūs m; (flowing) flux·us -ūs m

rupture s hernia f; seditio, dissensio f

rupture vt rumpĕre, abrumpĕre; vi rumpi

rural adj agrestis, rusticus

ruse s dolus m, fraus f

rush s (plant) juncus m; (charge) impet·us -ūs m

rush vt rapĕre; vi ruĕre, ferri; **to — forward** prorumpĕre, se proripĕre;

to — in inruĕre, incurrĕre; **to — out** erumpĕre, evolare

russet adj russus, rufus, ravus

rust s rubigo, aerugo f; (of iron) ferrugo f

rust vi rubiginem contrahĕre

rustic adj rusticus, agrestis

rustic s rusticus m, ruricola m & f

rustle vi crepitare, increpare

rustle s crepit·us -ūs m

rusty adj rubiginosus, aeruginosus; **to become —** rubigine obduci; (fig) desuescĕre

rut s (of wheel) orbita f

ruthless adj immisericors, inexorabilis, crudelis; **—ly** incrudeliter

rye s secale n

S

Sabbath s sabbata n pl

saber s acinaces m

sable adj pullus, ater, niger

sable s (fur) pellis zibellina f

sack s saccus m; (mil) direptio f

sack vt (mil) vastare, diripĕre

sackcloth s cilicium n

sacred adj sacer, sanctus, sacrosanctus

sacrifice s (act) sacrificium n, immolatio f; (victim) hostia, victima f; (fig) jactura f

sacrifice vt immolare, mactare, sacrificare; (fig) devovēre

sacrilege s sacrilegium n

sacrilegious adj sacrilegus

sad adj tristis, maestus, miserabilis; **—ly** maeste

sadden vt contristare, dolore afficĕre

saddle s ephippium n

saddle vt imponēre (with acc of thing and dat of person); **to — a horse** equum sternĕre

saddlebags s clitellae f pl

sadness s tristitia, maestitia f

safe adj tutus; (without hurt) incolumis; **— and sound** salvus; **—ly** tute

safe-conduct s tutela f, commeat·us -ūs m

safeguard s praesidium n, tutela f

safety s salus, incolumitas f; **in —** tuto

saffron adj croceus

sagacious adj sagax; **—ly** sagaciter

sagacity s sagacitas f

sage s (wise man) sapiens m

sage adj sapiens, prudens; **—ly** sapienter

sail s velum n; **to set —** vela dare

sail vi nave vehi, vela facĕre, navigare

sailing s navigatio f

sailor s nauta m

saint s vir sanctus m, femina sancta f

saintly adj sanctus, pius

sake s **for the — of** gratiā (with genit), causā (with genit), pro (with abl)

salad s acetaria n pl, moretum n

salamander s salamandra f

salary s salarium n, merces f

sale s venditio f; **for —** venalis; **to put up for —** venum dare

salesman s venditor m

salient adj prominens, saliens

saline adj salsus

saliva s saliva f, sputum n

sallow adj pallidus, luridus

sally s eruptio f, impet·us -ūs m

sally vi eruptionem facĕre, erumpĕre

salmon s salmo m

saloon s caupona f

salt s sal m

salt vt salire, sale condire

salting s salsura f

saltless adj insulsus

salt mine s salifodina f

salt shaker s salinum n

salt water s aqua marina f

salubrious adj salubris

salutary adj salutaris, utilis

salutation s salutatio, salus f

salute s salus, salutatio f

salute vt salutare

salvage vt servare, eripĕre

salvation s salus f

salve s unguentum n

same adj idem; **at the — time** eodem tempore, simul; **the very —** ipsissimus

sameness s identitas f

sample s exemplum, specimen n

sample vt libare

sanctify vt sanctificare, consecrare

sanctimonious adj sanctitatem affectans

sanction s comprobatio, auctoritas, confirmatio f

sanction vt ratum facĕre, sancire

sanctity s sanctitas, sanctimonia f

sanctuary s sanctuarium n; (refuge) asylum n

sand s (h)arena f

sandal s solea, crepida f

sandstone s tofus, tophus m

sandy adj (h)arenosus, sabulosus, (h)arenaceus; (in color) rufus

sane *adj* sanus

sanguinary *adj* sanguinarius, cruentus

sanguine *adj* sanguineus, alacer

sanitary *adj* salubris

sanity *s* sanitas, mens sana *f*

sap *s* sucus *m*

sap *vt* subruěre, haurire

sapling *s* surculus *m*

Sapphic *adj* Sapphicus

sapphire *s* sapphirus *f*

sarcasm *s* dicacitas *f*

sarcastic *adj* acerbus, mordax; —ally acerbe, amare

sarcophagus *s* sarcophagus *m*

sardine *s* sarda *f*

sardonic *adj* amarus

sash *s* cingillum *n*, zona *f*

Satan *s* Satanas, Satan *m*

satchel *s* sacculus *m*, pera *f*

satellite *s* satelles *m* & *f*

satiate *vt* satiare, saturare

satire *s* satura *f*

satirical *adj* acerbus, satiricus

satirist *s* derisor, saturarum scriptor *m*

satirize *vt* notare, perstringěre

satisfaction *s* compensatio *f*; *(feeling)* voluptas *f*

satisfactorily *adv* ex sententia (meā, tuā, *etc.*)

satisfactory *adj* idoneus, jucundus, gratus

satisfied *adj* contentus

satisfy *vt* satisfacěre *(with dat)*; *(to indemnify)* compensare; *(desires)* explēre

satrap *s* satrapes *m*

saturate *vt* saturare, imbuěre

satyr *s* satyrus *m*

sauce *s* condimentum *n*; *(of meat)* eliquamen *n*

saucer *s* patella, scutella *f*

saucily *adv* petulanter

saucy *adj* petulans, procax, protervus

saunter *vi* vagari, ambulari

sausage *s* farcimen *n*

savage *adj* ferus, efferatus; *(cruel)* saevus, atrox, immanis; —ly crudeliter, immaniter

save *vt* servare, conservare; *(from danger)* liberare, eripěre; **to — up** reservare

save *prep* praeter *(with acc)*

saving *s* conservatio *f*; —s peculium *n*

savior *s* servator, liberator *m*

Saviour *s* Salvator (mundi) *m*

savor *s* sapor, gust·us -ūs *m*

savor *vi* sapěre

savory *adj* sapidus

saw *s* *(tool)* serra *f*; *(saying)* proverbium *n*

saw *vt* serrā secare; *vi* serram ducěre

sawdust *s* scobis *f*

say *vt* dicěre; **that is to —** scilicet; **to — that . . . not** negare

saying *s* dictum, proverbium *n*

scab *s* crusta *f*

scabbard *s* vagina *f*

scaffold *s* tabulatum *n*, fala *f*

scald *vt* urěre

scale *s* *(of fish)* squama *f*; *(for weighing)* libra, trutina *f*; *(mus)* diagramma *n*; *(gradation)* grad·us -ūs *m*

scale *vt* *(fish)* desquamare; **to — a wall** murum per scalas ascenděre

scallop *s* pecten *m*

scalp *s* pericranium *n*

scaly *adj* squamosus, squameus

scamp *s* furcifer *m*

scamper *vi* cursare; **to — about** discurrěre, cursitare; **to — away** aufugěre

scan *vt* examinare, explorare; *(verses)* scanděre

scandal *s* ignominia *f*, opprobrium *n*

scandalize *vt* offenděre

scandalous *adj* probrosus, flagitiosus

scantily *adv* exigue, anguste

scanty *adj* tenuis, exiguus, exilis

scapegoat *s* piaculum *n*

scar *s* cicatrix *f*

scarce *adj* rarus; —ly vix, aegre

scarcity *s* paucitas, inopia *f*

scare *vt* terrēre, territare

scarecrow *s* terriculum *n*

scarf *s* fascia *f*, focale *n*

scarlet *s* coccum *n*

scarlet *adj* coccinus, coccineus

scathing *adj* acerbus, aculeatus

scatter *vt* spargěre, dispergěre, dissipare; *vi* dilabi, diffugěre

scavenger *s* cloacarius *m*

scene *s* prospect·us -ūs *m*, spectaculum *n*; *(on stage)* scaena *f*; *(place)* locus *m*

scenery *s* *(in theater)* scaenae apparat·us -ūs *m*; *(of nature)* species regionis *f*

scent *s* *(sense)* odorat·us -ūs *m*; *(of dogs)* sagacitas *f*; *(fragrance)* odor *m*

scent *vt* odorari

scented *adj* odoratus

scepter *s* sceptrum *n*

sceptic *s* scepticus *m*

sceptical *adj* dubitans, incredulus

schedule *s* ratio *f*

scheme *s* consilium *n*

scheme *vt* & *vi* moliri, machinari

schism *s* schisma, discidium *n*

scholar *s* litteratus *m*

scholarly *adj* litteratus, doctus

scholarship *s* litterae *f pl*, eruditio *f*

scholastic *adj* scholasticus

scholiast *s* scholiastes, interpres *m*

school *s* ludus *m*, schola *f*; *(group holding like opinions)* secta *f*

schoolboy *s* discipulus *m*

schoolmaster *s* magister *m*

schoolroom *s* schola *f*

science *s* scientia, doctrina, disciplina, ars *f*

scientific *adj* physicus; —ally physice; *(systematically)* ratione

scientist *s* physicus *m*

scimitar *s* acinaces *m*

scion *s* edit·us -ūs *m*, progenies *f*

scissors *s* forfex *f*

scoff *s* irrisio, derisio, cavillatio *f*

scoff *vi* cavillari; **to — at** irridēre, deridēre

scoffer *s* derisor, irrisor *m*

scold *vt* objurgare, increpare; *vi* desaevire

scolding *s* objurgatio *f*

scoop *s* trulla *f*

scoop *vt to* — **out** excavare

scope *s* campus *m*, spatium *n*

scorch *vt* adurĕre, torrēre

score *s* nota *f*; (*total*) summa *f*; (*twenty*) viginti; (*reckoning*) ratio *f*

score *vt* notare

scorn *s* contemptio *f*

scorn *vt* contemnĕre, spernĕre, aspernari

scornful *adj* fastidiosus; —**ly** fastidiose, contemptim

scorpion *s* scorpio, scorpius *m*

Soot *adj* Scoticus

Scotchman *s* Scotus *m*

Scotland *s* Scotia *f*

Scottish *adj* Scoticus

scoundrel *s* nebulo, furcifer *m*

scour *vt* (*to rub clean*) (de)tergēre; (*to range over*) pervagari, percurrĕre

scourge *s* flagellum *n*; (*fig*) pestis *f*

scourge *vt* verberare

scourging *s* verberatio *f*, verbera *n pl*

scout *s* explorator, speculator *m*

scout *vt* speculari, explorare

scowl *vi* frontem contrahĕre

scowlingly *adv* fronte contractā

scramble *vi to* — **up** scandĕre, escendĕre

scrap *s* fragmentum, frustum *n*

scrape *vt* radĕre, scabĕre; *to* — *together* corradĕre

scrape *s* difficultas *f*; (*quarrel*) rixa *f*

scraper *s* radula *f*

scraping *s* rasura *f*; —**s** ramenta *n pl*

scratch *s* levis incisura *f*

scratch *vt* radĕre, scalpĕre

scrawl *s* scriptio mala *f*

scrawl *vt & vi* male scribĕre

scream *s* ululat·us -ūs, clamor *m*; (*of an infant*) vagit·us -ūs *m*

scream *vi* ululare, clamitare

screech *s* stridor *m*

screech *vi* stridēre

screen *s* umbraculum *n*, obex *m*

screen *vt* protegĕre

screw *s* cochlea *f*

screw *vt* torquēre

scribble *vt & vi* scriptitare

scribe *s* scriba *m*

script *s* scriptum *n*; (*hand*) man·us -ūs *f*

scrofulous *adj* strumosus

scroll *s* volumen *n*, schedula *f*

scrub *vt* defricare, detergēre

scruple *s* scrupulus *m*, religio, dubitatio *f*

scrupulous *adj* religiosus, anxius; —**ly** religiose

scrutinize *vt* scrutari, perscrutari

scrutiny *s* scrutatio, perscrutatio *f*

scud *vi* celeriter aufugĕre

scuffle *s* rixa *f*

scuffle *vi* rixari

sculptor *s* sculptor, scalptor *m*

sculpture *s* (*art*) sculptura *f*; (*work*) opus, signum *n*

sculpture *vt* sculpĕre

scum *s* spuma *f*; (*fig*) sentina *f*

scurrilous *adj* scurrilis

scurvy *s* scorbutus *m*

scutcheon *s* scutum *n*

scythe *s* falx *f*

sea *s* mare, aequor *n*, pontus *m*

sea captain *s* navarchus *m*

seacoast *s* ora maritima *f*

seafaring *adj* maritimus, nauticus

sea gull *s* larus *m*

seal *s* sigillum, signum *n*; (*animal*) phoca *f*

seal *vt* signare; (*fig*) sancire; *to* — **up** obsignare

seam *s* sutura *f*

seaman *s* nauta *m*

seamanship *s* nauticarum rerum us·us -ūs *m*, ars navigandi *f*

sear *vt* adurĕre

search *s* investigatio, scrutatio *f*

search *vt* investigare, explorare; (*a person*) excutĕre; *vi to* — **for** quaerĕre, exquirĕre; *to* — **out** explorare

seasick *adj* nauseabundus; *to be* — nauseare

season *s* tempestas *f*, anni tempus *n*; (*proper time*) opportunitas *f*, tempus *n*; *in* — tempestive

season *vt* condire; (*fig*) assuefacĕre, durare

seasonable *adj* tempestivus, opportunus

seasoning *s* condimentum *n*

seat *s* sedes, sella *f*; (*dwelling*) sedes *f*, domicilium *n*

seat *vt* sede locare; *to* — **oneself** considĕre

seaweed *s* alga *f*

secede *vi* secedĕre

secession *s* secessio *f*

seclude *vt* secludĕre, removēre, abdĕre

secluded *adj* remotus, solitarius

seclusion *s* solitudo *f*, locus remotus *m*

second *adj* secundus, alter; **a** — **time** iterum; —**ly** deinde, tum

second *s* (*person*) adjutor *m*; (*of time*) punctum temporis *n*

second *vt* adesse (*with dat*), favēre (*with dat*), adjuvare

secondary *adj* secundarius, inferior

secondhand *adj* alienus, tritus

second-rate *adj* inferior

secrecy *s* secretum *n*; (*keeping secret*) silentium *n*

secret *adj* secretus, occultus, arcanus; *to keep* — celare; —**ly** clam

secret *s* secretum *n*, res arcana *f*; *in* — clam

secretary *s* scriba, amanuensis *m*

secrete *vt* celare, occultare, abdĕre

secretion *s* secretio *f*

sect *s* secta *f*

section *s* pars, sectio *f*

sector *s* sector *m*, regio *f*

secular *adj* profanus

secure *adj* tutus; —**ly** tuto

secure *vt* confirmare, munire; (*to obtain*) parare, nancisci; (*to fasten*) religare

security s salus, incolumitas f;
(*pledge*) satisdatio f, pignus n
sedan s lectica f
sedate adj gravis, sedatus; —**ly** graviter, sedate
sedentary adj sedentarius
sedge s ulva, carex f
sediment s sedimentum n, faex f
sedition s seditio, rebellio f
seditious adj seditiosus, turbulentus;
—**ly** seditiose
seduce vt seducěre, corrumpěre, depravare
seducer s corruptor m
seduction s corruptela f
seductive adj blandus; —**ly** blande
see vt & vi viděre, cerněre, conspicěre; (*to understand*) viděre, intellegěre, sentire; **to go to** — viśěre;
to — **to** curare
seed s semen n; (*offspring*) progenies
f; (*of fruit*) acinum n
seedling s surculus m
seek vt quaerěre, petěre; **to** — **to**
conari (*with inf*), laborare (*with inf*)
seem vi viděri
seeming adj speciosus; —**ly** in speciem, ut videtur
seemly adj decens, decorus
seep vi manare
seer s vates m
seethe vi fervěre, aestuare
segment s segmentum n
segregate vt segregare, secerněre
segregation s separatio f
seize vt prehenděre, arripěre, rapěre;
(*mil*) occupare; (*fig*) afficěre
seizure s comprehensio, occupatio f
seldom adv raro
select vt seligěre, eligěre, deligěre
select adj electus, lectus, exquisitus
selection s (*act*) selectio f; (*things
chosen*) electa n pl
self-confident adj sibi fidens, confidens
self-conscious adj pudibundus
self-control s continentia, temperantia f
self-denial s abstinentia f
self-evident adj manifestus
self-indulgent adj intemperans
selfish adj avarus
selfishness s avaritia f
self-respect s pudor m
sell vt venděre; vi venire
seller s venditor m
semblance s species, similitudo f
semicircle s hemicyclium n
semicircular adj semicirculus
senate s senat·us -ūs m; (*building*)
curia f
senator s senator m
senatorial adj senatorius
send vt mittěre; (*on public business*)
legare; **to** — **away** dimittěre; **to**
— **for** arcessěre; **to** — **forward**
praemittěre
senile adj senilis, aetate provectus
senior adj natu major
seniority s aetatis praerogativa f
sensation s sens·us -ūs m; (*fig*) mirum n
sense s (*faculty; meaning*) sens·us

-ūs m; (*understanding*) prudentia f;
(*meaning*) vis, significatio f
sense vt sentire
senseless adj absurdus, ineptus;
(*unconscious*) omni sensu carens
sensible adj sapiens, prudens
sensibly adv prudenter, sapienter
sensitive adj sensilis, patibilis;
(*touchy*) mollis
sensual adj voluptarius, libidinosus;
—**ly** libidinose
sensualist s homo voluptarius m
sensuality s libido f
sentence s (*gram*) sententia f; (*law*)
judicium n; **to pass** — judicare
sentence vt damnare, condemnare
sententious adj sententiosus; —**ly**
sententiose
sentiment s (*opinion*) sententia,
opinio f; (*feeling*) sens·us -ūs m
sentimental adj mollis, effeminatus
sentimentality s mollities animi f
sentinel s custos, vigil m
sentry s custos, vigil m; **sentries**
excubiae, stationes, vigiliae f pl
separable adj separabilis
separate adj separatus, disjunctus;
—**ly** separatim
separate vt separare, disjungěre, dividěre; vi separari, disjungi
separation s separatio, disjunctio f
September s (*mensis*) September m
sepulcher s sepulcrum n
sepulchral adj sepulcralis
sequel s exit·us -ūs m
sequence s ordo m, series f
seraph s seraphus m
serenade vt occentare
serene adj serenus, tranquillus; —**ly**
serene
serenity s serenitas, tranquillitas f
serf s servus m
serfdom s servitium n, servitus f
sergeant s optio m
series s series f, ordo m
serious adj serius, gravis; —**ly** serio
seriousness s gravitas f, serium n
sermon s oratio sacra f
serpent s serpens f, anguis m & f
servant s famulus m, famula f, servus m, serva f; (*public servant*)
minister m
serve vt servire (*with dat*); (*food*) ap-
poněre; (*to be useful to*) prodesse
(*with dat*); **to** — **a sentence** poenam subire; vi (*mil*) merěre, militare; (*to suffice*) sufficěre
service s (*favor*) officium n; (*mil*)
militia f, stipendia n pl; (*work*)
ministerium n; **to be of** — **to**
prodesse (*with dat*), bene merěri de
(*with abl*)
serviceable adj utilis
servile adj servilis, humilis
servility s humilitas f, animus abjectus m
servitude s servitus f
session s sessio f, convent·us -ūs m
set vt poněre, sistěre, collocare;
(*course*) dirigěre; (*example*) dare;
(*limit*) imponěre; (*sail*) dare; (*table*)
instruěre; **to** — **apart** secerněre,
seponěre; **to** — **aside** poněre; (*fig*)

rescindĕre; **to — down** deponĕre; *(in writing)* perscribĕre; **to — forth** exponĕre; **to — free** liberare; **to — in motion** ciēre; **to — in order** componĕre; **to — off** *(to adorn)* adornare; **to — on fire** incendĕre, accendĕre; **to — someone over** aliquem praeficĕre *(with dat)*; **to — up** statuĕre; *vi (of stars, etc.)* occidĕre; **to — in** *(to begin)* incipĕre; **to — out** proficisci

set *adj (fixed)* certus, praescriptus

set *s* congeries *f*

setting *s* occas·us -ūs *m*

settle *vt* statuĕre; *(business)* transigĕre; *(colony)* deducĕre; *(argument)* componĕre; *(debts)* solvĕre, expedire; *vi (to take up residence)* considĕre; *(to sink)* subsidĕre

settlement *s* constitutio *f*; *(agreement)* pactum *n*; *(colony)* colonia *f*; *(of liquids)* sedimentum *n*

settler *s* colonus *m*

seven *adj* septem; **— times** septies

sevenfold *adj* septemplex

seventeen *adj* septemdecim, decem et septem

seventeenth *adj* septimus decimus

seventh *adj* septimus; **the — time** septimum

seventieth *adj* septuagesimus

seventy *adj* septuaginta

sever *vt* separare; *vi* disjungi

several *adj* aliquot, complures; **—ly** singulatim

severe *adj* severus, gravis, durus; *(of weather)* asper; **—ly** severe, graviter

severity *s* severitas, gravitas *f*

sew *vt* suĕre; **to — up** consuĕre

sewer *s* cloaca *f*

sowing *s* sutura *f*

sex *s* sex·us -ūs *m*

sextant *s* sextans *m*

sexton *s* aedituus *m*

sexual *adj* sexualis

shabbily *adv* sordide, obsolete

shabbiness *s* sordes *f pl*

shabby *adj* sordidus, obsoletus

shackle *vt* compedibus constringĕre

shackles *s* vincula *n pl*, compedes *f pl*

shade *s* umbra *f*; **—s** *(of the dead)* manes *m pl*

shade *vt* opacare, adumbrare

shadow *s* umbra *f*

shadowy *adj* umbrosus, opacus; *(fig)* inanis, vanus

shady *adj* umbrosus, opacus

shaft *s (arrow)* sagitta *f*; *(of spear)* hastile *n*; *(of mine)* puteus *m*

shaggy *adj* hirsutus, villosus

shake *vt* quatĕre, concutĕre; *(head)* nutare; *vi* tremĕre; *(to totter)* vacillare

shaking *s* quassatio *f*; *(with cold, fear, etc.)* tremor, horror *m*

shaky *adj* instabilis

shallow *adj* brevis, vadosus; *(fig)* insulsus, levis

sham *s* dolus *m*, simulatio, species *f*

sham *adj* fictus, simulatus

shambles *s* laniena *f*, laniarium *n*

shame *s* pudor *m*; *(disgrace)* dedecus *n*, infamia, ignominia *f*

shame *vt* ruborem incutĕre *(with dat)*

shamefaced *adj* pudens, verecundus

shameful *adj* probrosus, turpis; **—ly** probrose, turpiter

shameless *adj* impudens; **—ly** impudenter

shamrock *s* trifolium *n*

shank *s* crus *n*

shanty *s* tugurium *n*

shape *s* forma, figura, facies *f*

shape *vt* formare, fingĕre

shapeless *adj* informis, deformis

shapely *adj* formosus

share *s* pars, portio *f*; *(of plow)* vomer *m*

share *vt* partire, impertire; particeps esse *(with genit)*

shark *s* p(r)istix *m*

sharp acutus; *(bitter)* acer, acerbus; *(keen)* acutus, acer, sagax; **—ly** acriter, acute; *(bitterly)* acerbe

sharpen *vt* acuĕre

shatter *vt* quassare, confringĕre; *(fig)* frangĕre

shave *vt* radĕre

shavings *s* ramenta *n pl*

shawl *s* amiculum *n*

she *pron* ea, illa, haec

sheaf *s* manipulus, fascis *m*

shear *vt* tondĕre

shearing *s* tonsura *f*

shears *s* forfices *f pl*

sheath *s* vagina *f*

sheathe *vt* in vaginam recondĕre

shed *vt* fundĕre, effundĕre

shed *s* tugurium *n*; *(mil)* vinea *f*

sheep *s* ovis *f*

sheepfold *s* ovile *n*

sheephook *s* pedum, baculum pastorale *n*

sheepish *adj* pudibundus; **—ly** pudenter

sheepskin *s* pellis ovilla *f*

sheer *adj* merus

sheet *s* linteum *n*; *(of paper)* plagula, scheda *f*; *(of metal)* lamina *f*

shelf *s* pluteus *m*, tabula *f*, pegma *n*

shell *s* concha, crusta *f*; *(husk)* folliculus *m*; *(of nuts, etc.)* putamen *n*

shell *vt* decorticare

shellfish *s* concha *f*

shelter *s* tegmen *n*; *(refuge)* refugium *n*; *(lodgings)* hospitium *n*

shelter *vt* tegĕre, defendĕre; *(refugee)* excipĕre

shepherd *s* pastor, opilio, pecorum custos *m*

shield *s* scutum *n*, parma *f*

shield *vt* tegĕre, protegĕre

shield bearer *s* scutigerulus, armiger *m*

shift *vt* mutare, amovĕre; *vi (as the wind)* vertĕre; *(to change position)* se movēre, mutari

shift *s (change)* mutatio *f*

shifty *adj* varius, mobilis

shin *s* tibia *f*, crus *n*

shine *s* nitor *m*

shine *vi* lucēre, fulgēre, nitēre; **to — forth** elucēre, enitēre, exsplen-

descēre; **to — on** or **upon** affulgēre (with dat)
shiny adj lucidus, fulgidus, nitidus
ship s navis f, navigium n
ship vt navi invehēre
shipbuilder s naupegus m
shipbuilding s architectura navalis f
shipmaster s navicularius m
shipwreck s naufragium n; **to suffer —** naufragium facēre
shipwrecked adj naufragus
shirk vt defugēre, detrectare
shirt s subucla, camisia f
shiver vi contremiscēre, horrēre
shoal s caterva f, grex m; (shallow) brevia n pl
shock vt percutēre, percellēre; (fig) offendēre
shock s concussio f, impet·us -ūs m; (fig) offensio f
shocking adj flagitiosus, atrox
shoe s calceus m
shoemaker s sutor m
shoot vt (missile) conjicēre, jaculari; (person) transfigēre; vi volare
shoot s surculus m
shooting star s fax caelestis f
shop s taberna, officina f
shopkeeper s tabernarius m
shore s litus n, ora f
short adj brevis; **to run — deficēre; —ly** brevi, mox
shortage s inopia f
shortcoming s defect·us -ūs m, delictum n
shorten vt coarctare, contrahēre; vi contrahi, minui
shorthand s notae breviores f pl
shortness s brevitas, exiguitas f; **— of breath** asthma n
short-sighted adj myops; (fig) improvidus, imprudens
short-winded adj anhelus
shot s ict·us -ūs m; (reach, range) jact·us -ūs m
should vi debēre; **I — go** mihi eundum est
shoulder s (h)umerus m; (of animal) armus m
shoulder vt suscipēre
shout s clamor m, acclamatio f
shout vt & vi clamare, acclamare, vociferari
shove vt trudēre, pulsare
shovel s pala f, rutrum n
shovel vt palā tollēre
show vt monstrare; (to display) exhibēre; (to teach) docēre; **to — off** ostendēre; vi **to — off** se jactare
show s (appearance) species f; (display) ostentatio f; (pretense) simulatio f; (entertainment) spectaculum n
shower s imber m
shower vt fundēre, effundēre
showy adj speciosus
shred s segmentum panni n; (scrap) frustum n
shrew s mulier jurgiosa f
shrewd adj acutus, astutus, callidus, sagax; **—ly** acute, callide, sagaciter
shrewdness s calliditas, astutia, sagacitas f

shriek s ululat·us -ūs m, ejulatio f
shriek vi ululare, ejulare
shrill adj peracutus, stridulus
shrimp s cancer pagurus m; (person) pumilio, homulus m
shrine s fanum, delubrum n
shrink vt contrahēre; vi contrahi; (to withdraw) refugēre; **to — from** abhorrēre ab (with abl), refugēre ab (with abl)
shrivel vt corrugare, torrefacēre; vi corrugari, torrescēre
shroud s integumentum n; (of ship) rudentes m pl
shroud vt involvēre, obducēre
shrub s frutex m
shrubbery s fruticetum n
shrug s (h)umerorum allevatio f
shrug vt **to — the shoulders** (h)umeros contrahēre or allevare
shudder vi horrēre; **to — at** horrēre
shuffle vt miscēre; vi claudicare
shun vt vitare, devitare, fugēre
shut vt claudēre, occludēre; **to — out** excludēre; **to — up** concludēre; vi **to — up** conticescēre
shutter s claustrum n, foricula f
shy adj timidus, pudibundus; **—ly** timide
shyness s timiditas, verecundia f
sibyl s sibylla f
sick adj (mentally or physically) aeger; (physically) aegrotus; **I am — of me** taedet (with genit), fastidio; **to be —** aegrotare
sicken vt fastidium movēre (with dat); vi in morbum incidēre, nauseare
sickle s falx f
sickly adj infirmus
sickness s morbus m, aegrotatio f
side s latus n; (direction) pars f; (district) regio f; (faction) partes f pl; (kinship) genus n; **of a — of a** latere (with genit); **on all —s** undique; **on both —s** utrimque; **on one —** unā ex parte; **on that —** illinc; **on the mother's —** materno genere; **on this — hinc; on this — of** cis (with acc), citra (with acc); **to be on the — of** stare ab (with abl), sentire cum (with abl)
side adj lateralis, obliquus
side vi **to — with** partes sequi (with genit), stare ab (with abl), sentire cum (with abl)
sideboard s abacus m
sidelong adj obliquus, transversus
sideways adv in obliquum, oblique
siege s obsessio, oppugnatio, obsidio f; **to lay — to** obsidēre
siesta s meridiatio f; **to take a — meridiare**
sieve s cribrum n; (little sieve) cribellum n
sift vt cribrare; (fig) scrutari
sigh s suspirium n
sigh vi suspirare; **to — for** desiderare
sight s (sense) vis·us -ūs m; (act of seeing) aspect·us -ūs m; (range) conspect·us -ūs m; (appearance) species f; (show) spectaculum n; **at**

first — primo aspectu; **to catch** — **of** conspicĕre; **to lose** — **of** e conspectu amittĕre

sight *vt* conspicari

sightless *adj* caecus

sightly *adj* decorus, decens

sign *s* signum, indicium *n*; (*mark*) nota *f*; (*distinction*) insigne *n*; omen, portentum *n*

sign *vt* (*e.g., a document*) subscribĕre, signare, consignare

signal *vi* signum dare; (*by a nod*) annuĕre

signal *s* signum *n*; (*mil*) classicum *n*

signal *adj* insignis, egregius

signature *s* signatura *f*, nomen *n*

signer *s* signator *m*

signet *s* sigillum *n*

significance *s* (*meaning*) significatio, vis *f*, sens·us -ūs *m*; (*importance*) momentum *n*

significant *adj* gravis, magnus, magni momenti (*genit*)

signify *vt* significare, portendĕre

silence *s* silentium *n*

silence *interj* tace!; (*to more than one person*) tacete!

silence *vt* comprimĕre; (*by argument*) refutare

silent *adj* tacitus, taciturnus; **to become** — conticescĕre; **to be** — tacēre; **—ly** tacite

silk *s* sericum *n*, bombyx *m & f*

silk *adj* sericus, bombycinus

silkworm *s* bombyx *m & f*

sill *s* limen inferum *n*

silly *adj* stultus, ineptus

silver *s* argentum *n*

silver *adj* argenteus

silversmith *s* faber argentarius *m*

silvery *adj* argenteus; (*of hair*) canus

similar *adj* similis; **—ly** similiter, pariter

similarity *s* similitudo *f*

simile *s* translatio, similitudo *f*

simmer *vi* lente fervēre

simper *vi* inepte ridēre

simple *adj* simplex; (*easy*) facilis; (*frank*) sincerus; (*silly*) stultus

simpleton *s* stultus, ineptus *m*

simplicity *s* simplicitas *f*

simplify *vt* faciliorem reddĕre

simply *adv* simpliciter; solum, tantummodo

simulate *vt* simulare

simulation *s* simulatio *f*

simultaneous *adj* eodem tempore; **—ly** simul, unā, eodem tempore

sin *s* peccatum, delictum *n*

sin *vi* peccare

since *prep* ex (*with abl*), ab (*with abl*), post (*with acc*); **ever** — usque ab (*with abl*)

since *adv* abhinc; **long** — jamdudum, jampridem

since *conj* (*temporal*) ex quo tempore, postquam, cum; (*causal*) quod, quia, quoniam, cum

sincere *adj* sincerus, candidus; **—ly** sincere, vere

sinew *s* nervus, lacertus *m*

sinewy *adj* nervosus, lacertosus

sinful *adj* impius, pravus; **—ly** impie, improbe

sing *vt & vi* canĕre, cantare

singe *vt* adurĕre, amburĕre

singer *s* cantator *m*, cantatrix *f*

singing *s* cant·us -ūs *m*

single *adj* solus, unicus, unus, singularis; (*unmarried*) caelebs; **not a** — **one** ne unus quidem

single *vt* **to** — **out** eligĕre

singly *adv* singulatim, viritim

singsong *s* canticum *n*

singsong *adj* canorus

singular *adj* unicus, singularis; (*outstanding*) egregius, eximius; **—ly** singulariter, unice, egregie

sinister *adj* infaustus, malevolus, iniquus

sink *vt* submergĕre, demergĕre, deprimĕre; (*money*) collocare; *vi* considĕre, subsidĕre; (*in water*) mergi; (*of morale, etc.*) cadĕre

sink *s* sentina *f*

sinless *adj* peccati expers

sinner *s* peccator *m*, peccatrix *f*

sinuous *adj* sinuosus

sip *vt* libare, sorbillare, degustare

siphon *s* sipho *m*

sir *s* (*title*) eques *m*

sir *interj* (*to a master*) ere!; (*to an equal*) bone vir!, vir clarissime!

sire *s* genitor *m*

siren *s* siren *f*

sister *s* soror *f*

sister-in-law *s* glos *f*

sisterly *adj* sororius

sit *vi* sedēre; **to** — **beside** assidēre (*with dat*); **to** — **down** considĕre; **to** — **on** insidēre (*with dat*); **to** — **up** (*to be awake at night*) vigilare

site *s* sit·us -ūs *m*

situated *adj* situs, positus

situation *s* sit·us -ūs *m*; (*circumstances*) res, conditio *f*

six *adj* sex; **— times** sexies

sixfold *adj* sextuplus

sixteen *adj* sedecim

sixteenth *adj* sextus decimus

sixth *s* sexta pars *f*

sixtieth *adj* sexagesimus

sixty *adj* sexaginta

size *s* magnitudo, mensura *f*

skein *s* glomus *n*

skeleton *s* sceletos *m*, ossa *n pl*

sketch *s* adumbratio, lineatio *f*

sketch *vt* adumbrare, delineare; (*fig*) describĕre

skiff *s* scapha *f*

skilful *adj* dexter, peritus, scitus; (*with hands*) habilis; **—ly** perite, scite

skill *s* sollertia, calliditas, peritia *f*

skilled *adj* peritus, doctus

skillet *s* cucumella *f*

skim *vt* despumare; (*fig*) percurrĕre, stringĕre

skin *s* (*of men*) cutis *f*; (*of animals*) pellis *f*; (*prepared*) corium *n*

skin *vt* pellem exuĕre (*with abl*)

skinny *adj* macilentus

skip *vt* praeterire; *vi* subsultare; **to** — **over** transilire

skirmish *s* concursatio, velitatio *f*

skirmish *vi* velitari

skirmisher s veles m

skirt s instita f; (*border*) fimbria f

skirt vt tangĕre, legĕre

skull s cranium, caput n

sky s caelum n, aether m; **under the open —** sub divo

slab s tabula, tessera f

slack adj remissus, laxus; (*fig*) piger, neglegens

slacken vt remittĕre, laxare, minuĕre; vi minui, remitti

slag s scoria f

slain adj occisus

slake vt exstinguĕre, sedare

slander s calumnia, obtrectatio f

slander vt obtrectare (*with dat*), calumniari

slanderer s obtrectator m

slanderous adj calumniosus, maledicus

slang s vulgaria verba n pl

slant vt acclinare; (*fig*) detorquĕre

slanting adj obliquus

slap s alapa f

slap vt alapam dare (*with dat*), palmā ferire

slash s (*cut*) caesura f; (*blow*) ict·us -ūs m; (*wound*) vulnus n

slash vt caedĕre, incidĕre

slaughter s caedes, trucidatio f

slaughter vt mactare, trucidare

slaughterhouse s laniena f

slave s servus m, serva f

slave dealer s venalicius, manciporum negotiator m

slavery s servitus f, servitium n

slave trade s venalicium n

slavish adj servilis; —**ly** serviliter

slay vt interficĕre, occidĕre, necare

slayer s necator, homicida m

sledge s traha, trahea f

sleek adj levis, politus, nitidus, pinguis

sleep s somnus m

sleep vi dormire

sleepless adj insomnis, pervigil

sleepy adj somniculosus, semisomnis; (*fig*) iners

sleet s nivosa grando f

sleeve s manica f

slender adj gracilis, tenuis

slice s segmentum, frustum n, offula f

slice vt secare

slide vi labi

slight adj levis, exiguus, tenuis; —**ly** leviter, paululum

slight s neglegentia, contemptio f

slight vt neglegĕre, contemnĕre

slily adv astute, callide, vafre

slim adj gracilis

slime s limus m

slimy adj limosus, mucosus, viscosus

sling s funda f; (*for arm*) fascia f

sling vt jaculari

slink vi to — **away** furtim se subducĕre

slip s laps·us -ūs m; (*of paper*) scheda f; (*in grafting*) surculus m; (*error*) peccatum n, culpa f

slip vt (*to give furtively*) furtim dare; vi labi; to let — omittĕre; to — **away** elabi

slipper s solea, crepida f

slippery adj lubricus; (*deceitful*) subdolus

slit s incisura f

slit vt incidĕre, discidĕre

slop s vilis pot·us -ūs m

slope s declivitas f, clivus m

slope vi proclinari, vergĕre

sloping adj declivis, pronus; (*upward*) acclivis

sloppy adj lutulentus, sordidus

slot s rima f

sloth s ignavia, pigritia, inertia f

slothful adj piger, segnis, iners; —**ly** pigre, segniter, ignave

slouch vi languide incedĕre

slough s (*of snake*) exuviae f pl; (*mire*) caenum n

slovenly adj sordidus, ignavus

slow adj tardus, lentus; (*gentle*) lenis; —**ly** tarde, lente, sensim

sluggard s homo piger m

sluggish adj piger, ignavus, segnis; —**ly** pigre, segniter

sluice s cataracta f

slumber s somnus, sopor m

slumber vi obdormiscĕre, dormitare

slur s macula f

slur vt inquinare; vi to — **over** extenuare, leviter attingĕre

slut s meretrix f

sly adj astutus, vafer, callidus; **on the —** clam; —**ly** astute, callide, vafre

smack s (*flavor*) sapor m; (*blow*) alapa f

smack vt (*to strike*) ferire; vi to — **of** sapĕre

small adj parvus, exiguus, tenuis

smart adj (*clever*) sollers, callidus; (*elegant*) lautus, nitidus; (*of pace*) velox; —**ly** callide; nitide

smart s dolor m

smart vi dolĕre

smash s concussio, fractura f

smash vt confringĕre

smattering s cognitio manca, levis scientia f

smear vt illinĕre, oblinĕre

smell s (*sense*) odorat·us -ūs m; (*odor*) odor m

smell vt olfacĕre, odorari; vi olēre; to — **of** olēre, redolēre

smelly adj olidus, graveolens

smelt vt (ex)coquĕre, fundĕre

smile s ris·us -ūs m; **with a —** subridens

smile vi subridēre; to — **at** arridēre (*with dat*)

smirk vi subridēre

smite vt ferire, percutĕre

smith s faber m

smithy s ferramentorum fabrica f

smock s tunica f

smoke s fumus m

smoke vt (*to cure by smoking*) infumare; vi fumare

smoky adj fumeus, fumidus, fumosus

smooth adj levis; (*of skin*) glaber; (*polished*) teres; (*calm*) placidus; (*of talk*) blandus; —**ly** leviter; blande

smooth vt polire, limare

smother vt suffocare, opprimĕre

smudge s sordes f

smudge *vt* inquinare, conspurcare

smug *adj* lautus, nitidus, sui contentus

smuggle *vt* furtim importare, sine portorio importare

smut *s* fuligo *f*

smutty *adj* obscenus; (*blackened*) fumosus

snack *s* portio, morsiuncula *f*

snail *s* cochlea *f*, limax *m & f*

snake *s* anguis *m & f*, serpens *f*

snap *vt* (*to break*) frangĕre; **to —** **the fingers** digitis concrepare; **to** **— up** corripĕre; *vi* disilire, frangi; **to — at** mordēre

snap *s* crepit·us -ūs *m*

snare *s* laqueus *m*, pedica *f*; (*fig*) insidiae *f pl*

snare *vt* illaquĕre, irretire

snarl *vi* (*as a dog*) ringĕre, hirrire

snatch *vt* rapĕre, corripĕre; **to —** **away** eripĕre; **to — up** surripĕre

sneak *s* perfidus *m*

sneak *vi* repĕre, serpĕre, latitare

sneer *s* rhonchus *m*, irrisio *f*

sneer *vi* irridēre, deridēre

sneeringly *adv* cum irrisione

sneeze *s* sternutamentum *n*

sneeze *vi* sternuĕre

sniff *vt* odorari, naribus captare

snip *vi* amputare; **to — off** decerpĕre, praecidĕre

snivel *s* mucus *m*

snivel *vi* mucum resorbēre

snob *s* homo arrogans *m*, homo fastidiosus *m*

snobbish *adj* fastidiosus

snore *s* rhonchus *m*

snore *vi* stertĕre

snort *s* fermit·us -ūs *m*

snort *vi* fremĕre

snout *s* rostrum *n*

snow *s* nix *f*

snow *vi* ningĕre; **it is snowing** ningit

snowball *s* glebula nivis *f*

snowdrift *s* niveus agger *m*

snowstorm *s* ningor *m*

snowy *adj* niveus, nivalis; (*full of snow*) nivosus

snub *vt* reprehendĕre, neglegĕre

snub *s* repulsa *f*

snuff *vt* **to — out** exstinguĕre

snug *adj* commodus; **—ly** commode

so *adv* sic, ita, (*before adjectives*) tam; **— far** eatenus, adhuc; **— much** tantum; **— so** mediocriter; **— that** ita ut; **— that not** ne; **— then** quare, quapropter

soak *vt* madefacĕre, macerare; *vi* madēre

soap *s* sapo *m*

soar *vi* in sublime ferri; (*of birds*) subvolare

sob *s* singult·us -ūs *m*

sob *vi* singultare

sober *adj* sobrius; (*fig*) moderatus, modestus; **—ly** sobrie; moderate

sobriety *s* sobrietas *f*; (*fig*) continentia *f*

sociable *adj* sociabilis, facilis, affabilis

social *adj* socialis, civilis, communis

society *s* societas *f*; **high —** optimates *m pl*; **secret —** sodalitas *f*

sock *s* pedale *n*, udo *m*

socket *s* (*in anatomy*) cavum *n*

sod *s* caespes *m*, glaeba *f*

soda *s* (*in natural state*) nitrum *n*; (*prepared*) soda *f*

sofa *s* lectulus, grabatus *m*

soft *adj* mollis, tener; (*fig*) delicatus, effeminatus; **—ly** molliter, leniter

soften *vt* mollire, mitigare; (*fig*) lenire, placare; *vi* mollescĕre; (*of fruits*) mitescĕre; (*fig*) mansuescĕre, mitescĕre

softness *s* mollitia, teneritas, lenitas *f*; (*effeminacy*) mollities *f*

soil *s* solum *n*, terra *f*

soil *vt* inquinare, contaminare

sojourn *s* commoratio, mansio *f*

sojourn *vi* commorari

solace *s* solatium *n*

solace *vt* consolari

solar *adj* solaris; solis (*genit*)

soldier *s* miles *m*

soldierly *adj* militaris

soldiery *s* miles *m*

sole *adj* solitarius; **—ly** solum, modo, tantum

sole *s* (*of foot*) planta *f*; (*of shoe*) solea *f*; (*fish*) solea *f*

solemn *adj* sollemnis; gravis; **—ly** sollemniter; graviter

solemnity *s* sollemne *n*, sollemnitas *f*; gravitas *f*

solemnization *s* celebratio *f*

solemnize *vt* celebrare

solicit *vt* rogare, flagitare

solicitation *s* flagitatio *f*

solicitor *s* flagitator *m*; (*law*) advocatus *m*

solicitous *adj* anxius, trepidus; **—ly** anxie, trepide

solicitude *s* sollicitudo, anxietas *f*

solid *adj* solidus; purus; (*fig*) verus, firmus; **—ly** solide

soliloquize *vi* secum loqui

soliloquy *s* soliloquium *n*

solitary *adj* solitarius; (*of places*) desertus

solitude *s* solitudo *f*

solstice *s* solstitium *n*

soluble *adj* dissolubilis

solution *s* dilutum *n*; (*fig*) solutio, explicatio *f*

solve *vt* solvĕre, explicare

solvency *s* facultas solvendi *f*

some *adj* aliqui; (*a certain*) quidam; nonnulli, aliquot

some *pron* aliqui; nonnulli; (*certain people*) quidam

somebody *pron* aliquis; **— or other** nescio quis

someday *adv* olim

somehow *adv* quodammodo, nescio quomodo, aliquā (*viā*)

someone *pron* aliquis; **— else** alius

something *pron* aliquid; **— else** aliud; **— or other** nescio quid

sometime *adv* aliquando

sometimes *adv* interdum, nonnumquam; **sometimes ... sometimes** modo ... modo

somewhat *adv* aliquantum; (*with comparatives*) aliquanto, paulo
somewhere *adv* alicubi; (*with motion*) aliquo; — **else** alibi; (*with motion*) alio
somnolence *s* somni cupiditas *f*
somnolent *adj* semisomnus
son *s* filius *m*
—**song** *s* cant·us -ūs *m*; (*tune*) melos *n*
son-in-law *s* gener *m*
sonorous *adj* sonorus, canorus; —**ly** sonore, canore
soon *adv* brevi tempore, mox; **as —as** simul, simulac, simulatque; **as — as possible** quamprimum; —**after** paulo post
sooner *adv* prius; (*preference*) potius; — **or later** serius ocius
soot *s* fuligo *f*
soothe *vt* permulcēre, mitigare, delenire
soothsayer *s* hariolus, sortilegus *m*
soothsaying *s* vaticinatio *f*
sooty *adj* fumosus
sop *s* offa, offula *f*
sophism *s* sophisma *n* cavillatio *f*
sophist *s* sophistes *m*
sophisticated *adj* urbanus, lepidus
sophistry *s* cavillatio captiosa *f*
soporific *adj* soporifer
sorcerer *s* magus *m*
sorceress *s* maga, saga *f*
sorcery *s* veneficium *n*
sordid *adj* sordidus, foedus; —**ly** sordide
sore *adj* (*aching*) tener; (*grievous*) atrox, durus; —**ly** graviter, vehementer
sore *s* ulcus *n*
sorrow *s* dolor, maeror, luct·us -ūs *m*
sorrow *vi* dolēre, lugēre
sorrowful *adj* luctuosus, tristis, maestus; —**ly** maeste
sorry *adj* (*pitiable*) miser; **I am — about** me paenitet (*with genit*); **I feel — for** me miseret (*with genit*), misereo (*with genit*)
sort *s* genus *n*, species *f*; **of that —** ejusmodi
sort *vt* digerēre, ordinare
sot *s* fatuus *m*; (*drunkard*) ebrius, potator *m*
sottish *adj* ebriosus
soul *s* (*principle of life*) anima *f*; (*principle of intellection and sensation*) animus *m*; (*person*) caput *n*
sound *adj* (*healthy*) validus, sanus; (*strong*) robustus; (*entire*) integer; (*in mind*) mentis compos; (*true, genuine*) verus; (*of sleep*) artus; (*valid*) ratus; —**ly** (*of beating*) vehementer, egregie; (*of sleeping*) arte
sound *s* sonus *m*; (*noise*) strepit·us -ūs, sonit·us -ūs *m*; (*of trumpet*) clangor *m*; (*strait*) fretum *n*
sound *vt* (*trumpet*) canēre; *vi* canēre, sonare; (*to seem*) vidēri
soundness *s* sanitas, integritas *f*
soup *s* jus *n*
sour *adj* acidus, acerbus; (*fig*) amarus, morosus; **to turn —** acescēre; (*fig*) coacescēre
source *s* fons *m*; (*of stream*) caput *n*;

(*fig*) origo *f*, fons *m*
South *s* meridies, auster *m*
southern *adj* australis, meridionalis
southward *adv* in meridiem, meridiem versus
south wind *s* auster, notus *m*
souvenir *s* monumentum *n*
sovereign *adj* supremus
sovereign *s* princeps, rex, regnator *m*
sovereignty *s* dominatio *f*, principat·us -ūs *m*
sow *s* sus *m* & *f*
sow *vt* serēre, seminare; (*a field*) conserēre
space *s* spatium *n*; (*of time*) intervallum *n*
spacious *adj* spatiosus, amplus
spade *s* ligo *m*, pala *f*
span *s* (*extent*) spatium *n*; (*measure*) palmus *m*
spangle *s* bractea *f*
spangle *vt* bracteis ornare
Spaniard *s* Hispanus *m*
Spanish *adj* Hispanicus, Hispaniensis
spar *s* tignum *n*
spar *vi* dimicare; (*fig*) digladiari
spare *vt* parcēre (*with dat*), parce uti (*with abl*)
spare *adj* parcus, frugalis, exilis
sparing *adj* parcus; —**ly** parce
spark *s* scintilla *f*; (*fig*) igniculus *m*
sparkle *vi* scintillare; (*as wine*) subsilire
sparkling *adj* coruscans
sparrow *s* passer *m*
Spartan *adj* Laconicus, Spartanus
spasm *s* spasmus *m*, convulsio *f*
spasmodically *adv* interdum
spatter *vt* aspergēre, inquinare
spatula *s* spatha *f*
spawn *s* ova *f* pl
spawn *vi* ova gignēre
speak *vt* & *vi* loqui, fari, dicēre; **to — of** dicēre de (*with abl*); **to — to** alloqui (*with acc*); **to — with** colloqui cum (*with abl*)
speaker *s* orator *m*
spear *s* hasta *f*
spear *vt* hastā transfigēre
special *adj* specialis, praecipuus; —**ly** specialiter, praecipue
specialty *s* proprietas *f*
species *s* species *f*, genus *n*
specific *adj* certus
specify *vt* enumerare, designare
specimen *s* specimen, exemplum *n*
specious *adj* speciosus
speck *s* macula *f*
speckle *vt* maculis variare
spectacle *s* spectaculum *n*
spectator *s* spectator *m*
specter *s* larva *f*, phantasma *n*
spectral *adj* larvalis
spectrum *s* spectrum *n*
speculate *vi* cogitare, conjecturam facēre; (*com*) foro uti
speculation *s* cogitatio, conjectura *f*; (*com*) alea *f*
speculative *adj* conjecturalis
speculator *s* contemplator *m*; (*com*) aleator *m*

speech s oratio f, sermo m; (*faculty*) lingua f

speechless adj mutus, elinguis; (*fig*) obstupefactus

speed s celeritas, velocitas f

speed vt accelerare, maturare; vi properare, festinare

speedily adv cito, celeriter

speedy adj citus, velox, celer

spell s incantamentum, carmen n

spelling s orthographia f

spelt s far n

spend vt impendĕre, consumĕre; (*to exhaust*) effundĕre; (*time*) agĕre

spendthrift s nepos, prodigus m

spew vt vomĕre

sphere s sphaera f, globus m; (*fig*) provincia f

spherical adj sphaericus, sphaeralis, globosus

sphinx s sphinx f

spice s condimentum n

spice vt condire

spicy adj conditus, aromaticus

spider s aranea f

spider web s araneum n

spigot s epistomium n

spike s clavus m

spill vt effundĕre, profundĕre

spin s (*thread*) nēre; to — round versare, circumagĕre; vi versari

spinach s spinacea oleracea f

spinal adj dorsalis

spine s spina f

spinster s innupta f

spiral adj intortus

spiral s spira, involutio f

spirit s spirit·us -ūs m, anima f; (*character*) ingenium n; (*ghost*) anima f; —s (*of the dead*) manes m pl

spirited adj animosus, alacer

spiritless adj piger, ignavus

spiritual adj animi (*genit*)

spit s veru n; (*spittle*) sputum n

spit vt & vi sputare, spuĕre

spite s livor m, malevolentia f, odium n

spite vt offendĕre

spiteful adj lividus, malevolus; —ly malevole

spittle s sputum n

splash vt aspergĕre

splash s fragor s

splendid adj splendidus; —ly splendide

splendor s splendor m

splint s ferula f

splinter s assula f

splinter vt assulatim findĕre

split s fissura f

split vt findĕre; vi findi

spoil vt spoliare; (*to mar*) corrumpĕre; (*to ruin*) perdĕre, depravare, vitiare

spoils s spolia n pl, praeda f

spoke s radius m

spokesman s orator m

spondee s spondeus m

sponge s spongia f

spongy adj spongiosus

sponsor s sponsor m

spontaneity s impuls·us -ūs m

spontaneous adj voluntarius; —ly sponte, ultro

spool s fusus m

spoon s cochleare n

spoonful s cochleare n

sport s ludus, lus·us -ūs m; (*mockery*) ludibrium n, irrisio f

sport vi ludĕre, lascivire

sportive adj jocosus; —ly jocose

sportsman s venator m

spot s macula f; (*stain*) macula, labes f; (*place*) locus m

spot vt (*to speckle*) maculis notare; (*to stain*) inquinare, maculare

spotless adj integer, purus, castus

spotted adj maculosus, maculis distinctus

spouse s conju(n)x m & f

spout s (*pipe*) canalis m; (*of jug*) os n; (*of water*) torrens m

spout vt ejaculare; (*speeches*) declamare; vi emicare

sprain vt intorquĕre, convellĕre

sprawl vi se fundĕre, prostratus jacĕre

spray s aspergo f

spray vt aspergĕre

spread vt pandĕre, distendĕre, extendĕre; diffundĕre; (*to make known*) divulgare; vi patēre; (*of news*) manare, divulgari; (*of disease*) evagari

sprig s ramusculus m, virgula f

sprightly adj alacer, vegetus

spring s (*season*) ver n; (*leap*) salt·us -ūs m; (*of water*) fons m, scaturgo f

spring adj vernus

spring vi (*to come from*) oriri, enasci; (*as rivers, etc.*) scatēre, effluĕre; (*to leap*) salire, exsilire

springtime s vernum tempus n

sprinkle vt spargĕre, aspergĕre; vi rorare

sprite s spectrum n

sprout s pullus, surculus m

sprout vi pullulare

spruce adj lautus, nitidus, comptus; —ly nitide

spur s calcar n; (*fig*) incitamentum n

spur vt calcaribus concitare; (*fig*) urgēre

spurious adj fictus, fucosus, spurius

spurn vt spernĕre, aspernari

spurt vi emicare

sputter vi balbutire

spy s explorator, speculator m

spy vt conspicĕre; vi speculari

squabble s jurgium n, rixa f

squabble vi rixari

squad s manipulus m, decuria f

squadron s (*of cavalry*) ala, turma f; (*of ships*) classis f

squalid adj squalidus, sordidus

squall s procella f

squalor s squalor m, sordes f

squander vt dissipare, effundĕre

squanderer s prodigus m

square adj quadratus; (*fig*) honestus, probus

square s quadratum n, quadra f; (*tool*) norma f

square vt quadrare; vi convenire, congruĕre

squash vt conterĕre, contundĕre

squat *vi* succumbĕre, recumbĕre, subsidĕre

squat *adj* parvus atque obesus

squeak *vi* stridĕre; (*as a mouse*) dintrire

squeak *s* stridor *m*

squeamish *adj* fastidiosus; **to feel —** fastidire

squeeze *vt* comprimĕre, premĕre; **to — out** exprimĕre

squint *vi* strabo esse

squint-eyed *adj* paetus

squire *s* armiger *m*; (*landowner*) dominus *m*

squirrel *s* sciurus *m*

squirt *vt* projicĕre; *vi* emicare

stab *s* ict·us -ūs *m*, puncta *f*

stab *vt* fodĕre, perforare

stability *s* stabilitas *f*

stabilize *vt* stabilĕre, firmare

stable *adj* stabilis, solidus

stable *s* stabulum *n*; (*for horses*) equile *n*; (*for cows, oxen*) bubile *n*

stack *s* acervus *m*, strues *f*

stack *vt* coacervare, cumulare

staff *s* baculum *n*, scipio *m*, virga *f*; (*of a magistrate*) consilium *n*; (*mil*) contubernales *m pl*

staff officer *s* contubernalis *m*

stag *s* cervus *m*

stage *s* (*in theater*) scaena *f*; (*degree*) grad·us -ūs *m*; (*on journey*) iter *n*

stagger *vt* obstupefacĕre; *vi* titubare

stagnant *adj* stagnans, torpens; (*fig*) iners

stagnate *vi* stagnare; (*fig*) refrigescĕre

stagnation *s* cessatio *f*, torpor *m*

staid *adj* gravis

stain *s* macula, labes *f*

stain *vt* maculare, contaminare; (*to dye*) tingĕre

stainless *adj* immaculatus, purus, integer

stair *s* scala *f*, grad·us -ūs *m*

staircase *s* scalae *f pl*

stake *s* palus *m*; (*wager*) depositum *n*; **to be at —** agi

stake *vt* deponĕre, appignerare

stale *adj* vetus, obsoletus; (*of bread*) secundus; (*of wine*) vapidus

stalk *s* (*of plant*) caulis, stipes *m*; (*of grain*) calamus *m*

stalk *vt* venari; *vi* incedĕre

stall *s* stabulum *n*

stall *vt* sistĕre; *vi* consistĕre

stallion *s* admissarius *m*

stamina *s* patientia *f*

stammer *vi* balbutire, linguā haesitare

stammering *adj* balbus

stammering *s* balbuties *f*

stamp *s* (*mark*) nota *f*; (*with the foot*) vestigium *n*; (*impression made*) impressio *f*

stamp *vt* imprimĕre, notare; (*money*) cudĕre; (*feet*) supplodĕre

stand *s* locus *m*, statio *f*; (*halt*) mora *f*; (*platform*) suggest·us -ūs *m*

stand *vt* (*to set upright*) statuĕre, constituĕre; (*to tolerate*) tolerare, perferre, sustinĕre; *vi* stare; **to —**

aloof abstare; **to — by** adesse (*with dat*); **to — fast** consistĕre; **to — for office** petĕre; **to — in awe of** in metu habĕre; **to — in need of** indigĕre (*with abl*); **to — on end** horrēre; **to — out** exstare, eminēre, prominēre; **to — still** consistĕre, subsistĕre

standard *adj* solitus

standard *s* (*mil*) vexillum, signum *n*; (*measure*) norma, mensura *f*

standard-bearer *s* vexillarius, signifer *m*

standing *s* stat·us -ūs, ordo *m*, conditio *f*; **of long —** vetus

standing *adj* perpetuus

standstill *s* **to be at a —** haerēre

stanza *s* tetrastichon *n*

staple *adj* praecipuus

star *s* stella *f*, sidus *n*; (*fig*) lumen *n*

starch *s* amylum *n*

starch *vt* amylare

stare *vi* obtut·us -ūs *m*, oculorum intentio *f*

stare *vi* stupēre; **to — at** intuēri

stark *adj* rigidus

stark *adv* omnino, penitus

starlight *s* siderum lumen *n*

starling *s* sturnus *m*

starry *adj* sidereus, stellatus

start *s* initium *n*; (*sudden movement*) salt·us -ūs *m*; (*of journey*) profectio *f*

start *vt* incipĕre, instituĕre; (*game*) excitare; *vi* (*to begin*) incipĕre, (*ex*)ordiri; (*to take fright*) resilire

starting gate *s* carceres *m pl*

startle *vt* terrēre, territare

starvation *s* fames *f*

starve *vt* fame interficĕre; *vi* fame confici

state *s* stat·us -ūs, locus *m*; (*pol*) civitas, respublica *f*; (*pomp*) magnificentia *f*

state *vt* declarare, dicĕre, affirmare

state *adj* publicus

stately *adj* grandis, lautus, splendidus

statement *s* affirmatio *f*, dictum *n*; testimonium *n*

statesman *s* vir reipublicae regendae peritus *m*

statesmanship *s* reipublicae regendae ars *f*

station *s* statio *f*, locus *m*

station *vt* locare, disponĕre

stationary *adj* stabilis, statarius, immotus

stationery *s* res scriptoriae *f pl*

statistics *s* cens·us -ūs *m*

statue *s* statua *f*, signum *n*

stature *s* statura *f*

statute *s* statutum, decretum *n*, lex *f*

staunch *adj* certus, firmus, fidus

staunch *vt* (*blood*) sistĕre

stave *vt* perrumpĕre; **to — off** arcēre

stay *vt* detinēre, sistĕre; (*to curb*) coercēre; *vi* manēre, commorari

stay *s* (*sojourn*) commoratio, mansio *f*; (*delay*) mora *f*; (*prop*) fulcrum *n*

steadfast *adj* constans, firmus, stabilis; **—ly** constanter

steadily *adv* constanter, firme, magis magisque

steadiness *s* stabilitas, constantia *f*

steady *adj* stabilis, firmus; (*fig*) constans, gravis

steak *s* offa, offula *f*

steal *vt* furari; *vi* furari; **to — away** se subducěre

stealing *s* furtum *n*

stealthily *adv* furtim

steam *s* vapor *m*

steam *vi* fumare

steed *s* equus bellator *m*

steel *s* chalybs *m*

steep *adj* arduus, praeceps, praeruptus

steep *vt* imbuěre, madefacěre

steeple *s* turris *f*

steepness *s* acclivitas, declivitas *f*

steer *s* juvencus *m*

steer *vt* gubernare, dirigěre

steering *s* gubernatio *f*

stem *s* stipes *m*; (*of ship*) prora *f*

stem *vt* obsistěre (*with dat*), cohibēre, reprimēre

stench *s* foetor *m*

step *s* pass·us -ūs, grad·us -ūs *m*; (*plan, measure*) ratio *f*; **flight of —s** scalae *f pl*; **— by —** gradatim, pededentim

step *vi* gradi

stepbrother *s* (*on father's side*) vitrici filius *m*; (*on mother's side*) novercae filius *m*

stepdaughter *s* privigna *f*

stepfather *s* vitricus *m*

stepmother *s* noverca *f*

stepson *s* privignus *m*

sterile *adj* sterilis

sterility *s* sterilitas *f*

sterling *adj* verus, bonus

stern *adj* durus, severus, torvus; **—ly** dure, severe, torve

stern *s* puppis *f*

sternness *s* severitas *f*

stew *s* carnes cum condimentis elixae *f pl*

stew *vt* lento igne coquěre

steward *s* procurator *m*; (*of estate*) vilicus *m*

stewardship *s* procuratio *f*

stick *s* fustis *m*; (*cane*) baculum *n*

stick *vt* affigěre; *vi* haerěre, haesitare

sticky *adj* viscosus, viscidus

stiff *adj* rigidus; (*fig*) severus, frigidus; **—ly** rigide

stiffen *vt* rigidum facěre; (*with starch*) amylare; *vi* obdurescěre

stifle *vt* suffocare; (*fig*) restinguěre

stigma *n* stigma *n*, nota *f*

stigmatize *vt* notare

still *adj* quietus, immotus, tranquillus

still *adv* (*adversative*) tamen, nihilominus; (*yet*) adhuc, etiamnum; (*with comparatives*) etiam

still *vt* pacare, sedare

stillborn *adj* abortivus

stillness *s* silentium *n*, taciturnitas *f*

stilts *s* grallae *f pl*

stimulant *s* irritamentum *n*, stimulus *m*

stimulate *vt* stimulare, excitare

stimulus *s* stimulus *m*

sting *s* aculeus *m*; (*fig*) (*of conscience*) angor *m*

sting *vt* pungěre, morděre

stinginess *s* avaritia *f*, sordes *f pl*

stingy *adj* avarus, sordidus

stink *s* foetor *m*

stink *vi* foetěre; **to — of** olēre (*with acc*)

stint *s* modus *m*

stint *vt* coercēre

stipend *s* salarium *n*, merces *f*

stipulate *vt* stipulari

stipulation *s* stipulatio, conditio, lex *f*

stir *vt* excitare; *vi* se movēre

stir *s* tumult·us -ūs *m*

stirring *adj* (*of a speech*) ardens

stitch *vt* suěre

stock *s* (*supply*) copia *f*; (*race*) stirps *f*, genus *n*; (*handle*) lignum *n*

stock *vt* instruěre; suppeditare

stockade *s* vallum *n*

stockbroker *s* argentarius *m*

stocking *s* tibiale *n*

Stoic *s* Stoicus *m*

stoical *adj* patiens, durus; **—ly** patienter

Stoicism *s* Stoica disciplina *f*

stole *s* stola *f*

stolen *adj* furtivus

stomach *s* stomachus *m*

stomach *vt* tolerare, perferre, pati

stone *s* lapis *m*, saxum *n*

stone *vt* lapidare

stonecutter *s* lapicida, lapidarius *m*

stone quarry *s* lapidicina *f*

stony *adj* (*full of stones*) lapidosus; (*of stone*) saxeus; (*fig*) durus

stool *s* scabellum *n*

stoop *vi* proclinare; (*fig*) se summittěre

stop *vt* sistěre, obturare, prohibēre; *vi* subsistěre; (*to cease*) desistěre

stop *s* mora, pausa *f*

stopgap *s* tibicen *m*

stoppage *s* obstructio *f*, impedimentum *n*

stopper *s* obturamentum *n*

store *s* (*supply*) copia *f*; (*shop*) taberna *f*

store *vt* conděre, reponěre

storehouse *s* promptuarium *n*; (*for grain*) horreum *n*; (*fig*) thesaurus *m*

stork *s* ciconia *f*

storm *s* tempestas, procella *f*

storm *vt* (*mil*) expugnare; *vi* desaevire

stormy *adj* turbidus, procellosus; (*fig*) tumultuosus

story *s* narratio, fabula *f*; (*lie*) mendacium *n*; (*of house*) tabulatum *n*

storyteller *s* narrator *m*; (*liar*) mendax *m*

stout *adj* corpulentus; (*brave*) fortis; (*strong*) firmus, validus; **—ly** fortiter

stove *s* focus, caminus *m*

stow *vt* conděre, reconděre; *vi* **to — away** in navi delitescěre

straddle *vi* varicare

straggle *vi* palari

straggler *s* palans *m*

straight *adj* rectus, directus

straight *adv* directo, rectā

straighten vt rectum facĕre; **to —
out** corrigĕre
straightforward adj apertus, simplex, directus
straightway adv statim
strain vt contendĕre; (muscle) luxare;
(to filter) percolare; vi eniti
strain s contentio f; (effort) labor m;
(mus) modus m
strained adj (style) arcessitus
strainer s colum n
strait adj angustus, artus
strait s fretum n; **—s** (fig) angustiae f pl
straiten vt contrahĕre, artare
strand s litus n; (of hair) floccus m
strand vt vadis illidĕre; vi impingi
strange adj insolitus, novus; mirus;
(foreign) peregrinus; **— to say** mi-
rabile dictu; **—ly** mirum in modum
strangeness s novitas f
stranger s advena, peregrinus m
strangle vt strangulare
strap s lorum n, strupus m
strapping adj robustus
stratagem s stratagema n; (trickery)
dolus m
strategic adj idoneus
strategy s consilium n
straw adj stramineus
straw s stramentum n; (for thatch)
stipula f
strawberry s fragum n
stray vi errare, aberrare
streak s linea f; (of character) vena f
streak vt lineis distinguĕre
stream s flumen n, amnis m
stream vi fluĕre, currĕre
streamer s vexillum n
street s via f; (narrow) vicus m
strength s robur n, vires f pl, nervi
m pl
strengthen vt roborare, confirmare;
munire
strenuous adj strenuus, sedulus;
—ly strenue
stress s (accent) ict·us -ūs m; (meaning) vis f, pondus n; (effort) labor m
stress vt exprimĕre
stretch vt tendĕre, extendĕre, distendĕre; **to — oneself** pandiculari;
to — out (hands) porrigĕre; (to
lengthen) producĕre; vi extendi, dis-
tendi; produci; patescĕre
stretch s spatium n
stretcher s lecticula f
strew vt spargĕre, sternĕre
stricken adj saucius, vulneratus
strict adj (severe) severus, rigidus;
(accurate) accuratus, exactus, diligens; **—ly** severe, diligenter; **—ly
speaking** immo
stricture s vituperatio f
stride s grad·us -ūs, pass·us -ūs m
stride vi varicare
strife s jurgium n, lis, pugna, discordia f
strike vt ferire, pulsare, percutĕre;
to — fear into incutĕre in (with
acc)
strike s cessatio operis f; (blow)
ict·us -ūs m
strikingly adv mirum in modum

string s filum n; (for bow) nervus m;
(for musical instrument) chorda f;
(fig) series f
string vt (bow) intendĕre
stringent adj severus
stringy adj fibratus
strip vt spoliare; denudare; (clothes)
exuĕre
strip s (of cloth) lacinia f; (of paper)
scheda f; (of land) spatium n
stripe s linea f; (blow) ict·us -ūs m;
(mark of blow) vibex f; (on toga)
clavus m
strive vi (e)niti, moliri, conari, laborare; **to — for** anniti, sectari
striving s contentio f, nis·us -ūs m
stroke s ict·us -ūs m, plaga f; (with
pen) pennae duct·us -ūs f; (of oar)
puls·us -ūs m
stroke vt (per)mulcēre
stroll s ambulatio f
stroll vi perambulare, spatiari
strong adj robustus, firmus, validus;
(smell) gravis; (powerful) potens;
(feeling) acer; (language) vehemens;
—ly valide, graviter, vehementer,
acriter
stronghold s arx f, castellum n
structure s structura f; (building)
aedificium n
struggle s certamen n, pugna f;
(fig) luctatio f
struggle vi contendĕre, (ob)niti, luctari
strumpet s scortum n, meretrix f
strut s incess·us -ūs m
strut vi turgēre, tumēre
stubble s stipula f
stubborn adj obstinatus, contumax,
pervicax; **—ly** obstinate, pervica-
citer
stubbornness s obstinatus animus
m, obstinatio, pertinacia f
stud s clavus m; equus admissarius m
student s discipulus m
studied adj meditatus; (style) exquisitus
studious adj studiosus discendi;
(careful) attentus
study s studium n; (room) bibliotheca f
study vt studēre (with dat); (to scrutinize) perscrutari
stuff s materia, materies f
stuff vt farcire; (with food) saginare
stuffing s (in cooking) fartum n; (in
upholstery) tomentum n
stultify vt ad irritum redigĕre
stumble vi offendĕre; **to — upon**
incidĕre in (with acc)
stumbling block s offensio f
stump s truncus, caudex m
stun vt stupefacĕre; (fig) confundĕre,
obstupefacĕre
stunted adj curtus
stupefy vt obstupefacĕre, perturbare
stupendous adj mirus, admirabilis
stupid adj stupidus, fatuus; **—ly**
stupide
stupidity s stupiditas, fatuitas f
stupor s stupor, torpor m
sturdiness s robur n, firmitas f
sturdy adj robustus, validus, firmus

sturgeon s acipenser m

stutter vi balbutire

sty s suile n, hara f

style s (literary) scribendi genus n; (rhetorical) dicendi genus n; (architectural) rit·us -ūs m; (of dress) habit·us -ūs m

style vt appellare, nominare

stylish adj speciosus, affectatus, elegans

suave adj suavis, urbanus

subdivide vt iterum dividěre

subdivision s pars f

subdue vt subjicěre, domare, vincěre

subject adj — to obnoxius (with dat), subjectus (with dat)

subject s homo subditus m; civis m; (topic) materia f, argumentum n; (matter) res f; (gram) subjectum n

subject vt subjicěre, subigěre

subjection s servitus f; patientia f

subjective adj proprius

subjugate vt subigěre, domare

subjunctive s subjunctivus modus m

sublime adj sublimis, excelsus; —ly excelse

sublimity s elatio, sublimitas f

submerge vt demergěre, inundare; vi se demergěre

submission s obsequium, servitium n, reverentia f

submissive adj summissus, obsequiosus; —ly summisse

submit vt (e.g., a proposal) referre; vi se deděre; to — to obtemperare (with dat)

subordinate vt subjicěre, supponěre

subordinate adj secundus, subjectus, inferior

suborn vt subornare

subscribe vt (to contribute) conferre; vi to — to assentiri (with dat)

subscriber s subscriptor m

subscription s collatio f

subsequent adj sequens, posterior, serior; —ly postea, deinde

subserve vt subvenire (with dat)

subservient adj obsequiosus

subside vi desiděre; (of wind) caděre; (of passion) defervescěre

subsidiary adj secundus

subsidy s subsidium n, collatio f, vectigal n

subsist vi subsistěre

subsistence s vict·us -ūs m

substance s substantia f; res f; (gist) summa f; (wealth) opes f pl

substantial adj solidus, firmus; (real) verus; (rich) opulentus; (important) magnus; —ly magnā ex parte, re

substantiate vt confirmare

substantive s nomen, substantivum n

substitute s vicarius m

substitute vt supponěre

substitution s substitutio f

subterfuge s effugium n, praetext·us -ūs m

subterranean adj subterraneus

subtle adj subtilis, tenuis; (shrewd) acutus, vafer

subtlety s subtilitas, tenuitas f;

(cleverness) astutia f

subtract vt subtrahěre, detrahěre, deducěre

subtraction s detractio, deductio f

suburb s suburbium n

suburban adj suburbanus

subversion s eversio f

subversive adj seditiosus

subvert vt evertěre

succeed vt succeděre (with dat), insequi, excipěre; vi (of persons) rem bene gerěre; (of activities) prospere evenire, succeděre

success s success·us -ūs, bonus event·us -ūs m, res secundae f pl

successful adj fortunatus, prosper; —ly fortunate, prospere

succession s successio f; (series) series f

successive adj continuus; —ly in ordine, continenter

successor s successor m

succinct adj succinctus, brevis, pressus; —ly presse

succor s subsidium, auxilium n

succor vt succurrěre (with dat), subvenire (with dat)

succulence s sucus m

succulent adj sucosus, suculentus

succumb vi succumběre

such adj talis; — . . . as talis . . . qualis

suck vt sugěre; to — in sorběre; to — up exsorběre, ebiběre; vi ubera ducěre

suckle vt nutricari

suction s suct·us -ūs m

sudden adj subitus, repentinus, inexpectatus; —ly subito, repente

sue vt litem intenděre (with dat); vi to — for orare, rogare, petěre

suffer vt pati, tolerare, sustiněre; vi dolěre, affici

sufferable adj tolerabilis, tolerandus

suffering s dolor m

suffice vi sufficěre, satis esse

sufficient adj satis (with genit); —ly satis

suffocate vt suffocare

suffocation s suffocatio f

suffrage s suffragium n

suffuse vt suffunděre

suffusion s suffusio f

sugar s saccharum n

sugar vt saccharo condire

sugar cane s arundo sacchari f

suggest vt suggerěre, subjicěre, admonēre

suggestion s suggestio, admonitio f

suicide s suicidium n; to commit — sibi mortem consciscěre

suit s lis, causa f; (clothes) vestit·us -ūs m

suit vt accommodare; convenire (with dat), congruěre (with dat)

suitable adj aptus, idoneus, congruus

suite s comitat·us -ūs m; (apartment) conclave n

suitor s procus m

sulfur s sulfur n

sulk vi aegre ferre

sulky adj morosus

sullen *adj* torvus, tetricus, morosus; **—ly** morose
sully *vt* inquinare, contaminare
sultry *adj* aestuosus, torridus
sum *s* summa *f*
sum *vt* **to — up** computare; (*to summarize*) summatim describĕre, breviter repetĕre
summarily *adj* breviter, summatim
summarize *vt* summatim describĕre
summary *adj* subitus, brevis
summary *s* epitome *f*, summarium *n*
summer *adj* aestivus
summer *s* aestas *f*
summit *s* culmen *n*; (*fig*) fastigium *n*
summon *vt* arcessĕre; (*a meeting*) convocare; **to — up courage** animum erigĕre, animum colligĕre
summons *s* vocatio *f*
sumptuary *adj* sumptuarius
sumptuous *adj* sumptuosus, lautus; **—ly** sumptuose
sun *s* sol *m*
sunbeam *s* radius *m*
sunburnt *adj* adustus
Sunday *s* Dominica *f*
sunder *vt* separare, sejungĕre
sundial *s* solarium *n*
sundry *adj* diversi, varii
sunlight *s* sol *m*
sunny *adj* apricus
sunrise *s* solis ort·us -ūs *m*
sunset *s* solis occas·us -ūs *m*
sunshine *s* sol *m*
sup *vi* cenare
superabundant *adj* nimius; **—ly** satis superque
superannuated *adj* emeritus
superb *adj* magnificus; **—ly** magnifice
supercilious *adj* superbus, arrogans
superficial *adj* levis; **—ly** leviter
superfluity *s* redundantia *f*
superfluous *adj* superfluus, supervacaneus
superhuman *adj* divinus, major quam humanus
superintend *vt* praeesse (*with dat*), administrare
superintendence *s* cura, curatio *f*
superintendent *s* praefectus, curator *m*
superior *adj* superior, melior; **to be — to** praestare (*with dat*)
superior *s* praepositus *m*
superiority *s* praestantia *f*
superlative *adj* eximius; (*gram*) superlativus
supernatural *adj* divinus
supernumerary *adj* ascripticius, accensus
supersede *vt* succedĕre (*with dat*)
superstition *s* superstitio *f*
superstitious *adj* superstitiosus
supervise *vt* procurare
supervision *s* cura, curatio *f*
supine *adj* supinus; **—ly** supine
supper *s* cena *f*; **after —** cenatus
supple *adj* flexibilis, flexilis
supplement *s* supplementum *n*, appendix *f*
supplement *vt* amplificare
suppliant *s* supplex *m & f*
supplicate *vt* supplicare
supplication *s* supplicatio, obsecratio *f*
supply *s* copia *f*; **supplies** (*mil*) commeat·us -ūs *m*
supply *vt* praebēre, suppeditare
support *s* (*prop*) fulcrum *n*; (*help*) subsidium *n*; (*maintenance*) alimentum *n*
support *vt* (*to hold up*) fulcire, sustinēre; (*to help*) adjuvare; (*to maintain*) alĕre
supportable *adj* tolerabilis
supporter *s* adjutor, fautor *m*
suppose *vt* opinari, putare, credĕre
supposition *s* opinio *f*
supremacy *s* dominat·us -ūs, principat·us -ūs *m*, imperium *n*
supreme *adj* supremus, summus; **—ly** unice, maxime
sure *adj* certus; (*faithful*) fidus; (*safe*) tutus; **—ly** certe, scilicet, profecto
surety *s* vas *n*; (*person*) sponsor *m*
surf *s* aest·us -ūs *m*
surface *s* superficies *f*; **the — of the sea** summum mare *n*
surfeit *s* satietas *f*; (*fig*) taedium *n*
surfeit *vt* saturare; (*fig*) satiare
surge *s* fluct·us -ūs, aest·us -ūs *m*
surge *vi* tumescĕre, surgĕre; **to — forward** proruĕre
surgeon *s* chirurgus *m*
surgery *s* chirurgia *f*
surgical *adj* chirurgicus
surly *adj* morosus, difficilis
surmise *s* conjectura *f*
surmise *vt* conjicĕre, suspicari
surmount *vt* superare, vincĕre
surmountable *adj* superabilis
surname *s* cognomen *n*
surpass *vt* superare, excedĕre, antecedĕre
surplus *s* reliquum, residuum *n*
surprise *s* (ad)miratio *f*; **to take by —** deprehendĕre
surprise *vt* admirationem movēre (*with dat*); (*mil*) opprimĕre; **to be surprised at** mirari, admirari
surprising *adj* mirus, mirabilis; inexpectatus; **—ly** mire, mirabiliter
surrender *s* (*mil*) deditio *f*; (*law*) cessio *f*
surrender *vt* dedĕre, tradĕre, cedĕre; *vi* se tradĕre, se dedĕre
surreptitious *adj* furtivus, clandestinus; **—ly** furtim, clam
surround *vt* circumdare, circumvenire, cingĕre
surroundings *s* vicinia *f*
survey *s* inspectio, contemplatio *f*; (*of land*) mensura *f*
survey *vt* inspicĕre, contemplari; (*land*) permetiri
surveyor *s* agrimensor, metator *m*
survival *s* salus *f*
survive *vt* supervivĕre (*with dat*); *vi* superstes esse
survivor *s* superstes *m & f*
susceptible *adj* mollis
suspect *vt* suspicari, suspicĕre; **to be suspected of** in suspicionem

venire quasi (*with verb in subjunctive*)
suspend *vt* suspendĕre, intermittĕre, differre
suspense *s* dubitatio *f*; in — suspensus
suspension *s* suspensio, dilatio *f*
suspicion *s* suspicio *f*; to throw — on suspicionem adjungĕre ad (*with acc*)
suspicious *adj* suspicax; (*suspected*) suspectus; —ly suspiciose
sustain *vt* sustinēre, sustentare; (*hardships, etc.*) ferre
sustenance *s* vict·us -ūs *m*
swab *s* peniculus *m*
swab *vt* detergēre
swaddling clothes *s* fasciae *f pl*, incunabula *n pl*
swagger *vi* se jactare
swaggerer *s* homo gloriosus *m*
swallow *s* (*bird*) hirundo *f*
swallow *vt* vorare, sorbēre; to — up devorare, absorbēre
swamp *s* palus *f*
swamp *vt* demergĕre
swampy *adj* paludosus
swan *s* cygnus *m*
swank *adj* lautus
swarm *s* examen *n*
swarm *vi* congregari
swarthy *adj* fuscus
swathe *s* fascia *f*
sway *s* dicio, dominatio *f*, imperium *n*
sway *vt* regĕre, movēre; *vi* vacillare
swear *vt* jurare; to — in sacramento adigĕre, sacramento rogare; *vi* jurare
sweat *s* sudor *m*
sweat *vi* sudare
sweep *vt* verrēre; to — out everrēre; *vi* to — by (*to dash by*) praetervolare; to — over (*to move quickly over*) percurrēre
sweet *adj* dulcis, suavis; (*fig*) blandus, jucundus; —ly suaviter
sweeten *vt* dulcem facĕre; (*fig*) lenire, mulcēre
sweetheart *s* deliciae *f pl*, amica *f*
sweetness *s* dulcedo, suavitas *f*
sweets *s* cuppedia *n pl*
swell *s* aest·us -ūs *m*, unda *f*
swell *vt* inflare, tumefacēre; *vi* tumēre
swelling *s* tumor *m*
swelter *vi* aestu laborare

swerve *vi* aberrare, vagari
swift *adj* celer, velox; —ly celeriter, velociter
swiftness *s* celeritas, velocitas *f*
swim *vi* natare, nare
swimmer *s* natator *m*
swimming *s* natatio *f*; (*of head*) vertigo *f*
swimming pool *s* piscina *f*
swindle *vt* fraudare, circumvenire
swindle *s* fraus *f*
swindler *s* fraudator *m*
swine *s* sus *m & f*
swineherd *s* suarius *m*
swing *s* oscillatio *f*
swing *vt* librare; *vi* oscillare
switch *s* (*stick*) virga, virgula *f*; (*change*) commutatio *f*
switch *vt* (*to flog*) flagellare; (*to change*) (com)mutare
swoon *vi* intermori, collabi
swoop *s* impet·us -ūs *m*
swoop *vi* incurrĕre; to — down on involare in (*with acc*)
sword *s* gladius, ensis *m*, ferrum *n*; with fire and — ferro ignique
sycamore *s* sycomorus *f*
sycophant *s* sycophanta, assentator *m*
syllable *s* syllaba *f*
syllogism *s* syllogismus *m*, ratiocinatio *f*
symbol *s* signum, symbolum *n*
symbolical *adj* symbolicus; —ly symbolice
symmetrical *adj* congruens, concinnus
symmetry *s* symmetria, concinnitas *f*
sympathetic *adj* concors, misericors
sympathize *vi* consentire; to — with miserēri (*with genit*)
sympathy *s* consens·us -ūs *m*, misericordia, concordia *f*
symphony *s* symphonia *f*, concent·us -ūs *m*
symptom *s* indicium, signum *n*
synagogue *s* synagoga *f*
syndicate *s* societas *f*
synonym *s* verbum idem declarans *n*
synonymous *adj* idem declarans, idem valens
synopsis *s* breviarium *n*, epitome *f*
syntax *s* syntaxis *f*
system *s* ratio, disciplina *f*
systematic *adj* ordinatus; —ally ratione, ordine

T

tab *vt* designare, notare
tabernacle *s* tabernaculum *n*
table *s* mensa *f*; (*list*) index *m*, tabula *f*
tablecloth *s* mantele *n*
table napkin *s* mappa *f*
tablet *s* tabula, tabella *f*, album *n*
tacit *adj* tacitus; —ly tacite
taciturn *adj* taciturnus

tack *s* clavulus *m*
tack *vt* to — on assuĕre, affigĕre; *vi* (*of ships*) reciprocari
tact *s* judicium *n*, dexteritas *f*
tactful *adj* prudens, dexter; —ly prudenter, dextere
tactician *s* rei militaris peritus *m*
tactics *s* res militaris, belli ratio *f*
tadpole *s* ranunculus *m*

tag s appendicula f
tail s cauda f
tailor s vestitor, textor m
taint s contagio f, vitium n
taint vt inficĕre, contaminare; (fig) corrumpĕre
take — vt capĕre, sumĕre, accipĕre; to — away demĕre, auferre, adimĕre; to — down (in writing) exscribĕre; to — for habēre pro (with abl); to — hold of prehendĕre; — in (e.g., a guest) recipĕre; (through deception) decipĕre; to — in hand suscipĕre; to — off exuĕre; to — out eximĕre; (from storage) promĕre; to — up suscipĕre; to — upon oneself sibi sumĕre; vi to — after similis esse (with genit or dat); to — off (to depart) abire; to — to amare, diligĕre
tale s fabula, narratio f
talent s talentum n; (fig) ingenium n
talented adj ingeniosus
talk s sermo m, colloquium n; idle — nugae f pl
talk vi loqui; to — with colloqui cum (with abl)
talkative adj loquax, garrulus
talker s (idle) gerro m
tall adj altus, celsus, procerus
tallow s sebum n
tally s tessera f
tally vi convenire
talon s unguis m
tambourine s tympanum n
tame adj cicur, mansuetus, domitus; —ly mansuete, leniter
tame vt domare, mansuefacĕre
tamer s domitor m
tamper vi to — with (persons) sollicitare; (writings) depravare
tan vt (by sun) adurĕre; (hides) perficĕre
tangible adj tractabilis
tangle s implicatio f, nodus m
tangle vt implicare
tank s lac·us -ūs m
tankard s cantharus m
tantalize vt vexare
tantamount adj par
tap s levis ict·us -ūs m
tap vt leviter ferire; (wine, etc.) relinĕre
tape s taenia f
taper s cereus m
taper vt fastigare; vi fastigari
tapestry s aulaeum, tapete n
taproom s taberna f
tar s pix f
tardily adv tarde, lente
tardiness s tarditas, segnitia f
tardy adj tardus, lentus
target s scopus m
tariff s portorium n
tarnish vt infuscare; vi infuscari
tarry vi commorari, cunctari
tart adj acerbus, amarus
tart s scriblita f, crustulum n
task s pensum, opus n; **to take to** — objurgare
taste s (sense) gustat·us -ūs m; (flavor) sapor m; (fig) judicium n
taste vt (de)gustare; vi sapĕre

tasteful adj elegans; —ly eleganter
tasteless adj insipidus; (fig) insulsus, inelegans; —ly insulse
tasty adj sapidus, dulcis
tattered adj pannosus
tatters s panni m pl
taunt s convicium n
taunt vt exprobrare
taut adj intentus
tavern s taberna, caupona f
tavern keeper s caupo m
tawdry adj fucatus, vilis
tawny adj fulvus
tax s vectigal, tributum n
tax vt vectigal imponĕre (with dat)
taxable adj vectigalis, stipendiarius
taxation s vectigalia n pl
tax collector s exactor m
teach vt docēre, instituĕre, erudire
teachable adj docilis
teacher s magister, praeceptor m; (of primary school) litterator m; (of secondary school) grammaticus m; (of rhetoric) rhetor m
teaching s institutio, eruditio f
team s jugales m pl; (of animals) jugum n
tear s lacrima f, flet·us -ūs m; (a rent) scissura f
tear vt scindĕre; to — apart discindĕre; to — in pieces dilacerare, dilaniare; to — off abscindĕre; to — open rescindĕre; to — out evellĕre; to — up convellĕre
tease vt vexare, ludĕre
teat s mamma f
technical adj (term) proprius; technicus, artificialis
technique s ars f
technology s officinarum artes f pl
tedious adj molestus; —ly moleste
tedium s taedium n
teem vi scatēre, redundare
teethe vi dentire
teething s dentitio f
tell vt narrare, memorare, referre; (to order) imperare (with dat), jubēre; — me the truth dic mihi verum
teller s numerator m
temerity s temeritas f
temper s temperatio f, animus m, ingenium n; (bad) iracundia f
temper vt temperare; (fig) lenire
temperament s animus m
temperance s temperantia f
temperate adj temperatus, moderatus, sobrius; —ly temperanter, sobrie
temperature s calor m, caloris grad·us -ūs m
tempest s tempestas f
tempestuous adj turbulentus, procellosus
temple s templum n, aedes f; (of forehead) tempus n
temporal adj humanus; profanus
temporarily adv ad tempus
temporary adj brevis
temporize vi tergiversari
tempt vt temptare, illicĕre
temptation s illecebra f
ten adj decem; — times decies

tenable *adj* defensibilis, stabilis
tenacious *adj* tenax, pertinax; —**ly** tenaciter, pertinaciter
tenacity *s* tenacitas, pertinacia *f*
tenancy *s* conductio *f*
tenant *s* conductor, colonus, incola *m*
tend *vt* curare; *vi* tendĕre, spectare
tendency *s* inclinatio *f*
tender *adj* tener, mollis; —**ly** tenere, indulgenter
tender *vt* offerre
tenderness *s* mollitia *f*; (*affection*) indulgentia *f*
tendon *s* nervus *m*
tendril *s* (*of vine*) pampinus *m*; (*of plants*) claviculus *m*
tenement *s* conductum *n*
tenement house *s* insula *f*
tenet *s* dogma *n*
tenfold *adj* decemplex, decuplus
tennis *s* **to play —** pilā ludĕre
tennis court *s* sphaeristerium *n*
tenor *s* tenor, sens·us -ūs *m*
tense *adj* intentus, attentus
tense *s* tempus *n*
tension *s* intentio *f*
tent *s* tentorium, tabernaculum *n*
tentative *adj* tentans
tenth *adj* decimus
tenth *s* decima pars *f*
tenuous *adj* tenuis, rarus
tenure *s* possessio *f*
tepid *adj* tepidus
term *s* (*word*) verbum *n*; (*limit*) terminus *m*; (*condition*) condicio, lex *f*
terminate *vt* terminare, finire; *vi* terminari, desinĕre; (*of words*) cadĕre
termination *s* terminatio *f*, finis, exit·us -ūs *m*
terrace *s* ambulatio *f*
terrestrial *adj* terrestris, terrenus
terrible *adj* terribilis
terribly *adv* horrendum in modum
terrific *adj* terrificus, terrens, formidabilis
terrify *vt* terrēre, perterrēre
territory *s* regio *f*, ager *m*, fines *m pl*
terror *s* terror *m*, formido *f*
terse *adj* brevis, pressus; —**ly** presse
test *s* probatio *f*, experimentum *n*
test *vt* probare, experiri
testament *s* testamentum *n*
testamentary *adj* testamentarius
testator *s* testator *m*
testify *vt* testificari, testari
testimonial *s* laudatio *f*
testimony *s* testimonium *n*
testy *adj* stomachosus, obstinatus, morosus
tether *s* retinaculum *n*
tether *vt* religare
text *s* verba *n pl*
textbook *s* enchiridion *n*
textile *adj* textilis
texture *s* textura *f*
than *adv* quam; atque, ac
thank *vt* gratias agĕre (*with dat*)
thankful *adj* gratus; —**ly** grate
thankless *adj* ingratus; —**ly** ingrate
thanks *s* gratiae, grates *f pl*
thanks *interj* gratias!
thanksgiving *s* grates *f pl*, gratula-

tio *f*; (*public act*) supplicatio *f*
that *adj* ille, is, iste
that *pron demonstrative* ille, is, iste; *pron rel* qui
that *conj* (*purpose, result, command*) ut; (*after verbs of fearing*) ne
thatch *s* stramentum *n*
thatch *vt* stramento tegĕre
thaw *vt* (dis)solvĕre; *vi* tabescĕre
the *article, not expressed in Latin*
the *adv* (*with comparatives*) **the . . . the** quo . . . eo
theater *s* theatrum *n*
theatrical *adj* scenicus, theatralis
thee *pron* te; **of —** de te; **to —** tibi; **with —** tecum
theft *s* furtum *n*
their *adj* illorum, eorum, istorum; **— own** suus
them *pron* eos, illos, istos; **to —** eis, illis, istis
theme *s* thema, argumentum *n*
themselves *pron reflex* se; **to —** sibi; **with —** secum; *pron intensive* ipsi
then *adv* (*at that time*) tum, tunc; (*after that*) deinde, inde; (*therefore*) igitur, ergo; **now and —** interdum, nonnumquam
thence *adv* inde, illinc; (*therefore*) ex eo, exinde
thenceforth *adv* ex eo tempore, dehinc
theologian *s* theologus *m*
theological *adj* theologicus
theology *s* theologia *f*
theoretical *adj* contemplativus
theory *s* ratio *f*
there *adv* ibi, illic; (*thither*) illuc; **— are** sunt; **— is** est
thereabouts *adv* circa, circiter, fere
thereafter *adv* deinde, postea
thereby *adv* ea re, eo
therefore *adv* itaque, igitur, idcirco, ergo
therefrom *adv* exinde, ex eo
therein *adv* in eo, in ea re
thereupon *adv* exinde, subinde
thesis *s* thesis *f*, propositum *n*
they *pron* ii, illi, isti
thick *adj* densus, spissus; —**ly** dense
thicken *vt* densare, spissare; *vi* concrescĕre
thicket *s* dumetum, fruticetum *n*
thickness *s* crassitudo *f*
thief *s* fur *m*
thievery *s* furtum *n*
thigh *s* femur *n*
thin *adj* tenuis, exilis, rarus; (*lean*) macer; —**ly** tenuiter, rare
thin *vt* attenuare; **to — out** rarefacĕre
thine *adj* tuus
thine *pron* tuus
thing *s* res *f*; **—s** (*possessions*) bona *n pl*; (*clothes*) vestimenta *n pl*
think *vt* cogitare; (*to believe, imagine, etc.*) putare, credĕre, opinari; **to — over** in mente agitare; *vi* **to — highly of** magni habēre
thinker *s* philosophus *m*
thinking *s* cogitatio *f*
thinness *s* tenuitas, raritudo *f*; (*of person*) macies *f*

third *adj* tertius; —**ly** tertio
third *s* tertia pars *f*
thirst *s* sitis *f*
thirst *vi* sitire; **to — for** sitire
thirstily *adv* sitienter
thirsty *adj* sitiens
thirteen *adj* tredecim, decem et tres
thirteenth *adj* tertius decimus
thirtieth *adj* tricesimus
thirty *adj* triginta
this *adj* hic
thistle *s* carduus *m*
thither *adv* illuc, istuc, eo
thong *s* lorum *n*
thorn *s* spina *f*, aculeus *m*
thorny *adj* spinosus; (*fig*) nodosus
thorough *adj* germanus, perfectus; —**ly** penitus, funditus
thoroughbred *adj* generosus, genuinus
thoroughfare *s* pervium *n*, via pervia *f*
though *conj* quamquam, quamvis
thought *s* (*act and faculty*) cogitatio *f*; (*product of thinking*) cogitatum *n*
thoughtful *adj* cogitabundus; providus; —**ly** anxie, provide
thoughtless *adj* inconsultus, improvidus; —**ly** temere, inconsulte
thousand *adj* mille; **a — times** millies
thousandth *adj* millesimus
thraldom *s* servitus *f*
thrall *s* servus *m*
thrash *vt* terěre; (*fig*) verberare
thrashing *s* verbera *n pl*
thread *s* filum *n*
thread *vt* inserěre
threadbare *adj* tritus, obsoletus
threat *s* minae *f pl*, minatio *f*
threaten *vt* minari (*with dat of person*); *vi* impendēre, imminēre
three *adj* tres; **— times** ter
threefold *adj* triplex, triplus
three-legged *adj* tripes
thresh *vt* terěre
threshing floor *s* area *f*
threshold *s* limen *n*
thrice *adv* ter
thrift *s* frugalitas, parsimonia *f*
thriftily *adv* frugaliter
thrifty *adj* parcus, frugalis
thrill *s* gaudium *n*, voluptas *f*; (*of fear*) horror *m*
thrill *vt* commovēre, percellěre
thrilling *adj* mirus, mirabilis
thrive *vi* virēre, vigēre, valēre
thriving *adj* vegetus, prosperus
throat *s* jugulum, guttur *n*, fauces *f pl*
throb *s* palpitatio *f*, puls·us -ūs *m*
throb *vi* palpitare
throes *s* dolor *m*
throne *s* solium *n*; (*fig*) regia dignitas *f*
throng *s* multitudo, turba, frequentia *f*
throng *vi* **to — around** stipare
throttle *vt* strangulare
through *prep* per (*with acc*); (*on account of*) ob (*with acc*), propter (*with acc*)
through *adv* render by compound verb with trans- or per-, e.g., **to**

read — perlegěre; — and — penitus, omnino
throughout *adv* prorsus, penitus
throughout *prep* per (*with acc*)
throw *vt* jacěre, conjicěre; (*esp. weapons*) mittěre, jaculari; **to — away** abjicěre; **to — back** rejicěre; **to — down** dejicěre; **to — open** patefacěre; **to — out** ejicěre; **to — together** conjicěre in unum; *vi* **to — up** vomēre
throw *s* jact·us -ūs *m*
thrush *s* turdus *m*
thrust *s* impet·us -ūs, ict·us -ūs *m*
thrust *vt* truděre, impellěre; (*with sword*) perfodēre
thumb *s* pollex *m*
thump *s* percussio *f*
thump *vt* tunděre
thunder *s* tonit·us -ūs *m*
thunder *vi* tonare
thunderbolt *s* fulmen *n*
thunderstruck *adj* attonitus, obstupefactus
thus *adv* ita, sic; **and —** itaque
thwart *vt* obstare (*with dat*), frustrari
thy *adj* tuus
tiara *s* diadema *n*
tick *s* (*insect*) ricinus *m*; (*clicking*) levis ict·us -ūs *m*
ticket *s* tessera *f*
tickle *vt & vi* titillare
tickling *s* titillatio *f*
ticklish *adj* periculosus
tide *s* aest·us -ūs *m*
tidings *s* nuntius *m*
tie *s* vinculum *n*; (*relationship*) necessitudo *f*
tie *vt* (al)ligare; (*in a knot*) nodare, nectěre
tier *s* ordo *m*
tiger *s* tigris *m*
tight *adj* strictus, astrictus, artus; —**ly** arte
tighten *vt* astringěre, adducěre, contenděre
tile *s* tegula, imbrex *f*
till *conj* dum, donec
till *prep* usque ad (*with acc*)
till *vt* colěre
tillage *s* agricultura *f*
tiller *s* (*person*) agricola *m*; (*helm*) gubernaculum *n*
tilt *vt* proclinare
timber *s* materia *f*, lignum *n*
time *s* tempus *n*, dies *f*; (*age, period*) aetas *f*; (*leisure*) otium *n*; (*opportunity*) occasio *f*; (*interval*) intervallum, spatium *n*; (*of day*) hora *f*; **another — alias; at the same — simul; for a — parumper; for a long — diu; for some — aliquamdiu; from — to — interdum; in a short — brevi; in — ad tempus; on — tempestive; what — is it?** quota hora est?
timely *adj* tempestivus, opportunus
timepiece *s* horarium, horologium *n*
timid *adj* timidus
timidity *s* timiditas *f*
timorous *adj* pavidus
tin *s* stannum, plumbum album *n*
tin *adj* stanneus

tincture s color m
tinder s fomes m
tinge vt tingĕre, imbuĕre
tingle vi formicare, verminare
tinkle vi tinnire
tinsel s bractea, bracteola f
tip s cacumen, acumen n, apex m
tip vt praefigĕre; (to incline) invertĕre
tipple vi potare
tippler s potor m
tipsy adj ebriolus, temulentus
tiptoe adv in digitos erectus
tire vt fatigare, lassare; vi defatigari
tired adj fessus, lassus; **I am — of**
me taedet (with genit); **— out** defessus
tiresome adj laboriosus; molestus
tissue s text·us -ūs m
titanic adj ingens
tithe s decuma f
title s titulus m; (of book) inscriptio
f; (of person) appellatio, dignitas f;
(claim) jus n
title page s index m
titter s ris·us -ūs m
to prep commonly rendered by the
dative; (motion, except with names
of towns, small islands and rus) ad
(with acc), in (with acc); **— and fro**
huc illuc
toad s bufo m
toast s (bread) panis tosti offula f;
(health) propinatio f; **to drink a**
— to propinare (with dat)
toast vt torrēre; (in drinking) propinare (with dat)
today adv hodie
today s hodiernus dies m
toe s digitus m
together adv simul, unā
toil s labor m, opera f
toil vi laborare
toilsome adj laboriosus, operosus
token s signum, pignus, indicium n
tolerable adj tolerabilis; mediocris
tolerably adv tolerabiliter; mediocriter
tolerance s patientia f
tolerant adj tolerans, indulgens, patiens; **—ly** indulgenter
tolerate vt tolerare, ferre
toleration s toleratio, indulgentia,
patientia f
toll s vectigal n; (at ports) portorium n
toll collector s exactor, portitor m
tomb s sepulcrum n
tombstone s lapis, cippus m
tomorrow adv cras
tomorrow s crastinus dies m; **the**
day after — perendie
tone s sonus m, vox f; (in painting)
color m
tongs s forceps m & f
tongue s lingua f; (of shoe) ligula f;
(pole of carriage) temo m
tonsils s tonsillae f pl
too adv nimis, nimium; (also) quoque,
insuper
tool s instrumentum n; (dupe) minister m
tooth s dens m; **— and nail** totis
viribus
toothache s dentium dolor m
toothless adj edentulus

toothpick s dentiscalpium n
tooth powder s dentifricium n
top adj summus
top s vertex, apex m; (of tree) cacumen n; (of house) fastigium n; (toy)
turbo m; **the — of the mountain**
summus mons m
top vt superare
topic s res f, argumentum n
topmost adj summus
topography s regionum descriptio f
topple vt evertĕre; vi titubare
torch s fax f
torment s tormentum n, cruciat·us
-ūs m
torment vt (ex)cruciare, torquēre
tormenter s tortor m
torpid adj torpens; **to be —** torpēre
torpor s torpor m
torrent s torrens m
torrid adj torridus
tortoise s testudo f
tortoise shell s testudo f
torture s tormentum n, cruciat·us
-ūs m
torture vt torquēre, (ex)cruciare
torturer s cruciator, tortor m
toss s jact·us -ūs m
toss vt jactare; vi jactari
total adj totus, universus; **—ly** omnino, prorsus
totality s summa, universitas f
totter vi vacillare, titubare
touch vt tangĕre, attingĕre; (to stir
emotionally) movēre, commovēre,
afficĕre; vi inter se contingĕre; **to**
— on attingĕre
touch s (con)tact·us -ūs m, tactio f
touching adj mollis, flexanimus
touchstone s (fig) obrussa f
touchy adj stomachosus
tough adj durus, lentus; (fig) strenuus; difficilis
tour s (rounds) circuit·us -ūs m;
(abroad) peregrinatio f
tourist s peregrinator m
tournament s certamen n
tow s stuppa f
tow vt remulco trahĕre
toward prep versus (with acc), ad
(with acc); (of feelings) erga (with
acc), in (with acc); (of time) sub
(with acc)
towel s mantele n; sudarium n
tower s turris f
tower vi **to — over** imminēre (with
dat)
towering adj excelsus, arduus
towline s remulcum n
town s urbs f; (fortified) oppidum n
town hall s curia f
townsman s oppidanus m
toy s crepundia n pl, oblectamentum
n
trace s vestigium n; (for horse) hel-
cium n
trace vt delinēre, describĕre; indagare, investigare; **to — back** repetĕre
track s vestigium n; (path) semita f,
calles m
track vt investigare
trackless adj avius, invius

tract s (*of land*) tract·us -ūs m, regio f; (*treatise*) tract·us -ūs m

tractable adj tractabilis, docilis, obsequiosus

trade s mercatura f, commercium n; (*calling*) ars f, quaest·us -ūs m

trade vt commutare; vi negotiari, mercaturas facĕre

trader s mercator m

tradesman s opifex m

tradition s traditio, fama, memoria f, mos majorum m

traditional adj patrius, a majoribus traditus

traduce vt calumniari, infamare

traffic s commercium n; (*on street*) vehicula n pl

tragedian s (*playwright*) tragoedus, tragicus poeta m; (*actor*) tragicus actor m

tragedy s tragoedia f

tragic adj tragicus; (*fig*) tristis, miserabilis; **—ally** tragice; miserabiliter

trail vt investigare; (*to drag*) trahĕre; vi trahi, verrĕre

trail s vestigium n; (*path*) calles m

train s (*line*) series f, ordo m; (*of robe*) instita f; (*retinue*) comitat·us -ūs m; (*of army*) impedimenta n pl

train vt educare, instruĕre, assuefacĕre

trainer s lanista, aliptes m

training s disciplina, institutio f; (*practice*) exercitatio f

trait s mos m

traitor s proditor m

traitorous adj perfidus; **—ly** perfide

trammel vt impedire, vincire, irretire

tramp s vagabundus, homo vagus m; (*of feet*) puls·us -ūs m

tramp vi gradi

trample vt calcare, conculcare; vi to — on obterĕre, proterĕre, opprimĕre

trance s stupor m, ecstasis f

tranquil adj tranquillus; **—ly** tranquille

tranquility s tranquillitas f, tranquillus animus m

tranquilize vt tranquillare

transact vt transigĕre, gerĕre

transaction s negotium n, res f

transcend vt superare, vincĕre

transcendental adj sublimis, divinus

transcribe vt transcribĕre

transcription s transcriptio f

transfer s translatio f; (*of property*) alienatio f

transfer vt transferre; (*property*) abalienare

transference s translatio f

transfigure vt transfigurare

transform vt vertĕre, commutare

transformation s commutatio f

transgress vt violare, perfringĕre; vi peccare, delinquĕre

transgression s violatio f, delictum n

transgressor s violator, maleficus m

transient adj transitorius, brevis, fluxus

transition s transitio f, transit·us

-ūs m

transitive adj transitivus; **—ly** transitive

transitory adj transitorius, brevis, fluxus

translate vt vertĕre, transferre

translation s translata n pl

translator s interpres m

transmission s transmissio f

transmit vt transmittĕre

transmutation s transmutatio f

transparent adj pellucidus; (*fig*) perspicuus

transpire vi perspirare, emanare; (*to happen*) evenire

transplant vt transferre

transport vt transportare, transvehĕre

transport s vectura f; (*ship*) navigium vectorium n, navis oneraria f; (*rapture*) sublimitas f

transportation s vectura f

transpose vt transponĕre

transposition s transpositio, trajectio f

trap s laqueus m, pedica f; (*fig*) insidiae f pl; to lay a — insidiari

trap vt (*to snare*) irretire; (*fig*) inlaqueare

trappings s ornamenta n pl, apparat·us -ūs m; (*of horse*) phalerae f pl

trash s scruta n pl; (*fig*) nugae f pl

trashy adj vilis; obscenus

travel vi iter facĕre; to — abroad peregrinari

traveler s viator, peregrinator m

traverse vt transire, peragrare, lustrare

travesty s perversa imitatio f

tray s ferculum n, trulla f

treacherous adj perfidus, dolosus; **—ly** perfidiose

treachery s perfidia f

tread vt calcare; vi incedĕre

tread s grad·us -ūs, incess·us -ūs m, vestigium n

treason s perduellio, proditio f

treasonable adj perfidus, proditorius

treasure s thesaurus m

treasure vt fovēre, magni aestimare

treasurer s aerarii praefectus m

treasury s aerarium n, fiscus m

treat vt uti (*with abl*), tractare; (*patient*) curare; (*topic*) tractare; (*to entertain*) invitare

treatise s libellus m, dissertatio f

treatment s tractatio f; (*by doctor*) curatio f

treaty s foedus, pactum n; to make a — foedus icĕre

treble adj triplex, triplus; (*of sound*) acutus

treble vt triplicare

tree s arbor f

trellis s clathrus m

tremble vi tremĕre, tremiscĕre

trembling adj tremulus

trembling s trepidatio f

tremendous adj immanis, ingens, vastus; **—ly** valde, maxime

tremulous adj tremulus, vacillans

trench s fossa f

trespass *vt* violare, offendĕre; *vi* delinquĕre

trespass *s* violatio, culpa *f*

tress *s* crinis, cirrus *m*

trestle *s* fulcimentum *n*

trial *s* tentatio, experientia *f*; *(test)* probatio *f*; *(trouble)* labor *m*; *(law)* judicium *n*, quaestio *f*

triangle *s* triangulum *n*

triangular *adj* triangulus, triquetrus

tribe *s* trib·us -ūs *f*

tribulation *s* tribulatio, afflictio *f*

tribunal *s* *(raised platform)* tribunal *n*; *(court)* judicium *n*

tribune *s* tribunus *m*

tribuneship *s* tribunat·us -ūs *m*

tributary *adj* vectigalis, stipendiarius

tributary *s* amnis in alium influens *m*

tribute *s* tributum, vectigal *n*

trick *s* dolus *m*, artificium *n*, fraus, ars *f*

trick *vt* fallĕre, decipĕre

trickle *s* guttae *f pl*

trickle *vi* stillare, manare

trickster *s* veterator, fraudator *m*

trident *s* tridens *m*

triennial *adj* triennis

trifle *s* res parvi momenti *f*, nugae *f pl*

trifle *vi* nugari

trifling *adj* levis, exiguus, frivolus

trill *s* sonus modulatus *m*

trill *vt* vibrare

trim *adj* nitidus, comptus, bellus

trim *vt* adornare; *(to prune)* putare, tondēre

trinket *s* tricae *f pl*

trip *s* iter *n*

trip *vt* supplantare; *vi* titubare; *(fig)* errare

tripartite *adj* tripartitus

tripe *s* omasum *n*

triple *adj* triplex

triple *vt* triplicare

tripod *s* tripus *m*

trireme *s* triremis *f*

trite *adj* tritus

triumph *s* *(entry of victorious Roman general)* triumphus *m*; *(victory)* victoria *f*

triumph *vi* triumphare; vincĕre; to — over devincĕre

triumphal *adj* triumphalis

triumphant *adj* victor; elatus, laetus

trivial *adj* levis, tenuis

triviality *s* nugae *f pl*

troop *s* turma, caterva *f*, grex, globus *m*; —s *(mil)* copiae *f pl*

trooper *s* eques *m*

trope *s* tropus *m*

trophy *s* tropaeum *n*

tropical *adj* tropicus

tropics *s* loca fervida *n pl*

trot *vi* tolutim ire

trouble *s* labor, dolor *m*, incommodum *n*, aerumna, molestia *f*

trouble *vt* turbare, vexare, angĕre

troublesome *adj* molestus, operosus

trough *s* alveus *m*

trounce *vt* *(to punish)* castigare; *(to defeat decisively)* devincĕre

troupe *s* grex *m*

trousers *s* bracae *f pl*

trout *s* tru(c)ta *f*

trowel *s* trulla *f*

truant *s* cessator *m*

truce *s* induciae *f pl*

truck *s* carrus *m*

truculent *adj* truculentus

trudge *vi* repĕre

true *adj* verus; *(genuine)* germanus; *(faithful)* fidus; *(exact)* rectus, justus

truism *s* verbum tritum *n*

truly *adv* vere, profecto

trump *vt* to — up effingĕre, ementiri

trumpet *s* tuba, bucina *f*

trumpeter *s* tubicen, bucinator *m*

truncheon *s* fustis *m*

trundle *vt* volvĕre

trunk *s* truncus *m*; *(for luggage)* cista *f*; *(of elephant)* proboscis *f*

trust *s* fiducia, fides *f*

trust *vt* fidĕre *(with dat)*, credĕre *(with dat)*; *(to entrust)* committĕre

trustee *s* fiduciarius, tutor *m*

trusteeship *s* tutela *f*

trustful *adj* credulus

trusting *adj* fidens; —ly fidenter

trustworthiness *s* integritas, fides *f*

trustworthy *adj* fidus; *(of witness)* locuples; *(of an authority)* bonus

trusty *adj* fidus

truth *s* veritas *f*, verum *n*; in — vero

truthful *adj* verax; —ly veraciter, vere

try *vt* tentare, probare, experiri; *(law)* cognoscĕre; *(to endeavor)* laborare; to — one's patience patientiā abuti

trying *adj* molestus, incommodus, gravis

tub *s* labrum, dolium *n*

tube *s* fistula *f*

tuck *vt* to — up succingĕre

tuft *s* floccus, cirrus *m*, crista *f*

tug *s* conat·us -ūs, nis·us -ūs *m*; *(ship)* navis tractoria *f*

tug *vt* trahĕre

tuition *s* tutela *f*

tumble *vi* corruĕre, collabi, volvi

tumbler *s* poculum vitreum *n*

tumor *s* tumor, tuber *m*

tumult *s* tumult·us -ūs *m*

tumultuous *adj* tumultuosus, turbulentus; —ly tumultuose

tune *s* tonus *m*, moduli *m pl*

tuneful *adj* canorus

tunic *s* tunica *f*

tunnel *s* canalis, cuniculus *m*

turban *s* mitra, tiara *f*

turbid *adj* turbidus, turbulentus

turbulence *s* tumult·us -ūs *m*

turbulent *adj* turbulentus; —ly turbulente

turf *s* caespes *m*

turgid *adj* turgidus

turkey *s* meleagris gallopavo *f*

turmoil *s* turba, perturbatio *f*, tumult·us -ūs *m*

turn *s* *(circuit)* circuit·us -ūs *m*; *(revolution)* conversio *f*, circumact·us -ūs *m*; *(change, course)* vicissitudo *f*; *(inclination of mind)* inclinatio

f, ingenium n; **a good —** officium,
beneficium n; **in —** invicem

turn vt vertĕre, convertĕre; (to twist)
torquĕre; (to bend) flectĕre; **to —
aside** deflectĕre; **to — away** avertĕre; **to — down** (refuse) recusare,
denegare, respuĕre; **to — into** mutare in (with acc), vertĕre in (with
acc); **to — over** (to hand over)
tradĕre, transferre; (property) alienare; (in mind) agitare; **to — one's
attention** to animadvertĕre; **to —
out** ejicĕre, expellĕre; **to — round**
volvĕre, circumagĕre, rotare; **to —
up** (with hoe) invertĕre; **to — up
the nose** nares corrugare; vi verti,
converti, versari; **to — against**
disciscĕre ab (with abl), alienari ab
(with abl); **to — aside** devertĕre,
se declinare; **to — away** discedĕre,
aversari; **to — back** reverti; **to —
into** (to be changed into) vertĕre in
(with acc), mutari in (with acc); **to
— out** cadĕre, evadĕre, contingĕre,
evenire; **to — round** converti; **to
— up** intervenire, adesse

turnip s rapum n

turpitude s turpitudo f

turret s turricula f

turtle s testudo f

turtledove s turtur m

tusk s dens m

tutelage s tutela f

tutor s praeceptor, magister m

tutor vt edocēre

tweezers s volsella f

twelfth adj duodecimus

twelve adj duodecim; **— times** duodecies

twentieth adj vicesimus

twenty adj viginti; **— times** vicies

twice adv bis

twig s surculus, ramulus m, virga,
virgula f

twilight s crepusculum n; (dawn) diluculum n

twin adj geminus

twin s geminus, gemellus m

twine s filum n, resticula f

twine vt circumplicare, contorquēre;
vi circumplecti

twinge s dolor m

twinkle vi micare, coruscare

twinkling s (of eye) nict·us -ūs m

twirl vt versare, circumagēre; vi versari

twist vt torquēre; vi flecti

twit vt exprobrare, objurgare

twitch s vellicatio f

twitch vt vellicare; vi micare

twitter vi minurire

two adj duo; **— at a time** bini; **—
times** bis

twofold adj duplex, duplus

type s (model) exemplum, exemplar
n; (class) genus n, forma, figura f

typhoon s turbo m

typical adj solitus, proprius

tyrannical adj tyrannicus, superbus;
—ly tyrannice, superbe

tyrannicide s (act) tyrannicidium n;
(person) tyranni interfector, tyrannicida m

tyrannize vi dominari

tyranny s tyrannis, dominatio f

tyrant s tyrannus, dominus superbus m

tyro s tiro m

U

udder s uber n

ugliness s deformitas, foeditas f

ugly adj deformis, turpis, foedus

ulcer s ulcus n

ulcerous adj ulcerosus

ultimate adj ultimus, extremus; **—ly**
tandem

umbrage s offensio f; **to take — at**
aegre ferre

umbrella s umbella f

umpire s arbiter, disceptator m

unabashed adj intrepidus

unabated adj integer

unable adj impotens, invalidus; **to
be — to** non posse, nequire

unaccented adj accentu carens

unacceptable adj ingratus, odiosus

unaccompanied adj incomitatus, solus

unaccomplished adj infectus, imperfectus

unaccountable adj inexplicabilis,
inenodabilis

unaccountably adv praeter opinionem, sine causa

unaccustomed adj insolitus, insuetus, inexpertus

unacquainted adj **— with** ignarus
(with genit), expers (with genit)

unadorned adj inornatus, incomptus,
simplex

unadulterated adj merus, integer

unaffected adj simplex, candidus

unafraid adj impavidus

unaided adj non adjutus, sine ope

unalterable adj immutabilis

unaltered adj immutatus

unanimous adj unanimus, concors;
—ly concorditer, consensu omnium

unanswerable adj irrefragabilis

unappeased adj implacatus

unapproachable adj inaccessus

unarmed adj inermis

unasked adj injussus, non vocatus

unassailable adj inexpugnabilis

unassuming adj modestus, moderatus, demissus

unattached adj liber, vacuus

unattainable adj arduus

unattempted adj inexpertus, inausus, intentatus

unattended adj incomitatus, sine comitibus

unattractive *adj* invenustus
unauthorized *adj* illicitus
unavailing *adj* inutilis, irritus
unavenged *adj* inultus
unavoidable *adj* inevitabilis
unaware *adj* inscius, nescius, ignarus
unbearable *adj* intolerabilis
unbeaten *adj* invictus
unbecoming *adj* indecorus, indecens; **it is** — dedecet
unbefitting *adj* indecorus
unbend *vi* animum remittĕre
unbending *adj* inflexibilis, inexorabilis
unbiased *adj* incorruptus, integer
unbidden *adj* injussus, ultro
unbleached *adj* crudus
unblemished *adj* integer, intactus
unblest *adj* infortunatus
unborn *adj* nondum natus
unbroken *adj* irruptus; integer; (*of horses*) indomitus
unbuckle *vt* refibulare
unburden *vt* exonerare
unbutton *vt* refibulare
unceasing *adj* constans, assiduus; **—ly** assidue
uncertain *adj* incertus, dubius; **—ly** incerte, dubie
uncertainty *s* dubium *n*, dubitatio *f*
unchangeable *adj* immutabilis
unchanged *adj* immutatus
unchanging *adj* integer, idem
uncharitable *adj* immisericors
unchaste *adj* impudicus, obscenus; **—ly** impudice, impure
uncivil *adj* inurbanus
uncivilized *adj* incultus
unclasp *vt* defibulare
uncle *s* (*father's brother*) patruus *m*; (*mother's brother*) avunculus *m*
unclean *adj* immundus
uncomfortable *adj* incommodus, molestus
uncommon *adj* rarus, insolitus, inusitatus; **—ly** raro, praeter solitum
unconcerned *adj* securus, incuriosus
unconditional *adj* absolutus, sine exceptione; **—ly** nulla condicione
unconnected *adj* disjunctus
unconquerable *adj* invictus
unconscionable *adj* iniquus, injustus, absurdus
unconscious *adj* omni sensu carens; **— of** ignarus (*with genit*), inscius (*with genit*)
unconstitutional *adj* illicitus; **—ly** contra leges
uncontrollable *adj* impotens
unconventional *adj* insolitus
unconvinced *adj* non persuasus
unconvincing *adj* non verisimilis
uncooked *adj* rudus
uncorrupted *adj* incorruptus
uncouth *adj* inurbanus, agrestis
uncover *vt* detegĕre, recludĕre, nudare
uncritical *adj* credulus
uncultivated *adj* incultus; indoctus
uncut *adj* intonsus
undamaged *adj* integer, inviolatus
undaunted *adj* impavidus, intrepidus

undecided *adj* incertus, dubius, anceps
undefended *adj* indefensus, nudus
undefiled *adj* purus, incontaminatus
undefined *adj* infinitus
undeniable *adj* haud dubius
under *adv* subter, infra
under *prep* (*position*) sub (*with abl*); (*motion*) sub (*with acc*); (*less than*) intra (*with acc*), infra (*with acc*)
underage *adj* impubes
underestimate *vt* minoris aestimare
undergarment *s* subucula *f*
undergo *vt* subire, pati
underground *adj* subterraneus
undergrowth *s* virgulta *n pl*
underhanded *adj* clandestinus, furtivus; **—ly** clam, furtive
underline *vt* subnotare
underling *s* minister, assecla *m*
undermine *vt* subruĕre, suffodĕre; (*fig*) labefacĕre, labefactare
underneath *adv* infra, subter
underneath *prep* (*position*) infra (*with acc*), sub (*with abl*); (*motion*) sub (*with acc*)
underrate *vt* minoris aestimare
understand *vt* intellegĕre, comprehendere
understanding *adj* prudens, sapiens
understanding *s* mens *f*, intellectus *—ūs m*; (*agreement*) consensus *—ūs m*; (*condition*) condicio *f*
undertake *vt* adire ac (*with acc*), suscipĕre; (*to begin*) incipĕre
undertaker *s* vespillo, libitinarius *m*
undertaking *s* inceptum, coeptum *n*
undervalue *vt* minoris aestimare
underworld *s* inferi *m pl*
undeserved *adj* immeritus, injustus; **—ly** immerito
undeserving *adj* indignus
undiminished *adj* imminutus
undiscernible *adj* imperceptus, invisus
undisciplined *adj* immoderatus; (*mil*) inexercitatus
undisguised *adj* apertus
undismayed *adj* impavidus, intrepidus
undisputed *adj* certus
undistinguished *adj* ignobilis, inglorius
undisturbed *adj* imperturbatus, immotus
undivided *adj* indivisus
undo *vt* (*knot*) expedire; (*fig*) infectum reddĕre; (*to ruin*) perdĕre
undone (*adj*) (*not completed*) infectus, imperfectus; (*ruined*) perditus
undoubted *adj* certus, haud dubius; **—ly** haud dubie
undress *vt* exuĕre; *vi* vestes exuĕre
undressed *adj* nudus; (*fig*) rudis
undue *adj* nimius, iniquus
undulate *vi* undare, fluctuare
undulation *s* undarum agitatio *f*
unduly *adv* nimis, plus aequo
undying *adj* aeternus, sempiternus
unearth *vt* detegĕre, effodĕre
unearthly *adj* humano major, divinus
uneasiness *s* sollicitudo, anxietas *f*

uneasy adj sollicitus, anxius
uneducated adj indoctus, illiteratus
unemployed adj vacuus, otiosus
unemployment s otium n, cessatio f
unencumbered adj expeditus
unending adj infinitus, perpetuus
unendurable adj intolerandus
unenjoyable adj injucundus
unenlightened adj ineruditus
unenviable adj non invidendus, miser
unequal adj inaequalis, dispar, impar; —ly inaequaliter, impariter, inique
unequaled adj singularis, eximius
unerring adj certus; —ly certe
uneven adj inaequalis, iniquus; (rough) asper
unexpected adj inopinatus, insperatus, improvisus; —ly de improviso
unexplored adj inexploratus
unfading adj semper recens
unfailing adj certus, perpetuus; —ly semper
unfair adj iniquus; —ly inique
unfaithful adj infidus, perfidus, infidelis; —ly perfide
unfamiliar adj ignotus, alienus
unfashionable adj obsoletus
unfasten vt laxare, resolvĕre
unfavorable adj adversus, iniquus, inopportunus
unfavorably adv male, inique
unfed adj impastus
unfeeling adj durus, crudelis; —ly dure, crudeliter
unfetter vt vincula demĕre (with dat)
unfinished adj imperfectus; (crude) rudis, impolitus
unfit adj inhabilis, ineptus, inutilis
unfold vt explicare, evolvĕre; (story) enarrare; vi dehiscĕre, patescĕre
unforeseeing adj imprudens, improvidus
unforeseen adj improvisus, insperatus
unforgiving adj inexorabilis
unfortified adj immunitus, nudus
unfortunate adj infelix, infortunatus, nefastus; —ly infeliciter
unfounded adj vanus, fictus
unfriendly adj parum amicus, inimicus, alienus
unfruitful adj infructuosus, sterilis, infecundus
unfulfilled adj infectus
unfurl vt pandĕre, solvĕre
unfurnished adj imparatus
ungainly adj ineptus, inhabilis
ungenerous adj illiberalis
ungentlemanly adj inurbanus, illepidus
ungird vt discingĕre
ungodly adj impius
ungovernable adj indomabilis, intractabilis
ungracious adj iniquus, asper
ungrateful adj ingratus; —ly ingrate
ungrudging adj non invitus; —ly sine invidia
unguarded adj incustoditus, indefensus; (of words) inconsultus
unhandy adj inhabilis

unhappily adv infeliciter, misere
unhappiness s tristitia, miseria, maestitia f
unhappy adj infelix, infortunatus, miser
unharness vt disjungĕre
unhealthiness s valetudo, gravitas f
unhealthy adj infirmus, morbosus; (unwholesome) gravis, insalubris
unheard-of adj inauditus
unheeded adj neglectus
unhelpful adj invitus, difficilis
unhesitating adj promptus, confidens; —ly confidenter
unhinge vt de cardine detrahĕre; (fig) perturbare
unholy adj impius, profanus
unhoped-for adj insperatus
unhurt adj incolumis, salvus
unicorn s monoceros m
uniform adj constans, aequabilis; —ly constanter, aequabiliter
uniform s vestit·us -ūs m; (mil) sagum n
uniformity s constantia, aequabilitas f
unify vt conjungĕre
unilateral adj unilaterus
unimaginative adj hebes
unimpaired adj integer, intactus
unimpeachable adj probatissimus
unimportant adj nullius momenti (genit), levis
uninformed adj indoctus
uninhabitable adj non habitabilis, inhabitabilis
uninhabited adj desertus
uninjured adj incolumis
uninspired adj hebes
unintelligible adj obscurus
uninteresting adj frigidus, jejunus
uninterrupted adj continuus, perpetuus
uninviting adj injucundus, non alliciens
union s (act) conjunctio f; (social) consociatio, societas f; (agreement) consens·us -ūs m; (marriage) conjugium n
unique adj unicus, singularis
unison s concent·us -ūs m
unit s monas f, unio m
unite vt conjungĕre, consociare; vi coalescĕre, coire; conjurare
unity s concordia f
universal adj universus, universalis; —ly universe, ubique
universe s mundus m, summa rerum f
university s academia, universitas f
unjust adj injustus, iniquus; —ly injuste, inique
unjustifiable adj indignus
unkempt adj incomptus, neglectus
unkind adj inhumanus; —ly inhumane
unknowingly adv insciens
unknown adj ignotus, incognitus
unlawful adj illegitimus, illicitus; —ly contra legem or leges
unless conj nisi
unlike adj dissimilis, dispar, diversus
unlikely adj parum verisimilis
unlimited adj infinitus, immensus
unload vt exonerare

unluckily *adv* infeliciter

unlucky *adj* infelix, infaustus

unmanageable *adj* intractabilis, contumax

unmanly *adj* mollis

unmannerly *adj* male moratus, inurbanus

unmarried *adj* (*man*) caelebs; (*woman*) innupta

unmask *vt* detegĕre

unmatched *adj* unicus, singularis

unmerciful *adj* immisericors; **—ly** immisericorditer

unmindful *adj* immemor

unmistakable *adj* certissimus

unmistakably *adv* sine dubio

unmoved *adj* immotus

unnatural *adj* (*event*) monstruosus; (*deed*) immanis, crudelis; **—ly** contra naturam

unnecessarily *adv* ex supervacuo, nimis

unnecessary *adj* haud necessarius, supervacaneus

unnerve *vt* debilitare

unnoticed *adj* praetermissus; **to go — latēre**

unobjectionable *adj* culpae expers, honestus

unoccupied *adj* vacuus; otiosus; (*of land*) apertus

unofficial *adj* privatus

unpack *vt* e cistis eximēre

unpaid *adj* (*of money*) debitus; (*of a service*) gratuitus

unpalatable *adj* amarus, insuavis

unparalleled *adj* unicus, singularis

unpardonable *adj* inexcusabilis

unpatriotic *adj* immemor patriae

unpitying *adj* immisericors, inexorabilis

unpleasant *adj* injucundus, incommodus; **—ly** injucunde, incommode

unpolluted *adj* impollutus; (*fig*) integer, intactus

unpopular *adj* invisus, invidiosus

unpracticed *adj* inexpertus, imperitus

unprecedented *adj* novus, inauditus

unprejudiced *adj* aequus

unpremeditated *adj* subitus, ex tempore

unprepared *adj* imparatus

unprincipled *adj* improbus

unproductive *adj* infecundus, infructuosus, sterilis

unprofitable *adj* vanus, inutilis

unprofitably *adv* inutiliter, frustra

unprotected *adj* indefensus

unprovoked *adj* non lacessitus, ultro

unpunished *adj* inpunitus, inultus

unqualified *adj* haud idoneus, inhabilis

unquenchable *adj* inexstinctus

unquestionable *adj* haud dubius, certissimus

unquestionably *adv* certe

unquestioning *adj* credulus

unravel *vt* retexēre; (*fig*) enodare, explicare

unreasonable *adj* rationis expers, absurdus; iniquus

unreasonably *adv* absurde, inique

unrefined *adj* rudis, crudus, incultus

unrelenting *adj* implacabilis, inexorabilis

unremitting *adj* assiduus, continuus

unrepentant *adj* impaenitens

unrestrained *adj* effrenatus, indomitus, effusus

unrighteous *adj* injustus, iniquus; **—ly** injuste

unripe *adj* immaturus, crudus

unroll *vt* evolvēre, explicare

unruliness *s* petulantia *f*

unruly *adj* effrenatus, turbulentus

unsafe *adj* intutus, periculosus

unsatisfactory *adj* non idoneus, malus

unsavory *adj* insipidus, insulsus, insuavis

unseasonable *adj* intempestivus, immaturis; incommodus, importunus

unseemly *adj* indecorus, indecens

unseen *adj* invisus

unselfish *adj* suae utilitatis immemor, liberalis; **—ly** liberaliter

unsettle *vt* turbare, sollicitare

unsettled *adj* incertus, inconstans; (*of mind*) sollicitus

unshaken *adj* immotus

unshaved *adj* intonsus

unsheathe *vt* destringĕre, e vagina educĕre

unsightly *adj* turpis, foedus

unskilful *adj* imperitus, inscitus; **—ly** imperite, inscite

unskilled *adj* imperitus, indoctus

unsophisticated *adj* simplex

unsound *adj* infirmus; (*mentally*) insanus; (*ill-founded*) vanus

unsparing *adj* inclemens; (*lavish*) prodigus, largus; **—ly** inclementer; prodige, large

unspeakable *adj* ineffabilis, inenarrabilis

unstable *adj* instabilis; (*fig*) levis, inconstans

unstained *adj* incontaminatus, purus

unsteadily *adv* inconstanter, instabiliter

unsteady *adj* inconstans, instabilis

unsuccessful *adj* infelix, infaustus; **—ly** infeliciter

unsuitable *adj* inhabilis, incommodus, alienus

unsuited *adj* haud idoneus

unsullied *adj* incorruptus

unsuspected *adj* non suspectus

untamed *adj* indomitus, ferus

untasted *adj* ingustatus

untaught *adj* indoctus, rudis

unteachable *adj* indocilis

untenable *adj* infirmus, inanis

unthankful *adj* ingratus

untie *vt* solvēre

until *conj* dum, donec, quoad

until *prep* usque ad (*with acc*), in (*with acc*); **— now** adhuc

untimely *adj* intempestivus, importunus, immaturus

untiring *adj* assiduus, indefessus

untold *adj* innumerus

untouched *adj* intactus, integer; (*fig*) immotus

untrained *adj* inexercitatus

untried adj inexpertus, intemptatus

untrodden adj non tritus, avius

untroubled adj placidus, tranquillus; (of sleep) levis

untrue adj falsus, mendax; (disloyal) infidus

untrustworthy adj infidus

unusual adj inusitatus, insolitus, insuetus; —ly praeter solitum, raro

unutterable adj infandus, inenarrabilis

unvarnished adj (fig) nudus, simplex

unveil vt detegĕre, patefacĕre

unversed adj imperitus

unwarranted adj injustus, iniquus

unwary adj imprudens, incautus

unwearied adj indefessus, impiger

unwelcome adj ingratus, injucundus

unwholesome adj insalubris

unwieldy adj inhabilis

unwilling adj invitus; —ly invite

unwind vt revolvĕre, retexĕre

unwise adj imprudens, insipiens; —ly imprudenter, insipienter

unworthy adj indignus

unwrap vt explicare, evolvĕre

unwritten adj non scriptus

unyielding adj inflexibilis, obstinatus

unyoke vt disjungĕre

up adv sursum; — and down sursum deorsum

upbringing s educatio f

upheaval s eversio f

uphold vt servare, sustinēre, sustentare

upkeep s impensa f

uplift vt sublevare

upon prep (position) super (with abl), in (with abl); (motion) super (with acc), in (with acc); (directly after) e(x) (with abl); (dependence) e(x) (with abl)

upper adj superus, superior

uppermost adj summus, supremus

upright adj erectus; (of character) honestus, integer; —ly recte; integre

uproar s tumult·us -ūs m, turba f

uproot vt eradicare, eruĕre

upset vt evertĕre, subvertĕre, percellĕre

upset adj perculsus

upstream adv adverso flumine

up to prep usque ad (with acc), ad (with acc); tenus (postpositive, with abl or genit)

upwards adv sursum, sublime; — of (of number) plus quam

urban adj urbanus, oppidanus

urge vt urgēre, impellĕre, hortari; to — on stimulare

urge s impuls·us -ūs m

urgency s gravitas, necessitas f

urgent adj gravis, instans, vehemens; to be — instare; —ly vehementer, magnopere, graviter

urn s urna f

us pron nos; to — nobis; with — nobiscum

usage s mos m, consuetudo f

use s us·us -ūs, mos m, consuetudo, usura f; no —! frustra!; to be of — usui esse, prodesse; to make — of uti (with abl)

use vt uti (with abl); (to take advantage of) abuti (with abl); to — something for aliquid adhibēre (with dat); to — up consumĕre, exhaurire; vi I used to solebam (with inf)

used adj usitatus; — to (accustomed to) assuetus (with dat)

useful adj utilis, commodus, aptus; —ly utiliter, commode, apte

useless adj inutilis, inhabilis; (of things) inanis; —ly inutiliter, frustra

usual adj usitatus, solitus, consuetus; —ly plerumque, fere, ferme; I — go soleo ire

usurp vt usurpare, occupare

usurper s usurpator m

usury s usura f; to practice — faenerari

utensils s utensilia, vasa n pl, supellex f

utility s utilitas f

utilize vt uti (with abl), adhibēre

utmost adj extremus, ultimus, summus; to do one's — omnibus viribus contendĕre

utter adj totus, extremus, summus; —ly omnino, funditus

utter vt eloqui, proferre, pronuntiare, edĕre

utterance s elocutio, pronuntiatio f, dictum n

uttermost adj extremus, ultimus

V

vacant adj vacuus, inanis; to be — vacare

vacation s vacatio f, feriae f pl

vacillate vi vacillare

vacuum s inane n

vagabond s vagabundus, grassator m

vagrant adj vagabundus, vagus

vague adj vagus, dubius, ambiguus; —ly incerte, ambigue

vain adj vanus, futilis; superbus, arrogans; in — frustra; —ly frustra

valet s cubicularius m

valiant adj fortis; —ly fortiter

valid adj validus, legitimus, ratus; (argument) gravis

valley s vallis f

valor s fortitudo f

valuable adj pretiosus

valuation s aestimatio f

value s pretium n, aestimatio f

value vt aestimare, ducĕre; to — highly magni aestimare, magni habēre

valueless adj vilis, inutilis

vanguard s (mil) primum agmen n

vanish *vi* vanescĕre, diffugĕre
vanity *s* gloria, ostentatio *f*
vanquish *vt* vincĕre, superare
vapor *s* vapor *m*, exhalatio *f*
variable *adj* commutabilis, varius
variation *s* varietas, commutatio, vicissitudo *f*
variety *s* varietas, diversitas, multitudo *f*
various *adj* varii, diversi; —**ly** varie, diverse
vary *vt* variare, mutare; *vi* mutari
vase *s* amphora *f*, vas *n*
vast *adj* vastus, ingens, immensus; —**ly** valde
vastness *s* immensitas *f*
vault *s* fornix, camera *f*; (*leap*) saltus·us -ūs *m*
vault *vi* salire
vaunt *vt* jactare; *vi* se jactare
veal *s* caro vitulina *f*
vegetable *s* holus *n*
vegetable *adj* holitarius
vehemence *s* vehementia, vis *f*, impetus·us -ūs *m*
vehement *adj* vehemens, violentus, fervidus; —**ly** vehementer, valde
vehicle *s* vehiculum *n*
veil *s* velamen *n*, rica *f*; (*bridal*) flammeum *n*; (*fig*) integumentum *n*
veil *vt* velare, legĕre
vein *s* vena *f*
velocity *s* velocitas, celeritas *f*
velvet *s* velvetum *n*
vend *vt* vendĕre
veneer *s* ligni bractea *f*; (*fig*) species *f*
venerable *adj* venerabilis
venerate *vt* venerari, colĕre
veneration *s* adoratio *f*, cultus·us -ūs *m*
vengeance *s* ultio, poena *f*; **to take — on** vindicare in (*with acc*), ulcisci
venom *s* venenum, virus *n*
vent *s* spiramentum, foramen *n*
vent *vt* aperire; **to — one's wrath on** iram erumpere in (*with acc*)
ventilate *vt* ventilare
venture *s* ausum *n*
venture *vt* periclitari; audĕre
veracious *adj* verax
veracity *s* veracitas *f*
verb *s* verbum *n*
verbal *adj* verbalis; —**ly** verbo tenus
verbatim *adv* ad verbum
verbose *adj* verbosus; —**ly** verbose
verdict *s* sententia *f*; **to deliver a —** sententiam pronuntiare
verge *s* margo, ora *f*; **to be on the — of** non procul abesse ut
verge *vi* vergĕre
verification *s* affirmatio *f*
verify *vt* ratum facĕre, confirmare
vermin *s* bestiolae *f pl*
versatile *adj* varius, agilis, versatilis
verse *s* versus·us -ūs *m*
versed *adj* peritus, exercitatus
version *s* forma, translatio *f*
vertex *s* vertex, vortex *m*
vertical *adj* rectus, directus; —**ly** ad lineam, ad perpendiculum
very *adj* ipse
very *adv* valde, admodum
vessel *s* vas *n*; (*ship*) navigium *n*
vest *s* subucula *f*

vestal *s* virgo vestalis *f*
vestige *s* vestigium, indicium *n*
vestment *s* vestimentum *n*
veteran *s* (*mil*) veteranus, vexillarius, emeritus *m*; (*fig*) veterator *m*
veterinarian *s* veterinarius *m*
veto *s* intercessio *f*, interdictum *n*
veto *vt* interdicĕre (*with dat*); (*as tribune*) intercedĕre (*with dat*)
vex *vt* vexare, sollicitare
vexation *s* vexatio, offensio *f*, stomachus *m*
via *prep* per (*with acc*)
vial *s* phiala *f*
vibrate *vi* tremĕre, vibrare
vibration *s* tremor *m*
vicar *s* vicarius *m*
vice *s* vitium *n*, turpitudo *f*
vicinity *s* vicinitas, vicinia *f*
vicious *adj* vitiosus, perditus; (*of temper*) ferox; —**ly** ferociter
vicissitude *s* vicissitudo *f*
victim *s* victima, hostia *f*; (*exploited*) praeda *f*
victimize *vt* circumvenire
victor *s* victor *m*, victrix *f*
victorious *adj* victor; (*of woman*) victrix; **to be —** vincĕre
victory *s* victoria *f*; **to win a —** victoriam reportare
vie *vi* certare, contendĕre; **to — with** aemulari (*with dat*)
view *s* aspectus·us -ūs, conspectus·us -ūs *m*; (*from above*) despectus·us -ūs *m*; (*opinion*) opinio, sententia *f*, judicium *n*; **in my —** me judice; **to have in —** praevidēre
view *vt* visĕre, conspicĕre, intuēri, inspicĕre
vigil *s* pervigilatio *f*, pervigilium *n*
vigilance *s* vigilantia, diligentia *f*
vigilant *adj* vigilans, diligens, intentus; —**ly** vigilanter, diligenter
vigor *s* vigor, impetus·us -ūs *m*, robur *n*
vigorous *adj* strenuus, acer, vegetus; —**ly** strenue, acriter
vile *adj* vilis, abjectus, perditus, flagitiosus
vilify *vt* infamare, calumniari
villa *s* villa *f*
village *s* vicus, pagus *m*
villager *s* vicanus, paganus *m*
villain *s* scelestus, nequam (*indecl*) *m*
villany *s* scelus *n*, improbitas, nequitia *f*
vindicate *vt* vindicare; (*to justify*) purgare; (*person*) defendĕre
vindictive *adj* ultionis cupidus
vine *s* vitis *f*
vinegar *s* acetum *n*
vineyard *s* vinea *f*, vinetum *n*
violate *vt* violare
violation *s* violatio *f*
violator *s* violator *m*
violence *s* violentia, vis *f*, impetus·us -ūs *m*; (*cruelty*) saevitia *f*
violent *adj* violentus, vehemens; —**ly** violenter, vehementer
virgin *adj* virginalis
virgin *s* virgo *f*
virile *adj* virilis
virility *s* virilitas *f*
virtually *adv* fere

virtue s virtus, probitas f; (power) vis f; **by — of** per (with acc), ex (with abl)

virtuous adj probus, honestus; (chaste) castus, pudicus; **—ly** honeste, caste

virulence s vis f, virus n; (fig) acerbitas f

visage s facies f, os n

viscous adj viscosus, lentus

visible adj aspectabilis, conspicuus, manifestus; **to be —** apparēre

visibly adv manifesto

vision s (sense) vis·us -ūs m; (apparition) visum n, visio f

visionary adj vanus, fictus, inanis

visit s salutatio f

visit vt visēre, visitare

visitor s salutator m, salutatrix f; advena, hospes m

visor s buccula f

vista s prospect·us -ūs m

visual adj oculorum (genit)

vital adj vitalis; (essential) necessarius; **—ly** praecipue

vitality s vis f, animus m

vitiate vt vitiare, corrumpěre

vituperate vt vituperare, reprehendēre

vituperative adj maledicus

vivacious adj vividus, alacer, hilaris; **—ly** acriter

vivacity s alacritas f

vivid adj vividus, acer; **—ly** acriter

vivify vt animare, vivificare

vocabulary s verborum copia f

vocal adj vocalis, canorus

vocation s officium, munus n

vociferous adj clamosus

vogue s mos m; **to be in —** in honore esse

voice s vox f, sonus m; (vote) suffragium n

void s inane, vacuum n

volatile adj levis, volaticus

volcanic adj flammas eructans

volcano s mons ignivomus m

volition s voluntas f

volley s conject·us -ūs m

voluble adj volubilis

volume s (book) volumen n; (quantity) copia, multitudo f; (size) amplitudo f

voluminous adj copiosus, amplus, magnus

voluntary adj voluntarius; (unpaid) gratuitus

volunteer s voluntarius m; (mil) miles voluntarius, evocatus m

volunteer vi sponte nomen dare

voluptuous adj voluptarius, voluptuosus, delicatus

vomit vt vomēre, evomēre

voracious adj vorax; **—ly** voraciter

voracity s voracitas f

vortex s vortex m

vote s suffragium n; (fig) (judgment) sententia f

vote vi suffragium ferre, suffragium inire; (of judge) sententiam ferre; (of senator) censēre; **to — against** antiquare; **to — for** suffragari (with dat)

votive adj votivus

vouch vi spondēre; **to — for** testificari, asseverare

voucher s (person) auctor m; (document) testimonium n

vow s votum n

vow vt (to promise) (de)vovēre, spondēre, promittēre

vowel s vocalis littera f

voyage s navigatio f

voyage vi navigare

voyager s navigator m

vulgar s vulgaris, communis; (low) plebeius, vilis

vulgarity s insulsitas f

vulnerable adj obnoxius

vulture s vultur m

W

wade vi per vada ire; **to — across** vado transire

wag vt vibrare, agitare

wage vt **to — war** bellum gerēre

wager vt deponēre; vi sponsionem facēre

wages s merces f, stipendium n

wagon s carrus m, plaustrum n

wail vi plorare, plangěre, ululare

wailing s plorat·us -ūs, planct·us -ūs m

waist s medium corpus n

wait vi manēre; **to — for** exspectare; **to — on** servire (with dat)

wait s mora f; **to lie in — for** insidiari (with dat)

waive vt decedēre de (with abl), remittěre

wake vt exsuscitare, excitare; vi expergisci

wake s vestigia n pl; **in the — of** post (with acc)

wakeful adj insomnis, vigil

waken vt exsuscitare, excitare; vi expergisci

walk s (act) ambulatio f; (place) ambulacrum n, xystus m; (covered) portic·us -ūs m; (gait) incess·us -ūs m

walk vi incedēre, ambulare, gradi

wall s (of house) paries f; (of town) moenia n pl, murus m

wall vt muro cingēre, moenibus munire

wallow vi volutari

walnut s juglans f

wan adj pallidus, exsanguis

wander vi vagari, errare; **to — about** pervagari; **to — over** pererrare

wanderer s erro, vagus m

wandering s erratio f

wane vi decrescěre, minui, tabescěre

want *s* egestas, inopia, indigentia, defectio *f*

want *vt* (*to wish*) velle; (*to lack*) egēre (*with abl*), indigēre (*with abl*), carēre (*with abl*); (*to miss*) desiderare

wanting *adj* (*defective*) vitiosus; (*missing*) absens; **to be —** deficĕre, deesse

wanton *adj* protervus, lascivus, petulans; **—ly** lascive, petulanter

war *s* bellum *n*; **to declare —** bellum indicĕre; **to declare — on** bellum indicĕre (*with dat*); **to enter —** bellum suscipĕre; **to wage —** bellum gerĕre

war *vi* bellare

war cry *s* ululat·us -ūs *m*

ward *s* (*of town*) regio *f*; (*guard*) custodia *f*; (*minor*) pupillus *m*, pupilla *f*

ward *vt* **to — off** arcēre, avertēre, defendēre

warden *s* custos *m*; (*of prison*) carcerarius *m*

warehouse *s* apotheca *f*

wares *s* merx *f*

warfare *s* bellum *n*, res bellica *f*

war horse *s* equus bellator *m*

warlike *adj* militaris, bellicosus

warm *adj* calidus; (*fig*) acer; **to be —** calēre; **—ly** ardenter, acriter

warm *vt* calefacĕre, tepefacĕre

warmth *s* calor, fervor *m*

warn *vt* monēre, praemonēre

warning *s* monitio *f*, monit·us -ūs *m*; (*object lesson*) exemplum *n*

warrant *s* auctoritas *f*, mandatum *n*

warrant *vt* praestare, promittĕre

warranty *s* satisdatio *f*

warrior *s* bellator, miles *m*, bellatrix *f*

wart *s* verruca *f*

wary *adj* cautus, providus, circumspectus

wash *vt* lavare; **to — away** abulĕre, diluĕre; **to — out** eluĕre; *vi* lavari

wash *s* (*clothes*) lintea lavanda *n pl*

washing *s* lavatio *f*, lotura *f*

wasp *s* vespa *f*

waste *s* detrimentum *n*, effusio, dissipatio *f*; (*of time*) jactura *f*

waste *adj* vastus, desertus; **to lay —** vastare, (de)populari

waste *vt* consumĕre, perdĕre, dissipare; (*time*) absumĕre, terĕre; *vi* **to — away** tabescĕre, intabescĕre

wasteful *adj* profusus, prodigus; **—ly** prodige

wasteland *s* solitudo, vastitas *f*

watch *s* (*guard*) vigilia *f*; (*sentry*) excubiae *f pl*; **to keep —** excubare; **to keep — over** invigilare (*with dat*), custodire

watch *vt* (*to observe*) observare, spectare, intuēri; (*to guard*) custodire; *vi* **to — out for** exspectare

watchful *adj* vigilans; **—ly** vigilanter

watchman *s* vigil, excubitor *m*

watchtower *s* specula *f*

watchword *s* tessera *f*, signum *n*

water *s* aqua *f*

water *vt* irrigare; (*animals*) adaquare

waterfall *s* cataracta *f*

watering place *s* aquarium *n*

watery *adj* aquaticus, aquosus

wave *s* unda *f*, fluct·us -ūs *m*

wave *vt* agitare, vibrare, jactare; *vi* undare, fluctuare

waver *vi* fluctuare, labare, dubitare

wavering *adj* dubius, incertus

wavy *adj* undans, undosus; (*of hair*) crispus

wax *s* cera *f*

wax *vt* incerare; *vi* crescĕre, augēri

waxen *adj* cereus

way *s* via *f*, iter *n*; (*manner*) ratio *f*, modus *m*; (*habit*) mos *m*; **all the — from** usque ab (*with abl*); **all the — to** usque ad (*with acc*); **to get in the — of** intervenire (*with dat*); **to give —** (*of a structure*) labare; (*mil*) pedem referre; **to give — to** indulgēre (*with dat*); **to stand in the — of** obstare (*with dat*)

wayfarer *s* viator *m*

waylay *vt* insidiari (*with dat*)

wayward *adj* inconstans, levis, mutabilis

we *pron* nos; **— ourselves** nosmet ipsi

weak *adj* infirmus, debilis, imbecillus; (*argument*) tenuis; (*senses*) hebes; **—ly** infirme

weaken *vt* infirmare, debilitare, enervare; *vi* labare, hebescĕre, infirmus fieri

weakness *s* infirmitas, debilitas *f*; (*of mind*) imbecillitas *f*; (*flaw*) vitium *n*; (*of arguments*) levitas *f*

wealth *s* divitiae, opes *f pl*; copia, abundantia *f*

wealthy *adj* dives, opulentus; abundans

wean *vt* ab ubere depellĕre; (*fig*) desuefacĕre

weapon *s* telum *n*

wear *vt* (*clothes*) gerĕre; **to — out** terĕre, exedĕre; *vi* durare

weariness *s* lassitudo *f*

wearisome *adj* molestus

weary *adj* lassus, fessus, fatigatus

weather *s* caelum *n*, tempestas *f*

weather *vt* **to — a storm** procellam superare

weave *vt* texĕre

web *s* (*on loom*) tela, textura *f*; (*spider's*) araneum *n*

wed *vt* (*a woman*) ducĕre; (*a man*) nubĕre (*with dat*); *vi* (*of husband*) uxorem ducĕre; (*of bride*) nubĕre

wedge *s* cuneus *m*

wedlock *s* matrimonium *n*

weed *s* herba inutilis *f*

weed *vt* eruncare

week *s* hebdomas *f*

weekly *adj* hebdomadalis

weep *vi* flēre, lacrimare; **to — for** deplorare

weeping *s* plorat·us -ūs *m*, lacrimae *f pl*

weigh *vt* pendĕre, ponderare, trutinari; (*fig*) meditari; **to — down** degravare; (*fig*) opprimĕre; *vi* **to — much** magni ponderis esse

weight s pondus n, gravitas f; (*influence*) (*fig*) auctoritas f; (*importance*) momentum n

weighty adj ponderosus, gravis

welcome s gratulatio, salutatio f

welcome vt salvēre jubēre, excipĕre

welcome interj salvei; (*to several*) salvēte!

weld vt (con)ferruminare

welfare s salus f

well s puteus, fons m

well adj sanus, validus, salvus

well adv bene, recte, probe; **very** — optime

well interj heia!

well-bred adj generosus, liberalis

well-known adj pervulgatus; notus, nobilis

welter s congeries, turba f

west s occidens, occas·us -ūs m

western adj occidentalis

westward adv in occasum, occasum versus

west wind s Zephyrus, Favonius m

wet adj humidus, uvidus, madidus

wet vt madefacĕre, rigare

whale s balaena f, cetus m

wharf s navale n, crepido f

what pron interrog quid, quidnam, ecquid

what adj interrog qui; — **sort of** qualis

whatever pron quisquis

whatever adj quicumque

wheat s triticum n

wheedle vt blandiri, delenire

wheedling adj blandus

wheel s rota f

wheelbarrow s pabo m

whelp s catulus m

when adv quando

when conj cum, ubi, ut

whence adv unde

whenever conj quandocumque, utcumque, quoties

where adv ubi

where conj quā, ubi

whereas conj quandoquidem

whereby adv re, quā viā, quo, per quod

wherefore adv quare, quamobrem, quapropter

wherein adv in quo, in quibus, ubi

whereof adv cujus, quorum; de quo, de quibus

whereto adv quo, quorsum

whereupon adv quo facto, post quae

wherever conj quacumque, ubicumque

whet vt acuĕre; (*fig*) exacuĕre

whether conj (*in single indirect question*) num, -ne, an; **whether . . . or** (*in multiple indirect questions*) utrum . . . an, -ne . . . an, . . . an; (*in disjunctive conditions*) sive . . . sive, seu . . . seu; **whether . . . or not** utrum . . . necne

whetstone s cos f

which pron interrog quis; (*of two*) uter; pron rel qui

which adj interrog qui; (*of two*) uter; adj rel qui

whichever pron quisquis, quicum-

que; (*of two*) untercumque

while s tempus, spatium n; **a little** — paulisper; **a long** — diu; **it is worth** — operae pretium est; **once in a** — interdum

while conj dum, quoad, donec

whim s libido f

whimper vi vagire

whimper s vagit·us -ūs m

whimsical adj levis, mobilis

whine vi miserabiliter vagire

whip s flagellum n, scutica f

whip vt flagellare, verberare

whirl vt torquēre, rotare; vi torquēri, rotari

whirlpool s vertex, gurges m

whirlwind s turbo, typhon m

whisper s susurrus m

whisper s & vi susurrare

whistle s (*pipe*) fistula f; (*sound*) sibilus m; (*of wind*) stridor m

whistle vi sibilare

white adj albus; (*brilliant*) candidus; (*of hair*) canus

whiten vt dealbare, candefacĕre; vi albescĕre, canescĕre

who pron interrog quis; pron rel qui

whoever pron quicumque, quisquis

whole adj totus, cunctus, integer

whole s totum n, summa f; **on the** — plerumque

wholesome adj saluber, salutaris

wholly adv omnino, prorsus

whose pron cujus; quorum

why adv cur, quare, quamobrem

wicked adj improbus, nefarius, impius; —**ly** improbe, nefarie

wickedness s nequitia, improbitas, impietas f, scelus n

wicker adj vimineus

wide adj latus, amplus; —**ly** late

widen vt dilatare, laxare, extendĕre; vi patescĕre, dilatari, laxari

widow s vidua f

widower s viduus m

widowhood s viduitas f

width s latitudo, amplitudo f

wield vt tractare, vibrare

wife s uxor, conju(n)x f

wifely adj uxorius

wig s capillamentum n

wild adj ferus; (*of trees, plants, etc.*) silvestris; (*of land*) vastus, incultus; (*of disposition*) saevus, amens, ferox; —**ly** saeve, ferociter

wilderness s vastitas, solitudo f, loca deserta n pl

wile s fraus f, dolus m

wilful adj pervicax, consultus; —**ly** de industria

will s voluntas f, animus m; (*intent*) propositum, consilium n; (*document*) testimonium n; (*of gods*) nut·us -ūs m; **at** — ad libidinem

will vt velle; (*legacy*) legare, relinquĕre

willing adj libens, promptus; **to be** — velle; —**ly** libenter

willow s salix f

wily adj vafer, astutus

win vt adipisci, nancisci, consequi, (*victory*) reportare; (*friends*) sibi conciliare; **to — over** conciliare; vi vincĕre, superare

wind s ventus m

wind vt circumvolvĕre, circumvertĕre, glomerare, torquĕre; **to — up** (to bring to an end) concludĕre; vi sinuare

windfall s (fig) lucrum insperatum n

winding adj sinuosus, flexuosus

windmill s venti mola f

window s fenestra f

windpipe s aspera arteria f

windy adj ventosus

wine s vinum n; (undiluted) merum n; (sour or cheap) vappa f; (new) mustum n

wing s ala f; (mil) cornu n

winged adj alatus, volucer

wink vi nictare, connivēre

winner s victor m

winning adj (fig) blandus, amoenus

winnings s lucrum n

winnow vt ventilare

winter s hiems f; **in the dead of —** media hieme; **to spend the —** hiemare

winter vi hiemare, hibernare

winter adj hibernus

winter quarters s hiberna n pl

wintry adj hiemalis, hibernus

wipe vt detergĕre; **to — away** abstergĕre; **to — out** delēre, abolēre, expungĕre

wire s filum aeneum n

wisdom s sapientia, prudentia f

wise adj sapiens, prudens; **—ly** s sapienter, prudenter

wise s modus m; **in no —** nequaquam

wish s optatum, votum n; **best —es** salus f

wish vt optare, velle, cupĕre; vi **to — for** exoptare, expetĕre

wisp s manipulus m

wistful adj desiderii plenus; **—ly** oculis intentis

wit s (intellect) ingenium n, argutiae f pl; (humor) sales m pl, facetiae f pl; (person) homo facetus m; **to be at one's —s' end** delirare; **to — scilicet**

witch s venefica, saga f

witchcraft s ars magica f, veneficium n

with prep cum (with abl); apud (with acc)

withdraw vt seducĕre, avocare; (words) revocare; vi recedĕre, discedĕre

wither vt torrēre, corrumpĕre; vi marcēre, arescĕre

withered adj marcidus

withhold vt retinēre, abstinēre, cohibēre

within adv intus, intra; (motion) intro

within prep intro (with acc), in (with abl); **— a few days** paucis diebus

without adv extra, foris; **from —** extrinsecus

without prep sine (with abl), absque (with abl), expers (with genit);

to be — carēre (with abl)

withstand vt obsistĕre (with dat), resistĕre (with dat)

witness s testis m & f; (to a signature) obsignator m; **to bear —** testificari; **to call to —** testari, antestari

witness vt testificari; (to see) intuēri, vidēre

witticism s sales m pl

witty adj facetus, salsus, acutus

wizard s magus, veneficus m

woe s dolor, luct·us -ūs m; **—s mala** n pl

woeful adj tristis, luctuosus, miser; **—ly** triste, misere

wolf s lupus m, lupa f

woman s mulier, femina f

womanhood s muliebris stat·us -ūs m

womanly adj muliebris

womb s uterus m

wonder s admiratio f; (astonishing object) miraculum, mirum n

wonder vi (ad)mirari; **to — at** admirari

wonderful adj mirabilis, admirandus; **—ly** mirabiliter, mirifice

wont adj **to be —** solēre (with inf)

woo vt petĕre

wood s lignum n; (forest) silva f, nemus n

wooded adj lignosus, silvestris

wooden adj ligneus

woodland s silvae f pl

woodman s lignator m

wood nymph s Dryas f

wooer s procus, amator m

wool s lana f

woolen adj laneus

word s verbum, vocabulum n; (spoken) vox f; (promise) fides f; (news) nuntius m; **in a —** denique; **to break one's —** fidem fallĕre; **to give one's —** fidem dare; **to keep one's —** fidem praestare; **for — for —** ad verbum

wordy adj verbosus

work s opera f, opus n; (trouble) labor m; (task) pensum n

work vt (to exercise) exercēre; (to till) colĕre; vi laborare, operari

workman s (unskilled) operarius m; (skilled) faber, opifex m

workmanship s opus n, ars f

workshop s officina f

world s (universe) mundus m, summa rerum f; (earth) orbis terrarum m; (nature) rerum natura f; (mankind) homines m pl

worldly adj profanus

worm s vermis, vermiculus m, tinea f

worm-eaten adj vermiculosus

worry s sollicitudo, cura f

worry vt vexare, sollicitare; vi sollicitari

worse adj pejor, deterior; **to grow —** ingravescĕre

worsen vi ingravescĕre

worship s veneratio f, cult·us -ūs m

worship vt venerari, adorare, colĕre

worshiper s cultor, venerator m

worst adj pessimus, deterrimus

worst vt vincĕre

worth s (*value*) pretium n; (*merit*) dignitas, virtus f; **to be —** valēre

worthless adj vilis, inutilis; (*of person*) nequam (*indecl*)

worthy adj dignus

wound s vulnus n

wound vt vulnerare; (*fig*) offendĕre, laedĕre

wounded adj saucius

wrap vt involvĕre; **to — up** complicare

wrath s ira, iracundia f

wrathful adj iratus, iracundus; **—ly** iracunde

wreak vt **to — vengeance on** ulcisci, vindicare

wreath s sertum n, corona f

wreathe vt (*to twist*) torquēre; (*to adorn with wreaths*) coronare, nectĕre

wreck s naufragium n

wreck vt frangĕre; (*fig*) perdĕre

wren s regulus m

wrench vt detorquēre, luxare

wrest vt extorquēre, eripĕre

wrestle vi luctari

wrestler s luctator, athleta m

wretch s miser, perditus, nequam (*indecl*) m

wretched adj miser, infelix, abjectus; **—ly** misere, abjecte

wretchedness s miseria, aerumna f

wring vt contorquēre, stringĕre; **to — the neck** gulam frangĕre

wrinkle s ruga f

wrinkle vt corrugare; **to — the forehead** frontem contrahĕre

wrinkled adj rugosus

writ s (*law*) mandatum n

write vt scribĕre, perscribĕre; (*poetry*) componĕre; (*history*) perscribĕre

writer s scriptor, auctor m

writhe vi torquēri

writing s (*act*) scriptio f; (*result*) scriptum n, scriptura f; (*hand*) man·us -ūs f

wrong adj pravus, perversus, falsus; (*unjust*) injustus, iniquus; **—ly** falso, male, perperam; **to be —** errare, falli

wrong s nefas n, injuria f, malum n; **to do —** peccare

wrong vt nocēre (*with dat*), injuriam inferre (*with dat*), laedĕre

wrought adj factus, confectus, fabricatus

wry adj distortus, obliquus

Y

yard s (*court*) area f; (*measure*) tres pedes m pl; **a — long** tripedalis

yawn vi oscitare, hiare; (*to gape open*) dehiscĕre

year s annus m; **every —** quotannis; **five —s** quinquennium n; **four —s** quadriennium n; **three —s** triennium n; **two —s** biennium n

yearly adj annuus, anniversarius

yearly adv quotannis

yearn vi **to — for** desiderare

yeast s fermentum n

yell s ululat·us -ūs m, ejulatio f

yell vi ululare, ejulare

yellow adj flavus, luteus, gilvus, croceus

yelp vi gannire

yes adv ita, immo, sane

yesterday adv heri

yet adv (*contrast, after adversative clause*) tamen, nihilominus; (*time*) adhuc; (*with comparatives*) etiam; **as — adhuc; not — nondum**

yield vt (*to produce*) ferre, parĕre, praebēre; (*to surrender*) dedĕre, concedĕre; vi cedĕre

yoke s jugum n; (*fig*) servitus f

yoke vt jugum imponĕre (*with dat*), conjungĕre

yonder adv illic

you pron (*thou*) tu; (*ye*) vos; **— yourself** tu ipse

young adj juvenis, adulescens; (*of child*) parvus; (*fig*) novus

younger adj junior, minor natu

youngster s adulescentulus m

your adj tuus; vester

yours pron tuus; vester

yourself pron reflex te; **to — tibi; with —** tecum; *intensive* tu ipse

yourselves pron reflex vos; **to — vobis; with —** vobiscum; *intensive* vos ipsi, vosmet ipsi

youth s (*age*) adulescentia f; (*collectively*) juventus f; (*young man*) juvenis, adulescens m

youthful adj juvenalis, puerilis; **—ly** juveniliter, pueriliter

Z

zeal s studium n, ardor, fervor m

zealous adj studiosus, ardens; **—ly** studiose, ardenter m

zenith s vertex m

zephyr s Zephyrus, Favonius m

zero s nihil, nihilum n

zest s (*taste*) sapor, gust·us -ūs m; (*fig*) gustat·us -ūs, impet·us -ūs m

zigzag adj tortuosus

zodiac s signifer orbis m

zone s zona, regio f

zoology s zoologia, animantium descriptio f